Morningside
Heights
and Harlem

*Central
Park*

*Upper
West
Side*

*Upper
East
Side*

*Upper
Midtown*

*Lower
Midtown*

EAST RIVER

PAGES 220–31
*Street Finder maps
19–20*

PAGES 166–81
*Street Finder maps
12, 13–14*

0 kilometers 1

0 miles 0.5

PAGES 150–65
*Street Finder maps
9, 12, 13*

PAGES 210–19
*Street Finder maps
11–12, 15–16*

PAGES 122–9
*Street Finder maps
8, 9*

PAGES 182–203
*Street Finder maps
12–13, 16–17*

PAGES 204–9
*Street Finder maps
12, 16*

PAGES 116–21
*Street Finder maps
4, 5*

EYEWITNESS TRAVEL

NEW YORK CITY

MAIN CONTRIBUTOR: ELEANOR BERMAN

DK

LONDON, NEW YORK,
MELBOURNE, MUNICH AND DELHI
www.dk.com

PROJECT EDITOR Fay Franklin
ART EDITOR Tony Foo
EDITORS Donna Dailey, Ellen Dupont, Esther Labi
DESIGNERS Steve Bere, Louise Parsons, Mark Stevens
EDITORIAL ASSISTANT Fiona Morgan

CONTRIBUTORS
Lester Brooks, Patricia Brooks, Susan Farewell

PHOTOGRAPHERS
Max Alexander, Dave King, Michael Moran

ILLUSTRATORS
Richard Draper, Robbie Polley, Hamish Simpson

This book was produced with the assistance of
Websters International Publishers.

Reproduced by Colourscan (Singapore)
Printed and bound by L.Rex Printing Co. Ltd, China.

First published in Great Britain in 1993
by Dorling Kindersley Limited
80 Strand, London WC2R 0RL

12 13 14 15 10 9 8 7 6 5 4 3 2 1

Reprinted with revisions 1994, 1995 (twice), 1997, 1999, 2000, 2001, 2002,
2003, 2004, 2005, 2006, 2007, 2008, 2009, 2010, 2011, 2012

Front cover main image: Empire State Building

MIX
Paper from
responsible sources
FSC
www.fsc.org   FSC™ C018179

◁ Towering skyscrapers in central New York

CONTENTS

HOW TO USE THIS GUIDE 6

Baseball star
Babe Ruth
(1895–1948)

INTRODUCING NEW YORK

South Manhattan skyline

NEW YORK CITY

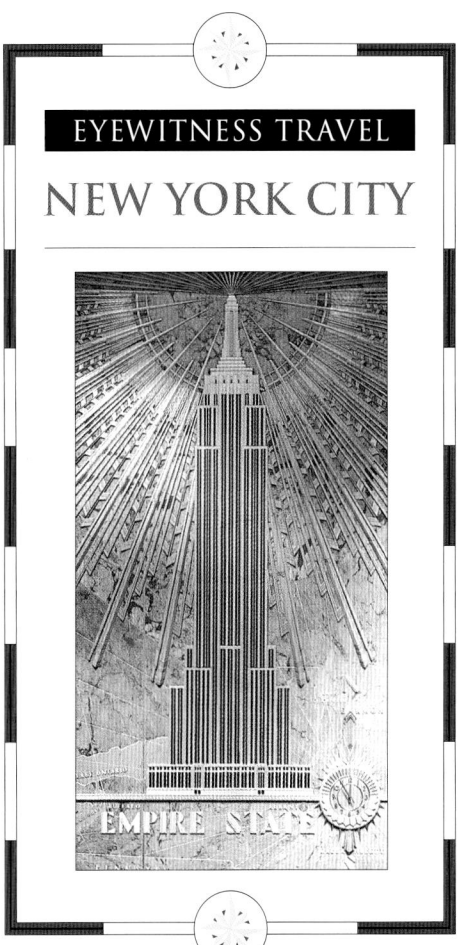

EMPIRE STATE

Chinatown, Lower East Side

Trump Tower, Upper Midtown

The New York City Ballet

Riverfront promenade in Brooklyn

TRAVELERS' NEEDS

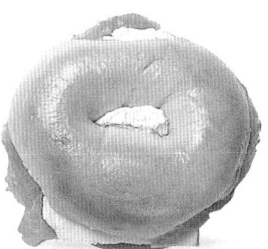

Bagel from a New York deli

SURVIVAL GUIDE

Solomon R. Guggenheim Museum, Upper East Side

HOW TO USE THIS GUIDE

This Eyewitness Travel Guide helps you get the most from your stay in New York with the minimum of practical difficulty. The opening section, *Introducing New York*, locates the city geographically, sets modern New York in its historical context and describes the highlights of the year. *New York at a Glance* is an overview of the city's attractions. Section two, *New York Area by Area*, guides you through the city's sightseeing areas. It describes all the main

sights with maps, photographs and detailed illustrations. In addition, seven planned walks take you step-by-step through special areas.

Well-researched tips on where to stay, eat, shop, and on sports and entertainment are in section three, *Travelers' Needs. Children's New York* lists highlights for young visitors, and section four, *Survival Guide*, shows you how to do everything from mailing a letter to using the subway.

NEW YORK AREA BY AREA

Manhattan has been divided into 15 sightseeing areas, each described separately. Each area opens with a portrait, summing up the area's character and history and listing all the sights to be covered. Sights are numbered and clearly located on an *Area Map*. After this comes a large-scale *Street-by-Street Map* focusing on the most interesting part of the area. Finding your way around each area is made simple by the numbering system. This refers to the order in which sights are described on the pages that follow.

Sights at a Glance lists the sights in the area by category, including: Historic Streets and Buildings, Modern Architecture, Museums and Galleries, Churches, Monuments, and Parks and Squares.

The area covered in greater detail on the *Street-by-Street Map* is shaded red.

Numbered circles pinpoint all the listed sights on the area map. Trump Tower, for example, is ❷

1 The Area Map
For easy reference, the sights in each area are numbered and located on an Area Map. *To help the visitor, the map also shows subway stations, heliports and ferry embarkation points.*

Photographs of facades and distinctive details of buildings help you locate the sights.

Color-coding on each page makes the area easy to find in the book.

Travel tips help you reach the area quickly by public transportation.

2 The Street-by-Street Map
This gives a bird's-eye view of the heart of each sightseeing area. The most important buildings are illustrated, to help you spot them easily as you walk around.

A locator map shows you where you are in relation to surrounding areas. The area of the *Street-by-Street Map* is shown in red.

Trump Tower ❷ is also shown on this map.

A suggested route for a walk takes you past some of the area's most interesting sights.

Stars indicate the sights that no visitor should miss.

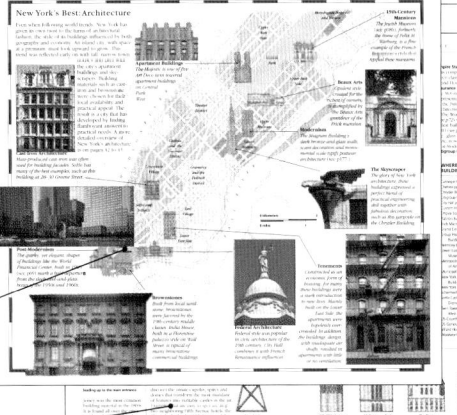

NEW YORK AT A GLANCE

Each map in this section concentrates on a specific theme: *Museums, Architecture, Multicultural New York,* and *Celebrated New Yorkers.* The top sights are shown on the map; other sights are described on the two pages following and cross-referenced to their full entries in the *Area by Area* section.

Each sightseeing area is color-coded.

The theme is explored in greater detail on the pages following the map.

3 Detailed information on each sight

All important sights in each area are described in depth here. They are listed in order, following the numbering on the opening Area Map. *Practical information is also provided.*

PRACTICAL INFORMATION

Each entry provides all the information needed to plan a visit to the sight. The key to the symbols is inside the back cover.

Map reference to Street Finder at back of book

Address

Sight Number

Trump Tower ➋

725 5th Ave. **Map** 12 F3.
Tel 832-2000. **M** 5th Ave-53rd St.
Garden level, shops open 10am–6pm
Mon–Sat. **Building open** 8am–10pm
daily. **Adm** free. See **Shopping** p311.
📷 ♿ *Concerts*. 🍴 🎭 🛍 🚻

Opening hours

Telephone number

Services and facilities available

Nearest subway station

4 New York's major sights

These are given two or more full pages in the sightseeing area in which they are found. Important buildings are dissected to reveal their interiors; museums have color-coded floor plans to help you find particular exhibits.

The Visitors' Checklist provides the practical information you will need to plan your visit.

The facade of each major sight is shown to help you spot it quickly.

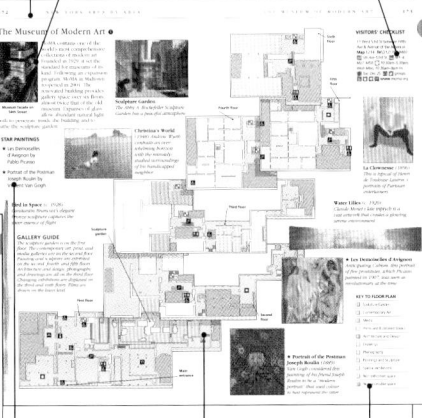

Stars indicate the most important exhibits or works of art on display inside, or the most interesting architectural details of the building.

A color key helps you find your way easily around the collection.

Floors are referred to in accordance with American usage, i.e., the "first floor" is at ground level.

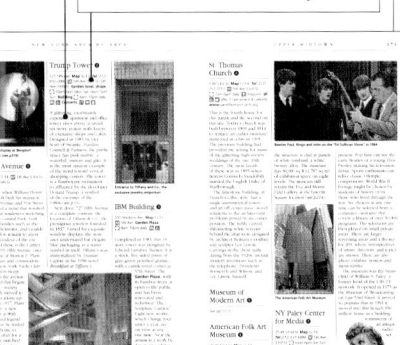

INTRODUCING NEW YORK

FOUR GREAT DAYS IN NEW YORK

At first glance New York may seem a bit overwhelming, but these four great days are planned to give you a taste of the Big Apple, with much of the city's best in architecture, shopping, museums, and fun. Each day offers a mix of things to see and do, and the schedules are not meant to

Chrysler pinnacle

be rigid – you'll find ample time to explore places that catch your fancy. All sights mentioned are cross-referenced so that you can find more information, check what's nearby, and tailor the day. Prices show the cost for two adults or for a family of two adults and two children including lunch.

CITY LANDMARKS

- A tour of the UN
- Modern, Art Deco, and Beaux Arts edifices
- Lights of Times Square
- Empire State Building

TWO ADULTS allow at least $140

Morning
Start at the East River with a guided tour of the **United Nations headquarters** (see pp160–63), with its striking modern architecture. Then head to 42nd Street, detouring into the unique residential enclave of **Tudor City** (see p158), and dropping in to admire the Art Deco interior of the **Chrysler Building** (see p155). Next is **Grand Central Terminal**, a great Beaux Art landmark (see pp156–7). Admire the Main Concourse and explore the shopping gallery, colorful food market, and a food court with everything from sushi to Southern barbecue to New York cheesecake. Another lunchtime option is chowder

or a platter of Long Island oysters at the **Grand Central Oyster Bar** (see p306).

Afternoon
Back on 42nd Street is another Beaux Arts creation, the **New York Public Library** (see p146; free one-hour tours at 11am and 2pm Tue–Thu). The marble halls, stairways, Main Reading Room and Periodicals Room are highlights. Check your e-mail for free in the Bill Blass Public Catalog Room. Look out also for current exhibits. Behind the library is **Bryant Park** (see p145), a welcome oasis of green in midtown. Ahead is New York's most famous crossroads, **Times Square** (see p147), gateway to the glittering neon of Broadway. Just beyond is 42nd Street, now a bright avenue of restored theaters, giant movie palaces, and Madame Tussaud's Wax Museum, with many true-to-life celebrities. Hail a cab to the **Empire State Building** (see pp136–7) and end the day with a fine twilight view of the city from the 86th-floor observatory.

Glistening Prometheus Statue and Lower Plaza at Rockefeller Center

ART AND SHOPPING

- A morning of modern art
- Lunch at Rockefeller Center
- Fifth Avenue shopping
- Tea at The Pierre

TWO ADULTS allow at least $135

Morning
The spectacular **Museum of Modern Art** (MOMA) (see pp172–5) will easily fill your morning with its wonderful art. Allow a couple of hours to enjoy its great works, including Van Gogh's *The Starry Night* and Claude Monet's *Water Lilies*, as well as Picasso's *Les Demoiselles d'Avignon*, to name just a few. Don't miss the design exhibits on floor three; one of MOMA's best-known facets. Leave the museum and stroll over to the **Rockefeller Center** (see p144) for lunch at the Rock Center Café, where you can watch the ice skaters in winter.

The neon lights of Times Square, the city's famous crossroads

◁ New York harbor and 42nd Street in 1946

In summer the rink is transformed into a leafy garden, where you can dine at the Rink Bar.

Afternoon
After lunch head for **St. Patrick's Cathedral** *(see pp178–9)*, the largest Catholic cathedral in the US and one of the city's finest places of worship. Then continue along **Fifth Avenue** for an afternoon of upscale shopping. Saks Fifth Avenue is just across the street from St. Patrick's at 50th Street. Heading uptown, the temptations include a dizzying variety of glitzy shops, such as Cartier (52nd St), Henri Bendel (55–56th sts), Prada, Tiffany (57th St), and Bergdorf Goodman (57–58 sts). End the day on 61st Street with a final splurge – enjoy a cocktail at **The Pierre** *(see p289)*.

Statue of Liberty

HISTORIC NEW YORK

- A boat trip to Ellis Island and the Statue of Liberty
- Lunch at Fraunces Tavern
- A tour of Old New York

TWO ADULTS allow at least $120

Morning
At Battery Park, board the ferry to the **Statue of Liberty** *(see pp74–5)* and on to **Ellis Island** *(see pp78–9)*, the point of arrival for many immigrants (round trip includes both stops). On your return, exit the park at **Bowling Green**, the city's oldest park *(see p73)*. Walk to the **Fraunces Tavern Block Historic District** *(see p76)*, New York's last block of 18th-century commercial buildings. The recreated Tavern includes a museum of the revolutionary period and a restaurant that

Central Park, a vast area of fun rides, animals, and places to play

is the perfect choice for an atmospheric lunch.

Afternoon
A block away is Stone Street Historic District, rebuilt after a fire in 1835. Look for **India House** *(see p56)*, once the New York Cotton Exchange, now **Harry's Café**. Take William Street to Wall Street and **Federal Hall** *(see p68)* with exhibits on the US Constitution. Nearby is the **New York Stock Exchange** *(see pp70–71)* and **Trinity Church** *(see p68)*, built in 1839. Go up Broadway to **St. Paul's Chapel** *(see p91)*, miraculously unscathed after the World Trade Center fell behind it. Ahead is **City Hall** *(see p90)*. Finally, head for the **South Street Seaport Historic District**, heart of the 19th-century port *(see pp82–3)*, with a view of the awesome **Brooklyn Bridge** *(see pp86–9)*.

A FAMILY FUN DAY

- A morning in Central Park
- Lunch at the Boathouse
- Dinosaurs at the American Museum of Natural History

FAMILY OF 4 allow at least $225

Morning
Central Park *(see pp205–9)* was made for family fun. Ride the vintage Carousel, watch model boats in action at Conservatory Pond, visit the Zoo, then watch the animal parade on the Delacorte clock on the half hour. There are themed playgrounds to please all ages: Safari at West 91st Street (2–5 years); Adventure at West 67th Street (6–12 years). The Swedish Cottage Marionette Theater, at West 79th, presents classic fairy tales at 10:30am and noon Tue–Fri (Wed also 2:30pm) and 1pm Sat; book ahead. Rent bikes or take a boat out on the lake, then lunch at the Boat House, which has a view of the lake. In winter, you can ice skate at the Wollman rink.

Afternoon
Depending on ages and interests, choose between the interactive **Children's Museum** *(see p219)*, or the famous dinosaurs and dioramas at the **American Museum of Natural History** *(see pp216–17)*. Finish up on West 73rd Street for a "wee tea" at Alice's Tea Cup.

Ellis Island, the view greeting early immigrants to New York

Putting New York on the Map

New York is a city of eight million people, covering 301 sq miles (780 sq km). The city gives its name to the state of New York, the capital of which is Albany, 156 miles (251 km) to the north. New York is also a good base from which to visit the historic towns of Boston and Philadelphia, as well as the nation's capital, Washington, DC.

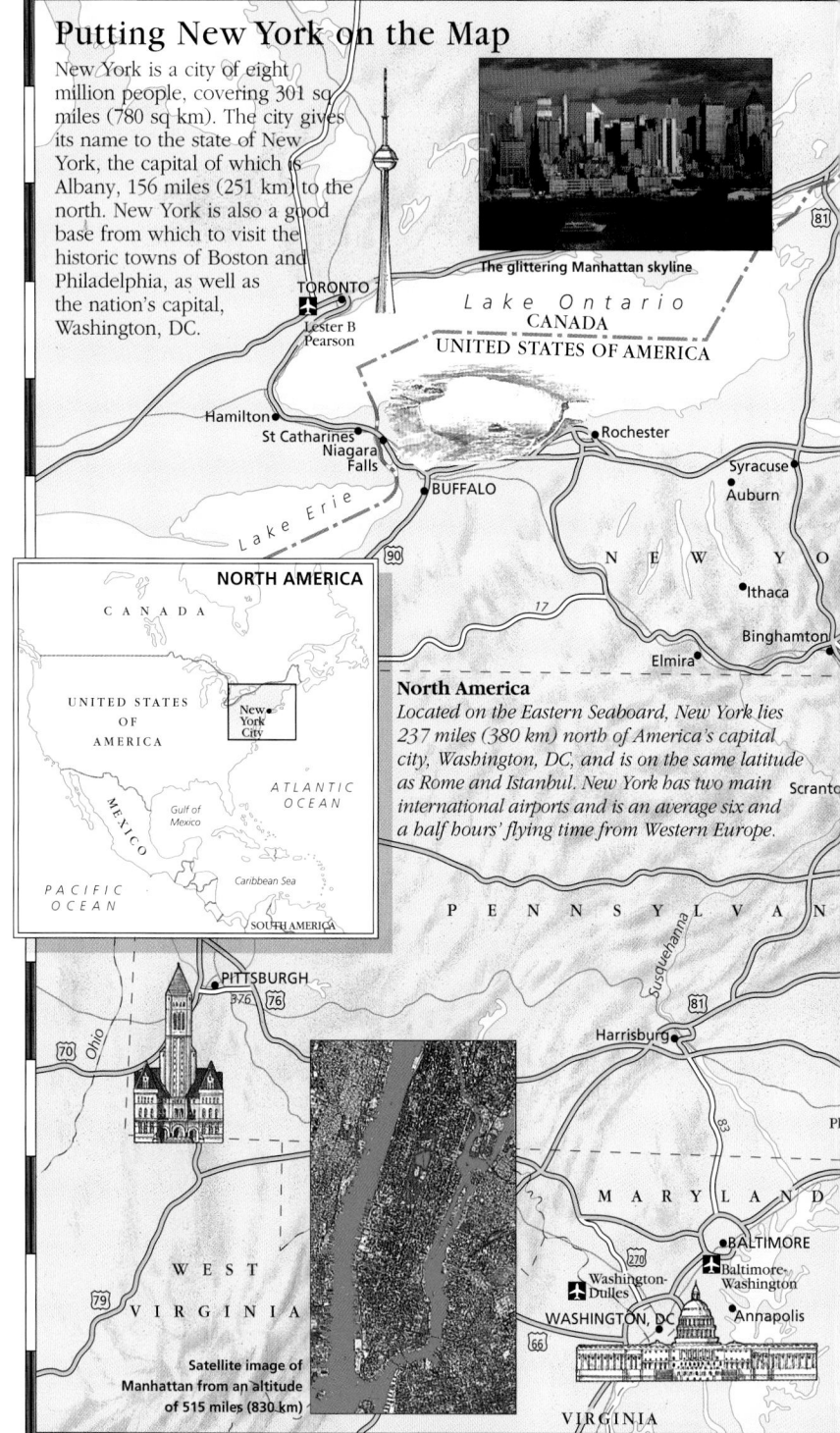

The glittering Manhattan skyline

Lake Ontario

CANADA
UNITED STATES OF AMERICA

TORONTO
Lester B Pearson

Hamilton
St Catharines
Niagara Falls
BUFFALO

Lake Erie

Rochester
Syracuse
Auburn

N E W Y O

Ithaca

Binghamton
Elmira

NORTH AMERICA

CANADA

UNITED STATES OF AMERICA

New York City

ATLANTIC OCEAN

MEXICO

Gulf of Mexico

Caribbean Sea

PACIFIC OCEAN

SOUTH AMERICA

North America

Located on the Eastern Seaboard, New York lies 237 miles (380 km) north of America's capital city, Washington, DC, and is on the same latitude as Rome and Istanbul. New York has two main international airports and is an average six and a half hours' flying time from Western Europe.

Scranton

P E N N S Y L V A N

Susquehanna

PITTSBURGH

Harrisburg

Ohio

M A R Y L A N D

BALTIMORE
Baltimore-Washington
Washington-Dulles
WASHINGTON, DC
Annapolis

W E S T
V I R G I N I A

Satellite image of Manhattan from an altitude of 515 miles (830 km)

VIRGINIA

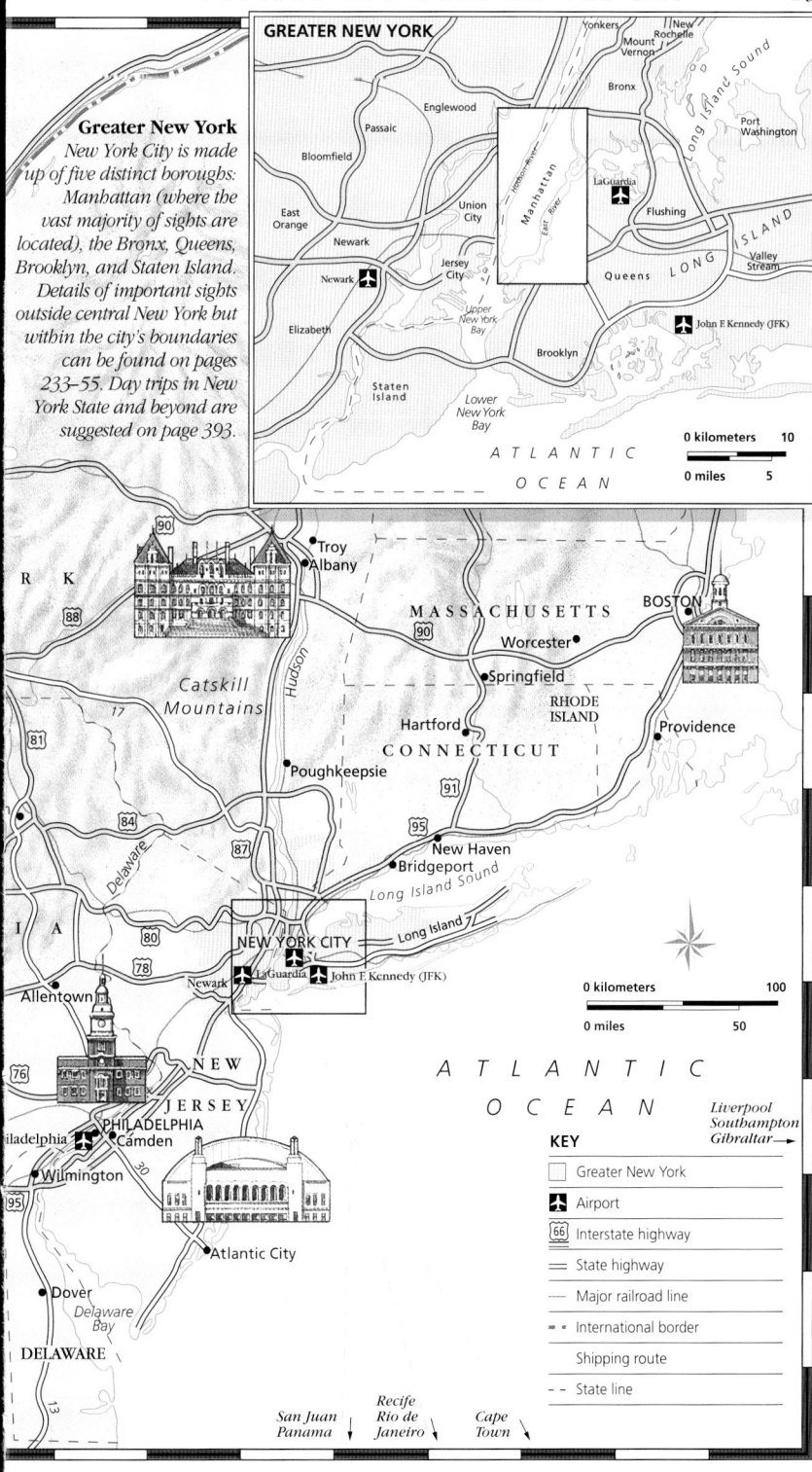

Greater New York

New York City is made up of five distinct boroughs: Manhattan (where the vast majority of sights are located), the Bronx, Queens, Brooklyn, and Staten Island. Details of important sights outside central New York but within the city's boundaries can be found on pages 233–55. Day trips in New York State and beyond are suggested on page 393.

GREATER NEW YORK

Yonkers · New Rochelle · Mount Vernon · Bronx · Port Washington · Englewood · Passaic · Bloomfield · East Orange · Union City · LaGuardia · Flushing · Newark · Jersey City · Queens · Valley Stream · Elizabeth · Upper New York Bay · John F Kennedy (JFK) · Brooklyn · Staten Island · Lower New York Bay

Long Island Sound · Manhattan · Hudson River · East River · LONG ISLAND

ATLANTIC OCEAN

0 kilometers 10

0 miles 5

Troy · Albany · MASSACHUSETTS · BOSTON · Worcester · Springfield · Catskill Mountains · RHODE ISLAND · Hartford · Providence · CONNECTICUT · Poughkeepsie · New Haven · Bridgeport · Long Island Sound · NEW YORK CITY · Long Island · Newark · LaGuardia · John F Kennedy (JFK) · Allentown · NEW JERSEY · PHILADELPHIA · Camden · Wilmington · Atlantic City · Dover · Delaware Bay · DELAWARE

Hudson · Delaware

ATLANTIC OCEAN

Liverpool · Southampton · Gibraltar →

0 kilometers 100

0 miles 50

KEY

- Greater New York
- ✈ Airport
- 66 Interstate highway
- State highway
- Major railroad line
- International border
- Shipping route
- State line

San Juan · Panama · Recife · Rio de Janeiro · Cape Town

Manhattan

This guide divides Manhattan into 15 areas, each with its own chapter. Many of New York's oldest and newest buildings rub shoulders in Lower Manhattan. It is from here, too, that you can take the Staten Island ferry, for breathtaking views of the city's famous skyline and the Statue of Liberty. Midtown includes the Theater District and Fifth Avenue's glittering shops. Museum Mile, alongside Central Park on Upper East Side, is a cultural paradise. To the north lies Harlem, America's most famous black community.

Grand Central Terminal
This Beaux Arts station has been a gateway to the city since 1913. Its concourse is a vast pedestrian area with a high-vaulted roof (see pp156–7).

Morgan Library & Museum
One of the world's finest collections of rare manuscripts, prints, and books is on display in this palazzo-style building (see pp164–5).

Statue of Liberty
Presented as a gift from the French to the American people in 1886, this towering statue has become a symbol of freedom throughout the world (see pp74–5).

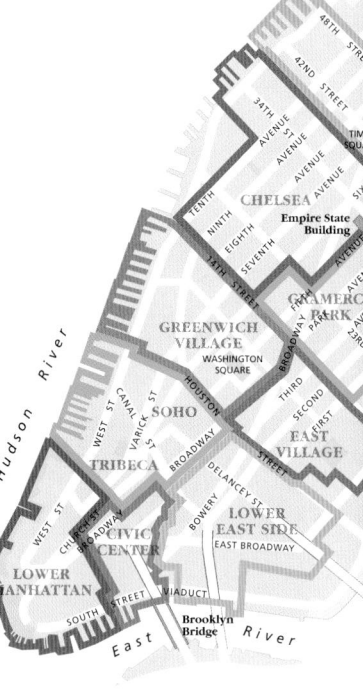

Cathedral of St. John the Divine
When it is finished, at some time after the mid-21st century, this great cathedral will be the largest in the world. It is also a theater and music venue (see pp226–7).

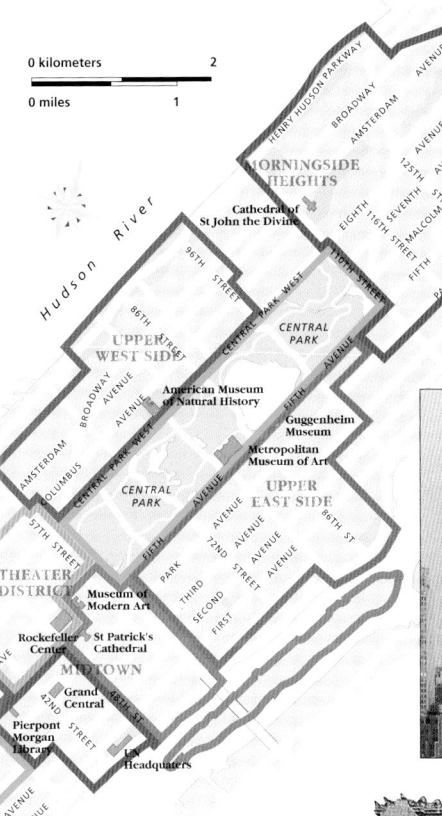

0 kilometers 2
0 miles 1

KEY

Major sight

United Nations
New York is the headquarters of the global organization set up to preserve world peace and security (see pp160–63).

Empire State Building
This is the tallest skyscraper in New York and a symbol of the city. Built in the 1930s, it has since attracted more than 110 million visitors (see pp136–7).

Metropolitan Museum of Art
With a stunning collection of artifacts dating from prehistoric times to the present, this is one of the world's greatest museums (see pp190–97).

Brooklyn Bridge
This bridge spans the East River between Manhattan and Brooklyn. Built in 1883, it was the largest suspension bridge and the first to be constructed of steel (see pp86–9).

Solomon R. Guggenheim Museum
A masterpiece of architecture by Frank Lloyd Wright, this unique building contains a fine collection of 19th- and 20th-century painting (see pp188–9).

THE HISTORY OF NEW YORK

From its first sighting almost 500 years ago by Giovanni da Verrazano, New York's harbor was the prize that all of Europe wanted to capture. The Dutch first sent fur traders to the area in 1621, but they lost the colony they called New Amsterdam to the English in 1664. The settlement was re-christened New York and the name stayed, even after the English lost the colony in 1783, at the end of the Revolutionary War.

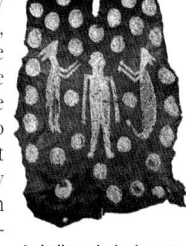

A shell-work cloak worn by an Indian chief

THE GROWING CITY

In the 19th century, New York grew rapidly and became a major port. Ease of shipping spawned manufacturing, commerce was king and great fortunes were made. In 1898, Manhattan was joined with the four outer boroughs to form the world's second-largest city. From 1800 to 1900, the population grew from 79,000 to 3 million people. New York City became the country's cultural and entertainment mecca as well as its business center.

THE MELTING POT

The city continued to grow as thousands of immigrants came seeking a better life. Overpopulation meant that many at first lived in slums. Today, the mix of cultures has enriched the city and become its defining quality. Its eight million inhabitants speak some 100 languages.

Manhattan's skyline took shape as the city grew skyward to make space for its ever-increasing population. Throughout its history, the city has experienced alternating periods of economic decline and growth, but in both good times and bad, it remains one of the world's most vital cities.

The following pages illustrate significant periods in New York's history.

A deed signed by New Amsterdam's last Dutch governor, Peter Stuyvesant, in 1664

◁ The southern half of Manhattan and part of Brooklyn in 1767

Early New York

Indian husk mask

Manhattan was a forested land populated by Algonquian-speaking Natives when the Dutch West India Company established a fur trading post called New Amsterdam in 1625. The first settlers built houses helter-skelter, so even today the streets of Lower Manhattan still twist. Broadway, then called by the Dutch name *Breede Wegh*, began as an Indian trail known as the Weekquaesgeek Trail. Harlem has also kept its Dutch name. The town was unruly until Peter Stuyvesant arrived to bring order. But the colony did not produce the expected revenues, and in 1664 the Dutch let it fall to the English, who renamed it New York.

GROWTH OF THE METROPOLIS

| ▨ 1664 | ☐ Today |

Seal of New Netherland
The beaver pelt and wampum (Indian shell beads) on the seal were the currency of the colony of New Netherland.

FIRST VIEW OF MANHATTAN (1626)
The southern tip of Manhattan resembled a Dutch town, down to the windmill. Although shown here, the fort had not yet been built.

The First New Yorkers
Algonquian-speaking Natives were the first inhabitants of Manhattan.

Iroquois Pot
Iroquois Indians were frequent visitors to early Manhattan.

Dutch ships

Indian Village
Some Algonquians lived in longhouses on Manhattan before the Dutch arrived.

Native canoe

Dutch Delftware
Colonists brought this popular tin-glazed earthen-ware pottery from Holland.

Manhattan Skyline
The Strand, now Whitehall Street, was the site of the city's first brick house.

Tiger timbers

WHERE TO SEE DUTCH NEW YORK

Dug up by workmen in 1916, these remnants of a Dutch ship, the *Tiger*, which burned in 1613, are the earliest artifacts of the period and are now in the Museum of the City of New York *(see p199)*. Rooms in this museum, as well as in the Morris-Jumel Mansion *(see p235)* and the Van Cortlandt House Museum *(see p240)*, display Dutch pottery, tiles and furniture.

Purchase of Manhattan
Peter Minuit bought the island from the Natives in 1626 for $24 worth of trinkets.

Dutch windmill

Fort Amsterdam

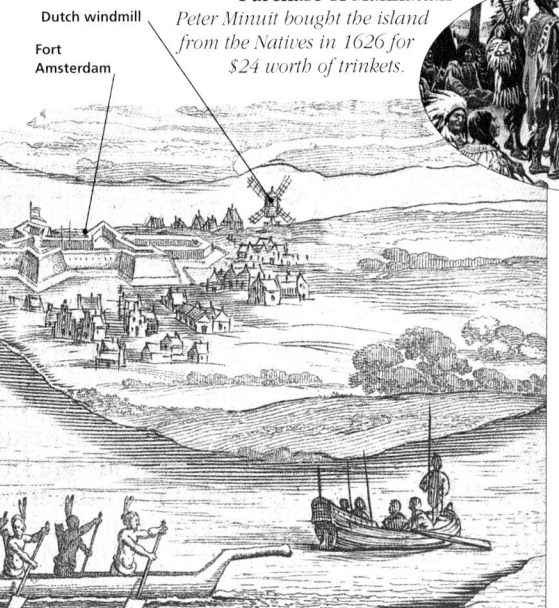

Peter Stuyvesant
The last Dutch governor was a tyrant who imposed strict laws – such as an edict closing all the city's taverns at 9 o'clock.

1660 First city hospital established

1664 British forces oust Dutch without a fight and change name to New York

1676 Great Dock built on East River

1698 Trinity Church dedicated

1660 **1680** **1700**

The surrender of New Amsterdam to the British

1680s Bolting Laws give New York exclusive right to process and ship grain

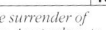

1683 First New York city charter established

1689 Merchant Jacob Leisler leads revolt against taxes and takes over the city for two years

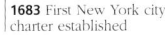

1693 Ninety-two cannons installed for protection; area becomes known as the Battery

1691 Leisler sentenced to death for treason

Colonial New York

Under British rule, New York prospered and the population grew rapidly. The bolting of flour (grinding grain) was the main commercial enterprise. Shipbuilding also flourished. As the city prospered, an elite emerged that could afford a more refined way of life, and fine furniture and household silver were made for use in their homes during the Colonial period. During more than a century of governing New York, Britain proved more interested in profit than in the welfare of the colony. The Crown imposed hated taxes, and the spirit of rebellion grew, although especially in New York, loyalties were divided. On the the eve of Revolution, New York was the second-largest city in the 13 colonies, with 20,000 citizens.

Colonial gentleman

Colonial currency

GROWTH OF THE METROPOLIS

| | 1760 | ☐ Today |

Bedroom

Colonial Street
Pigs and dogs roamed free on the streets of Colonial New York.

Dining room

Kas
This Dutch-style pine wardrobe was made in New York's Hudson River valley around 1720.

Shipping
Trade with the West Indies and Britain helped New York prosper. In some years, 200 or more vessels visited the port.

TIMELINE

1702 Lord Cornbury appointed Colonial governor; he often wore women's clothes

1711 Slave market set up at the foot of Wall Street

1720 First shipyard opens

| 1700 | 1710 | 1720 | 1730 |

1710 Iroquois chief Hendrick visits England

1732 First city theater opens

1725 *New York Gazette*, city's first newspaper, is established

Captain Kidd
*The Scottish pirate William Kidd
was a respected citizen, lending
a block and tackle to help build
Trinity Church (see p68).*

VAN CORTLANDT HOUSE

*Frederick Van Cortlandt built this
Georgian-style house in 1748 on a
wheat plantation in what is now the
Bronx. Today a museum (see p240),
it shows how a well-to-do Dutch-
English family once lived.*

WHERE TO SEE COLONIAL NEW YORK

Colonial buildings are open to
the public at Historic Richmond
Town on Staten Island *(see
p254)*. Fine examples of
Colonial silver and furniture are
on display at the Museum of the
City of New York *(see p199)*.

Richmond Town General Store

West parlor

Colonial Kitchen
*Plain white cheese, called "white meat," was
often served in place of meat. Waffles,
introduced by the Dutch, were popular. Fresh
fruit was rare, but preserved fruits were eaten.*

Pewter baby bottle

Cheese mold

Waffle iron

Decorative Carvings
*A face carved in stone peers
over each of the front windows.*

Sucket fork, for eating preserved fruits

1734 John Peter
Zenger's libel
trial upholds
freedom of the
press

1741 Slave uprising creates
hysteria; 31 slaves are
executed, 150 imprisoned

1754 French and
Indian War begins;
King's College (now
Columbia University)
founded

British soldier

1759 First
jail built

1740   **1750**   **1760**

1733 Bowling Green becomes
first city park;
first ferries
to Brooklyn

King's College

1762 First paid
police force

1763 War ends;
British gain control
of North America

Revolutionary New York

George Washington, Revolutionary general

Dug up into trenches for defense, heavily shelled by British troops and scarred by recurring fires, New York suffered during the American Revolution. But despite the hardships, many continued to enjoy cricket games, horse races, balls and boxing matches. After the British took the city in 1776, it became their headquarters. The Continental army did not return to Manhattan until November 25, 1783, two years after the fighting ended.

GROWTH OF THE METROPOLIS

▨ *1776*   ▢ *Today*

Battle Dress
The Continental (Patriot) army wore blue uniforms, while the British wore red.

British soldier

TOPPLING THE KING
New Yorkers tore down the statue of King George III in Bowling Green and melted it down to make ammunition.

Soldier's Haversack
American soldiers in the War of Independence carried their supplies in haversacks.

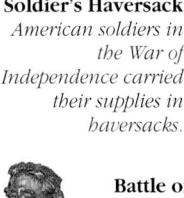

Battle of Harlem Heights
Washington won this battle on September 16, 1776. But he did not have enough troops to hold New York so retreated, leaving it to the British.

American soldier

Patriot

Death of a Patriot
While working behind British lines in 1776, Nathan Hale was captured and hanged by the British without trial for spying.

TIMELINE

1765 British pass Stamp Act; New Yorkers protest; Sons of Liberty formed

1767 New duties imposed with Townshend Act; after protests, the act is repealed

1770 Sons of Liberty fight British in the "Battle of Golden Hill"

1774 Rebels dump tea in New York harbor to protest taxes

1760

1770

1780

St. Paul's Chapel

1766 St. Paul's Chapel completed; Stamp Act repealed; Statue of George III erected on Bowling Green

General William Howe, commander in chief of the British troops

1776 War begins; 500 ships under General Howe assemble in New York harbor

Fire Fighters

Fires had long threatened the city, but during the war a series of fires nearly destroyed it. In the wake of the patriot retreat, on September 21, 1776, a devastating fire razed Trinity Church and 1,000 houses.

Leather fire bucket

Flags of the Revolution

Washington's army flew the Continental colors, with a stripe for each of the 13 colonies and a Union Jack in the corner. The Stars and Stripes became the official flag in 1777.

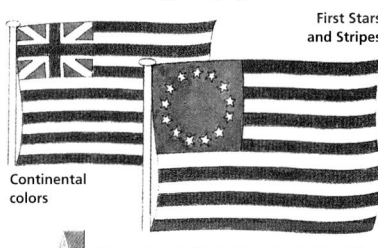

First Stars and Stripes

Continental colors

Statue of George III

General Washington Returns

Washington received a hero's welcome when he reentered New York on November 25, 1783, after the British withdrawal.

Cheering patriots

WHERE TO SEE THE REVOLUTIONARY CITY

In 1776, George Washington used the Morris-Jumel Mansion in upper Manhattan as a headquarters (*see p235*). He also slept at the Van Cortlandt House (*see p21 and p240*). After the war he bade farewell to his officers at Fraunces Tavern (*see p76*).

Morris-Jumel mansion

1783 Treaty of Paris signed, US wins independence; British evacuate New York

1784 Bank of New York chartered

1785 New York named US capital

1789 George Washington inaugurated as first president at Federal Hall

Washington's inauguration

1790 US capital is moved to Philadelphia

1790

1791 New York Hospital, city's oldest, opens

1792 Tontine Coffee House built – first home of the Stock Exchange

1794 Bellevue Hospital opens on the East River

1801 *New York Post* founded by Alexander Hamilton

1800

1804 Vice President Aaron Burr kills political rival Alexander Hamilton in a duel

New York in the 19th Century

Governor De Witt Clinton

Firmly established as the nation's largest city and preeminent seaport, New York grew increasingly wealthy. Manufacturing increased due to the ease of shipping; tycoons like John Jacob Astor made millions. The rich moved uptown; public transportation followed. With rapid growth came fires, epidemics and financial panics. Immigrants from Ireland, Germany, and other nations arrived. Some found prosperity; others crowded into slums in Lower Manhattan.

GROWTH OF THE METROPOLIS

▨ *1840* ☐ *Today*

Sheet Music
The Stephen Foster ballad Jeanie With the Light Brown Hair *was popular at this time.*

Croton Distributing Reservoir was built in 1842. Until then, New Yorkers had no fresh drinking water – they relied on deliveries of bottled water.

Omnibus
The horse-drawn omnibus was introduced for public transportation in 1832 and remained on New York streets until World War I.

Keeping Fit
Gymnasiums such as Dr. Rich's Institute for Physical Education were established in New York in the 1830s and 1840s.

TIMELINE

1805 First free state schools established in New York

1811 Randel Plan divides Manhattan into grid pattern above 14th Street

1812–14 War of 1812; British blockade New York harbor

The Constitution, *most famous ship in War of 1812*

1835 Much of old New York razed in city's worst fire

| 1810 | 1820 | 1830 |

1807 Robert Fulton launches first steamboat, on the Hudson River

1822 Yellow fever epidemic; people evacuate to Greenwich Village

1823 New York surpasses Boston and Philadelphia to become nation's largest city

1827 New York abolishes slavery

1837 New Yorker Samuel Morse sends first telegraph message

The Brownstone
Many brownstone row houses were built in the first half of the century. The raised stoop allowed separate entry to the parlor and ground-floor servants' quarters.

Crystal Palace was an iron and glass exhibition hall erected for the 1853 World's Fair.

NEW YORK IN 1855
Looking south from 42nd Street, Crystal Palace and the Croton Distributing Reservoir stood where the main public library and Bryant Park are today.

THE PORT OF NEW YORK
New York's importance as a port city grew by leaps and bounds in the early 19th century. Robert Fulton launched his first steamboat, the *Clermont*, in 1807. Steamboats made travel much quicker – it now took 72 hours to reach Albany, which was both the state capital and the gateway to the West. Trade with the West by steamboat and canal boat, and with the rest of the world by clipper ship, made the fortunes of many New Yorkers.

The steamboat *Clermont*

Crystal Palace in Flames
On October 5, 1858, New York's Crystal Palace exhibition hall burned to the ground, just as its predecessor in London did.

Grand Canal Celebration
Ships in New York harbor lined up to celebrate the 1825 Erie Canal opening. In connecting the Great Lakes with Albany, the state capital, on the Hudson River, the canal opened a water link between the Midwest and the Port of New York. New York realized huge profits.

FOR SAN FRANCISCO

FREE TRADE

The Age of Extravagance

Industrialist Andrew Carnegie

As New York's merchant princes grew ever wealthier, the city entered into a gilded era during which many of its most opulent buildings went up. Millions were lavished on the arts with the founding of the Metropolitan Museum, Public Library and Carnegie Hall. Luxury hotels like the Plaza and the original Waldorf-Astoria were built, and elegant department stores arose to serve the wealthy. Such flamboyant figures as William "Boss" Tweed, political strongman and king of corruption, and circus man Phineas T. Barnum were also larger than life.

GROWTH OF THE METROPOLIS
◼ *1890*   ☐ *Today*

Overlooking the Park
The Dakota (1880) was the first grand luxury apartment house on the Upper West Side (see p218).

Palatial Living
Mansions lined Fifth Avenue. When it was built in 1882, W.K. Vanderbilt's Italianate palace at 660 Fifth Avenue, was one of the farthest north.

Fashion City
Lord & Taylor built a new store on Broadway's Ladies' Mile; 6th Avenue between 14th and 23rd streets was known as Fashion Row.

BATHING SUITS.
A GREAT SPECIALTY AT
LORD & TAYLOR'S, Broadway and 20th Street, N.Y

THE ELEVATED RAILROAD
By the mid 1870s, elevated railroads or "Els" ran along 2nd, 3rd, 6th and 9th avenues. They made travel faster, but left noise, grime and pollution in their wake.

TIMELINE

1867 Brooklyn's Prospect Park completed

1868 First elevated railroad built on Greenwich Street

1870 J.D. Rockefeller founds Standard Oil

1871 The first Grand Central Depot opens on 42nd St.; "Boss" Tweed is arrested and imprisoned

1877 A.G. Bell demonstrates the telephone in New York

1865   **1870**   **1875**

1869 First apartment house built on 18th Street; Black Friday financial crisis hits Wall Street

The interior of the Stock Exchange

1872 Bloomingdale's opens

1873 Banks fail: Stock Exchange panics

1879 St. Patrick's Cathedral completed; first city telephone exchange opened on Nassau Street

Mark Twain's Birthday
Mark Twain, whose 1873 novel The Gilded Age *portrayed the decadent lifestyle of New Yorkers, celebrated his birthday at Delmonico's.*

WHERE TO SEE THE AGE OF EXTRAVAGANCE

The Gold Room in the Henry Villard Houses *(see p176)* is a good place to experience the city's past. Formerly the Music Room, it is now an upscale bar called Gilt. The Museum of the City of New York also has period rooms *(p199)*.

Elevated train

Bowery

Streetcar

Rural Fifth Avenue
This painting by Ralph Blakelock shows a shanty-town at 86th Street. Today it is one of New York's most expensive addresses.

The Tweed Ring
William "Boss" Tweed led Tammany Hall, which dominated city government. He stole millions in city funds.

Nast's cartoon of "Boss" Tweed

Tammany Tiger
The Museum of the City of New York has "Boss" Tweed's cane, which sports a gold Tammany Tiger mascot on its handle.

1880 Canned fruits and meats first appear in stores; Metropolitan Museum of Art opens; streets lit by electricity	**1883** Metropolitan Opera opens on Broadway; Brooklyn Bridge completed	**1886** Statue of Liberty unveiled

1880 **1885** **1890**

1891 Carnegie Hall opens

1888 Great Blizzard dumps 22 in (56 cm) of snow

1890 First moving picture shows appear in New York

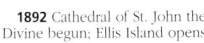

Grand display of fireworks over Brooklyn Bridge, 1883

1892 Cathedral of St. John the Divine begun; Ellis Island opens

New York at the Turn of the Century

Horse-drawn carriage

By 1900, New York was a hub of American industry: 70% of the country's corporations were based there, and the port handled two-thirds of all imported goods. The rich got richer, but in the crowded slums, disease spread. Even so, immigrants kept their rich traditions alive, and political and social reform emerged. In 1900, the International Ladies' Garment Workers' Union was founded to battle for the rights of the women and children who toiled in dangerous factories for low wages. The Triangle Shirtwaist Factory fire in 1911 also sped reform.

GROWTH OF THE METROPOLIS

▨ *1914*   ☐ *Today*

Gateway to America
Almost five times as crowded as the rest of New York, the Lower East Side was the most densely populated place in the world.

Crowded Conditions
Tenements were unhealthy and overcrowded. They often lacked windows, air shafts or proper sanitary facilities.

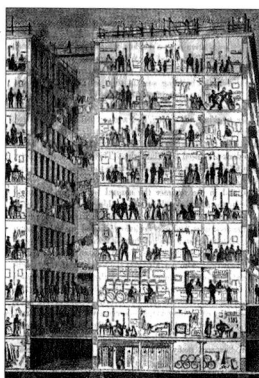

WHERE TO SEE TURN-OF-THE-CENTURY NEW YORK

The Lower East Side Tenement Museum (*see p97*) has exhibits on tenement life.

Tailor's scissors

Hip bath

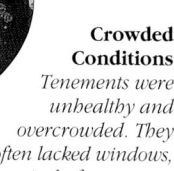

Inside a Sweatshop
Workers toiled long hours for low wages in the overcrowded sweatshops of the garment district. This view of Moe Levy's shop was taken in 1912.

Streetcars on Broadway

TIMELINE

1895 Olympia Theater is first to open in the Broadway area

1898 Five boroughs merge to form world's second-largest city

1901 Macy's opens Broadway department store

1895

1896 First bagel served in a Clinton Street bakery

1897 Waldorf-Astoria Hotel opens: the largest hotel in the world

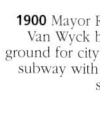

1900

1900 Mayor Robert Van Wyck breaks ground for city's first subway with silver shovel

1903 Lyceum Theater opens – oldest Broadway house still in use

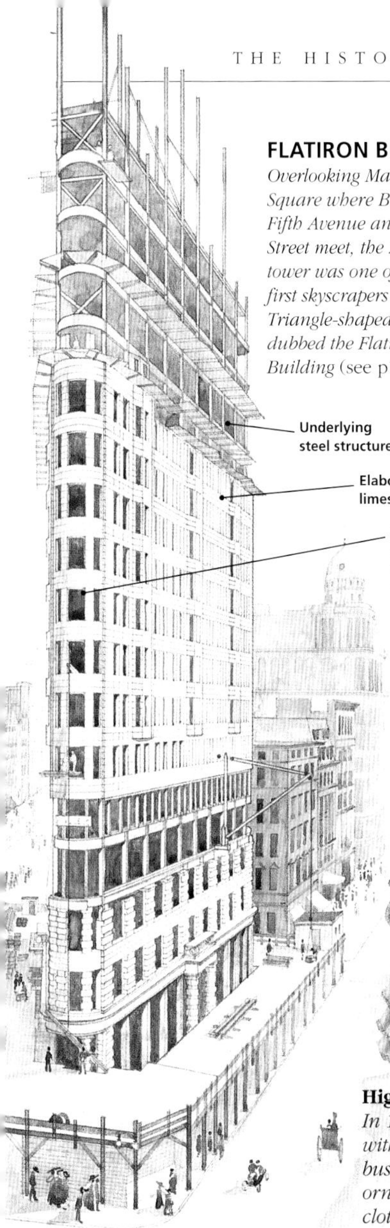

FLATIRON BUILDING

Overlooking Madison Square where Broadway, Fifth Avenue and 23rd Street meet, the 21-story tower was one of the city's first skyscrapers (1902). Triangle-shaped, it was dubbed the Flatiron Building (see p127).

Underlying steel structure

Elaborate limestone facade

Only 6 ft (185 cm) wide at apex of triangle

Supper in the Saddle

Decadent parties were all the rage. C.K.G. Billings's horseback dinner at Sherry's restaurant in 1903 was the talk of all New York.

Plaza Promenade

The section of Fifth Avenue in front of the Plaza Hotel was considered the most elegant in the city.

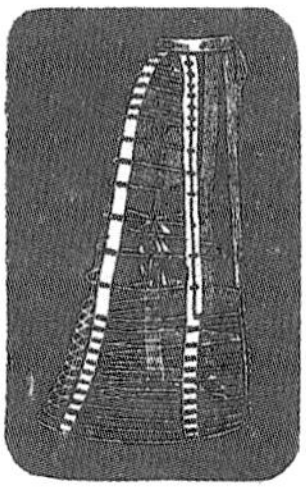

Ventilated hairpiece

High Fashion

In 1900 styles were stiff, with wire hoops and bustles worn beneath ornate dresses. Later, clothes became softer and more practical.

Long bustle

Wire hoops

1906 Architect Stanford White shot at Madison Square Garden, which he had built in 1890

1909 Wilbur Wright flies first plane over New York

1910 Pennsylvania Station opens

1913 Woolworth Building is world's tallest; new Grand Central Terminal opens; Harlem's Apollo Theater opens

1905

1910

1905 First crossing of the Staten Island Ferry

1907 First metered taxicabs; first Ziegfeld Follies

1911 Triangle Shirtwaist Factory fire kills 146 sweatshop workers; New York Public Library completed

Woolworth Building

New York Between the Wars

Entrance card to the Cotton Club

The 1920s were a time of high living for many New Yorkers. Mayor Jimmy Walker set the pace, whether squiring chorus girls, drinking in speakeasies or watching the Yankees. But the good times ended with the 1929 stock market crash. By 1932, Walker had resigned, charged with corruption, and one-quarter of New Yorkers were unemployed. With Mayor Fiorello La Guardia's 1933 election, New York began to recover and thrive.

GROWTH OF THE METROPOLIS

▨ 1933   ▢ Today

Exotic Costumes
Chorus girls were a major Cotton Club attraction.

THE COTTON CLUB
This Harlem nightclub was host to the best jazz in town, as first Duke Ellington and then Cab Calloway led the band. People flocked from all over the city to hear them.

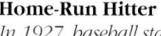

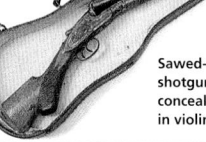

Defying Prohibition
Although alcohol was outlawed, speakeasies – semi-secret illegal drinking dens – still sold it.

Home-Run Hitter
In 1927, baseball star Babe Ruth hit a record 60 home runs for the Yankees. Yankee Stadium (see p241) became known as "the house that Ruth built."

Sawed-off shotgun concealed in violin case

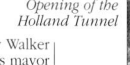

Gangsters
Dutch Schultz was the kingpin of an illegal booze racket.

TIMELINE

1918 End of World War I

1919 18th Amendment bans alcohol, launches Prohibition Era

1920 US women get the vote

Opening of the Holland Tunnel

1926 Jimmy Walker becomes mayor

1931 Empire State Building becomes world's tallest

| 1920 | 1925 | 1930 |

1924 Novelist James Baldwin is born in Harlem

1925 *The New Yorker* magazine is launched

1927 Lindbergh flies across the Atlantic; first talking movie, *The Jazz Singer,* opens; Holland Tunnel opens

1929 Stock market crash; Great Depression begins

1930 Chrysler Building completed

Big Band Leaders
Banned from many downtown clubs, black artists like Cab Calloway starred at the Cotton Club.

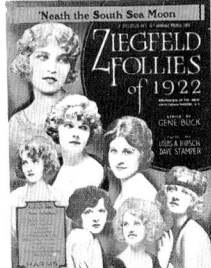

Broadway Melodies
The 1920s were the heyday of the Broadway musical, with a record number of plays opening.

THE GREAT DEPRESSION
The Roaring Twenties ended with the stock market crash of October 29, 1929, which set off the Depression. New York was hard hit: squatters' shacks sprang up in Central Park and thousands were out of work. But art flourished as artists went to work for the Works Projects Administration (WPA), creating outstanding murals and artworks throughout the city.

Waiting to receive benefits in 1931

Lindbergh's plane,
Spirit of St. Louis

Breakfast menu

Lindbergh's Flight
New Yorkers celebrated Lindbergh's nonstop solo flight across the Atlantic in 1927 in a variety of ways, including a breakfast in his honor.

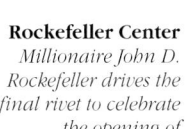

Rockefeller Center
Millionaire John D. Rockefeller drives the final rivet to celebrate the opening of Rockefeller Center on May 1, 1939.

Mass Event
Forty-five million people visited the 1939 World's Fair in New York.

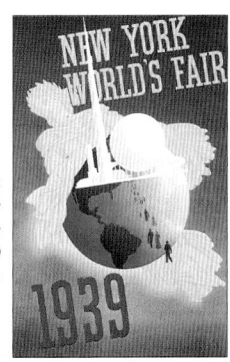

1933 Prohibition ends; Fiorello LaGuardia begins three terms as mayor

1935

1936 Parks Department headed by Robert Moses; new parks created

1939 Rockefeller Center is completed

1940 Queens-Midtown Tunnel opens

1940

1941 US enters World War II

1942 Times Square blacked out during World War II; Idlewild International Airport (now JFK) opens

1945

1944 Black leader Adam Clayton Powell elected to Congress

Postwar New York

Since World War II, New York has seen both the best of times and the worst. Although established as the financial capital of the world, the city itself almost went bankrupt in the 1970s. In 2008 the collapse of the Wall Street bank Lehman Brothers precipitated the worst financial crisis since 1929. Since the early 1990s, New York has seen a dramatic drop in the crime rate and an increase in the restoration of such landmarks as Grand Central Terminal and the "new" Times Square. This constant rebuilding is emblematic of the city's position as the cultural and financial hub of the United States.

1967 Hippie musical *Hair* opens on Off-Broadway, then transfers to the Biltmore Theater

1971 Pop artist Andy Warhol has a retrospective show of his work at the Whitney Museum

1975 Federal loan saves New York from bankruptcy

1953 Merce Cunningham founds dance company

1945 End of World War II

1954 Ellis Island closes

1966 Newspaper and transit strikes

1981 New York regains solvency

1946 UN headquarters established in New York

1959 Guggenheim Museum opens

1945	1950	1955	1960	1965	1970	1975	198
MAYORS:	IMPELLITERI	WAGNER		LINDSAY		BEAME	KOCH
1945	1950	1955	1960	1965	1970	1975	198

1947 Jackie Robinson, first black baseball player in the major leagues, signs with Brooklyn Dodgers

1963 Pennsylvania Station razed

1973 World Trade Center completed

1964 New York World's Fair; race riots in Harlem and Bedford-Stuyvesant; Verrazano Narrows Bridge links Brooklyn and Staten Island; Beatles play at Shea Stadium

Souvenir scarf

1968 20,000 anti-establishment hippies gather in Central Park; student sit-ins at Columbia University

Andy Warhol with actresses Candy Darling and Ultra Violet

1983 Economic boom: property prices skyrocket; Trump Tower completed by real estate tycoon Donald Trump, who symbolizes the "yuppie" wealth of the 1980s

1988 Twenty-five percent of New Yorkers live below the poverty line

1990 David Dinkins, New York's first black mayor, takes office; Ellis Island reopens as an immigration museum

2001 Terrorist attack on the World Trade Center; Mayor Giuliani is a great support to the people of New York. President George W Bush declares war on terrorism

1987 Stock market crash

1994 Rudolph Giuliani takes office as mayor

2003 A major power outage on August 14 leaves 50 million people in the North East (including New York City), mid-West, and ports of Canada, blacked out for up to 24 hours

1985	1990	1995	2000	2005	2010	2015

DINKINS   GIULIANI   BLOOMBERG

1985	1990	1995	2000	2005	2010	2015

2000 Population reaches just over 8 million

2009 US Airways flight 1549 crash-lands in the Hudson River. All 155 passengers survive

2013 Planned opening of 1 World Trade Center (formerly Freedom Tower)

1986 Shock of corruption scandals rock Mayor Koch's administration; Centennial of Statue of Liberty

2002 The lights go on in a regenerated 42nd Street, which crosses Broadway at Times Square. Along with neighboring Chelsea and its cutting-edge galleries, the area out-shines SoHo as the city's chic spot

1995 The neglected Chelsea Piers are renovated and open as a mammoth sports and entertainment complex (see p138)

NEW YORK AT A GLANCE

There are almost 300 places of interest described in the Area by Area section of this book. They range from the bustling New York Stock Exchange *(see pp70–71)* to Central Park's peaceful Strawberry Fields *(see p208)*, and from historic synagogues to dazzling skyscrapers. The following 14 pages provide a time-saving guide to New York's most interesting sights. Museums and architecture each have a section, and there are guides to the people and cultures that have given the city its unique character. Each sight is cross-referenced to its own full entry. Below are the top ten tourist attractions to start you off.

NEW YORK'S TOP TEN   TOURIST ATTRACTIONS

Ellis Island
See pp78–9.

Empire State Building
See pp136–7.

South Street Seaport
See pp82–4.

Rockefeller Center
See p144.

Museum of Modern Art
See pp172–5.

Central Park
See pp204–9.

Metropolitan Museum of Art
See pp190–97.

Statue of Liberty
See pp74–5.

Brooklyn Bridge
See pp86–9.

Chinatown
See pp96–7.

◁ Park Avenue's relentless flow of traffic

New York's Best: Museums

New York's museums range from the vast
scope of the Metropolitan Museum to the personal
treasures of financier J. Pierpont Morgan's own
collection. Several museums celebrate New York's
heritage, giving visitors an insight into the people
and events that made the city what it is today.
This map features some highlights, with a
detailed overview on pages 38 and 39.

Museum of Modern Art
Picasso's Goat (1950) is
among the impressive
collection in the
renovated and
expanded
Museum of
Modern
Art.

***Intrepid* Sea-Air-
Space Museum**
*This naval museum
also traces the
progress of
flight explo-
ration. The large air-
craft carrier housing the
museum returned to Pier 86
in late 2008 after renovation.*

**Morgan Library
& Museum**
*One of the world's
finest collections of
manuscripts, prints
and books includes
this rare French
Bible from 1230.*

**Merchant's
House
Museum**
*This perfectly
preserved
1832 house
belonged to
a wealthy
trader.*

Ellis Island
*This museum vividly re-
creates the experiences
of many millions of
immigrant families.*

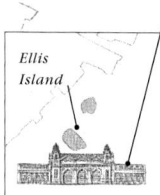

*Ellis
Island*

Theater
District

Chelsea
and the
Garment
District

Lower
Midtown

Gramercy
and the
Flatiron
District

Greenwich
Village

SoHo and
TriBeCa

East
Village

Lower East
Side

Lower
Manhattan

Seaport
and the
Civic
Center

Upper
West Side

0 kilometers   2

0 miles   1

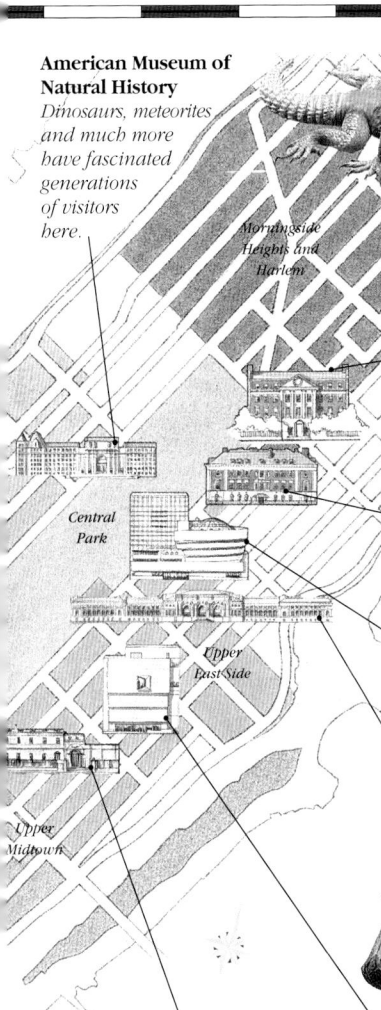

American Museum of Natural History
Dinosaurs, meteorites and much more have fascinated generations of visitors here.

Morningside Heights and Harlem

Central Park

Upper East Side

Upper Midtown

Museum of the City of New York
Costumes, works of art and household objects (such as this 1725 silver dish) create an intricate and detailed picture of New York's past.

Cooper-Hewitt Museum
A wealth of decorative arts is displayed in industrialist Andrew Carnegie's former Upper East Side mansion.

Solomon R. Guggenheim Museum
Painting and sculpture by almost all major avant-garde artists of the late 19th and 20th centuries fill Frank Lloyd Wright's stunningly renovated building.

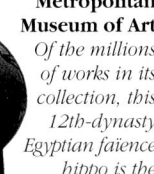

Metropolitan Museum of Art
Of the millions of works in its collection, this 12th-dynasty Egyptian faïence hippo is the museum's own mascot.

Frick Collection
The collection of 19th-century railroad magnate Henry Clay Frick is displayed in his former home. Masterpieces include St. Francis in the Desert *(about 1480) by Giovanni Bellini.*

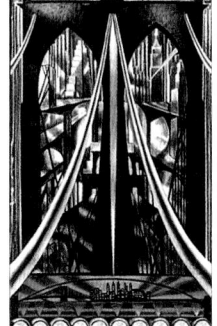

Whitney Museum of American Art
This exceptional collection includes many views of New York. One of the best is Brooklyn Bridge: Variation on an Old Theme *(1939), by Joseph Stella.*

Exploring New York's Museums

Richmond Town tobacco tin

You could devote an entire month to New York's museums and still not do them justice. There are more than 60 museums in Manhattan alone, and half as many again in the other boroughs. The wealth of art and the huge variety of offerings – from Old Masters to old fire engines, dinosaurs to dolls, Tibetan tapestries to African masks – is equal to that of any city in the world. Some museums close on Monday, as well as on another day. Many stay open late one or two evenings a week, and some have one evening when entry is free. Most museums charge for admission; for some, this is a suggested donation rather than a mandatory fee.

PAINTING AND SCULPTURE

New York is best known for its art museums. The **Metropolitan Museum of Art** houses an extensive collection of American art, as well as world-famous masterpieces. **The Cloisters**, a branch of the "Met" in Upper Manhattan, is a treasury of medieval art and architecture. The **Frick Collection** has a superb display of Old Masters. In contrast, the **Museum of Modern Art (MoMA)** houses Impressionist and modern paintings. **The Whitney Museum of American Art** and the **Solomon R. Guggenheim Museum** also specialize in modern art, the Whitney's biennial show being the foremost display of work by living artists. Today's cutting-edge art is at the **New Museum of Contemporary Art**, while the work of craft artists can be seen at the **American Folk Art Museum**. The **National Academy Museum** displays a collection of 19th- and 20th-century art, donated by academy members. In Harlem, the **Studio Museum** shows the work of black artists.

CRAFTS AND DESIGN

If you are interested in textiles, porcelain and glass, embroideries and laces, wallpaper, and prints, visit the **Cooper-Hewitt Museum**, the decorative arts outpost of Washington's Smithsonian Institution. The design collections at **MoMA** trace the history of design from clocks to couches. The **Museum of Arts and Design** offers the finest work of today's skilled artisans in mediums from furniture to pottery, and the **American Folk Art Museum** presents folk forms, from quilts to canes. Silver collections are notable at the **Museum of the City of New York**. The fine displays of native art at the **National Museum of the American Indian** include jewelry, rugs and pottery.

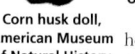

Corn husk doll, American Museum of Natural History

PRINTS AND PHOTOGRAPHY

The **International Center of Photography** is the only museum in New York that is totally devoted to this medium. Collections can also be seen at the **Metropolitan Museum of Art** and **MoMA**, and there are many examples of early photography at the **Museum of the City of New York** and **Ellis Island**.

Prints and drawings by such great book illustrators as Kate Greenaway and Sir John Tenniel are featured at the **Morgan Library & Museum**. The **Cooper-Hewitt Museum** has examples of the use of prints in the decorative arts.

FURNITURE AND COSTUMES

The annual exhibition of the Costume Institute at the **Metropolitan Museum of Art** is always worth a visit. Also impressive is the American Wing, with its 24 rooms of original furnishings tracing life from 1640 to the 20th century. Period rooms depicting New York in various settings, beginning with the 17th-century Dutch, are on display at the **Museum of the City of New York**. There are also some house museums that give a realistic picture of life and furnishings in old New York. The **Merchant's House Museum**, a preserved residence from 1832, was occupied by the same family for 98 years. **Gracie Mansion** was the residence of mayor Archibald Gracie, who bought it in 1798 from a shipping merchant, and it is open periodically for public tours. The **Theodore Roosevelt Birthplace** is the brownstone where the 26th president of the United States grew up, and the **Mount Vernon Hotel Museum** was an early 19th-century resort.

The Peaceable Kingdom (c.1840–45) by Edward Hicks, at the Brooklyn Museum

HISTORY

Palm pistol at the New York City Police Museum

American history unfolds at **Federal Hall**, the United States' first capitol, where George Washington took his oath as America's first president on the balcony in April 1789.

Visit the **Fraunces Tavern Museum** for a glimpse of colonial New York. **Ellis Island** and **Lower East Side Tenement Museum** re-create the hardships faced by immigrants. The **Museum of Jewish Heritage** in Battery City is a living memorial to the Holocaust. The **New York City Fire Museum** and the **New York City Police Museum** chronicle heroism and tragedy, while the **South Street Seaport Museum** re-creates early maritime history.

TECHNOLOGY AND NATURAL HISTORY

Forest-dwelling bonga, American Museum of Natural History

Science museums hold exhibitions from nature to space-age technology. The **American Museum of Natural History** has vast collections covering flora, fauna and cultures from around the world. Its Rose Center/Hayden Planetarium offers a unique view of space. The *Intrepid* **Sea-Air-Space Museum** is a repository of technology that chronicles military progress. It is based on the decks of an aircraft carrier.

If you missed a classic Lucille Ball sitcom or footage of the first man on the moon, the place to visit is the **The Paley Center for Media**, which holds these and many other classics of TV and radio.

ART FROM OTHER CULTURES

Egyptian mummy, Brooklyn Museum

Artwork of other nations is the focus of several special collections. Oriental art is the specialty of the **Asia Society** and the **Japan Society**. The **Jewish Museum** features major collections of Judaica and has changing exhibitions of various aspects of Jewish life. **El Museo del Barrio** is dedicated to the arts of Puerto Rico, including many Pre-Columbian Taino artifacts. For an impressive review of African-American art and history, visit the **Schomburg Center for Research in Black Culture**. Finally, the **Metropolitan Museum of Art** excels in its multicultural displays, ranging from the art of ancient Egypt to that of contemporary Africa.

LIBRARIES

New York's notable libraries, such as the **Morgan Library & Museum**, offer superb art collections as well as a chance to view pages from ancient manuscripts and rare books. The **New York Public Library**'s collection includes historic documents and manuscripts of many famous works.

BEYOND MANHATTAN

Other museums worth a visit include the **Brooklyn Museum of Art**, with a huge collection of artifacts from across the world and over one million paintings. The **Museum of the Moving Image** in Queens has a unique collection of motion-picture history. The **Jacques Marchais Museum of Tibetan Art** is a rare find on Staten Island as is **Historic Richmond Town**, a well-restored village dating from the 1600s.

FINDING THE MUSEUMS

New York's Best: Architecture

Even when following world trends, New York has given its own twist to the turns of architectural fashion, the style of its buildings influenced by both geography and economy. An island city, with space at a premium, must look upward to grow. This trend was reflected early on with tall, narrow town

houses and later with the city's apartment buildings and sky-scrapers. Building materials such as cast-iron and brownstone were chosen for their local availability and practical appeal. The result is a city that has developed by finding flamboyant answers to practical needs. A more detailed overview of New York's architecture is on pages 42–3.

Cast-Iron Architecture
Mass-produced cast iron was often used for building facades. SoHo has many of the best examples, such as this building at 28–30 Greene Street.

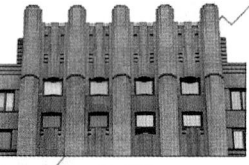

Apartment Buildings
The Majestic is one of five Art Deco twin-towered apartment buildings on Central Park West.

Theater District

Chelsea and the Garment District

Greenwich Village

Gramercy and the Flatiron District

SoHo and TriBeCa

East Village

Lower East Side

Lower Manhattan

Post-Modernism
The quirky, yet elegant, shapes of buildings like the World Financial Center, built in 1985 (see p69) mark a bold departure from the sleek steel-and-glass boxes of the 1950s and 1960s.

Brownstones
Built from local sand-stone, brownstones were favored by the 19th-century middle classes. India House, built in a Florentine palazzo style on Wall Street, is typical of many brownstone commercial buildings.

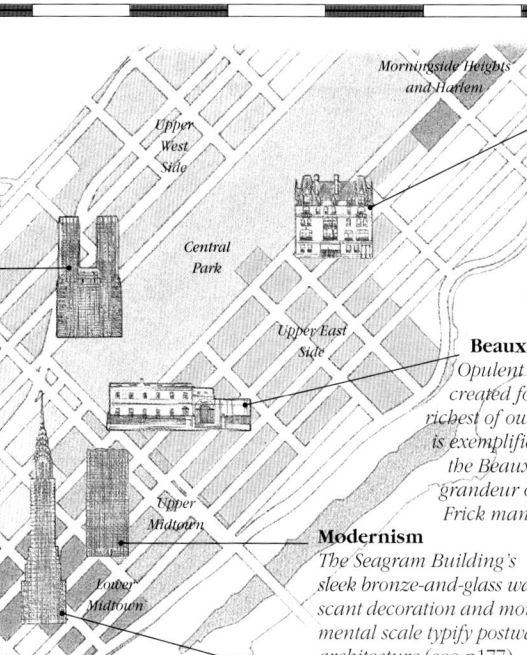

Morningside Heights
and Harlem

Upper
West
Side

Central
Park

Upper East
Side

Upper
Midtown

Lower
Midtown

E A S T R I V E R

0 kilometers   2

0 miles   1

19th-Century Mansions

The Jewish Museum (see p186), formerly the home of Felix M. Warburg, is a fine example of the French Renaissance style that typified these mansions.

Beaux Arts

Opulent style, created for the richest of owners, is exemplified by the Beaux Arts grandeur of the Frick mansion.

Modernism

The Seagram Building's sleek bronze-and-glass walls, scant decoration and monumental scale typify postwar architecture (see p177).

The Skyscraper

The glory of New York architecture, these buildings expressed a perfect blend of practical engineering skill and fabulous decoration, such as this gargoyle on the Chrysler Building.

Federal Architecture

Federal style was popular in civic architecture of the 19th century; City Hall combines it with French Renaissance influences.

Tenements

Constructed as an economic form of housing, for many these buildings were a stark introduction to new lives. Mainly built on the Lower East Side, the apartments were hopelessly overcrowded. In addition, the buildings' design, with inadequate air shafts, resulted in apartments with little or no ventilation.

Exploring New York's Architecture

A Federal-style front door

During its first 200 years, New York, like all of America, looked to Europe for architectural inspiration. None of the buildings from the Dutch colonial period survive in Manhattan today; most were lost in the great fire of 1776 or torn down to make way for new developments in the early 1800s. Throughout the 18th and 19th centuries, the city's major architectural trends followed those of Europe. With the advent of cast-iron architecture in the 1850s, the Art Deco period and the ever-higher rise of the skyscraper, New York's architecture came into its own.

FEDERAL ARCHITECTURE

This American adaptation of the Neoclassical Adam style flowered in the early decades of the new nation, featuring square buildings two or three stories tall, with low hipped roofs, balustrades and decorative elements – all carefully balanced. **City Hall** (1811, John McComb, Jr. and Joseph François Mangin) is a blend of Federal and French Renaissance influences. The restored warehouses of **Schermerhorn Row** (c. 1812) in the Seaport district are also in Federal style.

BROWNSTONES

Plentiful and cheap, the brown sandstone found in the nearby Connecticut River Valley and along the banks of the Hackensack River in New

A typical brownstone with stoop leading up to the main entrance

Jersey was the most common building material in the 1800s. It is found all over the city's residential neighborhoods, used for small homes or small apartments – some of the best examples of brownstone can be found in **Chelsea**. Because street space was limited, these buildings were very narrow in width, but also very deep. A typical brownstone has a flight of steps, called a stoop, leading up to the living floors. Separate stairs lead down to the basement, which was originally the servants' quarters.

TENEMENTS

Tenements were built to house the huge influx of immigrants who arrived from the 1840s up to World War I. The six-story blocks, 100 ft (30 m) long and 25 ft (8 m) wide, offered very little light and air except from tiny side-wall air shafts and windows at each end, leaving the middle rooms in darkness. The tiny apartments were called railroad flats after their similarity to railroad cars. Later designs had air shafts between buildings, but these helped the spread of fire. The **Lower East Side Tenement Museum** has scale models of the old tenements.

CAST-IRON ARCHITECTURE

An American architectural innovation of the 19th century, cast iron was cheaper than stone or brick and allowed ornate features to be prefabricated in foundries from molds and used as building facades. Today, New York has the world's largest concentration of full and partial cast-iron facades. The best, built in the 1870s, are in the **SoHo Cast-Iron Historic District**.

The original cast-iron facade of 72–76 Greene Street, SoHo

BEAUX ARTS

This French school of architecture dominated the design of public buildings and wealthy residential properties during New York's gilded age. This era (from 1880 to about 1920) produced many of the city's most prominent architects, including Richard Morris Hunt (**Carnegie Hall**, 1891; **Metropolitan Museum of Art**, 1895), who in 1845 was the first American architect to study in Paris; Cass Gilbert (**Custom House**, 1907; **New York Life Insurance**

ARCHITECTURAL DISGUISES

Some of the most fanciful forms on the New York skyline were devised by clever architects to disguise the city's essential but utilitarian – and rather unattractive – rooftop water tanks. Look skyward to discover the ornate cupolas, spires and domes that transform the most mundane of features into veritable castles in the air. Examples that are easy to spot are atop two neighboring Fifth Avenue hotels: the Sherry Netherland at 60th Street and the Pierre at 61st Street.

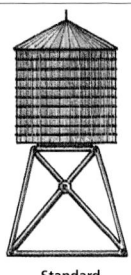

Standard water tower

The Dakota Apartments, built in 1884, on the Upper West Side across from Central Park

buildings resembled castles and châteaux, and were built around courtyards not visible from the street. Favorite landmarks are the five **Twin Towers** on Central Park West, the San Remo, Eldorado, Century, the Beresford, and the Majestic. Built during the peak of Art Deco (1929 to 1931), they create the distinctive skyline seen from the park.

Building, 1928; the **US Courthouse**, 1936); the teams of Warren & Wetmore (**Grand Central Terminal**, 1913; **Helmsley Building**, 1929); Carrère & Hastings (**New York Public Library**, 1911; **Frick Mansion**, 1914); and McKim, Mead & White, the city's most famous firm of architects (**Villard Houses**, 1884; **United States General Post Office**, 1913; **Municipal Building**, 1914).

APARTMENT BUILDINGS

As the city's population grew and space became ever more precious, family homes in Manhattan became much too expensive for most New Yorkers, and even the wealthy joined the trend toward communal living. In 1884 Henry Hardenbergh's Dakota *(see p218)*, one of the first luxury apartment buildings, started a spate of turn-of-the-century construction on the Upper West Side. Many of the

SKYSCRAPERS

Although Chicago gave birth to the skyscraper, New York has seen some of the greatest innovations. In 1902 Daniel Burnham, a Chicago architect, built the **Flatiron Building**, so tall at 300 ft (91 m) that skeptics said it would collapse. By 1913, the **Woolworth Building** had risen to 792 ft (241 m). Soon, zoning laws were passed requiring "setbacks" – upper stories were stepped back to allow light to reach street level. This suited the Art Deco style. The **Chrysler Building** (1930) was the world's tallest until the

Art Deco arched pattern on the spire of the Chrysler Building

Empire State Building (1931) was completed. Both are Art Deco classics, but it was Raymond Hood's **Group Health Insurance Building**, formerly the McGraw-Hill Building, that represented New York in 1932 in the *International Style* architectural survey.

The World Trade Center *(see p72)* was New York's tallest building until September 2001 *(see p54)*. It represented the "glass box" Modernist style, now superseded by the Post-Modern style, such as the **Citigroup Center** (1977).

WHERE TO FIND THE BUILDINGS

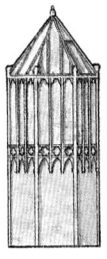

245 Fifth Avenue (Apartment Building)

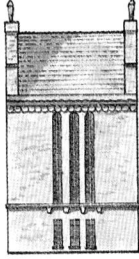

60 Gramercy Park North (Brownstone)

The Pierre (Beaux Arts)

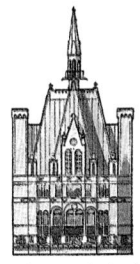

Sherry Netherland Hotel (Beaux Arts)

Multicultural New York

Wherever you go in New York, even in pockets of the hectic high-rise city center, you will find evidence of the richly ethnic flavor of the city. A bus ride can take you from Madras to Moscow, Hong Kong to Haiti. Immigrants are still coming to New York, though numbers are fewer than in the peak years from 1880 to 1910, when 17 million people arrived. In the 1980s, a million newcomers, largely from Caribbean countries and Asia, arrived and found their own special corner of the city. Throughout the year you will encounter crowds celebrating one of many festivals. To find out more about national celebrations and parades, see pages 50 to 53.

Hell's Kitchen
For a while called "Clinton" to reflect a new neighborhood mix, this was the first home of early Irish immigrants.

Little Ukraine
Services are held at T. Shevchenko Place as part of the May 17 festivities to mark the Ukrainians' conversion to Christianity.

Little Korea
Not far from Herald Square is a small Korean enclave with a variety of restaurants.

Little Italy
For ten days in September, the Italian community gathers around the Mulberry Street area, and the streets are taken over by the celebrations of the Festa di San Gennaro.

Theater District

Chelsea and the Garment District

Gramercy and the Flatiron District

Greenwich Village

SoHo and TriBeCa

East Village

Chinatown
Every year, in January or February, Mott Street is packed as residents celebrate the Chinese New Year.

Seaport and the Civic Center

Lower East Side

Lower Manhattan

The Lower East Side
The synagogues around Rivington and Eldridge streets reflect the religious traditions of this old Jewish area.

0 kilometers   2

0 miles   1

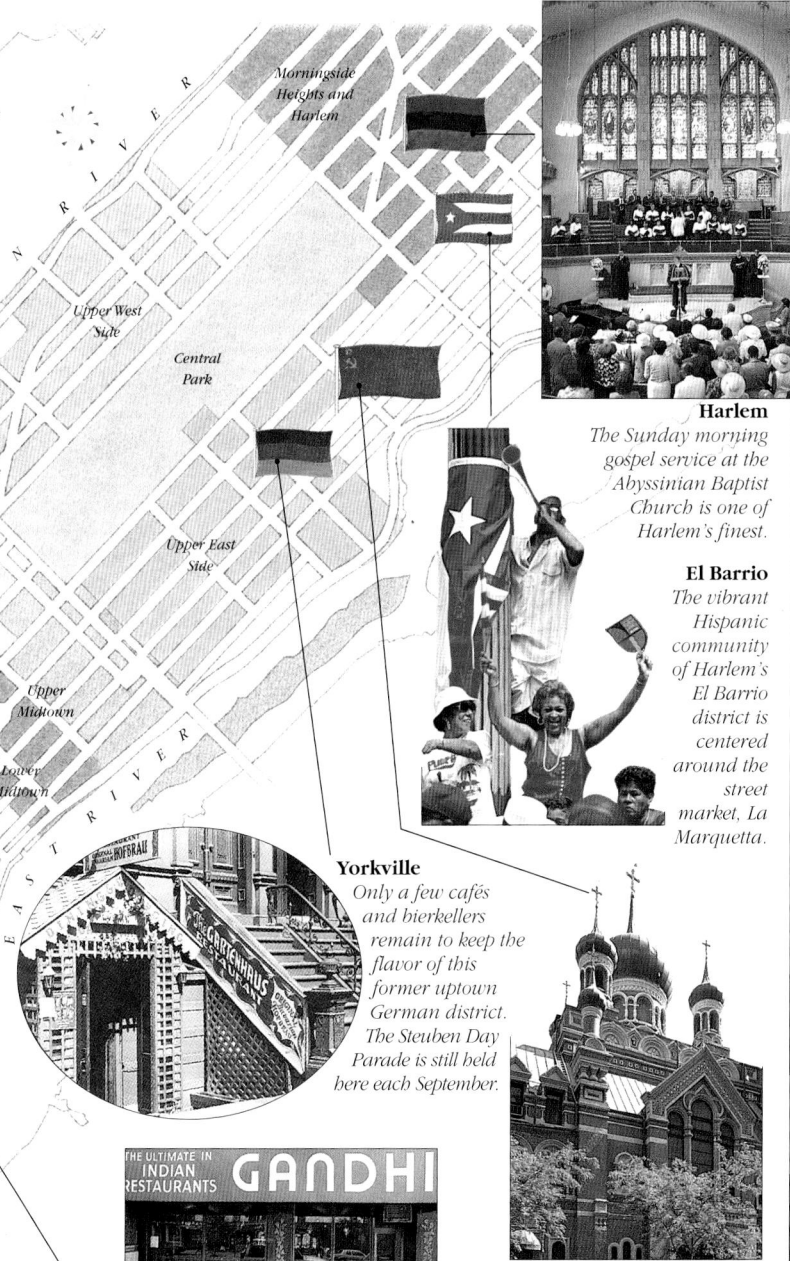

Harlem
The Sunday morning gospel service at the Abyssinian Baptist Church is one of Harlem's finest.

El Barrio
The vibrant Hispanic community of Harlem's El Barrio district is centered around the street market, La Marquetta.

Yorkville
Only a few cafés and bierkellers remain to keep the flavor of this former uptown German district. The Steuben Day Parade is still held here each September.

Upper East Side
The magnificent St. Nicholas Russian Orthodox Cathedral on East 97th Street is a reminder of the dispersed White Russian community. Mass is held in Russian each Sunday.

Little India
The restaurants of East 6th Street offer Eastern atmosphere at affordable prices.

Exploring New York's Many Cultures

Stained glass at the Cotton Club

Even "native" New Yorkers have ancestral roots in other countries. Throughout the 17th century, the Dutch and English settled here, establishing trade colonies in the New World. Soon America became a symbol of hope for the downtrodden elsewhere in Europe. Many flocked across the ocean, some penniless and with little knowledge of the language. The potato famine of the 1840s led to the first wave of Irish immigrants, followed by German and other European workers displaced by political unrest and the Industrial Revolution. Immigrants continue to enrich New York in countless ways, and today an estimated 100 languages are spoken.

the 1940s, they were the city's fastest-growing and most upwardly mobile ethnic group, extending the old boundaries of Chinatown and establishing new neighborhoods in parts of Brooklyn and Queens. Once a closed community, Chinatown now bustles with tourists exploring the streets and markets, and sampling the creative cuisine.

THE HISPANIC AMERICANS

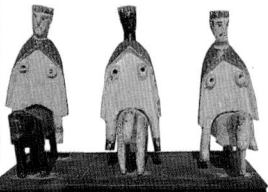

Hispanic religious carving at El Museo del Barrio *(see p231)*

Puerto Ricans were in New York as early as 1838, but it was not until after World War II that they arrived in large numbers in search of work. Most live in El Barrio, formerly known as Spanish Harlem. Professionals who fled Fidel Castro's Cuba have moved out of the city itself but are still influential in Hispanic commerce and culture. Parts of Washington Heights have large Dominican and Colombian communities.

THE IRISH

The Irish, who first arrived in New York in the 1840s, had to overcome harsh odds. Starving and with barely a penny to their names, they labored hard to escape the slums of Five Points and Hell's Kitchen, helping to build the modern city in the process. Many joined the police and fire-fighting forces, rising to high rank through dedication to duty. Others set up successful businesses, such as the Irish bars that act as a focus for the now-scattered New York Irish community.

Turkish immigrants arriving at former Idlewild Airport in 1963

THE JEWS

There has been a Jewish community in New York since 1654. The city's first synagogue, Shearith Israel, was established by refugees from a Dutch colony in Brazil and is still active today. These first settlers, Sephardic Jews of Spanish descent, included such prominent families as the Baruchs. They were followed by the German Jews, who set up successful retailing enterprises, like the Straus brothers at Macy's. Russian persecution led to the mass immigration that began in the late 1800s. By the start of World War I, 600,000 Jews were living on the Lower East Side. Today, this area is more Hispanic and Asian than Jewish, but it holds reminders of its role as a place of refuge and new beginnings.

THE GERMANS

The Germans began to settle in New York in the 18th century. From John Peter Zenger onward *(see p21)*, the city's German community has championed the freedom to express ideas and opinions. It has also produced giants of industry, such as John Jacob Astor, the city's first millionaire.

THE ITALIANS

Italians first came to New York in the 1830s and 1840s. Many came from northern Italy to escape the failing revolution at home. In the 1870s, poverty in southern Italy drove many more Italians across the ocean. In time, Italians became a potent political force in the city, exemplified by Fiorello La Guardia, one of New York's finest mayors.

THE CHINESE

The Chinese were late arrivals to New York. In 1880, the population of the Mott Street district was a mere 700. By

Eastern States Buddhist Temple, in central Chinatown *(see pp96–7)*

THE AFRICAN AMERICANS

Perhaps the best-known black inner-city community in the Western world, Harlem is noted for the Harlem Renaissance of writing *(see pp30–31)* as much as it is for great entertainment, gospel music and soul food. The move of black African Americans from the South to the North began with emancipation in the 1860s and increased markedly in the 1920s, when Harlem's black population rose from 83,000 to 204,000. Today Harlem is undergoing revitalization in many areas. The African American population has also dispersed throughout the city.

THE MELTING POT

Other New York cultures are not distinctly defined but are still easily found. Ukrainians gather in the East Village, around St. George's Ukrainian Catholic Church on East 7th Street. Little India can be spotted by the restaurants along East 6th Street. Koreans own many of the small grocery stores in Manhattan, but most tend to live in the Flushing area of Queens. The religious diversity of New York can be seen in the Islamic Center on Riverside Drive; the

A woman celebrating at the Greek Independence Day parade

Islamic Cultural Center on 96th Street – Manhattan's first major mosque; and the Russian Orthodox Cathedral on East 97th Street *(see p199).*

THE OUTER BOROUGHS

Brooklyn is by far the most international borough of New York. Caribbean newcomers from Jamaica and Haiti are

The New York police, a haven for Irish Americans

one of the fastest-growing immigrant groups. West Indians tend to cluster along Eastern Parkway between Grand Army Plaza and Utica Avenue, the route of the lavish, exotically costumed West Indian Day Parade in September. Recently arrived Russian Jewish immigrants have turned Brighton Beach into "Little Odessa by the Sea," and the Scandinavians and Lebanese have settled in Bay Ridge and the Finns in Sunset Park. Borough Park and Williamsburg are home to Orthodox Jews, and Midwood has an Israeli-Middle East accent. Italians live in the Bensonhurst area. Greenpoint is little Poland, and Atlantic Avenue is home to the largest Arab community in America.

The Irish were among the earliest groups to cross the Harlem River into the Bronx. Japanese executives favor the more exclusive Riverdale area. One of the most distinctive ethnic areas is Astoria, Queens, which has the largest Greek population outside the motherland. Jackson Heights is home to a large Latin American quarter, including 300,000 Colombians. Indians also favor this area and neighboring Flushing. But it is the Asians who have transformed Flushing, so much so that the local train is popularly known as "The Orient Express."

NEWCOMERS WHO MADE THEIR MARK *see also pp48–9.*

The dates mark the year these immigrants entered the US via New York.

- **1893** Irving Berlin (Russia), musician
- **1894** Al Jolson (Lithuania), singer
- **1896** Samuel Goldwyn (Poland), movie mogul
- **1902** Joe Hill (Sweden), labor activist
- **1903** Frank Capra (Italy), film director
- **1904** Hyman Rickover (Russia), developer of nuclear submarine
- **1906** "Lucky" Luciano (Italy), gangster (deported 1946)
- **1908** Bob Hope (England), comedian
- **1909** Lee Strasberg (Austria), theater director
- **1912** Claudette Colbert (France), film star
- **1913** Rudolph Valentino (Italy), film star
- **1921** Bela Lugosi (Hungary), star of *Dracula*
- **1923** Isaac Asimov (Russia), scientist and writer
- **1932** George Balanchine (Russia), ballet choreographer
- **1933** Albert Einstein (Germany), scientist
- **1938** von Trapp family (Austria), singers

1890	1895	1900	1905	1910	1915	1920	1925	1930	1935	1940

Remarkable New Yorkers

New York has nourished some of the best creative talents since the beginning of the 20th century. Pop Art began here, and Manhattan is still the world center for modern art. The alternative writers of the 1950s and '60s – known as the Beat Generation – took inspiration from the city's jazz clubs. And as it is the financial capital, many leading world financiers have made New York their home.

WRITERS

Novelist James Baldwin

Much great American literature was created in New York. *Charlotte Temple, A Tale of Truth,* first published in 1791 by Susanna Rowson (c. 1762–1824), was a tale of seduction in the city and a best-seller for 50 years.

America's first professional author was Charles Brockden Brown (1771–1810), who came to New York in 1791. The novels of Edgar Allan Poe (1809–49), the pioneer of the modern detective story, expanded the thriller genre. Henry James (1843–1916) published *The Bostonians* (1886) and became the master of the psychological novel, and his friend Edith Wharton (1861–1937) became known for her satirical novels about American society.

American literature finally won international recognition with Washington Irving's (1783–1859) satire, *A History of New York* (1809). It earned him $2,000. Irving coined the names "Gotham" for New York and "Knickerbockers" for New Yorkers. He and James Fenimore Cooper (1789–1851), whose books gave birth to the "Western" novel, formed the Knicker-

bocker group of US writers. Greenwich Village has always attracted writers, including Herman Melville (1819–91) whose masterpiece, *Moby Dick* (1851), was very poorly received at first. Jack Kerouac (1922–69), Allen Ginsberg, and William Burroughs all went to Colum- bia University and drank at the San Remo Café in Greenwich Village. Dylan Thomas (1914–53) lived at the Chelsea Hotel *(see p139).* Novelist Nathanael West (1902–40) worked in the Gramercy Park Hotel, and Dashiell Hammett (1894–1961) wrote *The Maltese Falcon* while living there. James Baldwin (1924–87), born in Harlem, wrote *Another Country* (1963) on his return to New York from Europe.

ARTISTS

The New York School of Abstract Expressionists founded the first influential American art movement. It was launched by Hans Hofmann (1880–1966) with Franz Kline and Willem de Kooning, whose first job in America was as a house- painter. Adolph Gottlieb, Mark Rothko (1903–70), and Jackson Pollock (1912–56) went on to popularize this style. Pollock, Kline and de Kooning all had their studios on the Lower East Side.

Pop Art began in New York in the 1960s with Roy Lichtenstein and

Pop artist Andy Warhol

Andy Warhol (1926–87), who made some of his cult films at 33 Union Square. Keith Haring (1958–90) was a very prolific graffiti artist who gained fame for his Pop Art murals and sculptures.

Robert Mapplethorpe (1946–89) acquired notoriety for his homoerotic photos of men. Jeff Koons was part of the Neo-Pop or Post-Pop movement of the 80s.

The illusionistic murals by Richard Haas enliven many walls throughout the city.

ACTORS

In 1849 the British actor Charles Macready started a riot by saying Americans were vulgar. A mob stormed the Astor Place Opera House, where Macready was playing Macbeth, police opened fire, and 22 rioters were killed.

In 1927 Mae West (1893–1980) spent 10 days in a workhouse on Roosevelt Island and was fined $500 for giving a lewd performance in her Broadway show *Sex.* Marc Blitzstein's radical pro-labor opera *The Cradle Will Rock* produced by Orson Welles (1915–85) and John Houseman (1902–88), was immediately banned and the show had to move to

Vaudeville actress Mae West

another theater. The actors managed to get around the ban by buying tickets and singing their roles from the audience.

The musical has been New York's special contribution to the theater. Florenz Ziegfeld's (1869–1932) *Follies* ran from 1907 to 1931. The opening of *Oklahoma!* on Broadway in 1943 began the age of musicals by the famous duo Richard Rodgers (1902–79) and Oscar Hammerstein, Jr. (1895–1960).

Off Broadway, the Provincetown Players at 33 MacDougal Street were the first to produce Eugene O'Neill's (1888–1953) *Beyond the Horizon* (1920). His successor as the major innovative force in US theater was Edward Albee, author of *Who's Afraid of Virginia Woolf?* (1962).

MUSICIANS AND DANCERS

Leonard Bernstein (1918–90) followed a long line of great conductors at the New York Philharmonic, including Bruno Walter (1876–1962), Arturo Toscanini (1867–1957) and Leopold Stokowski (1882–1977). Maria Callas (1923–77) was born in New York but moved to Europe.

Carnegie Hall *(see p148)* has featured Enrico Caruso (1873–1921), Bob Dylan and the Beatles. A record concert attendance was set in 1991 when Paul Simon drew a million people for his free concert in Central Park.

The legendary swinging jazz clubs of the 1930s and 1940s are now gone from 52nd Street. Plaques on "Jazz Walk" outside the CBS building honor such

Josephine Baker

famous performers as Charlie Parker (1920–55) and Josephine Baker (1906–75).

Between 1940 and 1965, New York became a world dance capital, with the establishment of George Balanchine's (1904–83) New York City Ballet and the American Ballet Theater. In 1958, choreographer Alvin Ailey (1931–89) set up the American Dance Theater, and Bob Fosse (1927–87) changed the course of musicals.

INDUSTRIALISTS AND ENTREPRENEURS

Tycoon Cornelius Vanderbilt

The rags-to-riches story is an American dream. Andrew Carnegie (1835–1919), "the steel baron with a heart of gold," started with nothing and died having given away $350 million. His beneficiaries included public libraries and universities throughout America. Many other foundations are the legacies of wealthy philanthropists. Some, like Cornelius Vanderbilt (1794–1877), tried to shake off their rough beginnings by patronizing the arts.

In business, New York's "robber barons" did what they liked with apparent impunity. Financiers Jay Gould (1836–92) and James Fisk (1834–72) beat Vanderbilt in the war for the Erie Railroad by manipulating stock. In September 1869 they caused Wall Street's first "Black Friday" when they tried to corner the gold market, but fled when their fraud was discovered. Gould died a happy billionaire, while Fisk was killed in a fight over a woman.

Modern entrepreneurs include Donald Trump *(see p33)*, owner of Trump Tower, and the late Leona and Harry Helmsley. After Leona passed away in August 2007, the bulk of the Helmsley's $4-billion estate was left to a charitable trust.

ARCHITECTS

Cass Gilbert (1858–1934), who built such Neo-Gothic skyscrapers as the Woolworth Building of 1913 *(see p91)* was one of the men who literally shaped the city. His caricature can be seen in the lobby, clutching a model of his masterpiece. Stanford White (1853–1906) was as well known for his scandalous private life as for his fine Beaux Arts buildings, such as the Players Club *(p128)*. For most of his life, Frank Lloyd Wright (1867–1959) spurned city architecture. When he was persuaded to leave his mark on the city, it was in the form of the Guggenheim Museum *(pp188–9)*. German-born Ludwig Mies van der Rohe (1886–1969), who built the Seagram Building *(p177)*, did not believe in "inventing a new architecture every Monday morning," although some might argue that this is just what New York has always done best.

Musical producer Florenz Ziegfeld

NEW YORK THROUGH THE YEAR

Springtime in New York sees Park Avenue filled with blooms, while Fifth Avenue goes green for St. Patrick's Day, the first of the year's many big parades. Summer in the city is hot and humid, but it is worth forsaking an air-conditioned interior to step outside, where parks and squares are the setting for free open-air music and theater. The first Monday in September marks Labor Day and the advent of the orange-red colors of autumn. Then, as Christmas nears, the shops and streets begin to sparkle with dazzling window displays.

Dates of the events on the following pages may vary. For details, consult the listings magazines *(see p377)*. NYC & Co., part of the New York Convention and Visitors Bureau *(see p371)*, issues a useful quarterly free calendar of events.

SPRING

Every season in New York brings its own tempo and temptations. In spring, the city shakes off the winter with tulips and cherry blossoms in the parks and spring fashions in the stores. Everyone window shops and gallery hops. The hugely popular St. Patrick's Day Parade draws the crowds, and thousands don their finery for the Easter Parade down Fifth Avenue.

Inventive Easter bonnets in New York's Easter Parade

MARCH

St. Patrick's Day Parade *(Mar 17)*, Fifth Ave, from 44th to 86th St. Green clothes, beer and flowers, plus bagpipes.
Greek Independence Day Parade *(Mar 25)*, Fifth Ave, from 49th to 59th St. Greek dancing and food.
New York City Opera Spring Season *(Mar–Apr)*, Lincoln Center *(p350)*.
Ringling Bros and Barnum & Bailey Circus *(Mar–Apr)*, Madison Square Garden *(p135)*.

EASTER

Easter Flower Show *(week before Easter)*, Macy's department store *(pp134–5)*.
Easter Parade *(Easter Sun)*, Fifth Ave, from 44th to 59th St. Paraders in costumes and outrageous millinery gather around St. Patrick's Cathedral.

APRIL

Cherry Blossom Festival *(late Mar–Apr)*, Brooklyn Botanic Garden. Famous for Japanese cherry trees and beautifully laid out ornamental gardens.
Earth Day Festival Activities *(varies)*.
Baseball *(Apr–late Sep/early Oct)*. Major league season starts for Yankees and Mets *(p360)*.
New York City Ballet Spring Season *(Apr–Jun)*, New York State Theater and Metropolitan Opera House in Lincoln Center *(p214)*.

MAY

Five Boro Bike Tour *(early May)*, a 42-mile (68-km) ride ending with a festival with live music, food and exhibitions.
Cuban Day Parade *(first Sun)*, a carnival on Sixth Ave, between 44th St and Central Park South.

Parading in national costume on Greek Independence Day

International Food Festival and Street Fair *(mid-May)*, from W 37th to W 57th St. Ethnic foods, music, and dance.
Washington Square Outdoor Art Exhibit *(usually last two weekends May; also Sep)*.
Memorial Day Activities *(last weekend)*. A parade down Fifth Ave, festivities at South Street Seaport.

Yellow tulips and cabs shine on Park Avenue

AVERAGE DAYS OF SUNSHINE PER MONTH

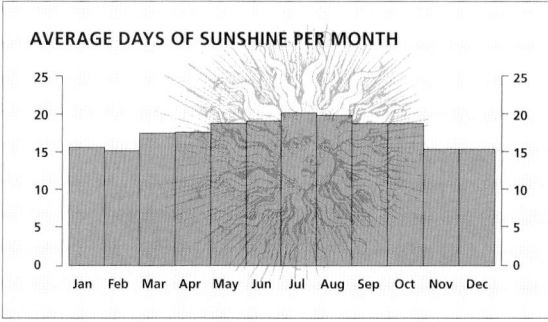

Jan Feb Mar Apr May Jun Jul Aug Sep Oct Nov Dec

Days of Sunshine
New York enjoys long hours of summer sun from June to August, with July the month of greatest sunshine. The winter days are much shorter, but many are clear and bright. Autumn has more sunshine than spring, although both are sunny.

SUMMER

New Yorkers escape the hot city streets when possible, for picnics, boat rides, and the beaches. Macy's fireworks light up the Fourth of July skies, and more sparks fly when the New York Yankees and Mets baseball teams are in town. Summer also brings street fairs, outdoor concerts, and free Shakespeare and opera in Central Park.

Policeman dancing in the Puerto Rican Day Parade

JUNE

Puerto Rican Day Parade *(early Jun)*, Fifth Ave, from 44th to 86th St. Floats and marching bands.
Museum Mile Festival *(second Tue)*, Fifth Ave, from 82nd to 105th St. Free entry to museums.
Central Park Summerstage *(Jun-Aug)*, Central Park. Music and dance of every variety, almost daily, rain or shine.
Metropolitan Opera Parks Concerts. Free evening concerts in parks throughout the city *(pp350–51)*.
Shakespeare in the Park *(Jun–Sep)*. Star actors take on the Bard at Delacorte Theater, Central Park *(p347)*.

JVC Jazz Festival *(mid–late Jun)*. Top jazz musicians perform in various halls in the city *(p353)*.
NYC Pride March *(late Jun)*, from 36th St along Fifth Ave to Christopher St past the Stonewall Inn *(p355)*.

JULY

Macy's Firework Display *(Jul 4)*, usually the East River. This is the undisputed high point of the city's Independence Day celebrations, featuring the best fireworks in town.
American Crafts Festival *(mid–Jun–early Jul)*, Lincoln Center *(p214)*. Displays of high-quality crafts.
Mostly Mozart Festival *(end Jul–end Aug)*, Avery Fisher Hall, Lincoln Center *(pp350–51)*.
NY Philharmonic Parks Concerts *(late Jul–early Aug)*. Free concerts in parks throughout the city *(p351)*.

Festivities at a summer street fair in Greenwich Village

Lincoln Center Festival *(Jul)*. Dance, opera, and other performing arts from around the world.

AUGUST

Harlem Week *(mid-Aug)*. Films, art, music, dance, fashion, sports, and tours.
Out-of-Doors Festival *(Aug)*, Lincoln Center. Free dance and theater performances *(p346)*.
US Open Tennis Championships *(late Aug–early Sep)*, Flushing Meadows *(p360)*.

Crowds of spectators flock to the US Open Tennis Championships

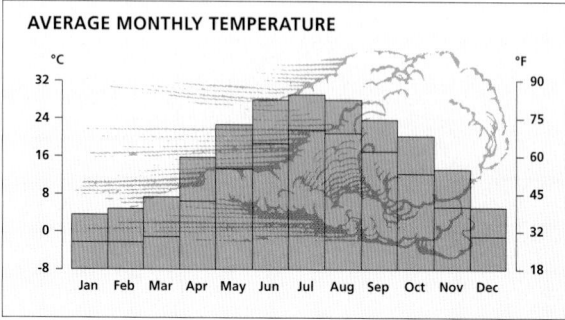

AVERAGE MONTHLY TEMPERATURE

Temperature
The chart shows the average minimum and maximum temperatures for each month in New York. With top temperatures averaging 84° F (29° C), the city can become hot and humid. In contrast, the months of winter, although rarely below freezing, can seem bitterly cold.

AUTUMN

Labor Day marks the end of the summer. The Giants and the Jets kick off the football season, the Broadway season begins and the Festa di San Gennaro in Little Italy is the high point in a succession of colorful neighborhood fairs. Macy's Thanksgiving Day Parade is the nation's symbol that the holiday season has arrived.

SEPTEMBER

Richmond County Fair
(Labor Day weekend), in the grounds of Historic Richmond Town *(p254)*. New York's only authentic county fair.
West Indian Carnival
(Labor Day weekend), Brooklyn. Parade, floats, music, dancing, and food.
Brazilian Festival
(early Sep), E 46th St, between Times Sq and Madison Ave.

Exotic Caribbean carnival costume in the streets of Brooklyn

Brazilian music, food, and crafts.
New York is Book Country *(mid–late Sep)*, Fifth Ave, from 48th to 59th Sts. Book fair.
Festa di San Gennaro *(third week)*, Little Italy *(p96)*. Ten days of festivities and processions.
New York Film Festival *(mid-Sep–early Oct)*, Lincoln Center *(p214)*. American films and international art films.
Von Steuben Day Parade *(third week)*, Upper Fifth Ave. German-American celebrations.
American Football *(season begins)*, Giants Stadium, home to the Giants and the Jets *(pp360–61)*.

OCTOBER

Columbus Day Parade *(2nd Mon)*, Fifth Ave, from 44th to 86th Sts. Parades and music to celebrate Columbus's first sighting of America.
Pulaski Day Parade *(Sun closest to Oct 5)*, Fifth Ave, from 26th to 52nd Sts. Celebrations for Polish-American hero Casimir Pulaski.
Rockefeller Center Ice Skating Rink *(Oct–Mar)*. Skate beneath the famous Christmas Tree.
Halloween Parade *(Oct 31)*, Sixth Avenue, Greenwich Village. Brilliant event with fantastic costumes.
Big Apple Circus *(Oct–Jan)*, Damrosch Park, Lincoln Center. Special themes are presented each year *(p365)*.
Basketball *(season begins)*, Madison Square Garden. Local team is the Knicks *(pp360–61)*.

Huge Superman balloon floating above Macy's Thanksgiving Day Parade

NOVEMBER

New York City Marathon *(first Sun)*. From Staten Island through all the city boroughs.
Macy's Thanksgiving Day Parade *(fourth Thu)*, from Central Park West and W 79th St to Broadway and W 34th St. A joy for children, this famous parade features floats, huge balloons, and even an appearance from Santa.
Christmas Spectacular *(Nov–Dec)*, Radio City Music Hall. Variety show, with the Rockettes.

Revelers in Greenwich Village's Halloween Parade

AVERAGE MONTHLY RAINFALL

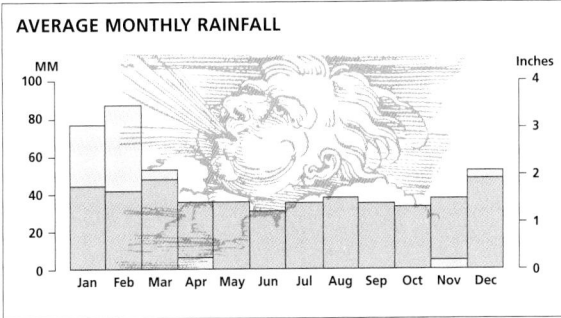

MM
100
80
60
40
20
0

Inches
4
3
2
1
0

Jan Feb Mar Apr May Jun Jul Aug Sep Oct Nov Dec

Rainfall

March and August are the months of heaviest rainfall in New York. Rainfall in spring is usually unpredictable, so be prepared. Sudden heavy snowfalls in winter can cause chaos in the city.

☐ Rainfall

☐ Snowfall

WINTER

New York is a magical place at Christmas – even the stone lions at the Public Library don wreaths for the occasion, and shops become works of art. From Times Square to Chinatown, New Year celebrations punctuate the season, and Central Park becomes a winter sports arena.

Statue of Alice in Wonderland in Central Park

DECEMBER

Tree-Lighting Ceremony *(early Dec)*, Rockefeller Center *(p144)*. Lighting of the giant Christmas tree in front of the RCA Building.
Messiah Sing-In *(mid-Dec)*, Lincoln Center *(p214)*. The audience rehearses and performs under the guidance of various conductors.
Hanukkah Menorah *(mid–late Dec)*, Grand Army Plaza, Brooklyn. Lighting of the huge menorah (candelabra) every night during the eight-day Festival of Lights.
New Year's Eve. Fireworks display in Central Park *(pp206–7)*; festivities in Times Square *(p147)*; 5-mile (8-km) run in Central Park; poetry reading in St. Mark's Church.

JANUARY

National Boat Show *(Jan)*, Jacob K. Javits Convention Center *(p138)*.
Chinese New Year *(late Jan/Feb)*, Chinatown *(pp96–7)*. Dragons, fireworks, and food.
Winter Antiques Show *(Jan)*, Seventh Regiment Armory *(p187)*. NYC's most prestigious antiques fair.

FEBRUARY

Black History Month. African-American events take place throughout the city.
Empire State Building Run-Up *(early Feb)*. Runners race to the 102nd floor *(pp136–7)*.
Lincoln and Washington Birthday Sales *(Feb 12–22)* Big department stores sales throughout the city.
Westminster Kennel Club Dog Show *(mid-Feb)*, Madison Square Garden *(p135)*. Major dog show.

Chinese New Year celebrations in Chinatown

PUBLIC HOLIDAYS

New Year's Day (Jan 1)
Martin Luther King Jr. Day (3rd Mon, Jan)
President's Day (3rd Mon, Feb)
Memorial Day (last Mon, May)
Independence Day (Jul 4)
Labor Day (1st Mon, Sep)
Columbus Day (2nd Mon, Oct)
Election Day (1st Tue, Nov)
Veterans Day (Nov 11)
Thanksgiving Day (4th Thu, Nov)
Christmas Day (Dec 25)

The giant Christmas tree and decorations at Rockefeller Center

The Southern Tip of Manhattan

This view of Lower Manhattan, seen from the Hudson River, encompasses some of the most striking modern additions to the city skyline, such as the distinctively topped quartet of the World Financial Center. You will also catch glimpses of earlier Manhattan: Castle Clinton set against the green space of Battery Park and, behind it, the Custom House building. From 1973 until September 2001 the area also boasted the World Trade Center. Its landmark towers were destroyed in a terrorist attack on the city. The 1 World Trade Center building (formerly known as Freedom Tower), on the northwest corner of the WTC site, is due for completion in late 2013.

WORLD TRADE CENTER REDEVELOPMENT SITE

On September 11, 2001, two planes bound for Los Angeles were hijacked and targeted at the World Trade Center. Hundreds of people died in the impact, but thousands more were killed when the twin towers collapsed. Two other planes were also hijacked that morning; the first struck the Pentagon, while the second came to ground near Pittsburgh. The death toll exceeded the number of troops killed in the Revolutionary War *(see pp22–3)*, and comparisons were made with the bombing of Pearl Harbor. Images of the destruction were seen across the world, drawing support for a "war against terrorism." Currently being constructed on the site is 1 World Trade Center (formerly called Freedom Tower). At 1,776 ft (541 m), its proposed height in feet refers to the year of the Declaration of Independence.

World Financial Center
At the heart of this complex is the Winter Garden – a place to shop, dine, be entertained, or just enjoy the Hudson River views (see p69).

1 World Trade Center
This and several further towers are planned for the WTC site.

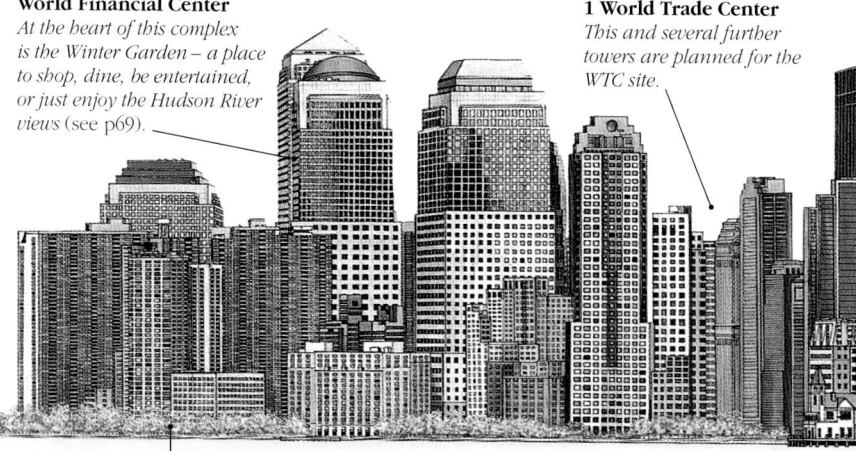

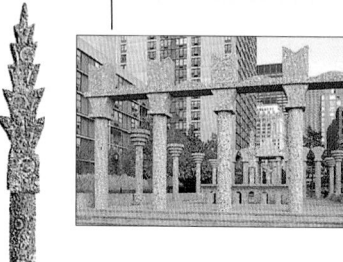

The Upper Room
This walk-around sculpture by Ned Smyth is one of many works of art in Battery Park City (see p72).

Detail from The *Upper Room*

An Earlier View
This 1898 photograph shows a skyline now changed beyond recognition.

Skyscraper Museum
Located at the southern tip of Battery Park City, the Skyscraper Museum celebrates and explores New York's rich architectural heritage.

US Custom House
This magnificent 1907 Beaux Arts building now houses the Museum of the American Indian (see p73).

East Coast War Memorial
In Battery Park, a huge bronze eagle by Albino Manca honors the dead of World War II.

26 Broadway
The tower of the former Standard Oil Building resembles an oil lamp. The interior is still decorated with company symbols.

Bank of New York

17 State Street

26 Broadway

1 Liberty Plaza

Liberty View

Castle Clinton

US Custom House

Shrine of Mother Seton
The first US-born saint lived here (see p76).

American Merchant Mariners' Memorial (1991)
This sculpture by Marisol is on Pier A, the last of Manhattan's old piers. The pier also has a clock tower that chimes the hours on ships' bells.

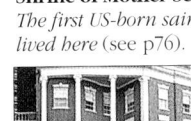

Lower Manhattan from the East River

At first sight, this stretch of East River shoreline, running up from the tip of Manhattan Island, is a seamless array of 20th-century office buildings. But from sea level, streets and slips are still visible, offering glimpses of old New York and the Financial District to the west. On the skyline itself, a few of the district's early skyscrapers still proudly display their ornate crowns above their more anonymous modern counterparts.

LOCATOR MAP

East River View

India House
The handsome brownstone at One Hanover Square is one of the finest of its kind.

Vietnam Veterans' Plaza
An engraved green-glass memorial dominates the former Coenties Slip, a wharf filled in to make a park in the late 19th century (see p76).

Hanover Square
A statue of one of the Dutch mayors, Abraham De Peyster, sits near the house where he was born in 1657.

One New York Plaza

55 Water Street

Barclay's Bank Building

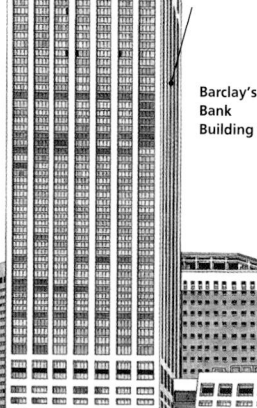

Downtown Heliport
Air-Sea Rescue and sightseeing flights operate from here.

Battery Maritime Building
This historic ferry terminal serves only Governors Island (see p77).

Delmonico's
This upscale steakhouse draws many carnivores.

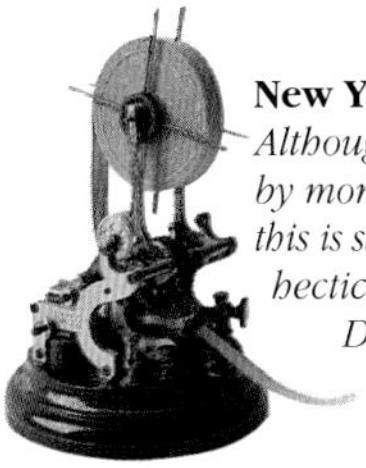

New York Stock Exchange
Although hidden from view by more modern edifices, this is still the hub of the hectic Financial District (see pp70–71).

Bank of New York
This serene 1928 interior is part of the bank set up in 1784 by Alexander Hamilton (see p23).

40 Wall Street
In the 1940s, the pyramid-topped tower of the former Bank of Manhattan was hit by a light aircraft.

70 Pine Street
Replicas of this elegant Gothic-style tower can be seen near the Pine and Cedar Street entrances.

Morgan Bank
Columns from lobby to rooftop are the theme of this striking modern building.

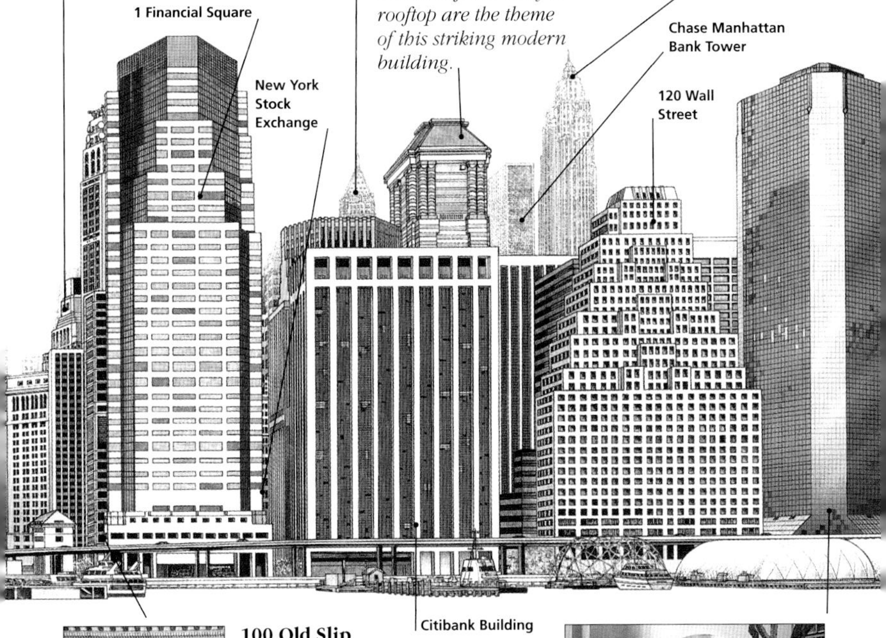

1 Financial Square

New York Stock Exchange

Chase Manhattan Bank Tower

120 Wall Street

Citibank Building

100 Old Slip
Now in the shadow of One Financial Square, the small palazzo-style First Precinct Police Department was the city's most modern police station when it was built in 1911.

Carved medallion, 100 Old Slip

***Queen Elizabeth* Monument**
The ocean liner that sank in 1972 is remembered here.

South Street Seaport

As the Financial District ends, the skyline, as seen from the East River or Brooklyn, changes dramatically. The corporate headquarters are replaced by the piers, low-rise streets and warehouses of the old seaport area, now restored as the South Street Seaport *(see pp82–3)*. The Civic Center lies not far inland, and a few of its monumental buildings can be seen. The Brooklyn Bridge marks the end of this stretch of skyline. Between here and midtown, apartment blocks make up the majority of riverside features.

LOCATOR MAP
South Street Area

Pier 17
A focal point of the Seaport, this traditional-style leisure pier is packed with shops, vendors, and restaurants.

Stonework on the Woolworth Building

Woolworth Building
The handsomely decorated spire marks the headquarters of F.W. Woolworth's empire. It is still the finest "cathedral of commerce" ever built (see p91).

Fleet Bank Building

Seaport Plaza

Transportation Building

Bogardus Building

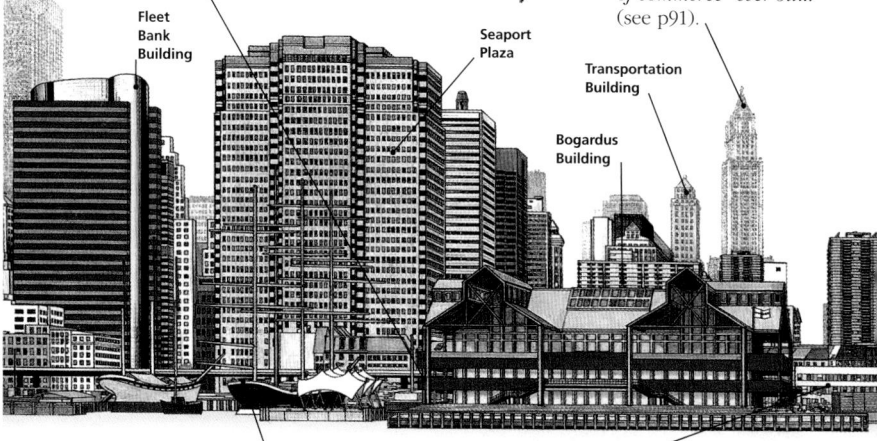

Maritime Crafts Center
At Pier 15, craftspeople demonstrate traditional seafaring skills such as woodcarving and modelmaking.

Titantic Memorial
The lighthouse on Fulton Street commemorates the sinking of the Titanic, the largest steam ship ever built.

Police Plaza
Five in One *(1971–4), in Police Plaza, is a sculpture by Bernard Rosenthal. It represents the five boroughs of New York.*

United States Courthouse
The Civic Center is marked on the skyline by the golden pyramid of architect Cass Gilbert's courthouse (see p85).

Municipal Building
Among the offices of this vast building is the Marriage Chapel, where weddings "at City Hall" actually take place. The copper statue on the skyline is Civic Fame *by Adolph Weinman (see p85).*

Surrogate's Court and Hall of Records
Archives dating back to 1664 are stored and displayed here (see p85).

Verizon Telephone Company

Police Plaza

Pace University

Southbridge Towers

Con Edison Mural
In 1975, artist Richard Haas re-created the Brooklyn Bridge on the side wall of a former electrical substation.

Brooklyn Bridge
Views of, and from, the bridge have made it one of New York's best-loved landmarks (see pp86–9).

Midtown Manhattan

The skyline of Midtown Manhattan is graced with some of the city's most spectacular towers and spires – from the familiar beauty of the Empire State Building's Art Deco pinnacle to the dramatic wedge shape of Citicorp's modern headquarters. As the shoreline progresses uptown, so the architecture becomes more varied; the United Nations complex dominates a long stretch, and then Beekman Place begins a strand of exclusive residential enclaves that offer the rich and famous some seclusion in this busy part of the city.

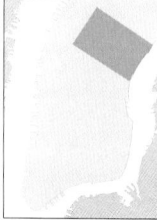

LOCATOR MAP

◻ *Midtown*

Chrysler Building
Glinting in the sun by day or lit up by night, this stainless-steel spire is, for many, the ultimate New York skyscraper (see p155).

Empire State Building
At 1,250 ft (381 m), this was the tallest building in the world for many years (see pp136–7).

Grand Central Terminal
Now dwarfed by its neighbors, this landmark building is full of period details, such as this fine clock (see pp156–7).

MetLife Building

The Highpoint

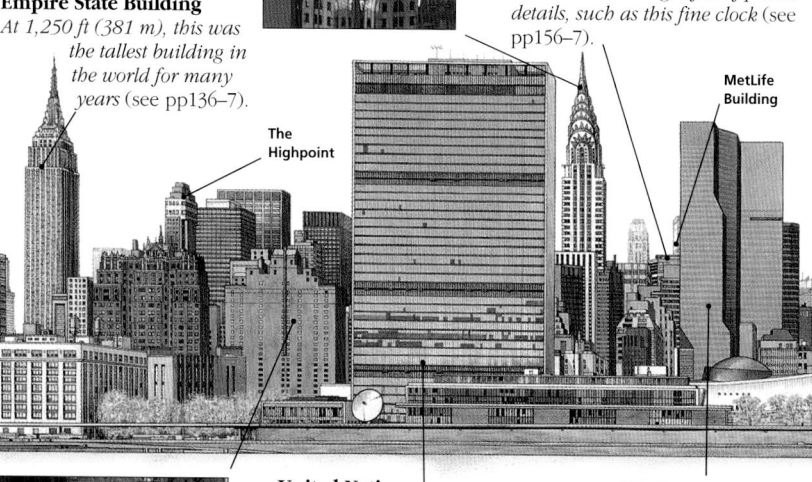

Tudor City
Built in the 1920s, this complex is mock Tudor on a grand scale, with over 3,000 apartments (see p158).

United Nations
Works of art from member countries include this Barbara Hepworth sculpture, a gift from Britain (see pp160–63).

1 and 2 UN Plaza
Angular glass towers house offices and the UN Millennium Plaza Hotel (see p158).

General Electric Building
Built of brick in 1931, this Art Deco building has a tall spiked crown that resembles radio waves. (see p176).

Waldorf–Astoria
The splendid interior of one of the city's finest hotels lies beneath twin copper-capped towers (see p177).

Citigroup Center
St. Peter's Church nestles in one corner of the Citigroup Center, with its raked tower (see p177).

Rockefeller Center
The outdoor skating rink and walkways of this complex of office buildings, shops, and eateries are a great place to people watch (see p144).

The Nail, by Arnaldo Pomodoro, St. Peter's Church, Citicorp Center

General Electric Building

100 UN Plaza

866 UN Plaza

Trump World Tower

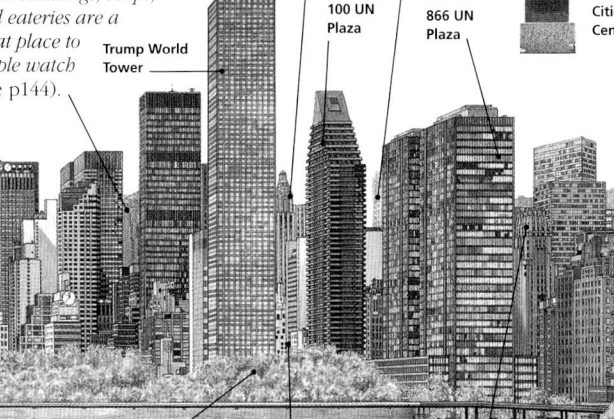

Japan Society
Japanese culture, from avant-garde plays to ancient art, can be seen here (see pp158–9).

St. Mary's Garden
The garden at Holy Family Church is a peaceful haven.

Beekman Tower
Now an all-suite hotel, this Art Deco tower was built in 1928 as a hotel for women who were members of US college sororities.

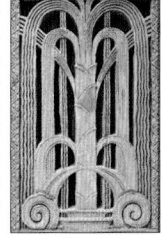

NEW YORK AREA BY AREA

LOWER MANHATTAN

The old and the new converge at Lower Manhattan, where Colonial churches and early American monuments stand in the shadow of skyscrapers. New York was born here, and this was the site of the nation's first capitol. Commerce has also flourished here since 1626, when Dutchman Peter Minuit purchased the island of Man-a-hatt-ta from the Algonquian Indians for goods valued at $24 *(see p19)*. A number of buildings are under development on the site of the World Trade Center *(see p54)*, including 1 World Trade Center. Upon completion, this will soar to 1,776 feet high. Visitors are advised to call all sights in the area to check opening times.

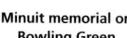

Minuit memorial on Bowling Green

Trinity Church at the head of Wall Street

SIGHTS AT A GLANCE

Historic Buildings and Important Sites
Battery Maritime Building 16
Federal Hall 2
Federal Reserve Bank 1
Fraunces Tavern Museum 13
New York Stock Exchange pp70–71 3
World Trade Center Site 6

Museums and Galleries
Castle Clinton National Monument 20
Ellis Island pp78–9 18
Museum of Jewish Heritage 21
Skyscraper Museum 8
US Custom House 11

Monuments and Statues
Charging Bull 9
Statue of Liberty pp74–5 17

Parks and Squares
Battery Park 19
Bowling Green 10
Vietnam Veterans' Plaza 14

Boat Trips
Staten Island Ferry 15

Churches
Saint Elizabeth Ann Seton Shrine 12
Trinity Church 4

Modern Architecture
Battery Park City 7
World Financial Center 5

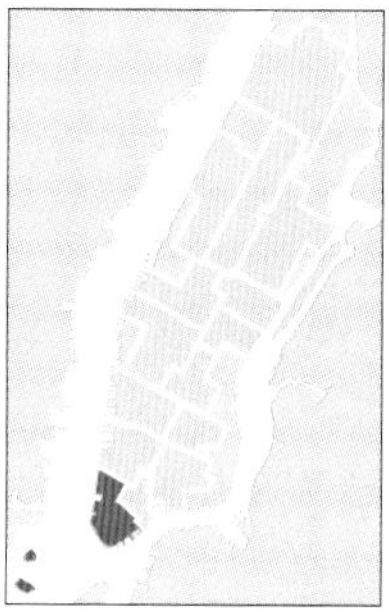

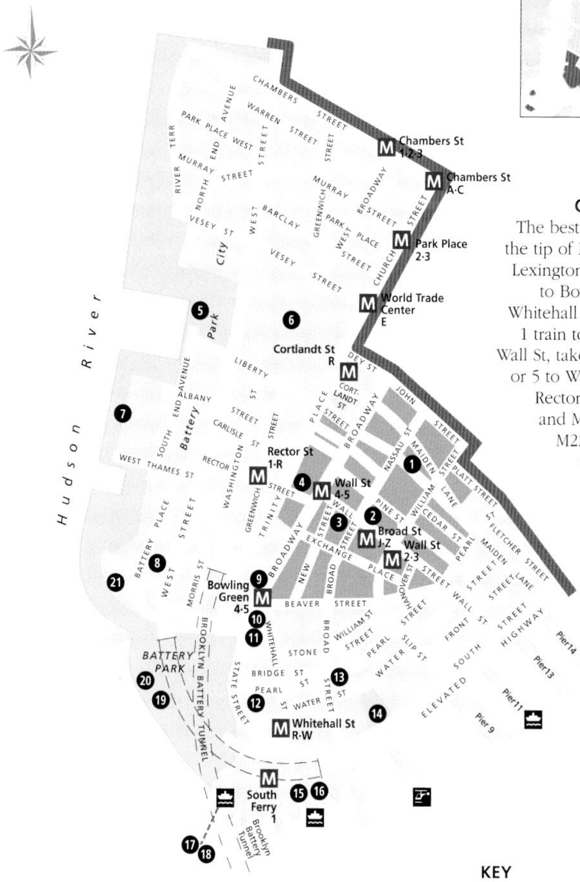

GETTING THERE

The best subway routes to the tip of Manhattan are the Lexington Ave 4 or 5 trains to Bowling Green; R to Whitehall St; or the 7th Ave 1 train to South Ferry. For Wall St, take subways 2, 3, 4, or 5 to Wall St, or 1 or R to Rector St. The M5, M15, and M20 buses and the M22 crosstown route all serve the area.

SEE ALSO

- ***Street Finder,*** maps 1, 2
- ***Where to Stay*** p280
- ***Restaurants*** p296

0 meters 500

0 yards 500

KEY

Street-by-Street map

[M] Subway station

⛴ Ferry boarding point

🚁 Heliport

Street by Street: Wall Street

No intersection has been of greater importance to the city, past or present, than the corners of Wall and Broad streets. Three important sites are located here. Federal Hall National Monument marks the place where, in 1789, George Washington was sworn in as president. Trinity Church is one of the nation's oldest Anglican parishes. The New York Stock Exchange, founded in 1817, is to this day a financial nerve center whose ups and downs cause tremors around the globe. The surrounding buildings are the very heart of New York's famous financial district.

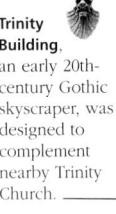

The Marine Midland Bank rises straight up 55 stories. This dark, glass tower occupies only 40% of its site. The other 60% is a plaza in which a large red sculpture by Isamu Noguchi, *Cube*, balances on one of its points.

Trinity Building, an early 20th-century Gothic skyscraper, was designed to complement nearby Trinity Church.

The Equitable Building (1915) deprived its neighbors of light, prompting a change in the law: skyscrapers had to be set back from the street.

★ Trinity Church
Built in 1846 in a Gothic style, this is the third church on this site. Once the tallest structure in the city, the bell tower is now dwarfed by the skyscrapers that surround it. Many famous early New Yorkers are buried in the churchyard **❹**

Wall Street subway (lines 4, 5)

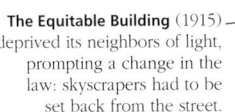

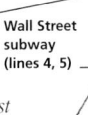

The Irving Trust Company, built in 1932, has an outer wall patterned to look like fabric. In the lobby is an Art Deco mosaic in shades of flame and gold.

26 Broadway was built as the home of the Standard Oil Trust. An oil lamp rests on top of it.

New York Stock Exchange ★
The hub of the world's financial markets is housed in a 17-story building constructed in 1903 **❸**

The Liberty Tower
is clad in white terra-cotta and is in the Gothic style. It was later turned into apartments.

The Chamber of Commerce
is a fine Beaux Arts building of 1901.

STAR SIGHTS

★ Federal Hall

★ Federal Reserve Bank

★ New York Stock Exchange

★ Trinity Church

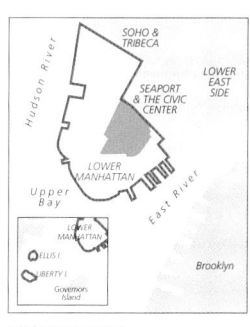

LOCATOR MAP
See Manhattan Map pp14–15

KEY

– – – Suggested route

0 meters	100
0 yards	100

Chase Manhattan Bank and Plaza has the famous Jean Dubuffet sculpture, *Four Trees*, located in the plaza.

★ Federal Reserve Bank
In the style of a Renaissance palace, this is a bank for banks. US currency is issued here ❶

Louise Nevelson Plaza
is a park containing Nevelson's sculpture *Shadows and Flags*.

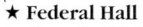

Wall Street is named for the wall that kept enemies and warring Indians out of Manhattan – the street is now the heart of the city's business center.

Wall Street in the 1920s

★ Federal Hall
Built as the US Custom House in 1842, this classical building, refurbished in 2006, houses an exhibit about the Constitution ❷

Federal Reserve Bank ❶

33 Liberty St. **Map** 1 C2. **Tel** (212) 720-6130. Ⓜ Fulton St–Broadway Nassau. ⭐ 9:30am–3:30pm on the half-hour. Free (book one week earlier). ⬤ pub hols. 📷 ♿ www.newyorkfed.org

Entrance to Federal Reserve Bank

This is a government bank *for* banks – it is one of the 12 Federal Reserve banks, and therefore issues US currency. You can identify bank notes originating from this branch by the letter B in the Federal Reserve seal on each note.

Five stories below ground is one of the largest storehouses for international gold. Each nation's hoard is stored in its own compartment within the subterranean vault, guarded by 90-ton doors. Payments between nations used to be made by physical transfers of gold. An exhibition of "The History of Money," with 800 items, runs from 10am to 4pm. Designed by York & Sawyer in the Italian Renaissance style, the 1924 building occupies a full block and is adorned with fine wrought-iron grillwork.

Federal Hall ❷

26 Wall St. **Map** 1 C3. **Tel** (212) 825-6888. Ⓜ Wall St. ⭐ 9am–5pm Mon–Fri. ⬤ public hols. 📷 ♿ ⭐ 10am, 1pm, 3pm. 📷 www.nps.gov/feha

A bronze statue of George Washington on the steps of Federal Hall marks the site where the nation's first president took his oath of office in 1789. Thousands of New Yorkers jammed Wall and Broad Streets for the occasion. They roared their approval when the Chancellor of the State of New York shouted, "Long live George Washington, President of the United States."

The present structure, renovated in 2006, was built between 1834 and 1842 as the US Customs House. It is one of the finest Classical designs in the city. Display rooms off the Rotunda include the Bill of Rights Room and an interactive computer exhibit about the Constitution.

Marble-columned rotunda within Federal Hall

New York Stock Exchange ❸

See pp70–71.

Trinity Churchyard

Trinity Church ❹

Broadway at Wall St. **Map** 1 C3. **Tel** (212) 602-0800. Ⓜ Wall St, Rector St. ⭐ 7am–6pm Mon–Fri, 8am–4pm Sat, 7am–4pm Sun (church); 7am–4pm Mon–Fri, 8am–3pm Sat & pub hols, 7am–3pm Sun (churchyard). 📷 12:05pm Mon–Fri, 9am & 11:15am Sun. 📷 except during services. ⭐ 2pm daily; also Sun after 11:15am service. **Concerts** see details online. 📷 📷 www.trinitywallstreet.org

This square-towered Episcopal church at the head of Wall Street is the third one on this site. Designed in 1846 by Richard Upjohn, it was among the grandest churches of its day, marking the beginning of the best period of Gothic Revival architecture in America. Richard Morris Hunt's design for the sculpted brass doors was inspired by Lorenzo Ghiberti's *Doors of Paradise* at the Baptistery in Florence.

Restoration has uncovered the original rosy sandstone, long buried beneath layers of city grime. The 280-ft (86-m) steeple, the tallest structure in New York until the 1860s, still commands respect despite its towering neighbors.

Many prominent early New Yorkers are buried in the graveyard: statesman Alexander Hamilton; steamboat inventor Robert Fulton; and William Bradford, founder of New York's first newspaper in 1725.

World Financial Center ❺

West St. **Map** 1 A2. *Tel* (212) 945-2600. Ⓜ Fulton St, WTC Station, Cortlandt St, Rector St.
🔲 ♿ 🍴 🖥 🛗
www.worldfinancialcenter.com

A model of urban design by Cesar Pelli & Associates, this development is a vital part of the revival of Lower Manhattan, and its damage in the World Trade Center attack was attended to as a matter of urgency. Four office towers soar skyward, housing the headquarters of some of the world's most important financial companies, including Dow Jones and American Express. At the heart of the complex lies the dazzling Winter Garden, a vast glass-and-steel public space (all 2,000 panes of glass had to be replaced), flanked by 45 restaurants and shops, opening onto a lively piazza and marina on the Hudson River. The sweeping marble staircase leading down to the Winter Garden often doubles as seating for free events,

Main floor of the Winter Garden

The atrium is a sparkling vault of glass and steel, 120 ft (36 m) high.

The "hourglass" staircase is used as extra seating during concerts in the Winter Garden.

An esplanade borders the Hudson.

Cafés and shops line the atrium.

varying from classical to contemporary in music, dance, and theater. Sixteen *Washingtonia robusta* palm trees, 40 ft (15 m) high, have been replaced in this contemporary version of the "palm court" of yesteryear.

Inaugurated in 1988, the building has been hailed as the Rockefeller Center of the 21st century.

World Financial Center viewed from the Hudson River

New York Stock Exchange ❸

In 1790, trading in stocks and shares took place haphazardly on or around Wall Street, but in 1792, 24 brokers who traded at 68 Wall Street signed an agreement to deal only with one another: the basis of the New York Stock Exchange (NYSE) was formed. The NYSE has weathered a succession of alternating slumps ("bear markets") and booms ("bull markets"), growing from a local market-place into a financial center of global importance. Membership is strictly limited. In 1817, a "seat" cost $25; in the "bullish" years of the late 1990s, the prices ran as high as $4 million. In 2006, the NYSE became a for-profit public company, and all the seats were exchanged for cash and stock settlements. Traders now buy one-year licenses.

Ticker-tape Machine
Introduced in the 1870s, these machines printed out up-to-the-minute details of purchase prices on ribbons of paper tape.

Computerized stock tickers
flash a steady stream of prices as fast as the human eye is able to read them.

WHAT A TRADING POST DOES

The 17 trading posts each consist of 22 groups, or "sections," of traders and technology, each trading the stock of up to 10 listed companies. Commission brokers work for brokerage firms, and rush between booth and trading post, buying and selling securities (stocks and bonds) for the public. A specialist trades in just one stock at a time, quoting bids to other brokers, and independent floor brokers handle orders for busy brokerage firms. Clerks process the orders that come into the trading post via SuperDOT computer into the Exchange's Market Data System. The pages help on the busy exchange floor, bringing orders from the booths to the brokers and specialists. Post display units

Trading post

show stock prices, and flat screens show prices and trades for the specialist. As of January 24, 2007, all NYSE stocks can also be traded via an electronic hybrid market.

The 48-Hour Day
During the 1929 Crash, stock exchange clerks worked nonstop for 48 hours. Their mood stayed cheerful despite the panic outside.

Public viewing gallery

Trading post

Members' entrance, Wall Street

Trading Floor
On a typical day, some 3.5 billion shares are traded for more than 2,000 listed companies. The advanced electronics that support the Designated Order Turnaround (SuperDOT) computer are carried above the chaos of the trading floor in a web of gold piping.

Great Crash of 1929
On Tuesday, October 29, over 16 million shares changed hands as the stock market crashed. Investors thronged Wall Street in bewilderment but, contrary to popular myth, traders did not leap from windows in panic.

TIMELINE

1792 Buttonwood Agreement signed on May 17

1844 Invention of the telegraph allows trading nationwide

1867 Ticker-tape machines introduced

1903 Present Stock Exchange building opens

1976 DOT system replaces ticker tape

1981 Trading posts upgraded with electronic units

1987 "Black Monday" crash, October 19. Dow Jones Index drops 508 points

1750	1800	1850	1900	1950	2000	2010

1817 New York Stock & Exchange Board created

Crowds gather outside during the 1929 Crash

1863 Name changed to New York Stock Exchange

1865 New Exchange Building opens at Wall and Broad Streets

1869 "Black Friday" gold crash, September 24

1929 Wall St. Crash, October 29

2001 After 8 years of bull markets, economy falters after September 11

2006 The NYSE merges with Archipelago Holdings to become a for-profit public company

World Trade Center Site ❻

Map 1 B2. Ⓜ *Chambers St, Rector St.* ◯ *Viewing wall on Church St.* **www**.panynj.gov/wtcprogress **www**.renewnyc.org **Tribute WTC Visitor Center** 120 Liberty St. *Tel* 1-866-737-1184. ◯ *10am–6pm Mon–Sat (from noon Tue), noon–5pm Sun.* 🈳 🅿 **www**.tributewtc.org

Immortalized by film-makers and photographers, the twin towers of the World Trade Center dominated the skyline of Manhattan for 27 years, until September 2001's terrorist attack *(see p54)*. The enormous weight of each building was supported by an inner wire cage, which melted from the heat of the fire caused by the two passenger aircraft that were flown into the towers.

These towers were part of a buildings complex consisting of six office blocks and a hotel, connected by a vast underground concourse lined with shops and restaurants. A bridge linked the complex to the World Financial Center *(see p69)*, which survived the attack. The World Trade Center was home to some 450 companies with 50,000 employees. Large numbers of visitors used to come to see the views from the observation deck or the rooftop promenade at Two World Trade Center. The elevator took 58 seconds to reach the 107th floor. At One World Trade Center, this speedy ascent could be taken to the Windows on the World restaurant on the 107th floor. One memorable day at the Center was on August 7, 1974, when Philippe Petit stepped onto a tightrope between the two towers and entertained crowds of office workers for almost an hour with a high-rise balancing act.

Buildings are beginning to reoccupy "Ground Zero". Plans to erect a skyscraper, designed by architect Daniel Libeskind, have been controversial. Several memorials and a museum are also being worked on and are planned to open in 2013.

The Tribute WTC Visitor Center, on the south side of the site, pays homage to the victims, survivors, and rescue efforts of September 11. They also offer walking tours.

Philippe Petit about to step out between the two towers in 1974

Battery Park City ❼

Map 1 A3. Ⓜ *Rector St.* 📷 ♿ 🍴 🏠 **www**.batteryparkcity.org

Governor Mario Cuomo set the tone for this project in

Battery Park City esplanade

1983 when he urged the developers, "Give it a social purpose – give it a soul." The ambitious neighborhood is on 92 reclaimed acres (37 ha) along the Hudson River. The restaurants, apartments, sculptures, and gardens are built on a human scale.

Battery Park City is designed to house more than 25,000 people. The most visible part of it is the World Financial Center *(see p69)* and total costs are estimated at $4 billion.

The 1.2-mile (2-km) walk along the river offers unobstructed views of the Statue of Liberty.

Skyscraper Museum ❽

39 Battery Pl. **Map** 1 A3. *Tel* (212) 968-1961. Ⓜ *Bowling Green, Rector St.* ◯ *noon–6pm Wed–Sun.* 🈳 🏠 **www**.skyscraper.org

Adjacent to the Ritz Carlton hotel, this museum celebrates New York's architectural heritage and examines the historical forces and individuals that shaped the city's skyline. There is a permanent exhibition on the World Trade Center and a digital reconstruction of how Manhattan has changed over time, as well as temporary exhibitions that analyze the various definitions of tall buildings: as objects of design, products of technology, sites of construction, real-estate investments, and places of work and residence.

The airy Skyscraper Museum

Arturo Di Modica's iconic bull statue, at the southern end of Broadway

Charging Bull **❾**

Broadway at Bowling Green.
Map 1 C4. Ⓜ *Bowling Green.*

At 1am on December 15, 1989, sculptor Arturo Di Modica and 30 friends unloaded his 7,000-lb (3,200-kg) *Charging Bull* bronze statue in front of the New York Stock Exchange. The group had eight minutes between police patrols to place the sculpture, but they managed to carry out the deed in just five. The bull was later taken away for obstructing traffic and lacking a permit. Due to the large outcry, however, the Parks Department gave it a "temporary" stomping ground on Broadway, just north of Bowling Green, where it remains to this day, the unofficial mascot of Wall Street.

Di Modica created the sculpture after the 1987 stock-market crash, to symbolize the "strength, power, and hope of the American people for the future." It took him two years to complete at a personal cost of $350,000.

Bowling Green **❿**

Map 1 C4. Ⓜ *Bowling Green.*

This triangular plot north of Battery Park was the city's earliest park, used first as a cattle market and later as a bowling ground. A statue of King George III stood here until the signing of the Declaration of Independence,

when, as a symbol of British rule, the statue was hacked to pieces and smelted for ammunition *(see pp22–3)*. The wife of the governor of Connecticut is said to have melted down enough pieces to mold 42,000 bullets.

The fence, erected in 1771, is still standing, but minus the royal crowns that once adorned it. They met the same fate as the statue. The Green was once surrounded by elegant homes. Beyond it is the start of Broadway, which runs the length of Manhattan and, under its formal name of Route 9, all the way north to the State capital in Albany.

Top of a column at the
US Custom House

Fountain at Bowling Green

US Custom House **⓫**

1 Bowling Green. **Map** 1 C4.
Ⓜ *Bowling Green.* **National Museum of the American Indian. Tel** *(212) 514-3700.*
⭘ *10am–5pm daily (to 8pm Thu).*
⬤ *Dec 25.* 🔲 🔲
www.nmai.si.edu

One of New York's finest Beaux Arts designs, this 1907 granite palace by Cass Gilbert is a fitting monument to the city's role as a great seaport, decorated by the best sculptors and artists of the time. Forty-four Ionic columns stand guard, with an ornate frieze. Heroic sculptures by Daniel Chester French depict four continents as seated women: Asia (contemplative), America (facing optimistically forward), Europe (surrounded by symbols of past glories) and Africa (still sleeping).

Inside, murals by Reginald Marsh decorate the fine marble rotunda, showing the progress of ships into the harbor. Opposite the entrance a portrait of movie star Greta Garbo giving a press conference on board ship. In 1973 the US Customs Service moved out, leaving the building empty but for a small bankruptcy court.

The Custom House took on a different function in 1994, when the George Gustav Heye Center of the **Smithsonian National Museum of the American Indian** was unveiled on three floors of the building. The museum's outstanding collection of about a million artifacts along with an archive of many thousands of photographs, spans the breadth of the native cultures of North, Central and South America.

Exhibitions include works by contemporary Native American artists as well as changing displays drawn from the permanent collection.

Statue of Liberty ⑰

A gift from the French to the American people, the statue was the brainchild of sculptor Frédéric-Auguste Bartholdi and has become a symbol of freedom throughout the world. In Emma Lazarus's poem, which is engraved on the base, Lady Liberty says: "Give me your tired, your poor,/ Your huddled masses yearning to breathe free." Unveiled by President Grover Cleveland on October 28, 1886, the statue was restored in time for its 100th anniversary in 1986. The crown and pedestal are closed for further renovation work until late 2012. The island remains open.

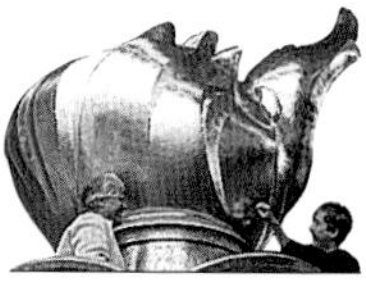

★ Golden Torch
In 1986, a new torch replaced the corroded original. The replica's flame is coated in 24-carat gold leaf.

The crown's seven rays represent the world's seas and continents.

The frame was designed by Gustave Eiffel, who later built the Eiffel Tower. The copper shell hangs on bars from a central iron pylon.

A central pylon anchors the 200-ton statue to its base.

354 steps lead from the entrance to the crown.

Observation deck

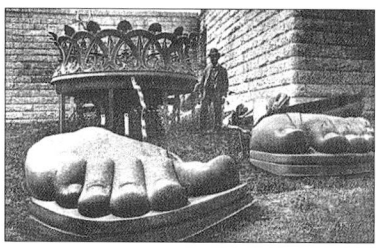

From Her Toes to Her Torch
Three hundred molded copper sheets riveted together make up Lady Liberty.

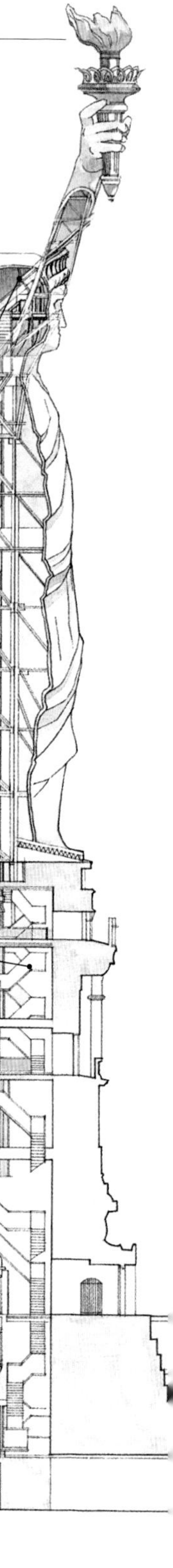

THE STATUE
With a height of 305 ft (93 m) from ground to torch, the Statue of Liberty dominates New York harbor.

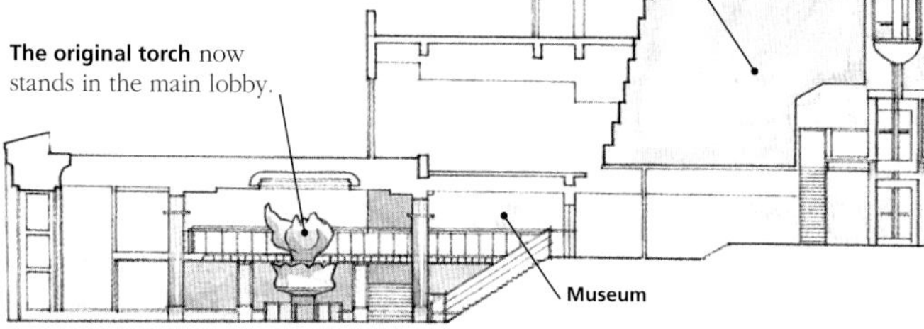

The pedestal is set within the walls of an army fort. It was the largest concrete mass ever poured.

★ Statue of Liberty Museum
Posters featuring the statue are among the items on display.

The original torch now stands in the main lobby.

Museum

★ Ferries to Liberty Island
Ferries cross New York Harbor to Liberty Island, where the Statue offers some of the city's finest views.

Portrait of Liberty
Bartholdi's mother was the model for Liberty. The seven rays of her crown represent the seven seas and seven continents.

Making the Hand
To mold the copper shell, the hand was made first in plaster, then wood.

A Model Figure
A series of graduated scale models enabled Bartholdi to build the largest metal statue ever constructed.

FREDERIC-AUGUSTE BARTHOLDI

The French sculptor who designed the Statue of Liberty intended it as a monument to the freedom he found lacking in his own country. He said "I will try to glorify the Republic and Liberty over there, in the hope that someday I will find it again here." Bartholdi devoted 21 years of his life to making the statue a reality, even traveling to America in 1871 to talk President Ulysses S. Grant and others into funding it and installing it in New York's harbor.

STAR FEATURES

★ Ferries to Liberty Island

★ Golden Torch

★ Statue of Liberty Museum

Restoration Celebration
On July 3, 1986, after a $100-million restoration, the statue was unveiled. The $2-million fireworks display was the largest ever seen in America.

Saint Elizabeth Ann Seton Shrine ⓬

7 State St. **Map** 1 C4. **Tel** (212) 269-6865. **M** Whitehall, South Ferry. ◯ 6:30am–5pm Mon–Fri. ✝ 8:05am, 12:15pm, 1:05pm Mon–Fri; 11am Sun. ◙

**Elizabeth
Ann Seton**

Elizabeth Ann Seton (1774–1821), the first native-born American to be canonized by the Catholic Church, lived here from 1801 to 1803. Mother Seton founded the American Sisters of Charity, the first order of nuns in the United States.

After the Civil War, the Mission of Our Lady of the Rosary turned the building into a shelter for homeless Irish immigrant women – 170,000 passed through on their way to a new life in America. The adjoining church was built in 1883. The Mission established and maintains the shrine to Mother Seton.

Fraunces Tavern Museum ⓭

54 Pearl St. **Map** 1 C4. **Tel** (212) 425-1778. **M** Wall St, Broad St, Bowling Green. ◯ noon–5pm Mon–Sat. ● public hols, day after Thanksgiving. ✂ ▣ groups only.

Lectures, films. ⏸ ▣
www.frauncestavernmuseum.org
NYC Police Museum 100 Old Slip, South St. **Map** 1 D3. **Tel** (212) 480-3100. ◯ 10am–5pm Mon–Sat. Donation suggested. ▣ groups only. **www**.nycpolicemuseum.org

New York's only remaining block of 18th-century commercial buildings contains an exact replica of the 1719 Fraunces Tavern where George Washington said farewell to his officers in 1783. The tavern had been an early casualty of the Revolution: the British ship *Asia* shot a cannonball through its roof in August 1775. The building was bought in 1904 by the Sons of the Revolution. Its restoration in 1907 was one of the first efforts to preserve the nation's heritage. The ground floor restaurant has wood-burning fires and great charm. An upstairs museum has changing exhibits interpreting the history and culture of early America. The **New York City Police Museum** *(see p84)* is at South Street. Exhibits include NYPD artifacts, interactive displays, seminars, and special events. Visit the Hall of Heroes and try your hand at the firearms training simulator.

Vietnam Veterans' Plaza ⓮

Between Water St and South St. **Map** 2 D4.
M Whitehall, South Ferry.

This multilevel brick plaza features, in its center, a huge wall of translucent green glass, engraved with excerpts from speeches, news stories, and moving letters to families from servicemen and women who died in the Vietnam war between 1959 and 1975.

Staten Island Ferry – one of the city's best bargains

Staten Island Ferry ⓯

Whitehall St. **Map** 2 D5. **Tel** 311. **M** South Ferry. ◯ 24 hrs. Free. ◙ ♿ **www**.siferry.com

The first business venture of a promising Staten Island boy named Cornelius Vanderbilt, who later became the railroad magnate, the ferry has operated since 1810, carrying island commuters to and from

The 18th-century Fraunces Tavern Museum and restaurant

the city and offering visitors an unforgettable close-up of the harbor, the Statue of Liberty, Ellis Island and lower Manhattan's incredible skyline. The fare is still the city's best bargain: it's free.

Battery Maritime Building ⑯

11 South St. **Map** 2 D4.
Ⓜ South Ferry. ⚫ to the public.

From 1909 to 1938, the municipal terminal for ferries to Brooklyn operated here on the site of a small wharf known as Schreijers Hoek, from which Dutch Colonial ships once set sail for the mother country. At the height of the ferry era, 17 lines made regular runs from these bustling piers, which are used now only by the Coast Guard service for Governors Island.
　The building was designed in 1907. Arriving boats face 300-ft (91-m) arched openings guarded by tall, ornately scrolled columns and adorned with latticework, molding, and rosettes typical of the Beaux Arts period. This is actually a false front of sheet metal and steel, painted green to resemble copper.

Ironwork railing on the Battery Maritime Building

Statue of Liberty ⑰

See pp74–5.

Ellis Island ⑱

See pp78–9.

Castle Clinton National Monument in Battery Park

Battery Park ⑲

Map 1 B4.
Ⓜ South Ferry, Bowling Green.

Named for the cannons that once protected the harbor, the park is one of the best places in the city for gazing out to sea. Over the years, landfill has extended the greenery far beyond its original State Street boundary.
　The park is rimmed with statues and monuments, such as the Netherlands Memorial

Beaux Arts subway entrance at the corner of Battery Park

Monument and memorials to New York's first Jewish immigrants and the Coast Guard. Fritz Koenig's *The Sphere*, a sculpture that once stood in the World Trade Center Plaza, is now here, serving as a memorial to those who died in the 9/11 terrorist attack.

Castle Clinton National Monument ⑳

Battery Park. **Map** 1 B4. **Tel** (212) 344-7220. Ⓜ Bowling Green, South Ferry. ◻ 8:30am–5pm daily. ⚫ Dec 25. ⊙ ♿ ☑ **Concerts.**
🏠 www.nps.gov/cacl

Castle Clinton was built in 1811 as an artillery defense post 300 ft (91 m) offshore,

connected to Battery Park by a causeway; but landfill gradually linked it to the mainland. None of its 28 guns was ever used in battle.
　The fort was enclosed in 1824 to become a fashionable theater, where Phineas T. Barnum introduced "Swedish nightingale" Jenny Lind in 1850. In 1855 it preceded Ellis Island as the city's immigration point, processing over 8 million newcomers. In 1896, it became the New York Aquarium, which moved to Coney Island in 1941 *(see p249)*.
　Now it is a monument and visitors' center for Manhattan's National Park Service sites, with historical panoramas of the city. The complex is the departure point for the Statue of Liberty–Ellis Island ferry *(see p386)*.

Museum of Jewish Heritage ㉑

36 Battery Place. **Map** 1 B4.
Tel (646) 437-4200. Ⓜ Bowling Green, South Ferry. 🚌 M5, M15, M20. ◻ 10am–5:45pm Sun–Thu (to 8pm Wed), 10am–3pm Fri and eve of Jewish holidays. ⚫ Sat, Jewish holidays, Thanksgiving. 🎦 ♿ 🎧 🏠 ☑ **Lectures.** www.mjhnyc.org

The museum has a core exhibition of more than 2,000 photographs, 800 artifacts, and 25 documentary films about Jewish life, before, during, and after the Holocaust. It also contains a state-of-the-art theater for films, lectures and performances; a memorial garden; classrooms; a resource center and library; a family history center; expanded gallery space for temporary exhibitions; offices; a café and event hall.

Ellis Island ⓲

Half of America's population can trace its roots to Ellis Island, which served as the country's immigration depot from 1892 until 1954. Nearly 12 million people passed through its gates and dispersed across the country in the greatest wave of migration the world has ever known.

The railroad office sold tickets onward to the final destination.

Main building

Centered on the Great Hall or Registry Room, the site today houses the three-story *Ellis Island Immigration Museum*. Much of this story is told with photos and the voices of actual immigrants, and an electronic database traces ancestors. Outside, the *American Immigrant Wall of Honor* is the largest wall of names in the world. No other place explains so well the "melting pot" that formed the character of the nation. Visit early to avoid the crowds.

Rail Ticket
A special fare for emigrants led many on to California.

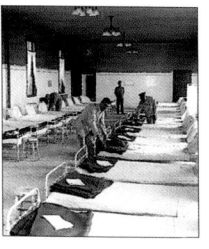

★ Dormitory
There were separate sleeping quarters for male and female detainees.

THE RESTORATION

In 1990 a $156-million project by the Statue of Liberty-Ellis Island Foundation, Inc., renewed several ruined build-ings, replacing the copper domes and restoring the interior with original fixtures.

The ferry office sold tickets to New Jersey.

★ Baggage Room *The immigrants' meager possessions were checked here on arrival.*

Great Hall ★
Immigrant families were made to wait for "processing" in the Registry Room. The old metal railings were replaced with wooden benches in 1911.

The metal and glass awning is a re-creation of the original.

Arrival *Steerage passengers crowd the deck as the ship approaches Ellis Island.*

Main entrance

Immigrant Family *An Italian mother and her children arrive in 1905.*

★ Medical Examining Rooms *Immigrants with contagious diseases could be refused entry and sent back home.*

STAR FEATURES

★ Baggage Room

★ Dormitory

★ Great Hall

VISITORS' CHECKLIST

Map 1 A5. ☎ (212) 363-3200.
Ⓜ 4, 5 to Bowling Green; 1 to South Ferry; R, W to Whitehall, then Statue Cruises Ferry from Battery Park. **Departures** every 20–30 mins 8:30am–4pm summer (winter hours vary).
Tel (877) 523-9849.
◯ 9:30am–5:15pm daily.
⬤ Dec 25. 🎫 ferry fee includes entry to Ellis Island and Liberty Island. ♿ 📷 🎁 🎧 🍴 🖥
www.nps.gov/elis
www.statuecruises.com

SEAPORT AND THE CIVIC CENTER

Manhattan's busy Civic Center is the hub of the city and the state, of the federal governments' court systems and the city's police department. In the 1880s it was the heart of the newspaper publishing business as well. The area is still a handsome enclave of imposing architecture with fine landmarks from every period in the city's history, from the 20th-century Woolworth Building to 19th-century City Hall and 18th-century St. Paul's Chapel, New York's oldest building in continuous use. Nearby is South Street Seaport. Called the "street of sails" in the 19th century because of the many ships that were moored there, the seaport underwent a decline when sailing ships became unprofitable. The area has been restored and is home to a museum and many shops and restaurants. The Brooklyn Bridge, once the largest suspension bridge in the world, lies to the north.

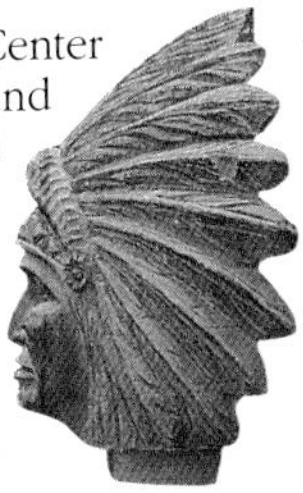

Ship's figurehead, South Street Seaport

SIGHTS AT A GLANCE

Historic Streets and Buildings
AT&T Building 14
Brooklyn Bridge pp86–9 3
City Hall 10
Criminal Courts Building 4
Municipal Building 7
New York County Courthouse 5
Old New York County Courthouse 9
Schermerhorn Row 2
South Street Seaport 1
Surrogate's Court, Hall of Records 8
United States Courthouse 6
Woolworth Building 12

Churches
St. Paul's Chapel 13

Parks and Squares
City Hall Park and Park Row 11

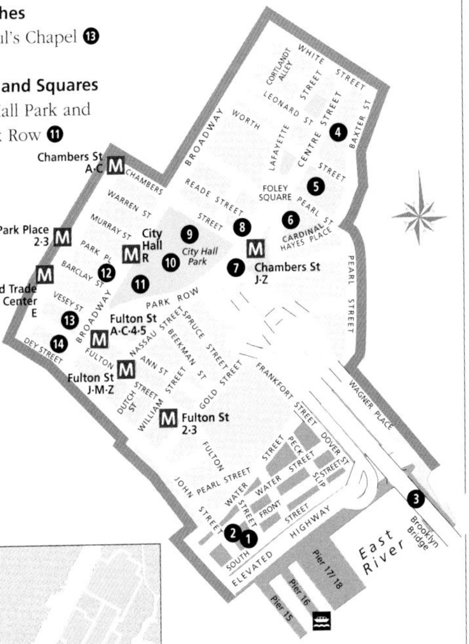

GETTING THERE

Many subway lines serve the area: the 7th Ave/Broadway 2 and 3 trains to Park Pl or Fulton St; the Lexington Ave 4, 5, and 6 to Brooklyn Bridge; the 8th Ave A and C to Chambers St; and the R to City Hall. By bus take the M9, M15, M103, or M22 crosstown.

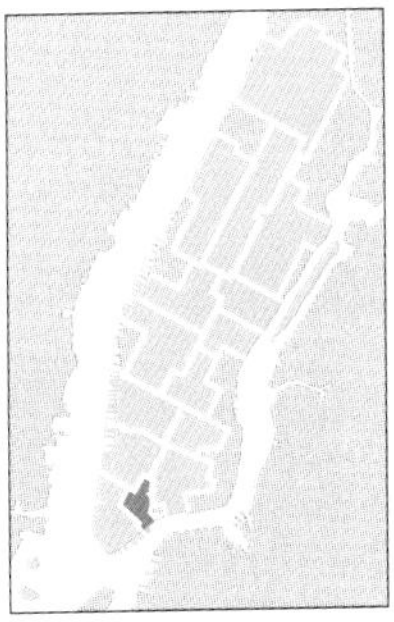

0 meters 500

0 yards 500

KEY

Street-by-Street map

[M] Subway station

Riverboat boarding point

SEE ALSO

- ***Street Finder,*** maps 1–2, 4
- ***Restaurants*** p296

◁ South Street Seaport

Street by Street: South Street Seaport

Part commercial and part historical, the
development of South Street Seaport
has transformed the former heart of the
19th-century port of New York, which
had long been neglected, into a lively
and pleasant part of the city. Tall ships
are once again moored here, and
shops, restaurants, and cafés abound.
The South Street Seaport Museum tells
the story of New York's maritime past
through craft demonstrations, ship tours,
and river cruises.

★ South Street Seaport
*Once full of sailors and sailing ships,
the seaport is now a lively complex of
shops, restaurants, and museums* ❶

Cannon's Walk is a 19th- and 20th-
century block of buildings, with an
outdoor café, shops, and a very
lively marketplace.

The Titanic Memorial is a
lighthouse built in 1913
in memory of those who
died on the *Titanic*. It
now stands on
Fulton Street.

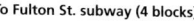
To Fulton St. subway (4 blocks)

Schermerhorn Row
*Built as warehouses in
1813 and due to house
The World Port New
York exhibit, the Row
contains the South
Street Seaport Museum
and Brookstone* ❷

**The Boat-
Building Shop**
lets you watch as skilled
craftspeople build and
restore small
wooden vessels

At the Maritime Crafts Center
woodcarvers and painters can
be seen at work on models,
ship carvings, and
figureheads.

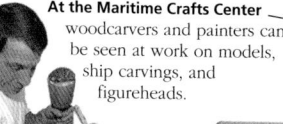

**Ship in a
bottle**

The Pilothouse
was originally from
a steam tugboat built
in 1923 by New York
Central. The Seaport's
admission and
information
center is to be
found here.

NEW YORK CENTRAL Nº 31

STAR SIGHTS

★ Brooklyn Bridge

★ South Street Seaport

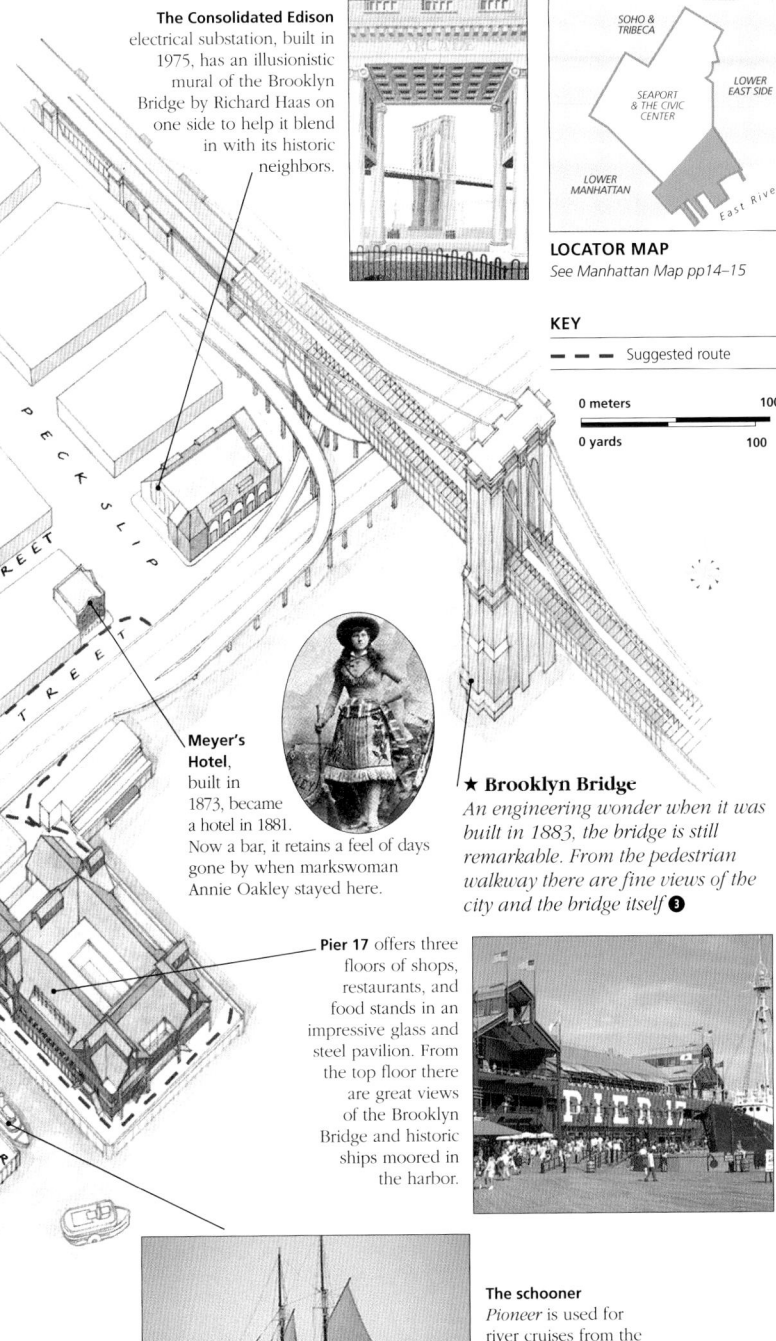

The Consolidated Edison electrical substation, built in 1975, has an illusionistic mural of the Brooklyn Bridge by Richard Haas on one side to help it blend in with its historic neighbors.

LOCATOR MAP
See Manhattan Map pp14–15

KEY

– – – Suggested route

0 meters 100

0 yards 100

Meyer's Hotel, built in 1873, became a hotel in 1881. Now a bar, it retains a feel of days gone by when markswoman Annie Oakley stayed here.

★ Brooklyn Bridge
An engineering wonder when it was built in 1883, the bridge is still remarkable. From the pedestrian walkway there are fine views of the city and the bridge itself ❸

Pier 17 offers three floors of shops, restaurants, and food stands in an impressive glass and steel pavilion. From the top floor there are great views of the Brooklyn Bridge and historic ships moored in the harbor.

The schooner
Pioneer is used for river cruises from the Seaport. The 1908 *Ambrose* lightship, which guided ships into port, is also moored here.

The Ambrose lightship at a South Street Seaport pier on the East River

South Street Seaport **0**

Fulton St. **Map** 2 E2. **Tel** (212) SEA-PORT. M Fulton St. ◯ Nov–Mar: 10am–7pm Mon–Fri, 11am–6pm Sun; Apr–Oct: 10am–9pm Mon–Sat, 11am–8pm Sun. 📷 🚻 📹 **Concerts.** 🚻
📷 **South Street Seaport Museum** 12 Fulton St. 📞 (212) 748-8600. ◯ Jan–Mar: 10am–5pm Fri–Mon; Apr–Dec: 10am–6pm Tue–Sun. ● Jan 1, Thanksgiving, Dec 25. 📷 🚻 📹 **Lectures, exhibits, films.** 🚻 📷 www.southstseaport.org

The heart of New York's 19th-century seaport has been given an imaginative new lease on life. In addition to several stores and restaurants, visitors will find seafaring craft, historic buildings, and museums, along with spectacular views of Brooklyn Bridge and the East River from the cobblestone streets. Historic ships berthed here range from the little tugboat *W.O. Decker* to the great four-masted sailing ship *Peking*. Mini-trips on the schooner *Pioneer* are a great way to see the river.

The **Museum** covers the 12 blocks of what was once America's leading port. Not only is it home to the largest fleet of privately maintained historic vessels in the US, but there are also artifacts, artworks, and documents from the 19th- and early 20th-century maritime world.

The New York City Police Museum *(see p76)* chronicles the history of law enforcement. Exhibits include weapons, the art of fingerprinting and forensics, and the arrest records of famous criminals.

Fulton Fish Market, a popular attraction at Seaport for more than 150 years, moved to the Bronx in 2006.

Schermerhorn Row **2**

Fulton and South Sts. **Map** 2 D3. M Fulton St.

This is Seaport's architectural showpiece. Constructed in 1811 by shipowner and chandler Peter Schermerhorn on land reclaimed from the river, the buildings were originally warehouses and counting-houses. With the opening of the Brooklyn Ferry terminus in 1814 and of Fulton Market in 1822, the block became desirable property.

The Row has been restored as part of the South Street development, and it now houses 24 museum galleries, as well as shops, and restaurants.

Restored buildings on Schermerhorn Row

Brooklyn Bridge **3**

See pp86–9.

Criminal Courts Building **4**

100 Centre St. **Map** 4 F5. M Canal St. ◯ 9am–5pm Mon–Fri. ● public hols. ♿

This 1939 building is Art Moderne in style, with towers reminiscent of a Babylonian temple. The three-story-high entrance is set back in a court, behind two huge, square, free-standing granite columns – an intimidating sight for the accused. The building also houses the Manhattan Detention Center for Men, which was formerly across the street in a building known as "The Tombs" because of its Egyptian-style architecture. The nickname has stuck, although the original is long gone. An aerial walkway, or "bridge of sighs," links the courts with the correctional facility across Centre Street.

The building also houses the night courts, where cases are generally heard from 5pm to 1am on weekdays.

Entrance to the Criminal Courts Building

New York County Courthouse **5**

60 Centre St. **Map** 2 D1. M Brooklyn Br-City Hall. ◯ 9am–5pm Mon–Fri. ● public hols. ♿

Built to replace the Tweed Courthouse *(see p90)*, this county supreme courthouse was completed in 1926.

The fluted Corinthian portico at the top of a wide staircase is the main feature of the hexagonal building. The austere exterior is offset by a circular-columned interior rotunda featuring Tiffany lighting fixtures and a series of rich marble and ceiling murals by Attilio Pusterla on themes of law and justice. Six wings radiate from the rotunda, each housing a single court and its facilities.

The courtroom drama *Twelve Angry Men,* starring Henry Fonda, was filmed here.

New York County Courthouse

United States Courthouse ❻

40 Centre St. **Map** 2 D1.
Ⓜ *Brooklyn Br-City Hall.* ◯ *9am–5pm Mon–Fri.* ⬤ *public hols.* ♿

This courthouse was the last project undertaken by noted architect Cass Gilbert, designer of the Woolworth Building *(see p91)*. Begun in 1933, the year before his death, it was finished by his son. The

United States Courthouse

31-story structure is a pyramid-topped tower set on a classical temple base. The bronzework on the doors is handsome, but the interior lacks the colorful decoration Gilbert had outlined in his sketchbooks. Aerial walkways link the building with its Police Plaza Annex.

Municipal Building ❼

1 Centre St. **Map** 1 C1.
Ⓜ *Brooklyn Br-City Hall.* ⬤ ♿

The Municipal Building, constructed in 1914, dominates the Civic Center and straddles Chambers Street. It was McKim, Mead & White's first skyscraper and houses government offices and a marriage chapel. The exterior, in harmony with City Hall, has no excess detail to detract from the earlier building. The most notable feature is the top, a fantasy of towers capped by Adolph Wienman's statue *Civic Fame.*

A railway passage (no longer in use) through the base, and the plaza joining the Municipal Building to the entrance of the IRT subway station were built as concessions to modern transportation needs. The building has had a far-reaching influence on architectural style; the main building at Moscow University is said to have been modeled on its design.

Surrogate's Court, Hall of Records ❽

31 Chambers St. **Map** 1 C1.
Ⓜ *City Hall.* ◯ *9am–5pm Mon–Fri.* ⬤ *public hols.* ⬤ ♿ ✍

A Beaux Arts triumph, the original Hall of Records was begun in 1899 and completed in 1911. The elaborate columned facade is of white Maine granite, with a high mansard roof. The figures by Henry K. Bush-Brown in the roof area represent life's stages from childhood to old age; the statues by Philip Martiny over the colonnade are of notable New Yorkers such as Peter

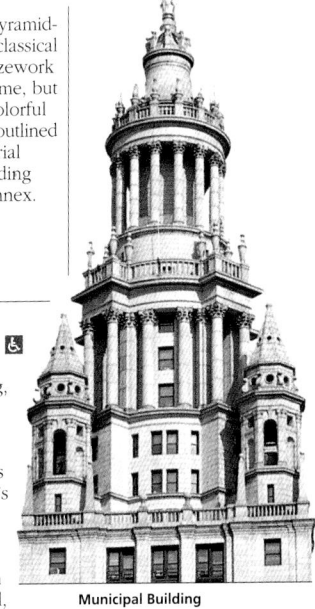

Municipal Building

Stuyvesant. Martiny also made the representations of New York in its infancy and New York in revolutionary times at the Chambers Street entrance.

The Paris Opéra Garnier was the inspiration for the twin marble stairways and painted ceiling of the dazzling central hall. The ceiling mosaic by William de Leftwich Dodge features the signs of the zodiac and symbols of record keeping.

The Hall of Records holds public records dating back to 1664. A permanent exhibition, *Windows on the Archives,* features historical papers, drawings, letters, and photographs illustrating what life was like in New York from 1626 to the present.

Surrogate's Court

Brooklyn Bridge ❸

Completed in 1883, the Brooklyn Bridge was the largest suspension bridge and the first to be constructed of steel. Engineer John A. Roebling conceived of a bridge spanning the East River while ice-bound on a ferry to Brooklyn. The bridge took 16 years to build, required 600 workers and claimed over 20 lives, including Roebling's. Most died of caisson disease (known as "the bends") after coming up from the underwater excavation chambers. When finished, the bridge linked Manhattan and Brooklyn, then two separate cities.

Souvenir medal cast for the opening of the bridge

BROOKLYN BRIDGE
From making the wire to sinking the supports, the bridge was built using new techniques.

Anchorage
The ends of the bridge's four steel cables are fastened to a series of anchor bars held in place by anchor plates. These are held down by giant granite vaults up to three stories high. Their vast interiors, once used for storage, are now used for summer art displays.

Granite vault

Cable to tower

Anchor bar

Anchor plate

Vault

Caisson
The towers rose up above caissons, each the size of four tennis courts, which provided a dry area for underwater excavation. As work went on, they sank deeper beneath the river.

Shaft

Anchor Plates
Each of the four cast-iron anchor plates holds one cable. The masonry was built up around them after they were placed in position.

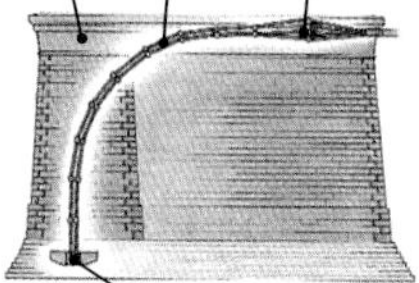

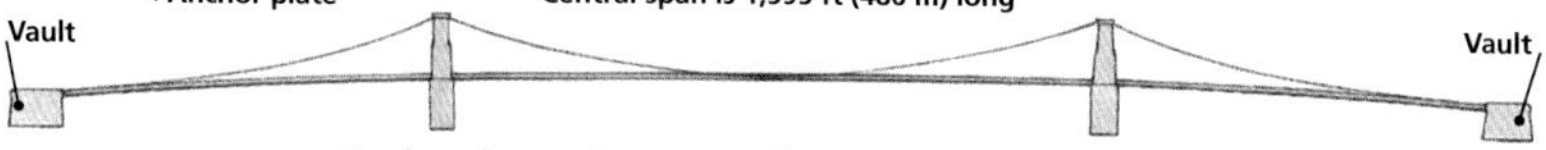

Anchor plates

Central span is 1,595 ft (486 m) long

Vault

Roadway from anchorage to anchorage is 3,579 ft (1,091 m)

First Crossing
Master mechanic E.F. Farrington in 1876 was the first to cross the river on the bridge-in-progress, using a steam-driven traveler rope. His journey took 22 minutes.

VISITORS' CHECKLIST

Map 2 D2. J, Z to Chambers St; 4 5, 6 to Brooklyn Bridge-City Hall (Manhattan side); A, C to High St (Brooklyn side). M9, M15, M22, M103.

Steel Cable Wire
Each cable contains 3,515 miles (5,657 km) of wire, galvanized with zinc for protection from the wind, rain, and snow.

Brooklyn Tower (1875)
Two Gothic double arches, each 271 ft (83 m) high, one in Brooklyn, the other in Manhattan, were meant to be the portals of the cities.

Inside the Caisson
Immigrant workers broke up rocks in the riverbed.

JOHN A. ROEBLING
The German-born Roebling designed the bridge. In 1869, just before construction started, his foot was crushed between an incoming ferry and the ferry slip. He died three weeks later. His son, Washington Roebling, finished the bridge, but in 1872 he was taken from a caisson suffering from the bends and became partly paralyzed. His wife, under his tutelage, then took over.

MAKING THE CABLES

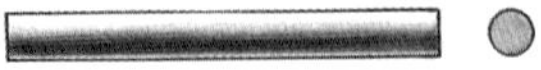

Thickness of steel wire (actual size)

End of wire

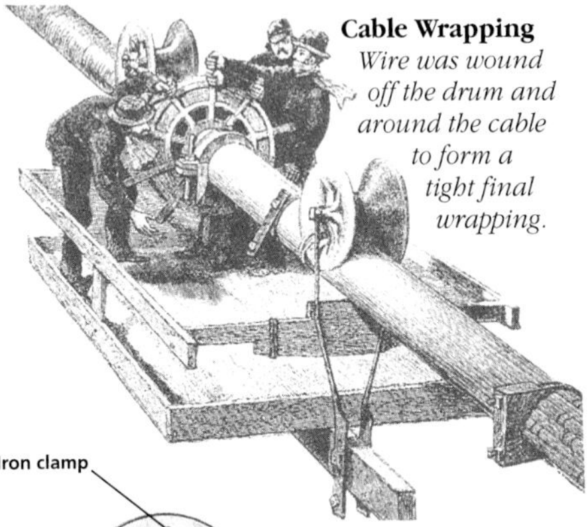

How the Cables Were Made
Each of the four main cables has 19 strands, each made of 278 steel wires. The wires were not twisted, but laid parallel.

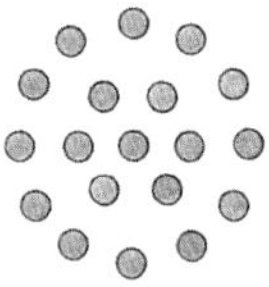

The 19 strands of a main cable

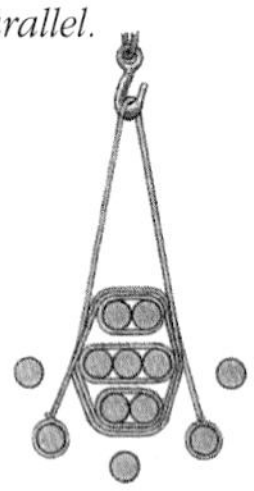

The strands were laid in order: after the bottom 12 strands were laid, the center strands were bound together.

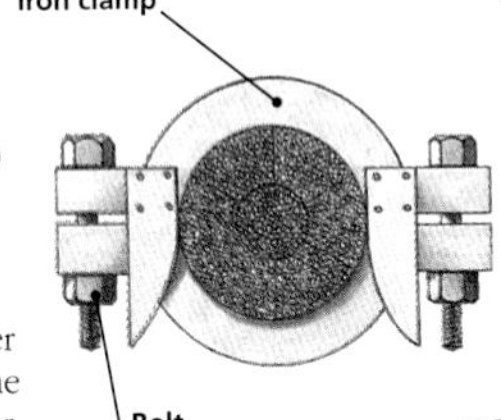

Iron clamp

Bolt

Cable Wrapping
Wire was wound off the drum and around the cable to form a tight final wrapping.

A massive iron clamp compressed all the strands into an even cylinder once they had been positioned.

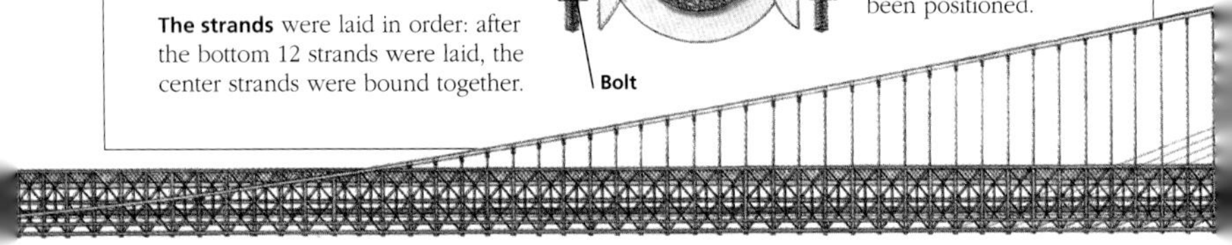

1983 Centennial Fireworks over the Brooklyn Bridge
Celebrating the bridge's 100th year, this display was awesome.

Bustling Bridge
This 1883 view from the Manhattan side shows the original two outer lanes for horse-drawn carriages, two middle lanes for cable cars, and the elevated center walkway.

Panic of May 30, 1883
After a woman tripped on the bridge, panic broke out. Of the estimated 20,000 people on the bridge, 12 were crushed to death.

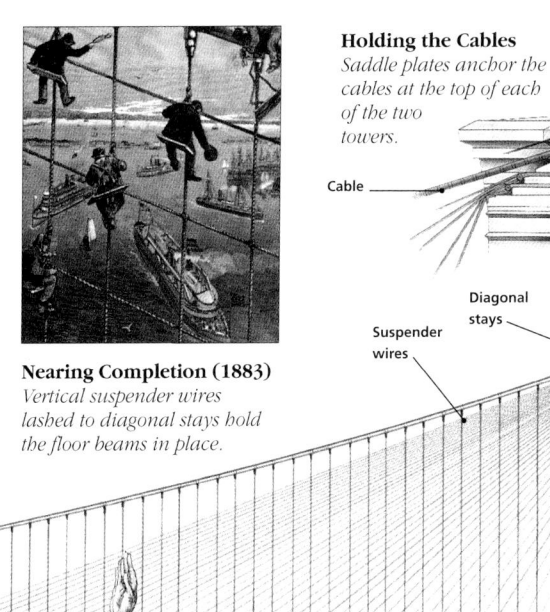

Nearing Completion (1883)
Vertical suspender wires lashed to diagonal stays hold the floor beams in place.

Holding the Cables
Saddle plates anchor the cables at the top of each of the two towers.

Cable

Diagonal stays

Suspender wires

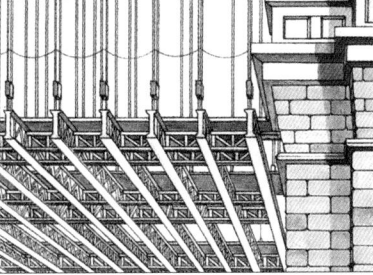

Floor Beams
The steel floor beams weigh 4 tons each.

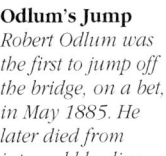

Odlum's Jump
Robert Odlum was the first to jump off the bridge, on a bet, in May 1885. He later died from internal bleeding.

Elevated Walkway
Poet Walt Whitman said that the view from the walkway – 18 ft (5.5 m) above the road – was "the best, most effective medicine my soul has yet partaken."

Old New York County Courthouse ❾

52 Chambers St. **Map** 1 C1.
Ⓜ *Chambers St-City Hall.*
⚑ *included in City Hall tour.*

This building is best known for the scandal it caused. It is nicknamed the "Tweed Courthouse" for the political boss who spent 20 times the budget for the building and pocketed $9 million of the total $14 million cost. "Boss" Tweed even bought a marble quarry and sold materials to the city at huge profit. Public outrage eventually led to his downfall in 1871 – ironically, he was tried in his own courthouse and died in a New York jail *(see p27)*.

After an $85 million restoration, including the 85-ft (26-m) rotunda and the grand staircase, this vibrant 19th-century landmark became the home of the Department of Education.

City Hall's imposing early 19th-century facade

City Hall ❿

City Hall Park. **Map** 1 C1. **Tel** 311.
Ⓜ *Brooklyn Br-City Hall Park Pl.*
◯ *for prearranged tours only.* 📷
♿ ⚑ *(212) NEW-YORK.*

City Hall has been the seat of the New York city government since 1812, and is one of the finest examples of early 19th-century American architecture. A stately Federal-style building (with some influences from the French Renaissance), it was

P.T. Barnum's museum blazes in 1865 as crowds watch from City Hall Park

designed by John McComb, Jr., the first prominent American-born architect, and the French emigré Joseph Mangin.

Marble cladding was not used for the building's rear, since it was not expected that the city would ever develop farther to the north. In 1954, a program of restoration remedied this and the interior was refurbished.

Mangin is usually given credit for designing the exterior, and McComb for the beautiful interior with its fine domed rotunda encircled by 10 columns. The space beneath it opens onto an elegant marble stairway, leading to the splendid second-floor City Council chambers and the Governor's Room, which houses a portrait gallery of early New York leaders. This magnificent entrance has welcomed rulers and heroes for nearly 200 years. In 1865 Abraham Lincoln's body lay in state in this hall.

Stand on the steps and look to your right to see a statue of Nathan Hale, a US soldier hanged by the British as a spy in September 1776 during the Revolutionary War. His last words – "My only regret is that I have not more lives than one to offer in the service of my country" – won him a permanent place in the history books and hearts of America.

City Hall Park and Park Row ⓫

Map 1 C2. Ⓜ *Brooklyn Br-City Hall Park Plc.*

This was New York's village green 250 years ago, complete with stocks and whipping post. It was the scene of pre-Revolution protests against English rule, and there is a memorial to the "Liberty Poles" (symbols of revolt) on City Hall's west lawn. The Declaration of Independence was read to George Washington and his troops here on July 9, 1776.

Later, Phineas T. Barnum's American Museum at the park's southern tip drew crowds from 1842 until it burned down in 1865. The Park Row building was the site of the Park Theater. From 1798 to 1848, the best actors of the day, such as Edmund Kean and Fanny Kemble, performed there. Park Row runs along the east side of City Hall Park. Once called "Newspaper Row," it was lined with the lofty offices of the *Sun, World, Tribune,* and other papers.

Statue of Benjamin Franklin in Printing House Square

Printing House Square has a statue of Benjamin Franklin with his *Pennsylvania Gazette*.

City Hall Park is a green space, used by those working nearby as a peaceful place to sit and relax.

Woolworth Building ⓬

233 Broadway. **Map** 1 C2. ◐ *to the public.* Ⓜ *City Hall Park Pl.*

Bas-relief caricature of architect Gilbert in the Woolworth lobby

In 1879, salesclerk Frank W. Woolworth opened a new kind of store, where shoppers could see and touch the goods, and everything cost five cents. The chain of stores that followed made him a fortune and changed retailing forever.

The 1913 Gothic headquarters of his empire was New York's tallest building until 1930. It set the standard for the great skyscrapers. Architect Cass Gilbert's soaring two-tiered design, adorned with gargoyles of bats and other wildlife, is topped with a pyramid roof, flying buttresses, pinnacles, and four small towers. The marble interior is rich with filigree, sculptured reliefs, and painted decoration, and has a high glass-tile mosaic ceiling that almost seems to glow. The lobby is one of the city's treasures. Gilbert showed his sense of humor here, in bas-relief caricatures of the founder counting out his fortune in nickels and dimes; of the real-estate broker closing a deal; and of Cass Gilbert himself cradling a large model of the building. Paid for with $13.5 million in cash, the building has never had a mortgage. Woolworth's went out of business in 1997. The building is now owned by the Witkoff Group.

St. Paul's Chapel ⓭

209–211 Broadway. **Map** 1 C2. *Tel* (212) 233-4164. Ⓜ *Fulton St.* ◐ *10am–6pm Mon–Sat, 9am–4pm Sun.* ◐ *most public hols.* 🕇 *12:30pm Wed; 8am, 10am Sun.* 📷 *by appt.* **Concerts** *1pm Mon.* www.saintpaulschapel.org

Miraculously untouched when the World Trade Center towers collapsed in 2001, St. Paul's is Manhattan's only extant church built before the Revolutionary

The Georgian interior of St. Paul's Chapel

War. It is a Georgian gem. The colorful interior, lit by Waterford chandeliers, is the setting for free concerts. The pew where newly inaugurated George Washington prayed has been preserved. In the churchyard, the Actor's Monument commemorates George F. Cooke, who played many great roles at the Park Theater; he drank himself to death at the Shakespeare Tavern on Fulton Street. The chapel's "Unwavering Spirit" exhibition chronicles the volunteer efforts after September 11.

AT&T Building ⓮

195 Broadway. **Map** 1 C2. Ⓜ *Broadway-Nassau Fulton St.* ◐ *office hours.*

This former headquarters was designed by Welles Bosworth from 1915 to 1922. The facade is said to have more columns than any other building in the world, and the interior of the building is a forest of marble pillars. The whole edifice looks like a gigantic square-topped layer cake.

A sea sprite above the door of the AT&T (American Telephone and Telegraph) Building

LOWER EAST SIDE

Nowhere does the strong ethnic flavor of New York come through more tangibly than in Lower Manhattan, where immigrants began to settle in the late 19th century. Here Italians, Chinese and Jews established distinct neighborhoods, preserving their languages, customs, foods and religions in the midst of a strange land. This neighborhood of

19th-century tin, Lower East Side Tenement Museum

low-rise buildings is steadily becoming gentrified, but the old flavor remains. The area brims with restaurants, bars, and trendy stores, but still offers some of the city's greatest bargains and has a spirit found nowhere else. The composer Irving Berlin, who grew up here, famously said: "Everybody ought to have a Lower East Side in their life."

SIGHTS AT A GLANCE

Historic Streets and Buildings
Chinatown ❹
Delancey Street ❿
East Houston Street ⓫
Engine Company No. 31 ⓮
Home Savings of America ❶
Little Italy ❸
Orchard Street ❽
Police Headquarters Building ❷

Puck Building ⓬

Parks and Squares
Columbus Park ❺

Museums and Galleries
FusionArts Museum ⓳
Lower East Side Tenement Museum ❼
New Museum of Contemporary Art ⓰

Shops and Markets
Economy Candy ⓱
Essex Street Market ⓴
The Pickle Guys ⓯

Churches and Synagogues
Angel Orensanz Center ⓲
Bialystoker Synagogue ❾
Eldridge Street Synagogue ❻
Old St. Patrick's Cathedral ⓭

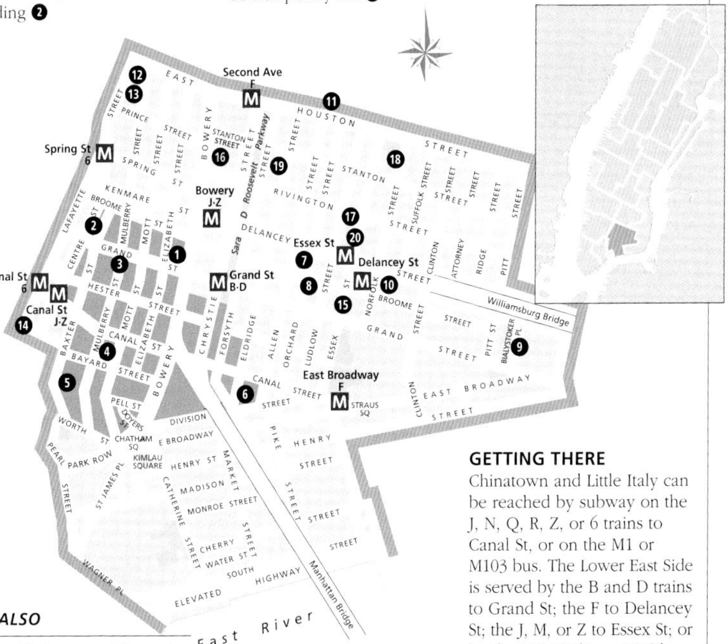

GETTING THERE
Chinatown and Little Italy can be reached by subway on the J, N, Q, R, Z, or 6 trains to Canal St, or on the M1 or M103 bus. The Lower East Side is served by the B and D trains to Grand St; the F to Delancey St; the J, M, or Z to Essex St; or by the M9, M14A, or M15 bus.

0 meters 500
0 yards 500

KEY
Street-by-Street map
M Subway station

◁ Dragon puppet in Chinatown at Chinese New Year

Street by Street: Little Italy and Chinatown

New York's largest and most colorful ethnic neighborhood is Chinatown, which is growing so rapidly that it is overrunning nearby Little Italy as well as the Lower East Side. Streets here teem with grocery stores, gift shops and hundreds of Chinese restaurants; even the plainest offer good food. What is left of Little Italy can be found at Mulberry and Grand streets, where old-world flavor abounds.

★ Little Italy
The scents of Italy still waft from the restaurants and bakeries of this area, once home to thousands of immigrants ❸

The Market on Canal Street has a wide range of bargains in new and used clothes and fresh produce.

Ⓜ **Canal Street** subway (lines R, W, N, Q, 6)

★ Chinatown
Home to a thriving – and still expanding – community of Chinese immigrants, this area is famous for its restaurants and hectic street life. The area truly comes alive around the Chinese New Year in January or February ❹

The Eastern States Buddhist Temple at 64b Mott Street contains over 100 golden Buddhas.

The Wall of Democracy on Bayard Street is covered with newspapers and posters describing the situation in China.

Columbus Park
Once a slum, this park now fills with residents playing mahjong ❺

Confucius Plaza is marked by sculptor Liu Shih's monument to the Oriental philosopher.

Chatham Square has a memorial to Chinese-American war dead.

Police Headquarters Building

The dome of this Baroque civic building towers over the City Hall area. In 1973, the police moved out; ten years later the building was turned into apartments ❷

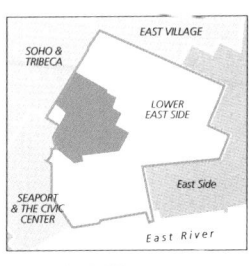

LOCATOR MAP
See Manhattan Map pp14–15

KEY

– – – Suggested route

Home Savings of America

Stanford White designed this in 1894 for the old Bowery Savings Bank ❶

Umbertos Clam House, known as the place where Mafia boss Joey Gallo was shot in 1972, once occupied this location on Mulberry Street.

```
0 meters          100
0 yards           100
```

★ **Eldridge Street Synagogue**
Built in 1887, this was the first large temple built in the US by European Jews ❻

STAR SIGHTS

★ Chinatown

★ Eldridge Street Synagogue

★ Little Italy

Bloody Angle, where Doyers Street turns sharply, was the gruesome site of many gangland ambushes during the 1920s.

Home Savings of America **❶**

130 Bowery. **Map** 4 F4.
Ⓜ *Grand St, Bowery.*

Imposing inside and out, this Classical Revival building was built for the Bowery Savings Bank in 1894. Architect Stanford White designed the ornamented lime-stone facade to wrap around the rival Butchers' and Drovers' Bank, which refused to sell the corner plot. The interior is decorated with marble pillars and a ceiling scattered with gilded rosettes.

By the mid-20th century, the bank was a contrast to the Bowery with its vagrants and flophouses. It is now the site of opulent Capitale, and open only for private functions.

Detail from Home Savings of America

Police Headquarters Building **❷**

240 Centre St. **Map** 4 F4.
Ⓜ *Canal St.* Ⓓ *to the public.*

Completed in 1909, this was a fitting home for the city's new professional police force. The main portico and end pavilions have Corinthian columns and the dome dominates the sky-line. However, lack of space meant the headquarters had to fit into a wedge-shaped site in the midst of Little Italy.

For nearly three-quarters of a century, this was where "New York's finest" came to work. During Prohibition, Grand Street from here to the Bowery was known as "Bootleggers' Row," and alcohol was easily obtained except when a police raid was due. The liquor merchants paid handsomely for a tip-off from inside police headquarters. The police moved to different head-quarters in 1973, and in 1985 the building was converted into a luxury cooperative apartment project.

Little Italy **❸**

Streets around Mulberry St.
Map 4 F4. Ⓜ *Canal St.*
www.littleitalynyc.com

The southern Italians who came to New York in the late 19th century found themselves living in the squalor of "dumbbell" apartments. These were built so close together that sunlight never reached the lower windows or backyards. With over 40,000 people living in 17 small, unsanitary blocks, diseases such as tuberculosis were rife.

Despite the privations of life on the Lower East Side, the community that grew up around Mulberry Street was lively with the colors, flavors, and atmosphere of Italy. These have lingered on, though the Italian population has dwindled to 5,000 and

Chinatown has encroached on the traditional "Little Italy."

The most exciting time to visit is during the Feast of San Gennaro around September 19 *(see p52)*. For nine days Mulberry Street is renamed Via San Gennaro. On the saint's day, his shrine and relics are paraded through the streets. Throughout the feast there is music, dancing, and sideshows, and stalls selling Italian food and drink, as well as other ethnic cuisines.

Little Italy's restaurants offer simple, rustic food served in friendly surroundings at reasonable prices. NoLIta, North of Little Italy, is filled with boutiques, shops, and cafés. The fashionable flock here for the coolest small labels.

A street scene in Little Italy

Chinatown **❹**

Streets around Mott St.
Map 4 F5. Ⓜ *Canal St.*
Eastern States Buddhist Temple
64b Mott St. Ⓞ *9am–6pm daily.*
www.explorechinatown.com

The Chinatown of the early 20th century was primarily a male community, made up of immigrants who had first gone to California. Wages were sent home to their families in China, who were prevented from joining them by US immigration laws. The men relaxed by gambling at mahjong. The community remained isolated from the rest of the city, financed and controlled by its own secret organizations, the Tongs.

Some of the Tongs were simply family associations who provided loans. Others, such as the On Leong and the Hip Sing, who were at war with one another, were criminal fraternities. Tiny, crooked Doyers Street was

Stonework figures adorning the Police Headquarters Building

A Chinese grocer tending his shop on Canal Street

called "Bloody Angle"; enemies were lured there and set upon by gang members waiting around the bend.

A truce between the Tongs in 1933 brought peace to Chinatown. By 1940 it was home to many middle-class families. Immigrants and businesses from Hong Kong also brought postwar prosperity to the community. Today over 80,000 Chinese-Americans live here.

Many visit the neighborhood to sample the cuisine, but there is more to do here than eat. There are galleries, antiques and curio shops, and Oriental festivals *(see p53)*. To glimpse another side of Chinatown, step into the incense-scented Eastern States Buddhist Temple at 64b Mott Street, where offerings are piled up and over 100 golden Buddhas gleam in the candlelight.

Columbus Park ❺

Map 4 F5. Ⓜ *Canal St.*

The tranquillity of Columbus Park today could not be further removed from the scene near this site in the early 1800s. The area, known as Mulberry Bend, was a red-light district, part of the infamous Five Points slum. Gangs with names like the Dead Rabbits and the Plug Uglies roamed the streets. A murder a day was common-place; even the police were afraid to pass through. Partly as a result of the writings of reformer Jacob Riis *(see p49)*, the slum was taken down in 1892. The park is now the only open space in Chinatown.

Eldridge Street Synagogue ❻

12 Eldridge St. **Map** 5 A5. *Tel (212) 219-0888.* Ⓜ *East Broadway.* ◻ *10am–5pm Sun–Thu, 10am–3pm Fri.* 🖼 🚫 🎞 *Every half hour from 10am until 3pm.* 🅰 **www**.eldridgestreet.org

When this house of worship was built by the Orthodox Ashkenazi from Eastern Europe in 1887, it was the most flamboyant temple in the neighborhood. But many immigrant Jews saw the Lower East Side as just the beginning of a new life, and later moved out of this massive synagogue.

In the 1930s, the huge sanctuary, rich with stained glass, brass chandeliers, marbleized wood paneling, and fine carving, was closed. Much later a group of citizens raised funds for preservation, and the main sanctuary was reopened in 2007. The syna-gogue has become a vibrant cultural center, with concerts and other special programs.

Even after years of neglect, the facade, with touches of Romanesque, Gothic and Moorish designs, is impressive. Inside, the Italian hand-carved ark and sculpted wooden balcony show why this build-ing was the pride of the area.

Lower East Side Tenement Museum ❼

108 Orchard St. **Map** 5 A4. **Tel** *(212) 431-0233.* Ⓜ *Delancey, Grand St.* ◻ *10am–6pm daily.* 🖼 *compulsory (book ahead). First tour: 10:30am; last tour: 5pm.* ● *Jan 1, Thanksgiving, Dec 25.* 🖼 🚫 🖼 *Lectures, films, videos.* 🅰 *(daily).* **www**.tenement.org

Street vendor's pushcart (1890s), Lower East Side Tenement Museum

The interior of this building was restored to re-create apartments as they appeared in the late 1870s, in 1916, 1918, and 1935. There were no regulations on tenement living conditions until 1879. Many rooms had no windows, and indoor plumbing was rare. The rooms give a sense of the cramped and deplorable conditions in which so many lived. The program includes the exhibit "Piecing It Together," about the area's garment history. The museum also offers superb walking tours.

Window, Eldridge Street Synagogue

Orchard Street ❽

Map 5 A3. Ⓜ *Delancey, Grand St.*
See ***Shopping** p320.*
www.lowereastsideny.com

Jewish immigrants founded
the New York garment
industry on this street, named
for the orchards that once
stood here on James De
Lancey's Colonial estate. For
years the street was filled with
pushcarts loaded with goods
for sale. The pushcarts are
long gone, and not all the
shopkeepers are Jewish, but
the flavor remains. On Sunday
there is an outdoor market,
and shoppers fill the street
from Houston to Canal,
looking for clothing bargains.
Orchard Street is also at the
heart of the Lower East Side's
gentrification. Boutiques and
vintage stores nestle alongside
bars, clubs, restaurants, and
the boutique Blue Moon
hotel, formerly a tenement.

Vegetable stall at an outdoor market in Canal Street

**Mural representing the zodiac sign
Cancer in Bialystoker Synagogue**

Bialystoker
Synagogue ❾

7–11 Willett St. **Map** 5 C4.
***Tel** (212) 475-0165.* Ⓜ *Essex St.*
✴ *frequent services.* ✔ *prearranged
only.* 📷 **www**.bialystoker.org

This 1826 Federal-style
building was originally the
Willett Street Methodist
Church. It was bought in
1905 by Jewish immigrants
from the Bialystok province
of Poland, who converted it
into a synagogue. For this
reason, it faces west in

the tradition of Christian
churches instead of east.
The synagogue has a
beautiful interior, with lovely
stained-glass windows, a
three-story carved wooden
ark, and murals representing
views of the Holy Land and
the signs of the zodiac,
including an interesting
oddity: a lobster meant to
represent Cancer, the crab.

Delancey Street ❿

Map 5 C4. Ⓜ *Essex St.*
See ***Shopping** p320.*
***Bowery Ballroom** 6 Delancey St.*
***Tel** (212) 533-2111. See website
for shows schedule.* 📷 *no flash.*
♿ **www**.boweryballroom.com

Once a majestic boulevard,
Delancey Street these days
is little more than an
obligatory entrance to the
Williamsburg Bridge. The
street was named for James
De Lancey, whose farm was

situated here in Colonial
days. During the American
Revolution *(see pp22–3)*,
De Lancey remained loyal
to King George III. After
the war, he fled to England,
and his land was seized.
At 6 Delancey sits the
Bowery Ballroom, a three-
story theater completed only
weeks before the stock
market crash of 1929 *(see
p31)*. Throughout the Great
Depression and World War II,
the building was deserted.
Later, it served as a retail
space, housing a haber-
dashery, a jeweler's boutique,
and Treemark Shoes, until
its resurrection as a live-
music venue in the late
1990s. Much of the theater's
original structure is still in
place, including such
decorative details as the
brass rails, the copper-
vaulted plaster ceiling
of the mezzanine bar,
and the brass and iron
exterior metalwork.

Live music at the Bowery Ballroom, in a stylish 1920s theater

East Houston Street ⓫

East Houston St. **Map** 4 F3, 5A3.
Ⓜ *Second Avenue.*

The dividing line between the Lower East Side and the East Village, East Houston between Forsyth and Ludlow streets clearly demonstrates

Trays of bagels at a traditional Jewish bakery in East Houston Street

the changing mix of old and new in the area. Between Forsyth and Eldridge streets is the Yonah Schimmel Knish Bakery, a fixture since 1890, still with its original showcases. Further down the block is the Sunshine Theater, constructed as a Dutch Church in the 1840s and later used as a boxing arena and a Yiddish vaudeville theater. Today it shows art films.

While much of the Jewish flavor of the Lower East Side has disappeared, there are two survivors farther along East Houston. Russ and Daughters is a culinary landmark, a third-generation family business that began on a pushcart, circa 1907. At this location since 1920, the store has seen its fortunes change with the neighborhood. It is famed for traditional smoked fish and herring, and has an impressive stock of caviar.

At the corner of Ludlow Street is perhaps the best-known survivor, the bustling Katz's Delicatessen *(see p297)*, well past its 100th

birthday and still packing them in for pastrami and corned beef sandwiches.

Puck Building ⓬

295–309 Lafayette St. **Map** 4 F3.
Ⓜ *Lafayette.* ◯ *to the public during business hours.* **Tel** *(212) 274-8900.*

This block-square architectural curiosity was built in 1885 by Albert and Herman Wagner. It is an adaptation of the German *Rundbogenstil*, a mid-19th-century style characterized by horizontal bands of arched windows and the skillful use of molded red brick.

From 1887 to 1916 the building housed the satirical magazine *Puck*, and at the turn of the century it was the largest building in the world devoted to lithography and publishing.

Today it is the site of some of New York's most stylish parties and artiest fashion-photography shoots. The only connection remaining to the mythical Puck is the gold-leaf statue on the corner of Mulberry and Houston, and the smaller version over the entrance on Lafayette Street.

Statue of Puck on the northeast corner of the Puck Building

Facade of Old St. Patrick's Cathedral, now a parish church

Old St. Patrick's Cathedral ⓭

263 Mulberry St. **Map** 4 F3.
Tel *(212) 226-8075.* Ⓜ *Prince St.*
◯ *8am–12:30pm & 3:30–6pm Thu–Tue.* ✝ *9am, noon Mon–Fri; 5:30pm Sat; 9:15am, 12:45pm Sun; Spanish: 11:30am Sun.*
www.oldsaintpatricks.com

The first St. Patrick's was begun in 1809, and it is one of the oldest churches in the city. When fire destroyed the original in the 1860s, it was rebuilt much as it is today. When the archdiocese transferred the see to the new St. Patrick's Cathedral uptown *(see pp178–9)*, Old St. Patrick's became the local parish church, and it has flourished despite a constantly changing ethnic congregation.

Below the church are vaults containing the remains of, among others, one of New York's most famous families of restaurateurs, the Delmonicos. Pierre Toussaint was also buried here, but in 1990 his remains were moved from the old graveyard beside the church to a more prestigious burial place in a crypt in the new St. Patrick's Cathedral. Born a slave in Haiti in 1766, Toussaint was brought to New York, where he lived as a free man and became a prosperous wig-maker. He later devoted himself to caring for the city's poor, also tending cholera victims and using his money to build an orphanage. The Vatican is now considering the philanthropic Toussaint for sainthood.

Engine Company No. 31 ⑭

87 Lafayette St. **Map** 4 F5.
Tel (212) 966-4510. Ⓜ Canal St.
⬤ to the public.

In the 19th century, fire stations were considered important enough to merit a building of architectural importance and the Le Brun firm was the acknowledged master of the art. This 1895 station is one of their best. The building resembles a Loire château, with its steep roof, dormers and towers, seeming almost fairy tale-like in this location.

The present-day tenant is the Downtown Community Television Center, which offers courses and workshops to members. However, the building is no longer open to the public.

Facade of Engine Company No. 31, in the style of a French château

The Pickle Guys ⑮

49 Essex St. **Map** 5 B4. **Tel** (212) 656-9739. Ⓜ Grand St. ◯ 9am–7pm Sun–Wed, 9am–8pm Thu, 9am–4pm Fri. **www**.nycpickleguys.com

The scent of pickles permeates this little section of Essex Street, just as it did in the early 1900s when Jewish pickle shops filled the area. True to the old Eastern European recipe, The Pickle Guys store their pickles in barrels filled with brine, garlic and spices; this mixture preserves the pickles for months on end. Pickle varieties include full sour, three-quarters sour, half sour, new, and hot.

Entrance to The Pickle Guys' store, with traditional pickling barrels

No chemicals or preservatives are added and the shop operates to strict Kosher rules.

The store also carries pickled tomatoes, pickled celery, olives, mushrooms, hot peppers, sun-dried tomatoes, sweet kraut, sauerkraut, and herring. It is run like a family business, with a friendly, chatty atmosphere, which perpetuates the neighborhood's traditions.

New Museum of Contemporary Art ⑯

235 Bowery St. **Map** 4 E3. **Tel** (212) 219-1222. Ⓜ Spring St, Bowery. ◯ 11am–6pm Wed–Sun (to 9pm Thu). 🎨 🚫 ♿ ✉ **Lectures, readings, music.** 🖥 **www**.newmuseum.org

Marcia Tucker left her post as the Whitney Museum's Curator of Painting and Sculpture in 1977 to found this museum. Her aim was to exhibit the kind of work she felt was missing from more traditional museums. She created one of New York's most cutting-edge exhibition spaces, which includes an innovative Media Lounge for digital art, video installations, and sound works.

The rotating collection features a wide range of art, from large-scale photographs of 1960s America to geometric abstracts. The museum takes an inclusive approach, showcasing both emerging and established artists, including Mark Rothko and Roy Lichtenstein.

The striking seven-story building, designed by Tokyo-based architects Sejima & Nishizawa, is a notable addition to this Manhattan street. It rises like a sculptural stack of glowing cubes and is the first art museum to be built in downtown Manhattan in over a century. It has 60,000 sq ft (5,574 sq m) of exhibition space, a theater, store, café, and a rooftop terrace offering stunning views of the city.

Sweets on the densely packed shelves at Economy Candy

Economy Candy ⑰

108 Rivington S. **Map** 5 B3. **Tel** 1-800 352-4544. Ⓜ Second Ave–Houston St. ◯ 10am–5pm Sat, 9–6pm Sun–Fri. **www**.economycandy.com

A Lower East Side landmark since 1937, this family-owned candy store stocks hundreds of varieties of candy, nuts, and dried fruit. Lined with floor-to-ceiling shelves packed with old-fashioned dispensers, the store is one of the few businesses on Lower East Side that has remained almost unchanged in name and specialty throughout the neighborhood's fluctuating fortunes over 50 years.

This is due in no small part to Jerry Cohen's enterprise in transforming his father's "Nosher's Paradise" from a penny candy store to a national company. The shop carries sweets and treats from all over the world, as well as numerous food items dipped in chocolate and 21 colors of candy-covered chocolate buttons.

Interior of the Angel Orensanz Center, once a large synagogue

Angel Orensanz Center ⑱

172 Norfolk St. **Map** 5 B3. **Tel** (212) 529-7194. Ⓜ Essex St, Delancey St. ⏰ 10am–6pm Mon–Fri and by appt. ♿ www.orensanz.org

Built in 1849, this cherry-red Neo-Gothic structure was once the oldest synagogue in New York. With ceilings 54 ft (15 m) high and seating for 1500, it was also the largest in the United States at the time. It was designed by the Berlin architect Alexander Saelzer in the tradition of the German Reform movement, and closely resembles Cologne Cathedral and the Friederichwerdeschekirche in the Mitte in Berlin.

After World War II and the decline of Lower East Side's Yiddish population, the synagogue was one of

many to close. In 1986, the building was acquired by the Spanish sculptor Angel Orensanz, who turned it into an art studio. It now serves as a spiritual and cultural center with a program of artistic, musical, and literary events.

FusionArts Museum ⑲

57 Stanton St. **Map** 5 A3. **Tel** (212) 995-5290. Ⓜ Second Ave-Houston St. ⏰ noon–6pm Tue–Fri & Sun. 📷 ♿ 🛗 www.fusionartsmuseum.org

With psychedelic metal sculptures that give a foretaste of the pieces displayed inside, the entrance to this museum is hard to miss. It is dedicated to showing "fusion art", defined as art in which various artistic disciplines, such as painting, sculpture, photography, and video, meld to form a distinct genre in themselves. The museum's location gives it access to an underground art scene that uptown contemporary art museums often neglect, and it also offers lesser-known artists the opportunity to exhibit their work in a reputable gallery.

Many New York City artists who have been creating fusion art on the Lower East Side for more than two decades have already shown their work in group exhibitions here.

Metal sculptures at the entrance of the FusionArts Museum

Essex Street Market ⑳

120 Essex St. **Map** 5 B3. **Tel** (212) 312-3603/388-0449. Ⓜ Essex St, Delancey St. ⏰ 8am–7pm Mon–Sat, 10am–6pm Sun. 📷 🍴 🛗 www.essexstreetmarket.com

The market was created in 1938 by Mayor Fiorello H. La Guardia to bring pushcart vendors together and out of the way of traffic, especially police cars and fire trucks that used the narrow streets.

Two dozen meat, cheese, produce, and spice stalls fill the market. One of the oldest vendors is Jeffrey's butcher store, which has been at the market since 1939. Also here are the Essex Restaurant, which servies Latin/Jewish fare, and Cuchifritos, an art gallery showing the work of the neighborhood's artists.

Cut of meat on a butcher's display at the indoor Essex Street Market

SOHO AND TRIBECA

Art and architecture are the twin lures that have transformed these formerly industrial districts. SoHo (south of Houston) was threatened with demolition in the 1960s until preservationists drew attention to the rare historic cast-iron architecture. The district was saved, and artists began to move into the loft spaces. Galleries, cafés, shops, and then boutiques followed. Brunch and gallery-hopping in SoHo is now a favorite weekend outing. As rents rose, many artists were priced out of SoHo and moved to TriBeCa (Triangle Below Canal). Now, trendy TriBeCa has galleries, many restaurants, and the Tribeca Film Festival in May.

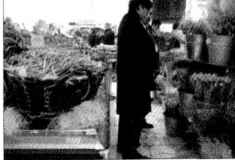

Gourmet food store Dean & DeLuca

SIGHTS AT A GLANCE

Historic Streets and Buildings

Greene Street 3
Harrison Street 8
Haughwout Building 1
St. Nicholas Hotel 2
Singer Building 4
White Street 9

Museums and Galleries

Children's Museum of the Arts 5
New York City Fire Museum 7
New York Earth Room 6

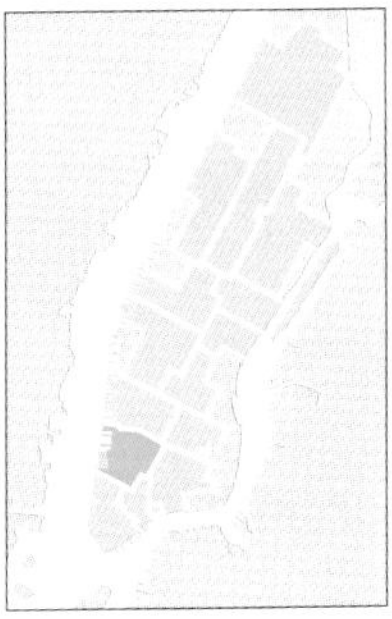

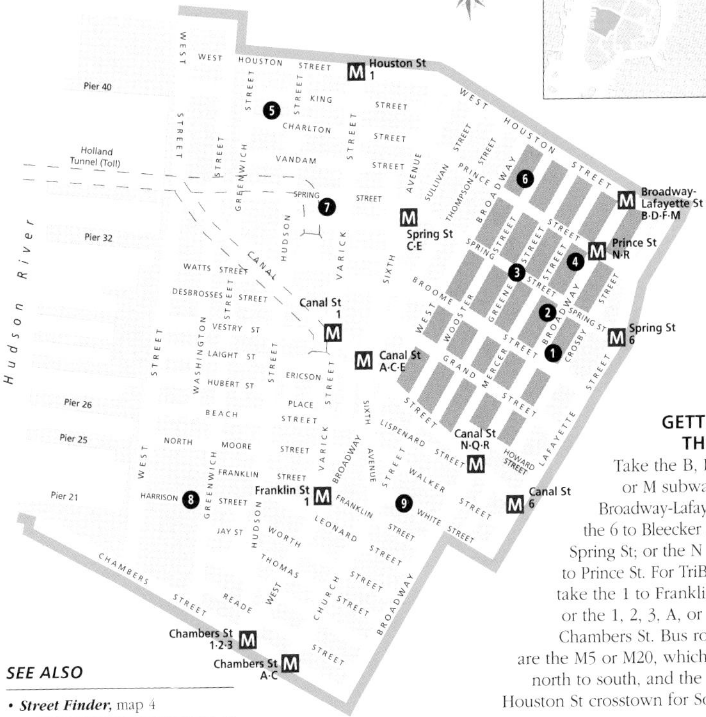

GETTING THERE

Take the B, D, F, or M subway to Broadway-Lafayette; the 6 to Bleecker St or Spring St; or the N or R to Prince St. For TriBeCa, take the 1 to Franklin St; or the 1, 2, 3, A, or C to Chambers St. Bus routes are the M5 or M20, which run north to south, and the M21 Houston St crosstown for SoHo.

SEE ALSO

- ***Street Finder,*** map 4
- ***SoHo Walk*** pp260–61
- ***Restaurants*** pp297–9
- ***Where to Stay*** p281

0 meters 500

0 yards 500

KEY

Street-by-Street map

Subway station

◁ Cast-iron facades on Greene Street

Street by Street: SoHo Cast-Iron Historic District

The largest concentration of cast-iron architecture in the world *(see p42)* survives in the area between West Houston and Canal streets. The heart of the district is Greene Street, where 50 buildings erected between 1869 and 1895 are found on five cobblestoned blocks. Most of their intricately designed cast-iron facades are in the Neo-Classical Revival style, with Corinthian columns and pediments. Mass-produced in a foundry, they were relatively inexpensive to produce and easy to erect and maintain. Now they are rare works of industrial art, well suited to the present character of this district.

West Broadway, as it passes through SoHo, combines striking architecture with a string of art galleries, shoe shops, designer boutiques, and small restaurants.

72–76 Greene Street, the "King of Greene Street," is a splendid Corinthian-columned building. It was the creation of Isaac F. Duckworth, one of the masters of cast-iron design.

The Broken Kilometer, at 393 West Broadway, is an installation by Walter De Maria *(see p107)*. Its 500 brass rods are arranged to play tricks with perspective. Laid end to end, the rods would measure 1 km.

Performing Garage is a tiny experimental theater that pioneers the work of avant-garde artists.

Canal Street-Broadway subway (2 blocks)

★ Greene Street
Of all Greene Street's fine cast-iron architecture, one of the best is 28–30, the "Queen," which was built by Duckworth in 1872, and has a tall mansard roof ❸

10–14 Greene Street dates from 1869. Note the glass circles in the risers of the iron stoop, which allowed daylight to reach the basement.

15–17 Greene Street is a late addition dating from 1895, in a simple Corinthian style.

★ **Singer Building**
This terra-cotta beauty was built in 1904 for the famous sewing machine company ❹

Richard Haas, the prolific muralist, has transformed a blank wall into a convincing cast-iron frontage.

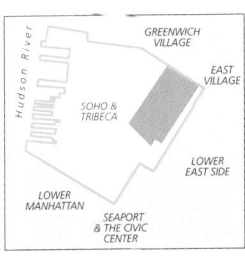

LOCATOR MAP
See Manhattan Map pp14–15

KEY
— — — Suggested route

Prince Street subway station (lines N, R)

Dean & DeLuca is one of the best gourmet food stores in New York. Its range includes a global choice of coffee beans *(see p336).*

101 Spring Street, with its simple, geometric facade and large windows, is a fine example of the style that led to the skyscraper.

Spring Street subway station

St. Nicholas Hotel
During the Civil War, this former luxury hotel was used as a headquarters for the Union Army ❷

0 meters   100
0 yards   100

STAR SIGHTS

★ Greene Street

★ Singer Building

Haughwout Building
In 1857 this was an elegant store, featuring the first Otis safety elevator ❶

Haughwout Building ❶

488–492 Broadway. **Map** 4 E4.
Ⓜ *Canal St, Spring St.*

Haughwout Building facade

This cast-iron building was erected in 1857 for the E.V. Haughwout china and glassware company, which once supplied the White House. Beneath the grime, the design is superb: rows of windows are framed by arches set on columns flanked by taller columns. Mass-produced sections repeat the pattern over and over. The building was the first to use a steam-driven Otis safety elevator, an innovation that made the skyscraper a possibility.

St. Nicholas Hotel ❷

521–523 Broadway. **Map** 4 E4.
Ⓜ *Prince St, Spring St.*

English parliamentarian W. E. Baxter, visiting New York in 1854, reported of the recently opened St. Nicholas Hotel: "Every carpet is of velvet pile; chair covers and curtains are made of silk or satin damask … and the embroidery on the mosquito nettings itself

St. Nicholas Hotel in its heyday in the mid-19th century

might be exhibited to royalty." It is small wonder, then, that it cost over $1 million to build – and with profits of over $50,000 for that year it must have seemed money well spent. Its glory was short-lived, however. In the Civil War it served as a Union Army head-quarters. Afterward, the better hotels followed the entertain-ment district uptown, and by the mid-1870s the St. Nicholas had closed. There is little left on the ground floor to attest to its former opulence, but look up to the remains of its once-stunning marble facade.

Greene Street ❸

Map 4 E4. Ⓜ *Canal St.*

Haas mural on Greene Street

This is the heart of SoHo's Cast-Iron District. Along five cobblestoned blocks are 50 cast-iron buildings dating from 1869 to 1895. The block between Broome and Spring streets has 13 full cast-iron facades and from 8–34 is the longest row of cast-iron buildings anywhere. Those at 72–76 are known as the "King of Greene Street," but 28–30, the "Queen," is considered to be the finest. The architecture is best appreciated as a streetscape, with row upon row of columned facades. Walk into any of the galleries housed within to see the spacious interior lofts.

At the corner of Greene and Prince streets, the illusionistic muralist Richard Haas has created an eye-catching work, disguising a plain brick side wall as a cast-iron frontage. Look for the detail of the little gray cat, which sits primly in an "open window."

Singer Building ❹

561–563 Broadway. **Map** 4 E3.
Ⓜ *Prince St.*

The "little" Singer Building built by Ernest Flagg in 1904 is the second and smaller Flagg structure by this name, and many critics think it superior to the 41-story tower on lower Broadway that was torn down in 1967. The charmingly ornate building is adorned with wrought-iron balconies and graceful arches painted in striking dark green. The 12-story facade of terracotta, glass and steel was advanced for its day, a forerunner of the metal and glass walls to come in the 1940s and 1950s. The building was an office and warehouse for the Singer sewing machine company, and the original Singer name can be seen cast in iron above the entrance to the store on Prince Street.

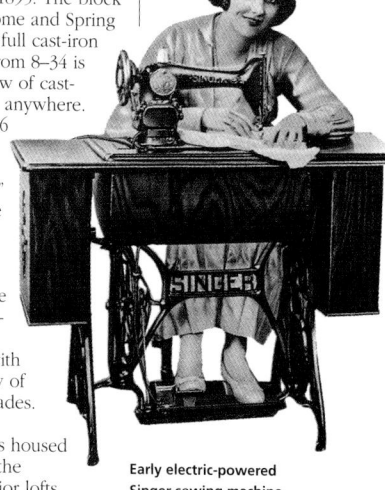

Early electric-powered Singer sewing machine

Children's Museum of the Arts ❺

103 Charlton St. **Map** 3 C4.
Tel *(212) 274-0986.* Ⓜ *Houston St.* 🚌 *M20, M21.* ◯ *noon–5pm Mon & Wed, noon–6pm Thu & Fri, 10am–6pm Sat & Sun .* 🖼 ♿ **www**.cmany.org

Founded in 1988, this innovative museum aims to make the most of children's artistic potential by providing plenty of hands-on activities, sing-alongs, workshops, and performances. Children aged 1–12 can busy themselves with paint, glue, paper and other messy materials to create their own drawings and sculptures. For inspiration, displays of work by

Brightly-colored exhibition space at the Children's Museum of the Arts

local artists are exhibited alongside examples of children's art from around the world. Kids can play around in the dressing-up room and the ball pond, and the museum also hosts a varied program of events appealing to children and families.

New York Earth Room ❻

141 Wooster St. **Map** 4 E3.
Tel *(212) 989-5566.* Ⓜ *Prince St.* ◯ *noon–3pm & 3:30–6pm Wed–Sun.* ♿ ⌀ **www**.earthroom.org

Of the three Earth Rooms created by conceptual artist Walter De Maria, this is the only one still in existence. Commissioned by the Dia Art Foundation in 1977, the interior earth sculpture consists

of 280,000 lbs (127,000 kg) of dirt piled 22 in (56 cm) deep in a 3,600 sq ft (335 sq m) room. *The Broken Kilometer*, another sculpture by De Maria, can be seen at 393 West Broadway (*see p104*). It is composed of 500 solid brass rods arranged in five parallel rows.

1901 La France horse-drawn steam pumper in the City Fire Museum

New York City Fire Museum ❼

278 Spring St. **Map** 4 D4.
Tel *(212) 691-1303.* Ⓜ *Spring St.* ◯ *10am–5pm Tue–Sat, 10am–4pm Sun.* 🌐 *public hols.* 🖼 📷 ♿ 📱 **www**.nycfiremuseum.org

This museum is housed in a Beaux Arts–style 1904 firehouse. New York City's unsurpassed collection of fire-fighting equipment and memorabilia from the 18th century to 1917 includes scale models, bells, and hydrants. Upstairs, fire engines are neatly lined up for an 1890 parade. An interactive fire simulation, available for groups, gives an insight into fire-fighting.
The museum's first floor features an exhibition on 9/11, filled with tributes.

Harrison Street ❽

Map 4 D5. Ⓜ *Chambers St.*

Surrounded by modern high-rise blocks, this rare row of eight beautifully restored Federal town houses, with their pitched roofs and distinctive dormer windows, almost seems like a stage set. The houses were constructed in the late 1700s and early 1800s. Two of the buildings were designed by John McComb, Jr., New York's first

major native-born architect, and were moved from Washington Street, their original site, for preservation purposes. The houses had previously been used as warehouses and were about to be razed to the ground, when, in 1969, the Landmarks Preservation Commission intervened to secure the necessary funding to enable them to be restored. They are now privately owned.
On the other side of the high-rise complex is Washington Market Park. This area was formerly the site of New York City's wholesale produce center. The market relocated to the Bronx in the 1970s.

White Street ❾

Map 4 E5. Ⓜ *Franklin St.*

While not as fine and intricate as some of the SoHo blocks, this sampling of TriBeCa cast-iron architecture shows a considerably wide range of styles. The house at No. 2 has carefully balanced Federal features and a rare gambrel roof, in contrast with the mansard roof of No. 17. Numbers 8 to 10 White, designed by Silesian-born Henry Fernbach, in 1869, have impressive Tuscan columns and arches, with Neo-Renaissance shorter upper stories to give an illusion of height. In contrast, 38 White is the home of neon artist Rudi Stern's gallery, Let There Be Neon.

Rudi Stern's Let There Be Neon gallery in White Street

GREENWICH VILLAGE

New Yorkers call it "the Village," and it began as a country village, an escape for city dwellers during the 1822 yellow fever epidemic. The random pattern of streets, reflecting early farm boundaries or streams, makes it a natural enclave that has been a bohemian haven and home to many artists and writers. A popular gay district is

Jazz club flag on West 3rd Street

here, but the area has become mainstream and expensive. Near Washington Square, it is dominated by New York University students. Once cheaper, the East Village attracts a trendy crowd from all over the city. The Meatpacking District, which still has a few meatpackers, has become overwhelmed with smart boutiques and restaurants.

SIGHTS AT A GLANCE

Historic Streets and Buildings
75½ Bedford Street **2**
Grove Court **3**
Isaacs-Hendricks House **4**
Jefferson Market Courthouse **7**
Meatpacking District **5**
New York University **14**

Patchin Place **8**
St. Luke's Place **1**
Salmagundi Club **10**
Washington Mews **13**

Museums and Galleries
Forbes Magazine Building **9**

Churches
Church of the Ascension **12**
First Presbyterian Church **11**
Judson Memorial Church **15**

Parks and Squares
Sheridan Square **6**
Washington Square **16**

GETTING THERE
By subway, take lines A, B, C, D, E, F, or M to West 4th St-Washington Sq; the 1 to Christopher St-Sheridan Sq or Houston St; or the N or R to 8th St. By bus, take the M1, M5, M20, or M8 crosstown.

SEE ALSO

• **Street Finder**, maps 3–4

• **Village Walk** pp260–61

• **Where to Stay** p281

• **Restaurants** pp299–301

KEY

Street-by-Street map

M Subway station

◁ **People enjoying relaxed café culture in leafy Greenwich Village**

Street by Street: Greenwich Village

A stroll through historic Greenwich Village is a feast of unexpected small pleasures – charming row houses, hidden alleys, and leafy courtyards. The often quirky architecture suits the bohemian air of the Village. Many famous people, particularly artists and writers, such as playwright Eugene O'Neill and actor Dustin Hoffman, have made their homes in the houses and apartments that line these old-fashioned narrow streets. By night, the Village really comes alive. Late-night coffeehouses and cafés, experimental theaters and music clubs, including some of the best jazz venues, beckon you at every turn.

The Lucille Lortel Theater is at No. 121 Christopher Street; it opened in 1955 with *The Threepenny Opera*.

Christopher Street, a part of New York's gay community, is lined with all kinds of shops, bookstores, and bars.

Twin Peaks at No. 102 Bedford Street began life in 1830 as an ordinary house. It was rebuilt in 1926 by architect Clifford Daily to house artists, writers, and actors. Daily believed that the quirky house would help their creativity flourish.

Grove Court
Six houses dating from 1853–4 are set at the back of a quiet leafy courtyard ❸

The building on the corner of Bedford and Grove streets was used as the characters' apartment block in the TV sitcom *Friends*.

No. 75½ Bedford Street
Built in 1873 in an alley, this is the city's narrowest house ❷

★ **St. Luke's Place**
This beautiful row of Italianate houses was built in the 1850s ❶

To Houston Street subway (2 blocks)

The Cherry Lane Theatre was founded in 1924. Originally a brewery, it was one of the first of the Off-Broadway theaters.

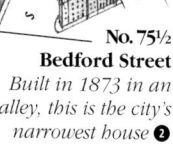

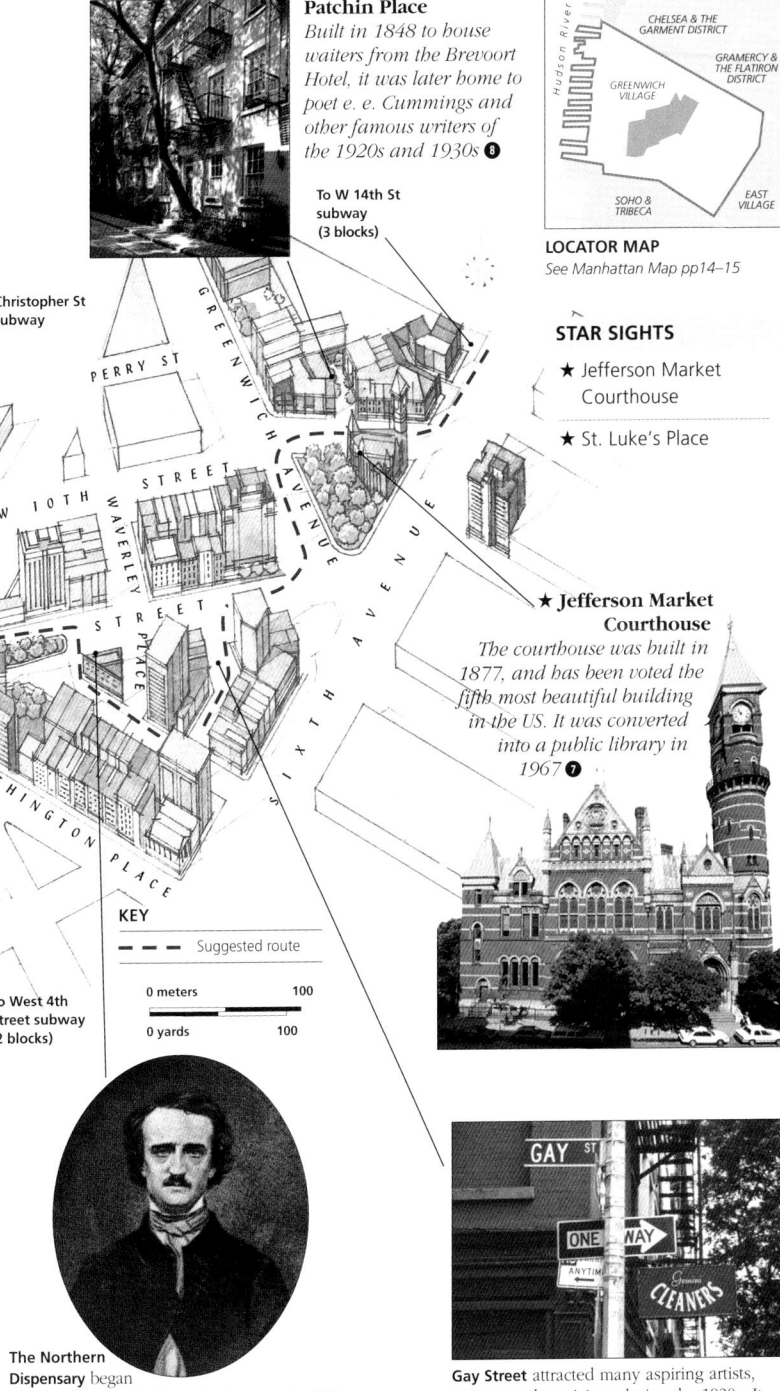

Patchin Place

Built in 1848 to house waiters from the Brevoort Hotel, it was later home to poet e. e. Cummings and other famous writers of the 1920s and 1930s ❽

To W 14th St subway (3 blocks)

Christopher St subway

PERRY ST

W 10TH STREET

WAVERLEY

STREET PLACE

SHINGTON PLACE

LOCATOR MAP
See Manhattan Map pp14–15

CHELSEA & THE GARMENT DISTRICT

Hudson River

GREENWICH VILLAGE

GRAMERCY & THE FLATIRON DISTRICT

SOHO & TRIBECA

EAST VILLAGE

STAR SIGHTS

★ Jefferson Market Courthouse

★ St. Luke's Place

★ Jefferson Market Courthouse

The courthouse was built in 1877, and has been voted the fifth most beautiful building in the US. It was converted into a public library in 1967 ❼

KEY

– – – Suggested route

0 meters   100
0 yards   100

To West 4th Street subway (2 blocks)

The Northern Dispensary began offering free medical care to the poor in 1827. Edgar Allan Poe was treated here for a cold in 1837. It is now a hostel for the disabled.

Gay Street attracted many aspiring artists, writers, and musicians during the 1920s. It was the setting for Ruth McKenney's novel, *My Sister Eileen*, and the film *Carlito's Way*.

Row houses on St. Luke's Place, a street with literary associations

St. Luke's Place ➊

Map 3 C3. Ⓜ *Houston St.*

Fifteen attractive row houses, dating from the 1850s, line the north side of this street. The park opposite is named for a previous resident of St. Luke's Place, Mayor Jimmy Walker, the popular dandy who ran the city from 1926 until he was forced to resign after a financial scandal in 1932.

In front of the house at No. 6 are the tall lamps that always identify a mayor's home in New York. The most recognizable house on the block is probably No. 10, the exterior of the Huxtable family home in *The Cosby Show* (although the series places it in Brooklyn). This is also the block where *Wait Until Dark* was filmed, starring Audrey Hepburn as a blind woman living at No. 4. Theodore Dreiser and the poet Marianne Moore are just two of the several writers who have lived here. Dreiser wrote *An American Tragedy* while living at No. 16. One block north, the corner of Hudson and Morton Streets marked the edge of the Hudson River in the 18th century.

Mayor's lamp at No. 6

75½ Bedford Street ➋

Map 3 C2. Ⓜ *Houston St.* ⬤ *to the public.* **www**.cherrylanetheatre.com

New York's narrowest home, just 9½ ft (2.9 m) wide, was built in 1893 in a former passageway. The poet Edna St. Vincent Millay lived here briefly, followed by the actor John Barrymore, and later Cary Grant. The three-story building, now renovated, is marked by a plaque.

Just around the corner, at 38 Commerce Street, Miss Millay founded the Cherry Lane Theater in 1924 as a site for avant-garde drama. It still premieres new works. Its biggest hit was the 1960s musical *Godspell*.

Grove Court ➌

Map 3 C2. Ⓜ *Christopher St/ Sheridan Sq.*

An enterprising grocer named Samuel Cocks built the six town houses here, in an area formed by a bend in the street. (The bends in this part of the Village originally marked divisions between colonial properties.) Cocks reckoned that having residents in the empty passage between 10 and 12 Grove Street would help his business at No. 18.

But residential courts, now highly prized, were not considered respectable in 1854, and the lowbrow residents attracted to the area earned it the nickname "Mixed Ale Alley." O. Henry later chose this block as the setting for his 1902 work *The Last Leaf*.

Isaacs-Hendricks House

Isaacs-Hendricks House ➍

77 Bedford St. **Map** 3 C2. Ⓜ *Houston St.* ⬤ *to the public.*

This is the oldest surviving home in the Village, built in 1799. The old clapboard walls are visible on the sides and rear; the brickwork and third floor came later. The first owner, John Isaacs, bought the land for $295 in 1794. Next came Harmon Hendricks, a copper dealer and associate of revolutionary Paul Revere. Robert Fulton, who used copper for the boilers in his steamboat, was one of Hendricks's customers.

Meatpacking District ➎

Map 3 B1 Ⓜ *14th St (on lines A, C, E); 8th Av L.*

Once the domain of butchers in blood-stained aprons hacking at sides of beef, these days (and particularly nights) the Meatpacking District is very different. Squeezed into an area south of 14th Street and west of 9th Avenue, the neighborhood is now dotted with trendy clubs, lounges, and boutique hotels that swell with New Yorkers out

The mid-19th-century town houses at Grove Court

for a good time. The neighborhood's hipness quotient rose when Soho House, the New York branch of the London private members' club, moved in, followed by the classy Hotel Gansevoort, with its rooftop swimming pool. Hip clothiers, including Stella McCartney and Marc Jacobs, have outlets here; upscale restaurants have opened; and new nightclubs and bars pop up every month.

The great allure of the Meatpacking District is, of course, that chic urbanites like some edginess to their nighttime recreation, and this is where the district delivers. The face of the neighborhood may be forever changed, but club-hoppers might still catch the occasional whiff of the meat-processing business that gave the area its name.

Sheridan Square **6**

Map 3 C2. M *Christopher St- Sheridan Sq.*

This square, where seven streets converge, is the heart of the Village. It was named for the Civil War General Philip Sheridan who became commander in chief of the US Army in 1883. His statue stands in nearby Christopher Park.

The Draft Riots of 1863 took place here. Over a century later, another famous disturbance rocked the square. The Stonewall Inn on Christopher Street was a gay bar that had stayed in business (it was then illegal for gays to gather in bars) by paying off the police. However, on June 28, 1969, the patrons rebelled, and in the pitched battle that ensued police officers were barricaded inside the bar. It was a landmark moral victory for the budding gay rights movement. The inn that stands today is not the original. The Village remains a focus for the city's gay community.

"Old Jeff," the pointed tower of Jefferson Market Courthouse

Jefferson Market Courthouse **7**

425 Ave of the Americas. **Map** 4 D1. *Tel* (212) 243-4334. M *W 4th St-Washington Sq.* □ noon–8pm Mon & Wed, 10am–6pm Tue, noon– 6pm Thu, 1–6pm Fri, 10am–5pm Sat. ● *public hols.* & **www**.nypl.org

This treasured Village landmark was saved from the wrecking ball and converted into a branch of the New York Public Library through a spirited preservation campaign that began at a Christmas party in the late 1950s.

The site became a market in 1833, named after former president Thomas Jefferson. Its fire lookout tower had a giant bell that was rung to alert the neighborhood's volunteer fire fighters. In 1865, the founding of the municipal fire department made the bell obsolete, and the Third Judicial District, or Jefferson Market, Courthouse was built. With its Venetian Gothic-style spires and turrets, it was named one of the 10 most beautiful buildings in the country when it opened in 1877. The old fire bell was installed in the tower. Here, in 1906, Harry Thaw was tried for Stanford White's murder (*see p126*).

By 1945, the market had moved, court sessions had been discontinued, the four-sided clock had stopped and the building was threatened with demolition. In the 1950s, preservationists campaigned first to restore the clock and then the whole building. Its renovation was undertaken by architect Giorgio Cavaglieri, who preserved many of the original details, including the stained glass and a spiral staircase that now leads to the library's dungeonlike reference room.

Facade and an ailanthus tree at Patchin Place

Patchin Place **8**

W 10th St. **Map** 4 D1. M *W 4th St- Washington Sq.*

One of many delightful and unexpected pockets in the Village is this tiny block of small residences. It is lined with ailanthus trees that were planted in order to "absorb the bad air." The houses were built in the mid-19th century for Basque waiters working at the Brevoort Hotel on Fifth Avenue.

Later the houses became fashionable addresses, with many writers living here. The poet e. e. Cummings lived at No. 4 from 1923 until his death in 1962. The English poet laureate John Masefield also lived on the block, as did the playwright Eugene O'Neill and John Reed, whose eyewitness account of the Russian Revolution, *Ten Days That Shook The World* was made into a film, *Reds*, directed by Warren Beatty.

Statue of General Sheridan in Christopher Park

Toy battleship from the Forbes Magazine Collection

Forbes Magazine Building ❾

60 5th Ave. **Map** 4 E1. **Tel** (212) 206-5548. Ⓜ 14th St–Union Sq. **Galleries** ◔ 10am–4pm Tue–Wed, Fri–Sat (times may vary). No strollers. 🎟 Thu: groups only. ♿ ◕ public hols.

Some architectural critics have called this 1925 limestone cube by Carrère & Hastings pompous. It was originally the headquarters of the Macmillan Publishing Company. When Macmillan moved uptown, the late Malcolm Forbes moved in with his financial magazine, *Forbes*. The Forbes Magazine Galleries here show Forbes's diverse tastes, with over 500 antique toy boats; Monopoly games; trophies; 12,000 toy soldiers; and a signed copy of Abraham Lincoln's Gettysburg Address, among other historical memorabilia. Paintings, from French to American Military works, are also on display.

Salmagundi Club ❿

47 5th Ave **Map** 4 E1. **Tel** (212) 255-7740. Ⓜ 14th St–Union Sq. ◔ 1–6pm Mon–Fri, 1–5pm Sat & Sun. 📷 www.salmagundi.org

America's oldest artists club resides in the last remaining mansion on lower Fifth Avenue. Built in 1853 for Irad Hawley, it now houses the American Artists' Professional League, the American

Watercolor Society and the Greenwich Village Society for Historic Preservation. Washington Irving's satiric periodical, *The Salmagundi Papers,* gave the club its name. Founded in 1871, the club moved here in 1917. Periodic art exhibits open the late 19th-century interior to the public.

Exterior of the Salmagundi Club

First Presbyterian Church ⓫

5th Ave at 12th St. **Map** 4 D1. **Tel** (212) 675-6150. Ⓜ 14th St–Union Sq. ◔ 11:45am–12:30pm Mon, Wed, Fri, 11am–12:30pm Sun. ✝ 6pm Wed in chapel. www.fpcnyc.org

Designed by Joseph C. Wells in 1846, this Gothic church was modeled on the Church of St Saviour in Bath, England. The church is noteworthy for its brownstone tower. The carved wooden plaques on the altar list every pastor since 1716. The south transept by McKim, Mead & White was added in 1893. The fence of iron and wood was built in 1844 and restored in 1981.

Church of the Ascension ⓬

5th Ave at 10th St. **Map** 4 E1. **Tel** (212) 254-8620. Ⓜ 14th St–Union Sq. ◔ noon–2pm, 5–7pm daily. ✝ 6pm Mon–Fri, 9am, 11am Sun. 📷 (except during services). www.ascensionnyc.org

Church of the Ascension

This English Gothic Revival church was designed in 1840–41 by Richard Upjohn, architect of Trinity Church. The interior was redone in 1888 by Stanford White, with an altar relief by Augustus Saint-Gaudens. Above the altar hangs *The Ascension*, a mural by John La Farge, who also designed some of the stained glass. The belfry tower is lit at night to show off the colors. In 1844 President John Tyler married Julia Gardiner here; she lived in nearby Colonnade Row *(see p120).*

Washington Mews ⓭

Between Washington Sq N and E 8th St. **Map** 4 E2. Ⓜ W 4th St.

Built originally as stables, this hidden enclave was turned into carriage houses around 1900. The south side was added in 1939. Gertrude Vanderbilt Whitney, founder of the Whitney Museum *(see pp200–01),* once lived here.

At No. 16 is NYU's French House, remodeled in a French style. Movies, lectures, and classes in French are held here.

New York University ⑭

Washington Sq. **Map** 4 E2.
Tel (212) 998-1212, (212) 998-4636. Ⓜ *W 4th St.* ◯ *8:30am–8pm Mon–Fri.* **www**.nyu.edu

Originally called the University of the City of New York, NYU was founded in 1831 as an alternative to Episcopalian Columbia University. It is now the largest private university in the US and extends for blocks around Washington Square.

Construction of the school's first building on Waverly Place sparked the Stone-cutters' Guild Riot of 1833: contractors protested the use of inmates from a state prison to cut stone. The National Guard restored order. The original building no longer exists, but a memorial with a piece of the original tower is on a pedestal set into the pavement on Washington Square South. Samuel Morse's telegraph, John W. Draper's first-ever photographic

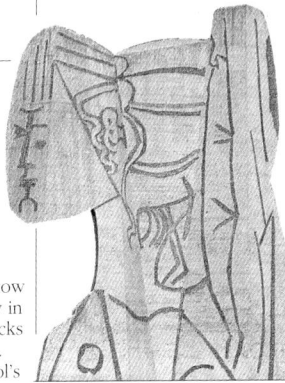

Bust of Sylvette **by Picasso, between Bleecker and West Houston streets**

portrait and Samuel Colt's six-shooter were invented here.

The Brown Building, on Washington Place near Greene Street, was the site of the Triangle Shirtwaist Company. In 1911, 146 factory workers died in a fire here, leading to new fire safety and labor laws.

A 36-ft (11-m) enlargement of Picasso's *Bust of Sylvette* is in University Village.

Judson Memorial Church ⑮

55 Washington Sq S. **Map** 4 D2.
Tel (212) 477-0351. Ⓜ *W 4th St.*
◯ *10am–1pm, 2–6pm Mon–Fri.*
🕇 *11am Sun.* **www**.judson.org

Built in 1892, this McKim, Mead & White church is an impressive Romanesque building with stained glass by John La Farge. Designed by Stanford White, it is named after the first American missionary sent to foreign soil, Adoniram Judson, who served in Burma in 1811. A copy of his Burmese translation of the Bible was put in the cornerstone when the building was dedicated.

It is the unique spirit of this church, not the architecture, that makes it stand out. Judson Memorial has played an active role in local and world concerns and has been the site of activism on issues ranging from AIDS to the arms race. It is also home to avant-garde art exhibitions and Off-Off Broadway plays.

Arch on the north side of Washington Square

Washington Square ⑯

Map 4 D2. Ⓜ *W 4th St.*

This vibrant open space was once marshland through which the quiet Minetta Brook flowed. By the late 1700s, the area had been turned into a public cemetery – when excavation began for the park, some 10,000 skeletal remains were exhumed. The square was used as a dueling ground for a time, then as a site

for public hangings until 1819. The "hanging elm" in the northwest corner remains. In 1826 the marsh was filled in and the brook diverted under-ground, where it still flows; a small sign on a fountain at the entrance to Two Fifth Avenue marks its course.

The magnificent marble arch by Stanford White, was completed in 1895 and replaced an earlier wooden arch that spanned lower Fifth Avenue to mark the centenary of George Washington's inauguration. A stairway is hidden in the right side of the arch. In 1916, a group of artists led by Marcel Duchamp and John Sloan broke in, climbed atop the arch, and declared the "free and independent republic of Washington Square, the state of New Bohemia."

Across the street is "the Row." Now part of NYU, this block was once home to New York's most prominent families. The Delano family, writers Edith Wharton, Henry James and John dos Passos, and artist Edward Hopper all lived here. Number 8 was once the mayor's official home.

Today students, families and free spirits mingle and enjoy the park side by side. A few drug dealers frequent the park, but it is safe by day.

Window on the corner of West 4th Street and Washington Square

EAST VILLAGE

Peter Stuyvesant had a country estate in the East Village, and in the 19th century, the Astors and Vanderbilts lived here. But around 1900, high society moved uptown, and immigrants moved in. The Irish, Germans, Jews, Poles, Ukrainians, and Puerto Ricans all left their mark in the area's churches and landmarks, and the city's most varied and least expensive ethnic restaurants. In the 1950s, low rents attracted the "beat generation." Later, hippies were followed by punks, and experimental music clubs and theaters still abound. Astor Place buzzes with students. To the east are Avenues A, B, C, and D, an area known as "Alphabet City," which, despite being somewhat gritty, has become one of the city's dining hotspots.

Mosaic, facade of St. George's Ukrainian Catholic Church

SIGHTS AT A GLANCE

Historic Streets and Buildings
Bayard-Condit Building ⑧
Colonnade Row ③
Cooper Union ①

Museums and Galleries
Merchant's House Museum ④

Churches
Grace Church ⑥
St. Mark's-in-the-Bowery Church ⑤

Parks and Squares
Tompkins Square ⑦

Famous Theaters
Public Theater ②

SEE ALSO
• *Street Finder,* maps 4, 5
• *Where to Stay* pp281–2
• *Restaurants* pp301–2

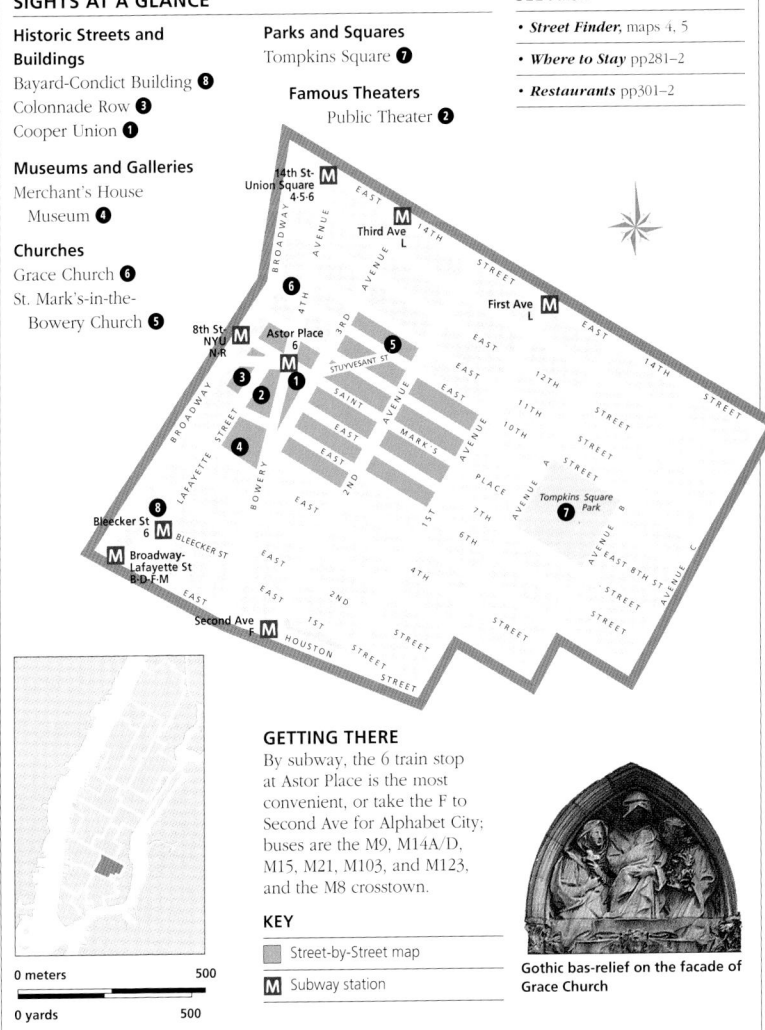

GETTING THERE
By subway, the 6 train stop at Astor Place is the most convenient, or take the F to Second Ave for Alphabet City; buses are the M9, M14A/D, M15, M21, M103, and M123, and the M8 crosstown.

KEY

▨	Street-by-Street map
Ⓜ	Subway station

0 meters 500
0 yards 500

Gothic bas-relief on the facade of Grace Church

◁ The interior of McSorley's Old Ale House

Street by Street: East Village

At the spot where Tenth and Stuyvesant streets now intersect, Peter Stuyvesant's country house once stood. His grandson, also named Peter, inherited most of the property and had it divided into streets in 1787. Among the prize sites of the St. Mark's Historic District are the St. Mark's-in-the-Bowery Church, the Stuyvesant-Fish house and the 1795 home of Nicholas Stuyvesant, both on Stuyvesant Street. Many other homes in the district were built between 1871 and 1890 and still have their original stoops, lintels and other architectural details.

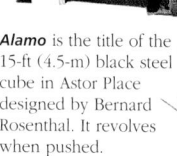

Astor Place subway (line 6)

Astor Place saw rioting in 1849. English actor William Macready, playing Hamlet at the Astor Place Opera House, criticized American actor Edwin Forrest. Forrest's fans revolted and there were 34 deaths.

Alamo is the title of the 15-ft (4.5-m) black steel cube in Astor Place designed by Bernard Rosenthal. It revolves when pushed.

Colonnade Row
Now in shabby disrepair, these buildings were once expensive town houses. The houses, of which only four are left, are unified by one facade in the European style. The marble was quarried by Sing Sing prisoners ❸

Public Theater
In 1965 the late Joseph Papp convinced the city to buy the Astor Library (1849) as a home for the theater. Now restored, it sees the opening of many famous plays ❷

STAR SIGHTS

★ Cooper Union

★ Merchant's House Museum

★ **Merchant's House Museum**
This museum displays Federal, American Empire, and Victorian furniture ❹

★ Cooper Union
This institution, known for its art and engineering programs, provides a free education to its students ❶

The Stuyvesant-Fish House (1803–04) was constructed out of brick. It is a classic example of a Federal-style house.

St. Mark's-in-the-Bowery-Church
The church was built in 1799 and the steeple added in 1828 ❺

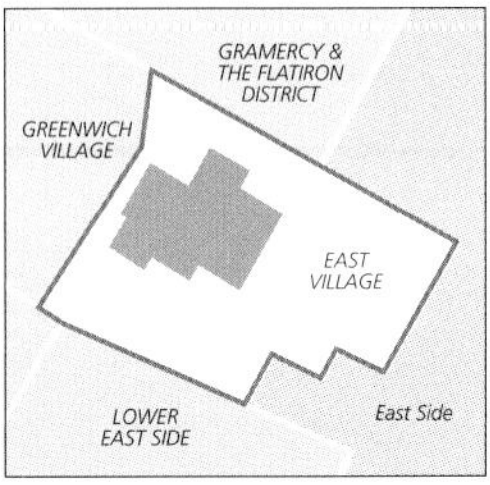

LOCATOR MAP
See Manhattan Map pp14–15

Renwick Triangle is a group of 16 houses built in the Italianate style in 1861.

Stuyvesant Polyclinic was founded in 1857 as the German Dispensary, and it is still a health clinic. The facade is decorated with the busts of many famous physicians and scientists.

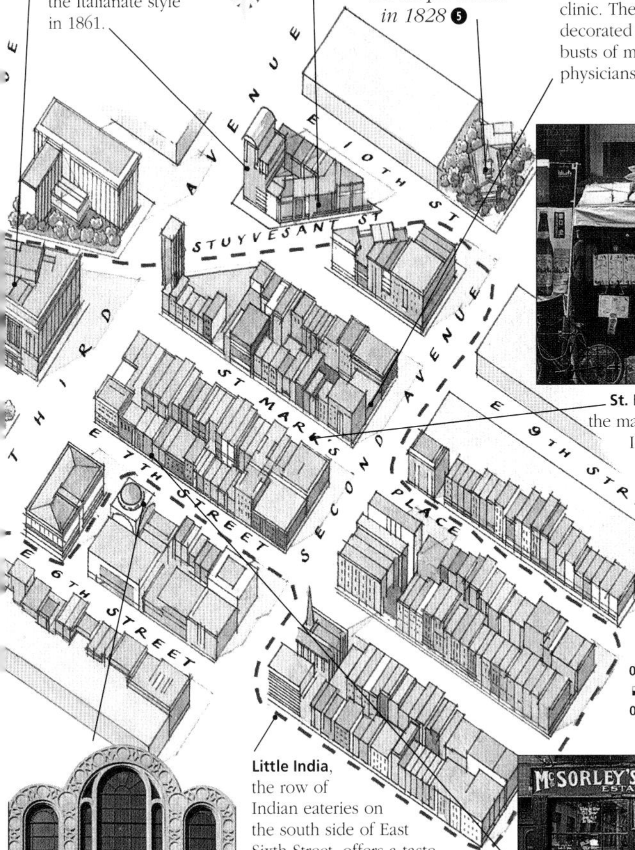

St. Mark's Place was once the main street of hippie life. It is still the hub of the East Village youth scene. Funky shops now occupy many of the basements.

0 meters 100

0 yards 100

Little India, the row of Indian eateries on the south side of East Sixth Street, offers a taste of India at budget prices.

KEY

— — — Suggested route

Little Ukraine is home to 30,000 Ukrainians. The hub is St. George's Ukrainian Catholic Church.

McSorley's Old Ale House still brews its own ale and serves it in surroundings virtually unchanged since it opened in 1854 *(see p317).*

Great Hall at Cooper Union, where Abraham Lincoln spoke

Cooper Union ❶

7 East 7th St. **Map** 4 F2.
Tel (212) 353-4000. Ⓜ Astor Pl.
⭘ 11am–7pm Mon–Fri, 11am–5pm
Sat, and for lectures and concerts in
Great Hall. ◐ Jun–Aug, public hols.
∅ ♿ **www**.cooper.edu

Peter Cooper, the wealthy industrialist who built the first US steam locomotive, made the first steel rails and was a partner in the first trans-atlantic cable venture, had no formal schooling. In 1859 he founded New York's first free, non-sectarian coeducational college specializing in design, engineering, and architecture. Still free, the school inspires intense competition for places. The six-story building, renovated in 1973–4, was the first with a steel frame, made of Cooper's own rails. The Great Hall was inaugurated in 1859 by Mark Twain, and Lincoln delivered his "Right Makes Might" speech there in 1860. Cooper Union still sponsors a Public Forum.

Public Theater ❷

425 Lafayette St. **Map** 4 F2. **Tel** (212) 967-7555 (tickets). Admin (212) 539-8500. Ⓜ Astor Pl. See also **Entertainment** p344. **www**.publictheater.org

This large redbrick and brown-stone building began its life in 1849 as the Astor Library, the city's first free library,

The Public Theater on Lafayette Street

now part of the New York Public Library. It is a prime American example of German Romanesque Revival style.

When the building was threatened with demolition in 1965, Joseph Papp, founder of the New York Shakespeare Festival, which became The Public Theater, persuaded New York City to buy it as a home for the company. Renovation began in 1967, and much of the handsome interior was preserved during conversion into six theaters. Although much of the work shown is experimental, The Public Theater was the original home of hit musicals *Hair* and *A Chorus Line* and hosts the popular Shakespeare in the Park (in Central Park) every summer.

Colonnade Row ❸

428–434 Lafayette St. **Map** 4 F2.
Ⓜ Astor Pl. ◐ to the public.

The Corinthian columns across these four buildings are all that remain of a once-magnificent row of nine Greek Revival town houses. They were completed in 1833 by developer Seth Geer and were known as "Geer's Folly" by skeptics who thought no one would live so far east. They were proved wrong when the houses were taken by such eminent citizens as John

Jacob Astor and Cornelius Vanderbilt. Washington Irving, author of *Rip Van Winkle* and other classic American tales, lived here for a time, as did two English novelists, William Makepeace Thackeray and Charles Dickens. Five of the houses were lost when the John Wanamaker Department Store razed them in the early 20th century to make room for a garage. The remaining buildings are falling to ruin.

Merchant's House Museum ❹

29 E 4th St. **Map** 4 F2. **Tel** (212) 777-1089. Ⓜ Astor Pl., Bleecker St.
⭘ noon–5pm Mon, Thu–Sun and
by appt. 📷 ∅ ⧖ 🚻
www.merchantshouse.com

The original 19th-century iron stove in the kitchen of the Merchant's House Museum

This remarkable Greek Revival brick town house, improbably tucked away on an East Village block, is a time capsule of a vanished way of life. It still has both its original fixtures and its kitchen, and is filled with the actual furniture, ornaments, and utensils of the family that lived here for almost 100 years. Built in 1832, it was bought in 1835 by Seabury Tredwell, a wealthy merchant, and stayed in the family until Gertrude Tredwell, the last member, died in 1933. She had maintained her father's home just as he would have liked it, and a relative opened the house as a museum in 1936. The first-floor parlors are very grand, a sign of how well New York's merchant class lived in the 1800s.

St. Mark's-in-the-Bowery Church **❺**

131 E 10th St. **Map** 4 F1. **Tel** (212) 674-6377. Ⓜ Astor Pl. ◯ 8:30am–4pm Mon–Fri (hours may vary). ✚ 6:30pm Wed, 11am Sun; in Spanish 5:30pm Sat.

One of New York's oldest churches, this 1799 building replaced a 1660 church on the *bouwerie* (farm) of Governor Peter Stuyvesant. He is buried here, along with seven generations of his descendants and many other prominent early New Yorkers. Poet W.H. Auden was a parishioner and is also commemorated here.

In 1878, a grisly kidnapping took place when the remains of department store magnate A.T. Stewart were removed from the site and held for $20,000 ransom.

The church rectory at 232 East 11th Street dates from 1900 and is by Ernest Flagg, who achieved renown for his Singer Building *(see p106)*.

Grace Church **❻**

802 Broadway. **Map** 4 F1. **Tel** (212) 254-2000. Ⓜ Astor Pl, Union Sq. 🚌 M1–3, M8, M101–3. ✚ Jul–Aug: 10am, 6pm Sun; Sep–Jun: 9am, 11am, 6pm Sun. ♿ 🅿 **Concerts.** **www**.gracechurchnyc.org

James Renwick, Jr., the architect of St. Patrick's Cathedral, was only 23 when he designed this church, yet many consider it his finest achievement. Its delicate early Gothic lines have a grace befitting the church's name. The interior is just as beautiful, with Pre-Raphaelite stained glass and a handsome mosaic floor.

The church's peace and serenity were briefly shattered in 1863, when Phineas T. Barnum

Tom Thumb and his bride at Grace Church

staged the wedding of midget General Tom Thumb here; the crowds turned the event into complete chaos.

The marble spire replaced a wooden steeple in 1888 amid fears that it might prove too heavy for the church – and it has since developed a distinct lean. The church is visible from afar, because it is on a bend on Broadway. Henry Brevoort forced the city to bend Broadway to divert it around his apple orchard.

Grace Church altar and window

Tompkins Square **❼**

Map 5 B1. Ⓜ 2nd Ave, 1st Ave. 🚌 M8, M9, M14A.

This English-style park has the makings of a peaceful spot, but its past has more often been dominated by strife. It was the site of America's first organized labor demonstration in 1874, the main gathering place during the neighborhood's hippie era of the 1960s and, in 1991, an arena for violent riots when the police tried to evict homeless people who had taken over the grounds. The square also contains a poignant monument to the neighborhood's greatest tragedy. A small statue of a boy

and a girl looking at a steamboat commemorates the deaths of over 1,000 local residents in the *General Slocum* steamer disaster. On June 15, 1904, the boat caught fire during a pleasure cruise on the East River. The boat was crowded with women and children from this then-German neighborhood. Many local men lost their entire families and moved away, leaving the area and its memories behind.

Bayard-Condict Building **❽**

65 Bleecker St. **Map** 4 F3. Ⓜ Bleecker St.

The graceful columns, elegant filigreed terra-cotta facade and magnificent cornice on this 1898 building mark the only New York work by Louis Sullivan, the great Chicago architect who taught Frank Lloyd Wright. He died in poverty and obscurity in Chicago in 1924.

Sullivan is said to have objected vigorously to the sentimental angels supporting the Bayard-Condict Building's cornice, but he eventually gave in to the wishes of Silas Alden Condict, the owner.

Because this building is squeezed into a commercial block, it is better appreciated from a distance. Cross the street and walk a little way down Crosby Street for the best view.

The Bayard-Condict Building

GRAMERCY AND THE FLATIRON DISTRICT

Four squares were laid out in this area by real estate developers in the 19th century to emulate the quiet, private residential areas in many European cities. Gramercy Park, still mainly residential, was one of them. The townhouses around this square were designed by some of the country's best architects, such as Calvert Vaux and Stanford White, and occupied by some of New York's most prominent citizens. Today, not far away, boutiques, trendy cafés, and high-rise apartments have taken over the stretch of lower Fifth Avenue just south of the famous Flatiron Building.

Lizard on a statue in Union Square

SIGHTS AT A GLANCE

Historic Streets and Buildings
Appellate Division of the Supreme Court of the State of New York ❸
Block Beautiful ⓫
Con Edison Headquarters ⓮
Flatiron Building ❺
Gramercy Park Hotel ⓬
Ladies' Mile ❻
The Library at the Players ❾
Metropolitan Life Insurance Company ❹

National Arts Club ❽
New York Life Insurance Company ❷

Museums and Galleries
Theodore Roosevelt Birthplace ❼

Churches
The Little Church Around the Corner ⓰

Parks and Squares
Gramercy Park ❿
Madison Square ❶
Stuyvesant Square ⓭
Union Square ⓯

SEE ALSO
• *Street Finder,* maps 8, 9
• *Where to Stay* p282
• *Restaurants* pp302–3

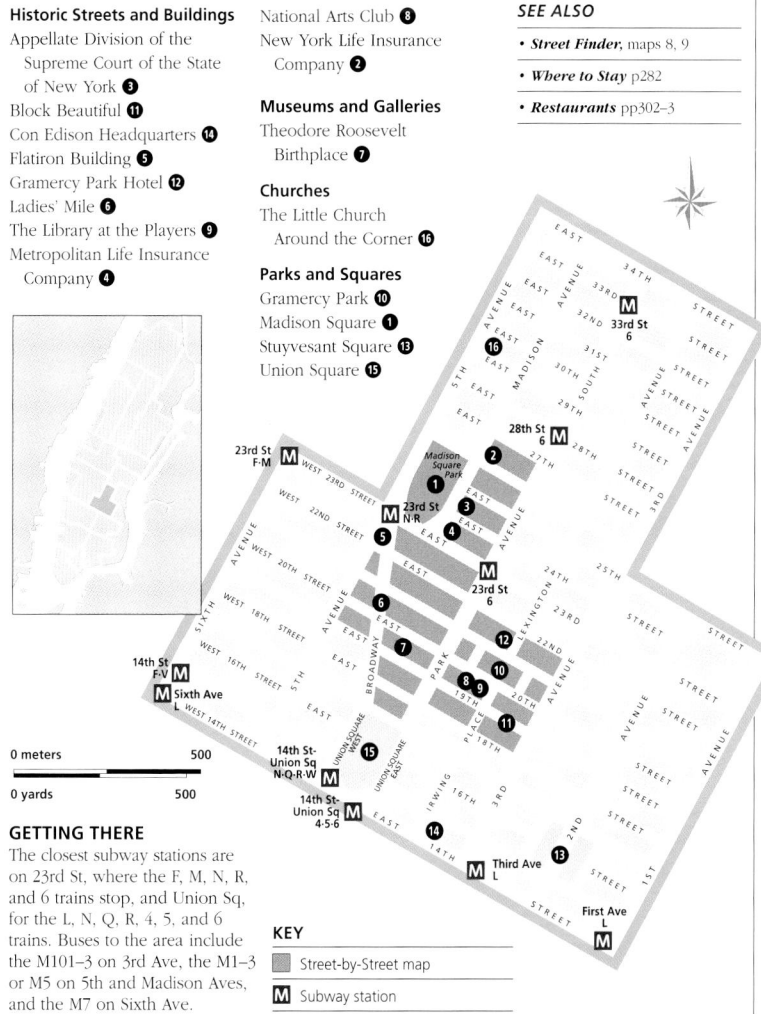

GETTING THERE
The closest subway stations are on 23rd St, where the F, M, N, R, and 6 trains stop, and Union Sq, for the L, N, Q, R, 4, 5, and 6 trains. Buses to the area include the M101–3 on 3rd Ave, the M1–3 or M5 on 5th and Madison Aves, and the M7 on Sixth Ave.

KEY

Street-by-Street map

Ⓜ Subway station

0 meters 500
0 yards 500

◁ **Con Edison Headquarters by night**

Street by Street: Gramercy Park

Gramercy Park and nearby Madison Square tell a tale of two cities. Madison Square is ringed by offices and traffic and is used mainly by those who work nearby, but the fine surrounding commercial architecture and statues make it well worth visiting. It was once the home of Stanford White's famous pleasure palace, the old Madison Square Garden, a place where revelers always thronged. Gramercy Park, however, retains the air of dignified tranquility it has become known for. Here, the residences and clubs remain, set around New York's last private park, for which only those who live on the square have a key.

★ Madison Square
The Knickerbocker Club played baseball here in the 1840s and was the first to codify the game's rules. Today office workers enjoy the park's many statues of 19th-century figures, among them Admiral David Farragut ❶

23rd Street subway (lines N, R)

Statue of Diana atop the old Madison Square Garden

M

★ Flatiron Building
The triangle made by Fifth Avenue, Broadway, and 22nd Street is the site of one of New York's most famous early skyscrapers. When it was built in 1903, it was the world's tallest building ❺

M

BROADWAY (LADIES MILE)

E 21ST STREET

A sidewalk clock found in front of 200 Fifth Avenue marks the very end of the once-fashionable shopping area, known as Ladies' Mile.

E 9TH ST

Ladies' Mile
Broadway from Union Square to Madison Square was once New York's finest shopping area ❻

Theodore Roosevelt Birthplace
The house is a replica of the one in which the 26th American president was born ❼

E 17TH ST

KEY

– – – Suggested route

0 meters	100
0 yards	100

National Arts Club
This is a private club for the arts, on the south side of the park ❽

Appellate Court
This small marble palace is said to be the world's busiest court-house ❸

MADISON AVENUE

E 26TH ST

AVENUE

23RD ST

Ⓜ 23rd Street subway (line 6)

The Library at the Players
Actor Edwin Booth founded this club in 1888 ❾

GRAMERCY PARK

IRVING PLACE

THIRD AVENUE

LOCATOR MAP
See Manhattan Map pp14–15

CHELSEA & THE GARMENT DISTRICT

LOWER MIDTOWN

East Side

GRAMERCY & THE FLATIRON DISTRICT

GREENWICH VILLAGE

EAST VILLAGE

New York Life Insurance Company
This spectacular building by Cass Gilbert bears his trade-mark pyramid-shaped top ❷

STAR SIGHTS

★ Flatiron Building

★ Madison Square

Metropolitan Life Insurance Company
Vast vaulted entrances mark each corner ❹

Gramercy Park
Only residents can use the park itself, but all can enjoy the peace and charm of the area around it ❿

The Brotherhood Synagogue was a Friends' Meeting House from 1859 to 1975, when it became a synagogue.

The Block Beautiful
This is a tree-lined stretch of East 19th Street. No particular house is outstanding, but the street as a whole is lovely ⓫

Pete's Tavern
has been here since 1864. Short story writer O. Henry, a well-known chronicler of the city, wrote "The Gift of the Magi" in the second booth.

Madison Square ❶

Map 8 F4. Ⓜ *23rd St.*

Farragut's statue, Madison Square

Planned as the center of a fashionable residential district, this square became a popular entertainment center after the Civil War. It was bordered by the elegant Fifth Avenue Hotel, the Madison Square Theater, and Stanford White's Madison Square Garden. The torch-bearing arm of the Statue of Liberty was exhibited here in 1884.

The Shake Shack is a top lunchtime spot for neighborhood office workers, while the surrounding park makes for a leisurely stroll to admire the sculptures. The 1880 statue of Admiral David Farragut is by Augustus Saint-Gaudens, with a pedestal by Stanford White. Farragut was the hero of a Civil War sea battle; figures representing Courage and Loyalty are carved on the base. The statue of Roscoe Conkling commemorates a US senator who died during the great blizzard of 1888. The Eternal Light flagpole, by Carrère & Hastings, honors the soldiers who fell during World War I.

New York Life Insurance Company ❷

51 Madison Ave. **Map** 9 A3.
Ⓜ *28th St.* ◯ *office hours.*

This imposing building was designed in 1928 by Cass Gilbert of Woolworth Building fame. The interior is a masterpiece, adorned with enormous hanging lamps, bronze doors and paneling, and a grand staircase leading, of all places, to the subway station.

Other famous buildings have stood on this site. Barnum's

Hippodrome was here in 1874, then the first Madison Square Garden opened in 1879. A wide range of entertainments were put on, including the prizefights of heavyweight boxing hero John L. Sullivan in the 1880s. The next Madison Square Garden – Stanford White's legendary pleasure palace – opened on the same site in 1890. Lavish musical shows and social events were attended by New York's elite, who paid over $500 for a box at the prestigious annual horse show.

The building had street-level arcades and a tower modeled on the Giralda in Seville. A gold statue of the goddess Diana stood atop the tower. Her nudity was shocking, but far more scandalous was the decadent life and death of White himself. In 1906, while watching a revue in the roof garden, he was shot dead by millionaire Harry K. Thaw, the husband of White's former mistress, showgirl Evelyn Nesbit. The headline in the journal *Vanity Fair* summed up popular feeling: "Stanford White, Voluptuary and Pervert, Dies the Death of a Dog." The ensuing trial's revelations about decadent Broadway high society leave modern soap operas far behind.

New York Life Insurance Company's golden pyramid roof

Appellate Division of the Supreme Court of the State of New York ❸

E. 25th St. at Madison Ave. **Map** 9 A4.
Ⓜ *23rd St.* ◯ *9am–5pm Mon–Fri (court in session from 2pm Tue–Thu, from 10am Fri).* ◉ *public hols.* ♿

Appeals relating to civil and criminal cases for New York and the Bronx are heard here, in what is widely considered to be the busiest court of its kind in the world. James Brown Lord designed the small yet noble Palladian Revival building in 1900. It is decorated with more than a

Statues of *Justice* and *Study* above the Appellate Court

dozen handsome sculptures, including Daniel Chester French's Justice flanked by Power and Study. During the week, the public is invited to step inside to admire the fine interior, designed by the Herter brothers, including the courtroom when it is not in session. Among the elegant details worth looking for are the fine stained-glass windows and dome, the murals, and the striking cabinetwork.

Displays in the lobby often feature some of the more famous –and infamous – cases that have been heard in this court. Among the celebrity names that have been involved in appeals settled here are Babe Ruth, Charlie Chaplin, Fred Astaire, Harry Houdini, Theodore Dreiser, and Edgar Allan Poe.

Clock tower of the Metropolitan Life Insurance Company building

Metropolitan Life Insurance Company ❹

1 Madison Ave. **Map** 9 A4.
Ⓜ 23rd St. 🕒 banking hours. 🚫

In 1909, the addition of a 700-ft (210-m) tower to this 1893 building ousted the Flatiron as the tallest in the world. The huge four-sided clock has minute hands said to weigh 1000 lb (454 kg) each. The building is lit up at night, and is a familiar part of the evening skyline. It served as the company symbol "the light that never fails." A series of historical murals by N.C. Wyeth, the famed illustrator of such classics as *Robin Hood*, *Treasure Island* and *Robinson Crusoe* (and the father of painter Andrew Wyeth), once graced the walls of the cafeteria. The building now houses First-Boston Crédit-Suisse.

Flatiron Building ❺

175 5th Ave. **Map** 8 F4. Ⓜ 23rd St.
🕒 office hours.

Originally named the Fuller Building after the construction company that owned it, this building by Chicago architect Daniel Burnham was the tallest in the world when it was completed in 1902. One of the first buildings to use a steel frame, it heralded the era of the skyscrapers.

It soon became known as the Flatiron for its unusual triangular shape, but some called it "Burnham's folly," predicting that the winds created by the building's shape would knock it down. It has withstood the test of time, but the winds along 23rd Street did have one notable effect. In the building's early days, they drew crowds of males hoping to get a peek at women's ankles as their long skirts got blown about. Police officers had to keep people moving along, and their call, "23-skidoo" became slang for "scram."

The stretch of Fifth Avenue to the south of the building, formerly rather run down, has come to life with chic shops such as Emporio Armani and Paul Smith, giving the area new cachet and a new name, "the Flatiron District."

Flatiron Building during its construction

Ladies' Mile ❻

Broadway (Union Sq. to Madison Sq.).
Map 8 F4–5, 9 A5. Ⓜ 14th St,
23rd St.

Arnold Constable store

In the 19th century, the "carriage trade" came here in shiny traps from their town houses nearby to shop at stores such as Arnold Constable (Nos. 881–887) and Lord & Taylor (No. 901). The ground floor exteriors have changed beyond recognition; look up to see the remains of once-grand facades.

President Teddy Roosevelt

Theodore Roosevelt Birthplace ❼

28 E. 20th St. **Map** 9 A5. **Tel** (212)
260-1616. Ⓜ 14th St.-Union Sq-
23rd St. 🕒 9am–5pm Tue–Sat (last
adm: 4pm). ● pub hols. 🎫 📷 📹
hourly. **Lectures, concerts, films,
videos.** 🖥 www.nps.gov/thrb

The reconstructed boyhood home of the colorful 26th president displays everything from the toys with which the young Teddy played to campaign buttons and emblems of the trademark "Rough Rider" hat that Roosevelt wore in the Spanish-American War. One exhibit features his explorations and interests; the other covers his political career.

Bas-relief faces of great writers at the National Arts Club

National Arts Club ❽

15 Gramercy Pk S. **Map** 9 A5. **Tel** (212) 475-3424. **M** 23rd St. ◐ noon–5pm Mon–Fri during exhibitions. **www**.nationalartsclub.org

This brownstone was the residence of New York governor Samuel Tilden, who condemned "Boss" Tweed (see p27) and established a free public library. He had the facade redesigned by Calvert Vaux in 1881–4. In 1906 the National Arts Club bought the home and kept the original high ceilings and stained glass by John La Farge. Members have included most leading American artists of the late 19th and early 20th century, who were asked to donate a painting or sculpture in return for life membership; these gifts form the permanent collection. The club is open to the public for exhibitions only.

The Library at the Players ❾

18 Gramercy Pk S. **Map** 9 A5. **Tel** (212) 228-7610. **M** 23rd St. ◑ except for pre-booked group tours. ◙

This two-story brownstone was the home of actor Edwin Booth, brother of John Wilkes Booth, President Lincoln's assassin. Architect Stanford White remodeled the

building as a club in 1888. Although intended primarily for actors, members have included White himself, author Mark Twain, publisher Thomas Nast and Winston Churchill, whose mother, Jennie Jerome, was born nearby. A statue of Booth playing Hamlet is across the street in Gramercy Park.

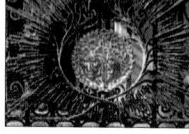

Decorative grille at The Players club

Gramercy Park ❿

Map 9 A4. **M** 23rd St, 14th St-Union Sq.

Gramercy Park is one of four squares (with Union, Stuyvesant and Madison) laid out in the 1830s and 1840s to attract society residences. It is the city's only private park, and residents in the surrounding buildings have keys to the park gate as the original owners once did. Look through the railings at the southeast corner to see Greg Wyatt's fountain, with giraffes leaping around a smiling sun.

The buildings around the square were designed by some of the city's most famous

Fountain with sun and giraffes by Greg Wyatt in Gramercy Park

architects, including Stanford White, whose house was located on the site of today's Gramercy Park Hotel. Particularly fine are 3 and 4, with graceful cast-iron gates and porches. The lanterns in front of 4 serve as symbols marking the house of a former mayor of the city, James Harper. Number 34 (1883) has been the home of the sculptor Daniel Chester French, the actor James Cagney and circus impresario John Ringling (who had a massive pipe organ installed in his apartment).

Block Beautiful ⓫

E 19th St. **Map** 9 A5. **M** 14th St-Union Sq, 23rd St.

House facade on the Block Beautiful on East 19th Street

This is a serene, tree-lined block of 1920s residences, beautifully restored. None of them is exceptional on its own, but together they create a wonderfully harmonious whole. Number 132 had two famous theatrical tenants: Theda Bara, silent movie star and Hollywood's first sex symbol, and the fine Shakespearean actress Mrs. Patrick Campbell, who originated the role of Eliza Doolittle in George Bernard Shaw's Pygmalion in 1914. The hitching posts outside 141 and the ceramic relief of giraffes outside 147–149 are two of the many details to look for as you walk along the block.

Gramercy Park Hotel ⑫

2 Lexington Ave at 21st St. **Map** 9 B4. **Tel** (212) 475-4320. Ⓜ 14th St-Union Sq, 23rd St. **www**.gramercyparkhotel.com

Located on the site of Stanford White's house, this hotel has, for more than 60 years, been a home away from home for many international visitors and New Yorkers alike. It is also right next to the only private park in Manhattan.

The shabby-chic hotel drew all types, from old matrons, to wealthy young rock stars. Then Ian Schrager, of Studio 54 fame, began a $200-million renovation, in which the 185-room hotel was given an "eclectic-Bohemian" look by artist Julian Schnabel. The conversion included 23 condominiums that range in price from $5 million to $10 million. The elegant Rose and Jade bars and a Chinese restaurant are open to the public.

Stuyvesant Square ⑬

Map 9 B5. Ⓜ 3rd Ave, 1st Ave.

This oasis, in the form of a pair of parks divided by Second Avenue, was part of Peter Stuyvesant's original farm in the 1600s. It was still in the Stuyvesant family when the park was designed in 1836; Peter G. Stuyvesant sold the land to the city for the nominal sum of $5 (much to the delight of those living nearby, who saw real estate values jump). A statue of Stuyvesant by Gertrude Vanderbilt Whitney stands in the park. The park separated the Stuyvesant area from the poorer Gas House district.

Con Edison Headquarters ⑭

145 E 14th St. **Map** 9 A5. Ⓜ 3rd Ave, 14th St-Union Sq. 🔲 to the public.

The clock tower of this building, which dates from 1911, is a local landmark. Originally conceived by Henry Hardenbergh, the

The towers of Con Edison (right), Metropolitan Life and the Empire State

architect best known for such buildings as the Dakota (see p218) and the Plaza (see p181). The 26-story tower was built by the same firm who designed Grand Central Terminal. Near the top of the tower, a 38-ft (11.6-m) bronze lantern was built as a memorial to Con Ed's employees who died in World War I. The tower itself is not as tall as nearby Empire State Building, but when it is lit up at night, it makes an attractive showpiece, in addition to a potent symbol of the company that keeps Manhattan and the other four boroughs shining.

Union Square ⑮

Map 9 A5. Ⓜ 14th St-Union Sq. **Farmers' Market** 🔲 8am–6pm Mon, Wed, Fri, Sat.

Greenmarket day at Union Square

Opened in 1839, this park joined Bloomingdale Road (now Broadway) with the Bowery Road (Fourth Avenue or Park), and hence its name. Later, the center of the square

was lifted up for a subway to run beneath it. The park became popular with soapbox orators. During the Depression in 1930, more than 35,000 unemployed people rallied here, before marching on to City Hall to demand jobs. The square hosts a greenmarket and is ringed by various shops from discount department stores to gourmet supermarkets.

The Little Church Around the Corner ⑯

1 E 29th St. **Map** 8 F3. **Tel** (212) 684-6770. Ⓜ 28th St. 🔲 8am–6pm daily. 🔲 12:10pm Mon–Fri; 8:30am, 11am Sun. ◻ ◻ ◻ Sun, after 11am service. **Lectures & concerts.** **www**.littlechurch.org

Built from 1849 to 1856, the Episcopal Church of the Transfiguration is a tranquil retreat. It has been known by its nickname since 1870 when Joseph Jefferson tried to arrange the funeral of fellow actor George Holland. The pastor at a nearby church refused to bury a person of so lowly a profession. Instead, he suggested "the little church around the corner." The name stuck and the church has had special ties with the theater ever since. Sarah Bernhardt attended services here.

The south transept window, by John La Farge, shows Edwin Booth playing Hamlet. Jefferson's cry of "God bless the little church around the corner" is commemorated in a window in the south aisle.

CHELSEA AND
THE GARMENT DISTRICT

This was open farmland in 1750. By the 1830s it was a suburb, and in the 1870s, with the coming of the elevated railroads *(see pp26–7)*, it had become commercial. Music halls and theaters lined 23rd Street. Fashion Row grew in the shadow of the El, with department stores serving middle-class New York. As fashion moved uptown, Chelsea drifted downhill. It became a warehouse district, until the Els were removed and New Yorkers rediscovered its town houses. When Macy's arrived at Herald Square to the north, the retailing and garment districts grew around it, along with the flower district. Today Chelsea is filled with art galleries and antique shops and has a large gay community.

Statue of garment worker, at 555 7th Avenue

The Empire State Building on Fifth Avenue, from Macy's department store on 34th Street

SIGHTS AT A GLANCE

Historic Streets and Buildings
Chelsea Art Galleries ⓫
Chelsea Historic District ⓭
Empire State Building
pp136–7 ❷

General Post
Office ❼

General Theological
Seminary ⓬
Hugh O'Neill Dry Goods
Store ⓯

Churches
Marble Collegiate Reformed
Church ❶
St. John the Baptist Church ❺

Modern Architecture
Chelsea Piers Complex ❿

Jacob K. Javits Convention
Center ❽
Madison Square Garden ❻

Monuments
Worth Monument ⓰

Parks and Squares
Herald Square ❸
High Line ❾

Landmark Hotels
Hotel Chelsea ⓮

Landmark Stores
Macy's ❹

GETTING THERE
To Chelsea, take the 1 subway train to 18th or 23rd St. The C and E trains go to 23rd St. Buses include the M11 and M20. For the area around Macy's, take the 1, or the 2 or 3 express trains to 34th St/ Penn Station. The A, C, and E trains also stop at 34th St, and the B, D, F, M, N, Q, and R trains stop at Herald Sq.

KEY

Street-by-Street map

Ⓜ Subway station

🚁 Heliport

SEE ALSO

• *Street Finder*, maps 7–8

• *Where to Stay* pp283–4

• *Restaurants* p304

Street by Street: Herald Square

Herald Square is named for the New York *Herald*, which had
its office here from 1894 to 1921. Today full of shoppers, the
area was once one of the raunchiest parts of New York. During
the 1880s and '90s, it was known as the Tenderloin District and
was filled with dance halls and bordellos. When Macy's opened
in 1901, the focus moved from flesh to fashion. New York's
Garment District now fills the
streets near Macy's around
Seventh Avenue, also
known as Fashion
Avenue. To the east on
Fifth Avenue is the
Empire State Building,
with the city's best
eagle's-eye views from
the observation deck.

Manhattan Mall, is
the former site of
Gimbel's, once
Macy's archrival.
It holds 90 stores,
a huge food court,
and a floor for
children's wares.

Fashion Avenue is another name for the
stretch of Seventh Avenue around 34th
Street. This area is the heart of New
York's garment industry. The streets are
full of men pushing racks of clothes.

**34th Street
subway (1, 2, 3)**

The Hotel Pennsylvania
was a center for the
1930s big bands –
Glenn Miller's song
"Pennsylvania 6-5000"
made its telephone
number
famous.

St. John
the Baptist Church
*A beautiful set of carved
Stations of the Cross is
hung on the walls
of the white marble
interior of this church* ❺

The SJM Building is at 130 West
30th Street. Mesopotamian-style friezes
adorn the outside of the building.

The Fur District is at the southern end
of the Garment District. Furriers ply their
trade between West 27th and 30th streets.

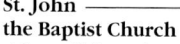

The Flower District,
around Sixth Avenue
and West 28th Street,
hums with activity in
the early part of the day
as florists pack their
vans with their highly
scented, brightly
colored wares.

**28th Street
subway
(lines N, R)**

★ Macy's
The biggest department store in the world has something for everyone ❹

The Greenwich Savings Bank (now the HSBC) is a Greek temple to banking with huge columns on three sides.

34th Street subway (lines B, D, F, M, N, Q, R)

Herald Square
The New York Herald Building's clock now is situated where Broadway meets Sixth Avenue ❸

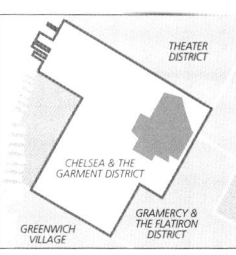

LOCATOR MAP
See Manhattan Map pp14–15

KEY

- - - Suggested route

0 meters 100
0 yards 100

Greeley Square is more of a traffic island than a square, but it does have a fine statue of Horace Greeley, founder of the New York *Tribune.*

★ Empire State Building
The observation deck of this quintessential skyscraper is a great place to view the city ❷

Little Korea is an area of Korean businesses. In addition to shops, there are restaurants nearby on West 31st and 32nd streets.

The Life Building at 19 West 31st Street housed *Life* magazine when it was a satirical weekly. Carrère & Hastings designed the building in 1894. It is now a hotel.

Marble Collegiate Church
This 1854 church was built in the Gothic Revival style. It became famous when Norman Vincent Peale was pastor here ❶

STAR SIGHTS

★ Empire State Building

★ Macy's

Marble Collegiate's Tiffany stained-glass windows

Marble Collegiate Reformed Church ❶

1 W. 29th St. **Map** 8 F3. **Tel** (212) 686-2770. Ⓜ 28th St. ⏰ 8:30am–8:30pm Mon–Fri, 9am–4pm Sat, 8am–3pm Sun. ⬤ public hols. ✝ 11:15am Sun. 🎥 during services. ♿ **Sanctuary** 3 W 29th St. ⏰ 10am–noon, 2–4pm Mon–Fri. **www**.marblechurch.org

This church is best known for its former pastor Norman Vincent Peale, who wrote *The Power of Positive Thinking*.

Another positive thinker, future US president Richard M. Nixon, attended services here when he was a lawyer in his pre-White House days.

The church was built in 1854 using the marble blocks that give it its name. Fifth Avenue was then no more than a dusty country road, and the cast-iron fence was there to keep livestock out.

The original white and gold interior walls were replaced with a stenciled gold *fleur-de-lis* design on a soft rust background. Two stained-glass Tiffany windows, depicting Old Testament scenes, were placed in the south wall in 1893.

Empire State Building ❷

See pp136–7.

Herald Square ❸

6th Ave. **Map** 8 E2. Ⓜ 34th St-Penn Station. See **Shopping** p321.

Named after the New York *Herald*, which occupied a fine arcaded, Italianate Stanford White building here from 1893 to 1921, the square was the hub of the rowdy Tenderloin district in the 1870s and 1880s. Theaters such as the Manhattan Opera House, dance halls, hotels, and restaurants kept the area humming with life until reformers clamped down on sleaze in the 1890s. The ornamental Bennett clock, named for James Gordon Bennett Jr., publisher of the *Herald*, is now all that is left of the Herald Building.

The Opera House was razed in 1901 to make way for Macy's and, soon after, other department stores followed, making Herald Square a mecca for shoppers. One such store was the now-defunct Gimbel Brothers Department Store, once archrival to Macy's. (The rivalry was affectionately portrayed in the New York Christmas movie *A Miracle on 34th Street*.) In 1988 the store was converted into a vertical mall with a glittery neon front. Most of the old names have gone, but Herald Square is still a key shopping district packed with chain stores. It also features a pedestrian plaza.

Macy's ❹

151 W. 34th St. **Map** 8 E2. **Tel** (212) 695-4400. Ⓜ 34th St-Penn Station. ⏰ 10am–9:30pm Mon–Sat, 11am–8:30pm Sun. ⬤ public hols. See **Shopping** p319. **www**.macys.com

The "world's largest store" covers a square block, and the merchandise inside includes any item you could imagine in every price range.

Macy's was founded by a former whaler named Rowland Hussey Macy, who opened a small store on West 14th Street in 1857. The store's red star logo came from Macy's tattoo, a souvenir of his sailing days.

By the time Macy died in 1877, his little store had grown to a row of 11 buildings. By 1902 Macy's had outgrown its 14th Street premises, and the firm acquired its present site, which covers about 2 million

Macy's 34th Street facade

The nave of St. John the Baptist Church

square feet (186,000 sq m) of floor space. The eastern facade has a modern entrance but still bears the bay windows and Corinthian pillars of the 1902 design. The 34th Street facade even has its original caryatids guarding the entrance, along with the clock, canopy, and lettering. Inside, many of the early wooden escalators are still in good working order. Unsurprisingly, Macy's is a designated National Historic Landmark.

Macy's sponsors New York's renowned Thanksgiving Day parade (see p52) and the Fourth of July fireworks (see p51). The store's popular Spring Flower Show draws thousands of visitors.

St. John the Baptist Church ❺

210 W 31st St. **Map** 8 E3. **Tel** (212) 564-9070. **M** 34th St-Penn Station. 6:15am–6pm daily. 8:45am, 10:30am, 5:15pm daily.

Founded in 1840 to serve a congregation of newly arrived immigrants, today this small Roman Catholic church is almost lost in the heart of

the Fur District. The exterior has a single spire. Although the brownstone facade on 30th Street is dark with city soot, many treasures lie within this dull exterior. The entrance is through the modern Friary on 31st Street.

The sanctuary by Napoleon Le Brun is a marvel of Gothic arches in glowing white marble surmounted by gilded capitals. Painted reliefs of religious scenes line the walls; sunlight streams through the stained-glass windows. Also off the Friary is the Prayer Garden, a small, green and peaceful oasis with religious statuary, a fountain and stone benches.

Madison Square Garden ❻

4 Pennsylvania Plaza. **Map** 8 D2. **Tel** (212) 465-6741. **M** 34th St-Penn Station. Mon–Sun, times vary according to shows. See **Entertainment** p360. www.thegarden.com

There's only one good thing to be said for the razing of the extraordinarily lovely McKim, Mead & White Pennsylvania Station building in favor of this undistinguished 1968 complex: it so enraged city preservationists that they formed an alliance to ensure that such a thing would never be allowed to happen again.

Madison Square Garden itself, which sits atop underground Pennsylvania Station, is a cylinder of precast concrete, functional enough as a 20,000-seat, centrally located home for the famous

New York Knickerbockers (the Knicks) basketball, Liberty (women's basketball), and New York Rangers hockey teams. It has a packed calendar of other events: rock concerts, championship tennis and boxing, outrageously staged wrestling, the Ringling Bros. and Barnum & Bailey Circus, an antiques show, a dog show and more. There is also a 5,600-seat theater.

Despite renovation work, Madison Square Garden lacks the panache of its earlier location, which combined a stunning Stanford White building with extravagant entertainment (see p126).

The massive interior of Madison Square Garden

General Post Office ❼

421 8th Ave. **Map** 8 D2. **Tel** (800) ASK-USPS. **M** 34th St-Penn Station. 24 hrs a day, every day (incl public hols). See **Practical Information** p377.

Designed by McKim, Mead & White in 1913, in a style to complement their 1910 Pennsylvania Station across the street, the General Post Office is a perfect example of a public building of the Beaux Arts period. The imposing, two-block-long structure has a broad staircase leading to a facade with 20 Corinthian columns and a pavilion at each end. The 280-ft (85-m) inscription across it is based on a description of the Persian Empire's postal service, from around 520 BC: "Neither snow nor rain nor heat nor gloom of night stays these couriers from the swift completion of their appointed rounds."

The Corinthian colonnade of the General Post Office

Empire State Building ❷

Empire State Building

The Empire State Building is the tallest skyscraper in New York. Named after the state's nickname, it has become an enduring symbol of the city. Construction began in March 1930, not long after the Wall Street Crash, and by the time it opened in 1931, space was so difficult to rent that it was nicknamed "the Empty State Building."

Only the immediate popularity of the observatories saved the building from bankruptcy; the observatories still attract more than 3.5 million visitors a year.

102nd-floor observatory

The Empire State was planned to be 86 stories high, but a then 150 ft (46 m) mooring mast for zeppelins was added. The mast, now 204 ft (62 m), transmits TV and radio to the city and four states.

CONSTRUCTION

The building was designed for ease and speed of construction. Everything possible was prefabricated and slotted into place at a rate of about four stories per week.

Symbols of the modern age are depicted on these bronze Art Deco medallions placed throughout the lobby.

The framework is made from 60,000 tons of steel and was built in 23 weeks.

Aluminum panels were used instead of stone around the 6,514 windows. The steel trim masks rough edges on the facing.

Ten million bricks were used to line the whole building.

Sandwich space between the floors houses the wiring, pipes and cables.

Over 200 steel and concrete piles support the 365,000-ton building.

Colored floodlighting of the top 30 floors marks special and seasonal events.

High-speed elevators travel at up to 1,000 ft (305 m) a minute.

Nine minutes 33 seconds is the record for racing up the 1,576 steps from the lobby to the 86th-floor observatory, in the annual Empire State Run-Up.

STAR FEATURES

★ Fifth Avenue Entrance Lobby

★ Views from the Observatories

★ **Views from the Observatories**
The 86th-floor observatory offers superb views, both from its indoor galleries and its 360-degree outdoor deck. The 102nd-floor observatory, 1,250 ft (381 m) high, requires an extra fee, payable at the second-floor Visitors' Center or online.

A Head for Heights
As the building took shape, construction workers often showed great bravery. Here, a worker clings to a crane hook. The Chrysler Building and other skyscrapers in the background appear surprisingly small.

Empire State 1454 ft (443 m) with mast

Eiffel Tower 1045 ft (319 m)

Great Pyramid 350 ft (107 m)

Big Ben 220 ft (67 m)

Pecking Order
New Yorkers are justly proud of their city's symbol, which towers above the icons of other countries.

Lightning Strikes
The Empire State Building is a natural lightning conductor, struck up to 100 times a year. The observation deck is open even during unfavorable weather.

★ **Fifth Avenue Entrance Lobby**
A relief image of the skyscraper is superimposed on a map of New York State in the marble-lined lobby.

ENCOUNTERS IN THE SKY

The Empire State Building has been seen in many films. However, the finale from the 1933 classic *King Kong* is easily its most famous guest appearance, as the giant ape straddles the spire to do battle with army aircraft. In 1945 a B-25 bomber flew too low over Manhattan in fog and struck the building just above the 78th floor. The luckiest escape was that of a young elevator operator whose cabin plunged 79 floors. The emergency brakes saved her life.

Jacob K. Javits Convention Center ❽

655 W. 34th St. **Map** 7 B2. **Tel** (212) 216-2000. Ⓜ 34th St-Penn Station, 42nd St. 🚌 M34, M42. ◯ only on show days – times vary. 📷 🚫 ♿ 👥 www.javitscenter.com

The Convention Center – modern New York architecture at its best

Strikingly modernistic in appearance, this glass building facing the Hudson River opened in 1986. It was designed by the Chinese-American architect I.M. Pei to give New York a new space for large-scale expositions, conventions, and trade shows. The 18-story building is constructed of 16,000 panes of glass, the two main halls can accommodate thousands of delegates, and the lobby is high enough to hold the Statue of Liberty.

In 1989 the construction of the Galleria River Pavilion provided an additional 40,000 sq ft (3,750 sq m) of open space to the building, and two outdoor terraces overlooking the river.

High Line ❾

Access at Gansevoort St, 14th St, 16th St, 18th St, and every two or three blocks to 30th St. **Map** 3 B1. **Tel** (212) 500-6035. Ⓜ 23rd St; 14th St (on lines A, C, E); 8th Av L; Christopher St/Sheridan Sq. ◯ 7am–10pm daily (to 8pm in winter). www.thehighline.org

This once-disused 1930s elevated railbed has been transformed into a slender city park. In 1999, local residents created the organization Friends of the High Line with the aim of saving the structure from demolition. Now extending from Gansevoort Street up Tenth Avenue to 30th Street, the park has played an important role in the gentrification of this neighborhood. The garden is planted with grasses, trees, and shrubs, and each section has different features – a mini-lawn, a sundeck, a steel flyover walkway – providing a totally unique experience.

Chelsea Piers Complex ❿

11th Ave (17th to 23rd Sts) **Map** 7 B5. **Tel** (212) 336-6666. Ⓜ14th St, 18th St, 23rd St. 🚌 M14, M23. ◯ daily. 🏃 www.chelseapiers.com

This mammoth complex converted four neglected piers into a center for a vast range of sports and leisure activities (see p33). The facilities include skating rinks, running tracks, a rock-climbing wall, a golf driving range, a marina, and TV and film production sound stages.

Aerial view of the Chelsea Piers Complex

Chelsea Art Galleries ⓫

Between W 21st St and W 27th St, around 10th and 11th Aves. **Map** 7 C4. Ⓜ 23rd St. ◯ usually 10am–6pm Tue–Sat. www.nygallerytours.com

Attracted by cheap rents, the many galleries that set up shop in Chelsea during the 1990s were a driving force in this area's resurgence. Between 150 and 200 venues are here, exhibiting work from up-and-coming artists in all manner of media. Check out P.P.O.W. or David Zwirner, which have a reputation for intriguing or provocative work. Try to avoid Saturdays, when art-crawler traffic is at its heaviest.

A 15th-century music manuscript in the General Theological Seminary

General Theological Seminary ⓬

175 9th Ave. **Map** 7 C4. **Tel** (212) 243-5150. Ⓜ 23rd St. ◯ noon–3pm Mon–Fri, 11am–3pm Sat. 🔔 11:45am Mon, Wed–Fri, 6pm Tue, Sun. 🚫 ♿ www.gts.edu

Founded in 1817, this block-square campus accepts 150 students at a time to train for the Episcopal priesthood. Clement Clarke Moore, a professor of Oriental Languages at what is today Columbia University (see p224), donated the site, officially known as Chelsea Square. The earliest remaining building dates from 1836; the most modern, St. Mark's Library, was built in 1960 and holds the largest collection of Latin Bibles in the world.

The campus can be entered from Ninth Avenue only. Inside, the garden is laid out in two quadrangles like an English cathedral close: it is especially lovely in the spring.

Chelsea Historic District ⓭

W. 20th St from 9th to 10th Aves. **Map** 8 D5. **M** *18th St.* **🚌** *M11.*

Although he is better known as the author of the poem "A Visit from St. Nicholas" than as an urban planner, Clement Clarke Moore owned an estate here and divided it into lots in the 1830s, creating handsome rows of town houses. Restoration has since rescued many of the original buildings here.

Of these, the finest are seven houses known as Cushman Row, running from 406–418 West 20th Street, which were built from 1839–40 for Don Alonzo Cushman. He was a merchant who also founded the Greenwich Savings Bank. He joined Moore and James N. Wells in the development of Chelsea. Rich in detail and intricate ironwork, Cushman Row is ranked with Washington Square North as a supreme example of Greek Revival architecture. Look for cast-iron wreaths around attic windows and the pineapples on the newel posts of two of the houses – old symbols of hospitality.

Farther along West 20th Street, from 446–450, there are fine examples of the Italianate style for which Chelsea is also renowned.

A house on Cushman Row

The detailed brickwork arches of windows and fanlights subtly implied the wealth of the owner, being able to afford this expensive effect.

Hugh O'Neill Dry Goods Store

Hotel Chelsea ⓮

222 W. 23rd St. **Map** 8 D4. **Tel** *(212) 243-3700.* **M** *23rd St.* **www**.hotelchelsea.com See **Where to Stay** p284.

Few hotels can match the Chelsea for artistic and literary heritage – and notoriety. Many former guests have been commemorated in the brass plaques on the hotel's

A guest's-eye view of the Hotel Chelsea's cast-iron stairwell

facade. They include Tennessee Williams, Mark Twain, Jack Kerouac, and Brendan Behan. Dylan Thomas spent his last years here. In 1966 Andy Warhol's movie *Chelsea Girls* was set here, reviving its cult status, and in 1978 punk band member Sid Vicious killed his girlfriend in the hotel. The Chelsea still draws musicians, artists, and writers who hope their names will one day be remembered. Stop by the bar to soak in the decadence of this creative atmosphere.

Hugh O'Neill Dry Goods Store ⓯

655–671 6th Avenue. **Map** 8 E4. **M** *23rd St.*

Though the store is long gone, the 1876 cast-iron columned and pilastered facade clearly shows the

scale and grandeur of the emporiums that once lined Sixth Avenue from 18th to 23rd streets, the area known as Fashion Row. O'Neill, whose sign can still be seen on the facade, was a showman and super-salesman whose trademark was a fleet of shiny delivery wagons. His customers came in droves via the conveniently close Sixth Avenue El. They were not the "carriage trade" enjoyed by Ladies' Mile *(see p127)*, but their numbers allowed the Row to flourish until the turn of the century, when the retailing district continued its move uptown. Now mostly restored, the buildings have turned into superstores and bargain places like T. J. Maxx.

Worth Monument ⓰

5th Ave and Broadway. **Map** 8 F4. **M** *23rd St-Broadway.*

Hidden away behind a water meter on a triangle amid city traffic is an obelisk erected in 1857 to mark the grave of the one public figure to be buried under the streets of Manhattan. That honor belongs to General William J. Worth, a hero of the Mexican wars of the mid-1800s. A cast-iron fence of swords embedded in the ground surrounds the monument.

The Worth Monument

THEATER DISTRICT

It was the move of the Metropolitan Opera House to Broadway at 40th Street in 1883 that first drew lavish theaters and restaurants to this area. In the 1920s, movie palaces added the glamour of neon to Broadway, the signs getting bigger and brighter until eventually the street became known as the "Great White Way." After World War II,

Lee Lawrie design in Rockefeller Center

the pull of the movies waned, and the glitter was replaced by grime. However, a redevelopment program has brought the public and the bright lights back. Pockets of calm also exist away from the bustle. Explore the Public Library or relax in Bryant Park. For the best of both worlds, though, visit the landmark Rockefeller Center.

The heart of the Theater District, around Times Square

SIGHTS AT A GLANCE

Historic Streets and Buildings
Alwyn Court Apartments **18**
Group Health Insurance Building **12**
New York Public Library **8**
New York Yacht Club **5**
Paramount Building **13**
Shubert Alley **14**
Times Square **10**

Museums and Galleries
International Center of Photography **9**
Intrepid Sea-Air-Space Museum **19**
Museum of Arts and Design **20**

Modern Architecture
MONY Tower **15**
Rockefeller Center **1**

Parks and Squares
Bryant Park **6**

Famous Theaters
Carnegie Hall **17**
City Center of Music and Dance **16**
Lyceum Theater **3**
New Amsterdam Theater **11**

Landmark Hotels and Restaurants
Algonquin Hotel **4**
Bryant Park Hotel **7**

Landmark Stores
Diamond Row **2**

GETTING THERE
Subway lines A, C, and E go to the Port Authority and connect to the 1, 2, 3, N, Q, R, S, and 7 at Times Sq. The B, D, F, and M stop at Rockefeller Center and Bryant Park, where you can catch the 7. The C, E, and 1 stop at 50th St, and the N and R stop at 49th St. Bus routes are the M1–5, M7, M10, M11, M16, M20, M31 and M104, and the M42, M50, and M57 crosstown.

SEE ALSO
- *Street Finder,* maps 8, 11–12
- *Where to Stay* pp284–7
- *Restaurants* pp304–6

KEY
Street-by-Street map
M Subway station
Riverboat boarding point

0 meters   500
0 yards   500

Street by Street:Times Square

Named for the 25-story New York Times Tower, which opened in 1906, Times Square has been at the heart of the city's theater district since 1899, when Oscar Hammerstein built the Victoria and Republic theaters. Since the 1920s, the glowing neon of theater billboards has combined with the *Times'* illuminated newswire and other advertising to create a spectacular lightshow. After a period of decline starting in the 1930s, which saw sex shows taking over many of the grand theatres, rejuvenation of the district began in the 1990s. Old-style Broadway glamour again rubs shoulders with modern entertainment in this enticing part of the city.

Paramount Hotel
Designed by Philippe Starck, this hotel is the hip haunt of the theater crowd who drink in the late-night Paramount Bar *(see p285).*

MTV Studios
Crowds gather outside around 3pm Monday through Friday to watch interviews being filmed in the second-floor studios. Roving cameras often seek reactions on the street.

Westin Hotel
This striking 45-story hotel consists of a prism split by a curving beam of light. Stunning views over the city.

Sardi's
In Times Square since 1921, Sardi's walls are lined with caricatures of Broadway stars of yesterday and today.

★ **E Walk**
This entertainment and retail complex has a multiplex cinema, restaurants, a hotel, and the BB King Blues Club.

★ **Times Square**
Every New Year's Eve at midnight, the famed crystal ball drops from the top of One Times Square. There are great views from the front of this New York landmark ❿

0 meters 100
0 yards 100

★ **New Victory Theater**
This classic Broadway theater is used as a young people's performance space.

Electronic Ticker Tape
The figures on the Morgan Stanley LED tickertape are 10 feet (3 m) high. It is one of the many eye-catching lighting displays that illuminate Times Square day and night. City ordinances require office buildings to carry neon advertising.

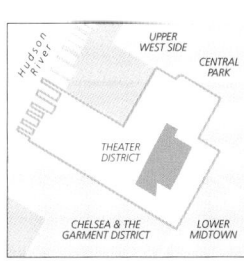

LOCATOR MAP
See Manhattan Map pp14–15

KEY

- - - Suggested route

STAR SIGHTS

★ E Walk

★ New Victory Theater

★ Times Square

McGraw-Hill Building

J.P. Stevens Tower

Celanese Building

Duffy Square
A statue of actor, composer, and writer George M Cohan, responsible for many of Broadway's hits, stands proud in this small square. Duffy Square is named for World War I hero, "Fighting" Father Duffy, immortalized in a statue. It is also home to the **TKTS** booth, where cut-price theater tickets are sold daily.

Times Square Information Center

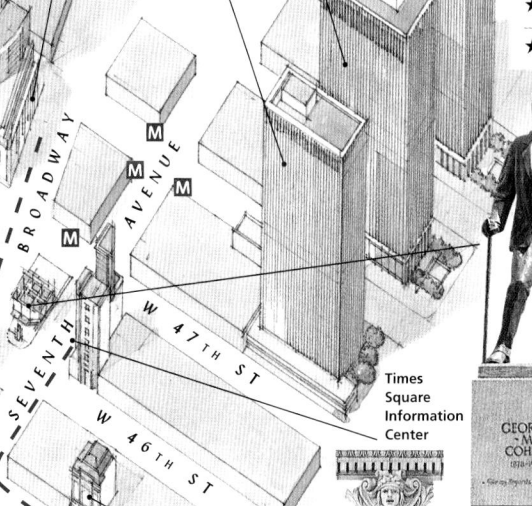

GEORGE
·M·
COHAN
1878–1942

Lyceum Theater
The oldest Broadway theater, the Lyceum has a beautifully ornate Baroque facade ❸

Belasco Theater
Built in 1907 by producer David Belasco, it was the most technically advanced theater of its time. Original Tiffany glass and Everett Shinn murals decorate the interior. It is rumored that Belasco's ghost still treads the boards some nights.

Rockefeller Center, looking toward the General Electric Building

Rockefeller Center ❶

Map 12 F5. Ⓜ *47th–50th Sts.* **Tel** *(212) 332-6868 (information).* ⊙ ♿ 🛗 🖥 ✆ *NBC, Rockefeller Center, daily.* **Tel** *(212) 664-7174 (reservations advised). Radio City Music Hall, daily.* **Tel** *(212) 247-4777. Top of the Rock, daily.* **Tel** *(212) 698-2000.* **www**.rockefellercenter.com **www**.nbc.com **www**.radiocity.com **www**.topoftherocknyc.com

When the New York City Landmarks Preservation Commission unanimously voted to declare Rockefeller Center a landmark in 1985, they rightly called it "the heart of New York . . . a great unifying presence in the chaotic core of midtown Manhattan."

It is the largest privately owned complex of its kind. The Art Deco design was by a team of top architects headed by Raymond Hood. Works by 30 artists can be found in foyers, on facades, and in the gardens. The site, once a botanic garden owned by Columbia University,

was leased in 1928 by John D. Rockefeller, Jr., as an ideal central home for an opera house. When the 1929 Depression scuttled these plans, Rockefeller, stuck with a long lease, went ahead with his own development. The 14 buildings erected between 1931 and 1940 provided jobs for up to 225,000 people during the Depression; by 1973 there were 19 buildings.

In December 1932, Radio City Music Hall opened within the complex. It still hosts its

Wisdom by Lee Lawrie, on the GE Building

famous Christmas and Easter shows here. Later, NBC opened its TV studios here. Rockefeller Plaza is home to a well-known ice-skating rink in winter; it is also the site of a famous Christmas tree.

The Top of the Rock, an observatory on the 67th–70th floors of the center, offers a dizzying 360° panoramic view of the city.

Diamond Row ❷

47th St, between 5th and 6th Aves. **Map** 12 F5. Ⓜ *47th–50th Sts. See* **Shopping** *p328.*

Most shop windows on 47th Street glitter with gold and diamonds. The buildings are filled with booths and workshops where jewelers vie for customers while, upstairs, vast sums of money change hands. Diamond Row was born in the 1930s, when the Jewish diamond cutters of Antwerp and Amsterdam fled to the US to escape Nazism. Even today, Jewish diamond dealers still predominate. Although mainly a wholesale district, individual customers are welcome. Bring cash, compare prices, haggle, and stay away if you know nothing about the value of diamonds.

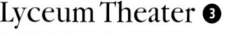

Diamond Row's main commodity

Lyceum Theater ❸

149 W 45th St. **Map** 12 E5. **Tel** *Telecharge (212) 239-6200.* Ⓜ *42nd, 47th St, 49th St. See* **Entertainment** *p345.*

The oldest active New York theater is a Baroque-style bandbox as frilly as a wedding cake. This 1903 triumph was the first theater by Herts and Tallant, later renowned for their extravagant style. The Lyceum made history with a record run of 1,600 performances of the comedy *Born Yesterday.* It was the first theater to be designated a historic landmark, and though the Theater District has shifted westward, there are still many shows here.

The Rose Room in the Algonquin Hotel

Algonquin Hotel ❹

59 W 44th St. **Map** 12 F5.
Tel (212) 840-6800. Ⓜ 42nd St.
See **Where to Stay** p285.
www.algonquinhotel.com

No other hotel captures the city's formidable literary history quite like the Algonquin Hotel. For more than a century it has played host to home-grown talent and international luminaries. In the 1920s, the Rose Room was home to America's best-known luncheon club, the Round Table, with literary lights such as Alexander Woollcott, Franklin P. Adams, Dorothy Parker, Robert Benchley, and Harold Ross. All were associated with the *New Yorker* (Ross was the founding editor), whose 25 West 43rd Street head-quarters had a back door opening into the hotel.

Renovations have preserved the old-fashioned, civilized feel of the Rose Room, as well as the cozy, paneled lobby where publishing types and theater-goers still like to gather for drinks, settling into comfortable armchairs and ringing a brass bell in order to summon the waiters.

New York Yacht Club ❺

37 W 44th St. **Map** 12 F5.
Tel (212) 382-1000. Ⓜ 42nd St.
⬤ to the public (members only).
www.nyyc.org

A whimsical 1899 creation, this private club has the carved sterns of 16th-century Dutch galleons in the three bay windows. The prows of the ships are borne up by sculpted dolphins and waves that spill over the window-sills and splash down to the pavement. This is the birthplace of the Americas Cup yacht race, which was based in the US from 1857 to 1983. That was the year the much coveted prize was taken from the table where it had stood for more than a century, when the *Australia II* sailed to a historic victory.

The Americas Cup, the coveted yachting prize

Bryant Park ❻

Map 8 F1. Ⓜ 42nd St.
www.bryantpark.org

In 1853, with the New York Public Library site still occupied by Croton Reservoir, Bryant Park (then Reservoir Park) housed a dazzling Crystal Palace, built for the World's Fair of that year *(see p25)*.

In the 1960s the park was a hangout for drug dealers and other undesirables. In 1989 the city renovated the park, reclaiming it for workers and visitors to relax in. In spring and fall, world-famous fashion shows take place here; in the summer, classic movies are screened. Over seven million books lie in storage stacks beneath the park.

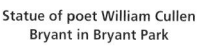

Statue of poet William Cullen Bryant in Bryant Park

Bryant Park Hotel ❼

40 W 40th St. **Map** 8 F1.
Tel (212) 869-0100. Ⓜ 42nd St.
www.bryantparkhotel.com

The American Radiator building (now the Bryant Park Hotel) was the first major New York work by Raymond Hood and John Howells, who went on to design the Daily News Building *(see p155)*, the McGraw-Hill building, and Rockefeller Center. The 1924 structure is reminiscent of one of Hood's best-known Gothic buildings, Chicago's Tribune Tower. Here, the design is sleeker, giving the building the illusion of being taller than its actual 23 stories. The black brick facade is set off by gold terra-cotta trim, evoking images of flaming coals: a comparison that would have suited its original owners well, since they made heating equipment. The building is now a luxury hotel *(see p288)* across the street from Bryant Park and boasts the New York outpost of trendy LA eatery Koi.

The Bryant Park Hotel, formerly the American Radiator Building

The New York Public Library ➑

5th Ave & 42nd St. **Map** 8 F1. **Tel** (212) 930-0830. Ⓜ 42nd St-Grand Central, 42nd St-5th Ave. ◯ 10am–6pm Mon–Sat, 1–5pm Sun. ⬤ public hols. ◉ ♿ ✓ **Lectures, readings.** ▯

Doorway leading to New York Public Library's Main Reading Room

In 1897 the coveted job of designing New York's main public library was awarded to architects Carrère & Hastings. The library's first director envisaged a light, quiet, airy place for study, where millions of books could be stored and yet be available to readers as promptly as possible. In the hands of Carrère & Hastings, his vision came true, in what is considered the epitome of New York's Beaux Arts period.

Built on the site of the former Croton Reservoir *(see p24)*, it opened in 1911 to immediate acclaim, despite having cost the city \$9 million.

Barrel vaults of carved white marble over the stairs in the Astor Hall

The vast, paneled Main Reading Room stretches two full blocks and is suffused with daylight from the two interior courtyards. Below it are 88 miles (140 km) of shelves, holding over seven million volumes. A staff of over 100 and a computerized dumb-waiter can supply any book within 10 minutes.

The Periodicals Room holds 10,000 current periodicals from 128 countries. On its walls are murals by Richard Haas, honoring New York's great publishing houses. The original library combined the collections of John Jacob Astor and James Lenox. Its collections today range from Thomas Jefferson's hand-written copy of the Declaration of Independence to T.S. Eliot's typed copy of "The Waste Land." More than 1,000 queries

The Main Reading Room, with its original bronze reading lamps

are answered daily, using the vast database of the CATNYP and LEO computer catalogs.

This library is the hub of a network of 82 branches, with nearly seven million users. Some branches are very well known, such as the New York Public Library for the Perform-ing Arts at the Lincoln Center *(see p212)* and the Schomburg Center in Harlem *(see p229)*.

One of the library's two stone lions, named Patience and Fortitude by Mayor LaGuardia

International Center of Photography ❾

1133 Avenue of the Americas (43rd St). **Map** 8 F1. *Tel (212) 857-0000.* Ⓜ *42nd St.* ◐ *10am–6pm Tue–Thu, Sat & Sun; 10am–8pm Fri.* ◉ *major hols.* 🅿 ♿ 🛈 *10am–5pm Tue–Sun.* 💻 **www**.icp.org

This museum was founded by Cornell Capa in 1974 to conserve the work of such photojournalists as his brother Robert, who was killed on assignment in 1954. The collection of 12,500 original prints contains work by top photographers such as Ansel Adams, Henri Cartier-Bresson, and W. Eugene Smith. Special exhibitions are organized from the ICP'S archive as well as from outside sources. There are also films, lectures, and classes.

Times Square ❿

Map 8 E1. Ⓜ *42nd St-Times Sq.* 🛈 *Times Square Visitor Center, 1560 Broadway (46th St) 9am–8pm daily (from 8am Sat & Sun).* 🎫 *noon Fri, (212) 869-1890.* **www**.timessquarenyc.org

The 1990s saw a transformation in Times Square, reversing a decline that began during the Depression. The square is now a safe and vibrant place where Broadway traditions comfortably coexist with modern innovations.

Although the *New York Times* has moved on from its original headquarters at the south end of the square, the glistening ball (now of Waterford crystal) still drops at midnight on New Year's Eve, as it has since the building opened with fanfare and fireworks in 1906. New buildings, such as the Bertelsmann and the fashionably minimalist Condé Nast offices, sit comfortably alongside the classic Broadway theaters.

Broadway's fortunes have also revived. Many theaters have been renovated and are again housing new productions; theatergoers throng the area's bars and restaurants each evening.

One of the newer landmarks is the 57-story skyscraper designed by Miami architects Arquitectonica, that tops the E Walk entertainment and retail complex at 42nd Street and Eighth Avenue *(see p142).* Other attractions include an outpost of Madame Tussaud's Wax Museum at 42nd Street, between Seventh and Eighth Avenues; a massive Disney Store; Bowlmor Lanes bowling alley; a pedestrian plaza; and Toys 'R' Us at 1514 Broadway.

W.C. Fields (far left) and Eddie Cantor (holding top hat, right) in the 1918 *Ziegfeld Follies* at the New Amsterdam Theater

New Amsterdam Theater ⓫

214 W 42nd St. **Map** 8 E1. *Tel (212) 282-2900.* Ⓜ *42nd St-Times Sq.* 🎫 *10am–3pm Mon–Tue, 10am–11am Thu–Sat, 10am Sun; (212) 282-2907.*

This was the most opulent theater in the United States when it opened in 1903, and the first to have an Art Nouveau interior. It was owned for a time by Florenz Ziegfeld, who produced his famous *Follies* revue here between 1914 and 1918 – with Broadway's first $5 ticket price. He remodeled the roof garden into another theater, the Aerial Gardens. This is one of the fine early theaters on 42nd Street that fell on hard times. With the rehabilitation of Times Square its fortunes rose again and it is once more in Show Business.

Art Deco top of the Paramount Building

Group Health Insurance Building ⓬

330 W 42nd St. **Map** 8 D1. Ⓜ *42nd St-8th Ave.* ◐ *office hours.*

This 1931 design by Raymond Hood was the only New York building selected for the influential International Style survey of 1932 *(see p43).* Its unusual design gives it a stepped profile seen from east and west, but a slab effect viewed from the north and south. The exterior's horizontal bands of blue-green terra-cotta have earned it the nickname "jolly green giant." Step inside to see the classic Art Deco lobby of opaque glass and stainless steel.

One block west is Theater Row, a pleasant group of Off-Broadway theaters and cafés.

Paramount Building ⓭

1501 Broadway. **Map** 8 E1. Ⓜ *34th St.*

The fabulous ground-floor movie theater where bobby-soxers stood in line in the 1940s to hear Frank Sinatra perform is gone, but there's still a theatrical feel to the massive building designed by Rapp & Rapp in 1927. On each side 14 symmetrical setbacks rise to an Art Deco crown – a tower, clock, and globe. In the heyday of the "Great White Way," the tower was lit, with an observation deck at the top. The Hard Rock Cafe is now here, along with a retail store and a concert area.

Shubert Alley ⓮

Between W 44th and W 45th St. **Map** 12 E5. Ⓜ *42nd St-Times Sq. See* ***Entertainment*** *p342.*

The playhouses on the streets west of Broadway are rich in theater lore – and in notable architecture. Two classic theaters built in 1913 are the Booth (222 West 45th Street), named after actor Edwin Booth, and the Shubert (225 West 44th), after theater baron Sam S. Shubert. They form the west wall of Shubert Alley, where aspiring actors lined up, hoping for a casting in a Shubert play.

A Chorus Line ran at the Shubert until 1990, for a record 6,137 performances; Katharine Hepburn starred earlier in *The Philadelphia Story.* Across from the 44th Street end of the alley is the St. James, where Rodgers and Hammerstein made their debut with *Oklahoma!* in 1941, followed by *The King and I.* Nearby is Sardi's, the restaurant where actors waited for opening-night reviews. Irving Berlin staged *The Music Box Revue* opposite the other end of the alley in 1921. His Music Box Theater has since housed many famous shows.

The tiled Moorish facade of the City Center of Music and Dance

MONY Tower ⓯

1740 Broadway. **Map** 12 E4. Ⓜ *57th St-Seventh Ave.* ☒ *to the public.*

Built in 1950, the head office of the Mutual of New York insurance company (now MONY Financial Services) has a weather vane that tells you everything except the wind direction. The mast turns green for fair, orange for cloudy, flashing orange for rain and white for snow. Lights moving up the mast mean warmer weather; lights going down mean get out your overcoat!

City Center of Music and Dance ⓰

131 W 55th St. **Map** 12 E4. **Tel** (212) 581-1212. Ⓜ *57th St-Seventh Ave.* ☒ ♿ *See* ***Entertainment*** *p346.* www.citycenter.org

This highly ornate Moorish structure with its dome of Spanish tiles was designed in 1924 as a Masonic Shriners' Temple. It was saved from the developers by Mayor LaGuardia, becoming home to the New York City Opera and Ballet in 1943. When the troupes moved to Lincoln Center, City Center lived on as a major venue for dance. Renovation work has preserved the delightful excesses of the architecture.

Carnegie Hall ⓱

154 W 57th Street. **Map** 12 E3. **Tel** (212) 247-7800. Ⓜ *57th St-Seventh Ave.* **Museum** ⬜ *11am–4:30pm daily & during concert intermissions.* ⬤ *Wed.* ☒ ♿ ◪ *11:30am, 12:30pm, 2pm & 3pm Mon–Fri; 11:30am & 12:30pm Sat; 12:30pm Sun.* ◪ *See* ***Entertainment*** *p350.* www.carnegiehall.org

Financed by millionaire philan-thropist Andrew Carnegie, New York's first great concert hall opened in 1891. The terracotta and brick Renaissance-style building has among the best acoustics in the world. On opening night, Tchaikovsky was a guest conductor and New York's

Auditorium of the Shubert Theater, built by Henry Herts in 1913

Carnegie Hall offering some of the best acoustics in the world

finest families attended. For many years Carnegie Hall was home to the New York Philharmonic, under conductors such as Arturo Toscanini, Bruno Walter, and Leonard Bernstein. Playing Carnegie Hall quickly became an international symbol of success for both classical and popular musicians.

In the 1950s, a campaign by violinist Isaac Stern saved the site from redevelopment, and in 1964 it was made a national landmark. Renovation in 1986 brought the bronze balconies and the ornamental plaster back to their original splendor. In 1991, a museum opened next to the first-tier level, telling the story of the first 100 years of "The House that Music Built." In 2003, the Judy and Arthur Zankel Hall reestablished the lower level as a performance venue.

Top orchestras and performers from around the world still fill Carnegie Hall, and the corridors are lined with memorabilia of artists who have performed here.

Millionaire Andrew Carnegie

Alwyn Court Apartments ⑱

180 W 58th St. **Map** 12 E3. Ⓜ *57th St-Seventh Ave.* ◐ *to the public.*

You can't miss it – not with the fanciful crowns, dragons, and other French Renaissance-style terra-cotta carvings covering the exterior of this 1909 Harde and Short apartment building. The ground floor has lost its cornice, but the rest of the building is intact, and it's one of a kind in the city.

The facade follows the style of François I, whose symbol, a crowned salamander, can be seen above the entrance to the building.

The interior courtyard features a dazzling display of the illusionistic skills of artist Richard Haas, in which plain walls are transformed into "carved" stonework.

The crowned salamander, symbol of François I, on Alwyn Court

Intrepid Sea-Air-Space Museum ⑲

Pier 86, W 46th St. **Map** 11 A5. Ⓖ *(877) 957-SHIP.* ▨ *M42, M50.* ◐ *Apr–Sep: 10am–5pm Mon–Fri; 10am–6pm Sat, Sun and hols; Oct–Mar: 10am–5pm Tue–Sun and hols.* ▨ Ⓐ www.intrepidmuseum.org

Exhibits on board this World War II aircraft carrier include fighter planes from the 1940s, the A-12, the world's fastest spy plane, and the *Growler*, a guided-missile submarine.

The workings of today's super-carriers are traced in Stern Hall, while Technologies Hall looks at the rockets of the future and includes two flight simulators. Mission Control offers live coverage of NASA shuttle missions.

Photographs, film footage, and archive material explore the lives of the crew.

The flight deck of the Intrepid with fighter and spy planes on display

Museum of Arts and Design ⑳

2 Columbus Circle. **Map** 12 D3. **Tel** *(212) 956-3535.* Ⓜ *59th St-Columbus Circle.* ◐ *10am–6pm Tue, Wed, Fri–Sun; 11am–9pm Thu.* ◐ *public hols.* ▨ ◐ Ⓐ Ⓕ **Lectures, films.** Ⓐ www.madmuseum.org

The leading American cultural institution of its kind, this museum housed in a modern, bold, eye-catching building is dedicated to contemporary objects in an array of media, from clay and wood to metal and fiber. The collection has over 2,000 artifacts by international craftsmen and designers. Items by top-class American craftsmen are also on sale.

LOWER MIDTOWN

From Beaux Arts to Art Deco, this section of midtown boasts some fine architecture. Quiet, residential Murray Hill was named for a country estate that once occupied the site. By the turn of the century, it was home to many of New York's first families, including the financier J.P. Morgan, whose library,

Brass door, Fred F. French Building

now a museum, reveals the grandeur of the age. The commercial pace quickens at 42nd Street, near Grand Central Terminal, where tall office buildings line the streets. However, few of the newer buildings have equaled the Beaux Arts Terminal itself or such Art Deco beauties as the Chrysler Building.

SIGHTS AT A GLANCE

Historic Streets and Buildings
Chanin Building **4**
Chrysler Building **5**
Daily News Building **6**
Fred F. French Building **12**
Grand Central Terminal pp156–7 **2**
Helmsley Building **8**
Home Savings of America **3**
Sniffen Court **15**
Tudor City **7**

Museums and Galleries
Japan Society **11**
Morgan Library & Museum pp164–5 **14**

Modern Architecture
MetLife Building **1**
Nos. 1 and 2 United Nations Plaza **9**
United Nations pp160–63 **10**

Churches
Church of the Incarnation **13**

GETTING THERE
By subway, take the crosstown S or 7, or the Lexington Avenue 4, 5, or 6 trains to 42nd Street–Grand Central. Buses M1–5, M15, and M101–3 run along the area's avenues, while the M16, M34, and M42 are the crosstown buses.

SEE ALSO

• **Street Finder,** maps 9, 12, 13

• **Where to Stay** pp287–8

• **Restaurants** p306

KEY

Street-by-Street map

M Subway station

◁ **The stainless-steel–coated spire of the Chrysler Building**

Street by Street: Lower Midtown

A walk in the neighborhood allows you to see an eclectic mix of New York's architectural styles. Step back to appreciate the contours of the tallest skyscrapers, and step inside to experience the many fine interiors, from modern atriums such as those in the Philip Morris Building and Ford Foundation buildings to the ornate details of the Home Savings Bank and the soaring spaces of Grand Central Terminal.

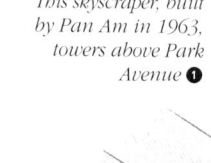

MetLife Building
This skyscraper, built by Pan Am in 1963, towers above Park Avenue ❶

★ Grand Central Terminal
The vast, vaulted interior is a splendid reminder of the heyday of train travel. This historic building also features specialty shops and gourmet restaurants ❷

Grand Central-42nd St. subway (lines S, 4, 5, 6, 7)

STAR SIGHTS

- ★ Chrysler Building
- ★ Daily News Building
- ★ Grand Central Terminal
- ★ Home Savings of America

Chanin Building
Built for self-made real estate mogul Irwin Chanin in the 1920s, this building has a fine Art Deco lobby ❹

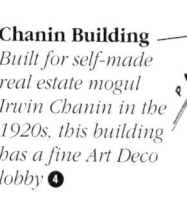

PARK AVENUE

E 41ST ST

LEXINGTON AVENUE

The Mobil Building
has a self-cleaning stainless steel facade that is embossed in geometric patterns to prevent it from warping. It was built in 1955.

Brass door, Home Savings Bank

★ Home Savings of America
Formerly the headquarters of the Bowery Savings Bank, this is one of the finest bank buildings in New York. Architects York & Sawyer designed it to resemble a Romanesque palace ❸

Helmsley Building

Straddling Park Avenue between 45th and 46th, its ornate entrance symbolized the wealth of its first occupants, New York Central Railroad ➑

Mailbox in the Chrysler Building

LOCATOR MAP
See Manhattan Map pp14–15

THEATER DISTRICT — UPPER MIDTOWN

LOWER MIDTOWN

GRAMERCY & THE FLATIRON DISTRICT — East Side — East River

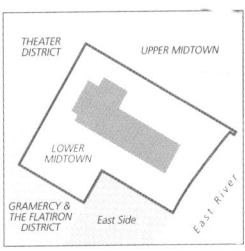

KEY

– – – Suggested route

| 0 meters | 100 |
| 0 yards | 100 |

★ Chrysler Building

Ornamented with automotive motifs, this Art Deco delight was built in 1930 for the Chrysler car company ➎

Worker resting during construction of the Chrysler Building

The Ford Foundation Building is the headquarters of Ford's philanthropic arm. It has a lovely interior garden surrounded by a cube-shaped building made of pinkish gray granite, glass, and steel.

Ralph J. Bunche Park

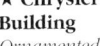

E 42ND STREET

3RD AVENUE

SECOND AVENUE

FIRST AVENUE

★ Daily News Building

The Art Deco former home of the newspaper has a revolving globe in the lobby ➏

Tudor City

This 1928 private residential complex has 3,000 apartments. Built in the Tudor style, it features fine stonework details ➐

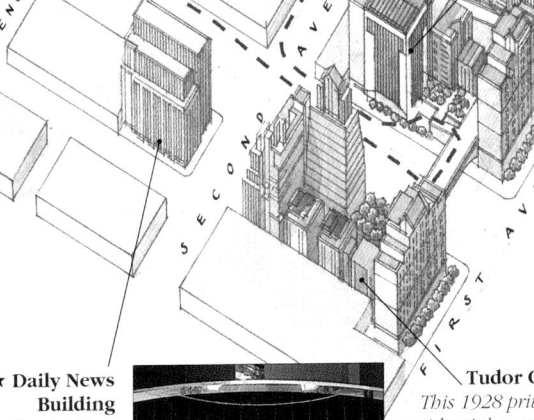

MetLife Building ❶

200 Park Ave. **Map** 13 A5.
Ⓜ *42nd St-Grand Central.*
◯ *office hours.* 🔽 🔢

Lobby of the MetLife Building

Once, the sculptures atop the Grand Central Terminal stood out against the sky. Then this colossus, formerly called the Pan Am Building and designed by Walter Gropius, Emery Roth and Sons, and Pietro Belluschi, rose up in 1963 to block the Park Avenue view. It dwarfed the terminal and aroused universal dislike. At the time it was the largest commercial building in the world, and the dismay over its scale helped thwart a later plan to build a tower over the terminal itself.

It is ironic that the New York skies were blocked by Pan Am, a company that had opened up the skies as a means of travel for millions of people. When the company began in 1927, Charles Lindbergh, fresh from his solo trans-atlantic flight, was one of their pilots and an adviser on new routes. By 1936, Pan Am managed to introduce the first trans-Pacific passenger route, and in 1947 they introduced the first round-the-world route.

The building's famous roof-top heliport was abandoned in 1977 after a freak accident showered debris on to the surrounding streets. Now Pan Am itself has gone, too, and in 1981 the entire building was sold to the Metropolitan Life organization.

Grand Central Terminal ❷

See pp156–7.

Home Savings of America ❸

110 E 42nd St. **Map** 9 A1. Ⓜ *42nd St-Grand Central.* ◯ *by appt only.*
Cipriani *Tel* (646) 723-0826.

Many consider this 1923 building the best work of the best bank architects of the 1920s. York & Sawyer chose the style of a Romanesque basilica for the uptown offices of the venerable Bowery Savings Bank (now Home Savings of America). An arched entry leads into the vast banking room, with a high beamed ceiling, marble mosaic floors, and marble columns that support the stone arches that soar overhead.

Facade of Home Savings of America building

Between the columns are unpolished mosaic panels of marble from France and Italy. The rich detailing includes symbolic animal motifs, such as a squirrel representing thrift and a lion for power.

Chanin Building ❹

122 E 42nd St. **Map** 9 A1.
Ⓜ *42nd St-Grand Central.*
◯ *office hours.*

Stonework detail on the Chanin Building

Once the headquarters of Irwin S. Chanin, one of New York's leading real estate developers, the 56-story tower was the first skyscraper in the Grand Central area, a harbinger of things to come. It was designed by Sloan & Robertson in 1929 and is one of the best examples of the Art Deco period. A wide bronze band, patterned with birds and fish, runs the full length of the facade; the terracotta base is decorated with a luxuriant tangle of stylized leaves and flowers. Inside, Radio City's sculptor René Chambellan worked on the reliefs and the bronze grills, elevator doors, mailboxes, clocks, and pattern of waves in the floor. The vestibule reliefs chart the career of Chanin, who was a self-made man.

Carved detail in the banking hall of Home Savings of America

Chrysler Building ❺

405 Lexington Ave. **Map** 9 A1.
Tel (212) 682-3070. M 42nd St-
Grand Central. ⬜ office hours
(7am–6pm), lobby only. 📷 ♿

**Stainless-steel
gargoyle on the
Chrysler Building**

Walter P. Chrysler began his
career in a Union Pacific
Railroad machine shop, but
his passion for the motor
car helped him rise
swiftly to the top
of this industry, to
found, in 1925, the
corporation bearing
his name. His wish for
a headquarters in New
York that symbolized
his company led to
a building that will
always be linked with
the golden age of
motoring. Following
Chrysler's wishes, the
stainless-steel Art
Deco spire resembles
a car radiator grill;
the building's series
of stepped setbacks
are emblazoned with
winged radiator caps,
wheels and stylized
automobiles; and there
are gargoyles modeled
on hood ornaments
from the 1929
Chrysler Plymouth.

It stands at 1,046ft
(320 m) but it lost the
title of tallest building
in the world to the
Empire State Building
a few months after its
completion in 1930.
William Van Alen's
77-story Chrysler Building and
its shining crown are still
among the city's best-known
and most-loved landmarks.

The crowning spire was
kept a secret until the last
moment, when, having been

built in the fire shaft, it was
raised into position through
the roof, ensuring that the
building would be higher
than the Bank of Manhattan,
then just completed down-
town by Van Alen's great
rival, H. Craig
Severance.

Van Alen was
poorly rewarded
for his labors.
Chrysler accused him
of accepting bribes from
contractors and refused to
pay him. Van Alen's career
never recovered from the slur.

The stunning lobby, once
used as a showroom for
Chrysler cars, was perfectly
restored in 1978. It is lavishly
decorated with patterned
marbles and granite from
around the world and has
chromed steel trim. A vast
painted ceiling by Edward

Elevator door at the Chrysler Building

Trumball shows transportation scenes of the late 1920s.

Although the Chrysler Corporation never occupied the
building as their headquarters,
their name remains, as firm a
fixture as the gargoyles.

Entrance to the Daily News Building

Daily News
Building ❻

220 E 42nd St. **Map** 9 B1.
M 42nd St-Grand Central.
⬜ 8am–6pm Mon–Fri.

The *Daily News* was founded
in 1919, and by 1925 it was a
million-seller. It was known,
rather scathingly, as "the
servant girl's bible," for its
concentration on scandals,
celebrities, and murders, its
readable style and heavy use
of illustration. Over the years
it has stuck to what it does
best, and the formula paid
off handsomely. It revealed
stories such as the romance
of Edward VIII and Mrs.
Simpson, and has become
renowned for its punchy
headlines. Its circulation
figures are still among the
highest in the United States.

Its headquarters, designed
by Raymond Hood in 1930,
has rows of brown and
black brick alternating with
windows to create a vertical
striped effect. Hood's lobby
is familiar to many as that of
the *Daily Planet* in the 1980s
Superman movies. It includes
the world's largest interior
globe, and bronze lines on
the floor indicate the direction
of world cities and the
position of the planets. At
night, the intricate detail over
the front entrance of the
building is lit from within
by neon. The newspaper's
offices are now on West
33rd Street, but this building
has been designated as a
national historic landmark.

Grand Central Terminal ❷

In 1871 Cornelius Vanderbilt opened a railway station on 42nd Street. Although often revamped, it was never large enough and was finally demolished. The present station opened in 1913. This Beaux Arts gem has been a gateway to and symbol of the city ever since. Its glory is the soaring main concourse and the way it separates pedestrian and train traffic. The building has a steel frame covered with plaster and marble. Reed & Stern were in charge of the logistical planning; Warren & Wetmore for the overall design. The restoration by architects Beyer Blinder Belle is awesome.

42nd Street colonnaded facade

Statuary on the 42nd Street Facade
Jules-Alexis Coutans sculptures of Mercury, Hercules, and Minerva crown the main entrance.

Main Concourse Level

Circumferential Road

Subway

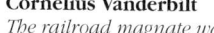

Cornelius Vanderbilt
The railroad magnate was known as the "Commodore."

As many as 750,000 people pass through the terminal each day. An escalator leads up into the MetLife Building, where there are specialty shops and restaurants.

Vanderbilt Hall, adjacent to the Main Concourse, is a good example of Beaux Arts architecture. It is decorated with gold chandeliers and pink marble.

STAR SIGHTS

★ Central Information

★ Grand Staircases

★ Main Concourse

Grand Central Oyster Bar
This popular spot (see p306), with its yellow Guastavino tiles, is one of the many eateries in the station. The dining concourse is enormous, with food, snacks, and drinks to suit all tastes.

★ Main Concourse
This vast area with its vaulted ceiling is dominated by three great arched windows on each side.

VISITORS' CHECKLIST

E 42nd St at Park Ave.
Map 13 A5.
Tel *(212) 532-4900.*
M 4, 5, 6, 7, S to
Grand Central.
M1–5, M42, M50,
M101–103, Q32.
5:30am–1:30am daily.
12:30pm Wed,
*suggested donation $10,
(212) 935-3960; 12:30pm Fri,
free, (212) 883-2420.*
Lost & found (212) 340-2555.
www.grandcentralterminal.com

Vaulted Ceiling
A medieval manuscript provided the basis for French artist Paul Helleu's zodiac design containing over 2,500 stars. Lights pinpoint the major constellations.

The Lower Level
is linked to the other levels by stairways, ramps, and escalators.

Grand Staircase
There are now two of these double flights of marble steps, styled after the staircase in Paris' Opera House, and a vivid reminder of the glamorous days of early rail travel.

★ Central Information
This four-faced clock tops the travel information booth on the main concourse.

Tudor City ❼

E 41st–43rd St between 1st and
2nd Aves. **Map** 9 B1. Ⓜ *42nd St-Grand Central.* 🚌 *M15, M42, M50.*
www.tudorcity.com

Dating from 1925–8, this early
urban renewal effort by the
Fred F. French Company was
designed as a middle-class
city within the city. Rents were
modest, thanks to the "large-scale production." There
are 12 buildings containing
apartments, a hotel, shops,
restaurants, a post office, and
two small private parks, all
built in the Tudor Gothic style.

In the mid-19th century the
area was the haunt of gangs
and criminals and was known
as Corcoran's Roost, after
Paddy Corcoran, the leader
of the notorious "Rag Gang."
The East River shore was lined
with glue factories, slaughter-houses, breweries, and a
gasworks. Some were still
there when Tudor City was
planned, so its buildings have
only a few outward-facing
windows from which residents
might enjoy what is
now a great view
of the river.

Upper stories of Tudor City

Helmsley Building ❽

230 Park Ave. **Map** 13 A5.
Ⓜ *42nd St-Grand Central.*
◯ *office hours.*

One of the great New York
views looks south down Park
Avenue to the Helmsley
Building straddling the busy
traffic flow beneath. There is
just one flaw – the monolithic
MetLife Building (which was
built by Pan Am as its
corporate headquarters

Performance at the Japan Society

in 1963) that towers behind
it, replacing the building's
former backdrop, the sky.

Built by Warren & Wetmore
in 1929, the Helmsley Building
was originally the headquarters
of the New York Central Rail-road Company. Its namesake,
the late Harry Helmsley,
was a billionaire
who began his
career as a New
York office boy
for $12 per
week. His wife
Leona, who
passed away
in 2007, was
a prominent
feature
in all the
advertise-ments for their hotel chain –
until her imprisonment in
1989 for tax evasion on a
grand scale. Many observers
believe that the extravagant
glitter of the building's face-lift is due to Leona's over-blown taste in decor.

1 & 2 United Nations Plaza ❾

Map 13 B5. Ⓜ *42nd St-Grand Central.*
🚌 *M15, M42, M50.*

These two great
columns of blue-green mirrored
glass are set at an
angle to each other;
the play of light and reflec-tions on their gleaming sides
and sloping setbacks make
them seem a giant, ever-changing, work of modern
art. The marble and
mirrored interiors are also
stunning. They house
streamlined modern
offices and, in No. 1,
the Millennium
United Nations
Plaza Hotel.
Here, the
guest list frequently includes
many UN delegates from all
over the world as well as a
number of visiting heads of
state. Even the stresses of
international diplomacy must
ease when one is floating
lazily in the glassed-in
swimming pool, enjoying the
bird's-eye views of the city
and the United Nations itself.

United Nations ❿

See pp160–63.

Japan Society ⓫

333 E 47th St. **Map** 13 B5.
***Tel** (212) 832-1155.* Ⓜ *42nd St-Grand Central.* 🚌 *M15, M50.*
***Gallery** ◯ 11am–6pm Tue–Thu,
11am–9pm Fri, 11am–5pm Sat–Sun.*
🚫 ♿ 🎥 **www**.japansociety.org

The headquarters of the Japan
Society, founded in 1907 to
foster understanding and
cultural exchange
between Japan
and the US,
was built with
the help of

Roman gods reclining against the Helmsley Building clock

John D. Rockefeller III, who underwrote costs of some $4.3 million. The striking black building with its delicate sun grilles was designed by Tokyo architects Junzo Yoshimura and George Shimamoto in 1971. It includes an auditorium, a language center, a research library, a museum gallery, and traditional Oriental gardens.

Changing exhibits include a variety of Japanese arts, from swords to kimonos to scrolls. The society offers programs of Japanese performing arts, lectures, language classes, and many business workshops for American and Japanese executives and managers.

Fred F. French Building ⑫

521 5th Ave. **Map** 12 F5.
Ⓜ *42nd St-Grand Central.*
◯ *office hours.*

Built in 1927 to house the best-known real estate firm of the day, this is a fabulously opulent creation.

It was designed by French's chief architect, H. Douglas Ives, in collaboration with Sloan & Robertson, whose

Tiffany stained-glass window in the Church of the Incarnation

other work included the Chanin Building *(see p154).* They handsomely blended Near Eastern, ancient Egyptian and Greek styles with early Art Deco forms.

Multicolored faïence ornaments decorate the upper facade, and the water tower is hidden in a false top level of the building. Its disguise is an elaborate one, with reliefs showing a rising sun flanked by griffins and bees and symbols of virtues such as integrity and industry. Winged Assyrian beasts ride on a bronze frieze over the entrance. These exotic themes continue into the vaulted lobby, with its elaborate polychrome ceiling decoration and 25 gilt-bronze doors.

This was the first building project to employ members of the Native Canadian Caughnawaga tribe as construction workers. They did not fear heights and soon became highly sought-after as scaffolders for many of the city's most famous skyscrapers.

Lobby of the Fred F. French Building

Church of the Incarnation ⑬

209 Madison Ave. **Map** 9 A2. **Tel** (212) 689-6350. Ⓜ *42nd St-Grand Central, 33rd St.* ◯ *11:30am–2pm Mon–Fri (also 4–7pm Tue, 5–7pm Wed), 1–4pm Sat, 8:15am–12:30pm Sun.* ✝ *12:15pm & 6:30pm Wed, 12:45pm Fri, 8:30am & 11am Sun.* 📷 ♿ ✉ *By appointment.* **www**.churchoftheincarnation.org

This Episcopal church dates from 1864, when Madison Avenue was home to the elite. Its patterned sandstone and brownstone exterior is typical of the period. The interior has an oak communion rail by Daniel Chester French; a chancel mural by John La Farge; and stained-glass windows by La Farge, Tiffany, William Morris and Edward Burne-Jones.

Morgan Library & Museum ⑭

See pp164–5.

Sniffen Court ⑮

150–158 E 36th St. **Map** 9 A2.
Ⓜ *33rd St.*

Here is a delightful, intimate courtyard of ten brick Romanesque revival carriage houses, built by John Sniffen in the 1850s. They are perfectly and improbably preserved off a busy block in modern New York. The house at the south end was used as a studio by the American sculptor Malvina Hoffman, whose plaques of Greek horsemen decorate the exterior wall.

Malvina Hoffman's studio

United Nations ⑩

Founded in 1945 with 51 members, the United Nations now numbers 189 nations. Its aims are to preserve world peace, to promote self-determination, and to aid economic and social well-being around the globe. New York was chosen as the UN headquarters, and John D. Rockefeller, Jr.

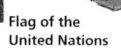

Flag of the United Nations

donated $8.5 million for the purchase of the site. The chief architect was American Wallace Harrison, who worked with an international Board of Design Consultants. The 18-acre (7-ha) site is an international zone, with its own stamps and post office. In 2006, the UN's General Assembly approved a $1.6-billion renovation of the complex that will take several years to complete; visitors should phone ahead to check access.

United Nations headquarters

Secretariat building

The Conference Building houses meeting rooms for the Security Council, the Trusteeship Council and the Economic and Social Council.

★ Security Council
Delegates and their assistants confer around the horseshoe-shaped table while verbatim reporters and other UN staff members sit at the long table in the center.

Trusteeship Council

Economic and Social Council

STAR FEATURES

★ General Assembly

★ Peace Bell

★ Reclining Figure

★ Security Council

★ Peace Bell
Cast from the coins of 60 nations, this gift from Japan hangs on a cypress pagoda shaped like a Shinto shrine.

Rose Garden
Twenty-five varieties of roses adorn the manicured gardens on the East River.

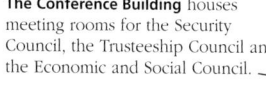

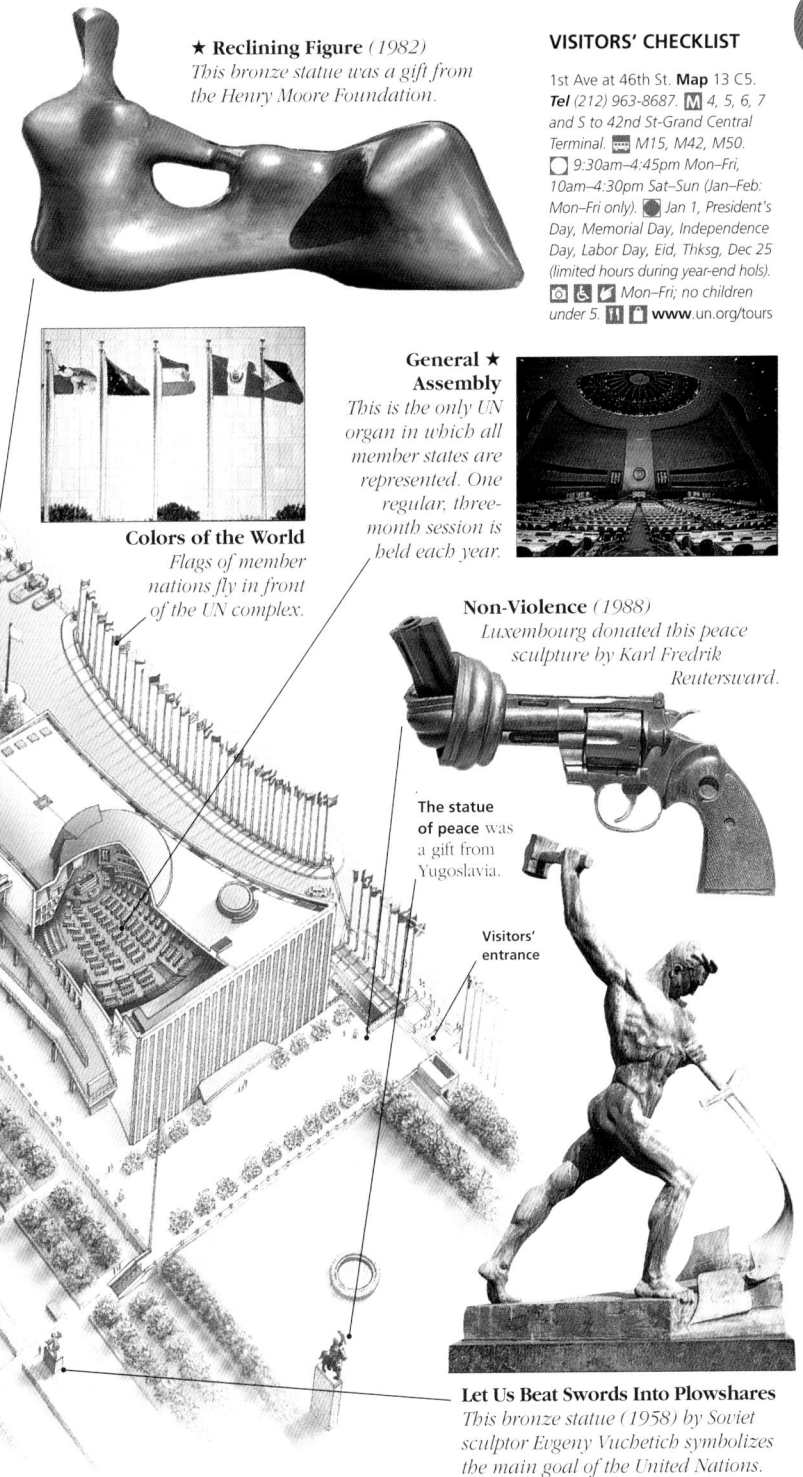

★ **Reclining Figure** *(1982)*
This bronze statue was a gift from the Henry Moore Foundation.

General ★ Assembly
This is the only UN organ in which all member states are represented. One regular, three-month session is held each year.

Colors of the World
Flags of member nations fly in front of the UN complex.

Non-Violence *(1988)*
Luxembourg donated this peace sculpture by Karl Fredrik Reutersward.

The statue of peace was a gift from Yugoslavia.

Visitors' entrance

Let Us Beat Swords Into Plowshares
This bronze statue (1958) by Soviet sculptor Evgeny Vuchetich symbolizes the main goal of the United Nations.

The Work of the United Nations

The goals of the United Nations are pursued by three UN councils and a General Assembly comprising all of its member nations. The Secretariat carries out the administrative work of the organization. Guided tours allow visitors to see the Security Council Chamber. Often there is a chance to briefly observe a meeting.

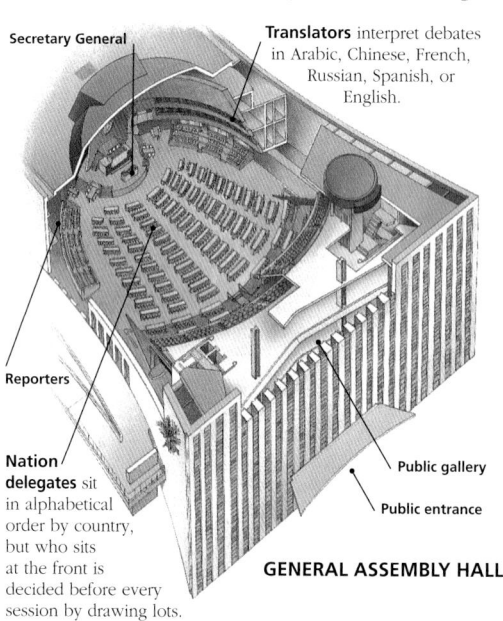

Secretary General

Translators interpret debates in Arabic, Chinese, French, Russian, Spanish, or English.

Reporters

Nation delegates sit in alphabetical order by country, but who sits at the front is decided before every session by drawing lots.

Public gallery

Public entrance

GENERAL ASSEMBLY HALL

GENERAL ASSEMBLY

The General Assembly is the governing body of the UN and has regular sessions each year from mid-September to mid-December. Special sessions are also held when the Security Council or a majority of members request one. All member states are represented with an equal vote, regardless of size. The General Assembly may discuss any international problem raised by the members or by other UN bodies. Although it cannot enact laws, recommendations strongly influence world opinion; these require a two-thirds majority vote.

Lots are drawn before each session to determine the seating in the chamber for the delegations. All 1,898 seats in the chamber are equipped with earphones that offer simultaneous translations in several languages. The General Assembly also appoints the Secretary General (on the recommendation of the Security Council), approves the UN budgets and elects the non-permanent members of

Foucault's Pendulum **(Holland); its slowly rotating swing is proof of the earth's rotation on its axis**

the Councils. Together with the Security Council, it also appoints the judges of the International Court of Justice, based in the Netherlands.

SECURITY COUNCIL

The most powerful part of the UN is the Security Council. It strives to achieve international

Mural symbolizing peace and freedom by Per Krohg (Norway)

peace and security and intervenes in crises such as the fighting in Iraq and Afghanistan. It is the only body whose decisions member states are obliged to obey as well as the only one in continuous session.

Five of its members – China, France, the Russian Federation, the United Kingdom, and the United States – are permanent. The other nations are elected by the General Assembly to serve two-year terms.

When international conflicts arise, the Council first tries to seek agreement by mediation. If fighting breaks out, it may issue cease-fire orders and impose military or economic sanctions. It could also decide to send UN peace-keeping missions into troubled areas to separate opposing factions until issues can be resolved through diplomatic channels.

Military intervention is the Council's last resort. UN forces may be deployed, and peace-keeping forces are resident in such places as Cyprus and the Middle East.

TRUSTEESHIP COUNCIL

The smallest of the councils, this is the only UN body whose workload is decreasing. The council was established in 1945 with the goal of fostering peaceful independence for non-self-governing territories or colonies. Since then, more than 80 colonies have gained self-rule, and the number of people living in dependent territories has been reduced from 750 million to about 3 million. The Trusteeship Council consists of the five permanent members of the Security Council.

Zanetti mural (Dominican Republic) in the Conference Building depicting the struggle for peace

Trusteeship Council Chamber

ECONOMIC AND SOCIAL COUNCIL

The 54 members of this Council work to improve the standard of living and social welfare around the world, goals that consume 80% of the UN's resources. It makes recommendations to the General Assembly, to each member nation and to the UN's specialized agencies. The Council is assisted by commissions dealing with regional economic problems, human rights abuses, population, narcotics, and women's rights. It also works with the International Labor Organization, the World Health Organization, UNICEF, and other global welfare organizations.

SECRETARIAT

An international staff of 16,000 works for the Secretariat to carry out the day-to-day work of the United Nations. The Secretariat is headed by the Secretary General, who plays a key role as a spokesperson in the organization's peacekeeping efforts. The Secretary General is appointed by the General Assembly for a five-year term. On January 1, 2007, Ban Ki-moon of South Korea became the latest Secretary General.

IMPORTANT EVENTS IN UN HISTORY

Soviet premier Krushchev speaking to the General Assembly in 1960

The UN depends on voluntary compliance and military support from its members to keep the peace in the event of disputes. In 1948, the UN declared South Korea the legitimate government of Korea; two years later, it played a major role in defending South Korea against North Korea. In 1949, the UN helped negotiate a cease-fire between Indonesia and the Netherlands and set up a conference that led to the Dutch granting independence to Indonesia.

In 1964 a UN military force was sent to Cyprus to keep peace between the Greeks and Turks, and still remains. Persistent issues in the Middle East have kept UN forces in the area since 1974, the year that China – long refused membership in favor of Taiwan – gained UN membership. In the 1990s, the UN was involved in the break-up of Yugoslavia, and more recently in the conflicts in Afghanistan and Libya. A 2004 UN mission to Congo was plagued by accusations of sexual abuse by UN peace-keepers. In 2006–7 there were arrests over kickbacks in the UN oil-for-food program to Iraq.

At any given time at least half a dozen missions are active somewhere in the world. The UN was awarded the Nobel Peace Prize in 1988 and 2001.

WORKS OF ART AT THE UN

The UN Building has acquired numerous works of art and reproductions by major artists; many have been gifts from member nations. Most of them have either a peace or international friendship theme. The legend on Norman Rockwell's *The Golden Rule* reads "Do unto others as you would have them do unto you." Marc Chagall designed a large stained-glass window as a memorial to former Secretary General Dag Hammarskjöld, who was accidentally killed while on a peace mission in 1961. There is a Henry Moore sculpture in the grounds (limited access) and many other sculptures and paintings by the artists of many nations.

The Golden Rule (1985), a large mosaic by Norman Rockwell

Morgan Library & Museum ⑭

The Morgan Library's collection, accumulated by banker Pierpont Morgan, is housed in a magnificent palazzo-style 1902 building by architects McKim, Mead & White. Morgan's son, J. P. Morgan, Jr., made it a public institution in 1924. One of the world's finest collections of rare manuscripts, drawings, prints, books, and bindings is on display in a complex that includes the original library and the home of Pierpont Morgan.

Exterior of the original library building

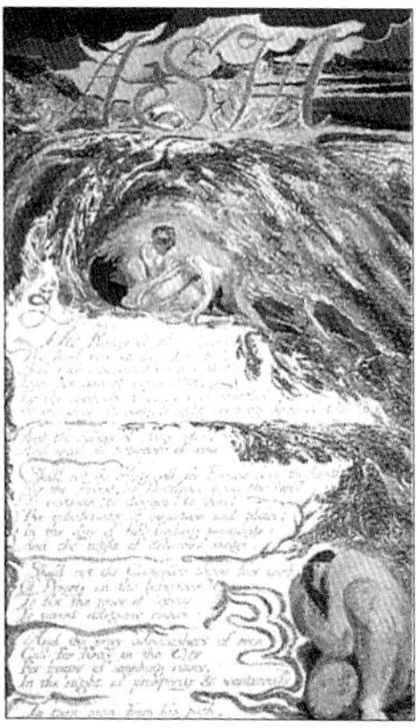

The Song of Los *(1795)*
Mystic poet William Blake designed and engraved this plate for one of his most innovative works.

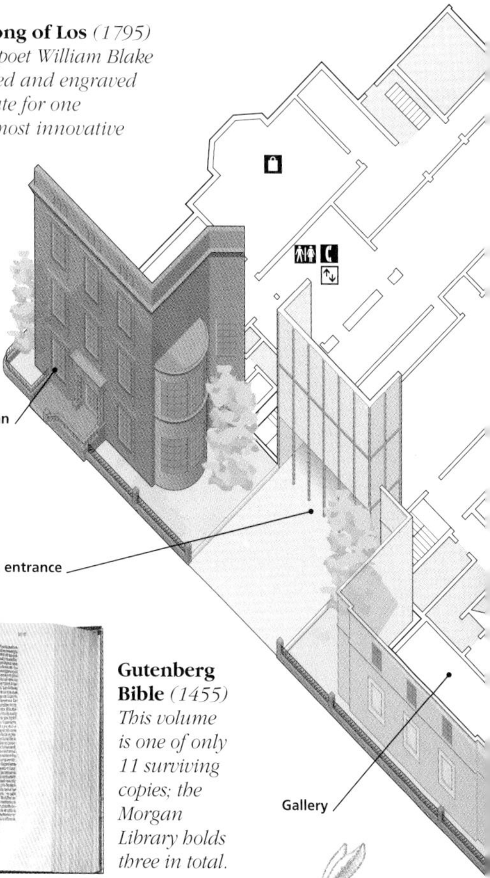

Morgan House

KEY TO FLOOR PLAN

☐ Exhibition space

▨ Non-exhibition space

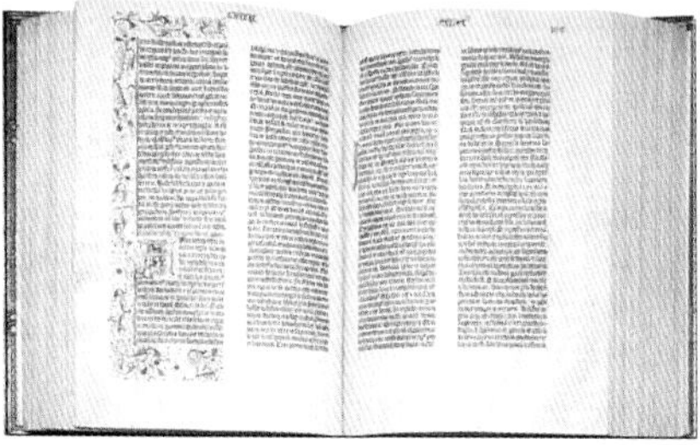

Main entrance

Gutenberg Bible *(1455)*
This volume is one of only 11 surviving copies; the Morgan Library holds three in total.

Gallery

The Nursery Alice
Lewis Carroll's characters are immortalized in John Tenniel's classic illustrations (c. 1865).

STAR EXHIBITS

★ The West Room

★ The Rotunda

★ East Room

LIBRARY GUIDE

Mr. Morgan's Study and the original library contain some of his favorite paintings, objets d'art and rare acquisitions. Changing exhibitions feature a wide variety of impressive cultural artifacts.

Mozart's Horn Concerto in E-flat Major

The six surviving leaves of this score are written in different colored inks.

VISITORS' CHECKLIST

225 Madison Ave. **Map** 9 A2.
Tel (212) 685-0008.
M 6 to 33rd St; 4, 5, 6, 7,
S to Grand Central Terminal;
B, D, F, V to 42nd St.
M1–5, and M16, M34
crosstown. ◯ 10:30am–5pm
Tue–Thu, 10:30am–9pm Fri,
10am–6pm Sat, 11am–6pm
Sun. ● Mon, Jan 1,
Thanksgiving, Dec 25. free
7–9pm Fri.
www.themorgan.org

West Room
(Mr. Morgan's
study)

★ **East Room**
The walls are lined from floor to ceiling with triple tiers of bookcases. Murals show historical figures and their muses, and signs of the zodiac.

★ **The Rotunda** *(1504)*
The entrance foyer of the Library has marble columns and pilasters; the marble floor is modeled on the floor in Villa Pia in the Vatican gardens.

★ **The West Room**
Renaissance art and an antique, Florentine wooden ceiling adorn this room.

PIERPONT MORGAN

Pierpont Morgan (1837–1913) was not only a leading financier but also one of the great collectors of his time. Rare books and original manuscripts were his passion, and inclusion in his collection was an honor. In 1909, when Morgan requested the donation of the manuscript of *Pudd'nhead Wilson*, Mark Twain responded, "One of my high ambitions is gratified."

UPPER MIDTOWN

pscale New York in all its diversity is here, in this district of churches and synagogues, clubs and museums, grand hotels and famous stores, as well as trend-setting skyscrapers and pockets of luxury living. For almost 30 years from 1833, Upper Midtown was home

1946 Cisitalia in the MoMA

to society names such as Astor and Vanderbilt. In the 1950s, architectural history was made when the Lever and Seagram buildings were erected. These first great modern towers marked midtown Park Avenue's change from a residential street to a prestigious office address.

SIGHTS AT A GLANCE

Historic Streets and Buildings
Beekman Place **18**
Fuller Building **21**
General Electric Building **11**
Roosevelt Island **19**
Sutton Place **17**
Villard Houses **9**

Modern Architecture
Citigroup Center **15**
IBM Building **3**
Lever House **13**
Seagram Building **14**
Trump Tower **2**

Museums and Galleries
American Folk Art Museum **6**
Museum of Modern Art (MoMA) pp172–5 **5**

The Paley Center for Media **7**

Churches and Synagogues
Central Synagogue **16**
St. Bartholomew's Church **10**
St. Patrick's Cathedral pp178–9 **8**
St. Thomas Church **4**

Landmark Hotels
Plaza Hotel **22**
Waldorf–Astoria **12**

Landmark Stores
Bloomingdale's **20**
Fifth Avenue **1**

Roosevelt Island

East River (West channel)

Roosevelt Island

| 0 meters | 500 |
| 0 yards | 500 |

KEY

Street-by-Street map

M Subway station

SEE ALSO

GETTING THERE
Take the 6 subway to 51st St; the 4, 5, 6, N, or R to 59th St; or the E or M to 53rd St-Fifth Ave or 53rd St-Lexington. Bus routes are the M1–5, M15, M101–3, and Q32. Crosstown buses are the M27, M31, M50, and M57.

◁ The façade of St. Patrick's Cathedral on Fifth Avenue

Street by Street: Upper Midtown

The luxury stores that are synonymous with Fifth Avenue first blossomed as society moved on uptown. In 1917, Cartier's acquired the mansion of banker Morton F. Plant in exchange for a string of pearls, setting the style for other retailers to follow. But this stretch of midtown is not simply for shoppers. There are three distinctive museums and an equally diverse assembly of architectural styles to enjoy, too.

Fifth Avenue
The popular carriage rides offer tourists a taste of past elegance and a leisurely way to view some of the main sights around this thoroughfare ❶

The University Club was built in 1899 as an elite club for gentlemen.

W 55TH ST

St. Thomas Church
Much of the interior carving was designed by sculptor Lee Lawrie ❹

★ **Museum of Modern Art**
One of the world's finest collections of modern art ❺

The Paley Center for Media
Exhibitions, seasons of special screenings, live events and a vast library of historic broadcasts are offered at this media museum ❼

Fifth Avenue subway (lines E, V)

FIFTH AVENUE

Saks Fifth Avenue has offered goods in impeccable taste to generations of New Yorkers. *(See p319.)*

★ **St. Patrick's Cathedral**
This, the largest Catholic cathedral in the United States, is a magnificent Gothic Revival building ❽

Olympic Tower
combines offices, apartments and a skylit atrium within its sleek walls.

Villard Houses
Five handsome brownstone houses now form part of the New York Palace Hotel ❾

STAR SIGHTS

★ Museum of Modern Art

★ St. Patrick's Cathedral

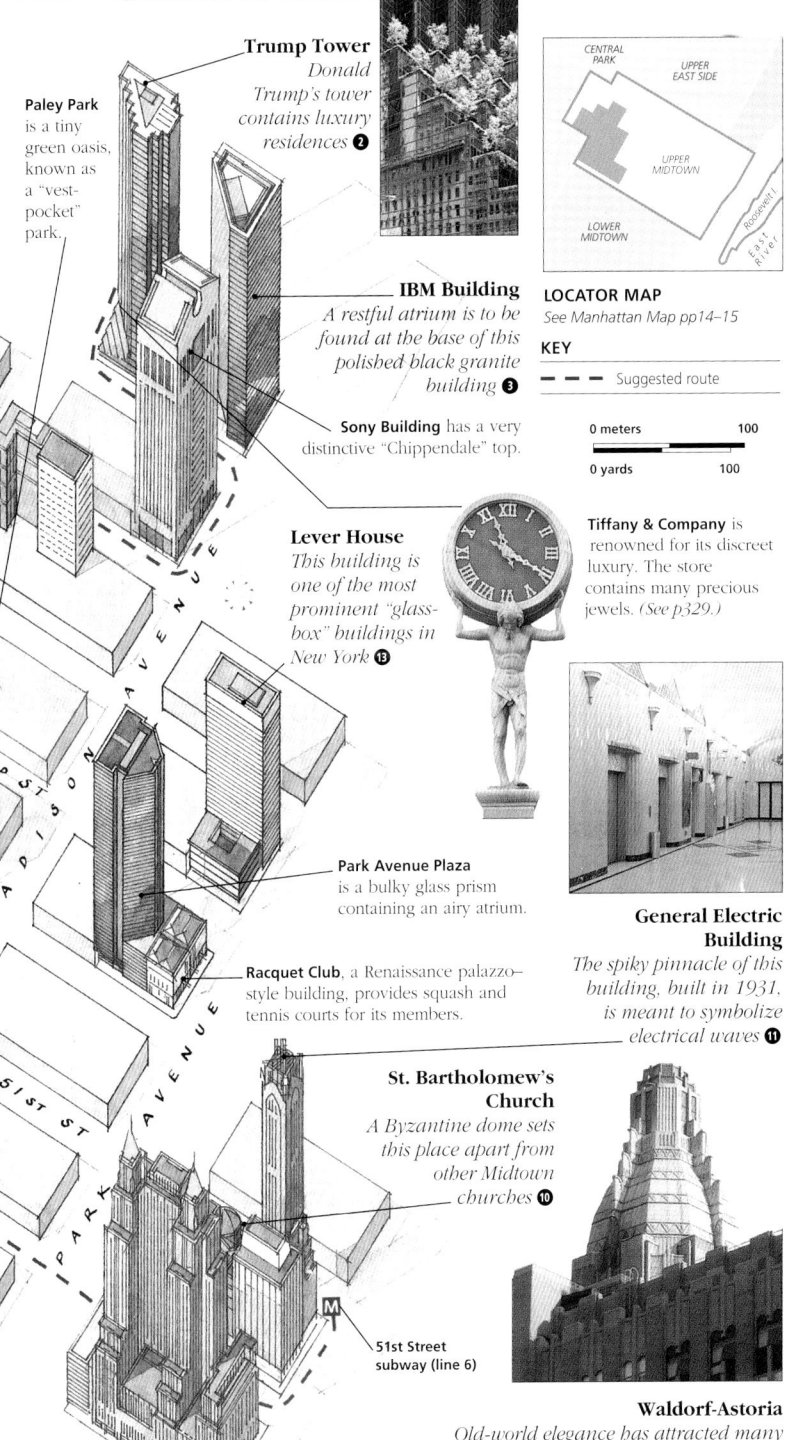

Trump Tower
Donald Trump's tower contains luxury residences ❷

Paley Park is a tiny green oasis, known as a "vest-pocket" park.

IBM Building
A restful atrium is to be found at the base of this polished black granite building ❸

Sony Building has a very distinctive "Chippendale" top.

LOCATOR MAP
See Manhattan Map pp14–15

KEY

– – – Suggested route

| 0 meters | 100 |
| 0 yards | 100 |

Lever House
This building is one of the most prominent "glass-box" buildings in New York ❸

Tiffany & Company is renowned for its discreet luxury. The store contains many precious jewels. *(See p329.)*

Park Avenue Plaza is a bulky glass prism containing an airy atrium.

Racquet Club, a Renaissance palazzo–style building, provides squash and tennis courts for its members.

General Electric Building
The spiky pinnacle of this building, built in 1931, is meant to symbolize electrical waves ⓫

St. Bartholomew's Church
A Byzantine dome sets this place apart from other Midtown churches ⓾

51st Street subway (line 6)

Waldorf-Astoria
Old-world elegance has attracted many famous guests to this hotel, including the late Duke and Duchess of Windsor ⓬

Window display at Bergdorf
Goodman (see p319)

Fifth Avenue ❶

Map 12 F3–F4. Ⓜ *5th Ave-53rd St, 5th Ave-59th St.*

In 1883, when William Henry Vanderbilt built his mansion at Fifth Avenue and 51st Street, he started a trend that resulted in palatial residences stretching as far as Central Park, built for top families such as the Astors, Belmonts, and Goulds. Only a few remain to attest to the grandeur of the era.

One of these is the Cartier store at 651 Fifth Avenue, once the home of Morton F. Plant, millionaire and commodore of the New York Yacht Club. As retailers swept north up the avenue – a trend that began in 1906 – society gradually moved uptown. In 1917, Plant moved to a mansion at 86th Street, and legend has it that he traded his old home to Pierre Cartier for a perfectly matched string of pearls.

Fifth Avenue has been synonymous with luxury goods ever since. From Cartier at 52nd Street to Henri Bendel at 56th and Tiffany and Bergdorf Goodman at 57th, you will find many brands symbolizing wealth and social standing today, just as Astor and Vanderbilt did over a century ago.

Trump Tower ❷

725 5th Ave. **Map** 12 F3. *Tel (212) 832-2000.* Ⓜ *5th Ave-53rd St, 5th Ave–59th St.* **Garden level** ☐ *10am–6pm Mon–Sat, noon–5pm Sun.* **Building** ☐ *8am–10pm daily.*
🗗 ♿ 🍴 🚻 🛗

This glittering, exorbitantly expensive apartment and office tower rises above a lavish six-story atrium. Designed in 1983 by Der Scutt of Swanke, Hayden, Connell & Partners, the public space has pink marble, mirrors and glitz throughout. There is an impressive 80-ft (24-m) high indoor waterfall, while the exterior is lined with hanging gardens. The tower is a flamboyant monument to affluence by the developer Donald Trump, a symbol of the excesses and grandeur of the 1980s (*see p33*).

Next door, 727 Fifth Avenue is a complete contrast: the location of Tiffany & Co., the prestigious jewelers founded in 1837. Famed for exquisite window displays, the store uses understated but elegant blue packaging as a status symbol in itself. Tiffany's was immortalized by Truman Capote in his 1958 novel *Breakfast at Tiffany's.*

Entrance to Tiffany & Co., the exclusive jewelry emporium

IBM Building ❸

590 Madison Ave. **Map** 12 F3. Ⓜ *5th Ave.* **Garden Plaza** ☐ *8am–10pm daily.* 🗗 ♿

Completed in 1983, this 43-story tower was designed by Edward Larrabee Barnes. It is a sleek, five-sided prism of gray-green polished granite, with a cantilevered corner at 57th Street. The **Garden Plaza**, with its bamboo trees, is open to the public and has been redubbed "The Sculpture Garden." Eight new works, which change four times a year, are on view at any one time. Near the atrium is a work by American sculptor Michael Heizer, entitled *Levitated Mass.* Inside a low, stainless-steel tank is a huge slab of granite that seems to float on air.

On the corner of 57th Street and Madison Avenue is *Saurien,* a bright-orange abstract sculpture by Alexander Calder.

Interior of the Trump Tower atrium

St. Thomas Church ❹

1 W 53rd St. **Map** 12 F4. **Tel** (212)
757-7013. Ⓜ 5th Ave-53rd St.
🕐 7am–6pm daily. 🚻 frequent. 📷
♿ 🎦 after 11am service & concerts.
www.saintthomaschurch.org

This is the fourth home for
this parish and the second on
this site. Today's church was
built between 1909 and 1914
to replace an earlier structure
destroyed in a fire in 1905.
The previous building had
provided the setting for many
of the glittering high-society
weddings of the late 19th
century. The most lavish
of these was in 1895 when
heiress Consuelo Vanderbilt
married the English Duke of
Marlborough.

The limestone building, in
French–Gothic style, has a
single asymmetrical tower
and an off-center nave, novel
solutions to the architectural
problems posed by its corner
position. The richly carved,
shimmering white screens
behind the altar were designed
by architect Bertram Goodhue
and sculptor Lee Lawrie.
Carvings in the choir stalls,
dating from the 1920s, include
modern inventions such as
the telephone, Presidents
Roosevelt and Wilson, and
Lee Lawrie himself.

Museum of Modern Art ❺

See pp172–5.

American Folk Art Museum ❻

45 W 53rd St. **Map** 12 F4.
Tel (212) 265-1040. Ⓜ 5th Ave-
53rd St. 🕐 10:30am–5:30pm
Tue–Sun (7:30pm Fri). 🎦 ♿ 🎦
🖥 🛈 www.folkartmuseum.org

The permanent home for
the appreciation and study
of American folk art is here,
in the first free-standing art
museum built in New York
since 1966. Designed by the
innovative architectural firm
of Tod Williams Billie Tsien &
Associates and built in 2001,

Beatles Paul, Ringo and John on the "Ed Sullivan Show" in 1964

the structure is clad in panels
of white tombasil, a white
bronze alloy. The museum
has 30,000 sq ft (2,787 sq m)
of exhibition space on eight
levels. The museum still
retains the Eva and Morris
Feld Gallery at the Lincoln
Square location (see p214).

The American Folk Art Museum

The Paley Center for Media ❼

25 W 52nd St. **Map** 12 F4.
Tel (212) 621-6800. Ⓜ 5th Ave-
53rd St. 🕐 noon–6pm Wed–Sun
(to 8pm Thu). ● public
hols. 🎦 📷 ♿ 🎦 🛈
www.paleycenter.org

In this one-of-a-kind
repository museum,
visitors can watch and
listen to news and a
collection of entertainment
and sports documentaries
from radio and
television's earliest
days to the present.
Pop fans can see the

early Beatles or a young
Elvis Presley making his
television debut. Sports
enthusiasts can relive classic
Olympic competitions.
World War II footage might
be chosen by students of
history or by those who
lived through the war. Six
choices at any one time
can be selected from a
computer catalogue that
covers a library of over
50,000 programs. The
selections are then played
on small private areas.
There are larger screening
areas and a theater for 200,
where retrospectives of
artists and directors are
shown. There are also photo
exhibits and memorabilia.

The museum was the brain-
child of William S. Paley, a
former head of the CBS TV
network. It opened in 1975 as
the Museum of Broadcasting
on East 53rd Street. It proved
so popular that in 1991 it
moved into this hi-tech $50
million home in a building
reminiscent of
an antique
radio
set.

1960s television star Lucille Ball

The Museum of Modern Art ❺

MoMA contains one of the world's most comprehensive collections of modern art. Founded in 1929, it set the standard for museums of its kind. Following an expansion program, MoMA in Midtown reopened in 2004. The renovated building provides gallery space over six floors, almost twice that of the old museum. Expanses of glass allow abundant natural light both to penetrate inside the building and to bathe the sculpture garden.

Museum facade on 54th Street

Sculpture Garden
The Abby A. Rockefeller Sculpture Garden has a peaceful atmosphere.

STAR PAINTINGS

★ Les Demoiselles d'Avignon by Pablo Picasso

★ Portrait of the Postman Joseph Roulin by Vincent Van Gogh

Christina's World
(1948) Andrew Wyeth contrasts an over-whelming horizon with the minutely-studied surroundings of his handicapped neighbor.

Bird in Space *(c. 1928)*
Constantin Brancusi's elegant bronze sculpture captures the sheer essence of flight.

GALLERY GUIDE

The sculpture garden is on the first floor. The contemporary art, print, and media galleries are on the second floor. Painting and sculpture are exhibited on the second, fourth, and fifth floors. Architecture and design, photography, and drawings are all on the third floor. Changing exhibitions are displayed on the third and sixth floors. Films are shown on the lower level.

Sculpture garden

First floor

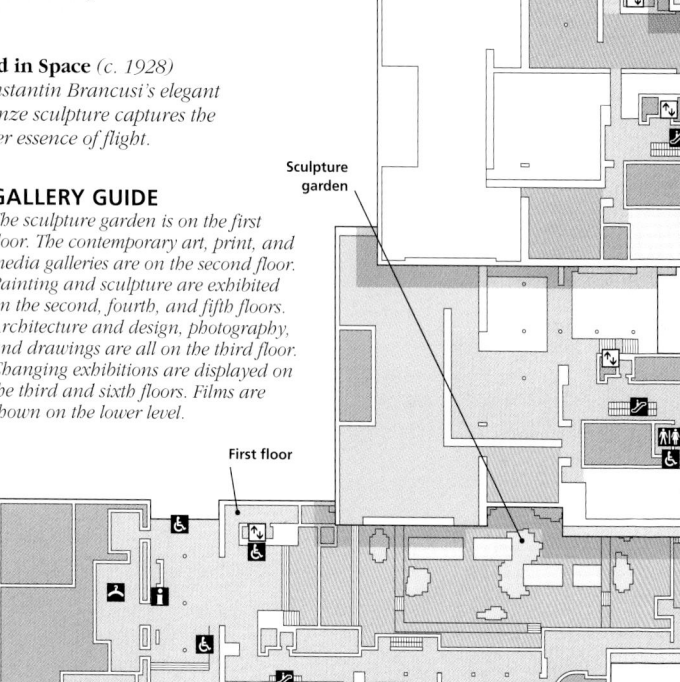

Main entrance

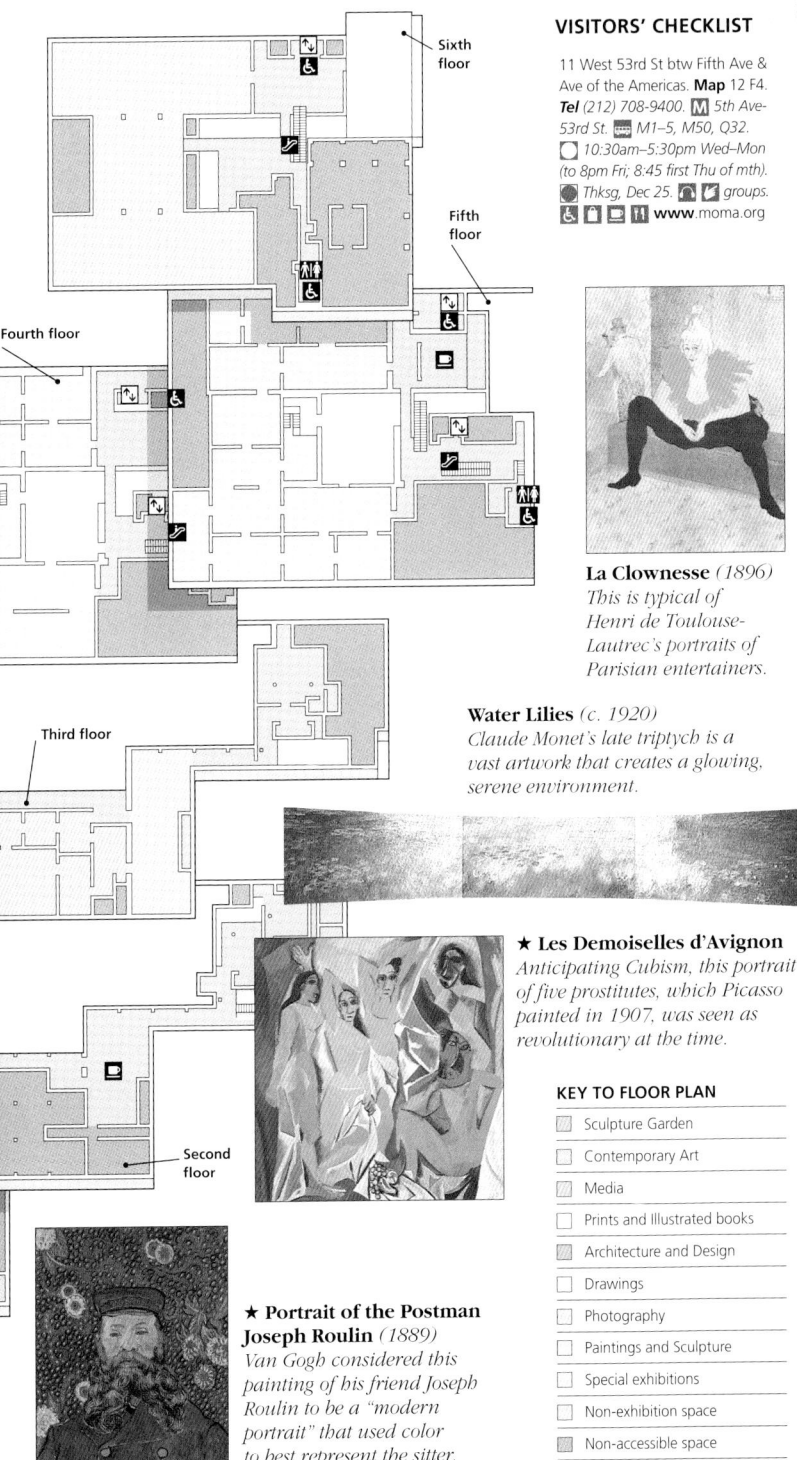

VISITORS' CHECKLIST

11 West 53rd St btw Fifth Ave &
Ave of the Americas. **Map** 12 F4.
Tel *(212) 708-9400.* M *5th Ave-
53rd St.* M1–5, M50, Q32.
10:30am–5:30pm Wed–Mon
(to 8pm Fri; 8:45 first Thu of mth).
Thksg, Dec 25. groups.
www.moma.org

La Clownesse *(1896)*
*This is typical of
Henri de Toulouse-
Lautrec's portraits of
Parisian entertainers.*

Water Lilies *(c. 1920)*
*Claude Monet's late triptych is a
vast artwork that creates a glowing,
serene environment.*

★ Les Demoiselles d'Avignon
*Anticipating Cubism, this portrait
of five prostitutes, which Picasso
painted in 1907, was seen as
revolutionary at the time.*

KEY TO FLOOR PLAN

	Sculpture Garden
	Contemporary Art
	Media
	Prints and Illustrated books
	Architecture and Design
	Drawings
	Photography
	Paintings and Sculpture
	Special exhibitions
	Non-exhibition space
	Non-accessible space

**★ Portrait of the Postman
Joseph Roulin** *(1889)*
*Van Gogh considered this
painting of his friend Joseph
Roulin to be a "modern
portrait" that used color
to best represent the sitter.*

Exploring the Collection

The Museum of Modern Art has approximately 150,000 works of art ranging from Post-Impressionist classics to an unrivaled collection of modern and contemporary art, from fine examples of design to early masterpieces of photography and film.

1880S TO 1940S PAINTING AND SCULPTURE

The Persistence of Memory by the Surrealist Salvador Dalí (1931)

Paul Cézanne's monumental *The Bather* and Vincent Van Gogh's *Portrait of the Postman Joseph Roulin* are two of the seminal works in the museum's collection of late-19th-century painting. Both Fauvism and Expressionism are well represented with works by Matisse, Derain, Kirchner, and others, while Pablo Picasso's *Les Demoiselles d'Avignon* marks a transition to the Cubist style of painting.

The collection also has an unparalleled number of Cubist paintings, providing an overview of a movement that radically challenged our perception of the world. Among the vast range are Picasso's *Girl with a Mandolin,* Georges Braque's *Man with a Guitar* and *Soda,* and *Guitar and Flowers* by Juan Gris. Works by the Futurists, who brought color and movement to Cubism to depict the dynamic modern world, include *Dynamism of a Soccer Player* by Umberto Boccioni, plus works by Balla, Carrà, and Villon. The geometric

abstract art of the Constructivists is included in a strong representation of Lissitzky, Malevich, and Rodchenko; De Stijl's influence is seen in paintings by Piet Mondrian, such as *Broadway Boogie Woogie.* There is a large body of work by Matisse, such as *Dance I* and *The Red Studio.* Dalí, Miró, and Ernst feature among the bizarre, strangely beautiful Surrealist works.

POSTWAR PAINTING AND SCULPTURE

The extensive collection of postwar art includes works by Bacon and Dubuffet, and has a particularly strong representation of American artists. The collection of Abstract Expressionist art, for example, includes Jackson Pollock's *One [Number 31, 1950],* Willem de Kooning's *Women, I,* Arshile Gorky's *Agony,* and *Red, Brown,*

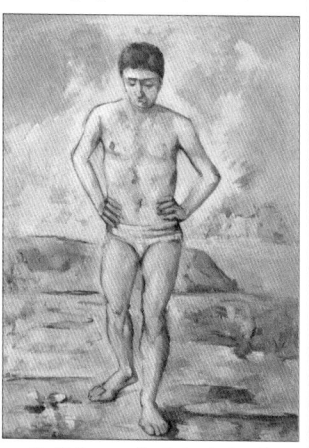

The Bather, an oil painting by French Impressionist artist Paul Cézanne

and Black by Mark Rothko. Other notable works include Jasper Johns' *Flag,* Robert Rauschenberg's *First Landing Jump,* composed of urban refuse, and *Bed,* which consists of bed linen. The Pop Art collection includes Roy Lichtenstein's *Girl with Ball* and *Drowning Girl,* Andy Warhol's famous *Gold Marilyn Monroe,* and Claes Oldenburg's *Giant Soft Fan.*

Works after about 1965 include pieces by Judd, Flavin, Serra, and Beuys, among many others.

DRAWINGS AND OTHER WORKS ON PAPER

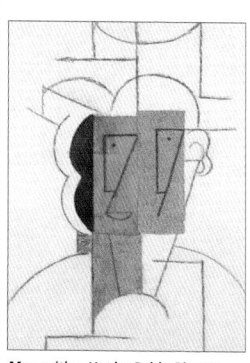

Man with a Hat by Pablo Picasso (1912), a collage with charcoal

More than 7,000 artworks ranging in size from tiny preparatory pieces to large mural-sized works are among MoMA's holdings. Many drawings use conventional materials, such as pencil, charcoal, pen and ink, pastel, and watercolor. However, there are also collages and mixed-media works composed of paper ephemera, natural products, and man-made goods.

The collection provides an overview of Modernism, from the late 19th century to the present day, including movements such as Cubism, Dadaism, and Surrealism. Drawings by famous and well-established artists, such as Picasso, Miró, and Johns, are exhibited alongside a growing number of works by talented emerging artists.

PRINTS AND ILLUSTRATED BOOKS

American Indian Theme II by Roy Lichtenstein (1980)

All significant art movements from the 1880s onward are represented in this extensive collection, which provides a fascinating overview of printed art. With more than 50,000 items in the department's holdings, there are wide-ranging examples of historical and contemporary printmaking. Works created in such traditional media as etchings, lithographic prints, screenprints, and woodcuts are displayed alongside pieces created using more experimental techniques.

There are some particularly fine examples of works by Andy Warhol, who is widely considered to be the most important printmaker of the 20th century. There are also many illustrations and prints by other artists including Redon, Munch, Matisse, Dubuffet, Johns, Lichtenstein, Freud, and Picasso.

PHOTOGRAPHY

The photography collection begins with the invention of the medium around 1840. It includes pictures by fine artists, journalists, scientists, and entrepreneurs, as well as amateur photographers.

Among the highlights of the collection are some of the best-known works by American and European photographers including Atget, Stieglitz, Lange, Arbus, Steichen, Cartier-Bresson, and Kertesz. There is also a range of contemporary practitioners,

FILM DEPARTMENT

With a collection of over 22,000 films and four million stills, the collection can offer a wide range of programs, including retrospectives of individual directors and actors, films in specific genres and experimental work, as well as a broad range of other exhibitions. Film conservation is a key part of the department's work. Today's top directors are donating copies of their films to help fund this expensive but vital work.

Film still of Charlie Chaplin and Jackie Coogan in The Kid (1921)

most notably Friedlander, Sherman, and Nixon.

The photographers have covered an extensive variety of subject matter in both colour and black and white–delicate landscapes, scenes of urban desolation, abstract imagery, and stylish portraiture, including some

Sunday on the Banks of the Marne, photographed by Henri Cartier-Bresson in 1939

beautiful silver-gelatin print nudes by the French Surrealist Man Ray. Together, they form a complete history of photographic art and represent one of the finest collections in existence.

ARCHITECTURE AND DESIGN

The Museum of Modern Art was the first art museum to include utilitarian objects in its collection. These range from household appliances such as stereo equipment, furniture, lighting, textiles, and glassware to industrial ball bearings and silicon chips. Architecture is represented in the collection of photographs, scale models, and drawings of buildings that have been or might have been built.

Graphic design is shown in typography and posters. Larger exhibits that look as if they belong in a museum of transportation include Willys-Overland Jeep and the Bell helicopter.

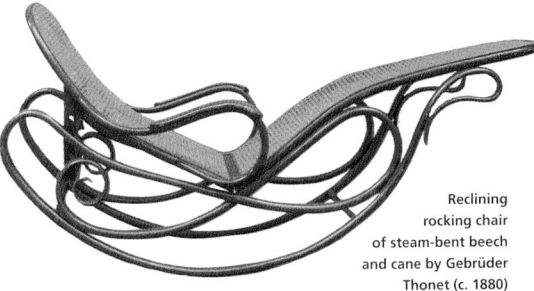

Reclining rocking chair of steam-bent beech and cane by Gebrüder Thonet (c. 1880)

St. Patrick's Cathedral 8

See pp178–9.

Villard Houses 9

457 Madison Ave (New York Palace Hotel). **Map** 13 A4. **Tel** *(800) NY PALACE.* M *51st St.* **www.**newyork palace.com **Municipal Art Sociey Urban Center** ☐ *10am–7pm Mon–Thu, 10am–6pm Fri, 10am–5:30pm Sat.* **Tel** *(212) 935 3960.* ⊙ ⴴ ⴴ **www.**mas.org

Henry Villard was a Bavarian immigrant who became publisher of the *New York Evening Post* and founder of the Northern Pacific Railroad. In 1881, he bought the land opposite St. Patrick's Cathedral and hired McKim, Mead & White to design town houses on the site. The inspired result has six four-story houses set round a central court opening to the street and the church, though financial difficulties forced Villard to sell and ownership passed to the Roman Catholic archdiocese. When the church outgrew its space in the 1970s the houses were saved when the Helmsley chain purchased air rights for the 51-story Helmsley (now New York) Palace Hotel.

The center wing comprises the hotel's formal entrance and the Villard Bar & Lounge. The **Municipal Art Society Urban Center** occupies the north wing, and its bookshop is the best place in New York for architectural books on the city. The Municipal Art Society also organizes excellent architectural tours, from Harlem to Brooklyn and Staten Island.

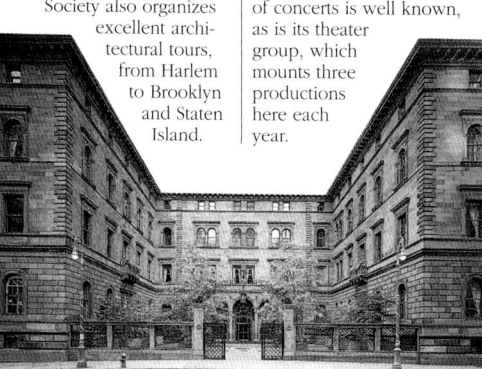

Villard Houses, now the entrance to the New York Palace Hotel

St. Bartholomew's Church

St. Bartholomew's Church 10

109 E 50th St. **Map** 13 A4. **Tel** *(212) 378-0222.* M *51st St.* ☐ *8am–6pm daily (to 7:30pm Thu & 8:30pm Sun).* ⴴ *frequent.* ⊙ ⴴ **Lectures, concerts.** ⴴ ⴴ *after 11am Sunday services.* ⴴ *(212) 888-2664.* **www.**stbarts.org

Known fondly to New Yorkers as "St. Bart's," this Byzantine structure with its ornate detail, pinkish brick, open terrace and a polychromed gold dome brought color and variety to Park Avenue in 1919.

Architect Bertram Goodhue incorporated into the design the Romanesque entrance portico created by Stanford White for the original 1903 St. Bartholomew's on Madison Avenue, and marble columns from the earlier church were used in the chapel.

St. Bartholomew's program of concerts is well known, as is its theater group, which mounts three productions here each year.

General Electric Building 11

570 Lexington Ave. **Map** 13 A4. M *Lexington Ave.* ⊙ *to the public.*

In 1931 architects Cross & Cross were commissioned to design a skyscraper that would be in keeping with its neighbor, St. Bartholomew's Church. Not an easy task, but the result won unanimous acclaim. The colors were chosen to blend and contrast, and the design of the tower complemented the church's polychrome dome.

The General Electric Building on Lexington Avenue

View the pair from the corner of Park and 50th to see how well it works. However, the General Electric is no mere backdrop but a work of art in its own right and a favorite part of the city skyline. It is an Art Deco gem from its chrome and marble lobby to its spiky "radio waves" crown.

Walk one block north on Lexington Avenue to find a place much cherished by movie fans. It is right at this spot that Marilyn Monroe, in a billowing white frock, stood so memorably in the breeze from the Lexington Avenue subway grating in the movie *The Seven-Year Itch.*

Waldorf–Astoria ⑫

301 Park Ave. **Map** 13 A5.
Tel (212) 355-3000. 🅜 Lexington
Ave, 53rd St. See **Where to Stay**
p288. **www**.waldorf.com

This Art Deco classic, which covers an entire city block, was designed by Schultze & Weaver in 1931. The original Hotel at 34th Street was demolished to make way for the Empire State Building.

Winston Churchill and New York philanthropist Grover Whalen at the Waldorf–Astoria in 1946

Still deservedly one of New York's most prestigious hotels, the Waldorf–Astoria serves, too, as a reminder of a more glamorous era in the city's history. The 625-ft (190-m) twin towers, where the Duke and Duchess of Windsor lived, have hosted numerous celebrities, including every US president since 1931. The giant lobby clock, executed for the Chicago World's Fair of 1893, is from the original hotel, and the piano in the Peacock Alley cocktail lounge belonged to Cole Porter when he was a resident of the hotel's exclusive Towers.

Lever House ⑬

390 Park Ave. **Map** 13 A4.
🅜 5th Ave-53rd St. **Lobby and
building** 🔘 to the public. 🔳

Imagine a Park Avenue lined with sturdy, residential buildings – and then imagine the sensation when they were suddenly reflected here in the first of the city's glass-walled skyscrapers, one of the most influential buildings of the modern era. The design, by Skidmore, Owings & Merrill, is simply two

The pool at the Four Seasons in the Seagram Building

rectangular slabs of stainless steel and glass, one laid horizontally, the other stacked to stand tall above it, to allow light in from every side. The crisp and bright design was intended to symbolize many of the Lever Brothers' products – they make soaps and other cleaning products. Revolutionary though it was in 1952, Lever House is now dwarfed by its many imitators, but its importance as an architectural pacesetter remains undiminished. The Lever House restaurant is a VIP scene.

Lever House on Park Avenue

Seagram Building ⑭

375 Park Ave. **Map** 13 A4. 🅜 5th
Ave-53rd St. 🔘 9am–5pm Mon–Fri.
🔳 See **Where to Eat** p307.

Samuel Bronfman, the late head of Seagram distillers, was prepared to put up an ordinary commercial building until his architect daughter, Phyllis Lambert, intervened and persuaded him to go to the best – Mies van der Rohe.

The result, which is widely considered the finest of the many Modernist buildings of the 1950s, consists of two rectangles of bronze and glass that let the light pour in.

Within is the exclusive Four Seasons Restaurant *(see p.307)*, a landmark in its own right. Designer Philip Johnson has created a remarkable space, with the centerpiece of one room a pool, and another a bar topped by a quivering Richard Lippold sculpture.

Office workers at lunch in the spacious Citigroup Center atrium

Citigroup Center ⑮

153 E 53rd St. **Map** 13 A4. 🅜 53rd
St-Lexington Ave. 🔘 7am–11pm
daily. 🔳 🔳 **St. Peter's Lutheran
Church** 619 Lexington Ave. *Tel* (212)
935-2200. 🔘 9am–9pm daily. 🔳
12:15pm Mon–Fri, 6pm Wed, 8:45am
& 11am Sun. **Jazz vespers** 5pm
Sun. **Concerts** noon Wed. **York
Theater at St. Peter's;** *Tel* (212)
935-5820. **www**.saintpeters.org

An aluminum-clad spire built on ten-story stilts with a sliced-off roof, Citigroup Center is unique; it caused a sensation when it was completed in 1978. The unusual base design had to incorporate St. Peter's Lutheran Church. The church is separate both in space and design, a granite sculpture below a corner of the tower. Step inside to see the striking interior and the Erol Beker Chapel by sculptor Louise Nevelson. The church is well known for its organ concerts, jazz vespers, and theater presentations. Citigroup's slanting top never functioned as a solar panel as intended, but it is an unmistakable landmark on the skyline.

St. Patrick's Cathedral ⑧

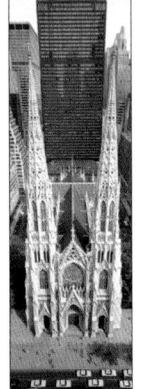

The cathedral's Fifth Avenue facade

The Roman Catholic Church originally intended this site for use as a cemetery, but in 1850 Archbishop John Hughes decided to build a cathedral instead. Many thought that it was foolish to build so far beyond the (then) city limits, but Hughes went ahead anyway. Architect James Renwick built New York's finest Gothic Revival building, the largest Catholic cathedral in the United States. The cathedral, which seats 2,500 people, was completed in 1878, though the spires were added from 1885 to 1888.

★ Lady Chapel
This chapel honors the Blessed Virgin. The stained-glass windows portray the mysteries of the rosary.

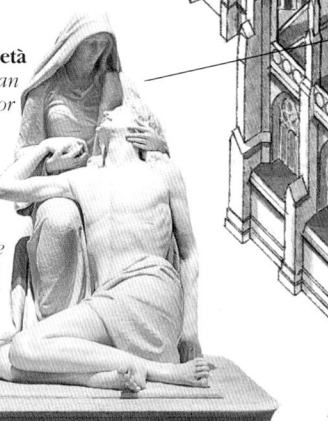

Pietà
American sculptor William O. Partridge created this Pietà in 1906. The statue stands at the side of the Lady Chapel.

★ Baldachin
The great baldachin rising over the high altar is made entirely of bronze. Statues of the saints and prophets adorn the four piers supporting the canopy.

STAR FEATURES

★ Baldachin

★ Great Bronze Doors

★ Great Organ and Rose Window

★ Lady Chapel

Cathedral Facade
The exterior wall is built of white marble. The spires rise 330 ft (101 m) above the pavement.

Stations of the Cross
Carved of Caen stone in Holland, these reliefs won first prize in the field of religious art at the Chicago World's Fair in 1893.

VISITORS' CHECKLIST

5th Ave and 50th St. **Map** 12 F4. **Tel** (212) 753-2261. 6 to 51st St; E, V to Fifth Ave. M1–5, M50, Q32. 7:30am–8:45pm daily. frequent Mon–Sat; 7, 8, 9, 10:15am & noon, 1, 4 (in Spanish) & 5:30pm Sun. *Concerts, recitals, lectures.* **www.**saintpatrickscathedral.org

Saint Elizabeth Ann Seton Shrine
The bronze statue and screen depict the life of the first American to be canonized a saint. She founded the Sisters of Charity (see p76).

★ Great Organ and Rose Window
Measuring 26 ft (8 m) in diameter, the rose window shines above the great organ, which has more than 7,000 pipes.

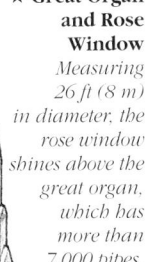

Main entrance

★ Great Bronze Doors
The massive doors weigh 20,000 lb (9,000 kg) and are adorned with important religious figures in New York.

Central Synagogue 🔟

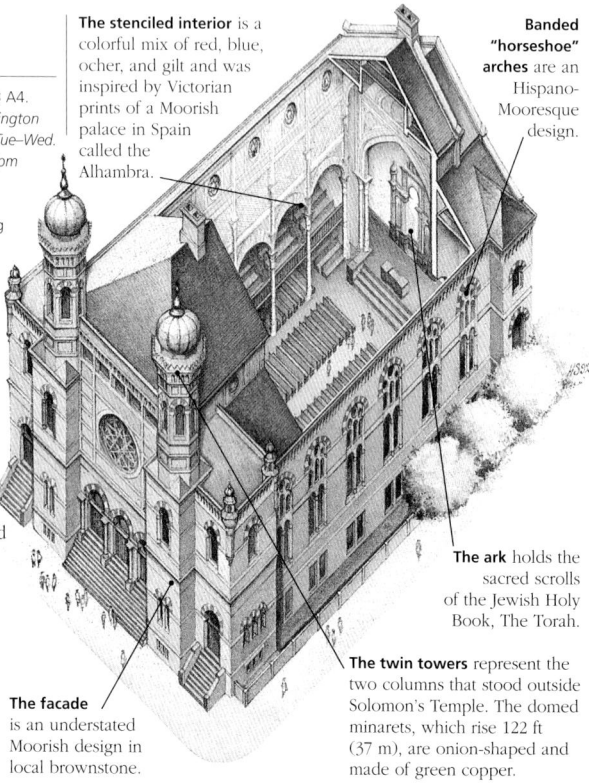

652 Lexington Ave. **Map** 13 A4.
Tel *(212) 838–5122.* M *Lexington Ave-53rd St.* ⬤ *noon–2pm Tue–Wed.* ◪ *12:45pm Wed.* ⬤ ⬤ *6pm Fri, also 10am Sat (Jul–Aug), 10.30am Sat (Sep–Jun).*
www.centralsynagogue.org

This is New York's oldest building in continuous use as a synagogue. It was designed in 1870 by Silesian-born Henry Fernbach, America's first prominent Jewish architect. He also designed some of SoHo's finest cast-iron buildings. Restored after a 1999 fire, the Synagogue is considered the city's best example of Moorish-Islamic Revival architecture. The congregation was founded in 1846 as Ahawath Chesed (Love of Mercy) by 18 immigrants, most of them from Bohemia, on Ludlow Street on the Lower East Side.

The stenciled interior is a colorful mix of red, blue, ocher, and gilt and was inspired by Victorian prints of a Moorish palace in Spain called the Alhambra.

Banded "horseshoe" arches are an Hispano-Mooresque design.

The ark holds the sacred scrolls of the Jewish Holy Book, The Torah.

The twin towers represent the two columns that stood outside Solomon's Temple. The domed minarets, which rise 122 ft (37 m), are onion-shaped and made of green copper.

The facade is an understated Moorish design in local brownstone.

Sutton Place 🔟

Map 13 C3. M *59th St, 51st St.* 🚌 *M15, M31, M57.*

Sutton Place is a posh and pleasant neighborhood, delightfully devoid of busy traffic, made up of elegant low-rise apartment houses and town houses designed by noted architects. The arrival of New York society in the 1920s transformed an area that had once been the province of factories and tenements. Three Sutton Square is the residence of the secretary-general of the United Nations. Look beyond Sutton Square and 59th Street for a glimpse of Riverview Terrace, a private street of five ivy-covered brownstones fronting on the river. The tiny parks at the end of 55th Street and jutting out at 57th Street offer views of the river and the Queensboro Bridge.

After much neighborhood opposition, Bridgemarket opened in 2000. Located between the huge vaults under the Queensboro Bridge, there is an upscale Terence Conran's for housewares and a Food Emporium supermarket.

Park at Sutton Place, looking toward Queensboro Bridge and Roosevelt Island

Beekman Place 🔟

Map 13 C5. M *59th St, 51st St.* 🚌 *M15, M50.*

Smaller than Sutton Place, and even more tranquil, is Beekman Place, a virtually private two-block enclave of 1920s town houses and small-scale apartments. Famous residents here have included Gloria Vanderbilt, Rex Harrison, Irving Berlin and members of the large Rockefeller family.

At Turtle Bay Gardens, restored brownstone houses dating from the 1860s hide a charming Italianate garden. Among the residents enticed by this privacy have been the film stars Tyrone Power and Katharine Hepburn, composer Stephen Sondheim, and writer E.B. White.

Roosevelt Island ⑲

Map 14 D2. Ⓜ *59th St. Tram, Roosevelt Island station (F).*
www.rioc.com

Since 1976 a Swiss cable car departing from Second Avenue at 60th Street has offered a quick, thrilling ride across the East River to Roosevelt Island, with eagle's-eye views of the city and the Queensboro Bridge. The island is now also serviced by the F subway line.

Near the tram station are the remains of the Blackwell farmhouse, which stood from 1796 to 1804 and gave the island its name until real estate development began in the 1920s. From then until the 1970s, the island housed a succession of hospitals, an almshouse, a jail, a workhouse, and an insane asylum, and became known as Welfare Island. In 1927, Mae West was held in the penitentiary here after a "lewd performance." The ruins of 19th-century hospitals still remain, as does an 1872 lighthouse built by an asylum inmate.

The clock statues above the Fuller Building entrance

Bloomingdale's store sign

Bloomingdale's ⑳

1000 3rd Ave. **Map** 13 A3. **Tel** (212) 705-2000. Ⓜ 59th St. ◯ 10am–8:30pm Mon–Fri, 10am–7pm Sat, 11am–7pm Sun. See **Shopping** p319. **www**.bloomingdales.com

For a while in the booming 1980s, "Bloomies" was synonymous with the good life. Founded by Joseph and Lyman Bloomingdale in 1872, this famous department store had a bargain-basement image until the 3rd Avenue El was taken down in the 1960s. Then came the store's transformation to the epitome of trendy, sophisticated shopping. But the late 1980s brought new ownership and eventual bankruptcy. While not as flashy as in the past, Bloomingdale's is open every day and remains one of the city's best-stocked stores. A second store has opened in SoHo at 504 Broadway.

Fuller Building ㉑

41 E 57th St. **Map** 13 A3. *Peter Findlay Gallery.* **Tel** (212) 644-4433; *James Goodman Gallery.* **Tel** (212) 593-3737. ◯ 10am–6pm Tue–Sat. Ⓜ 59th St.

This slim-towered black, gray and white 1929 beauty by Walker & Gillette is a prime example of geometric Art Deco design. The striking statues on either side of the clock above the entrance are by Elie Nadelman. Step inside to admire the intricate mosaic tile floors; one panel shows the Fuller Company's former home in

the famous Flatiron Building on Fifth Avenue *(see 127).* The Fuller Building is a hive of exclusive art galleries, most of which are open to the public daily.

French Renaissance–style facade of the Plaza Hotel

Plaza Hotel ㉒

5th Ave & Central Park South. **Map** 12 F3. Ⓜ Fifth Ave-59th St.

The city's grande dame of hotels was designed by Henry J. Hardenbergh, known for the Dakota *(see p218)* and the original Waldorf–Astoria. Completed in 1907 at the exorbitant cost of $12.5 million, the Plaza was proclaimed "the best hotel in the world," with 800 rooms, 500 baths, a two-story ballroom, five marble staircases, and 14- to 17-room apartments for such families as the Vanderbilts and the Goulds *(see p49).*

The 18-story cast-iron structure resembles a French Renaissance château. Much of the interior decoration came from Europe. The Palm Court still has mirrored walls and Italian carvings of the four seasons, and is a lovely place for afternoon tea.

Already lavishly restored by its former owner Donald Trump, the building underwent a $400-million conversion into a mix of apartments, hotel condominiums, and a 130-room hotel. There are also six floors of luxury retail and upscale dining, including the famous Oak Room.

UPPER EAST SIDE

At the turn of the century, New York society moved to the Upper East Side – and stayed. Many of the Beaux-Arts mansions in this district are now museums and embassies, but the well-to-do still occupy the grand apartment buildings on Fifth and Park avenues. Chic shops and galleries line

African urn, Metropolitan Museum of Art

Madison Avenue. Farther east, the area includes what is left of German Yorkville in the East 80s, Hungarian Yorkville to the south, and little Bohemia, with its Czech population, below 78th Street. Although many of these ethnic groups no longer inhabit the area, their churches, restaurants, and shops still remain.

Bird's-eye view of the lobby at the Solomon R. Guggenheim Museum

SIGHTS AT A GLANCE

Historic Streets and Buildings
Gracie Mansion **16**
Henderson Place **14**
Park Avenue Armory **10**

Museums and Galleries
Asia Society **9**
Cooper-Hewitt National Design Museum **3**
Frick Collection pp202–3 **8**
Jewish Museum **2**
Metropolitan Museum of Art pp190–97 **6**
Mount Vernon Hotel Museum and Garden **13**
Museum of the City of New York **19**
National Academy Museum **4**
Neue Galerie New York **1**
Society of Illustrators **12**
Solomon R. Guggenheim Museum pp188–9 **5**
Whitney Museum of American Art pp200–1 **7**

Churches and Synagogues
Church of the Holy Trinity **17**
St. Nicholas Russian Orthodox Cathedral **18**
Temple Emanu-El **11**

Parks and Squares
Carl Schurz Park **15**

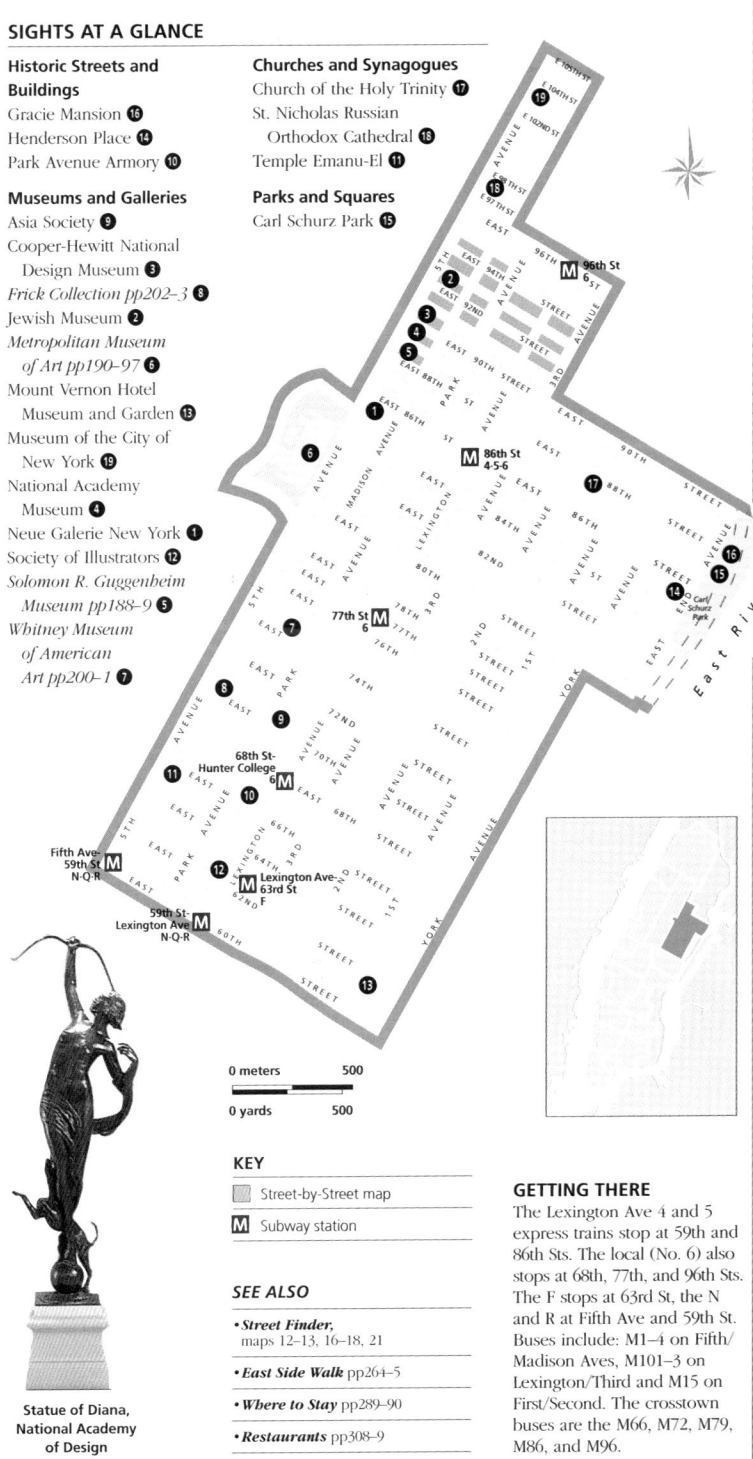

KEY

▨ Street-by-Street map

Ⓜ Subway station

SEE ALSO

• *Street Finder,* maps 12–13, 16–18, 21

• *East Side Walk* pp264–5

• *Where to Stay* pp289–90

• *Restaurants* pp308–9

Statue of Diana, National Academy of Design

GETTING THERE
The Lexington Ave 4 and 5 express trains stop at 59th and 86th Sts. The local (No. 6) also stops at 68th, 77th, and 96th Sts. The F stops at 63rd St, the N and R at Fifth Ave and 59th St. Buses include: M1–4 on Fifth/Madison Aves, M101–3 on Lexington/Third and M15 on First/Second. The crosstown buses are the M66, M72, M79, M86, and M96.

Street by Street: Museum Mile

Many of New York's museums are clustered on the Upper East Side, in homes ranging from the former Frick and Carnegie mansions to the modernistic Guggenheim, designed by Frank Lloyd Wright. The displays are as varied as the architecture, running the gamut from Old Masters to photographs to decorative arts. Presiding over the scene is the vast Metropolitan Museum of Art, America's answer to the Louvre. Some of the museums stay open late one day a week.

Jewish Museum
The most extensive collection of Judaica in the world is housed here. It includes coins, archaeological objects, and ceremonial and religious artifacts ❷

★ Cooper-Hewitt National Design Museum
Ceramics, glass, furniture and textiles are well represented here ❸

The Church of the Heavenly Rest was built in 1929 in the Gothic style. The madonna in the pulpit is by sculptor Malvina Hoffman.

National Academy Museum
The Academy, founded in 1825, moved here in 1940. Its fine collection includes paintings and sculptures by its members ❹

Graham House is an apartment building with a splendid Beaux Arts entrance. It was built in 1892.

★ Solomon R. Guggenheim Museum
Architect Frank Lloyd Wright's building, which is in the form of a spiral, is floodlit at dusk. The best way to see one of the world's premier collections of modern art is to take the elevator to the top and walk down ❺

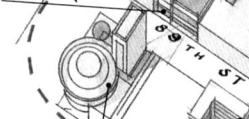

STAR SIGHTS

★ Cooper-Hewitt Museum

★ Solomon R. Guggenheim Museum

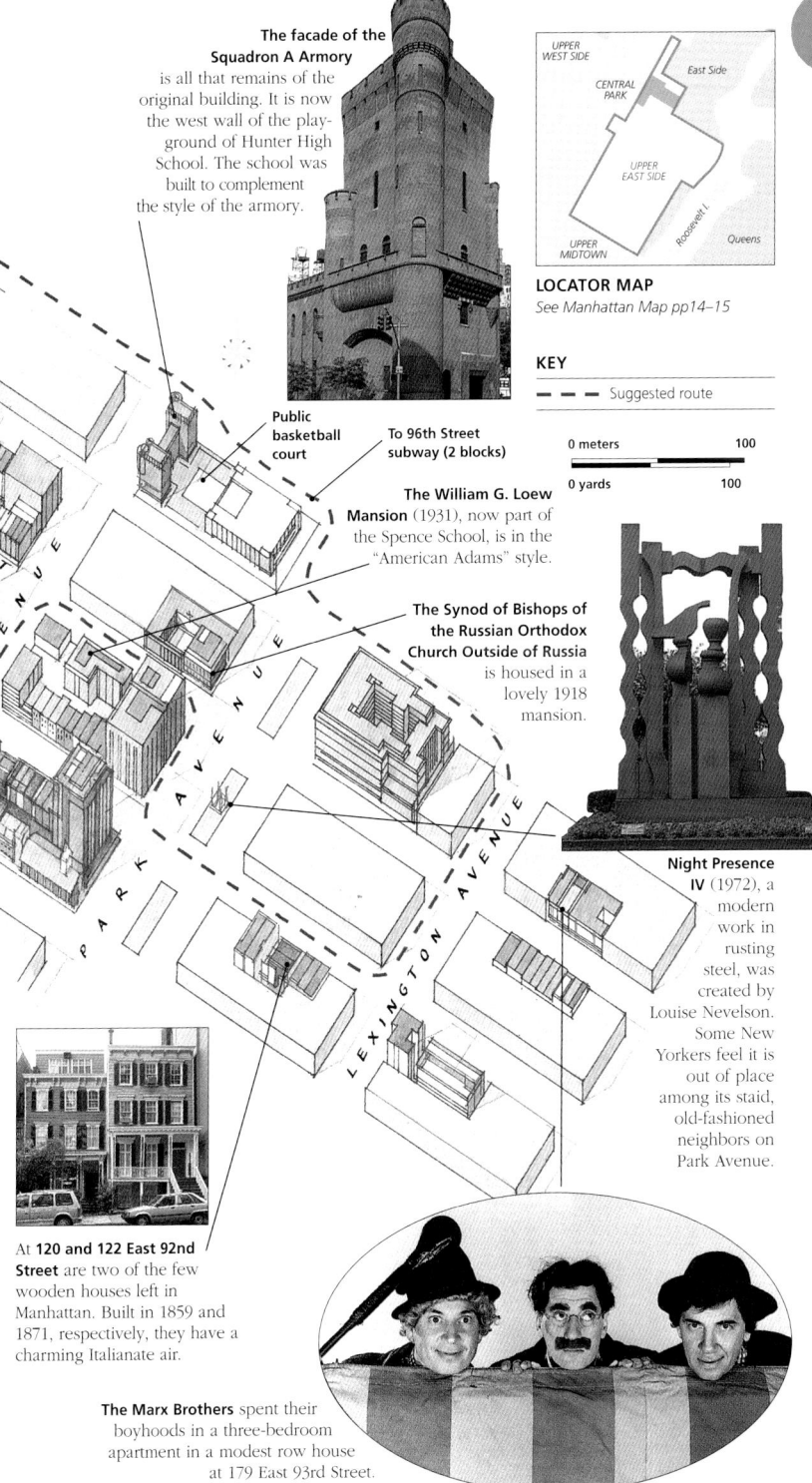

The facade of the Squadron A Armory is all that remains of the original building. It is now the west wall of the playground of Hunter High School. The school was built to complement the style of the armory.

LOCATOR MAP
See Manhattan Map pp14–15

UPPER WEST SIDE

East Side

CENTRAL PARK

UPPER EAST SIDE

Roosevelt I.

Queens

UPPER MIDTOWN

KEY

- - - Suggested route

0 meters   100
0 yards   100

Public basketball court

To 96th Street subway (2 blocks)

The William G. Loew Mansion (1931), now part of the Spence School, is in the "American Adams" style.

The Synod of Bishops of the Russian Orthodox Church Outside of Russia is housed in a lovely 1918 mansion.

Night Presence IV (1972), a modern work in rusting steel, was created by Louise Nevelson. Some New Yorkers feel it is out of place among its staid, old-fashioned neighbors on Park Avenue.

At **120 and 122 East 92nd Street** are two of the few wooden houses left in Manhattan. Built in 1859 and 1871, respectively, they have a charming Italianate air.

The Marx Brothers spent their boyhoods in a three-bedroom apartment in a modest row house at 179 East 93rd Street.

Neue Galerie New York ●

1048 5th Ave at E 86th St. **Map** 16
F3. **Tel** (212) 628-6200. Ⓜ 86th St.
🚌 M1–4. 🕐 11am–6pm Thu–Mon.
● public hols. 🖾 🛍 Ⓜ Ⓜ Café
9am–6pm daily (to 9pm Thu–Sun).
🚻 🛗 www.neuegalerie.org

This museum was founded by
art dealer Serge Sabarsky and
philanthropist Ronald Lauder.
Its objective is to collect,
research, and exhibit the
fine and decorative arts of
Germany and Austria from
the early 20th century.
   The Louis XIII-style Beaux-
Arts structure was completed
in 1914 by Carrère & Hastings,
who also designed the New
York Public Library (see p146).
The building, a designated
landmark, is considered one
of the most distinguished
buildings on Fifth
Avenue. Once
occupied by Mrs.
Cornelius Vanderbilt
III, the mansion was
purchased by Lauder and
Sabarsky in 1994. The
ground floor houses the
entrance, a bookshop, and
the Café Sabarsky, which
draws its inspiration from the
Viennese cafés of old and
also plays host to chamber,
cabaret, and classical music
concerts. The second floor
is devoted to the works of
Klimt, Schiele, and Wiener
Werkstätte objects. The upper
floors feature works from
Der Blaue Reiter (artists
such as Klee, Kandinsky),
the Bauhaus (Feininger,
Schlemmer), and Die Brücke
(Mies van der Rohe, Breuer).

Jewish Museum ●

1109 5th Ave. **Map** 16 F2. **Tel** (212)
423-3200. Ⓜ 86th St, 96th St.
🚌 M1–4. 🕐 11am–5:45pm Thu–Tue
(to 8pm Thu, to 4pm Fri). ● public
& Jewish hols. 🖾 🛍 🛗 Ⓜ 🚻
www.thejewishmuseum.org

The exquisite château-like
residence of Felix M. Warburg,
financier and leader of the
Jewish community, was
designed by C. P. H. Gilbert
in 1908. It now houses one of

the world's largest collections
of Jewish fine and ceremonial
art, and historical Judaica. The
stonework in an extension is
by the stonemasons of St. John
the Divine (see pp226–7).
   Objects have been brought
here from all over the world,
some at great risk of persecution to the donors. Covering
4,000 years, artifacts include
Torah crowns, candelabras,
kiddush cups, plates, scrolls,
and silver ceremonial objects.
   There is a Torah ark from
the Benguiat Collection, the
exquisite faience entrance
wall of a 16th-century Persian
synagogue, and the powerful
Holocaust by sculptor George
Segal. Changing exhibitions
reflect Jewish life and
experience around
the world.

**19th-century
ewer and basin from Istanbul
at the Jewish Museum**

Cooper-Hewitt National Design Museum ●

2 E 91st St. **Map** 16 F2. **Tel** (212)
849-8400. Ⓜ 86th St, 96th St.
🚌 M1–4. 🕐 10am–5pm Mon–Sat
(to 6pm Sat), 11am–6pm Sun.
● Jan 1, Thksg, Dec 25. 🖾 🛍 🛗
🛗 🚻 🛗 www.cooperhewitt.org

One of the largest design
collections in the world, this
museum occupies the former
home of industrialist Andrew
Carnegie. The collection was
amassed by the Hewitt sisters,
Amy, Eleanor, and Sarah. The
museum opened in 1897 at
Cooper Union (see p120);
the Smithsonian Institution acquired the collections in 1967,
and the Carnegie Corporation
offered the mansion.
   Carnegie asked for "the most
modest, plainest, and most
roomy house in New York,"
but the house set new trends

Cooper-Hewitt Museum entrance

with central heating, private
elevator, and air-conditioning.
Note the wooden staircase,
rich paneling and carving,
and the sunny solarium.

National Academy Museum ●

1083 5th Ave. **Map** 16 F3. **Tel** (212)
369-4880. Ⓜ 86th St. 🚌 M1–4.
🕐 noon–5pm Wed–Thu, 11am–6pm
Fri–Sun. ● public hols. 🖾 🛍 🛗
🚻 www.nationalacademy.org

More than 6,000 paintings,
drawings, and sculptures,
including works by Thomas
Eakins, Winslow Homer,
Raphael Soyer, and Frank
Lloyd Wright, comprise the
collection of the National
Academy Museum, founded
in 1825 by a group of artists.
The group's mission was
(and is) to train artists and
exhibit their work.
   In 1940, Archer Huntington,
an art patron and philan-
thropist, donated his house,
an attractive building with
patterned marble floors and
decorative plaster ceilings.
The grand entrance foyer has
a statue of Diana by sculptor
Anna Hyatt Huntington.

**Statue of Diana in the National
Academy Museum entrance foyer**

Solomon R. Guggenheim Museum ❺

See pp188–9.

Metropolitan Museum of Art ❻

See pp190–97.

Whitney Museum of American Art ❼

See pp200–01.

Frick Collection ❽

See pp202–03.

Asia Society ❾

725 Park Ave. **Map** 13 A1. *Tel* (212) 288-6400. Events: (212) 517-ASIA. M 68th St. 11am–6pm Tue–Sun (to 9pm Fri). public hols. 2pm Tue–Sat, 6:30pm Fri. www.asia society.org

Founded by John D. Rockefeller III in 1956 to increase understanding of Asian culture, the society is a forum for 30 countries from Japan to Iran, Central Asia to Australia.

The 1981 eight-story building was designed by Edward Larrabee Barnes and is made of red granite. After a renovation in 2001, the museum has increased gallery space. One gallery is permanently devoted to Rockefeller's own collection of Asian sculptures, amassed by him and his wife on frequent trips to the East.

Changing exhibits show a wide variety of Asian arts, and the society has a full program of films, dance, concerts, and lectures and a well-stocked bookshop.

South Asian sculpture at the Asia Society

Entrance hall of the Park Avenue Armory

Park Avenue Armory ❿

643 Park Ave. **Map** 13 A2. *Tel* (212) 616-3930. M 68th St. call for opening times. www.armoryonpark.org

From the War of 1812 through two world wars, the Seventh Regiment, an elite corps of "gentlemen soldiers" from prominent families, has played a vital role. Within the fortress-like exterior of their armory are extraordinary rooms filled with lavish Victorian furnishings, *objets d'art*, and regimental memorabilia.

The design by Charles W. Clinton, a veteran of the regiment, had offices facing Park Avenue, with a vast drill hall stretching behind to Lexington Ave. The reception rooms include the Veterans' Room and the Library by Louis Comfort Tiffany. The drill hall is now the site of the Winter Antiques Show *(see p53)* and a favorite venue for charity balls. A massive renovation is under way, after which the Armory will open its doors as a center for arts and education.

Temple Emanu-El ⓫

1 E 65th St. **Map** 12 F2. *Tel* (212) 744-1400. M 68th St, 63rd St. 10am–5pm Sun–Fri (last adm on Fri 3:30pm), 12:30–4:45pm Sat. Jewish hols. 5:30pm Sun–Thu, 5:15pm Fri, 10:30am Sat. www.emanuelnyc.org

This impressive limestone edifice of 1929 is the largest synagogue in the world, with seating for 2,500 in the main sanctuary alone. It is home to the oldest Reform congregation in New York, and the wealthiest members of Jewish society worship here.

Among the synagogue's many fine details are the bronze doors of the Ark, which represent an open Torah scroll. The Ark also has stained glass depicting biblical scenes and showing the tribal signs of the houses of Israel. These signs also appear on a great recessed arch that frames a magnificent wheel window, the dominant feature of the Fifth Avenue facade.

The synagogue stands on the site of the palatial home of Mrs. William Astor, the legendary society hostess. Lady Astor moved to the Upper East Side after a feud with her nephew, who lived next door. Her wine cellar and three marble fireplaces still remain at the synagogue.

The Ark at Temple Emanu-El

Solomon R. Guggenheim Museum ❺

Home to one of the world's finest collections of modern and contemporary art, the building itself is perhaps the museum's greatest masterpiece. The exterior of the museum was beautifully restored in celebration of the 50th anniversary of the building in 2009. Designed by Frank Lloyd Wright, the shell-like facade is a veritable New York landmark. The spiral ramp curves down and inward from the dome, passing works by major 19th-, 20th-, and 21st-century artists along the way.

Fifth Avenue facade

Paris Through the Window
The vibrant colors of Marc Chagall's 1913 masterpiece illumine the canvas, conjuring up images of a magical and mysterious city where nothing is quite what it appears to be.

Small Rotunda

Sackler Center for Arts Education

ℹ

THE SOLOMON

Main entrance

Woman Ironing *(1904)*
A work from Pablo Picasso's Blue Period, this painting is his quintessential image of hard work and fatigue.

Yellow Cow *(1911)*
Franz Marc's late work focused on nature and color.

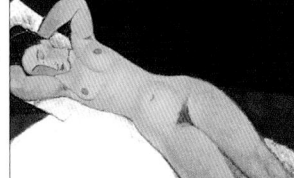

Nude *(1917)*
This sleeping figure is typical of Amedeo Modigliani's stylized work.

MUSEUM GUIDE

The Great Rotunda features special exhibitions. The Small Rotunda shows some of the museum's Impressionist and Post-Impressionist holdings. The Tower galleries (also known as The Annex) hold exhibitions of work from the permanent collection, as well as contemporary pieces. The permanent collection is shown on a rotating basis, and only parts of it are on display at any one time.

Tower

Great Rotunda

Café

Before the Mirror *(1876) In trying to capture the flavor of 19th-century society, Edouard Manet often used the image of the courtesan.*

VISITORS' CHECKLIST

1071 5th Ave at 89th St.
Map 16 F3. **Tel** *(212) 423-3500.*
M 4, 5, 6 to 86th St. M1-4.
10am–5.45pm Fri–Wed (to 7.45pm Sat). Thksgv, Dec 25.
Performing art series, concerts, lectures.
www.guggenheim.org

Woman Holding a Vase *Fernand Léger incorporated elements of Cubism into this work from 1927.*

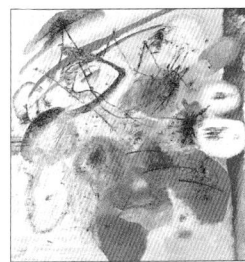

Black Lines *(1913) This is one of Vasily Kandinsky's earliest examples of his work in "non-objective" art.*

Woman with Yellow Hair *(1931) The gentle, voluptuous figure of Picasso's mistress often appears in his work.*

FRANK LLOYD WRIGHT

During his lifetime, Wright was considered the great innovator of American architecture. Characteristic of his work are Prairie-style homes and office buildings of concrete slabs, glass bricks, and tubing. Wright received the Guggenheim commission in 1942 and it was completed after his death in 1959, his only New York building.

Interior of the Guggenheim's Great Rotunda

Metropolitan Museum of Art ❻

Founded in 1870 by a group of artists and philanthropists who dreamed of an American art institution to rival those of Europe, this collection is thought to be the most comprehensive in the Western world. Works date from prehistoric times to the present. The museum opened here in 1880 and houses collections from all continents. The Greek and Roman galleries on the first floor are especially popular.

The entrance of the Metropolitan Museum of Art

★ Jeanne Hébuterne
(1919) Amedeo Modigliani's mistress, Hébuterne, appears in over 20 of his works. She killed herself the day after he died in 1920.

Ground floor

Pendant Mask
The kingdom of Benin (now part of Nigeria) was renowned for its art. This mask was made in the 16th century.

Seated Man with Harp
This statuette was made in the Cyclades c. 2,800 BC.

GALLERY GUIDE

Most of the collections are housed on the two main floors. Works from 19 curatorial areas are in the permanent galleries, with designated sections for temporary exhibitions. Central on the first and second floors are European painting, sculpture, and decorative art. The Costume Institute is situated on the ground level, directly below the Egyptian galleries on the first floor.

The Marriage Feast at Cana
This rare 16th-century panel painting by Juan de Flandes is part of the Linsky Collection

Bust of Diderot (1773)
Jean Antoine Houdon's bust was made for a Russian count.

★ Portrait of the Princesse de Broglie
This portrait, painted in 1853, was J.A.D. Ingres' last.

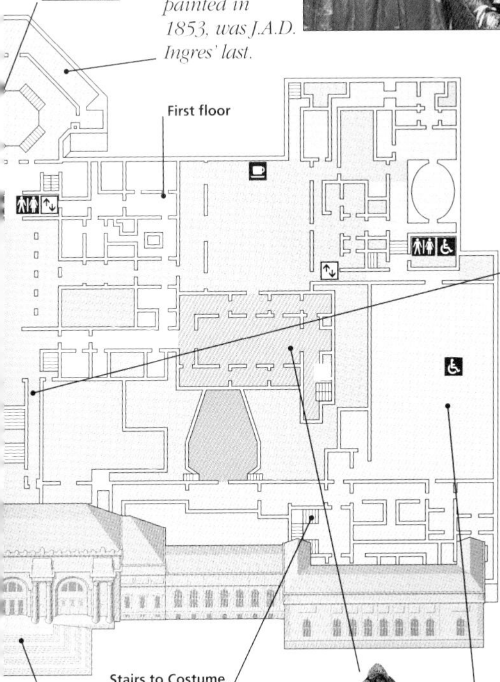

VISITORS' CHECKLIST

1000 Fifth Ave. **Map** 16 F4.
📞 (212) 535-7710. Ⓜ 4, 5, 6 to 86th St. 🚌 M1–4. ⬜ 9:30am–5:30pm Tue–Thu & Sun, 9:30am–9pm Fri–Sat. ⬤ Jan 1, Thanksgiving, Dec 25. 📷 ⬜ 🔶 **Concerts, lectures, classes, seminars, film & video presentations.** **www**.metmuseum.org

First floor

Byzantine Galleries
This marble panel with a griffin is from Greece or the Balkans (c.1250). It is just one of the pieces on display in the Byzantine Galleries.

STAR EXHIBITS

★ Byzantine Galleries

★ Jeanne Hébuterne by Amedeo Modigliani

★ Portrait of the Princesse de Broglie by Ingres

★ Temple of Dendur

Stairs to Costume Institute

Main entrance

KEY TO FLOOR PLAN

- ☐ Robert Lehman Collection
- ☐ European painting, sculpture and decorative arts
- ☐ Art of Africa, Oceania, and the Americas
- ☐ Modern art
- ☐ American art
- ☐ Egyptian art
- ☐ Greek and Roman art
- ☐ Medieval and Byzantine art
- ☐ Arms and armor
- ☐ Grace Rainey Rogers Auditorium
- ☐ Non-exhibition space

English Armor
This was made for Sir George Clifford around 1580.

★ Temple of Dendur (15 BC)
The Roman emperor Augustus built this three-room temple. He is shown in its reliefs making offerings.

Metropolitan Museum of Art: Upper Levels

Card Players (1890)
Paul Cézanne departed here from his traditional landscapes, still lifes, and portraits to paint this scene of peasants intently playing cards.

Sculpture Garden
These modern sculptures, on the roof of the Modern Art wing, are changed annually.

Gertrude Stein (1905–6)
This portrait of the American writer is by Pablo Picasso. The masklike face is evidence of his debt to African and Roman art.

★ Cypresses (1889)
Vincent Van Gogh painted this the year before he died. The heavy brushstrokes and the swirling style mark his later work.

First floor

Second floor

STAR EXHIBITS

★ Cypresses by
Vincent Van Gogh

★ Diptych by
Jan van Eyck

★ George Washington
Crossing the Delaware
by Leutze

★ Self-portrait (1660)
by Rembrandt

**Eagle-headed Winged
Being Pollinating the
Sacred Tree** (about 900 BC)
This relief comes from an
Assyrian palace.

★ Diptych *(1425–30)*
Flemish painter Jan van Eyck was one of the earliest masters of oil painting. These scenes of the Crucifixion and Last Judgment show him to be a forerunner of realism, too.

★ Washington Crossing the Delaware
In 1851 Emanuel Gottlieb Leutze painted this romanticized – and inaccurate – view of the famous crossing.

KEY TO FLOOR PLAN

- European painting, sculpture, and decorative arts
- Ancient Near Eastern art
- Modern art
- American art
- Asian art
- Cypriot art
- Musical instruments
- Drawings, prints, and photographs
- Non-exhibition space
- Art of Arab Lands, Turkey, Iran, Central Asia, and Later South Asia

Astor Court

The Death of Socrates *(1787)*
Jacques-Louis David shows Socrates about to take poison rather than renounce his beliefs.

★ Self-portrait *(1660)*
Rembrandt painted almost 100 self-portraits. This one shows him at the age of 54.

THE ASTOR COURT

In 1979, 27 craftspeople from China, responsible for the care of Souzhou's historic gardens, came to New York to replicate a Ming-style scholar's garden in the Metropolitan Museum. They used centuries-old techniques and handmade tools that had been passed down for generations. It was the first cultural exchange between the United States and the People's Republic of China. The result is a quiet garden for meditation, a Western parallel to Souzhou's Garden of the Master of the Fishing Nets.

Exploring the Metropolitan

The treasures of "the Met" include a vast collection of American art and more than 2,500 European paintings, including masterpieces by Rembrandt and Vermeer. There are also many Islamic exhibits, plus the greatest collection of Egyptian art outside Cairo.

AFRICA, OCEANIA, AND THE AMERICAS

A painted gold funerary mask (10th–14th century) from the necropolis of Batán Grande, Peru

Nelson Rockefeller built the Michael C. Rockefeller Wing in 1982 in memory of his son, who lost his life on an art-finding expedition in New Guinea. The wing showcases a superb collection of over 1,600 objects from Africa, the islands of the Pacific and the Americas.

Among the African works, the ivory and bronze sculptures from the royal kingdom of Benin (Nigeria) are outstanding, as is the wooden sculpture by the Dogon, Bamana and Senufo peoples of Mali. From the Pacific come carvings by the Asmat people of New Guinea and decorations and masks from the Melanesian and Polynesian islands. From Mexico and Central and South America come pre-Columbian gold, ceramics and stonework. The wing also contains fine Native American artifacts by the Inuit and other groups.

AMERICAN ART

Gilbert Stuart's portrait of George Washington, George Caleb Bingham's *Fur Traders Descending the Missouri*, John SingerSargent's notorious portrait of *Madame X,* and the monumental *Washington Crossing the Delaware* by

Emanuel Leutze are among the icons in the American Wing. It holds not only one of the world's finest collections of American painting and sculpture but also of decorative arts from Colonial times to the beginning of the 20th century. Highlights range from elegant Neo-Classical silver vessels made by Paul Revere to innovative glassware by Tiffany & Co. In the furniture section are settees, dining chairs, tables, bookcases, and desks from major centers of American cabinetmaking such as Boston, Newport, and Philadelphia.

Period rooms, with their original decorative woodwork and furnishings, range from the saloon hall in which George Washington celebrated his last birthday to the elegant prairie-style living room from the house that Frank Lloyd Wright designed for Francis W. Little in Wayzata, Minnesota, in 1912.

The Charles Engelhard Court is an indoor sculpture garden with large-scale architectural elements, including the lovely stained-glass and mosaic loggia from Louis Comfort Tiffany's Long Island estate and the facade of an 1824 United States Branch Bank that once stood on Wall Street.

ANCIENT NEAR EASTERN AND ISLAMIC ART

Massive stone sculptures of winged, human-headed animals, once the guardians of the 9th-century BC Assyrian

Mysterious in identity and origin, a rare 5,000-year-old copper head from the Near East

palace of Ashurnasirpal II, stand at the entrance to the Ancient Near Eastern galleries. Inside is a collection spanning 8,000 years, rich in Iranian bronzes, Anatolian ivories and Sumerian sculptures, and Achaemenian and Sassanian silver and gold. An adjacent area contains Islamic art of the 7th to the 19th centuries; glass and metalwork from Egypt, Syria and Meso-potamia; royal miniatures from Persia and Mughal India; 16th- and 17th-century rugs; and an 18th-century room from Syria.

ARMS AND ARMOR

Mounted knights in full armor charge at each other across the equestrian court here. These galleries are a favorite with children and anyone moved by medieval romance or thrilled by power.

There are suits of armor, rapiers and sabers with hilts of precious stones and gold, firearms inlaid with ivory and mother-of-pearl, plus colorful heraldic banners and shields.

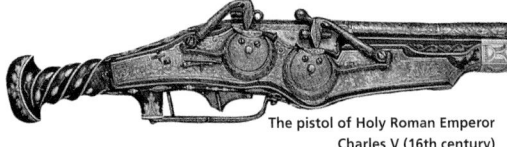

The pistol of Holy Roman Emperor Charles V (16th century)

Highlights include the armor of gentleman-pirate Sir George Clifford, a favorite of Queen Elizabeth I. The rainbow-colored armor of a 14th-century Japanese shogun and a collection of Wild West revolvers that once belonged to gunmaker Samuel Colt are also exhibited here.

ASIAN ART

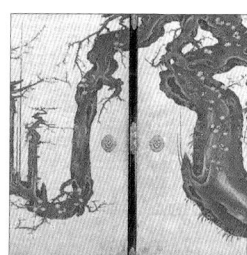

The Old Plum, a Japanese paper screen from the early Edo period (about 1650)

Many outstanding galleries contain masterpieces of Chinese, Japanese, Korean, Indian, and Southeast Asian art, dating from the second millennium BC to the 20th century. A full-scale Ming-style Chinese scholar's garden was built by craftspeople from Souzhou as part of the first cultural exchange between the United States and the People's Republic of China. The museum also has one of the finest collections of Sung and Yuan paintings in the world, Chinese Buddhist monumental sculptures, fine Chinese ceramics and jade, and an important display of the arts of ancient China.

The full range of Japanese arts is represented in a breathtaking suite of 11 galleries featuring chronological and thematic displays of Japanese lacquer, ceramics, painting, sculpture, textiles, and screens. Indian, Southeast Asian, and Korean galleries display superb sculptures and other arts from these regions.

COSTUME INSTITUTE

The 31,000-piece collection of costumes and accessories has expanded by over 23,000 items under an agreement with the Brooklyn Museum (see pp250–53). There is no permanent display due to the fragility of the objects, but there are two special exhibitions a year.

The collection spans five centuries from the 17th century to the present and is a definitive compendium of fashionable dress, from the elaborately embroidered dresses of the late 1600s to gowns from the Napoleonic era. The designs of Elsa Schiaparelli, Worth, and Balenciaga are also included, along with Ballets Russes costumes and even David Bowie's sequined jockstrap.

The *Art of Dress* audio tour, narrated by actress Sarah Jessica Parker, focuses on how artists have used clothing to express identity and power.

The Institute is sophisticated in its understanding of conservation techniques, with a state-of-the-art laboratory.

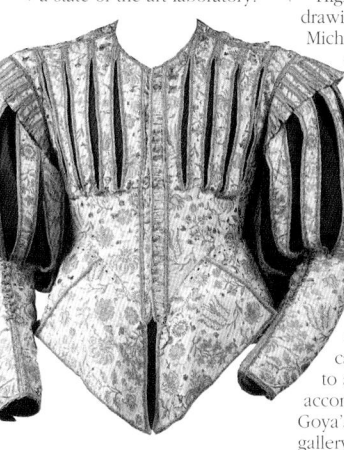

A 17th-century European silk-and-satin doublet

DRAWINGS, PRINTS, AND PHOTOGRAPHS

This eclectic gallery regularly displays selections from the museum's incredible holdings of drawings, prints, etchings, and photographs. The

Michelangelo's studies of a Libyan Sibyl for the ceiling of the Sistine Chapel (1508)

drawings collection is especially rich in Italian and French art from the 15th to the 19th century. Specific exhibits of the drawings in this collection are shown on a rotating basis because of the light-sensitive nature of works on paper.

Highlights among the 11,000 drawings include works by Michelangelo, Leonardo da Vinci, Raphael, Ingres, Goya, Rubens, Rembrandt, Tiepolo, and Seurat.

The encyclopedic print collection of nearly 1.5 million images and over 14,000 illustrated books includes major works by virtually every master printmaker, from an early German woodcut called *Virgin and Child* to some of Dürer's most accomplished works and Goya's *The Giant*. Influential gallery-owner Alfred Stieglitz's donation of his own extensive collection of photographs brought here such gems as Edward Steichen's *The Flatiron*. It formed the core of a photography collection that is now also particularly strong in Modernist works dating from between the world wars.

Ephemera such as posters and advertisements form another part of this collection.

EGYPTIAN ART

One of the museum's best-loved areas is the ancient Egyptian wing, which displays every one of its thousands of holdings – from the prehistoric period to the 8th century AD. Objects range from the fragmented jasper lips of a 15th-century BC queen to the massive Temple of Dendur. Other amazing archaeological finds, most of them originating from museum-sponsored expeditions undertaken early in the 20th century, include sculptures of the notorious Queen Hatshepsut, who seized the Theban throne in the 16th century BC; 100 carved reliefs of Amenhotep IV's reign; and tomb figures like the blue faïence hippo that has become the museum's mascot.

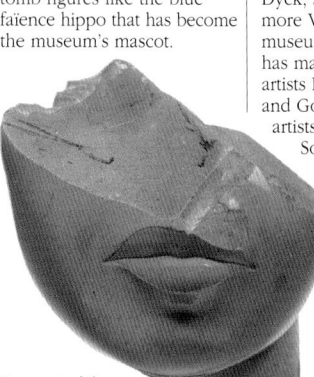

Fragment of the head of a pharoah's queen

EUROPEAN PAINTING, SCULPTURE, AND DECORATIVE ARTS

The heart of the museum is its awe-inspiring collection of over 3,000 European paintings. The Italian works include

Young Woman with a Water Jug (1660) by Johannes Vermeer

Botticelli's *Last Communion of Saint Jerome* and Bronzino's *Portrait of a Young Man*. The Dutch and Flemish canvases are among the world's finest, with Brueghel's *The Harvesters*, several works by Rubens, Van Dyck, and Rembrandt, and more Vermeers than any other museum. The collection also has masterpieces by Spanish artists El Greco, Velázquez, and Goya, and by French artists Poussin and Watteau. Some of the finest Impressionist and Post-Impressionist canvases reside here: 34 Monets, including *Terrace at Sainte-Adresse;* 18 Cézannes; and several Van Goghs, including *Cypresses.* In the Kravis wing and adjacent galleries are works from the 60,000-object collection of European sculpture and decorative arts, such as Tullio Lombardo's marble statue of Adam; a bronze statuette of a rearing horse, after a model by Leonardo; and dozens of pieces by Degas and Rodin. Period settings include the patio from a 16th-century

Spanish castle and a series of ornate 18th-century French domestic interiors known as the Wrightsman Rooms. The Petrie European Sculpture Court features French and Italian sculpture in a beautiful garden setting reminiscent of Versailles in France.

GREEK AND ROMAN ART

A Roman sarcophagus from Tarsus, donated in 1870, was the first work of art in the Met's collections. It can still be seen in the museum's Greek and Roman galleries, along with breathtaking wall panels from a villa that was buried under the lava of Vesuvius in AD 79, Etruscan mirrors, Roman portrait busts, exquisite objects in glass and silver, and hundreds of Greek vases. A monumental 7th-century BC statue of a youth shows the movement toward naturalism in sculpture, and the Hellenistic *Old Market Woman* demonstrates how the Greeks had mastered realism by the 2nd century BC.

An amphora by Exekias, showing a wedding (6th century BC)

LEHMAN COLLECTION

What had been one of the the finest private art collections in the world, that of investment banker Robert Lehman, came to the museum in 1969. The Lehman Wing is a dramatic glass pyramid housing an extraordinarily varied collection rich in Old Masters and 19th-century French paintings, drawings, bronzes,

EGYPTIAN TOMB MODELS

In 1920, a Met researcher's light illuminated a room, which had been closed for 2,000 years, in the tomb of the nobleman Meketre. Within were 24 tiny, perfect replicas of his daily life: his house and garden, fleet of ships and herd of cattle. Meketre is there, too, on his boat, inhaling a lotus's scent and enjoying the music of his singer and harpist. The museum has 13 of these delightful replicas.

A panel from the stained-glass *Death of the Virgin* window, from the 12th-century cathedral of Saint Pierre in Troyes, France

Renaissance majolica, Venetian glass, furniture, and enamels. Among the canvases are works by north-European masters; Dutch and Spanish paintings, French masterworks, Post-Impressionists and Fauves.

MEDIEVAL ART

The Metropolitan's medieval collection includes works dating from the 4th to the 16th century, roughly from the fall of Rome to the beginning of the Renaissance. The collection is split between the main museum and its uptown branch, the Cloisters *(see pp236–9)*. In the main building are a chalice once thought to be the Holy Grail, six silver Byzantine plates showing scenes from the life of David, a 1301 pulpit by Giovanni Pisano in the shape of an eagle, and several monumental sculptures of the Virgin and Child. Other exhibits include Migration jewelry, liturgical vessels, stained glass, ivories, and 14th- and 15th-century tapestries.

MUSICAL INSTRUMENTS

The world's oldest piano, Andrés Segovia's guitars and a sitar shaped like a peacock are some of the features of a broad and sometimes quirky collection of musical instruments that spans six continents and dates from prehistory to the present. The instruments illustrate the history of music and performance, and most of them are conserved to remain in playable condition.

Worth particular mention are instruments from the European courts of the Middle Ages and the Renaissance; rare violins; harpsichords; instruments inlaid with precious materials; and a fully equipped traditional violin-maker's work-shop; there are also African drums, Asian *pi-pas*, or lutes; and Native American flutes. Visitors can use audio equipment to hear many of the instruments playing the music of their day.

Stradivari violin from Cremona, Italy (1691)

MODERN ART

Since its foundation in 1870, the museum has been acquiring contemporary art, but it was not until 1987 that a permanent home for 20th-century art was built – the Lila Acheson Wallace Wing. Other museums in New York have larger collections of modern art, but this display space is considered among the finest. European and American works from 1900 onward are featured on three levels, starting with Europeans such as Picasso, Kandinsky, Braque, and Bonnard. The collection's greatest strength lies in its collection of modern American art, with works by New York school "The Eight," including John Sloan; such Modernists as Charles Demuth and Georgia O'Keeffe; American Regionalist Grant Wood; Abstract Expressionists Willem de Kooning; and such Color Field painters as Clyfford Still.

Grant Wood's view of *The Midnight Ride of Paul Revere* (1931)

Special areas of the wing house Art Nouveau and Art Deco furniture and metalwork; a large collection of works on paper by Paul Klee; and the Sculpture Gallery, with its large-scale sculptures and canvases.

Gems of the collection include Picasso's portrait of Gertrude Stein, Matisse's *Nasturtiums* and *"Dance, 1"* Demuth's *I Saw the Figure 5 in Gold*, Jackson Pollock's *Autumn Rhythm*, and Andy Warhol's last self-portrait.

Each year the Cantor Roof Garden at the top of the wing features a new installation of contemporary sculpture, especially dramatic against the backdrop of the New York skyline and Central Park.

Book cover (1916) by illustrator N. C. Wyeth

Society of Illustrators

128 E 63rd St. **Map** 13 A2.
Tel (212) 838-2560. M Lexington
Ave. ☐ 10am–8pm Tue, 10am–5pm
Wed–Fri, noon–4pm Sat. ● public
hols. ◙ & restricted. ▢ ▢
www.societyillustrators.org

Established in 1901, this
society was formed to
promote the illustrator's art.
Its notable roster included
Charles Dana Gibson, N. C.
Wyeth, and Howard Pyle. It
was at first concerned with
education and public service,
and still holds monthly
lectures. In 1981, the Museum
of American Illustration
opened in two galleries.
Changing thematic exhibitions
show the history of book and
magazine illustration, with an
annual exhibition of the year's
finest American illustrations.

Mount Vernon Hotel Museum

421 E 61st St. **Map** 13 C3. **Tel** (212)
838-6878. M Lexington Ave,
59th St. ☐ 11am–4pm Tue–Sun.
● Aug, public hols. ▢ ▢ ▢ ▢
www.mvhm.org

Built in 1799, the Mount
Vernon Hotel Museum and
Garden was once a country
day hotel for New Yorkers

who needed to
escape from the
crowded city, then
only at the south
end of the island.
The stone building
sits on land once
owned by Abigail
Adams Smith,
daughter of Presi-
dent John Adams.
   It was acquired
by the Colonial
Dames of America
in 1924 and turned
into a charming re-
creation of a Federal
home. Costumed
guides show visitors
through the rooms,
which exhibit
Chinese porcelain,
Sheraton chests, and
a Duncan Phyfe
sofa. One bedroom
even contains a baby's cradle
and children's toys. An 18th-
century-style garden has been
planted around the house.

Henderson Place

Map 18 D3. M 86th St.
🚌 M31, M79, M86.

**Queen Anne row houses
at Henderson Place**

Now surrounded by modern
apartment blocks, this enclave
of 24 red-brick Queen Anne
row houses was built in 1882.
The row houses were
commissioned by John C.
Henderson, a hat-maker, as
a self-contained community.
The elegant Lamb & Rich
design has gray slate roof
gables, pediments, parapets,
chimneys and dormer
windows forming patterns,
and a turret marking the
corner of each block.

Carl Schurz Park promenade

Carl Schurz Park

Map 18 D3. M 86th St.
🚌 M31, M79, M86.

Laid out in 1891, this park
along the East River has a wide
promenade over the East River
Drive. It offers fine vistas of
the river and the turbulent
waters of Hell Gate, where
the river meets Long Island
Sound. It is named after Carl
Schurz, a native who became
Secretary of the Interior
(1869–75). The first part of the
promenade is the John Finlay
Walk, named for an editor of
the *New York Times* known for
his hiking prowess. One of
the city's most pleasant green
escapes, the park's grassy
areas are filled with basking
New Yorkers on sunny days.

Gracie Mansion

East End Ave at 88th St. **Map** 18 D3.
Tel (212) 639-9675. M 86th St.
🚌 M31, M79, M86. ☐ 10am, 11am,
1pm, 2pm most Weds for prebooked
guided tours only. ▢ ▢ & ▢

This gracious, balconied
wooden 1799 country home
is the official mayor's
residence. Built by wealthy
merchant Archibald Gracie,
it is one of the best Federal
houses left in New York.
   Acquired by the city in
1887, it was the first home of
the Museum of the City of
New York. In 1942 it became
the official Mayoral Residence.
When Fiorello LaGuardia

Front view of Gracie Mansion

moved in after nine years in office, preferring it to a 75-room palace on Riverside Drive, he said that even the modest Gracie Mansion was too fancy for him. "The Little Flower" (from Fiorello) had fought corruption in the city.

Church of the Holy Trinity ⑰

316 E 88th St. **Map** 17 B3. *Tel* (212) 289-4100. Ⓜ 86th St. ◯ 9am–5pm Mon–Fri, 7:30am–2pm Sun. ✝ 8:45am Tue, Thu; 8am, 10:30am, 6pm Sun. 🅾
www.holytrinity-nyc.org

Arched doorway of the Church of the Holy Trinity

Delightfully placed in a serene garden setting, this church was constructed in 1889 of glowing golden brick and terracotta in French Renaissance style. It boasts one of New York's best bell towers, which holds a handsome wrought-iron clock with brass hands. The arched doorway is richly decorated with carved images of the saints and prophets.

The complex was donated by Serena Rhinelander in memory of her father and grandfather. The land was part of the Rhinelander farm, which the family had owned for 100 years.

Farther down at 350 E. 88th Street is the Rhinelander Children's Center, also a gift, and the headquarters of the Children's Aid Society.

St. Nicholas Russian Orthodox Cathedral ⑱

15 E 97th St. **Map** 16 F1. *Tel* (212) 876-2190. Ⓜ 96 St. ◯ by appt. ✝ throughout the week, including 10am & 6pm Wed & Sun. 🅾
www.russianchurchusa.org

Built in Muscovite Baroque style in 1902, this church has five onion domes crowned with crosses, and blue and yellow tiles on a red brick and white stone facade. Among the early worshipers were White Russians who had fled the first uprisings at home, mostly intellectuals and aristocrats who soon became a part of New York society. Later, there were more waves of refugees, dissidents, and defectors.

The cathedral now serves a scattered community, and the congregation is small. Mass is celebrated in Russian with great pomp and dignity.

The cathedral is filled with the scent of incense. The high central sanctuary has marble columns with blue and white trim above. Ornate wooden screens trimmed with gold enclose the altar. It is unique, an unexpected find on a side street in this staid part of Manhattan.

Facade and domes of St. Nicholas Russian Cathedral

Facade of the Museum of the City of New York

Museum of the City of New York ⑲

1220 5th Ave at 103rd St. **Map** 21 C5. *Tel* (212) 534-1672. Ⓜ 103rd St. ◯ 10am–5pm Tue–Sun. ● Jan 1, Thanksgiving, Dec 25. 🎥 🅾 ♿ 🎞
📷 🏪 **www**.mcny.org

Founded in 1923 and at first housed in Gracie Mansion, this museum is dedicated to New York's development from its earliest beginnings up to the present and on to the future.

Housed in a handsome Georgian Colonial building since 1932, the museum has expanded its public space, with special exhibitions throughout the year. These cover subjects such as fashion, architecture, theater, social and political history, and photography. In addition there is a collection of toys, including the famed Stettheimer Dollhouse, with original works of art in miniature, painted by such luminaries as Marcel Duchamp and Albert Gleizes.

A core exhibition of the museum is the film *Timescapes: A Multimedia Portrait of New York* (every 30 mins, 10:15am–4:45pm). It uses images from the museum's collection and historic maps to chart the growth of New York, from its early days as a tiny settlement to its current status as one of the largest cities in the world.

Whitney Museum of American Art ❼

The Whitney Museum is the foremost showcase for American art of the 20th and 21st centuries. It was founded in 1930 by sculptor Gertrude Vanderbilt Whitney after the Metropolitan Museum of Art turned down her collection of works by living artists such as Bellows and Hopper. In 1966 the museum moved to the present inverted-pyramid building designed by Marcel Breuer. The Whitney Biennial, held in even years, is the most significant survey of new trends in American art.

The cantilevered facade of the Whitney Museum

Green Coca-Cola Bottles
Andy Warhol's 1962 work is a commentary on mass production and monopoly.

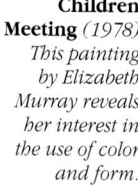

Children Meeting (1978)
This painting by Elizabeth Murray reveals her interest in the use of color and form.

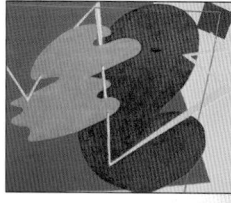

Little Big Painting
The 1965 work by Roy Lichtenstein is a comic critique of Abstract Expressionist painting.

Early Sunday Morning (1930)
Edward Hopper's paintings often convey the emptiness of American city life.

MUSEUM GUIDE

The second and fifth floors showcase exhibitions from the permanent collection, which may include works by the likes of Calder, O'Keeffe, and Hopper. Changing exhibitions occupy the third and fourth floors.

Dempsey and Firpo
In 1924, George Bellows depicted one of the most famous prizefights of the century.

Three Flags *(1958)*
Jasper Johns's use of familiar objects in an abstract form was influential in the development of Pop Art.

Painting Number 5
The early modernist artist Marsden Hartley painted this oil on canvas between 1914 and 1915.

Circus *(1926–31)*
Alexander Calder's fanciful creation is usually on display.

Tango *(1919)*
This is considered Polish-born Elie Nadelman's greatest work of wood sculpture.

Gertrude Vanderbilt Whitney *(1916)*
Robert Henri's oil shows the Whitney Museum's founder.

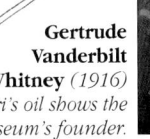

Frick Collection ❽

The art collection of steel magnate Henry Clay Frick (1849–1919) is exhibited in a residential setting amid the furnishings of his opulent mansion, which provides a rare glimpse of how the extremely wealthy lived in New York's gilded age. Henry Frick intended the collection to be a memorial to himself, and on his death he bequeathed the entire house to the nation. The collection includes important Old Master paintings, major works of sculpture, French furniture, rare Limoges enamels, and beautiful Oriental rugs.

★ Lady Meux (1881)
Before marrying a brewery baron, the coquettish young Lady Meux was an actress. This was Whistler's second of three portraits of her.

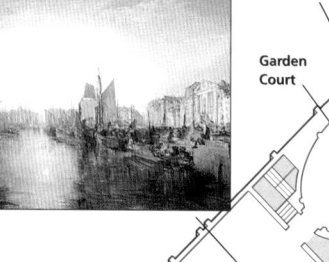

The Harbor of Dieppe *(1826)*
J.M.W. Turner was criticized by some skeptical contemporaries for depicting this northern European port suffused with light.

Garden Court

Library

West Gallery

The Polish Rider
The identity of the rider in this equestrian portrait, painted by Rembrandt in 1655, is unknown. The somber, rocky landscape creates an eerie atmosphere of unknown danger.

STAR PAINTINGS

- ★ Lady Meux by James McNeill Whistler

- ★ Officer and Laughing Girl by Johannes Vermeer

- ★ Mall in St. James's Park by Thomas Gainsborough

- ★ Sir Thomas More by Hans Holbein

★ Sir Thomas More *(1527)*
Holbein's portrait of Henry VIII's Lord Chancellor was painted eight years before More's execution for treason.

Living Hall

GALLERY GUIDE

Of special interest are the West Gallery, with oils by Vermeer, Hals, and Rembrandt; the East Gallery, featuring Van Dyck and Whistler; the Oval Room, featuring Gainsborough; the Library and Dining Room, with English works; and the Living Hall, with works by Titian and Holbein.

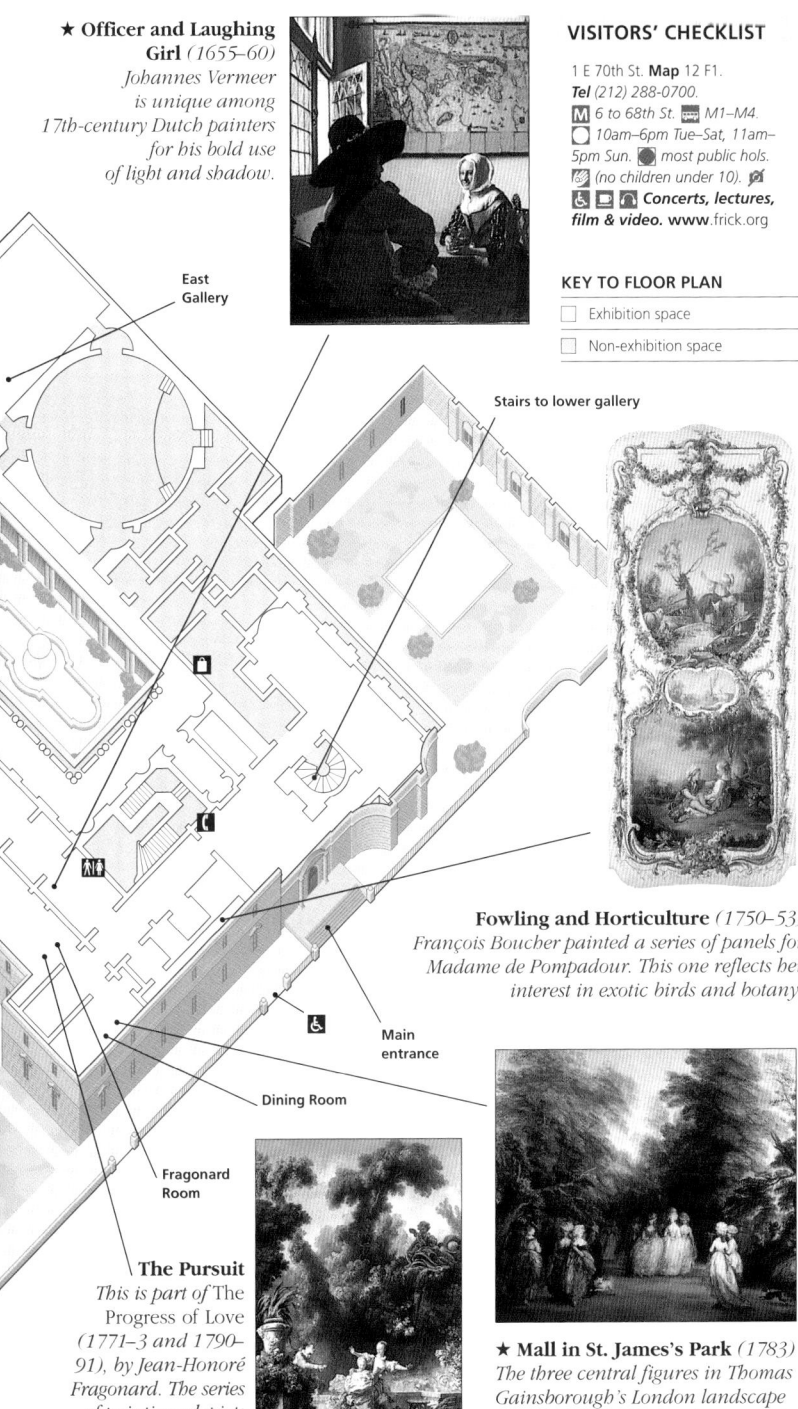

★ Officer and Laughing Girl *(1655–60)*
Johannes Vermeer is unique among 17th-century Dutch painters for his bold use of light and shadow.

East Gallery

VISITORS' CHECKLIST

1 E 70th St. **Map** 12 F1.
Tel (212) 288-0700.
M 6 to 68th St. M1–M4.
10am–6pm Tue–Sat, 11am–5pm Sun. most public hols.
(no children under 10).
Concerts, lectures, film & video. www.frick.org

KEY TO FLOOR PLAN

☐ Exhibition space

☐ Non-exhibition space

Stairs to lower gallery

Fowling and Horticulture *(1750–53)*
François Boucher painted a series of panels for Madame de Pompadour. This one reflects her interest in exotic birds and botany.

Main entrance

Dining Room

Fragonard Room

The Pursuit
This is part of The Progress of Love *(1771–3 and 1790–91), by Jean-Honoré Fragonard. The series of paintings depicts the events of an idealized courtship.*

★ Mall in St. James's Park *(1783)*
The three central figures in Thomas Gainsborough's London landscape may be the daughters of George III.

CENTRAL PARK

The city's "backyard" was created in 1858 by Frederick Law Olmsted and Calvert Vaux on an unpromising site of quarries, pig farms, swampland, and shacks. Five million cubic yards of stone, earth, and topsoil turned it into the lush 843-acre (340-ha) park of today. There are scenic hills, lakes and lush meadows, dotted throughout with outcrops of Manhattan bedrock, and planted with more than 500,000 trees and shrubs. Over the years the park has blossomed, with playgrounds, skating rinks, ball fields, and spaces for every other activity, from chess and croquet to concerts and events. Cars are not allowed on weekends, giving bicyclists, in-line skaters, and joggers the right-of-way.

Statues, Delacorte Theater *(see p206)*

SIGHTS AT A GLANCE

Historic Buildings
Belvedere Castle ❸
The Dairy ❶

Monuments and Statues
Bethesda Fountain and Terrace ❺
Bow Bridge ❹
Strawberry Fields ❷

Lakes and Gardens
Central Park Zoo ❼
Conservatory Garden ❽
Conservatory Water ❻

SEE ALSO

• **Street Finder**, maps 12, 16, 21

• **www**.centralparknyc.org

GETTING THERE

Subway lines B and C run the length of the park on the Upper West Side, with stops at 59th, 72nd, 81st, 86th, 96th, 103rd, and 110th Sts. The 59th St/Columbus Circle stop is served by the 1; the 2 and 3 stop at 72nd and 110th Sts; the N, Q, and R stop at 57th St and Fifth Ave at the southern end of the park. Bus routes M1–4 run along the eastern edge of the park, M10 along the west, and M5 along the south.

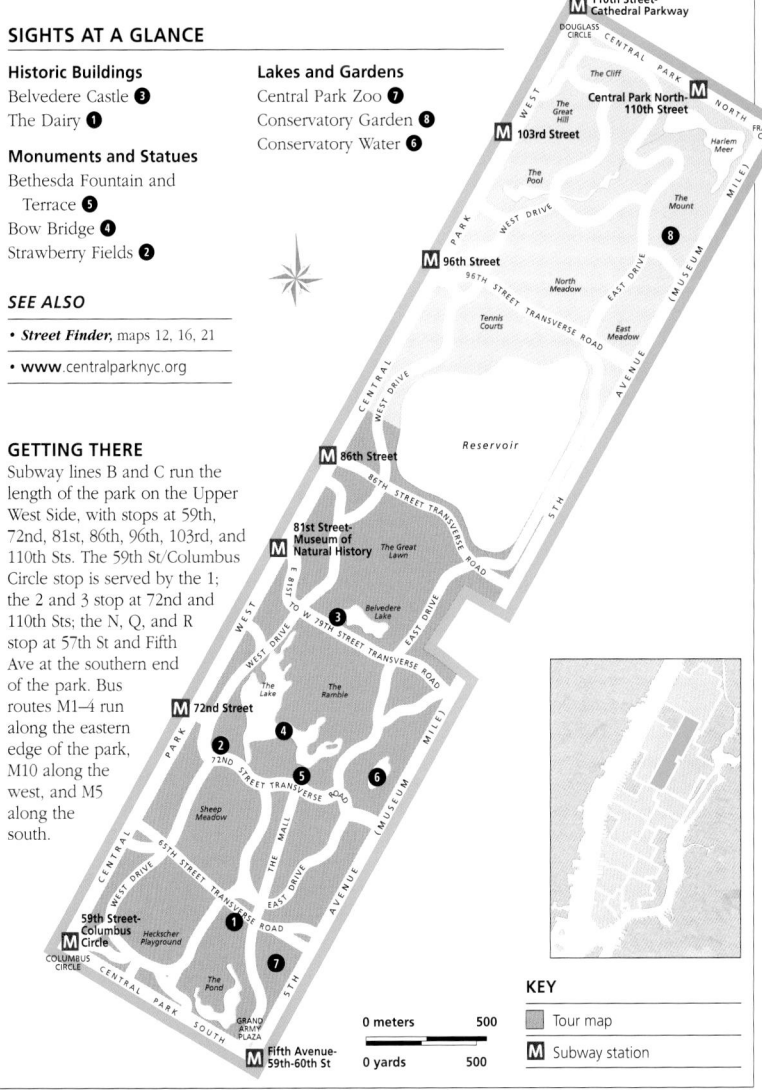

KEY

▢	Tour map
Ⓜ	Subway station

0 meters 500
0 yards 500

◁ **Bird's-eye view of the park**

A Tour of Central Park

On a short visit, a walking tour from 59th to 79th streets takes in some of Central Park's loveliest features, from the dense, wooded Ramble to the open formal spaces of Bethesda Terrace. Along the way are man-made lakes and more than 30 graceful bridges and arches that link around 68 miles (109 km) of footpaths, bridle paths, and roads in the park. In summer the park is often several degrees cooler than the city streets around it, and thus is a favorite retreat.

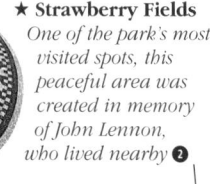

★ **Strawberry Fields**
One of the park's most visited spots, this peaceful area was created in memory of John Lennon, who lived nearby ❷

★ **Bethesda Fountain and Terrace**
The richly ornamented formal terrace overlooks the Lake and the wooded shores of the Ramble ❺

Wollman Rink was restored in the 1980s for future generations of skaters by tycoon Donald Trump.

Central Park Zoo
Three climate zones are home to more than 150 species of animals ❼

The Pond

Plaza Hotel
(see p181)

Frick Collection
(see pp202–3)

★ **The Dairy**
This Victorian Gothic building houses one of the park's visitor centers. Make it your first stop and pick up a calendar of park events ❶

Hans Christian Andersen's statue is a favorite Central Park landmark for children. It is on the west side of Conservatory Water and is a popular site for story-telling in the summer.

Bow Bridge
This cast-iron bridge links the Ramble with Cherry Hill by a graceful arch, 60 ft (18 m) above the Lake ❹

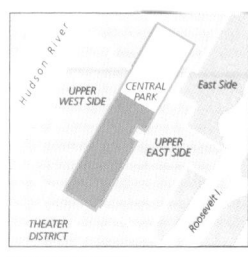

LOCATOR MAP
See Manhattan Map pp14–15

Alice in Wonderland is immortalized in bronze at the northern end of Conservatory Water, along with her friends the Cheshire Cat, the Mad Hatter and the Dormouse. Children love to slide down her toadstool seat.

STAR SIGHTS

★ The Dairy

★ Strawberry Fields

★ Belvedere Castle

★ Bethesda Fountain

★ Conservatory Water

Dakota Building *(see p218)*

San Remo Apartments *(see p214)*

American Museum of Natural History *(see pp216–17)*

GREAT LAWN

Metropolitan Museum *(see pp190–97)*

Obelisk

The Ramble is a wooded area of 37 acres (15 ha), crisscrossed by paths and streams. It is a paradise for birdwatchers. More than 275 species of birds have been spotted in the park, which is on the Atlantic migration flyway.

Reservoir

Guggenheim Museum *(see pp188–9)*

★ **Belvedere Castle**
From the terraces, there are unequaled views of the city and surrounding park. Within the stone walls is a visitor center ❸

★ **Conservatory Water**
From March to November, this is the scene of model boat races. Many of the tiny craft are stored in the boathouse that adjoins the Lake ❻

The Carousel, part of the park's Children's District

The Dairy ❶

Map 12 F2. **Tel** (212) 794-6564.
M Fifth Ave. ⏱ 10am–5pm daily.
Slide show. 📷
www.centralparknyc.org

Now used as Central Park's Visitor Center, this charming building of natural stone was planned as part of the "Children's District" of the park, which included a playground, the Carousel, a Children's Cottage, and stable. In 1873, there were cows grazing on the meadows in front of the Dairy, a ewe and her lambs feeding nearby, and chickens, guinea fowl, and peacocks roaming the lawn. City children could get fresh milk and other refreshments here. Over the years, the Dairy deteriorated, being used as a shed until restoration in 1979, done according to original photographs and drawings. The Dairy is the place to begin exploring the lush and leafy park; maps and details of events can be obtained here. The less energetic can rent chess and checkers sets for use on the pretty inlaid boards of the *kinderberg*, the charming little "children's hill" nearby.

Strawberry Fields ❷

Map 12 E1. **M** 72nd St.

The restoration of this teardrop-shaped section of the park was Yoko Ono's tribute in memory of her slain husband, John Lennon. They lived in the Dakota apartments overlooking this spot (see p218). Gifts for the garden came from all over the world. A mosaic set in the pathway, inscribed with the word *Imagine* (named for Lennon's famous song), was a gift from the city of Naples in Italy.

This broad expanse of the park's landscape was designed by Vaux and Olmsted. Now it is an international peace garden, with 161 species of plants (one from every country of the world), including jetbead, roses, witch hazel, birches – and strawberries.

Belvedere Castle ❸

Map 16 E4. **Tel** (212) 772-0210.
M 81st St. ⏱ 10am–5pm Tue–Sun.
⬤ Tue in winter. 📷 ♿ to main floor only.

This stone castle atop Vista Rock, complete with tower and turrets, offers one of the best views of the park and the city from its lookout on the rooftop. Inside is the Henry Luce Nature Observatory, with a delightful exhibit telling inquisitive young visitors about the surprising variety of wildlife to be found in the park.

The view to the north from the castle allows you to look down into

Belvedere Castle with its lookout over the park

the Delacorte Theater, home to the free productions of Shakespeare in the Park every summer, often featuring bigname stars (see p347). The theater was the gift of George T. Delacorte. Publisher and founder of Dell paperbacks, Delacorte was a delightful philanthropist who was responsible for many of the park's pleasures.

Bow Bridge ❹

Map 16 E5. **M** 72nd St.

This is one of the park's seven original cast-iron bridges and is considered one of the finest. It was designed by Vaux as a bow tying together the two large sections of the Lake. In the 19th century, when the Lake was used for ice skating, a red ball was hoisted from a bell tower on Vista Rock to signal that the ice was safe. The bridge offers expansive views of the park and the buildings bordering it on both the east and west sides.

A tranquil scene in Central Park, overlooked by exclusive apartments

An 1864 print of Bethesda Fountain and Terrace

Bethesda Fountain and Terrace ❺

Map 12 E1. Ⓜ️ *72nd St.*

Situated between the Lake and the Mall, this is the architectural heart of the park, a formal element in the naturalistic landscape. The fountain was dedicated in 1873. The statue, *Angel of the Waters*, marked the opening of the Croton Aqueduct system in 1842, bringing the city its first supply of pure water; its name refers to a biblical account of a healing angel at the pool of Bethesda in Jerusalem. The Spanish-style detailing, such as the sculptured double staircase, tiles, and friezes, is by Jacob Wrey Mould.

The terrace is one of the best spots to relax and take in some people-watching.

Conservatory Water ❻

Map 16 F5. Ⓜ️ *77th St.*

Better known as the Model Boat Pond, this stretch of water is home to model yacht races every weekend.

At the north end of the lake, a sculpture of Alice in Wonderland is a delight for children. It was commissioned by George T. Delacorte in honor of his wife. He himself is immortalized in caricature as the Mad Hatter. On the west bank, free story hours are held at the Hans Christian Andersen statue. The author is portrayed reading from his own story, "The Ugly Duckling," while its hero waddles at

his feet. Children like to climb on the statue and snuggle in the author's lap. Conservatory Water's literary links continue into adolescence: it is here that J. D. Salinger's Holden Caulfield comes to tell the ducks his troubles in *The Catcher in the Rye*.

Each spring, birdwatchers gather at the pond to see the city's most famous red-tailed hawk, Pale Male, nest on the roof of 927 Fifth Avenue.

Central Park Zoo ❼

Map 12 F2. **Tel** *(212) 439-6500.* Ⓜ️ *Fifth Ave between 63rd and 66th sts.* 🕙 *10am–5pm Mon–Fri, 10am–5:30pm Sat–Sun & hols; Nov–Mar: 10am–4:30pm daily. Last adm: 30 mins before closing.* 🎟️ 📷 ♿ 🖥️ 📱 www.centralparkzoo.com

This imaginative zoo has won plaudits for its creative and humane use of small space. More than 150 species of animals are represented in three climate zones, the Tropics, the Polar Circle, and the California coast. An equatorial rain forest is home to monkeys and free-flying birds, while penguins and polar bears populate an Arctic landscape that allows views both above and under water.

At the Tisch Children's Zoo children can get close to goats, sheep, alpacas, cows, and pot-bellied pigs. By its entrance is the much-loved Delacorte Clock, which plays nursery rhymes every half hour, as bronze musical animals (such as a goat playing pan pipes) circle around it. Toward Willowdell Arch is another favorite – the memorial to Balto, leader of a team of huskies that made a heroic journey across Alaska with serum for a diphtheria epidemic.

Statue of Balto, the heroic husky dog, Central Park Wildlife Center

Conservatory Garden ❽

Map 21 B5. Ⓜ️ *Central Pk N, 103rd St.* **Tel** *(212) 860-1382.* 🕙 *8am–dusk.* ♿

The Vanderbilt Gate on Fifth Avenue is the entry to a 6-acre (2.4-ha) park containing three formal gardens. Each one represents a different national landscape style. The Central Garden, with a large lawn, yew hedges, crabapple trees, and a wisteria pergola recreates an Italian style. The South Garden, spilling over with perennials, represents an English style, with a bronze statue in the reflecting pool of Mary and Dickon, from Frances Hodgson Burnett's *The Secret Garden*. Beyond is a slope with thousands of native wildflowers, spreading into the park beyond. The North Garden, in the French style, centers around the bronze *Fountain of the Three Dancing Maidens*. It puts on a brief but brilliant display of annuals each summer.

Polar bear in the Central Park Zoo

UPPER WEST SIDE

This district of New York became residential in the 1870s, when the Ninth Avenue elevated railroad *(see pp26–7)* made commuting to midtown possible. The Dakota, the city's first luxury apartment house, was built here in 1884, and the streets were graded and leveled. Buildings sprang up on Broadway and Central Park West, and cross streets, dating from the 1890s, still retain fine brownstone row houses. The area is bustling and diverse, with many cultural institutions, including the American Museum of Natural History, Lincoln Center, and Columbus Circle complex for Time Warner and CNN.

Indian mask, Museum of Natural History

SIGHTS AT A GLANCE

Historic Streets and Buildings

The Ansonia 16
Columbus Circle 7
The Dakota 9
The Dorilton 17
Hotel des Artistes 8
Pomander Walk 13
Riverside Drive and Park 14
Twin Towers of Central Park West 1
Metropolitan Opera House 4
New York State Theater 3

Museums and Galleries

American Museum of Natural History pp216–17 11
Children's Museum of Manhattan 15
New-York Historical Society 10
Rose Center for Earth and Space 12

Famous Theaters

Avery Fisher Hall 6
Lincoln Center for the Performing Arts 2
Lincoln Center Theater 5

GETTING THERE

By subway, take the A, B, C, D, or 1 to Columbus Circle; the 1, 2, or 3 along Broadway; or the B or C along Central Park West. Buses are the M5, M7, M10 (Central Park West), M11, and M104, and the M66, M72, M79, and M86 crosstown.

SEE ALSO

• ***Street Finder,*** maps 11, 15
• ***Where to Stay*** pp290–91
• ***Restaurants*** pp309–10

KEY

Street-by-Street map
[M] Subway station

◁ **The facade of 14 Riverside Drive**

Street by Street: Lincoln Center

Lincoln Center was conceived when both the Metropolitan Opera House and the New York Philharmonic required homes, and a large tract on Manhattan's west side was in dire need of revitalization. The notion of a single complex where different performing arts could exist side by side seems natural today, but in the 1950s it was considered both daring and risky. Today Lincoln Center has proved itself by drawing audiences of five million each year. Proximity to its halls prompts both performers and arts lovers to live nearby.

★ **Lincoln Center for the Performing Arts**
Dance, music, and theater come together in this fine contemporary complex. It is also a great place to sit around the fountain and people-watch ❷

Lincoln Center Theater
The Vivian Beaumont and the Mitzi E. Newhouse theaters are both housed in this building ❺

Composer Leonard Bernstein's famous musical *West Side Story,* which was based on the Romeo and Juliet theme, was set in the impoverished neighborhood that was razed to make room for Lincoln Center. Bernstein was later instrumental in setting up the large music complex.

The Guggenheim Bandshell in Damrosch Park is the site of free concerts.

The New York State Theater
This is the home of the New York City Ballet, as well as an opera company ❸

The College Board Building is an Art Deco delight that now houses condominiums and the administrative offices of the College Board, developers of the college entrance exam.

Metropolitan Opera House
Lincoln Center's focus is the Opera House. The café at the top of the lobby offers wonderful plaza views ❹

American Folk Art Museum
Quilting, pottery, and furniture are some of the arts displayed here.

Early American quilt

James Dean once lived in a one-room apartment on the top floor at 19 West 68th Street.

★ **Hotel des Artistes**
Artists Isadora Duncan, Noël Coward, and Norman Rockwell once lived here **8**

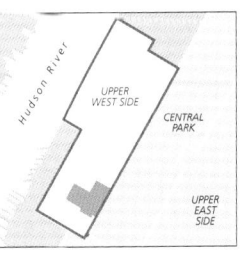

LOCATOR MAP
see Manhattan Map pp14–15

KEY

— — — Suggested route

0 meters   100
0 yards   100

To 72nd Street subway (4 blocks)

An ABC-TV sound stage for soap operas is housed in this castle-like building, formerly an armory.

55 Central Park West is the Art Deco apartment building that featured in the film *Ghostbusters*.

The Society for Ethical Culture was one of the city's first Art Nouveau buildings. It also houses a school.

To 59th Street subway (2 blocks)

Central Park West is home to many celebrities, who like the privacy of its exclusive apartments.

W 67TH STREET
65TH STREET
CENTRAL PARK WEST

STAR SIGHTS

★ Lincoln Center

★ Hotel des Artistes

Century Apartments
The Century's twin towers are visible from the park, making it a New York landmark **1**

The San Remo, a twin-towered apartment house designed by Emery Roth

Twin Towers of Central Park West ❶

Map 12 D1, 12 D2, 16 D3, 16 D5. Ⓜ *59th St-Columbus Circle, 72nd St, 81St, 86th St.* ☐ *to the public.*

A familiar landmark on the New York skyline, the four twin-towered apartment houses on Central Park West were built between 1929 and 1931, before the Great Depression halted all luxury construction. They are among the most sought-after residences in New York.

Admired today for their grace and architectural detail, they were designed in response to a city planning law allowing taller apartments if setbacks and towers were used.

Emery Roth designed the San Remo (145 CPW), whose tenants have included Dustin Hoffman, Paul Simon, and Diane Keaton. Turned down by the residents' committee, Madonna went to live close by at 1 West 64th Street. The towers of the Eldorado (300 CPW), also by Roth, were home to Groucho Marx, Marilyn Monroe, and Richard Dreyfuss. The Majestic (115 CPW) and the Century (25 CPW) are both sleek classics by Art Deco designer Irwin S. Chanin.

Lincoln Center for the Performing Arts ❷

Map 11 C2. **Tel** *(212) 546-2656.* Ⓜ *66th St.* ♿ ☎ *(212) 875-5350.* 🍴 ☐ *See* **Entertainment** *pp350–51.* **www**.lincolncenter.org

In May 1959, President Eisenhower traveled to New York to turn a shovelful of earth, Leonard Bernstein lifted his baton, the New York Philharmonic and the Juilliard

Central plaza at Lincoln Center

Choir broke into the Hallelujah Chorus – and the city's major cultural center was born. It soon covered 15 acres (6 ha) on the site of the slums that had been the setting for Bernstein's classic musical *West Side Story.* The plaza fountain is by Philip Johnson, and the sculpture, *Reclining Figure,* is by Henry Moore.

Jazz at the Lincoln Center has developed a state-of-the-art facility dedicated to a wide range of jazz performances. It forms part of a major complex at Columbus Circle *(see p215).*

New York State Theater ❸

Lincoln Center. **Map** 11 D2. **Tel** *(212) 870-5570.* Ⓜ *66th St.* ♿ ☎ 🍴 ☐ *See* **Entertainment** *pp346–7.* **www**.nycballet.com

The home base for the highly acclaimed New York City Ballet and the New York City Opera, a troupe devoted to presenting opera at popular prices, is a Philip Johnson design. It was inaugurated in 1964.

Gargantuan white marble sculptures by Elie Nadelman dominate the vast four-story foyer. The theater seats 2,800 people. Because of its rhinestone lights and chandeliers both inside and out, some have described the theater as "a little jewel box."

Metropolitan Opera House ❹

Lincoln Center. **Map** 11 D2. **Tel** *(212) 362-6000.* Ⓜ *66th St.* ♿ ☎ ☐ *See* **Entertainment** *pp350–51.* **www**.metopera.org; **www**.abt.org

Home to the Metropolitan Opera Company and the American Ballet Theater, "the Met" is the most spectacular of Lincoln Center's buildings. Five great arched windows offer views of the opulent foyer and two murals by Marc Chagall. (You can't see them in the mornings when they are protected from the sun.) Inside there are curved white marble stairs, red carpeting, and exquisite starburst crystal chandeliers that are raised to the ceiling

Concert at Guggenheim Bandshell, Damrosh Park, near the Met

just before each performance. All the greats have sung here, including Maria Callas, Jessye Norman, and Luciano Pavarotti. First nights are glittering, star-studded occasions.

The Guggenheim Bandshell, in Damrosch Park next to the Met, is a popular concert site. The high point of the season is the Lincoln Center Out-of-Doors Festival, which takes place in August and features global music, dance, and spoken-word performances.

Lincoln Center Theater ❺

Lincoln Center. **Map** 11 C2. **Tel** *(212) 362-7600 (Beaumont and Newhouse), (212) 870-1630 (Library). 800-432 7250 (tickets).* M *66th St.* See **Entertainment** *pp350–51.* **www**.lct.org

Two theaters make up this innovative complex, where eclectic and often experimental drama is presented.

The theaters are the 1,000-seat Vivian Beaumont and the more intimate 280-seat Mitzi E. Newhouse. Works by some of New York's best modern playwrights have featured at the Beaumont. Among these was Arthur Miller's *After the Fall*, the theater's inaugural performance in 1962.

The size of the Newhouse suits workshop-style plays, but it can still make the news with theatrical gems such as Robin Williams and Steve Martin in a production

of Samuel Beckett's *Waiting for Godot*. The complex also houses the New York Public Library for the Performing Arts, which has exhibits including audio cylinders of early Met performances and original scores and playbills.

Avery Fisher Hall ❻

Lincoln Center. **Map** 11 C2. **Tel** *(212) 875-5030.* M *66th St.* See **Entertainment** *pp350–51.* **www**.newyorkphilharmonic.org

Located at the northern end of the Lincoln Center Plaza, Avery Fisher Hall is home to America's oldest orchestra, the New York Philharmonic. It also provides a stage for some of the Lincoln Center's own performers, and the Mostly Mozart Festival.

When the venue opened in 1962 as the Philharmonic Hall, critics initially complained about the acoustics. Several structural modifications, however, have rendered the hall an acoustic gem, comparing favorably with other great classical concert halls around the world. For a small fee, the public can attend rehearsals on Thursday mornings in the 2,738-seat auditorium.

Columbus Circle ❼

Columbus Circle, New York. **Map** 12 D3. M *59th St.* **Concerts** *(212) 258-9800.* **www**.jazzatlincolncenter.org

Presiding over this urban plaza at the corner of Central Park is a marble statue of explorer Christopher Columbus, perched on top of a tall granite column in the center of a fountain and plantings. The statue is one of the few remaining original features in this circle – it has become one of the largest building projects in New York's history.

Multi-use skyscrapers have been erected, attracting national and

international businesses. Global media company Time Warner has its headquarters in an 80-story skyscraper. The 2.8 million sq ft (260,000 sq m) building provides a retail, entertainment, and restaurant facility. Facilities include shops such as Hugo Boss, Williams-Sonoma, Borders Books, and Whole Foods Market; dining at Per Se and Masa; and a Mandarin Oriental hotel.

The Time Warner Center is also home to Jazz at the Lincoln Center. The two venues here – The Frederic P. Rose Concert Hall and The Allen Room – together with a jazz club and education center, comprise the world's first performing arts facility dedicated to jazz.

Other notable buildings in Columbus Circle include Hearst House, designed by British architect Norman Foster, Trump International Hotel, the Maine Monument, and the eye-catching Museum of Arts and Design, formerly the American Craft Museum.

Hotel des Artistes ❽

1 W 67th St. **Map** 12 D2. **Tel** *(212) 877-3500 (café).* M *72nd St.*

Built in 1918 by George Mort Pollard, these two-story apartments were intended to be working artists' studios, but they have attracted a variety of interesting tenants, including Alexander Woollcott, Norman Rockwell, Isadora Duncan, Rudolph Valentino, and Noël Coward. The base of the building's facade is decorated with figures of artists.

Decorative figure on the Hotel des Artistes

American Museum of Natural History ⓫

This is one of the world's largest natural history museums. Since the original building opened in 1877, the complex has grown to cover four city blocks, and today holds more than 30 million specimens and artifacts. The most popular areas are the dinosaurs and the Milstein Hall of Ocean Life. The Rose Center for Earth and Space includes the Hayden Planetarium (see p218).

The facade on 77th Street

STAR EXHIBITS

★ Barosaurus

★ Blue Whale

★ Great Canoe

★ Star of India

★ Star of India
This 563-carat gem is the world's largest blue star sapphire. Found in Sri Lanka, it was given to the museum by J. P. Morgan in 1900.

GALLERY GUIDE
Enter at Central Park West onto the second floor to view the Barosaurus exhibit, African, Asian, Central and South American peoples and animals. First floor exhibits include ocean life, meteors, minerals and gems, and the Hall of Biodiversity. North American Indians, birds, and reptiles occupy the third floor. Dinosaurs, fossil fishes, and early mammals are on the fourth floor.

★ Blue Whale
The blue whale is the largest animal, living or extinct. Its weight can exceed 100 tons. This replica is based on a female captured off South America in 1925.

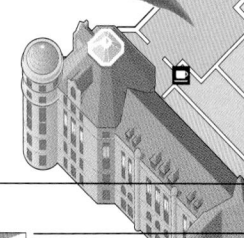

★ Great Canoe
This 63-ft (19.2-m) seafaring war canoe from the Pacific Northwest was carved from the trunk of a single cedar. It stands in the Grand Gallery.

Entrance on W. 77th St

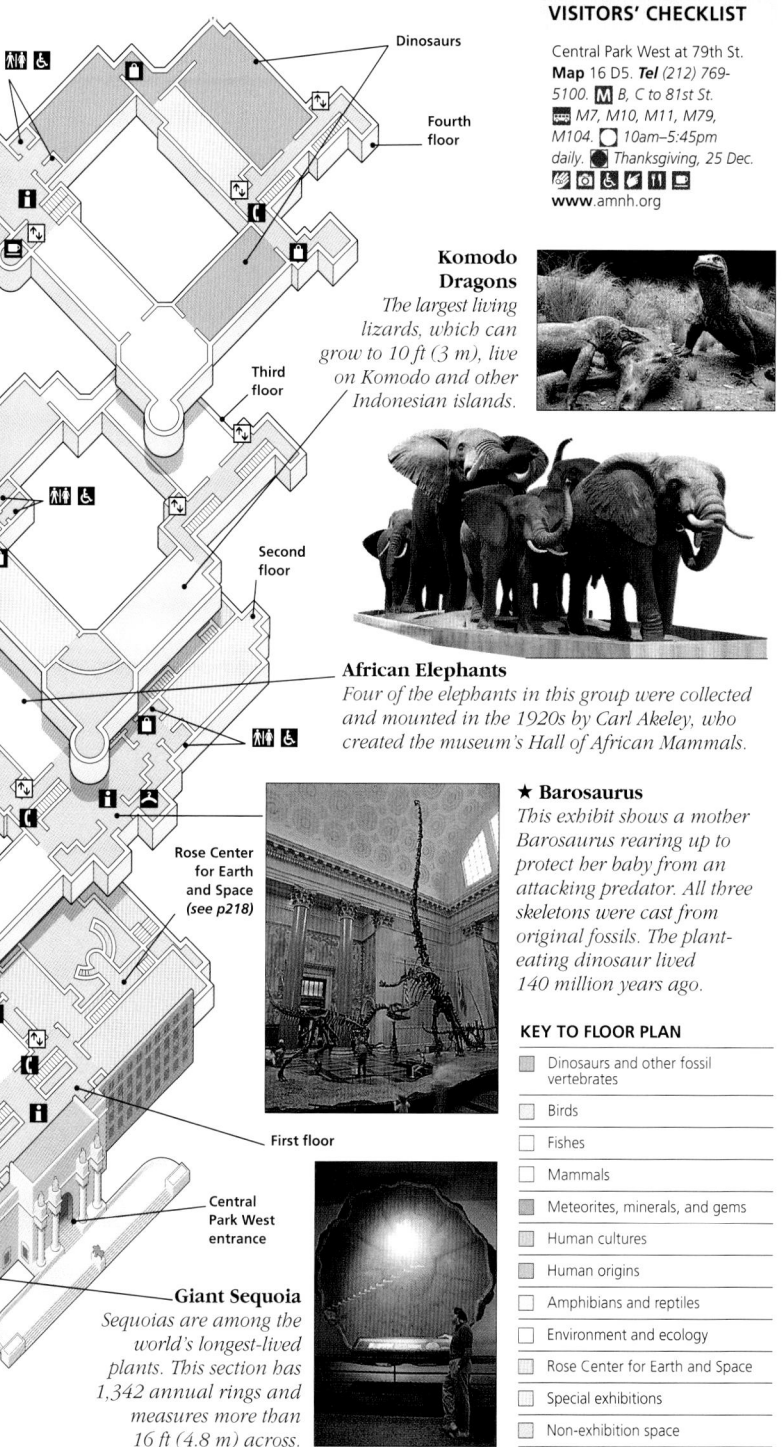

VISITORS' CHECKLIST

Central Park West at 79th St.
Map 16 D5. **Tel** (212) 769-
5100. **M** B, C to 81st St.
M7, M10, M11, M79,
M104. ☐ 10am–5:45pm
daily. ☐ Thanksgiving, 25 Dec.
www.amnh.org

Dinosaurs

Fourth floor

Third floor

Second floor

Rose Center for Earth and Space
(see p218)

First floor

Central Park West entrance

Komodo Dragons

The largest living lizards, which can grow to 10 ft (3 m), live on Komodo and other Indonesian islands.

African Elephants

Four of the elephants in this group were collected and mounted in the 1920s by Carl Akeley, who created the museum's Hall of African Mammals.

★ Barosaurus

This exhibit shows a mother Barosaurus rearing up to protect her baby from an attacking predator. All three skeletons were cast from original fossils. The plant-eating dinosaur lived 140 million years ago.

KEY TO FLOOR PLAN

	Dinosaurs and other fossil vertebrates
☐	Birds
☐	Fishes
☐	Mammals
	Meteorites, minerals, and gems
	Human cultures
	Human origins
☐	Amphibians and reptiles
☐	Environment and ecology
	Rose Center for Earth and Space
☐	Special exhibitions
☐	Non-exhibition space

Giant Sequoia

Sequoias are among the world's longest-lived plants. This section has 1,342 annual rings and measures more than 16 ft (4.8 m) across.

The Dakota ❾

1 W 72nd St. **Map** 12 D1.
Ⓜ *72nd St.* ⬤ *to the public.*

The name and style reflect the fact that this apartment building was truly "way out West" when Henry J. Hardenbergh, the architect responsible for the Plaza Hotel, designed it in 1880–84. It was New York's first luxury apartment house and was originally surrounded by squatters' shacks and wandering farm animals. Commissioned by Edward S. Clark, heir to the Singer sewing machine fortune, it is one of the city's most prestigious addresses.

The Dakota's 65 luxurious apartments have had many famous owners, including Judy Garland, Lauren Bacall, Leonard Bernstein, and Boris Karloff, whose ghost is said to haunt the place. It was the setting for the film *Rosemary's Baby,* and the site of the tragic murder of former Beatle John Lennon. His widow, Yoko Ono, still lives here.

Carved Indian head over the entrance to the Dakota

New-York Historical Society ❿

170 Central Park West. **Map** 16 D5.
Tel *(212) 873-3400.* Ⓜ *81st St.*
Galleries ⬤ *10am–6pm Tue–Sat (to 8pm Fri), 11am–5:45pm Sun.* 🖼
Library ⬤ *10am–5pm Tue–Sat (Tue–Fri in summer).* ⬤ *public hols.* 🚫
♿ 📷 💻 📷 **www**.nyhistory.org

Founded in 1804, this society houses a distinguished research library and the city's oldest

museum. Its collections include historical material relating to slavery and the Civil War, an outstanding collection of 18th-century newspapers, all 435 watercolors of Audubon's *Birds of America,* and the world's largest collection of Tiffany lamps and glasswork. There are also fine displays of American furniture and silver.

American Museum of Natural History ⓫

See pp216–17.

Rose Center for Earth and Space ⓬

Central Park West at 81st St.
Map 16 D4. **Tel** *(212) 769-5100.*
Ⓜ *81st St.* ⬤ *10am–5:45pm daily.*
IMAX show: every hour on the half-hour 10:30am–4:30pm; Space show: every half-hour 10:30am–4:30pm (from 11am Wed, to 5pm Sat & Sun).
www.amnh.org/rose

On the northern side of the American Museum of Natural History *(see pp216–17)* is the spectacular Rose Center for Earth and Space. Housed within an 87-ft (26-m) sphere, the center contains the technologically advanced Space Theater; the Cosmic Pathway, a 350-ft (107-m) spiral ramp with a timeline chronicling 13 billion years of evolution; and the Big Bang Theater, where the origins of the universe are explained.

The Hall of Planet Earth, centered around rock samples and using state-of-the-art computer and video displays explaining how the Earth works, explores our geologic history. Exhibits in the Hall of the Universe

The Rose Center for Earth and Space

present the discoveries of modern astrophysics. Four zones have hands-on interactive exhibits. Seen from the street at night, the Rose Center is breathtaking; the exhibits inside prove that, as Carl Sagan said, "We are starstuff."

Pomander Walk ⓭

261–7 W 94th St. **Map** 15 C2.
Ⓜ *96th St.*

Look through the gate for a delightful surprise – a double row of tiny town houses built in 1921 to look like the London mews setting of a popular play of the same name. It was much favored as a home by movie actors, including Rosalind Russell, Humphrey Bogart, and the Gish sisters.

Facade of a house on Pomander Walk

Riverside Drive and Park ⓮

Map 15 B1–B5, 20 D1–D5.
Ⓜ *79th St, 86th St, 96th St.*

Riverside Drive is one of the city's most attractive streets – broad, with shaded and lovely views of the Hudson River. It is lined with the opulent original town houses, as well as more modern apartment buildings. At 40–46, 74–77, 81–89, and 105–107 Riverside Drive are houses designed in the late 19th century by local architect Clarence F. True. The curved gables, bays and

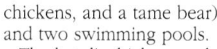

arched windows seem to suit the curves of the road and the flow of the river.

The bizarrely named Cliff Dwellers' Apartments at 243 (between 96th and 97th streets) is a 1914 building with a frieze showing early Arizona cliff dwellers, complete with masks, buffalo skulls, mountain lions, and rattlesnakes.

Riverside Park was designed by Frederick Law Olmsted in 1880. He also laid out Central Park *(see pp204–7)*.

Soldiers' and Sailors' monument in Riverside Park

Children's Museum of Manhattan ⓯

212 W 83rd St. **Map** 15 C4.
***Tel** (212) 721-1234.* Ⓜ *79th St, 81st St, 86th St.* ◯ *10am–5pm Tue–Sun.* ● *Jan 1, Thanksgiving, Dec 25.* 🖼 🅿 ♿ 🏠
www.cmom.org

This particularly imaginative participatory museum was founded in 1973 and is based on the premise that children learn best through play. The exhibit called "Eat, Sleep, Play" links food, the digestive system, and healthy living, while in "Block Party" children can build castles, towns, and bridges out of wooden blocks. Kids also delight in the exhibits on cartoon favorites Curious George and Dora the Explorer and her adventurous cousin Diego, where they learn about

Children's Museum entrance

travel and cultures around the world.

On weekends and holidays there are guest performers, from puppeteers to storytellers, in the 150-seat theater. There is also a gallery for free events, like "Pajama Day," as well as lively, theme-based tours of the museum.

The Ansonia ⓰

2109 Broadway. **Map** 15 C5.
Ⓜ *72nd St.* ● *to the public.*

This Beaux Arts gem was built in 1899 by William Earl Dodge Stokes, heir to the Phelps Dodge Company fortune, who brought French architect Paul E.M. Duboy to design a building to rival the Dakota. The hotel was converted to a condominium in 1992. The most prominent features are the round corner tower and the two-story mansard roof adorned with single and double dormers. The building had a roof garden (complete with Dodge's menagerie: ducks,

chickens, and a tame bear) and two swimming pools.

The hotel's thick, soundmuffling walls soon made it a favorite with the musical stars of yesteryear. Florenz Ziegfeld, Arturo Toscanini, Enrico Caruso, Igor Stravinsky, and Lily Pons were once regular guests there.

The Dorilton ⓱

171 W 71st St. **Map** 11 C1.
Ⓜ *72nd St.* ● *to the public.*

Opulent detail and an impressive high mansard roof adorn this apartment house. On the West 71st Street side of the building is a nine-story-high gateway. To the modern eye, the Dorilton is gloriously elaborate, but when it was first built in 1902 it provoked this reaction, reported by the *Architectural Record*: "The sight of it makes strong men

Balcony on the Dorilton, supported by groaning figures

swear and weak women shrink affrighted."

What would the critics have made of the Alexandria Condominium, at 135 West 70th Street, just a block away? Built in 1927 as the Pythian Temple, its current name stems from the lavish Egyptian-style motifs that adorned this former Masonic lodge. Many were stripped away when the building was converted to a condominium, but you can still see what the polychrome designs were like. There are lotus leaves, hieroglyphics, ornately carved columns, mythical beasts, and, in majestic splendor on the roof, two seated pharaohs.

Distinctive rounded turret of the Ansonia Hotel

MORNINGSIDE HEIGHTS AND HARLEM

Morningside Heights, near the Hudson River, is home to Columbia University and two of the city's finest churches. Farther east is Hamilton Heights, situated on the border of Harlem, America's most famous black community. One way to see the district's highlights, which are spread over a large area, is by taking one of the tours offered, including a Sunday morning tour *(see p387)*. Many tours start in Hamilton Heights, move east to the St. Nicholas Historic District, stop to enjoy the gospel choir at the Abyssinian Baptist Church, and end with a Southern-style brunch at Sylvia's, Harlem's best-known restaurant.

St. Francis of Assisi, Museo del Barrio

Louis Armstrong in a stained-glass window at the Cotton Club

SIGHTS AT A GLANCE

Historic Streets and Buildings
City College of the City
  University of New York **7**
Columbia University **1**
Grant's Tomb **6**
Hamilton Grange National
  Memorial **8**
Hamilton Heights
  Historic District **9**
Low Library **3**
Mount Morris
  Historic District **17**
St. Nicholas
  Historic District **10**
St. Paul's Chapel **2**

Museums and Galleries
Museo del Barrio **19**
Schomburg Center for Research
  into Black Culture **12**
Studio Museum in Harlem **16**

Famous Theaters
Apollo Theater **15**
Harlem YMCA **13**

Churches
Abyssinian Baptist Church **11**
*Cathedral of St. John
  the Divine pp226–7* **4**
Riverside Church **5**

Parks and Squares
Marcus Garvey Park **18**

Landmark Restaurants
Sylvia's **14**

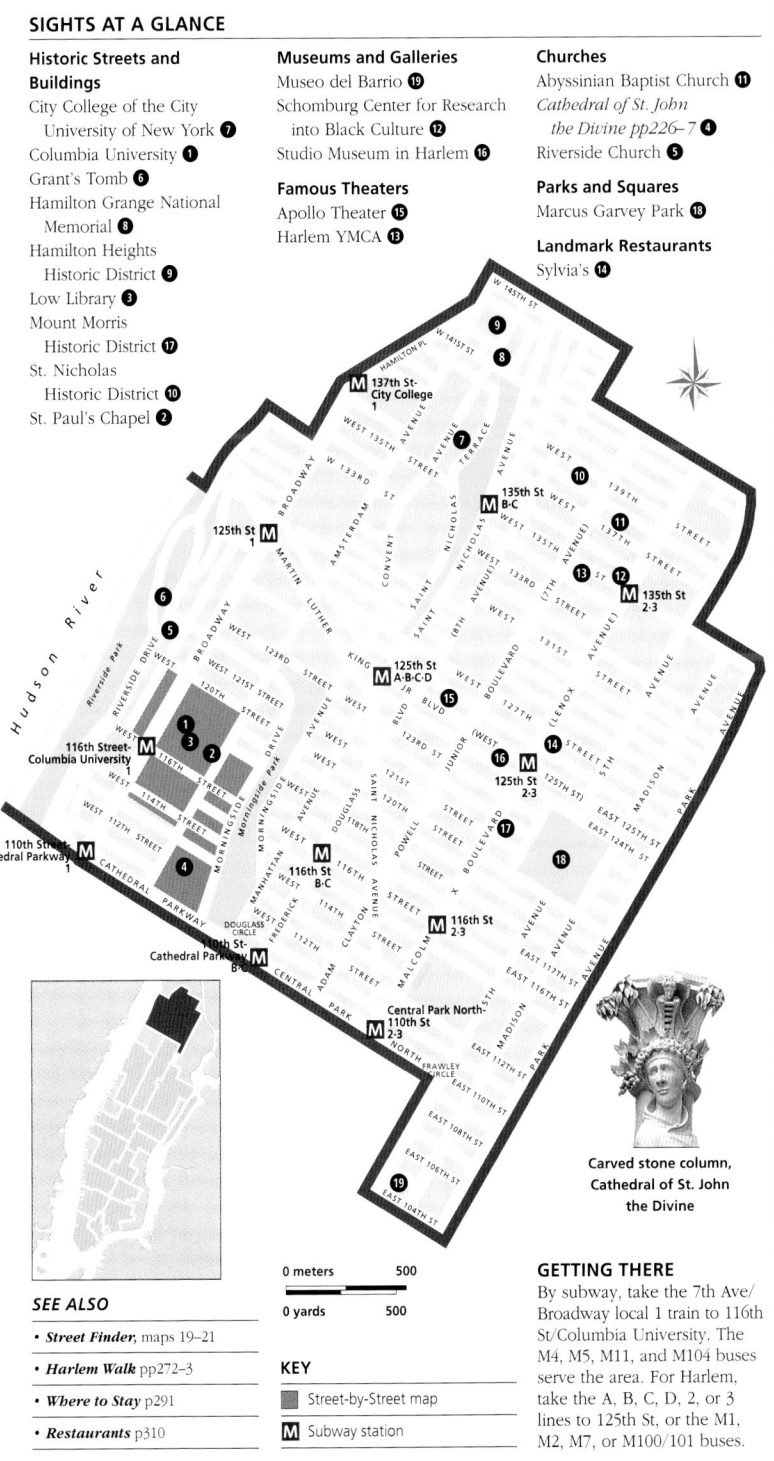

Carved stone column,
**Cathedral of St. John
the Divine**

0 meters   500
0 yards   500

KEY
  Street-by-Street map
M Subway station

GETTING THERE
By subway, take the 7th Ave/
Broadway local 1 train to 116th
St/Columbia University. The
M4, M5, M11, and M104 buses
serve the area. For Harlem,
take the A, B, C, D, 2, or 3
lines to 125th St, or the M1,
M2, M7, or M100/101 buses.

Street by Street: Columbia University

A great university is as much spirit as buildings. After admiring the architecture, linger awhile on Columbia's central quadrangle in front of the Low Library, where you will see the jeans-clad future leaders of America meeting and mingling between classes. Across from the campus on both Broadway and Amsterdam Avenue are the coffee-houses and cafés where students engage in lengthy philosophical arguments, debate the topics of the day or simply unwind.

Alma Mater was sculpted by Daniel Chester French in 1903 and survived a bomb blast in the 1968 student demonstrations.

ALMA MATER

116th St/Columbia University subway (line 1) — Ⓜ

The School of Journalism is one of Columbia's many McKim, Mead & White buildings. Founded in 1912 by publisher Joseph Pulitzer, it is the home of the Pulitzer Prize awarded for the best in letters and music.

Butler Library is Columbia's main library.

Low Library
With its imposing façade and high dome, the library dominates the main quadrangle. McKim, Mead & White designed it in 1895–97 ❸

★ Central Quadrangle
Columbia's first buildings were designed by McKim, Mead & White and built around a central quadrangle. This view looks across the quad toward Butler Library ❶

St. Paul's Chapel
*Designed by the architects Howells &
Stokes in 1907, this church is known
for its fine woodwork and magnificent vaulted interior. It is full of
light and has fine acoustics* ❷

The Sherman
Fairchild
Center was
built in 1977
to house the
university's
life sciences
departments.

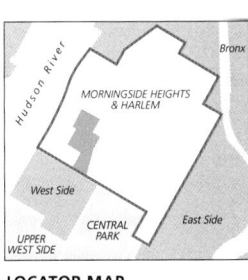

LOCATOR MAP
See Manhattan Map pp14–15

KEY

– – – Suggested route

| 0 meters | 100 |
| 0 yards | 100 |

Student demonstrations put Columbia
University in the news in 1968.
The demonstrations were sparked
by the university's plan to build a
gymnasium in nearby Morningside
Park. The protests forced the
university to build elsewhere.

The Église de Notre Dame was built for a
French-speaking congregation. Behind
the altar is a replica of the grotto at
Lourdes, France, the gift of a woman
who believed her son was healed there.

**★ Cathedral of St.
John the Divine**
*If this Neo-Gothic
cathedral is ever
finished, it will be
the largest in the
world. Although one third of the
structure has not yet been built, it
can hold 10,000 parishioners* ❹

**Carved
stonework**
decorates the
facade of the
Cathedral.

STAR SIGHTS

★ Cathedral of
  St. John the Divine

★ Central
  Quadrangle

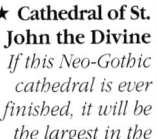

Alma Mater statue at the Low Library, Columbia University

Columbia University ❶

Main entrance at W 116th St and Broadway. **Map** 20 E3. **Tel** *(212) 854-1754.* Ⓜ *116th St-Columbia University.* **Visitors' Center**. ◯ *9am–5pm Mon–Fri.* 🗓 *1pm Mon–Fri.* **www**.columbia.edu

This is the third location of one of America's oldest universities. Founded in 1754 as King's College, it was first situated close to where the World Trade Center stood.

In 1814, when a move uptown was proposed, the university approached the authorities for funding but was instead given a plot of land valued at $75,000, on which to build a new home. The university never built on the land itself, but leased it out and spent the years from 1857 to 1897 in buildings nearby. It finally sold the plot in 1985 to the leaseholders, Rockefeller Center Inc., for $400 million.

The present campus was begun in 1897 on the site of the Bloomingdale Insane

Asylum. Charles McKim, the architect, placed the university on a terrace, serenely above street level. Its spacious lawns and plazas still create a sense of contrast in the busy city.

Columbia is noted for its law, medicine, and journalism schools. Its distinguished faculty and alumni, past and present, include over 50 Nobel laureates. Famous alumni include Isaac Asimov, J.D. Salinger, James Cagney, and Joan Rivers. Across the street is the affiliated Barnard College, a highly selective liberal arts college for women.

St. Paul's Chapel ❷

Columbia University. **Map** 20 E3. **Tel** *(212) 854-1487, for concert info.* Ⓜ *116th St-Columbia Univ.* ◯ *10am–11pm Mon–Sat (term time), 10am–4pm (breaks).* 🗓 *Sun.* 📷 ♿

Interior brick vaulting of St. Paul's Chapel dome

Columbia's most outstanding building, built in 1904, is a mix of Italian Renaissance, Byzantine, and Gothic. The interior Guastavino vaulting is of intricate patterns of aged red brick; the whole chapel is bathed in light from above.

The free organ concerts are an exceptionally fine way to appreciate the beauty and acoustics of this church. The Aeolian-Skinner pipe organ is renowned for its fine tone.

Facade of St. Paul's Chapel

Low Library ❸

Columbia University. **Map** 20 E3. Ⓜ *116th St-Columbia University.*

A Classical, columned building atop three flights of stone stairs, the library was donated by Seth Low, a former mayor and college president. The statue in front of it, *Alma Mater* by Daniel Chester French, became familiar as the backdrop to the many 1968 anti-Vietnam War student demonstrations. The building is now used as offices, and its rotunda for a variety of academic and ceremonial purposes. The books were moved in 1932 to the Butler Library, across the quadrangle. The university's library collections total more than six million volumes.

Cathedral of St. John the Divine ❹

See pp226–7.

Riverside Church ❺

490 Riverside Dr at 122nd St. **Map** 20 D2. **Tel** *(212) 870-6700.* Ⓜ *116th St-Columbia Univ.* ◯ *7am–10pm daily.* 🗓 *10:45am Sun.* 📷 *with prior permission.* ♿ 📷 ***Carillon bell concerts***; *(212) 870-6784; 10:30am, 12:30pm & 3pm Sun.* ***Theater***; *(212) 864-2929.* 🖥 **www**.theriversidechurchny.org

A 21-story steel frame with a Gothic exterior, the church design was inspired by the cathedral at Chartres. It was lavishly funded by John D. Rockefeller, Jr., in 1930. The Laura Spelman Rockefeller Memorial Carillon (in honor

Columbia University's main courtyard and the Low Library

of Rockefeller's mother) is the largest in the world, with 74 bells. The 20-ton Bourdon, or hour bell, is the largest and heaviest tuned carillon bell ever cast. The organ, with its 22,000 pipes, is among the largest in the world.

At the rear of the second gallery is a figure by Jacob Epstein, *Christ in Majesty*, cast in plaster and covered in gold leaf. Another Epstein statue, *Madonna and Child*, stands in the court next to the cloister. The panels of the chancel screen honor eight men and women whose lives have exemplified the teachings of Christ. They range from Socrates and Michelangelo to Florence Nightingale and Booker T. Washington.

For quiet reflection, enter the small, secluded Christ Chapel, patterned after an 11th-century Romanesque church in France. For views, take the elevator to the 20th floor and then walk the 140 steps to the top of the 392-ft (120-m) bell tower for a fine panorama of Upper Manhattan from the observation deck.

Mosaic mural in Grant's Tomb showing Grant (right) and Robert E. Lee

Grant's Tomb ❻

W 122nd St and Riverside Dr. **Map** 20 D2. **Tel** *(212) 666-1640.* **M** *116th St-Columbia Univ.* M5. ◯ *9am–5pm daily.* ● *in bad weather (call ahead), Jan 1, Thanksgiving, Dec 25.* ⊙ ☑ 🛇 www.nps.gov/gegr

This grandiose monument honors America's 18th president, Ulysses S. Grant, the commanding general of the Union forces in the Civil War.

The mausoleum contains the coffins of General Grant and his wife, in accordance with the president's last wish that they be buried together. After Grant's death in 1885, more than 90,000 Americans contributed $600,000 to build the sepulcher, which was inspired by Mausoleus's tomb at Halicarnassus, one of the Seven Wonders of the Ancient World.

General Grant on a Civil War campaign

The tomb was dedicated on what would have been Grant's 75th birthday, April 27, 1897. The parade of 50,000 people, along with a flotilla of 10 American and 5 European warships, took more than seven hours to pass in review.

The interior was inspired by Napoleon's tomb at Les Invalides in Paris. Each sarcophagus weighs 8.5 tons. Two exhibit rooms feature displays on Grant's personal life and his presidential and military career. Surrounding the north and east sides of the building are 17 sinuously curved mosaic benches that seem totally out of keeping with the formal architecture of the tomb. They were designed in the early 1970s by the Chilean-born Brooklyn artist Pedro Silva and were built by 1,200 local volunteers, who worked under his supervision. The benches were inspired by the work of Spanish architect Antonio Gaudi in Barcelona. The mosaics depict subjects ranging from the Inuit to New York taxis to Donald Duck.

A short walk north of Grant's Tomb is another monument. An unadorned urn on a pedestal marks the resting place of a young child who fell from the riverbank and drowned. His grieving father placed a marker that simply reads: "Erected to the memory of an amiable child, St. Clair Pollock, died 15 July 1797 in his fifth year of his age."

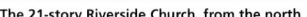

The 21-story Riverside Church, from the north

Cathedral of St. John the Divine ❹

Cram's Gothic West Front

Started in 1892 and still only two-thirds finished, this will be the largest cathedral in the world. The interior is over 600 ft (180 m) long and 146 ft (45 m) wide. It was originally designed in Romanesque style by Heins and LaFarge; Ralph Adams Cram took over the project in 1911, devising a Gothic nave and west front. Medieval construction methods, such as stone-on-stone supporting buttresses, continue to be used to complete the cathedral, which also serves as a venue for theater, music, and avant-garde art.

Choir
Each of the choir's columns is 55 ft (17 m) tall and made of polished gray granite.

Nave
Rising to a height of over 100 ft (30 m), the piers of the nave are topped by graceful stone arches.

Rose Window ★
Completed in 1933, the stylized motif of the Great Rose is symbolic of the many facets of the Christian Church.

★ West Front Entrance
The portals of the cathedral's west front are adorned with many fine stone carvings. Some are recreations of medieval religious sculpture, but others have modern themes. This apocalyptic vision of New York's skyline, by local stonemason Joe Kincannon, seems almost to predict the events of September 11, 2001 (see p54).

STAR FEATURES

- ★ Bay Altars
- ★ Peace Fountain
- ★ Rose Window
- ★ West Front Entrance

★ Peace Fountain
The sculpture is the creation of Greg Wyatt and represents nature in its many forms. It stands within a granite basin on the Great Lawn, south of the cathedral.

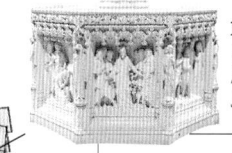

Baptistry
The Gothic Baptistry has Italian, French and Spanish influences.

THE FINISHED DESIGN

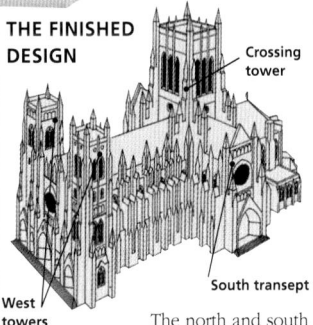

Crossing tower

West towers

South transept

The north and south transepts, the crossing tower, and the west towers have yet to be finished. When the money to fund their construction is raised, the proposed design will still take at least another 50 years to complete.

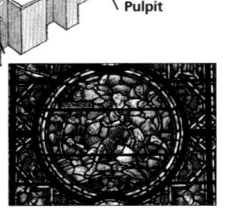

★ Bay Altars
The bay altar windows are devoted to human endeavor. The sports window shows feats of skill and strength.

Pulpit

Bishop's Chair
This is a copy from the Henry VII chapel in Westminster Abbey.

St. Ambrose Chapel
Named after a 4th-century Italian bishop, the chapel is decorated with Renaissance-style ironwork.

TIMELINE

	1800	1850	1900	1950	2000	2010
	1823 Cathedral planned for Washington Square	**1891** Site chosen and designated Cathedral Parkway	**1909** Pulpit designed by Henry Vaughan **1911** Cram design replaces earlier ones		**2001** Major fire destroys interior and roof of north transept	
	1873 Charter granted **1888** Competition to design cathedral won by Heins & LaFarge **1892** December 27 (St. John's Day), cornerstone laid		**1916** Ground broken for nave **1941** Work halted by World War II and does not resume until 1978		**1978–89** Third phase of building. Stonemasons' Yard opened and south tower heightened	

City College of the City University of New York ⓞ

Main entrance at W 138th St and Convent Ave. **Map** 19 A2. **Tel** *(212) 650-7000.* Ⓜ *137th St-City College.* **www**.ccny.cuny.edu

Set high on a hill adjoining Hamilton Heights, the original Gothic quadrangle of this college, built between 1903 and 1907, is very impressive. The material used for the buildings is Manhattan schist, a stone that had been excavated in building the IRT subway. Later, contemporary buildings were added to the school, which enrolls nearly 15,000 students.

Once free to all residents of New York, City College still offers an education at low tuition rates. Three-quarters of the students are from minority groups, and a large number of them are the first in their families to attend college.

Shepard Archway at City College of the City University of New York

Hamilton Grange National Memorial ⓞ

Saint Nicholas Park, 414 W 141st St. **Map** 19 A1. **Tel** *(212) 283-5154.* Ⓜ *137th St-City College.* ⊙ *9am–5pm Fri–Sun.* ⬤ *public hols.* ⬛ ⬛ *hourly.* **www**.nps.gov/hagr

Squeezed between a church and apartments is the 1802 country home of Alexander Hamilton. He was one of the architects of the federal government system, First Secretary of the treasury and founder of the National Bank. His face is on the $10 bill.

Statue of Alexander Hamilton at Hamilton Grange

Hamilton lived in The Grange for the last two years of his life. He was killed in a duel with political rival Aaron Burr in 1804.

In 1889, St. Luke's Episcopal Church acquired the site, and the building was moved four blocks west. A second relocation in 2006–2011 moved the building to its current site in St. Nicholas Park.

Hamilton Heights Historic District ⓞ

W 141st–W 145th St and Convent Ave. **Map** 19 A1. Ⓜ *137th St-City College.*

Originally this was a setting for the impressive country estates of the wealthy. Also known as Harlem Heights, it was developed during the 1880s following the extension of the El line *(see p26)* into the neighborhood. The privacy of the enclave, on a high hill above Harlem, made it a very desirable location.

The section of Hamilton Heights known as Sugar Hill was highly favored by Harlem's elite – US Supreme Court Justice Thurgood Marshall, notable jazz musicians Count Basie, Duke

Ellington, and Cab Calloway, and world champion boxer Sugar Ray Robinson have all lived there.

The handsome three- and four-story stone row houses were built between 1886 and 1906 mixing Flemish, Romanesque and Tudor influences. In fine condition, many are used as residences by the faculty of City College.

Row houses in Hamilton Heights

St. Nicholas Historic District ⓞ

202–250 W 138th & W 139th St. **Map** 19 B2. Ⓜ *135th St (B, C).*

A startling contrast to the rundown surroundings, the two blocks here, known as the King Model Houses, were built in 1891 when Harlem was considered a neighborhood for New York's gentry. They still comprise one of the city's most distinctive examples of row townhouses.

The developer, David King, chose three leading architects, who succeeded in blending their different styles to create a harmonious whole. The most famous of these was the firm of McKim, Mead & White,

Houses in St. Nicholas district

Adam Clayton Powell, Jr. addressing a civil rights campaign

designers of the Pierpont Morgan Library *(see pp164–5)* and Villard Houses *(see p176)*, who were responsible for the northernmost row of solid brick Renaissance palaces. Their homes featured ground floor entrances rather than the typical New York brownstone stoops. Also, the elaborate parlor floors have ornate wrought-iron balconies below, as well as carved decorative medallions above their windows.

The Georgian buildings designed by Price and Luce are built of buff brick with white stone trim. James Brown Lord's section of buildings, also Georgian in architectural style, feels much closer to Victorian, with outstanding red-brick facades and bases constructed of brownstone.

Successful blacks were attracted here in the 1920s and 1930s, giving it the nickname Strivers' Row. Among them were celebrated musicians W. C. Handy and Eubie Blake.

Abyssinian Baptist Church ⓫

132 W 138th St. **Map** 19 C2. *Tel* (212) 862-7474. **M** 135th St (B, C, 2, 3). 🚹 9am, 11am Sun. Groups of 10 or more need reservations. **www**.abyssinian.org

Founded in 1808, New York's oldest black church became famous through its charismatic pastor Adam Clayton Powell, Jr. (1908–72), a congressman

and civil rights leader. Under his leadership it became the most powerful black church in America. A room in the church houses memorabilia from his life.

The church, a fine 1923 Gothic building, welcomes properly dressed visitors to Sunday services and to hear its superb gospel choir.

Schomburg Center for Research into Black Culture ⓬

515 Malcolm X Blvd. **Map** 19 C2. **M** 135th St (2, 3). *Tel* (212) 491-2200. ⏱ noon–8pm Tue–Thu, 10am–6pm Fri & Sat. ● public hols. 🎥 (212) 491-2207. ♿ 🅿 **www**.schomburgcenter.org

Housed in a sleek contemporary complex opened in 1991, this is the largest research center of black and African culture in the United States. The immense collection was assembled by the late Arthur Schomburg, a black man of Puerto Rican descent, who was told by a teacher that there was no such thing as

Kurt Weill, Elmer Rice, and Langston Hughes at the Schomburg Center

"black history." The Carnegie Corporation bought the collection in 1926 and gave it to the New York Public Library; Schomburg was made curator in 1932.

The library was the unofficial meeting place for writers involved in what later became known as the Harlem Renaissance of the 1920s, including Langston Hughes, W.E.B. Du Bois, and Zora Neale Hurston. It also hosted many poetry readings and literary gatherings.

The Schomburg Library has excellent facilities for conserving and making available the archive's treasures, which include rare books, photos, movies, art, and recordings. The library was planned and designed to double as a cultural center and includes a theater and two art galleries, which feature changing shows of art and photography.

Harlem YMCA ⓭

180 W 135th St. **Map** 19 C3. *Tel* (212) 281-4100. **M** 135th St (2, 3).

Sociologist W. E. B. Du Bois

Paul Robeson and many others made their first stage appearances here in the early 1920s. The Krigwa Players, organized by W.E.B. Du Bois in the basement in 1928, was founded to counter the derogatory images of blacks often presented in Broadway reviews of the time. The "Y" also provided temporary lodgings for some notable new arrivals in Harlem, including writer Ralph Ellison.

Gospel singers performing at Sylvia's during Sunday brunch

Sylvia's ⑭

328 Lenox Ave. **Map** 21 B1.
Tel (212) 996-0660. Ⓜ 125th St
(2, 3). **www**.sylviassoulfood.com

Harlem's best-known soul food restaurant serves up Southern-fried or smothered chicken, spicy ribs, black-eyed peas, collard greens, candied yams, sweet potato pie, and other comforting Southern

delicacies. Sunday brunch here is served to the accom-paniment of Gospel singers.
Take some time to explore the market at the corner of 125th Street and Lenox Avenue (opposite Sylvia's), extending for a block or more in either direction. Vendors sell African clothing, jewelry, and art of varying quality.

Apollo Theater ⑮

253 W 125th St. **Map** 21 A1.
Tel (212) 531-5304/5 (events);
(212) 531-5337 (tours).
Ⓜ 125th St. ◯ at showtimes.
🎦 Groups only. ♿ 🚻
See **Entertainment** p353.
www.apollotheater.com

The Apollo opened in 1913 as a whites-only opera house. Its great fame came when Frank Schiffman, a white entrepreneur, took over in

1934. He then opened the theater to all races and turned it into Harlem's best-known showcase, with great artists such as Bessie Smith, Billie Holiday, Duke Ellington, and Dinah Washington.
Wednesday Amateur Nights,

Apollo Theater

(begun in 1935) with winners determined by audience applause, were famous, and there was a long waiting list

for performers. These amateur nights launched the careers of Sarah Vaughan, Pearl Bailey, James Brown, and Gladys Knight, among others, and they still attract hopefuls.
The Apollo was *the* place during the swing band era; following World War II, a new generation of musicians, such as Charlie "Bird" Parker, Dizzy Gillespie, Thelonius Monk, and Aretha Franklin, continued the tradition.
Rescued from decline and refurbished in the 1980s, the Apollo once again features top black entertainers and hosts Amateur Nights.

Studio Museum in Harlem ⑯

144 W 125th St. **Map** 21 B2.
Tel (212) 864-4500. Ⓜ 125th St
(2, 3). ◯ noon–6pm Thu, Fri, & Sun,
10am–6pm Sat. ● public hols.
💲 Donations. 🎦 ♿ 🎦 **Lectures,
children's programs, films,
video presentations.** 🚹 🖼
www.studiomuseum.org

The museum was founded in 1967 in a loft on upper Fifth Avenue with the mission of becoming the premier center for the collection and exhibition of the art and artifacts of African-Americans.
The present premises, a five-story building on Harlem's main commercial street, was donated to the museum by the New York Bank for Savings in 1979. There are galleries on two levels for changing exhibitions featuring artists and cultural themes, and three galleries are devoted to the permanent collection of works by major black artists.
The photographic archives comprise one of the most

Exhibition space at the Studio Museum in Harlem

complete records in existence of Harlem in its heyday. A side door opens onto a small sculpture garden.

In addition to its excellent exhibitions, the Studio Museum also maintains a national artist-in-residence program, and offers regular lectures, seminars, children's programs, and film festivals. An excellent shop sells a range of books, unique prints, and various African crafts.

Mount Morris Historical District ⑰

W 119th–W 124th Sts. **Map** 21 B2. Ⓜ *125th St (2, 3)*.

You can plainly see that the late 19th-century Victorian-style town houses near Marcus Garvey Park were once grand. This was a favorite neighborhood of German Jews moving up in the world from the Lower East Side. Time has not been kind, and this district shows how the area has deteriorated.

A few impressive churches, such as St. Martin's Episcopal Church, remain. There are also some interesting juxtapositions of faiths to be seen: the columned Mount Olivet Baptist Church, at 201 Lenox Avenue, was once Temple Israel, one of the most imposing synagogues in

St. Martin's Episcopal Church on Lenox Avenue

the city; and at the Ethiopian Hebrew Congregation, 1 West 123rd Street, housed in a former mansion, the choir sings in Hebrew on Saturdays.

Marcus Garvey Park ⑱

120th–124th Sts. **Map** 21 B2. Ⓜ *125th St (2, 3)*.

The flamboyant black nationalist leader Marcus Garvey

This hilly, rocky, two-block square of green is the site of New York's last fire watchtower, an open cast-iron structure built in 1856, with spiral stairs leading to the observation deck. The bell below the deck sounded the alarm. It may be best to view it from a distance, however, if you have any doubts about your safety.

Previously known as Mount Morris Park, it was renamed in 1973 in honor of Marcus Garvey. He came to Harlem from Jamaica in 1916 and founded the Universal Negro Improvement Association, which promoted self-help, racial pride and a back-to-Africa movement.

Museo del Barrio ⑲

1230 5th Ave. **Map** 21 C5. ***Tel*** *(212) 831-7272*. Ⓜ *103rd St, 110th St.* ◻ *11am–6pm Tue–Sat (to 9pm Wed), 1–5pm Sun.* ● *Jan 1, Jul 4, Thanksgiving, Dec 25.* 🖼 🎫 🚫 ♿ 🟥 **www.elmuseo.org**

Founded in 1969, this was North America's first museum devoted to Latin American art. It specializes in the culture of Puerto Rico. Exhibitions feature contemporary painting and sculpture, folk art, and historical artifacts. The stars of the collection are about 240 wooden Santos (carved figures of saints) and a reconstructed *bodega*, or Latino corner grocery. Exhibits change often, but some of the Santos are often on display. The Pre-Columbian collection contains rare artifacts from the Caribbean. Situated at the far end of Museum Mile, this unusual museum attempts to bridge the gap between the lofty Upper East Side and Spanish Harlem.

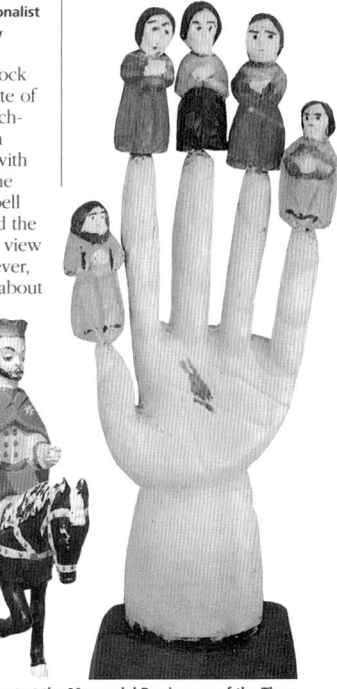

Folk art at the Museo del Barrio: one of the Three Wise Men (left) and the Omnipotent Hand

FARTHER AFIELD

Though officially part of New York City, the boroughs outside Manhattan are quite different in feel and spirit. They are residential and don't have the famous skyscrapers that are associated with New York. The difference is evident even in the way residents describe a trip to Manhattan as "going into the city." Yet the outlying areas boast many attractions, including the city's biggest zoo, botanical gardens, museums, beaches, and sports arenas. For a guided walk around Brooklyn, see pages 266–7.

SIGHTS AT A GLANCE

Historic Streets and Buildings
Alice Austen House **27**
George Washington Bridge **3**
Grand Army Plaza **18**
Historic Richmond Town **24**
Morris-Jumel Mansion **2**
Park Slope Historic District **19**
Wave Hill **5**
Yankee Stadium **10**

Museums and Galleries
Audubon Terrace **1**
Brooklyn Children's Museum **16**
Brooklyn Museum pp250–53 **21**

Jacques Marchais Museum of Tibetan Art **25**
MoMA PS1, Queens **15**
Museum of the Moving Image and Kaufman Astoria Studio **14**
New York Hall of Science **13**
Snug Harbor Cultural Center **26**
The Cloisters Museum pp236–9 **4**
Van Cortlandt House Museum **6**

Parks and Gardens
Bronx Zoo pp244–5 **9**
Brooklyn Botanic Garden **22**
Flushing Meadow-Corona Park **12**

New York Botanical Garden pp242–3 **8**
Prospect Park **20**

Famous Theaters
Brooklyn Academy of Music **17**

Cemeteries
Woodlawn Cemetery **7**

Beaches
City Island **11**
Coney Island **23**
Jamaica Bay Wildlife Refuge Center **28**
Jones Beach State Park **29**

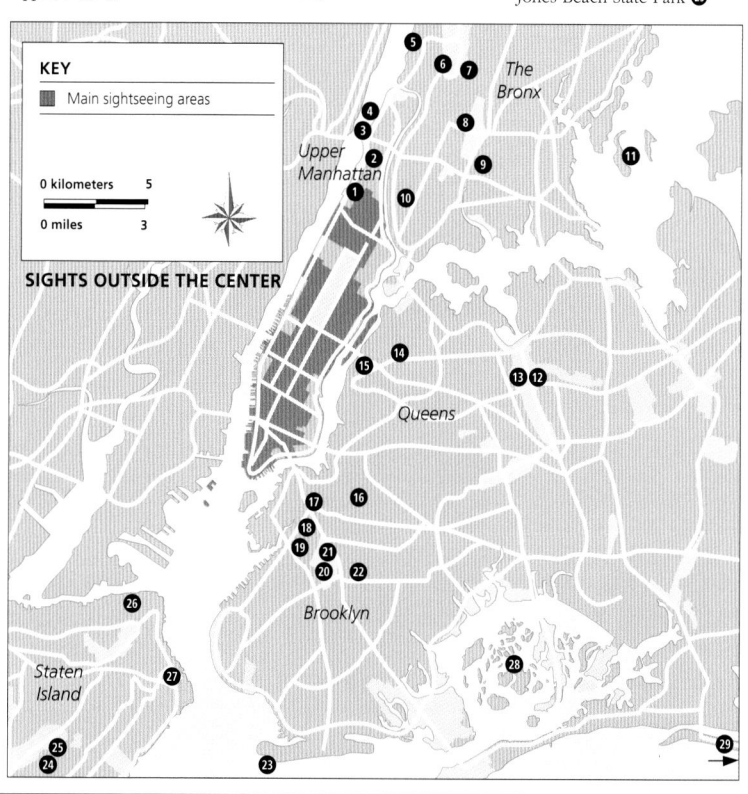

KEY

▢ Main sightseeing areas

0 kilometers   5
0 miles   3

SIGHTS OUTSIDE THE CENTER

◁ Jamaica Bay

Upper Manhattan

It was in Upper Manhattan that the 18th-century Dutch settlers established their farms. Now a suburban area with little of the bustle of downtown Manhattan, it is a good place to escape the inner city for some relaxed museum and landmark sightseeing. The Cloisters (*see pp236–9*) displays a magnificent collection of medieval art, housed within original European buildings of the period. A piece of New York history is found at the Morris-Jumel Mansion in north Harlem. From his headquarters here, George Washington mounted the defense of Manhattan in 1776.

Audubon Terrace ❶

Broadway at 155th St. **M** *157th St.*
American Academy of Arts and Letters; *(212) 368-5900.* ◗ *1–4pm Thu–Sun.* ◙ **Hispanic Society of America**; *(212) 926-2234.* ◗ *10am– 4:30pm Tue–Sat, 1–4pm Sun.* ◉ *public hols.* **Donations**. ◙ ◙ *2pm Sat.* ◙ www.hispanicsociety.org

This 1908 complex of Classical Revival buildings by Charles Pratt Huntington is named for the great naturalist John James Audubon, whose estate once included this land. Audubon is buried in nearby Trinity Cemetery. His gravestone, a Celtic cross, bears the symbolic images of his adventurous career: the birds he painted, his palette and brushes, and his rifles.

Facade of the American Academy of Arts and Letters

The complex was funded by the architect's cousin, civic benefactor Archer Milton Huntington. His dream was that it should be a center of culture and study. A central plaza contains statues by his wife, sculptress Anna Hyatt Huntington.

Audubon Terrace contains two themed museums that are worth seeking out. The American Academy of Arts and Letters was set up to honor American writers, artists, and composers, and 75 honorary members from overseas. On this illustrious roll are writers John Steinbeck and Mark Twain, painters Andrew Wyeth and Edward Hopper, and composer

Aaron Copland. Exhibitions feature members' work. The library (for scholars, by appointment) has old manuscripts and first editions.

The Hispanic Society of America is a public museum and library based upon a personal collection amassed by Archer M. Huntington. The main gallery, in Spanish Renaissance style, holds works by Goya, El Greco, and Velázquez. There are also extensive collections of Spanish sculpture, decorative arts, prints, and photographs, with changing exhibits throughout the year.

Bronze door, American Academy

Nearby, the Church of Our Lady of Esperanza stands on a knoll at 624 W 156th Street, which was once part of Audubon Park. It was built at the instigation of Señora de Barril, wife of the Spanish Consul-General in New York, as a church for the Spanish-speaking peoples of New York City. Built with funds provided by railroad magnate Archer Milton Huntington, the church was completed in 1912, and enlarged in the 1920s.

Statue of El Cid by Anna Hyatt Huntington at Audubon Terrace

Morris-Jumel Mansion ➋

Corner W 160th St and Edgecombe Ave. *Tel* (212) 923-8008. **M** 163rd St. ⬛ 10am–4pm Wed–Sun. ⬤ public hols. 📷 📷 📷 noon Sat by appt. 🔲 www. morrisjumel.org

This is one of New York's few pre-Revolutionary buildings. Now a museum with nine restored period rooms, it was built in 1765 for Roger Morris. His former military colleague George Washington used it as temporary headquarters while defending Manhattan in 1776. In 1810 it was bought and updated by Stephen Jumel, a merchant of French-Caribbean descent, and his wife Eliza.

The pair furnished the house with souvenirs of their many visits to France. Her boudoir has a "dolphin" chair, reputedly bought from Napoleon. Eliza's social climbing and love affairs scandalized New York society. It was rumored that she let her husband bleed to death in 1832 so she could inherit his fortune. She later married Aaron Burr, aged 77, and divorced him three years later on the day he died.

The exterior of the Palladian-style, wood-sided Georgian house with classical portico and octagonal wing has been restored. The museum exhibits include many original Jumel pieces.

The 3,500-ft (1,065-m) span of the George Washington Bridge

George Washington Bridge ➌

M 175th St. www.panynj.gov

French architect Le Corbusier called this "the only seat of grace in the disordered city." While not as famous a landmark as its Brooklyn equivalent, this bridge by engineer Othmar Ammann and his architect Cass Gilbert has its own character and history. Plans for a bridge linking Manhattan to New Jersey had been in the pipeline for more than 60 years before the Port of New York Authority raised the $59 million to fund the project. It was Ammann who suggested a road bridge rather than the more expensive

The lighthouse under Washington Bridge

rail link. Work began in 1927 and the bridge was opened in 1931: first across were two young roller skaters from the Bronx. Today it is a vital link for commuter traffic and is in constant use.

Cass Gilbert had plans to clad the two towers with masonry but funds did not permit it, leaving an elegant skeletal structure 600 ft (183 m) high and 3,500 ft (1,065 m) long.

Ammann had also allowed for a second deck in his plan, and this lower deck was added in 1962, increasing the bridge's capacity enormously. Now the eastbound toll collection shows a traffic level of over 53 million cars per year.

Below the eastern tower is a lighthouse that was saved from possible demolition in 1951 by public pressure. Many thousands of young New Yorkers and children all around the world have loved the bedtime story *The Little Red Lighthouse and the Great Gray Bridge*, and wrote letters to save the lighthouse. Author Hildegarde Hoyt Swift wove the tale around her two favorite New York landmarks.

The bridge is also home to the world's largest free-flying American flag, which is hung out on major federal holidays.

The Cloisters Museum ➍

See pp236–9.

Morris-Jumel Mansion, built in 1765, with its original colossal portico

The Cloisters Museum ❹

The Cloisters seen from Fort Tryon Park

This world-famous museum of medieval art resides in a building constructed from 1934 to 1938, incorporating medieval cloisters, chapels, and halls. Sculptor George Grey Barnard founded the museum in 1914; John D. Rockefeller, Jr. funded the Metropolitan Museum of Art's 1925 purchase of the collection and donated the site at Fort Tryon Park and also the land on the New Jersey side of the Hudson River, directly across from The Cloisters.

Tomb Effigy of Jean d'Alluye
This tomb immortalizes the 13th-century crusader.

Langon Chapel

Pontaut Chapter House

Gothic Chapel

★ **Unicorn Tapestries**
The set of beautiful tapestries, woven in the Netherlands around 1500, depicts the quest and capture of the mythical unicorn.

STAR EXHIBITS

- ★ Annunciation Triptych by Robert Campin
- ★ Belles Heures de Jean, Duc de Berry
- ★ Unicorn Tapestries

Boppard Stained-Glass Lancets *(1440–47)*
Below the lancet of St. Catherine, angels display the arms of the coopers' guild, of which Catherine was patron.

Bonnefort Cloister

Glass Gallery

Trie Cloister

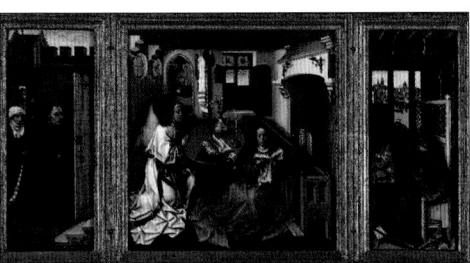

★ **Annunciation Triptych** *(about 1425)*
The Campin Room is the location of this small Robert Campin of Tournai triptych, a magnificent example of early Netherlandish painting.

Saint-Guilhem Cloister
Intricate floral ornamentation can be found on the capitals of this cloister.

Romanesque Hall

Upper floor

Lower floor

Virgin and Child Frescoes
This 12th-century fresco is from the Catalan Church of the Virgin.

KEY TO FLOOR PLAN

☐	Exhibition space
☐	Non-exhibition space

Cuxa Cloister
The reconstructed 12th-century cloister features Romanesque architectural detail and motifs.

Enthroned Virgin and Child
This elaborately carved ivory sculpture was made in England during the late 13th century.

Main entrance

GALLERY GUIDE
The museum is organized roughly in chronological order. It starts with the Romanesque period (AD 1000) and moves to the Gothic (1150 to 1520). Sculptures, stained glass, paintings, and the gardens are on the lower floor. The Unicorn Tapestries are on the upper floor.

★ Belles Heures
This book of hours, commissioned by Jean, Duc de Berry, is among a rotating installation of exquisite illuminated books and folios.

Exploring The Cloisters Museum

Known particularly for its Romanesque and
Gothic architectural sculpture, The Cloisters
Museum's collection also includes illuminated
manuscripts, stained glass, metalwork, enamels,
ivories, and paintings. Among its tapestries is the
renowned *Unicorn* series. The Cloisters' splendid
medieval complex is unrivaled in North America.

A 16th-century Flemish boxwood
rosary bead from the Treasury

ROMANESQUE ART

A lifesized 12th-century Spanish
crucifix portraying Christ as the
King of Heaven

Fanciful beasts and people,
acanthus blossoms and
scrollwork top the columns
around The Cloisters Museum.
Many are in the Romanesque
style that flourished in the
11th and 12th centuries.
The museum has numerous
masterpieces of Romanesque
art and architecture, showing
the style's powerful rounded
arches and intricate details.
Highly embellished capitals
and warm, pink marble typify
the 12th-century Cuxa Cloister
from the Pyrenees in France.
A griffin, a dragon, a centaur,
and a basilisk are among the
creatures parading over the
Narbonne Arch nearby.

In a more solemn style,
the apse from the church of
Saint-Martín in Fuentidueña,
Spain, is a massive rounded
vault constructed from 3,300
blocks of limestone. It is
decorated with a 12th-century
fresco of the Virgin and Child
and has a golden-crowned
Christ depicted as triumphant
over death.

More than 800 years ago,
Benedictine and Cistercian
monks sat on the cold stone
benches in the Pontaut Chapter
House. By the 19th century it
had become so neglected that
it was used as a stable. Its
ribbed vaulting is a foretaste
of the Gothic style to come.

GOTHIC ART

Where Romanesque art was
solid, the Gothic style that
followed (from 1150 to
around 1520) was open, with
pointed arches, glowing
stained-glass windows, and
three-dimensional sculpture.
Gothic depictions of the
Virgin and Child display
exquisite craftsmanship.

The Gothic Chapel's
brilliantly colored windows
show scenes and figures from
biblical stories. Lifesized tomb
sculptures include the effigy
of the Crusader knight Jean
d'Alluye. During the 1790s,

Vaulted ceiling of the Pontaut Chapter House

the statue's original home, La Clarté-Dieu Abbey in France, was vandalized, and the statue was used to bridge a stream.

In the Boppard Room, the lives of the saints are told in marvelous late Gothic stained glass from Germany.

Robert Campin's Flemish masterwork, the *Annunciation* altarpiece, is the focus of the Campin Room. It is an intimate room with furnishings that might have belonged to a wealthy 15th-century family.

THE TAPESTRIES

The Cloisters' tapestries are full of rich imagery and symbolism, and are among the museum's most highly prized treasures. The four *Nine Heroes Tapestries* bear the coat of arms of Jean, Duc de Berry, who was a brother of the King of France and one of the greatest art patrons of the Middle Ages. These tapestries are one of only two sets that survived from the late 14th century; the other set belonged to Jean's brother, Louis, Duc d'Anjou.

Nine great heroes of the past – three pagan, three Hebrew, three Christian – are shown with members of the medieval court, from cardinals, knights, and damsels to musicians.

In an adjacent room is the magnificent *Hunt of the Unicorn*, a series of seven tapestries woven in the Netherlands around 1500. It depicts the symbolic hunt of the mythical unicorn and capture by a maiden.

Although they were misused in the 19th century to protect fruit trees from frost damage,

MEDIEVAL GARDENS

More than 300 varieties of plants grown in the Middle Ages can be found in The Cloisters' gardens. The Bonnefont Cloister has many species of aromatic, magic, medicinal, and culinary herbs. The Trie Cloister features plants shown in the *Unicorn Tapestries* and reveals the use of flowers in medieval symbolism: roses (for the Virgin Mary), pansies (the Holy Trinity), and daisies (the eye of Christ).

Bonnefont Cloister

the tapestries are remarkably well preserved. They are also astonishing in detail, with

Julius Caesar, entertained by court musicians, in a *Nine Heroes* tapestry

literally hundreds of minutely observed plants and animals. Their story can be read as a tale of courtly love, but the series is also an allegory of the Crucifixion and the Resurrection of Christ.

THE TREASURY

In medieval times, precious objects were stored for safe-keeping in sanctuaries. At The Cloisters, they are found in the Treasury.

The collection includes several Gothic illuminated "books of hours." These were used for the private devotions of the nobility, such as the Limbourg brothers' *Belles Heures*, made for Jean, Duc de Berry, in 1410, and the tiny, palm-sized version by Gothic master Jean Pucelle for the Queen of France, around 1325.

Other religious artifacts range from a 13th-century English ivory Virgin to the 14th-century silver gilt and enamel reliquary shrine thought to have belonged to Queen Elizabeth of Hungary, along with censers, chalices, candlesticks, and crucifixes.

Curiosities here include the "Monkey Cup," an enameled beaker probably made for the 15th-century Burgundian court, showing mischievous monkeys robbing a sleeping peddler; an intricately carved rosary bead the size of a walnut; a 13th-century boat-shaped, jeweled saltcellar; and a full set of playing cards dating to the 15th century.

        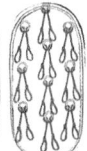

Hunting images and symbols depicted on a 15th-century deck of playing cards

The west parlor of the Van Cortlandt House Museum

The Bronx

Once a prosperous suburb with a famous Grand Concourse lined with apartment buildings for the wealthy, the Bronx has now become an unfortunate symbol of urban decay. Still, diverse ethnic communities, unique resources, and charming areas, such as Riverdale at the northern end, remain.

Two main attractions are the Bronx Zoo and New York Botanical Garden. There is also a golf course at Ferry Point Park, and Fulton Fish Market has relocated here. The much-loved Yankees baseball team's *(see p360)* main stadium is located here.

Wave Hill **5**

W 249th St and Independence Ave, Riverdale. **Tel** (718) 549-3200. **M** 231st St, then bus Bx7, 10, or museum shuttle bus hourly 9:10am–3:10pm. ◯ 10am–5:30pm Tue–Sun (to 4:30pm mid-Oct–mid-Apr). 🎫 free Tue (Jul, Aug & Nov–Apr), 9am–noon Tue (May, Jun, Sep & Oct), 9am–noon Sat (all year). 🏛 2pm Sun. 🏠 www.wavehill.org

This 28-acre (11-ha) oasis of beauty boasts fine views over to the New Jersey Palisades across the Hudson River. The former estate of financier and conservationist George W. Perkins, Wave Hill has had many distinguished tenants,

including Theodore Roosevelt, Mark Twain, and Arturo Toscanini. Perkins also owned neighboring estates, underneath which he built a recreation center complete with bowling alley, and a tunnel leading into the main building.

The house is frequently used for concerts. They often take place in the grand Armor Hall, designed in 1928 for Bashford Dean, who was then the curator of the collection of arms and armor at the Metropolitan Museum of Art.

The gardens were originally designed by Viennese land-scape gardener Albert Millard. There are also greenhouses, lawns, an herb garden, and woodlands. Exhibitions range from sculpture to horticulture.

The adjoining Riverdale Park, which is also open to the public, has attractive woodland and paths along the river.

The interior of the grand Armor Hall at Wave Hill

Van Cortlandt House Museum **6**

Van Cortlandt Park. **Tel** (718) 543-3344. **M** 242nd St, Van Cortlandt Park. ◯ 10am–3pm Tue–Fri, 11am–4pm Sat, Sun (last adm: 30 mins before closing). ● public hols & Nov 26. 🎫 free Wed. 📷 ✔ 🏠 See **The History of New York** pp20–21. **www**.vancortlandthouse.org

The facade of Van Cortlandt House

A restored 1748 Georgian Colonial country manor built of rough stone, the Bronx's oldest building was the family home of Frederick Van Cortlandt, a New Yorker who inherited great wealth and was related to many influential families of his day.

The dining room was used as one of General George Washington's headquarters; the ground behind the house was once the scene of skirmishing during the Revolutionary War.

The interior has American period furnishings as well as a superb collection of delft-ware and a complete 17th-century Dutch bedroom.

On the exterior, look for the carved faces in the keystones over the windows.

Woodlawn Cemetery ❼

Webster Ave and E 233rd St.
Tel (718) 920-0500. Ⓜ Woodlawn.
◐ 8:30am–5pm daily.
◑ public hols. ⦿ 🅱 🅲
www.thewoodlawncemetery.org

Established in 1863, Woodlawn Cemetery is the burial place of many a wealthy and distinguished New Yorker.

Entrance to the Woolworth mausoleum

Memorials and tombstones are set in beautiful grounds. F.W. Woolworth and many members of his family are interred in a mausoleum only a little less ornate than the building that carries the family name. The pink marble vault of meat magnate Herman Armour is oddly reminiscent of a ham.

Other New York notables buried here include Mayor Fiorello LaGuardia; Rowland Hussey Macy, the founder of the great department store; author Herman Melville; and jazz legend Duke Ellington.

New York Botanical Garden ❽

See pp242–3.

Bronx Zoo/Wildlife Conservation Park ❾

See pp244–5.

Yankee Stadium ❿

E 161st St at River Ave, Highbridge.
Tel (718) 293-6000. Ⓜ 161st St.
🅲 noon daily (except on game afternoons); reservation advised.
See **Sport** p360. **www**.yankees.com

This has been the home of the New York Yankees baseball team since 1923. Among Yankee heroes are two of the greatest players of all time: Babe Ruth and Joe DiMaggio (who was also famous for marrying the actress Marilyn Monroe in 1954). In 1921 left-hander Babe Ruth, wearing the Yankees' distinctive pinstripes, hit the stadium's first home run – against the Boston Red Sox, his former team. The stadium was completed two years later by Jacob Ruppert, the owner of the Yankees, and became known as "the house that Ruth built".

Joe DiMaggio in action at Yankee Stadium in 1941

Yankee Stadium had a facelift in the mid-1970s to seat up to 54,000 people. One of the largest annual gatherings has been that of the Jehovah's Witnesses, and in 1950, 123,707 people attended in a single day. In 1965 Pope Paul VI celebrated mass before a crowd of more than 80,000. It was the first visit to North America by a pope – the second was made in 1979 when John Paul II also visited the stadium.

A new Yankee Stadium, located parallel to the old site, at 161st and 164th streets, opened in April 2009.

The Yankees remain one of the top teams in the American League. There are five Yankee Clubhouse stores in New York, where tickets for tours and games can be purchased.

City Island ⓫

Ⓜ 6 to Pelham Bay Park, then Bx29 to City Island.
Museum 190 Fordham St.
◐ 1–5pm Sat & Sun. **Tel** (718) 885-0008. **www**.cityislandmuseum.org

Situated off the northeast shore of the Bronx and surrounded by Long Island Sound, City Island is a small nautical outpost with a very New England feel and offers a refreshing change of pace. Its scenic marinas are filled with sailboats, and its seafood restaurants would satisfy any sailor's appetite. Several Americas Cup winners have been built in its boatyards.

The **City Island Museum** is in one of the island's most historic buildings, the old Public School 17, built on an Indian burial ground at a high point on the island. City Island is linked to the Bronx by bridge. To the north on the mainland is Orchard Beach, a crescent of white sand edged with bathing huts. The beach is popular with area residents, and it can be crowded.

An old tugboat moored at one of City Island's piers

The New York Botanical Garden ❽

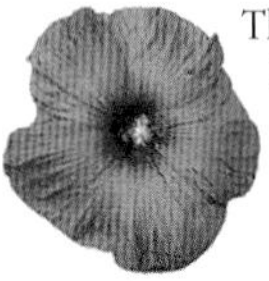

Hibiscus

The New York Botanical Garden is 250 acres (100 ha) of dazzling beauty and hands-on enjoyment. From the nation's most glorious Victorian glasshouse to the 12-acre (5-ha) Everett Children's Adventure Garden, it is alive with things to discover. One of the oldest and largest botanical gardens in the world, it has 50 gardens and plant collections, and 50 acres (20 ha) of uncut forest. The spectacular Enid A. Haupt Conservatory has been wonderfully restored as *A World of Plants*, with misty tropical rain forests and dramatic deserts.

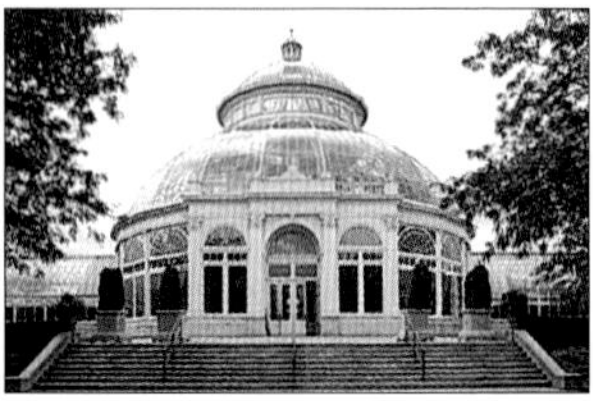

Entrance to Enid A. Haupt Conservatory

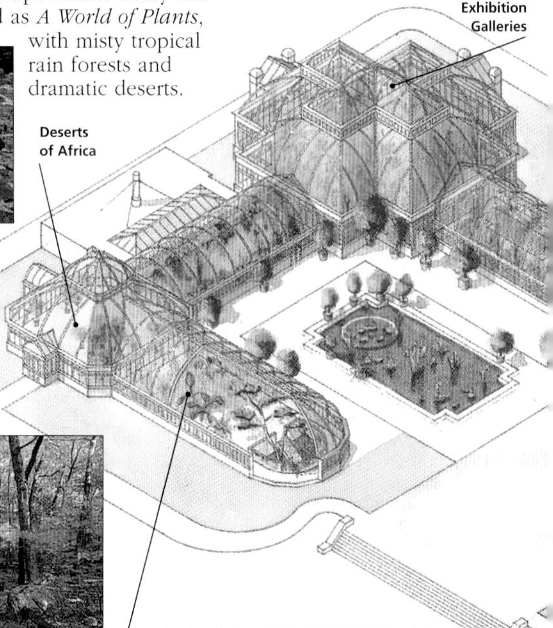
Seasonal Exhibition Galleries
Deserts of Africa
Deserts of the Americas

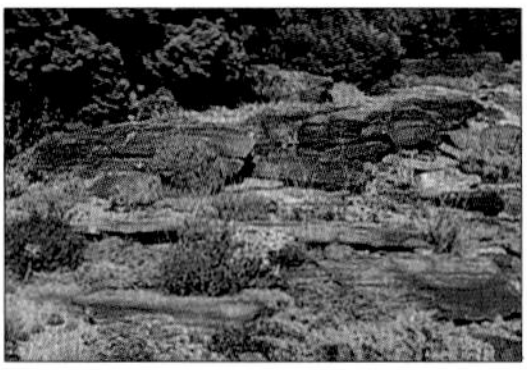

Rock Garden
Rock outcroppings, streams, a waterfall, and a flower-rimmed pond create an alpine habitat for plants from around the world ④

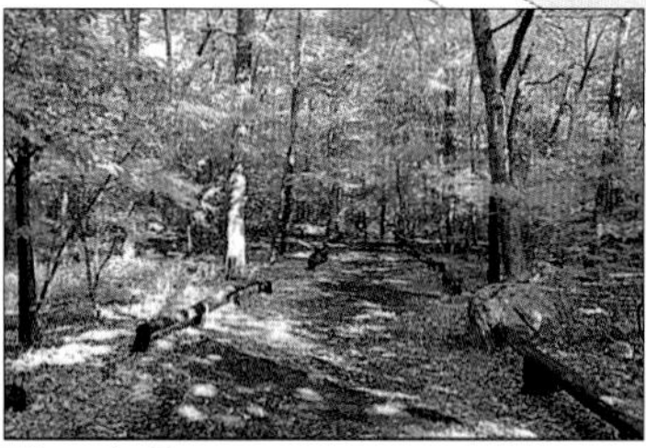

Historic Forest
One of New York City's last surviving natural forest areas includes red oak, white ash, tulip trees, and birch ⑤

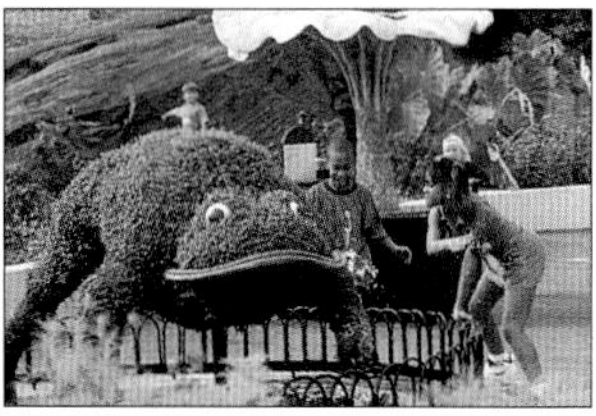

Everett Children's Adventure Garden *Kids can discover the wonders of ecology and plants* ⑧

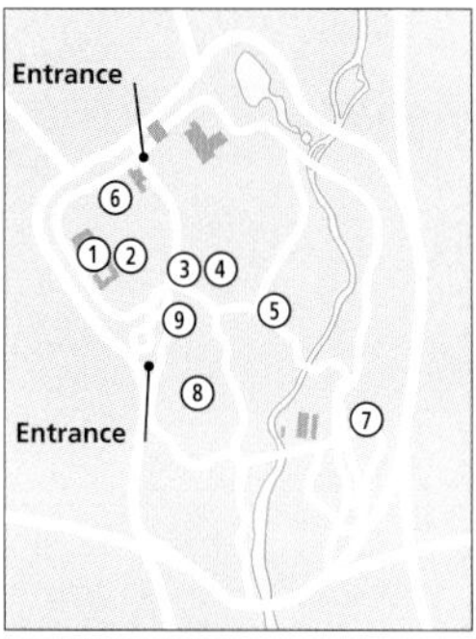
Entrance
⑥
①②
③④
⑨
⑤
⑧
⑦
Entrance

LOCATOR MAP

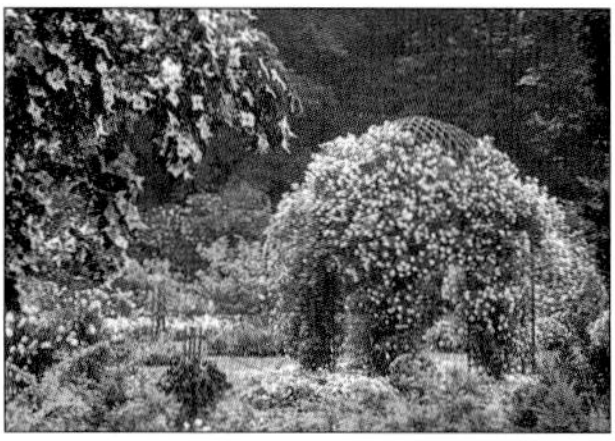

Peggy Rockefeller Rose Garden
Over 2,700 rose bushes have been planted in the Rose Garden, laid out in 1988 according to the 1916 design ⑦

Palms of the Americas Gallery
100 majestic palms soar into a 90-ft (27-m) glass dome. A tranquil reflecting pool is surrounded by tropical plants.

VISITORS' CHECKLIST

Kazimiroff Blvd, Bronx River Parkway (Exit 7W). **Tel** (718) 817-8700. Ⓜ 4, B, D to Bedford Park Blvd. 🚌 Bx26. ◯ 10am–6pm Tue–Sun (until 5pm mid-Jan–Feb). ● public hols. 🎫 Free all day Wed & 10am–noon Sat. 📷 ♿ ✍ ▭ 🎭 **Lectures.** www.nybg.org

The Enid A. Haupt Conservatory consists of 11 interconnecting glass galleries housing *A World of Plants*, including rain forests, deserts, aquatic plants, and seasonal exhibitions ①

Garden Cafe
This is a delightful spot to enjoy a meal. You can eat outside on terraces overlooking beautiful gardens ⑥

Conservatory

Jane Watson Irwin Perennial Garden
Flowering perennials are arranged in dramatic patterns according to height, shade, color and blooming time ②

Tropical Lowland Rain Forest Gallery

Courtyard Pool

Leon Levy Visitor Center
This modern pavilion has a shop, a café, and a visitor orientation facility ⑨

Aquatic Plants and Vines Gallery

Tropical Upland Rainforest Gallery

Tram
The half-hour tour of the gardens provides information about horticultural, educational, and botanical research programs. Passengers can alight at a number of stops to explore the gardens before reboarding ③

Bronx Zoo ⑨

Opened in 1899, the Bronx Zoo is the largest urban zoo in the United States. It is home to more than 4,000 animals of 500 species, which live in realistic representations of their natural habitats. The zoo is a leader in the perpetuation of endangered species, such as the Indian rhinoceros and the snow leopard. Its 265 acres of woods, streams, and parklands include, in season, a children's zoo, the Butterfly Garden, the Wild Asia Monorail, and camel rides. Other attractions include daily sea lion feedings, primate training at the Monkey House, a one-of-a-kind bug carousel, and a 4-D theater experience.

★ The Congo Gorilla Forest
This award-winning replica of a central African rainforest is home to the largest population of Western Lowland gorillas in the US, as well as a family of pygmy marmosets, the world's smallest monkeys.

★ African Plains
Wild dogs, zebras, lions, giraffes, and gazelles roam the African Plains. Predators and prey are separated by a moat.

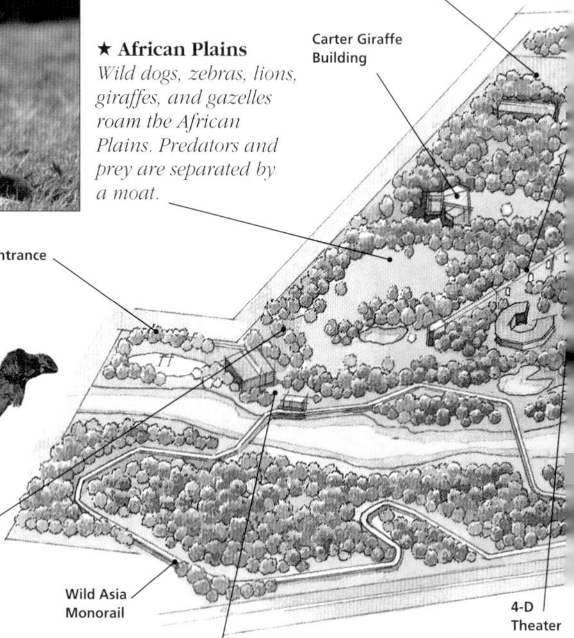

Carter Giraffe Building

Asia entrance

Camel Rides
Children enjoy such seasonal experiences as camel rides and other attractions.

Wild Asia Monorail

4-D Theater

★ JungleWorld
A climate-controlled tropical rain forest harbors mammals, birds, and reptiles from South Asia. The animals are kept apart from visitors by ravines, streams and cliffs.

Monkeys in JungleWorld

Baboon Reserve
Visitors walk along a dry riverbed to see wildlife in an Ethiopian mountain habitat.

Children's Zoo
Kids can crawl through a prairie dog tunnel, try on a turtle shell, and pet and feed the animals.

VISITORS' CHECKLIST

Fordham Rd/Bronx River Pkwy. *Tel* (718) 367-1010. Ⓜ 2, 5 to E Tremont Ave. ℝ to Fordham. 🚌 Bx9, Bx12, Bx19, Bx22, Bx39, BxM11, Q44. ◯ 10am–5pm Mon–Fri, 10am–5:30pm Sat & Sun (Nov–Mar: 4:30pm daily). 🎟 by donation Wed; separate fees may apply to some exhibits. 📷 ♿ 🎦 🍴 🏛 **Children's Zoo** ◯ Apr–Oct. **www**.bronxzoo.com

STAR FEATURES

★ African Plains

★ Congo Gorilla Forest

★ JungleWorld

★ Tiger Mountain

★ Wild Asia Monorail

★ World of Birds

World of Reptiles

The Zoo Center

Butterfly Garden

Southern Boulevard entrance

Madagascar!

Aquatic Bird House

Sea Bird Colony

fowl sh

Rainey Gate entrance

Monkey House

★ World of Birds
Exotic birds soar free in the lush surroundings of a rain forest. An artificial waterfall rushes down a 50-ft (15-m) fiberglass cliff in this walk-through habitat.

Great hornbill

Mouse-House

Bronx Parkway entrance

Himalayan Highlands
Endangered species, such as snow leopards and red pandas, are here.

★ Wild Asia Monorail
From May to October, the monorail journeys through forests and meadows, where rhinos, tigers, and Mongolian wild horses roam free.

★ Tiger Mountain
Amur tigers are on view all year. Only one inch of glass separates visitors from these magnificent wild cats.

Queens

A big, sprawling borough, Queens has a wide variety of attractions and residential and commercial areas, including Long Island City, where exciting museums and restaurants are springing up all over. Development of the borough accelerated after 1909, when the construction of Queensboro Bridge made commuting easier. The city's main airports are here, and there are many different ethnic enclaves including the Greek neighborhood of Astoria and the various Asian communities in Flushing.

A 1900 Mutoscope at the Museum of the Moving Image

Flushing Meadow–Corona Park ⑫

🅼 Willets Point-Shea Stadium. See **Sports** p361.

The site of New York's two World's Fairs now offers expansive waterside picnic grounds and a multitude of attractions. These include the 41,000-seat Citi Field stadium, home of the New York Mets baseball team, and a popular site for rock concerts. Flushing Meadow is also home to the US Tennis Center, where the prestigious United States Open is played. The courts are open for would-be Clijsters, Federers, and Nadals for the remainder of the year. In the 1920s this area was known as the Corona Dump, a nightmarish place of salt marshes and great piles of smoldering trash. In *The Great Gatsby*, author F. Scott Fitzgerald dubbed it the "valley of ashes." It reeked of rotting garbage and glowed red at night. New York's Parks' Commissioner Robert Moses was the driving force behind its transformation. A whole mountain of trash was removed and the river was totally re-channeled. The marsh was drained, and sewage works were built, helping to restore the area. This site was to serve as the location for the 1939 World's Fair, at which a world on the brink of war saluted the elusive notion of world peace.

The Unisphere, symbol of the 1964 fair, still dominates the remains of the fairground. This giant hollow ball of green steel, built by the US Steel Corporation, is 12 stories high and weighs a massive 350 tons.

The 1964 World's Fair Unisphere at Flushing Meadow-Corona Park

New York Hall of Science ⑬

46th Ave and 111th St Flushing Meadow, Corona Park. **Tel** (718) 699-0005. 🅼 111th St. 🕐 Sep–Jun: 9:30am–2pm Mon–Thu, 9:30am–5pm Fri, 10am–6pm Sat & Sun; Jul–Aug: 9:30am–5pm Mon–Fri, 10am–6pm Sat & Sun. 🔴 Labor Day, Dec 25. 🈳🅿️♿🔼🔊 **www**.nysci.org

The science pavilion was built for the 1964 World's Fair, with stained glass set in concrete. It is now a hands-on museum of science and technology, with exhibits on color, light, and physics. Kids love the giant video screens and laser optical exhibits.

The concrete curtain wall of the New York Hall of Science

Museum of the Moving Image and Kaufman Astoria Studio ⑭

35th Ave at 36th St, Astoria. **Museum** (718) 784-0077. 🅼 36th St. **Steinway Museum** 🕐 10:30am–5pm Tue–Sun (to 8pm Fri, to 7pm Sat & Sun). Screenings: 7:30pm Fri, afternoon and eves Sat & Sun. 🎟️ (free 4–8pm Fri). 🎬 2pm Sat & Sun. 🔴 Memorial Day, Thnksgv, Dec 25. **Studio** 🔴 to public. 🅿️♿ 🖥️🔼 **www**.movingimage.us

In New York's filmmaking heyday, Rudolph Valentino, W.C. Fields, the Marx Brothers, and Gloria Swanson all made films in the Astoria Studio, which was opened in 1920 by Paramount Pictures. When the movies went west, the army took over, making training films from 1941 to 1971. The complex stood empty until 1977 when Astoria Motion Picture and Television

Poster at the Museum of the Moving Image

Foundation was created to preserve it. *The Wiz*, a musical starring Michael Jackson and Diana Ross, was made here, helping to pay for restoration.

Today, the studios house the largest moviemaking facilities on the East Coast.

In 1981 one of the studio buildings was transformed into the Museum of the Moving Image, with interactive displays on production and theaters for the screening of movies and television, as well as a special lecture hall.

There is a lot of memorabilia on display, from Ben Hur's chariot to *Star Trek* costumes. The main gallery draws from the permanent collection of over 85,000 movie artifacts. A major expansion of the museum has created a state-of-the-art facility, with a 254-seat theater, a video-screening ampitheater, and an educational 71-seat screening room.

MoMA PS1, Queens ⓯

22–25 Jackson at 46th Ave, Long Island City. *Tel* (718) 784-2084. Ⓜ E, M to 23rd St-Ely Ave; 7 to 45 Road-Courthouse Square; G to Court Sq or 21 St-Van Alst. 🚌 B61, Q67. ◯ noon–6pm Thu–Mon. ● Jan 1, Dec 25. 🔲 🔲 🔲 www.ps1.org

Housed in an elementary school, PS1 was founded in 1971 under a scheme to transform abandoned New York City buildings into exhibition, performance, and studio spaces for artists. The museum is affiliated to the Museum of Modern Art *(see pp172–5)* and is one of the oldest art organisations in the US devoted solely to modern art. Temporary exhibitions are hosted alongside permanent works and many pieces are interactive. In summer, music is performed in the courtyard.

Brooklyn

The bandstand at Prospect Park (see p248)

If Brooklyn were a separate city, it would be the country's fourth largest. It has a character all of its own. Many entertainment greats – Mel Brooks, Phil Silvers, Woody Allen, and Neil Simon among them – celebrate their birthplace with great affection and humor. Brooklyn is a veritable melting pot, with West Indians, Hasidic Jews, Russians, Italians, and Arabs living side by side. Among the diverse neighborhoods are the historic residential districts of Park Slope and Brooklyn Heights.

Brooklyn Children's Museum ⓰

145 Brooklyn Ave. *Tel* (718) 735-4400. Ⓜ Kingston (C, 3). ◯ 10am–5pm Tue–Sun. ● public hols. **Rooftop Theater** ◯ 6:30–8pm Fri, 10am–5pm Sat & Sun. ● public hols. 🔲 🔲 🔲 🔲 www.bchildmus.org

The Brooklyn Children's Museum was the first to be designed especially for children and was founded in 1899. Since then, it has been a model, inspiration, and consultant to the development of more than 250 museums for children across the country and all over the world. Housed in a high-tech, specially designed underground building dating from 1976, it is one of the most imaginative children's museums anywhere.

The layout of the building, which has doubled in size and is a maze of complex interconnected passageways running off the main "people tube" – a huge drainage pipe that connects the four levels. The emphasis here is on involvement and hands-on exhibits and everywhere you look there are curiosities to be discovered, experienced, made, or played with. There is even a walk-on piano like the one in the film *Big* – children of every age find it quite irresistible.

Special exhibitions and events are designed to help children learn about the planet, resolve their fears or problems, understand other cultures, and discover the past. The squeals of laughter that are always heard are a sign of this museum's success in teaching both children and the young at heart.

A mask at the Brooklyn Children's Museum

The facade of the Brooklyn Academy of Music

Brooklyn Academy of Music ⑰

30 Lafayette Ave. *Tel (718) 636-
4100.* Ⓜ *Atlantic Ave, Nevins St
(M, N, Q, R, 2, 3, 4, 5).* 🅿 ♿
📧 🚻 www.bam.org *See Classic
and Contemporary Music p350.*

Home to the Brooklyn Philharmonic, the Academy of
Music (BAM) is Brooklyn's
leading cultural venue and
the oldest, founded in 1858.
It offers outstanding performances, often tending toward
the innovative and avant-garde.

The classic 1908 building,
designed by Herts & Tallant,
was inaugurated with a
production of Gounod's opera
Faust featuring the Neapolitan
tenor Enrico Caruso. Among
the greats who have performed
here are actress Sarah Bernhardt, ballerina Anna Pavlova,
musicians Pablo Casals and
Sergei Rachmaninoff, poets
Edna St. Vincent Millay and
Carl Sandburg, and statesman
Winston Churchill. Many
international touring groups
have made appearances here,
including Britain's Royal
Shakespeare Company.

The BAM Next Wave Festival,
which usually runs over the
last three months of the year,
has presented contemporary
artists such as musicians

David Byrne and
Philip Glass and
choreographers
Pina Bausch and
Mark Morris. The
BAM also runs the
Harvey Theater
nearby, a movie
theater now used
for dance, drama, and music
events. BAM Rose Cinemas
show first-run independent
films and BAMcinématek
has classics, retrospectives,
festivals, and sneak previews.

Grand Army Plaza ⑱

Plaza St at Flatbush Ave.
Ⓜ *Grand Army Plaza (2, 3).*
Arch ⬜ *for occasional exhibitions.*

**The Soldiers' and Sailors' Arch at
Grand Army Plaza**

Frederick Law Olmsted and
Calvert Vaux laid out this
grand oval in 1870 as a gateway to Prospect Park. The
Soldiers' and Sailors' Arch
and its sculptures were
added in 1892 as a tribute
to the Union Army. The bust
of John F. Kennedy here is
the only official New York
monument to him.

In June, the plaza is the
center of the Welcome Back
to Brooklyn Festival for the
famous – and not-so-famous –
people born in Brooklyn.

Park Slope Historic District ⑲

Streets from Prospect Park W below
Flatbush Ave, to 8th/7th/5th Aves. Ⓜ
Grand Army Plaza (2, 3), 7th Ave (F).

Relief work on the Montauk Club

This wonderful enclave of
beautiful Victorian town
houses was developed on the
edge of Prospect Park in the
1880s. It served the upper-
middle-class professionals
who were able to commute
into Manhattan after the
Brooklyn Bridge was opened
in 1883. The shady streets
are lined with two- to five-
story houses in every
architectural style popular in
the late 19th century, some
with the towers, turrets, and
curlicues so representative
of the era. Particularly fine
examples are in Romanesque
Revival style, with rounded
entry arches.

The Montauk Club at 25
Eighth Avenue combines
the style of Venice's Ca'
d'Oro palazzo with the
friezes and gargoyles of the
Montauk Indians, for whom
this popular 19th-century
gathering place was named.

Prospect Park ⑳

Ⓜ *Grand Army Plaza, Prospect Park
(B, Q).* 🅿 *& information (718) 287-
3400.* 📧 🚻 www.prospectpark.org

Olmsted and Vaux considered
this park, opened in 1867,
better than their earlier Central
Park *(see pp203–09)*. The
Long Meadow, a sweep of
broad lawns and grand vistas,
is the longest unbroken swath
of green space in New York.

Olmsted's belief was that
"a feeling of relief is experienced by entering them [the
parks] on escaping from the
cramped, confining and
controlling circumstances
of the streets of the town."

The facade of the Brooklyn Public Library on Grand Army Plaza

That vision is still as true today as it was a century ago.

Among the many notable features are Stanford White's colonnaded Croquet Shelter, and the pools and weeping willows of the Vale of Cashmere. The Music Grove bandstand shows Japanese influences and hosts both jazz and classical music concerts throughout the summer.

A favorite feature of the park is the Camperdown Elm, an ancient and twisted tree planted in 1872. The Friends of Prospect Park raise money to keep it and all the park trees healthy. This old elm has inspired many poems and paintings. Prospect Park has a wide variety of landscapes, from classical gardens dotted with statues to rocky glens with running brooks. A guided tour with a ranger is the best way to see the park.

Carousel horse in Prospect Park

Brooklyn Museum ㉑

See pp250–53.

Brooklyn Botanic Garden ㉒

900 Washington Ave. **Tel** *(718) 623-7200.* Ⓜ *Prospect Pk (B, Q), Eastern Pkwy (2, 3).* **Grounds** ☐ *Apr–Sep: 8am–6pm Tue–Fri (10am Sat, Sun, & public hols), Oct–Mar: 8am–4:30pm (10am Sat, Sun, & public hols).* ☐ *Jan 1, Labor Day, Thanksgiving, Dec 25.* 🅿 *Mar–mid-Nov: free Tue & 10am–noon Sat; mid-Nov–late Feb: free for under-16s Mon–Fri.* 📷 ♿ 🚻 🍴 ☐ www.bbg.org

Though it is not vast, you will find that this 50-acre (20-ha) garden holds many delights. The area was designed by the

An Atlantic green turtle at the New York Aquarium, on Coney Island

Olmsted Brothers in 1910 and features an Elizabethan-style "knot" herb garden and one of North America's largest collections of roses.

The central showpiece is a Japanese hill-and-pond garden, complete with a teahouse and Shinto shrine. In late April and early May the park promenade is aglow with delicate Japanese cherry blossoms, which have prompted an annual festival featuring typical Japanese culture, food, and music. April is also the time for tourists to appreciate Magnolia Plaza, where some 80 trees display their beautiful, creamy blossoms against a backdrop of daffodils on Boulder Hill.

The Fragrance Garden is planted in raised beds, where the heavily scented, textured and flavored plants are all labeled in Braille, giving blind visitors an opportunity to identify them as well.

The conservatory houses one of America's largest bonsai collections and some rare rain forest trees, whose extracts allow scientists to produce life-saving drugs.

Brooklyn Botanic Garden lily pond

Coney Island ㉓

Ⓜ *Stillwell Ave (D, F, N, Q), W 8th St (F, Q).* **New York Aquarium** *Surf Ave and W 8th St.* **Tel** *(718) 265-FISH.* ☐ *10am–5pm daily (to 5:30pm Sat, Sun, & hols). (Jun–Aug: to 6pm Mon–Fri & 7pm Sat, Sun & hols; Nov–Mar: to 4:30pm daily).* 🅿 *last adm: 45 mins before closing.* ☐ www.nyaquarium.com **Coney Island Museum** *1208 Surf Ave, nr W 12th St.* **Tel** *(718) 372-5159.* ☐ *noon–5pm Sat & Sun.* 🅿 www.coneyislandusa.com

In the mid-1800s, Brooklyn poet Walt Whitman composed many of his works on Coney Island, at that time untamed Atlantic coastline. By the 1920s, Coney Island was billing itself as the "World's Largest Playground," with three huge fairgrounds providing hair-raising rides. The subway arrived in 1920, and the 1921 boardwalk ensured Coney Island's popularity throughout the Depression.

A major attraction is the **New York Aquarium**, with over 350 species. The **Coney Island Museum** has memorabilia, souvenirs, and relics of old rides. Coney Island is in the process of being modernized, much to the chagrin of local residents, who fear that its character will be lost. However, the boardwalk still yields lovely ocean views, and the Cyclone roller coaster has been designated an official city landmark. The Mermaid Parade in June is a major annual event.

Brooklyn Museum ㉑

When it opened in 1897, the
Brooklyn Museum building,
designed to be the largest cultural
edifice in the world, was the
greatest achievement of New York
architects McKim, Mead & White.

North facade, designed by McKim, Mead & White

Though only one-sixth completed, the museum
is today one of the most impressive cultural institutions
in the United States, with a permanent encyclopedic
collection of some one million objects, which are housed
in a grand structure of 560,000 sq ft (41,805 sq m).

KEY TO FLOOR PLAN

- Arts of Africa and the Americas
- Asian art
- Prints, drawings, and photographs
- Williamsburg Murals
- Egyptian and Classical art
- Decorative arts
- Painting and sculpture
- Special exhibitions
- Non-exhibition space

★ Female Figurine
*This 5,000-year-old rare
statuette is a highlight of
the museum's impressive
Egyptian collection.*

Iris and B. Cantor
Auditorium

Chinese Jar
*Cobalt blue fishes and
water plants adorn this
14th-century Yuan
dynasty blue-and-white
ceramic jar.*

★ Beaded Crown
*This 19th-century
crown from
Nigeria is
the ultimate
symbol of
Yoruba
kingship.*

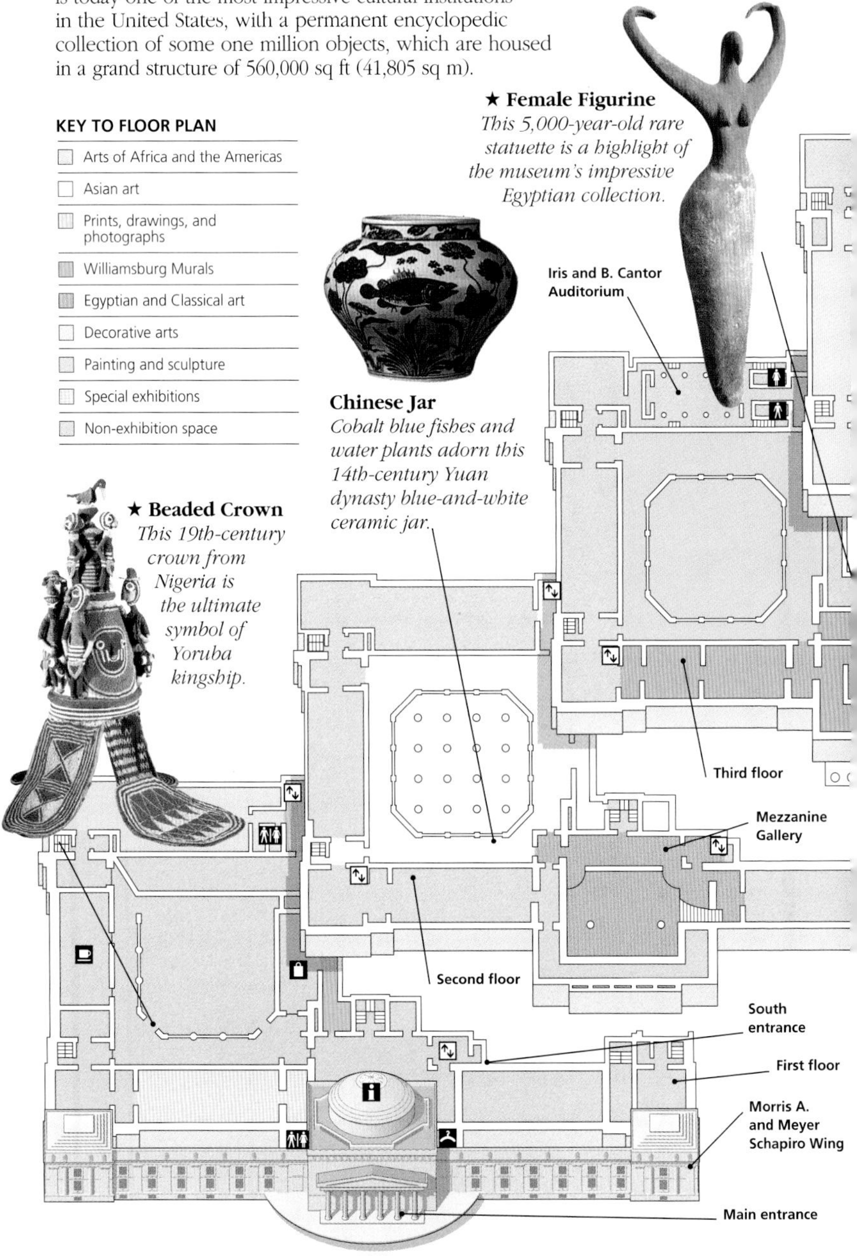

Third floor

Mezzanine
Gallery

Second floor

South
entrance

First floor

Morris A.
and Meyer
Schapiro Wing

Main entrance

★ An Out of Doors Study (1889)
*Sargent's portrait of French artist
Paul Helleu and his wife Alice was
painted during the couple's visit to
the Sargent family at Fladbury.*

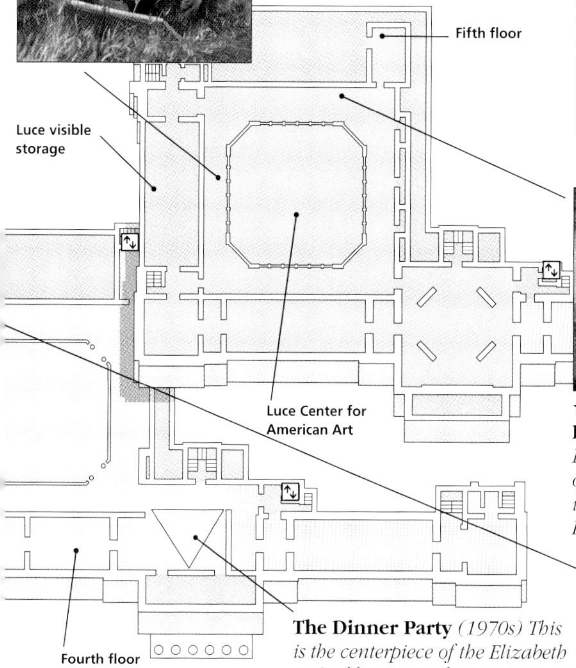

Fifth floor

Luce visible
storage

Luce Center for
American Art

Fourth floor

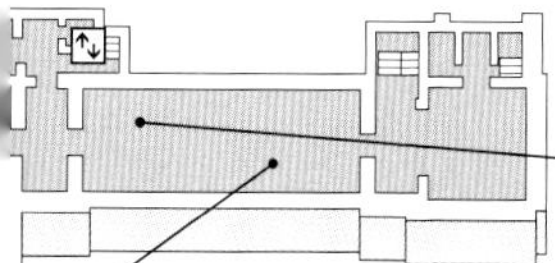

Alexander the Great
*The military leader was
portrayed in alabaster
in the 1st
century
BC.*

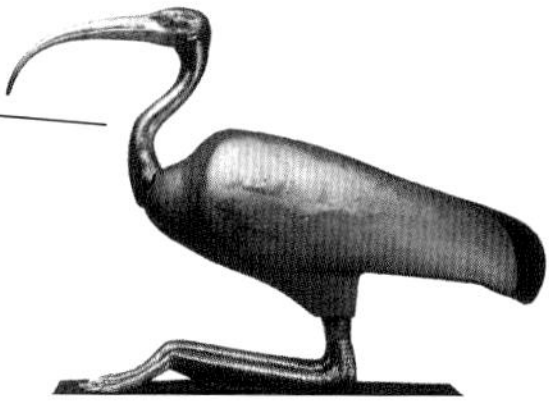

Ibis Coffin (332–330 BC)
*The sacred bird of ancient
Egypt merited a splendid
coffin of gold leaf and silver.*

The Dinner Party (1970s) *This
is the centerpiece of the Elizabeth
A. Sackler Center for Feminist Art.*

VISITORS' CHECKLIST

200 Eastern Pkwy, Brooklyn.
Tel (718) 638-5000. Ⓜ 2, 3 to
Eastern Parkway/Brooklyn
Museum. 🚌 B41, B45, B67,
B69. ◻ 11am–6pm Wed–Sun
(to 10pm Thu & Fri); 1st Sat of
each month: 11am–11pm (free).
● Jan 1, Thanksgiving, Dec 25.
Donation expected. 📷 🚻 🎧
🎫 🛍 🍴 **Concerts, lectures.**
www.brooklynmuseum.org

**★ Winter Scene in
Brooklyn** (1820)
*Francis Guy's depiction
of downtown Brooklyn
is from the American
Identities Collection.*

**Moorish Smoking
Room** (1865)
*This room is from a
house on West 54th
Street, bought by J. D.
Rockefeller in 1884.*

STAR EXHIBITS

★ An Out of Doors
   Study, by John
   Singer Sargent

★ Beaded Crown

★ Female Figurine

★ Winter Scene
   in Brooklyn,
   by Francis Guy

GALLERY GUIDE
*The collection is on five floors,
with African and New World
art on the first; prints,
drawings, and Asian art on the
second; Egyptian, Classical,
and European painting and
sculpture on the third; decorative art on the fourth; and
American art on the fifth.
There is special exhibition space
on the first and fourth floors.*

Exploring the Collection

The Brooklyn Museum houses one of the finest art collections in the United States. Its strengths include an outstanding collection of Native American art from the Southwest; American period rooms; exquisite pieces of ancient Egyptian and Islamic art; and important American and European paintings.

Seated Buddha torso in limestone, from India (late 3rd century AD)

ARTS OF AFRICA, THE PACIFIC, AND THE AMERICAS

The Brooklyn Museum set a precedent in the United States in 1923 by exhibiting African objects as works of art rather than as artifacts. Since then, the African art collection has grown steadily in both importance and size.

Exhibits include a rare intricately carved ivory gong from the Benin kingdom of 16th-century Nigeria, one of only five in existence.

The museum also has a notable collection of Native American work, including totem poles, textiles, and pottery. A 19th-century deer-skin shirt, once worn by a chief of the Blackfoot tribe, depicts his brave and daring exploits in battle.

Ancient American artistic traditions are represented by Peruvian textiles, Central American gold, and Mexican sculpture. A beautifully preserved tunic from Peru, dating from AD 600, is so tightly woven that its vibrant symbolic designs appear to have been painted onto the cloth rather than woven in the traditional manner.

The Oceanic collection includes sculpture from the Solomon Islands, Papua New Guinea, and New Zealand.

ASIAN ART

Changing exhibitions from the museum's permanent collection of Chinese, Japanese, Korean, Indian, Southeast Asian, and Islamic art are always on display. Japanese and Chinese paintings, Indian miniatures, and Islamic calligraphy complement the Asian sculpture, textiles, and ceramics. The collections of Japanese folk art, Chinese cloisonné (enamel work), and Oriental carpets are of particular note. Good examples of Buddhist art range from a variety of Chinese, Indian, and Southeast Asian Buddhas to a mandala-patterned temple banner from 14th-century Tibet, painted in rich, luminous watercolors.

Blackfoot tribe deerskin shirt, decorated with porcupine quills and glass beads (19th century)

DECORATIVE ARTS

The decorative arts collection reflects changes in domestic life and design from the 17th century to the present.

The Moorish Smoking Room, from John D. Rockefeller's brownstone house, embodies elegant New York living in the 1880s. There is also a 1928–30 Art Deco study from a Park Avenue apartment, including a walk-in bar that was hidden behind paneling during the Prohibition era *(see pp30–31)*.

More than 350 items from the museum's collection of silver, furniture, ceramics, and textiles are featured in the Luce Center for American Art. Although centered mostly on American art, the selection also includes pieces of Native American and Spanish colonial art.

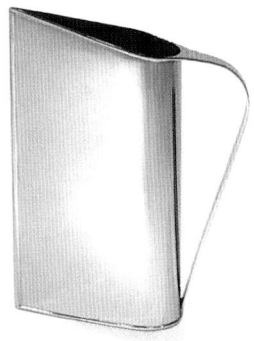

Normandie chrome pitcher, by Peter Müller-Munk (1935)

The Luce galleries are arranged thematically and explore crucial moments and ideas in American visual culture over the past 300 years. Among the collection are pieces by John Singer Sargent, Frank Lloyd Wright, and Georgia O'Keeffe.

EGYPTIAN, CLASSICAL, AND ANCIENT MIDDLE EASTERN ART

Recognized as among the world's finest, the Egyptian collection holds many masterpieces. It begins with an early female figure dating from 3500 BC, and encompasses sculptures, statues, tomb paintings, and reliefs as well as funerary paraphernalia. Of the latter, the most unusual is the coffin of an ibis, probably recovered from the vast animal cemetery of Tuna el-Gebel in Middle Egypt. The ibis was a sacred bird representing the god Thoth, and this coffin is made of solid silver and wood overlaid with gold leaf, with rock crystal for the bird's eyes. These galleries have been renovated into a state-of-the-art, high-tech installation.

Among the artifacts from the Greek and Roman civilizations are statuary, pottery, bronzes, jewelry, and mosaics.

Among the Ancient Near and Middle Eastern exhibits are an extensive collection of pottery and 12 alabaster reliefs from the Assyrian palace of King Ashurnasirpal II. These date from around 883–859 BC and depict the king fighting, overseeing his crops, and purifying the "sacred tree," a major icon in Assyrian religion.

PAINTING AND SCULPTURE

This section contains works from the 14th century to the present, including a well-known and outstanding 19th-century French art collection with works by Degas, Rodin, Monet, Cézanne, Matisse, and Pissarro. It also boasts one of the largest holdings of Spanish

Pierre de Wiessant (about 1886) by Auguste Rodin, from his *Burghers of Calais* group

Colonial paintings and one of the best collections of North American paintings to be found in the United States.

The museum's 20th-century American collection includes, appropriately, *Brooklyn Bridge* by Georgia O'Keeffe.

The Sculpture Garden holds architectural ornamentation taken from demolished New York buildings, including statues rescued from the original Penn Station, and a replica of the Statue of Liberty.

PRINTS, DRAWINGS, AND PHOTOGRAPHS

The museum has an important collection of prints, drawings, and photographs that are constantly rotated for conservation purposes. The range includes a rare woodcut print by Dürer entitled *The Great Triumphal Chariot* and works by Piranesi. The Impressionist and Post-Impressionist collection includes works by Toulouse-Lautrec and Mary Cassatt, the only American woman associated with the Impressionist movement. There are lithographs by James McNeill Whistler, Winslow

Rotherhithe, an etching by James McNeill Whistler (1860)

Homer engravings, and a superb selection of drawings by Fragonard, Paul Klee, Van Gogh, Picasso, and Gorky, among others, many of them in black and white.

The photography collection consists mainly of works by major 20th-century American photographers, including a 1924 portrait of Mary Pickford by Edward Steichen and work by Margaret Bourke-White, Berenice Abbott, and Robert Mapplethorpe.

Sandstone reliefs from Thebes in Egypt (around 760–656 BC), depicting the great god Amun-Re and his consort Mut

Staten Island

Apart from the famous ferry ride, Staten Island and its attractions are not well known to New Yorkers in general. Residents feel so ignored, in fact, that they've talked about seceding from the city. Visitors who venture beyond the ferry terminal, however, will be pleasantly surprised to find hills, lakes, and greenery, with expanses of open space, amazing harbor views, and well-preserved early New York buildings. One of the biggest surprises here is a cache of Tibetan art that is hidden away in a replica of a Buddhist temple.

Historic Richmond Town ㉔

441 Clarke Ave. **Tel** (718) 351-1611.
🚌 S74 from ferry. ☐ Sep–Jun:
1–5pm, Wed–Sun; Jul–Aug: 10am–
5pm Wed–Sat, 1–5pm Sun.
⬤ Jan 1, Easter Sun, Thanksgiving,
Dec 25. 🎟️ 📷 ♿ 🎬 🚻 🏪
www.historicrichmondtown.org

There are now 29 buildings, 14 of which are open to the public, in New York's only restored village and outdoor museum. The village was first named Coccles-town, after the local shellfish, but was soon corrupted to "Cuckoldstown," much to the annoyance of the

Cologne at the General Store

residents. By the end of the Revolutionary War the alternative name of Richmondtown had been adopted. It was the county seat until Staten Island was made part of the city in 1898, and has been preserved as an example of an early New York settlement.

The Voorlezer House, built in the Dutch era before 1696, is the oldest elementary

school to be found in the country. The Stephens General Store, which opened in 1837, doubled as the local post office. It has been well restored, right down to the contents of the shelves. The complex, set on 100 acres (40 ha), includes wagon sheds, a courthouse built in 1837, houses, several shops, and a tavern. There are also seasonal workshops where traditional rural crafts are demonstrated to visitors.

The Voorlezer House at Richmond Town

St. Andrew's Church, dating to 1708, and its old graveyard are just across the Mill Pond stream, and the Historical Society Museum is in the County Clerk's and Surrogate's Office. The toy room is a delight.

Jacques Marchais Museum of Tibetan Art ㉕

338 Lighthouse Ave. **Tel** (718) 987-3500. 🚌 S74 from ferry. ☐ 1–5pm
Wed–Sun. ⬤ public hols. 🎟️ 📷 🎬
🎬 **www**.tibetanmuseum.org

A hilltop provides a tranquil setting for one of the largest collections of privately owned Tibetan art of the 15th to the 20th centuries outside Tibet. The main building is a replica of a mountain monastery with an authentic altar in three

Sacred sculpture at the Jacques Marchais Center of Tibetan Art

tiers, crowded with gold, silver, and bronze figures.

The second building is used as a library. The soothing garden has some stone sculptures, including life-size Buddhas. The museum was built in 1947 by Mrs. Jacques Marchais, a dealer in Asian art. The Dalai Lama paid his first visit here in 1991.

A gazebo at the Snug Harbor Cultural Center

Snug Harbor Cultural Center ㉖

1000 Richmond Terrace.
Tel (718) 448-2500. 🚌 S40 from ferry to Snug Harbor Gate.
Grounds ☐ dawn–dusk daily.
Art Gallery ☐ 10am–5pm Tue–Sun.
🎟️ donation. **Children's Museum**
☐ noon–5pm (summer 11am–5pm)
Tue–Sun. ⬤ Jan 1, Thanksgiving,
Dec 25. ♿ limited. 🎬 🏪
www.snug-harbor.org

Founded in 1801 as a haven for aged sailors, Snug Harbor is now an arts center, with a complex of 28 buildings in various stages of restoration. There are five stately Greek Revival gems dating from 1831 to 1880, the finest such collection in the US. The oldest, the Main Hall, is the

Visitors' Center. This leads through to the **Newhouse Center for Contemporary Art**, but the ships in the stained-glass windows are a reminder of its origins. Other buildings house the award-winning **Staten Island Children's Museum** and Veterans Memorial Hall, used for indoor performances. A sculpture festival and summer shows are held on the lawns. The Staten Island Botanical Garden has a noted orchid collection and a beautiful rose garden.

Snug Harbor is the legacy of a Scottish sailor, Robert Richard Randall, who became rich in the Revolutionary War and bequeathed this property to be used by seamen, enabling them to enjoy its harbor views.

Clear Comfort, Alice Austen's lifetime residence

Alice Austen House ㉗

2 Hylan Blvd. **Tel** (718) 816-4506.
🚌 S 51 from ferry to Hylan Blvd.
🕐 noon–5pm Thu–Sun; grounds: to dusk. 🌙 Jan, Feb, public hols.
📷 **Donation** 📷 ♿ limited. 📷
🌐 www.aliceausten.org

This small cottage built around 1690 has the delightful name of Clear Comfort. It was the home of the photographer

Alice Austen, who was born in 1866 and who lived in this house for most of her life. She documented life on the island, in Manhattan, and also on trips to other parts of the country and on her travels to Europe. She lost all her money in the stock market crash of 1929, and her poverty forced her into a public poorhouse at the age of 84. One year later, her photographic talent was finally recognized by *Life* magazine, which published an article about her, earning her enough money to enter a nursing home. She left 3,500 negatives dating from 1880 to 1930. Today, the Friends of Alice Austen House mounts exhibitions of her best work.

Even Farther Afield

The village of Broad Channel at Jamaica Bay

Jamaica Bay Wildlife Refuge Center ㉘

Cross Bay Blvd at Broad Channel. **Tel** (718) 318-4340. 🚇 Broad Channel (A). 🕐 sunrise to sunset; visitor center: 8:30am–5pm daily. 🌙 seasonal (call ahead) www.nps.gov/gate

The marshes and uplands of the Refuge cover an area almost the size of Manhattan. Over 300 species of birds live here either seasonally or all year round. On the main Atlantic migratory path, the Refuge is at its best in spring and autumn, when the skies are filled with skeins of geese and ducks. The park rangers lead hikes and nature walks for weekend visitors – wear

suitable shoes and clothes, and take along a zoom-lens camera or binoculars to get the best from your visit. The only village is Broad Channel, a small collection of houses on pilings on the Cross Bay Boulevard. The Refuge and a 10-mile (16-km) stretch of beach and boardwalk at Rockaway, are accessible by subway from Manhattan.

Jones Beach State Park ㉙

Beaches. 🕐 all year. 📷 late May–Labor Day. **Tel** (516) 785-1600. www.nysparks.state.ny.us/parks 📷 Long Island Railroad: Penn Station to Jones Beach; train schedule (late May–Labor Day); (718) 217-5477. **Jones Beach Theater**; (516) 221-1000. ♿ www.jonesbeach.com

Jones Beach was the creation of Robert Moses, New York's Parks' Commissioner *(see p246)*, who transformed this narrow spit of land into Long Island's most accessible and popular beach in 1929. There

are sand dunes, surf on the Atlantic side, and sheltered water in the bay. There is also miniature golf, swimming pools, restaurants, and the **Jones Beach Theater**, which hosts concerts in the summer.

Robert Moses State Park is on the next island to the east, Fire Island, which is over 30 miles (48 km) long, yet less than 900 yds (800 m) across. Areas of the island are totally unspoiled, with long stretches of white sands, making it a great place for walking and bicycling in peaceful surroundings. Fire Island also has one of the few remaining forests on the Eastern Seaboard.

Fire Island's communities are small and varied. Some are favored by singles looking for the company of the opposite sex, others are sedate and family-orientated, and still others are favorites with New York's large gay community.

Sunbathers basking at Jones Beach

SEVEN GUIDED WALKS

alking in New York is an excellent way to discover the human scale of the city. The following 16 pages explore the unique character and charm of New York through seven thematic walks. These range from an exploration of Greenwich Village and SoHo's literary and artistic connections *(see pp260–61)* to a trip across the Brooklyn Bridge for spectacular views and a glimpse of 19th-century New York *(see pp266–7)*.

In addition, each of the 15 areas of Manhattan described in the *Area by Area* section of this book has a

Sculpture outside US Custom House, Lower Manhattan

short walk on its *Street-by-Street* map, taking you past many of the interesting sights in that area.

Various organizations run walking tours of the city. These range from serious appraisals of architectural history to a guide to the ghosts of Broadway. Details of tour organizers are listed on page 387. Although New York's crime rate has dropped to a record low, as in any major city take extra care of your personal belongings while walking *(see p372–3)*. Plan your route ahead and walk only during daylight hours.

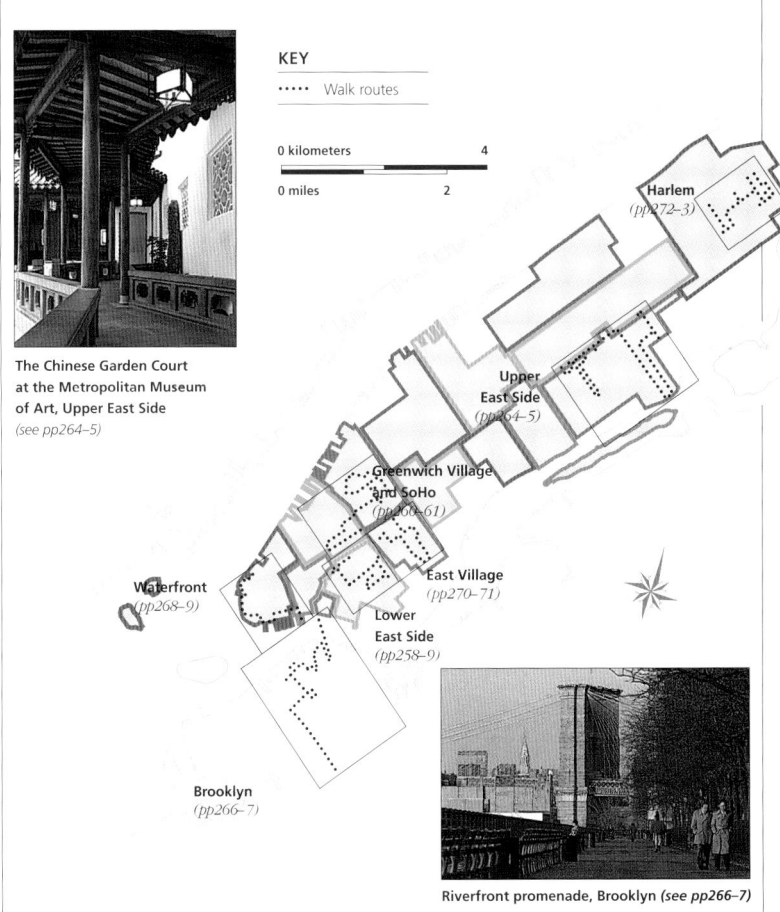

The Chinese Garden Court at the Metropolitan Museum of Art, Upper East Side *(see pp264–5)*

KEY

····· Walk routes

0 kilometers 4

0 miles 2

Harlem *(pp272–3)*

Upper East Side *(pp264–5)*

Greenwich Village and SoHo *(pp260–61)*

Waterfront *(pp268–9)*

East Village *(pp270–71)*

Lower East Side *(pp258–9)*

Brooklyn *(pp266–7)*

Riverfront promenade, Brooklyn *(see pp266–7)*

◁ **Relaxing on Grove Street, Greenwich Village** *(see pp260–61)*

A 90-Minute Walk in the Lower East Side

This walk is through old immigrant neighborhoods that have given New York its unique flavor, and illustrates the ever-changing texture of the city as neighborhoods are rediscovered and one set of newcomers replaces another. Along the way you can experience a variety of cultures and cuisines. Sunday is the best day for local color. See more about Lower East Side on pages 92–101.

The Lower East Side

Begin on East Houston Street, the border between the Lower East Side (LES) and the East Village, where some of the best traditional Jewish cuisine can be found at Yonah Schimmel Knish Bakery [1] (137). In the same location since 1920, Russ & Daughters, [2] (179) is run by the great-grandson of the founder and famed for smoked fish and caviar. Katz's Delicatessen [3] (205) has been a fixture for over 100 years. Continue to Norfolk Street and turn right to see the Angel Orensanz Center [4] (172), housed in New York's oldest synagogue building.

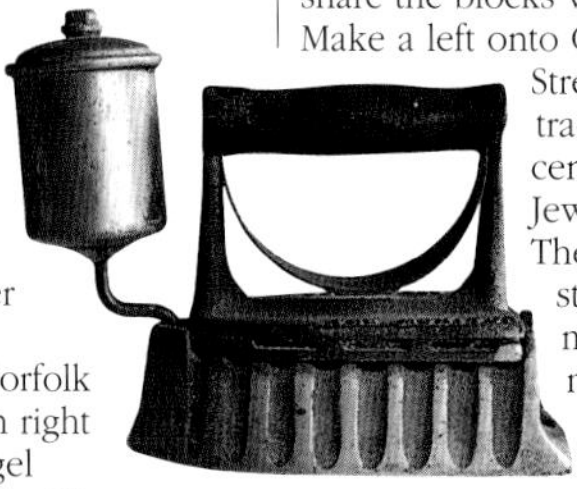

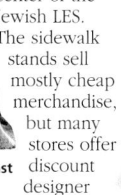

An 1885 iron from the Lower East Side Tenement Museum [6]

TIPS FOR WALKERS

Starting point: *East Houston St.*
Length*: 2 miles (3.2 km).*
Getting there: *Take the subway F or V to Second Avenue; exit East Houston at Eldridge. Other stops: F to Delancey; J, M, Z to Essex. The M15 bus stops on East Houston and on the corner of Delancey and Allen Streets; M14A and M9 run along Essex Street. Returning from Chinatown-Little Italy, Canal Street station is served by the J, N, Q, R, and 6 trains.*
Stopping-off points: *Little Italy's cafés are perfect for coffee and cakes. For more substantial fare, Sweet-n-Tart at 20 Mott Street is good for Chinese food, or for Italian on Mulberry Street, Il Cortile (125) or Il Palazzo (151). Il Laboratorio del Gelato, at 188 Ludlow Street, is a popular spot in summer, offering dozens of flavors of ice cream and sorbet.*

Turn right on Rivington Street for the Shaarai Shomoyim First Romanian-American Congregation [5] (89), a synagogue in a handsome 1890 brick building.

The LES has been discovered by hip young New Yorkers and is now home to cutting-edge boutiques, trendy clubs, and restaurants. On Rivington Street, cool fashion shops share the blocks with the old. Make a left onto Orchard Street, the traditional center of the Jewish LES. The sidewalk stands sell mostly cheap merchandise, but many stores offer discount designer leather and fashion. All are closed on Saturday, so Sunday is the busiest day.

A must stop for historians is the Lower East Side Tenement Museum [6] (108). An original tenement has been restored to show how three immigrant families lived from 1874 to the 1930s.

Take a short detour to the right down Broome Street for another unique survivor, the Kehila Kedosha Janina Synagogue and Museum [7] (280), a small but fascinating congregation with a little up-stairs museum.

Return to Orchard Street, continuing along to the right. A left at Grand Street will bring you into New York's former "pickle district" on Essex. Step into The Pickle Guys store [8] (49), where you can sample sour, half-sour, and hot pickles.

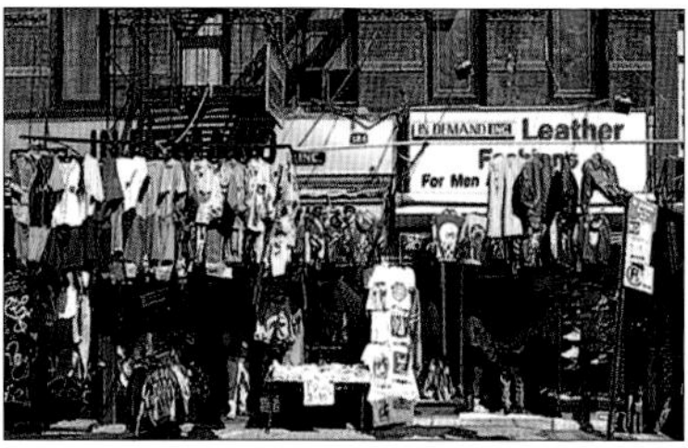

Clothes vendors at Orchard Street market

Head back along Grand Street, taking a left on Eldridge Street, which will take you, beyond Canal Street, to the grand Eldridge Street Synagogue [9] (12), the first Eastern European synagogue in New York, which also houses a museum on the Jewish community.

KEY

••• Walk route

✳ Good viewing point

[M] Subway station

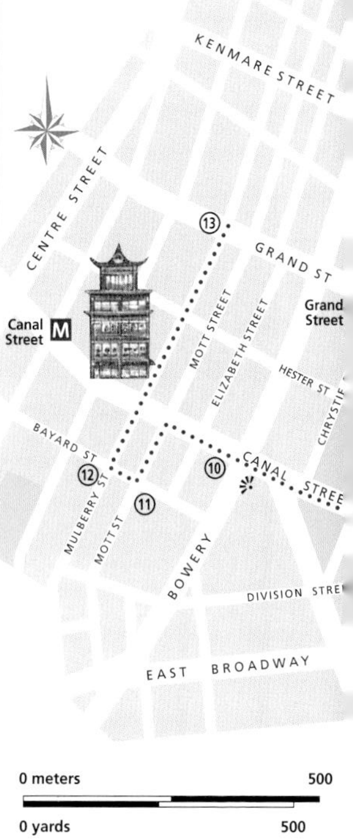

Russ & Daughters ②

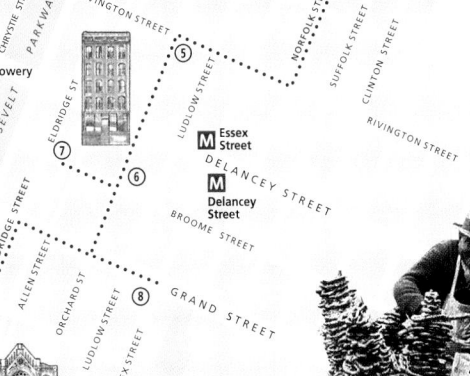

Bowery

East Broadway

Kam Man Food Products at
200 Canal Street

Chinatown

Turn around and return to Canal Street, pausing to admire the spire of the Chrysler Building and the city skyline in view in the distance from Eldridge. Turn left and cross the Bowery, where many jewelry shops are found, remnants of the city's original Diamond District ⑩ (1). As you continue, the shops give way to stalls selling an exotic array of vegetables, and butcher shops with rows of roast ducks in the windows. At 200 Canal Street is Kam Man Food Products. One of the largest Chinese markets in the area, it is a fascinating place to

Pretzel seller on Orchard Street

explore. Turn left from Canal to Mott Street, and you'll know you are right in the heart of Chinatown by all the Chinese neon signs. There are hundreds of restaurants here, from holes-in-the-wall to haute cuisine, all offering a chance to taste unusual fare. For spiritual sustenance. visit the Eastern States Buddhist Temple ⑪ in Mott Street (64b).

At Bayard Street, stop for an ice cream at the Chinatown Ice Cream Factory (65), which

offers decidedly unusual flavors such as black sesame, taro, and zen butter, as well as traditional ones. While still on Bayard, have a look at all the Chinese political posters and messages on the Wall of Democracy, then turn back and walk to Mulberry Street. The curve next to Columbus Park was Mulberry Bend ⑫, once notorious for gang murders and mayhem.

An Italian deli in Little Italy ⑬

Little Italy

Walk up Mulberry Street toward Grand Street, and you are suddenly in Little Italy ⑬. Small in area though it is, and encroached on by Chinatown, this is a colorful few blocks of Old-World restaurants, coffee shops, and stores selling home-made pasta, sausages, breads, and pastries. The Italian population has dwindled over the years, but a staunch group of merchants remain, determined to retain the area's Italian atmosphere. Their stronghold is Mulberry Street, between Broome and Canal streets, with a few shops holding their own on Grand Street near Mulberry. If you continue to walk on Grand, however, you are quickly back into Chinatown.

The big event of the year is the Feast of San Gennaro, named for the patron saint of Naples. For 11 nights in September, Mulberry Street is jammed with locals and visitors enjoying the parades and the Italian food, with rows of sizzling sausages stalls.

A 90-Minute Walk in Greenwich Village and SoHo

A stroll through the patchwork quilt of streets in Greenwich Village takes you to where New York's best-known writers and artists have lived, worked, and played. It ends with a tour of SoHo's galleries and museums, where established artists show their work. For more details on sights in Greenwich Village, see pages 108–15, and for SoHo sights, *see pages 102–07.*

Facade in Washington Mews ⑬

Author Mark Twain, who lived on 10th Street

West 10th Street

The junction of 8th Street and 6th Avenue ① has many book, music, and clothing stores nearby. Walk up Sixth to West Ninth Street to see (on the left at 425) Jefferson Market Courthouse ②.

Turn right at West 10th Street ③ to the Alexander Onassis Center for Hellenic Studies (58). A passageway at the front once led up to the Tile Club, a gathering place for the artists of the Tenth Street Studio, where Augustus Saint-Gaudens, John LaFarge, and Winslow Homer lived. Mark Twain lived at 24 West 10th Street, and Edward Albee at 50 West 10th.

Back across Sixth Avenue is Milligan Place ④, with 19th-century houses, and Patchin Place ⑤, where the poets E. E. Cummings and John Masefield both lived. Farther on is the site of the Ninth Circle bar ⑥ which when it opened in 1898 was known as "Regnaneschi's." It was the subject of John Sloan's painting *Regnaneschi's Saturday Night.* Playwright Edward Albee first saw the question "Who's afraid of Virginia Woolf?" scrawled on a mirror here.

TIPS FOR WALKERS

Starting point: *8th St/6th Ave.*
Length: *2 miles (3.2 km).*
Getting there: *Take subway train A, B, C, D, E, or F to West 4th Street-Washington Square station (8th Street exit). Fifth Avenue buses M2 and M3 stop at 8th Street. From here, walk one block west to 6th. The M5 bus loops near Washington Square along 8th Street and up Sixth Avenue.*
Stopping-off points: *The Pink Tea Cup, 88 Seventh Ave South, is good for lunch. Fanelli's Café, 94 Prince Street, has been serving customers since 1847 and was once a speakeasy.*

The unusual exterior of Twin Peaks ⑨

Greenwich Village

Turn left at Waverly Place past the Three Lives Bookstore (154 West 10th St), a typical literary gathering spot, to Christopher Street and the Northern Dispensary ⑦.

Follow Grove Street along Christopher Park to Sheridan Square, the busy hub of the Village. The Circle Repertory Theater ⑧, which premiered plays by Pulitzer Prizewinner Lanford Wilson, is now closed.

Cross Seventh Avenue and bear left on to Grove Street. At the corner of Bedford Street, you can't miss "Twin Peaks" ⑨ (102 Bedford), a home for artists in the 1920s. Turn back around to look at the northeast corner of Bedford and Grove streets ⑩: the exterior of this edifice had a recurring role in the TV sitcom *Friends* as the characters' apartment building. 75½ Bedford is the narrowest house in the Village, and was once the home of feminist poet Edna St. Vincent Millay.

Walk up Carmine to Sixth Avenue and turn right at Waverly Place. At 116 Waverly ⑪, Anne Charlotte Lynch, an English teacher, held weekly gatherings in her town house for such eminent friends as Herman Melville and Edgar Allan Poe, who gave his first reading of *The Raven* here.

A detour left of just half a block will bring you to MacDougal Alley ⑫, a lane of carriage houses in which Gertrude Vanderbilt Whitney had her studio. She opened the first Whitney Museum here in 1932, just behind the studio.

Washington Square

Back on MacDougal, turn left to Washington Square North, to see the finest Greek Revival houses in the United States. Built of red brick, they have marble balustrades and entrances flanked by columns. Writer Henry James set his *Washington Square* in No. 18, his grandmother's home.

Washington Square Park and Arch

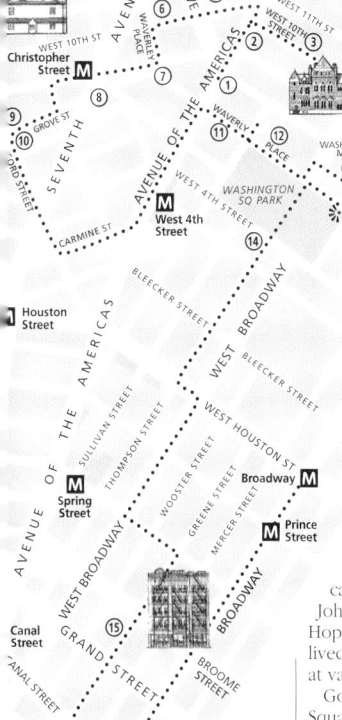

Pause at Fifth Avenue to look back at Washington Square Park, with its famous Washington Square Arch. Go across to Two Fifth Avenue; opposite is Washington Mews ⑬, an elegant carriage house complex. John Dos Passos, Edward Hopper, and Rockwell Kent lived in the studio at No. 14a at various times.

Go back up Washington Square North, past some elegant houses. Writer Edith Wharton lived at 7 Washington Square North. Now walk beneath the arch and across Washington Square Park. On the left as you leave the park, is the fine Judson Memorial Church and Tower ⑭ by Stanford White and the NYU Loeb Student Center. The Center was once a boarding house, known as the "house of genius," and is where Theodore Dreiser wrote *An American Tragedy*.

SoHo

Walk south on Thompson, a typical Village street lined with bars, cafés, and shops. Turn left at Houston, SoHo's northern limit, and right on West Broadway, lined with some of the city's most famous galleries along with a large number of chic and arty boutiques.

Turn left at Spring Street for yet more tempting shops, then right at Greene Street ⑮, which is the heart of the Cast-Iron Historic District. Many of these fine buildings now house art galleries.

Turn left at the end of Greene Street to Canal Street, the end of SoHo, to see how quickly the atmosphere of New York can change. This noisy street is full of hawkers and discount electronics stores. You can explore bargains for the next two blocks and then turn left up Broadway. Keen shoppers can turn right on Spring Street and head for the NoLita district, featuring clothes by trendy, aspiring designers.

Cast-iron facade, Greene Street ⑮

| 0 meters | 500 |
| 0 yards | 500 |

KEY

• • • Walk route

☀ Good viewing point

Ⓜ Subway station

Entrance to subway station in wintertime, near Bryant Park ▷

A Two-Hour Walk in the Upper East Side

A promenade along upper Fifth Avenue and its environs will take you past the best remaining examples of New York's turn-of-the-century gilded age. A detour through the old German district of Yorkville leads to a riverside stroll to Gracie Mansion, official residence of the city's mayor, dating from 1799. For details on Upper East Side sights, *see pages 182–203*.

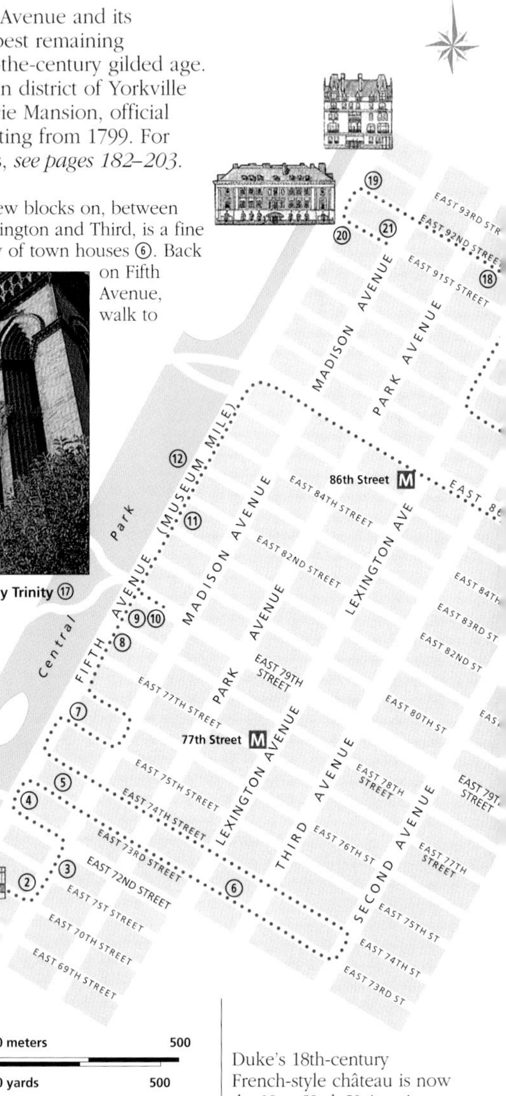

From the Frick to the Met

Begin at the Frick mansion ①, built in 1913–14 for coal magnate Henry Clay Frick and home to an exquisite art collection *(pp202–3)*. Many such mansions were built as New York's first families outdid each other with miniature Versailles châteaux and Venetian palazzos. Most of those still standing have now become either institutions or museums. The apartment building opposite the Frick is typical of those where today's affluent New Yorkers live.

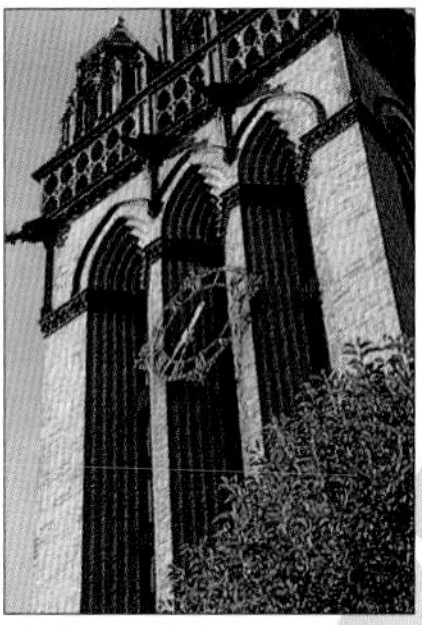

Church of the Holy Trinity ⑰

East on 70th are two of the city's top art galleries, Knoedler & Co (19) and Hirschl & Adler ② (21). Walk up Madison to the corner of 72nd Street, to the big Polo-Ralph Lauren store ③, the 1898 French Renaissance home of Gertrude Rhinelander Waldo. Wander inside to see the elegant restored interior.

Walk back toward Fifth on the north side of 72nd, past two limestone beauties that once housed the Lycée Français de New York ④. Continue along Fifth Avenue to 73rd Street. Turn east to 11, Joseph Pulitzer's former home ⑤.

A few blocks on, between Lexington and Third, is a fine row of town houses ⑥. Back on Fifth Avenue, walk to 75th Street, to see No. 1, the former residence of Edward S. Harkness, son of a founder of Standard Oil. It is now the Commonwealth Fund ⑦. At 1 East 78th, the tobacco millionaire James B. Duke's 18th-century French-style château is now the New York University Institute of Fine Arts ⑧.

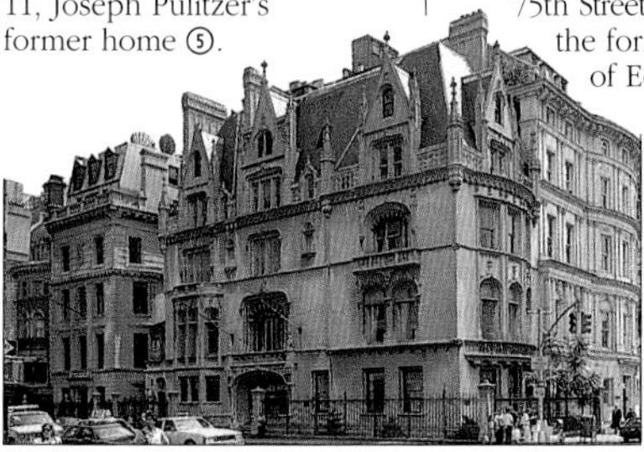

Ukrainian Institute of America ⑩

At 79th Street and Fifth, the former home of financier Payne Whitney, is the French Embassy ⑨, and 2 East 79th is the Ukrainian Institute of America ⑩. On the southeast corner of 82nd Street is Duke-Semans House ⑪, one of the few grand Fifth Avenue residences that are still privately owned. Save another full day for The Metropolitan Museum of Art ⑫ at 82nd.

Carl Schurz Park Promenade

TIPS FOR WALKERS

Starting point: *Frick Collection.*
Length: *3 miles (4.8 km).*
Getting there: *Take subway train 6 to 68th Street and Lexington, then walk west (left) three blocks to Fifth Avenue. Or take the M1, M2, M3, or M4 bus up Madison Avenue to 70th Street and walk one block west.*
Stopping-off points: *Try the cafés at the Whitney and Guggenheim museums. Head to Café Sabarsky at the Neue Galerie (5th Ave/ 86th St) for Austrian food, or try the Heidelberg Café (2nd Ave off 86th St) for authentic Bavarian. Madison Avenue between 92nd and 93rd has many places to eat, including Sarabeth's Kitchen, with its excellent weekend brunch.*

Yorkville

Turn east on 86th Street for what is left of German Yorkville – Bremen House ⑬, cross Second Avenue, then turn right to the Heidelberg Café and German deli Schaller & Weber ⑭ for a break, or try Papaya King's hot dogs (179 East 86th Street).

East River and Gracie Mansion

Henderson Place ⑮ at East End Avenue is a cluster of 24 Queen Anne town houses. Carl Schurz Park opposite was named for the city's most prominent German immigrant, editor of *Harper's Weekly* and the *New York Post*. The park promenade atop East River Drive leads to a view of Hell Gate, where the Harlem River, Long Island Sound, and New York harbor meet. From the walkway you can see the back of Gracie Mansion ⑯, the mayor's official residence. Walk west on 88th Street past the Church of the Holy Trinity ⑰ and at Lexington Avenue go to 92nd Street and west past two of the few wooden houses left in Manhattan ⑱.

The Cooper-Hewitt Museum ⑳

Carnegie Hill

Back on Fifth Avenue, turn downtown past the Felix Warburg Mansion of 1908, now the Jewish Museum ⑲, and continue to 91st Street and the huge Andrew Carnegie home, now the Cooper-Hewitt Museum ⑳. Built in 1902 in the style of an English country manor, it gave the area the unofficial name of Carnegie Hill. The James Burden House ㉑ at 7 East 91st Street, built for Vanderbilt heiress Adele Sloan in 1905, has a spiral staircase under a stained-glass skylight that was known in society as "the stairway to heaven." At 1 East 91st, the financier Otto Kahn's Italian Renaissance-style residence was a show-place with a drive-through porch and interior courtyard. It is now the Convent of the Sacred Heart School.

Wooden houses on 92nd Street ⑱

A Three-Hour Walk in Brooklyn

A trip across New York's most famous crossing leads to Brooklyn Heights, the city's first suburb. This neighborhood has a 19th-century feel, mixed with a hint of Middle Eastern cultures. The riverfront promenade has unrivaled views of Manhattan. For more details on sights in Brooklyn, *see pages 247–53.*

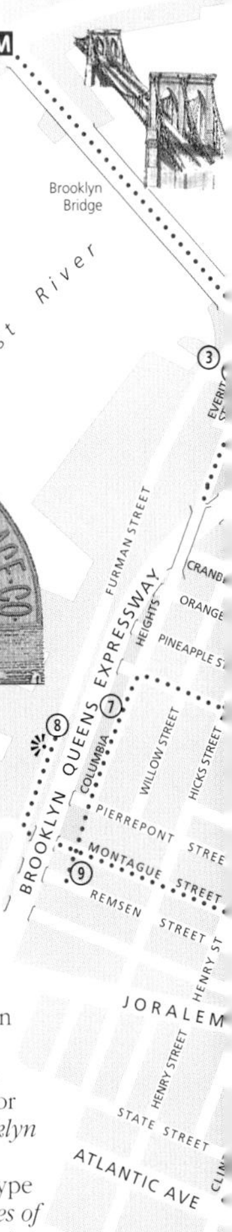

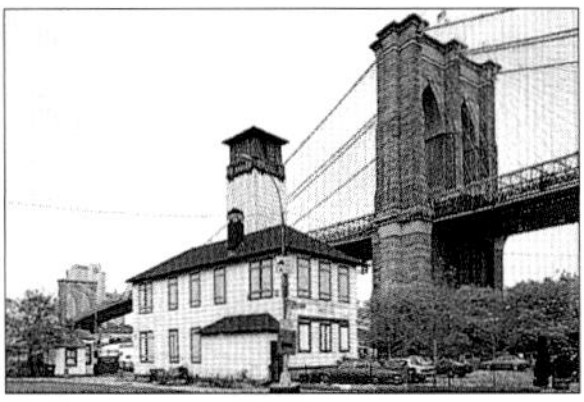

Fire Station on Old Fulton Street

Fulton Ferry Landing

About 3,580 ft (1 km) long, the Brooklyn Bridge span yields thrilling views of the lower New York skyline and prize photo opportunities. Take a taxi, or if you have time, walk across to Brooklyn.

On the far side, follow the Tillary Street sign to the right, turn right at the bottom of the stairs, then take the first path through the park and walk down Cadman Plaza West ① under the Brooklyn-Queens Expressway; here Cadman becomes Old Fulton Street. You can see the bridge on the right as you head to the river at Water Street and the Fulton Ferry landing ②. During the Revolutionary War, George Washington's troops fled to Manhattan from here. In 1814, this was the depot for the ferry connecting Brooklyn and Manhattan Island. This transformed Brooklyn Heights from a predominantly farming area to a residential district. The area is full of character and is still a very popular place to live. To the right is the River Café ③. This restaurant's fine cuisine and spectacular views of the Manhattan skyline make it one of New York's most exceptional dining spots. Double back past the former Eagle Warehouse ④ of 1893.

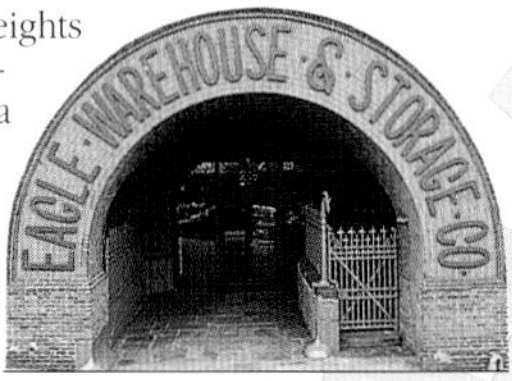

Eagle Warehouse ④

Brooklyn Heights

From the landing, turn right to steep Everitt Street up Columbia Heights, on to Middagh Street, and along the streets of Brooklyn Heights. 24 Middagh ⑤ is one of the oldest, built in 1824.

Next turn right on Willow and left on Cranberry; here the town houses range from wooden clapboards to brick Federal-style to brownstones. Except for cars and a few modern buildings, you could be in the 19th century.

Many famous people have lived here. Truman Capote wrote *Breakfast at Tiffany's* and *In Cold Blood* in the basement of 70 Willow, and Arthur Miller once owned 155 Willow. Walt Whitman lived on Cranberry Street when he was editor of the *Brooklyn Eagle*. He set the type for his *Leaves of Grass* at a print shop near the corner of Cranberry and Fulton. The town houses now on the site are called Whitman Close.

Turn right along Hicks. The Hicks family, local farmers, inspired the name "hick" for a yokel. Turn left on Orange Street to the Plymouth Church ⑥, home of Henry Ward Beecher, an antislavery preacher. His sister, Harriet

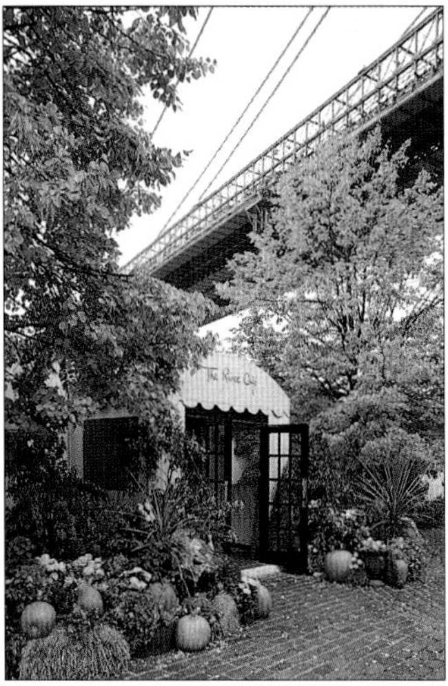

Entrance to the River Café ③

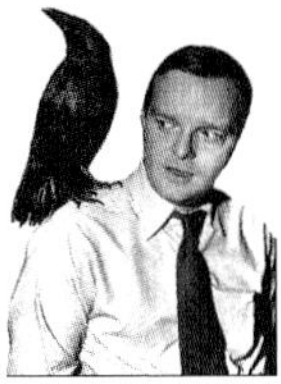

Truman Capote with feathered friend

Beecher Stowe, wrote *Uncle Tom's Cabin*. Meander along Henry and Pineapple streets. At Clark Street are marquees of once-luxurious hotels, such as the Towers. Follow Clark Street to 142 Columbia Heights, where Norman Mailer lived ⑦. Washington Roebling, architect of the Brooklyn Bridge, lived at 110.

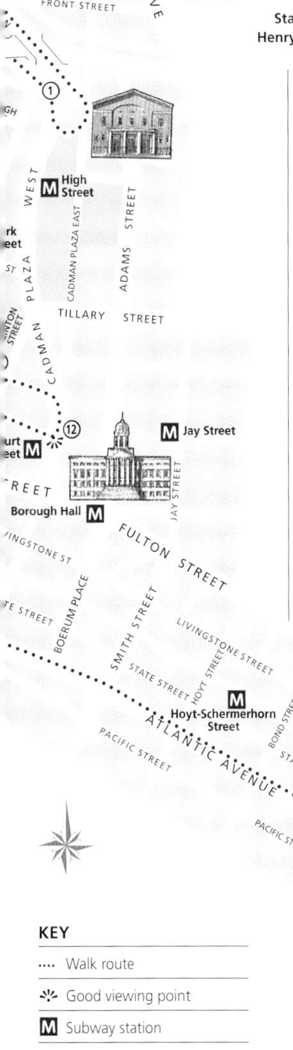

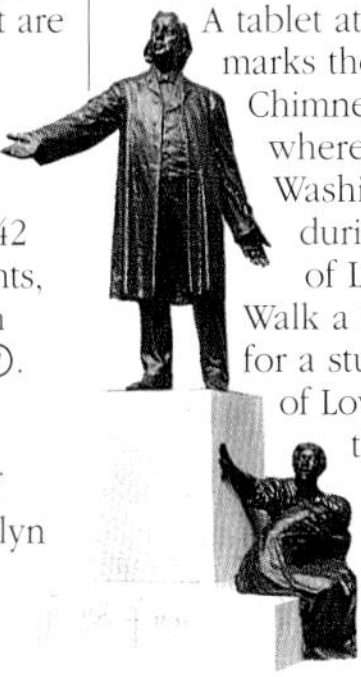

Statue of preacher Henry Ward Beecher ⑥

The Promenade

At Montague, turn onto the riverfront Promenade ⑧. A tablet at the entrance marks the site of Four Chimneys, the house where George Washington lived during the Battle of Long Island. Walk a little farther for a stunning view of Lower Manhattan that will make you catch your breath in awe. Savor this scene, then turn inland again, on Montague. Here, make a quick detour right to 1 Montague Terrace ⑨ where the English poet W. H. Auden lived. Thomas Wolfe finished *Of Time and the River* while he was living at 5 Montague.

TIPS FOR WALKERS

Starting point: *Brooklyn Bridge.*
Length: *3½ miles (5.5 km).*
Getting there: *Take subway train 4, 5, or 6 on the Lexington Ave line to Brooklyn Bridge-City Hall (nearest stop to the bridge). The M15 Second Ave bus also stops at City Hall. Returning to Manhattan, take train 2, 3, 4, 5, M, N, or R from Borough Hall; or 2, 3, 4, 5, M, N, R, or Q from Atlantic Ave.*
Stopping-off points: *Teresa's, 80 Montague St, has Polish dishes at reasonable prices. Try Henry's End, 44 Henry St, for fine dining in Brooklyn Heights; Mile End, 97A Hoyt St, for deli favorites; or Iris Café, 20 Columbia Place, for light meals.*

The old Montague Street trolley, which led to the river and the ferry

Montague and Clinton Streets

Once back on Montague Street, walk to the heart of Brooklyn Heights, with all its cafés and boutiques. The baseball team, the Brooklyn Dodgers, got their name from dodging the trolley cars that once ran down the street. Walk to the intersection of Montague and Clinton to see the stained glass of the 1834 Church of St. Ann and the Holy Trinity ⑩. Walk a block left on Clinton to Pierrepont Street for the Brooklyn Historical Society ⑪. A block farther, at Court Street, is the 1849 Borough Hall ⑫, and the subway taking you back to Manhattan.

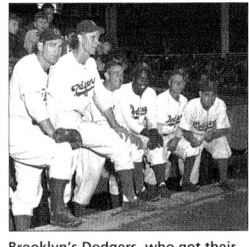

Brooklyn's Dodgers, who got their name from dodging trolley cars

Atlantic Avenue

Another option is to stay on Clinton Street and walk the five short blocks to Atlantic Avenue. A left turn here leads to a whole string of Middle Eastern emporia, such as Sahadi Imports ⑬ at 187 Atlantic Avenue, which stocks a huge selection of foods. The Damascus Bakery at 195 makes the most delicious filo pastries. Various other shops here sell Arabic books, tapes, DVDs, and CDs.

At Flatbush Avenue, look left to the Brooklyn Academy of Music ⑭ and the grand front of the Williamsburg Savings Bank. Watch for signs to the subway for your journey back to Manhattan.

KEY

···· Walk route

⁎⁎ Good viewing point

Ⓜ Subway station

0 meters 500

0 yards 500

A 90-Minute Waterfront Walk

From the breezy Battery Park City Esplanade with its sweeping river views and upscale condos to the magnificent schooners moored at South Street Seaport, this waterfront amble introduces you to New York's formidable maritime legacy. The concrete jungle may lie just a few blocks inland, yet it seems worlds away, as the bleating horns and hiss of the crosstown buses are blessedly muffled. Stroll the green tip of Battery Park for a startling reminder that Manhattan is, in fact, an island. For more details on sights in Lower Manhattan, *see pp64–79.*

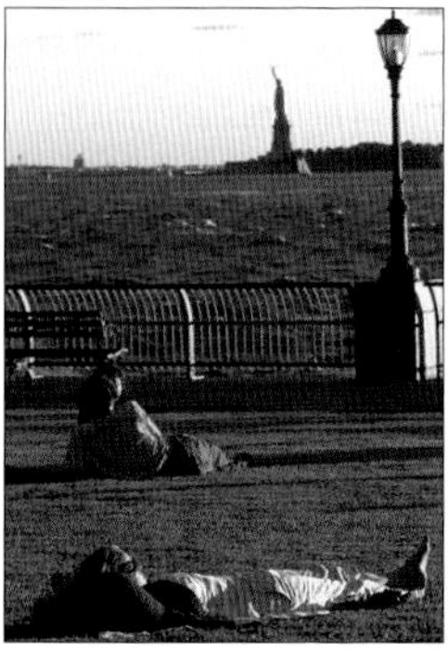

View of the Statue of Liberty from the waterfront promenade

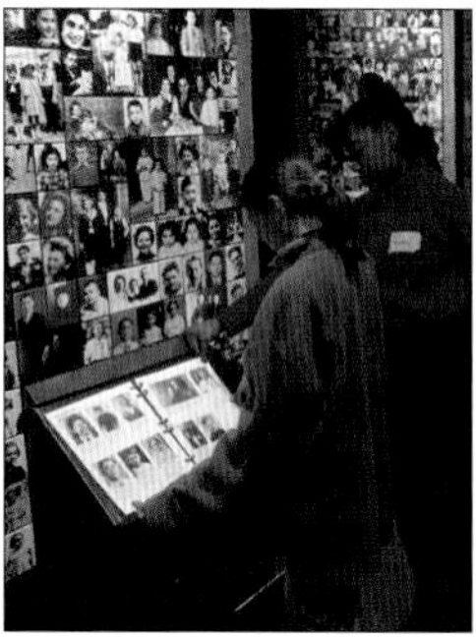

The many photographs at the Museum of Jewish Heritage ⑤

Battery Park City

Begin your walk on the Esplanade ① near Rector Place Park, west of the Rector Street subway stop. Across the Hudson River looms the New Jersey skyline. Stroll toward the South Cove ②, where you'll catch sight, as did more than 100 million immigrants on their arrival, of Lady Liberty herself. Explore Robert F. Wagner, Jr. Park ③, named after a former New York City mayor. The leafy acres of grassy slopes, linden trees, and inviting pavilions are an important link in Lower Manhattan's waterfront "greenbelt". Climb to the Wagner Park lookout point ④ for vistas of the Hudson River. Here, information panels chronicle New York City's seafaring history, when grand schooners and coastal packets plied these waters.

Battery Place

On Battery Place, visit the Museum of Jewish Heritage ⑤ *(see p77)* and its outdoor Garden of Stones, a calm, elegant space of dwarf oak saplings growing out of boulders. Since Manhattan is the undisputed king of tall buildings, pay homage at the sleek Skyscraper Museum ⑥, a marvel in stainless steel. Admire skyscraper history and contemporary designs from around the world, as well as the original model, created in 1971, of the former World Trade Center.

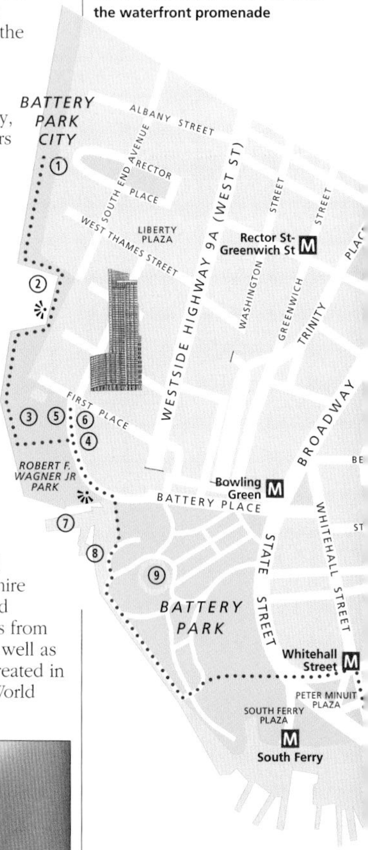

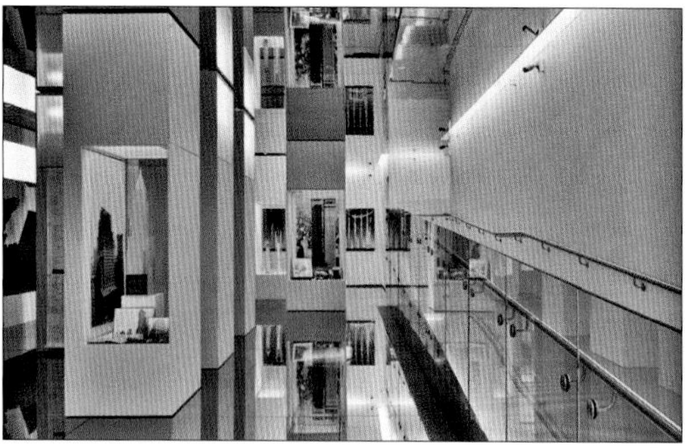

Shiny surfaces and sharp angles at the Skyscraper Museum ⑥

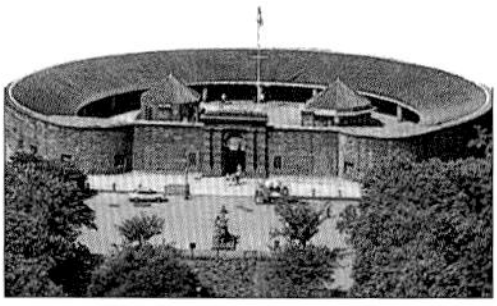

Castle Clinton, an early 19th century fort built to defend the harbor ⑨

Battery Park

On your way to nearby Battery Park, check out Pier A ⑦, which is all that remains of the 1886 grand marine firehouse. Important visitors who arrived by sea were once greeted with festive jets of water pumped into the sky by the fireboats. The clock on the pier tower used to keep time to the maritime system – eight bells and all's well. Continue along the waterfront, looking out for the American Merchant Mariners Memorial ⑧, a haunting sculpture of soldiers pulling a desperate comrade out of the waters, based on photographs of a World War II attack on an American ship. Head past Castle Clinton

Enjoying a well-earned rest at a café, South Street Seaport ⑬

monument ⑨, a fort built during the War of 1812. It later became an opera house, theater, and aquarium, but is now a museum. Stroll through the park where you can relax on benches in the shade of trees. Continue on to State Street, turn right on Whitehall, and then left onto South Street, passing the graceful Beaux Arts Battery Maritime Building ⑩.

South Street Seaport

Follow South Street, with the Brooklyn Bridge in the distance. Walk through the Vietnam Veterans Memorial Plaza ⑪ with its glass memorial etched with the poignant words from soldiers to their loved ones. Head north on Water Street, so named because it marks what was once the water's edge, and past Old Slip; all streets named "slip" are where boats used to dock between piers. Look west up the famed Wall Street ⑫ (see pp66–7) as you

cross it, for a view of the spires of Trinity Church (see p68). Turn right at Maiden Lane, then left onto the quaint and cobblestoned Front Street, which feeds into South Street Seaport ⑬ (see pp82–5), marked by the wooden masts and sails of the tall ships in the harbor. Explore New York's seafaring history at the South Street Seaport Museum, and then wander the shop-lined Fulton Street to Water Street. Take a peek into Bowne & Co Stationers at 211 ⑭, a charming old-fashioned print shop with 19th-century antique hand presses. Amble toward Pier 16 for a further glimpse of the past at the Maritime Crafts Center ⑮ where painters and carvers work at figureheads and carvings. Continue on to Pier 17 ⑯, bustling with shops and cafés. As you walk the wooden pier, look back for a memorable view of Manhattan – the masts of ancient schooners against the city's towering skyscrapers. Finish up at the inviting Paris Café in the 1873 Meyer's Hotel (see p83).

TIPS FOR WALKERS

Starting point: The Esplanade near Rector Place.
Length: 2 miles (3.2 km).
Getting there: Take subway train 1 or R to Rector Street. Head west on Rector Street, cross the bridge over West Street to Rector Place, and walk to the Esplanade.
Stopping-off points: Gigino, on Wagner Park at 20 Battery Place, offers savory Italian fare outdoors.

KEY

• • • Walk route

☀ Good viewing point

Ⓜ Metro station

0 meters   300

0 yards   300

A 90-Minute Walk in the East Village

Originally the farm or *bouwerie* of the Stuyvesant family, this historic area now has a different appeal with its musical and artistic associations, as well as many of the city's interesting and affordable ethnic bars and restaurants. It also manages to balance a peaceful residential area with business and creativity, which is reflected in the constantly changing funky record shops, vegan cafés, craft stores, and live music clubs. For more details on sights in the East Village, *see pp116–21*.

Astor Place

Adjacent to the Astor Place subway stop is a black steel cube called the *Alamo* ① – a meeting point for students and skateboarders. Walk towards Third Avenue through the large buildings that comprise Cooper Union ② *(see p120)*. This scholarship college was founded in 1859 by Peter Cooper, an illiterate but successful businessman and proponent of free education. Across the street is the Continental ③, a live music venue that has hosted groups such as Iggy Pop and Guns N' Roses. In the East Village, 8th Street becomes St. Mark's Place ④, a former jazz, then hippie, then punk hangout. With so many sidewalk cafés and street vendors, this is one of the busiest pedestrian areas of Manhattan. St. Mark's Ale House ⑤ on the right, formerly The Five Spot, was where musicians and poets got together in the 1960s. A few steps down is Trash and Vaudeville ⑥, a punk/goth clothing store that was once the Bridge Theater. The venue was repeatedly shut down due to controversial acts, then reopened. Yoko Ono held "happenings," and the US flag was burned as an anti-war protest in 1967. At 19–25 St. Mark's Place ⑦, there was a Jewish hangout, then the Italian mafia ruled, until Andy Warhol turned the space into the infamous nightclub Electric Circus in the 1960s. The Velvet Underground was among the bands who played here. If you would like to check out their albums, make sure to stop at Kim's Video ⑧ nearby, which stocks obscure music and movies.

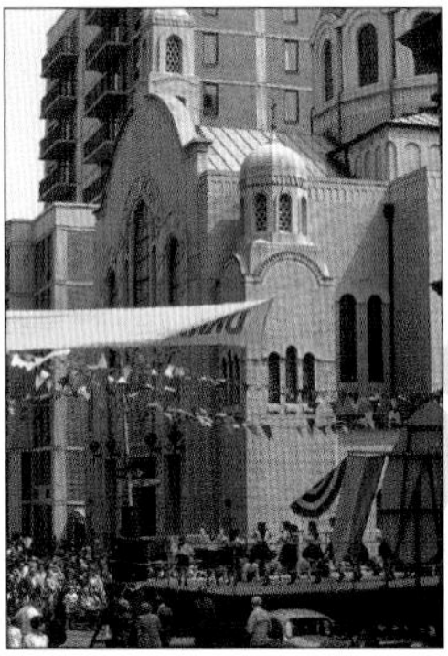

Locals enjoying celebrations on Ukrainian Day

Little Ukraine

Turn left onto Second Avenue, home of the largest and longest-standing Ukrainian population in the US, with restaurants, bars, and centers

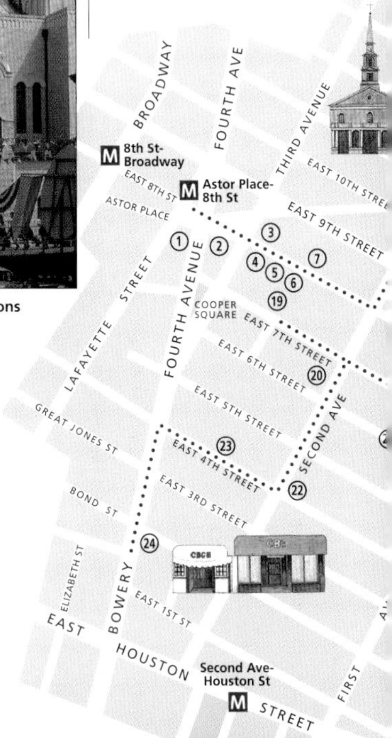

TIPS FOR WALKERS

Starting point: *The Alamo.*
Length: *1.75 miles (2.8 km).*
Getting there: *Take the subway train 6 to Astor Place. Or take M101, M102, or M103 buses.*
Stopping-Off Points: *Many good-value places on St. Mark's Place, but try Jules Bistro (French) between 1st and 2nd avenues, and Caracas Arepa Bar (cheap Venezuelan) at 93½ East 7th St.*

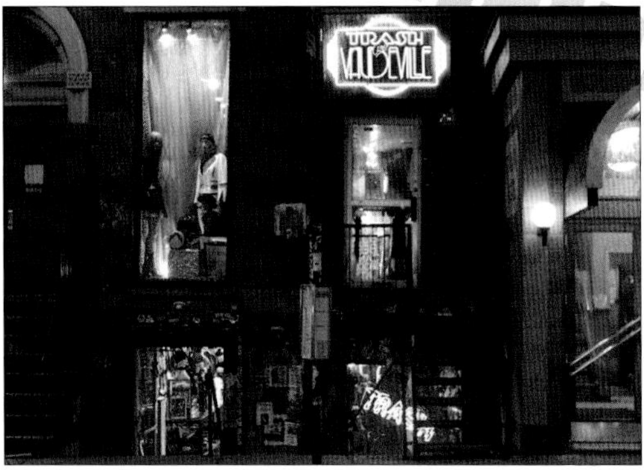

Trash and Vaudeville store, once a venue known for controversial acts ⑥

The style and elegance of an earlier century at Veniero's ⑫

Tompkins Square Park

Built in 1834, this square has seen political activism of all kinds. It is also where a sacred elm tree in the middle of the park ⑮ commemorates the first Hare Krishna ceremony on American soil. Jazz great Charlie Parker lived across the street from the park from 1950–55 ⑯. Walk to the southwestern corner on 7th Street where 7A ⑰ serves breakfast 24 hours a day. Down the block, Turntable Lab 04 ⑱ sells DJ equipment and vinyl. If thirsty, continue west toward Second Avenue to McSorley's Old Ale House ⑲, one of the oldest bars in the city. Then get back onto Second Avenue and turn right to see where the old Fillmore East Auditorium ⑳ used to be (105). This classic rock scene featured such legends as The Doors, Jimi Hendrix, Janis Joplin, and Pink Floyd. The Who even premiered their rock opera *Tommy* here. Look left at 6th Street – "Indian Restaurant Row" ㉑ – where Bengali curry houses compete for business. Go down Second Avenue to number 80 ㉒; this was the home of Joe "The Boss" Masseria, head of the Italian mob in the 1920s. Turn right onto 4th Street where KGB bar ㉓, on the right, is a literary institution. A final left on Bowery leads to the former site (315) of CBGB & OMFUG ㉔, or Country, Bluegrass, Blues & Other Music For Uplifting Gormandizers, birthplace of American rock band Talking Heads.

such as the Ukrainian National Home ⑨ on the right (140), and the good-value, 24-hour Ukrainian eaterie Veselka ⑩ on the corner. Farther up Second Avenue, at East 10th Street, sits the St. Mark's-in-the-Bowery Church ⑪ *(see p121)*. Erected in 1795, this church was Dutch governor Peter Stuyvesant's private chapel and he is buried here. More recently, the Black Panthers and Young Lords gathered here, and Allen Ginsberg and other notable writers contributed to The Poetry Project that exists to this day. A right on 11th Street leads to Veniero's ⑫, a stylish Italian bakery that still has many of its original details, such as hand-stamped metal ceilings. Make a right and then a left onto 10th Street, past the three-story Russian and Turkish Bath House ⑬, to the northern edge of Tompkins Square Park ⑭ *(see p121)*.

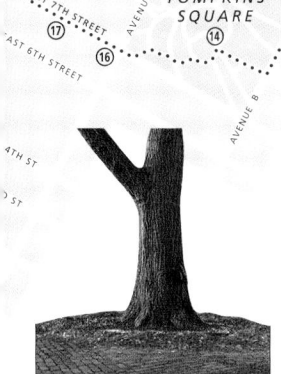

Elm tree in Tomkins Square Park, a Hare Krishna memorial ⑮

KEY

• • • Walk route

Ⓜ Metro station

```
0 meters      200
0 yards       200
```

"Indian Restaurant Row", lined with curry houses ㉑

A 90-Minute Walk in Harlem

Few neighborhoods in New York are as rich in cultural history as Harlem, a haven for African-American heritage. This walk starts in Strivers' Row, one of the few areas that provided affordable housing during the 1920s and 1930s when the area flourished with creative and intellectual expression. It takes you past renowned gospel churches, jazz and blues clubs, and ends at the Apollo Theater, Harlem's famous showcase for new artists. For more details on sights in Harlem, *see pp220–31.*

An ornate doorway in Strivers' Row ①

Strivers' Row

The tree-lined area on 138th Street between Seventh and Eighth avenues is the St. Nicholas Historic District, commonly known as Strivers' Row ①. In the 1920s and 1930s wealthy and influential black professionals aiming for better lives moved into homes designed by such great architects as James Brown Lord and McKim, Mead & White. Signs on some of the gates still read "Private road walk your horses." A short detour left on Seventh Avenue (Adam Clayton Powell, Jr. Boulevard) and right on 139th Street leads to West 139th Street ②, where in 1932 16-year-old Billie Holiday moved into No. 108 shortly before landing her first singing job at a club in nearby "Jungle Alley."

Abyssinian Baptist Church

Turn right at Lenox Avenue and right back onto 138th Street toward the striking Abyssinian Baptist Church ③ *(see p229)*, which is internationally renowned for its magnificent Sunday gospel service. Founded in 1921 and named for the East African Americans of its first congregation, this church has hosted such notable pastors as Adam Clayton Powell, Jr. A stone's throw away on West 137th Street is the Mother Zion church ④, New York's first black church and one of America's oldest. While part of the Underground Railroad (an escape route for slaves), it acquired the nickname "Freedom Church." Continue to the Countee Cullen Regional Library where Madam C.J. Walker founded the Walker School of Hair ⑤. With her successful cosmetics line and hair-smoothing system, Walker was one of the first self-made female millionaires in the country. An active philanthropist, she donated to many African-American charities such as the National Association of Colored People (NAACP) and Tuskegee Institute. After her death in 1919, her daughter A'Leila turned the salon into an intellectual center for artists, scholars, and activists. It was named "The Dark Tower" after Harlem writer Countee Cullen's protest poem. Around the corner on Lenox Avenue is the Schomburg Center for Research into Black Culture ⑥ *(see p229)*, a national research library named for the Puerto Rican-born black scholar who donated his personal collection to the library and served as its curator for six years. Down West 136th Street is Montgomery ⑦, a whimsical women's clothing store with one-of-a-kind designs. Farther down at No. 267 is "Niggerati Manor" ⑧, an artist's rooming house, so-named by Zora Neale Hurston, who lived here while collaborating with Wallace Thurman, Aaron Douglas, and Bruce Nugent on *Fire!!*, a magazine devoted

APOLLO
APOLLO
AMATEUR NITE EVERY WED $1
WELCOME JESSE JACKSON
FUNDRAISER SAT FEB 18 8PM
RAISIN IN THE SUN & THE FAMILY

Apollo Theater, famous for televised shows and legendary acts ⑭

ST NICHOLAS PARK
SAINT NICHOLAS AVE
FREDERICK DOUGLASS
WEST 126TH
WEST 125TH STR
WEST 124TH STREET
WEST 123RD STREET
125th Street
⑭

The famous Sylvia's restaurant, providing authentic soul food ⑪

to young black artists. Get back on Adam Clayton Powell, Jr. Boulevard and follow it down to "Jungle Alley" ⑨, the former highlight of Harlem nightlife, which once contained numerous bars, clubs, cabarets, and speakeasies. A detour across 131st Street will bring you to Marcus Garvey's house ⑩ (235), a major leader and fierce proponent of black unity, economic independence, and

Art displays at the Schomberg Center for Research into Black Culture ⑥

have all performed. It is also home to the Zebra Room, a jazz spot that James Baldwin and Malcolm X frequented. In the middle of the next block is The Studio Museum in Harlem ⑬ (see pp230–31), with a variety of contemporary art exhibits, programs, lectures, and performances by artists of African descent. Its store is also worth a browse for its array of posters and books.

The great jazz singer Billy Holiday ②

Apollo Theater
On West 125th Street is the famous Apollo Theater ⑭ (see p230), where since 1934, "stars are born and legends are made." These performers have ranged in style from Ella Fitzgerald to James Brown. Since 1987, "Amateur Night at the Apollo" has been televised nationwide and the theater has become the third-most popular tourist destination in Manhattan.

"Jungle Alley," where Billie Holiday first performed ⑨

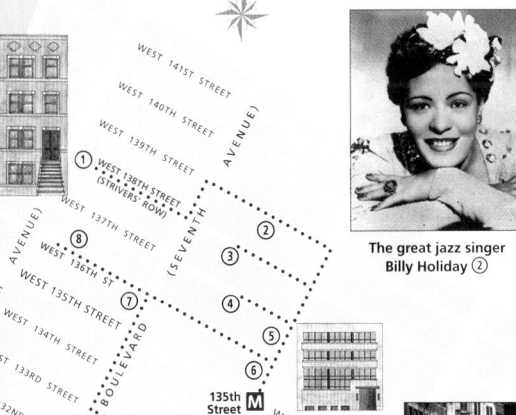

0 meters 200
0 yards 200

pride. Return to Adam Clayton Powell, Jr. Boulevard and make a left on 127th Street until you reach Sylvia's Restaurant ⑪ (see p230), the self-proclaimed "Queen of Soul Food." Family-owned since 1962, Sylvia's serves authentic southern favorites, such as fried chicken, catfish, and BBQ ribs. Stay on Lenox Avenue until 125th Street; here you'll find Lenox Lounge ⑫ where Billie Holiday, Miles Davis, and John Coltrane

TIPS FOR WALKERS

Starting point: Strivers' Row.
Length: 1.75 miles (2.8 km).
Getting there: Take subway train 2 or 3 to 135th St and Lenox Ave, then walk north to 138th St and west to Seventh Ave. Or take M2, M7, or M10 bus to 135th St and walk to Seventh Ave.
Stopping-off Points: Sylvia's on 127th and Lenox is the famous soul food place in Harlem. It is the perfect place to refuel.

KEY

• • • Walk route

Ⓜ Metro station

TRAVELERS' NEEDS

WHERE TO STAY

With over 75,000 hotel rooms available, New York offers something for everyone. The city's top hotels are the most expensive in the US, but the best news for visitors is the increase in budget and mid-priced hotels. While many of these are basic rather than charming, they offer good value. Other budget options are furnished apartments and studios, and bed and breakfasts, as well as youth hostels and YMCAs. From an inspection of over 200 hotels in New York, we have selected the best of their kind. The hotels listed on pp280–91 contain detailed descriptions of facilities, which will help you select the one best suited to your needs. Most hotels have a website address to enable you to book a room online.

Cole Porter's piano, in the Waldorf Astoria bar *(see p288)*

Rooftop terrace at the Peninsula New York *(see p289)*

WHERE TO LOOK

The East Side, roughly between 59th and 77th Streets, is the traditional location for luxury hotels. The renovation of certain landmark midtown properties by famous hotel chains, however, such as the St. Regis by Starwood, and the former Gotham Hotel, which is now The Peninsula New York, has considerably increased the competition in this price range.

Business travelers tend to favor midtown, especially the moderately priced hotels lining Lexington Avenue near Grand Central Terminal.

Those seeking relative quiet with access to midtown should look in the Murray Hill area, while theater-lovers should note the revival of the Times Square area, where there are many hotels within walking distance of the bustling Theater District.

There are a number of good, inexpensive hotels around Herald Square, which is convenient for shopping.

Trendy boutique hotels have flourished in SoHo and the Meatpacking District, where there are also plenty of good bars, restaurants, and upscale shops *(see pp320–21)* as well as trendy nightclubs.

New York & Co. (the Convention and Visitors Bureau) publishes a free, annually updated leaflet called "The New York Hotel Guide," listing current rates and toll-free numbers. Staff will offer advice about hotels but do not make reservations on your behalf.

HOTEL PRICES

Some hotels offer seasonal promotional rates and other off-peak reductions. For example, business travelers vacate hotels at the end of the working week, and you can take advantage of bargain weekend deals, even in luxury hotels, as prices drop *(see Special Rates p278).* There are a growing number of good value all-suite hotels available in every price category. Suites offer extra space plus cooking facilities and a refrigerator. Most suites can accommodate up to four people, which makes them popular with families.

HIDDEN EXTRAS

When calculating the cost of hotels in New York, it is not enough simply to take into consideration the quoted room price. Hotel rooms have long been subject to extra taxes, but the former sliding scale, which favored rates under $100, has now given way to a blanket 13.375% hotel tax, plus $3.50 per night per room fee.

Several hotels now include continental breakfast in the room price. This is a big saving, since standard hotel continental breakfast prices, before tax and tip, start at about $10 and soar to around

Antique furnishings, Inn at Irving Place *(see p283)*

◁ Tourists consult map on busy New York street

The Tribeca Grand lobby *(see p281)*

$25 in some of the luxury hotels. To save money, head for the nearest deli or coffee shop and leave the hotel to business people having power breakfasts.

Hotel telephone charges are always high; it is much less expensive to use the pay phone in the lobby, particularly when you are calling overseas.

Tips are expected. Staff who take your luggage to the room are usually tipped a minimum of $1 per bag – more in a luxury hotel. The concierge need not be tipped for normal services such as arranging transportation or making dinner reservations, but should be rewarded for exceptional services. When

you order from room service, a service charge will usually be included in the bill; if not, a 15–20% tip is customary. Solo travelers will find that single room rates are usually at least 80% of the double rate and are sometimes the same as for two people.

FACILITIES

Although you'd expect hotel rooms in New York City to be noisy, most windows are double- or even triple-glazed to keep out the noise. Air-conditioning is a standard feature, so there is no need to open the windows in hot weather. Even so, some rooms are obviously quieter than others, especially if they are at the back of the hotel or overlooking a courtyard – check when reserving. Light sleepers may also want to request a room away from the elevator.

Television, radio, and at least one telephone are usually provided in every room, even in modest lodgings, and most hotel bedrooms have private bathrooms. In budget and mid-priced hotels, a shower, rather than a tub, is the norm. Many hotels offer Internet access (often with free Wi-Fi), a business center, and a health club or exercise room. Luxury facilities include minibars in the room, dual phones, private phone message systems, and electronic checkout.

Most of the hotels listed here are within a few minutes' walk of shops and restaurants. Few hotels have their own parking, but valets may park your car in nearby garages. A reduced (but still expensive) daily parking fee is normally offered. If there is no concierge at the hotel, front desk staff will always help to answer any queries.

Understated elegance at the stylish Kitano *(see p288)*

DIRECTORY

HOW TO RESERVE

It is advisable to make hotel reservations at least one month in advance, otherwise you may well find that the best rooms and suites have been taken. The busiest periods are at Easter, the New York Marathon week in late October or early November, Thanksgiving and Christmas.

Reserve directly with the hotel online, or by telephone, letter, or fax. Internet bookings on Expedia.com and Hotels. com yield the best deals. Written confirmation of your telephone booking will be required, probably with a deposit as a guarantee of your arrival; any cancellation fees may be deducted from this. You can pay by credit card, international bank draft or money order, or US traveler's check. Advise the staff if you are going to arrive at the hotel after 6pm or you will lose your reservation, unless you have prepaid with a credit card.

You can also book a hotel through your travel agent or airline. Most hotels have a toll-free telephone number for use in the United States, but these numbers do not work from Europe and the UK. If the hotel is part of an international chain, an affiliated hotel in your country should be able to reserve a room for you.

SPECIAL RATES

Hotels are busiest during the week, when business travelers are in the city, so most of them offer budget weekend packages. It's often possible to move from a standard to a luxury room for the weekend at the same rate. A lower corporate rate is usually available to employees of large companies. Quite often, reservation clerks will grant corporate discounts on request without asking for a company affiliation. It is also worth checking a hotel website for special deals and promotions.

Some reservation agencies offer discount rates. A good travel agent should be able to get the best rates, but compare prices by contacting directly a discount reservation service such as Hotel con-x-ions or Quikbook *(see p277)*, which offers discounts of 20–50%, depending on the time of year. You reserve by credit card and receive a voucher, which you present to the hotel. Sites such as www.kayak.com offer "private sales" of discounted hotel rooms.

Package tours can also provide savings. Their rates may not oblige you to stay with a tour group, only to use their air and hotel arrangements. They may also include airport transfers, an additional saving. Airlines frequently have special deals, particularly during slow travel seasons. A knowledgeable travel agent should be able to tell you the current best deals, but newspapers often advertise special, limited offers that can be booked directly. At off-peak times you may net even bigger savings than with the package plans.

Lobby of the St. Regis Hotel *(see p289)*

DIRECTORY

DISABLED TRAVELERS

By law, new hotels must provide facilities for disabled visitors. Many older buildings have also been renovated so as to comply with this regulation.

To find out which hotels offer the best facilities, check their websites. These are provided for all the hotels listed on pp280–91. When booking, let the hotel know of any specific needs. Guide dogs are allowed in most hotels, but it is also advisable to check in advance.

The **Mayor's Office for People With Disabilities** also offers information about hotels.

TRAVELING WITH CHILDREN

American hotels are generally very welcoming toward children. Cots or cribs as well as lists of reliable baby-sitters are usually available, and most hotel restaurants are happy to cater to young guests.

Traveling with children can be cheaper than anticipated. Many hotels do not charge for children if they stay in their parents' room, or make only a small charge for an extra bed. There is usually a limit of one or two children per room in these cases, and most hotels stipulate that the children must be under a certain age, most often 12. Parents of older children are expected to pay the full price, although the age limit is occasionally extended to 18. Ask about family rates when you make your reservation.

BED-AND-BREAKFAST

An increasing number of bed-and-breakfast accommodations in private apartments is available in New York. These can vary from a room in an apartment with an owner-host in residence to an entire self-contained apartment with its own kitchen and bathroom, which you have to yourself while the owner is away.

Staying in a private apartment has certain advantages. It enables you to feel at home in a New York neighborhood and to visit local restaurants,

Entrance to the Peninsula Hotel (see p289)

which are usually far more reasonably priced than those in tourist areas.

Bed-and-breakfast lodgings can be found through many free booking services. Some booking agencies have a two-or-more-night minimum.

Rates for unhosted apartments vary from about $100 to $300, and for a double room start at $100 a night, depending on whether you have a private bathroom. There is a wide range of apartments, from spacious and luxurious to cramped and dowdy. Be aware that, if the address is remote or inconveniently far from bus routes or subway stations, your costs will rise, as you will need frequent cabs. Ask about location and amenities when you reserve.

YOUTH AND BUDGET ACCOMMODATIONS

New York's youth hostel and its many **YMCA** dormitories offer lodgings for those on a tight budget. For the longer-term visitor, the **92nd Street Y**, a nonsectarian hostel in the Upper East Side, has good-value rooms, with prices starting from around $35 to $50 a night.

Sky-high swimming pool at a luxury hotel

There are no campsites in Manhattan, and, sadly, youth hostels are not as prevalent in New York as they are in large European cities.

For budget-minded travelers looking for the bare essentials, inexpensive rooms are available in several areas of New York, particularly in Chelsea, the Garment District, and the Upper West Side, and to a lesser extent in such prime neighborhoods as the Upper Midtown. Although some of these budget-price rooms are reasonably comfortable, with private baths or showers, others may be rather small, perhaps with no air conditioning, and you may have to share a bathroom.

Other interesting sources for budget lodgings are websites like www.couchsurfing.com, which has many member-hosts in New York, and www.airbnb.com, where locals offer accommodation in their homes for a very reasonable fee.

Finally, another way to make your budget go further is to avoid having breakfast in your hotel. Even its coffee shop is likely to be more expensive than an outside coffee shop or deli.

BEYOND MANHATTAN

As New York City becomes safer – and Manhattan more expensive – accommodation options are emerging in the outer boroughs for savvy travelers. Indeed, areas such as Williamsburg and Dumbo in Brooklyn have become destinations in their own right over the past few years, thanks to a rising number of cool bars, good restaurants, and trendy stores.

For a little over $300, which buys an average room in Manhattan, you can book a king room at the Marriott Brooklyn Bridge in Brooklyn Heights *(see p291)*, or a room with flat-screen TV and wireless internet access at the four-star boutique hotel Le Bleu, in the up-and-coming area of Gowanus, close to Park Slope (www.hotellebleu.com).

As always, cheaper deals can often be negotiated or found on hotel websites.

Choosing a Hotel

These hotels have been selected across a wide price range for their good value, excellent facilities, and location. This chart lists the hotels by area of the city in the same order as the rest of the guide. Within each area, entries are listed alphabetically within each price category, from the least expensive to the most expensive.

PRICE CATEGORIES
For a standard double room per night, inclusive of breakfast, service charges, and any additional taxes:

$ under $150
$$ $150–$250
$$$ $250–$350
$$$$ $350–$450
$$$$$ over $450

LOWER MANHATTAN

Best Western Seaport Inn Downtown
$$

33 Peck Slip, 10038 **Tel** *(212) 766-6600* **Fax** *(212) 766-6615* **Rooms** *72*   Map *2 D2*

You'll feel like you're stepping into a 19th-century sailor's haunt at this property with views of Brooklyn Bridge. Families enjoy the deluxe breakfast and the lounge with coffee and tea. The 24-hour fitness center is large. Upgrade to a room with a terrace if you can. **www.seaportinn.com**

Conrad New York
$$$

102 North End Ave, 10282 **Tel** *(212) 945-0100* **Fax** *(212) 945-3012* **Rooms** *463*   Map *1 A2*

This all-suite hotel is a great bet for families. Two-room accommodations feature fold-out couch beds. Fantastic views of the harbor and discounted weekend rates. The hotel is located near Battery Park City and the Statue of Liberty ferry, but is quite far from the subway. **http://conradhotels1.hilton.com**

Gild Hall
$$$

15 Gold St, 10038 **Tel** *(212) 232-7700* **Fax** *(212) 425-0330* **Rooms** *126*   Map *2 D2*

This luxury hotel boasts, among other features, a bi-level private library, an elegant champagne bar, a modern English tavern, and über-sleek guest rooms. The mini bars are stocked by Dean & DeLuca, and the king suites even have chandeliers. **www.thompsonhotels.com**

Marriott New York City Financial Center
$$$

85 West St, 10006 **Tel** *(212) 385-4900* **Fax** *(212) 227-8136* **Rooms** *497*   Map *1 B3*

This hotel in the heart of Financial District is modern and grand, and even offers an indoor pool. All rooms have luxurious bedding, and some offer views of the Statue of Liberty and New York Harbor. Primarily a business hotel, this property sometimes offers great weekend rates. **www.nycmarriottfinancial.com**

Ritz Carlton Battery Park
$$$

2 West St, 10004 **Tel** *(212) 344-0800* **Fax** *(212) 344-3801* **Rooms** *298*   Map *1 B4*

Telescopes in the elegantly modern rooms offer spectacular close-up views of the Statue of Liberty and New York Harbor. Bathrooms are sleek and large, while business travelers are well catered for with numerous programs and amenities. Afternoon tea is served in the bar. **www.ritzcarlton.com**

The Wall Street Inn
$$$

9 South William St, 10004 **Tel** *(212) 747-1500* **Fax** *(212) 747-1900* **Rooms** *46*   Map *1 C3*

Rates can drop to bargain levels on weekends at this business-targeted hotel. The early-American interiors keep it from feeling stuffy, and the professional service is first class. While rooms can feel small, the beds are comfortable. Score a corner room for a whirlpool tub. Continental breakfast included. **www.thewallstreetinn.com**

LOWER EAST SIDE

Off SoHo Suites Hotel
$$

11 Rivington St, 10002 **Tel** *(212) 979-9808* **Fax** *(212) 979-9801* **Rooms** *38*   Map *5 A3*

Trendy downtown neighborhoods have enveloped this budget spot making it a good choice for those wanting to be near SoHo or the Lower East Side. Small suites share facilities, while the larger ones come with private bathrooms and full kitchens, making it a good choice for bigger groups or families. **www.offsoho.com**

Blue Moon Hotel
$$$

100 Orchard St, 10002 **Tel** *(212) 533-9080* **Fax** *(212) 533-9148* **Rooms** *22*   Map *5 A3*

The spacious rooms, views, and amenities would amaze former residents of this one-time Lower East Side tenement. Located on a historic block, it mixes memorabilia and nostalgia with modern luxuries that include hydro-massage baths, flatscreen TVs, and free Wi-Fi. A good base for exploring a resurgent neighborhood. **www.bluemoon-nyc.com**

Key to Symbols *see back cover flap*

The Gem

135 East Houston St, 10002 **Tel** *(212) 358-8844* **Fax** *(212) 473-3500* **Rooms** *46* **Map** *5 A3*

This hotel offers small yet clean budget rooms for checking out the trendy cafés and boutiques just outside. Steps away from the subway line and cheap eats, the location for young hipsters is hard to beat. Some rooms have microwaves and small fridges. The famous Katz's Deli is just a block away. **www.thegemhotel.com**

Hotel on Rivington

105 Rivington St, 10002 **Tel** *(212) 475-2600* **Fax** *(212) 475-5959* **Rooms** *110* **Map** *5 A3*

Even the glass-enclosed showers have a view in this chic, 21-story tower offering oversize rooms with floor-to-ceiling windows and a 360-degree vista. Guests enjoy a private lounge, a state-of-the-art fitness center, and many other amenities. A sign of the changes on the Lower East Side. **www.hotelonrivington.com**

SOHO AND TRIBECA

Cosmopolitan Hotel

95 West Broadway, 10007 **Tel** *(212) 566-1900* **Fax** *(212) 566-6909* **Rooms** *125* **Map** *1 B1*

This budget gem is located in the heart of trendy TriBeCa. While rooms are small, they are well maintained, with equally tiny but clean bathrooms; most have complimentary Wi-Fi. The many top restaurants nearby and easy access to public transport make this a top budget recommendation. Also great for shopping. **www.cosmohotel.com**

Duane Street Hotel

130 Duane St, 10013 **Tel** *(212) 964-4600* **Fax** *(212) 964-4800* **Rooms** *45* **Map** *1 B1*

This intimate hotel features sleek, minimalist decor. Rooms have flatscreen TVs, all the latest amenities, and walk-in showers. The Mehtaphor restaurant, offering "Asian urban" fare, is small and inviting. Convenient for City Hall and the many restaurants of TriBeCa, plus SoHo and Chinatown. **www.duanestreethotel.com**

Holiday Inn SoHo

138 Lafayette St, 10013 **Tel** *(212) 966-8898* **Fax** *(212) 941-5832* **Rooms** *227* **Map** *4 F5*

This basic property is a longtime favorite of those wishing to be close to New York's bustling downtown area. SoHo, Chinatown, the Lower East Side, and Little Italy are just steps away with boutique shops and restaurants galore. Rooms are simple but comfortable, and the in-house restaurant is good at a pinch. **www.hidowntown-nyc.com**

Smyth Tribeca

85 West Broadway, 10007 **Tel** *(212) 587-7000* **Rooms** *100* **Map** *1 B1*

Smyth Tribeca features a sleek modern design with classic touches. A high-ceilinged lobby with plush, fabric walls gives way to ample rooms with pale and dark woods, crisp linens, and marble bathrooms. Ease into the evening over a cocktail at the elegant hotel bar. **www.thompsonhotels.com**

Tribeca Grand Hotel

2 Sixth Ave, 10013 **Tel** *(212) 519-6600* **Fax** *(212) 519-6700* **Rooms** *203* **Map** *3 E5*

The atrium lobby gives this hotel a grand look. The private screening room downstairs has long made this a favorite of celebrities. Rooms are sleekly designed and the bathroom amenities first-rate. Score a corner room or studio suite for the most space, and make sure to sip a drink in the lounge to maximize star sightings. **www.tribecagrand.com**

60 Thompson

60 Thompson St, 10012 **Tel** *(877) 431-0400* **Fax** *(212) 431-0200* **Rooms** *100* **Map** *4 D4*

This chic boutique hotel has an excellent Thai restaurant, Kittichai, and a summertime rooftop lounge/deck available only to guests and certain trendsetters. Rooms are minimalist yet comfortable with a pleasing palette tone, and have all the latest high-tech gadgets. Location is the star here. **www.60thompson.com**

SoHo Grand Hotel

310 West Broadway, 10013 **Tel** *(212) 965-3000* **Fax** *(212) 965-3200* **Rooms** *363* **Map** *4 E4*

Entertainment moguls and celebrities as well keep returning to this boutique favorite. Located in the middle of happening SoHo, the rooms are small and can seem dark despite the high windows offering views of downtown. A 24-hour room service and pet amenities keep guests happy. **www.sohogrand.com**

Greenwich Hotel

377 Greenwich St, 10013 **Tel** *(212) 941-8900* **Fax** *(212) 941-8600* **Rooms** *88* **Map** *1 B1*

Robert DeNiro and partners spared nothing in their luxurious eight-story hotel, which opened in 2008. Part rustic, part elegant eclectic style mixes Tibetan rugs, Moroccan tiles, old wood beams, and antique Asian art. Rooms are light and spacious, and there's a large salon and an outdoor terrace. Worth the splurge. **www.thegreenwichhotel.com**

The Mercer Hotel

147 Mercer St, 10012 **Tel** *(212) 966-6060* **Fax** *(212) 965-3838* **Rooms** *75* **Map** *4 E3*

This discreet boutique property comes at luxury prices, and celebrities seeking a bit more privacy often make this their choice. Rooms are designed as lofts with exposed brick and wooden floors. Bathroom tubs are large enough for two. Children are welcome – cribs featuring Frette linens are available. **www.mercerhotel.com**

GREENWICH VILLAGE

Washington Square Hotel
$$

103 Waverly Place, 10011 **Tel** *(212) 777-9515* **Fax** *(212) 979-8373* **Rooms** *160*   **Map** *4 D2*

Just steps away from NYU, this hotel faces bustling Washington Square Park. The marble lobby leads to fresh, boutique-like rooms. The central location means higher-than-average rates, but great bars and restaurants are just around the corner. The on-site restaurant also offers good meals. **www.wshotel.com**

Abingdon Guest House
$$$

13 Eighth Ave, 10014 **Tel** *(212) 243-5384* **Fax** *(212) 807-7473* **Rooms** *9*   **Map** *3 C1*

This lovely guesthouse is located on one of the West Village's most beautiful brownstone- and boutique-lined streets. Each room has unique decor and is fitted with classic comforts. No on-site full-time staff means this gem is best suited to independent travelers. No breakfast, but there are coffee facilities. **www.abingdonguesthouse.com**

Gansevoort Hotel
$$$$

18 Ninth Ave, 10014 **Tel** *(212) 206-9700* **Fax** *(212) 255-5858* **Rooms** *210*   **Map** *3 B1*

A 45-ft (13.5-m) rooftop pool and Ono, an indoor-outdoor restaurant, are among the features that draw models and celebrities to this sleek, high-rise addition to the hip Meatpacking District. Rooms are a good size with plush feather beds, while bathrooms are luxurious, and the hotel spa lavish. **www.hotelgansevoort.com**

Soho House
$$$$$

59 Ninth Ave, 10014 **Tel** *(646) 253-6122* **Rooms** *24*   **Map** *3 B1*

Sister to London's exclusive private club, the New York version is also a hotel where guests enjoy all facilities, including rooftop pool, sitting rooms, library, restaurant, and the Cowshed spa. Rooms with names like Playpen and Playground range from large to gigantic, with prices to match. **www.sohohouseny.com**

EAST VILLAGE

Union Square Inn
$

209 East 14th St, 10003 **Tel** *(212) 614-0500* **Fax** *(212) 614-0512* **Rooms** *40*   **Map** *4 F1*

All the standard comforts come at reasonable prices in this hotel. Rooms have no views and are nothing to write home about, but the beds are comfortable and bathrooms clean. European breakfast is on offer at the in-house café (limited hours). Union Square nearby is great for peoplewatching and shopping. **www.unionsquareinn.com**

The Bowery Hotel
$$$$

335 Bowery, 10003 **Tel** *(212) 505-9100* **Rooms** *135*   **Map** *4 F3*

From the same duo who developed the Maritime in Chelsea comes this luxury lodging. An opulent 17-story hotel, it features lobby fireplaces and wood-paneled elevators, floor-to-ceiling windows in every room, and seven rooms with private terraces, hot tubs, and outdoor showers. The bar attracts a VIP scene. **www.theboweryhotel.com**

Cooper Square Hotel
$$$$$

25 Cooper Square, 10003 **Tel** *(212) 475-5700* **Rooms** *145*   **Map** *4 F2*

The sleek, modernist Cooper Square Hotel is slightly out of character with its edgy, counter-culture East Village neighborhood – much like the striking Carlos Zapata-designed tower. The hotel offers its guests a number of perks, including a good restaurant, complimentary Wi-Fi, and gym passes. **www.thecoopersquarehotel.com**

GRAMERCY AND THE FLATIRON DISTRICT

Hotel 17
$

225 East 17th St, 10003 **Tel** *(212) 475-2845* **Fax** *(212) 677-8178* **Rooms** *120*   **Map** *9 B5*

Young travelers love the location of this very basic budget option. Rooms are tiny with not much flair and some share baths. Woody Allen popularized this hotel in *Manhattan Murder Mystery* and supposedly Madonna stayed here as a young singer. Some cheap eats are nearby as is good mainstream shopping. **www.hotel17ny.com**

Hotel 31
$

129 East 31st St, 10016 **Tel** *(212) 685-3060* **Fax** *(212) 532-1232* **Rooms** *60*   **Map** *9 A3*

This sister property to Hotel 17 features 60 rooms, each decorated differently, although the style is typical chic floral print. Rooms have the basics such as air-conditioning, televisions with cable, and some share baths. This area is a little quieter at night. **www.hotel31.com**

Key to Price Guide *see p280* **Key to Symbols** *see back cover flap*

Gershwin Hotel

$$

7 East 27th St, 10016 **Tel** *(212) 545-8000* **Fax** *(212) 684-5546* **Rooms** *150*

Map *8 F3*

An original Andy Warhol *Campbell's Soup Can* in the lobby sets the tone of this pop art-inspired hotel. More art can be found on every floor. Rooms are bright and stylishly decorated. A tourist bargain, as it's just steps to the Empire State Building. Many reasonable restaurants nearby. **www.gershwinhotel.com**

Thirty Thirty

$$

30 East 30th St, 10016 **Tel** *(212) 689-1900* **Fax** *(212) 689-0023* **Rooms** *253*

Map *9 A3*

The stylish rooms here are perfect for sophisticated travelers on a budget. While small, the rooms are quite comfortable with many twin-bedded rooms available as well as some with kitchenettes. The restaurant and lounge add to its attractions. Several trendy restaurants and shops nearby as well. **www.thirtythirty-nyc.com**

Hotel Roger Williams

$$$

131 Madison Ave, 10016 **Tel** *(212) 448-7000* **Fax** *(212) 448-7007* **Rooms** *193*

Map *9 A3*

A stylish option for those with a little more to spend, and the amenities make it worth the price – free breakfast, all-day serve-yourself coffee and treats, and a DVD library. The rooms are soothing in blond woods and warm colors. Fifteen rooms have garden terraces. Seasonal discounts can make this more affordable. **www.hotelrogerwilliams.com**

Hotel Giraffe

$$$$

365 Park Ave South, 10016 **Tel** *(212) 685-7700* **Fax** *(212) 685-7771* **Rooms** *73*

Map *9 A4*

Perhaps the Flatiron District's finest full-service luxury hotel, the rooms are decorated with custom furnishings invoking the Moderne style. Suites have French doors opening onto a Juliet balcony. A restaurant two doors down from the hotel offers superb cuisine and potent cocktails with a lounge scene. **www.hotelgiraffe.com**

Inn at Irving Place

$$$$

56 Irving Place, 10003 **Tel** *(212) 533-4600* **Fax** *(212) 533-4611* **Rooms** *12*

Map *9 A5*

Edith Wharton would be proud of these antique brownstones buildings, run impeccably as a luxury inn. Each room features beautiful bathrooms, as well as modern technology such as CD players. Complimentary breakfast is served in the salon, and don't miss the high tea. **www.innatirving.com**

The Marcel at Gramercy

$$$$

201 East 24th Street, 10010 **Tel** *(212) 696-3800* **Fax** *(212) 696-0077* **Rooms** *135*

Map *9 B4*

The Marcel reopened in 2008 after a makeover that added four floors, the Polar restaurant, and an airy lounge. Rooms have clean, modern decor; many were combined to offer larger spaces. Compact baths have walk-in showers with rainfall shower heads. Complimentary morning newspaper and coffee. **www.marcelatgramercy.com**

Gramercy Park Hotel

$$$$$

2 Lexington Ave, 10010 **Tel** *(212) 920-3300* **Fax** *(212) 673-5890* **Rooms** *185*

Map *9 A4*

The Gramercy Park Hotel is an "eclectic-Bohemian" extravagance, oozing modern art, wood paneling, velvet, and state-of-the-art gadgets. Guests can relax on the private rooftop garden at the elegant Rose and Jade bars or in Gramercy Park itself (yes, the keys are available). **www.gramercyparkhotel.com**

CHELSEA AND THE GARMENT DISTRICT

Americana Inn

$

69 West 38th St, 10018 **Tel** *(212) 840-6700* **Fax** *(212) 840-1830* **Rooms** *50*

Map *8 F1*

This is the place for the budget-minded traveler looking for the bare minimum essentials. Rooms have private sinks, and each floor features a shared kitchenette. The central location and friendly staff make a winning combination. Just be aware that the area is always busy and can get hectic and loud. **www.theamericanainn.com**

Chelsea International Hostel

$

251 West 20th St, 10011 **Tel** *(212) 647-0010* **Fax** *(212) 727-7289* **Rooms** *57*

Map *8 D5*

Considered one of the city's best hostels, this complex features a series of low-rise buildings looking out on a central courtyard. Both private bunked rooms and shared dorm beds are available; all bathrooms are shared. Facilities include two fully-equipped kitchens, laundry machines, and TVs. **www.chelseahostel.com**

Chelsea Lodge

$

318 West 20th St, 10011 **Tel** *(212) 243-4499* **Fax** *(212) 243-7852* **Rooms** *22*

Map *8 D5*

A lovingly restored townhouse in the Chelsea Historic District is the setting for this budget find. The small rooms have private sinks and showers, so guests only share toilet facilities. Perfect for independent travelers looking for a true NYC experience. **www.chelsealodge.com**

Chelsea Star Hotel

$

300 West 30th St, 10011 **Tel** *(212) 244-7827* **Fax** *(212) 279-9018* **Rooms** *34*

Map *8 D3*

The interiors of this hotel are bright and upbeat if a bit garish. A life-size statue of Betty Boop greets you at the lobby, and there are plenty of contemporary art galleries nearby. Rooms here range from dormitory style to more upscale chic with four-poster beds and DVD players. Free Wi-Fi. **www.starhotelny.com**

Colonial House Inn
🕻   Ⓢ

318 West 22nd St, 10011 **Tel** *(212) 243-9669* **Fax** *(212) 633-1612* **Rooms** *20*   **Map** *8 D4*

While the owners of this lovely brownstone-turned-inn cater mostly to a gay male clientele, everyone is welcome. The well-maintained rooms have modern decor and Wi-Fi; almost half have private baths, and a few feature working fireplaces. Seasonal discounts apply. **www.colonialhouseinn.com**

Broadway Plaza Hotel
🔗 P 🕻   ⓈⓈ

1155 Broadway, 10001 **Tel** *(212) 679-7665* **Fax** *(212) 679-7694* **Rooms** *69*   **Map** *8 F3*

You might not know it from the neon signs outside, but inside, the rooms of this reasonably priced hotel are cozy and tastefully decorated, with high-speed Internet access. Complimentary breakfast. The neighborhood can be noisy, but the location within sight of the Empire State Building makes up for it. **www.broadwayplazahotel.com**

Chelsea Savoy Hotel
🔗   ⓈⓈ

204 West 23rd St, 10011 **Tel** *(212) 929-9353* **Fax** *(212) 741-6309* **Rooms** *90*   **Map** *8 E4*

One of the more modern options in Chelsea, this hotel has a devoted following of those who appreciate the consistent service. The rooms are pleasant though lacking in any extra touches. A good choice for those who appreciate the Chelsea restaurant, bar, and club scene. **www.chelseasavoynyc.com**

Comfort Inn Chelsea
🔗 🍽 🍸   ⓈⓈ

18 West 25th St, 10010 **Tel** *(212) 645-3990* **Fax** *(212) 633-8952* **Rooms** *121*   **Map** *8 F4*

Budget travelers enjoy the location of this modest find in hip Chelsea. The 1901 brick building offers clean rooms with TVs and refrigerators. The restaurant and coffee bar in the lobby are a draw, as are the nearby restaurants and art galleries. The suites, which sleep up to six, are a bargain. **www.choicehotels.com**

Hotel Chelsea
🔗 🍽   ⓈⓈ

222 West 23rd St, 10011 **Tel** *(212) 243-3700* **Fax** *(212) 675-5531* **Rooms** *400*   **Map** *8 E4*

Music history was made when punk legend Sid Vicious killed girlfriend Nancy Spungen here. Since then, famous personalities such as Sandra Bernhardt and post-Uma Ethan Hawke have stayed in the hotel. Some claim the large rooms and privacy are the draw, while others enjoy the bohemian, if somewhat dusty, furnishings. **www.hotelchelsea.com**

Hotel Metro
🔗 🍽 🍸 🕻   ⓈⓈ

45 West 35th St, 10001 **Tel** *(212) 947-2500* **Fax** *(212) 279-1310* **Rooms** *179*   **Map** *8 F2*

This Art Deco-inspired jewel is one of the best-priced mid-range hotels in midtown. Rooms are large and better decorated than most in this range. Rates include breakfast, and many enjoy the restaurant ambience and food. The real draw is the rooftop terrace with dramatic views of the Empire State Building. **www.hotelmetronyc.com**

Hotel Wolcott
🔗 🍸 🕻   ⓈⓈ

4 West 31st St, 10001 **Tel** *(212) 268-2900* **Fax** *(212) 563-0096* **Rooms** *250*   **Map** *8 F3*

The large rooms, low rates, and central location makes this a good choice for budget-minded travelers. While the rooms are plain, they are clean, and internet access is available. There are laundry facilities on the premises, and though there is no restaurant, cheap eats abound in the area. **www.wolcott.com**

Herald Square Hotel
🔗 🚴 🕻   Ⓢ

19 West 31st St 10001 **Tel** *(212) 279-4017* **Fax** *(212) 643-9208* **Rooms** *100*   **Map** *8 F3*

This charming, reasonably priced Beaux Arts hotel was once the headquarters of *Life* magazine *(see p133)*, and the original *Life* magazine collection is available for guests to look at. Rooms are tastefully decorated with traditional furniture and have all essential amenities. No breakfast, but hot drinks are available. **www.heraldsquarehotel.com**

Ace Hotel
🔗 P 🍽   ⓈⓈⓈ

20 West 29th St, 10001 **Tel** *(212) 679-2222* **Rooms** *260*   **Map** *8 F3*

The Ace Hotel channels a youthful rock-n-roll vibe: many of the large rooms come with vintage furniture, full-size refrigerators, and even turntables and guitars. The loft corner room has a large bathroom with claw-foot tub. Those on a budget can opt for the bunkbed rooms. Many locals come here for its trendy restaurants. **www.acehotel.com**

Four Points by Sheraton
🔗 🍽 🚴 🍸 🕻   ⓈⓈⓈ

160 West 25th St, 10001 **Tel** *(212) 627-1888* **Fax** *(212) 627-1611* **Rooms** *158*   **Map** *8 E4*

This budget-conscious hotel appeals to sophisticated travelers and business executives who are willing to spend a little more. Rooms are well designed and some have balconies with views of downtown, plus good service as you'd expect from this chain. **www.starwoodhotels.com/fourpoints**

The Maritime
🔗 🍽 🍸 🕻   ⓈⓈⓈ

363 West 16th St, 10011 **Tel** *(212) 242-4300* **Fax** *(212) 242-1188* **Rooms** *125*   **Map** *8 D5*

You can't help noticing the nautical theme of this hotel, since every room is centered around a porthole window with views of the Hudson River. This hip and happening place has rooms that are small but well designed, and several restaurants and bars, including the noted Matsuri. Lots of outdoor space too. **www.themaritimehotel.com**

Radisson/Martinique on Broadway
🔗 🍽 🍸 🕻   ⓈⓈⓈ

49 West 32nd St, 10001 **Tel** *(212) 736-3800* **Fax** *(212) 277-2702* **Rooms** *532*   **Map** *8 F3*

The landmarked French-Renaissance building houses this outpost of the reliable Radisson chain. Past the ornate lobby, the rooms have been restored to an elegant finish. Affordable Asian dining lines the blocks around the hotel, just steps away from some of the best tourist sites on the island. **www.radisson.com/newyorkny_broadway**

Key to Price Guide *see p280* **Key to Symbols** *see back cover flap*

THEATER DISTRICT

Best Western President Hotel

234 West 48th St, 10036 **Tel** *(212) 246-8800* **Fax** *(212) 974-3922* **Rooms** *334*

Map *12 E5*

Families prefer the junior suites with fold-out sofas for children, while the standard rooms work well for the typical traveler. This outpost of the chain hotel is well run with simple but clean rooms in a good location. Be aware that the area is always busy, so light sleepers might look elsewhere. **www.bestwestern.com**

Big Apple Hostel

119 West 45th St, 10036 **Tel** *(212) 302-2603* **Fax** *(212) 302-2605* **Rooms** *39*

Map *12 E5*

For prime location, this hostel is perfect for young travelers. While most beds are dormitory style (both single-sex and co-ed), a few private rooms with queen-size beds are available. Full kitchen facilities, and the backyard garden provide a respite from the harried streets of Manhattan. Book well in advance. **www.bigapplehostel.com**

Park Savoy Hotel

158 West 58th St, 10019 **Tel** *(212) 245-5755* **Fax** *(212) 765-0668* **Rooms** *70*

Map *12 E3*

While this very plain hotel offers the most basic of accommodation, it does so only a block away from Central Park. The rooms are clean, but they tend to be a little ragged and spartan. Expect friendly but limited service at the front desk. Grab a sandwich to go at one of the delis nearby and head to the park. **www.parksavoyhotelny.com**

414 Hotel

414 West 46th St, 10036 **Tel** *(212) 399-0006* **Fax** *(212) 957-8716* **Rooms** *22*

Map *11 C5*

This small and stylish hotel has accommodating staff and complimentary Wi-Fi. King-size rooms tend to be nicer than the double rooms, with better beds and linens. Make sure you snag a room overlooking the private garden courtyard for less noise. **www.414hotel.com**

Amsterdam Court Hotel

226 West 50th St, 10019 **Tel** *(212) 459-1000* **Fax** *(212) 265-5070* **Rooms** *125*

Map *12 D4*

This property is perfect for travelers who value style but travel on a budget. Rooms are decorated in soothing whites and khakis and offer Belgian linens with down comforters and CD players. A rooftop terrace is delightful in summer. There are many good restaurants nearby, on Ninth Avenue. **www.nychotels.com**

Belvedere Hotel

319 West 48th St, 10036 **Tel** *(212) 245-7000* **Fax** *(212) 245-4455* **Rooms** *400*

Map *12 D5*

This quality mid-range hotel is a great choice over many hotels in this price range and location. Rooms are larger than average and relatively attractive. A very popular Brazilian steakhouse is located on the premises, a good addition to the many quality eateries just outside. A family favorite. **www.belvederehotelnyc.com**

Da Vinci Hotel

244 West 56th St, 10019 **Tel** *(212) 489-4100* **Fax** *(212) 399-0434* **Rooms** *20*

Map *12 D3*

This European-style, intimate boutique property prides itself on good service. Rooms are on the small side, but well stocked and comfortable. A good choice for those who want to be close to the theater and don't mind the heavily touristed street. Meals in this area can be pricey, so opt for coffee shops and diners. **www.davincihotel.com**

Holiday Inn New York City-Midtown-57th St

440 West 57th St, 10019 **Tel** *(212) 581-8100* **Fax** *(212) 581-7739* **Rooms** *596*

Map *11 C3*

This solid choice from the famous American chain is a favorite with families thanks to the outdoor pool, and the fact that children enjoy a free breakfast. The rooms are all that you'd expect – clean, comfortable, and wired for internet access. Just blocks away from Central Park and the Theater District. **www.hi57.com**

Hotel Skyline

725 10th Ave, 10019 **Tel** *(212) 586-3400* **Fax** *(212) 582-4604* **Rooms** *230*

Map *11 C5*

Unique in the area, this motel-style inn is ideal for families, offering spacious rooms, a big heated indoor swimming pool, and moderate prices. Broadway shows and many restaurants are a short stroll away. The on-site facility has the city's lowest parking rates. **www.skylinehotelnyc.com**

Algonquin

59 West 44th St, 10036 **Tel** *(212) 840-6800* **Fax** *(212) 944-1419* **Rooms** *174*

Map *12 F5*

The home of Dorothy Parker's literary "Round Table" of the 1920s has been fully refurbished and still draws literati to its doors. The comfortable rooms are small, so if possible, splurge on a literary-themed suite. The well-preserved mahogany-paneled lobby provides access to the legendary Oak Room cabaret. **www.algonquinhotel.com**

Blakely Hotel

136 West 55th St, 10019 **Tel** *(212) 245-1800* **Fax** *(212) 582-8332* **Rooms** *115*

Map *12 E4*

This hotel has been done up in a boutique tradition with an eye on service. From the duo who developed Mercer, the Blakely offers superb value and location in this price range. The nicely appointed rooms include details such as Egyptian linens, while the restaurant serves top-notch Italian fare. **www.blakelynewyork.com**

Casablanca Hotel
$$$ | Map 8 E1

147 West 43rd St, 10036 **Tel** *(212) 869-1212* **Fax** *(212) 391-7585* **Rooms** *48*

This Moroccan-themed hotel is ideal for theatergoers. The rooms are small, and feature fun touches such as polished rattan fixtures. Complimentary breakfast is served in the fireplace lounge. Great peoplewatching for the fashionistas heading in and out of *Vogue* headquarters across the street. **www.casablancahotel.com**

Chambers
$$$ | Map 12 F3

15 West 56th Street, 10019 **Tel** *(212) 974-5656* **Fax** *(212) 974-5657* **Rooms** *77*

A little downtown style livens up this strip of midtown with a sleek design. The smallish rooms feature original modern art, Frette bathrobes, and cashmere throws. The excellent Town restaurant downstairs serves modern French cuisine. A perfect spot to take a break from shopping on Madison Avenue. **www.chambershotel.com**

Hotel Mela
$$$ | Map 12 D5

120 West 44th St, 10036 **Tel** *(877) 452-MELA* **Fax** *(212) 704-9680* **Rooms** *228*

This hotel aims to offer boutique luxury that reminds its guests of home, beginning with a foyer that is less "hotel" and more a discreet welcoming area. The rooms are small but clean, with comfortable beds, nice bathroom amenities, flatscreen TVs, and complimentary wireless internet access. **www.hotelmela.com**

Mansfield
$$$ | Map 12 E5

12 West 44th St, 10036 **Tel** *(212) 277-8700* **Fax** *(212) 764-4477* **Rooms** *124*

This 1905 hotel has been made over as a boutique property with rooms featuring complimentary internet access and down comforters. The bar is a quiet spot for a drink after a hectic New York day. Tucked away on a busy street, the hotel's location is very convenient to theatergoers. **www.mansfieldhotel.com**

Michelangelo
$$$ | Map 12 F4

152 West 51st St, 10019 **Tel** *(212) 765-0505* **Fax** *(212) 581-7618* **Rooms** *178*

Italian Renaissance is the name of the game at this boutique gem that features classic rugs and weavings throughout the property. Italian espresso and pastries for breakfast start the day and Baci chocolates at bedtime finish it off. Bathrooms make good use of Italian marble. We say *la dolce vita*. **www.michaelangelohotel.com**

Millennium Broadway
$$$ | Map 12 E5

145 West 44th St, 10036 **Tel** *(212) 768-4400* **Fax** *(212) 768-0847* **Rooms** *752*

Comfortable rooms are good value at this business-orientated skyscraper hotel that is also ideally located for Broadway. The separate Premier Tower is a more luxurious option, and also has a women's floor. The bar is a nice stop for after-theater drinks. **www.millennium-hotels.com**

Roosevelt Hotel
$$$ | Map 13 A5

45 East 45th St, 10017 **Tel** *(212) 661-9600* **Fax** *(212) 885-6161* **Rooms** *1013*

Built in 1924 and meticulously renovated and restored for its 80th birthday, this "grand dame of Madison Avenue" is still a favorite of business and leisure travelers. Rooms are well appointed with comfortable beds, and the lobby will make you feel like you've stepped into history. **www.theroosevelthotel.com**

The Time
$$$ | Map 12 D5

224 West 49th St, 10019 **Tel** *(212) 320-2900* **Fax** *(212) 245-2305* **Rooms** *200*

The Time has been renovated by the celebrated designer Adam Tihany, who has used a primary-color palette to create a multi-sensory experience. Some of the rooms are small, especially for the price. The lobby bar can be a scene, so stop by for a cocktail. Some can find the noise level too distracting. **www.thetimeny.com**

Doubletree Guest Suites
$$$$ | Map 12 E5

1568 Broadway, 10036 **Tel** *(212) 719-1600* **Fax** *(212) 921-5212* **Rooms** *460*

What this all-suite hotel lacks in charm, it more than makes up for in location and superior facilities. Some suites are designed for families, while others are perfect for business travelers. A special kids' play area makes it a favorite of families with toddlers, and the NYC Visitors' Center is right downstairs. **www.nyc.doubletreehotels.com**

Hilton Times Square
$$$$ | Map 8 E1

234 West 42nd St, 10036 **Tel** *(212) 840-8222* **Fax** *(212) 840-5516* **Rooms** *444*

You could easily miss this oasis of serenity in the midst of the Times Square madness, but don't. The design of the hotel goes way beyond chain mentality with oversize rooms and modern amenities. Rooms begin on the 23rd floor, assuring great views of the area. The upscale restaurant is a winner. **www.timessquare.hilton.com**

Le Parker Meridien
$$$$ | Map 12 E3

118 West 57th St, 10019 **Tel** *(212) 245-5000* **Fax** *(212) 307-1776* **Rooms** *730*

With outstanding service, one of the best restaurants in town, and an excellent gym, this sleek and modern hotel offers the best value in this price category. Try the cheap, in-house burger joint after going for a rooftop swim. Rooms are large, with high design and the latest technology. **www.parkermeridien.com**

The London, NYC
$$$$ | Map 2 E4

151 West 54th St, 10019 **Tel** *(212) 307-5000* **Fax** *(212) 765-6530* **Rooms** *561*

A charming mural of Hyde Park marks this 54-story tower, an all-suite hotel with some of the city's largest accommodations, and smartly refurbished by British designer David Collins. The London, NYC boasts the well-reviewed debut in the United States of British star chef Gordon Ramsay. **www.thelondonnyc.com**

Sofitel
❄ [P] 🍴 🍸 [W] $$$$

45 West 44th St, 10036 **Tel** *(212) 354-8844* **Fax** *(212) 354-2480* **Rooms** *398* **Map** *12 F5*

This 30-story property blends modern and classic design and was an instant hit in the Theater District, with warm decor, helpful service, and a pleasant brasserie. High floor rooms facing the front have fabulous views and some of the top tier suites have terraces. A favorite with both business and leisure travelers. **www.sofitel.com**

W Times Square
❄ 🍴 👪 🍸 [W] $$$$

1567 Broadway, 10036 **Tel** *(212) 930-7400* **Fax** *(212) 930-7500* **Rooms** *507* **Map** *12 E5*

This hip hotel from the Starwood Group continues to draw crowds and fans because of its high-design and ultra-modern rooms. Although somewhat dark, they offer fantastic views of midtown. The lounges and restaurants are always happening places. Make sure to check out Blue Fin for great sushi. **www.whotels.com**

Ritz-Carlton, New York, Central Park
❄ 🍴 👪 🍸 [W] $$$$$

50 Central Park South, 10019 **Tel** *(212) 308-9100* **Fax** *(212) 207-8831* **Rooms** *260* **Map** *12 F3*

Fans rave that this is the best hotel for service in the entire Ritz-Carlton chain. Traditional in style, the large rooms are extremely comfortable and filled with the latest technology. The full-service spa and location across from Central Park make it a true winner. **www.ritzcarlton.com**

LOWER MIDTOWN

Hotel Grand Union
❄ 👪 $

34 East 32nd St, 10016 **Tel** *(212) 683-5890* **Fax** *(212) 689-7397* **Rooms** *95* **Map** *9 A3*

Extreme budget travelers of all ages find the Grand Union of good value for the level of service it offers. While rooms can be downright unattractive, they are well maintained and have all the necessary comforts. Some rooms are large enough for families. **www.hotelgrandunion.com**

Courtyard New York
❄ 🍴 👪 🍸 [W] $$

3 East 40th St, 10016 **Tel** *(212) 447-1500* **Fax** *(212) 683-7839* **Rooms** *185* **Map** *8 F1*

The neighborhood can be pricey, but this hotel, a member of the Marriott chain, offers good value for its price range. Families appreciate the location, since it is close to the New York Public Library and the Theater District, but without the noise. The on-site Salmon River restaurant serves excellent seafood dishes. **www.courtyard.com**

70 Park
❄ 🍴 👪 🍸 [W] $$$

70 Park Ave, 10016 **Tel** *(212) 973 2400* **Fax** *(212) 973-2401* **Rooms** *205* **Map** *9 A1*

This smart addition in the boutique category from the well-regarded Kimpton Group is stylish and well executed. Pets are welcome, and they provide extra amenities for the little critters. Business travelers appreciate the free extras such as Wi-Fi and high-speed internet. Rooms can be small, but comfortable. **www.70parkave.com**

Affinia Dumont
❄ 👪 🍸 [W] $$$

150 East 34th St, 10016 **Tel** *(212) 481 7600* **Fax** *(212) 889-8856* **Rooms** *248* **Map** *9 A2*

This all-suite hotel is perfect for travelers who want space and comfortable design. Amenities include full kitchens with microwave ovens, and the helpful staff will even do grocery shopping for you. The on-site spa is excellent and will help travelers stay refreshed. **www.affinia.com**

Dylan
❄ 🍴 🍸 [W] $$$

52 East 41st St, 10017 **Tel** *(212) 338-0500* **Fax** *(212) 338-0569* **Rooms** *107* **Map** *9 A1*

This boutique property is the former home of the Chemists Club, a 1903 Beaux-Arts building. The lobby may feel a little antiseptic, but the rooms are spacious by city standards. A decent steakhouse is on the premises, which is good, because there aren't too many good options nearby. **www.dylanhotel.com**

Library Hotel
❄ [W] $$$

299 Madison Ave, 10017 **Tel** *(212) 983-4500* **Fax** *(212) 499-9099* **Rooms** *60* **Map** *9 A1*

This unique boutique hotel features cleverly designed rooms organized around a library theme. From fairy tales to erotic literature, choose your room based upon mood, and you'll get the books to go with it. A lovely rooftop terrace and all-day snacks make this a winning choice. **www.libraryhotel.com**

W The Court / W The Tuscany
❄ 🍴 👪 🍸 [W] $$$

120–130 East 39th St, 10016 **Tel** *(212) 686-1600* **Fax** *(212) 779-8352* **Rooms** *320* **Map** *9 A1*

This matched set of club-like properties offers boutique-style hotels with much better service. Rooms are equipped with the latest technology, and many offer free movie downloads. The Court has a trendier lounge scene, while the Tuscany is a little more relaxed. Both are recommended in this price range. **www.whotels.com**

Bryant Park
❄ 🍸 [W] $$$$

40 West 40th St, 10018 **Tel** *(212) 869-0100* **Fax** *(212) 869-4446* **Rooms** *128* **Map** *8 F1*

Wonderful pedigree and great location makes this midtown find a winner. The stunning American Radiator Building (with all the gold leaf) is home to minimalist design luxury across from Bryant Park. The Cellar Bar is filled with fashionistas; it also has a 70-seat screening room. **www.bryantparkhotel.com**

Fitzpatrick Grand Central Hotel
🖼️🛗 $$$$
141 East 44th St, 10017 **Tel** *(212) 351-6800* **Fax** *(212) 818-1747* **Rooms** *155*   **Map** *13 A5*

An elegant hotel with charming service only steps away from Grand Central Terminal. Rooms go beyond business comforts with luscious colors, and some have canopied beds. An on-site pub offers after-hours fun. Its location near many subway lines make it a good base for exploring. **www.fitzpatrickhotels.com**

Kitano
🖼️🍴🛗🅦 $$$$
66 Park Ave, 10016 **Tel** *(212) 885-7000* **Fax** *(212) 885-7100* **Rooms** *149*   **Map** *9 A2*

Buttoned-up Japanese-style service is the name of the game at this elegant midtown hotel, which caters primarily to a business crowd. Hotel rooms are havens of serenity with complimentary Japanese green tea. The restaurant also draws a crowd. This part of Park Avenue can seem amazingly serene. **www.kitano.com**

UPPER MIDTOWN

Hotel 57
🖼️🍴 $$
130 East 57th St, 10022 **Tel** *(212) 753-8841* **Fax** *(212) 869-9605* **Rooms** *220*   **Map** *13 A3*

The hotel lives up to the label "cheap chic," effortlessly combining high design with low prices. While the rooms can be narrow and often share baths in the hallway, it's hard to beat the price with such a great midtown location, close to all major shopping. Great views from the 17th-floor bar. **www.hotel57.com**

The Pod Hotel
🖼️ $$
230 East 51st St, 10022 **Tel** *(212) 355-0300* **Fax** *(212) 755-5029* **Rooms** *320*   **Map** *13 B4*

The Pod's prices are very reasonable, especially for the prime neighborhood. Be sure to inquire about private baths and the exact size of the room, as many can be tiny. But all are clean, and the hotel runs exceedingly well. Single rooms are a bargain. There is also a rooftop terrace. **www.thepodhotel.com**

Courtyard by Marriott Midtown East
🖼️📺🅦 $$$
866 Third Ave, 10022 **Tel** *(212) 644-1300* **Fax** *(212) 317-7940* **Rooms** *308*   **Map** *13 B4*

The spacious rooms make this a good choice for families that need to be in this neighborhood. Rooms are modern and have in-room coffee makers and free high-speed internet access. Free Wi-Fi is available in a special lounge. The neighborhood can be much quieter at night. **www.marriott.com**

Doubletree Metropolitan Hotel
🖼️🍴🛗📺 $$$
569 Lexington Ave, 10022 **Tel** *(212) 752-7000* **Fax** *(212) 758-6311* **Rooms** *722*   **Map** *13 A4*

This former Loews property is now being managed by the Doubletree group, which means service remains strong with a special catering to families. Rates are reasonable, and while rooms can be small, they are well cared for. Restaurants on-site are good family dining options. **www.metropolitanhotelnyc.com**

Kimberly Hotel
🖼️🍴🛗 $$$
145 East 50th St, 10022 **Tel** *(212) 755-0400* **Fax** *(212) 486-6915* **Rooms** *185*   **Map** *13 A5*

For large space and great value, this low-profile establishment is perhaps the best choice. The one- and two-bedroom suites feel like apartments, with full-size kitchens and well-appointed furniture. The location is wonderful for a little peace and quiet, yet close to good shopping. **www.kimberlyhotel.com**

Roger Smith
🖼️🛗🅦 $$$
501 Lexington Ave, 10022 **Tel** *(212) 755-1400* **Fax** *(212) 758-4061* **Rooms** *130*   **Map** *13 A5*

This unassuming property has a few high-design touches that separate it from the rest of the pack. Rooms are larger than normal and individually decorated. Rates include breakfast. Draws a diverse crowd, from businessmen to arty folk. The neighborhood calms down a bit when the sun goes down. **www.rogersmith.com**

The Benjamin
🖼️🍴🛗📺🅦 $$$$
125 East 50th St, 10022 **Tel** *(212) 715-2500* **Fax** *(212) 715-2525* **Rooms** *209*   **Map** *13 A4*

The modern rooms in this low-key hotel are designed for comfort. The work stations are perfect for business travelers. Each room has a kitchenette, and comes with a varied pillow menu to guarantee you a perfect night's sleep. Restaurant and small spa on site as well. **www.thebenjamin.com**

Omni Berkshire Place
🖼️🛗📺🅦 $$$$
21 East 52nd St, 10022 **Tel** *(212) 753-5800* **Fax** *(212) 754-5018* **Rooms** *396*   **Map** *12 F4*

The decor is designed for comfort at this understated hotel. Service earns high marks and the wealth of business facilities make it a great choice for the business traveler. But the hotel also caters to families, so make sure you check for discounted weekend rates. The area is a little less hectic than most. **www.omnihotels.com**

Waldorf-Astoria / Waldorf Towers
🖼️🛗📺🅦 $$$$
301 Park Ave, 10022 **Tel** *(212) 355-3000* **Fax** *(212) 872-7272* **Rooms** *1,242*   **Map** *13 A5*

This New York legend is still kicking, despite complaints about indifferent service. Rates can be reasonable because the hotel is enormous, but it does have a historical feel about it. Rooms are large, and if you score one in the exclusive Towers, you can expect 24-hour butler service. **www.waldorfastoria.com**

Key to Price Guide *see p280* **Key to Symbols** *see back cover flap*

Four Seasons New York

🔲 🅿 🍴 � 📺 $$$$$

57 East 57th St, 10022 **Tel** *(212) 758-5700* **Fax** *(212) 758-5711* **Rooms** *368*   **Map** 13 A3

One of the crown jewels in the Four Seasons chain is this I.M. Pei-designed tower that rises 52 stories above midtown – the tallest hotel in Manhattan. The lobby reeks of New York power and elegance and is worth a look. Rooms are large and extremely comfortable with fabulous views of Central Park. **www.fourseasons.com/newyorkfs**

New York Palace

🔲 🍴 � 📺 ⓦ $$$$$

455 Madison Ave, 10022 **Tel** *(212) 888-7000* **Fax** *(212) 303-6000* **Rooms** *896*   **Map** 13 A4

This splendid hotel, housed in a landmark 1882 house, is a wonderfully lavish establishment with old-world style and good service. Many think it's the most serene and calming spot in NYC. The location is terrific and the views, notably of St. Patrick's Cathedral, are splendid. **www.newyorkpalace.com**

Peninsula New York

🔲 〰 � 📺 ⓦ $$$$$

700 Fifth Ave, 10019 **Tel** *(212) 956-2888* **Fax** *(212) 903-3949* **Rooms** *239*   **Map** 12 F4

Expect legendary Peninsula service at the small Asian chain's Big Apple outpost. Rooms are designed for ultimate comfort with the latest technology integrated seamlessly. The spa is one of the best in New York, and the rooftop bar and terrace is a prime choice for sunset drinks. Highly recommended. **www.peninsula.com**

The Plaza

🔲 🅿 🍴 📺 ⓦ $$$$$

Fifth Ave and Central Park South, 10019 **Tel** *(212) 759-3000* **Fax** *(212) 759-3001* **Rooms** *282*   **Map** 12 F3

New York's 1907 Grande Dame has emerged from a $400-million face-lift agleam with Baccarat chandeliers, vast expanses of marble, and large, luxurious rooms. Additions include a condominium tower, elaborate spa, and a two-story shopping center. The Palm Court, Oak Room, and Oak Bar remain. **www.fairmonthotels.com/theplaza**

St. Regis New York

🔲 🅿 🍴 � 📺 ⓦ $$$$$

2 East 55th St, 10022 **Tel** *(212) 753-4500* **Fax** *(212) 787-3447* **Rooms** *408*   **Map** 12 F4

This 1904 Beaux-Arts landmark is filled with luxury and old-world glamour, with chandeliers, expensive rugs, and a butler assigned to each floor. Service is very formal, but you would expect this of a grand dame. A favorite spot for weddings. The historic King Cole bar is known for its splendid Bloody Marys. **www.stregis.com**

UPPER EAST SIDE

Franklin

🔲 ⓦ $$$

164 East 87th St, 10128 **Tel** *(212) 369-1000* **Fax** *(212) 369-8000* **Rooms** *50*   **Map** 17 A3

Rooms may be tiny at this modern hotel, but they are well appointed with romantic canopied beds, flatscreen TVs, complimentary Wi-Fi, and the like. The limited space makes it the choice for short-term travelers or light packers. Continental breakfast included. Check for seasonal rates. **www.franklinhotel.com**

Hotel Wales

🔲 🍴 � 📺 $$$

1295 Madison Ave, 10028 **Tel** *(212) 876-6000* **Fax** *(212) 860-7000* **Rooms** *88*   **Map** 17 B2

A cozy, comfortable hotel that is well located for Museum Mile. The decor and furnishing feature some nice touches, such as mahogany furniture, Belgian linen on the beds, and fresh flowers in the rooms. There are some wonderful city views from the rooftop terrace. **www.waleshotel.com**

Surrey Hotel

🔲 🍴 � $$$$

20 East 76th St, 10021 **Tel** *(212) 288-3700* **Fax** *(212) 628-1549* **Rooms** *130*   **Map** 17 A5

This all-suite hotel is a lovely choice for those willing to spend extra on dramatically more space. Each suite has a fully-equipped kitchen, but the reason to stay here is the in-suite dining from the famous Café Boulud downstairs. Cheaper diners and pizzerias are all around the area. **www.thesurrey.com**

Carlyle

🔲 🍴 � 📺 $$$$$

35 East 76th St, 10021 **Tel** *(212) 744-1600* **Fax** *(212) 717-4682* **Rooms** *187*   **Map** 17 A5

You'll feel like a true Upper Eastsider in a room at this legendary hotel. The elegant rooms and phenomenal service have drawn heads of state and movie stars alike. Afternoon tea attracts the who's who of New York socialites. Central location just one block from Central Park but away from the hustle and bustle. **www.thecarlyle.com**

The Pierre

🔲 🍴 � 📺 ⓦ $$$$$

2 East 61st St, 10021 **Tel** *(212) 838-8000* **Fax** *(212) 940-8109* **Rooms** *203*   **Map** 12 F3

Inviting service makes this sophisticated hotel seem not so intimidating. The interiors are grand, but the rooms have a residential feel. Royalty would feel right at home here, with gloved elevator operators. The bar and restaurant are both recommended. **www.tajhotels.com/pierre**

Sherry-Netherland

🔲 🍴 � 📺 ⓦ $$$$$

781 Fifth Ave, 10022 **Tel** *(212) 355-2800* **Fax** *(212) 319-4306* **Rooms** *50*   **Map** 12 F3

A little less stuffy than next-door neighbor The Pierre, this old-world style hotel defines residential living in New York City. Suites are enormous, and the service is top-of-the-class. Breakfast at the downstairs Cipriani's is included in the price, if you can handle sitting with fellow powerbrokers. **www.sherrynetherland.com**

UPPER WEST SIDE

Amsterdam Inn $

340 Amsterdam Ave, 10024 **Tel** *(212) 579-7500* **Fax** *(212) 545-0103* **Rooms** *25*   **Map** *15 C5*

All rooms are well cared for in this budget establishment, but the rooms can be narrow. Some share baths, but the private ones are good value. Be sure to verify that a "double" is actually a real bed for two, rather than a single and pull-out trundle. Excellent location near Upper West Side museums. **www.amsterdaminn.com**

Hostelling International – New York $

891 Amsterdam Ave, 10025 **Tel** *(212) 932-2300* **Fax** *(212) 932-2574* **Rooms** *628*   **Map** *20 E5*

You will feel like you've gone back to college in this mammoth building that feels exactly like a dormitory. The good news is that it features all the upside of campus living – cafeteria, game room, laundry, internet access, and picnic tables. The establishment is at least 18 years old. **www.hinewyork.org**

Hotel Newton $

2528 Broadway, 10025 **Tel** *(212) 678-6500* **Fax** *(212) 678-6758* **Rooms** *110*   **Map** *15 C2*

One of the best options for the price, this well-run hotel has clean and attractive rooms with nice bathrooms. Service is pleasant and professional. Guests have access to a state-of-the-art fitness club across the street. While there's no restaurant on the premises, there are many options up and down Broadway. **www.thehotelnewton.com**

Jazz on the Park $

36 West 106th St, 10025 **Tel** *(212) 932-1600* **Fax** *(212) 932-1700* **Rooms** *220*   **Map** *21 A5*

This arty hostel is extremely popular and brings a downtown feel to the sometimes staid Upper West Side. Don't miss the coffeehouse with live music that can be a little rowdy. Dorm rooms are very basic and so are the bathrooms. Very international crowd. The area keeps getting better and better. **www.jazzonthepark.com**

Milburn $

242 West 76th St, 10023 **Tel** *(212) 362-1006* **Fax** *(212) 721-5476* **Rooms** *114*   **Map** *15 C5*

This all-suite hotel is exceedingly well priced and offers all the comforts of home, including size. While not particularly smart, the rooms come with well-equipped kitchenettes and nice bathrooms. Staff are helpful and laundry facilities are also available. Good restaurants around the corner. **www.milburnhotel.com**

West End Studios $

850 West End Ave, 10025 **Tel** *(212) 749-7104* **Fax** *(212) 865-5130* **Rooms** *85*   **Map** *15 B1*

Blocks away from Riverside Park, this is a good budget choice for those who want to experience neighborhood living. A little way from the main subway lines, the hotel offers very basic and quite small rooms with shared baths. The family room comes with two beds and a bunkbed. **www.westendstudios.com**

Excelsior Hotel $$

45 West 81st St, 10024 **Tel** *(212) 362-9200* **Fax** *(212) 580-3972* **Rooms** *200*   **Map** *16 D4*

Welcoming Old World ambience awaits at this traditional hotel with comfortable rooms, a warm library/sitting room/ breakfast room, and a well-equipped fitness center. The American Museum of Natural History is across the street, Central Park and a subway to midtown are on the corner. A good family choice. **www.excelsiorhotelnyc.com**

Hotel Beacon $$

2130 Broadway, 10023 **Tel** *(212) 787-1100* **Fax** *(212) 724-0839* **Rooms** *236*   **Map** *15 C5*

Families enjoy the extra-large rooms and laundry facilities on offer at this great-value hotel. The rooms aren't the best in town, but they have kitchenettes and often can accommodate four people. Larger groups should inquire about the two-bedroom/two-bath suites. **www.beaconhotel.com**

Lucerne $$

201 West 79th St, 10024 **Tel** *(212) 875-1000* **Fax** *(212) 579-2408* **Rooms** *184*   **Map** *15 C4*

This lovely jewel of a mid-priced hotel is housed in an elegant 1903 building. The rooms are very well maintained and feature Americana furnishings. Rates include Continental breakfast, and don't miss the live jazz and blues in the stylish bar and grill. Other good restaurant options are just blocks away. **www.thelucernehotel.com**

On the Ave $$

2178 Broadway, 10024 **Tel** *(212) 362-1100* **Fax** *(212) 787-9521* **Rooms** *251*   **Map** *15 C5*

Style is the name of the game at this mid-range budget hotel filled with modern design. Rooms have modular furniture in natural hues. A great deck offers beautiful views of the city. If possible, spring for a deluxe room, otherwise you might be too cramped. Good dining options up and down the avenue. **www.ontheave-nyc.com**

6 Columbus $$$

6 Columbus Circle, 10019 **Tel** *(212) 204-3000* **Fax** *(212) 204-3030* **Rooms** *88*   **Map** *12 D3*

The former West Park Hotel has been transformed by the trendy Thompson Hotel group with retro 1960s decor, four added floors and an uptown outpost of SoHo's popular Blue Ribbon Sushi restaurant. The Time Warner Center and Central Park are very close, Broadway and Lincoln Center a short walk away. **www.thompsonhotels.com**

Empire Hotel ❄ [P] 🍴 💼 🍸 [W] $$$

44 West 63rd St, 10023 **Tel** *(212) 265-7400* **Fax** *(212) 265-7401* **Rooms** *420* **Map** *12 D2*

Only the 1920s metal canopy remains of the old Empire, there is now a dramatic entry, chic lobby and bar, stunning rooftop setting for cocktails, and an outdoor plunge pool for guests. Modernistic room decor is in earth tones. Most baths have shower only, but they are walk-ins with rain shower heads. **www.empirehotelnyc.com**

Inn New York City [W] $$$$

266 West 71st St, 10023 **Tel** *(212) 580-1900* **Fax** *(212) 580-4437* **Rooms** *4* **Map** *11 C1*

Nothing but the best will do at this small, intimate, and charming guesthouse. A renovated 19th-century townhouse, it has four suites, each with its own theme – Opera, Library, Vermont, or Spa. All rooms are equipped with top-notch amenities, and the in-suite breakfast is delightful. An over-the-top treat to be sure. **www.innnewyorkcity.com**

Mandarin Oriental New York ❄ 🍴 💼 🏋 🍸 [W] $$$$$

80 Columbus Circle, 10023 **Tel** *(212) 805-8800* **Fax** *(212) 805-8888* **Rooms** *248* **Map** *12 D3*

Asian opulence comes at quite a price in this dramatic hotel. Rooms are modern-Oriental and feature terrific views of Central Park and the Hudson, if on a high floor. The spa is wonderful, but pricey. The bar and restaurants offer the same view and can be quite a scene in the evening. **www.mandarinoriental.com**

Trump International Hotel & Tower ❄ 🍴 🏋 🍸 [W] $$$$$

1 Central Park West, 10023 **Tel** *(212) 299-1000* **Fax** *(212) 299-1150* **Rooms** *167* **Map** *12 D3*

This modern luxury hotel tower prides itself on its exclusivity, discretion, and style. Lovely rooms are decorated in soothing tones and offer the latest technology. The unobstructed views of Central Park is the real draw, as is the Jean-Georges restaurant downstairs. **www.trumpintl.com**

MORNINGSIDE HEIGHTS AND HARLEM

Astor on the Park ❄ $

465 Central Park West, 10025 **Tel** *(212) 866-1880* **Fax** *(212) 316-9555* **Rooms** *112* **Map** *21 A5*

On Central Park West at 106th Street, the convenient location of this hotel more than makes up for the small, basic rooms. It is an ideal choice for visitors on a budget who plan to be out for most of the day (and night!). The bathrooms are clean, and the staff friendly.

Morningside Inn Hotel ❄ $

235 West 107th St, 10025 **Tel** *(212) 316-0055* **Fax** *(212) 864-9155* **Rooms** *96* **Map** *20 E5*

This hotel is modern and fresh, although it still retains the air of a dormitory. Best for students or single travelers, try and score a double deluxe, which will assure you a private bath and air-conditioning. All rooms are clean and well cared for. **www.morningsideinn-ny.com**

Sugar Hill Harlem Inn $$

460 West 141st St, 10031 **Tel** *(212) 234-5432* **Fax** *(212) 234-5432* **Rooms** *5* **Map** *19 A2*

Attractive rooms in this Victorian town house have names like Miles and Ella for the jazz greats who once favored this neighborhood. Two accommodations are studios with kitchens, one is a two-bedroom apartment. Most have fireplaces; all have private bathrooms, TV, DVD player, and air-conditioning. **www.sugarhillharleminn.com**

FARTHER AFIELD

BROOKLYN Best Western Gregory Hotel Brooklyn ❄ $$

8315 Fourth Ave, 11209 **Tel** *(718) 238-3737* **Fax** *(718) 680-0827* **Rooms** *70*

While this hotel is quite off the beaten path, it is a good choice for those who need to be in Brooklyn. The subway is only a few blocks away. Rooms can be small, but are well maintained. Past service problems seem to have been fixed with a change in management. Several cheap eats around the corner. **www.bestwestern.com**

BROOKLYN Marriott Brooklyn Bridge ❄ [P] 🍴 💼 🍸 [W] $$

333 Adams St, 11201 **Tel** *(718) 246-7000* **Fax** *(718) 246-0563* **Rooms** *355*

The only full-service hotel in Brooklyn, this is a wonderful option for business and leisure travelers who want to explore this borough but be close to Financial District. Nine major subway lines converge outside the hotel, and the rooms are nicely decorated. Lobby is grand, and there's a large fitness center with a pool. **www.marriott.com**

QUEENS Sheraton LaGuardia East Hotel ❄ [P] 🍴 🍸 [W] $$

135–20 39th Ave, 11354 **Tel** *(718) 460-6666* **Fax** *(718) 445-2655* **Rooms** *173*

A comfortable, full-service 16-story hotel in the heart of Flushing's booming Chinatown, offering free transportation to LaGuardia airport and easy access to Mets games at Citi Field or the Arthur Ashe Tennis Center. Features include fitness and business centers, in-room coffee makers, and free Wi-Fi. **www.sheraton.com/laguardia**

RESTAURANTS AND BARS

New Yorkers love to eat well, and in the five boroughs there are more than 25,000 restaurants catering to their wishes. City dwellers avidly read restaurant reviews in magazines such as *New York* to ensure that they are seen in the latest fashionable eatery. "In" places and cuisine change with great regularity, while some favorite places simply remain popular.

The classic
Manhattan cocktail

The restaurants cited in our listings have been selected as the best that New York can offer across a wide price range. While the information on pages 296–311 will help you to select a suitable restaurant, there are details of lighter refreshments on pages 312–14. *New York's Bars* on pages 315–17 highlights some of the city's best drinking spots.

RESTAURANT MENUS

Meals in most of the better restaurants consist of three courses: an appetizer (starter), an entrée (the main course), and a dessert. In some fine restaurants you may be offered a complimentary appetizer, such as a small dollop of mousse or a tiny triangle of quiche. Appetizers at the better restaurants are often the chef's most creative dishes – some diners request two appetizers and no entrée. Italian menus offer a pasta

Street-corner hot dog stand

dish as a course before the main course, but in many places pasta is seen as a main course. Coffee or tea and a dessert ordinarily conclude the meal in restaurants above the coffee-shop level. Your coffee cup may be refilled until you refuse any more. Some of the better establishments feature a cheeseboard on the menu.
   To get a sense of a restaurant's cuisine, visit www.menupages.com, which features the menus of several thousand Manhattan eateries. Other local websites, including the weekly *New York* magazine's (www. nymag.com), often have links to restaurant menus.

PRICES

You will always find a restaurant in New York to suit your budget. At inexpensive coffee shops, diners and fast-food chains, $10–$15 will buy you a filling meal. There are also hundreds of acceptable, even first-rate, restaurants where you can eat well at a moderate cost – around $25 per person for a filling and decent meal, not including drinks – in attractive surroundings.
   For dinner at a trendy New American venue with a star chef, the bill could be upward of $80 to $100 per person, excluding drinks. Many top restaurants do, however, offer fixed-price (or, as they are known in New York, prix-fixe) meals. This is normally a much cheaper way of enjoying a good meal than choosing dishes from the à la carte menu. Lunch is also less expensive than dinner in such places and, because of the profusion of business diners, lunch is often the busiest period of the day.

TAXES AND TIPPING

New York city sales tax of 8.625% will be added to your bill. Service is not usually included. Tipping can run from 10% at a coffee shop to 20% at the fanciest places, with 15% an average fair tip. Many people just double the sales tax to work out a tip.

A typical New York deli *(see p312)*

The bill is known as the "check" in the US. The most commonly accepted credit cards are VISA, MasterCard and American Express. Traveler's checks are taken in many restaurants. Diners and coffee shops may accept cash only. In fast-food chains, you order at the counter and pay cash in advance. Some other types of establishment also take only cash.

DINING ON A BUDGET

Despite the tales of $200 business lunches, there are ways to stretch a meal budget in New York.
   Order fewer courses than you would normally. American portions are huge, and an appetizer is often big enough for a light main course. You could share one with your companion or choose two appetizers and no entrée.
   Ask your waiter if there is a prix-fixe menu. Many of the more expensive restaurants offer this at lunch and dinner – in the early evening it may be called the pre-theater menu. Or try a prix-fixe lunch buffet. These are popular in Indian

McSorley's Old Ale House *(see p316)* restaurants and

other places and make for very reasonably priced meals.

Other options for a quick, tasty, and restorative meal are the less expensive Chinese, Thai, and Mexican restaurants. Italian pizzerias and French bistros, as well as the small eateries that serve hamburgers or sandwiches and desserts, also offer good value. Alternatively, go to bars featuring "happy hours." They often offer a variety of substantial hors d'oeuvres, like Spanish *tapas*, which can make a meal in themselves.

If you simply want to see inside the restaurants every visitor has heard about, just go to have a drink and soak up the atmosphere. Many restaurants post their menus or will let you see them before you are seated, good for checking prices in advance. During Restaurant Week (usually in January and July), you can dine in some of the city's restaurants for a fraction of the usual cost – visit www.nycgo.com/restaurantweek.

Poolside dining at Four Seasons (see p307)

HOURS

Breakfast hours are usually from 7 to 10:30 or 11am. Sunday brunch, a popular meal, is served at most better restaurants between about 11am and 3pm. Lunch runs from 11:30am or noon to 2:30pm at most places, but the busiest time of the day is 1pm. Dinner is usually served from 5:30 or 6pm onward. The most popular time is around 7:30 or 8pm.

Some restaurants stop serving at 10pm during the week, or 11pm on Friday and Saturday. Certain informal restaurants are open from 11:30am to 10pm. Coffee shops are open long hours, from 7am to midnight or even 24 hours.

Dining in style at the Oyster Bar in Grand Central Terminal *(see p306)*

DRESS CODES

Few restaurants demand that male diners dress formally, though a jacket is required at classy restaurants, and a jacket and tie at the very best. At most restaurants, for both men and women, smart "business casual" suffices.

Women tend to dress up when dining at the more expensive restaurants. If you are unsure, check what the dress code is when you make your reservation.

RESERVATIONS

It is wise to make reservations at any restaurant above the diner/fast-food level, especially on weekends. Some of the trendiest restaurants won't accept bookings, or won't take them less than two months in advance. Be sure to make reservations for lunch at a midtown restaurant. Note that you may still have to wait at the bar, even if you have booked. Waits of an hour at the most popular spots are not unusual.

SMOKING

Smoking is illegal in all bars and restaurants in New York. The only exceptions are owner-operated bars that have special smoking rooms.

CHILDREN

When eating out with children, ask if there's a child's menu with half-portions. The prices are reduced, sometimes by half. Children are accepted in most New York restaurants,

but if yours are unpredictable stick to casual spots, Chinatown Chinese or family-run Italian restaurants, burger bars, delis, cafés, fast food chains and diners. A few of the better restaurants have facilities for babies or toddlers; others may not be so well equipped. Dining out in the more formal New York restaurants is certainly not a family affair.

WHEELCHAIR ACCESS

While many restaurants may be able to accommodate a wheelchair, always mention your requirements when making your reservation. Many of the smaller places cannot cater to disabled customers because of lack of space.

CELEBRITY CHEFS

New York City attracts top chefs from around the world, all of whom are determined to make their mark and win over the local diners and the *New York Times*' influential restaurant reviewer.

A meal in a top restaurant will not come cheaply, but it can be worth the splurge. Booking a table can be difficult, and reservations should be made as early as two months in advance. Some reservations can be made online through Opentable (www.opentable.com).

Among the best names and signature venues are Thomas Keller (Per Se), Daniel Bouley (Daniel), Gordon Ramsay (London NYC), Jean-Georges Vongerichten (Jean-Georges), Mario Batali (Babbo), Alain Ducasse (Adour), and Nobu Matsuhisa (Nobu New York).

The Flavors of New York

Few cities can match the diversity of New York's restaurants. Reflecting the city's melting pot of nationalities, foods range from the "hautest" of French and continental cuisine to the freshest sushi outside of Tokyo. Caribbean, Mexican, Thai, Vietnamese, Korean, Greek, Indian – all are well represented, and every block seems to have an Italian restaurant. The quality of the city's top restaurants is unsurpassed and their chefs are superstars, as well-known and revered as movie idols. Yet, because so many nationalities are represented in its culinary culture, only a few foods are native to the city itself.

Dim sum

Fresh, local produce on display at the Greenmarket

DELI DINING

A large Jewish population has given rise to some of New York's best known specialties, now enjoyed by all – overstuffed corned beef and pastrami sandwiches, dill pickles, matzo ball soup, herrings, blintzes, and bagels served with cream cheese

and smoked salmon. The bagel, once synonymous with New York, has become a universal American food, but a true New York bagel is nothing like the bready imitations found in the hinterlands. It is shaped by hand, and the dough is cooked briefly in boiling water before being baked, resulting in a unique firm and chewy texture. A relative, and another New York specialty, is the bialy,

a flat, chewy flour-dusted roll with a center indentation filed with toasted onions. The finest examples of each are to be found in the kosher bakeries of the Lower East Side *(see pp92–101)*.

THE GREENMARKET

You may well find yourself next to a well-known chef browsing at New York's greenmarkets, open-air markets where farmers from

Pastrami on rye **Blintzes** **Dill pickles** **Bagels with smoked salmon and cream cheese** **Pickled herrings**

Selection of classic foods available at any New York deli

NEW YORK SPECIALTIES

While New York dining may span all nations, a few special dishes are closely associated with the city. Manhattan Clam Chowder, prepared with tomatoes rather than cream, has been popular ever since it was introduced at Coney Island beach stands in the 1880s. In the city's many steak houses, a prime selection is the "New York strip steak," a boneless sirloin cut from the short loin, the tenderest portion of beef. Italian cuisine has often been given a New York spin. Rich and creamy New York cheesecake is made with cream cheese rather the Italian ricotta. And, since traditional wood-burning ovens were impractical in New York, the first Italian immigrant chefs used coal ovens. Though these are rare today, purists still insist they are necessary for a true New York pizza.

Pretzels

Manhattan clam chowder
This is a rich blend of potatoes, onions, tomatoes, oyster crackers crumbs and clams.

Fast food cart on a Manhattan street corner, selling hots dogs and sodas

upstate New York sell fresh-picked fruits and vegetables, as well as meat, poultry and dairy products. Over 105 city restaurants patronize the greenmarkets, so you'll find ultra-fresh local produce on many menus in the city. As many as 70 vendors attend the biggest of the markets in Union Square on Monday, Wednesday, Friday, and Saturday *(see p129)*.

STREET FOOD

Street food is a favorite choice in a fast-moving city. Hot dogs and oversize soft pretzels are classic New York choices, along with some surprisingly good food cart specialties, from falafel to soup to barbecue to Texas chile, all ready to eat on the run. In winter, vendors all over town offer hot roasted chestnuts.

SOUL FOOD

Harlem is America's largest African-American community, and restaurants here are the place to sample specialties from the Deep South, such as fried chicken, ribs, collard

An Oriental produce store in New York's Chinatown

greens, yams, flaky biscuits or cornbread. A popular Harlem dish, fried chicken and waffles, is said to have originated to serve musicians leaving jazz clubs in the wee hours.

ASIAN FOOD RIVALS

Chinese restaurants and dim sum parlors have long been found throughout the city, but lately they have been challenged by the arrival of many excellent Thai and Vietnamese restaurants. All these, however, take second place to the multiplying sushi bars and high-profile, highly praised Japanese chefs.

DELICATESSEN CLASSICS

Babkas Slightly sweet, yeasted coffee cakes.

Blintzes Crêpes filled with sweetened soft white cheese and/or fruit and sautéd.

Chopped liver Chicken livers mashed with minced onion, hard-cooked eggs and *schmaltz* (chicken fat).

Gefilte fish Minced white fish dumplings poached in fish broth. A holiday dish.

Knishes Soft dough shells filled with oniony mashed potatoes.

Latkes Grated potato, onion and matzo-meal pancakes.

Rugelach Rich, cream-cheese-dough pastries filled with jam, chopped nuts and raisins.

New York-style pizza *Thick- or thin-crusted, a true New York pizza must be baked in a coal-fired oven.*

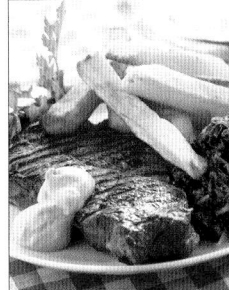

New York Strip Steak *Served with creamed spinach, fries or hash-browns, this tender steak is hard to beat.*

New York cheesecake *This is a dense, rich, baked cake with a crust of pastry or graham crackers (digestives).*

Choosing a Restaurant

The restaurants in this section have been selected for their good value and exceptional food. Within each area, entries are listed alphabetically within each price category, from the least to the most expensive. Details of *Light Meals and Snacks* are on pages 312–14 and for some of New York's best *Bars* see pages 315–17.

PRICE CATEGORIES
The following price ranges are for a three-course meal for one, including a glass of house wine and all unavoidable charges including sales tax:

$ under $25
$$ $25–$40
$$$ $40–$60
$$$$ $60–$80
$$$$$ over $80

LOWER MANHATTAN

George's New York
89 Greenwich St, 10006 **Tel** (212) 269-8026

$

Map 1 B1

Literally hundreds of dishes can be found on George's menu, which ranges from classic American diner regulars to more exotic fare like honey Dijon chicken and Romanian steak. Expect this place to be crowded at lunchtime, when it draws both businesspeople who work locally and tourists. Open 6am–10pm daily.

Adrienne's Pizza Bar
87 Pearl St, 10004 **Tel** (212) 248-3838

$$

Map 1 C4

The setting on a quaint street straight out of Old New York adds to the appeal of this popular spot, which is known for its thin-crust rectangular pizzas. An ideal stop for a tasty, inexpensive lunch while touring Lower Manhattan, but if you happen to be in the neighborhood at dinner, the mood is more serene.

Les Halles
15 John St between Broadway and Nassau St, 10038 **Tel** (212) 285-8585

$$

Map 1 C2

The Financial District meets a Parisian-style brasserie at this sister restaurant of the Park Avenue Les Halles, made famous by its celebrity chef Anthony Bourdain. Expect well-executed dishes such as mussels and *frites*. A heaven for carnivores, with a wide selection of grilled meats.

Battery Gardens
17 State St, Battery Park, 10004 **Tel** (212) 809-5508

$$$

Map 1 C4

It's worth a trip to the tip of Manhattan for the fantastic vistas of the harbor and the Statue of Liberty from this haven in Battery Park. The American-Continental menu is adequate, but the view is the lure. On a balmy day when you can sit on the terrace, there's no place like it.

Fraunces Tavern
54 Pearl St, corner of Broad Street, 10004 **Tel** (212) 968-1776

$$$

Map 1 C4

This historic tavern has been in operation since 1762 and was where George Washington bid a fond farewell to his officers, on the eve of his retirement in 1783. Classic American steak and fish dishes are on offer, along with wholesome pot roasts and soups. In winter warm up in the snug lounge.

Harry's Café
1 Hanover Sq, 10004 **Tel** (212) 785-9200

$$$

Map 1 C3

The former Bayard's has been restyled as a clubby steakhouse offering first-rate food and wine. If you don't have an expense account and your budget is limited, you can still enjoy the atmosphere of this landmark heritage building by choosing from a short and reasonably priced café menu. One of the few Wall Street spots open at the weekend.

SEAPORT AND THE CIVIC CENTER

Acqua at Peck Slip
21–23 Peck Slip, 10038 **Tel** (212) 349-4433

$$$

Map 2 D2

Amid the tourist traps of South Street Seaport, this Italian restaurant stands out like a beacon, serving up New American-tinged Italian dishes prepared with organic ingredients. Service can be a little slow, so just sit back and enjoy the vaulted ceilings and warm earthy tones that make this a cozy, romantic spot. The lasagna is fantastic.

Bridge Café
279 Water St at Dover St, 10038 **Tel** (212) 227-3344

$$$

Map 2 D2

A charming café located just below the Brooklyn Bridge, this age-old restaurant is worth a visit while in the area. Adventurers should try the specialty – buffalo steak with gnocchi. For the tamer, there are still plenty of options – from lobster pot pie and fresh fish to a grilled vegetables and goat's cheese plate.

Key to Symbols *see back cover flap*

Stella Maris
213 Front St, 10038 **Tel** *(212) 233-2437*   **Map** *2 D2*

A welcome find in the Seaport area, Stella Maris is a pleasant bistro with sleek decor. The seasonal modern European menu puts the emphasis on seafood, including a superb black sole, and offers a few pub favorites. The Raw Bar features oysters, clams, and treats such as poached lobster. The outdoor terrace is a great place for brunch.

LOWER EAST SIDE

Grand Sichuan
125 Canal St at Bowery, 10002 **Tel** *(212) 625-9212*   **Map** *4 E5*

A never-ending menu with all kinds of Sichuan, Hunang, and "Chinese-food American style," as well as all types of hot (including spicy) and cold noodles and fried rice. It also offers a wide variety of vegetarian dishes. Spotty service and scant decor may be the reason for the quite affordable prices.

Katz Delicatessen
205 East Houston St, 10002 **Tel** *(212) 254-2246*   **Map** *5 A3*

A New York City classic, this Jewish deli continues to serve the best towering pastrami and corned beef sandwiches. Don't expect much from service or decor – it's all in the pastrami and the very affordable prices. Famous for sending salami to the army, way before *that* scene from *When Harry Met Sally* (which is commemorated with a sign).

Teany Café
90 Rivington St, 10002 **Tel** *(212) 475-9190*   **Map** *5 A3*

Rock star Moby owns this famous café offering all vegan and vegetarian sandwiches, salads, and nibblers. Great desserts, too, such as the chocolate peanut butter bomb and the warm rhubarb pie. The "afternoon tea service" for one or two is worth a try.

Il Palazzo
151 Mulberry St, 10013 **Tel** *(212) 343-7000*   **Map** *4 F4*

Il Palazzo ranks among Little Italy's few good Italian restaurants, especially when it comes to service. A glassed-in garden boosts its charm. Home-made pastas and risotti are always good and inexpensive choices. Popular desserts include cannoli and tiramisu.

Joe's Shanghai
9 Pell St, 10013 **Tel** *(212) 233-8888*   **Map** *4 F5*

When visiting this famous local restaurant, don't miss the crab and pork soup dumplings. This dish is the main reason for long lines especially on weekends, but it's worth it. The rest of the menu is hit and miss but it's good value. Other locations may have better decor/service at the expense of food quality.

Sammy's Roumanian
157 Chrystie St, 10002 **Tel** *(212) 673-0330*   **Map** *5 A4*

The Jewish-inspired menu at Sammy's Roumanian offers traditional fare such as *latkes*, chopped liver, mashed potatoes with *schmaltz* (chicken fat), and a large selection of meat cuts. Try the garlic sausage with ice-cold vodka. Impromptu entertainment and singalongs add to the fun factor.

Macondo
157 E Houston St, 10002 **Tel** *(212) 473-9900*   **Map** *5 A3*

Despite the simple "Mexican beach-shack" look, Macondo has a lot to offer. The elevated street food from Spain and Central and South America – think tacos, tapas, arepas, and ceviches – is finger-licking good, and the spirited atmosphere and potent, tangy cocktails are hard to resist.

The Orchard
162 Orchard St, 10002 **Tel** *(212) 353-3570*   **Map** *5 A3*

Imaginative New American food is served up to a hip and young LES crowd. The decor is stylish, with subdued lighting. Don't miss the steak tartare flatbread. Wines come at a good range of price points, ensuring there is something for every budget.

The Stanton Social
99 Stanton St, 10002 **Tel** *(212) 995-0099*   **Map** *5 A3*

Groovy and gorgeous sums up the scene at this restaurant, where the atmosphere almost overshadows the food. The eclectic tapas menu has many mouthwatering options, from French onion soup and dumplings to mini burger "sliders" – but beware: the cost adds up quickly. The cocktails are equally inviting.

wd-50
50 Clinton St, 10002 **Tel** *(212) 477-2900*   **Map** *5 B3*

Wylie Dufresne, a pioneer in molecular gastronomy and the man behind the LES's food revolution, serves serious food in a casual setting that suits the neighborhood. His eclectic modern American cuisine is known for innovative touches, like lamb flavored with banana consommé. If you can't get a reservation, walk-ins are welcome for bar dining.

SOHO AND TRIBECA

Lombardi's
32 Spring St, 10012 **Tel** *(212) 941-7994*

Map 4 F4

Among the top pizzerias of the city, the brick-oven baked pies come thin, charred, and oozing a delectable mozzarella. Lombardi's pays the price for its popularity with big crowds and long lines, but a very welcome expansion now allows you and your friends to share the joy faster.

Peanut Butter & Co.
240 Sullivan St, 10012 **Tel** *(212) 677-3995*

Map 4 D2

A sandwich shop worth the trip to see the unbelievable combinations available with peanut butter. Yes, you can even get the famous Elvis Presley-inspired sandwich. Thankfully, you can get milk too, and plenty of other yummy desserts. Invite friends and bring your kids and your wallet won't even notice it.

Pho Pasteur
85 Baxter St, 10013 **Tel** *(212) 608-3656*

Map 4 F5

A tiny restaurant in the midst of Chinatown, offering a cheap and fast choice of noodles. Try the Vietnamese rolls with lettuce leaves and rice noodles. You can even see yourself sweat in the mirrored walls in case you order any of their spicy dishes. Also try the large variety of Asian beverages.

Aquagrill
210 Spring St, 10012 **Tel** *(212) 274-0505*

Map 4 D4

Aquagrill is a seafood-lovers' paradise with very fresh ingredients. An oyster bar selection to die for, a reliable kitchen, and courteous service are all ingredients for success adding up to a busy dining room. The mussel soup with saffron comes highly recommended.

Balthazar
80 Spring St, 10012 **Tel** *(212) 965-1414*

Map 4 E4

The jewel in restaurateur Keith McNally's crown remains a popular draw, thanks to the Parisian brasserie setting, good-quality food, superb wine selection, and lively bar scene – you'll find SoHo literati, VIPs, and tourists rubbing shoulders here. Balthazar is a good choice for both brunch and late-night dining. There is also an excellent on-site bakery.

The Harrison
355 Greenwich St, 10013 **Tel** *(212) 274-9310*

Map 4 D5

A New England seafront house in the midst of TriBeCa offering good "re-engineered" American fare such as biscuits and gravy with chorizo and clams and a crispy chicken with chestnut stuffing. Very popular with the area's 30-somethings, which means long lines at times.

L'Ecole
462 Broadway, 10012 **Tel** *(212) 219-3300*

Map 4 E4

This small and charming SoHo restaurant is used by the students of the French Culinary Institute to do their hands-on training. The place offers different tasting menus at reasonable prices considering the good quality of the food and unfailingly courteous service.

Lupa
170 Thompson St, 10012 **Tel** *(212) 982-5089*

Map 4 F3

An Italian *trattoria* courtesy of celebrity chef Mario Batali offering a cheaper alternative to its flagship Babbo. Expect a wide variety of dishes such as smoked eggplant, excellent fresh pastas, and accomplished entrées such as pork *saltimbocca*. Excellent Italian wine list.

Minetta Tavern
113 MacDougal St, 10012 **Tel** *(212) 475-3850*

Map 4 D2

This Italian bistro manages to be both casual and celebrity-friendly. The menu is short but perfectly formed, and each dish is prepared with great flair, from the *petite omelette*, frog's legs, and tasty bone marrow to the incredible range of steaks. Open only in the evenings (5:30pm–1am). Reservations recommended.

Odeon
145 West Broadway, 10013 **Tel** *(212) 233-0507*

Map 1 B1

One of the first restaurants to open in TriBeCa back in the 1980s, this "faux-bistro" offers good quality French-American fare. Don't miss the steak tartare, but note that the burgers are also top notch. The decor is simple and the place is always packed with a mixed crowd.

Peep
177 Prince St, 10012 **Tel** *(212) 254-7337*

Map 4 D3

A hip SoHo single set descends on this hot-pink restaurant for tasty Thai and exotic cocktails. Be sure to stop by the bathrooms that give the restaurant its name – don't worry, the mirrors are only one-way (looking out). Prix-fixe lunches and dinner specials are a bargain.

Key to Price Guide *see p296* **Key to Symbols** *see back cover flap*

Petite Abeille
$$$

134 West Broadway, 10013 **Tel** *(212) 791-1360* **Map** *1 B1*

European cartoon favorite Tintin lends charm to the decor at this branch of a reasonably priced Belgian mini-chain. The most popular dish is mussels and French fries, especially the all-you-can-eat offerings on Wednesdays. The list of imported beers is impressive. Also open for breakfast and weekend brunch, when Belgian waffles are a favorite.

Public
$$$

210 Elizabeth St, 10012 **Tel** *(212) 343-7011* **Map** *4 F3*

A taste of modern Down Under food with inventive creations such as Meyer lemon ceviche, and grilled kangaroo on falafel. Try fusion cocktails or the Australian beer on offer and enjoy the industrial-chic, high-ceilinged space that fills nightly with a stylish SoHo crowd.

Kittichai
$$$$

60 Thompson St, 10012 **Tel** *(212) 219-2000* **Map** *4 D4*

A high-end Thai restaurant in a beautifully designed space of the 60 Thompson hotel *(see p281)*, Kittichai is a definite place to be seen. The menu offers an expensive selection, including "Thai tapas," as well as seafood dishes such as monkfish with ginger, and desserts like banana spring rolls drizzled with a burnt honey sauce.

Nobu
$$$$

105 Hudson St, 10013 **Tel** *(212) 219-0500* **Map** *4 D5*

Chef Nobu Matsuhisa offers a menu of fantastic reach for those who can afford it and get a reservation. The menu features items such as tuna toro tartar, Peruvian-influenced ceviches and tempuras, not to mention a lengthy sushi menu. This high-profile spot attracts celebrities and mortals alike.

Bouley
$$$$$

163 Duane St, 10013 **Tel** *(212) 668-5829* **Map** *1 C1*

The modern French cuisine of famed chef David Bouley has an impressive TriBeCa home, with vaulted ceilings and elegant decor worthy of the fine fare. For those who cannot manage the hefty tab, the four-course prix-fixe lunch menu is a worthy sampling of the master's talents.

Corton
$$$$$

239 West Broadway, 10013 **Tel** *(212) 219-2777* **Map** *4 E5*

After a 20-year reign in TriBeCa, the much-loved Montrachet has become Corton (named after a noted wine district in Burgundy) and given a revamped look and menu. The decor is cool and modern, and the chef has introduced modern French cuisine – like foie gras with beets and blood orange – that has critics singing. A worthwhile splurge.

Megu
$$$$$

62 Thomas St, 10013 **Tel** *(212) 964-7777* **Map** *1 B1*

Joining the latest trend in behemoth Japanese restaurants, Megu has an impressively decorated menu offering an outrageous option of dishes to be shared. Prime ingredients can quickly add up in the tab but some consider it the equivalent of dinner and a show. Can be noisy, especially on weekends.

GREENWICH VILLAGE

A Salt & Battery
$

112 Greenwich Ave, 10011 **Tel** *(212) 691-2713* **Map** *3 B1*

Come here for the best fish-and-chips this side of the pond at rock-bottom prices. There are many different combinations of fish and platters to choose from. A vast selection of other side dishes as well makes the trip worth it, especially that infamously delicious deep-fried Mars bar.

Corner Bistro
$

331 West 4th St, 10014 **Tel** *(212) 242-9502* **Map** *3 C1*

The line outside indicates this isn't your typical bistro food, but a dive that has developed a cult following for the juiciest and messiest burgers and the cheapest beer in town. Grab a spot in line that sometimes snakes by the bar and outside. Food is served on paper plates with lots of napkins.

Moustache
$$

90 Bedford St, 10014 **Tel** *(212) 229-2220* **Map** *3 C2*

Middle-Eastern casual eatery with consistently good and cheap food, including Turkish *pitzas*, merguez sausages, and grilled lamb. The space is often too small for the crowd, and service can be slow. Try the sibling East Village spot at 265 East 10th Street, which includes an indoor garden.

Westville
$$

210 West 10th St, 10014 **Tel** *(212) 741-7971* **Map** *3 C2*

A no-thrills, narrow eatery offering great-value meals of regional American cooking – comfort food staples such as cod po'boys, burgers, mac 'n' cheese, and BLTs. Westville is so popular, it has spawned two sister restaurants – one in the East Village and another in Chelsea.

10 Downing
10 Downing St, 10014 **Tel** *(212) 255-0300*   **Map** *4 D3*

Dine on *nouveau* French cuisine at this sleek restaurant that fills with a lively crowd of locals and visitors. Try the hearty *cassoulet* tossed with mini duck meatballs or *agnelotti* topped with peekytoe crab. For dessert the rich chocolate cake with a malt-flavored ice cream center is a real treat.

Blue Ribbon Bakery
33 Downing Street, 10014 **Tel** *(212) 337-0404*   **Map** *4 D3*

An extensive tapas-style menu made out of cheeses and cold cuts with fantastic bread is complemented with soups, salads, and entrées such as filet mignon and burgers. An accessible wine list makes this an ideal place to pass time with friends and family.

Centro Vinoteca
74 Seventh Ave, 10011 **Tel** *(212) 367-7470*   **Map** *8 E5*

This buzzing, split-level restaurant, with whitewashed brick walls and large picture windows, features creative Italian fare. Ease into the evening with *piccolino* (small plates), including fried cauliflower in a parmesan crust, followed by meaty main dishes such as lamb bolognese or rabbit stuffed with sausage and pine nuts.

One
1 Little West 12th St, 10014 **Tel** *(212) 255-9717*   **Map** *3 B1*

The New American menu is designed around plates for one and plates to share, with a large selection of seafood platters as a group option. Most people come here for the hopping, trendy scene rather than the food, however. There are three different lounge areas: choose one according to your mood.

Otto
1 Fifth Ave, 10003 **Tel** *(212) 995-9559*   **Map** *4 E1*

An upscale and fashionable pizzeria from chef Mario Batali. An amazing wine list and an array of side dishes and antipasti can quickly raise your tab in this usually crowded and upbeat place. Try the famous lardo pizza, which is exactly what it sounds like – pig lard slathered on pizza crust. Don't miss the olive oil ice cream.

Pastis
9 Ninth Ave, 10014 **Tel** *(212) 929-4844*   **Map** *3 B1*

Among the pioneers in the Meatpacking District, this gorgeous Parisian bistro offers good-quality French fare in large portions. The noise level can be high on weekends, with plenty of celebrity sightseeing. It also serves a good weekend brunch. If you can't get a reservation, just show up and take your chances.

Pearl Oyster Bar
18 Cornelia St, 10014 **Tel** *(212) 691-8211*   **Map** *4 D4*

Very successful raw bar in the Village with top-of-the-line fresh ingredients and bold flavors. The lobster roll is a smash hit, as are the Prince Edward Island mussels. The daily specials are listed on the blackboard, and service is amicable too, but be prepared for long lines at rush hours.

The Spotted Pig
314 West 11th St, 10014 **Tel** *(212) 620-0393*   **Map** *3 B2*

Britons will feel at home in English chef April Bloomfield's Italian take on gastropub fare. This tiny spot fills up quickly, so get there early during peak times and enjoy drinks at the bar. Hand-cask beer from Brooklyn Brewery is great with the first-rate shepherd's pie.

The Waverly Inn and Garden
216 Bank St (Waverly Place), 10014 **Tel** *(212) 243-7900*   **Map** *3 C1*

The quaint name belies the social scene, which on any given night might include celebrities, fashion editors, and VIPs. The homespun, well-priced menu features a selection of American classic dishes: clam chowder, pork chops with roasted apples, and the much-talked-about mac and cheese with shaved truffles.

Babbo
110 Waverly Place, 10011 **Tel** *(212) 777-0303*   **Map** *4 D2*

Chef Mario Batali's flagship restaurant is housed in this beautiful Village duplex – paradise for high-quality pasta and offal lovers alike. Hard to get reservations and service could see some improvement given the prices. A winning wine list and trendy crowd add the magic touch to a great dining experience.

Blue Hill
75 Washington Place, 10011 **Tel** *(212) 539-1776*   **Map** *4 E4*

This New American kitchen is obsessed with the quality of its ingredients, especially with the addition of its own Stone Barns produce from upstate New York. The limited menu is a guarantee of the freshness and liveliness of the seasonal dishes. Taste the poached foie gras or the Berkshire pork with chestnuts.

Da Silvano
260 Sixth Ave, 10014 **Tel** *(212) 982-2343*   **Map** *4 D3*

This Tuscan restaurant is popular more for the celebrities who dine here than the food itself, which covers a wide range of pastas, some seafood antipasti, salads, and traditional entrées such as lamb chops and stewed rabbit. The coveted outdoor seats are perfect for people watching in the summer months.

One if by Land, Two if by Sea

17 Barrow St, 10014 **Tel** *(212) 228-0822*

Map *3 C3*

Aaron Burr's carriage house made famous in the American Revolution is one of the most romantic and historical spots in town. To some, the decor seems a tad kitsch. The three-course prix-fixe of casual American dining is served right next to the fireplace and candles. Piano music daily.

Spice Market

403 West 13th St, 10014 **Tel** *(212) 675-2322*

Map *3 B1*

A beautiful behemoth of a place featuring Asian-inspired "street food" by chef Jean Georges Vongerichten. With a club-like atmosphere, it is *the* place for beautiful people (including waiters) to sip fancy cocktails. The menu, however, is a hit-and-miss affair.

Gotham Bar & Grill

12 East 12th Street, 10003 **Tel** *(212) 620-4020*

Map *4 E1*

A New York classic of modern American cuisine showcasing revolutionary chef Alfred Portale's creations such as gingerbread crusted foie gras or roasted pheasant in a ginger and juniper marinade. Some consider the place somewhat past its prime but the bargain $25 prix-fixe lunch is worth a try.

EAST VILLAGE

Blue 9 Burger

92 Third Ave, 10003 **Tel** *(212) 979-0053*

Map *4 F1*

Tasty griddle hamburgers in the East Village at very affordable prices for when you get those fast-food cravings but don't want to visit a chain. Plus, they offer a mango-chili sauce with your fries. Grab it to go and head to a park nearby for a good people-watching picnic.

Dumpling Man

100 St Mark's Place, 10009 **Tel** *(212) 505-2121*

Map *5 A1*

Tiny yet trendy bar in the East Village, offering a wide variety of dumplings to meet your imagination. You get to watch what goes on behind the bar as the cooks handle the steamed or fried treasures. With rock-bottom prices, it doesn't get better than this dinner and a show.

Minca Ramen Factory

536 East 5th St, 10009 **Tel** *(212) 505-8001*

Map *5 B2*

Minca is a Ramen-style noodle joint that is far away from your memories of microwave noodle cups. You can choose a variety of noodles with beef, pork, vegetarian, and more. Perfect spot for cold weather after a stroll through the East Village hip boutiques.

Caracas Arepa Bar

91 East 7th St, 10009 **Tel** *(212) 228-5062*

Map *5 A2*

A kitschy restaurant with delicious Venezuelan fast food and slow service. *Arepas* (savoury corn cakes with a variety of fillings), sandwiches, and *tamales* are great fillers at rock-bottom prices. The premises are unbelievably small but the food keeps people coming. They also have a Brooklyn location.

Counter

105 First Ave, 10003 **Tel** *(212) 982-5870*

Map *5 A2*

Inventive vegetarian cuisine worth the trip for non-vegetarians in a sophisticated dining room. An inviting environmentally sound, organic or biodynamic, wine list is also highly recommended. Caring but nevertheless spotty service from time to time.

Great Jones Café

54 Great Jones St, 10012 **Tel** *(212) 674-9304*

Map *4 F2*

Get your fix of New Orleans cooking in this inexpensive, family-friendly, jukebox-equipped hole-in-the-wall. Staples include fried shrimp po'boys, andouille sausages, and jambalaya. Definitely down it all with a beer. Look for the colorful Elvis likeness in the window.

Il Bagatto

192 East 2nd St, 10009 **Tel** *(212) 228-0977*

Map *5 B2*

Trendy and popular Italian eatery with inexpensive and well-executed food that has New Yorkers flocking to the East Village. However, be warned of long lines and rushed service as a consequence. The reservation policy is a bit of mystery, so call ahead and see. If staying locally, order take-away.

La Palapa

77 St. Marks Place, 10003 **Tel** *(212) 777-2537*

Map *5 A1*

Mexico City-style and regional Mexican cooking with authentic ingredients make this a good fiesta destination in the beautifully decorated dining room. It's easy on the wallet and serves great margaritas too. Don't miss the Zihuatanejo-style catfish or the duck in black mole sauce.

Lil' Frankies

$$$

19–21 First Ave, 10003 **Tel** *(212) 420-4900* **Map** *5 A2*

Lil' Frankies is a neighborhood pizzeria with an oven that claims to have lava from Vesuvius! Despite the boasting, cheap and very good pizzas draw a hip young crowd. The place features a backyard garden for alfresco dining, and service is friendly, if a bit on the slow side.

Zum Schneider

$$$

107 Avenue C, 10009 **Tel** *(212) 598-1098* **Map** *5 B2*

Oktoberfest all year round in this neighborhood favorite Bier Garten. Bring your lederhosen and enjoy the relaxed atmosphere and great sausages. Family-friendly, it usually draws big crowds on weekends when the service can be slow. As you might expect, a great selection of beer on tap from all over the world.

Casimir

$$$$

103 Avenue B, 10009 **Tel** *(212) 358-9683* **Map** *5 B2*

Packed French bistro in the happening area of Alphabet City. Authentic fare brought by good-looking, not necessarily speedy, waiters includes black pudding sausage and steak *frites*. Try grabbing a table at the little outside garden for extra charm, and make sure to bring your American Express (the only card accepted).

Dirt Candy

$$$$

430 East 9th St, 10009 **Tel** *(212) 228-7732* **Map** *5 B1*

Chef/owner Amanda Cohen's vegetarian dishes are brilliant on every level. High-concept inventions such as the mint and tarragon zucchini pasta, the cube of portobello mushroom mousse, and the jalapeño hush puppies are colorful, sexy, and extremely tasty. Open 5:30–11pm Tue–Sat.

Jules

$$$$

65 St. Marks Place, 10003 **Tel** *(212) 477-5560* **Map** *5 A2*

A candle-lit Parisian brasserie vibe and live jazz nightly with no cover charge (a New York rarity) make this a fine East Village choice. The menu has familiar bistro offerings like steak *frites* as well as more classic French dishes. The swinging young crowd adds to the ambience. Be prepared; the band will ask for tips.

The Mermaid Inn

$$$$

96 Second Ave, 10003 **Tel** *(212) 674-5870* **Map** *5 A2*

This hip seafood restaurant attracts a young foodie crowd delighting in a prime, fresh raw bar and New England-style fare such as lobster sandwiches and chowder. A no-reservation policy usually comes with long lines attached, but stick them out: it is worth it.

Momofuku Noodle Bar

$$$$

171 First Ave, 10003 **Tel** *(212) 475-7899* **Map** *5 A1*

Celebrated Korean-American chef David Chang is at the helm of this airy restaurant. The menu changes daily and might include steamed pork buns or duck confit salad. The signature ramen comes soaked in a fragrant stock made from pork bones and chicken legs, and then laden with pork belly, snowpeas, and a poached egg.

Hearth

$$$$$

403 East 12th St, 10009 **Tel** *(212) 602-1300* **Map** *5 A1*

A Tuscan-American restaurant with high-quality and audacious food in a romantic and chic-rustic setting. Chef Marco Canora offers interesting dishes such as *ribollita* (bean and cabbage soup), New Zealand venison, and olive oil cake. Tasting menu available.

Jewel Bako

$$$$$

239 East 5th St, 10003 **Tel** *(212) 979-1012* **Map** *4 F2*

The battle for New York's best sushi got more heated with this high-end Japanese restaurant offering fresh-from-the-sea ingredients beautifully prepared. Courteous but erratic service and the extremely tiny premises take some shine out of the expensive experience. A more casual spot just opened around the corner.

GRAMERCY AND THE FLATIRON DISTRICT

Chat 'n' Chew

$$$

10 East 16th St, 10003 **Tel** *(212) 243-1616* **Map** *8 F5*

Kitschy comfort food destination in the Union Square area that fills the spot and is gentle on the wallet. Staples include mac 'n' cheese, a year-round Thanksgiving roast-turkey dinner, and mama's meatloaf. Don't forget the mashed potatoes, and a changing selection of cakes and pies for dessert. Good brunch spot.

Chennai Garden

$$$

129 East 27th St, 10016 **Tel** *(212) 689-1997* **Map** *9 A3*

The area known as "Curry Hill" has many Indian restaurants but this inviting spot is a bit different, offering well-prepared South Indian fare that also happens to be vegetarian and kosher. Although the decor is nothing special, the bargain-priced all-you-can-eat lunch buffet definitely impresses with its variety and freshness.

Key to Price Guide *see p296* **Key to Symbols** *see back cover flap*

Pipa

🈂️♿ $$

38 East 19th St, 10003 **Tel** *(212) 677-2233*   **Map** 9 A5

Popular Pipa features a spacious dining room with wooden tables, aged mirrors, heavy draperies, and twinkling chandeliers. The zesty Spanish *tapas* include *coca*, a Catalan flatbread topped with tart artichokes and *sobrasada*, a spicy Mallorcan sausage; and sautéed spinach studded with raisins. There are also pitchers of potent sangria.

Tong Thai Brasserie

$$

39 East 13th St, 10003 **Tel** *(212) 253-2696*   **Map** 4 F1

A former lumber store transformed into an elegant two-level Thai restaurant, Tong Thai offers an array of creative dishes, including mussels resting on pillows of rice batter, and salt-baked chicken sweetened with strips of mango. For a warm finish, sip aromatic tea served in little iron teapots.

Bamiyan

🏃♿ $$$

358 Third Ave, 10016 **Tel** *(212) 481-3232*   **Map** 9 B3

This Afghan restaurant offers a pleasant change of pace, with windows featuring tribal rugs and pillow seats around traditional low tables. The authentic menu features tasty curries, charcoal-grilled kebabs and yogurt dishes, along with more unusual dishes for adventurous diners.

Blue Smoke

🏃 $$$

116 East 27th St, 10016 **Tel** *(212) 447-7733*   **Map** 9 A3

Danny Meyer does down south BBQ in this hip joint. Expect luscious heavy-duty pulled pork sandwiches, full racks of ribs, corn muffins, and hushpuppies (deep-fried cornmeal batter). The place features a jazz club downstairs. The large bar offers beer from around the US, and is great for large groups.

Devi

♿ $$$

8 East 18th St, 10003 **Tel** *(212) 691-1300*   **Map** 8 F5

A trendy newcomer from chefs Suvi Saran and Hemant Mathur, showcasing authentic regional Indian cuisine in a gracious environment full of Indian textiles and woodcarvings. Dishes include tandoori lamb chops with pear chutney and Masala-fried quail, and don't miss the delectable cauliflower!

I Trulli

🈂️🍴 $$$

122 East 27th St, 10010 **Tel** *(212) 481-7372*   **Map** 9 A3

An upscale Italian restaurant specializing in Pugliese (Southern Italian) cuisine, I Trulli is the ideal spot for a romantic dinner by the fireplace in winter or in the garden during summer. A great wine list is available both here and at Enoteca I Trulli, its wine bar next door.

Pure Food and Wine

🏃🈂️ $$$

54 Irving Place, 10003 **Tel** *(212) 477-1010*   **Map** 9 A5

New York's first restaurant dedicated to the raw-vegan movement – no food heated above 118°F. Expect produce with pedigree in creative dishes at this smart venue. A few examples include coconut noodles, cauliflower samosas, and an amaranth-crust pizza with hummus.

Tamarind

♿ $$$

41–43 East 22nd St, 10010 **Tel** *(212) 674-7400*   **Map** 8 F4

A modern Indian restaurant with minimalist decorations, fantastic china, and friendly service. While pricier than your average Indian eatery, the quality of the ingredients and mix of flavors will transport you to India promptly. Ask the waiter to help you pair something from their extensive wine list.

Craft

🏃♿ $$$$

43 East 19th St, 10003 **Tel** *(212) 780-0880*   **Map** 9 A5

Executive chef Tom Colicchio offers a "deconstructed" menu of vibrant quality in this sleekly decorated venue. Diners have the option to "create" their entrées with a combination of ingredients and sides that can quickly push up the tab. If it seems stressful, just ask the waiter for advice.

Gramercy Tavern

♿ $$$$

42 East 20th St, 10003 **Tel** *(212) 477-0777*   **Map** 9 A5

Acclaimed chef Michael Anthony prepares outstanding food in a comfortable, always-hopping, rustic ambience of a country inn house. An ideal place for a sophisticated dining experience without stuffy pretense. This is consistently one of the best dining experiences in the city.

Mesa Grill

🏃♿ $$$$

102 Fifth Ave, 10011 **Tel** *(212) 807-7400*   **Map** 8 F5

Star chef Bobby Flay's flagship restaurant showcases modern Southwestern cuisine and has pleased crowds since 1991. The creative menu includes cornmeal-crusted oysters, a "deconstructed" lamb taco, and chile- and honey-glazed salmon. The special margaritas are quite something, and the bar scene alone can get quite lively.

Tocqueville

♿ $$$$

1 East 15th St, 10003 **Tel** *(212) 647-1515*   **Map** 8 F5

This tucked-away gem in Union Square offers French cuisine with Japanese touches, in a simple yet elegant and intimate room. Husband-and-wife team Marco Moreira and Jo-Ann Makovitsky put out well-executed quality ingredients. Great for a special occasion that does not require a house mortgage.

Union Square Café

$$$$ ⬧ 🏷️

21 East 16th Street, 10003 **Tel** *(212) 243-4020*

Map *9 A5*

Among the most popular of New York City restaurants, this Danny Meyer flagship serves modern American cuisine in comfortable surroundings, drawing ingredients from the greenmarket in Union Square. The prices are anything but market level. Courteous service.

11 Madison Park

🚶 ⬧ 🏷️ $$$$$

11 Madison Ave, 10010 **Tel** *(212) 889-0905*

Map *9 A4*

The Art Deco dining room with soaring ceilings and views of historic Madison Square Park make this the most elegant of Danny Meyer's restaurant empire. The chef has introduced a modern French menu that gets high marks from critics. Note, however, that the haute cuisine comes at a correspondingly high price.

Veritas

$$$$$ ⬧ 🏷️

43 East 20th St, 10010 **Tel** *(212) 353-3700*

Map *9 A5*

A small sleek restaurant in the Flatiron District dedicated to wine. Wine-lovers may have a coronary when reading the 2,700 plus wine list. However, the food rises to the occasion with jewels such as foie gras with a quince-Armagnac sauce and a fragrant bouillabaisse of monkfish, skate, cauliflower, and saffron. Prix-fixe only.

CHELSEA AND THE GARMENT DISTRICT

Bottino

🏷️ $$$

246 Tenth Ave, 10001 **Tel** *(212) 206-6766*

Map *7 C4*

A Northern Italian restaurant in a restored 100-year-old hardware shop with minimalist decor. The place attracts a stylish crowd especially to its lovely backyard garden to enjoy traditional salads, pastas, and grilled meats. Try tasty dishes like spinach pasta with ricotta cheese or juicy New York strip steak with cannellini beans.

The Red Cat

$$$

227 Tenth Ave, 10011 **Tel** *(212) 242-1122*

Map *7 C4*

Modern American food in a gorgeous barnhouse setting with red- and white-painted wood that will transport you to New England. The menu features some of the best quality dishes in the neighborhood such as crispy fried oysters, wild striped bass in white wine butter, and delicious risotto fritters with blueberries.

Sueños

🚶 $$$

311 West 17th St, 10011 **Tel** *(212) 243-1333*

Map *8 D5*

Traditional Mexican regional cuisine served in a colorful mid-sized space. Great tequila and margarita bar and inventive food creations, including a chile-tasting menu, provide the necessary ingredients for a pleasant, if slightly above average-priced, dining experience.

Trestle on Tenth

⬧ 🏷️ $$$

242 Tenth Ave, 10001 **Tel** *(212) 645-5659*

Map *7 C4*

The exceedingly convivial Trestle is an elegant establishment that wants its customers to dine in relaxed, comfortable surroundings and leave well fed. Swiss specialties – including rosti and pork dishes – share the menu with European-leaning staples. In summer, visitors opt for the breezy garden out back instead of the charming brick-lined dining room.

Buddakan

⬧ $$$$

75 Ninth Ave, 10011 **Tel** *(212) 989-6699*

Map *8 D5*

Philadelphia restaurateur Stephen Starr is repeating his success with a series of New York establishments. Buddakan is the jewel in his crown, featuring jaw-dropping decor in the main hall and a series of more intimate, smaller spaces. The Asian fusion cuisine is tasty, but not the main draw to this Chelsea restaurant. Hopping bar scene.

Matsuri

🏷️ $$$$

369 West 16th St, 10011 **Tel** *(212) 243-6400*

Map *8 D5*

An enormous and noisy dining space in the Maritime Hotel *(see p284)*, Matsuri features high-quality Japanese fare from chef Tadashi Ono. He offers a range of dishes prepared with prime ingredients such as Kobe beef, sweet shrimp, and sake-soaked black cod. There is also a great sake list.

THEATER DISTRICT

Burger Joint at Le Parker Meridien

🍽️ 🚶 ⬧ $

119 West 57th St, 10019 **Tel** *(212) 708-7414*

Map *12 E3*

This kitsch joint inside the Parker Meridien hotel *(see p286)* serves freshly cooked, mouthwatering burgers, fries, shakes, beer, and little else at rock-bottom prices. There's nothing uptight about this midtown gem hidden behind curtains in the lobby.

Key to Price Guide *see p296* **Key to Symbols** *see back cover flap*

Carnegie Deli

854 Seventh Ave, 10019 **Tel** *(212) 757-2245*

Map *12 E4*

You'll have to wait in long lines to glimpse one of this deli's gargantuan sandwiches and history-making cheesecakes. You'll also have to endure hostile waiters in order to experience this "quintessential" New York experience. While expensive, you probably won't eat for over a week.

Carve Unique Sandwiches

760 Eighth Ave, 10036 **Tel** *(212) 730-4949*

Map *12 D5*

A small shop where you can get all your sandwich cravings fulfilled on the cheap in the Theater District. Hefty sandwiches include grilled lemon chicken, and a tomato, basil, and mozzarella combo. Lines are exasperatingly long at lunchtime, so try it in off hours.

Pam Real Thai Food

404 West 49th St, 10019 **Tel** *(212) 333-7500*

Map *11 C5*

If you are looking for good, inexpensive Thai food in the area, and don't care about decor, then this is the place. The usual assortment of curries, soups, pad Thai and noodle and rice dishes come in a variety of spicy degrees to order. No reservations means long waits at rush hour.

Kodama Sushi

301 West 45th St, 10036 **Tel** *(212) 582-8065*

Map *12 D5*

The convenient location, reliably fresh sushi, and other well-prepared Japanese favorites at good prices make Kodama a popular pre-theater choice. Regulars recommend the menu of rolls, with inventive ingredient combinations. Fast service ensures you will make the show on time, even at busy times.

Norma's

118 West 57th St, 10019 **Tel** *(212) 708-7460*

Map *12 E3*

Brunch reaches its zenith here in Le Parker Meridien hotel *(see p286)*. The elaborate and creative menu, from lobster and asparagus omelette to chocolate French toast, will fulfill all of your desires. Pricey, but you won't eat anything else for the rest of the day, or have brunch anywhere quite like it. Weekends can see long lines. Very family-friendly.

Virgil's Real Barbecue

152 West 44th St, 10036 **Tel** *(212) 921-9494*

Map *12 E5*

Hopping BBQ joint in the heart of Times Square with an always-bustling clientele and fast service. Ideal for pre-theater dining, provided that the heavy meal doesn't make you sleepy. Staples include over 10 different meat platters (with BBQ varieties from various US regions), and tasty side dishes such as biscuits, collard greens, grits, and mac 'n' cheese.

Becco

355 West 46th St, 10036 **Tel** *(212) 397-7597*

Map *11 D5*

Chef Lidia Bastianich is a co-owner of this standard Italian *trattoria* on restaurant row offering a decent selection of antipasti, salads, pastas, and main courses, as well as pre-theater menus. The $25 wine list is a great deal as well; for those with more to spend, check out the more extensive regular wine list.

Marseille

630 Ninth Ave, 10036 **Tel** *(212) 333-3410*

Map *12 D5*

Good dining in the Theater District is indeed possible at this romantic restaurant serving French-Mediterranean cuisine, with modern twists, including roasted monkfish with a cream-and-green-apple purée. The vegetarian-friendly menu is served by a courteous staff. Check out the funky French surfer bar, Réunion, downstairs.

Molyvos

871 Seventh Ave, 10019 **Tel** *(212) 582-7500*

Map *12 E4*

An upscale Greek restaurant near Carnegie Hall. The warm Mediterranean decor is the perfect setting for fresh seafood and other Greek specialties justifying the above-average prices. Try the flashy (and flaming) saganaki appetizer for your own pre-theater experience. Prix-fixe available.

Osteria al Doge

142 West 44th St, 10036 **Tel** *(212) 944-3643*

Map *12 E5*

Venetian cuisine in a rustic dining room with a successful power-lunch clientele and popular with early evening theater-goers. Service is expeditious and warm. The menu includes pizza, great salads, and carpaccio as well as fresh pastas at prices and quality better than other venues in the area.

Blue Fin

1567 Broadway, 10036 **Tel** *(212) 918-1400*

Map *12 E5*

Among the coolest places in the area, this is dedicated to seafood in a big way, including a raw and sushi bar. The two-story restaurant is always hopping and some may complain about the noise level, not just from the live music. A good place to flex the expense account.

db Bistro Moderne

55 West 44th St, 10036 **Tel** *(212) 391-2400*

Map *8 F1*

Home of the famous $32 burger (filled with foie gras and wine-braised short ribs). This lively midtown restaurant offers another glimpse of Daniel Boulud's fine-dining experience with less damage to the wallet. Popular for power lunches with the publishing executive crowd who can afford it. Nice choice for upscale pre-theater dinner.

Esca ♿ ☀ $$$$

402 West 43rd St, 10036 ***Tel*** *(212) 564-7272* ***Map*** *8 D1*

An upscale Italian seafood restaurant from the Batali-Bastianich partnership. A large variety of appetizers is followed by other dishes that reflect the great quality of its ingredients. Service can be unreliable and some think the atmosphere is a bit stale. A little formal, so not the best place for children.

Gordon Ramsay ♿ 🍸 $$$$

151 West 54th St, 10019 ***Tel*** *(212) 468-8888* ***Map*** *12 E4*

Despite UK chef Gordon Ramsay's brash reputation, his first US venture is a subdued affair. The 45-seat restaurant focuses on exquisite French cuisine with Asian accents, including roasted striped bass with bak choi and caramelized sweetbreads. The prix-fixe lunch is a bargain. Book well in advance, especially for the eight-seat kitchen table.

Osteria del Circo ♿ $$$$

120 West 55th St, 10019 ***Tel*** *(212) 265-3636* ***Map*** *12 E4*

Northern Italian restaurant from the Maccioni family known for Le Cirque. The Adam Tihany-designed dining room is spacious and comfortable and the food is well executed amid very affable service. Save space for desserts, including the Tuscan doughnuts with cappuccino cream.

Triomphe ♿ $$$$

49 West 44th St, 10036 ***Tel*** *(212) 453-4233* ***Map*** *12 F5*

A charming oasis of quiet from the bustle of Times Square, this French restaurant in the Iroquois Hotel pairs excellent food and wine with impeccable service. Tasting menus are available, as well as quirkier events, such as gathering between 10 and 20 of your friends to enjoy dinner and a movie in the private room.

Le Bernardin ♿ 🍸 $$$$$

155 West 51st St, 10019 ***Tel*** *(212) 554-1515* ***Map*** *12 E4*

A dream-come-true for seafood- and fish-lovers. This superb and elegant longstanding restaurant offers an outstanding dining experience with French haute cuisine from chef Eric Ripert. Service is flawless, including the sommelier advice. It's the place to propose.

Milos Estiatorio 👶 ♿ $$$$$

125 West 55th St, 10019 ***Tel*** *(212) 245-7400* ***Map*** *12 E4*

Formidable Greek food with fresh-out-of-the-water seafood set in a spartan, airy dining room where guests select the fish from a beautifully decorated stand. The catch of the day depends on the luck of the fishermen purveyors for this upscale restaurant. Prices are some of the most expensive in town.

LOWER MIDTOWN

Ali Baba 👶 ♿ ☀ $$

212 East 34th St, 10016 ***Tel*** *(212) 683-9206* ***Map*** *9 B2*

Kebabs and lamb dishes are the favorites at this unpretentious Turkish standby offering good food at moderate prices. Pita pizzas are among the house specialties, and all of the *meze* (appetizers), hot and cold, are tasty, as are the main dishes, such as the lamb kebabs. The outdoor dining area hidden in the back is a welcome oasis in midtown.

Artisanal 👶 ♿ $$$

2 Park Ave, 10016 ***Tel*** *(212) 725-8585* ***Map*** *9 A2*

Sparkling upscale French bistro, where the main topic is cheese, including a large selection to taste either by themselves or in fondues. Non-cheese lovers need not be afraid, as there are plenty of dairy-free selections available. Note that reservations aren't always respected on time.

Grand Central Oyster Bar 👶 ♿ $$$

Grand Central, Lower Level, 42nd St, 10017 ***Tel*** *(212) 490-6650* ***Map*** *9 A1*

Cavernous space inside Grand Central, where you'll be transported to the past. The very fresh seafood in simple preparations is not too pricey, and the menu features a long list of over a dozen kinds of oysters. The setting and decor are casual, so leave the fur coats at home and bring your appetite.

Convivio 👶 ♿ $$$$

45 Tudor City Place, 10017 ***Tel*** *(212) 599-5045* ***Map*** *9 B1*

The former L'Impero restaurant has become the more colorful, less formal, Convivio. While the mood is more casual, the excellent southern Italian menu is as good as ever, and the pasta dishes continue to please. The prix-fixe is reasonable for this quality. Still a special occasion choice and a good excuse to discover hidden Tudor City.

Michael Jordan's The Steakhouse NYC 👶 ♿ $$$$

Grand Central, North Balcony, 10017 ***Tel*** *(212) 655-2300* ***Map*** *9 A1*

The celebrity player's steakhouse located at the mezzanine of Grand Central Terminal. Expect high-quality (and high-priced) dry-aged cuts. Avoid a hot summer day, because the terminal is not air-conditioned. Service is casual but knowledgable, and you can't beat the view of the hectic train passengers below.

Key to Price Guide *see p296* **Key to Symbols** *see back cover flap*

UPPER MIDTOWN

La Bonne Soupe 👪 ♿ $
48 West 55th St, 10019 ***Tel*** *(212) 586-7650* ***Map*** *12 F4*

A cozy haven for the thrifty, with a French bistro menu including quiches, omelettes, soups, steaks, fondues, and crêpes. There are daily changing specials and a reasonably priced set three-course menu. La Bonne Soupe features a small terrace for outdoor dining in the warm months. A great low-cost option in this pricey and upscale neighborhood.

BLT Steak 👪 ♿ $$$
106 East 57th St, 10022 ***Tel*** *(212) 752-7470* ***Map*** *13 A3*

Bistro Laurent Tourondel (BLT) offers fancy steaks with prime ingredients and your choice of sauces, from tangy three-mustard to creamy Béarnaise, for your Angus-certified protein. A stylish room with toffee-colored booths, a zinc bar, and other eye-catching elements draws a hip, fashion-conscious crowd.

Dawat 👪 ♿ $$$
210 East 58th St, 10022 ***Tel*** *(212) 355-7555* ***Map*** *13 B3*

An attractive Indian restaurant with recipes from none other than famous Indian chef Madhur Jaffrey. Signature dishes include salmon rubbed with a coriander chutney and baked in a banana leaf. The clever touch is a snack car that parades to your table. If you're not an Indian food expert, ask the helpful staff for advice.

Rue 57 👪 ♿ ⛱ $$$
60 West 57th St, 10019 ***Tel*** *(212) 307-5656* ***Map*** *12 F3*

The fusion fever does not stop at Rue 57, which offers a combination of a sushi bar and French cuisine in a popular sophisticated bistro. The succulent duck à l'orange comes highly recommended. It's good value as a breakfast option as well. Sidewalk tables available – a great people-watching spot in warm months.

Shun Lee Palace 👪 ♿ $$$
155 East 55th St, 10022 ***Tel*** *(212) 371-8844* ***Map*** *13 A4*

A handsome dining room considered one of the city's premier Chinese restaurants. The menu is a Cantonese/Szechuan blend with casserole specialties. The Grand Marnier prawns can become a serious addiction. Another location is near Lincoln Center at 43 West 65th Street.

Insieme $$$$
77 Seventh Ave, 10019 ***Tel*** *(212) 582-1310* ***Map*** *12 E4*

Chef Marco Canova introduces his inventive Italian cuisine to this corner of midtown. The spare, cool-toned restaurant features weathered white-oak tables, raw-silk drapes, and a menu that lists traditional Italian dishes on one side and modern, quirky takes on the other.

Marea $$$$
240 Central Park South, 10019 ***Tel*** *(212) 582-5100* ***Map*** *12 D3*

This Italian seafood palace features a superb menu – with a location to match, situated as it is at the crossroads of Central Park South and Columbus Circle. Delicacies include salt-crusted sea bass and razor clams with fennel fronds. There is also a small selection of non-fish dishes. Marea offers brunch on Sundays. Closed Sat lunch.

Pampano 👪 ⛱ $$$$
209 East 49th St, 10017 ***Tel*** *(212) 751-4545* ***Map*** *13 B2*

A lovely, modern Mexican restaurant from chef Richard Sandoval and opera legend co-owner Placido Domingo. Inventive and fresh creations in a chic dining room will make you want to sing an aria or two. Don't miss the smoked swordfish appetizer or the halibut Pampano. A beautiful terrace is also available.

Aquavit ♿ [T] $$$$$
65 East 55th St, 10022 ***Tel*** *(212) 307-7311* ***Map*** *13 A4*

The minimalist space for Aquavit serves as the home of inventive Scandinavian creations, including smoked Arctic char, from chefs Nils Noren and Marcus Samuelsson, with prime ingredients and several tasting menus available. The signature Aquavit cocktails are also a must.

Felidia [T] $$$$$
243 East 58th St, 10022 ***Tel*** *(212) 758-1479* ***Map*** *13 B3*

TV star chef Lidia Bastianich offers upscale Italian fare in this charming, wood-paneled town house with exposed bricks and flower arrangements. Conducive to romance, the seasonal menu is creative and well executed. In line with Lidia's other restaurants, an impressive wine list is also available.

Four Seasons ♿ $$$$$
99 East 52nd St, 10022 ***Tel*** *(212) 754-9494* ***Map*** *13 A4*

Restaurants come and go, but this gracious New York institution with landmark decor by Philip Johnson seems to go on forever, always among the top-rated for American-Continental food. The Grill Room is still the prime place for power lunches, and the Pool Room is a perfect setting for special-occasion dinners.

La Grenouille
$$$$$

3 East 52nd St, 10022 **Tel** *(212) 752-1495*   **Map** *12 F4*

One of the last remaining classic French restaurants in the city, with outstanding food. The dining room walls are laden with silk and velvet banquettes, and beautiful floral arrangements abound, making the eating experience a memorable one. A place for special occasions.

L'Atelier de Joel Robuchon
$$$$$

57 East 57th St, Four Seasons Hotel, 10022 **Tel** *(212) 350-6658*   **Map** *13 A3*

Chef Joel Robuchon has brought his exquisite Asian-influenced French cuisine to the Four Seasons Hotel *(see p289)*. Just be prepared to pay dearly for these "small plates" of near perfection, from plump scallops in seaweed butter to quail stuffed with foie gras. A seat at the counter gives a view of the culinary team at work in the open kitchen.

The Modern
$$$$$

9 West 53rd St, 10019 **Tel** *(212) 333-1220*   **Map** *12 F4*

In a clean, modern space at the Museum of Modern Art, this restaurant serves an impeccable array of New American and French dishes, alongside an extensive wine list. Expect a high level of service. The tasting menu is popular and can be enjoyed with a wine pairing if your wallet can take the strain; if not, you can eat in the more casual Bar Room.

Oceana
$$$$$

1221 Sixth Ave, 10020 **Tel** *(212) 759-5941*   **Map** *12 E5*

Ease into the evening with a crisp white wine and a platter of fresh seafood at this stylish vaulted restaurant. The menu features American cuisine with influences from as far afield as the Mediterranean and Asia. Excellent dishes include *branzino* (sea bass) stuffed with mushrooms, spinach, and black olives. There is also a Raw Bar.

UPPER EAST SIDE

Brother Jimmy's BBQ
$$

1485 Second Ave, 10021 **Tel** *(212) 288-0999*   **Map** *17 B5*

The original of the Brother Jimmy's chain promises a rowdy evening and some "finger-lickin'" ribs and Southern favorites. All-you-can-eat specials are a popular option. This is a good destination for carnivores, though there are a few options for vegetarians. Some quieter tables can be found at the rear.

Shanghai Pavilion
$$

1378 Third Ave, 10021 **Tel** *(212) 585-3388*   **Map** *17 B5*

Offering Shanghai cuisine, as authentic as you can get outside of Chinatown, the menu here has plenty of options at reasonable prices, making it a good value in this neighborhood. The service is friendly. Great dim sums, noodle dishes, and specialties such as velvet sea bass or lobster tropicana.

Via Quadronno
$$

25 East 73rd St, 10021 **Tel** *(212) 650-9880*   **Map** *12 F1*

A cute Italian-style "bar paninoteca" with a rainbow of delicious prime-ingredient sandwiches and salads worth a stop after a Museum Mile extravaganza. The small space inspired by a Milan paninoteca translates into waiting lines at peak hours. Definitely splurge on a glass of wine to go with the meal.

Beyoglu
$$$

1431 Second Ave, 10028 **Tel** *(212) 650-0850*   **Map** *17 B5*

Everyone raves about the *meze*, delicious Turkish appetizers, at this whimsically decorated, always crowded neighborhood favorite. Regulars make a meal of a selection of small treats like *borek* (filo stuffed with feta cheese), stuffed grape leaves, calf's liver, and eggplant salad; the daily seafood specials and lamb are also recommended.

Maya
$$$

1191 First Ave, 10021 **Tel** *(212) 585-1818*   **Map** *13 C2*

Chef Richard Sandoval serves sophisticated and delicate main courses at this upbeat Mexican restaurant in a peach-hued setting. The drawback comes in the sound level; dine early to avoid the din. Many rave about the seafood tacos, margaritas, and guacamole.

Sfoglia
$$$

1402 Lexington Ave, 10128 **Tel** *(212) 831-1402*   **Map** *17 A2*

This popular restaurant specializes in Italian farmhouse fare. Start out with a bowl of plump, complimentary olives, followed by a pot of wild mussels steeped in garlic or braised duck with dried apricots. Top off the evening with a fine Italian wine, and don't miss the superb desserts, including home-made cookies and tangy gelato.

Café Boulud
$$$$

20 East 76th St, 10021 **Tel** *(212) 772-2600*   **Map** *16 F5*

Chef Daniel Boulud creates a less formal dining room with solid creations inside the Surrey hotel. An interesting array of dinner options will keep any diner intrigued – "Le Tradition" (classic French), "Le Voyager" (world cuisines), "Le Potager" (vegetarian), and "La Saison" (seasonal specialties).

Key to Price Guide *see p296* **Key to Symbols** *see back cover flap*

Daniel
♿ 👔 $$$$$

60 East 65th St, 10021 ***Tel*** *(212) 288-0033* ***Map*** *13 A2*

Chef Daniel Boulud's flagship restaurant features a Venetian Renaissance-inspired dining room, one of the most luscious settings in town. His highly acclaimed creations celebrate the seasons: summer brings forth corn crêpes stuffed with chanterelles, while in autumn there are mushrooms in a white truffle sauce. Beware of the sky-high prices.

David Burke Townhouse
👔 $$$$$

133 East 61st St, 10021 ***Tel*** *(212) 813-2121* ***Map*** *13 A3*

Creative New American dishes from chef/owner David Burke. Diners cross a glamorous, white, gloss-and-stone bar to proceed to a cool dining area in bold colors and lacquered surfaces. Save room for the signature cheesecake "lollipop" dessert. The Townhouse is also renowned for its weekend brunches.

UPPER WEST SIDE

Whole Foods Market
🧒 ♿ $

Time Warner Center, 10 Columbus Circle, 10019 ***Tel*** *(212) 823-9600* ***Map*** *12 D3*

An enormous, environment-friendly supermarket with an impressive food hall stocking all sorts of cuisine from sushi to pizzas. The ideal spot to shop for your inexpensive picnic adventures in Central Park or eat in at the booths. A wine shop is available inside too. Beware of crowds at peak times. There are other branches throughout New York.

Gennaro
💳 🧒 ♿ $$

665 Amsterdam Ave, 10025 ***Tel*** *(212) 665-5348* ***Map*** *15 C2*

An inexpensive small café serving consistently good Italian food with large servings. With a no-reservation policy, there can be lines at busy times. All the usuals are available here, including daily pasta specials and a wine list that is pretty reasonable. When busy, service can be annoyingly slow.

Olympic Flame Diner
🧒 ♿ $$

200 West 60th St, 10023 ***Tel*** *(212) 581-5259* ***Map*** *11 C3*

A classic New York diner, Olympic Flame is a find in the Lincoln Center area, where reasonable prices and tables without reservations are hard to come by. The enormous menu offers everything from omelettes, salads, and burgers to pastas, Greek specialties, and regular entrées. The efficient waiters will get you out in time for the curtain.

BLT Market
👔 $$$

Ritz-Carlton Hotel, 1430 Sixth Ave, 10019 ***Tel*** *(212) 521-6125* ***Map*** *12 E3*

French chef Laurent Tourandel's epicurean empire expands with this venture that pays homage to seasonal produce and local purveyors. The impressive result is rustic fare with a French twist, from stuffed Amish chicken with shoestring potatoes to black cod with butternut squash purée. Breakfast is served daily. Open 5:30–10pm Tue–Sun.

Boathouse Restaurant Central Park
🧒 ♿ ⛱ $$$

Central Park, East 72nd St & Park Drive North, 10023 ***Tel*** *(212) 517-2233* ***Map*** *12 E1*

The setting by Central Park's lake could not be any lovelier than this boathouse. An ideal place for brunch or lunch, and a romantic dinner is available April through October. Given the prices, it's unfortunate that the inevitable touristy nature has limited its potential to serve above-average food.

Café Fiorello
🧒 $$$

1900 Broadway, 10023 ***Tel*** *(212) 595-5330* ***Map*** *12 D2*

Boasting that it's "the longest running show on Broadway" this noisy Italian place features a bountiful antipasto bar. You can sample enough for a whole meal before crossing the street to the Lincoln Center. The menu also includes pizzas and standard Italian fare. Great for peoplewatching in the seasonal outside tables.

Café Frida
🧒 ⛱ $$$

368 Amsterdam Ave, 10025 ***Tel*** *(212) 749-2929* ***Map*** *15 C1*

This lively Mexican joint serves all the usual suspects – *chile relleno*, quesadillas, fajitas, tacos – along with heavier, more serious options and a few surprises, such as Mexican cheese fondue and *ceviche*. Visit during brunch for a Mexican take on eggs Benedict. No American Express.

Café Luxembourg
🧒 $$$

200 West 70th St, 10023 ***Tel*** *(212) 873-7411* ***Map*** *11 C1*

A classic Art Deco Parisian bistro with a zinc-topped bar, antique mirrors, and a loyal, hip clientele with the occasional celebrity sighting. Standard bistro fare with weekly specials available but don't expect flawless service. The crowd and decor make it a good choice for business dinners.

Calle Ocho
🧒 ♿ $$$

446 Columbus Ave, 10024 ***Tel*** *(212) 873-5025* ***Map*** *16 D4*

It's a never-ending party in this loud and colorful Cuban restaurant filled with beautiful 20-somethings. The menu is an amalgam of Latin American dishes, all with varying degrees of success. A small kids' menu is also available. Located close to the American Museum of Natural History.

Pasha
🚸 $$$

70 West 71st St, 10023 **Tel** *(212) 579-8751* **Map** *12 D1*

A serene and spacious, skylit, Turkish restaurant with friendly service ideal for a good conversation amid well-executed food. The lamb dumpling appetizers are delicious as well as the eggplant dishes, in particular the smoky *patlican salatasi*, mashed with garlic, olive oil, and lemon.

Rosa Mexicano
🚸 ♿ $$$

61 Columbus Ave, 10023 **Tel** *(212) 977-7700* **Map** *12 D2*

Popular and trendy upscale Mexican fine dining drawing a crowd of hip diners near Lincoln Center. Awesome pomegranate margaritas and sparkling sangrias, plus guacamole made to order at your table. Try the *cochinita pibil* tacos (achiote rubbed pork steamed in banana leafs) or the Veracruz fish in tomato sauce.

Ouest
🚸 ♿ $$$$

2315 Broadway, 10024 **Tel** *(212) 580-8700* **Map** *15 C4*

Chef Tom Valenti offers his version of New American comfort cuisine – it's an elegant restaurant that still makes you feel comfortable. The menu features nightly specials such as traditional meatloaf and other creative dishes such as poached squab with foie gras *agnolotti*. An outstanding wine list is available as well.

Asiate
♿ 👔 $$$$$

80 Columbus Circle, 35th Floor, 10019 **Tel** *(212) 805-8881* **Map** *12 D3*

Stellar views of Central Park are available from this Asian-influenced restaurant at the Mandarin Oriental hotel. Highlights include pan-seared foie gras with steamed sea eel and tamarind sauce and Wagyu beef with oxtail sauce. The bar includes an interesting array of cocktails.

Jean-Georges
♿ 👔 $$$$$

1 Central Park West at Columbus Circle and West 60th St, 10023 **Tel** *(212) 299-3900* **Map** *12 D3*

Chef Jean-Georges's flagship temple for modern French cuisine with Asian nuances. An austere yet elegant, Adam Tihany-designed room is the stage for an impressive array of delicate dishes. Service is courteous and knowledgeable. One of the most memorable fine dining experiences in New York.

Masa
♿ 👔 $$$$$

Time Warner Center, 10 Columbus Circle, 10019 **Tel** *(212) 823-9800* **Map** *12 D3*

Chef Masayoshi Takayama, of the famed LA Ginza Sushi-ko, has moved to New York to break the record of most expensive meal ever. It consists of a never-ending *kaiseki*-style (tasting) menu chosen by Mr Masa using incredibly fresh ingredients. Take a seat by the sushi bar to savor the show in every detail.

Per Se
♿ 👔 $$$$$

Time Warner Center, 10 Columbus Circle, 10019 **Tel** *(212) 823-9335* **Map** *12 D3*

Call at least two months in advance to score a seat in the critically acclaimed restaurant from Thomas Keller of California's French Laundry fame. The tasting menus change daily, and many think the vegetarian option is the best. Plus, it offers spectacular views of Central Park. Service is impeccable.

Picholine
👔 $$$$$

35 West 64th St, 10023 **Tel** *(212) 724-8585* **Map** *12 D2*

Terrance Brennan's elegant French-Mediterranean restaurant a few steps away from the Lincoln Center. Several prix-fixe, *à la carte*, and even tasting menus available with dishes such as John Dory with grapes, chanterelles, and truffle vinaigrette. Save room for their famous artisanal cheeses.

MORNINGSIDE HEIGHTS AND HARLEM

Sylvia's
🚸 ♿ $$

328 Lenox Ave, 10027 **Tel** *(212) 996-0660* **Map** *21 B1*

Soul food at its best can be found at this Harlem classic, named after the owner and decorated with portraits of jazz greats and famous visitors. Think fried or smothered chicken with waffles, spare ribs, catfish, collard greens, and sweet potatoes. Be sure to save room for Southern desserts like peach cobbler and "red velvet" chocolate cake.

FARTHER AFIELD: BROOKLYN

Chip Shop
🍴 🚸 $

383 Fifth Ave, 11215 **Tel** *(718) 832-7701*

An outpost of British comfort food in New York City, this inexpensive shop offers fish and chips, bangers and mash, and kidney pies in a kitschy dining room. Great to sit back with a group of friends and enjoy a pint of beer. Family-friendly as well. Don't forget to try the yummy fried Mars bar. There are several other locations in Brooklyn.

Key to Price Guide *see p296* **Key to Symbols** *see back cover flap*

Grimaldi's

19 Old Fulton St, 11201 **Tel** *(718) 858 4300*

Unbelievably good coal-oven pizzas made from the milkiest mozzarella and the freshest sauce. Definitely try the pepperoni. This place is worth the trip to Brooklyn and a walk back across the bridge. Bring your family and wait in line to taste the inexpensive pies at this buzzing pizzeria.

Prime Meats

465 Court St (Carroll Gardens), 11231 **Tel** *(718) 254-0327*

Frank Castronovo and Frank Falcinelli have built a small empire with a few ingredient-led restaurants and a cookbook or two, gathering much respect from the dining community. Their seasonal menu is informed by German favorites. The titled meats are the stars, from the Sürkrüt Garnie (a wurst and pork belly sampler plate) to pork schnitzel.

Rye

247 South 1st St, 11211 **Tel** *(718) 218-8047*

Williamsburg's (and Manhattan's) culinary star Cal Elliott brought an old factory back to life with a 100-year-old oak bar and his high-quality, low-price American dishes. The meatloaf sandwich and the wild mushroom lasagna stand out. Rye also offers great handcrafted cocktails. Open for dinner seven nights a week and for brunch on Sundays.

The Grocery

288 Smith St, 11231 **Tel** *(718) 596-3335*

A charming 30-seat restaurant in Carroll Gardens, offering a delightful seasonal menu such as whole boneless trout stuffed with spaetzle and asparagus or braised duck breast with bulghur, Swiss chard, and caramelized red wine. The romantic venue also features a lovely summer garden.

Peter Luger Steakhouse

178 Broadway, 11211 **Tel** *(718) 387-7400*

A New York institution serving "the discerning steak connoisseur" since 1887. Try their out-of-this-world meat. Just be aware that the decor's ambience is much like a beer-hall and the waiters can be snippy. Reserve ahead and still expect to wait for a table.

River Café

One Water St, 11201 **Tel** *(718) 522-5200*

Unrivaled for its location featuring stunning Manhattan skyline views, this upscale Brooklyn standout offers a New American three-course, prix-fixe menu. A tasting menu is also available. An unbeatable romantic place for special occasions. Save room for their signature chocolate Brooklyn Bridge dessert.

Chef's Table at Brooklyn Fare

200 Schermerhorn St, 11201 **Tel** *(718) 243-0050*

The Chef's Table, an 18-seat counter in a space adjacent to the Brooklyn Fare grocery store, has received two Michelin stars thanks to Cesar Ramirez's painstaking small-plate preparations (20 courses in all). Because of its popularity, it is wise to make reservations a few weeks in advance. Bring your own bottle.

FARTHER AFIELD: QUEENS

Il Bambino

34–08 31st Ave, Astoria 11106 **Tel** *(718) 626-0087*

Unlike many Astoria eateries, the casual and cheery Bambino has no aspirations of cultural authenticity. The panini (featuring intriguing combinations), salads, and Italian meat-and-cheese plates are flavorful and surprisingly filling. Stop by for the famous peanut butter hot chocolate on a cold winter morning, or at the end of a night out.

Jackson Diner

37–47 74th St, 11372 **Tel** *(718) 672-1232*

This spacious Indian cafeteria-style restaurant pulls out all the stops for well-prepared Northern Indian (spicy) and Southern Indian (less spicy) food at very cheap prices and well worth the visit when you are at Jackson Heights. Magnificent lamb and tandoori chicken and prawn dishes, as well as samosas and great *lassi* to wash it all down.

Sripraphai

64-13 39th Ave, Woodside, 11377 **Tel** *(718) 899-9599*

Many believe the best, most authentic, and least expensive Thai food in New York is found in this plain café, 20 minutes from Manhattan, not far from the Woodside stop on the No.7 subway line. Well worth the trip, especially on a balmy night when you can enjoy the very pretty garden out back.

Elias Corner

24–02 31st St, 11102 **Tel** *(718) 932-1510*

Among the more popular Greek restaurants with a huge following and long lines. This no-thrills, expanded restaurant serves some of the freshest fish in town, prepared simply. A large garden also makes this a good place for group gatherings, if you don't mind the wait at rush hours, especially weekends.

Light Meals and Snacks

You can get a snack almost anywhere and anytime in Manhattan. New Yorkers seem to eat endlessly – on street corners, in bars, luncheonettes, delis, before and after work, and long into the night. Casual eating in New York might include soft pretzels or char-roasted chestnuts from a corner stand; a huge sandwich from a deli; a Greek gyro sandwich (roasted lamb in pita bread) from street vendors; a pre-theater snack at a café or coffee bar; or a post-party binge at an all-night diner or bistro. While street fare is generally cheap, the quality and culinary skills vary greatly.

DELIS

Delicatessens are a New York institution, not to mention a great source for a hefty lunchtime sandwich. Any visitor to the city should definitely try a deli's wonderful corned beef and pastrami sandwiches. While **Carnegie Delicatessen** in the Theater District is perhaps New York's most famous deli, **Katz's Deli** on the Lower East Side is much more authentic – and cheaper. Also deservedly popular is **Second Avenue Deli**, with its superb pastrami on rye and oozing blintzes.

Most deli business is takeout, and as a result, delis are bustling places serving huge sandwiches at relatively cheap prices. Counter staff are typically surly and impatient, and rudeness has almost become a trademark of the **Stage Deli**, which is now more of a tourist stop than the showbiz favorite it used to be.

For New York ethnic Jewish flavor, try **Barney Greengrass**, on the Upper West Side. In operation since 1929, the "Sturgeon King" serves up lox, salmon, pastrami, and, of course, sturgeon. **Zabar's** is a takeout heaven for yuppies who put up with the crowds for superb smoked fish, pickles, and salads.

CAFÉS, BISTROS, AND BRASSERIES

Cafés, bistros, and the larger brasseries have become "in" places in New York. Try the upscale **Balthazar** on Spring Street for "brilliantly faux" everything except the menu, which is stellar. Even more trendy is Balthazar's sister bistro, **Pastis**, in the Meatpacking District. **Café Centro**, above Grand Central, is particularly busy and noisy during lunchtime, and is a favorite with business types. The Centro's Provençal/Mediterranean fare includes fish soups and some succulent desserts. **Brasserie** on East 53rd, a longtime landmark, has had an elegant remodeling. **Bistro du Nord** on Madison Avenue has a variety of French/American fare with an inventive flair. Downtown, **Odeon** is a TriBeCa favorite for its brasserie menu and late hours. **Raoul's** in SoHo is a French bistro with a relaxed ambience that keeps artists and other habitués coming back for reliable, informal food. **Elephant and Castle**, a minimally decorated café, is a Greenwich Village standby for soup-salad-omelette lunches and other light snacks. Its real forte is breakfast and brunch, served in ample portions at modest prices. The bar scene is lively too. Tiny **Chez Jacqueline** is also a favored Village spot. Its French bistro fare and proximity to several off-Broadway theaters make it popular with the young, hip, and international crowd for a moderately priced dinner or late supper.

In the Theater District, try the Cuban **Victor's Café**. Large, lively, and Latin, it is known for authentic Cuban food served in giant portions at medium prices. **Chez Josephine** is an exuberant bistro-cabaret with live jazz piano playing. The scene is the main attraction here, and the French food is excellent.

La Boite en Bois, small but delightfully French, serves delicious French bistro food and is conveniently close to Lincoln Center. In the same vicinity is **Vince and Eddie's**, a tiny gem known for reliable, often superb American food.

Sarabeth's, on the Upper West Side, defies categorizing, but might best be dubbed a café. Breakfast or weekend brunch is the best time to try waffles, French toast, pancakes, and omelettes.

The Gramercy Park area's **Les Halles** is about as all-out French bistro as New York gets. At its late-night peak, the decibel level is high, but regulars think the *frites* and beef dishes are worth the noise and crowds.

PIZZERIAS

Pizza is available all over New York, from street stands and fast-food places that sell it by the slice to a traditional Neapolitan pizzeria.

Some pizzerias offer something more. **Arturo's Pizzeria** uses a coal oven for crisp, thin-crusted bases with the added inducement of live jazz. **Mezzogiorno** has a Tuscan menu and wonderful pizzas with unusual toppings. **Lombardi's** oven-baked pizzas are considered among the finest in Manhattan. The crowded **Mezzaluna** also specializes in brick-oven, thin-crusted pizza, as does **John's Pizzeria**, whose fans, including Woody Allen, consider it Manhattan's best. At **Two Boots**, specialty pies are named for characters in movies and TV shows, such as The Newman, from *Seinfeld*, and The Dude, from *The Big Lebowski*.

Brooklyn boasts a top pizzeria in Coney Island's **Totonno Pizzeria**, which is well worth the trip for real pizza aficionados, though it also has a Manhattan branch. **Joe's Pizza** has made a name for itself in Brooklyn and Manhattan. It's often busy, but the lines move quickly.

Generally, pizza parlors are good places to go for a cheap, simple meal, particularly with children. Most places won't take reservations, so popular ones may have long lines.

HAMBURGER PLACES

Apart from the hot dog stands on the street, New York has many places selling better quality burgers, even though prices for a top grade all-beef burger can go up to $10.

Burgers have even gone "upscale" with famed New York restaurateur Danny Meyer creating the **Shake Shack**, which has several locations around Manhattan, including one at Madison Square Park. It offers good-value eats all year round. In Midtown, the stylish Le Parker Meridien Hotel houses the **Burger Joint**, which looks like a truck-stop, and has some of the best burgers in town.

Bright and basic, the five outlets of **Jackson Hole** offer fat, juicy, meaty burgers in 28 varieties popular with kids. Adults might prefer less glare and smarter decor, but they will like the low prices. Alternatively, sink your teeth into the juicy burgers on offer at the **Five Guys** chain.

The **Corner Bistro** in Greenwich Village offers New York's best burgers, tasty and reasonably priced. The beer selection is good, too, and the 4am closing makes this a great late-night stop.

DINERS AND LUNCHEONETTES

Diners and luncheonettes, also called sandwich or coffee shops, can be found all over New York City. Food is mostly bland but served in huge, cheap platefuls. They are usually open from breakfast until late evening, and you can stop in at almost any hour.

A favorite trend with diners has seen 1990s replicas of the old 1930s cheap-eats places. One such retro diner is **Chock Full o' Nuts**, a

relaunch of a chain of coffee-branded cafés. A brighter, higher-energy option can be found near Carnegie Hall, in the **Brooklyn Diner**.

Theatergoers love **Junior's** diner in Brooklyn which is famous for its delicious cheesecake. **Big Nick's** on Broadway is the best place for a pizza, hamburger, or breakfast on the Upper West Side. The **Coffee Shop** in Union Square serves Brazilian-American fare and is open all night.

On the Upper East Side, Eli Zabar's **E.A.T.** sells excellent but pricey Jewish favorites – such as mushroom-barley soup and challah bread, as well as some sinful desserts. Another popular UES spot is **EJ's Luncheonette**, offering classic kid-friendly meals in a retro 1950s setting.

Devotees swear by **Viand**, a spic-and-span East Side luncheonette, with cheap, ample American breakfasts, good burgers, egg creams, and the best turkey sandwiches in town. **Veselka**, not the usual New York sandwich shop, serves Polish/Ukrainian food at rock-bottom prices and also has a second outlet, **Little Veselka**.

TEA ROOMS

The only place you can be absolutely sure of getting a cup of real, brewed tea is at a formal, prix-fixe afternoon tea in a lounge at one of New York's pricier hotels, from 3pm to 5pm.

For an extra-stylish tea, on Chippendale furniture, visit **Carlyle** in the Upper East Side. Another good buy in hotel prix-fixe tea is **Hotel Pierre**. Tea at the **Waldorf-Astoria** comes with Devonshire cream, while the elegant tea at **Stanhope** on Fifth Avenue is abundant enough to carry you through to a late dinner.

A variation on tea themes can be found in a chain of teahouses called **Saint's Alp**. These delightful spots, serving frothy, flavored, colorful tea drinks poured over crushed ice, can be found at 51 Mott Street

near Chinatown and in the East Village and Times Square areas. Teatime can also be enjoyed at **Tea & Sympathy**, in the Village, on Greenwich Avenue.

COFFEE AND CAKES

You can get a decent cup of coffee for as little as 75 cents, with endless free refills, at most diners, luncheonettes, and coffee shops. There is a popular trend for coffee bars that serve a variety of specialty coffees, such as cappuccino, espresso, and caffè latte. Ice-cream parlors and patisseries also serve good coffee, along with sinfully luscious pastries.

People wait in line at **Magnolia Bakery** to sample the decadent cakes. Magnolia has now opened a second spot on the Upper West Side. **Joe** boasts the world's best espresso machine, while **Caffè Ferrara**, going strong since 1892, has moderately priced Italian pastries, good coffee, and outdoor seating.

The Hungarian Pastry Shop has a range of Austro-Hungarian delights and views of St. John the Divine. Located in the Hotel Edison, **Café Edison** offers reasonably priced food in an Art Nouveau setting. **Sant Ambroeus** is a luxurious outpost of the Milanese pasticceria selling sumptuous desserts. In addition to home delivery of pies or cakes, **Dessert Delivery** has a nifty café for tasting the pastries and coffee. Try **Serendipity 3**, famous for its Victoriana, ice-cream creations – if you're an ice-cream aficionado don't miss the frozen hot chocolate – as well as coffee, and mid-afternoon snacks.

Barnes & Noble Café is a happy refuge for coffee and a pastry while browsing the bookstore. **Mudspot** is the permanent counterpart to the mobile, bright orange "Mudtrack" van that sells potent coffee. And, like them or not, you can't ignore **Starbucks**, which has dozens of locations around town.

DIRECTORY

LOWER MANHATTAN

Pastis
9 9th Avenue. **Map** 3 B1.

LOWER EAST SIDE

Caffè Ferrara
195 Grand St. **Map** 4 F4.

Katz's Deli
205 E Houston St.
Map 5 A3.

Saint's Alp
51 Mott St. **Map** 4 F4.

Two Boots
384 Grand St. **Map** 5 B4.

SOHO AND TRIBECA

Lombardi's
32 Spring St. **Map** 4 F4.

Mezzogiorno
195 Spring St. **Map** 4 D4.

Odeon
145 W Broadway.
Map 1 B1.

Raoul's
180 Prince St. **Map** 4 D3.

GREENWICH VILLAGE

Arturo's Pizzeria
106 W Houston St.
Map 4 E3.

Balthazar
80 Spring St. **Map** 4 E4.

Chez Jacqueline
72 MacDougal St.
Map 4 D2.

Corner Bistro
331 W 4th St. **Map** 3 C1.

Elephant and Castle
68 Greenwich Ave.
Map 3 C1.

Five Guys
296 Bleecker St.
Map 3 C3.

Joe
141 Waverly Place.
Map 3 C1.

Joe's Pizza
7 Carmine St. **Map** 4 D3.

Magnolia Bakery
401 Bleecker St.
Map 3 C2.
200 Columbus Ave.
Map 12 D1.

Sant Ambroeus
259 W 4th St.
Map 3 C1.

Tea & Sympathy
108 Greenwich Ave.
Map 3 C1.

EAST VILLAGE

Little Veselka
75 E 1st St.
Map 4 F3.

Mudspot
307 E 9th St. **Map** 4 F1.

Veselka
144 2nd Ave. **Map** 4 F1.

GRAMERCY AND THE FLATIRON

The Coffee Shop
29 Union Square West
Map 9 A5.

Les Halles
411 Park Ave South
Map 9 A3.

Shake Shack
Madison Square Park.
Map 8 F4.

CHELSEA AND THE GARMENT DISTRICT

Chock Full o' Nuts
25 W 23rd St.
Map 8 F4.

THEATER DISTRICT

Café Edison
Edison Hotel,
228 W 47th St.
Map 12 D5.

Carnegie Delicatessen
854 7th Ave.
Map 12 E4.

Chez Josephine
414 W 42nd St.
Map 7 B1.

Junior's
Shubert Alley,
enter on 45th St.
Map 12 E5.

Stage Deli
834 7th Ave.
Map 12 E4.

Victor's Café
236 W 52nd St.
Map 11 B4.

EAST SIDE MIDTOWN

Second Avenue Deli
162 E 33rd St.
Map 9 B2.

UPPER MIDTOWN

Barnes & Noble Café
Citicorp Building,
160 E 54th St.
Map 13 A4.

Brasserie
100 E 53rd St.
Map 13 A4.

Brooklyn Diner
212 W 57th St.
Map 12 E3.

Burger Joint
Le Parker Meridien Hotel,
118 W 57th St.
Map 12 E3.

Waldorf-Astoria
301 Park Ave.
Map 13 A5.

UPPER EAST SIDE

Bistro du Nord
1312 Madison Ave.
Map 17 A2.

Carlyle
35 E 76th St. **Map** 17 A5.

Dessert Delivery
350 E 55th St.
Map 13 B4.
Tel 838-5411.

E.A.T.
1064 Madison Ave.
Map 17 A4.

EJ's Luncheonette
1271 3rd Ave.
Map 13 B1.

Hotel Pierre
2 E 61st St.
Map 12 F3.

Jackson Hole
232 E 64th St.
Map 13 B2.
One of five branches.

John's Pizzeria
408 E 64th St.
Map 13 C2.
One of three branches.

Mezzaluna
1295 3rd Ave.
Map 17 B5.

Serendipity 3
225 E 60th St.
Map 13 B3.

Stanhope
995 5th Ave.
Map 17 A4.

Viand
1011 Madison Ave.
Map 17 A5.
One of four branches.

UPPER WEST SIDE

Barney Greengrass
541 Amsterdam Ave.
Map 15 C3.

Big Nick's
2175 Broadway
at 77th St.
Map 15 C5.

La Boite en Bois
75 W 68th St.
Map 11 C1.

Sarabeth's
423 Amsterdam Ave.
Map 15 C4.

Whitney Museum
945 Madison Ave.
Map 17 A5.

Vince and Eddie's
70 W 68th St.
Map 11 C1.

Zabar's
2245 Broadway.
Map 15 C2.

MORNINGSIDE HEIGHTS AND HARLEM

The Hungarian Pastry Shop
Amsterdam & 109th St.
Map 20 E4.

BROOKLYN

Totonno Pizzeria
1524 Neptune Ave.
Map 7 C5.

New York Bars

New York bars play a huge role in the life and culture of the city. Many New Yorkers spend the evening in a succession of bars, because each usually offers something more than just alcohol. There may be additional inducements, like excellent food, live music, dancing, or a particularly large selection of beers. Brew pubs, which serve meals and brew beer on the premises, are also popular. Bars suiting every taste and budget are to be found in every corner.

RULES AND CONVENTIONS

Bars generally remain open from around 11am until 2am. Some stay open to 4am, when they must close by law. Many bars have a "happy hour" between 5pm and 7pm, when they offer twofers (two drinks for the price of one) and free snacks. Bartenders can refuse to serve anyone they consider having had too much to drink. Smoking is banned and is only allowed outside or in specially ventilated rooms.

The legal minimum drinking age is 21; if the bartender suspects you are younger, you'll be "carded," or asked for identification. Children aren't usually allowed in.

It is common to "run a tab" by giving the bartender a credit card and paying your bill just before you leave. Tipping the bartender is expected – 15 percent of the bill or about $1 per drink. Shots are not pre-measured, so if you want a bigger drink, it can help to "belly up" to the bar and tip the bartender accordingly for his or her generosity. You may even be poured a free drink if you tip handsomely. If you sit at a table, you'll be served there and charged more. A round of drinks can be expensive. Save money by buying a quart (95 cl) or a half gallon (190 cl) pitcher of beer.

Many bars have obtained liquor licenses under an oscure cabaret law that prohibits dancing. Bars are regularly closed down for ignoring this rule, so if staff ask you to refrain from dancing to music, they are serious and should be obeyed.

WHAT TO DRINK

Mainstream bars serve standard beers from big producers, such as Budweiser, Coors, and Miller, as well as high-profile imports including Becks, Heineken, and draft Guinness. Old pubs and chic bars have a much wider variety of beers, imported and small domestics. These include flavorful beers, usually based on traditional European styles, made by some of New York's microbreweries. The locally brewed Brooklyn Lager is highly rated.

Other popular drinks include "designer," or "fusion," cocktails, rum and coke, vodka-and-tonic, gin-and-tonic, dry Martinis, and Scotch or bourbon – either "straight up" (without ice) or "on the rocks" (with ice). The "Cosmopolitan" is very New York: vodka, cranberry juice, triple sec, and lime. Most of the bars serve a range of Martinis made with vodka.

Wine is widely available at bars, and the "wine bar" concept has made a comeback, with options all over the city.

FOOD

Some bars serve food such as burgers, fries, salads, sandwiches, and spicy chicken wings throughout the day. If you are visiting the bar of a popular restaurant, you can often order bar snacks. Most bar kitchens stop serving food just before midnight.

FASHIONABLE BARS

To get into a hip bar, you will need to look glamorous and be prepared to wait in line, unless you arrive early. The Meatpacking District is lined with lively bars, including **Cielo**, a strobe-lit bar and club with potent cocktails and a soundtrack with everything from 1980s pop to hip-hop. Within stumbling distance is **Buddha Bar NYC**, a spinoff of the Paris original. The enormous restaurant has a bar that draws a hip crowd. The only serene elements are the massive Buddha and the jellyfish-stocked aquariums. Also incorporating a giant Buddha is **Tao Bar**, located in a former theater next to the Four Seasons Hotel. The venue is spread over three floors: the top two are devoted to pan-Asian cuisine and overlook the bar below.

The nightlife in the Lower East Side (LES) is growing in leaps and bounds, with numerous bars and clubs opening their doors. Enjoy cocktails and conversation at the lively **Schiller's Liquor Bar**. Formerly the Bowery Bar, the **B-Bar** still attracts a stylish crowd, though some claim its glory days are over. In the summer, the enormous outdoor space can't be beaten. **Pravda** is another favorite in nearby NoLIta. Subdued lighting creates a degree of calm in this subterranean spot decorated in Soviet chic. **The Odeon** on Broadway captures the lively SoHo-TriBeCa scene.

BARS WITH VIEWS

Top of the Tower, on the 26th floor of the Art Deco Beekman Tower, offers unsurpassed views of the city and great piano music. Also with great views are the **Rooftop Bar and Lounge** at the Empire Hotel, **Stone Rose Lounge** in the Time Warner Center, and **Rise** at the Ritz-Carlton in Battery Park. In warm weather, **Bryant Park Café** is a popular midtown scene, or you can sip cocktails and soak up the dazzling skyline views on **230 Fifth**'s vast wrap-around terrace.

HISTORIC AND LITERARY BARS

If you sample only one New York bar, it should probably be **McSorley's Old Ale House**, an Irish saloon often dubbed "McSurly's" because of its staff. It opened in 1854, and is one of the city's oldest bars.

The Ear Inn dates from 1812 when the first tavern opened on this SoHo site. Its cramped interior and long wooden bar ooze authenticity. Another SoHo favorite is **Fanelli's Café**, a former speakeasy that opened its doors in 1922 (though locals have been visiting the watering hole on this site since 1847).

Greenwich Village has some of the city's oldest bars, such as Dylan Thomas's favorite, the **White Horse Tavern**, an unpretentious 1880s landmark still crowded with literary and collegiate types. It also has an outdoor café for warm weather. **Peculier Pub** is a beer-lover's paradise, with over 360 varieties of beer.

A good, if touristy, place for a drink in the financial district is **Fraunces Tavern**, first built in 1719 *(see p76)*.

Pete's Tavern in the Gramercy Park area dates to 1864. Busy until 2am, it is known for Victoriana and the house brew called Pete's Ale. The typical Irish pub **Old Town Bar** has been serving stout since 1892, and is now favored largely by advertising types. No longer the celebrity scene it once was, **Sardi's** still appeals to *New York Times* reporters, and serves generous portions.

Hidden away in the balcony of Grand Central Terminal is **The Campbell Apartment**, the former private office of 1920s tycoon John W. Campbell. The spectacular space resembles a 13th-century Florentine palace. On the Upper East Side, the **Uptown Lounge** draws large crowds with its potent cocktails, tasty nibbles, and lively dance tunes.

A bustling saloon with Irish bartenders, **P. J. Clarke's** has been New York's favorite since the 1890s. **Elaine's**, also on the East Side, remains a haunt of mainly visiting literary types, though the food is so-so.

Near Carnegie Hall is **P. J. Carney's**, a watering hole for musicians and artists since 1927. It serves Irish ales and a good shepherd's pie.

YOUNG HANGOUTS

Brew pubs, where the house beer is brewed on the premises, are all the rage with the 20- and 30-somethings, as are bars that stock a variety of microbrews and imported beers. The **Chelsea Brewing Company** is a large, fun-filled brew pub in the Chelsea Piers sports complex. In the Gramercy neighborhood, you will find the **Heartland Brewery**, a bustling brew pub with five beers, including the outstanding India Pale Ale, and many seasonals, such as pumpkin ale. The cozy bar at **The Room**, in SoHo, has a good selection of beers and wine.

Serious beer drinkers will enjoy the 170 draft and bottled Belgian beers on offer at **Burp Castle**, while homesick Brits will likely head to **Manchester**. In a cozy, publike setting, you'll find Watneys or Newcastle Brown Ale on tap, just two of the 18 draft beers, and 40 bottled ones not widely available in New York.

In the East Village is bustling **d.b.a.**, which has 14 draft beers on tap, along with scores of microbrews and 50 single-malt whiskeys to choose from.

A popular beer stop uptown for the college-age crowd is the loud and noisy **Brother Jimmy's BBQ**, where you can snack on old-fashioned southern barbequed ribs.

Park Slope Ale House in Brooklyn is another brew pub favored by the young for its home brews and seasonal beers, as well as its decent pub grub and lively ambience.

GAY AND LESBIAN BARS

Gay bars can be found in Greenwich Village, Chelsea, and the East Village with a few on the Upper East and West Sides. Lesbian bars are mostly in Greenwich Village and East Village. For current listings, check the free weekly gay publication *Next* (www.nextmagazine.com).

HOTEL BARS

Centrally located, the **Algonquin Hotel** *(see p145)* was a famous literary haunt in the 1920s and early 1930s. Its Lobby Bar and Blue Bar are good places for a quiet pre-dinner or pre-theater drink.

The minimalist **Bar 44** in the lobby lounge of the Royalton Hotel is a perfect spot for a drink while watching the theatrical crowds drifting in and out. Also in the Theater District, the **Paramount Bar** has floor-to-ceiling windows and is usually frequented by fashion and theater types. In Upper Midtown there's the **Gilt Bar**, where you can recline on soft, plush red velvet seats.

The **Bull and Bear** in the Waldorf-Astoria, dating back to the Prohibition era, exudes comfort, charm, and a sense of history.

The stylish **King Cole Room** at St. Regis Hotel is named after a colorful mural behind the bar, by Maxfield Parrish.

Relax to downtempo tunes at the **Grand Bar**. One of New York's trendiest nightspots, the Soho Grand's bar is a good place to people-watch. Its sister hotel, the Tribeca Grand, also draws a crowd to its **Church Lounge**.

With dark-wood panels, navy-blue color scheme, and a kitschy seafaring theme, the Maritime Hotel's **Lobby Bar** draws a young, trendy crowd. Special attractions include a roaring fire in winter and an outdoor terrace in summer.

The glass-floored **Hudson Bar** at Ian Schrager's trendy Hudson Hotel is a regular hot-spot. The **Rose** and **Jade** bars, in Schrager's Gramercy Park Hotel, are filled with fashion-istas drinking in the "eclectic-Bohemian" vibe. Equally popular are **Thom Bar** at the 60 Thompson Hotel and **Bookmarks** at the Library Hotel; both attract a sophisticated scene. For those interested in joining the *Sex and the City* crowd, there's Rande Gerber's **Whiskey Blue Bar** in one of the boutique W Hotels.

DIRECTORY

LOWER MANHATTAN

Fraunces Tavern
54 Pearl St. **Map** 1 C4.
www.fraucestavern.com

Rise
2 W St. **Map** 1 B4.

SOHO AND TRIBECA

Church Lounge
Tribeca Grand, 2 6th Ave.
Map 4 D4.
www.tribecagrand.com

The Ear Inn
326 Spring St. **Map** 3 C4.
www.earinn.com

Fanelli's Café
94 Prince St. **Map** 4 E3.

The Grand Bar
Soho Grand, 310
W Broadway. **Map** 4 E4.
www.sohogrand.com

The Odeon
145 W Broadway.
Map 1 B1. **www**.the
odeonrestaurant.com

Pravda
281 Lafayette St.
Map 4 F3.
www.pravdany.com

The Room
144 Sullivan St. **Map** 4 D3.

Thom Bar
60 Thompson Hotel, 60
Thompson St. **Map** 4 D4.
www.60thompson.com

GREENWICH VILLAGE

Buddha Bar NYC
25 Little W 12th St.
Map 3 B1.
www.buddhabarnyc.com

Cielo
18 Little W 12th St.
Map 3 B1.
www.cieloclub.com

Peculier Pub
145 Bleecker St.
Map 4 D3.
www.peculierpub.com

White Horse Tavern
567 Hudson St.
Map 3 C1.

EAST VILLAGE AND LOWER EAST SIDE

B-Bar
40 E 4th St. **Map** 4 F2.
www.bbarandgrill.com

Burp Castle
41 E 7th St.
Map 4 F2.
http://burpcastlenyc.
wordpress.com

d.b.a.
41 1st Ave. **Map** 5 A1.
www.drinkgoodstuff.com

McSorley's Old Ale House
15 E 7th St. **Map** 4 F2.
www.mcsorleys
newyork.com

Schiller's Liquor Bar
131 Rivington St.
Map 5 B3.

GRAMERCY

Heartland Brewery
35 Union Square W.
Map 9 A5.
www.heartland
brewery.com

Jade Bar
Gramercy Park Hotel,
2 Lexington Ave.
Map 9 A4.
www.gramercypark
hotel.com

Old Town Bar
45 E 18th St.
Map 8 F5.
www.oldtownbar.com

Pete's Tavern
129 E 18th St.
Map 9 A5.
www.petestavern.com

Rose Bar
Gramercy Park Hotel,
2 Lexington Ave.
Map 9 A4.
www.gramercypark
hotel.com

CHELSEA AND THE GARMENT DISTRICT

Chelsea Brewing Company
Pier 59, 11th Ave.
Map 7 B5. **www**.chelsea
brewingco.com

Lobby Bar
Maritime Hotel, 363
W 16th St. **Map** 8 D5.
www.themaritime
hotel.com

THEATER DISTRICT

Bar 44
Royalton Hotel, 44 W
44th St. **Map** 12 F5.

Bryant Park Café
Bryant Park. **Map** 8 F1.
www.bryantpark.org

Hudson Bar
Hudson Hotel, 356 W
58th St. **Map** 12 D3.
www.hudsonhotel.com

Paramount Bar
Paramount Hotel, 235 W
46th St. **Map** 12 E5.

P. J. Carney's
906 7th Ave. **Map** 12 E3.
www.pjcarneys.com

Sardi's
234 W 44th St. **Map**
12 F5. **www**.sardis.com

LOWER MIDTOWN

230 Fifth
230 Fifth Ave. **Map** 8 F3.

Bookmarks
The Library Hotel, 299
Madison Ave. **Map** 9 A1.

The Campbell Apartment
Grand Central Terminal,
15 Vanderbilt Ave.
Map 9 A1.

UPPER MIDTOWN

Bull and Bear
Waldorf-Astoria Hotel,
Lexington Ave. **Map** 13
A5. **www**.bullbearbar.com

Gilt Bar
New York Palace Hotel,
455 Madison Ave.
Map 13 A4.
www.giltnewyork.com

King Cole Room
St. Regis Hotel, 2 E 55th
St. **Map** 12 F5.

Manchester
920 2nd Ave.
Map 13 B5.

P. J. Clarke's
915 3rd Ave.
Map 13 B4.

Stone Rose Lounge
10 Columbus Circle,
4th Floor.
Map 12 D3.
www.gerberbars.com

Tao Bar
42 E 58th St.
Map 13 A3.
www.taorestaurant.com

Top of the Tower
Beekman Tower,
3 Mitchell Place.
Map 13 C5.
www.thebeekman
hotel.com

Whiskey Blue Bar
541 Lexington Ave.
Map 13 A2.
www.gerberbars.com

UPPER EAST SIDE

Brother Jimmy's BBQ
1485 2nd Ave.
Map 17 B5.
www.brotherjimmys.com

Elaine's
1703 2nd Ave.
Map 17 B4.

Uptown Lounge
1576 Third Ave.
Map 17 B3.
http://uptownlounge
nyc.com

UPPER WEST SIDE

Rooftop Bar and Lounge
Empire Hotel, 44
W 63rd St.
Map 12 D2.
www.empirehotel
nyc.com

BROOKLYN

Park Slope Ale House
356 6th Ave at 5th St.

SHOPPING

Visitors to New York will inevitably include shopping in their action plans. The city is the consumer capital of the world: a shopper's paradise and a constant source of entertainment, with dazzling window displays and a staggering variety of goods for sale. Anything can be found here, from high fashion to rare children's books, state-of-the-art electronics, and a mouthwatering array of exotic food. If you are looking for a personal Hovercraft, read-in-the-dark eyeglass attachments, a designer bed for your pet gerbil, or a Wurlitzer jukebox, this is the city of your dreams. Whether you have $50,000 or $5, New York is the place to spend it.

Tiffany's clock

BEST BUYS

New York is a bargain hunter's dream, with huge discounts on anything from household goods to designer clothes. Some of the best shops are on Orchard Street and Grand Street on the Lower East Side, where designer goods are sold at considerably lower

The 1920s-style Henri Bendel store (see p319)

than the retail price. You can find just about every imaginable item of clothing here, in addition to tableware, shoes, home furnishings, and electronics. Some shops in this area are closed on Saturday – the Jewish Sabbath – but are usually open all day Sunday.

Another great area for fashion bargain hunters is the Garment District, roughly between Sixth and Eighth avenues from 30th to 40th Street. The main hub, Seventh Avenue, was renamed Fashion Avenue in the early 1970s. Several designers and manufacturers have showrooms here, some of which are open to the public. Many of their samples are put up for sales, announced on notices posted around the area. The best

time to visit them is just before one of the major gift-giving holidays. Top Button (www.topbutton.com) has comprehensive sales listings.

SALES

One word you'll come across all over the city, anytime of the year, is "sale." So check the sale goods before you pay full price for any purchase. The best sales are during New York's sale seasons, which generally run from June until end-July and from December 26 until February. Look up the local papers for ads. Along midtown Fifth Avenue you'll see signs announcing "Lost Our Lease" sales. Avoid them, as these signs have been up for years at many shops. Also keep your eyes peeled for "Sample Sales," where the top designers sell to the public the sample outfits they have created to show store buyers. Sample sales occur at different locations throughout the city, and are generally not advertised, so your best bet is to keep a lookout for signs announcing sample sales, particularly on Fifth Avenue and on Broadway.

The Bulgari entrance at Hotel Pierre (see p289)

HOW TO PAY

Most shops accept major credit cards, although there will often be a minimum purchase price. If you want to use your traveler's checks, identification is needed. Personal checks drawn in another currency will be refused. Some stores only take cash, especially during sales.

OPENING HOURS

Most shops are open from 10am to 6pm, Monday to Saturday. Many department stores are open through Sunday, and until 9pm at least two nights a week. Lunch hours (noon to 2:30pm), Saturdays, sales, and holidays will be the most crowded times.

Designer dress at a New York sale

TAXES

The New York City sales tax is 8.625 percent, although clothing and shoes under $110 are exempt. However, sales tax will be waived if the goods are shipped home.

SHOPPING TOURS

If you dread braving the stores alone, shopping tours are a good, reasonably priced option. Apart from the main department stores, you could visit private designer show-rooms, auction houses, or fashion shows. Some operators will customize tours to suit your requirements.

DEPARTMENT STORES AND MALLS

Most of the large department stores are in midtown Manhattan. Explore them at your

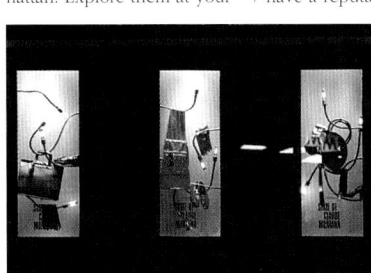

Window displays at Bloomingdale's *(see p181)*

leisure, since all these stores tend to be enormous, with a great range of goods. If possible, avoid weekends and vacation times, when the crowds can be overwhelming. Prices are often high, but you may find some bargains during sales.

Stores such as Saks Fifth Avenue, Bloomingdale's, and Macy's provide a diverse and extraordinary range of shopping services, including actually shopping for you.

One of the biggest malls in Manhattan is the **Shops at Columbus Circle** in the Time Warner Center. Its stores include Williams-Sonoma, Coach, and men's clothier Hugo Boss. Chelsea has the **Limelight Marketplace**. Previously a church, then a raucous nightclub, it is

now a temple to upscale fashion and food, with about 50 vendors.

Barney's New York, favored by young professionals, spe-cializes in excellent, though expensive, designer clothes.

Luxurious, elegant, and understated, **Bergdorf Goodman** sells contemporary clothes by European designers at high prices. The men's store is across the street.

Bloomingdale's *(see p181)* is the Hollywood film star of the department stores, with many eye-catching displays and seductive goods. New Yorkers young and old come here to seek out the latest in fashion. The linen and fine china departments have a reputation for quality, and the gourmet food section features a shop devoted entirely to caviar. Extensive shopping services and amenities include a noted restau-rant, Le Train Bleu, with its view of the Queensboro Bridge. There is also a SoHo branch on Broadway. Though much smaller than the main store, it stocks a similar selection of luxury goods.

At the exclusive **Henri Bendel**, everything from the Art Deco jewels to beautiful handmade shoes is displayed as a priceless work of art. The store, laid out in a series of 1920s-style boutiques, sells an excellent range of innovative women's fashions.

Lord & Taylor is renowned for its classic and much more conservative fashions for men and women, with an empha-sis on US designers.

Macy's, the self-proclaimed largest store in the world *(see p134–5)*, has ten floors selling everything imaginable from can openers to antiques.

A magnificent display offering household goods

Saks Fifth Avenue, known for style and elegance, has long been considered one of the city's best department stores, with service to match. It sells stunning designerwear for adults as well as children.

ADDRESSES

Barney's New York
660 Madison Ave. **Map** 13 A3.
Tel (212) 826-8900.

Bergdorf Goodman
754 5th Ave. **Map** 12 F3.
Tel (212) 753-7300.

Bloomingdale's
1000 3rd Ave. **Map** 13 A3.
Tel (212) 705-2000.
504 Broadway. **Map** 4 E4.
Tel (212) 729-5900.

Convention Tours Unlimited
Tel (212) 545-1160.

Elegant Tightwad
Tel (800) 808-4614.

Guide Service of New York
Tel (212) 408-3332.

Henri Bendel
712 5th Ave. **Map** 12 F4.
Tel (212) 247-1100.

Limelight Marketplace
656 6th Ave. **Map** 8 E5.
Tel (212) 226-7585.

Lord & Taylor
424 5th Ave. **Map** 8 F1.
Tel (212) 391-3344.

Macy's
151 W 34th St. **Map** 8 E2.
Tel (212) 695-4400.

Saks Fifth Avenue
611 5th Ave. **Map** 12 F4.
Tel (212) 753-4000.

Shop Gotham
Tel (866) 795-4200 or (212) 209-3370 to purchase tour tickets.

Shops at Columbus Circle
Time Warner Center. **Map** 12 D3.
Tel (212) 823-6300.

New York's Best: Shopping

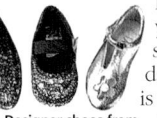

Designer shoes from Madison Avenue

In a city where you can literally shop 24 hours a day, the best plan is to shop the way New Yorkers do, by neighborhood. Each has its own character and specialties. Here are highlights of the best shopping districts – where they are and what you will find in each. If time is very tight, head for one of the huge department stores *(see p319)*, or if window shopping is your preference, stroll along Fifth Avenue, home to Manhattan's most glittering stores *(see opposite)*. For great bargains in a truly ethnic area, try the Lower East Side.

Greenwich Village and the Meatpacking District
Quaint, eclectic, and antique choices in the Village, and gourmands will enjoy the myriad speciality food stores. Meander over to Meatpacking District for high fashion shopping (see pp112–13).

SoHo
The area bordered by Sixth Avenue, Lafayette, Houston, and Canal streets is bustling with antiques, crafts, and clothes from designer flagships. Weekend brunchtime gallery-hopping is very popular. Cross Broadway to NoLIta for even trendier, cutting-edge fashion (see pp104–5).

East Village and Lower East Side
Explore around St Mark's Place for shoes, avant-garde fashions, and ethnic goods (see pp118–19). Bargains are becoming harder to find in the Lower East Side, but trendy options are increasing (see pp94–5).

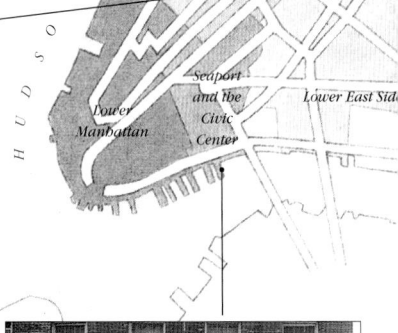

South Street Seaport
This is a browser's paradise of crafts, gifts, souvenirs, books, and antiques with a seafaring connection (see pp82–3).

Columbus and Amsterdam avenues
These are New York hot spots for exclusive but trendy designer clothes, quirky antiques, esoterica, and upscale gift shops (see pp212–13).

Madison and Lexington avenues
Shoppers come here for classics in art and antiques, designer clothes, and shoes. The Whitney Museum shop is nearby (see pp184–5).

East 57th and 59th streets
Exclusive antiques and high fashion are found on 57th Street – and be sure not to miss Bloomingdale's (see p181).

0 kilometers 2
0 miles 1

Herald Square and the Garment District
Here you will find Macy's, a store that occupies an entire block. The surrounding area (especially Seventh Avenue) is the fashion wholesale center with major discounts during sales – but some stores accept only cash (see pp132–3).

FIFTH AVENUE'S PRESTIGIOUS STORES
(see pp168–70)

Harry Winston

Saks Fifth Avenue

Tiffany's

Cartier

From Saks to Tiffany's
Leading retailers have their flagship store on world-famous Fifth Avenue.

Harry Winston
(see p328)

New York Originals

New York is a city where just about any kind of shop, no matter how esoteric, will always attract customers. Dozens of tiny shops scattered around the city specialize in unusual merchandise, from butterflies and bones to traditional Tibetan treasures and Shamrock sprigs from Ireland. Coming across these in some tucked-away corner is what makes shopping in New York such an entertaining and invigorating experience.

SPECIALTY SHOPS

For beautiful brass, onyx, and pewter chess sets, and the opportunity to play a decent game, make a move to the **Chess Shop**. For every type of pen **Arthur Brown & Bros.** stocks an enormous range, including such names as Mont Blanc and Schaeffer. For those with a bit more energy, **Blades Board & Skate** sells and rents out skates and also the trendiest skateboards plus all the safety equipment.

If you're looking for different or unusual buttons, a visit to **Tender Buttons**, which stocks millions, is a must. Whether you want enamel, wood, or Navajo silver buttons – or perhaps want your own buttons made into cuff links or earrings – here you'll find just what you want – and more. **Trash & Vaudeville** has been supplying punk and goth gear to New Yorkers for decades and is the HQ of Astor Place fashion.

Leo Kaplan Ltd. is the place to go if you are a keen collector of paperweights, while **Rita Ford's Music Boxes**, a 19th-century style shop, stocks a tuneful and extensive range of music boxes.

The **New York Firefighter's Friend** sells an intriguing range of items related to fire-fighting, including toy fire engines, firemen's jackets, badges, stuffed toy dalmatians and a wide selection of T-shirts, including a popular one with FDNY (Fire Department New York) on one side and "Keep back 200 feet" on the other.

Spies and conspiracy theorists will be enthralled with the extensive offering at **Quark Spy**, where you can simple choose from survival kits and camera pens up to audio intelligence rooms.

For the true romantic who wants to impress, everything sold by **Only Hearts** is heart-shaped, including pillows, soap, and jewelry. If you are artistic, or if you wish to buy a present for someone who is, visit **Pearl Paint**, which stocks everything you could need, from easels and brushes to modeling clay. **Forbidden Planet** is a science-fiction megastore with everything from comics to models for the true fan.

Cologne made especially for George Washington and the official soap of the White House during the Eisenhower era are just some of the many fascinating items for sale at **Caswell-Massey Ltd.**, which is the oldest pharmacy in the city.

Guitar gurus will want to visit **Rudy's**, **Manny's**, or **Sam Ash's** guitar shop. Not only is there a chance you'll bump into Eric Clapton or Lou Reed – both have their guitars made in this area – but you'll find the widest and best choice of instruments in the city.

Bibliophiles will find a range of gifts in both the **New York Public Library Shop** *(see p146)* (such as bookends of the lions guarding the main entrance) and the **Morgan Library Shop** *(see pp164–5)*, including bookmarks and writing paper.

University logos and college colors dominate the many knickknacks and accessories at **The Yale Club** gift shop and **The Princeton Club**.

Weisburg Religious Articles carries one of the largest selections of Jewish religious items in the city.

The Cathedral Shop at the Cathedral of St. John the Divine on Amsterdam Avenue is a large store selling books, artworks, herbs, jewelry, and religious items made locally.

MEMORABILIA

At Lincoln Center, the **Metropolitan Opera Shop** has records, cards, librettos, small binoculars, and many other opera-related items. For theater fans, everything from scripts and vocal scores to CDs can be found at **One Shubert Alley**. For thousands of rare and classic film stills and posters visit **Jerry Ohlinger's Movie Material Store** on 242 W 14th Street.

The **Carnegie Hall Shop** carries musically themed cards, T-shirts, games, posters, tote bags, and much more. For something truly original and very American, be sure to visit **Lost City Arts** and **Urban Archaeology** in SoHo. Between these two shops, you'll unearth all sorts of relics from America's past, from Barbie Doll lunch boxes to salvaged furniture, including antique, claw footed bath tubs.

TOYS, GAMES, AND GADGETS

For children's gifts, don't miss the legendary **F.A.O. Schwarz**. This is a massive store crammed with luxury toy cars, enormous stuffed animals and every kind of electronic toy imaginable. There are shoulder-to-shoulder crowds at Christmas, when you might have to line up to get in.

The **Children's General Store** is one of the city's smarter toy stores, with a focus on educational and classic goods, while a trip to the **American Girl Place** doll store could entertain a young girl all day, with options such as a café, photo studio, and hair salon.

Penny Whistle Toys sells a huge selection of quality toys, games, and all kinds of dolls. **Red Caboose** is for fans of model railways. On three floors, the **Toys 'R' Us** flagship glass building on Broadway is the largest toy store in the world, with a 60-ft (20-m) ferris wheel.

Dinosaur Hill on Second Avenue offers handmade

puppets and toys, mobiles, and beautifully made children's clothes. It's expensive but worth it. Since 1848, **Hammacher Schlemmer** have been encouraging shoppers to buy gadgets for home, office, and recreation that they didn't know they wanted. The quirky **Kidrobot** in SoHo draws both kids and collectors for its urban, cartoony action figures and memorabilia.

MUSEUM SHOPS

Some of New York's best souvenirs can be found in the city's many museum shops. In addition to the usual range of books, posters, and cards, there are reproductions of the exhibits on display, including jewelry and sculpture. The **Museum of Arts & Design** (see p149) has an excellent selection of American crafts as well as original works for sale. In addition to realistic model dinosaurs, rubber animals, minerals, and rocks, the **American Museum of Natural History** (see pp216–17) has a variety of recycled products and earth-awareness gifts,

which include posters, bags, and T-shirts with environmental messages, and a large selection of Native American handicrafts. There is also a kids' shop with reasonably priced items such as shell sets, magnets, and toys.

The **Asia Society Bookstore and Gift Shop** (see p187) has a striking selection of Oriental prints, posters, art books, toys, and jewelry. Items related to interior design are offered at the **Cooper-Hewitt** (see p186). One of New York's largest collections of Jewish ceremonial objects, including menorahs and Kiddush cups, books, and jewelry, is found in the small shop at the **Jewish Museum** (see p186).

For reproduction prints of famous paintings and other exquisite gifts a visit to the **Metropolitan Museum of Art** (see pp190–97) gift shop is a must. There is also an enormous book department and a children's gift shop. The traditional **American Folk Art Museum** (see p171) prides itself on its American country crafts, including wooden toys, quilts, and weathervanes, which are

mostly original. Works by craftspeople who currently have pieces on display in the museum are also sold.

The **Museum of the City of New York** (see p199), specializes in pictures of old New York as well as books and unique prints and posters. The **Museum of Modern Art/MOMA Design Store** (see pp172–75) has a highly praised selection of innovative home furnishings, toys, and kitchenware inspired by international designers such as Frank Lloyd Wright and Le Corbusier.

For a selection of nautical items, including charts, maps, model ships, and scrimshaw, go to the **South Street Seaport Museum Shops** (see pp82–85). The **Whitney Museum's Shop** (see pp200–201) stocks American-made items, including jewelry, wooden toys, books, and posters complementing current exhibitions. The **Museum of Jewish Heritage** (see p77) has a gift shop with an unusual array of gifts, souvenirs, and educational material about Jewish life. Open to ticketed visitors only.

THE BEST OF THE IMPORTS

New York is a massive melting pot of ethnic groups, nationalities, and cultures. Many ethnic shops specialize in food or goods of a particular group. **Alaska on Madison** has a collection of Eskimo art and Northwest prints and hangings, as does **Alaska House** in SoHo. The **Chinese Porcelain Company** sells exquisite Chinese decorative arts and furniture. **Pearl River Mart** has been a staple for Asian goods for thirty years, from novelty items to tea and tote-bags, and **Himalayan Crafts and Tours** stocks everything from paintings to Tibetan rugs. **Sweet Life**, on the Lower East Side, is a tiny, old-fashioned candy shop with delicacies from around the world. **Things Japanese**

has beautifully made crafts and unusual books. **Surma** is a Ukrainian general store that sells hand-painted eggs and linens. **Common Ground** sells Native American arts, and **Astro Gems** has a large collection of jewelry and mineral specimens from Africa and Asia. Nearby, Chinatown is packed with shops selling everything from souvenirs to leather goods, all at low prices.

ADDRESSES

Alaska House
109 Mercer St. **Map** 4 E3.
Tel (212) 431-1580.

Alaska on Madison
937 Madison Ave. **Map** 17 A1.
Tel (212) 879-1782.

Astro Gems
185 Madison Ave. **Map** 9 A2.
Tel (212) 889-9000.

Chinese Porcelain Company
475 Park Ave. **Map** 13 A3.
Tel (212) 838-7744.

Common Ground
55 W 16th St. **Map** 8 F5.
Tel (212) 989-4178.

Himalayan Crafts and Tours
2007 Broadway. **Map** 11 C1.
Tel (212) 787-8500.

Pearl River Mart
477 Broadway. **Map** 4 E4.
Tel (212) 431-4770.

Sweet Life
63 Hester St. **Map** 5 B4.
Tel (212) 598-0092.

Surma
11 E 7th St. **Map** 4 F2.
Tel (212) 477-0729.

Things Japanese
127 E 60th St. **Map** 13 A3.
Tel (212) 371-4661.

DIRECTORY

SPECIALTY SHOPS

Arthur Brown & Bros.
2 W 46th St. **Map** 12 F5.
Tel (212) 575-5555.

Blades Board & Skate
120 W 72nd St.
Map 12 D1.
Tel (888) 552-5233.
One of several branches.

Caswell-Massey Ltd.
518 Lexington Ave.
Map 13 A5.
Tel (212) 755-2254.

The Cathedral Shop
Cathedral of St. John the
Divine, 1047 Amsterdam
Ave. **Map** 20 E4.
Tel (212) 316-7540.

Leo Kaplan Ltd.
114 E 57th St.
Map B A3.
Tel (212) 355-7212.

Morgan Library Shop
Madison Ave at 36th St.
Map 9 A2.
Tel (212) 685-0008.

New York Firefighter's Friend
263 Lafayette St.
Map 4 F3.
Tel (212) 226-3142.

New York Public Library Shop
5th Ave at 42nd St.
Map 8 F1.
Tel (212) 930-0869.

Only Hearts
386 Columbus Ave.
Map 15 D5.
Tel (212) 724-5608.

Pearl Paint
308 Canal St. **Map** 4 E5.
Tel (212) 431-7932.

The Princeton Club
15 W 43rd St. **Map** 8 F1.
Tel (212) 596-1200.

Quark Spy
240 E 29th St. **Map** 9 B3.
Tel (212) 683-9100.

Rita Ford's Music Boxes
19 E 65th St. **Map** 12 F2.
Tel (212) 535-6717.

Rudy's
169 W 48th St.
Map 12 E5.
Tel (212) 391-1699.

Tender Buttons
143 E 62nd St.
Map 13 A2.
Tel (212) 758-7004.

The Chess Shop
230 Thompson St.
Map 4 D3.
Tel (212) 475-9580.

Trash & Vaudeville
4 St. Mark's Pl.
Map 5 A4.
Tel (212) 982-3590.

Weisburg Religious Articles
45 Essex St. **Map** 5 B4.
Tel (212) 674-1770.

The Yale Club
50 Vanderbilt Ave.
Map 13 A5.
Tel (212) 661-2070.

MEMORABILIA

One Shubert Alley
1 Shubert Alley.
Map 12 E5.
Tel (212) 944-4133.

The Carnegie Hall Shop
881 7th Ave. **Map** 12 E3.
Tel (212) 903-9610.

Forbidden Planet
840 Broadway.
Map 4 E1.
Tel (212) 473-1576.

Jerry Ohlinger's Movie Material Store
253 W 35th St.
Map 8 D2.
Tel (212) 989-0869.

Lost City Arts
18 Cooper Square.
Map 4 F2.
Tel (212) 375-0500.

Metropolitan Opera Shop
Metropolitan Opera
House, Lincoln Center, 136
W 65th St. **Map** 11 C2.
Tel (212) 580-4090.

Urban Archaeology
143 Franklin St.
Map 4 D5.
Tel (212) 431-4646.

TOYS, GAMES, AND GADGETS

American Girl Place
609 Fifth Ave.
Map 12 F5.
Tel (877) 247-5223.

The Children's General Store
Lexington Concourse,
Grand Central Station.
Map 9 A1.
Tel (212) 682-0004.

Dinosaur Hill
306 E 9th St, 2nd Ave.
Map 4 F1.
Tel (212) 473-5850.

F.A.O. Schwarz
767 5th Ave.
Map 12 F3.
Tel (212) 644-9400.

Hammacher Schlemmer
147 E 57th St.
Map 13 A3.
Tel (212) 421-9000.
One of two branches.

Kidrobot
126 Prince St.
Map 4 E3.
Tel (212) 966-6688.

Penny Whistle Toys
448 Columbus Ave.
Map 16 D4.
Tel (212) 873-9090.
One of several branches.

Red Caboose
23 W 45th St.
Map 12 F5.
Tel (212) 575-0155.

Toys 'R' Us
1514 Broadway,
Times Square.
Map 8 E2.
Tel (646) 366-8800.

MUSEUM SHOPS

Museum of Arts & Design
40 W 53rd St.
Map 12 F4.
Tel (212) 956-3535.

American Folk Art Museum
45 W 53rd St.
Map 12 F4.
Tel (212) 265-1040.

American Museum of Natural History
W 79th St at Central
Park W. **Map** 16 D5.
Tel (212) 769-5100.

Asia Society Bookstore and Gift Shop
725 Park Ave.
Map 13 A1.
Tel (212) 288-6400.

Cooper-Hewitt
2 E 91st St. **Map** 16 F2.
Tel (212) 849-8400.

Jewish Museum
1109 5th Ave.
Map 16 F2.
Tel (212) 423-3200.

Metropolitan Museum of Art
5th Ave at 82nd St.
Map 16 F4.
Tel (212) 535-7710.

Museum of the City of New York
5th Ave at 103rd St.
Map 21 C5.
Tel (212) 534-1672.

Museum of Jewish Heritage
18 1st Place, Battery Park
City. **Map** 1 B4.
Tel (646) 437-4200.

Museum of Modern Art/MOMA Design Store
44 W 53rd St.
Map 12 F4.
Tel (212) 767-1050.

South St. Seaport Museum Shops
12 Fulton St.
Map 2 D2.
Tel (212) 748-8600.

The Whitney Museum's Store Next Door
943 Madison Ave.
Map 13 A1.
Tel (212) 570-3676.

Fashion

Whether you're looking for a secondhand pair of 501s or the kind of ballgown Ivana Trump would be proud to wear, you're sure to find it in New York. The city is the fashion capital of America and an important center of clothing manufacture and design. New York's clothing stores, like its restaurants, reflect the city's dramatically different styles and cultures. To save time it's probably best to visit one area at a time and wander from store to store. Alternatively, visit one of the major department stores for an excellent selection of fashion for everyone.

AMERICAN DESIGNERS

Many American designers sell their creations in boutiques within the large department stores, or have exclusive shops of their own. One of the most famous is Michael Kors, known for sophisticated looks that are classic and comfortable.

Bill Blass is the king of American fashion whose clothes feature loads of different colors, wild patterns, innovative shapes, and a lot of wit. Liz Claiborne's designs are always elegantly simple, casual, and reasonably priced, including everything you could possibly need from tennis whites to casual professional wear for women.

Marc Jacobs, known for his sportswear, has his own label and store in Greenwich Village. James Galanos is an exclusive designer for the rich and famous, making one-of-a-kind *couture* clothes, and Betsey Johnson is popular with women able to wear figure-hugging fashions in fabulous fabrics.

In the last decade, Donna Karan has become a name that appears everywhere. Her simple, stylish, and great-looking designs work for everything from work-out clothes to black tie wear. Calvin Klein now has his name on place settings and sunglasses in addition to underwear, jeans, and a whole range of clothes. He is renowned for comfortable, sensuous, and well-fitting – as well as very hip – looks. Ralph Lauren is very well known for his aristocratic and expensive clothes, a

"look" favored by the exclusive and posh Ivy League, horsey set. For those with a taste for more experimental designs, Joan Vass specializes in moderately priced but exciting, colorful, and innovative knitwear.

DISCOUNT DESIGNER CLOTHES

If you're on the lookout for discount designer clothes, **Designer Resale**, **Encore**, and **Michael's** sell a wide range. Oscar de la Renta, Ungaro, and Armani are just some of the leading labels available. Clothes are either new or worn but near-perfect.

The designer discount emporium **Century 21** in Lower Manhattan sells European and American designer fashions discounted up to an amazing 75 percent off regular retail prices. **Filene's Basement**, one of Manhattan's longest-running discount department stores, offers designer clothes, shoes, and accessories at bargain prices. **Loehmann's** offers discounted fashion clothes, and it's the place to shop if you want top-of-the-line fashions at unbelievable discounts.

MEN'S CLOTHES

In the center of midtown, you'll find two of the city's most highly regarded mens-wear stores: **Brooks Brothers** and **Paul Stuart**. Brooks Brothers is something of a New York institution, famous for its traditional, conservative clothing such as smart button-down shirts and Chinos. There's an ultra-conservative

woman's line too. Paul Stuart prides itself on its very British look and offers a stylish array of superbly tailored fashions. Go to the high-quality department store **Bergdorf Goodman Men** to find beautifully made Turnbull & Asser shirts and marvelous suits by Gianfranco Ferré or Hugo Boss.

Barney's New York has one of the most comprehensive men's departments in America, with a truly massive range of clothes and accessories.

The Custom Shop Shirtmakers specializes in custom-made suits and shirts in beautiful materials. Go to **Burberry Limited** if you are looking for classic British trenchcoats and traditional outdoor wear.

J. Press sells classic, conservative yet elegant clothes while **John Varvatos** is famous for luxurious, sporty designs with superb detail. Uptown designer menswear boutiques include the renowned **Beau Brummel** with a selection of very stylish European clothes and **Thomas Pink** whose bright colors and fine fabrics make this store a celebrity favorite. Many of these men's stores also carry striking women's fashions. The **Hickey Freeman** store on Fifth Avenue sells a wide range of men's traditional clothing.

CHILDREN'S CLOTHES

In addition to an excellent selection within the large department stores, there are several shops around the city that sell children's clothing exclusively. A good example is **Bonpoint**, which has a world of French-style charm. Also stocked with delightful outfits is **Bundle**, in SoHo.

GapKids and **BabyGap** shops, often in the **Gap** shops, have comfortable, long-lasting cotton overalls, sweat pants, denim jackets, sweatshirts, and leggings. Actress Phoebe Cates has opened a hip kids' clothing store on Madison Avenue called **Blue Tree**. **Space Kiddets** has everything from booties to Western wear.

WOMEN'S CLOTHES

Women's fashion is subject to design trends, and New York stores keep pace with them all. Most of the city's most fashionable shops are found in the midtown area around Madison and Fifth Avenues. These include some of the major department stores (see p319), which stock a range of American designers, including Donna Karan, Ralph Lauren and Bill Blass.

Leading international names such as **Chanel** and **Valentino** also have shops here, as does one of the outstanding American designers, **Michael Kors**. There is also a handful of popular ready-to-wear stores, including **Ann Taylor**, which is much favored by young, busy professionals looking for stylish, comfortable clothing.

Right at the heart of this area stands the pink-marbled Trump Tower, which houses a selection of exclusive shops.

Madison Avenue is packed with designers for the smart set, who have everything you could ever need, including **Givenchy**, who sells show-stopping formal gowns at phenomenal prices; Valentino, who has classic Italian clothes; and **Emanuel Ungaro**, who generally has something to suit most tastes and physiques from beautifully tailored jackets to more matronly full-figured and boldly patterned print dresses. **Missoni** is famous for richly textured sweaters in sumptuous wools and colorful patterns. **Yves St Laurent Rive Gauche** has evening gowns, one-of-a-kind jackets, silks and extravagant blouses, and beautifully cut pants suits.

Sophisticated Italian looks are also available from Italian style kings **Giorgio Armani** and **Gianni Versace**. **Dolce & Gabbana** sells unique, one-of-a-kind Italian clothing. **Gucci**, one of the oldest Italian shops in America, is only for the wealthy and status-conscious.

The Upper West Side has many shops competing for attention with contemporary fashions, including **Betsey Johnson**'s shop, with her whimsical, relatively inexpensive designs. **Calvin Klein** now has a store on the East Side, specializing in ultra-hip, casual fashions. **French Connection** is known for its affordable separates, both casual and for the office. **Scoop** is *the* place to get a little black dress.

The villages – the East Village in particular – are the best places to go for secondhand clothing and 1950s rock 'n' roll gear, with ever-changing interesting shops run by new and young designers and art school graduates. For a range of affordable, well-cut clothes from classic to casual, try **APC**.

Cheap Jack's carries a huge selection of secondhand Levi's as well as hundreds of denim and leather jackets. **Screaming Mimi's** is where

you could unearth that pair of velvet bell-bottoms or go-go boots you've always dreamed of having. A more mainstream shop is **The Gap**, a chain store selling lots of moderately-priced, casual and comfortable clothes for men, women, and children.

Sotto and Notto/Nolita rival Madison Avenue for designer boutiques specializing in expensive but interesting clothes – the fashions here are far more avant-garde. The playful boutique **Kirna Zabete**, for example, features a unique range of clothes as well as accessories. You'll also find **Yohji Yamamoto** in this area, among other exclusive stores. **Comme des Garçons** in the Garment District sells minimalist Japanese chic.

Cynthia Rowley is a prominent New York designer who sells flirty fashions for women and **What Comes Around Goes Around** on West Broadway is the place to go for vintage jeans.

SIZE CHART

For Australian sizes follow the British and American conversions.

Children's clothing

American	2–3	4–5	6–6x	7–8	10	12	14	16 (size)
British	2–3	4–5	6–7	8–9	10–11	12	14	14+ (years)
Continental	2–3	4–5	6–7	8–9	10–11	12	14	14+ (years)

Children's shoes

American	7½	8½	9½	10½	11½	12½	13½	1½	2½
British	7	8	9	10	11	12	13	1	2
Continental	24	25½	27	28	29	30	32	33	34

Women's dresses, coats and skirts

American	4	6	8	10	12	14	16	18
British	6	8	10	12	14	16	18	20
Continental	38	40	42	44	46	48	50	52

Women's blouses and sweaters

American	6	8	10	12	14	16	18
British	30	32	34	36	38	40	42
Continental	40	42	44	46	48	50	52

Women's shoes

American	5	6	7	8	9	10	11
British	3	4	5	6	7	8	9
Continental	36	37	38	39	40	41	44

Men's suits

American	34	36	38	40	42	44	46	48
British	34	36	38	40	42	44	46	48
Continental	44	46	48	50	52	54	56	58

Men's shirts

American	14	15	15½	16	16½	17	17½	18
British	14	15	15½	16	16½	17	17½	18
Continental	36	38	39	41	42	43	44	45

Men's shoes

American	7	7½	8	8½	9½	10½	11	11½
British	6	7	7½	8	9	10	11	12
Continental	39	40	41	42	43	44	45	46

DIRECTORY

DISCOUNT DESIGNER CLOTHES

Century 21 Department Store
22 Cortland St.
Map 1 C2.
Tel (212) 227-9092.

Designer Resale
324 E 81st St.
Map 17 B4.
Tel (212) 734-3639.

Encore
1132 Madison Ave.
Map 17 A4.
Tel (212) 879-2850.

Filene's Basement
4 Union Square South.
Map 9 A5.
Tel (212) 358-0169.
One of several branches.

Loehmann's
101 7th Ave. **Map** 8 E1.
Tel (212) 352-0856.

Michael's
1041 Madison Ave.
Map 17 A5.
Tel (212) 737-7273.

MEN'S CLOTHES

Barney's New York
660 Madison Ave.
Map 13 A3.
Tel (212) 826-8900.

Beau Brummel
347 W Broadway.
Map 4 E3.
Tel (212) 219-2666.
One of several branches.

Bergdorf Goodman Men
754 5th Ave.
Map 12 F3.
Tel (212) 753-7300.

Brooks Brothers
346 Madison Ave.
Map 9 A1.
Tel (212) 682-8800.

Burberry Limited
9 E 57th St.
Map 12 F3.
Tel (212) 757-3700.

The Custom Shop Shirtmakers
618 5th Ave.
Map 12 F4.
Tel (212) 245-2499.
One of several branches.

Hickey Freeman
666 Fifth Ave.
Map 12 F4.
Tel (212) 586-6481.

J. Press
7 E 44th St. **Map** 12 F5.
Tel (212) 687-7642.

John Varvatos
149 Mercer St. **Map** 4 E3.
Tel (212) 965-0700.

Paul Stuart
350 Madison Ave.
Map 13 A5.
Tel (212) 682-0320.

Polo/Ralph Lauren
Madison Ave at 72nd St.
Map 13 A1.
Tel (212) 606-2100.

Thomas Pink
520 Madison Ave.
Map 13 A4.
Tel (212) 838-1928.

CHILDREN'S CLOTHES

Blue Tree
1283 Madison Ave.
Map 17 A2.
Tel (212) 369-2583.

Bonpoint
1269 Madison Ave.
Map 17 A3.
Tel (212) 722-7720.

Bundle
128 Thompson St.
Map 4 D3.
Tel (212) 982-9465.

GapKids
60 W 34th St. **Map** 8 F2.
Tel (212) 760-1268.
One of several branches.

Space Kiddets
46 E 21st St.
Map 8 F4.
Tel (212) 420-9878.

WOMEN'S CLOTHES

Ann Taylor
645 Madison Ave.
Map 13 A3.
Tel (212) 832-2010.
One of several branches.

APC
131 Mercer St.
Map 4 E3.
Tel (212) 966-9685.

Betsey Johnson
248 Columbus Ave.
Map 16 D4.
Tel (212) 362-3364.
One of several branches.

Calvin Klein
654 Madison Ave.
Map 13 A3.
Tel (212) 292-9000.

Chanel
15 E 57th St.
Map 12 F3.
Tel (212) 355-5050.

Cheap Jack's
841 Broadway.
Map 4 E1.
Tel (212) 777-9564.

Comme des Garçons
520 W 22nd St.
Map 8 F3.
Tel (212) 604-9200.

Cynthia Rowley
376 Bleecker St.
Map 3 C2.
Tel (212) 242-3803.

Dolce & Gabbana
434 W Broadway.
Map 4 E3.
Tel (212) 965-8000.

Emanuel Ungaro
792 Madison Ave.
Map 13 A2.
Tel (212) 249-4090.

French Connection
700 Broadway.
Map 4 E2.
Tel (212) 473-4486.
One of several branches.

The Gap
250 W 57th St.
Map 12 D3.
Tel (212) 315-2250.
One of many branches.

Gianni Versace
647 5th Ave. **Map** 12 F4.
Tel (212) 317-0224.

Giorgio Armani
760 Madison Ave.
Map 13 A2.
Tel (212) 988-9191.
717 5th Ave.
Map 12 F3.
Tel (212) 207-1902.

Givenchy
710 Madison Ave.
Map 13 A1.
Tel (212) 688-4005.

Gucci
685 5th Ave.
Map 12 F4.
Tel (212) 826-2600.

Kirna Zabete
96 Greene St.
Map 4 E4.
Tel (212) 941-9656.

Michael Kors
974 Madison Ave.
Map 17 A5.
Tel (212) 452-4685.

Missoni
1009 Madison Ave.
Map 13 A1.
Tel (212) 517-9339.

Saks Fifth Avenue
611 5th Ave.
Map 12 F4.
Tel (212) 753-4000.

Scoop
532 Broadway
(near Spring St).
Map 4 E4.
Tel (212) 925-2886.
One of two branches.

Screaming Mimi's
382 Lafayette St.
Map 4 F2.
Tel (212) 677-6464.

Valentino
747 Madison Ave.
Map 13 A2.
Tel (212) 772-6969.

What Comes Around Goes Around
351 W Broadway.
Map 4 E4.
Tel (212) 343-9303.

Yohji Yamamoto
103 Grand St.
Map 4 E4.
Tel (212) 966-9066.

Yves St Laurent Rive Gauche
855 Madison Ave.
Map 13 A1.
Tel (212) 517-7400.

Accessories

In addition to the following shops, all of the major Manhattan department stores have extensive accessory departments stocking a range of hats, gloves, bags, jewelry, watches, scarves, shoes, and umbrellas.

JEWELRY

Midtown Fifth Avenue is where to find the most dazzling jewelers. By day, windows glisten with gems from around the world; by night they are empty – the jewels safely locked away. The most sensational shops are all within a couple of blocks of one another and include the museum-like **Harry Winston**, which show-cases its coveted jewels from around the world. **Buccellati** is well respected for its innovative Italian creations and excellent workmanship. **Bulgari** has an impressive collection that ranges in price from a couple of hundred to over a million dollars.

Housed in a Renaissance-style palazzo, **Cartier** is a jewel in itself and sells its beautiful baubles at unthinkable prices. **Tiffany & Co.** has ten floors of glittering crystal, diamonds, and other jewels just waiting to be packed up for you and taken away in the store's signature sky blue boxes.

Diamond Row, a one-block area on 47th Street (between Fifth and Sixth Avenues), is lined with shops displaying hundreds of thousands of dollars worth of diamonds, gold, pearls, and other exotic jewels from around the world. Try not to miss the **Jewelry Exchange**, a complex where 60 different crafts-people sell their ware direct to the public. Boisterous bargaining is very much alive here, so be prepared to play the game.

HATS

New York's oldest hat shop is **Worth & Worth**, which also has the largest collection of hats in the city. You can get anything here, from original Australian bush hats to silk toppers, to slouch hats and boaters. **Suzanne Millinery** is the hat-maker to the stars, as she has proved very popular with celebrities such as Ivana Trump and Whoopi Goldberg. **Lids** sells baseball caps in dozens of varieties, with logos ranging from sports teams to the evergreen "I HEART NY". For a wide range of fabulous headgear, stop by **The Hat Shop**, where you can find everything from classic to contemporary styles.

UMBRELLAS

The minute it starts to rain in New York, hundreds of street vendors selling umbrellas seem to sprout like mushrooms. Their umbrellas, which sell at just a few dollars, are without doubt the cheapest in the city, but unlikely to last much longer than the downpour itself. For good-quality umbrellas, you'll find a fine selection of Briggs of London at **Worth & Worth**. There is a wide range of different sizes, trendy patterns, and traditional tartans and stripes at **Barney's New York**, and there's always **Macy's** (see p319) for the usual sizes and styles. World-famous **Gucci** has umbrellas to match its ties. Subway-themed ones can be found at the **NY Transit Museum Store**.

HANDBAGS AND BRIEFCASES

Twice a year, during the January and August sales, a serpentine line of buyers wraps around the corner of 48th Street and Madison Avenue waiting to get into **Crouch & Fitzgerald**, an old New York institution, selling handbags, briefcases, and luggage. All the well-known brands are sold here, including Judith Leiber, Ghurka, Dooney & Bourke, and Louis Vuitton, as well as the firm's own line. Elsewhere in the city are such exclusive shops as **Bottega Veneta**, and **Prada**, where handbags are displayed like precious art, with prices to match. Younger and trendier places include **Furla**, well-respected for its Italian designs, and the stylish **Il Bisonte**. Current must-have designer Rafé Totengco's soft suede pastel pouches are found at **TG-170**. **The Coach Store** is known for its simple, classic leather handbags. Designer **Kate Spade's** stylish yet practical rectangular handbags, in a plethora of prints and colors, have become modern classics, and add a chic touch to any woman's wardrobe. **Jack Spade** designs similarly unique bags for men.

For discount designer handbags try the legendary **Fine & Klein**, and for bargain briefcases from slim enve-lopes to thick lawyer's bags, a visit to the **Altman Luggage Company** is a must.

SHOES AND BOOTS

Manhattan shoe stores are famous for their extensive selections of shoes and boots, and if you shop around, you are sure to find what you want at a reasonable price.

Most of the large depart-ment stores in New York also have shoe departments where you can find designer-label shoes in addition to other brands. **Bloomingdale's** (see p181) has a huge women's footwear department, and **Brooks Brothers** has one of the best selections of tradi-tional men's shoes in the city.

For both men's and women's shoes, the most exclusive shops are around the midtown area. **Ferragamo** sells classic styles crafted in Florence. Go to **Botticelli** for whimsical shoe fashions. For stylish shoes at decent prices, head for **Sigerson Morrison** in Little Italy.

For cowboy boots, head for **Billy Martin's**. There's a huge selection of handmade boots, from basic, no-frills "ropers," which real American cowboys wear, to crocodile leather boots that sell for thousands of dollars. Billy Martin's stocks western garb and accessories, so you can dress in western gear from head to toe. For beautiful custom-made boots, try **Buffalo Chips Bootery**.

Sneaker collectors should make a stop at **Alife Rivington Club** on the Lower East Side, which stocks several hard-to-find styles.

For the best in children's shoes, **East Side Kids** stocks the trendiest fashions for kids, while **Shoofly** has imported shoes in all styles.

The **Jimmy Choo** boutique offers a plethora of sexy, stylish heels. Popular among Manhattan's chic set are the beautiful women's shoes,

particularly the flattering heels, at **Manolo Blahnik**. **Christian Louboutin** rounds out the stiletto heavyweights. Spain's most popular brand, **Camper**, has an airy SoHo store featuring their signature comfy, funky, and colorful shoes for women and men.

For discounted shoes, go to West 34th Street and West Eight Street between Fifth and Sixth Avenues, and Orchard Street on the Lower East Side. The **DSW** store, on the third floor of 40 E 14th Street, sells brand-name shoes and boots at a fraction of the regular price. There's also a branch near Battery Park.

LINGERIE

Expensive imports from Europe, which are sexy yet elegant, can be found at **La Petite Coquette**.

More affordable is **Victoria's Secret** on 57th Street or SoHo, which offers beautifully made lingerie in satin, silk, and many other fine fabrics. **Henri Bendel's** lingerie department offers a sumptuous array of lingerie, from naughty to nice. The Italian **La Perla** features seductive lingerie and undergarments in sensual fabrics from tulle and chiffon to satin.

DIRECTORY

JEWELRY

Buccellati
46 E 57th Ave. **Map** 12 F3.
Tel (212) 308-2900.

Bulgari
730 5th Ave. **Map** 12 F3.
Tel (212) 315-9000.

Cartier
653 5th Ave. **Map** 12 F4.
Tel (212) 753-0111.

Harry Winston
718 5th Ave. **Map** 12 F3.
Tel (212) 245-2000.

Jewelry Exchange
15 W 47th St. **Map** 12 F5.

Tiffany & Co
5th Ave. **Map** 12 F3.
Tel (212) 755-8000.

HATS

The Hat Shop
120 Thompson St. **Map** 4
D3. *Tel (212) 219-1446.*

Lids
243 W 42nd St. **Map** 8
E1. *Tel (212) 575-1717.*

Suzanne Millinery
27 E 61st St. **Map** 13 A3.
Tel (212) 593-3232.

Worth & Worth
45 W 57th St, 6th floor,
Suite Le02. **Map** 12 F3.
Tel (212) 265-2887.

UMBRELLAS

Barney's New York
See p319.

Gucci
See p327.

NY Transit Museum Store
Grand Central Terminal.
Map 9 A1.
Tel (212) 878-0106.

HANDBAGS AND BRIEFCASES

Altman Luggage Company
135 Orchard St. **Map** 5 A3.
Tel (212) 254-7275.

Il Bisonte
120 Sullivan St. **Map** 4
D4. *Tel (212) 966-8773.*

Bottega Veneta
635 Madison Ave. **Map** 13
A3. *Tel (212) 371-5511.*

The Coach Store
595 Madison Ave. **Map** 13
A3. *Tel (212) 754-0041.*

Crouch & Fitzgerald
400 Madison Ave.
Map 13 A5.
Tel (212) 755-5888.

Fine & Klein
119 Orchard St. **Map** 5
A3. *Tel (212) 674-6720.*

Furla
598 Madison Ave.
Map 13 A3.
Tel (212) 755-8986.
One of two branches.

Jack Spade
56 Greene St. **Map** 4 E4.
Tel (212) 625-1820.

Kate Spade
454 Broome St. **Map** 4
E4. *Tel (212) 274-1991.*

Prada
49 E 57th St. **Map** 12 F3.
Tel (212) 308-2332.

TG-170
170 Ludlow St. **Map** 5 A3.
Tel (212) 995-8660.

SHOES AND BOOTS

Alife Rivington Club
158 Rivington St. **Map** 5
B3. *Tel (212) 375-8128.*

Billy Martin's
220 E 60th St. **Map** 13
B3. *Tel (212) 861-3100.*

Botticelli
620 5th Ave. **Map** 12 F4.
Tel (212) 582-6313.

Bloomingdale's
See p319.

Brooks Brothers
See p327.

Buffalo Chips Bootery
355 W Broadway. **Map**
4 E4. *Tel (212) 625-8400.*

Camper
125 Prince St. **Map** 4 E3.
Tel (212) 358-1842.

Christian Louboutin
941 Madison Ave.
Map 17 A5.
Tel (212) 396-1884.

DSW
40 E 14th St. **Map** 9 A5.
Tel (212) 674-2146.

East Side Kids
1298 Madison Ave. **Map**
17 A2. *Tel (212) 360-5000.*

Ferragamo
655 5th Ave. **Map** 12 F3.
Tel (212) 759-3822.

Jimmy Choo
645 5th Ave. **Map** 12 F4.
Tel (212) 625-1820.

Manolo Blahnik
31 W 54th St. **Map** 12 F4.
Tel (212) 582-3007.

Shoofly
42 Hudson St. **Map** 1 B1.
Tel (212) 406-3270.

Sigerson Morrison
28 Prince St. **Map** 4 F3.
Tel (212) 219-3893.

LINGERIE

Henri Bendel
See p319.

La Perla
93 Greene St. **Map** 4 E3.
Tel (212) 219-0999.

La Petite Coquette
51 University Place. **Map** 4
E1. *Tel (212) 473-2478.*

Victoria's Secret
34 E 57th St. **Map** 12 F3.
Tel (212) 758-5592.
591–593 Broadway.
Map 4 E3.
Tel (212) 219-3643.

Beauty, Manicures and Pedicures, and Hair Salons

You can shop 'til you drop in New York City – and when you do, rest assured that rejuvenation (and a heavenly foot massage) is just around the corner. There are plenty of well-stocked beauty stores, manicure and pedicure specialists, and sleek hair salons. Many of the manicurists and salons cater to New Yorkers and their hectic schedules, so they often accept same-day appointments that can easily fitted in between rounds of sightseeing and shopping. After a pamper session or two (or three…), you'll be ready to hit the shops again, this time with the prettiest toes and silkiest hair around.

BEAUTY STORES

The French-owned **Sephora** is a cosmetics megastore that offers its shoppers row upon row of beauty products, from skin cleansers to cosmetics and fragrances, and, thankfully, a no-pressure sales staff. For all-natural essences and products, try **Erbe** ("herbs" in Italian), a soothing sanctuary with a plethora of hypo-allergenic products, all made with fresh herbs and free from mineral oils, animal products, waxes, synthetic fragrances, or dyes. The royal jelly nutrient moisturizer and Pennywort exfoliating cream are popular choices.

The high-ceilinged **MAC Cosmetics** store is always busy. Their face powders, particularly the Studio Fix line, are unsurpassed. The promise of creamy Swedish skin (at a reasonable price) lures shoppers to **FACE Stockholm**, where they stock natural, botanical skin products plus lipstick and nail polish in a rainbow of colors. Since 1851, **Kiehl's** has been creating cleansers, toners, balms, and masques "in purposefully utilitarian" packaging as the natural ingredients speak for themselves.

The nature-friendly **Fresh** sells fragrant body creams and fruity perfume. **Sabon** sells a luxurious range of bath and beauty products that are 100 percent natural and irresistibly scented. Soaps can be bought by the pound here, and they are gift-wrapped for free.

For good quality makeup that stands the test of time, visit SoHo's stylish **Make Up for Ever**, which stocks everything from liquid face foundations and creamy lipsticks, to sparkling body powders. Head to earthy **Origins** and select from their plethora of plant-based lotions, an antioxidant moisturizer made with white tea, and body creams sensitive enough for a baby's skin. British beauty maven Nicky Kinnaird has opened her first outlet of **Space.NK** in SoHo. The shop also offers beauty services.

Most of New York's large department stores, including **Bloomingdale's**, **Lord & Taylor**, **Saks Fifth Avenue**, **Barney's New York**, and **Macy's** offer well-stocked makeup counters.

MANICURES AND PEDICURES

Young Korean entrepreneur Ji Baek's **Rescue Beauty Lounge** started out as a cozy SoHo salon, but it proved so popular that she had to open a second outpost. As well as manicures and pedicures, you can have waxing and browse hard-to-find makeup lines. **Eve's** may look somewhat bland and institutional, but appearances can be deceiving. Their long-lasting manicures and pedicures are top-notch. **Dashing Diva** not only offers excellent manicures and pedicures at a bargain price (starting at $10). The whole experience is made all the more alluring, however, as they offer treats with their treatments. On Thursdays and Fridays, they serve Cosmopolitans and turn up the music.

Experience the ultimate in hand and nail care at **Sweet Lily Natural Nail Spa & Boutique**. The range includes an intoxicating blend of warm milk and almond oil for your hands, and a moisturizing honey walnut mask with a honey walnut manicure ($40). The hot lavender cream manicure includes a wonderful conditioning treatment for cuticles that contains tea tree and citrus oil. The boutique is not just for adults, as there is also a manicure for little girls: the Little Miss Mani includes a choice of nail art.

HAIR SALONS

If you're in the mood for a new hair do, or just want to refresh your current cut, try one of New York City's cutting-edge hair salons.

The stylists at the downtown **Arrojo Studio** will update your style, so that you walk out of the salon looking as hip as they do. Arrojo colorists are also top-notch, and the salon offers a wide range of exellent color treatments. Follow the celebrities, and get your hair cut, styled, and/or colored by stylist Frederic Fekkai or one of his associates at the chic **Frederic Fekkai Beaute de Provence**. This top salon is very much a cut above the rest.

Korean stylist Younghee Kim, formerly of Vidal Sassoon, offers hip cuts and colors, as well as "hair spa treatments" and thermal conditioning, starting at $110 at her eponymous hair salon, **Younghee Salon** in TriBeCa. The stylists at the **Rumor Salon** are well-known to be czars with scissors, creating simple yet fashionable and flattering cuts amid a spare salon awash in warm lighting. Set in a classy, sun-flooded loft, the **Aveda Institute** offers superb cuts, colors, and scalp massages. Pick up one of their plant-based beauty and bath products. The institute also offers the opportunity to receive a discount haircut by one of the trainee hairdressers.

A great choice for men is **La Boite a Coupe**, whose clientele includes many advertising and media personalities. Moroccan-French stylist Laurent De Louya has been cutting hair here since 1972. The upscale, Asian-accented **Le Salon Chinois**, never fails to create a sleek cut that will turn heads.

They also offer excellent scalp treatments, hair aromatherapy, and effective "Japanese straightening." Head to the lovely **TwoDo Salon**, where you can get an expert cut and color amid a rustic, colorful decor of fresh flowers and brick walls hung with paintings by local artists.

Styling stalwart **Vidal Sassoon** is still going strong. Visit the elegant downtown salon on Fifth Avenue where accomplished stylists and colorists – all of whom have gone through the company's rigorous training – turn out

impeccable, eye-catching cuts and colors. **Toni & Guy**, a premiere hair salon from the UK, is renowned for its consistently good cuts. The NYC salon is the US training headquarters, where creative stylists offer the boldest cuts around. Toni & Guy colorists have also been lauded for their tinting and highlighting skill.

For more great cuts and colors, try the hip favorites **Antonio Prieto** and **Bumble & Bumble**, the refined **John Masters Organics**, and the elite **Oscar Blandi**.

DIRECTORY

BEAUTY STORES

Erbe
196 Prince St. **Map** 4 D3.
Tel (212) 966-1445.

FACE Stockholm
10 Columbus Circle.
Map 12 D3.
Tel (212) 823-9415.

110 Prince St, SoHo.
Map 4 E3.
Tel (212) 966-9110.

Fresh
57 Spring St at Lafayette St. **Map** 4 F4.
Tel (212) 925-0099.
One of five branches.

John Masters Organics
77 Sullivan St near Broome St. **Map** 4 D4.
Tel (212) 343-9590.

Kiehl's
109 3rd Ave. **Map** 9 B5.
Tel (212) 677-3171.

MAC Cosmetics
113 Spring St. **Map** 4 E4.
Tel (212) 334-4641.

Make Up for Ever
409 W Broadway at Spring St. **Map** 4 E4.
Tel (212) 941-9337.

Origins
175 5th Ave at 23rd St.
Map 8 F4.
Tel (212) 677-9100.

Sabon
93 Spring St. **Map** 4 E4.
Tel (212) 925-0742.
One of three branches.

Sephora
555 Broadway.
Map 4 E3.
Tel (212) 625-1309.
One of several branches.

Space.NK
99 Greene St, near Spring St. **Map** 4 E4.
Tel (212) 941-9200.

MANICURE AND PEDICURES

Barney's New York
660 Madison Ave.
Map 13 A3.
Tel (212) 826-8900.

Bloomingdale's
1000 3rd Ave.
Map 13 B3.
Tel (212) 705-2000.

Bloomingdale's SoHo
504 Broadway.
Map 4 E4.
Tel (212) 729-5900.

Dashing Diva
41 E 8th St. **Map** 4 E2.
Tel (212) 673-9000.

Eve
400 Bleecker St.
Map 3 C2.
Tel (212) 807-8054.

Lord & Taylor
424 5th Ave. **Map** 8 F1.
Tel (212) 391-3344.

Macy's
151 W 34th St.
Map 8 E2.
Tel (212) 695-4400.

Rescue Beauty Lounge
8 Centre Market Pl.
Map 4 F4.
Tel (212) 431-0449.
34 Gansevoort St.
Map 3 B1.
Tel (212) 206-6409.

Saks Fifth Avenue
611 5th Ave. **Map** 12 F4.
Tel (212) 753-4000.

Sweet Lily Natural Nail Spa & Boutique
222 W Broadway, between N Moore & Franklin sts. **Map** 4 E5.
Tel (212) 925-5441.

HAIR SALONS

Antonio Prieto
25 19th St, between 5th & 6th aves. **Map** 8 F5.
Tel (212) 255-3741.

Arrojo Studio
180 Varick St.
Map 4 D3.
Tel (212) 242-7786.

Aveda Institute
233 Spring St. **Map** 4 D4.
Tel (212) 807-1492.

La Boite a Coupe
18 W 55th St.
Map 12 F4.
Tel (212) 246-2097.

Bumble & Bumble
415 13th St, near 9th Ave. **Map** 3 B1.
Tel (212) 521-6500.

Frederic Fekkai Beaute de Provence
15 E 57th St.
Map 12 F3.
Tel (212) 753-9500.

Oscar Blandi
746 Madison Ave.
Map 13 A2.
Tel (212) 988-9404.

Le Salon Chinois
44 W 55th St, 4th Floor. Between 5th & 6th aves.
Map 12 F4.
Tel (212) 956-1200.

Rumor Salon
15 E 12th St, 2nd Floor.
Map 4 E1.
Tel (212) 414-0195.

Toni & Guy
673 Madison Ave, Suite 2 at 61st St.
Map 13 A3.
Tel (212) 702-9771.

TwoDo Salon
210 W 82nd St, between Broadway & Amsterdam. **Map** 15 C4.
Tel (212) 787-1277.

Vidal Sassoon
90 5th Ave, Suite 90. Between 14th & 15th sts.
Map 8 F5.
Tel (212) 229-2200.

Younghee Salon
64 N Moore St.
Map 4 D5.
Tel (212) 334-3770.

Books and Music

As the publishing capital of America, it's not surprising that New York has the country's best selection of bookstores. These range from vast general interest stores to hundreds of esoteric bookstores specializing in everything from sci-fi to suspense, selling new books and old. Music lovers will also find sounds for all tastes at reasonable prices, plus thousands of rare recordings.

GENERAL INTEREST BOOKSTORES

One of the most well-known of New York's bookstores – for best prices as well as selection of titles – is **Barnes & Noble** on Fifth Avenue, reputedly the world's largest bookstore and packed high with over three million books on every imaginable subject. There are branches all over the City, plus the sales annex across the street, with amazing bargains.

Several blocks away is the main branch of New York's famous **Strand Book Store**, with an astonishing two million copies of new and secondhand books spread out over several floors of crowded bookshelves and passageways. There is also a large rare book room for first editions.

Westsider Bookshop is as comprehensive as its music counterpart, as it stocks an enormous collection of used books and country/bluegrass LPs. **12th Street Books** has a good selection of new and used books, and art books. **Housing Works Bookstore Café** is a lovely, high-ceilinged bookstore-café with a wide range of gently used books. The friendly **McNally Jackson** stocks classics and contemporary fiction, and also has a café.

Rizzoli has a big selection of photography, foreign language, music, and art books, plus children's books and videos. **Shakespeare & Co.** offers a sensational selection of titles and is open late every night.

SPECIALTY BOOKSTORES

For the best selection of art books in the city, visit **Hacker-Strand Art Books**. **Urban Center Books** has titles on urban planning and other conservation issues. The city's largest selection of theatrical books and publications is found at **Drama Book Shop**. Jewish books and music abound at **J. Levine Judaica**. Rare books, books out-of-print, and old books about New York are the *raison d'être* of **JN Bartfield Books**. The **Biography Bookshop** is the only midtown store specializing in diaries, letters, biographies, and autobiographies. Theater buffs should try **Applause Theater & Cinema Books**.

Books on murder and suspense are the focus of **Mysterious Bookshop**.

Try **Forbidden Planet** for old and new science-fiction books and comics. **Midtown Comics** has two spacious locations and offers a good range of comics at affordable prices, mostly from the late 1980s to the present. Vintage collectors might prefer **Jim Hanley's Universe**, across from the Empire State Building. Collectible merchandise here ranges from reasonable to "ask Santa" in price.

Bank Street Book Store has one of the best selections of current children's books; they also host storytime and other engaging events for kids. Visit **Books of Wonder** for a variety of hardcover and rare children's books.

The Complete Traveler stocks a wide selection of brand-new and antique travel books and guides for your trip. The staff is very knowledgeable and more than helpful.

For an excellent range of maps visit the **Hagstrom Map & Travel Store**. Cookbooks are on the menu at **Kitchen Arts & Letters**, with many out-of-print books and first editions. Radicals should head for **Revolution Books** or **St. Mark's Bookstore**, which also has an excellent selection of literary and art titles. **Idlewild** is a travel-centric bookstore where everything is arranged by destination.

Lots of educational toys and their book tie-ins can be found in the airy and bright **Scholastic Store**, downstairs from the publisher's SoHo offices.

RECORDS AND COMPACT DISCS

J&R Music World is a complete home-entertainment store with one of the best CD selections in the city.

For out-of-print records, go to **Westsider Records**, a treasure trove for collectors, with an excellent choice of classical, jazz, and opera recordings. **House of Oldies** has a massive stock of deleted and rare records to suit all tastes. **Bleecker Bob's Golden Oldies** record shop has everything from imports, rock, and punk to rare jazz. **Academy Records** is another excellent choice, with second-hand CDs, LPs, and DVDs.

DJs and vinyl lovers still have options for deep house, breakbeat, and electronica. Check out **Turntable Lab** in Manhattan, while in Brooklyn there is **Earwax** or the lively **Halcyon**. True music enthusiasts should head to **Other Music**, which stocks obscure gems, from hot electronica to 1970s free jazz. **Disc-O-Rama** has some of the cheapest CD prices around.

SHEET MUSIC

Just behind Carnegie Hall is one of the best stores for classical sheet music, **Joseph Patelson Music House**. The **Frank Music Company** has a huge collection of classical music scores. **Charles Colin Publications** specializes in jazz. For chart music and pop tunes try **Colony Music Center** in the Brill Building on Broadway.

DIRECTORY

GENERAL INTEREST BOOKSTORES

Barnes & Noble
105 5th Ave. **Map** 8 F5.
Tel (212) 807-0099.
One of several branches.

Housing Works Bookstore Café
126 Crosby St. **Map** 4 F3.
Tel (212) 334-3324.

McNally Jackson
52 Prince St. **Map** 4 F3.
Tel (212) 274-1160.

Rizzoli
31 W 57th St.
Map 12 F3.
Tel (212) 759-2424.

Shakespeare & Co.
716 Broadway.
Map 4 E2.
Tel (212) 529-1330.
One of several branches.

Strand Book Store
828 Broadway.
Map 4 E1.
Tel (212) 473-1452.

12th Street Books
11 East 12th St.
Map 4 F1.
Tel (212) 645-4340.

Westsider Bookshop
2246 Broadway.
Map 15 C4.
Tel (212) 362-0706.

SPECIALTY BOOKSTORES

Applause Theater & Cinema Books
19 W 21st St.
Map 8 F4.
Tel (212) 575-9265.

Bank Street Book Store
610 W 112th St.
Map 21 A4.
Tel (212) 678-1654.

Biography Bookshop
400 Bleecker St.
Map 3 C2.
Tel (212) 807-8655.

Books of Wonder
16 W 18th St.
Map 8 E5.
Tel (212) 989-3270.

The Complete Traveler
199 Madison Ave.
Map 9 A2.
Tel (212) 685-9007.

Drama Book Store
250 W 40th St.
Map 8 E1.
Tel (212) 944-0595.

Forbidden Planet
840 Broadway.
Map 4 E1.
Tel (212) 473-1576.

Hacker-Strand Art Books
45 W 57th St.
Map 12 F3.
Tel (212) 688-7600.

Hagstrom Map & Travel Store
57 W 43rd St.
Map 8 F1.
Tel (212) 398-1222.

Idlewild
12 W 19th St. **Map** 8 F5.
Tel (212) 414-8888.

Jim Hanley's Universe
4 W 33rd St.
Map 8 F2.
Tel (212) 268-7088.

J. Levine Judaica
5 W 30th St.
Map 8 F3.
Tel (212) 695-6888.

JN Bartfield Books
30 W 57th St.
Map 12 F3.
Tel (212) 245-8890.

Kitchen Arts & Letters
1435 Lexington Ave.
Map 17 A2.
Tel (212) 876-5550.

Midtown Comics
200 W 40th St.
Map 8 E1.
459 Lexington Ave.
Map 13 A5.
Tel (212) 302-8192.

Mysterious Bookshop
58 Warren St.
Map 1 B1.
Tel (212) 582-1011.

Revolution Books
9 W 19th St.
Map 7 C5.
Tel (212) 691-3345.

St. Mark's Bookshop
31 3rd Ave.
Map 5 A2.
Tel (212) 260-7853.

The Scholastic Store
577 Broadway.
Map 4 E4.
Tel (212) 343-6166.

Urban Center Books
457 Madison Ave.
Map 13 A4.
Tel (212) 935-3592.

RECORDS AND COMPACT DISCS

Academy Records
12 W 18th St. **Map** 7 C5.
Tel (212) 242-3000.
One of several branches.

Bleecker Bob's Golden Oldies
118 W 3rd St.
Map 4 D2.
Tel (212) 475-9677.

Disc-O-Rama
186 W 4th St.
Map 4 D2.
Tel (212) 206-8417.

Earwax
218 Bedford Avenue,
Brooklyn.
Tel (718) 486-3771.

Halcyon The Shop
57 Pearl St at Water St,
Dumbo, Brooklyn.
Map 2 F2.
Tel (718) 260-WAXY.

House of Oldies
35 Carmine St.
Map 4 D3.
Tel (212) 243-0500.

J&R Music World
23 Park Row.
Map 1 C2.
Tel (800) 806-1115.

Other Music
15 E 4th St.
Map 4 F2.
Tel (212) 477-8150.

Turntable Lab
120 E 7th St.
Map 5 A2.
Tel (212) 677-0675.

West Sider Records
233 W 72nd St.
Map 11 D1.
Tel (212) 874-1588.

SHEET MUSIC

Charles Colin Publications
315 W 53rd St.
Map 12 D4.
Tel (212) 581-1480.

Colony Music Center
1619 Broadway.
Map 12 E4.
Tel (212) 265-2050.

Frank Music Company
244 W 54th St.
Map 12 D4.
Tel (212) 582-1999.

Joseph Patelson Music House
160 W 56th St.
Map 12 E4.
Tel (212) 757-5587.

Art and Antiques

Any art-loving visitor to New York could easily spend several days gallery-hopping around the several hundred galleries found throughout New York. Antique lovers can find an exciting variety of goods, including Americana and many bargains, at the many flea markets; or they can browse through European and American fine antiques in one of the more exclusive antiques centers. To find out what's happening, pick up the free monthly *Art Now Gallery Guide*, available at most galleries, or check the local papers.

ART GALLERIES

One of the city's best-known galleries is **Leo Castelli**, an important showcase for Pop Art during the early 1960s and now spotlighting new artists. **Mary Boone Gallery** features Neo-Expressionist artists such as Julian Schnabel. **Pace Wildenstein Gallery** exhibits current stars, especially well-known painter-photographers. **Postmasters** features impressive changing shows of emerging artists. **Marian Goodman Gallery** focuses on the European avant-garde.

In Chelsea, the **Mathew Marks Gallery** and **Marianne Boesky Gallery** are usually worth a visit. **Paula Cooper** often hosts controversial shows in her beautiful loft space. The **Gagosian Gallery** exhibits paintings by modern masters, with great works by Lichtenstein and Johns. It also has an outlet in the Upper East Side where you can find **Knoedler & Company**, and the **Hirschl & Adler Galleries** with a good selection of European and American fine art. **Max Protech** is very architecture-friendly, while **Esso** displays Pop Art. **Barbara Gladstone** is another heavy hitter in the art scene, and **Exit Art** is famed for its multimedia exhibitions. The airy **Agora Gallery** shows memorable local and international works, including Art Nouveau pieces.

AMERICAN FOLK ART

If you're in the market for American folk art, **Susan Parrish Antiques** has a wide selection of hooked rugs and other Americana, but is open only by appointment. Similar goods are at **Laura Fisher Quilts** in Manhattan Art & Antiques Center, who sells everything from decoys to hooked rugs.

ANTIQUES CENTERS AND SECONDHAND ANTIQUES

In addition to hundreds of small shops selling everything from tiger teeth to multimillion-dollar paintings, Manhattan is home to **The Manhattan Art & Antiques Center**, which has dozens of dealers under one roof. The **Showplace Antique and Design Center** in Chelsea, featuring four floors of antiques, retro furnishings, and memorabilia, is also well worth a visit.

AMERICAN FURNITURE

For furniture from the 17th-, 18th-, and 19th-centuries, try **Bernard & S. Dean Levy**, or **Leigh Keno American Furniture**. **Judith & James Milne** sell early American country furniture as well as a splendid collection of quilts. Alternatively, go to **Woodard & Greenstein American Antiques & Quilts** for a truly wonderful selection of Shaker pieces.

Collectors of Art Deco or Art Nouveau furniture should pay a visit to **Alan Moss**, which is full of furniture and decorative items of all kinds. **Macklowe Gallery** on Madison Avenue has a massive collection of fine Art Nouveau furniture. Just a few blocks away, **Lillian Nassau** has Tiffany lamps and many Art Nouveau and Art Deco pieces.

New York has a handful of retro shops, including **Depression Modern**, which has treasures from the 1930s and 1940s.

INTERNATIONAL ANTIQUES

If you're looking for English antiques, try **Florian Papp** and **Kentshire Galleries**. For European pieces, you'll have plenty of choices; try **Betty Jane Bart Antiques**, **Kurt Gluckselig Antiques**, **Linda Horn Antiques**, and **Les Pierres**. La Belle Epoque stocks antique posters. Oriental dealers include luxury **Doris Leslie Blau**, **E. & J. Frankel**, and **Flying Cranes Antiques**.

FLEA MARKETS

New York has a number of year-round weekend markets. Most flea markets officially open at 9 or 10am. If you arrive early, you could unearth some valuable piece of cultural Americana like a Barbie lunch box or a Soupy Sales record.

Visit the **Annex Antiques Fair and Flea Market** for everything from secondhand clothing to antique furniture. The **Columbus Avenue Flea Market** has new and second-hand clothing and furniture. For information on all street fairs and flea markets, check Friday's *The New York Times* or *The Village Voice*.

AUCTION HOUSES

Manhattan's two most celebrated auction houses are **Christie's** and **Sotheby's**, selling collectibles ranging from coins, jewels, and vintage wines to fine and decorative arts. Also worth a try are **Doyle New York** and **Phillips de Pury & Co.** both well-respected names for fine art, jewelry, and antiques. Bear in mind that items for sale are previewed several days before the auctions, so check the Friday and Sunday *Times* beforehand to see what's coming up. The venerable **Swann Galleries** auctions prints, books, maps, posters, autographs, and photographs.

DIRECTORY

ART GALLERIES

Agora Gallery
530 W 25th St. **Map** 7
C4. **Tel** (212) 226-4151.

Barbara Gladstone
515 W 24th St.
Map 7 C4.
Tel (212) 206-9300.

Esso Gallery
531 W 26th St, 2nd Floor.
Map 7 C4.
Tel (212) 560-9728.

Exit Art
475 10th Ave. **Map** 7 C2.
Tel (212) 966-7745.

Gagosian Gallery
555 W 24th St.
Map 7 C4.
Tel (212) 741-1111.
One of several galleries.

**Hirschl & Adler
Galleries**
21 E 70th St.
Map 12 F1.
Tel (212) 535-8810.

**Knoedler &
Company**
19 E 70th St.
Map 13 A1.
Tel (212) 794-0550.

Leo Castelli
18 E 77th St.
Map 17 A5.
Tel (212) 249-4470.

**Marian Goodman
Gallery**
24 W 57th St.
Map 12 F3.
Tel (212) 977-7160.

**Marianne Boesky
Gallery**
535 W 22nd St.
Map 7 C4.
Tel (212) 680-9889.

Mary Boone Gallery
745 5th Ave.
Map 12 F3.
Tel (212) 752-2929.
One of two galleries.

**Mathew Marks
Gallery**
523 W 24th St.
Map 7 C4.
Tel (212) 243-0200.

Max Protech
511 W 22nd St.
Map 7 C4.
Tel (212) 633-6999.

**Pace Wildenstein
Gallery**
534 W 25th St.
Map 7 C4.
Tel (212) 929-7000.
One of two galleries.

Paula Cooper
534 W 21st St.
Map 7 C4.
Tel (212) 255-1105.

Postmasters
459 W 19th St.
Map 7 C5.
Tel (212) 727-3323.

AMERICAN FOLK ART

Laura Fisher Quilts
Manhattan Art
& Antiques Center,
1050 2nd Ave.
Map 13 B4.
Tel (212) 838-2596.

**Susan Parrish
Antiques**
Tel (212) 807-1561.
By appointment only.

ANTIQUE CENTERS AND SECOND-HAND ANTIQUES

**The Manhattan
Arts & Antiques
Center**
1050 2nd Ave.
Map 13 A3.
Tel (212) 355-4400.

**The Showplace
Antique and Design
Center**
40 W 25th St. **Map** 8 F4.
Tel (212) 633-6063.

AMERICAN FURNITURE

Alan Moss
436 Lafayette St.
Map 4 F2.
Tel (212) 473-1310.

**Bernard &
S. Dean Levy**
24 E 84th St.
Map 16 F4.
Tel (212) 628-7088.

Depression Modern
150 Sullivan St.
Map 4 D3.
Tel (212) 982-5699.

**Judith & James
Milne**
506 E 74th St. **Map** 17
C5. **Tel** (212) 472-0107.
One of two branches.

**Leigh Keno
American Furniture**
127 E 69th St.
Map 17 A5.
Tel (212) 734-2381.

Lillian Nassau
220 E 57th St.
Map 13 B3.
Tel (212) 759-6062.

Macklowe Gallery
667 Madison Ave.
Map 13 A3.
Tel (212) 644-6400.

**Woodard &
Greenstein
American Antiques**
506 E 74th St.
Map 17 A5.
Tel (212) 988-2906.

INTERNATIONAL ANTIQUES

La Belle Epoque
280 Columbus Ave.
Map 12 D1.
Tel (212) 362-1770.

**Betty Jane Bart
Antiques**
1225 Madison Ave.
Map 17 A3.
Tel (212) 410-2702.

Doris Leslie Blau
724 5th Ave. **Map** 12 F3.
Tel (212) 586-5511.
By appointment only.

E. & J. Frankel
1040 Madison Ave.
Map 17 A5.
Tel (212) 879-5733.

Florian Papp
962 Madison Ave.
Map 17 A5.
Tel (212) 288-6770.

**Flying Cranes
Antiques**
1050 2nd Ave.
Map 13 B4.
Tel (212) 223-4600.

Kentshire Galleries
37 E 12th St. **Map** 4 E1.
Tel (212) 673-6644.

**Kurt Gluckselig
Antiques**
200 E 58th St. **Map** 13 B3.
Tel (212) 758-1805.

**Linda Horn
Antiques**
1015 Madison Ave.
Map 17 A5.
Tel (212) 772-1122.

Les Pierres
369 Bleecker St.
Map 3 C2.
Tel (212) 243-7740.

FLEA MARKETS

**Annex Antiques
Fair and Flea
Market**
26th St at 6th Ave, 112
W 25th St (Annex). **Map**
8 E4. **Tel** (212) 243-5343.
Open Sat and Sun.

**Columbus Avenue
Flea Market**
Columbus Ave, between
76th and 77th St.
Map 16 D5. **Tel** (631)
873-4790. Open Sun.

AUCTION HOUSES

Christie's
20 Rockefeller Plaza.
Map 12 F5.
Tel (212) 636-2000.

Doyle New York
175 E 87th St.
Map 17 A3.
Tel (212) 427-2730.

**Phillips de
Pury & Co.**
450 W 15th St.
Map 7 C5.
Tel (212) 940-1200.

Sotheby's
1334 York Ave.
Map 13 C1.
Tel (212) 606-7000.

Swann Galleries
104 E 25th St.
Map 9 A4.
Tel (212) 254-4710.

Gourmet Groceries, Specialty Food, and Wine Shops

New York's striking cultural and ethnic diversity is celebrated in its food – the city's food shops provide a truly international feast. There is also a dazzling array of coffee stores and wine shops available almost everywhere you turn.

GOURMET GROCERIES

Scattered around town are several famous food emporiums that are tourist attractions in themselves. Remember, too, to visit the department stores, which often rival the specialty food stores.

At **Dean & DeLuca** on Broadway, a chic delicatessen, food has been elevated to an art form – don't miss the huge selection of take-out food. **Russ & Daughters** on Houston Street, one of the oldest gourmet shops, is known as an "appetizing" store, full of ethnic food and famous for smoked fish, cream cheese, chocolates, and bagels. The **Gourmet Garage** on Broome Street sells all kinds of delicious fresh food, in particular organic produce. **Zabar's** on Broadway is perhaps the finest food store in the world, with huge crowds jostling for the excellent smoked salmon, bagels, caviar, nuts and candies, cheese, and coffee.

William Poll on Lexington Avenue offers picnic hampers as well as a great variety of prepared dishes. For pâté de foie gras, Scottish smoked salmon, beluga, and caviar, go to **Caviarteria**.

Whole Foods, famed for their superb selection of natural, organic, wholesome foods, draws devoted shoppers throughout the city. The Whole Foods in Columbus Circle is now the largest supermarket in Manhattan, with row upon gleaming row of quality food "in its purest state" with no artificial additives. There's also a popular central Whole Foods on Union Square. **Fairway Market** on Broadway offers premium groceries from fresh produce to smoked fish and baked goods.

SPECIALTY FOOD

Fabulous bread and cake shops abound but one of the best is **Poseidon Greek Bakery**, renowned for its filo pastry. **H & H Bagels** bakes 60,000 of the finest bagels every day. Try the delicious Chinese pastries at **Fung Wong**, or the pretzel croissants and great tarts at **City Bakery**. Instantly recognizable by the line of happy customers at the door, **Magnolia Bakery** is famed for its beautifully decorated and superb-tasting cupcakes. It has three locations in Manhattan.

Great confectionery shops include **Li-Lac** for handmade chocolates and **Mondel Chocolates** for chocolate animals. **Economy Candy** has a huge range of dried fruit but for a real treat go to **Teuscher Chocolates**, which has fresh champagne truffles flown in direct from Switzerland.

Myers of Keswick imports English food. For something more exotic, **Kam Man Market** is an Oriental grocery selling Chinese, Thai, and other Oriental products. The **Italian Food Center** has great olive oils, dried pastas, and sausages. Go to **Jefferson Market** for meat and fish, and **Citarella** for its fine seafood. **Penzey's**, in the Grand Central Terminal, has a wide variety of herbs and spices, as does the Middle Eastern shop **Kalustyan's**.

For a wide choice of cheese, as well as olives and *charcuterie*, visit **Murray's Cheese Shop**. The intoxicating wafts that greet you at the front door are sure to lure you in. Named New York's Best Cheese Shop by many of the city's newspapers, it is heaven for cheese-lovers, with over 250 types of cheese from around the world, from bloomy rinds like Camembert to moist Ricotta. Feel free to sample; the friendly staff happily offers tastings from the mind-boggling selection. Make a picnic out of it, and pick up some of their fresh breads and olives to accompany your pungent purchases.

If you are looking for true old Eastern European pickle recipes then **The Pickle Guys** is the right place. In addition to pickles, they also store pickled tomatoes, mushrooms, olives, hot peppers, sweet kraut, sauerkraut, herring, and sun-dried tomatoes.

For fruit and vegetables at reasonable prices, visit a farmers' green market, but get there early if you want the pick of the crop. Among the most popular are **Upper West Side**, **St. Mark's in-the-Bowery**, and **Union Square**. For information on the city's markets, phone: (212) 788-7476.

COFFEE STORES

New York also has many fine coffee stores. Among the best are **Oren's Daily Roast** and **Porto Rico Importing Company**, each with a mouth-watering selection. **The Sensuous Bean** features a superb range of gourmet coffees and teas, as does the cozy **McNulty's Tea & Coffee Company**, one of the nation's oldest coffee stores.

WINE SHOPS

Acker, Merrall & Condit have been selling wines since 1820 and have an excellent selection. Go to **Garnet Liquors** for fine wines and champagnes at bargain prices. **Spring Street Wine Shop**, in the heart of SoHo, is a convenient, well-stocked spot to pop in for a bottle of fine wine. **Sherry-Lehmann** is New York's leading wine merchant. **Astor Wines & Spirits**, New York's largest wine store, features a massive selection of premium and discount wines and spirits. Every month they highlight their Top 10 choices under $10 – great for superb bargains. **Union Square Wines and Spirits** offers terrific a variety of wines, and features tastings every week.

DIRECTORY

GOURMET GROCERIES

Caviarteria
502 Park Ave.
Map 13 A3.
Tel (212) 759-7410.

Dean & DeLuca
560 Broadway.
Map 4 E3.
Tel (212) 226-6800.
One of several branches.

Fairway Market
2127 Broadway.
Map 15 C5.
Tel (212) 595-1888.

Gourmet Garage
453 Broome St.
Map 4 E4.
Tel (212) 941-5850.
One of several branches.

Russ & Daughters
179 E Houston St.
Map 5 A3.
Tel (212) 475-4880.

Whole Foods
10 Columbus Circle.
Map 12 D3.
Tel (212) 823-9600.
One of several branches.

William Poll
1051 Lexington Ave.
Map 17 A5.
Tel (212) 288-0501.

Zabar's
2245 Broadway.
Map 15 C4.
Tel (212) 787-2000.

SPECIALTY FOOD

Citarella
2135 Broadway.
Map 15 C5.
Tel (212) 874-0383.

City Bakery
3 W 18th St.
Map 8 F5.
Tel (212) 366-1414.

Economy Candy
108 Rivington St.
Map 5 A3.
Tel (212) 254-1531.

Fung Wong
41 Mott St.
Map 4 F3.
Tel (212) 267-4037.

H & H Bagels
2239 Broadway.
Map 15 C4.
Tel (212) 595-8003.
One of two branches.

Italian Food Center
186 Grand St.
Map 15 C4.
Tel (212) 925-2954.

Jefferson Market
450 Ave of the Americas.
Map 12 E5.
Tel (212) 533-3377.

Kalustyan's
123 Lexington Ave.
Map 9 A3.
Tel (212) 685-3451.

Kam Man Market
200 Canal St.
Map 4 F5.
Tel (212) 571-0330.

Li-Lac
40 Eighth Ave. **Map** 3 C1.
Tel (212) 924-2280.

Magnolia Bakery
401 Bleecker St.
Map 3 C2.
Tel (212) 462-2572.

Mondel Chocolates
2913 Broadway.
Map 20 E3.
Tel (212) 864-2111.

Murray's Cheese Shop
257 Bleecker St.
Map 4 D2.
Tel (212) 243-3289.
One of two branches.

Myers of Keswick
634 Hudson St.
Map 3 C2.
Tel (212) 691-4194.

Penzey's
Grand Central Terminal.
Map 9 A1.
Tel (212) 972-2777.

The Pickle Guys
49 Essex St.
Map 5 B4.
Tel (212) 656-9739.

Poseidon Greek Bakery
629 9th Ave.
Map 12 D5.
Tel (212) 757-6173.

St. Mark's in-the-Bowery Greenmarket
E 10th St at 2nd Ave.
Map 4 F1.
Open Tue.

Teuscher Chocolates
25 E 61st St.
Map 12 F3.
Tel (212) 751-8482.
620 5th Ave.
Map 12 F4.
Tel (212) 246-4416.

Union Square Greenmarket
E 17th St & Broadway.
Map 8 F5.
Open Mon, Wed, Fri, and Sat.

Upper West Side Greenmarket
Columbus Ave
at 77th St.
Map 16 D5.
Open Sun.

COFFEE STORES

McNulty's Tea & Coffee Company
109 Christopher St.
Map 3 C2.
Tel (212) 242-5351.

Oren's Daily Roast
1144 Lexington Ave.
Map 17 A4.
Tel (212) 472-6830.
One of several branches.

The Sensuous Bean
66 W 70th St.
Map 12 D1.
Tel 1-800-238-6845.

Porto Rico Importing Company
201 Bleecker St.
Map 3 C2.
Tel (212) 477-5421.
One of several branches.

WINE SHOPS

Acker, Merrall & Condit
160 W 72nd St.
Map 11 C1.
Tel (212) 787-1700.

Astor Wines & Spirits
399 Lafayette St.
Map 4 F2.
Tel (212) 674-7500.

Garnet Liquors
929 Lexington Ave.
Map 13 A1.
Tel (212) 772-3211.

Sherry-Lehmann
679 Madison Ave.
Map 13 A3.
Tel (212) 838-7500.

Spring Street Wine Shop
187 Spring St.
Map 4 D4.
Tel (212) 219-0521.

Union Square Wines and Spirits
33 Union Square West.
Map 9 A5.
Tel (212) 675-8100.

Electronics and Housewares

From flat-screen TVs and top-of-the-line sound systems to swanky designer home furnishings, New York City abounds with electronics and housewares stores. Perhaps the most competitive retailers in New York are the ones that sell electronics, so it pays to shop around. Be particularly careful with electronics stores on the heavily touristed streets and those around the major tourist sights, such as Fifth Avenue near the Empire State Building. Many of these stores sell mediocre, sometimes faulty equipment at inflated prices, and it's a hassle or near impossible to get a refund once you've returned home. If you're buying electronic goods to take to Europe, make sure they have compatible voltages and formats (many in the US are made to different standards).

SOUND SYSTEMS AND EQUIPMENT

For the latest in cutting-edge stereo equipment, head to **Sound by Singer**. **J&R Music World** sells competitively priced equipment and has the best jazz CD collection in the city. The Danish **Bang & Olufsen** showcases a range of sleek, minimalist sound systems that can dress up even the humblest flat. **Harvey Electronics** sells top-notch stereos and electronics with the bonus of a friendly, informative staff. Browse the quality systems at **Lyric Hi-Fi**, a longtime favorite that's been around since 1959. The perennially jam-packed **Sony Style** delivers on its wide assortment of top-shelf sound systems and plenty of impulse-buy gizmos. True to its name, the chain store **Best Buy** does offer some of the best buys on an enormous range of stereo systems and home-entertainment products. For high-end stereo equipment and components, check out **Innovative Audio Video Showrooms**. Also stop to look around at the wide range of both used and new stereos at the friendly **Stereo Exchange**.

PHOTOGRAPHY

B & H Photo is where amateur and professional photographers can find everything they need. **Willoughby's** has decent sales on photographic equipment and supplies. The appropriately named **Olden Camera** on Broadway eschews anything digital offering instead quality, old-school cameras and gear. Head to Chelsea's **Foto Care** for a wide range of cameras and accoutrements. **Alkit Pro Camera** offers a large assortment of cameras, components, and lighting equipment plus rentals and film developing and processing. Make for **Adorama** in the Flatiron District, and browse the spectacular displays of digital cameras and accessories, point-and-shoots, and disposables, and also affordable prices on film developing and processing. Don't miss the quality, high-end cameras and equipment at the elegant **The Photo Village**.

COMPUTERS

There are several Macintosh meccas in Manhattan, including the immense, airy **Apple Store SoHo** and the new, gleaming cube of a store on Fifth Avenue. Mac-philes flock to both to peruse and test-drive the latest models, plug in to iPods, and attend seminars geared to both novices and experts.

If you brought your computer from home and find that you need a repair, head to **Amnet PC Solutions**, where a tech whiz will – keep your fingers crossed – be able to fix whatever ails your computer. If you'd rather not haul your computer across town in a cab, they also do house calls starting at $125 an hour. The specialty at **Tekserve** is Mac repairs, where you can get a free estimate and also browse for upgrades.

KITCHENWARE

Most of the department stores offer a wide range of household goods. For a specialized shop, try **Broadway Pan-handlers** on Broome Street, a cook's heaven with outstanding baking and pastry-making equipment. **Bridge Kitchenware** is a household name among most restaurateurs. **Williams-Sonoma** has a wide range of kitchenware, utensils, and cookbooks. The East Village, particularly on and around Bowery Street, has long been the nucleus for restaurant supply stores, where you can find top-quality kitchenware at bargain prices. **Leader Restaurant Equipment & Supplies** sells all the kitchenware you can think of, from heavy cutlery to sushi platters and chopsticks.

HOUSEWARES AND FURNISHINGS

Baccarat, **Lalique**, and **Villeroy & Boch** are where you'll find the finest crystal, china, and silverware. **Orrefors Kosta Boda** has beautiful glassware, from vases to candlesticks, and **Tiffany & Co.** is also a fashionable spot. Go to **Avventura** for crystal and china and, for the best of inexpensive, utilitarian china, visit **Fishs Eddy**. Try **Ceramica**, which stocks lovely handmade Italian pottery, and **La Terrine** and **Stuben Glass** for hand-painted ceramics. Browse the hip SoHo showcase of designer **Jonathan Adler**, whose eye-catching pottery of natural shades and primitive and organic shapes will stand out from everything else in your living room. His collection includes a "family" of playful decanters in the shapes of man, woman, and child, plump vases of smiling suns and fish plates, and a menagerie of pottery animals, including bookends shaped like the front and back of a charging bull. **ABC Carpet & Home** on Broadway has an enviable reputation for home furnishings. For low prices on housewares, shop on **Grand Street** on the Lower East Side.

For elegant furniture, from soft leather sofas to luxurious beds, and sleek tableware, try Giorgio Armani's posh **Armani Casa**. **Dune** on Franklin Street in TriBeCa

offers chic furniture by contemporary designers, including wool sofas and convertible lounges. **Design Within Reach** is the source for fully licensed classics, such as Saarinen, Eames, and Bertoia. If you lean toward retro, make a beeline for **Restoration Hardware** on Broadway, where you can choose from updated Art Deco furnishings, lighting fixtures, and patinated bronze accessories.

LINENS

Linens can be found in most department stores, but for silk sheets and luxurious linens, visit **Porthault** and **Pratesi**. The Italian **Frette**, on Madison Avenue, sells thick towels and robes and wonderfully soft cotton sheets and bedding. **Bed, Bath & Beyond** offers a varied selection of bed linens, kitchen, and bath accessories.

DIRECTORY

SOUND SYSTEMS AND EQUIPMENT

Bang & Olufsen
952 Madison Ave.
Map 17 A5.
Tel (212) 879-6161.

Best Buy
60 W 23rd St. **Map** 8 E4.
Tel (212) 366-1373.

Harvey Electronics
2 W 45th St. **Map** 12 F5.
Tel (212) 575-5000.

Innovative Audio Video Showrooms
150 58th St. **Map** 13 A4.
Tel (212) 634-4444.

J & R Music World
31 Park Row. **Map** 1 C2.
Tel (212) 238-9100.

Lyric Hi-Fi
1221 Lexington Ave.
Map 17 A4.
Tel (212) 439-1900.

Sony Style
550 Madison Ave.
Map 13 A4.
Tel (212) 833-5336.

Sound by Singer
18 16th St. **Map** 8 F5.
Tel (212) 924-8600.

Stereo Exchange
627 Broadway.
Map 4 E3.
Tel (212) 505-1111.

PHOTOGRAPHY

Adorama
42 18th St. **Map** 8 F5.
Tel (212) 741-0466.

Alkit Pro Camera
222 Park Ave S.
Map 9 A5.
Tel (212) 674-1515.

B & H Photography
420 9th Ave. **Map** 8 D2.
Tel (212) 444-6615.

Foto Care
136 W 21st St. **Map** 8 E4.
Tel (212) 741-2990.

Olden Camera
1263 Broadway, 4th floor.
Map 8 F3.
Tel (212) 725-1234.

The Photo Village
1133 Broadway, Suite 824.
Map 8 F4.
Tel (212) 989-1252.

Willoughby's
298 5th Ave.
Map 8 F3.
Tel (800) 378-1898.

COMPUTERS

Amnet PC Solutions
229 E 53rd St.
Map 13 B4.
Tel (212) 593-2425.

Apple Store Fifth Avenue
767 5th Ave. **Map** 12 F3.
Tel (212) 336-1440.

Apple Store SoHo
103 Prince St. **Map** 4 E3.
Tel (212) 226-3126.

Tekserve
119 W 23rd St. **Map** 8 E4.
Tel (212) 929-3645.

KITCHENWARE

Bridge Kitchenware
214 E 52nd St.
Map 13 B4.
Tel (212) 688-4220.

Broadway Panhandlers
477 Broome St. **Map** 4 E4.
Tel (212) 966-3434.

Leader Restaurant Equipment & Supplies
191 Bowery. **Map** 4 F4.
Tel (212) 677-1982.

Williams-Sonoma
10 Columbus Circle.
Map 12 D3.
Tel (212) 823-9750.
One of several branches.

HOUSEWARES & FURNISHINGS

ABC Carpet & Home
888 Broadway. **Map** 8 F5.
Tel (212) 473-3000.

Armani Casa
97 Greene St. **Map** 4 E3.
Tel (212) 334-1271.

Avventura
463 Amsterdam Ave.
Map 15 C4.
Tel (212) 769-2510.

Baccarat
625 Madison Ave.
Map 13 A3.
Tel (212) 826-4100.

Ceramica
59 Thompson St. **Map** 4 D4. *Tel (800) 270-0900.*

Design Within Reach
142 Wooster St. **Map** 4 E3. *Tel (212) 475-0001.*
One of several branches.

Dune
88 Franklin St. **Map** 4 E5.
Tel (212) 925-6171.

Fishs Eddy
889 Broadway. **Map** 8 F5.
Tel (212) 420-9020.

Grand Street
Lower East Side.
Map 4 E5.

Jonathan Adler
47 Greene St. **Map** 4 E4.
Tel (212) 941-8950.

Lalique
712 Madison Ave.
Map 13 A3.
Tel (212) 355-6550.

Orrefors Kosta Boda
200 Lexington Ave.
Map 9 A2.
Tel (212) 684-5455.

Restoration Hardware
935 Broadway. **Map** 8 F4.
Tel (212) 260-9479.

Stuben Glass
667 Madison Ave.
Map 13 A3.
Tel (212) 752-1441.

La Terrine
1024 Lexington Ave.
Map 13 A1.
Tel (212) 988-3366.

Tiffany & Co.
See p329.

Villeroy & Boch
41 Madison Ave.
Map 9 A4.
Tel (212) 213-8149.

LINENS

Bed, Bath & Beyond
620 Ave of the Americas.
Map 8 F5.
Tel (212) 255-3550.

Frette
799 Madison Ave.
Map 13 A1.
Tel (212) 988-5221.

Porthault
18 E 69th St. **Map** 12 F1.
Tel (212) 688-1660.

Pratesi
829 Madison Ave. **Map** 13 A2. *Tel (212) 288-2315.*

ENTERTAINMENT IN NEW YORK

New York City is a non-stop entertainment extravaganza, every day, all year round. Whatever your taste, you can be sure the city will satisfy it on both a grand and an intimate scale. The challenge is to take advantage of as many of the entertainments as possible. If it's theater, you can enjoy a mainstream success on Broadway or take a chance on an experimental production in a loft. If it's music, there's the magnificence of opera at the Met or a jazz group blowing in a club in the Village. You can catch a spectacle of avant-garde dance in a café or try your own avant-garde dancing in one of the city's warehouse-sized clubs. Movie theaters abound. But perhaps best of all is wandering and watching the vast show that is New York.

Performance by the New York City Ballet

PRACTICAL INFORMATION

Find out what events there are to choose from in the arts and leisure listings of *The New York Times* and the *Village Voice* newspapers and in *Time Out New York*, *New York*, and

TKTS discount ticket booth

The New Yorker magazines. Listings are updated on the websites of these magazines, such as www.nymag.com and http://newyork.timeout.com. At your hotel ask for *Where*, a free weekly magazine with maps and information on the many attractions.

Hotel staff may be able to answer some of your questions and should also carry a wide selection of brochures and leaflets. In addition, they may be willing to reserve tickets for you. Some hotel TVs have a New York visitor information channel.

At **NYC & Company**, touch-screen kiosks provide information and sell tickets to the city's top attractions. Multi-lingual counselors, discount coupons, free maps, brochures, tour information, and ATMs are available. **Broadway Inner Circle** gives brief descriptions of current

shows, schedules, and prices; **Moviefone** gives online information on all the films; and **ClubFone** has up-to-date information on nightlife.

BOOKING TICKETS

Popular shows may be sold out for weeks ahead, so book early. Box offices are open daily, except Sundays, from 10am until one hour after the performance begins. Call in person, or phone the box office or a ticket agency and order your seats by credit card. The biggest agencies are **Telecharge**, **Ticketmaster**, and **Ticket Central**; they charge a small fee. An independent ticket agent may also be able to find seats for you – try **Prestige Entertainment**; others are listed in the Yellow Pages. Fees vary according to demand. Broadway Ticket Center in

A band playing at a cozy New York jazz club

the Times Square Information Center (*see p371*) sells full-price tickets.

DISCOUNT TICKETS

Established in 1973 to the advantage of theaters and theatergoers alike, the non-profit **TKTS** company sells unsold tickets on the day of performance for all Broadway shows. Discounts range from 25 to 50 percent, but the price will include a small handling fee and must be paid for in cash or by traveler's check.

The **TKTS** booth in Times Square (at Duffy Square under the red steps) sells matinée tickets from 10am to 2pm every Wednesday and Saturday, and from 11am to 3pm on Sundays; evening tickets are sold from 3pm to 8pm, and Sunday tickets from 11am until closing. The booths at Front and John streets, where lines are often shorter, sell evening tickets from 11am to 6pm Monday to Saturday. All matinée tickets and Sunday performances are sold the day before. There is also a TKTS booth in downtown Brooklyn.

The **Broadway Ticket Center** in Times Square offers same-day and advance tickets for both Broadway and Off-Broadway shows. They also have seating charts and, occasionally, video previews to help you choose a show.

You can purchase day-of-performance tickets from **Ticketmaster** at

The Booth Theater on Broadway *(see p345)*

discounts of 10 to 25 percent (with a small commission fee) by telephone. The **Hit Show Club** sells vouchers to its members (it's free to join) that can be exchanged at box offices for discounted tickets. Some shows offer standing-room tickets on the day at a bargain price. It's often the only way to catch a sold-out show on short notice, but you might not get the best view. You can also get discount tickets for shows at **Broadway Bucks**. **StubHub!** is the largest ticket resale site. Tickets for sports, music, and Broadway events are FedExed to you.

"SCALPERS" AND TOUTS

If you buy from a "scalper" (a ticket tout), you risk getting tickets for the wrong day, counterfeit tickets, and paying outrageous prices. The police often monitor sports and theater venues for scalpers and their customers.

FREE TICKETS

Free tickets to TV shows, concerts, and special events are sometimes offered at **NYC & Co.** (New York Convention & Visitors Bureau), which is open from 8:30am to 6pm Monday to Friday and 9am to 5pm on weekends. Free or deeply discounted tickets to film or theater premieres are often advertised in *The New York Times*, *Daily News*, or

Time Out New York. The "Cheap Thrills" section in the *Village Voice* lists poetry readings, recitals, and experimental films. The Shakespeare Festival at the **Delacorte Theater** in Central Park offers free tickets – one per person – on a first-come, first-served basis (be prepared to queue).

Neon lights of theaters in the heart of Broadway

DISABLED ACCESS

Broadway theaters reserve a few spaces and cut-price tickets for the disabled. Call **Ticketmaster** or **Telecharge** well in advance for information and to reserve your tickets. For Off-Broadway theaters, call their box offices. Some theaters offer special equipment for their hearing-impaired patrons. **Tap** can arrange sign language for Broadway theaters.

USEFUL CONTACTS

Broadway Bucks
226 W 47th St. **Map** 12 E5.
Tel 1-800-223-7565, ext. 214.
www.bestofbroadway.com

Broadway Inner Circle
Tel (212) 563-2929.
www.broadwayinnercircle.com

Broadway Ticket Center
Times Square Information Center,
1560 Broadway. **Map** 12 E5.

ClubFone
Tel (212) 777-2582.
www.clubfone.com

Delacorte Theater
Entrance via 81st St at Central Park W. **Map** 16 E4.
Tel (212) 539-8750.
www.publictheater.org
Summer time only.

Hit Show Club
Tel (212) 581-4211.
www.hitshowclub.com

Movie Tickets Online
www.movietickets.com
www.fandango.com
www.moviefone.com

NYC & Co.
810 7th Ave. **Map** 12 E4.
Tel (212) 484-1222.
www.nycvisit.com

Prestige Entertainment
Tel 1-800-243-8849.

StubHub!
Tel (866) STUB-HUB.
www.stubhub.com

Tap (Theatre Access Project)
Tel (212) 221-1103 (Voice).
www.tdf.org

Telecharge
*Tel (212) 239-6200,
1-800-432-7250.*
www.telecharge.com

Ticket Central
Tel (212) 279-4200.
www.ticketcentral.org

Ticketmaster
*Tel (212) 307-4100,
1-800-755-4000.*
www.ticketmaster.com

TKTS
Tel (212) 221-0013.
Front & John Sts. **Map** 2 D2.
Duffy Square, Times Square.
47th St & Broadway. **Map** 12 E5.
Tel (212) 221-0885, ext. 446.
www.tdf.org/TKTS

New York's Best: Entertainment

Greenwich Village jazz club

New York is one of the great entertainment capitals of the world. Top names in every branch of the arts are drawn here to perform and often to live and work. Major sports events are a huge attraction and live music, theater, and comedy can be found throughout the year. In terms of nightlife, New York truly lives up to its reputation as "the city that never sleeps." From the huge choice offered, there are some venues and events that stand out as classics of their kind; this selection has been chosen from the listings on pages 344 to 363 as among those not to be missed. Even if you experience only one of them, you will have been part of something as essentially New York as the Empire State Building or the Brooklyn Bridge.

Madison Square Garden
Top sporting action is found at "the Garden," including home games for basketball's New York Knicks and ice hockey's Rangers, plus the Golden Gloves boxing tournament (see p360).

Film Forum
At New York's most stylish arts movie theater you can see the latest foreign and American independent releases or catch up with a classic in a wide range of retrospectives (see p349).

Village Vanguard
The jazz clubs of Greenwich Village have played host to all the great names in jazz. Fans can catch the stars of today and tomorrow at the world-famous Village Vanguard and the Blue Note (see p352).

Thea Distr

Chelsea and the Garment District

Greenwich Village

Soho and TriBeCa

Lower East Side

Seaport and the Civic Center

Lower Manhattan

HUDSON RIVER

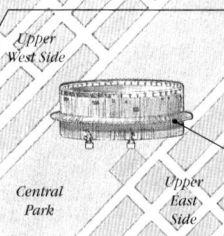

Upper
West Side

Central
Park

Upper
East
Side

Upper
Midtown

Gramercy
and the
Flatiron
District

E A S T   R I V E R

Philharmonic Rehearsals
*The Wednesday- and
Thursday-morning rehearsals
at Avery Fisher Hall are often
open to the public at a fraction
of the normal ticket price
(see p350).*

Metropolitan Opera House
*Reserve well ahead and prepare
to pay high prices to see the giants
of the opera world (see p350).*

Shakespeare in
Central Park
*If you are a
summer visitor,
set aside a time
to get one of
the rare free
tickets for the
Delacorte
Theater's open-air Shakespeare
featuring top Hollywood and
Broadway names (see p344).*

The Nutcracker
*The Christmas event for children of
every age is performed each year at
Lincoln Center by the New York City
Ballet (see p346).*

0 kilometers   2
0 miles   1

Public Theater
*Founded in 1954,
the Public has a
mandate to create
theater for all New
Yorkers. Its year-
round Shakespeare
Festival is part of
a commitment to
classical works,
but new plays are
also developed
here (see p120).*

Carnegie Hall
*Conveniently situated in the
Theater District, Carnegie Hall is
famous the world over as a showcase for the best in the musical arts.
A backstage tour gives a fascinating insight into "the house that
music built" (see p350).*

Theater and Dance

New York is famous for its extravagant musicals and its ferocious critics. It is one of the world's greatest theater and dance centers, featuring every kind of production imaginable. Whether your preference is for the glitz and glamour of a Broadway blockbuster or something truly experimental, you'll find it here.

BROADWAY

Broadway has long been synonymous with New York's Theater District, but the majority of Broadway theaters are actually scattered between 41st and 53rd streets and from Sixth to Ninth Avenues, with a few around the much-improved Times Square. Most were built between 1910 and 1930, during the heyday of vaudeville and the famous Ziegfeld Follies. The **Lyceum** (*see p144*) is the oldest theater still in operation (1903), the **American Airlines Theater**, permanent home of the Roundabout Theater Co., is the newest, and the historic **Biltmore Theater** opened in 2003 after a 14-year closure.

Many Broadway theaters went through a slump in the 1980s but are now enjoying a revival, using big names to draw in the crowds. This is where you will find the "power productions" – the big, highly publicized dramas, musicals and revivals starring Hollywood luminaries in (it is hoped) sure-fire earners. Hits have included imports such as *Les Misérables;* New York originals such as *Cats* and *The Producers;* the popular children's favorite *The Lion King;* and great revivals like *42nd Street.* There have also been glitzy adaptations from popular movies, such as *Hairspray;* shows celebrating 60s and 70s pop favorites, such as ABBA in *Mamma Mia*! and Monty Python's *Spamalot.*

OFF-BROADWAY AND OFF-OFF-BROADWAY

There are about 20 Off-Broadway stages and 300 Off-Off-Broadway stages whose works will sometimes transfer to Broadway. Off-Broadway theaters have from 100 to 499 seats, and Off-Off-Broadway showplaces have fewer than 100. Both range from the well-appointed to the improvised, sited in lofts, churches, and even garages. Off-Broadway became very popular during the 1950s as a reaction to the commercialism of Broadway. It was also an ideal place for cautious producers to try out works considered too avant-garde for Broadway at lower operating costs. During the past two decades, Off-Off-Broadway theaters have staged more experimental pieces by these same producers.

Off-Broadway theaters are found all over Manhattan – from the **Douglas Fairbanks Theater**, where the irreverent *Forbidden Broadway* plays, to Central Park's open-air **Delacorte Theater**. Some are even in the Broadway district, such as the **Manhattan Theater Club**. Farther afield are the **Brooklyn Academy of Music (BAM)** (*see p248*), and the **92nd Street Y**. In these venues you will find lively, unusual, and experimental showcases for new talent as well as lots of uninhibited productions.

The Off-Broadway theaters mounted the first productions in New York of the works of playwrights Eugene O'Neill, Tennessee Williams, Eugene Ionesco, Sean O'Casey, Jean Genet, and David Mamet. Samuel Beckett's *Happy Days* premiered at the **Cherry Lane Theatre** in 1961, a venue that still promotes cutting-edge writing. Off-Broadway theaters host modern and often irreverent treatments of the classics.

Sometimes a more intimate, smaller Off-Broadway stage suits a production better than a larger more established theater would, as proved by such long-running successes as *The Fantasticks* along with the *Threepenny Opera*, which has been shown at the **Lucille Lortel Theater** since 1955.

PERFORMANCE THEATERS

This extremely avant-garde art form can be found in several Off- and Off-Off-Broadway locations. Accurate descriptions and categorizations are almost impossible, but expect the bizarre and outlandish. The most likely venues to find this are **La MaMa Experimental Theatre Club, P.S. 122, HERE, Baruch Performing Arts Center, 92nd Street Y, Symphony Space**, and the **Joseph Papp Public Theater** (*see p120*). The latter is perhaps the most influential theater in New York. It was founded in the 1950s by the late director Joseph Papp, who introduced neighborhood tours to bring theater to people who had never seen it before.

The Public Theater created hits such as *A Chorus Line;* and *Hair;* it is most famous for its free summer performances of Shakespeare at the Delacorte Theater in Central Park (*see p208*). It usually has several productions running, and at 6pm on the day of performance, "Quiktix" tickets (limited to two per person) are sold in the Public Theater lobby.

THEATER SCHOOLS

New York is the best place in the country to see actors learning their trade. Foremost among the acting schools is **The Actors' Studio**. The late Lee Strasberg, the advocate of method acting – in which the actor aims for complete identification with the character being played – was its guru. His students included Dustin Hoffman, Al Pacino, and Marilyn Monroe. "In progress" productions feature trainees and are open to the public and free. Sandy Meisner trained many actors, including the late Lee Remick, at the **Neighborhood Playhouse School of the Theater**. Its plays are not open to the public. The **New Dramatists** began in 1949 to develop new playwrights, helping the careers of the likes of William Inge. Play readings are open to the public and free.

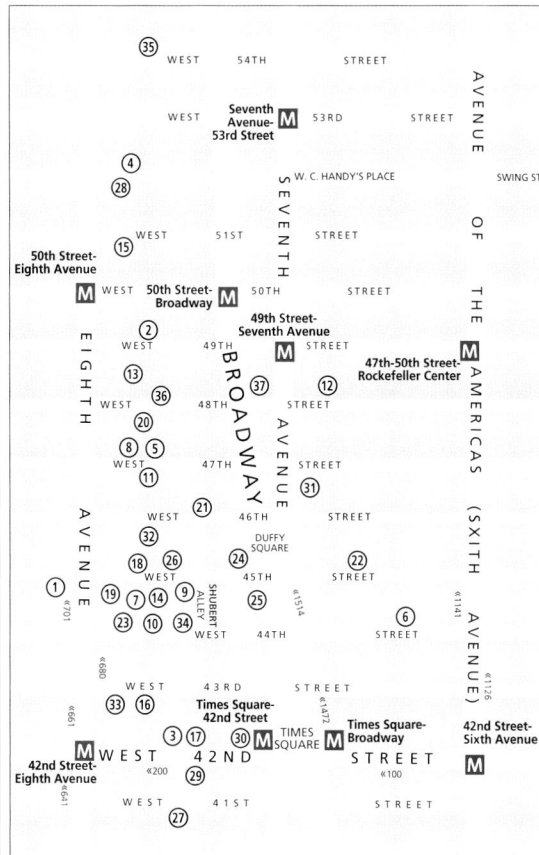

BROADWAY THEATERS

① **Al Hirschfield**
302 W. 45th St.
Tel (212) 239-6200.

② **Ambassador**
219 W. 49th St.
Tel (212) 239-6200.

③ **American Airlines Theater**
227 W. 42nd St.
Tel (212) 719-1300.

④ **August Wilson**
245 W. 52nd St.
Tel (212) 239-6200.

⑤ **Barrymore**
243 W. 47th St.
Tel (212) 239-6200.

⑥ **Belasco**
111 W. 44th St.
Tel (212) 239-6200.

⑦ **Bernard B Jacobs**
242 W. 45th St.
Tel (212) 239-6200.

⑧ **Biltmore**
261 W. 47th St.
Tel (212) 239-6200.

⑨ **Booth**
222 W. 45th St.
Tel (212) 239-6200.

⑩ **Broadhurst**
235 W. 44th St.
Tel (212) 239-6200.

⑪ **Brooks Atkinson**
256 W. 47th St.
Tel (212) 307-4100.

⑫ **Cort**
138 W. 48th St.
Tel (212) 239-6200.

⑬ **Eugene O'Neill**
230 W. 49th St.
Tel (212) 239-6200.

⑭ **Gerald Schoenfeld**
236 W. 45th St.
Tel (212) 239-6200.

⑮ **Gershwin**
222 W. 51st St.
Tel (212) 307-4100.

⑯ **Helen Hayes**
240 W. 44th St.
Tel (212) 239-6200.

⑰ **Hilton**
213 W. 42nd St.
Tel (212) 307 4100.

⑱ **Imperial**
249 W. 45th St.
Tel (212) 239-6200.

⑲ **John Golden**
252 W. 45th St.
Tel (212) 239-6200.

⑳ **Longacre**
220 W. 48th St.
Tel (212) 239-6200.

㉑ **Lunt–Fontanne**
205 W. 46th St.
Tel (212) 307-4747.

㉒ **Lyceum**
149 W. 45th St.
Tel (212) 239-6200.

㉓ **Majestic**
247 W. 44th St.
Tel (212) 239-6200.

㉔ **Marquis**
211 W. 45th St.
Tel (212) 307-4100.

㉕ **Minskoff**
200 W. 45th St.
Tel (212) 307-4100.

㉖ **Music Box**
239 W. 45th St.
Tel (212) 239-6200.

㉗ **Nederlander**
208 W. 41st St.
Tel (212) 307-4100.

㉘ **Neil Simon**
250 W. 52nd St.
Tel (212) 307-4100.

㉙ **New Amsterdam**
214 W. 42nd St.
Tel (212) 307 4100.

㉚ **New Victory**
209 W. 42nd St.
Tel (212) 239-6200.

㉛ **Palace**
1564 Broadway.
Tel (212) 307-4100.

㉜ **Richard Rodgers**
226 W. 46th St.
Tel (212) 307-4100.

㉝ **St. James**
246 W. 44th St.
Tel (212) 239-6200.

㉞ **Shubert**
225 W. 44th St.
Tel (212) 239-6200.

㉟ **Studio 54**
254 W. 54th St.
Tel (212) 719 3100.

㊱ **Walter Kerr**
219 W. 48th St.
Tel (212) 239-6200.

㊲ **Winter Garden**
1634 Broadway.
Tel (212) 239-6200.

For other theaters
see p347.

BALLET

At the heart of the dance world is Lincoln Center *(see p214)*, where the New York City Ballet performs pieces in the **New York State Theater**. This company was created by the legendary brilliant choreographer George Balanchine *(see p49)* and is probably still the best in the world. The current director, Peter Martins, was one of Balanchine's best dancers and continues the strict policy of ensemble dancing rather than "star turns." The season runs from November to February and late April to early June. The ballet school at the **Juilliard Dance Theater** also presents a spring workshop every year, and this is a good chance to see budding stars.

The American Ballet Theater appears at the **Metropolitan Opera House**, which also hosts many visiting foreign companies, such as the Kirov, Bolshoi, and Royal ballets. Its repertoire includes 19th-century classics, such as *Swan Lake,* and works by modern choreographers such as Twyla Tharp and Paul Taylor.

CONTEMPORARY DANCE

New York is the center of many of the most important movements in modern dance. The **Dance Theater of Harlem** is world famous for its modern, traditional, and ethnic productions. Other havens of experimental dance include the **92nd Street Y** and the **Merce Cunningham Studio** in Greenwich Village. The unique **Dance Theater Workshop** features contemporary dance and performance from around the world. **The Kitchen**, **La MaMa**, **Symphony Space**, and **P.S. 122** are all multimedia venues with the latest in contemporary dance, performance art and avant-garde music. Choreographer Mark Morris's company performs at the **Mark Morris Dance Center** in Brooklyn; **City Center** *(see p148)* is a favorite spot for dance fans. It used to house the New York City

Ballet and the American Ballet Theater before Lincoln Center was built. As well as featuring the Joffrey Ballet, City Center has held performances by all the great contemporary artists, including Alvin Ailey's blend of modern, jazz, and blues, and the companies of modern dance masters Merce Cunningham and Paul Taylor. Avoid the mezzanine, as the view is restricted.

The city's single most active venue for dance is probably the **Joyce Theater**, where such well-established companies as the Feld Ballet, along with bold newcomers and visiting troupes, perform.

Each spring the Festival of Black Dance at the **Brooklyn Academy of Music (BAM)** *(see p248)* features everything from ethnic dance to hip-hop. During autumn the "Next Wave" festival of music and dance is held, celebrating international and American avant-garde dance and music. During winter, the American Ballet Festival is held here.

During June, **New York University** *(see p115)* holds a Summer Residency Festival with lecture-demonstrations, rehearsals, and performances, and **Dancing in the Streets** organizes summertime dance performances all over the city.

Throughout the month of August, **Lincoln Center Out of Doors** has a program of free dance events on the plaza, with such experimental groups as the American Tap Dance Orchestra.

The **Duke Theater** presents many contemporary dance companies and participates in events such as the New York Tap Festival.

At different times of the year, **Radio City Music Hall** holds several spectacular shows, with different companies from all over the world. At Christmas and Easter, it features the famously precise Rockettes dance troupe.

Choreographers and dance companies frequently present works-in-progress and recitals to the public. Among the most interesting venues for these is the **Joan Weill Center for Dance** , which is one of the country's largest dance

facilities and was created by the Alvin Ailey American Dance Theater to promote black cultural expression. The **Hunter College Dance Company** performs new works by its student choreographers, and the **Isadora Duncan Dance Foundation** recreates Duncan's original dances. To see contemporary choreographers, the best place to go is **Juilliard Dance Theater**.

PRICES

Theater is extremely expensive to produce, and ticket prices tend to reflect this. Even Off- and Off-Off-Broadway tickets are not cheap anymore. Preview tickets are easier to get hold of, though, and it's fun to see a show before the reviews are in so you're able to make up your own mind.

For a Broadway theater ticket you can expect to pay $80 or more; for musicals, up to $100; Off-Broadway, $25 to $60. For dance, $20 to $50 is the usual range, with up to $115 for the American Ballet Theater.

TIMES OF PERFORMANCE

The general rules for theater-hours are: closed on Mondays (except for most musicals), with matinees on Wednesdays, Saturdays, and sometimes Sundays. Matinees usually begin at 2pm, with evening performances at 8pm. Be sure to check the correct dates and times of the performance beforehand, as tickets are usually non-refundable if you fail to turn up at the correct time.

BACKSTAGE TOURS AND LECTURES

For those interested in the mechanics and anecdotes of the theater, your best bet is to go on one of the theater tours. The **92nd Street Y** organizes insider's views of the theater, with famous directors, actors, and choreographers taking part. Writers are invited along to read or discuss their current works. **Radio City Music Hall** also holds tours.

DIRECTORY

OFF-BROADWAY

92nd Street Y
1395 Lexington Ave.
Map 17 A2.
Tel (212) 415-5500.

Baruch Performing Arts Center
55 Lexington Ave.
Map 9 A4.
Tel (646) 312-4085.

Brooklyn Academy of Music
30 Lafayette Ave,
Brooklyn.
Tel (718) 636-4100.

Cherry Lane Theatre
38 Commerce St.
Map 3 C2.
Tel (212) 239-6200.

HERE Art Center
145 6th Ave.
Map 4 D4.
Tel (212) 647-0202.

Circle in the Square
1633 Broadway.
Map 12 E4.
Tel (212) 307-0388.

Delacorte Theater
Central Park. (81st St.)
Map 16 E4.
Tel (212) 539-8750.
Summer time only.

Douglas Fairbanks Theater
432 W 42nd St.
Map 7 C1.
Tel (212) 239-6200.

Lambs Theater
130 W 44th St.
Map 12 E5.
Tel (212) 575-0300.

Lucille Lortel Theater
121 Christopher St.
Map 3 C2.
Tel (212) 924-2817.

Manhattan Theater Club
311 W 43rd St.
Map 8 D1.
Tel (212) 399-3000.

New York Theater Workshop
79 E 4th St. **Map** 4 F2.
Tel (212) 460-5475.

Public Theater
425 Lafayette St.
Map 4 F2.
Tel (212) 539-8500.

Symphony Space
2537 Broadway.
Map 15 C2.
Tel (212) 864-5400.

Vivian Beaumont
Lincoln Center.
Map 11 C2.
Tel (212) 362-7600.

OFF-OFF-BROADWAY

Bouwerie Lane Theater
330 Bowery.
Map 4 F2.
Tel (212) 677-0060.

The Kitchen
512 W 19th St.
Map 7 C5.
Tel (212) 255-5793.

Performing Garage
33 Wooster St.
Map 4 E4.
Tel (212) 966-3651.

York Theater at St. Peter's Church
Citigroup Center,
619 Lexington Ave.
Map 13 A4.
Tel (212) 935-5820.

PERFORMANCE THEATER

La MaMa Experimental Theatre Club
74a E 4th St.
Map 4 F2.
Tel (212) 475-7710.

P.S. 122
150 First Ave.
Map 5 A1.
Tel (212) 477-5288.

Public Theater
See Off-Broadway.

THEATER SCHOOLS

The Actors' Studio
432 W 44th St.
Map 11 B5.
Tel (212) 757-0870.

New Dramatists
424 W 44th St.
Map 11 C5.
Tel (212) 757-6960.

DANCE

92nd Street Y
See Off-Broadway.

Brooklyn Academy of Music
See Off-Broadway.

City Center
130 W 56th St.
Map 12 E4.
Tel (212) 581-1212.

Dance Theater of Harlem
466 W 152nd St.
Tel (212) 690-2800.

Dance Theater Workshop
219 W 19th St. **Map** 8 E5.
Tel (212) 924-0077.

Dancing in the Streets
55 6th Ave (offices).
Tel (212) 625-3505.

Hunter College Dance Company
695 Park Ave.
Map 13 A1.
Tel (212) 772-4490.

Isadora Duncan Dance Foundation
141 W 26th St.
Map 20 D2.
Tel (212) 691-5040.

Joan Weill Center for Dance
405 W 55th St.
Map 11 D4.
Tel (212) 405-9000.

Joyce Theater
175 Eighth Ave at 19th St.
Map 8 D5.
Tel (212) 242-0800.

Juilliard Dance Theater
60 Lincoln Center Plaza,
W 65th St.
Map 11 C2.
Tel (212) 769-7406.

PERFORMANCE VENUES

Duke Theater
229 W 42nd St.
Map 8 E1.
Tel (646) 223-3000.

The Kitchen
See Off-Off-Broadway.

La MaMa Experimental Theatre Club
See Performance Theater.

Lincoln Center Out of Doors
Lincoln Center, Broadway
at 64th St. **Map** 11 C2.
Tel (212) 362-6000.

Manhattan Center
311 W 34th St. **Map** 8 D2.
Tel (212) 279-7740.

Mark Morris
3 Lafayette Ave. (Brooklyn)
Tel (718) 624-8400.

Merce Cunningham Studio
55 Bethune St. **Map** 3 B2.
Tel (212) 255-8240.

Metropolitan Opera House
Lincoln Center, Broadway
at 65th St. **Map** 11 C2.
Tel (212) 362-6000.

New York State Theater
Lincoln Center, Broadway
at 65th St. **Map** 11 C2.
Tel (212) 870-5570.

New York University
Tisch School of the Arts
(TSOA), 111 2nd Ave.
Map 4 F1.
Tel (212) 998-1920.

P.S. 122
See Performance Theater.

Radio City Music Hall
50th St at Ave of the
Americas. **Map** 12 F4.
Tel (212) 307-7171.

Symphony Space
See Off-Broadway.

BACKSTAGE TOURS

92nd Street Y
See Off-Broadway.

Radio City Music Hall
Tel (212) 307-7171.

Events Guide
www.playbill.com
www.newyork.
citysearch.com

Movies

New York is a film buff's paradise. Apart from new US releases, which show months in advance of other countries, many classic and foreign films are screened here.

The city has always been the testing ground for new developments in films, and it continues to be a hotbed of young and innovative talent. Many of the movies' most famous directors – Spike Lee, Martin Scorsese, and Woody Allen – were born and raised in New York, and the city's influence is perceptible in many of their films. They, and others, can often be seen filming on the streets of the city; many of New York's landmarks have become famous after appearing in films. Most of the TV networks based in New York offer free tickets to the recordings of their shows. Watching a show such as *The Late Show with David Letterman* is a popular activity for visitors.

FIRST-RUN MOVIES

New York reviews and box office returns are so vital to a film's success that most major American films have their premieres in Manhattan's theaters. First-run films are shown mainly at the City Cinema chains, AMC Loews, United Artists, and Cineplex Odeon, which are scattered around the city. Some theaters have recorded information giving the names and duration of the different films showing, with starting times and ticket prices.

Programs start at 10am or 11am and are repeated every two to three hours until midnight. You should expect to line up for most evening and weekend performances of the more popular films. Making reservations using a credit card is possible at some theaters for an additional charge

of about $2 per ticket. Matinees (usually before 4pm) are easier to get into. Senior citizens pay a reduced price for tickets: the required age may be over 60, 62, or 65 depending on the policy of the theater.

NEW YORK FILM FESTIVAL

A high point of the year for film buffs is the New York Film Festival, now in its third decade. Organized by the **Film Society of Lincoln Center**, the festival starts in late September and continues for two weeks at the many Lincoln Center theaters. Outstanding new films from the US and abroad are entered in a competition for the huge prestige of winning an award. Many of the films shown during the festival are later released and can usually be seen only in art houses.

The **TriBeCa Film Festival**, created in part by director and actor Robert De Niro, was launched in 2002 to celebrate New York City as a filmmaking capital and to contribute to the long-term recovery of Lower Manhattan. The festival showcases a wide range of films, including classics, documentaries, and premieres, and usually takes place in late April and early May. Every spring, **Docfest** (the New York International Documentary Festival) presents five days of film and video documentaries from around the world, followed by panel discussions with the filmmaker.

FILM RATINGS

Films in the United States are graded as follows:
G General audiences; all ages admitted;
PG Parental guidance suggested; some material unsuitable for children.
PG-13 Parents strongly cautioned; some material inappropriate for children under age 13.
R Restricted. Children under 17 need to be accompanied by a parent or an adult guardian.
NC-17 No children under 17 admitted.

ON LOCATION

Many New York locations have played starring roles in films. Here are a few:

The Brill Building (1141 Broadway) contained Burt Lancaster's penthouse in *Sweet Smell of Success.*
The Brooklyn Bridge was a great backdrop in Spike Lee's *Mo' Better Blues.*
Brooklyn Heights and the **Metropolitan Opera** appeared in *Moonstruck.*
Central Park has shown up in countless films, including *Love Story* and *Marathon Man.*
55 Central Park West will be remembered as Sigourney Weaver's home in *Ghostbusters.*
Chinatown played a major role in *Year of the Dragon.*
The Dakota was where Mia Farrow lived in the classic *Rosemary's Baby.*
The Empire State Building is still standing after *King Kong*'s last battle. The observation deck is where Cary Grant waited in vain in *An Affair to Remember;* here Meg Ryan finally met Tom Hanks in *Sleepless in Seattle.*
Grand Central Station is famous for Robert Walker's meeting with Judy Garland in *Under the Clock* and for the magical ballroom sequence in *The Fisher King.*
Harlem hosted the jazz musicians and dancers in *The Cotton Club.*
Katz's Deli was the setting for the café scene between Billy Crystal and Meg Ryan in *When Harry Met Sally...*
Little Italy appeared in *The Godfather I* and *II.*
Madison Square Garden was the setting for the dramatic climax of *The Manchurian Candidate.*
Tiffany & Co. was Audrey Hepburn's favorite shop in *Breakfast at Tiffany's.*
The United Nations Building featured in *North by Northwest* and *The Interpreter.*
Washington Square Park was where Robert Redford and Jane Fonda walked *Barefoot in the Park.*

FOREIGN FILMS AND ART HOUSES

For the latest foreign and independent films, go to the **Angelika Film Center**, which also has an upscale coffee bar. Other good places are the **Rose Cinemas** at the BAM, the **Film Forum**, and **Lincoln Plaza Cinema**. The Plaza has a busy program of art and foreign films. For Asian, Indian, and Chinese films, you should visit the **Asia Society**. The **French Institute** screens many French films with English subtitles on Tuesdays. The **Quad Cinema** shows a wide selection of foreign films, often quite rare. **Cinema Village** runs special film events, such as the Festival of Animation.

The **Walter Reade Theater** houses the Film Society of the Lincoln Center, offering retrospectives of international movies as well as celebrations of contemporary works, such as the popular annual Spanish Cinema Now festival.

CLASSIC FILMS AND MUSEUMS

Retrospectives of films by particular directors or featuring specific actors are shown at the **Public Theater** and the **Whitney Museum of American Art** (see pp200–201). The **Museum of the Moving Image** (see p246) screens old films and also has many exhibits of memorabilia from the film industry. The **Paley Center for Media** (see p171) has regular screenings of classic films; you can also see or hear specific television or radio programs. Students interested in classic, new and experimental movies will appreciate the collection of the **Anthology Film Archives**.

The shows at the **Rose Center for Earth and Space** at the **American Museum of Natural History** are well worth a whole day's visit.

On summer evenings in Bryant Park, you can watch free classic movies, and on Saturday mornings, the **Film Society of Lincoln Center,** where special children's shows are held.

TELEVISION SHOWS

A number of TV programs originate in New York. The popular *David Letterman* and *Saturday Night Live* shows are almost impossible to get tickets for, but tickets for many other shows can be obtained online, by calling the networks such as **NBC**, **ABC**, and **CBS**, or sometimes on standby.

Another good source of free tickets is the Times Square Information Bureau (see p368). On weekday mornings on Fifth Avenue around **Rockefeller Plaza**, free tickets for a number of TV programs are sometimes distributed by the program's production staff. There's absolutely no way that you can plan for this. It's simply a matter of good luck and being in the right place at the right time.

For those who want to get a glimpse behind the scenes of TV, NBC organizes tours of the studios, from 8:30am to 4:30pm Mon–Thu (depart every 30 mins), 9:30am to 5:30pm Fri–Sat, and 9:30am to 4:30pm on Sunday (depart every 15 mins).

CHOOSING WHAT TO SEE

If you feel bewildered by the huge range of films offered in New York, check the listings in *New York* magazine, the *New York Times*, the *Village Voice* and *The New Yorker*. The following Internet guides give show times and locations:
www.moviefone.com
www.movietickets.com

DIRECTORY

ABC
Tel (212) 580-5176.
www.abc.com.

American Museum of Natural History
Central Park W at 79th St.
Map 16 D5.
Tel (212) 769-5100.

Angelika Film Center
18 W Houston St.
Map 4 E3.
Tel (212) 995-2000.

Anthology Film Archives
32 2nd Ave at 2nd St.
Map 5 C2.
Tel (212) 505-5181.

Asia Society
725 Park Ave. **Map** 13 A1.
Tel (212) 517-2742.

CBS
Tel (212) 247-6497.

Cinema Village
22 E 12th St. **Map** 4 F1.
Tel (212) 924-3363.

Docfest
Tel (212) 668-1100.
www.docfest.org

Film Forum
209 W Houston St.
Map 3 C3.
Tel (212) 727-8110.

French Institute
55 E 59th St. **Map** 12 F3.
Tel (212) 355-6160.

Lincoln Plaza Cinema
1886 Broadway.
Map 12 D2.
Tel (212) 757-2280.

Museum of Modern Art
11 W 53rd St. **Map** 12 F4.
Tel (212) 708-9480.

Museum of the Moving Image
35th Ave & 36th St. Astoria, Queens.
Tel (718) 784-0077.

NBC
30 Rockefeller Plaza at 49th St.
Tel (212) 664-3056.
www.nbc.com

The Paley Center for Media
25 W 52nd St. **Map** 12 F4.
Tel (212) 621-6600.

Public Theater
425 Lafayette St.
Map 4 F4.
Tel (212) 539-8500.

Quad Cinema
34 W 13th St.
Map 4 D1.
Tel (212) 255-8800.

Rockefeller Plaza
47th–50th St, 5th Ave.
Map 12 F5.

Rose Cinemas
Brooklyn Academy of Music (BAM), 30 Lafayette Ave, Brooklyn.
Tel (718) 636-4100.

TriBeCa Film Festival
Tel (212) 941-2400.
www.tribecafilmfestival.org

Walter Reade Theater
70 Lincoln Center Plaza.
Map 12 D2.
Tel (212) 875-5600.

Whitney Museum of American Art
945 Madison Ave.
Map 13 A1.
Tel 1-800-WHITNEY.

Classical and Contemporary Music

New Yorkers have a voracious appetite for music. Live concerts by the world's most celebrated musical performers may be enjoyed at famous halls throughout the year, and younger, newer artists, and exotic imports always find receptive audiences.

TICKETS

Find out what you can choose from in New York by checking out the listings in the *New York Times* and the *Village Voice* and in *Time Out New York* and *The New Yorker* magazines.

CLASSICAL MUSIC

The orchestra in residence at **Avery Fisher Hall** in Lincoln Center *(see p215)* is the New York Philharmonic. It is also the annual site for the popular "Mostly Mozart" series and Young People's Concerts. **Alice Tully Hall**, in Lincoln Center, is an acoustic gem and home to the Chamber Music Society.

One of the world's premier concert halls is the revamped **Carnegie Hall** *(see p148)*. Upstairs in the Weill Recital Hall there are quality performances for reasonable prices.

The **Brooklyn Academy of Music (BAM)** *(see p248)* is the home of the Brooklyn Philharmonic. Classical music, dance, opera, jazz, and world music all find an audience at the **New Jersey Performance Arts Center** in Newark.

The **Merkin Concert Hall** is host to some top chamber ensembles and soloists. For really excellent acoustics, go to the **Town Hall**. The **92nd Street Y's** Kaufmann Concert Hall also offers a lively menu of music and dance. There's also the **Frick Collection** and **Symphony Space**, both of which offer a varied program

ranging from gospel to Gershwin, classical to ethnic. The beautiful Grace Rainey Rogers Auditorium in the **Metropolitan Museum of Art** is for chamber music and soloists, while the well-equipped **Florence Gould Hall**, at the Alliance Française, presents a varied program of chamber music, orchestral pieces, concerts, and even classic French films.

The **Juilliard School of Music** and the **Mannes College of Music** are both considered excellent. Their students and faculties give free recitals, and there are shows by leading orchestras, chamber music groups, and opera companies. The **Manhattan School of Music** offers an excellent program of over 400 events per year, from classical to jazz.

At 9:45am on the Thursdays of the New York Philharmonic concerts, the evening show is rehearsed at **Avery Fisher Hall** in Lincoln Center. Audiences are often admitted to listen, and rehearsal tickets are available at low prices. The **Kosciuszko Foundation** hosts the annual Chopin Competition. **Corpus Christi Church** has an active concert schedule, presenting such groups as the Tallis Scholars.

OPERA

Dominating the city's operatic scene is **Lincoln Center** *(see p212)*, home to the New York City Opera, and the **Metropolitan Opera House**, which has its own opera company. The Met is the jewel in the crown, offering top international performers. More accessible and dynamic is the New York City Opera. Its performances range from *Madame Butterfly* to *South Pacific*, with subtitles above the stage to help the audience understand the plot. Lower-priced quality performances

are staged by the up-and-coming singers at the **Village Light Opera Group**, the **Amato Opera Theater**, the **Kaye Playhouse** at Hunter College, and the students at the **Juilliard Opera Center** in Lincoln Center.

CONTEMPORARY MUSIC

New York is one of the most important places in the world for contemporary music. Exotic, ethnic, and experimental music is played in many first-rate venues. The **Brooklyn Academy of Music (BAM)** is the standard-bearer of the avant-garde. Each autumn the Academy holds a festival of music and dance called "Next Wave," which has helped launch many musical careers.

An annual festival of serious modern music called "Bang on a Can" is performed at the **Ethical Culture Society Hall** and features works by Steve Reich, Pierre Boulez, and John Cage. Experimentalists, such as Davie Weinstein with his "audio-visual acid test" music – a mix of CD players, amplified instruments, keyboards, and sound effects – perform at the **Dance Theater Workshop**. Other venues include the **Asia Society** *(see p187)*, with its jewel of a theater for many visiting Asian performers, and **St. Peter's Church**.

BACKSTAGE TOURS

Behind-the-scenes tours are offered by **Lincoln Center** and **Carnegie Hall**.

RELIGIOUS MUSIC

Few experiences are more moving than an Easter concert in the vast **Cathedral of St. John the Divine** *(see pp226–7)*. Seasonal music is also offered at many of the city's museums and in almost every other available space – from **Grand Central Terminal**'s main concourse *(see pp156–7)* to bank and hotel lobbies. For jazz vespers in a stunning modern building, visit **St. Peter's Church** *(see p177)*.

CLASSICAL RADIO

New York has three FM radio stations that broad-cast classical music: WQXR at 96.3, the National Public Radio station WNYC at 93.9 and WKCR 89.9.

Most of these concerts are free, but you are encouraged to contribute.

ALFRESCO

Free outdoor summer concerts occur in **Bryant Park**, **Washington Square**, and **Lincoln Center's Damrosch Park**. The annual concerts on Central Park's Great Lawn and in Brooklyn's Prospect Park are performed by the New York Philharmonic and the Metropolitan Opera. In good weather, strolling musicians perform at South Street Seaport, on the steps of the **Metropolitan Museum**

of Art *(see pp190–97)*, and in the area around Washington Square.

MUSIC FOR FREE

Free musical performances are given at **The Cloisters** *(see pp236–9)* and the **Whitney Museum**'s Philip Morris Building *(see p152)*. Sunday-afternoon recitals are held at Rumsey Playfield and the Naumburg Bandshell in Central Park *(see p208)*, as well as the Summerstage. Call **The Dairy** for more information. You will also find music in the **Federal Hall** *(see p68)*, while at **Lincoln Center**, don't

miss the exciting free performances held in the **Juilliard School of Music**. Other popular venues include the **Greenwich House Music School** (free student recitals) and the **Winter Garden** at the World Financial Center *(see p69)*. Numerous free concerts and talks take place in the city's churches, including **St. Paul's Chapel**, **Trinity Church** *(see p68)*, and St. Thomas Church *(see p171)*.

INTERNET EVENTS GUIDE

www.nymag.com
www.nytoday.com
www.newyork.citysearch.com
http://newyork.timeout.com

DIRECTORY

92nd Street Y
1395 Lexington Ave.
Map 17 A2.
Tel (212) 415-5500.

Amato Opera Theater
319 Bowery at 2nd St.
Map 4 F2.
Tel (212) 228-8200.

Asia Society
725 Park Ave.
Map 13 A1.
Tel (212) 517-2742.

Brooklyn Academy of Music
30 Lafayette Ave, Brooklyn.
Tel (718) 636-4100.

Bryant Park
Map 8 F1.
Tel (212) 768-4242.

Carnegie Hall
881 7th Ave. **Map** 12 E3.
Tel (212) 247-7800.

Cathedral of St. John the Divine
1047 Amsterdam Ave & 112th St. **Map** 20 E4.
Tel (212) 316-7540.

The Cloisters
Fort Tryon Park.
Tel (212) 923-3700.

Corpus Christi Church
529 W 121st St.
Map 20 E2.
Tel (212) 666-9350.

The Dairy
Central Park at 65th St.
Map 12 F2.
Tel (212) 794-6564.

Dance Theater Workshop
See Dance p347.

Ethical Culture Society Hall
2 W 64th St.
Map 12 D2.
Tel (212) 874-5210.

Federal Hall
26 Wall St.
Map 1 C3.
Tel (212) 825-6888.

Florence Gould Hall (at the Alliance Française)
55 E 59th St.
Map 13 A3.
Tel (212) 355-6160.

Frick Collection
1 E 70th St. **Map** 12 F1.
Tel (212) 288-0700.

Greenwich House Music School
46 Barrow St. **Map** 3 C2.
Tel (212) 242-4770.

Kaye Playhouse (Hunter College)
695 Park Ave. **Map** 13 A1.
Tel (212) 772-4448.

Kosciuszko Foundation
15 E 65th St. **Map** 12 F2
Tel (212) 734-2130.

Lincoln Center
155 W 65th St.
Map 11 C2.
Tel (212) 546-2656.
Tours of various venues at Lincoln Center can be arranged by calling:
Tel (212) 875-5350.

Alice Tully Hall
Tel (212) 875-5050.

Avery Fisher Hall
Tel (212) 875-5030.

Damrosch Park
Tel (212) 875-5000.

Juilliard Opera Center
Tel (212) 769-7406.

Juilliard School of Music
Tel (212) 799-5000.

Metropolitan Opera House
Tel (212) 362-6000.

Manhattan School of Music
120 Claremont Ave.
Map 20 E2.
Tel (212) 749-2802.

Mannes College of Music
150 W 85th St.
Map 15 D3.
Tel (212) 580-0210.

Merkin Hall
129 W 67th St.
Map 11 D2.
Tel (212) 501-3330.

Metropolitan Museum of Art
1000 5th Ave at 82nd St.
Map 16 F4.
Tel (212) 535-7710.

New Jersey Performance Arts Center
1 Center St, Newark, NJ.
Tel 1-888-466-5722.

St. Paul's Chapel
Broadway at Fulton St.
Map 1 C2.
Tel (212) 233-4164.

St. Peter's Church
619 Lexington Ave.
Map 13 A4.
Tel (212) 935-2200.

Symphony Space
2537 Broadway.
Map 15 C2.
Tel (212) 864-5400.

Town Hall
123 W 43rd St.
Map 8 E1.
Tel (212) 997-1003.

Trinity Church
Broadway at Wall St.
Map 1 C3.
Tel (212) 602-0800.

Village Light Opera Group
Perform at: Haft Auditorium, Fashion Institute of Technology, 227 W 27th St.
Map 8 E3.
Tel (212) 352-3101.

Washington Square
Map 4 D2.

Whitney Museum
Philip Morris Building, 120 Park Ave at 42nd St.
Map 9 A1.
Tel 1-800-944-8639.

Winter Garden
World Financial Center, West St.
Map 1 A2.
Tel (212) 945-2600.

Rock, Jazz, and World Music

There's every imaginable form of music in New York, from international stadium rock to the sounds of the 1960s, from Dixieland jazz or country blues, soul, and world music to talented street musicians. The city's music scene changes at a dizzying pace, with many new arrivals (and departures) almost daily, so there's no way to predict what you may find when you arrive. Musical standards also vary.

PRICES AND PLACES

At clubs, expect to pay a cover charge and possibly a one- or two-drink minimum (at $7 or more) requirement. The prices for concerts range from $50 to $150 for the major venues. Many of the smaller concert venues are arranged for seating in certain areas and dancing in others – often with different prices for each.

The top international bands are usually to be found in the huge arenas at the **Meadowlands** or **Madison Square Garden** *(see p135)*. Here the likes of Elton John, Bruce Springsteen, and Madonna perform. Tickets for these events sell out very fast, so buy as many as you need as soon as you hear of a concert, unless you don't mind paying a lot for them through an agent or a scalper *(see p341)*. During the summer, big outdoor concerts are held at Jones Beach *(see p255)* and **Central Park SummerStage**.

Medium-sized venues for mainstream bands include the Art Deco palace of **Radio City Music Hall**, the **Manhattan Center** (formerly the Hammerstein Ballroom), and the **Beacon Theater**. Booking an impressive lineup of acts is the **Nokia Theater** in Times Square. This state-of-the-art venue is known for its top-notch acoustics. The most popular live-music venues are in the Upper West Side area.

Many leading rock venues are basically bars with music. They will often book different bands every night, so check the listings in the *New York Times*, *Village Voice*, or *Time Out New York* or phone the place to find out what's happening and at what time during that particular week.

ROCK MUSIC

Rock comes in many forms: gothic, industrial, techno, psychedelic, post-punk funk, indie, and alternative music are among the latest crazes. If you prefer to see more of a band than a giant video screen, the following venues have a much more intimate, friendly atmosphere.

The **Knitting Factory Brooklyn** has new music, while the **Mercury Lounge** is one of the most happening music spots, featuring hot new bands being groomed for MTV. **Irving Plaza** is where relatively unknown and sometimes known rock groups play, as do the occasional famous country and blues musicians.

The **Bowery Ballroom**, in the Lower East Side, boasts superior acoustics and sightlines and usually books well-known touring acts and local bands.

A converted bodega, **Arlene's Grocery** attracts a loyal crowd thanks to acts ranging from rock to country and comedy. Its Live Rock and Roll Karaoke on Monday nights is also popular. **Joe's Pub** draws those who appreciate the eclectic roster of rock, jazz, hip-hop, and lounge music. A more upscale venue, **Crash Mansion** showcases up-and-coming talents of any musical persuasion, from rock and punk to Brazilian and jazz, as well as featuring established performers such as Norah Jones.

JAZZ

The original Cotton Club and Connie's Inn, which were once crucibles of jazz, are long gone, as are the former speakeasies of West 52nd Street. However, many talented performers carry on the old traditions of Dave Brubeck, Les Paul, Duke Ellington, Count Basie, and other big bands. In Harlem, the stylish yet informal **Lenox Lounge** features contemporary jazz on the weekends.

In Greenwich Village, jazz temples from the 1930s survive and continue to foster great music. Foremost among them is the **Village Vanguard**, where some of the most highly revered jazz memories linger, and newer ones are being fashioned by such groups as the McCoy Tyner and Branford Marsalis trios. **Blue Note** hosts big bands at high prices but has a great atmosphere. **Smalls** offers cutting-edge jazz, with four sets a night from two different bands (Mon–Sat).

Smoke is an intimate nightspot offering a divergent roster of musicians, and **Birdland** features ex-Mingus alumni and musicians such as Bud Shank.

Café Carlyle, an East Side spot once famed for late jazz pianist and singer Bobby Short, now sometimes features clarinetist-filmmaker Woody Allen playing with Eddy Davis and his New Orleans Jazz Band. **Jazz Standard**, with an ample underground performance space, showcases top-notch jazz performers most nights of the week.

A sophisticated club and restaurant, **Iridium** features progressive jazz. If you're in New York in June, don't miss the annual **JVC Jazz Festival**, where famous jazz and blues icons play at various clubs all around Manhattan.

Jazz at Lincoln Center events are scheduled throughout the year, including concerts by the renowned Lincoln Center Jazz Orchestra under the direction of Wynton Marsalis. The music ranges from Duke Ellington's New York sounds to Johnny Dodds' traditional New Orleans-style jazz. Jazz at Lincoln Center now has its own home since it moved into the world's first performing arts center specifically for jazz. It is housed in the Time Warner Center – a multiroom facility on Columbus Circle, perched above Central Park, with bandstands posed against sparing walls of glass and a dance floor beneath the moon and stars *(see p215)*. Finally, Friday night at the **Rose Center** (at **AMNH**) offers live jazz concerts.

FOLK AND COUNTRY MUSIC

Folk, rock music, and R&B (rhythm and blues) can be found at the rather faded **Bitter End**, which once showcased James Taylor and Joni Mitchell but now

specializes in promising new talent, as does **Kenny's Castaways**. Also worth checking out is the **Sidewalk Café**, with its wide range of emerging performers.

BLUES, SOUL, AND WORLD MUSIC

For blues, soul, and world music, options include the **Apollo Theater** in Harlem *(see p230)*. For more than 60 years the near-legendary Wednesday Amateur Nights have been responsible for discovering and launching stars, including James Brown and Dionne Warwick.

The **Cotton Club** is no longer located in its original spot, but the modern venue offers good blues, jazz, and a

Sunday real Gospel brunch on Harlem's main street. The **B.B. King's Blues Club** lineup often features legendary jazz and gospel performers. Food is also served, but can be pricy. Don't miss "Mambo Mondays" with Nestor Torres at **SOB's** (Sounds of Brazil), a world music club specializing in Afro-Latin rhythms.

Terra Blues's bar doubles as an interesting music venue. The blues artists that appear here range from authentic Chicago acoustic players to modern blues acts. In the East Village, **The Stone** showcases an eclectic range of artsy acts. Part community center and café, part jazz and experimental music space, the **5C Café** is a throwback to old New York and has a laidback vibe.

DIRECTORY

MUSIC VENUES

Beacon Theater
2124 Broadway.
Map 15 C5.
Tel (212) 465-6500.

Central Park SummerStage
Rumsey Playfield.
Map 12 F1.
Tel (212) 360-2777.

Madison Square Garden
7th Ave & 33rd St.
Map 8 E2.
Tel (212) 465-6741.

Manhattan Center
311 W 34th St. **Map** 8 D2. *Tel (212) 279-7740.*

Meadowlands
50 Route 120 E
Rutherford, NJ.
Tel (201) 935-3900.

Nokia Theater
1515 Broadway.
Map 12 E5.
Tel (212) 930-1959.

Radio City Music Hall
See p347.

ROCK MUSIC

Arlene's Grocery
95 Stanton St. **Map** 5 A3.
Tel (212) 995-1652.

Bowery Ballroom
6 Delancey St. **Map** 4 F3.
Tel (212) 533-2111.

Crash Mansion
199 Bowery. **Map** 4 F3.
Tel (212) 982-7767.

Irving Plaza
17 Irving Pl. **Map** 9 A5.
Tel (212) 777-6800.

Joe's Pub
Public Theater, 425
Lafayette St. **Map** 4 F2.
Tel (212) 539-8770.

Knitting Factory Brooklyn
361 Metropolitan Ave.
Tel (347) 529-6696.

Mercury Lounge
217 E Houston St.
Map 5 A3.
Tel (212) 260-4700.

JAZZ

Birdland
315 W 44th St. **Map** 12 D5. *Tel (212) 581-3080.*

Blue Note
131 W 3rd St. **Map** 4 D2.
Tel (212) 475-8592.

Café Carlyle
95 E 76th St. **Map** 17 A5.
Tel (212) 744-1600.

Iridium
1650 Broadway. **Map** 12 D2. *Tel (212) 582-2121.*

Jazz at Lincoln Center
Tel (212) 258-9800.

Jazz Standard
116 E 27th St. **Map** 9 A3
Tel (212) 576-2232.

JVC Jazz Festival
www.festivalnetwork.com

Lenox Lounge
288 Malcolm X Blvd.
Map 21 B2.
Tel (212) 427-0253.

Rose Center
79th St at CPW. **Map** 16 D5. *Tel (212) 769-5100.*

Smalls
183 W 10th St. **Map** 3 C2. *Tel (212) 252-5091.*

Smoke
2751 Broadway. **Map** 20 E5. *Tel (212) 864-6662.*

Village Vanguard
178 7th Ave S. **Map** 3 C1. *Tel (212) 255-4037.*

FOLK AND COUNTRY

Bitter End
147 Bleecker St. **Map** 4 E3. *Tel (212) 673-7030.*

Kenny's Castaways
157 Bleecker St.
Map 4 E3.
Tel (212) 979-9762.

Sidewalk Café
94 Ave A. **Map** 5 B2.
Tel (212) 473-7373.

BLUES, SOUL, AND WORLD MUSIC

5C Café
68 Avenue C. **Map** 5 C2.
Tel (212) 477-5993.

Apollo Theater
253 W 125 St.
Map 19 A1.
Tel (212) 531-5305.

B.B. King's Blues Club
237 W 42nd St.
Map 8 E1.
Tel (212) 997-4144.

Cotton Club
656 W 125th St. **Map** 22 F2. *Tel (212) 663-7980.*

SOB's
204 Varick St. **Map** 4 D3.
Tel (212) 243-4940.

The Stone
Avenue C at 2nd St.
Map 5 C2.
www.thestonenyc.com

Terra Blues
149 Bleecker St.
Map 4 E3.
Tel (212) 777-7776.

Clubs, Dance Halls, and Gay and Lesbian Venues

New York's nightlife and club scene is legendary, and deservedly so. Whatever your preference – be it for a noisy disco, stand-up comedy, or the soothing melodies of a Harry Connick, Jr. sound-alike in a piano bar – you'll really be amazed at the choice. There was a rash of big discos in the 1980s, but relatively few of these have survived the trend toward the comfort and style of supper clubs.

WHEN AND WHERE

The best and hippest time for clubbing is during the week – it's also a lot cheaper. Take a fair amount of money and some ID to prove that you're old enough to drink (which is over 21) – but beware, all the drinks are very expensive.

The trendiest clubs roll on until 4am or later. Fashions and club nights change all the time, so go to Tower Records on Broadway for all the latest leaflets, check club details in the listings magazines *(see p340)* and read the *Village Voice*. The most interesting places nowadays are often popularized by word of mouth. Your best bet is to go somewhere like Pacha and hope someone will tell you where to go on to. It's a well-known spot and often invitations to other clubs are given out there.

DANCING

New Yorkers thrive on music and dancing. The dance floors available all around the city range from the ever-popular **SOB's** – for jungle, reggae, soul, jazz, and salsa – to a few huge basketball-court-sized places, such as **Roseland**. This has ballroom dancing every Thursday and Sunday and is New York's classic Broadway ballroom, revealing a tantalizing glimpse of older Broadway culture. It also has a good megasize, 700-seater, restaurant with a fully stocked bar.

The legendary club **Pacha**, which started out in Ibiza, has opened a swanky four-floor venue in the heart of Times Square and is consistently booking top international DJs to make the most of the colossal sound system installed here. This is the place for those who enjoy pounding music, sweaty dance floors, and a lively crowd. **Marquee** is another A-list spot in Chelsea, with a glass-enclosed VIP mezzanine that draws Hollywood starlets. Bring some models if you want to be sure of getting in.

The botanically themed **Greenhouse** has a spacious interior decorated and lit by thousands of tiny, colored bulbs. It is also eco-conscious and LEED- (Leadership in Energy and Environmental Design) certified. Fashion and film events are often held here, and savvy clubbers have made it one of their top destinations. Another venue that's always packed is **Webster Hall**, an elder statesman of NYC nightlife that offers four floors of R&B, pop, electro, or house (when it's not hosting a special event). By comparison, **Cielo** is embracing the 21st century. This sleek, upscale room aimed mostly at those who love electronica boasts a killer sound system that envelops dancers as they jostle in a sunken living-room dance floor.

Those who are seriously interested in music and dancing head to **The Sullivan Room**, which draws the cream of techno talent and boasts a top-notch sound system and plenty of seating; or **Santos Party House**, which is basically two large, square, and black-painted rooms, where people go to get wild. Santos is part-owned by rocker Andrew W.K.

NIGHTCLUBS

Nightclubs are the places to see a show. NY shows are less flashy than in the 1940s and 1950s but they still boast a wide variety of acts. Expect to pay a cover charge; many of the clubs also require that you have at least two drinks.

The **Oak Room** at the Algonquin Hotel helped launch the careers of Harry Connick, Jr. and Diana Krall, among others. The chic **Supper Club** surrounds you with gold lamé draperies and features big-band music downstairs. Cabaret singers perform upstairs in their intimate Blue Room. **Joe's Pub** at the Public Theater has decent food and a wonderful array of performances and musical acts. **Feinstein's at the Regency** is the epitome of classic cabaret. Come here to enjoy everything from tinkling live piano shows to Broadway tributes and jazz trios.

GAY AND LESBIAN VENUES

The past two decades have seen the arrival of clubs and restaurants specifically geared to gay and lesbian clientele. Popular gay cabarets include the **Duplex**, which has a mix of stand-up comics, comedy sketches and singers. Often adorned with year-round Christmas lights, the long-running **Pieces** heats up most nights of the week with everything from drag shows to karaoke.

The very fashionable nightclubs and bars for men include the trendy, older-skewing uptown **Town House**, a piano bar with restaurant, and **Don't Tell Mama**, a long-established gay bar that presents good musical revues and spoofs. Even more elite is the **Hiro Ballroom** at the Maritime Hotel, a Sunday night must for the beautiful set. There are two levels to this Japanese-themed restaurant, with ample seating for poseurs who wish to see and be seen. **Henrietta Hudson** caters solely to women, as does the imaginatively decorated **Cubby Hole**, a cozy lesbian bar where regulars often sing along to the jukebox.

Magazines such as the *Village Voice* and *Next* have good listings of what's happening in the gay communities, and the *Gay Yellow Pages* covers the gay scene. If you need more information, phone the **Gay and Lesbian Switchboard**.

The Chelsea neighborhood, particularly around Eighth Avenue, is the bustling heart of New York's gay life. The Hell's Kitchen area, around the mid-40s between Eighth and 10th avenues, also thrums with gay nightlife – **Barrage** is a hopping bar featuring a popular Friday happy hour. The inviting and stylish **G Lounge** serves a potent selection of cocktails and flavored coffees, and is the perfect spot for a drink before hitting the clubs. Lively **Barracuda** features drag

shows and draws a diverse crowd of regulars and newcomers, while **Gym** caters to those into sporting events. **Stonewall Inn**, the famed site of the Stonewall riots and birth of the modern gay movement, has undergone a multimillion-dollar refurbishment. The comfy neighborhood lounge **Posh** pulls in a friendly crowd for the popular happy hour 4–8pm, and no visit to NYC would be complete without the spectacle of loud and flashy **Splash Nightclub**,.

DIRECTORY

DANCING

Cielo
18 Little West 12th St.
Map 3 B1.
Tel (212) 645-5700.

Greenhouse
150 Varick St.
Map 4 D4.
Tel (212) 807-7000.

Marquee
289 10th Ave.
Map 7 C4.
Tel (646) 473-0202.

Pacha
618 W 46th St.
Map 12 E5.
Tel (212) 209-7500.

Roseland
239 W 52nd St.
Map 12 E4.
Tel (212) 247-0200.

Santos Party House
96 Lafayette St.
Map 4 F5.
Tel (212) 714-4646.

SOB's
204 Varick St.
Map 4 D3.
Tel (212) 243-4940.

Sullivan Room
218 Sullivan St.
Map 4 D2.
Tel (212) 252-2151.

Webster Hall
125 E 11th St.
Map 4 F1.
Tel (212) 353-1600.

NIGHTCLUBS

Feinstein's at the Regency
540 Park Ave.
Map 13 A3.
Tel (212) 339-4095.

Joe's Pub
425 Lafayette St.
Map 4 F2.
Tel (212) 539-8777.

The Oak Room
Algonquin Hotel,
59 W 44th St.
Map 12 F5.
Tel (212) 419-9331.

The Supper Club
240 W 47th St.
Map 12 D5.
Tel (212) 921-1940.

GAY AND LESBIAN VENUES

Barracuda
275 W 22nd St.
Map 8 D4.
Tel (212) 645-8613.

Barrage
401 W 47th St.
Map 12 D5.
Tel (212) 586-9390.

The Cubby Hole
281 W 12th St.
Map 3 C1.
Tel (212) 243-9041.

Don't Tell Mama
343 W 46th St.
Map 12 D5.
Tel (212) 757-0788.

Duplex
61 Christopher St.
Map 3 C2.
Tel (212) 255-5438.

G Lounge
223 W 19th St.
Map 8 E5.
Tel (212) 929-1085.

Gay and Lesbian Switchboard
Tel (212) 989-0999.

Gym
167 Eighth Ave.
Map 8 D5.
Tel (212) 337-2439.

Henrietta Hudson
438 Hudson St.
Map 3 C3.
Tel (212) 924-3347.

Hiro Ballroom
The Maritime Hotel,
371 W 16th St.
Map 8 D5.
Tel (212) 727-0212.

Pieces
8 Christopher St.
Map 4 D2.
Tel (212) 929-9291.

Posh
405 W 51st St.
Map 11 C4.
Tel (212) 957-2222.

Splash
50 W 17th St. **Map** 8 F5.
Tel (212) 691-0073

Stonewall Inn
53 Christopher St.
Map 3 C2.
Tel (212) 488-2705.

Town House
236 E 58th St.
Map 13 B4.
Tel (212) 754-4649.

Comedy, Cabaret, and Literary Events

From Jack Benny and Rodney Dangerfield to Woody Allen and Jerry Seinfeld, New York has spawned almost as many comics as it has jokes about itself, including the requisite quips: on crime – "In New York crime is getting worse. When I was there the other day, the Statue of Liberty had both hands up"; and on driving – "Always look both ways when running a red light." Comedy is a cut-throat business here. This is good news for punters, because it means that no matter what comedy club you walk into, you'll be howling after just a few sets. NYC is also a consummate romancer, judging by its plethora of cabarets and lounges. An unforgettable New York experience is to be serenaded by a lounge singer in a dusky piano bar. New York also boasts a booming literary scene, with superb weekly readings and lectures.

COMEDY SHOWCASES

Many of New York's best current comedy clubs or showcases have evolved from earlier "improvisational" comedy. Part of the allure of New York comedy clubs is that you never know who might get behind the mic to deliver their spiel. Anyone from Dennis Miller and Roseanne Barr to Robin Williams could show up. A word of caution: if you don't want to be singled out and made fun of, sit away from the stage. Many of the larger comedy clubs offer meals, and at the more popular clubs, it's always a good idea to make reservations to ensure admission.

Leading the comedy club pack is the **Broadway Comedy Club** in the Theater District, which has formed from a merger of Chicago City Limits and NY Improv. As the city's largest club, it draws big names nightly. **Caroline's** also has big-name comics perform in elegant surroundings. The famous catchphrase of the bug-eyed New York comedian Roger Dangerfield was "I get no respect," but judging from the lasting fame of his **Dangerfield's Comedy Club**, which draws top acts from around the country, he seems to have gotten respect after all. The **Upright Citizens Brigade Theatre** has sassy, Chicago-style improvisation on various days of the week.

Many of the UCB's weekly late shows are free. The **Gotham Comedy Club** in the Flatiron District, presents a wide range of comics in a sophisticated setting. **Comic Strip Live**, on the East Side, has hosted a slew of top comics, including Eddie Murphy, and continues to introduce many new comics to the scene. The basement-level **Comedy Cellar** in Greenwich Village presents a nightly lineup of new and established comics. Also good are **Stand-Up NY**, **NY Comedy Club**, and **Laugh Lounge NYC**, which showcases two comedy shows a night, as well as offering nicely priced cocktails. **Underground Lounge** and **The Laugh Factory** are also good value.

CABARETS AND PIANO BARS

Cabarets have become a New York institution. Such cozy, just-for-listening places are often called "rooms" and are located in hotels. Most operate from Tuesday to Saturday (usually with a cover charge or a drink minimum), and most take credit cards.

The Algonquin's **Oak Room** has song stylists. For a classic piano lounge with a pano-ramic Manhattan view, visit the **Top of the Tower** at the Beekman Tower Hotel. The "long-distance hummer" award goes to the late Bobby Short, who played his piano for over 25 years at the Café Carlyle in the **Carlyle Hotel**. Now Woody Allen plays there on Mondays with Eddy Davis's New Orleans Jazz Band.

Also in the Carlyle is **Bemelman's Bar**, with its whimsical murals; it attracts a relaxed crowd who enjoy first-class crooners. A jacket is required if you visit the **5757 Bar** at the Four Seasons Hotel, but the opulence of the place makes it worth dressing up.

The spirited cabaret **Don't Tell Mama** showcases emerging and established performers who belt out their songs with equal gusto. **Ars Nova** in Hell's Kitchen is an informal, anything-goes cabaret where you may see show tunes and experimental comedy, and has attracted the likes of Liza Minnelli and Tony Kushner.

For Manhattan's choicest cabaret, kick back and enjoy the show at lively **Duplex**, the longest-running cabaret venue in New York City. Relax to the tinkling of keys at the downstairs piano bar, or head upstairs for superlative classic cabaret shows, one-act plays, and top-notch comedy. A mixed crowd, including the talented staff, croons along at **Brandy's Piano Bar**. For a memorable evening of song and music, head to **Feinstein's at the Regency Hotel**, where top-of-the-line performers entertain an appreciative crowd. Enjoy sultry cabaret, theater, and musical ensembles at the plush showroom in **Dillon's Restaurant and Lounge**, nestled in the heart of the Theater District.

LITERARY EVENTS AND POETRY SLAMS

As the birthplace of some of the greatest American writers, from Herman Melville to Henry James, and the adopted home of countless others, New York has long been a writer's city. The literary tradition is celebrated throughout the year, with readings and talks that take place at bookstores, libraries, cafés, and community centers across the city. Readings are usually free, but expect long lines for the better known names. The **92nd Street Y** hosts readings by some of the greatest writers to pass through New York, including many Nobel- and Pulitzer-prize winning authors. Most NYC bookstores present a weekly or monthly reading series, including **Barnes & Noble** (the Fifth Avenue and Union Square branches usually attract high-profile authors). The **Mid-Manhattan Library** also presents readings, as does **Strand Bookstore**. Enjoy

spirited readings by playwrights at the **Drama Book Shop**. Check out *The New Yorker* magazine, available in bookstores and at many newsstands, for current listings of readings and talks.

Poetry slams (also known as Spoken Word), are just what the name implies – an evening of freeform poems, raps, and storytelling, usually raucous and entertaining, often unpredictable, and never boring. The **Nuyorican Poets Café** in Alphabet City, often heralded as the progenitor of spoken word in New York,

serves up a nightly mix of poetry slams, readings, and performances. Faculty and staff at Columbia and CUNY and writing professionals can be found at **KGB Bar**'s series of literary events. The **Bowery Poetry Club**, established as a performance space for spoken word in all its incarnations, presents an eclectic range of performances, from poetry jams to various performance arts. The **Poetry Project** at St. Mark's Church also hosts contemporary poetry readings, events, and workshops.

DIRECTORY

COMEDY SHOWCASES

Broadway Comedy Club
318 W 53rd St.
Map 12 E4.
Tel (212) 757-2323.

Caroline's
1626 Broadway.
Map 12 E5.
Tel (212) 757-4100.

Comedy Cellar
117 MacDougal St.
Map 4 D2.
Tel (212) 254-3480.

Comic Strip Live
1568 2nd Ave.
Map 17 B4.
Tel (212) 861-9386.

Dangerfield's
1118 1st Ave.
Map 13 C3.
Tel (212) 593-1650.

Gotham Comedy Club
208 W 23rd St.
Map 8 D4.
Tel (212) 367-9000.

The Laugh Factory
303 W 42 St.
Map 8 D1.
Tel (212) 586-7829.

Laugh Lounge NYC
151 Essex St.
Map 5 B3.
Tel (212) 614-2500.

NY Comedy Club
241 E 24th St.
Map 9 B4.
Tel (212) 696-5233.

Stand-up NY
236 W 78th St.
Map 15 C5.
Tel (212) 595-0850.

Underground Lounge
955 W End Ave.
Map 20 E5.
Tel (212) 531-4759.

Upright Citizens Brigade Theatre
307 W 26th St.
Map 8 D4.
Tel (212) 366-9176.

CABARETS AND PIANO BARS

5757 Bar
Four Seasons Hotel,
57 E 57th St.
Map 12 F3.
Tel (212) 758-5700.

Ars Nova
511 W 54th St.
Map 12 E4.
Tel (212) 489-9800.

Brandy's Piano Bar
235 E 84th St.
Map 17 B4.
Tel (212) 650-1944.

Carlyle Hotel
35 E 76th St.
Map 17 A5.
Tel (212) 744-1600.

Dillon's Restaurant and Lounge
245 W 54th St.
Map 12 D4.
Tel (212) 307-9797.

Stand-up NY

Don't Tell Mama
343 W 46th St.
Map 12 D5.
Tel (212) 757-0788.

Duplex
61 Christopher St.
Map 3 C2.
Tel (212) 255-5438.

Feinstein's at the Regency Hotel
540 Park Ave.
Map 13 A3.
Tel (212) 759-4100.

Oak Room
Algonquin Hotel,
59 W 44th St.
Map 12 F5.
Tel (212) 840-6800.

Top of the Tower
Beekman Tower Hotel,
3 Mitchell Pl.
Map 13 C5.
Tel (212) 355-7300.

LITERARY EVENTS AND POETRY SLAMS

92nd Street Y
1395 Lexington Ave.
Map 17 A2.
Tel (212) 415-5729.

Barnes & Noble
555 Fifth Ave.
Map 12 F5.
Tel (212) 697-3048. 33 E 17th St.
Map 9 A5.
Tel (212) 253-0810.

Bowery Poetry Club
308 Bowery.
Map 4 F3.
Tel (212) 614-0505.

Drama Book Shop
250 W 40th St.
Map 8 E1.
Tel (212) 944-0595.

KGB Bar
85 E 4th St.
Map 4 F2.
Tel (212) 505-3360.

Mid-Manhattan Library
455 Fifth Ave at 40th St.
Map 8 F1.
Tel (212) 340-0833.

Nuyorican Poets Café
236 E 3rd St.
Map 5 B2.
Tel (212) 505-8183.

Poetry Project
St. Mark's Church,
131 E 10th St.
Map 4 F1.
Tel (212) 674-0910.

Strand Bookstore
828 Broadway.
Map 4 E1.
Tel (212) 473-1452.

Late-Night New York

New York is indeed a city that never sleeps. If you wake up in the middle of the night – with a craving for fresh bread, a need to be entertained, or an urge to watch the sun rise over the Manhattan skyline – there are always plenty of options to choose from.

BARS

The best and friendliest bars are often the Irish ones. **O'Flanagan's** or **Scruffy Duffy's** are both loud, have late-night dancing, and cater to regulars. Go for a late-night dry martini at the **Temple Bar**. The best piano bars are in the hotels: try the Café Carlyle in the **Carlyle Hotel**, **Feinstein's at Loews Regency** (see p357), or the Oak Room in the **Algonquin Hotel**.

For hot American jazz until 4am, go to **Joe's Pub** or the **Blue Note**. **Cornelia Street Café** is a lively nook for prose, poetry, and theater readings. Poetry, theater, and Latin music can be found at the **Nuyorican Poets Café**. If you're in the Village, stop in at **Rose's Turn** for open mike, piano bar, and late-night ambience.

MIDNIGHT MOVIES

Special midnight showings and a youthful crowd can be found at the Angelika Film Center and the Film Forum (see p349). New multi-plexes often show movies at midnight on weekends.

SHOPS

Shakespeare & Company Booksellers on Broadway and the St. Mark's Bookshop are open until late. The **Apple Store** on Fifth Ave is open 24 hours and well worth a visit at any time of the day. In the evening, DJs bring the store to life, while during the day, more than 300 Mac specialists are available for training and consultations. In SoHo, **H&M** sells affordable fashion until 9pm Monday to Saturday and until 8pm on Sundays.

Among the many Village clothing stores that stay open late is **Trash and Vaudeville** (open till 8pm Mon–Sat); **Macy's** at Herald Square

is open daily until 9:30pm. For health essentials, numerous **Duane Reade**, **CVS**, and **Rite Aid** pharmacies are open 24 hours.

TAKE-OUT FOOD AND GROCERIES

A few take-out food stores are open 24 hours a day, including numerous **Gristedes** emporiums and the **West Side Supermarket**. Many Korean greengrocers also stay open all night. The **Food Emporium** is a supermarket chain usually open until midnight. Liquor stores are usually open until 10pm and many deliver.

For the best in bagels, go to **H & H Bagels**, **Bagels On The Square**, and **Jumbo Bagels and Bialys**. Many pizzerias and Chinese restaurants stay open late.

DINING

The trendy set often frequent **Balthazar**, and **Les Halles** for good French dishes. Twentysomethings will seek out the **Coffee Shop** for late-night beer and Brazilian food. You'll find delicious and legendary sandwiches at the **Carnegie Deli**. **Caffè Reggio** in Greenwich Village has been a favorite for late-night coffee and desserts since 1927. Other good options include **Blue Ribbon** and **Odeon**. **The Dead Poet** is a real Upper West Side neighborhood hangout, with a jukebox, a lively bar, and late-night bar food. Downtown, the party crowds flock to **Bereket Turkish Kebab House** for excellent kebabs, or to the **Moonstruck Diner** in Chelsea. Both are open 24 hours a day.

SPORTS

There is late-night play at **Slate Billiards** until 4am on weekends. Have late-night beers and burgers with the

New York University crowd at **Bowlmor Lanes** bowling alley. Also popular is the **Lucky Strike Lanes and Lounge**, featuring cocktails, bowling, and music in a retro atmosphere. **24–7 Fitness Club** offers a no-frill gym around the clock.

SERVICES

Midnight Express Cleaners picks up garments in Manhattan until midnight and has them ready the next day. Note that this service does not pick up or deliver to major hotels. On Thursdays hairdresser **George Michael of Madison Avenue/Madora** is open until 9pm and will also make house calls. Primarily for women, the no-nonsense Korean spa **Juvenex** provides massages and saunas at any time. If you are locked out, try **Mr Locks Inc**. For stamps, head to the General Post Office, open 24 hours. Upscale grocer **Dean & DeLuca**'s Kip's Bay branch is open till 10pm.

TOURS AND VIEWS

One of New York's most enjoyable walks is along the Hudson River at the World Financial Center's **Battery Park City**, open (and safe) at all hours. Piers 16 and 17 at South Street Seaport attract strollers and revelers all night long and the **Harbour Lights** restaurant on Pier 17 is often open until 2am for a middle of the night pick-me-up. Enjoy the city lights by taking a **Circle Line** two-hour tour of the nighttime harbor.

Try the Riverview Terrace at Sutton Place: the benches offer a peaceful place to watch the sun rise over the East River, Roosevelt Island, and Queens. Two of the most sensational views with the Manhattan backdrop are (looking west) from the **River Café** and (looking east) from **Arthur's Landing** restaurant.

Take a trip on the **Staten Island Ferry** (see p76) to see the Statue of Liberty and the Manhattan skyline in the dawn light, or a take a taxi across Brooklyn Bridge (see *pp86–9*) to watch the sun rise over New York Harbor. Go to the **Beekman Tower Hotel**'s Top of the Tower for some panoramas of the city's East Side up to 1am. The ultimate view is from the **Empire State Building**: its observation decks *(see pp136–7)* stay open until 2am. **Top of the**

Rock's observation decks *(see p144)* are open until midnight. **Rise**, the 14th-floor bar of the Ritz-Carlton Hotel in Battery Park has great views of the harbor and Statue of Liberty.

Château Stables has rides in horse-drawn carriages and **Liberty Helicopters** run flights

over the city at sunset. If you want something a little bit different, try **Marvelous Manhattan Tours**' escorted evening barhopping walks. And if you still can't sleep, stroll along the Upper West Side and grab a couple of hot dogs at the famous **Gray's Papaya**.

DIRECTORY

BARS

Algonquin Hotel
See p357.

Blue Note
See p353.

Carlyle Hotel
See p357.

Cornelia Street Café
29 Cornelia St.
Map 4 D2.
Tel (212) 989-9318.

Joe's Pub
See p353.

Nuyorican Poets Café
236 E 3rd St. **Map** 5 A2.
Tel (212) 505-8183.

O'Flanagan's
1215 1st Ave. **Map** 13 C2.
Tel (212) 439-0660.

Rose's Turn
See p357.

Scruffy Duffy's
743 8th Ave. **Map** 12 D5.
Tel (212) 245-9126.

Temple Bar
332 Lafayette St.
Map 4 F4.
Tel (212) 925-4242.

SHOPS

Apple Store
767 5th Ave. **Map** 12 F3.
Tel (212) 336-1440.

CVS Pharmacy
158 Bleecker St. **Map** 4
D3. **Tel** (212) 982-3133.

Duane Reade Drugstores
224 W 57th (Broadway).
Map 12 D3.
Tel (212) 541-9708.

1279 3rd Ave at E 74th St.
Map 17 B5.
Tel (212) 744-2668.

H&M
558 Broadway. **Map** 4
E4. **Tel** (212) 343-2722.

Macy's
See p134.

RiteAid Pharmacy
See p373.

Trash and Vaudeville
See p324.

TAKE-OUT FOOD AND GROCERIES

Bagels On The Square
7 Carmine St. **Map** 4 D3.
Tel (212) 691-3041.

Gristedes Food Emporium
See the Yellow Pages
for locations.

H & H Bagels
Broadway at 80th St.
Map 15 C4.
Tel (212) 595-8003.

H & H Midtown Bagels East
1551 2nd Ave. **Map** 17
B4. **Tel** (212) 734-7441.

Jumbo Bagels and Bialys
1070 2nd Ave. **Map** 13
B3. **Tel** (212) 355-6185.

West Side Market
2171 Broadway.
Map 15 C5.
Tel (212) 595-2536.

DINING

Balthazar
80 Spring St. **Map** 4 E4.
Tel (212) 965-1414.

Bereket Turkish Kebab House
187 E Houston St. **Map** 5
A3. **Tel** (212) 475-7700.

Blue Ribbon
See p300.

Caffè Reggio
119 MacDougal St. **Map**
4 D2. **Tel** (212) 475-9557.

Carnegie Deli
See p314.

Coffee Shop
See p314.

The Dead Poet
450 Amsterdam Ave. **Map**
15 C4. **Tel** (212) 595-5670.

Gray's Papaya
Broadway at 72nd St.
Map 11 C1.
Tel (212) 260-3532.

Les Halles
See p314.

Moonstruck Diner
400 W 23rd St.
Map 7 C4.
Tel (212) 752-1711.

Odeon
See p298.

SPORTS

24–7 Fitness Club
47 W 14th St. **Map** 4 D1.
Tel (212) 206-1504.

Bowlmor Lanes
110 University Pl. **Map** 4
E1. **Tel** (212) 255-8188.

Lucky Strike Lanes and Lounge
624–660 West 42nd St.
Map 7 B1.
Tel (646) 829-0170.

Slate Billiards
See p361.

SERVICES

Dean & DeLuca
576 2nd Ave. **Map** 9 B3.
Tel (212) 696-1369.
One of several branches.

General Post Office
See p135.

George Michael of Madison Avenue/Madora
422 Madison Ave. **Map** 13
A5. **Tel** (212) 752-1177.

Juvenex Spa
25 W 32nd St, Fifth Floor.
Map 8 F3.
Tel (646) 733-1330.

Midnight Express Cleaners
Tel (718) 392-9200.

Mr Locks Inc
Tel (866) 675-6257.

TOURS AND VIEWS

Arthur's Landing
Port Imperial Marina,
Pershing Circle,
Weehawken, NJ.
Tel (201) 867-0777.

Battery Park City
West St. **Map** 1 A3.

Beekman Tower Hotel
1st Ave & 49th St. **Map** 13
C5. **Tel** (212) 355-7300.

Château Stables
608 W 48th St. **Map** 15
B3. **Tel** (212) 246-0520.

Circle Line
W 42nd St. **Map** 15 B3.
Tel (212) 563-3200.

Harbour Lights
89 South St Seaport.
Pier 17. **Map** 2 D2.
Tel (212) 227-2800.

Liberty Helicopters
Tel (212) 487-4777.

Marvelous Manhattan Tours
Tel (718) 846-9308.

Rise
Ritz-Carlton, Battery Park.
Map 1 B4.
Tel (212) 344-0800.

River Café
See p311.

Staten Island Ferry
See p76.

Top of the Rock
See p144.

Sports

Many New Yorkers are ardent sports fans, and you'll find a range of sports events, both to watch and participate in, going on throughout the year. The city boasts two professional baseball teams, two hockey teams, a basketball team, and two football teams. Madison Square Garden plays host to an extraordinary variety of spectator sports, including basketball, hockey, boxing, and track and field events. Tennis fans can take in the US Open and Virginia Slims tournaments, and those who follow track and field events swarm to the Millrose Games, where top runners and other athletes compete.

TICKETS

The easiest way to get hold of tickets is through **Ticketron** or **Ticketmaster**. For the big games, you may need a ticket agent. You can also buy tickets at the stadium box office itself, though these tickets often sell out quickly, so you'll have to call or stop by far in advance. Keep your eyes peeled for ticket offers in the free entertainment weeklies that are distributed throughout town, and check the local newspapers for upcoming sporting events.

FOOTBALL

The city's two professional football teams are the New York Giants and the New York Jets. They both play their home games across the river at the **Giants Stadium** in New Jersey. Tickets for the Giants, a popular team with an impressive number of NFL and Super Bowl champion-ships under their belt, are near-impossible to obtain, but they may be available for the Jets, who are seen by some as perpetual also-rans but are no less beloved by their fans. Their last championship win was in 1969.

BASEBALL

To capture the essence of this American institution, baseball fans should try to see the famed New York Yankees, who play at **Yankee Stadium**. The team's legendary accomplishments are manifold, and include winning the most World Series titles and boasting such celebrated players as Joe DiMaggio and Jackie Robinson. The New York Mets, the other major baseball team, play at **Citi Field** in Queens. Catching a game of "America's favorite pastime" on a crisp summer day is a memorable event, from the crack of the bat and the baseball soaring into the clear blue sky to the seem-ingly effortless slides into base and the roar of the crowd. If you can, try and catch a game when the Yankees are playing their archrivals the Boston Red Sox. The baseball season runs from April to October.

BASKETBALL

The New York Knicks play their home games at **Madison Square Garden**; tickets are pricey and difficult to attain, so you'll need to reserve far in advance through Ticketron or Ticketmaster. The ever-popular Harlem Globetrotters also play their games at The Garden.

BOXING

Professional boxing matches are more often seen on Paramount's wide TV screen than in the flesh at Madison Square Garden. Also at the Garden are the Daily News Golden Gloves in mid-April, the largest and oldest amateur boxing tournament in the US, with boxers from New York's five boroughs competing. Past Golden Glove winners, many of whom have gone on to become Olympic gold medal-ists and world champions, have included Sugar Ray Robinson and Floyd Patterson.

HORSE RACES

A day at the races may not be quite the lavish affair it once was, but the high-stakes races still draw the society crowd – hats, summer dresses and all – along with lively crowds who have come to cheer, jeer, and bet on their lucky horse. Harness racing, in which horses pull sulkies (small carts), takes place year-round at the **Yonkers Raceway**. Flat races are held daily, except Tuesday, October to May, at the **Aqueduct Race Track** in Queens, and May to October at the **Belmont Park Race Track** in Long Island.

ICE HOCKEY

Fists and ice fly when the New York Rangers meet their competition at Madison Square Garden. The New York Islanders are also fierce hockey contenders, with exciting matches at the **Nassau Coliseum** in Long Island. The hockey season runs from October to April.

ICE-SKATING

There are a variety of good places to go ice skating out of doors. One is the **Rockefeller Plaza Rink**, which looks beauti-ful at Christmas. The others are in Central Park: **Wollman Memorial Rink** and **Lasker Ice Rink**. For indoor sites, try the Sky Rink at **Chelsea Piers**.

MARATHON

To be one of the 30,000 who enter the New York Marathon, you have to sign up six months in advance. The race is held on the first Sunday in November. Phone (212) 423-2249 for information.

TENNIS

The top tennis tournament in New York is the US Open, played each August at the **National Tennis Center**. Also good is the women's Virginia Slims Championships in November at **Madison Square Garden** (see p135). If you want to play tennis rather than watch it, look in the telephone directory under "Tennis Courts: Public and Private." For private courts, you can expect to pay about $50–70 an hour. The **Manhattan Plaza Racquet Club** offers both courts and lessons by the hour. For public courts, you will need a $50 permit, available from the **NY City Parks & Recreation Department**. You will also need an identity card and a reservation coupon.

TRACK AND FIELD

The Millrose Games, which draws top athletes from around the world, are normally held in early February at **Madison Square Garden**. The 100-meter sprint, pole vault, and high jump competitions are particularly exciting. The Amateur Athletic

Union (AAU) championships, where many renowned student athletes compete, are held in late February at the Garden. Chelsea Piers also has a complete track and field complex.

SPORTS BARS

New York City is crammed with sports bars, often unmissable for their big screens, sports banners, and cheering (or booing), beer-guzzling patrons. For a slice of American sports life, step into a sports bar when a big game is on, and you'll soon be whooping it up with the rest of them. Try **Mickey Mantle's**, which has a giant scoreboard. **ESPN Zone**, in Times Square, offers a plethora of screens so that you can follow the action no matter where you are. **Bounce**,

on the Upper East Side, is a boisterous sports lounge with drinks specials through the week. **Bar None** and the friendly, Irish **Pioneer Bar** are also favorites, and for soccer, try the amiable **Nevada Smith's** in the East Village, with friendly, Guinness-fueled crowds.

OTHER ACTIVITIES

In Central Park, options include renting rowboats from **Loeb Boathouse** or playing chess – pick up the pieces from The Dairy *(see p208)*. Rent rollerblades at **Blades Board & Skate** and have a free lesson on stopping at Central Park before making a circuit. Bowling is available at **Chelsea Piers** and a few other lanes throughout the city. **Slate Billiards** and many bars offer pool and darts.

DIRECTORY

Aqueduct Race Track
Ozone Park, Queens.
Tel (718) 641-4700.

Bar None
98 3rd Ave. **Map** 4 F1.
Tel (212) 777-6663.

Belmont Park Race Track
Hempstead Turnpike, Long Island.
Tel (718) 641-4700.

Blades Board & Skate
120 W 72nd St.
Map 12 D1.
Tel (212) 787-3911.

Bounce
1403 Second Ave.
Map 13 B1.
Tel (212) 535-2183.

Chelsea Piers Sports & Entertainment Complex
Piers 59–62 at 23rd St & 11th Ave (Hudson River).
Map 7 B4–5.
Tel (212) 336-6000.
www.chelseapiers.com

Citi Field
126th St at Roosevelt Ave, Flushing, Queens.
Tel (718) 507-8499.

ESPN Zone
1472 Broadway at W 42nd St.
Map 8 E1.
Tel (212) 921-3776.

Giants Stadium
Meadowlands, E Rutherford, NJ.
Tel (201) 935-8111.
www.giants.com
Tel (516) 560-8200.
www.newyorkjets.com

Lasker Ice Rink
Central Park Drive East at 108th St.
Map 21 B4.
Tel (212) 534-7639.

Loeb Boathouse
Central Park.
Map 16 F5.
Tel (212) 517-2233.

Madison Square Garden
7th Ave at 33rd St.
Map 8 E2.
Tel (212) 465-6741.
www.thegarden.com

Manhattan Plaza Racquet Club
450 W 43rd St.
Map 7 C1.
Tel (212) 594-0554.

Mickey Mantle's
42 Central Park South.
Map 12 E3.
Tel (212) 688-7777.

Nassau Coliseum
1255 Hempstead Turnpike.
Tel (516) 794-9303.
www.nassau coliseum.com

National Tennis Center
Flushing Meadow Park, Queens.
Tel (718) 595-2420.
www.usta.com

Nevada Smith's
74 3rd Ave.
Map 4 F1.
Tel (212) 982-2591.

NY City Parks & Recreation Department
Arsenal Building, 64th St & 5th Ave.
Map 12 F2.
Tel (212) 408-0100.
www.nycgovparks.org

Pioneer Bar
218 Bowery. **Map** 4 F3.
Tel (212) 334-0484.

Plaza Rink
1 Rockefeller Plaza, 5th Ave. **Map** 12 F5.
Tel (212) 332-7654.

Slate Billiards
54 W 21st St.
Map 8 E4.
Tel (212) 989-0096.

Ticketmaster
Tel (212) 307-4100.
www.ticketmaster.com

Ticketron
Tel (212) 239-6200, 1-800-432-7250.
www.telecharge.com

Wollman Memorial Rink
Central Park, 5th Ave at 59th St.
Map 12 F2.
Tel (212) 439-6900.

Yankee Stadium
161st and 164th sts, The Bronx.
Tel (718) 293-4300.

Yonkers Raceway
Yonkers, Westchester County.
Tel (914) 968-4200.

Fitness and Wellbeing

New York City may be (in)famous for its concrete, crowds, and cacophony, but the urban jungle is a boon for sports and fitness aficionados. A host of possibilities beckon, from pedaling on the sun-washed riverfront and jogging under the shadow of Manhattan's signature skyline at the Central Park Reservoir to scaling a soaring climbing wall at one of the city's many upscale gyms, indulging in a massage at gorgeous spa strewn with rose petals and finding your inner Om in the lotus position at a yoga class.

CYCLING

There's nothing like being stuck in midtown traffic to make you long for pedaling the open road. While Manhattan may be one of the most crowded islands on the planet, it offers a surprising 120 km (75 miles) of bike trails. At the last count, Manhattan boasted more than 110,000 everyday cyclists. One of the most pleasant places to cycle is in Central Park during the weekend, when it's closed to cars. Bikes may be rented from **Central Park Bike Rentals** on Columbus Circle. If you would like to feel the river breeze in your hair, pedal the well-maintained bike path along the West Side Highway that runs parallel to the Hudson River, or hit the bike trails in Riverside Park. On summer weekends, the paths can get exasperatingly congested, but if you go early or late in the day, or in the winter months, you can often coast solo.

The friendly folks at **Bicycle Habitat** on Lafayette Street rent bikes and dole out tips on getting around New York by bike.

FITNESS CENTERS, GYMS, AND HEALTH CLUBS

In New York, a weekly workout has become almost de rigueur for even the most extreme workaholics. Gyms and health clubs have sprouted across the city to accommodate the demand, and serious sweating goes on at all hours, day and night. The options are endless: Get your aggression out with a punch bag, increase your heart rate on the stairmaster, or pump iron. Most major hotels have fitness centers. Many commercial gyms and health clubs are open only to members, but an increasing number of gyms now offer day passes. Check out the **Chelsea Piers Sports & Entertainment Complex** on Piers 59–62 near Hudson River; there's something for everyone at this enormous facility. It's one-stop shopping at the multilevel **May Center for Health, Fitness, and Sport at the 92nd Street Y**, with exercise studios, weight-training, racquetball courts, a boxing room, and an indoor track. Day passes start at around $35. With its well-maintained gym along with an array of personal diet and exercise programs, the **Casa Spa & Fitness at the Regency Hotel** on Park Avenue lives up to its promise to be "your health and fitness oasis when you're away from home".

You can enjoy a wide range of activities at **YMCA** (one in West Side and the other on 47th Street) fitness centers. The state-of-the-art training equipment, a number of gymnasiums, swimming pools, aerobics studios, running/walking tracks, and various courts for different games, add to your enthusiasm of working out. The center also has special programs for elderly people designed to suit their physical stature for a healthy life.

GOLF

Practice your swing at **Randalls Island Golf Center** on Randalls Island, **Chelsea Golf Club**, or play mini-golf at the **Wollman Memorial Rink** in Central Park. The city owns several courses in the boroughs, such as **Pelham Bay Park** in the Bronx and **Silver Lake** on Staten Island.

JOGGING

Some parks are safe for joggers, others are not, so be guided by your concierge. None is safe after dark, at dusk or before dawn. The most popular and beautiful route is around the reservoir in Central Park. The **NY Road Runners** on 89th Street have weekly running clinics and races, as does **Chelsea Piers Sports & Entertainment Complex**.

PILATES

All you have to lose are your love handles. Work your abs and torso for lean, toned muscles at a Pilates class. The philosophy behind Pilates is based on the premise that the body's core is the "powerhouse" for the peripheral parts of the body. Challenge your muscles at a **Grasshopper Pilates** class, which is taught by a professionally trained dancer in a TriBeCa loft. **Power Pilates** also hold strengthening classes throughout the city.

YOGA

It's easier to get in touch your spiritual center when you can do it in a place like the airy **Exhale Mind Body Spa** on Madison Avenue, with its high ceilings and hard-wood floors. "Journey into the Core", "Ride the Vinyasa Wave", and "Dance into Trance" at a variety of yoga sessions, the ideal antidote to the city's madness. And, lest you should think yoga isn't enough of a workout, then you haven't tried the core fusion power pack abs session. **YogaMoves** on Sixth Avenue also offers a wide range of yoga classes, from beginner to advanced.

SPAS

Pamper yourself at one of New York City's choice spas and you'll emerge fresh as a daisy – and ready to take on the urban jungle once again. Most spas offer packages where you can enjoy several treatments at a lower price. If you're travelling with your significant other, bond over a couples' massage. The intoxicating wafts of incense that greet you at the front door of the fragrant, low-lit **Clay** are just a hint of the luxurious massage that awaits within.

At the comfy, casual **Oasis Day Spa** at Union Square, select from six aromatherapy massages ($100) in aromas of uplift, refresh, balance, passion, calm, or relief. Men's specials include a Dead Sea salt scrub, an algae facial, or a muscle meltdown massage ($100 for an hour). For a slice of heaven, Bali style, disappear into the **Acqua Beauty Bar** on 14th Street and enjoy a botanical purifying facial ($115), orchid pedicure ($45), or Indonesian ritual of beauty ($170), where your skin is scrubbed with ground rice and kneaded with fragrant oils. Enter **Bliss** on 57th Street and you'll soon discover that there's nothing a carrot and sesame body buff ($195) or fully loaded facial ($195) can't cure. Top it off with a decadent double chocolate pedicure, accompanied by a cup of creamy cocoa. Pure bliss.

Celebrities including Antonio Banderas and Kate Moss swear by **Mario Badescu** on 52nd Street whose facials and body scrubs, including the fresh fruit body scrub, with plump raspberries and strawberries, are as legendary as the beauty products, which are perfect to bring home as gifts.

SWIMMING

Many Manhattan hotels have pools with free access during your stay. It is also possible to purchase a day pass to use a hotel swimming pool and facilities – for example, at Le Parker Meridien *(see p286)*. You can also swim and surf at the Surfside 3 Maritime Center at **Chelsea Piers**. For a day trip, go to Jones Beach State Park *(see p255)* along Long Island's shoreline.

INDOOR SPORTS

Chelsea Piers has it all: roller rinks, bowling, indoor soccer, basketball, rock-climbing walls, fitness centers, golf, a field house for gymnastics, sports medicine, spa centers, and of course, swimming pools. This huge complex, which is spread over four old West Side piers, is open to everyone.

Apart from providing fitness centers, gymnasium facilities, and indoor sports activities **YMCA** also offers exercise, balance, and flexibility classes; organizes day trips; special events; and sports and volunteer opportunities. If you are planning an adventurous day out for your children with fitness on the agenda or for burning extra calories then the club is worth a visit.

DIRECTORY

Acqua Beauty Bar
7 E 14th St. **Map** 8 F5.
Tel (212) 620-4329.

Bicycle Habitat
244 Lafayette St.
Map 4 F3.
Tel (212) 431-3315.

Bliss
19 E 57th St.
Map 12 F3.
Tel (212) 219-8970.
(Also has a SoHo location).

Casa Spa & Fitness at the Regency Hotel
540 Park Ave.
Map 13 A3.
Tel (212) 223-9280.

Central Park Bike Rental
2 Columbus Circle.
Map 12 D3.
Tel (212) 541-8759.

Chelsea Piers Sports & Entertainment Complex
Piers 59–62 at 23rd St & 11th Ave (Hudson River).
Map 7 B4–5.
Tel (212) 336-6000.
www.chelseapiers.com

Clay
25 W 14th St.
Map 4 D1.
Tel (212) 206-9200.

Exhale Mind Body Spa
980 Madison Ave.
Map 17 A5.
Tel (212) 561-6400.

Grasshopper Pilates
116 Franklin St.
Map 4 E5.
Tel (212) 431-5225.

NY Road Runners
9 E 89th St.
Map 17 A3.
Tel (212) 860-4455.

Mario Badescu
320 E 52nd St.
Map 13 B4.
Tel (212) 758-1065.

May Center for Health, Fitness, and Sport at the 92nd Street Y
1395 Lexington Ave.
Map 17 A2.
Tel (212) 415-5729.

Oasis Day Spa
108 E 16th St.
Map 9 A5.
Tel (212) 254-7722.
One of several branches.

Pelham Bay Park
The Bronx,
870 Shore Rd.
Tel (718) 885-1461.

Power Pilates
49 W 23rd St,
10th floor.
Map 8 F4.
Tel (212) 627-5852.

Randalls Island Golf Center
Randalls Island.
Map 22 F2.
Tel (212) 427-5689.

YMCA West Side
1395 Lexington Ave.
Map 17 A2.
Tel (212) 415-5500.

Silver Lake
915 Victory Blvd.
Staten Island.
Tel (718) 447-5686.

Wollman Memorial Rink
Central Park, 5th Ave at 59th St. **Map** 12 F2.
Tel (212) 439-6900.

YMCA 47th St
224 E 47th St.
Map 13 B5.
Tel (212) 756-9600.

YogaMoves
1026 6th Ave.
Map 8 E1.
Tel (212) 278-8330.

CHILDREN'S NEW YORK

Young visitors soon catch the contagious excitement in the air in New York. Attractions for all ages abound, and plenty are designed especially for children. More than a dozen theater companies, two zoos, and plenty of imaginative museums are for just the young, backed up with special events at many museums and parks. The chance to visit a TV studio is a treat, and New York's own Big Apple Circus is a perennial delight. With more to do than can ever be squeezed into a single visit, you'll never hear the cry "I'm bored!" Best of all, there's no need to spend a fortune to have fun.

A young visitor making New York his very own playground

PRACTICAL ADVICE

New York is family-friendly. Many of its hotels allow children in parents' rooms free, and will supply cots or cribs if needed. Most museums charge half price or less for children, while others are free. Children under 112 cm (44 in) also ride free on subways and buses when accompanied by an adult. Travel between 9am and 4pm to avoid rush hours.

Supplies such as diapers and medicines are readily available, and the Rite Aid Pharmacy *(see p373)* is open 24 hours a day. Finding changing tables in public toilets is less easy, but no one objects if a counter is used. Best bets are the facilities in libraries, hotels, and department stores. Most hotels will arrange baby-sitters; try **Baby Sitters' Guild** or **Pinch Sitters**.

To find out more about the range of current activities for children, get a copy of the free

quarterly calendar of events, available from the New York Convention and Visitors Bureau *(see p368)*. Weekly listings can be found in *New York* magazine or *Time Out New York*.

NEW YORK ADVENTURES

The city can seem like a giant amusement park for youngsters. Elevators whisk you sky-high for bird's-eye views from atop the world's highest buildings. You can set sail on the classic **Circle Line** tour around Manhattan; the sailboat **Pioneer** *(see p84)*, or charter your own paddle-wheeler from the marina at E. 23rd St; or the free round-trip on the Staten Island Ferry *(see p76)*. The Roosevelt Island Tram *(see p181)* is a Swiss cable car offering an airborne ride over the East River. Central Park *(see pp204–9)* is a source of rides of every kind – from the old-fashioned charm of the carousel to real horseback and ponycart rides. Children who prefer a faster

Skating with Santa at Rockefeller Center

pace can join the skate-boarders and in-line skaters who cruise around the traffic-free park every weekend.

Cooling off in a playground in Central Park

MUSEUMS

While many of New York's museums appeal to all ages, some are designed just for the young. High on the list are the Children's Museum of Art *(see p107)*, where kids can paint and sculpt, and the Children's Museum of Manhattan *(see p219)*, a multimedia world in which children produce their own videos and newscasts. Farther afield are the **Staten Island Children's Museum**, where a huge climb-through anthill is one of the favorite items, and the Brooklyn Children's Museum *(see p247)*. The *Intrepid* Sea-Air-Space Museum *(see p149)* is a real aircraft carrier. Finally, don't miss the dinosaur display at the American Museum of Natural History *(see pp216–17)*.

OUTDOOR FUN

In summer, all of New York comes out to play. Central Park is a child's wonderland, from skating rinks to boating lakes, bicycle paths to miniature golf. The park offers free entertainment – such as guided walks by park rangers on Saturdays, toy sailboat races and summer storytelling. The Central Park Wildlife Center and the Tisch Children's Zoo are favorites.

Children of all ages will be fascinated by the Bronx Zoo/ Wildlife Conservation Park which is home to over 500 species (see pp244–5).

Coney Island (see p249) is just a subway ride away. Winter brings the chance to skate at Rockefeller Center (see p144) or in Central Park on a rink fringed with views of skyscrapers.

INDOOR FUN

New York children's theater is of a quality and variety matching that for adults. Some favorite companies are the **Paper Bag Players** and **Theaterworks USA**, whose shows sell out fast; get schedules and reserve seats early.

The **Swedish Marionette Theater** in Central Park has shows at 10:30am and noon Tuesdays through Fridays, and Saturdays until 1pm.

The New York City Ballet's annual Christmas production of *The Nutcracker* at Lincoln Center (see p212) opens at the same time that the **Big Apple Circus** sets up its tent nearby. Ringling Brothers and Barnum & Bailey Circus is in action at Madison Square Garden (see p135) each spring.

Opportunities for youngsters to work off energy in winter are many, from indoor skating rinks to mini-golf and bowling alleys at **Chelsea Piers**. Kids can create video games, movies, and music for free at **Sony Wonder Technology Lab**.

Centerpiece clock at toy store F.A.O. Schwarz

SHOPPING

There will be no complaints about shopping trips if they include the huge **F.A.O. Schwarz** or **Toys 'R' Us** for a vast range of wonderful toys and other items. For more information on other toystores see New York Originals on pages 322–4. Youngsters are welcomed for storytelling sessions at **Books of Wonder**.

EATING OUT

Hamburger-and-pasta joint **Ottomanelli's Café** is very popular with children, and even adults find it hard to finish their huge burgers. The colorful **S'Mac**, where the specialty is creamy macaroni and cheese, is also a hit with youngsters. The lively **Hard Rock Café** is also popular, and most children enjoy the foods sold around Chinatown and Little Italy. Drop into the **Chinatown Ice Cream Factory** for some strange and wonderful flavors. For a quick hot snack, try pizza-by-the-slice or pretzels and hot dogs from street vendors.

DIRECTORY

PRACTICAL ADVICE

Baby Sitters' Guild
Tel (212) 682-0227.

Pinch Sitters
Tel (212) 260-6005.

ADVENTURES

Circle Line
Pier 83, W 42nd St. **Map** 7 A1.
Tel (212) 563-3200.

MUSEUMS

Staten Island Children's Museum
1000 Richmond Terr, Staten Is.
Tel (718) 273-2060.

INDOOR FUN

Big Apple Circus
Tel (212) 268-2500.

Chelsea Piers
Tel (212) 336-6800.
www.chelseapiers.com

Paper Bag Players
Tel (212) 663-0390.

Sony Wonder Technology Lab
550 Madison Ave. **Map** 13 A3.
Tel (212) 833-8100.

Swedish Cottage Marionette Theater
Tel (212) 988-9093.

Theaterworks USA
787 7th Ave. **Map** 12 E4.
Tel (212) 627-7373.

SHOPPING

Books of Wonder
16 W 18th St. **Map** 8 C5.
Tel (212) 989-3270.

F.A.O. Schwarz
767 5th Ave. **Map** 12 F3.
Tel (212) 644-9400.

Toys 'R' Us
See p324.

EATING OUT

Chinatown Ice Cream Factory
65 Bayard St. **Map** 4 F5.
Tel (212) 608-4170.

Hard Rock Café
1501 Broadway. **Map** 8 E1.
Tel (212) 343-3355.

Ottomanelli's Café
1626 York Ave. **Map** 17 C3.
Tel (212) 772-7722.

S'Mac
345 E 12th St. **Map** 5 A1.
Tel (212) 358-7912.

Storytelling session at South Street Seaport

SURVIVAL GUIDE

PRACTICAL INFORMATION

New York is one of the most diverse and exciting cities in the world. The fast pace of Manhattan may seem daunting at first, but there are many services to help tourists, and you will find the city is safe and easy to explore. Midtown streets are straight and mostly laid out in an easy-to-follow grid pattern. Buses and subway trains *(see pp388–91)* are reliable and cheap; there are plenty of cash machines *(see p374)*, and money can be easily exchanged at banks and hotels. The wide range of prices offered by the many hotels *(see pp280–91)*, restaurants *(see pp296–311)*, and entertainment venues *(see pp340–65)* in the city means that your New York trip can be both fun and affordable.

NYC & Company
nycgo.com

New York City tourist office logo

Skaters at an ice rink in Central Park

WHEN TO GO

September and October are the prize months in New York, offering warm days, cool nights, and colorful leaves in the city parks. Late spring is also appealing, when the city is less crowded and humid. Summers can be unpleasantly hot, but there are attractions such as outdoor concerts, plays, and sporting events to keep visitors busy. Christmas in the city is wonderful, although you will have to share your experience with thousands of other tourists. Weather-wise, any season can be unpredictable; always pack layers, and be prepared for changes.

VISAS AND PASSPORTS

All visitors to the United States require passports valid for at least six months after the dates of travel. Citizens of Great Britain, Australia, New Zealand, and 32 other countries, including most EU countries, do not need visas if they are staying in the US for 90 days or less. However, they must apply and pay for entry online via the Electronic System for Travel Authorization (ESTA). The ESTA is valid for up to two years and can be used for multiple entries into the US (https://esta.cbp.dhs.gov/).

Canadians must show their passports when entering the US by air, and a passport or an enhanced driver's license proving citizenship when arriving by land or sea.

Those requiring a visa should apply in person at the nearest US embassy or consulate in their own country. It is vital to begin the process early, allowing sufficient time for processing the application. Some services will expedite the process for a fee. Visit http://travel.state.gov for more details.

CUSTOMS INFORMATION

Customs allowances per person when you enter the US are 200 cigarettes, 100 cigars, or 4.4 lb (2 kg) of tobacco; no more than 2 pints (1 liter) of alcohol; and gifts worth no more than $100. Many foods, including fruits and vegetables, are prohibited from entering the United States. Baked items, candy, chocolate, and cured cheese are exceptions, as are canned goods (other than those containing meat or poultry products) if being imported for personal use.

Upon arrival at one of New York's airports, follow signs stating "other than American passports" to immigration counters, where your passport will be stamped. Next, reclaim your bags from the appropriate area and proceed to a customs officer, who will examine the customs declaration that you should have received and filled in on your flight.

TOURIST INFORMATION

Advice on any aspect of life in New York City is available from the New York Convention & Visitors Bureau, known as **NYC & Co.** Its 24-hour touch-tone phone service *(see p371)* offers help

New York tourist information office

outside office hours. New York City has another free phone and Internet service, **311**, which provides government information and non-emergency general assistance. Calls are answered by a team 24 hours a day, with a translation service.

SMOKING AND ETIQUETTE

It is illegal to smoke in any public place or building in New York, including restaurants, and this law is taken very seriously.

When boarding buses, New Yorkers generally form a line rather than pushing to enter. Subway boarders are not so polite at rush hours, but do stand aside to let passengers exit before rushing in. Turning off cell phones in theaters, cinemas, and museums is expected. Casual wear is accepted in many places in New York City, but some establishments may require formal dress; check when you make a reservation.

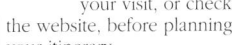

The New York Pass and CityPASS

ADMISSION PRICES

New York can be expensive for visitors, though you may often find a way to avoid high charges. Museum prices can run from $12 to $20, but some galleries, such as the Metropolitan Museum, call their charge a "suggested donation," leaving it to the visitor to decide what to pay. On Friday evenings (Saturdays for the Guggenheim), the Museum of Modern Art, Whitney Museum, and Folk Art Museum are open late and are free or have a "pay what you wish" policy. The Jewish Museum is free all day Saturday, while the Brooklyn Museum offers free art and entertainment on the first Saturday of the month (5–11pm). Consult local listings for museums of interest to you. The **New York Pass** and **CityPASS** *(see p370)*, offer discounted entry to some 50 attractions.

OPENING HOURS

Business hours are generally from 9am to 5pm, with no lunchtime closing. Many midtown stores stay open until 7pm to accommodate people in full-time jobs, and they may close even later on Thursdays, at 8:30 or 9pm. Most stores are also open from noon to 6pm on Sundays.

Typical banking hours run from 9am to 6pm, Monday to Friday; some banks also open on Saturdays from 9am to 3pm. ATM machines are available 24 hours for credit and debit card cash withdrawals *(see p374)*.

Closing days vary for the major museums, as do the evenings they are open late, although most tend to be closed on a Monday. The Museum of Modern Art is closed on Tuesdays, however, while the Guggenheim closes on Thursdays. Phone ahead of your visit, or check the website, before planning your itinerary.

New York's traffic rush hours extend roughly from 8 to 10am and 4:30 to 6:30pm, Monday to Friday. During these times, every form of public transportation will be crowded, as will pedestrian streets.

PUBLIC CONVENIENCES

New York City does not provide public bathrooms. Free restrooms can be found at city information centers,

The entrance to the Guggenheim Museum *(see pp188–9)*

department stores, large bookstores (such as Barnes & Noble), and big restaurant chains (Starbucks, McDonald's), as well as at hotels. Bathrooms are also available in train and bus stations, but these are not always the most pleasant options.

TAXES AND TIPPING

Sales tax in New York is 8.875%, and it is added to all purchases (including meals), except for clothing under $100. Tipping is an integral part of New York life: taxi drivers expect 10–15%; cocktail waiters 15%, hotel room service 10% (when not added to the bill); coat check $1; hotel maids $1 or $2 per day after the first day; hotel bellhops about $1 per bag; hairstylists 15–20%, and barbers 10–20%. Waiters generally receive 15–20% of the bill, not including tax. A quick way to calculate restaurant tips is simply to double the tax, adding up to about 18%.

Many stores have late opening hours to accommodate workers

City bus with access ramp lowered for a disabled passenger

TRAVELERS WITH SPECIAL NEEDS

All city buses have ramps for easy access. Subways, however, are a challenge for the disabled, as most stations are accessed via steps from the street. Only the busiest stops and stations, such as Grand Central and Penn stations and the Port Authority Bus Terminal, have elevators. A list of accessible stations is available on the Metropolitan Transit Authority website (www.mta.info).

Most hotels, restaurants, and attractions are equipped for disabled visitors, but do check in advance. It is also wise to ask about accessibility to the restrooms.

Some museums offer tours for deaf, blind, or disabled visitors, and all Broadway theaters have devices for the hearing-impaired. The *Official Accessibility Guide*, available free from the **Mayor's Office for People with Disabilities**, is a great resource, as is *Access for All*, published by **Hospital Audiences**. Both detail disabled access at public places such as museums, landmarks, theaters, and stadiums.

SENIOR TRAVELERS

Seniors are welcomed in New York, and they are eligible for many offers. They travel half-fare on all subways and buses and get discounted prices at museums, movie theaters, and many sightseeing attractions. City buses can lower the entry steps to make it easier for older passengers to board.

GAY AND LESBIAN TRAVELERS

New York has a large gay and lesbian population. Gay Pride Week in June brings celebrants from around the world for parties and a big parade, and the annual Halloween parade in Greenwich Village also has a large gay following. The **Lesbian, Gay, Bisexual & Transgender Community Center** is a good first stop for general information. Christopher Street in Greenwich Village is the birthplace of New York's gay scene. Eighth Avenue around Chelsea is the epicenter of activity today, with Hell's Kitchen becoming increasingly popular; Park Slope in Brooklyn is a hotspot for the lesbian community. **Next** (www.next magazine.com) is a free weekly publication that can be found in these areas. The monthly **GO Magazine** (www.gomag.com) covers the lesbian scene, and *Time Out New York (see p377)* and the *New York* magazine website (www.nymag.com) have gay and lesbian listings.

Sign for the Lesbian, Gay, Bisexual & Transgender Community Center

STUDENT TRAVELERS

Many museums and theaters in New York offer discounted admission for students. To receive this, however, you will need to show proof of your student status. An **International Student Identity Card (ISIC)** can be purchased quite cheaply, provided you have the right credentials, from **STA Travel**, which has two branches in New York. At the same time, ask for a copy of the *ISIC Student Handbook*, which lists places and services that offer discounts to cardholders, including selected accommodations, various museums, tours, theaters,

attractions, nightclubs, and restaurants.

Although it is very difficult to obtain permission to work in the US, students are eligible to work as part of exchange programs or as interns. Again, STA Travel can provide you with further details.

Note that the minimum age for drinking in New York is 21, and patrons may be asked for proof of age.

International Student Identity Card

TRAVELING ON A BUDGET

There are many ways to take advantage of the best of New York while on a budget. The TKTS booth *(see p341)*, near Times Square, offers half-price admission to same-day Broadway shows, while pre-theater prix-fixe meals save on dining. The David Rubenstein Atrium, across from Lincoln Center *(see p214)*, offers discount tickets for same-day performances, in addition to a free concert in the Atrium itself on Thursdays at 8:30pm. The New York Philharmonic invites visitors to rehearsals for just $16, and the Juilliard School *(see p214)* also presents free concerts. In summer, free Shakespeare plays and music by the Philharmonic and the Metropolitan Opera are performed in Central Park. Many TV shows produced in the city are free to watch live if you request tickets in advance. The **New York Pass**, while not cheap, is good value for those who plan to do a lot of sightseeing. It offers free entry to over 50 attractions, from museums to the Empire State Building and river cruises. The **New York CityPASS** gives holders admission to six must-see sights in the city.

TIME

New York is on Eastern Standard Time from early November to mid-March.

Eastern Daylight Time moves the American clock forward 1 hour the rest of the year.

Add 5 hours for the time in London, 8 hours for Moscow, 14 hours for Tokyo, and 16 hours for Sydney.

ELECTRICAL APPLIANCES

All American electric current flows at a standardized 110 to 120 volts AC (alternating current). You will need to bring an adapter plug and a voltage convertor that fits standard US electrical outlets. US plugs have two flat prongs.

Most New York hotels provide wall-mounted electric hair dryers in bathrooms. In addition, some hotels have wall plugs capable of powering both 110- and 220-volt electric shavers, but little else – not even radios. It can, in fact, be dangerous to connect anything more powerful.

Some New York hotel rooms provide coffee-makers; however, most have radios and clocks, and a large number have iPod docking stations. If you require an iron and ironing board, but they are not in the room, ask room service.

CONVERSION CHART

Bear in mind that 1 US pint (0.5 liter) is a smaller measure than 1 UK pint (0.6 liter).

Imperial to Metric
1 inch = 2.5 centimeters
1 foot = 30 centimeters
1 mile = 1.6 kilometers
1 ounce = 28 grams
1 pound = 454 grams
1 US pint = 0.47 liter
1 US gallon = 3.8 liters

Metric to Imperial
1 millimeter = 0.04 inch
1 centimeter = 0.4 inch
1 meter = 3 feet 3 inches
1 kilometer = 0.6 mile
1 gram = 0.04 ounce

RESPONSIBLE TOURISM

New York is increasingly aware of "green issues." Proper recycling bins, with separate areas for paper and plastic, are widely available. Most hotels encourage guests to be ecologically aware and not request fresh towels every day. Shoppers tend to carry reusable cloth shopping bags, which are sold in almost every department store and

Fresh local produce for sale at one of New York's Greenmarkets

supermarket. Most markets carry organic foods, and the city's many neighborhood Greenmarkets are popular sources of locally grown produce. The **Greenmarket at Union Square** (Mon, Wed, Fri, and Sat) is one of the best. Opening times vary.

You can contribute to these green efforts by patronizing restaurants that use locally grown produce. **5 Points** and **Gramercy Tavern** are two popular restaurants that have been given the **Slow Food NYC** seal of approval.

DIRECTORY

EMBASSIES AND CONSULATES

Australia
150 E 42nd St. **Map** 9 A1.
Tel (212) 351-6500.
www.australianyc.org

Britain
845 Third Ave. **Map** 13 B4.
Tel (212) 745-0200.
www.britainusa.com/ny

Canada
1251 Sixth Ave at 50th St.
Map 12 E4.
Tel (212) 596-1628.
www.canada-ny.org

Ireland
345 Park Ave. **Map** 13 A4.
Tel (212) 319-2555.
www.consulateofireland
newyork.org

New Zealand
37 Observatory Circle, NW,
Washington, DC, 20008.
Tel (202) 328-4800.
www.nzembassy.org

TOURIST INFORMATION

311
Tel 311. **www**.nyc.gov/311

NYC & Co.
810 Seventh Ave. **Map** 12
E4. *Tel* (212) 484-1222.
www.nycgo.com

New York CityPASS
www.citypass.com/city/ny

New York Pass
www.newyorkpass.com

Times Square Information Center
1560 Broadway.
Map 12 E5.
www.timessquarenyc.org

TRAVELERS WITH SPECIAL NEEDS

Hospital Audiences
Tel (212) 575-7676.
www.hospital
audiences.org

Mayor's Office for People with Disabilities
Tel (212) 788-2830.
www.nyc.gov/mopd

GAY AND LESBIAN TRAVELERS

Lesbian, Gay, Bisexual & Transgender Community Center
208 West 13th St. **Map** 3
C1. *Tel* (212) 620-7310.
www.gaycenter.org

STUDENT TRAVELERS

International Student Identity Card (ISIC)
www.isic.org

STA Travel
30 Third Avenue.
Map 4 F1.
Tel (212) 473-6100.

Also at: 2871 Broadway.
Map 20 E4.
Tel (212) 865-2700.
www.statravel.com

BUDGET TRAVEL
www.nycgo.com/free
www.nyc.gov/nyculture

RESPONSIBLE TOURISM

5 Points
31 Great Jones St. **Map** 4
F2. *Tel* (212) 253-5700.
www.fivepoints
restaurant.com

Gramercy Tavern
42 East 20th St. **Map** 9 A5.
Tel (212) 477-6777.
www.gramercytaven.com

Greenmarket at Union Square
Union Square. **Map** 9 A5.
www.cenyc.org

Slow Food NYC
www.slowfoodnyc.org

Personal Security and Health

Police badge

New York is one of the US's safest large cities. There is a good level of security in midtown, the transportation system, and at airports, and the city's police force is very much in evidence around Manhattan. As in any major metropolis, there are places where travelers would be foolish to venture after dark alone, such as city parks and quiet streets. But if you keep your wits about you and stick to the following guidelines, you should enjoy a trouble-free and pleasant visit to New York City.

New York City police officers patrolling the streets

POLICE

The New York Police Department has around-the-clock foot, horse, bike, and car patrols. These are concentrated in specific areas at critical times – for instance, the Theater District after show times. There is also a police presence on the subways and buses, and this is reflected in the dramatic drop in crime statistics.

LOST AND STOLEN PROPERTY

There is no city-wide lost-and-found service, but the Metropolitan Transit Authority (MTA) *(see p391)* has a lost-and-found department for city buses and subways, and the Taxi Commission *(see p387)* will help passengers who have left their belongings in a cab. The lost-and-found rooms at Grand Central and Penn stations are well run, with helpful staff. If you don't

know who to contact, phone 311 for guidance.

In the event of loss or theft of valuables, report all missing items to the police, or **Crime Victims Hot Line** and make sure you get a copy of the police report for your insurance claim. It is wise to keep the receipts of expensive items as proof of possession.

If your passport is stolen, report the theft immediately to your consulate *(see p371)*. Lost or stolen credit cards should also be reported promptly so that your account can be blocked. American Express *(see p375)* has offices in the city where new cards can be processed quickly, and other card companies can often provide replacements. It is always a good idea to separate your credit and debit cards so that if a wallet is lost, you have a backup card.

WHAT TO BE AWARE OF

Manhattan has become quite a safe place to roam, but pickpockets do operate and common sense still rules, as

in any big city. Be alert, and walk as if you know where you're going. Avoid eye contact and confrontations with down-and-outs. If someone asks you for money, be careful and do not be drawn into conversation.

It is better to avoid deserted locations late at night. Even if there is no actual danger, empty streets may make you feel uneasy. Neighborhoods such as parts of the Lower East Side, Chinatown, or midtown west of Broadway bustle through dinner hours but feel empty after 10pm or so. The Financial District is deserted after business hours, and even the very trendy TriBeCa and SoHo areas are empty late at night. Subways stay crowded until around 11pm, but many may not be advisable later. If you can't find or afford a taxi, try to travel with a group and keep to the main streets.

Parks are not recommended after dark, unless there is a concert or other event. If you want to go for a jog, ask your hotel concierge for a map of safe routes. In crowds, take precautions to avoid being pickpocketed.

When walking in the street, keep your wallet in an inconspicuous place, never in a back pocket, and have your MetroCard or change handy for bus fares – it's best not to have to dig into your purse or wallet while standing in line. Never stop to count your money on the street, and be aware of strangers watching

It is best to travel in groups and stick to the main streets and avenues

Police car

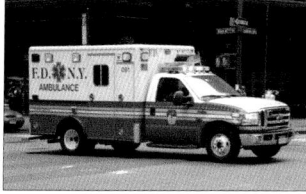
Ambulance

Fire engine

at bank ATMs. Defeat purse snatchers by carrying your bag with the clasp facing toward you and the shoulder strap across your body.

Wise travelers always leave valuable jewelry at home or stored at the hotel. Do not allow anyone except hotel and airport personnel to carry your luggage or parcels, and stow your valuables and camera in a locked suitcase or a closet safe when you leave your hotel room.

IN AN EMERGENCY

If you should be involved in a medical emergency, proceed at once to a hospital emergency room. Dial **411**, and ask the operator to give you the number of the nearest hospital. Should you need an ambulance, telephone **911**, and one will be sent. If you have time and a choice, avoid the crowded city-owned hospitals listed in the Blue Pages telephone book. Instead, choose one of the many private hospitals listed in the Yellow Pages (*see also Directory box*).

If your travel medical insurance is in order, you won't have to worry about costs, but remember that national insurance in other countries is not valid in the US.

If the situation is not urgent, ask your hotel to call a doctor or dentist to visit you in your room or to recommend one. You can find one yourself through the **NY Hotel Urgent Medical Services** or **NYU Dental Care**. The Beth Israel Medical Center has an excellent walk-in clinic, **DOCS**. For more general advice and information, call **Travelers' Aid**, a national organization geared to helping travelers. Note that the cost of prescriptions may be higher than in your home country.

HOSPITALS AND PHARMACIES

If you must visit a doctor or hospital, be prepared to undergo an expensive experience: some of the city's practitioners and facilities are among the best in the country, and they charge accordingly. The best way to protect yourself against large medical costs is with comprehensive travel insurance. Note that you will have to pay and then reclaim the money. Hospitals accept most credit cards, but physicians and dentists are more likely to want payment in cash. The city has many 24-hour pharmacies, some will often fill a prescription while you wait.

A 24-hour pharmacy, one of several in the city

TRAVEL INSURANCE

Travel insurance is highly recommended, mainly because of the high cost of medical care. There are many types and levels of coverage, with prices dependent on the length of your trip and the number of people covered.

Among the most important features are emergency medical and dental care, trip cancellation, baggage and travel-document loss, and accidental dismemberment or death. Many policies will cover all of these items.

DIRECTORY

POLICE

All Emergency Services
Tel 911 (or 0).

Crime Victims Hot Line
Tel (212) 577-7777.

IN AN EMERGENCY

DOCS
55 E 34th St. **Map** 8 F2.
Tel (212) 252-6000.
One of three branches.

NY Hotel Urgent Medical Services
Tel (212) 737-1212.

NYU Dental Care
345 E 24th St/First Ave.
Map 9 B4. *Tel (212) 998-9800,*
(212) 998-9828 (weekends and after 9pm).

Travelers' Aid
JFK Airport, Terminal 410.
Tel (718) 656-4870.

HOSPITALS AND PHARMACIES

Duane Reade
4 Times Square, near Broadway.
Map 8 E1. *Tel (646) 366-8047.*

Midtown Hospital Emergency Rooms
11th St and Seventh Ave.
Map 3 C1. *Tel (212) 604-7998.*

NYU Medical Center
560 First Avenue at 33rd Street.
Map 9 C3. *Tel (212) 263-5550.*

Rite Aid
50th St/Eighth Ave. **Map** 12 D4.
Tel (212) 247-8384.

St. Luke's Roosevelt
58th St and Ninth Ave. **Map** 12 D3.
Tel (212) 523-6800.

Banks and Currency

New York is the nation's banking center. It has a wealth of local, regional, and major national banks, plus some retail branches of the leading foreign banks. HSBC and Barclays are well represented in the city; the banks of Australia, Canada, Ireland, Scotland, Japan, and Turkey also all have offices or branches. Exchange bureaux are located in airports, the major train stations, and in various locations throughout the city, though you will probably get a better rate of exchange from a bank.

American Express charge cards

BANKING

New York banks are generally open weekdays from 9am to 6pm. Several banks open earlier or close later in the evening to suit commuters' needs, and many now stay open on Saturday 9am–3pm. Tellers are available to help customers inside the bank, or you can use a cash withdrawal machine (ATM). At most banks, all the tellers will cash traveler's checks and exchange your currency.

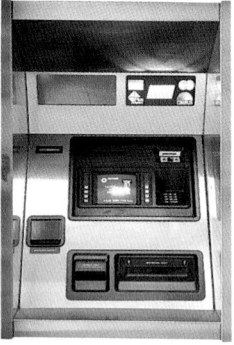

ATM (machine) for cash withdrawal

ATMS

Automated teller machines (ATMs) can be found in most bank lobbies. They enable you to obtain American currency 24 hours a day from your bank account using a debit card. ATMs usually issue American banknotes in $20 denominations. Among the many advantages of ATMs is the swift, secure exchange of your money at the whole-sale rate used between the banks. Bank fees are generally much lower than those charged by money-exchange offices. Before you leave for New York, ask your

bank which New York City banks and ATM systems will accept your bank card and what fees and commissions will be charged on each transaction. Most ATMs are part of either the Cirrus or the Plus network. They accept various US bank cards, MasterCard and Visa cards, and certain others.

On a more cautionary note, always be aware of your surroundings when using an ATM. Make sure you shield your PIN, and, if available, use a machine located within the bank. Be careful when removing your card at the machine.

CREDIT CARDS AND TRAVELER'S CHECKS

MasterCard, **American Express**, **Visa**, and **Diners Club** cards are widely accepted throughout the United States, regardless of which company or bank issued them. These cards can also be used for purchases, as well as to obtain cash advances from ATMs. Before you travel, it is a good idea to phone your card provider and inform them that you will be abroad, or you may find that your card gets blocked when you start using it in New York. Charges may be higher when using a credit card – check with your bank before you leave.

In the United States, you can use a credit card to pay for most purchases in store and online. Major expenses such as tours, travel packages, and expensive rentals are all best paid for by credit card. Using a card also means that you can avoid carrying large sums of money around with you.

Traveler's checks issued in dollars by American Express and **Thomas Cook** are widely accepted without a fee by most department stores, shops, hotels, and restaurants in New York. Traveler's checks in other currencies, including sterling, are not universally accepted. Major hotels may have cashiers that will exchange traveler's checks, but more often than not you will need to visit a bank. Exchange rates for foreign currency are printed daily in *The New York Times* and *Wall Street Journal* and may be posted in bank windows. American Express checks may also be exchanged without a fee at American Express offices.

Among the most well-established foreign-exchange brokers are **Travelex Currency Services Inc.** and American Express. All brokers are listed in the Yellow Pages under "Foreign Money Brokers." When you use the services of a foreign-exchange broker, you will have to pay a fee, which will vary widely from one place to the next. There will also be a commission.

Banking company **Chase** has over 400 locations where you can exchange money, and there are scores of hole-in-the-wall check-cashing shops in Manhattan. **TD Bank** also has branches throughout Manhattan, many of which are open on Saturdays and until 8pm on weekdays. Both Chase and TD Bank are listed in the Yellow Pages.

WIRING MONEY

In emergencies, you can arrange to have money wired to you through **MoneyGram** or **Western Union**, though there is a considerable fee.

Coins

American coins come in 1-, 5-, 10-, 25- and 50-cent pieces. A gold-tone $1 coin is also in circulation, as are the State quarters, which feature a historical scene on one side. One-dollar coins are not popular, however, and you will receive them mainly as change from vending machines. Each value of coin has a popular name: 25-cent pieces are called quarters, 10-cent pieces are called dimes, 5-cent pieces are called nickels, and 1-cent pieces are called pennies.

| 1-cent coin (a penny) | 5-cent coin (a nickel) | 10-cent coin (a dime) | 25-cent coin (a quarter) |

Bank Notes (Bills)

The units of currency in the United States are dollars and cents. There are 100 cents to a dollar. Bank notes come in the following denominations: $1, $5, $10, $20, $50, and $100. Security features include subtle color hues and improved color-shifting ink in the lower right hand corner of the face of each note.

1-dollar bill ($1)

5-dollar bill ($5)

10-dollar bill ($10)

20-dollar bill ($20)

50-dollar bill ($50)

100-dollar bill ($100)

DIRECTORY

CREDIT CARDS AND TRAVELER'S CHECKS

American Express
Tel (212) 758-6510.
www.americanexpress.com

Chase
www.chase.com

Diners Club
www.dinersclubus.com

MasterCard
Tel (800) 424-7787 (ATM locator).
www.mastercard.com

TD Bank
www.tdbank.com

Thomas Cook
www.thomascook.com/money

Travelex Currency Services Inc.
Tel (212) 265-6063.
www.travelex.com

Visa
Tel (800) 843-7587.
www.visa.com

WIRING MONEY

MoneyGram
www.moneygram.com

Western Union
www.westernunion.com

Communications and Media

Sign for public payphones

The wide use of cellular telephones and the Internet has changed the communications picture in most of the world, and New York is no exception. Though some public telephones may still be found in hotel lobbies, they have disappeared from city streets. Visitors will find the city is well supplied with mobile telephone stores, Internet cafés, and public access to computers and Wi-Fi. The variety of readily available local newspapers and magazines makes it easy for visitors to keep up with world news as well as the latest dining and entertainment options in the city. New York 1, the all-local TV outlet found at Channel 1, is a quick source for up-to-the minute weather reports and news.

Using a laptop in the New York Public Library

REACHING THE RIGHT NUMBER

- Five area codes are used in New York: 212, 646, 917 (cell phones) are for Manhattan; the other boroughs use 718 and 347. Calls to 800, 888, 866, and 877 numbers are free.
- To call any number in Manhattan, even in your same area code, you must first dial 1.
- To make an international direct call, dial 011 followed by the country code (Australia: 61; New Zealand: 64; UK: 44), then the city or area code (minus the first 0) and the local number.
- International Directory Inquiries are on 00. International operator assistance is on 01.

INTERNET

Visitors will find many ways to access the Internet in New York. The **Times Square Information Center** provides free use, as does the **New York Public Library** at its main facilities and all 85 branches. Almost all hotels offer the use of computers, but some hotel business centers can be expensive. Most hotels also have Wi-Fi, though you may be charged to use it. (In hotels' public areas, however, Wi-Fi is often complimentary.) **FedEx Office Center** locations around town have computer rentals at 30 cents per minute. Rates are better at Internet cafés, which abound. Some, such as the **easyInternet café**, are huge; others, including **Cyber Café**, give more emphasis to the snacks and coffee available. Expect to pay about $6 for 30 minutes. **Web2Zone** offers cheap rates at quiet times.

There is free Wi-Fi at all libraries, Barnes & Noble stores, and in most city parks and plazas below 59th Street, including Bryant Park and Union Square. Cafés such as Starbucks has Wi-Fi for around 10 cents per minute.

CELL PHONES

Visitors who wish to use their own cell phone in the US will need a tri-band phone and a SIM card that has been set up for "roaming." Ask your cell-phone provider if you are unsure whether your phone is ready to be used abroad.

Note that you are charged for the calls you receive as well as for the calls you make. However, some cell-phone companies offer "bundles" of calls to save costs while you are away.

If you are going to be in New York for some time, buy a sim card for better rates on local calls or rent a telephone. **Cellhire** offers rentals for $19 per week, with charges of 20 cents per minute and overseas rates from 49 cents.

PUBLIC TELEPHONES

If you can find a public telephone, you will see that the setup is standard. Few use credit cards, but you can buy prepaid phone cards from newsstands for long-distance calls; they can be bought in $5, $10, and $25 amounts. The cards offer good savings compared to standard rates. Most phones are coin-operated and take 5-, 10-, and 25-cent coins. In some locations the pay phone may belong to an independent company. The independents are often more expensive and less reliable. Regulations require each public pay phone to post information about charges, toll-free numbers, and how to make calls using other carriers. Look for the Verizon logo on the box to be sure the phone will reach all numbers at standard rates. Within all boroughs of New York City, the standard charge, around 25 cents, buys 3 minutes' talking time. International rates for calls dialed from a land line vary.

US Postal Service logo

POSTAL SERVICES

The city's main **General Post Office** is open 24 hours a day. Stamps can be bought here, from branch offices, and from some drugstores and news-stands. As well as at post offices, letters can be mailed at your hotel's concierge desk (which usually sells stamps too); in letter slots in office-building lobbies; and in street mailboxes. These are usually painted blue, or red, white, and blue. The mail is generally not picked up on Sundays. Post offices are shown on the Street Finder maps *(see pp394–5)*.

All letters are sent first class. The post office also offers several special-delivery services: Express Mail service, for next-day delivery; Global Express Guaranteed, which delivers overseas in one–three days; and Express Mail International, with delivery in three–five days. Private express services such as **FedEx**, **UPS**, or **DHL** can be arranged through hotels. Online services are available.

NEWSPAPERS AND MAGAZINES

New York has one major daily newspaper, *The New York Times*, and two colorful tabloids, *The Daily News* and the *New York Post*. Two free morning tabloids are also available, *AM New York* and *Metro*. Both are useful for local events and a brief rundown of the news. The best entertainment listings are found in the Friday and Sunday editions of *The New York Times* and in weekly magazines such as *Time Out New York, New York*, and *The New Yorker*. The *Village Voice*, a free weekly newspaper, also has entertainment listings, geared largely to a younger audience.

The free weekly *Where*, distributed through hotel concierges, lists major museums, their opening hours, locations, and any exhibitions. *Art Now/New York Gallery Guide*, also free, is released in art galleries monthly. It lists current exhibitions and has maps showing where they are located.

You can buy foreign newspapers at **Universal News & Magazine**, **Hotalings**, **Barnes & Noble** bookstores, airports, and some hotels.

TELEVISION AND RADIO

TV program schedules for each day can be found in the local dailies. *The Daily News* on Sunday has a useful pull-out section of the next week's programs. The choice of TV stations in New York is vast. Major networks include CBS on channel 2, NBC on channel 4, ABC on channel 7, and WNYW (Fox) on channel 5. PBS offers cultural and educational fare on channel 13. Cable TV offers everything from the Arts & Entertainment Network (channel 46) to sports on ESPN (channel 28) and public-access programs.

AM radio stations include WCBS News (880AM), WINS News (1010AM), and WFAN Sports (660AM). Some FM stations are WWFS–contemporary (102.7FM), WBGO–jazz (88.3FM), and WQXR–classical (105.9FM).

DIRECTORY

USEFUL NUMBERS

Directory Inquiries
Tel 411 or 10-10-9000.
www.bigyellow.com
www.switchboard.com

CELL PHONES

Cellhire
45 Broadway, 20th Floor.
Map 1 C3. *Tel (888) 950-9391.*
www.cellhire.com

INTERNET

Cyber Café
250 W 49th St. **Map** 11 B5.
Tel (212) 333-4109.

easyInternetcafé
234 W 42nd St. **Map** 8 D1.

FedEx Office Center
www.fedex.com

Library for the Performing Arts
40 Lincoln Center Plaza.
Map 11 C2. *Tel (212) 870-1630.*

New York Public Library
5th Avenue and 42nd Street.
Map 8 F1. *Tel (212) 939-0653.*

Times Square Information Center
1560 Broadway. **Map** 12 E5.
www.timessquarenyc.org

Web2Zone
54 Cooper Square. **Map** 4 F2.

POSTAL SERVICES

DHL
Tel (800) 782-7892.

FedEx
Tel (800) 225-5345.

General Post Office
421 Eighth Ave. **Map** 8 D2.
Tel (800) ASK-USPS or (800) 222-1811.
Priority and Express Mail: *Tel (800) 463-3339.* **www**.usps.com

UPS
Tel (800) 742-5877.

NEWSPAPERS AND MAGAZINES

Barnes & Noble
1972 Broadway at 68th Street.
Map 11 C1.

Hotalings
630 W 52nd St. **Map** 11 B4.

Universal News & Magazine
977 Eighth Ave. **Map** 12 D3.

Express Mail **Priority Mail** **Standard Mail**

GETTING TO NEW YORK

A lot of global airlines run direct flights to New York. The city is also very well served by charter and domestic services. Price wars between airlines have reduced fares, and domestic flights are an affordable form of national travel. Early reservation and seat selection are good ways to ensure a more comfortable flight. New York City is also a regular docking point for many cruise ships.

Delta Airlines flight arriving in New York

The train network across the United States is not as extensive as that found in Europe, but Amtrak, the national carrier, has several comfortable and clean long-distance trains that run from New York. Interstate and long-distance buses are a cheaper way to travel and usually have air-conditioning and on-board toilets. For information on arriving in New York, see the map on *pages 382–3*.

Taxis heading into LaGuardia airport

AIR TRAVEL

New York can be reached by air direct from most major cities. The flight from London takes about 8 hours, however, there are no direct flights from Australia or New Zealand. Instead, the airlines fly to the West Coast or Asia, which takes around 10–14 hours, land, refuel, and then continue on to New York.

Allow extra time at the airport, for both arriving and departing, and for the careful passport and security checks in the United States.

Among the main airline carriers to New York are **Air Canada**, **Delta**, **British Airways**, **American Airlines**, **Virgin Atlantic**, and **United Airlines**. All international flights arrive at either JFK Newark airports.

TICKETS AND FARES

APEX (Advance Purchase Excursion) tickets for the scheduled airlines are usually the cheapest return fares apart from package tours. They must be bought at least

14 days in advance and are valid for a stay of 7–30 days. The least expensive international air fares to and from Europe are found from November to March, excluding holiday periods. Budget airlines flying within the US – such as **Southwest Airlines**, **JetBlue**, and **AirTran** – often have better fares than the major airlines.

Booking online can help save money. Websites such as www.lastminute.com, www.priceline.com, and www.expedia.com have flight-and-hotel deals that tend to be cheaper than booking the two separately. Search engines like www.kayak.com are useful for comparing the costs of all the different airlines and online travel stores.

ON ARRIVAL

Be prepared for extra security precautions when you visit the United States. Make sure that you leave ample time for checking in – ask your flight carrier what time you need to arrive at the airport for your flight. They can also give you details about any restrictions on hand luggage.

The airline you are flying with will give you an I-94 form to fill out before you land. It asks simple questions such as your name, birth date, country of citizenship, passport number, and current address.

Have this form and your passport ready for the Customs and Border Protection officer who will inspect your documents (get in the line that says "non-US passports"). The officer may ask you questions such as why you are visiting and how long and where you will stay. Your fingerprints will be taken, and you will be photographed with a digital camera. The I-94 is in two parts; one part will be for you to keep. This part must be returned on departing.

AirTrain en route to JFK

JOHN F. KENNEDY AIRPORT (JFK)

Every year, some 41 million passengers pass through New York's main airport, JFK. It serves over 100 airlines in nine terminals and is the main New York entry for international flights. JFK lies 15 miles (24 km) southeast of Manhattan, in the borough of Queens, about 45–60 minutes from midtown. However, airport traffic is often heavy, so the trip can take longer.

Larger carriers like American Airlines, British Airways, Delta, and United Airlines

Planes arriving at Newark airport

have their own arrivals and departure terminals, which they may share with some of their partners. Terminal 4 is the main arrival area for over 50 international airlines, and Terminal 1 serves many foreign carriers, including Air China, Air France, Alitalia, and Japan Airlines.

Foreign-exchange offices and ATMs are located in all terminals, and each terminal has a service desk to help book hotels and answer any transportation questions. Courtesy phones are also provided by car-rental companies.

Dispatchers regulate the line for the yellow taxis waiting outside each terminal. There is a flat fee of $45, plus tolls and tip. New York Airport buses go to Grand Central, Penn Station, and the Port Authority; tickets start at $13. The Express Shuttle Service ($14) stops at many midtown hotels. **SuperShuttle** runs shared vans that will go to specific addresses for about $23 for the first guest and $10 for each additional passenger. Advance reservations are needed for the trip back to the airport. Air-Link has a similar service for $19. Round-trip fares are cheaper.

A light-rail system, AirTrain JFK connects to the A train at Howard Beach, and to the E, J, and Z trains and Long Island Rail Road (for Penn Station) at Jamaica. The AirTrain costs $5, the subway $2.25.

If you are feeling rich **Helicopter Flight Services** offer a 10-minute helicopter ride for $850 to East 34th Street.

NEWARK LIBERTY AIRPORT (EWR)

Newark, New York's second-largest international airport, is about 16 miles (26 km) southwest of Manhattan, in New Jersey.

Most international flights into Newark arrive at Terminal B. Baggage trolleys are free for passengers arriving on international flights. Foreign-exchange desks and ATMs can also be found in the terminal, but there is no left-luggage room.

The Ground Transportation Services desk can help arrange private onward travel. Courtesy phones are provided by limousine and car-rental firms. Many of these have a free shuttle service to their rental offices.

As with JFK, there are taxi stands located outside most arrival areas, and uniformed taxi dispatchers will help you hail a cab. The taxi ride into Manhattan takes about 40–60 minutes and will cost you up to $50, plus tolls and tip.

Olympia Airport Express buses to Manhattan stop at the Port Authority Bus Terminal, 42nd Street near 5th Avenue, and Grand Central Station. The journey time is no longer than a cab, but the fare is only $15. Round-trip fares are cheaper.

AirTrain Newark takes about 10 minutes to link to NJ Transit and Amtrak trains, which then take around 25 minutes to arrive at Penn station. The total journey costs about $12 on NJ Transit, or $32 on Amtrak.

Hotels can be booked on arrival through courtesy phones

in all terminals at Newark that link directly to various Manhattan hotels. Knowledgeable staff are on hand to help you make the best choice.

LAGUARDIA AIRPORT (LGA)

LaGuardia is a busy airport serving domestic carriers from all over the US. It lies 8 miles (13 km) east of Manhattan, on the north side of Long Island, in Queens. The trip to Manhattan averages 30 minutes.

Upon arrival, you can rent luggage trolleys from the baggage-claim area next to the luggage carousels. Skycaps, people who check in your luggage for you, are on hand to assist you. Baggage can also be left in the Tele-Trip business center on the departure level. A foreign-currency exchange desk and ATMs are located in the Central Terminal. A free bus service runs between each of the terminals and parking areas from 5am to 2am.

Buses and taxis into the city and its suburbs depart from the front of the terminal buildings. If you are approached by other taxis offering you transportation, do not accept. These drivers have no insurance, and you will be overcharged. A taxi fare starts at $2.50 and increases by $0.40 every fifth of a mile. A single bus ride is $2.25. The cost of tolls, plus a peak-hour surcharge of $1 (4–8pm) weekdays or a night surcharge of 50 cents (8pm–6am), will be added to the taxi fare shown on the meter.

Terminal at LaGuardia airport

Ocean liner anchored in Manhattan

ARRIVING BY SEA

Cruising past the Statue of Liberty into New York Harbor is a thrilling experience. The city's three cruise ports are popular stopping-off points for many major cruise lines sailing to the Caribbean, Bermuda, Canada, and Europe.

The main **New York Cruise Terminal**, on 12th Avenue between 46th and 54th streets, serves Carnival, Silversea, Holland America, MSC, and NCL lines. Taxis are available at the vehicle entrance, located at 55th Street and 12th Avenue. The M57 and M31 crosstown buses provide convenient, inexpensive access to midtown, and it is only a 15–20-minute walk to the heart of Manhattan.

The state-of-the-art **Brooklyn Cruise Terminal** was opened in 2006 in Red Hook. It is the port of choice for Cunard and Princess Cruise lines and the home port of the *QM2*, which sails to New York from Southampton several times a year. You can also take the *QM2* from New York to Australia and New Zealand. Taxis from the terminal can drop you in Manhattan or at convenient subway stops into the city.

Royal Caribbean and Celebrity cruise ships use the **Cape Liberty Cruise Port** in Bayonne, on the New Jersey side of New York Harbor. It is 7 miles (11 km) from New York City and about 15 minutes from Newark International Airport. The Hudson–Bergen Light Rail station at 34th Street, an easy taxi ride just 2 miles (3 km) from the port, connects to PATH trains, New Jersey Transit at Hoboken, and ferry services to and from New York. Visit www.njtransit.com for more information.

Passengers arriving by ship who remain in New York receive the same I-94 form as air passengers and go through the same procedures; *see p378* for more details.

ARRIVING BY LONG-DISTANCE BUS

Long-distance buses from all over the US arrive at the **Port Authority Bus Terminal**, on Eighth Avenue, between 40th and 42nd streets. The location is convenient to midtown, and many hotels are within walking distance. Taxis can be found on the Eighth Avenue side of the terminal; the A and C subway stops are located on the lower floors in the terminal; and a one-block-long tunnel leads to Times Square station and other subway connections. The M42 crosstown bus stops at the corner of Eighth Avenue and 42nd Street, and uptown buses are available on Eighth Avenue. Buses from the Port Authority connect with all three airports, and the terminal also serves many busy commuter bus lines to New Jersey. With over 6,000 buses arriving and departing daily, the atmosphere can be hectic at rush hour.

Buses can be an economical way to see the US. **Greyhound Lines** offer a Discovery Pass priced at $199 for seven days ($299 for 15 days). No advance reservations are necessary. Buses are comfortable and air-conditioned, and they have reclining seats, ample legroom, and usually bathrooms. Greyhound **NeOn** buses, available from New York to Boston, Toronto, and Montreal, are equipped with free Wi-Fi and plug-ins for devices such as iPods. The trip to Boston takes 4½ hours, to Montreal 8½ hours, and to Toronto 11½ hours.

Greyhound has a ticket office in the Port Authority Bus Terminal, but it is cheaper to buy tickets over the phone or online. APEX tickets save 25% off the regular price on shorter trips purchased at least 14 days in advance, and 10% (or more) for tickets bought seven days in advance. "Friends and family" rates offer savings of 50% for up to three companions with the purchase of a regular adult fare. Seniors, students, and military personnel have special discounts.

ARRIVING BY TRAIN

Amtrak, the US passenger rail service, connects New York with the rest of the country and Canada. Amtrak trains use **Penn Station** as their New York headquarters *(see p392)*. The Metro-North train service and the daily commuter service from upstate New York and Connecticut arrive at Grand Central Terminal *(see p392)*

Amtrak has its own section in Penn Station for ticket sales and separate waiting rooms for coach and high-speed passengers. Tickets can be purchased in advance by phone or online and picked up at the station at the ticket

Imposing entrance hall of Grand Central Terminal

window or at automated kiosks. If you pick up tickets at the window, a photo ID will be requested.

Taxis are available from the station, and buses run downtown on Seventh Avenue and uptown on Eighth. The Lexington and Broadway lines also serve the station.

Amtrak trains are very comfortable, with ample legroom and snack-bar services, as well as dining cars on longer routes. Sleeping compartments are available on long-distance trips, some with showers and toilets ensuite.

Amtrak's USA Rail Pass allows unlimited travel for 15 days for $389; children pay half-fare. The most used train service from New York is Amtrak's Northeast Corridor route between Boston, New York, Philadelphia, and Washington, DC. Most of the trains on this route have unreserved seating, but high-speed Acela Express trains offer an hourly service with reserved first-class and business-class seating and electrical outlets for laptops.

ARRIVING BY CAR

Manhattan is an island, so it must be approached via bridge or tunnel. From the

Traffic approaching the George Washington Bridge

south, the entries are from New Jersey via the Holland Tunnel to the Financial District, or the Lincoln Tunnel to midtown. A more scenic approach is the George Washington Bridge, which arrives at 178th Street to the north of the city.

The Robert Kennedy Bridge (formerly known as the Triborough Bridge) has branches from two boroughs connecting to Manhattan. The bridge from Queens, east of the city, is used by those arriving at LaGuardia or JFK airports. The second branch, from the Bronx, approaches Manhattan from the north. The two bridges merge into one and offer a

striking view of the city skyline on the approach.

Those driving in from Queens can avoid tolls by taking the 59th Street Bridge. Queens is also connected to Manhattan by the Midtown Tunnel, which feeds into the Long Island Expressway.

The most famous approach to New York is via the Brooklyn Bridge, with its vistas of the skyscrapers of the downtown Financial District. Brooklyn is also connected to the city by the Brooklyn Battery tunnel.

BRIDGE AND TUNNEL TOLLS

Most of the major access routes in and out of New York City levy tolls. Tolls for the tunnels to and from Long Island and Brooklyn cost $6.50, as does the Robert Kennedy Bridge. The Lincoln Tunnel, Holland Tunnel, and the George Washington Bridge between New York and New Jersey are free for those leaving New York, but they charge $8 coming into the city. Tolls must be paid in cash. Avoid E-Z Pass lanes, marked with purple signs, which are only for holders of pre-paid passes.

DIRECTORY

AIR TRAVEL

Air Canada
Tel (888) 247-2262.
www.aircanada.ca

Airport Information Service
Tel JFK: (718) 244-4444.
EWR: (973) 961-6000.
LGA (718) 533-3400.
www.panynj.gov/airports

AirTran
Tel (800) 247-8726.
www.airtran.com

American Airlines
Tel (800) 433-7300.
www.aa.com

British Airways
Tel (800) AIRWAYS.
www.british-airways.com

Delta
Tel (800) 241-4141.
www.delta.com

Helicopter Flight Services
Tel (212) 355-0801.
www.heliny.com

JetBlue
Tel (800) 538-2583.
www.jetblue.com

Olympia Airport Express
Tel 877-863-9275.
www.coachusa.com

Southwest Airlines
Tel (800) 435-9792.
www.southwest.com

SuperShuttle
Tel (212) 209-7000.
www.supershuttle.com

United Airlines
Tel (800) 241-6522.
www.united.com

Virgin Atlantic
Tel (800) 862-8621.

ARRIVING BY SEA

Brooklyn Cruise Terminal
Pier 12, Building 112,
Bowne Street, Red Hook.
Tel (718) 246-2794.
www.nycruise.com

Cape Liberty Cruise Port
14 Port Terminal Blvd,
Bayonne.
Tel (201) 823-3737.
www.cruiseliberty.com

New York Cruise Terminal
Pier 90, 711 12th Avenue.
Map 11 B4.
Tel (212) 246-5450.
www.nycruise.com

ARRIVING BY LONG-DISTANCE BUS

Greyhound Lines
Tel (800) 231-2222.
www.greyhound.com

NeOn
www.neonbus.com

Port Authority Bus Terminal
Eighth Ave and W 40th St.
Map 8 D1.
Tel (212) 564-8484.
www.panynj.gov

ARRIVING BY TRAIN

Amtrak
Tel (800) 872-7245.
www.amtrak.com

Penn Station
Eighth Ave and 31st St.
Map 8 E3.
www.amtrak.com

Arriving in New York

This map shows the links between New York's three airports and the center of Manhattan. It also illustrates rail connections linking New York to the rest of the United States and Canada. Travel information, including times for bus, rail, and helicopter services, and connections to subway lines, is listed in each information box. The passenger ship terminal, New York's key point of arrival for the flood of post-war immigrants, is located on 55th Street. Port Authority Bus Terminal, on the West Side, provides services across the city.

Ships at the passenger terminal

🚢 PASSENGER SHIP TERMINAL
Piers 88–92 for some cruise ships. Cunard and Princess services use Brooklyn Cruise Terminal.

Passenger Ship Terminal ⭕

KEY

🛫	Airport *see pp378–9*
🚢	Seaport *see p380*
🚆	Rail link *see pp380–81*
🚌	Bus station/link *see p380*
🚁	Helicopter links *see p379*
▬	New York Airport Service and Super Shuttle *see pp378–9*
▬▬	Helicopters *see p379*
▭▭	Long Island Rail Road *see pp392–3*
▭▭	New Jersey Transit buses *see p379*
▭▭	Olympia Airport Express *see p379*
▬▬	AirTrain *see p379*
▬	Subway A *see p389*

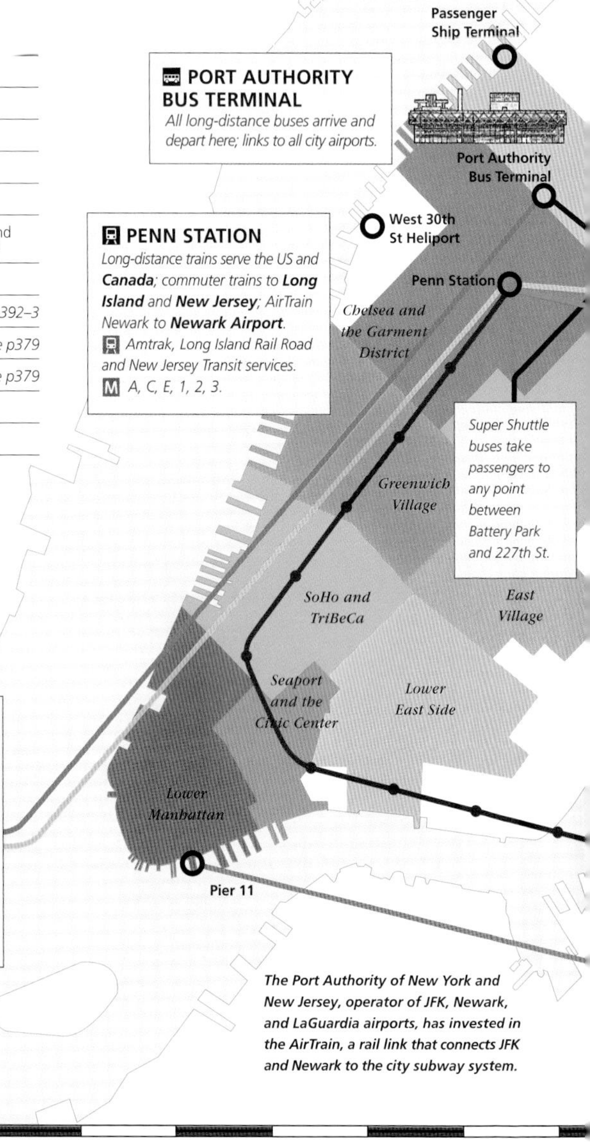

🚌 PORT AUTHORITY BUS TERMINAL
All long-distance buses arrive and depart here; links to all city airports.

Port Authority Bus Terminal

⭕ **West 30th St Heliport**

Penn Station ⭕

🚆 PENN STATION
*Long-distance trains serve the US and **Canada**; commuter trains to **Long Island** and **New Jersey**; AirTrain Newark to **Newark Airport**.*
🚆 *Amtrak, Long Island Rail Road and New Jersey Transit services.*
Ⓜ *A, C, E, 1, 2, 3.*

Chelsea and the Garment District

Super Shuttle buses take passengers to any point between Battery Park and 227th St.

Greenwich Village

East Village

SoHo and TriBeCa

Seaport and the Civic Center

Lower East Side

Lower Manhattan

Pier 11 ⭕

🛫 NEWARK
🚌 *Olympia Airport Express 4am–11pm, every 20–30 mins to **Penn Station, Grand Central** and **Port Authority**.*
🚌 *New Jersey Transit Every 15–20 mins to **Port Authority**.*
🚆 *New Jersey Transit or Amtrak to **Penn Station** 5am–midnight, every 5–20 mins Mon–Fri; every 50 mins Sat & Sun.*

The Port Authority of New York and New Jersey, operator of JFK, Newark, and LaGuardia airports, has invested in the AirTrain, a rail link that connects JFK and Newark to the city subway system.

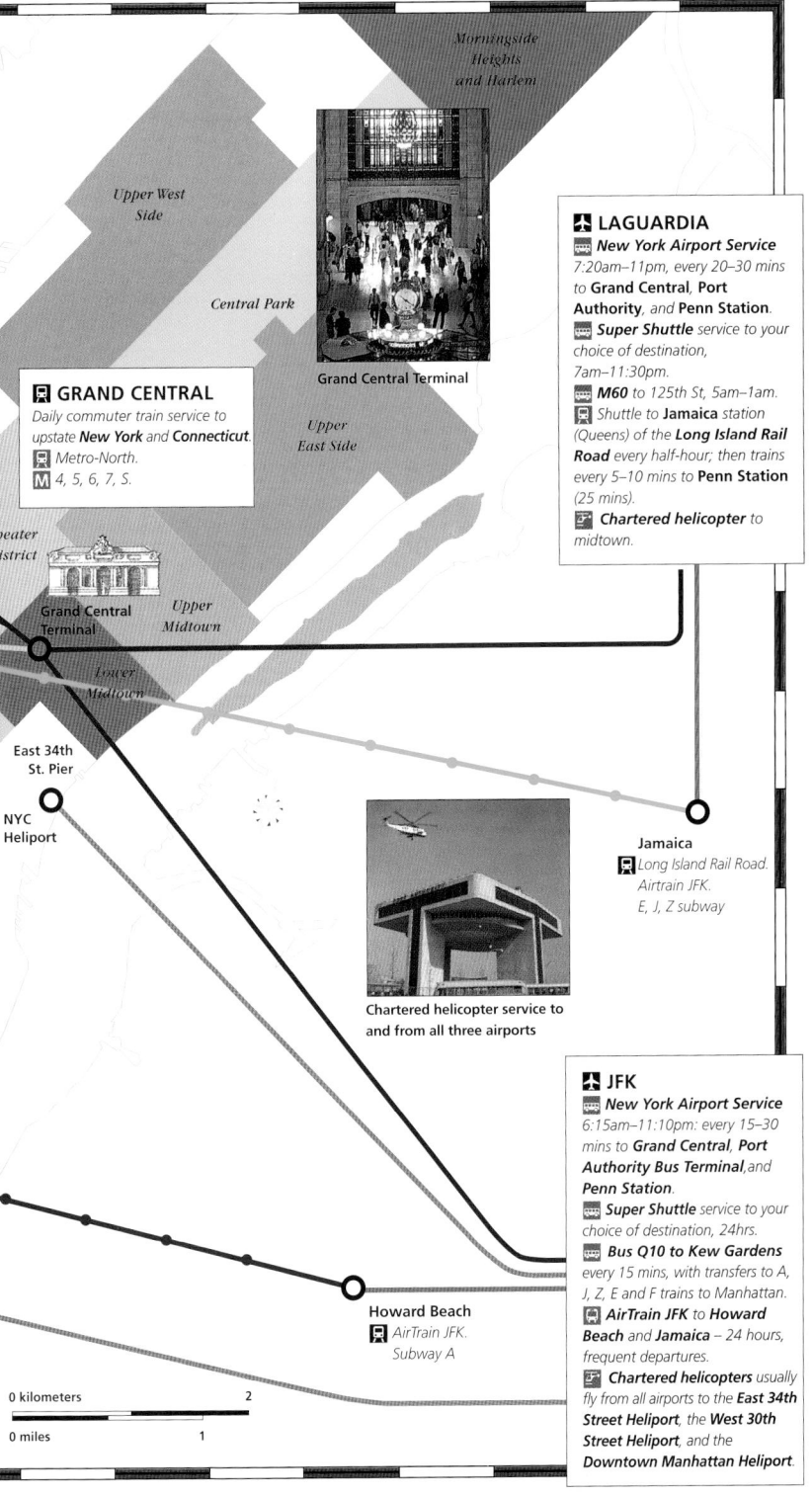

Morningside Heights and Harlem

Upper West Side

Central Park

Grand Central Terminal

Upper East Side

R GRAND CENTRAL
Daily commuter train service to upstate **New York** *and* **Connecticut**.
M Metro-North.
M 4, 5, 6, 7, S.

heater district

Grand Central Terminal

Upper Midtown

Lower Midtown

East 34th St. Pier

NYC Heliport

✈ LAGUARDIA
🚌 **New York Airport Service**
7:20am–11pm, every 20–30 mins to **Grand Central**, **Port Authority**, *and* **Penn Station**.
🚌 **Super Shuttle** *service to your choice of destination, 7am–11:30pm.*
🚌 **M60** *to 125th St, 5am–1am.*
🚇 *Shuttle to* **Jamaica** *station (Queens) of the* **Long Island Rail Road** *every half-hour; then trains every 5–10 mins to* **Penn Station** *(25 mins).*
🚁 **Chartered helicopter** *to midtown.*

Jamaica
🚇 *Long Island Rail Road. Airtrain JFK. E, J, Z subway*

Chartered helicopter service to and from all three airports

Howard Beach
🚇 *AirTrain JFK. Subway A*

✈ JFK
🚌 **New York Airport Service**
6:15am–11:10pm: every 15–30 mins to **Grand Central**, **Port Authority Bus Terminal**, *and* **Penn Station**.
🚌 **Super Shuttle** *service to your choice of destination, 24hrs.*
🚌 **Bus Q10 to Kew Gardens** *every 15 mins, with transfers to A, J, Z, E and F trains to Manhattan.*
🚇 **AirTrain JFK to Howard Beach** *and* **Jamaica** *– 24 hours, frequent departures.*
🚁 **Chartered helicopters** *usually fly from all airports to the* **East 34th Street Heliport**, *the* **West 30th Street Heliport**, *and the* **Downtown Manhattan Heliport**.

0 kilometers   2
0 miles   1

GETTING AROUND NEW YORK

With more than 6,000 miles (9,650 km) of streets, getting around New York might seem a problem, but the city is actually a network of small neighborhoods that are connected via subway or bus. Each one is also quite walkable or easy to get around on public transportation. Midtown Manhattan, for example, with many of the major sights, runs 25 blocks from 34th to 59th streets, and if you should tire, you can hop on a bus that goes down Fifth Avenue or up Sixth. Subways are the quickest way to get around. Service is frequent, they are inexpensive and reliable, and they make stops throughout Manhattan. The city's bus service is also reliable and convenient but can be slow in traffic. Weekly or unlimited MetroCards, valid for all public transportation, provide excellent value. Taxis are the best option for door-to-door transit, but they can be expensive if you are held up by traffic.

Signs on a street corner

GREEN TRAVEL

New York is working hard to be more energy-efficient for those traveling around town. Back in the 1990s, the city was a pioneer in launching an alternative-fuel vehicle program aimed at cutting emissions and making its bus fleet one of the cleanest in the world. It was the first in the US to switch all diesel buses to ultra-low sulfur fuel. Cleaner-burning engines have been installed, and buses have been equipped with filters, cutting emissions by as much as 95 per cent. The MTA currently has around 2,000 hybrid-electric buses in operation. Numerous bicycle lanes have also been added around town for those brave enough to use them amid the heavy city traffic.

When it comes to leaving the city, the US train system is quite limited, but New York has some of the better connections, especially Amtrak's East Coast Metroliner and Acela trains *(see pp381 and 393)*.

Cyclist in Central Park

FINDING YOUR WAY AROUND NEW YORK

Manhattan's avenues run north to south; New Yorkers say "uptown" and "downtown." Streets (except in the older areas) run east to west, and are referred to as "crosstown." Fifth Avenue is the divider between East and West street addresses.

Most streets in midtown are one-way. In general, traffic is eastbound on even-numbered streets and westbound on odd-numbered streets. Avenues also tend to be one-way. First, Third (above 23rd Street), Madison, Avenue of the Americas (Sixth), Eighth, and Tenth avenues are northbound, while Second,

FINDING AN ADDRESS

A useful formula has been devised to help pinpoint any avenue address. By dropping the last digit of the address, dividing the remainder by 2, then adding or subtracting the key number given here, you will discover the nearest cross street. For example: to find No. 826 Lexington Avenue, you have to drop the 6; divide 82 by 2, which is 41; then add 22 (the key number). Therefore, the nearest cross street is 63rd Street.

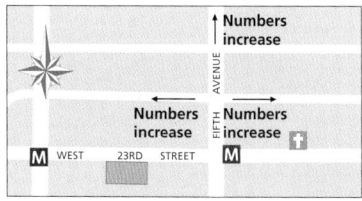

Avenue Address	Key Number	Avenue Address	Key Number
1st Ave	+3	9th Ave	+13
2nd Ave	+3	10th Ave	+14
3rd Ave	+10	Amsterdam Ave	+60
4th Ave	+8	Audubon Ave	+165
5th Ave, up to 200	+13	Broadway above	
5th Ave, up to 400	+16	23rd St	-30
5th Ave, up to 600	+18	Central Park W, divide	
5th Ave, up to 775	+20	full number by 10	+60
5th Ave 775–1,286,		Columbus Ave	+60
do not divide by 2	-18	Convent Ave	+127z
5th Ave, up to 1500	+45	Lenox Ave	+110
5th Ave, up to 2000	+24	Lexington Ave	+22
(6th) Ave of the		Madison Ave	+26
Americas	-12	Park Ave	+35
7th Ave below		Park Ave South	+8
110th St	+12	Riverside Drive, divide	
7th Ave above		full number by 10	+72
110th St	+20	St Nicholas Ave	+110
8th Ave	+10	West End Ave	+60

Walking through Chelsea

Lexington, Fifth, Seventh, and Ninth avenues and Broadway below 59th Street are southbound. There is two-way traffic on York, Park, 11th, and 12th avenues and on Broadway above 60th Street.

The grid of streets is rectangular rather than square, so crosstown blocks are longer than north–south avenue blocks. To gauge distances, 20 north–south city blocks equal about 1 mile (1.6 km); it takes only about five to eight crosstown (east–west) blocks to make up that distance.

Some streets have more than one name – for example, Avenue of the Americas is better known as Sixth Avenue. Park Avenue is called Park Avenue South below 34th Street and Fourth Avenue below 14th Street. The maps in this guide give the names most often used.

PLANNING YOUR JOURNEY

Buses and subways are busiest during the rush hours: 8–10am and 4:30–6:30pm, Monday to Friday. Throughout these periods, it may be easier to face the crowds on foot than attempt any journey by bus, taxi, or subway. At other times of day and during certain holiday periods (see p53), the traffic is often much lighter, and you should reach your destination quickly.

There are, of course, a few exceptions. When the president or other political celebrities visit, security measures can cause major disruption to the traffic. The area around Seventh Avenue, south of 42nd Street, is likely to be busy during the day with the truck and handcart traffic of New York's garment industry.

Avoid Fifth Avenue on parade days, which often take place in spring and fall. On these days, and during the New York Marathon, it is difficult to get across town as bus services are disrupted. If such events are scheduled during your visit, plan to see other areas of the city on that day. Subway traffic will not be affected, though trains may be more crowded than usual.

DRIVING IN NEW YORK

Heavy traffic, lack of parking, and expensive rental cars make driving in New York a frustrating experience. If you decide to drive, you must wear a seat belt by law. Driving is on the right, and the speed limit is usually 30 mph (48 kmh) in midtown. Most streets are one-way, and there are traffic lights at almost every corner. Unlike the rest of New York State, you can never turn right on a red light unless there is a sign indicating otherwise.

To rent a car, you must be at least 25 years old. You will need a valid driver's license (foreign visitors need an International Driver's License), a passport, and a credit card.

CAR INSURANCE

Unless you are adequately covered by your own insurance policy, you should take out damage and liability protection when renting a car. Check with your insurance company before you travel.

Your car-rental agency will be able to provide you with a policy if necessary.

PARKING

Parking in Manhattan is costly and difficult. You can use parking garages, or see if your hotel includes overnight parking, but both options are very expensive.

The busiest streets in midtown do not allow parking. Other streets may have curbside meters for short-term (20–60 minutes) parking. Yellow street and curb markings mean no parking.

"Alternate-side" parking applies on most of the city's side streets. Cars may usually be left all day and night, but they must be moved to the other side of the street before 8am the next day. For specific information, call 311.

Car-rental logos

PENALTIES

If you receive a parking ticket, you have seven days to pay the fine or to appeal. If you have any queries about your ticket, call the **Parking Violations Bureau**.

If you cannot find your car, call 311 to find out if it has been towed. The **Traffic Department Tow Pound** is open 24 hours a day, Monday to Saturday. Redeeming your car will cost $185 towing fee, $70 execution fee, and $10–15 per day storage fee. Traveler's checks, certified checks, money orders, and cash are accepted. If you have rented the car, the contract must be produced, and only the authorized driver may redeem the vehicle.

Traffic passing through Times Square at night

Taxis driving through an intersection in SoHo

TAXIS

There are more than 12,000 yellow cabs in New York, easily identified by their color, the distinctive logo on the door, and the light on top. A taxi can carry up to four passengers, with a single fare covering everyone on board. All taxis are metered and can issue printed receipts. Taxis can be hailed anywhere on the street, but taxi stands are scarce. The best places to find waiting cabs are outside Penn and Grand Central stations. Cabs indicate that they are available by turning on the top light. This goes off if the cab is occupied or if the side lights indicate "off duty."

Licensed taxis undergo periodic inspections and are insured against accidents and losses. Non-licensed, or "gypsy," cabs are unlikely to have these safeguards. They will have no meters and charge what they please.

Once the cab driver accepts a passenger, the meter starts ticking at $2.50, plus a state tax surcharge of 50 cents. The fare increases 40 cents after each additional one-fifth of a mile (292 yards/267 meters) or every 60 seconds of waiting time. There is an additional 50-cent charge from 8pm to 6am, and a $1 extra charge from 4 to 8pm on weekdays. It is customary to tip the driver about 15%. Taxi drivers will accept credit cards.

Make sure your driver understands where you want to go before you start your ride. If you have a map of the area, mark the locations you want. A driver should not ask you your destination until after you've sat down, and by law, they must take you anywhere in the city. They must follow your requests not to smoke or talk on a cell phone, to open or close a window, and to pick up or drop off passengers as you direct. Each yellow cab displays the driver's photograph and registered number next to the meter. If drivers don't comply with your requests, you can report them to the **Taxi & Limousine Commission**.

As an expensive alternative, radio-dispatched sedans can be hired for $40 per hour with a two hour minimum.

WALKING

All intersections have lamp-posts with clearly marked street names; most have electric traffic signals. The lights show red (stop) and green (go) for vehicles, and "Walk/Don't Walk" signals for pedestrians. Crossing while the "Don't Walk" sign is showing is not recommended, nor is crossing mid-block, referred to in the US as "jay-walking."

Vehicles in the US drive on the right, and there are no markings on the road for pedestrians indicating the direction of traffic. It is best to look both ways before you cross, and beware of cars, trucks, and taxis turning the corner behind you as you start to cross the street.

Signs in midtown

Midtown has several small parks and plazas where visitors can rest. In the Broadway area you can have a rest with a Times Square view on the high tier of steps behind the TKTS booth (Broadway and 47th St). Some of the surrounding blocks are traffic-free and furnished with chairs. The traffic islands around the Lincoln Center also offer seating *(us on p370)*.

FERRIES

The **Circle Line** runs several ferry services a day to the Statue of Liberty and Ellis Island from Battery Park, at the southern tip of Manhattan. The 24-hour **Staten Island Ferry**, also from Battery Park, travels the channel and offers splendid views of lower Manhattan, the Statue of Liberty, Ellis Island, the bridges, and Governors Island. The round trip is the best bargain in New York; it's free.

WATER TAXIS

The **New York Water Taxi** is mainly a commuter service, but it also offers various tours and a weekend hop-on/hop-off sightseeing boat (mid-Apr–mid-Oct). The route is around New York Harbor, between West 44th and East 34th streets, with stops including Chelsea Pier, World Financial Center, Battery Park, South Street Seaport, the Brooklyn river-front, and Long Island City. In summer, water taxis provide a service to a couple of man-made beaches in Long Island City and on Governors Island.

A water taxi crossing New York Harbor

GUIDED TOURS

Whichever way you choose to see New York – with the help of a knowledgeable guide, a photographer, a pre-recorded walk, or an exciting trip in a helicopter, boat, or horse-drawn carriage – organized sightseeing trips can save a lot of time and effort. Walking tours give in-depth background information about specific neighborhoods and the city's history and architecture that you might not get on your own. The **Municipal Art Society** is renowned for its knowledge-able guides. Fascinating behind-the-scenes tours are available for the New York Public Library, Metropolitan Opera, and Radio City Music Hall. Bus tours are also a great way to see the city, as you can hop on/hop off as you please *(see also p391).*

CYCLING

Hoping to cut down on auto traffic, the city is making a real effort to create bike paths, which cover over 90 miles (145 km) in Manhattan. It takes courage to travel beside heavy traffic on busy midtown streets; however, trails along the East River and far west side are pleasant and very popular, as are the many roads for bikers in Central Park, where auto traffic is banned on week-ends. Visit www.nycbike maps.com for maps of bike routes. You can rent bikes at Columbus Circle or the Loeb Boathouse in Central Park *(see p362).*

DIRECTORY

CAR RENTAL AGENCIES

Avis
Tel (800) 331-1212.
www.avis.com

Budget
Tel (800) 527-0700.
www.drivebudget.com

Hertz
Tel (800) 654-3131.
www.hertz.com

National
Tel (800) CAR RENT.
www.nationalcar.com

PARKING

Alternate Side Park-ing Information
Tel 311.

Parking Violations and Towing Information
Tel 311.

Parking Violations Bureau
Tel (718) 802-3636.

Police
Tel 911.

Traffic Department Tow Pound
Pier 76, W 38th St and 12th Ave. **Map** 7 B1.
Tel 311.

TAXIS

Taxi & Limousine Commission
Tel 311.

Taxi Lost and Found
Tel 311.

Transportation Department
Tel 311.

FERRIES

Circle Line
www.circleline.com

Staten Island Ferry
www.siferry.com

WATER TAXIS

New York Water Taxi
Tel (212) 742-1969.
www.nywatertaxi.com

GUIDED TOURS

Bicycle Tours: Bite of the Apple Tours
2 Columbus Circle, 59th St & Broadway. **Map** 12 D3.
Tel (212) 541-8759.

Boat Tours: Circle Line Sightseeing Yachts
Pier 83, W 42nd St. **Map** 7 A1. *Tel (212) 563-3200.*

Spirit of New York
W 23rd and Eighth Ave. **Map** 8 D4.
Tel (866) 211-3805.

World Yacht, Inc.
Pier 81, W 41st St. **Map** 7 A1. *Tel (212) 630-8100.*

Building Tours: Grand Central Terminal
E 42nd St at Park Ave. **Map** 13 A5.
Tel (212) 883-2420.
www.grandcentral terminal.com

Heritage Trails
Federal Hall, 26 Wall St. **Map** 1 C3.
www.nps.gov/feha/

Metropolitan Opera Tours
Lincoln Center. **Map** 11 C2. *Tel (212) 769-7020.*
www.metoperafamily.org

NBC Studio Tour
30 Rockefeller Plaza. **Map** 12 F5. *Tel (212) 664-7174.* www. rockefellercenter.com

New York Public Library
Fifth Ave and 42nd St. **Map** 8 F1.
Tel (917) 275-6975.
www.nypl.org

Radio City Music Hall Stage Door Tours
Sixth Ave. **Map** 12 F4.
Tel (212) 247-4777.

Walkin' Broadway
1619 Broadway. **Map** 12 E5. *Tel (212) 997-5004.*

Bus Tours: Gray Line of New York
42nd St and Eighth Ave. **Map** 8 D1.
Tel (212) 397-2620.

Carriage Tours
59th St at Fifth Ave and along Central Park S. **Map** 12 F3.

Helicopter Tours: Liberty
W 30th St and 12th Ave, South Ferry. **Map** 7 B3.
Tel (212) 967-6464.

Walking Tours: Adventures on a Shoestring
300 W 53rd St. **Map** 12 E4. *Tel (212) 265-2663.*

Big Apple Greeters
1 Centre St, Suite 2035.
Map 4 F4.
Tel (212) 669-8159.

Big Onion Walking Tours
76 13th St, Brooklyn.
Tel (212) 439-1090.
http://bigonion.com

Eldridge Street Synagogue
12 Eldridge St. **Map** 5 A5.
Tel (212) 227-8780.

Harlem Spirituals, Inc.
690 Eighth Ave. **Map** 8 D1. *Tel (212) 391-0900.*

Lower East Side Tenement Museum
108 Orchard St. **Map** 5 A4. *Tel (212) 431-0233.*

Municipal Art Society
457 Madison Ave. **Map** 13 A4. *Tel (212) 980-1297.*
www.mas.org

Wall Street Walks
Tel (212) 209-3379.
www.wallstreetwalks.com

CYCLING

Central Park Bike Rental
203 West 58th St.
Map 12 E3.
Tel (212) 541-8759.
www.centralpark biketour.com

Traveling by Subway

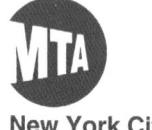

New York City Subway

New York subway logo

The subway is the quickest and most reliable way to travel in the city. The vast system extends over 233 route miles (375 km) and has 468 stations. Most routes operate 24 hours a day throughout the year. In the past few years, the subway system has been upgraded, and the trains are now air-conditioned, well lit, safer, and (unless you are riding at rush hour) more comfortable. Since the 1980s, a portion of all station-improvement funds has gone to the Arts for Transit project, with some notable results. Keep an eye out for the mosaics, sculptures, and art that decorate many stations.

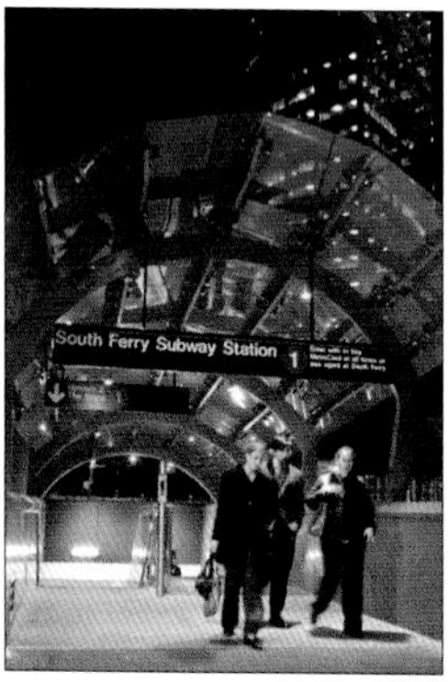
South Ferry Subway Station 1

Passengers exiting from South Ferry Subway Station

TICKETS AND FARES

A MetroCard must be purchased in order to enter the subway. The fare is $2.25 no matter how far you travel; if you buy a single-use ticket, though, the price rises to $2.50. One money-saving ticket is the 7-day ($29) Unlimited Ride MetroCard. If you purchase a Pay-Per-Ride MetroCard and put $10 or more on it, you will receive a 7 per cent bonus credit. MetroCards, which can also be used on buses *(see pp390–91)*, are sold at newsstands, drugstores, and other locations around the city, as well as at all subway stations, where you can pay with cash. The machines take cash and debit and credit cards. One transfer per ride is allowed between the subway and bus; it must be used within 2 hours.

USING THE SUBWAY

Enter the subway by swiping your MetroCard at the turnstiles; the card is not needed to exit. Look for signs for uptown (northbound) and downtown (southbound) trains. Note that there are two types of trains: local trains stop at all stations, while faster express trains make fewer stops. Express lines have different letters or numbers than local ones; both types of stops are distinguished on every subway map.

SUBWAY STATIONS

Many subway entrances are marked by illuminated spheres: green where the station booth is manned around the clock, red where there is restricted entry. Others are marked simply by a sign bearing the name of the station and the numbers or letters of the routes passing through it. Although the subway system runs 24 hours a day, not all routes operate at all times. The basic service is between 6am and midnight. The most crowded periods are the weekday rush hours (6–8:30am and 4:30–6:30pm); it is best to avoid these times if you can. If not, during

READING THE SUBWAY MAP

Each route is identified on the subway map *(see inside back cover)* by color, by the names of the stations at each end of the line, and by a letter or number. Local and express stops and interchange points are also identified. The letters and numbers below the station names indicate which routes serve that particular station. A letter or number in heavy type indicates that trains on that route stop there between 6am and midnight; letters in lighter type mean that the route is served by a part-time service only; a boxed letter or number shows the last stop on the line. Express trains are indicated on subway maps with a white (rather than solid) circle. The maps posted in all the subway stations have a comprehensive guide that explains the trains and timetable of each route. Note that New Yorkers refer to subway lines by letter or number, not by color.

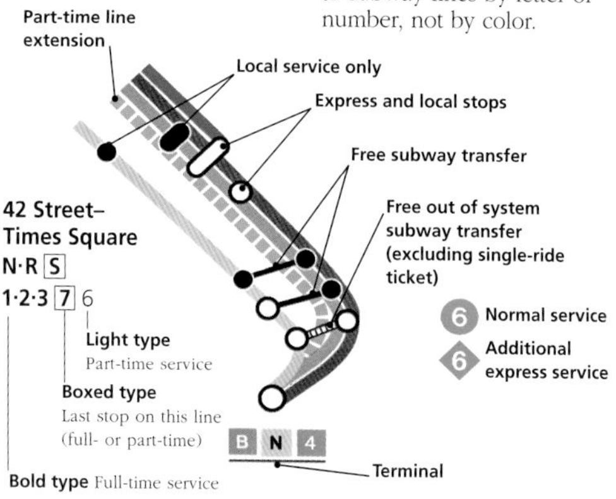
Part-time line extension
Local service only
Express and local stops
Free subway transfer
Free out of system subway transfer (excluding single-ride ticket)
42 Street–Times Square
N·R [S]
1·2·3 [7] 6
Light type
Part-time service
Boxed type
Last stop on this line (full- or part-time)
Bold type Full-time service
[6] Normal service
[6] Additional express service
B N 4
Terminal

TRAVELING BY SUBWAY

Subways run north–south up and down the city; the N, R, E, F, V, and W trains run east–west from Midtown to Queens. See "Subway Lines" for the most useful routes.

1 There is a map of the subway system on the back inside cover of this book. Large-scale maps are also positioned in prominent areas in every station. Maps are also available at www.mta.info and at subway stations.

3 Use MetroCard to pass through the turnstile onto the platform.

6 On every platform, you will find a line map, while on each train there is a system map next to the door on both sides of the car. Newer trains have electronic route maps for that line that light up overhead. Stops are announced on the public address system, and you will see station names at each platform. The doors are operated by the conductor.

2 Buy a MetroCard from a station subway booth or MetroCard vending machine. The machines accept most credit and debit cards and bills up to $50, but no pennies. Vending machines can also be used to refill MetroCards.

4 Follow the directions for the train you want. For safety, stay in sight of the booth as you wait for your train; at night, stay in one of the yellow off-hours waiting areas.

5 Each train displays its route number or letter in the appropriate color and the names of the terminal stations.

7 After leaving the train, look for signs giving directions to the exit. If you need to change trains, just follow the signs to the connecting platforms.

---

crowded times the first and last cars are usually less busy.

The subway is generally quite safe, but visitors may feel more secure riding during the day and until around 10pm, when there are many other passengers around. If you feel unsure, stand in the "Off-Hours Waiting Area" on the platforms. Avoid traveling alone late at night, but if you have no choice, use the central cars. In an emergency, contact either the station agent in the station booth or a member of the train crew, who are located in the first car and in the middle of the train.

SUBWAY LINES

Subways run north–south on Lexington, Sixth Avenue, Seventh Avenue/Broadway, and Eighth Avenue. The #7 train runs west–east into Queens, while the E, F, M, N, Q, and R travel south–north until around midtown, and then east into Queens. A shuttle train connects Grand Central-42nd Street to Times Square-42nd Street. Trains mostly run along one avenue, but some stations, such as those at Times Square, Union

Square, and Columbus Circle, are convenient transfer points where several lines converge.

Each subway line has a distinct color, while the routes on each line are identified either by letter or number. For example, the Lexington Avenue line is green and the #6 is a local train, while #4 and #5 run express. The Eighth Avenue line is blue, and the A train is the express, while C and E are local trains. First and last stops are posted on track signs and on each car. Large system maps are posted in all stations. Free individual subway maps are usually available from booth attendants.

Some lines are especially useful for visitors. The Lexington Line is the only one serving the East Side and its many museums. The #6 train stops near the Guggenheim, the Metropolitan Museum of Art, and the Frick Collection. The red #1 Broadway/Seventh Avenue line on the West Side takes you to Lincoln Center,

Number 6 train at Brooklyn Bridge–City Hall station

MOMA, Times Square, Greenwich Village, SoHo, the Financial District, and South Ferry, where you can catch a ferry to the Statue of Liberty.

Track work at weekends can cause changes to the schedule. When you enter, ask the booth attendant about changes that may affect your journey.

DIRECTORY

MetroCard Customer Service
Tel (212) 638-7622.

MTA Automated Travel Planner
http://tripplanner.mta.info/

Subway Information
Tel (718) 330-1234.
www.mta.info

Traveling by Bus

Traveling by bus is a good way to take in many of New York's sights. The city's 4,000-plus blue-and-white buses cover more than 200 routes in the five boroughs. Many run 24 hours a day, every day. The buses are modern, clean, air-conditioned, and energy-efficient. They are also quite safe and tend not to get crowded, except during rush hours. Smoking and eating are forbidden on all public buses, and only service animals (guide dogs) are allowed on board.

Bus stop in midtown Manhattan

TICKETS AND FARES

You can pay the $2.25 fare on a bus using a MetroCard (see p388), or exact change in coins. Bus drivers cannot make change, and fare boxes do not accept dollar bills, half-dollars, or pennies. You can buy a MetroCard at any subway station booth or machine and at many other outlets around the city.

If you need to take more than one bus to reach your destination, you are eligible for a free transfer. If you pay your fare with a MetroCard, transfers to bus or subway are automatically placed electronically on the card. If you use cash, ask the driver for a transfer ticket when you pay. Transfers are good for 2 hours.

Senior citizens with proof of age and the disabled pay half-fare. All buses can "kneel," lowering the steps to help elderly people to board (see p370). They are also accessible to wheelchairs via a lift with ramp, at the rear or front depending on the bus design.

BUS STOPS

Buses will stop only at designated bus stops. They follow north–south routes on the major avenues, stopping every two or three blocks. Crosstown buses run east–west and usually stop at every block, with the exception of Park Avenue, which is skipped by some lines. Many routes run a 24-hour daily service.

Bus stops are marked by red, white, and blue signs, and yellow paint along the curb. Most also have bus shelters; newer shelters provide seating and helpful signs giving the location. A route map and schedule is posted at each stop. Buses use letters to indicate the boroughs they serve: M for Manhattan, B for Brooklyn, Bx for the Bronx, and Q for Queens. Bus stops often serve several routes, so check the maps at the stop for your route, then look for that route number posted on the lighted strip above the windshield on the front of the bus.

Some buses will be marked "Limited," indicated by a flashing sign in the route number space and by a card in the front window. These buses are faster since they make fewer stops, but be sure the stops they do make are near your destination. Limited buses do stop at streets connecting to crosstown buses.

Free city bus maps are often available on board; ask the driver for a copy.

USING BUSES

Most buses run every 3–5 minutes during the morning and evening rush hours, and every 7–15 minutes from noon to 4:30pm and from 7 to 10pm. Bad traffic or adverse weather conditions can cause delays. Service is reduced on weekends and holidays.

Enter the bus at the front door. If you are unsure of your route, ask the driver if they will be stopping at your destination or close to it. The majority of New York's bus drivers are helpful and will call out your stop if you ask when you board. Put your MetroCard in the slot or drop the correct coins in the fare box, then look for a seat.

To request a stop when traveling on the bus, press the yellow vertical call strip between the windows. Some newer buses also have stop buttons on center poles. A "Stop Requested" sign near the driver will then light up. If the bus is crowded, it is wise to start moving toward the exit door when you are a few blocks from your stop.

Leave through the double door located toward the rear of the bus. The driver will activate the door release as soon as the bus has stopped, and a green light will go on above the door. You then push the yellow stripe on the door, and the doors will open automatically; they will stay open long enough for everyone to leave. If the strip does not work properly, just push the door and then hold it open for the passenger behind you as you leave.

The M86 crosstown bus traveling through Central Park

NIGHT BUSES

Most lines run 24 hours, but be sure to check the schedule posted at your stop. After 10pm, many buses run every 20 minutes or so. From midnight to 6am, expect to wait 30–60 minutes for a bus.

BUS TOURS

One of the most popular ways to see the sights is aboard a hop-on/hop-off bus tour that allows you to get off wherever you like, stay as long as you want, and catch another bus when you are ready. Gray Line *(see p387)* is the best-known company offering these tours aboard double-decker buses. Routes include a Downtown Loop, Uptown Loop, Brooklyn Loop, and Night/Holiday Lights Tour (not hop-on/hop-off). Buy a 48- or 72-hour pass, and you can see a great deal of New York. While you ride, narration is available in several languages through rented headsets.

MTA TRIP PLANNER

The MTA website has a useful feature known as the Trip Planner, which provides a map and directions by bus and/or subway between any two points in New York. Enter your starting and ending points, the time you expect to travel, preferred mode of transportation, how far you are willing to walk, and whether you need accessible vehicles, and you will get clear directions. Visit http:// travel.mtanyct.info to access the planner; www.hopstop. com offers a similar service.

DIRECTORY

Lost Property on Buses:
Tel (212) 712-4500.

MTA Travel Information
Tel (718) 330-1234.
www.mta.info

Route Maps
Available from MTA/NYCT,
Customer Service Center,
3 Stone Street, Lower Manhattan.
Map 1 C4.

SIGHTSEEING BUSES

For a pleasant and cheap alternative to a tour bus, hop on a city bus and see New York with the New Yorkers. Recommended bus routes include route M2, which runs down Fifth Avenue alongside Central Park and stops near the Guggenheim and the Metropolitan. It then returns north on Madison Avenue (via the Empire State Building and the Rockefeller Center), where it runs alongside the M5, which continues south to SoHo and Greenwich Village. From Broad Street, head north on the M15 to visit Brooklyn Bridge and the United Nations, or take route M7 or M20 along Eighth Avenue for Times Square and Madison Square Garden.

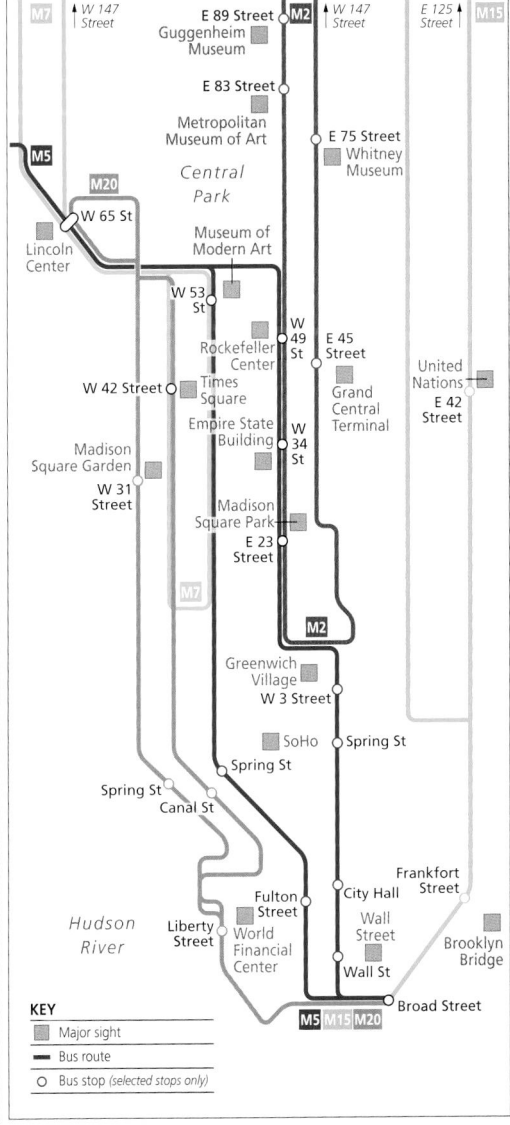

Day Trips from New York

For a change of pace and some beautiful scenery, it is worth taking a day trip from New York City to the surrounding areas. Public transport links are excellent, and there are many convenient and easy ways to travel to nearby destinations (see pp232–55).

Departure board at Penn Station

MAIN TRAIN STATIONS

New York has two main train stations, serving commuters as well as long-distance travelers.

Grand Central Terminal (see pp156–7), on Park Avenue at 42nd Street, is the main terminal for **Metro-North Railroad** trains (Hudson, New Haven, and Harlem lines), which run north and east of New York and serve southwest Connecticut and Westchester, Dutchess, and Putnam counties (see pp380–81). From Grand Central, you can travel by train to the Bronx Zoo (see pp244–5), the New York Botanical Garden, President Franklin D. Roosevelt's Hyde Park estate, and other mansions and towns overlooking the Hudson River.

The 4, 5, and 6 trains on the Lexington line and number 7 on the Flushing line serve Grand Central subway station. A shuttle train service links Grand Central to Times Square. Many bus lines stop near Grand Central, and taxis can usually be found in front of the station on 42nd Street or across from the side entrance on Vanderbilt Avenue at 43rd Street.

Penn Station, between Seventh and Eighth avenues and from 31st to 33rd streets, is a somewhat cramped underground terminal that was rebuilt in 1963 underneath the Madison Square Garden complex (see p135). **Long Island Rail Road** (LIRR) and **New Jersey Transit** commuter trains, plus **Amtrak** trains from Canada and other parts of the US, terminate at this station. There are no luggage trolleys, but redcap porters will help.

Taxis can be found at street level. Buses run downtown on Seventh Avenue and uptown on Eighth Avenue. The Eighth Avenue subway lines A, C, and E run on the Eighth Avenue side of the station; the Broadway lines 1, 2, and 3 run on the Seventh Avenue side of the station.

COMMUTER RAIL LINES

Metro-North lines to upstate New York and Connecticut depart from Grand Central Station. These are mostly commuter trains but may be useful for trips to New Haven or Hartford, Connecticut, or to destinations along the Hudson River.

Long Island Rail Road and New Jersey Transit commuter rail lines depart from Penn Station. They can take you to New Jersey or Long Island beach resorts, or to the casinos at Atlantic City, New Jersey.

Long Island Rail Road

Long Island Rail Road logo

PATH trains are used mainly by commuters. They operate around the clock between New Jersey stations and Penn Station. From Penn Station they make stops at Christopher Street; the World Trade Center; Ninth, 14th, 23rd, and 33rd streets; and Avenue of the Americas.

TICKETS AND FARES

Train tickets are based on a one-way fare; a return fare is twice the single fare. Peak commuter fares are for trains arriving in New York weekdays between 6 and 10am or departing between 4 and 8pm. All other hours and weekend days are considered off peak and cost much less.

The Long Island Rail Road has many One-Day Getaway packages, with discounted rail fares and admissions to places such as the Hamptons, vineyards, historic sites, and New York Mets baseball games.

Metro-North and LIRR cars are all one class and have no reserved seating, while Amtrak trains offer both services. The conductor will ask to see your ticket after the train has left the station.

Long Island Rail Road train

BOOKING TICKETS

Ticketing offices at all train stations will accept most credit and debit cards, as well as cash. When there are lines for tickets, you can use the automated machines, which accept credit cards. Tickets can be purchased online by credit card. Savings are offered for those who buy in advance. Note that there is a surcharge for buying tickets after you board the train.

Yale University in New Haven, Connecticut

DAY TRIPS BY TRAIN

Many destinations near New York are well worth a visit and easily reached by train. Below is a list of some recommended sights; for further details, call NYC & Co. *(see p371)*.

Stony Brook is a peaceful North Shore village and the entrance to the Three Villages historic district. The journey takes 2 hours from Penn Station on a LIRR train.

The chic bars, clubs, and boutiques of the Hamptons are just under 3 hours from New York. Take a LIRR train from Penn Station.

Westbury House, John Phipps's 1906 re-creation of a Charles II mansion with English formal gardens, is 40 minutes from Manhattan. Take a LIRR train from Penn Station to Old Westbury.

Kykuit, the Rockefeller mansion; Washington Irving's home "Sunnyside;" and Jay Gould's mansion, "Lyndhurst", are all in Tarrytown. Take a Metro-North train from Grand Central Station, then a taxi. The journey should take 40–50 minutes.

Two hours outside of Manhattan is Hyde Park, where you can visit Franklin D. Roosevelt's Springwood estate and the Vanderbilt mansion. Take a Metro-North train from Grand Central to Poughkeepsie, then a bus.

Cold Spring, New York, is an antiquing mecca on the Hudson. The scenic riverside journey takes 70 minutes from Grand Central on the Metro-North Hudson Line.

New Haven, Connecticut, is home to the world-famous Yale University. The journey takes 1 hour and 45 minutes, again on a Metro-North train from Grand Central.

DAY TRIPS BY BUS

Many appealing destinations can be reached by bus from the Port Authority Bus Terminal *(see p381)* on Eighth Avenue. **Short Line Bus** offers popular day-out packages to the US Military Academy at West Point, Franklin D. Roosevelt's home at Hyde Park, and the Storm King Art Center. Also on offer is shopping at the Woodbury Common Outlet Center. Rates include round-trip bus fare and any admissions.

New Jersey Transit buses go to the casinos at Atlantic City; they also have stops on the Jersey shore. **Trans-Bridge Lines** has services to charming antiquing meccas such as Lambertville, New Jersey, and New Hope, Pennsylvania.

A number of budget bus lines have inexpensive fares to Philadelphia, a historic city with many attractions that is only 100 miles (160 km) from New York. Among the most reliable and comfortable of these are **Megabus** and **Bolt Bus**, both of which offer free Wi-Fi on board. For those with time to travel farther afield, these companies also serve Boston and Washington, DC.

Bus tickets are on sale in the main concourse of the Port Authority. The long-distance bus companies Greyhound *(see p381)*, **Peter Pan**, and **Adirondacks** and the Short Line, Trans-Bridge, and New Jersey Transit commuter lines have their own ticket counters. No reservations are taken on any of these bus lines.

DAY TRIPS BY SUBWAY OR CITY BUS

The outer boroughs, served by New York's subway and bus system, are also worth exploring. Head for the Coney Island beaches *(see p249)* and the New York Aquarium on the D train, or take the M4 bus to the last stop and visit The Cloisters *(see pp236–9)*, high above the Hudson River.

New York's fascinating ethnic neighborhoods are also easily reached by subway. At Grand Central Station, take the 7 Queens train to 74th Street in Jackson Heights, where you'll find a slice of India. Nearby, 37th Avenue is home to New York's Latin-American community. If you stay on the 7 train to the end of the line, you can explore a Chinatown that some say rivals the one in Manhattan, as well as the city's largest Korean neighbourhood.

In Brooklyn, the D train will take you to the Russian enclave of Brighton Beach, while the G train will let you sample a bit of Poland in Greenpoint. Take the N train to go Greek or Egyptian in Astoria, or the M train to the city's largest Orthodox Jewish community in Borough Park.

DIRECTORY

TRAIN INFORMATION

Amtrak
Tel (800) USA-RAIL or (800) 872-7245. **www**.amtrak.com

Long Island Rail Road (LIRR)
Tel (718) 217-LIRR. www.mta.info

Metro-North Railroad
Tel (212) 532-4900. www.mta.info

New Jersey Transit
Tel (973) 275-5555. www.njtransit.com

PATH
Tel (800) 234-7284. www.panynj.com

BUS INFORMATION

Adirondacks
Tel (518) 846-8016. **http**://visitadirondacks.com

Bolt Bus
Tel (877) 265-8287. www.boltbus.com

Megabus
Tel (877) 462-6342. www.megabus.com

Peter Pan
Tel (800) 343-9999. www.peterpanbus.com

Short Line Bus
Tel (201) 529-3666. www.coachusa.com/shortline

Trans-Bridge Lines
Tel (610) 868-6001. www.transbridgelines.com

STREET FINDER

The map references given with all sights, hotels, restaurants, bars, shops, and entertainment venues described in this book refer to the maps in this section (*see* How the Map References Work *opposite*). These maps cover the whole of Manhattan. A complete index of street names and all the places of interest marked on the maps can be found on the following pages.

The key map *(below)* shows the areas covered by the *Street Finder*, within the various districts. The maps include all of Manhattan's sight-seeing areas (which are color-coded), with all the districts important for hotels, restaurants, bars, shops, theaters, and entertainment.

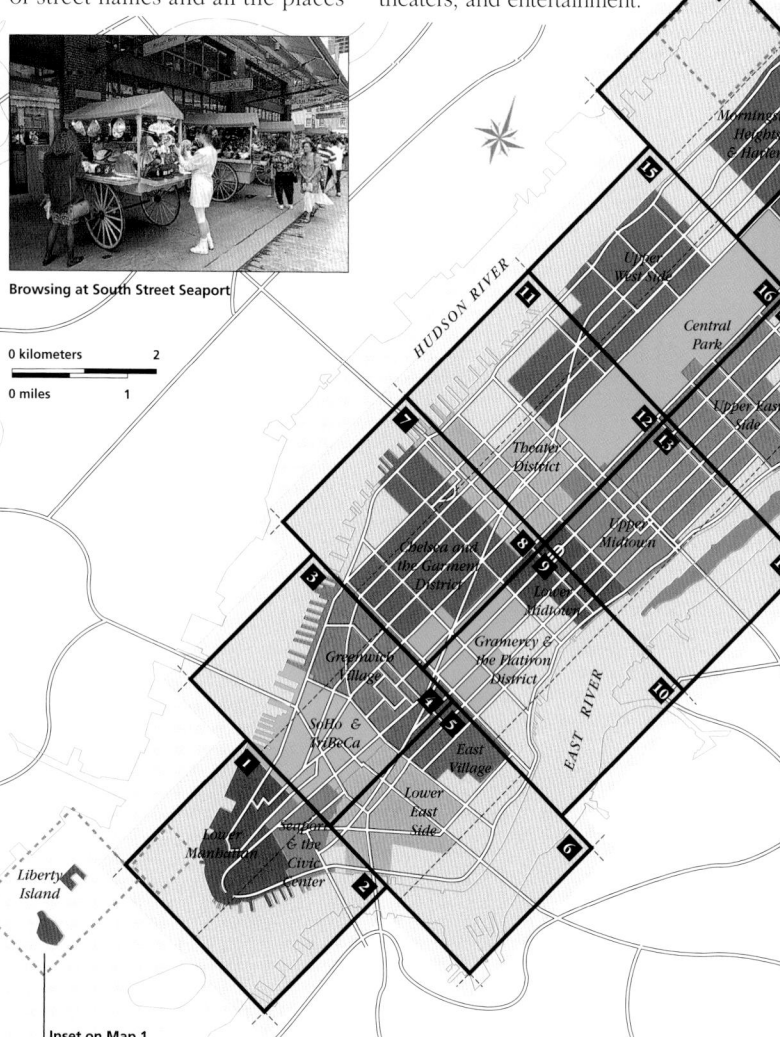

Browsing at South Street Seaport

0 kilometers 2

0 miles 1

Inset on Map 1

Inset on Map 19

KEY TO STREET FINDER

Major sight

Other sight

Station building

M Subway station

Heliport

Ferry terminal

Bus terminal

P Parking

Tourist information office

Hospital with emergency room

Police station

Church

Synagogue

Post office

Railroad line

Pedestrian street

SCALE OF MAP PAGES

0 meters	200	
		1:11,500
0 yards	200	

HOW THE MAP REFERENCES WORK

The first figure tells you which Street Finder map to turn to.

Theodore Roosevelt Birthplace ❼

28 E 20th St. **Map 9 A5.** *Tel* 260-1616. **M** *14th St-Union Sq.* 9am–5pm Wed–Sun (last adm: 4:30pm). *public hols.* **Lectures, concerts, films & video** **www**.nps.gov/thrb

A letter and number give the grid reference. Letters go across the map's top and bottom, numbers on its sides.

The map continues on map 5 of the *Street Finder.*

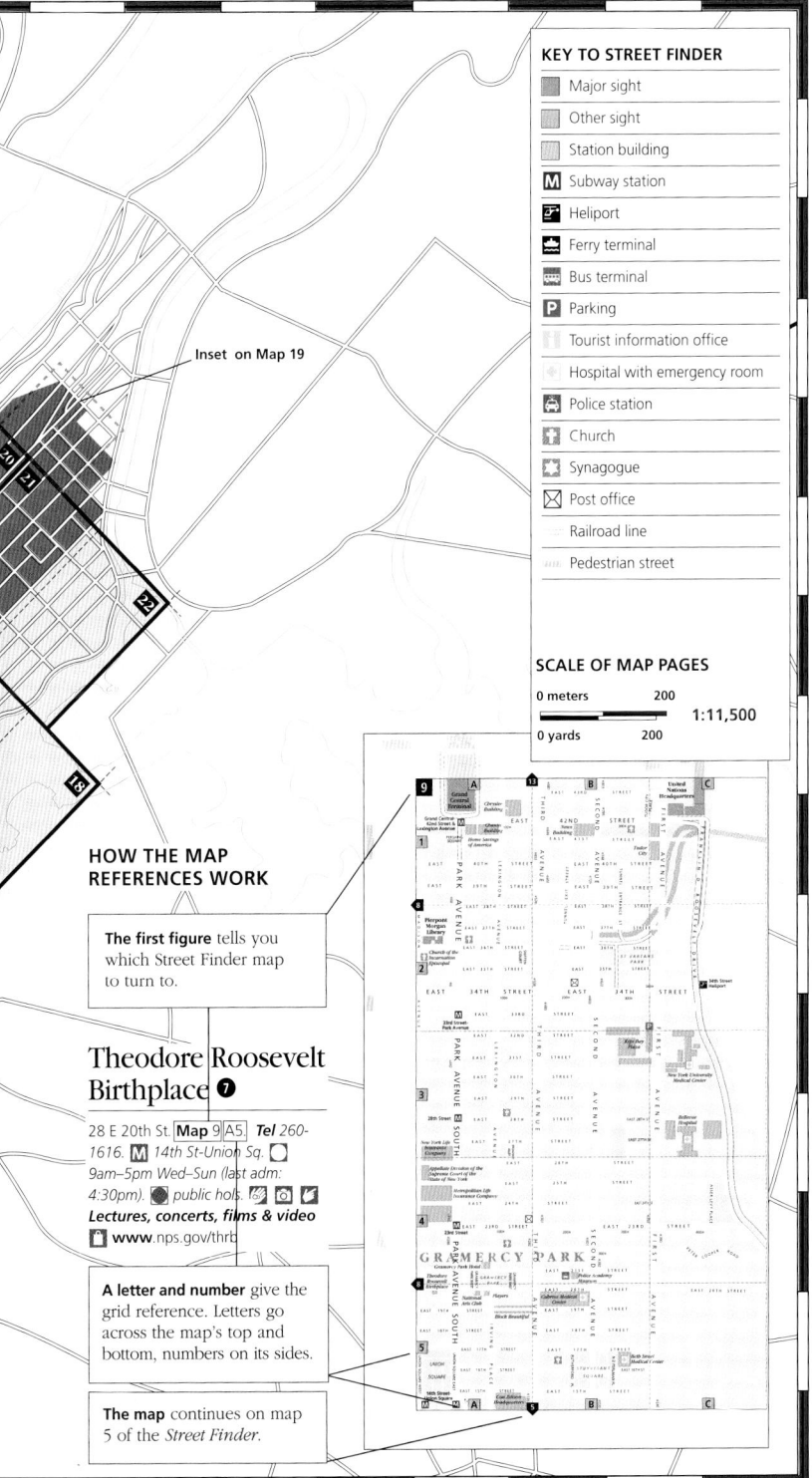

Street Finder Index

Each place name is followed by its borough (unless in Manhattan) and then by its Street Finder reference

Each place name is followed by its borough (unless in Manhattan) and then by its Street Finder reference

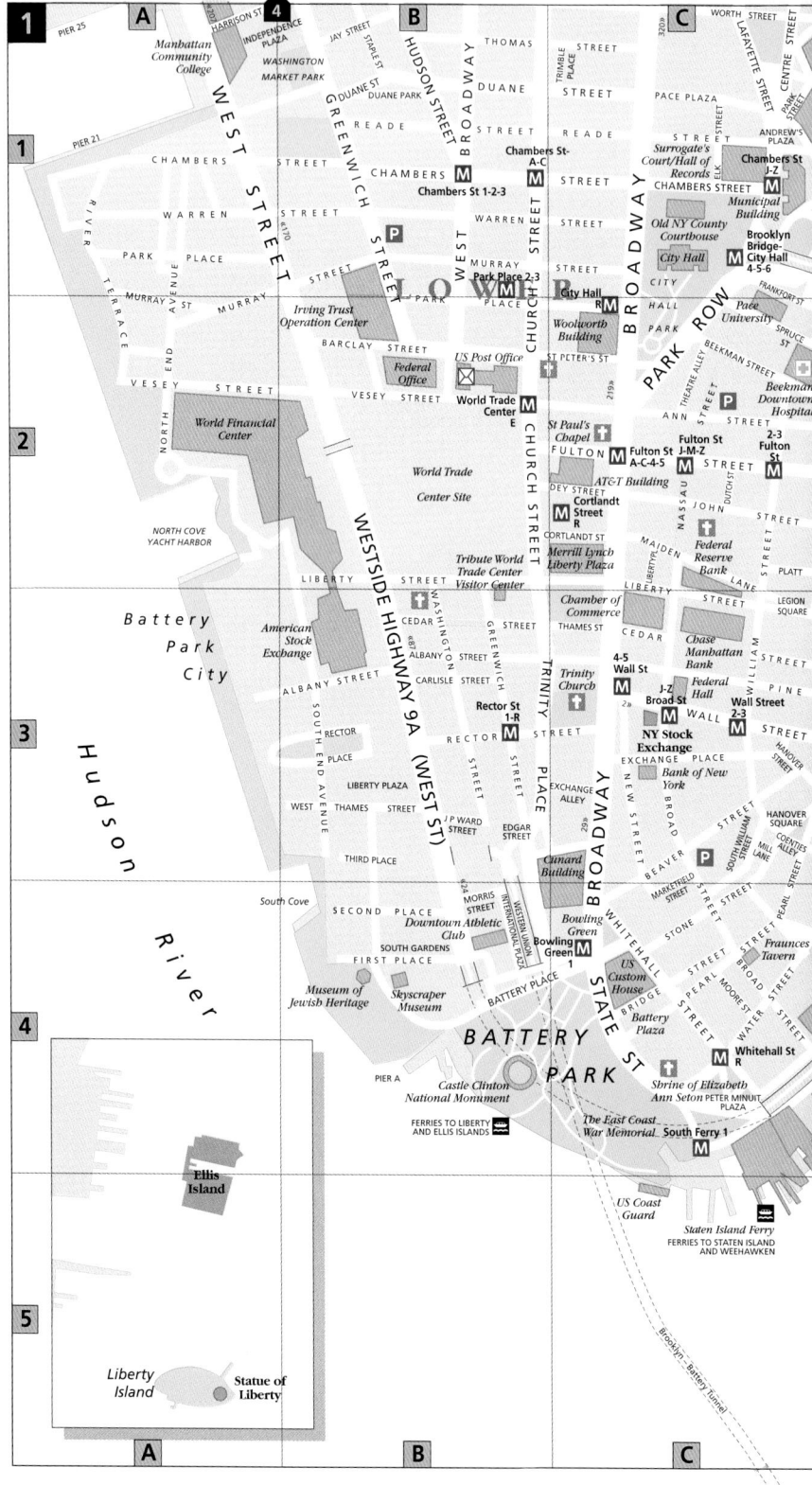

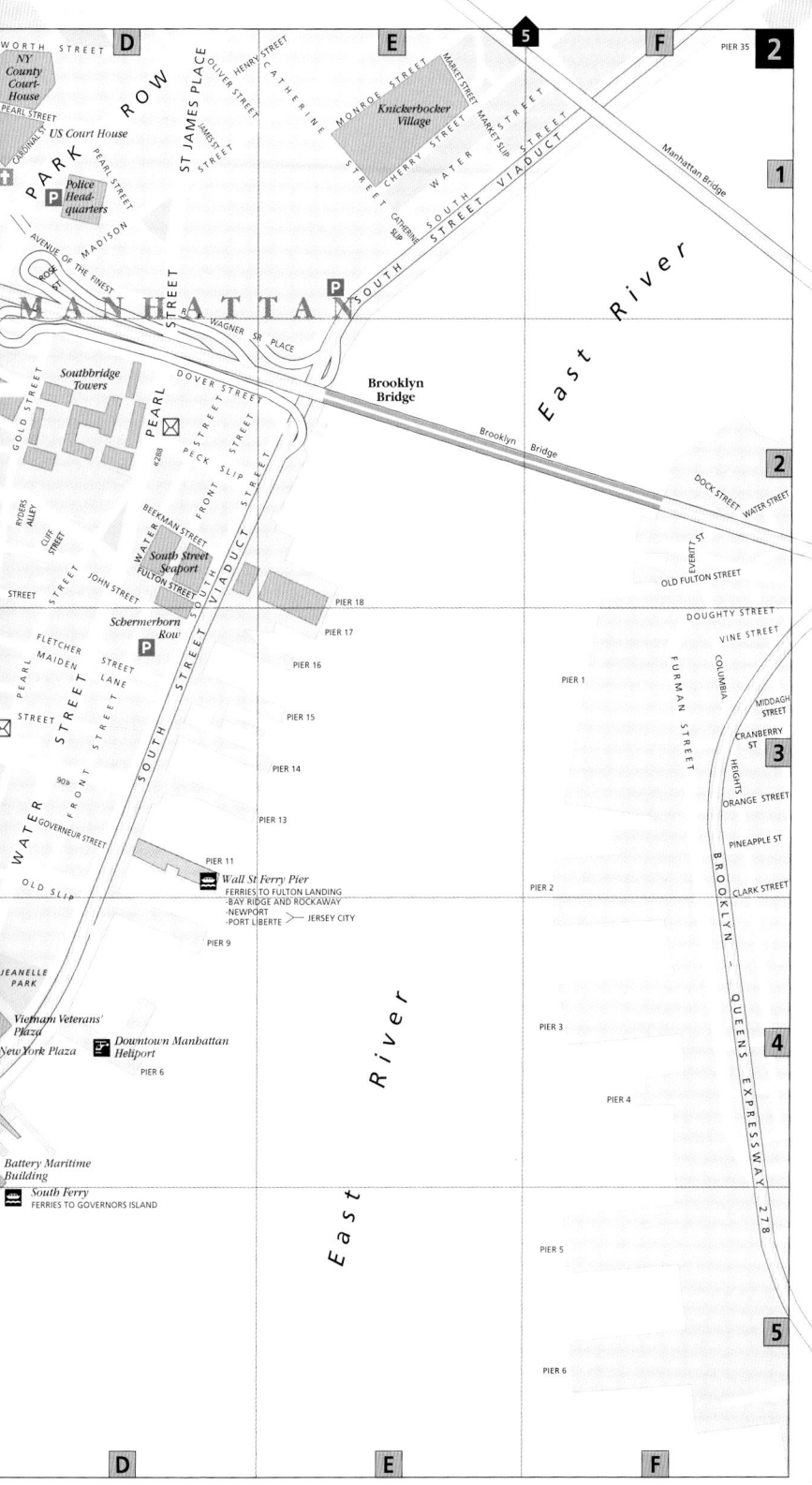

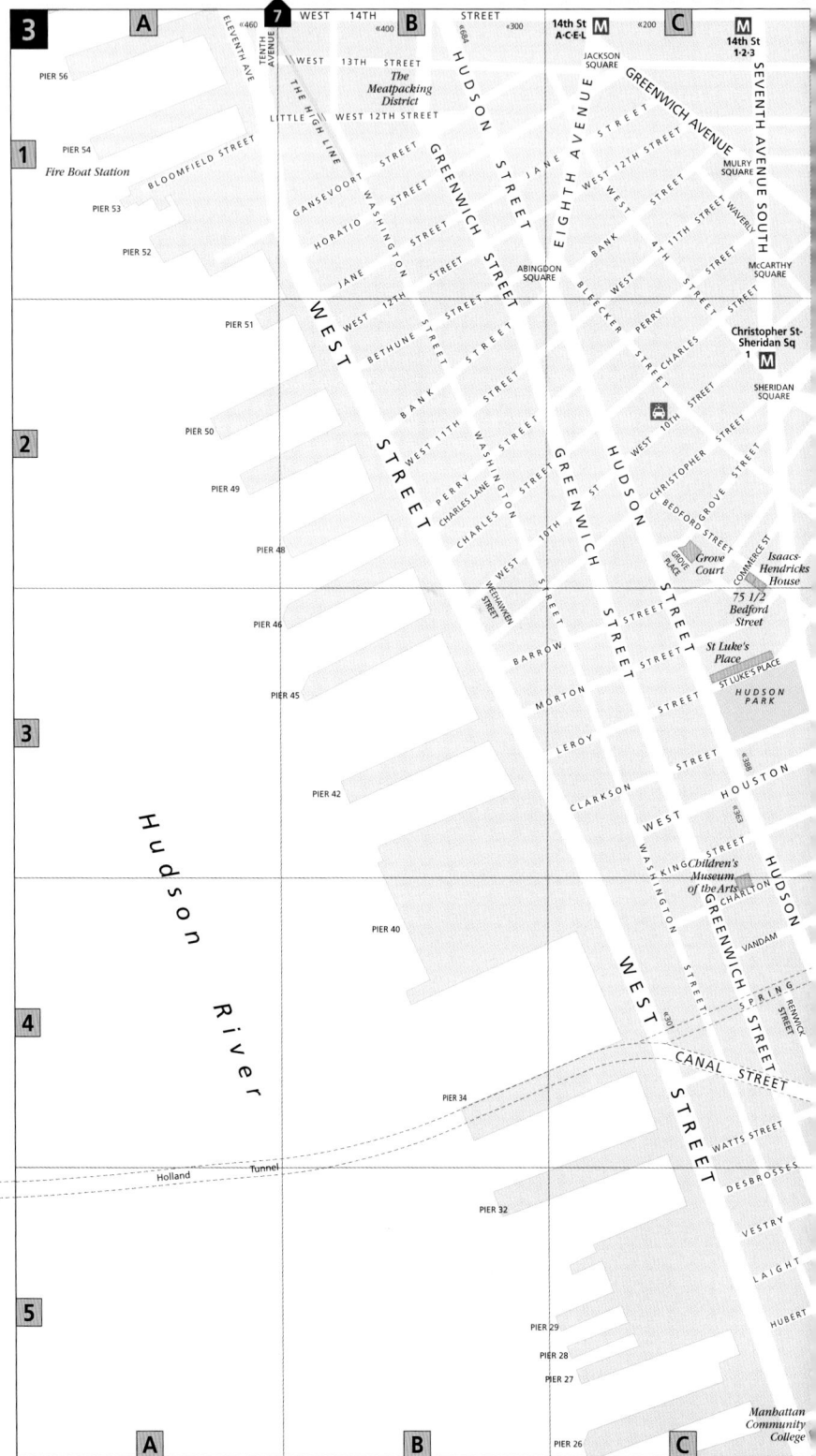

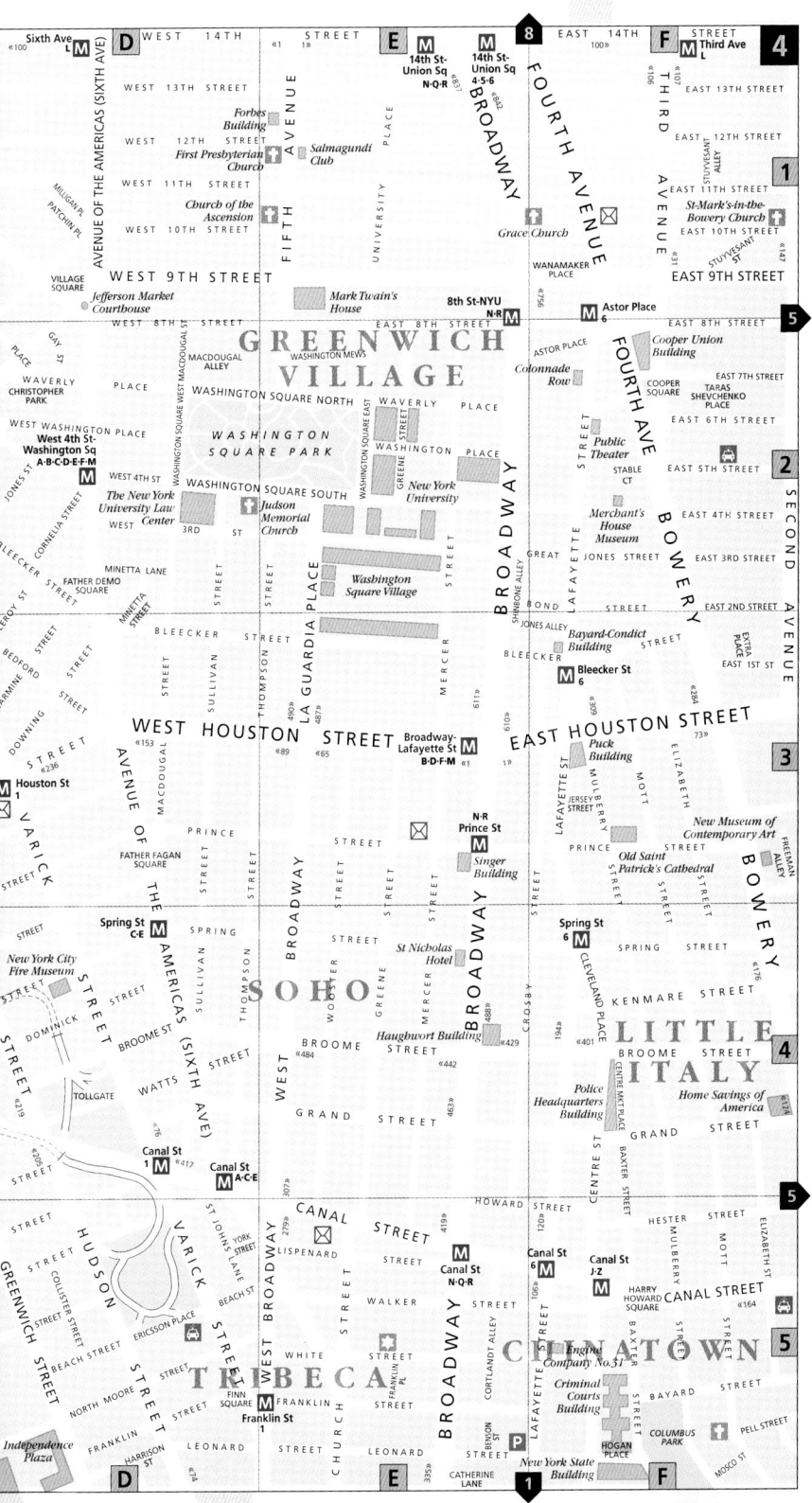

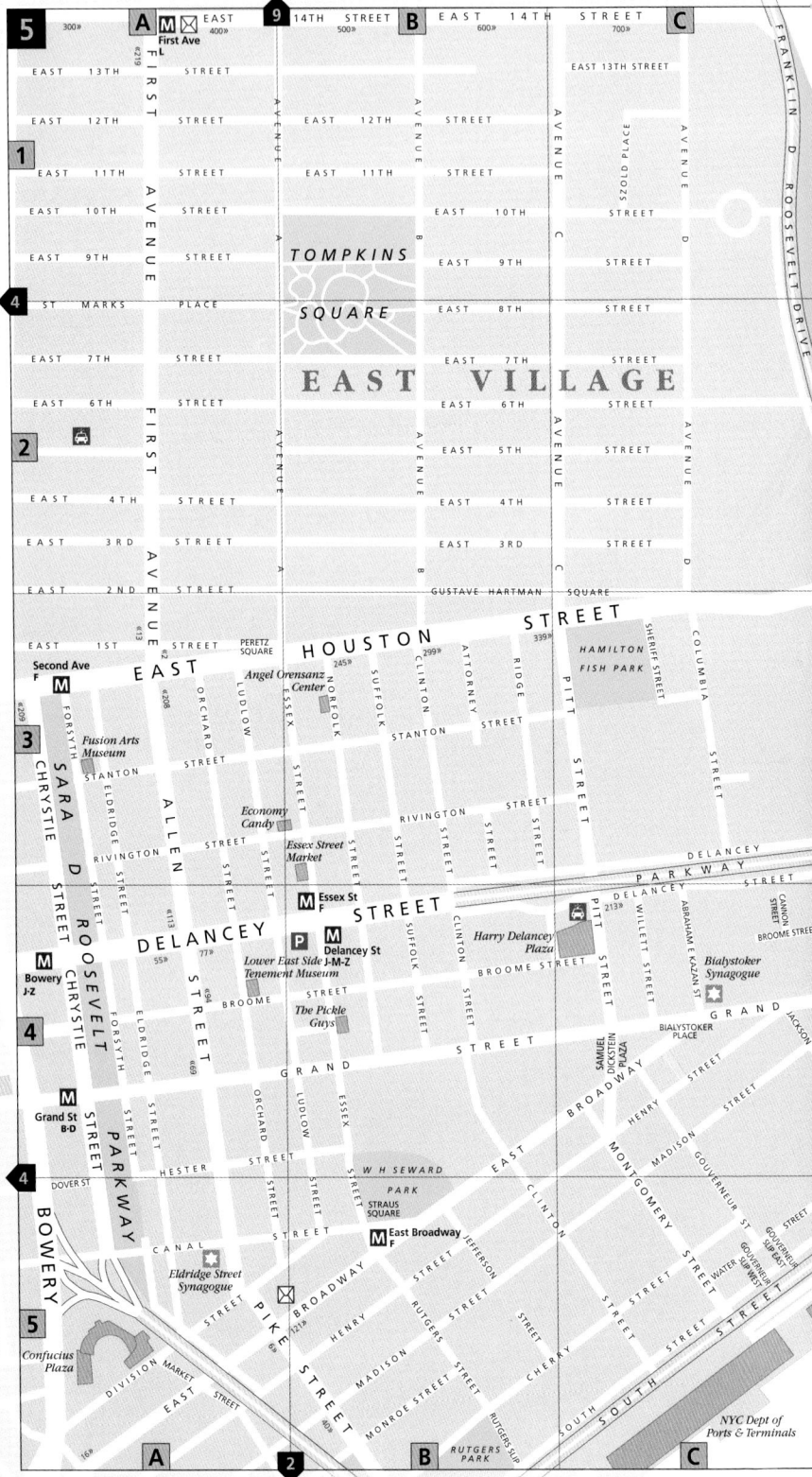

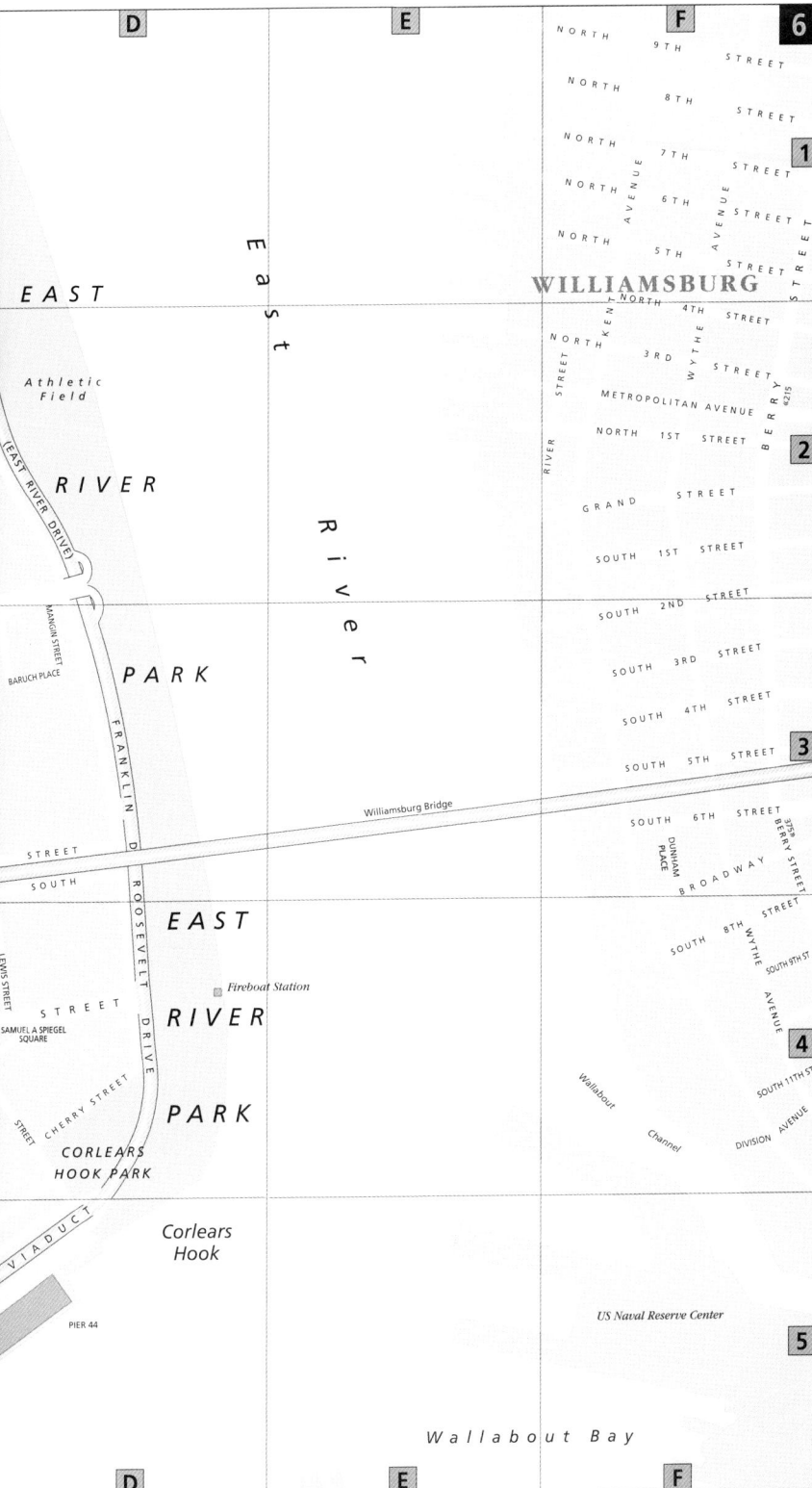

WILLIAMSBURG

EAST

East River

River

Athletic Field

RIVER

PARK

(EAST RIVER DRIVE)

MANGIN STREET

BARUCH PLACE

FRANKLIN D ROOSEVELT DRIVE

STREET

SOUTH

LEWIS STREET

EAST

Fireboat Station

STREET

SAMUEL A SPIEGEL SQUARE

RIVER

CHERRY STREET

STREET

PARK

CORLEARS HOOK PARK

VIADUCT

Corlears Hook

PIER 44

NORTH 9TH STREET
NORTH 8TH STREET
NORTH 7TH STREET
NORTH 6TH AVENUE STREET
NORTH 5TH STREET
NORTH AVENUE
KENT STREET
BERRY STREET #215
NORTH 4TH STREET
WYTHE STREET
NORTH 3RD STREET
METROPOLITAN AVENUE
RIVER STREET
NORTH 1ST STREET
GRAND STREET
SOUTH 1ST STREET
SOUTH 2ND STREET
SOUTH 3RD STREET
SOUTH 4TH STREET
SOUTH 5TH STREET

Williamsburg Bridge

SOUTH 6TH STREET
DUNHAM PLACE
375R BERRY STREET
BROADWAY
SOUTH 8TH STREET
WYTHE STREET
SOUTH 9TH ST
AVENUE
SOUTH 11TH ST
Wallabout Channel
DIVISION AVENUE

US Naval Reserve Center

Wallabout Bay

D · E · F

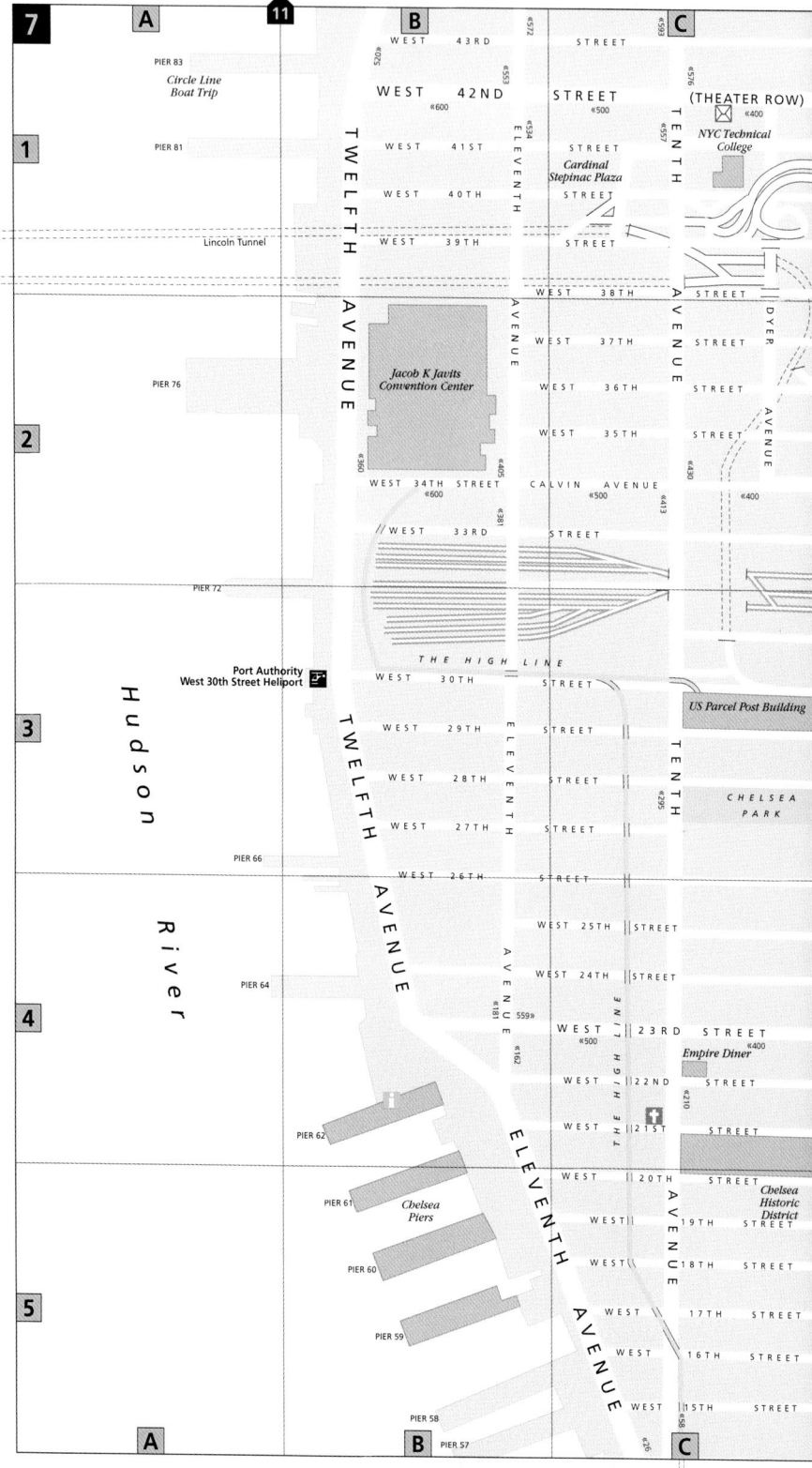

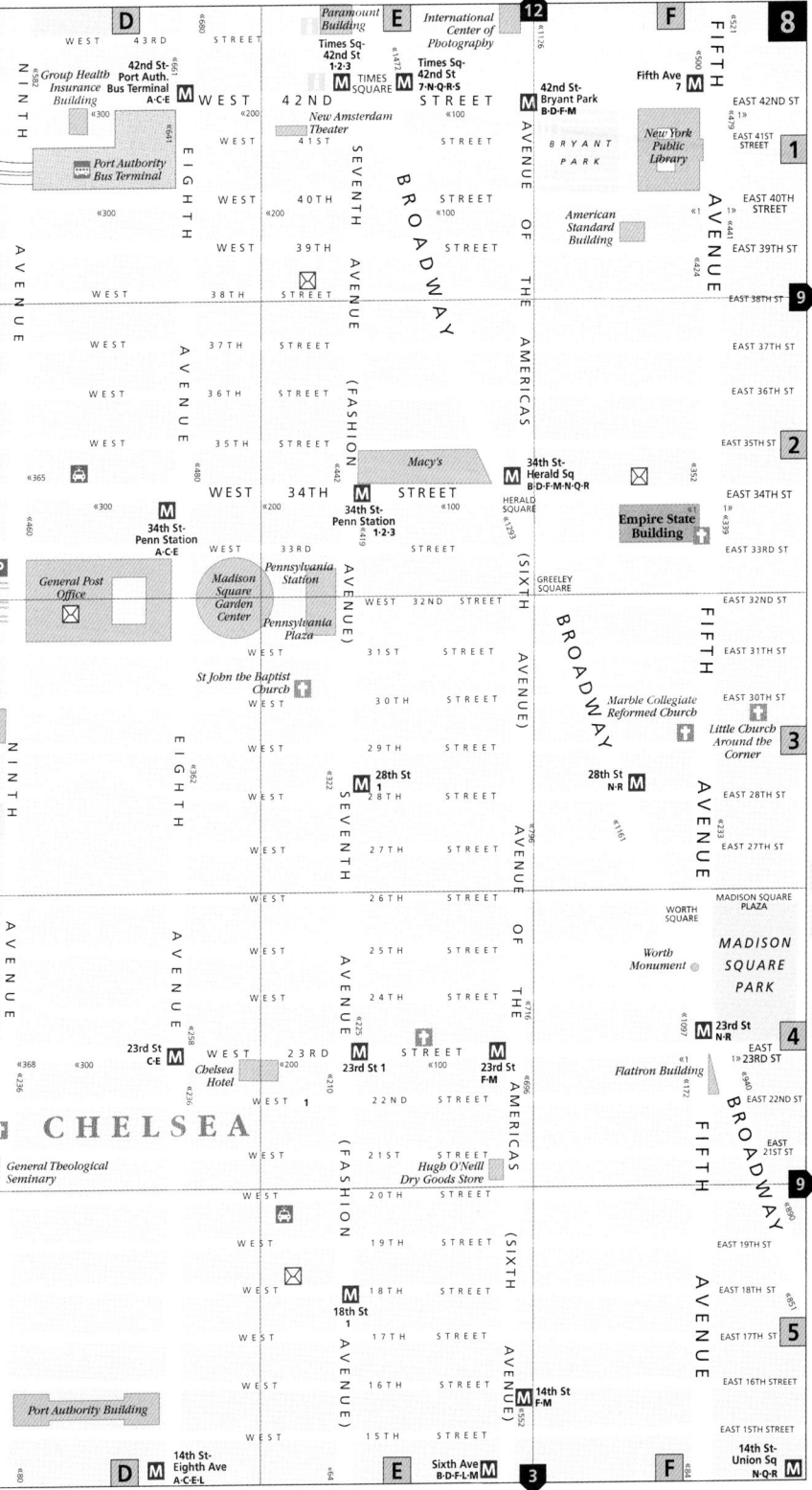

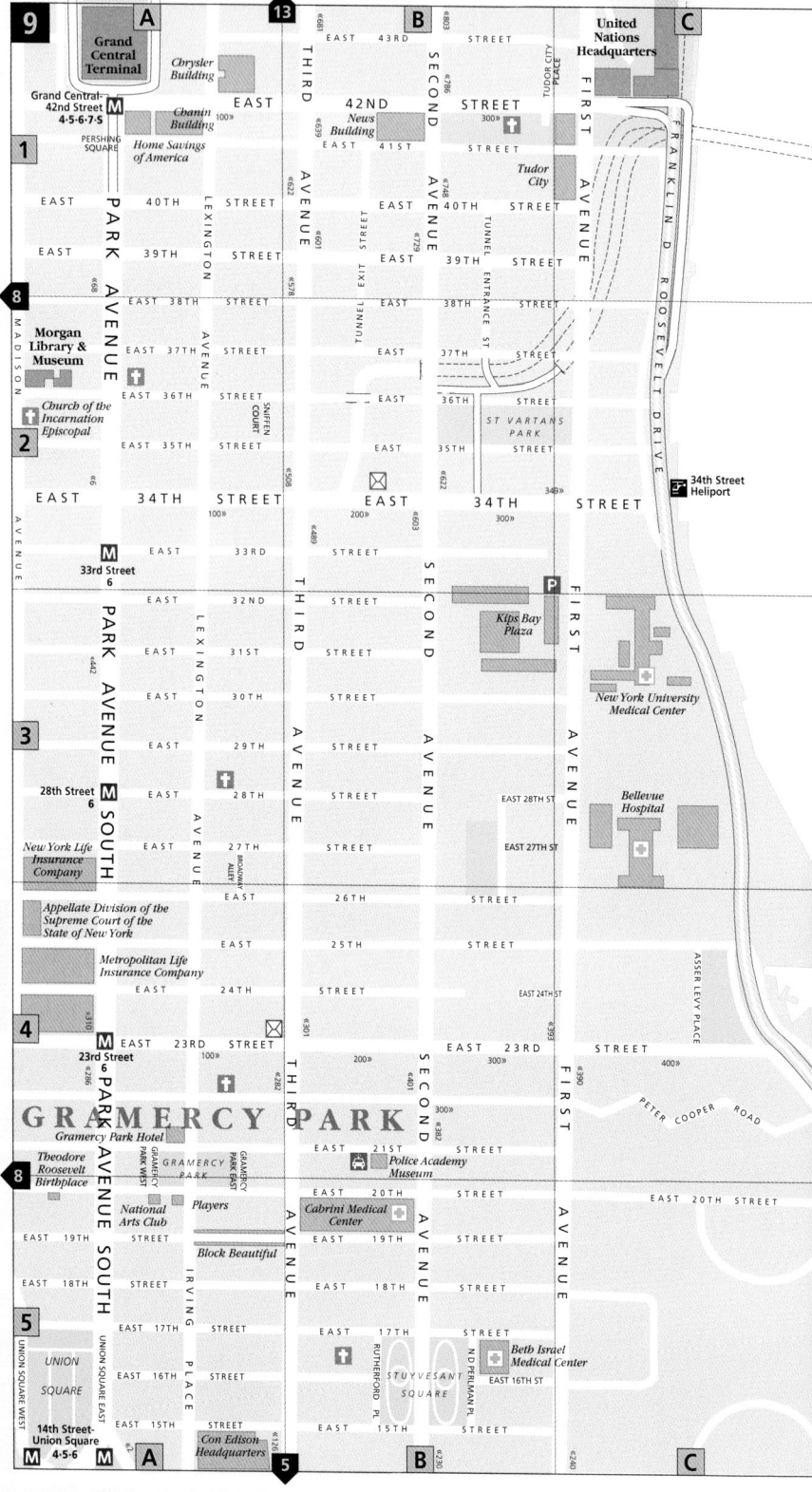

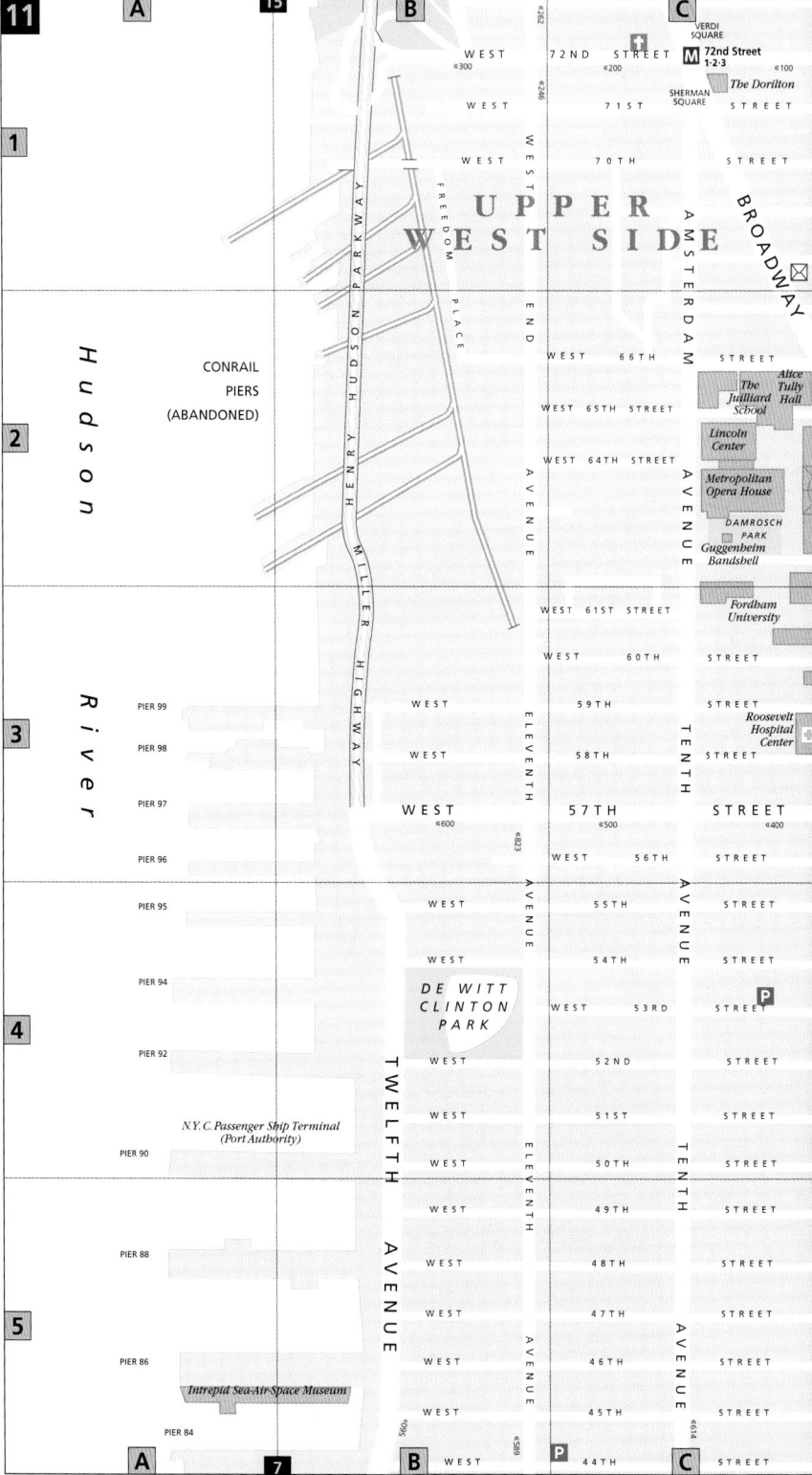

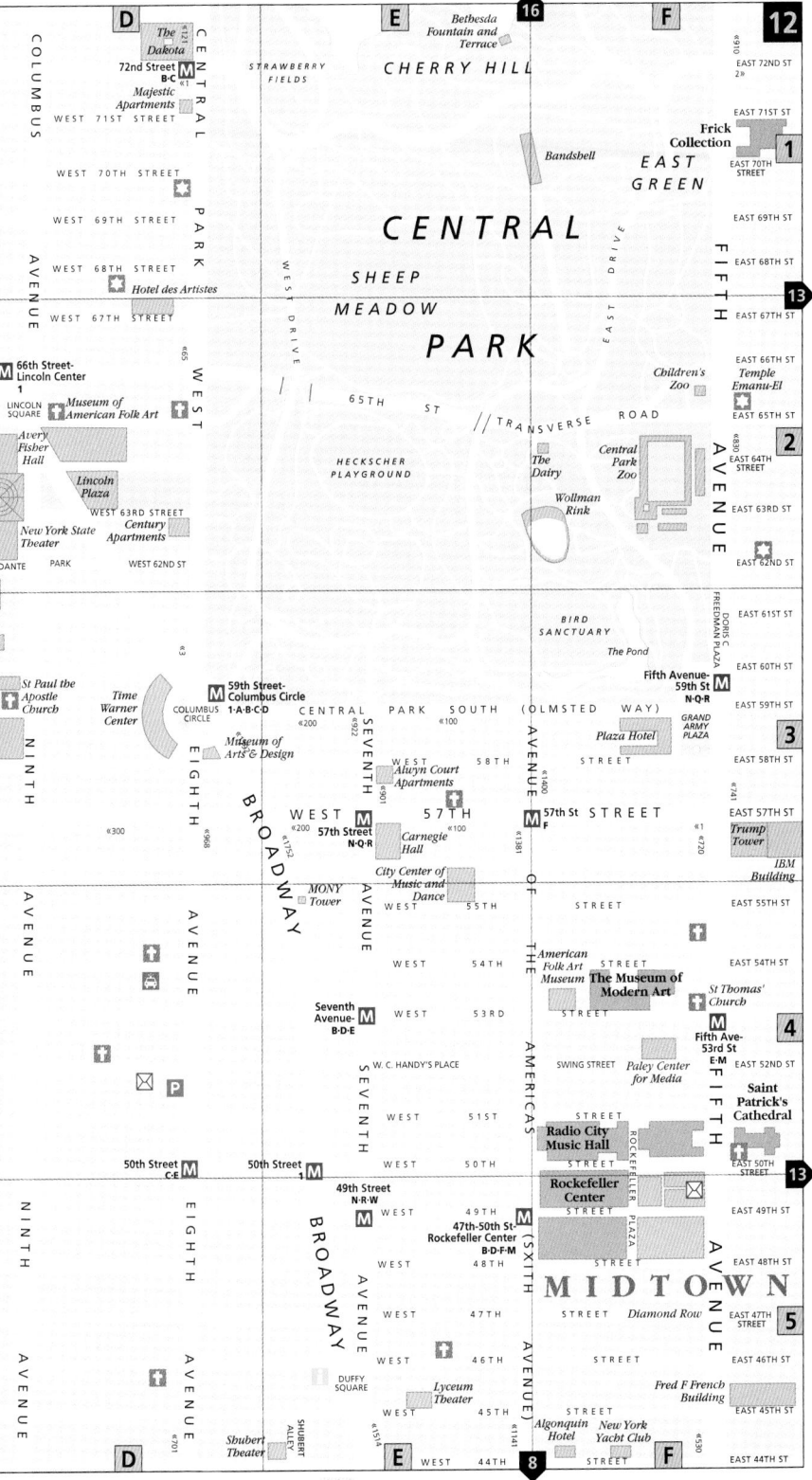

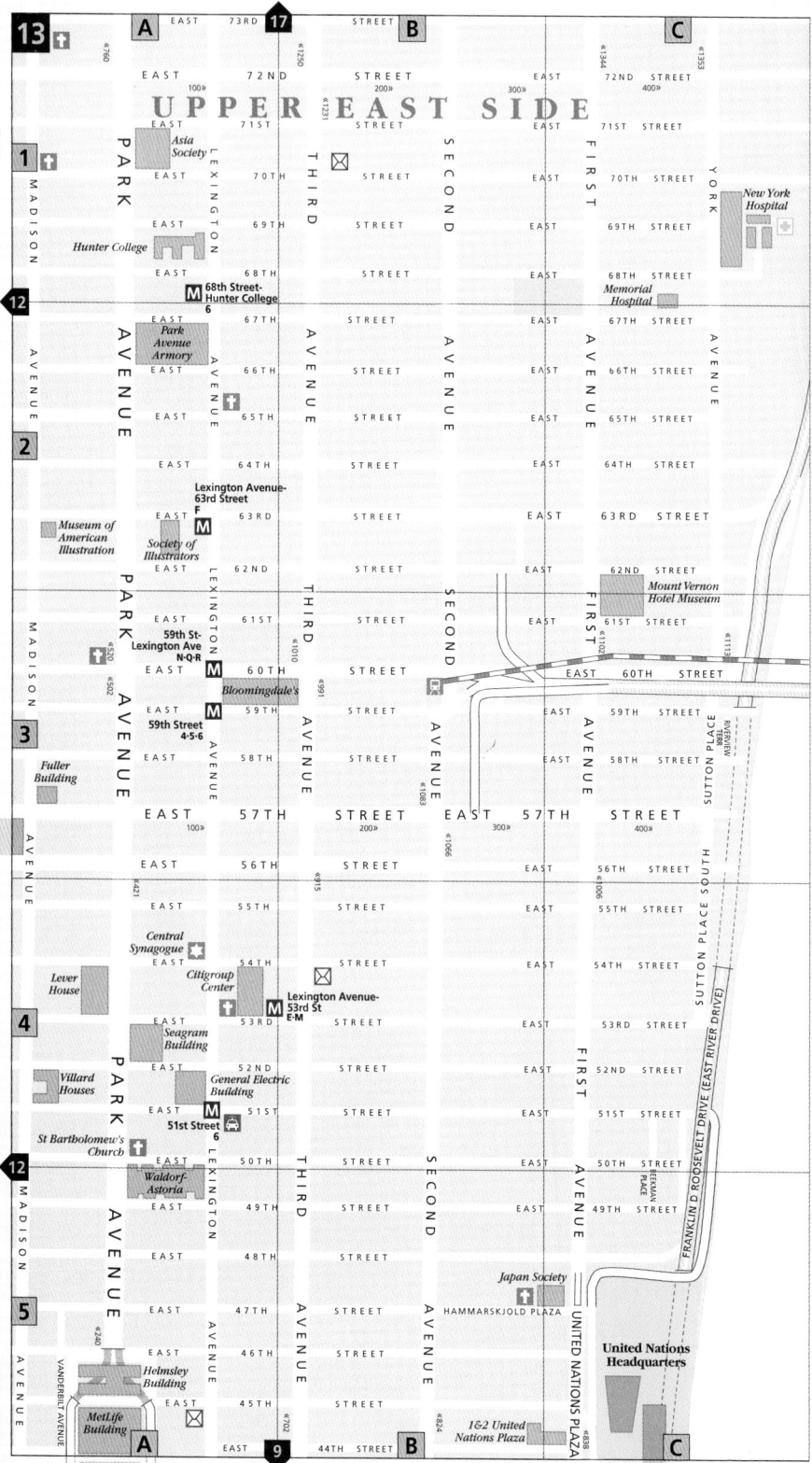

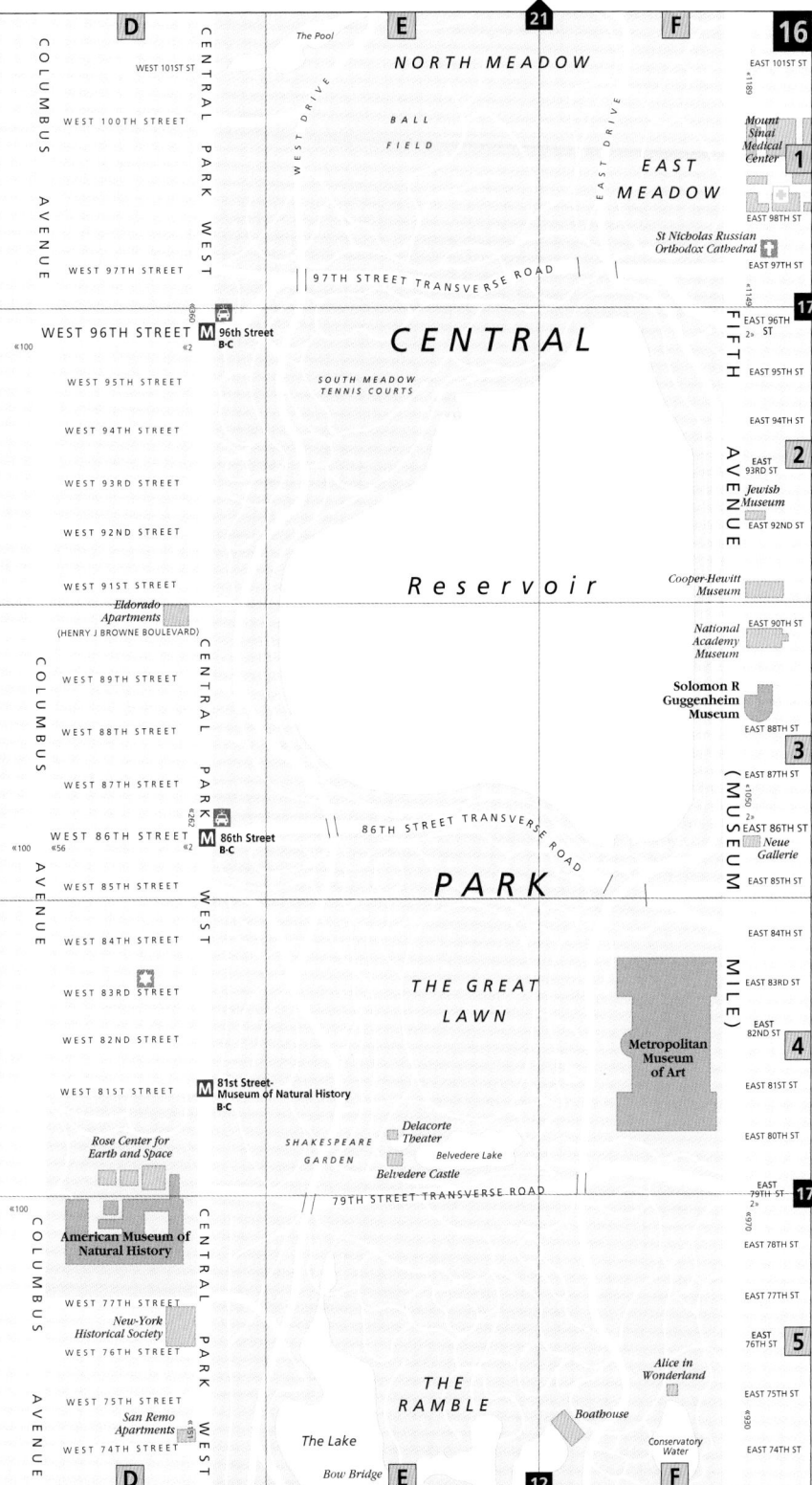

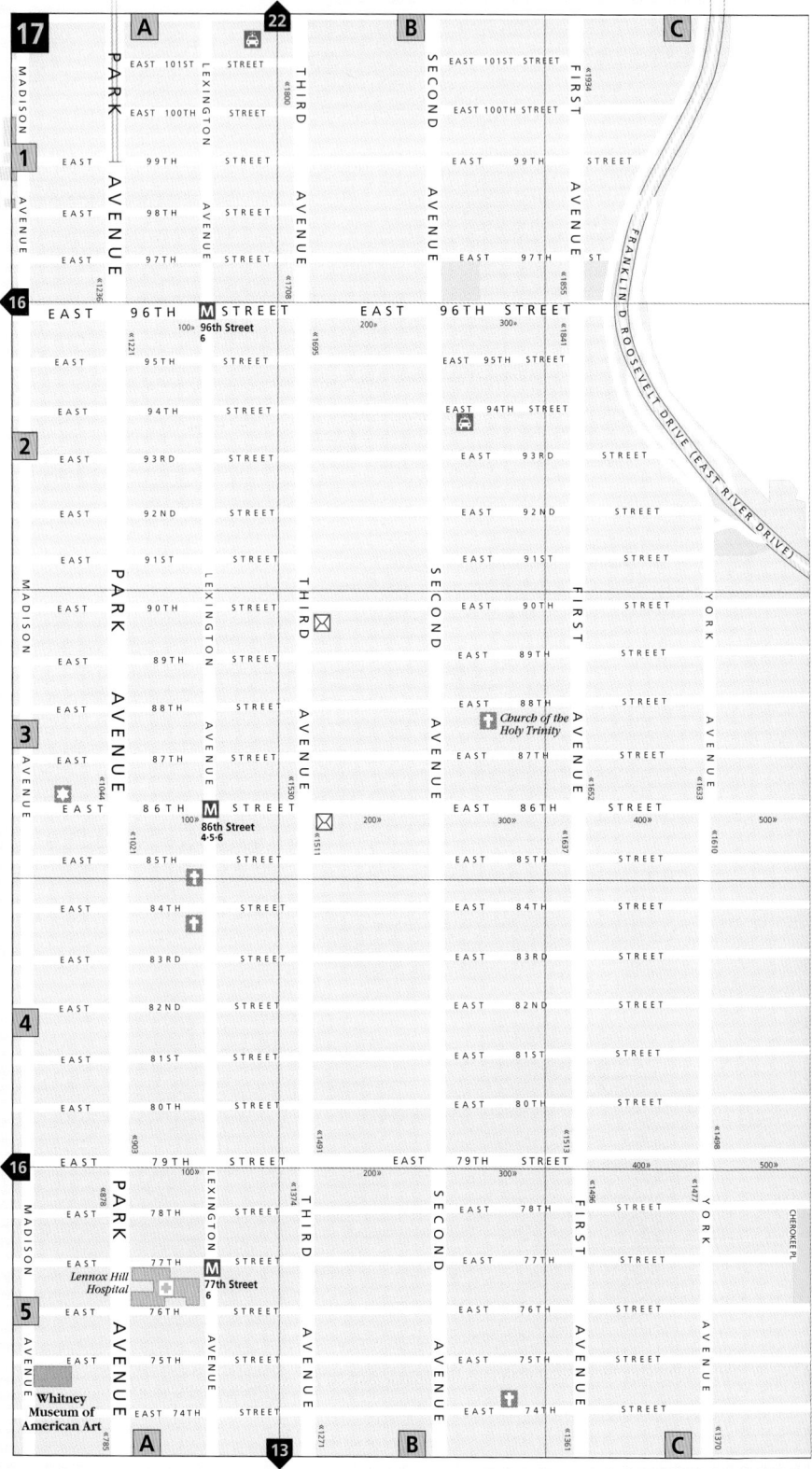

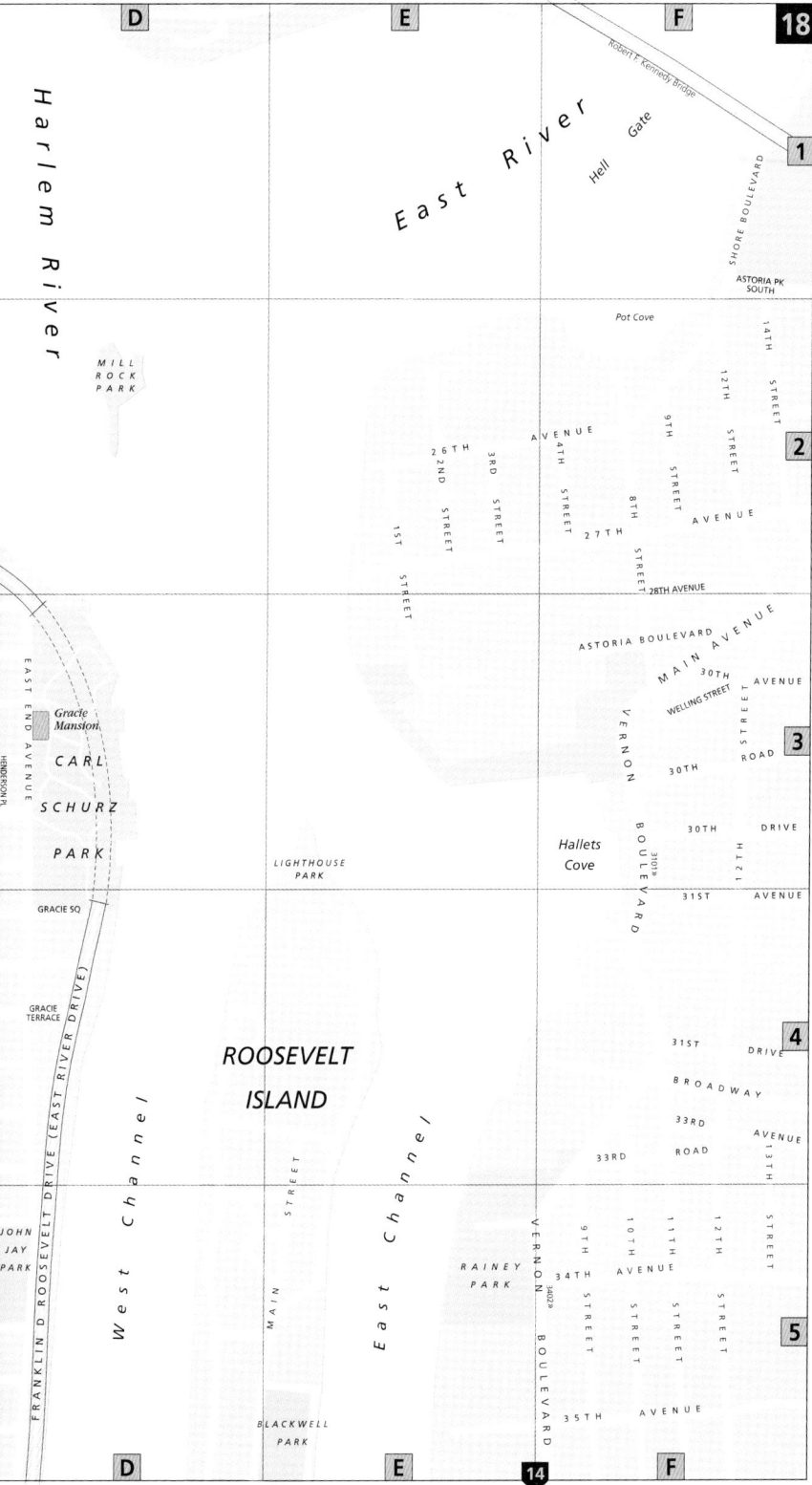

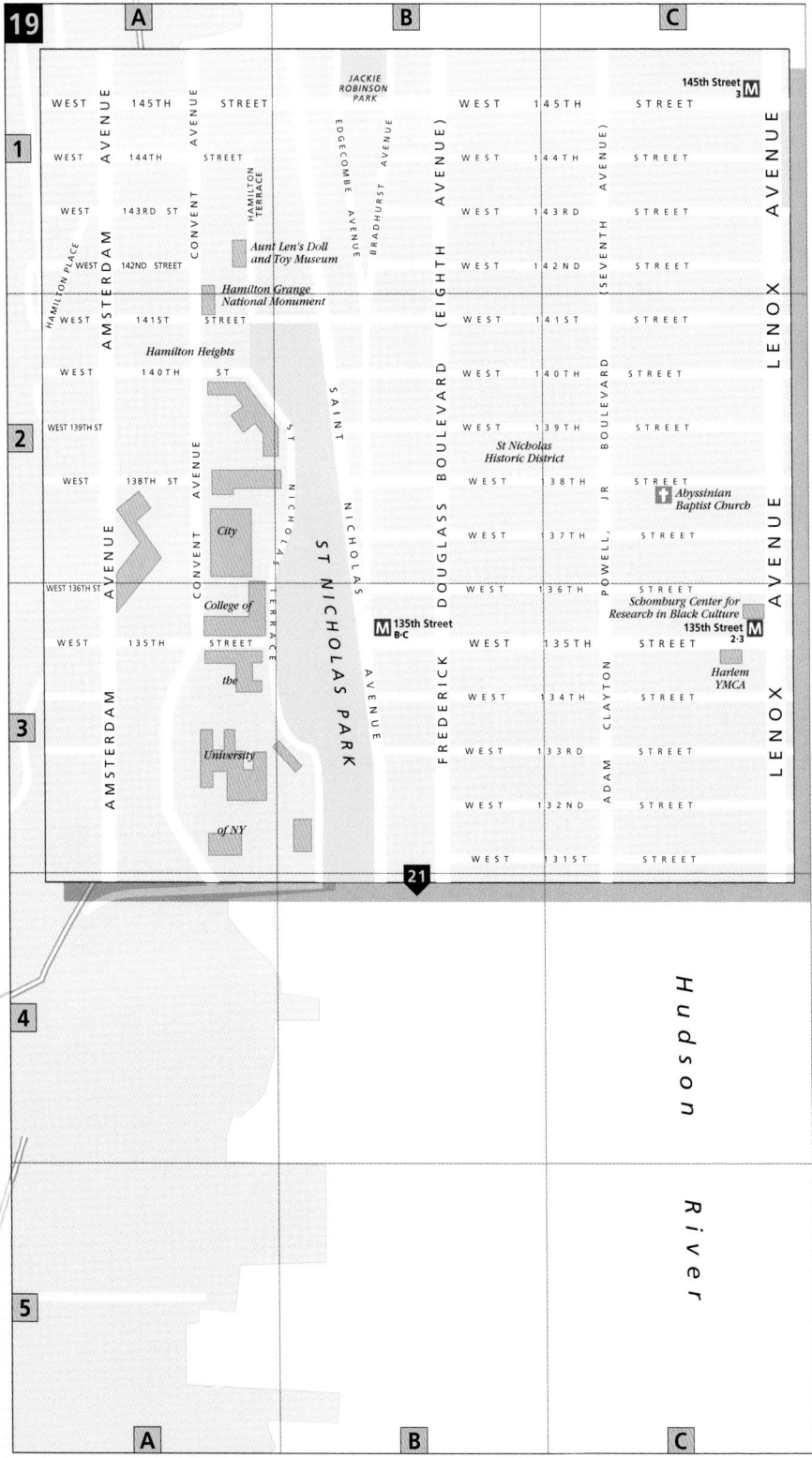

Acknowledgments

Dorling Kindersley would like to thank the many people whose help and assistance contributed to the preparation of this book.

Main Contributor
Eleanor Berman has lived in New York for almost 40 years. Her travel articles are widely published and she is the author of *Away for the Weekend: New York*, a favorite since 1982. Her other books include *Away for the Weekend* guides for the Mid-Atlantic, New England and Northern California, *Travelling on Your Own* and *Reflections of Washington, DC.*

Museum Contributors
Michelle Menendez, Lucy O'Brien, Heidi Rosenau, Elyse Topalian, Sally Williams.

Dorling Kindersley wishes to thank editors and researchers at Websters International Publishers: Sandy Carr, Matthew Barrell, Sara Harper, Miriam Lloyd, Ava-Lee Tanner, Celia Woolfrey.

Additional Photography
Rebecca Carman, Rachel Feierman, Andrew Holigan, Edward Hueber, Eliot Kaufman, Karen Kent, Dave King, Norman McGrath, Howard Millard, Angus Oborn, Ian O'Leary, Rough Guides/Nelson Hancock, Susannah Sayler, Paul Solomon, Chuck Spang, Chris Stevens, Peter Wilson.

Additional Illustrations
Steve Gyapay, Arshad Khan, Kevin Jones, Dinwiddie MacLaren, Janos Marffy, Chris D. Orr, Nick Shewring, John Woodcock.

Cartography
Maps Uma Bhattacharya, Andrew Heritage, Suresh Kumar, James Mills-Hicks, Chez Picthall, John Plumer (Dorling Kindersley Cartography), Kunal Singh. Advanced Illustration (Cheshire), Contour Publishing (Derby), Europmap Ltd (Berkshire). Street Finder maps: ERA-Maptec Ltd (Dublin) adapted with permission from original survey and mapping by Shobunsha (Japan).

Cartographic Research
Roger Bullen, Tony Chambers, Ruth Duxbury, Ailsa Heritage, Jayne Parsons, Laura Porter, Donna Rispoli, Joan Russell, Jill Tinsley, Andrew Thompson.

Design and Editorial
Managing Editor Douglas Amrine
Managing Art Editors Stephen Knowlden, Geoff Manders
Senior Editor Georgina Matthews
Series Design Consultant Peter Luff
Editorial Director David Lamb
Art Director Anne-Marie Bulat
Production Controller Hilary Stephens
Picture Research Susan Mennell, Sarah Moule
Dtp Designer Andy Wilkinson
Keith Addison, Emma Anacootee, Lydia Baillie, Eleanor Berman, Vandana Bhagra, Jon Paul Buchmeyer, Ron Boudreau, Linda Cabasin, Rebecca Carman, Michelle Clark, Sherry Collins, Carey Combe, Diana Craig, Maggie Crowley, Guy Dimond, Nicola Erdpresser, Rhiannon Furbear, Fay Franklin, Tom Fraser, Anna Freiberger, Jo Gardner, Camilla Gersh, Alex Gray, Michelle Haimoff, Marcus Hardy, Sasha Heseltine, Rose Hudson, Pippa Hurst, Kim Inglis, Jaqueline

Jackson, Stuart James, Claire Jones, Priya Kukadia, Mathew Kurien, Maite Lantaron, Shahid Mahmood, Susan Millership, Jane Middleton, Todd Obolsky, Catherine Palmi, Helen Partington, Pollyanna Poulter, Leigh Priest, Pamposh Raina, Nicki Rawson, Alice Reese, Marisa Renzullo, Amir Reuveni, Ellen Root, Liz Rowe, Sands Publishing Solutions, Anaïs Scott, Shailesh Sharma, Meredith Smith, AnneLise Sorensen, Anna Streiffert, Clare Sullivan, Andrew Szudek, Alka Thakur, Shawn Thomas, Conrad Van Dyk, Ros Walford, Lucilla Watson.

Special Assistance
Beyer Blinder Belle, John Beatty at the Cotton Club, Peter Casey at the New York Public Library, Nicky Clifford, Linda Corcoran at the Bronx Zoo, Audrey Manley at the Morgan Library, Jane Fischer, Deborah Gaines at the New York Convention and Visitors Bureau, Dawn Geigerich at the Queens Museum of Art, Peggy Harrington at St. John the Divine, Pamela Herrick at the Van Cortlandt House, Marguerite Lavin at the Museum of the City of New York, Robert Makla at the Friends of Central Park, Gary Miller at the New York Stock Exchange, Laura Mogil at the American Museum of Natural History, Fred Olsson at the Shubert Organization, Dominique Palermo at the Police Academy Museum, Royal Canadian Pancake House, Lydia Ruth and Laura I. Fries at the Empire State Building, David Schwartz at the American Museum of the Moving Image, Joy Sienkiewicz at the South Street Seaport Museum, Barbara Orlando at the Metropolitan Transit Authority, the staff at the Lower East Side Tenement Museum, Msgr. Anthony Dalla Valla at St. Patrick's Cathedral.

Research Assistance
Christa Griffin, Bogdan Kaczorowski, Steve McClure, Sabra Moore, Jeff Mulligan, Marc Svensson, Vicky Weiner, Steven Weinstein.

Photographic Reference
Duncan Petersen Publishers Ltd.

Photography Permissions
Dorling Kindersley would like to thank the following for their kind permission to photograph at their establishments: American Craft Museum, American Museum of Natural History, Aunt Len's Doll and Toy Museum, Balducci's, Home Savings of America, Brooklyn Children's Museum, The Cloisters, Columbia University, Eldridge Street Project, Federal Hall, Rockefeller Group, Trump Tower.

Picture credits
a = above; b = below/bottom; c = center; f = far; l = left; r = right; t = top.

Works of art have been reproduced with the permission of the following copyright holders:
© ADAGP, Paris and DACS, London 2011: 67ca (April 1971–July 1972, by Jean Dubuffet), 107cl, 162tr (donated by the Norwegian Government, 1952), 172bl, 188cl, 189cra, 189crb; © ARS, NY and DACS, London 2011:185cr, 201crb; Jose de Creeft ©DACS, London/VAGA, New York 2011: 53cl, 207cl; © DACS, London 2011: 161cr, 163tc; *Charging Bull* © Arturo Di Modica 1998 73tl; © Sucession Picasso/DACS, London 2011: 36tr, 115tc, 173cb, 174cr, 188bl, 189bl, 192cl; DK IMAGES: Judith Miller/Wallis & Wallis, Sussex 58br; © Kingdom of Spain, Gaia - Salvador Dali Foundation, DACS, London 2011: 174cl; © Marisol Escobar/DACS, London/VAGA, New York

2011: 55bc; © Jasper Johns/DACS, London/VAGA, New York 2011: 201ca; ©The Estate of Roy Lichtenstein/DACS, London 2011: 175tl, 200clb; © 1993 Frank Stella/ARS, New York and DACS, London: 192tr; By permission of E Jan Nadelman: 201br; Printed by permission of the Norman Rockwell Family Trust © 1961 the Norman Rockwell Family Trust: 163br; © Licensed by The Andy Warhol Foundation for the Visual Arts, Inc/ARS, New York and DACS, London 2011: 200cla; © The Whitney Museum of American Art: 37br, 200bl.

The Publishers are grateful to the following museums, companies and picture libraries for permission to reproduce their photographs:

AGENCE FRANCE PRESSE: Doug Kanter 33tr; ALAMY IMAGES: Ambient Images Inc./Joseph A. Rosen 171c; Sandra Baker 370tl; Peter Cavanagh 373cla; Comstock Images 295c; Wendy Connett 96cr; Eye Ubiquitous/Jon Hicks 130c; Kevin Foy 73tl; Jeff Greenberg 268cla; Blaine Harrington III 379tl; Bob Jones 111b; Richard Levine 381tc; Yadid Levy 366–7; Ian Marlow 373cl; Ellen McKnight 378cl; PCL 295tl; Pictures Colour Library 108; Alex Segre 294cla; Lana Sundman 373tl; tbkmedia.de 340bc; Hugh Threlfall 372cla; ALGONQUIN HOTEL, N.Y: 280bl; AMERICAN MUSEUM-HAYDEN PLANETARIUM, NY: D. Finnin 218t; AMERICAN MUSEUM OF THE MOVING IMAGE: Carson Collection © Bruce Polin 247t; AMERICAN MUSEUM OF NATURAL HISTORY, NY: 39bl, 216ca; D. Finnin 216bl; Angel Orensanz Center: Laszlo Regas 101cl; Aquarius, UK: 171tr; Ashmolean Museum, Oxford: 17tc; THE ASIA SOCIETY, NY: 187cl; ATTACHÉ COMMUNICATIONS: 392crb; AVERY FISHER HALL: © N McGrath 1976 351tr. AVIS BUDGET GROUP: 385crb; © THE GEORGE BALANCHINE TRUST: *Apollo*, choreography by George Balanchine, photo by P Kolnik 5tc; *Stravinsky Violin Concerto*, choreography by George Balanchine, photo by P Kolnik 340tc; George Balanchine's *The Nutcracker*, SM, photo by P Kolnik 343cb; The BETTMANN ARCHIVE, NY: 18bcl, 19cra, 19cr, 19bl, 20cl, 22cbr, 22bl, 22–23, 25br, 27cra, 28cla, 28cra, 28crb, 32cla, 33tl, 43tl, 45cbl, 49c, 54–55b, 71tl, 74cla, 79crb, 79br, 111bl, 177cla, 185br, 209t, 212cl, 225cr, 231t, 241tr, 267tr; Bettmann Newsphotos/Reuters: 33tr; Bettmann/ UPI: 29cra, 29bc, 30bcr, 31br, 32cra, 32bl, 32br, 46cl, 48cl, 49bl, 72c, 78cl, 153c, 163c, 266br, 267cr; BLOOMINGDALE'S: 29cbr; © Roy Export Company Establishment 173tr; THE BRITISH LIBRARY, London: 16; BROOKLYN HISTORICAL SOCIETY: (detail) 89tl; THE BROOKLYN MUSEUM: 38bl, 39c, 250c, 250cra, 250bl, 251t, 251cra, 251c, 251bl, 251b, 252t, 252br, 253cr, 253bl; Lewis Wick Hine, *Climbing Into The Promised Land*, 1908 – 36clb; J Kerr 250c, 252bl; P Warchol: 251cr; The Cantor Collection 253cl; Adam Husted 250t; BROWN BROTHERS: 67br, 71bl, 82cra, 90t, 106br. CAMERA PRESS: 30cbr, 30bl, 33cb, 127cr; R Open 48tr; T Spencer 32cb; THE CARLYLE HOTEL, NY: 281tr; CARNEGIE HALL: © H. Grossman 343br; J ALLAN CASH: 33bl; CATHEDRAL OF ST. JOHN THE DIVINE: Greg Wyatt 1985, 227tl; CBS ENTERTAINMENT/DESILU TOO: "Vacation from Marriage" 171br; CHELSEA PIERS: Fred George 33bl; CHILDREN'S MUSEUM OF THE ARTS: 107cl; CityPASS 369c; COLORIFIC!: Colorific/ Black Star: 79cra; T Cowell 223cr; R Fraser 74t; D Moore 31bl; T Spiegel 15cr, 364tr; CORBIS: Bettmann 137cl, 273ca, 383c; Jacques M. Chenet 272tl; Randy Duchaine 99cl; Kevin Fleming 271tl; Bob Krist 10cra; Todd Gipstein 75t; David Lehman: 138bl; Gail Mooney 207b, 269tr, 271br;

Bill Ross 12t; Michael Setboun 268tr; Steven E. Sutton 51b; Bo Zaunders 376cl; Mike Zens 262–3. CULVER PICTURES, INC: (inset) 9, 19crb, 20cbl, 21bl, 23tl, 23br, 26tl, 26cl, 29cb, 29bl, 48br, 49tr, 74bl, 75cra, 75cb, 76tl, 78crb, 83c, 121bl, 124tc, 127bl, 137cr, 147c, 149cl, 229t, 229bc, 229cr, 261crb. DAILY EAGLE: (detail) 89cl; DAILY NEWS: 370tl, 370tr. ESTO: P Aaron 342bl; DELTA AIRLINES INC. CORPORTAE COMMUNICATIONS EMEA: 378tc; DOLLAR THRIFTY AUTOMOTIVE GROUP, Inc.: 385cra; MARY EVANS PICTURE LIBRARY: 24br, 87br, 106bl; CHRIS FAIRCLOUGH COLOUR LIBRARY: 385bcl; THE FORBES MAGAZINE COLLECTION, NY: 114tl; FOUR SEASONS HOTEL: Peter Vitale 281cr; FRAUNCES TAVERN MUSEUM, NY: From the exhibit "Come All You Gallant Heroes" The World of the Revolutionary Soldier December 4, 1991 to August 14, 1992: 22cla; Copyright THE FRICK COLLECTION, NY: 37bl (*St Francis In The Desert* by Giovanni Bellini), 202ca, 202cl, 202clb, 202b, 202tr, 203ca, 203cr, 203bc, 203br. GARRARD THE CROWN JEWELLERS: 145c; GETTY IMAGES: AFP/Stan Honda 392cla; Mitchell Funk 341cb; Michael Grimm 386tl; GREENMARKET FARMERS MARKET: 371tr; THE SOLOMON R GUGGENHEIM MUSEUM, NY: photo by D Heald 188tl, 188bl, 188bc, 188br, 189t, 189cra, 189crb, 189bl; ROBERT HARDING PICTURE LIBRARY: 378tc; HARPERS NEW MONTHLY MAGAZINE: 87tl; HARPERS WEEKLY: 367c; MILTON HEBALD: *Prospero and Miranda* 205t, *Romeo and Juliet* 343cr. THE IMAGE BANK: front endpaper bl, 89br; M Melford 393tl; P Miller 383tr; A Satterwhite 75br. THE JEWISH MUSEUM: NY: 184tr, 186c; THE KOBAL COLLECTION: 213tc; LEBRECHT MUSIC: Toby Wales 149t; THE LEISURE PASS GROUP: 369cla; THE LESBIAN, GAY, BISEXUAL & TRANSGENDER COMMUNITY CENTER: 370c; FRANK LESLIE'S ILLUSTRATED NEWSPAPER: 86br, 87tr, 275c; LIBRARY OF CONGRESS: 20bc, 23cla, 27bl, 27br; LIFE MAGAZINE © TIME WARNER INC/KATZ/A FEININGER: 8–9; Georg John Lober: *Hans Christian Andersen*, 1956, 206br; LEONARDO MEDIA LTD: 276br, 276cl, 277crb, 277tl; THE LOWELL HOTEL, NY: 281cl; MARY ANN LYNCH: 318bc, 372cl. MADISON SQUARE GARDEN: 134r, 342cr; MAGNUM PHOTOS: © H Cartier-Bresson 175c; Erwitt 35cr; G Peres 14br, 92; JACQUES MARCHAIS CENTER OF TIBETAN ART: 254bc; MASTERFILE UK: Gail Mooney 33br; METRO-NORTH COMMUTER RAILROAD: F English 156tr, 156cla; THE METROPOLITAN MUSEUM OF ART, NY: 35bl (*Young Woman With A Waterjug* by Johannes Vermeer), 37crb (*Figure of a Hippopotamus*, faience, Egypt, 12th Dynasty), 182tc, 190cla, 190clb, 190bc, 190br, 191tl, 191tr, 191cr, 191bl, (photo Al Mozell) 191br, 192tr, 192c, 192bl, 192br, 193tl, 193tr, 193c, 193bl, 194tl, 194tr, 194b, (detail) 195tl, 195tr, 195b, 196t, 196cl, 196cr, 196b, 197tl, 197cr, 197bl, 236tr, 236cl, 236cr, 236b, 237ca, 237cr, 237bl, 237br, 238tl, 238tr, 239tr, 239c, 239b; METROPOLITAN TRANSIT AUTHORITY: 388tl, 392bl; MTA/Patrick Cashin 388cl, all 389, 390tr, 390bl; COLLECTION OF THE MORGAN LIBRARY, NY: 36cr (*Blanche of Castille and King Louis IX of France, author dictating to a scribe,* moralized Bible, c1230), 164br, *Song of Los* David A. Loggie (gift of Mrs Landon K Thorne) 164la, *Biblia Latina* David A. Loggie 164lb, 165tl, 165c, 165bl, 165br; Morris-Jumel Mansion, Inc NY: 19tl; A Rosario 23crb; THE MUSEUM OF THE CITY OF NEW YORK: 17b, 18cra, 18–19, 19tr, 20ca, 21crb (photo J Parnell), 22tl, 22cbl, 24tl (attributed to Samuel Lovett Waldo), 24cla, 24clb, 25cr, 25crb, 25bc, 26cb, 27tl, 27crb, 27cb, 28bl, 29tr, 30tl, 30cr, 31tc, 31c, 32tr, 57tr (silver porringer), 87cr (Talfour); THE MUSEUM OF MODERN ART, NY:

172c, 172bl, 173tc, 173cra, 173crb, 173cb, 173bl, 174cl, 174cr, 175tl, 175b; *The Bather*, c. 1885, Paul Cézanne 174bc; Cisitalia "202" GT car 167tc; © 2004 Photo Elizabeth Felicella, architectural rendering Kohn Pedersen Fox Associates, digital composite Robert Bowen 172tl; ©2005 Timothy Hursley 168cr, 172tr; *The Goat* by Pablo Picasso, 1950, 36t; *Portrait of the Postman Joseph Roulin* by Vincent Van Gogh, 1889, 35ca. NATIONAL BASEBALL LIBRARY, COOPERSTOWN, NY: 4tr, 25bl, 30cl; NATIONAL CAR RENTAL: 385cr; NATIONAL MUSEUM OF THE AMERICAN INDIAN/SMITHSONIAN INSTITUTION: 18c; NATIONAL PARK SERVICE: Ellis Island Immigration Museum 78ca, 78br; Statue of Liberty National Monument 75bl; THE NEW MUSEUM OF CONTEMPORARY ART, NY: 107cl; NEW YORK BOTANIC GARDEN: Tori Butt 242b, 243t/cl/b; Jason Green 242cr; Muriel Weinerman 243b; NEW YORK CITY FIRE DEPARTMENT: 359br; NEW YORK CITY TRANSIT AUTHORITY: 390bc; Phil Bartley 391tc, 391ca, 391cl; THE NEW YORKER MAGAZINE INC: Cover drawing by Rea Irvin, © 1925, 1953, All rights reserved, 30bcl; THE NEW YORK PALACE, NY: 27tr; NEW YORK POST: 370tl; NEW YORK PUBLIC LIBRARY: Special Collection Office, Schomburg Center for Research in Black Culture 30ca, 31cla; Stokes Collection 23tr; NEW YORK STATE DEPARTMENT OF MOTOR VEHICLES: 386b; NEW YORK STOCK EXCHANGE: 71ra; THE NEW YORK TIMES: 370tl; NPA: © CNES 1993 12b; NYC & COMPANY: 368br, 368tc; Julienne Schaer, 2009 372br; Stefano Giovannini 369br; THE PENINSULA, NY: 279bc; PERFORMING ARTS LIBRARY: Clive Barda 212bl; The Pickle Guys: Alan Kaufman 100bl; PHOTOLIBRARY: Renaud Visage 166; PLAZA HOTEL, NY: 280tr; POPPERFOTO: 31cra, 31cr, 262cla; THE PORT AUTHORITY OF NEW YORK & NEW JERSEY: 379br; COLLECTION OF THE QUEENS MUSEUM OF ART: purchased with funds from the George and Mollie Wolfe World's Fair Fund 31cbr; Official souvenir, purchase 32cbr; RENSSELAER POLYTECHNIC INSTITUTE: 86–87, 87bl; REX FEATURES LTD: Sipa-Press 52tr, 52br; Courtesy of the Rockefeller Center © THE ROCKEFELLER GROUP, Inc: 31cbl. LUIS SANGUINO: *The Immigrants*, 1973, 258b; THE ST. REGIS, NY: 278c; Scientific American: 18 May 1878 edition 86tr; 9 November 1878 edition 88bl; THE SHERMAN GROUP/NEW YORK WATER TAXI: 386br; SKIDMORE, OWINGS & MERRILL LLP, Chicago: 54cr; SKYSCRAPER MUSEUM: Robert Polidori 55tl; 72br; 268bl; THE SOCIETY OF ILLUSTRATORS: 198tl; SOUTH STREET SEAPORT MUSEUM: R.B. Merkel 83bl, 84bl; FRANK SPOONER PICTURES: Gamma 160cl; Liaison/Gamma/ Anderson front endpaper clb, 160tl, 161cla; Liaison/Levy/Halebian: 44tr, 47c; STA TRAVEL GROUP: 370br; THEATER DEVELOPMENT FUND: David LeShay 340cl; TURNER ENTERTAINMENT COMPANY: 137br, 185br. UNITED NATIONS, NY: 161cra, 162tr, 162bc, 163tc, 163cla,

163br; UNITED NATIONS PHOTO: 160tr; Used with permission UN PLAZA HYATT HOTEL, NY: 281bl. © JACK VARTOOGIAN, NY: 61bc, 158t. JUDITH WELLER: *The Garment Worker* 130t; LUCIA WILSON CONSULTANCY: Ivar Mjell 2–3, 15br; COLLECTION OF THE WHITNEY MUSEUM OF AMERICAN ART, NY: 200cla, 200clb, 201t, 201ca, 201crb (purchase with funds from a public fundraising campaign in May 1982. One half of the funds were contributed by the Robert Wood Johnson Jr. Charitable Trust. Additional major donations were given by The Lauder Foundation; the Robert Lehman Foundation, Inc.; the Howard and Jean Lipman Foundation, Inc; an anonymous donor; The TM Evans Foundation, Inc.; MacAndrews & Forbes Group Incorporated; the DeWitt Wallace Fund, Inc; Martin & Agnes Gruss; Anne Phillips; Mr and Mrs Laurance S. Rockefeller; the Simon Foundation, Inc.; Marylou Whitney; Bankers Trust Company; Mr and Mrs Kenneth N Dayton; Joel and Anne Ehrenkranz; Irvin and Kenneth Feld; Flora Whitney Miller. More than 500 individuals from 26 states and abroad also contributed to the campaign), 201br (purchased with funds from the Mr and Mrs Arthur G Altschul Purchase Fund, the Joan and Lester Avnet Purchase Fund, the Edgar William and Bernice Chrysler Garbisch Purchase Fund, the Mrs Robert C Graham Purchase Fund in honour of John I H Baur, the Mrs Percy Uris Purchase Fund and the Henry Schnakenberg Purchase Fund in honor of Juliana Force); 200tr Krause/Johansen; 201bc gift of Flora Whitney Miller 86.70.3; 200c purchase, with funds from the Louis and Bessie Adler Foundation, Inc., Seymour M. Klein, President 78.34; 201cr gift of an anonymous donor 58.65. WHEELER PICTURES: 78t; WILDLIFE CONSERVATION SOCIETY, BRONX ZOO: Dennis DeMello 244bl; Julie Maher 244tr, 244cl, 245br, 245bl; ROBERT WRIGHT: 43t, 140b, 142tr, 142cr, 142bl; 143tl/br, 156br, 157tl/r, 293tr. YU YU YANG: *Untitled*, 1973, 57br.

All other images © Dorling Kindersley.
See www.dkimages.com for further information.

Front Endpapers
ALAMY IMAGES: Eye Ubiquitous/Jon Hicks Ltl; Pictures Colour Library ftl; MAGNUM PHOTOS: G. Per bl; PHOTOLIBRARY: Renaud Visage tr.
Map cover: GETTY IMAGES: Photographer's Choice/ Brian Lawrence.
Jacket
Front - GETTY IMAGES: Photographer's Choice/Brian Lawrence. Back - ALAMY IMAGES: Patrick Batchelder cla; Russell Kord clb; DORLING KINDERSLEY: Robert Wright tl; GETTY IMAGES: Photographer's Choice/Rich LaSalle bl. Spine - GETTY IMAGES: Photographer's Choice/Brian Lawrence t.

SPECIAL EDITIONS OF DK TRAVEL GUIDES

DK Travel Guides can be purchased in bulk quantities at discounted prices for use in promotions or as premiums. We are also able to offer special editions and personalized jackets, corporate imprints, and excerpts from all of our books, tailored specifically to meet your own needs.

To find out more, please contact:
(in the United States) **SpecialSales@dk.com**
(in the UK) **TravelSpecialSales@uk.dk.com**
(in Canada) DK Special Sales at **general@tourmaline.ca**
(in Australia) **business.development@pearson.com.au**

Series in Health and Social Justice

Series Editors

Mercedes Becerra
Aviva Chomsky
Shelly Errington
Paul Farmer
Kenneth Fox
Jennifer Furin
Alec Irwin
Jim Yong Kim
Joyce V. Millen
Joe Rhatigan
Haun Saussy

"In an era in which the globalization of corporate enterprises has become prominent, this volume examines globalization's consequences for the health and welfare of poor people. Through sound scholarship, *Dying for Growth* documents widening economic disparities. Yet the book also demonstrates how equitable public policies can help achieve good health programs even in the face of economic adversity. By showing that increased suffering among the poor is not an inevitable byproduct of our modern economy, it is a book that offers hope. For all those interested in equity and social justice this is an important volume which should have a large audience."

> Julius B. Richmond, M.D.
> Assistant Secretary for Health and
> U.S. Surgeon General, 1977-1981

"Through documented evidence and careful analysis, *Dying for Growth* shatters the myth that the prevailing form of globalization is inevitable and shows that economic growth alone will not cure our ailing world. The poor, the ill, and the landless take center stage in this work. They speak of the need to move beyond the tunnel vision of unbridled economic growth and journey on a path that will bring food, education, and adequate health care to all. Bravo to the Institute for Health and Social Justice for exposing the human consequences of unjust global economic policies."

> Jean-Bertrand Aristide
> Former President of Haiti and
> Author of *Eyes of the Heart: Seeking a*
> *Path for the Poor in the Age of Globalization*

"*Dying for Growth*'s compelling case studies document how globalization—largely uncontrolled by nations but carefully controlled by corporations—is a major cause of global deterioration in the health and well-being of millions of people. Anyone concerned about this rapidly growing problem needs to read this excellent book, which brings together in one place, for the first time, an abundance of timely and important information with thousands of listed references."

> Sidney Wolfe, M.D.
> Director of Public Citizen's Health Research Group

"This impressive book is for all those who are puzzled by the failures of trickle down economics. In highly accessible prose, *Dying for Growth* explains why, amid extraordinary growth in world wealth, hundreds of millions still lack resources to secure adequate food, shelter, and healthcare. Through meticulous research, the authors trace how political and economic policies, such as structural adjustment programs, exacerbate global disparities and render the poorest people even more vulnerable to disease. *Dying for Growth* offers countless insights to students, policy makers, and health care workers. It will serve as an invaluable resource guide for all those interested in working to improve the health and well being of the entire global community."

> Johanna P. Daily, M.D.
> Division of Infectious Disease, Brigham and Women's Hospital
> Harvard Medical School and School of Public Health

Dying for Growth

Global Inequality
and the Health of the Poor

Edited by

Jim Yong Kim
Joyce V. Millen
Alec Irwin
John Gershman

Common Courage Press

Monroe, Maine

Library of Congress Cataloging-in-Publication Data

Dying for growth : global inequality and the health of the poor / edited by Jim Yong
Kim ... [et al.].
    p. cm.
  Includes index.
  ISBN 1-56751-161-9 (cloth) -- ISBN 1-56751-160-0 (pbk.)
   1. Poor--Medical care--Case studies. 2. Poor--Health and hygiene--Case studies. 3.
Poor--Medical care--Economic aspects--Developing countries--Case studies. 4.
Poor--Developing countries--Health aspects--Case studies. I. Kim, Jim Yong.

RA418.5.P6 D95 1999
362.1'086'942--dc21   98-054695

Common Courage Press
P.O. Box 702
Monroe, ME 04951
207-525-0900
fax: 207-525-3068
www.commoncouragepress.com

The Institute for Health and Social Justice
Partners In Health
113 River Street
Cambridge, MA 02139
(617) 441-6288
pih.org

First Printing

Contents

PART III

POWERFUL PLAYERS, HARMFUL CONSEQUENCES:
TRANSNATIONAL CORPORATIONS,
INEQUALITY, AND HEALTH

Acknowledgments

This book and the series of which it is a part are projects of the Institute for Health and Social Justice (IHSJ). The Institute is a nonprofit center for education and research that seeks to examine contemporary health problems from a social justice perspective. It counts among its affiliates activist scholars and community workers from diverse disciplines, who work as research fellows, affiliated professors, physicians, interns, work-study students, and volunteers. Some are involved in the Institute's Cambridge office, while others work in far corners of the country and the globe—participating with us in an ongoing effort to understand the causes and manifestations of poverty and inequality.

Dying for Growth is a work of scholarship, but also of passion. The book grows out of a passionate desire to shed light on the complex relationship between global economics and poor people's health. This same shared determination has knit together the members of the Institute for Health and Social Justice since the organization was founded. Virtually all the Institute's associates have assisted us in the production of this volume, which is the culmination of over three years of collective work. Most have had to step beyond the security of their disciplinary boundaries. All have been generous and patient, showing through their various contributions an immutable dedication to the critical analysis of current political and economic change and its implications for poor people's lives. Without the active contributions of the whole IHSJ community, this volume could not have been completed.

Among the 27 authors who wrote *Dying for Growth*, many have lived, married, raised families, and worked for decades in poor communities locally and throughout the world. In these settings, hundreds of courageous people have shared with us stories about their illnesses, options for care, and treatments. Many of them were our patients; others were colleagues and friends in our partner programs in Haiti, Peru, Mexico, and the United States. Some were strangers who took the time to explain their struggles and offer their often penetrating analyses. Our intention in producing this book was to put their collective struggles into context: to seek explanations for how and why in this age of extraordinary wealth and technological advancement people routinely suffer and die from preventable and easily treatable diseases. We are grateful to all of those who shared their stories with us, and thereby, with the readers of this book. We dedicate *Dying for Growth* to them.

Many Thanks

For their intellectual realism, spiritual optimism, and inspiration to us and to the world, we extend our gratitude to Noam Chomsky, Gustavo Gutiérrez, and Sister Ruth Rosenbaum.

Within the IHSJ community, one person stands out for his commitment to this project. Evan Lyon joined us during a difficult phase of the project when we found ourselves overwhelmed by the logistics involved in coordinating the work of so many busy scholars. Evan brought a willingness to take on logistics and to tackle the task of checking and then rechecking the thousands of sources used in the book. We are grateful to him.

Appreciation also goes to several of the series' editors who were encouraging and helpful since the idea of *Dying for Growth* first began to take shape: Paul Farmer, Haun Saussy, Shelly Errington, and Jennifer Furin. Several of the book's authors stepped out beyond the call of duty and graciously took the time to provide feedback on other chapters. For these efforts and their patient commitment, we thank David Kotz, Aaron Shakow, Jennifer Ross, Joel Brenner, Heena Patel, Tim Holtz, Arnie Chien, Avi Chomsky, Brooke Schoepf, Ken Fox, and Janie Simmons.

We thank our old friends, Kristin Nelson and Roger Grande, for their early guidance, and Anna Donald, Latyr Diouf, and Erika Barth, who made significant scholarly contributions to the project. Vaughn Mankey deserves thanks for his careful reading of chapters and his master indexing. We are indebted to our friend, Bill Rodriguez, who stepped in on several occasions as an on-call final reader. And for their essential and expert feedback, we extend our appreciation to Sally Zierler, Aaron Cohen, Chuck Levenstein, Diane Millen, and Bill Millen.

For coming in at the last hour and working diligently with us to complete final chapters, enormous gratitude goes to Dorothy Fallows, Heather Rensberry, Jonathan Welch, Julie Rosenberg, and Ian Costello.

We are indebted to many other colleagues, interns, and friends who ran back and forth to libraries, read chapters, provided helpful comments, and committed their time to a variety of other endeavors. Appreciation goes to David Devine, Peter Smith, Monica Chierici, Susan Krumplitsch, Nazli Parvizi, Stephanie Oppenheimer, Tim Surrly, Rebecca Wolfe, Catherine Crosland, Meg Doherty, Moupali Das, R. Jay Magill, Caitlin Clark, Ariane Bradley, Eileen Kim, Matthew Tripp, Naomi Shank, Sarah Pomerantz, Asmita Jayendra, Arthur Lever, Marna Schwartz, Henry Epino, Stephan Buttenweiser, Miriam Shakow, Jill Petty, Ana Blohm, Chengetto Mukonoweshuro, Katy Farmer, Bob Dellinger, and Louise Badiane.

Tom White, as always, continues to challenge and inspire us in our search for the causes of the suffering he so faithfully works to alleviate through his generosity and leadership.

For their dependable support, we are grateful to the intellectual godparents of the Institute for Health and Social Justice: Howard Hiatt, Arthur Kleinman, Leon Eisenberg, Mary-Jo DelVecchio Good, Byron Good, Kris Heggenhougen. And we thank our other colleagues in Harvard Medical School's Department of Social Medicine.

We would also like to acknowledge the support of the John D. and Catherine T. MacArthur Foundation, Harvard Medical School, and the W. K. Kellogg Foundation; their contributions have helped to keep the IHSJ afloat and provide the means for its members to engage in collective critical reflection.

For courageously and patiently embarking upon this project with us, we applaud our publishers Greg Bates, Flic Shooter, Arthur Stamoulis, and the rest of the Common Courage family. And for calming the final maelstrom with his meticulous editing and typesetting, we are grateful to William Oppenheimer.

We cannot begin to inventory the generous assistance we received from our Partners in Health and our life partners. Thank you to Ophelia Dahl, Carole Mitnick, Jen Singler, Loune Viaud, Jaime Bayona, Sonya Shin, Maria Contreras, Heidi Behforouz, Anne Hyson, Mercedes Becerra, Matthew Olins, Cassis Henry, Kathryn Kempton, Summer Pierre, Kim Houston, Sergeline Lucien, Elizabeth Foley, Mary Kay Smith Fawzi, Lydia Mann-Bondat, Chris Douglas, Sarah Widmer, Alicia Ingalls, Jane Kim, Lovely Benoit, Yusuf Karacaoglu, Jenny Severin, and Marshall Fordyce.

Last, though by no means least, we thank Laurie Wen and Deborah Yashar for supporting the *Dying for Growth* endeavor, and Younsook Lim for shouldering so many extra burdens to help us through to the end of this lengthy journey. And for believing in this book, editing its chapters, sacrificing for it any semblance of a normal life, and riding the waves and hiking the valleys of its endless production with grace, patience, and love, we embrace Dave Harrison.

Joyce V. Millen
Alec Irwin
Jim Yong Kim
John Gershman

Foreword by Paul Farmer

Ours is a time of unprecedented wealth. Politicians and their patrons ceaselessly tell us that we live in an era of limited resources (meaning by this that the welfare state is necessarily on its last legs). Surprisingly, this cry has been taken up by those responsible for formulating social policy. But most fail to observe that the resources they are talking about happen to be less limited now than ever before in human history. It is a fact that "rising tides" of affluence, driven by a growing and globalizing market economy, have *not* lifted all boats. Instead, expanding world wealth has been linked to a sharp rise in inequality—in particular, to increases in the numbers of people living in extreme poverty.

What does the combination of rising affluence and increasing poverty mean for the health of the one billion people who are unable to secure food and water, the most basic measure of disease prevention? What do these trends mean for those who have lost out in this "new world order"? These questions have guided us in compiling *Dying for Growth*, the second volume in the Series in Health and Social Justice.

WHY DID WE WRITE THIS BOOK?

Why would a group primarily concerned with the provision of direct health-care services write a book about economic policies? In a sense, the answer is simple: because the experiences of our patients, who for the most part live in poverty, have spurred us to do so. In the clinic, each day brings a harvest of tales of woe. In a wealthy city in the United States, we hear of hard choices between heating an apartment and filling prescriptions. In a dreary village in rural Haiti, we hear of families going hungry in order to purchase the most basic medical services. Even if we had balked at making the connection between economic policy and illness experience, our patients have been quick to point out these links. When the sick in El Salvador or Haiti insist, "I'm sick because I lost my land," is it far-fetched to discern in such claims the impact of ill-advised decisions about land tenure and agricultural policy? All those who participated in the writing of this volume have been forced to consider health and sickness as economic outcomes. And we found this to be a universal concern, no matter where we traveled or with whom we spoke.

But this book is not merely a report from the clinic and the field. It has a program of theoretical investigation as well. Some of us, prompted by our patients, have long asked how large-scale social forces come to have their effects on the bodies of the poor and marginalized. Others in our group have critically explored the "immodest claims of causality" staked by officialdom, by academics, and by others who tread the corridors of power. The first book in this series sought to apply precisely these perspectives to the topic of *Women, Poverty, and AIDS*.

These books are written by scholars—anthropologists, epidemiologists, historians, and political economists—but they are prompted by the concerns of doctors and patients. If questions about economic policy are legitimately posed by patients and healers, from what vantage might these questions best be explored? As historians, we prize a convincing example: certain times and places afford a clear view of the impact of poverty and inequality on the health of vulnerable groups. Ironically, perhaps, so-called "boom times" offer the best opportunity for questioning the optimism that proclaims, "A rising tide lifts all boats." And *deserted places* are the ones in which to discern, at first hand, the impact of economic policies. Squatter settlements, refugee camps, and slums show to best advantage the physical vulnerability of the whole species, first experienced by the poor. They remain our mine-shaft canaries.

Dying for Growth contains a set of case studies written from the margins.[1] Sometimes, these are the edges or pockets of poverty sitting hard against enormous wealth; sometimes, these margins are more vast, a sea of unrelenting poverty far from plenty. But whether written from Roxbury, Massachusetts, or from a village in rural Senegal, the cases were sifted through the same filter of collegiality as they were being written and edited. That is, a group of us worked together for over three years in order to help one another think through a diverse set of data and experiences. We sought to discern what was similar and what was dissimilar. Although not everyone could agree on the best route to growth with equity, we could agree that growing *inequality* was central to the problems faced by communities inhabiting these margins.

In part a report from these communities, the book's chapters move from urban inequalities in Peru and the United States to beleaguered rural villages in Senegal and Haiti. They examine challenges to Cuba's health-care system and the "demographic disaster" now facing post-*perestroika* Russia. Exploring labor and environmental health crises owing to expanding transnational corporate power, other chapters in *Dying for Growth* reveal the inner workings of an electronics factory in a Mexican border town, and the aftermath of the Bhopal industrial disaster. Finally, the last section of the book highlights examples of national and local efforts to resist the seemingly ineluctable pull of inequality.

SOCIAL INEQUALITY AND PATHOGENESIS

The notion that social inequality has in and of itself a noxious effect is not a new insight; this has been the refrain of the oppressed from time immemorial. And those who care for oppressed peoples concur. William Budd, one of the great doctors of the Victorian era, was best known for his treatise on typhoid fever. Typhoid is transmitted through contaminated food and, especially, contaminated water; it is an affliction that seems to seek out misery and strike at the weakest. In Budd's time, London each year offered up a significant number of its slum-dwellers to typhoid. But no one, Budd warned in 1874, could be expected to be spared all risk:

> This disease not seldom attacks the rich, but it thrives among the poor. But by reason of our common humanity we are all, whether rich or poor, more nearly related here than we are apt to think. The members of the great human family are, in fact, bound together by a thousand secret ties, of whose existence the world in general little dreams.
>
> And he that was never yet connected with his poorer neighbor, by deeds of charity or love, may one day find, when it is too late, that he is connected with him by a bond which may bring them both, at once, to a common grave.[2]

The "thousand secret ties" still connect the poor and the wealthy, despite all the barriers our age has set up to separate them. They are, in fact, less secret (though, for many, effectively censored into invisibility) in the age of the telecommunications revolution.

Recent years have seen a number of studies devoted to the subject of health and inequality. Drawing generously on this corpus of work, *Dying for Growth* attempts to add the vitality of practice to what remains an experience-distant literature. That is, the authors of these 16 chapters work quite far from the circles in which economic policy is formulated. But our engagement with the destitute sick offers us an important vantage point from which to interrogate both the policies purporting to promote economic growth and the larger trends in which these policies are embedded. This vantage point is a fitting one, since the price of market-driven economic growth is, in almost every case, paid chiefly by those least able to shoulder new burdens.

"BOOKS WITH ATTITUDE"

When we inaugurated this series, we promised "books with attitude," but failed to mention precisely *what* attitude we had in mind. Since writing *Dying for Growth* was fundamentally a collective exercise, it is perhaps important to bring into relief the shared hermeneutic behind the exercise. Looking back on the results of our discussions, we see our shared engagement revealing itself, throughout these studies, in three central concerns:

1. Compassion

In referring to the *vitality of practice*, we mean that most of us benefit from close contact with those who endure the conditions we deplore in these pages. The word "compassion" *means* "suffering with," and although respect for the sufferers guards us (we hope) from pity and immodest identification, we do share an overwhelming sense of compassion for the victims of unbridled growth. Editing such sentiments out of our essays has seemed, at times, an error: the studied "neutrality" of scholarly prose amounts, too often, to a passive or heartless endorsement of the plans of the powerful.

2. *Dismay*

Something between dismay and anger fuels many of these chapters. The fecklessness of the powerful is manifest throughout the margins inhabited by those we serve, and in our daily work we often hear the bitter recriminations of the powerless. Exactly how much of this bitterness to remove from these pages has been the subject of debate among contributors. I can say, in rereading the chapters, that expunging any more of these sentiments would have come close to editorial whitewashing. The Hippocratic dictum *primum, non nocere*—"above all, do no harm"—should be rapidly incorporated into the policies of the international financial institutions. If this book can make visible and audible the pain that accompanies "growth at any cost," one of its chief aims will have been reached.

3. *Humility*

No matter how you slice it, there is ample cause for humility in ventures such as ours. *Dying for Growth* attempts to fill a gap in the literature, and the existence of the gap shames us into wanting to say: "Sorry. We should have done this years ago." Modesty is not a great virtue among economic forecasters (least of all those with a program to peddle). The case studies are rife with accounts of predictions gone awry, and those who promised future prosperity for the poor need to acknowledge that not all of their projections have come true. Many "development" policies have clearly harmed the most vulnerable, even as they fed the fortunes of the already empowered. We, in turn, are reminded of the limits of our wisdom as we contemplate the difficult policy decisions that we, as scholars in service to community, do not have to make. Most of all, we feel humility before the suffering of the destitute sick. We offer up this book as a small token of gratitude for all they've taught us.

To anchor a book suffused with what are, for most scholars, repressed sentiments, we have sought to carefully document our claims. Often, we have retreated from a forceful position or interpretation because we were unable to support that position with adequate data. Some will feel that too much effort was expended in buttressing the case studies with scholarship, and not enough in shortening them. But *Dying for Growth* is, to our knowledge, the first attempt to pull together such a vast array of studies attempting to answer questions of enormous importance—enormous, that is, to all who agree that the needless suffering and shameful deaths documented in these pages merit more than passing notice.

Selected Abbreviations

AFDC	Aid to Families with Dependent Children
AIDS	acquired immune deficiency syndrome
AIP	Apparel Industry Partnership
APEC	Asia Pacific Economic Cooperation
ARDS	acute respiratory distress syndrome
BCCI	Bank of Credit and Commerce International
BIP	Border Industrialization Program (Mexico)
BOOP	bronchiolitis obliterans with organizing pneumonia
CDC	Centers for Disease Control *or* California Department of Corrections
CDCP	Centers for Disease Control and Prevention
CEC	Commission for Environmental Cooperation
CEO	chief executive officer
CETA	Comprehensive Employment and Training Act
CP	community participation
CPI	consumer price index
DALY	disability-adjusted life year
DAWN	Drug Abuse Warning Network
DDT	dichlorodiphenyl trichloroethane
DEA	Drug Enforcement Administration
DFG issues	dying for growth issues
DHF	dengue hemorrhagic fever
DHHS	Department of Health and Human Services
DSS	Department of Social Services *or* dengue shock syndrome
EAP	economically active population *or* employee-assistance program
ECA	Economic Commission for Africa
ECLAC	Economic Commission for Latin America and the Caribbean
EIU	Economist Intelligence Unit
EPA	Environmental Protection Agency
EPZ	export processing zone
EU	European Union

FAO	Food and Agriculture Organization
FBI	Federal Bureau of Investigation
FDA	Food and Drug Administration
FDI	foreign direct investment
FSC	foreign sales corporation
FTAA	Free Trade Area of the Americas
FTZ	free trade zone
G-7	Group of Seven*
G-8	Group of Eight**
GAO	General Accounting Office
GATT	General Agreement on Tariffs and Trade
GDI	Gender-Related Development Index
GDP	gross domestic product
GM	genetic modification
GNP	gross national product
HDI	Human Development Index
HIPC	heavily indebted poor country
HIV	human immunodeficiency virus
HMO	health maintenance organization
HOPE	Human Rights, Opportunity, Partnership, and Empowerment (for Africa)
HPI	Human Poverty Index
ICC	International Chamber of Commerce
ICCPR	International Covenant on Civil and Political Rights
ICCR	Interfaith Center on Corporate Responsibility
ICESCR	International Covenant on Economic, Social, and Cultural Rights
ICFTU	International Confederation of Free Trade Unions
IDB	Inter-American Development Bank
IFAD	International Fund for International Development
IFI	international financial institution
ILO	International Labour Organization
IMF	International Monetary Fund
IMR	Infant Mortality Rate
IOCU	International Organization of Consumers Unions
IRD	integrated rural development project
ISI	import substitution industrialization
LDC	less developed country
LSCF	large-scale commercial farm

---

*Canada, France, Germany, Italy, Japan, United Kingdom, United States
**Canada, France, Germany, Italy, Japan, Russia, United Kingdom, United States

MAI   Multilateral Agreement on Investment
MCH   maternal and child health
MDB   multilateral development bank
MDR-TB   multidrug-resistant tuberculosis
MMS   mandatory minimum sentencing

NAAEC   North American Agreement on Environmental Cooperation
NAALC   North American Agreement on Labor Cooperation
NAFTA   North American Free Trade Agreement
NGO   nongovernmental organization
NIC   newly industrialized country
NIDA   National Institute on Drug Abuse
NIP   New Industrial Policy
NPE   New Political Economy

OAU   Organization of African Unity
ODA   overseas development assistance
OECD   Organization for Economic Cooperation and Development
OPEC   Organization of Petroleum Exporting Countries
OPIC   Overseas Private Investment Corporation
OSHA   Occupational Safety and Health Administration
Oxfam   Oxford Committee for Famine Relief

PAC   political action committee
PAHO   Pan American Health Organization
PHC   primary health care
PHN   population, health, and nutrition
PPP   purchasing power parity

SAP   structural adjustment program
SIF   social investment fund
SILICS   severely indebted low-income country
SSA   sub-Saharan Africa
STD   sexually transmitted disease

TB   tuberculosis
TNC   transnational corporation
TRIM   trade-related investment measure

UDHR   Universal Declaration of Human Rights
UN   United Nations
UNCED   United Nations Conference on Environment and Development
UNCTAD   United Nations Conference on Trade and Development
UNCTC   United Nations Commission on Transnational Corporations

UNDP	United Nations Development Programme
UNICEF	United Nations Children's Fund
	(*formerly* United Nations International Children's
	Emergency Fund)
UNRISD	United Nations Research Institute for International Development
USAID	United States Agency for International Development
USDA	United States Drug Administration
WHO	World Health Organization
WTO	World Trade Organization

PART I

Introduction
to the Problem

Guatemala City, Guatemala. Living in the refuse of other people's more privileged existence. (photo by Jerry Berndt)

CHAPTER ONE

Introduction:
What is Growing?
Who is Dying?

Joyce V. Millen, Alec Irwin, and Jim Yong Kim

T he image on the facing page records an encounter that we would hope to re-create for every reader of this book. The photographer who took the little girl's picture met her while walking on the edge of a garbage dump not far from a major urban center in Central America. The girl held a tattered book in her hand. She asked the photographer if he would please teach her how to read. She beckoned for him to follow her into the mountains of garbage.

Stumbling over mangled tires, skidding on piles of cans, and breathing the sour odors of decaying waste, the photographer and his guide reached a clearing on the side of a small hill. It took a moment for the photographer to grasp that he had just entered the girl's home. The walls of her home and the implements of her survival were quite literally garbage: the refuse of other people's more privileged existence.

Dying for Growth asks about the causes and consequences of the discrepancy between this girl's life and the lives of those whose waste she dwells in, wears, and eats. Focusing on health rather than other traditional indicators of wealth, we explore a world of inequality and analyze political and economic forces that maintain that inequality. The goal of our study is to show how the structure and current rules of today's market-led economic globalization widen the chasm between the privileged and the destitute, imperiling the lives of the world's poor.

GLOBAL HEALTH: WINNERS AND LOSERS

Considering the lives of people who dwell in desperate conditions, like the girl living in the garbage dump, we can easily sense connections between poverty, denial of basic life necessities, and illness.[1] Disease proliferates in communities lacking adequate housing, food, sewage, waste disposal, drainage, and clean water for drinking, cooking, and cleaning. With such basic needs unmet, members of these communities are vulnerable to the spread of air- and water-borne diseases such as diphtheria, tuberculosis, cholera, typhoid, infectious hepatitis, yellow fever, and malaria—to name but a few.

Yet many of us believe such living conditions and diseases to be rather uncommon today—more typical of life in previous centuries. After all, by most accounts the world's health is improving. We now have the technical capacity to eradicate nearly all nutritional deficiencies and infectious diseases. Widely published indicators reflect important gains in public health on an international scale. The World Health Organization's (WHO's) 1998 annual report, commemorating the organization's fiftieth anniversary, celebrated the many health successes of the last half century. Among them:

- Average worldwide life expectancy increased from 48 years in 1955 to 66 years in 1998.

- In 1955 the worldwide infant mortality rate was 148 per 1,000 live births. In 1995 that rate had been reduced to 59 per 1,000 births.

- In 1955 approximately 21 million children died before they reached age five. In 1997 slightly fewer than 11 million children died before their fifth birthday.[2]

Given these trends, one might consider superfluous a book that explores connections between global economics and health among the poor. Because the health of the world's population is plainly getting better, shouldn't we simply continue to promote the strategies that brought about these improvements? Regrettably, the situation is not so simple.

Closer examination shows that the signs of dramatic improvements in international health are deceptive in important respects. Gains in some areas are counterbalanced by stagnation and decline in others. Aggregate statistics mask the fact that health improvements are unevenly distributed. In particular, many of the significant gains made over the last 50 years are marred by growing health disparities between the world's wealthy and the world's poor. At the close of 1998, the WHO director declared:

> Never have so many had such broad and advanced access to healthcare. But never have so many been denied access to health. The developing world carries 90 percent of the disease burden, yet poorer countries have access to only 10 percent of the resources that go to health.[3]

While the successes indicated earlier and the many more cited in the "cautiously optimistic" WHO report are encouraging, these gains cannot obscure equally dramatic losses illustrating the negative side:

- More than 50 percent of the people in the world's 46 poorest countries are without access to modern health care.[4]

- Approximately three billion people in developing countries do not have access to sanitation facilities.[5]

- More than one billion individuals in developing countries do not have access to safe drinking water.[6]

- At least 600 million urban dwellers in Africa, Asia, and Latin America live in what the WHO calls life- and health-threatening homes and neighborhoods.[7]

- In 1998, two-fifths of all the people who died in the world died prematurely.[8]

Looking further into the WHO annual report, we find that of the 10 million deaths among children under five in 1997, 97 percent occurred in developing countries and the majority could have been prevented. While the rate of infant mortality in the world has declined steadily in the last 50 years, there is a 16-fold difference between the present rate in the 26 wealthiest countries and the rate found in 48 of the least developed countries.[9]

Recognizing the central role nutrition plays in preventing disease, the WHO report observed that the world's food supply has nearly doubled in the last 40 years, a rate of increase well in excess of population growth.[10] Yet 11.2 million people in the United States cannot afford enough food for their families, and 828 million people in the developing world are chronically undernourished. Of the 31,000 children under five who die every day in the world, 50 percent die from hunger-related causes.[11] In sub-Saharan Africa since the mid-1980s, the number of undernourished people has more than doubled. In south-central Asia, about 50 percent of children under the age of five are malnourished.[12]

Clearly the encouraging world health figures do not mean improved health for all. It is not merely a matter of lagging progress; indeed, significant reversals are occurring in a number of countries. While the overall life expectancy in the world has increased by 17 years over the last half century, in several African countries life expectancy is falling dramatically due to the linked pandemics of AIDS and tuberculosis, exacerbated in part by externally imposed economic programs that intensify the effects of poverty.[13] For example, by the end of the 1990s, Zimbabwe will see a ten-year reduction in the life expectancy of a child born in 1990.[14] Early in the next decade, children in Botswana can expect to live on average only to age 40; without AIDS the life expectancy would be closer to 70.[15]

Countries on other continents have also seen declines in health indicators. In the late 1970s and 1980s, Nicaragua had achieved impressive improvements in infant mortality, access to health care, and immunization coverage. These gains have now been reversed: hunger and malnutrition in that country are on the rise.[16] Russia is currently experiencing some of the world's most dramatic health reversals. Since the early 1990s, Russia, an industrialized country that formerly enjoyed a sophisticated and extensive health-care system, has experienced an alarming drop in life expectancy and a surge in the incidence of infectious and parasitic diseases.[17] Prior to 1991, for example, Russia had lowered its tuberculosis rates by 5 to 7 percent per year.[18] Since 1991, reported tuberculosis cases in the country have more than doubled, and active cases are growing by at least 10 percent each year.[19]

THE GOALS OF THIS BOOK

The conviction guiding this book is that the gains in world health should not be evaluated merely by comparing today's aggregate health indicators with those of 50 years ago. Rather, recent gains should be put into perspective by asking why they have not been even greater given the unprecedented wealth and technological innovation currently available. We now have a more complete understanding of the roles diet, exercise, smoking, and alcohol play on health than we did 50 years ago. We possess a greater number of vaccines and drugs to prevent and cure major diseases; far more accurate diagnostic methods; more effective and less invasive medical interventions; and more sophisticated ways of distributing medical information. And though we are often reminded, usually by the privileged, that we live in a world of limited financial resources, such resources are less limited now than ever before in human history. Despite these enabling factors, while the proportion of people in good health today may be greater than 50 years ago, the absolute number of people suffering from preventable diseases with little or no access to health care has risen dramatically in this same period.[20] This paradox—that poverty, vulnerability, and suffering should flourish even as wealth and technological power increase—frames our questioning in *Dying for Growth*.

The scholars, physicians, and activists who came together to write this book aimed to share the insights provided by their different disciplines, and to uncover commonalities in the struggles, sufferings, and successes of those with whom they have worked in the Americas, Africa, Asia, and Eastern Europe. All of us have seen evidence of connections between changes in the global economy and the health crises now facing poor communities; *Dying for Growth* was conceived to clarify this relationship and explore the factors that link health to current socioeconomic policy and development strategies.

While the idea that health is influenced by political and economic forces is not new, the actual practice of documenting these connections remains rare. Scholars and health workers regularly explain that the well-being of communities and the health of individuals are linked to "structural forces," "systemic factors," and "global circumstances." But analyses that trace in detail causal relationships between economic realities and actual health outcomes are still scarce. This book seeks to fill an important gap in knowledge by examining the documentable health effects of economic development policies and strategies promoted by the governments of wealthy countries and by international agencies such as the World Bank, the International Monetary Fund (IMF), and the World Trade Organization (WTO). It is clear that our work here is only a first step and that much research remains to be undertaken before these issues are fully understood. Yet first steps, however tentative, must be made. When facts conflict with conventional wisdom, that wisdom must be questioned.

GROWTH FOR WHOM?

At the heart of current conventional wisdom in economics, we find the concept of *growth* and a number of assumptions about the relationship between *economic growth* and quality of life.[21] *Economic growth* usually refers to the real (inflation-adjusted) annual percentage change in a country's gross domestic product (GDP).[22] Strong GDP growth is commonly taken as the primary vital sign of a healthy economy and the best proof that a society is "developing." Worldwide, economic and political policy over the last several decades has been driven by the perceived imperative to achieve and sustain growth. The conviction that enhanced economic growth automatically brings with it increased prosperity and a better life for all—not only the already affluent but, in the long run, the disadvantaged members of society as well—is widespread, and until recently, virtually unquestionable.

The idea that robust economic growth will automatically lead to a better life for everybody is comforting. Unfortunately, it is also wrong. The concrete effects of decades of political and economic policies designed to promote and sustain growth contradict the hypothesis that corporate-led economic growth is the only path to reducing poverty and improving the quality of life for all people. The studies in this book present evidence that the quest for growth in GDP and corporate profits has in fact worsened the lives of millions of women and men. Our authors show, through a series of detailed case studies, how specific growth-oriented policies have not only failed to improve living standards and health outcomes among the poor, but also have inflicted additional suffering on disenfranchised and vulnerable populations.[23]

The ideology most responsible for promoting a vision of economic growth as good in and of itself has also shaped development discourse and policy choices among key international institutions since the late 1970s. Historically, this ideology has been known under various names: "neoliberalism," "the Washington consensus," "Reaganism," "the New Right agenda," and "corporate-led economic globalization," to name a few.[24] This view asserts that economic growth is by definition good for everyone and that economic performance is optimized when governments refrain from interfering in markets. Thus, for the good of all citizens, governments should grant the greatest possible autonomy to individual market actors—companies in particular. Unsurprisingly, the main advocates of neoliberal policies—governments of wealthy countries, banks, corporations, and investors—are also those who have profited most handsomely from their application.

The proponents of neoliberal principles argue that economic growth promoted in this way will eventually "trickle down" to improve the lives of the poor.[25] Increasingly, however, such predictions have proved hollow. In many cases, economic policies guided by neoliberal agendas have worsened the economic situation of the middle classes and the poor. Today, per capita income in more than 100 countries is lower than it was 15 years ago. At the close of two decades of neoliberal dominance in international finance and development, more than 1.6 billion people are worse off economically in the late 1990s than they were in the early 1980s.[26] While most of the world's poor are dying—in the sense of *yearning*—to reap some of the benefits of this growth, others are literally dying from the austerity measures imposed to promote it.

Even where neoliberal policy measures have succeeded in stimulating economic growth, growth's benefits have not gone to those living in "dire poverty"—one-fourth of the world's population, according to the WHO.[27] Rather, the gains of growth have been concentrated disproportionately in the hands of the already well-off.[28] In poor countries, economic benefits have flowed largely to the most affluent 20 percent of the population and to foreign corporations and banks. In the United States, where a significant percentage of transnational corporate profits come to rest, the wealthiest one percent of the population more than doubled its ownership of private wealth between 1976 and 1997, from 19 to 39 percent of total U.S. private wealth.[29] In its 1998 annual report, the United Nations Development Programme (UNDP) calculated that it would take less than four percent of the combined wealth of the 225 richest individuals in the world to achieve and maintain access to basic education, basic health care, reproductive health care, adequate food, safe water, and adequate sanitation for all people living on the planet.[30]

In the face of such disparities and the anxiety provoked by recent financial crises in Asia, Eastern Europe, and Latin America, an increasingly widespread dissatisfaction with neoliberalism has emerged. Critical reflections on neoliberal dogma and its associated reckless market practices now appear in mainstream publications, and it seems that changes in the architecture of the international economy may be forthcoming.[31] Our concern is that these changes may bring simply more of the same to poor people. The replacement of neoliberalism by some new "ism" will not in itself make poor people's lives better, nor render them less vulnerable to deprivation and disease. Reforming international market mechanisms so as to guarantee greater stability and predictability for the investors and firms that operate in those markets may be laudable, but it is insufficient. The economic, political, and moral challenge to which our studies point goes deeper. That challenge is to make improved health for poor people a central goal and a binding measure in the planning, execution, and evaluation of economic and social policy on the local, national, and international levels.

THE HEALTH OF THE POOR AS AN EVALUATIVE CRITERION

The case studies in this book do more than simply demonstrate interconnections between health outcomes and political and economic policies; they also attempt to assess policies, using as a yardstick the health of the poor. If a strategy designed to increase a country's GDP actually achieves this goal, should we call the strategy a success? If GDP growth itself is seen as the only relevant criterion, then obviously the answer is yes. But if our measure also includes assessment of trends in the health of the poor, and if we see that poor people's health suffers because of the strategy, then we believe the strategy must be considered a failure. Using the health of the poor as a gauge by which to judge development strategies, trade agreements, or the elements of structural adjustment programs, we ask if these programs and strategies work to protect the health of the most vulnerable people affected by them, and we argue that to ensure such protection is a moral duty.

To evaluate policies using the health of the poor as a chief criterion is a complicated endeavor. Such analysis requires attention not only to historical factors (such as the legacy of colonialism, global trends, and the sociopolitical dynamics within countries) but also to the accuracy of indicators used.[32] We cannot simply identify a policy measure, chart the duration of its implementation within a country, and then, observing changes in health and social indicators through time, deduce the effects of the policy on the poor. The causal relationships at work are vastly more complicated. Aware of these difficulties, we attempt to provide strong qualitative evidence for associations between different policies and health outcomes, and then underscore the implications of these associations for the everyday struggles and health problems of the poor. Our analyses reflect our own intimate experiences with those suffering the effects of the political and economic processes we examine.

We are conscious that in many of the cases discussed in this volume, the available data do not permit absolutely unambiguous conclusions. Critics may be quick to suggest that the lines of causality we have drawn are open to alternative interpretations. We welcome such challenges, *inasmuch as they motivate the critics themselves and others to pursue further research*, clarifying the questions raised in *Dying for Growth* and adding to our shared knowledge on these questions. Among the main reasons for publishing this book is precisely to stimulate further basic research on the neglected topic of how specific economic policies impact poor people's health. Again and again in the process of research and writing, the authors of this volume have had to face the frustrating paucity of reliable data that would permit clear insight into the links between, for example, particular activities undertaken by transnational corporations (TNCs) and health trends in poor communities situated close to sites of TNC operations. Much work remains to be done, and we hope that the discussions provoked by *Dying for Growth* will give further impetus to this research. In the meantime, the fact that the available data are incomplete does not prevent us from formulating reasonable conclusions.[33] Interpreting current data as accurately and conscientiously as possible, we aim not to say the last word but, on the contrary, to galvanize debate on a topic that is for millions of people very literally a matter of life and death.

THE CHAPTERS

Dying for Growth comprises five thematic parts, each including one or several chapters. In the interest of flow, we have relegated much valuable supporting data and detail to the endnote section of the book. We encourage readers to make full use of the material in the endnotes.

The first section of the volume introduces the themes, problems, and terms pivotal to an analysis of economics and health. Within this section, Chapter Two provides a history of the issues at stake in debates about development, particularly the relationship between growth, poverty, and inequality. Chapter Three explores the evolution and possible inadequacies of terms and concepts prominent in discussions of the global economy.

The second section addresses national responses and local effects of specific economic development approaches. Whereas widespread health reversals are most often attributed to war, natural disasters, or epidemics, the chapters in this section demonstrate that even these proximal causes of widespread suffering and disease cannot be divorced from their historic foundations nor from the economic policies and political choices that pattern them. Chapter Four traces a rural Haitian community's heightened vulnerability to violence and disease back to the country's long history of oppression. Ongoing external involvement in Haitian development endeavors and the country's recent political upheaval are shown to be conjoined factors in that vulnerability. Chapter Five describes how the combined effects of colonialism's legacy and externally imposed structural adjustment programs exacerbate the already precarious conditions of poor farmers and urban dwellers in several African countries. Chapter Six examines the privatization of health care in Peru, arguing that privatization strategies, increasing in popularity worldwide, risk serious health consequences for the poor. Chapter Seven concerns Russia, where we see for the first time a major industrial country suffering significant setbacks in health care and health outcomes in the absence of major wars or natural disasters.

Section Three moves beyond national-level policies to examine how the growth of TNCs, coupled with increased trade and investment liberalization, affects the health and well-being of vulnerable populations. Focusing on labor practices, environmental effects, promotion and marketing activities, and corporate political influence, Chapters Eight and Nine explore connections between TNC operations and health. Scrutinizing the aftermath of the Bhopal gas disaster of 1984, Chapter Ten explains how TNCs apply double standards to their operations in rich and poor countries, demonstrating that corporations harm and kill residents of poor communities yet incur relatively little social or even financial penalty. In Chapter Eleven, the authors show that for Mexican industrial workers, such as those in assembly plants on the U.S. border, trade liberalization has meant a more polluted environment and decreased power to negotiate living wages and healthy working conditions.

The single chapter in Section Four is a provocative reinterpretation of the conventional wisdom about a major U.S. public health problem and the policy measures that have been taken to contain it. This chapter (Twelve) looks beyond the proximate causes of drug use and abuse by observing how private economic interests drive U.S. drug policy at home and abroad.

The concluding section offers intellectual and practical alternatives to the problems described in the preceding chapters. Using Cuba as an example, Chapter Thirteen makes the case that when leaders prioritize social equity and the fundamental right of all citizens to health care, even economically strapped governments can achieve improved and more equitable health outcomes. Documenting the troubled relationship between nongovernmental community health organizations and the post-war Salvadoran State, Chapter Fourteen exposes a fundamental flaw in neoliberal health policy reform efforts. In Chapter Fifteen, we bring together the volume's principal themes and reflect on ways to inform our own work as students, scholars, health providers, and activists by reference to the needs and experiences of the poor. The final chapter is a resource guide for readers who would like to engage further in "pragmatic solidarity" with poor communities. The book, and especially the last chapter, is intended to be a useful tool, but "whether it will play that role or not will be determined by what you do after you put this book down."[34]

CHAPTER TWO

Getting a Grip on the Global Economy

John Gershman and Alec Irwin

I sometimes wonder whether there is any way of making poverty terribly infectious. If that were to happen, its general elimination would be, I am certain, remarkably rapid.[1]

Nobel Laureate Amartya Sen

Poverty, inequality, and patterns of economic change directly and indirectly shape health policy and health outcomes. This chapter investigates the economic side of these relationships. We focus on five interwoven themes—poverty, inequality, development, growth, and globalization—aiming to clarify the meaning of these terms and to analyze relationships among them.

This chapter is a selective discussion of concepts and tools that will be helpful in understanding the themes explored in the remainder of *Dying for Growth*. Later chapters present specific case studies of how the health of poor communities is affected by processes like privatization, trade liberalization, and deregulation, as well as by actors such as transnational corporations (TNCs), international financial institutions (IFIs), bilateral foreign aid agencies, and nongovernmental organizations (NGOs).[2] Specific local cases take on their full meaning, however, when we see their relation to wider patterns. Our goal here is to provide conceptual grounding and historical context for understanding how broad economic forces and institutions interact with individuals and local communities.

Economic development, conflated with economic growth, is often presented today as the necessary and sufficient solution to the problem of poverty. We aim to develop critical tools for assessing this claim and the ideological assumptions on which it rests. We question the presumption that assuring strong economic growth is all that is needed to combat poverty and inequality. In raising these issues, we join a growing number of critics challenging the notion that there is only one effective pathway for growth and development, that of the currently dominant model of free-market capitalism.[3]

Amidst the current global economic turmoil, there is increasing recognition by mainstream analysts and economic actors that changes are necessary in the institutions and practices that compose the world economy. As one journalist noted after the 1998 annual World Bank-IMF meetings, the "global economic crisis" has undermined the long-unquestioned dominance of "Western-style free market economics." Prominent mainstream economists like Paul Krugman and Jeffrey Sachs, as well as the World Bank's Chief Economist Joseph Stiglitz and high-profile billionaire George Soros, have entered the debate. In response to the ongoing Asian crisis, increasingly explicit disagreements have emerged between analysts at the World Bank, the International Monetary Fund (IMF), and the U.S. Treasury Department. Meanwhile, citizens in Asian countries have actively resisted government policies mandated by the IMF. These trends illustrate what a senior international financial official describes as "a growing cultural clash over the economics of Western-driven globalization."[4]

Even with the emerging challenges to long-held assumptions, "growth" still remains for many (economists and non-economists) a word charged with almost magical power. Yet international development organizations have begun to acknowledge that growth must follow particular patterns if it is to benefit the poor. This realization itself, however, raises new questions. If the pattern of growth is so important, what kind of pattern should we look for? Can beneficial patterns be expected to emerge naturally, through the action of intrinsic market mechanisms, or will they have to be created by sustained political effort? Who would stand to gain from such effort, and whose interests might be threatened? How do our assumptions about the benefits of economic growth square with the actual economic history of the past several decades? How is the current trajectory of globalization likely to affect poverty and inequality in the years ahead? This chapter does not answer all these complex questions, but does provide a framework for exploring them critically.

It should be clear from the outset that our goal is not to assert that economic growth is unimportant or irrelevant to struggles against poverty. Yet we argue that growth, as such, is an insufficient objective. Joining other critics of the current conventional wisdom in economics, we want to move toward alternative ways of assessing development and evaluating policies that aim to advance development. Our claim in this book is that concrete effects on the health and well-being of the poor provide decisive criteria by which the value of development efforts must be analyzed and judged. Who will actually benefit from new policies or institutions created at the national or international levels? How will these policies and structures affect the poor? These questions should be central to discussions of global economic change.

To pose questions in this way is to connect development economics and poverty issues explicitly with politics. More so, it is to suggest that economic processes cannot be properly understood independent of political structures and choices. Yet economic analysis and politics both draw their orientation from an awareness of history. To understand today's politics of growth it is vital to have a sense of the history of ideas and ideologies of growth. When we speak of getting an analytic grip on the world economy, all these factors are involved: the realization that economic "laws" and market forces do not function independently of political choices; the understanding that economic principles and institutions we take for granted are in fact the products of a particular history; and the conviction that critical analysis and political struggle are required for a more equitable distribution of the benefits of growth.

The framework we have just considered determines the structure of our argument in this chapter. We begin by examining some basic concepts associated with poverty and development in order to arrive at a clearer sense of the scope and nature of poverty. We then turn to an examination of the history of poverty and development in the post-World War II era, focusing on such crucial episodes as the "Debt Crisis" of the 1980s and the subsequent period of "structural adjustment." We explore the implications of the new relationships emerging at this time between poor countries and the international financial institutions that took the lead in responding to a situation of global financial crisis. The final section of the chapter turns to today's world economy, at a time in which the buzzwords "globalization" and "competitiveness" have become ubiquitous. We survey selected aspects of the current economic landscape, seeking to discern those traits that will be especially pertinent for ongoing debates on poverty, inequality, and growth.

POVERTY AND THE PANACEA OF GROWTH
Conventional Wisdom and Complex Realities

To deplore the magnitude of human suffering caused by poverty is a familiar ritual for our public figures, from spiritual leaders to heads of state to TV talk-show hosts. We have no trouble denouncing poverty as a problem. Moreover, in recent years a consensus seems to have taken shape among many economists, political leaders, and businesspeople about the most effective way to combat poverty. Poverty will be reduced—and can *only* be significantly reduced, it is argued—through the long-term benefits of sustained economic growth. The inequalities that characterize our world will diminish, albeit gradually, as more countries enter and become competitive in the market-driven global economy. Thus, those committed to fighting poverty and narrowing inequality must make growth, economic globalization, and modernization their priorities.

Such claims are a part of the conventional wisdom of our era. However, as we try to bring the relations between poverty, inequality, and economic growth more clearly into focus, conventional wisdom seems problematic. This may be, in part, because the exact meanings of the key terms remain elusive. What do sweeping terms like "poverty" and "global inequality" actually refer to? First, some quantitative measures:

- An estimated three billion people today survive on the equivalent of under $2 a day, 1.3 billion of them on less than $1 a day.[5] Every day, some 840 million people go hungry. Of the 4.4 billion people in developing countries, nearly three-fifths lack basic sanitation. Almost a third, well over 1 billion people, lack access to clean water. A quarter of these 4.4 billion people do not have adequate housing. Nearly a third of the people in the least developed countries—most of them in sub-Saharan Africa—will die before reaching the age of 40.[6]

- 100 countries have undergone grave economic decline over the past three decades. Per capita income in these 100 countries is now lower than it was 10, 15, 20, or in some cases even 30 years ago. In Africa, the average household consumes 20 percent less today than it did 25 years ago. Worldwide, more than

1 billion people saw their real incomes fall during the period 1980-1993. Meanwhile, according to the United Nations Development Program's (UNDP's) 1998 *Human Development Report*, the 15 richest people in the world enjoy combined assets that exceed the total annual gross domestic product (GDP) of sub-Saharan Africa. At the end of the 1990s, the wealth of the three richest individuals on earth surpassed the combined annual GDP of the 48 least developed countries.[7]

- In 1960, the poorest 20 percent of the world's people received 2.3 percent of global income. By 1991, their share had sunk to 1.4 percent. Today, the poorest 20 percent receive only 1.1 percent of global income. The ratio of income of the wealthiest 20 percent of the people to that of the poorest 20 percent was 30 to 1 in 1960. By 1995, that ratio stood at 82 to 1. The 20 percent of the world's people who live in the highest-income countries account for 86 percent of total worldwide private consumption expenditures; the poorest 20 percent, only 1.3 percent. These global disparities are mirrored within many countries. In Brazil, for example, the poorest 50 percent of the population received 18 percent of the national income in 1960, falling to 11.6 percent in 1995. The richest ten percent of Brazilians received 54 percent of national income in 1960; by 1995 this proportion had risen to 63 percent.[8]

What do such figures and descriptions reveal? First, that poverty kills. The World Health Organization (WHO) underscores that poverty signifies brutal suffering and premature death for those in its grasp. Poverty is the "main reason why babies are not vaccinated, clean water and sanitation [are] not provided, and curative drugs and other treatments [remain] unavailable." Around the world, poverty is the chief cause "of reduced life expectancy, of handicap and disability, and of starvation."[9] Furthermore, it is a major contributor to mental illness, stress, suicide, family disintegration, and substance abuse.[10]

The figures we have just seen reveal, too, that poverty and inequality are growing worse today in many parts of the world despite decades of effort to stimulate economic growth and despite recent favorable economic figures in countries like the United States. Even in regions where economic performance has been strong, the anticipated benefits of growth have failed to materialize for many people.

Finally, implicit in these quantitative indicators are issues of *power*. In distributing wealth, economic structures both assign and respond to power. Within these structures, certain interests are privileged, and resources are distributed for the benefit of some groups at the expense of others. We see the political character of decisions that determine, for example, whether a poor country's limited resources will be used to construct local health clinics or will go instead to purchase new weapons for the military. The political dimension emerges again when poor countries slash funding for social services in order to make payments on staggering foreign debts. And again when U.S. health corporations reap record profits while an increasing number of American citizens find themselves unable to afford basic health insurance. The relationship between health and the economy cannot be separated from questions of power—who wields it, how, and to what ends.

Growth As Miracle Drug

The solution to the complex problem of poverty routinely proffered over the last half century by leading economic analysts in the world's most powerful countries is disarmingly simple: *development*, defined primarily in terms of *economic growth*. The consensus among influential thinkers concerning this notion—even among thinkers whose political, social, and philosophical views are otherwise sharply opposed—has been little short of miraculous. At the root of this consensus lies the belief that growth and development are virtually synonymous. This tendency takes hold not only in the minds of analysts and policymakers, but also among the general public. We have been taught to believe that economic growth automatically translates into greater prosperity and a better life for all—even when this assumption is contradicted by daily experience in a country like the United States, where relatively robust economic growth in recent years has gone hand in hand with a palpable erosion of the quality of life for many citizens.[11]

How is growth measured? The usual indicator for growth—and thus, it is assumed, for progress in development—is annual increase in real (inflation-adjusted) per capita GDP.[12] Gross domestic product is similar to but distinct from gross national product (GNP). Gross domestic product measures the value of all goods and services produced within a country, regardless of the nationality of the producers. In contrast,

---

Box 2.1: Measuring Poverty

For technical and statistical purposes, poverty is usually measured by establishing a *poverty line*, set at some multiple of the income necessary to purchase a basic food basket that provides sufficient nutrition for an active, productive life. People whose income is below the level necessary to purchase even that basic food basket are called *absolutely poor*, or *in deprivation*. A significant degree of arbitrariness is involved in setting poverty lines. The World Bank has established a line for absolute poverty at $1 per day, as measured by relative purchasing power parity.[13] Using this poverty line, the Bank estimates that some 1.3 billion people are absolutely poor. If the Bank had used a line of $2 per day, the figure would be 3 billion. At whatever level the line is set, the number of people who fall below the line is called the *headcount index*, usually represented as a percentage of the population.

By themselves, the poverty line and headcount index don't tell us anything about the severity of poverty. Are most poor people living just below the poverty line, earning approximately 95 cents a day, or are they living in extreme poverty, earning just 12 cents a day? The *poverty gap* shows the depth of poverty by measuring how far (on average) those living in poverty are from the poverty line. The gap is expressed as the percent difference between the average income of those living in poverty and the set poverty line. For example, according to figures published by the World Bank in 1997, the 1993 poverty gap in the Middle East and North Africa was 0.6 percent, while in South Asia it was 12.6 percent and in sub-Saharan Africa, 15.3 percent—showing that the average person living in poverty in sub-Saharan Africa fell further below the poverty line than in most other parts of the world.[14]

Box 2.2: Measuring Social Inequality

When looking at the nature and effects of poverty, we must also focus on questions of income inequality. The conventional measure of inequality is the *Gini coefficient*. The coefficient is a number between zero and one, where zero represents perfect income equality (all people have equal incomes) and one represents perfect inequality (all income is received by one person). Graphically, the Gini coefficient measures the area between the curve that plots existing income distribution (known as the *Lorenz curve*) and a line reflecting perfect equality; the higher the coefficient, the greater the inequality.

Explaining disparities in wealth and income requires examining factors like geography, gender, race, and ethnicity, as well as economics. For example, an estimated 70 percent of people living in absolute poverty today are women, while in the Americas, indigenous communities suffer disproportionately.[15]

While quantitative measures of poverty reveal important trends, we must also be attentive to the risks involved in measuring poverty primarily according to income. The work of economist and philosopher Amartya Sen highlights the limits of an income-based approach. Sen argues for understanding human beings not merely as "recipients of income" but as "people attempting to live satisfactory lives."[16] In this more inclusive framework, the struggle against poverty involves more than raising incomes, vital as such improvements in income are. It also entails efforts or contributions that may not in fact "show up in production and growth figures, and are not achieved by economic growth."[17] Examples include safe drinking water, adequate nutrition, and improved schooling.

The concept of *vulnerability* (or *insecurity*), as distinguished from the concept of poverty, helps us analyze the exposure of particular social groups to external risks, shocks, and stresses, and assess their capacity to respond to these challenges. Subsistence farmers who diversify their crop selection, for example, may be poor without being vulnerable. If, on the other hand, they enter the market by selling high-risk export crops, their income may rise, but their vulnerability may also increase. As with vulnerability to economic fluctuation, vulnerability to disease reflects the severity of poverty, and contributes to its perpetuation as well. Examining vulnerability can highlight structural and institutional factors that are important to understanding the effects of different health policies—as well as of particular patterns of growth—on poverty and inequality.

Some recent analyses of poverty have focused on the concept of social exclusion: the "process through which individuals or groups are wholly or partially excluded from full participation in the society in which they live."[18] Social exclusion further expands the dimensions along which poverty is measured and analyzed. Many analysts believe social exclusion is an analytical tool that can be used in both poor and rich countries, whereas income poverty is sometimes thought to have a more limited application in wealthy countries.

We can see that analysts' decisions about which economic and social indicators to use carry important consequences. Specific indicators can clarify some

> dynamics and processes while obscuring others. We need to pay close attention to the indicators different sources select as we seek to evaluate the claims made for or against particular development policies.

GNP is the value of the total output of goods and services generated by a country's citizens, whether they reside in that country or abroad. Thus, for example, GNP does not include the value of goods and services produced by foreign workers living on a country's soil. However, wages and corporate profits generated within a country's territory by foreign workers and companies are counted as part of the host country's GDP, even when these sums are remitted abroad.[19]

Per capita GDP can be an important predictor of health and life quality in a country. A very strong relationship appears to exist between per capita GDP and certain crucial health indicators, such as life expectancy and infant mortality. However, per capita GDP does not tell the whole story. As an average indicator, per capita GDP tells us nothing about the distribution of either wealth or income; that is, whether the benefits of growth are shared widely among the population or are restricted to a narrow elite. A genuine understanding of the effect of growth on the poor demands a "thicker" reading of human experiences and socioeconomic relationships.[20] As the UNDP's *Human Development Report* of 1997 acknowledges, what is needed is growth consciously crafted and shaped for a "pro-poor" impact. "In too many countries, growth has failed to reduce poverty, either because growth has been slow or stagnant *or because its quality and structure have been insufficiently pro-poor.*"[21]

Growth *can* benefit the poor. Yet there is no *guarantee* that growth in per capita GDP will translate into improvements in income for the poorest and most vulnerable groups in society. Still less automatic "are the links between economic growth and reduction in other aspects of human poverty—such as illiteracy, a short lifespan, ill health, lack of personal security." The UNDP is correct in stressing that "[d]istribution, government policies and public provision" decisively affect the translation of a given level of consumption and growth into effective poverty reduction.[22]

Unfortunately, GDP growth today remains the most commonly used indicator of progress toward the reduction of poverty, and, more generally, of the overall economic health of a given society. Many economists and political leaders (including the vast majority of those with direct influence over policy decisions in wealthy countries) continue to affirm some version of the theory that has been summed up in the adage that a "rising tide lifts all boats." For decades, this theory has been used to legitimize growth-oriented economic policies in the United States and elsewhere. Conventional economic wisdom continues today to consist of variations on this theme. Empirically, however, it appears evident that in most cases the "rising tide" of growth lifts some boats while capsizing and sinking others.

To understand where and why growth fails to fulfill the promises made about its beneficial effects, we must pay attention not only to GDP but to the *pattern* of growth as it expresses itself in human experience at various economic levels within a society. This pattern influences and is influenced by social conditions and government policies, including commitment to health as a fundamental political imperative. Significant factors influencing the way growth circulates through the complex structures of a living society include the following: initial asset distributions (land, human capital, natural resources, and so forth); the redistributive nature of government programs; and the extent to which growth is more labor- or capital-intensive.[23] Therefore, to discern patterns and their consequences correctly, we must pay attention to (in)equality of asset ownership; to government services' success or failure in reaching the poor; and to the degree to which growth is labor-intensive, because labor power is typically the poor's most significant asset.

Yet if economic growth *per se* is actually a relatively unreliable indicator of improvement in life quality for poor people, how did growth become so widely accepted as the royal road to reducing poverty? To understand how an uncritical ideology of growth came to occupy a dominant position in contemporary economic theory and political discourse, we need to look at the history of development economics.

HISTORICAL PERSPECTIVES ON GROWTH: THE "GOLDEN AGE" AND BEYOND

Development Discourse in the Golden Age

Early writing on development economics as a field of its own coincided with the post-World War II era and the identification of the majority of the world as "underdeveloped."[24] The fundamental assumption linking the ideologically heterogeneous writings produced in this early phase of development was a version of the "rising tide" principle. Following the classical economists, most development economists viewed the accumulation of physical capital (if it embodied technical progress) as leading quasi-automatically to a reduction in poverty.[25] As technical progress and the accumulation of physical capital generated an expansion of economic activity, economic growth would *ipso facto* create greater wealth, which would eventually be distributed through market interactions to all segments of the population. As this process unfolded, "developing" nations would pass through socioeconomic and demographic transitions, some of which might be painful in the short term, but which would eventually yield greater wealth and higher quality of life for all.

The period of rapid expansion of the world economy between 1945 and the mid-1970s has been broadly referred to as the "Golden Age." During this period, industrialized economies grew at almost 5 percent annually, nearly double the industrialized countries' long-term historical rate. The Golden Age brought prosperity to many citizens of established industrial powers and increased wealth dramatically, even in certain parts of the world where economic modernization was more recent. In Taiwan and South Korea, for example, growth brought improvements in the standard of living for most of the population, though development in these countries involved government repression, restriction of personal freedoms, and severe environmental degradation.[26]

Three key international institutions emerged during the Golden Age, and have continued to play a pivotal role in the world economy. These are the

International Monetary Fund (IMF), the World Bank, and the General Agreement on Tariffs and Trade (GATT), with the latter giving birth to the World Trade Organization (WTO) in 1994.[27] The IMF and World Bank are also known as the Bretton Woods Institutions, because plans for their establishment were drawn up at a conference in Bretton Woods, New Hampshire, in July 1944. The original mission of the IMF, conceived in the aftermath of the Great Depression, was to constitute a permanent international body capable of coordinated action to prevent or contain economic crises like those that marked the 1930s. The IMF strove to eliminate trade restrictions and the destructive economic policies, such as competitive currency devaluations, that had paralyzed investment and trade in the 1930s.[28] Maintaining a fixed exchange rate system, the IMF would facilitate the conversion of currencies and smooth the way for orderly international commerce. The World Bank, originally called the International Bank for Reconstruction and Development, began operations in 1946-47. As the name suggests, the Bank's first purpose was to aid in the reconstruction of economies devastated by the Second World War, primarily economies of Western European countries and Japan. Rapidly, however (beginning in 1948), the Bank began providing development loans to poor countries.[29] The GATT was an integrated set of trade agreements aimed at the reduction of tariffs and other barriers to trade. Signed in 1947 by 23 countries, the GATT was originally intended as an interim arrangement, but sustained itself through several decades as an effective instrument for trade liberalization in manufactured goods.

The overarching objective associated with the IMF, the World Bank, and the GATT was to shape and then maintain a system of what has come to be termed "embedded liberalism." This framework encouraged free trade at the international level combined with restrictions on capital mobility and a domestic social contract sufficient to maintain relative peace between labor and capital.[30] The reconstructed global economy, it was hoped, would nurture growth in the underdeveloped world while protecting the interests of the dominant capitalist powers. Broad, stable prosperity ensured by the vigilance of the multilateral institutions was seen as the most reliable defense against the encroachments of communism.[31]

The question of how economic development related to social equality or inequality concerned some development economists from the beginning. It was widely assumed that growth in low-income countries would necessarily be inequitable at first, and that economic disparities would probably have to increase initially while the process of growth was launched and gathered momentum.[32] Current research has called this model into question. The earlier view assumed that growth initially demands a certain degree of inequality and routinely (though temporarily) exacerbates inequality as growth starts to unfold. In contrast, recent studies suggest that greater initial *equality*, not inequality, is beneficial for growth itself. Initial equality also enhances the degree to which GDP growth enables poverty reduction. One study estimates that annual per capita GDP growth of 10 percent "would reduce the incidence of income poverty by 30 percent in relatively egalitarian societies...and by only 10 percent in less equal societies."[33] A significant aspect of these findings is their suggestion that government policies—as opposed to some "natural" process of economic development or an intrinsic "law" of market forces—play a key role in shaping the interaction of growth, poverty, and inequality.

The economic achievements of the Golden Age sparked the imagination and the rhetorical passions of national and international elites. A series of initiatives expressed hope for universal access to those basic services and resources that seemed to represent the foundation of a dignified life: services and resources promised by the proponents of growth as the reward for pressing forward on the path of development. It was in this context that the 1978 Alma Ata declaration "Health for All by the Year 2000" was launched.[34] By 1978, however, the Golden Age of (relative) prosperity for both rich and poor countries was in fact already over. The oil crisis of 1973 is often seen as symbolically marking the conclusion of the era of rapid expansion and economic optimism.[35] Since that year, the GDP growth rates for the 29 wealthy countries that make up the Organization for Economic Cooperation and Development (OECD), and the rates for the world as a whole, have been nearly halved.[36]

Three decisive developments marked the conclusion of the Golden Age: the decline in growth rates in the OECD countries and "stagflation" (high levels of both inflation and unemployment) in the United States in the 1970s; the election of rhetorically anti-statist governments in Great Britain (Thatcher), the United States (Reagan), and Germany (Kohl); and, in the early 1980s, the Debt Crisis.[37]

The Debt Crisis and its aftermath require detailed examination. This episode reshaped the global economic landscape and redefined relationships between developing countries and the major international financial institutions. The lasting effects of the crisis have played an important role in configuring the power dynamics of the new era of globalization and economic restructuring.

Crisis and Adjustment

The *Debt Crisis* refers to the panic generated in international financial and political circles in the late 1970s to mid-1980s, when it began to appear that a substantial number of heavily indebted Third World countries would be unable to continue making payments on their debts to commercial banks in wealthy countries. In the preceding decade, commercial banks had furnished vast amounts of capital in loans to the developing world. Thus, it was feared the looming default of debtor countries, toppling the banks, might produce a collapse of the global financial system. This collapse was averted by the energetic intervention of wealthy countries, acting through the World Bank and the IMF. These institutions took center stage in the resolution (or perhaps more accurately, the effective displacement) of the crisis. "Solving" the Debt Crisis involved imposing structural adjustment programs (SAPs) on the economies of debtor countries, thus allowing these economies to "return to growth" and, most importantly, to continue making interest payments on their foreign loans.[38]

Before exploring the consequences of structural adjustment schemes and in particular their effects on health outcomes among the poor, we need to look back briefly at the historical roots of the Debt Crisis. Only in so doing can we begin to refute the all too common and convenient assumption among some economists and politicians that the crisis was primarily the result of mismanagement and "corruption" in poorer countries.

The economic problems of heavily indebted poor countries reached crisis proportions under the combined impact of three principal factors:

- **Changes in the international economy.** The oil price increases spurred by OPEC (the Organization of Petroleum Exporting Countries) in and after 1973 created new pressures for foreign exchange among oil importing countries worldwide. Because commodity prices remained stable and interest rates low throughout the 1970s, poorer countries did not face immediate difficulties with maintaining payments on their external debts. But interest rates skyrocketed after 1979 with the shift in monetary policy by the U.S. Federal Reserve system under its newly appointed board chairman, Paul Volcker. The rise in U.S. interest rates increased debt service for countries that had U.S. dollar-denominated loans—in other words, most borrowing countries—because the cost of their loans went up.[39] This effect—combined with the recession and declining commodity prices of the early 1980s—meant developing countries were caught between higher debt payments, smaller markets for their exports, and reduced inflows of foreign loans.

- **Expanded bank lending.** The enormous revenues generated by OPEC countries (Saudi Arabia, Kuwait, and the United Arab Emirates, for example) required a mechanism to circulate the capital, much of which was deposited with commercial banks. The OPEC monies joined a larger, growing supply of dollars not deposited in U.S. banks but held by financial institutions in other parts of the world: the so-called "Eurodollar" market. This capital was available to fund foreign investment by private as well as public agents. Third World governments, in need of foreign exchange to promote industrialization in the face of declining demand in the developed countries, were prime clients for the "petrodollars." The commercial banks began a virtual orgy of lending.[40]

- **Development strategies in crisis.** Many poorer countries had pursued development strategies that relied heavily on state intervention in the economy to promote industrialization through mechanisms like state-owned corporations, subsidies to urban consumers, and restrictions on foreign trade and investment. These strategies had led to significant growth and industrialization in some parts of the Third World. In parts of the world where industries never became internationally competitive, however, countries were unable to earn foreign exchange by exporting their goods overseas. The combination of three factors— small domestic markets for those industrial goods that were produced; increased foreign exchange demands for oil and petroleum-related imports; and increasing pressure from the poor and middle classes for greater redistribution of the benefits of economic growth—posed challenges to these political regimes. In the 1970s, by and large, governments responded to these challenges with increased borrowing from abroad.

While some countries had already technically defaulted on their loans in the late 1970s and early 1980s, the Debt Crisis is usually symbolically dated to August 1982, when Mexican leaders informed the U.S. government that Mexico was unable to make payments on its external debt. The United States organized a rescue package, less out of neighborly benevolence than fear of the consequences a possible Mexican default would have on North American financial institutions and corporations.

Worldwide, initial responses to the Debt Crisis, led largely by the IMF, were based on the then-prevalent belief that the crisis was merely a short-term problem of liquidity.[41] Soon, however, it became clear that the damaged economies were not rebounding, nor was foreign capital flowing back into developing countries. So the World Bank and IMF, pushed by their most powerful shareholders—the United States, Great Britain, and Germany—intervened more dramatically to address the crisis. A consensus eventually emerged among policy-makers in the development institutions and their backer governments: what was required was nothing less than the radical restructuring of Third World economies.

The policy objectives of this restructuring were linked to ideological changes among leading rich-country governments—represented most dramatically by the Thatcher, Reagan, and Kohl administrations—and among some Third World, particularly Latin American, technocrats and elites. Their prescription for poorer countries became known as "structural adjustment" when implemented as programs by the World Bank and IMF, or, more broadly, as the "Washington Consensus" or "neoliberalism."[42] This shift reflected the emergence of a new conventional wisdom regarding development and growth, the consequences of which have been far-reaching.

Spokespersons of the new consensus shared a profoundly cynical view of the state, or at least of state power in developing countries (neoliberal free-market rhetoric often contrasted sharply with the actual policies of the Reagan and Thatcher governments at home).[43] Neoliberal thinkers' diagnosis of the problems facing poor countries was that the state played too great a role in the economy, inhibiting markets and firms from operating in a manner that would raise overall welfare. They saw state failure (that is, state intervention that prevented markets from acting efficiently) as the key reason why countries were, and remained, poor. Even when market mechanisms did go wrong, these economists believed state intervention was undesirable, because the costs of state action might outweigh the benefits. They believed government's legitimate role in the economy was limited to protecting property rights, enforcing contracts, and (in some cases) investing in human capital.[44] Its initial debacles in places like Chile notwithstanding, the neoliberal analysis had an understandable appeal.[45] The Debt Crisis required an explanation; neoliberal economics provided one. The diagnosis was that excessive state intervention had bred uncompetitive, inefficient industries sheltered behind protectionist walls, and that such state interference had distorted markets and prices.

The Mechanics of Adjustment

Adjustment was expected to unfold in a debtor country according to roughly the following pattern. The first step in treating the ailing economy was stabilization, through a form of "shock therapy" if the economic system was in the midst of hyperinflation, or a more traditional IMF package if inflation was not wildly out of control. The objective of stabilization was to reduce inflation and even out the country's balance of payments; that is, the relationship between foreign exchange garnered from exports and the demand for imports. Such goals could, in theory, be achieved by reducing demand for goods and services in the economy (by cutting government spending or lowering wages, for example). These methods are known as "demand-side" measures; they focus on a quick reduction in the effective demand in an economy. Once stabilization is achieved, the free market's own self-regulating mechanisms are trusted with the job of adjusting to provide the necessary cure for previous distortions, which are understood to have been largely the result of state interference.[46]

The structural adjustment prescription was (and is) usually seen as embracing three interrelated aims and processes:

- Reduce the role of the state relative to the market in the economy;

- Enhance economic efficiency by allowing prices to be determined by market forces, such as exchange rates, interest rates, and real wages;

- Integrate the national economy into the world economy by lifting barriers to trade and investment.[47]

In short, the policies comprise *privatization*, *liberalization*, and *deregulation*.

Privatization involves the sale of state-owned enterprises, and in some cases means shifting the provision of social services that were previously state-administered—for example, social security, education, and health care—from the public sector to the private sector (either to for-profit firms or nonprofit NGOs). *Liberalization* requires reducing barriers to the free flow of trade and investment, as well as reducing or eliminating government subsidies that keep the prices of certain essential goods low. Cutting subsidies, allowing the market to set prices, and reducing barriers to the free flow of goods, services, and capital will, according to the model, ensure that the "prices are right." Prices will reflect the actual value of goods, as measured by the market. Capital (investment) will flow to those sectors of the economy that are most productive and profitable. Liberalizing trade and investment is a means of integrating the national economy more closely with the world economy through the reduction of tariff and non-tariff barriers (quotas, licenses, and so forth) to imports. The idea behind integration is to provide a rapid relay between prices in the world economy and the domestic economy. In theory, this will raise social welfare by making cheaper goods and services available to consumers through imports, at the same time forcing producers in the country to be more "competitive." *Deregulation* means reducing the level of state control over the flow of capital, goods, services, and, increasingly, domestic labor markets.[48] These key theoretical commitments shaped structural adjustment programs in their early phases; their influence continues to be felt today.

The involvement of the World Bank and IMF in molding the policies of countries in Latin America, Africa, and parts of Asia expanded dramatically in the 1980s. By the end of 1991, 75 countries had received adjustment loans worth more than the equivalent of $41 billion. Of those 75 countries, 30 were in Africa. Most of those 30 had had near-continuous programs with the IMF and the World Bank since the early 1980s. Meanwhile, there were 107 World Bank-IMF programs in 18 Latin American countries during the 1980s.[49]

How adequately did these programs work in practice? Was structural adjustment an effective tool for addressing the Debt Crisis and its consequences? Clearly, adjustment worked very well to manage one dimension of the crisis: ensuring repayment of debts to lending institutions in wealthy countries. Between 1983 and 1989, poor countries paid $242 billion more to creditors than they received in new loans. And the net transfer of resources from developed to developing countries changed from a positive flow of nearly $43 billion in 1981 to a negative flow of $33 billion in 1988.[50]

On the other hand, structural adjustment did not reduce debts, cut poverty, nor return countries to the path of growth.[51] The external debt stock of developing countries increased from $616 billion in 1980 to an estimated $2.2 trillion at the end of 1997.[52] Moreover, the absolute dollar value of debt reveals nothing about the amount of debt in relation to the size of poor countries' economies. The ratio of debt stock to GDP and the ratio of debt service to earnings from exports give a clearer picture of the daunting scale of the debt problem many poor countries face, relative to the actual size and strength of their economies.[53] The ratio of external debt to GNP for developing countries as a whole peaked in 1987, fell slightly, rose again in the early 1990s, and stood at 34.9 percent in 1997.[54] This is roughly 50 percent higher than where the ratio stood in 1982, at the start of the Debt Crisis.

To understand the Debt Crisis it is also important to distinguish between *official debt* and *commercial debt*. *Official debt* is debt owed to governments or multilateral institutions, such as the IMF, World Bank, and regional development banks. *Commercial debt* is debt owed to private commercial banks. Whereas in the early 1980s commercial banks were poorer countries' main creditors, governments and international institutions now play a dominant lending role. Worldwide, multilateral institutions like the World Bank and IMF accounted for 17 percent of long-term finance in 1997, with bilateral sources (governments of developed countries) contributing a further 31 percent, together nearly equaling all private loans.[55] In many cases, the increase in official debt has represented the socialization of previously private debt, as governments have either used official loans to pay off commercial creditors, or actually transformed private commercial debt into public debt.

The level of official versus commercial debt varies sharply by region. In sub-Saharan Africa, multilateral and bilateral creditors have an especially decisive position in the debt picture. In 1997, the World Bank estimated the region's long-term debt at $179.2 billion, of which 74 percent was owed to official creditors. Over half of that official debt was owed to other governments, while the remainder was owed to multilateral agencies like the World Bank and the IMF. In Latin America and the Caribbean, a third of long-term debt is owed to official creditors; of that, just over half is owed to governments.[56] This shift makes the continuation of the Debt Crisis more explicitly a function of political choices. When commercial debt was dominant, it would have been harder (if not impossible) to manage large-scale debt write-offs or reductions, given the power that banking interests exercise in the industrialized countries. Now, creditor governments and their citizens have greater power to forgive these debts directly. In fact, there is some historical precedent for canceling large amounts of debt.[57]

The debt problem of poor countries continues to exact a cruel toll in deteriorating life quality, massive physical and psychological suffering, and squandered human potential, as urgently needed social investment in health and education takes a back seat to debt service. Some figures help give a sense of the human deprivation associated with crushing debt burdens:

- In Africa as a whole, governments transfer to northern creditors four times more in debt payments than they spend on the health and education of their citizens.[58]

- In Mozambique, debt servicing for 1996 absorbed twice the amount allocated to the combined current budgets for health and education. This, in a country where one-quarter of all children die before the age of five as a result of infectious disease, and where two-thirds of the population is illiterate.

- In Niger, the country at the bottom of the UNDP's Human Development Index, life expectancy averages 47 years and only 14 percent of the population is literate, but debt servicing absorbs more than the combined budgets for health and education.

- In Nicaragua, where three out of every four people live below the poverty line; where one-quarter of the under-five population suffers nutritional deficiency; and where 35 percent of the population is illiterate, debt repayments exceed the total social-sector budget.

- In Bolivia, where greater than 80 percent of the highland population lives in poverty; where only 16 percent of that population has access to safe water; and where more than one-third of all women are illiterate, debt repayments for 1997 accounted for three times the spending allocated for rural poverty reduction.[59]

Nearly two decades after the Debt Crisis began, halting steps toward debt reduction for the poorest, most heavily indebted countries are emerging.[60] Yet progress has been agonizingly slow. In September 1996, the Heavily Indebted Poor Countries (or HIPC) Initiative was launched, targeted at reducing the debt burdens of the 41 poorest, heavily indebted countries.[61]

By April 1998, the boards of the World Bank and IMF had reviewed ten countries' eligibility for the initiative. Six of these countries—Bolivia, Burkina Faso, Côte d'Ivoire, Guyana, Mozambique, and Uganda—had qualified under the HIPC Initiative for debt relief totaling about $3 billion in net present-value terms. This was equivalent to nominal debt relief of about $5.7 billion, the amount needed to reduce these countries' debt to a sustainable level, as defined by the HIPC Initiative. The Group of Seven (G-7) Cologne Debt Relief Initiative (June 1999) promised substantive debt cancelation to a larger group of poor countries, and explicitly acknowledged a close connection between debt relief, poverty reduction, and sustainable development.[62] Important as such a step may be for the countries participating in this initiative, it stops far short indeed of addressing the full dimensions of the crisis. The Cologne Initiative continues to make debt relief contingent upon poor countries' implementation of IFI-sanctioned austerity policies that perpetuate poverty and exacerbate environmental degradation. This selective response is inadequate, given the human costs of debt burdens. External debt for many countries continues to grow, and this legacy from the 1980s will likely shape the beginning of the new millennium for many citizens of the world's poorest countries.

Economists continue to debate the "lost decade" of the 1980s and the role of structural adjustment within it. The World Bank has conducted major studies of the impact of structural adjustment, several with specific reference to Africa.[63] The Bank's first review of adjustment lending in 1988 found that countries receiving adjustment loans over several years out-performed comparable countries "on most indicators, but with some rather significant exceptions: low-income countries, heavily indebted countries, and sub-Saharan Africa."[64] With "exceptions" like these, one might wonder, why bother to state a rule? The Bank's more recent studies on Africa, meanwhile, have come under fire for statistical manipulation.[65]

The Many Faces of Structural Adjustment

Around the same time as the World Bank's initial review of adjustment policies, analysts associated with UNICEF published the first major critique of adjustment, entitled *Adjustment with a Human Face* (1987). UNICEF's analysis focused on how the poor, in particular women and children, bear a disproportionate share of the costs of adjustment. The study stressed the need to incorporate compensatory programs for those negatively affected by economic change. As one analyst noted, the text's claim "was neither particularly original nor politically daring."[66] Yet the publication of *Adjustment with a Human Face* stirred heated debates. A decade later, it is time to take stock of the adjustment debate and its aftermath.

Initially, it is difficult to isolate the specific impact of structural adjustment programs on poverty. Poverty itself is complex, as we have seen, and structural adjustment affects a society on many levels. As one way of approaching the issue, we can bracket some of our own critical questions and concede, for the sake of discussion, the general premise that encouraging economic growth is one important component of a realistic poverty-reduction program. We can then consider how adjustment affects growth.

Public investment is a key determinant of growth (though of course not the only such determinant). One point on which virtually all studies agree is the correlation between structural adjustment and declining public investment.[67] This is especially important because public investment funds social infrastructure and other needs that are unlikely to be adequately addressed by the private sector: for example, sanitation, drinking water, schools, and health clinics. Clearly, not all public investment is inherently or necessarily beneficial. Governments have, in fact, bankrolled notorious development disasters, such as large dams that have uprooted communities and wrought environmental havoc.[68] Yet adequate, properly managed public investment is vital to a society's long-term viability and to the well-being of its citizens, particularly the poor.

It is empirically well established that IMF programs are associated with a significant decline in public investment.[69] This is not surprising. If an IMF program aims to strengthen the balance of payments in the short term by reducing aggregate demand relative to supply, then the brunt of the change will fall upon government spending, of which public investment is a significant component. Faced with pressure to reduce spending, it is politically easier for a government to cut monies for building new roads or sanitation systems, or to reduce maintenance on existing facilities, than to cut other types of direct consumption expenditures. This falling public investment undermines the prospects for future growth. This produces a destructive contradiction, in that the hope of finding ways to increase their rate of economic growth is a major reason countries seek IMF assistance in the first place. In the 1980s, the IMF was already supposed to have shifted its policies to respond to this problem, but a number of studies suggest that "the changes in practice have been minimal, if not indiscernible."[70]

The World Bank itself notes that "when structural adjustment issues came to the fore little attention was paid to the effects on the poor."[71] The injury to the poor has come in two main forms: lower incomes and declining access to quality social services. And all reviews agree that poverty increased in both absolute and relative terms over the 1980s in Africa, Latin America, and the Caribbean.

The distributional impact of adjustment within a country depends significantly on the extent of initial equality of asset ownership. In rural areas, for example, if land ownership is highly concentrated, the benefits of adjustment (typically, reducing the negative term of trade against agriculture) will flow to the landed elite; this was the case in Ecuador and Malawi, for example.[72] Adjustment has its most significant effect through its impact on employment, which is almost "invariably negative in the short run."[73] Under "stabilization" programs in Latin America, observers have noted a "strong and consistent pattern of reduction of labor's share in income."[74] In the 1990s, the continued evolution of these patterns in Latin America and the Caribbean has given little cause for rejoicing among the region's poor and disenfranchised.[75]

Growth has rebounded in Latin America in the 1990s (to an average 3.5 percent annual increase in GDP), yet neither its level nor its pattern has been sufficient to alter severe inequalities, nor reduce the number of poor. The Inter-American Development Bank (IDB) concedes, in a chilling understatement, that "the relatively well-off groups of Latin American society appear to have benefited from the recovery of the 1990s somewhat more than the poorest classes."[76] In Africa, home to 25 of the 32 countries classified by the World Bank as severely indebted low-income countries, the situation is even bleaker. Sub-Saharan Africa receives less than 1 percent of global private capital flows, and so remains dependent on financial flows from official sources: wealthy-country governments and the international financial institutions. From 1990 to 1993, sub-Saharan Africa transferred $13.4 billion annually to its external creditors, more than it spent on education and health combined.[77] The IMF notably remains an enormous drain. From 1987 to 1993, the net transfer of resources from Africa to the IMF was $3.8 billion.[78]

In sum, the poor were often suffering in the period of economic crisis immediately prior to the adjustment program; often they suffered even more severely as adjustment proceeded and access to publicly funded social services dwindled. Significantly, however, this rule did not hold in all cases. Some countries, such as Costa Rica and Malaysia, were able to combine adjustment with increasing shares of government expenditures in the social sectors. This more positive outcome was largely a function of political factors. In some cases, policy-makers committed themselves to poverty alleviation, whether for reasons of conviction or to purchase political stability. Alternately or in addition to that commitment, some countries saw groups of poor people organize to voice demands and effectively advance their interests.[79]

A number of reviews describing the economic situation in Latin America in the 1980s suggest that the distribution of the costs of adjustment was not determined by immutable laws of economics. Rather, the distribution was significantly shaped by the (in)equality of asset distribution, the extent and strength of social safety nets prior to the crisis, the nature of the political regime (democratic or authoritarian), and the relative political power exercised by unions, business, and other groups.[80] The existence of these differences suggests that the negative effects of adjustment on the poor were not inevitable. That is, political forces influenced the extent to which the costs of adjustment were borne disproportionately by the disadvantaged. This shows us that simply focusing on designing a better mousetrap (or, in this case, a better adjustment program) is insufficient. Such a narrow reform effort ignores the broader political and economic structures that decisively configure growth, poverty, and inequality.

The 1990s: A New Poverty Agenda

The debates over the costs of adjustment and the decade-long decline of many economies in Africa and Latin America in the 1980s pushed poverty back onto the international agenda. This new trend was underscored by two publications in 1990: the UNDP's first *Human Development Report* and the World Bank's *World Development Report* on poverty.

In the *World Development Report*, the World Bank announced a shift toward "poverty reduction" as its overarching objective, and described a three-pronged strategy to attain this goal: labor-intensive growth; investing in the poor via the development of human capital (mainly in the health and education sectors); and the promotion of safety nets and targeted social programs. The other regional development banks quickly followed with explicit poverty-reduction agendas. Targets and criteria for antipoverty operations were established, aiming in particular to retain or garner support for replenishments of the multilateral development banks' concessional, or "soft," loan windows.[81]

We will have more to say about specific aspects of the World Bank's antipoverty agenda shortly. For the moment, we can note that several general trends distinguish the current climate from the earlier era of "defensive modernization," during which the World Bank sought to "give people a stake, however minimal, in the system,"[82] primarily in order to undercut demands for more radical types of political change. In the Bank's new stance on poverty, more attention is given to direct targeting of resources to the poor and underserved, as opposed to a belief that growth itself will automatically trickle down to benefit the poor.[83] The current approach focuses on providing public goods that benefit poor people, rather than emphasizing, for example, agricultural development *per se*, because elite groups often capture the credit and other input subsidies provided under integrated rural development programs. Thus, World Bank analysts are now expected to examine the composition of public spending with an eye for the effects of social spending on the poor. Analysts now ask, for example, whether health spending is targeted toward the poor or the urban elite, and if resources for education fund primary schools in poor regions or college education for the urban middle class.

Despite these positive developments, the World Bank's approach continues to exhibit significant problems. A 1996 World Bank report on poverty-reduction efforts in sub-Saharan Africa (*Taking Action for Poverty Reduction in Africa*) found that in reality, "few projects provide for monitoring or evaluating their effects on the poor."[84] Another World Bank review of poverty indicators for the fiscal years 1988-1993 found that, for World Bank-assisted projects described as poverty-targeted and for program credits focused on poverty reduction, one-third of staff appraisal reports did not mention the use of indicators beyond those appropriate for routine project management— meaning that these evaluations gave no specific attention to the question of how the poor were affected.[85] *Taking Action's* review of 96 investment and adjustment projects approved by the World Bank in fiscal years 1992-94 found that "at best 30 percent of the Bank-assisted investment and adjustment projects committed to enabling long-term growth had pro-poor components."[86] The World Bank clearly has some ways to go in developing approaches to policy and lending that genuinely reduce poverty by promoting equitable patterns of growth.

A crucial thrust of the World Bank's new poverty agenda is the orientation of expenditures to human capital (health and education), based on the view that efficient and equitable delivery of social services (particularly primary education and basic health care) can actually contribute to economic growth as well as promote equity.[87] These particular World Bank policies affect the health of the poor in at least three dimensions: economic policies shaped by the Bank's structural and sectoral adjustment loans; lending targeted specifically to the health sector; and the Bank's role in promoting particular kinds of health-care policies, represented most clearly in the publication of *Investing in Health*, the World Bank's 1993 World Development Report.[88] The appearance of this study marked, according to the *Lancet*, a shift in leadership on international health from the World Health Organization to the World Bank.[89] The Bank has increased its lending and research output to the health sector as part of its antipoverty agenda. World Bank lending in the population, health, and nutrition (PHN) sectors has increased in absolute terms from an annual average of $103 million in the 1981-84 period, to $1.3 billion in the fiscal 1991-94 period, and to $1.8 billion in fiscal years 1995-97. Population, health, and nutrition loans currently comprise about 7 percent of the Bank's total lending.[90] The publication of the Bank's *Investing in Health* was applauded by health advocates for its emphasis on primary care, but has also been criticized for its promotion of market-oriented health-care systems (including managed care), its reluctance to identify the weaknesses of such systems, and its emphasis on cost recovery.

The World Bank's policy dialogue with borrowing countries has at least as great an impact on health policy as do World Bank-sponsored projects. In the 1980s, World Bank-approved adjustment programs focused on cutting government expenditures with little attention to the impact that such cuts would have on the poor. In the 1990s, the Bank's policy recommendations, outlined in *Investing in Health*, include: shifting public health expenditures from tertiary to primary care;

developing more targeted interventions, such as micro-nutrient programs and early childhood interventions; decentralization; and the use of "cost recovery" mechanisms, such as user fees.

The World Bank has played an important role in the debate over shifting health policy from public to private financing. In 1987, *Financing Health Services in Developing Countries: An Agenda for Reform* directly challenged the idea of free, universally available health care: "The…common approach to health care in developing countries has been to treat it as a right of citizenry and to attempt to provide free services for everyone. This approach does not usually work. It prevents the government health system from collecting revenues that many patients are both able and willing to pay."[91] In line with this stance, a typical component of adjustment programs has been cutbacks in government spending and the introduction of user fees for social services such as health care. More than 30 countries in Africa now operate national cost-recovery systems in health care. Not coincidentally, in large areas of sub-Saharan Africa, the quality of care as measured by attendance levels in hospitals and clinics has been falling since the late 1980s. Recent studies in Zaire, Nigeria, and Zimbabwe all found that previously stable attendance rates at medical facilities plummeted after the introduction of user fees.[92]

The impact on Zimbabwe was important precisely because Zimbabwe had been seen as an example of a state attempting to provide wide-ranging health services, and because Zimbabwe's health indicators compared favorably with those elsewhere in sub-Saharan Africa. User-fee targets and the policy framework for health reform were shaped by two World Bank reports on Zimbabwe's health system.[93] While the World Bank did not explicitly include the implementation of cost recovery as a condition for Zimbabwe's receiving its adjustment loans, World Bank research suggested that user fees could fund an increased share of the health budget, from 3 percent to as much as 33 percent.[94] In part as a response to previous criticisms of the negative impact of adjustment programs on social services, the Bank claimed that it had negotiated a pledge from the Zimbabwean government to "protect" real expenditures in the health budget during the adjustment program. However, budget allocations for health fell as a percentage of the total budget; as a percentage of GDP; and in real per capita terms.[95] The World Bank has recognized that health measures such as the control of communicable diseases and public health education are basic public goods that will likely be undersupplied by the market. Yet, despite this recognition of the market's failure to guarantee health care, the World Bank still promotes market-driven policies, such as cost recovery.[96]

We now turn our attention briefly to the third main component of the World Bank's antipoverty agenda, the targeting of social services and safety nets.[97] The issue of targeting emerged in part because of the recognition that the benefits of some universal social programs (like general food subsidies) were received disproportionately by the non-poor.[98] Two distinct but related approaches to targeting developed. One was expenditure-shifting within social service programs like health and education to those services most likely to be used by the poor. This meant, for example, shifting the education budget away from university education to primary schools and moving health-care funds from urban hospitals toward rural primary care. The second type of targeting consisted of developing specific programs for the poor, either through reform of an existing general subsidy or through the adoption of a new program.

A number of problems confront programs that shift from universal provision to "targeted" benefits. One is the increased administrative cost associated with a targeted program. Another is the impact of reduced political support for targeted programs. The political argument around targeting is the more important consideration. Universal programs tend to have greater popular support. In Sri Lanka, for example, when general food subsidies were replaced by means-tested food stamps, middle class support evaporated. By 1984, the level of income transferred through the program fell to half its 1979 level, and coverage of the poor declined.[99]

Social Investment Funds (SIFs) represent another strategy emerging in response to criticisms of the anti-poor effects of adjustment policies. Social funds are targeted antipoverty funds often disbursed to projects proposed by grassroots NGOs or local governments. Much has been made of some social funds' demand-based approach. This has enabled communities with strong civil society organizations to use fund resources to promote accountable and broad-based community development. Transparently organized social funds that are responsive, accountable, and honest can build upon existing social capital resources in communities to support pro-poor infrastructure or social service investments. However, in areas where local politics are characterized by "clientelism" and authoritarianism, these funds can be captured by local elites and can reinforce clientelism and exclusionary development, as Jonathan Fox has shown for parts of Mexico, and Carol Graham argues for Peru and Senegal.[100]

Moreover, these organizations rarely represent the poorest of the poor. As Carol Graham notes in her broad review of SIFs: "The most evident drawback of the social fund approach is that the poorest groups, which tend to be weakly organized, are the least equipped to solicit benefits from demand-based programs."[101] For poor women for example, "the record of the supply-oriented government schemes in terms of reaching poor women and providing them with paid work is far better than that of the demand-driven social funds."[102]

Our survey of poverty-reduction efforts in the 1990s shows a mixture of positive intentions and inconclusive, sometimes negative results. At a minimum, it can be said that enormous challenges remain unresolved, and that current strategies appear inadequate to meet those challenges. The World Bank drafts a new *World Development Report* on poverty every ten years, with the next scheduled to appear in late 2000. These reports effectively serve to represent and legitimate the consensus view of powerful development actors. Hence they play an important role in defining the limits of the "possible" and the "reasonable" in development thinking and policy-making. Amidst the current global economic instability, gaps and uncertainties have emerged in what was the conventional wisdom of the 1980s and 1990s. These provide some new (albeit small) opportunities to bring new questions, issues, and voices into the development debate.[103]

Redistribution and Politics: Restoring the Missing Links

As several analysts have argued, adding safety nets and social funds long after adjustment has begun—ten years in some cases—does not constitute the creation of a new antipoverty agenda. Without a sustained effort to redistribute economic resources among the members of society, antipoverty interventions will be piecemeal, fragile, and often ineffectual. Economist Michael Lipton observes that:

> Calories are less unequally distributed than food, food than consumption, consumption than income, and income than assets...[T]he richest decile can well be, at most, four times better placed than the poorest to meet calorie requirements for a full and active life—yet three hundred times better placed in respect of asset ownership.

This vast discrepancy "naturally focuses...the attention of fighters of wars against poverty" on the issue of asset redistribution.[104] The missing link in both the World Bank's changing poverty agenda and in UNICEF's *Adjustment with a Human Face* is the question of redistribution on grounds of both social justice and economic efficiency. Lipton suggests that the "constriction of the ability of the poor to operate in the marketplace may help explain why the unprecedented decline in world poverty from 1945-[19]80 appears to have stopped and not to have resumed, though growth has....Though set up as caricature enemies, redistributive and market reforms need each other if they are to accelerate growth or help the poor."[105] Recent research by IDB Vice-President Nancy Birdsall and her collaborator Juan Luis Londoño also highlights this gap in the analysis and policy advocacy of the World Bank. Birdsall, formerly on the World Bank staff, notes that while the new World Bank poverty agenda has belatedly identified social spending as a key element of a pro-poor growth agenda, "World Bank and other development economists have neglected...a second key determinant of poverty reduction and aggregate growth: the distribution of assets," including both physical assets and human capital. "More concern earlier with the causes and the consequences of income inequality would have called greater attention to a fundamental constraint on poverty reduction: the poor's lack of access to the assets necessary for increased productivity and income."[106]

Under these circumstances, there is a tendency in some quarters simply to blame the IFIs for the impacts of adjustment. Yet there is plenty of blame to go around, and others deserve their fair share. First, the IFIs depend on their major donor governments, above all the members of the G-7 countries, and the larger group of OECD economies. The policies of the IFIs are in many cases shaped and in others simply eclipsed by the political, diplomatic, and sometimes military interventions of the United States and other countries. Such interventions seek in some cases to prevent "untrustworthy" states (Chile under Allende, for example, or Sandinista Nicaragua) from gaining access to IFI support. In other instances, the powerful countries want to ensure that their allies receive IFI assistance on the most favorable terms (Marcos in the Philippines, or the recent bailout in Mexico).[107] In general, the research and policy agenda of the World Bank is substantially shaped by the need to appease the Bank's main shareholders (particularly the United States) and thus in turn by the major powers' desire to maintain access to global financial markets.[108] A second and related point is that the foreign economic policies of the rich countries (including their bilateral aid programs) have an even larger impact than the World Bank and the IMF in some countries. Third, it is sometimes politically convenient for Third World elites to pin blame on the IMF and the World Bank when these elites want to be perceived by their fellow citizens as pursuing certain reform policies unwillingly. Whipping up nationalist sentiment against the Bank and the IMF can become a useful mantle under which elites implement adjustment measures to their own advantage while exempting themselves from blame for the painful consequences. Here we must recall that many Third World elites implemented liberalization with an enthusiasm that exceeded even that of the World Bank, privatizing, liberalizing, and deregulating faster than SAP conditionalities mandated. This was clearly the case in Mexico and Chile.[109]

Yet, while it is clearly simplistic to assign all blame for the negative effects of structural adjustment programs and their successors to the IFIs, it is equally apparent that the concrete operations and policy analyses of institutions like the World Bank need to evolve considerably in order to support pro-poor patterns of growth and development. A commitment to redistribution is vital if we are to change a pattern in which the health of markets has routinely taken unquestioned priority over the health and lives of poor people.

Past and Present

Our survey of some major episodes in recent economic history—in particular the Debt Crisis and its aftermath—has yielded a number of important lessons. We have seen how an ideological notion of economic growth as a supreme, unquestioned value took shape in the post-World War II "Golden Age"; but we also noted evidence casting doubt on theories that argued that strong growth, at least in its initial phases, requires (and will probably exacerbate) socioeconomic inequalities. Reviewing the history of the structural adjustment programs imposed on poor countries in the wake of the Debt Crisis, we concluded that the disproportionately destructive effects of these programs on poor communities were not inevitable, but were the result of political choices (whether explicit or tacit). The World Bank itself, recognizing grave flaws in its earlier approach, has more recently articulated an antipoverty framework that represents a theoretical step forward from previous policies, though a considerable gap still separates theory from practice. However, even in theory the Bank's modified strategies leave much to be desired in terms of their capacity to protect the health of the poor. We have argued that to prevent the poor from bearing a disproportionate share of the social costs of economic restructuring, the theme of redistribution must be reintroduced as the "missing link" in current discussions of market reform and growth.

Perhaps most importantly, this brief retrospective survey reminds us that the economic principles most of us tend to regard as self-evident and in some sense "natural" are in fact the products of a quite specific history. There is nothing natural about the notion of a free market, nor about the thesis that economic growth will benefit (sooner or later) all members of a given society. But to expose the historical roots of these notions does not mean we think they are irrelevant to current realities. On the contrary, these historically embedded ideas continue to shape the present and, surely, will exert a powerful influence on our collective future. Many of the assumptions and theories we have encountered in exploring the early phases of development economics, the Debt Crisis, and the policies of structural adjustment remain active in the current global economy, the evolution of which preoccupies scholars, the media, and ordinary people.[110]

In the last part of this chapter, we now turn our attention to the economic "new world order" emerging under the impact of a relatively broad consensus whose watchwords include "globalization," "free markets," and "competitiveness." We examine some of the main architectural features of the global economy as a prologue to tracing their implications for the health of the poor in subsequent chapters.

GLOBALIZATION AND THE NOT-TERRIBLY-NEW WORLD ORDER

It has become a truism to say that we live in a global economy. While global economic patterns have been developing since at least the sixteenth century, "globalization" is now increasingly deployed in the United States and Europe, both as a description and as an explanation of social phenomena. In the United States, for example, the debate about globalization fuses with discussions of job loss and of the growth in trade and trade agreements (such as the North American Free Trade Agreement, or NAFTA). Worries over imports from developing countries, as well as "runaway" firms seeking pollution havens abroad, have coincided with growing domestic inequality and falling real wages since the late 1970s, generating a new level of public concern about globalization and its consequences.

This concern is not unreasonable, though it would be a serious mistake to blame trade *per se* for American social ills. Many of these ills have their roots in other areas: policies that enable and even encourage corporations to abandon local communities in pursuit of increased profits; tax structures favorable to corporations; the lack of adaptive programs such as job retraining to assist laid-off workers; and the promotion of labor-displacing technologies. In the late 1990s, despite its wealth and its status as the largest economy in the world, the United States registers poverty rates and inequalities of both wealth and income among the highest of all OECD countries.[111]

We cannot, of course, analyze the intricacies of the global economy in a few pages. In what follows, we touch on a few crucial aspects of global capitalism that will be useful in interpreting the specific cases examined in later chapters: the growth of "free" trade; the role of TNCs; and the mingling of expanding, accelerated capital flows with the impacts of privatization. These trends are endorsed as the route to success and (eventually) an improved life for all in the new world economy: the idolatry of growth has broadened to include globalization as a companion deity. Current developments pose new challenges—but possibly also new opportunities—for an agenda that advocates redistribution as the missing link in development policy.

Trade, Free and Otherwise

A cornerstone of the emerging global economic order is free trade—the unhindered movement of goods and services on an international scale. Yet "free" trade is not as simple an idea as it may seem, and the global triumph of market freedom is not without its ambiguities.[112] Though theoretically at liberty to roam the globe, most trade today remains concentrated among the OECD countries; the European Union (EU), the United States, and Japan combined have nearly the same share of world merchandise exports and imports (46.3 percent of exports and 46.4 percent of imports) as does the rest of the world combined.[113] A first fact to keep in mind, then, is that most trade in the world is conducted between rich countries.

A second fact to consider is that the new global trade does not look like classic textbook models of trade. Indeed, a significant amount of "trade" (estimates range from 30 to 40 percent) actually consists of transactions within the same (transnational) firm. The United Nations Conference on Trade and Development (UNCTAD) estimates that roughly equal shares of world trade are accounted for by transnational corporations trading with their own affiliates, TNC trade with non-affiliates, and trade among domestic firms.[114]

The expansion of TNCs has been a major source of the proliferation of trade. The rise of processing and assembly operations under the aegis of TNCs has spurred trade growth, while at the same time highlighting the key role played by transactions among and within TNCs as a significant percentage of world trade. For example, *maquiladora* exports rose from 33 percent of Mexico's exports in 1990 to nearly 40 percent in 1995, while the *maquiladoras'* share of imports rose from 25 percent in 1990 to more than 35 percent in 1995. In China, comparable operations constituted nearly 50 percent of all exports and 45 percent of imports.[115]

Has the expansion in world trade benefited developing countries? This is a difficult question to answer because the differential impact of trade on wealthy and poorer countries reflects, in part, differences in what the respective traders bring to the market. While most wealthy countries export manufactured goods and services, many developing countries rely most heavily on the export of primary commodities like unprocessed agricultural products, minerals, oil, wood, or fish. A higher proportion of exports composed of manufactured goods is associated with higher growth. Developing countries in which manufactured exports made up at least 50 percent of total exports grew four times as fast as countries that were predominately commodity exporters. Today, developing countries as a group account for about 25 percent of world exports in manufactured goods, compared to 5 percent in the early 1970s. However, three-quarters of this growth in manufacturing for export is accounted for by the East Asian Newly Industrialized Countries (NICs): South Korea, Taiwan, Hong Kong, and Singapore. While primary commodities are of diminishing significance in world trade flows, some countries remain heavily dependent upon them. About 30 countries in Africa and 18 in Latin America rely upon primary commodity exports for more than half of their export earnings. In some cases, the export economy depends on a single crop. Coffee exports, for example, constitute greater than 75 percent of the export earnings of Uganda and Ethiopia.[116] The reliance on primary commodity exports renders such countries vulnerable to world commodity price fluctuations; hampers their growth potential; and ultimately limits the degree to which they can benefit from expanding international trade.

The growth in world trade and investment has generated a search for new ways to govern "free" economic exchange. It may seem contradictory to suggest that increasing free trade requires increased regulation. Yet this paradox is at the heart of the contemporary global economy.

On January 1, 1995, at the conclusion of the Uruguay round, the WTO was created to succeed the GATT and assume the role of managing the world trade system. One of the primary goals of the WTO is to establish a mechanism whereby member countries can hold other members accountable to commitments they have made regarding trade liberalization. The WTO has no autonomous power to enforce compliance, but constitutes a venue in which member countries can cite violations by another member country and have the dispute settled. The system aims to restrict the use of arbitrary trade sanctions by one country against another, a strategy often employed by the United States. The WTO also guarantees a more stable playing field for transnational corporations with operations in many different countries. What one country views as unjustified trade barriers, however, may be another country's health, safety, environmental, and/or labor standards; conflicts in this area are likely to be ongoing.

While the WTO is the primary site of global trade negotiations, there are also initiatives at the regional level aimed at liberalizing trade, and in some cases investment flows. The WTO counted at least 100 regional trade groupings formed by the end of 1994, nearly one-third of which had organized within the previous five years. Nearly all members of the WTO participate in at least one such structure.[117] We can begin to see that "free trade" actually involves a particular way of *managing* trade. It is a misrepresentation to say that free trade demands only deregulation. In fact, "free" trade and "free" markets require extensive sets of regulations: recognition of patents, copyrights, and other intellectual property rights; the ability to enforce contracts; and so forth. Given the importance of TNCs in world trade, it is moreover not surprising that so-called free trade agreements include numerous provisions reflecting the interests of corporations concerned, above all, with maximizing their own profitability. Harvard economist Robert Lawrence notes that such agreements are "motivated by the desire to facilitate international investment and the operations of multinational firms as much as to promote trade."[118]

Transnationals: Big Players in the Global Game

The role of transnational corporations in promoting free trade agreements reflects their growing power within the global economy as a whole. Of the world's 100 largest economies, 49 are countries, and 51 are corporations. The United Nations Conference on Trade and Development estimates that TNCs account for over 73 million jobs worldwide—only about 3 percent of the world's total labor force. However, if we exclude agriculture, TNCs employ approximately 20 percent of the world's labor force.[119] The increasing dominance of transnational corporations over international economic activity is one of the most salient features of the global economy.[120]

The role of TNCs has expanded due to the combination of several factors: advances in information processing, communications, and transportation technologies that enable production to be coordinated on a global scale; a shift toward more export-oriented development strategies; and, finally, the growing liberalization of trade and foreign investment regulations, which has spurred a new round of foreign direct investment.[121] These technological and economic patterns have intertwined with political developments in complex ways. Governments in fact have funded many of the key infrastructural investments useful to TNCs, indicating once again the important role that government intervention, as opposed to "natural" laws of economics, plays in shaping patterns of investment. Governments' role in providing tax breaks and other incentives to TNCs (such as bans on union-organizing or strikes) illustrates how the logic of competitiveness, or of "creating a good investment climate" to promote growth, may work against the well-being of workers and citizens. Meanwhile, TNCs have become increasingly involved as the main lobbyists behind free trade agreements and initiatives to liberalize investment flows. (For more on these topics, see Chapter Nine.)

Negotiations for a Multilateral Agreement on Investment (MAI), which would resemble the agreements that created the WTO, began under the auspices of the OECD in May 1995. As drafted, the MAI would have provided a global charter restricting how governments could regulate foreign investment (defined broadly as foreign direct investment, as well as stocks and bonds, real estate, and intellectual property). The draft contained strict limits on governments' right to place obligations on foreign investors, and would have enshrined the free transfer and repatriation of profits and capital. At the end of 1998, negotiations for the MAI stalled within the OECD, due to opposition by a number of members, particularly France. The issue now is whether these debates will be continued within a broader forum, such as the WTO. The MAI would legally anchor full capital mobility along with free trade at the center of the world economy for the twenty-first century. For developing countries, the implications of a radical and definitive loosening of controls on capital movements could be dramatic, as the post-1997 Asian financial crisis helps us understand.[122] The Multilateral Agreement on Investment is discussed in detail in Chapter Nine, Box 9.1.

Some recent authors have popularized the dramatic vision of a global economic system entirely at the mercy of fickle, fast-moving capital. While relatively accurate for currency flows and forms of financial capital, this vision is less useful for thinking about foreign direct investment and TNCs and is in any case far from universally accepted.[123] In understanding TNC decision-making, the emphasis on profitability rather than just low-cost production is an important consideration. The widely held belief that firms invest abroad solely to reduce production costs (particularly wages) or to avoid more costly environmental and safety regulations may be true for some sectors, such as textiles and garments, where labor costs constitute a significant percentage of production expenses; however, in other industries (automobiles, for example), profitability considerations are more complex. These considerations include concern for market share and for access to skilled labor and markets, along with an interest in political and social stability.[124] Since 1990, nearly three-quarters of foreign direct investment in poor countries has been concentrated in just ten countries.[125] If labor costs were *the* defining feature, many more low-wage countries, such as Haiti and Bangladesh, would be swamped with foreign investment.

Overall flows of foreign direct investment are concentrated among the wealthy countries and then, secondarily, among the wealthier developing countries and those countries which provide opportunities for higher profits. While the industrialized countries dominate both inward and outward stocks of foreign direct investment, "emerging market" economies have grown considerably as both sources and destinations of investment. By the end of 1996, emerging market groups accounted for about 30 percent of global inward stocks and 10 percent of outward stocks of foreign direct investment. Net foreign direct investment flows continue to be the largest component of external resource flows to developing countries in the 1990s, dwarfing foreign aid by almost three times in 1997.[126] Influxes of private capital into developing countries are usually applauded as harbingers and catalysts of future prosperity. Yet the current disproportion between foreign aid and private investment also signifies that poor countries and their citizens are increasingly dependent upon corporations seeking profits, rather than on governments and donor agencies whose concern (at least nominally) is with enhancing the well-being of people. As global investment figures rise while health indicators decline in many poor communities, we must re-examine the prevalent assumption that increased levels of corporate investment in developing countries' economies will naturally bring improvements in life-quality to these countries' disadvantaged and vulnerable citizens.

Finance Capital and Globalization

While many of the contemporary debates on globalization focus on free trade agreements like NAFTA and on the growth of foreign direct investment by TNCs, the most dramatic globalization of economic activity has been in the movement of finance capital. In financial markets around the world, networks of traders now shift currency, bonds, and stocks twenty-four hours a day. At first glance, the activities of international speculators using advanced technology to navigate the digitalized global marketplace seem unrelated to the struggles of poor people lacking adequate food and shelter. Yet as far apart as their respective worlds appear, international traders exert an increasingly direct influence over the lives of the poor. Indeed, the increasing vulnerability of poor communities to shocks and fluctuations emanating from the world of global finance is a key trait of the global economy.

While advocates of free trade are dominant among the world's most powerful economic policy managers, the extension of the principle of free trade to capital (let alone labor) is much more contested, even among mainstream economists.[127] Until the Asian (and, subsequently, global) economic crisis that began in mid-1997—foreshadowed by the Mexican crisis of 1995—the position that what was good for goods and services was also good for capital seemed to be winning adherents. The recent wave of crises from Asia to Russia to Brazil has now made capital mobility and capital controls an explicitly political issue. (Meanwhile, of course, the idea that labor should have the same rights and protections as the movement of goods and services has little hearing.)

The speed, ubiquity, and sheer volume of international financial transactions have exploded in the last 25 years. The trend is especially visible in the area of currency trading. Typical daily trading in foreign exchange (*currencies*) soared from $10-20 billion in 1973, to $60 billion in 1983, $1.2 trillion by mid-1995, and an estimated $1.5 trillion by April 1998. Systematic monitoring of other forms of currency derivative and interest rate derivative instruments began only in the mid-1990s, but transactions in this category have grown from $196 billion in 1995 to an estimated $362 billion in 1998.[128] At the same time, the foreign reserves that central bankers have to intervene in currency markets have steadily declined as a percentage of overall trading volume. In 1983, five major central banks (Switzerland, Japan, the

United States, Germany, and Great Britain) held $139 billion in foreign currency reserves, while average daily turnover in the markets was in the $39 billion range. By 1986, the values were about equal. By 1992, the same five central banks held $278 billion, against $623 billion in daily trading activity. This expansion in global currency flows is only partially due to transactions required by an increase in trade: the ratio of the value of foreign exchange transactions to world trade rose from 10:1 in 1983 to more than 60:1 in 1992.[129]

The Mexican economic crisis of 1994-95 and the continuing instability in Asia since mid-1997 highlight the importance of what are known as *portfolio investment flows*. These are investments in stocks and bonds, some of which have boomed in the 1990s. Worldwide stock market capitalization is now estimated to be $17 trillion, three times the value a decade ago ($5.6 trillion at the end of 1986). The U.S. stock market alone is valued at $7.7 trillion (roughly the same as the U.S. annual GDP).[130] Meanwhile, from 1980-1994, the movement of U.S. money into stocks across borders increased sixteenfold, to $1.5 trillion.[131]

Portfolio investment is sometimes called "hot money" because it is relatively easy to move from country to country, unlike, for example, foreign direct investment in factories. "Hot money" shuttles electronically and instantaneously from one market to another. This accelerates the impact of the contagious panics that are intrinsic to deregulated capital markets. At the touch of a computer button, investors can move billions of dollars in or out of countries, undermining the stability of national economies. As a consequence, governments find themselves increasingly at the mercy of individuals seeking large short-term profits.[132] The resulting patterns have led commentators to compare the global economy to a casino, but one where the gaming rules are written by and for the wealthiest gamblers.[133] Poor-country governments operating in such an uncertain economic environment therefore have an increasingly difficult time making the long-term budgetary commitments necessary for real improvements in health and welfare.

Portfolio investment in the so-called emerging markets of the developing world increased significantly in the early 1990s. The volatility of those investments has been implicated in a series of recent economic crises: in Mexico and Latin America in 1994-95 and again in 1998; in Asia since June of 1997; and in Russia in 1998.[134] The historically unprecedented development of stock markets in developing countries in the last 15 years has been shaped by external financial liberalization (sometimes as part of sectoral or structural adjustment programs) and inflows of portfolio capital (sometimes linked to the privatization of public enterprises). Net portfolio investment in developing countries grew from an annual average of $3.4 billion in 1983-88 to $44 billion from 1989-1995; in 1997, it was an estimated $32.5 billion.[135]

The privatization of state-owned corporations in wealthier countries, and later in developing countries (often as a result of structural adjustment programs), provided an important impetus to portfolio investment. Britain pioneered the sell-off of state firms in the 1980s under Margaret Thatcher.[136] The largest value of privatizations remains in the OECD countries, although the proportion of privatizations in non-OECD (developing) countries has been increasing, rising from 17 percent in 1990 to

22 percent in 1996. In 1990, world privatizations totaled almost $30 billion, while in 1996 they reached $88 billion, the largest annual total yet.[137]

The media celebrates the expansion of mutual funds and stock markets as the democratization of capitalism. For example, the proportion of U.S. households with mutual fund ownership increased from 6 percent in 1980 to 30 percent in 1995, a development that has been widely cited. The crucial issue, nonetheless, remains the exercise of functional control over these investments.[138] However widely shares may be owned, a smaller number of investors (whether individuals or firms) effectively determine the actual flows of capital. As the IMF notes: "The investor base in securities markets in industrialized countries, and increasingly in developing countries, is dominated by a relatively small number of large institutional investors."[139]

In the United States, institutional investors in 1995 controlled almost 40 percent of household assets, in contrast to 20 percent in 1980.[140] In October 1996 the total assets of U.S. mutual funds stood at $3.39 trillion, up from $2.16 trillion in 1994 and $241 billion in 1980. The assets of Fidelity Research and Management, the largest mutual fund company, increased one hundred-fold from 1972 to 1995, to $390 billion.[141] The percentage of U.S. corporate stock held by institutions rose from 16 percent in 1965 to 46 percent in 1990.[142] Institutional investors control 63 percent of the largest 250 companies, up from 54.8 percent at the beginning of the decade. Nearly one-fifth of the largest American companies have 80 percent or more of their shares controlled by institutions; in 1990 only 3 percent of the largest companies found themselves in this position. Health care is one of the sectors with the highest level of institutional ownership.[143]

These developments suggest that in contrast to the image of growing democratization of corporate capitalism, control over capital is in fact in some respects increasingly centralized. This means that decisions about where capital will flow are often determined by people far from the places where the consequences of these choices will be felt most acutely. This tendency complicates the challenge of shaping capital investment to obtain pro-poor patterns of growth.

The increased mobility of international capital in the present world economy is a dramatic shift from the so-called Golden Age period, in which trade flows increased, but international capital flows were relatively smaller. In the 1980s, wealthy countries began removing restrictions on inflows and outflows of capital, and by the 1990s capital flows among the OECD countries were largely deregulated. In recent years the IMF has been preparing to amend its charter in order to adopt the liberalization of capital controls as one of its main organizational objectives. This is a radical departure from the original Bretton Woods vision of promoting free trade while restricting the mobility of capital. The Mexican and Asian crises of the mid- to late 1990s suggest that there is a real need for a fundamental debate over the international financial regime that has taken shape since the 1970s. A number of proposals have emerged, including Nobel laureate James Tobin's proposal for a tax on currency transactions.[144] The current World Bank chief economist has voiced strong criticisms of today's economic orthodoxy in light of the Asian Crisis, even if World Bank practice has not changed.[145] In any event, as social scientist Robert Wade suggests, "We should keep at the forefront of discussion the absence of empirical evidence that capital account convertibility is good for developing countries, and the abundance of historical evidence that free international capital markets are prone to excesses that inflict huge social costs."[146]

The scope and human meaning of these costs are illustrated by recent events in Indonesia. Since July 1997, Indonesia has been in the grip of economic crisis. Among the breakdown's important causal factors was a development strategy heavily dependent on the influx of "hot" foreign capital. When, amidst the general Asian shake-up of 1997, foreign portfolio investment began a panicked flight from the Indonesian market, the country's economy underwent a dizzying collapse. Viewed from afar by foreign investors, the Indonesian crisis appears primarily in the form of plunging stock prices and shrinking corporate profits. For the country's poor, the events wear a different face. Indonesia's economic implosion has brought massive unemployment and spiraling inflation. The government's Central Bureau of Statistics predicted in July 1998 that by the end of the year, 95.8 million Indonesians (48 percent of the country's total population of 202 million) would be living below the poverty line.[147] As a result, child malnutrition, once virtually vanquished, has re-emerged as a pervasive public health threat.

As the national economy disintegrates, the situation faced by Sumirah, a 36-year-old mother of two interviewed by the *Jakarta Post*, is grimly typical:

> Sumirah is daydreaming. The 36-year-old mother is wishing that the days when she could properly feed her two under-five children were back. "Every day I ask myself what I can give my children to eat," she said numbly, while watching the children, aged 2 and 4, play in front of their house in Rembang....[Sumirah's] husband is a pedicab driver who earns a mere Rp 3,000 (30 U.S. cents) a day. The income is far from enough to support the family of four with the price of rice having soared as high as Rp 4,000 per kilo. "Often my husband and I have to eat cassava so that we can get money to buy rice and tempeh for the children," she said. "We will do everything to ensure they don't get skinny."
>
> The Suparlans, Sumirah's neighbors, are in the same boat. The parents eat cassava as the economic crisis bites deeper. Rice is only for their three children. "My wife and I can stand hunger, and we don't want to see our children underfed, with distended bellies," said Suparlan, a hawker of children's bamboo toys. The deteriorating economic abyss has left him wondering how his family can survive and how his children, in their tender years, can grow normally if they lack vital nutrition.[148]

Sumirah and the Suparlans are people whose lives have been directly and brutally affected by the transformations associated with development strategies founded upon the unreflective pursuit of economic globalization and the unrestricted electronic mobility of capital. Their stories remind us that the manipulation of money, even in its "hottest" and most disembodied forms, has consequences for real human bodies: for the health and indeed the very survival of vulnerable individuals, families, and communities. Traders risk vast sums of money in the international financial marketplace. Development experts and politicians risk their professional standing and their share of power. But for the poor, the stakes in the economic casino are infinitely higher. Financial and political fortunes can be, and routinely are, won back again after an initial defeat. The life of a child is a different sort of gambling chip. Once lost, it is gone forever.

Examples like Sumirah's story show that as we analyze trends in the evolving global economy and consider how economic patterns should interact with political structures, our thinking must be multilayered. Responsible economic analysis must systematically interrelate quantitative data and the "laws" of the market with the level of human experience where international capital movements translate into hunger and despair for people like Sumirah and the Suparlans.

CONCLUSION: THE IDOLATRY OF GROWTH

This chapter has tried to put in place conceptual tools and historical background for an investigation of relations between global economic patterns and the health of poor people. We have also sought to raise fundamental questions that provide context for the specific case studies presented in this book. We have tried to bring into relief the presuppositions that underlie today's conventional wisdom on relations between poverty, inequality, economic growth, and globalization.

The notion of economic development, understood as equivalent to strong growth in annual per capita GDP, is often construed today as the necessary and sufficient solution to the problem of poverty. This belief forms a part of that fund of common-sense knowledge that, in the words of M.I.T. economist Paul Krugman, "everyone knows to be true" without even having to think about it. Yet precisely "because it is known to be the truth," such an idea "has a profound influence on actual policies in the real world."[149] Our rapid survey of the recent history of development economics suggested that the influence of this particular idea of economic development on "actual policies in the real world" has been pronounced, durable, and in many instances destructive. We saw, on the one hand, that economic policies intended to stimulate growth often fail to do so, and, on the other, that even where GDP growth is strong, there is no guarantee that this improvement in broad economic indicators will translate into improvements in the health and well-being of poor people. Growth as such does not automatically make poor people's lives better, and policies legitimated by the perceived need to generate growth at all costs have often made the living conditions of poor and middle-income people demonstrably worse.

Economic growth can bring important benefits for the poor. Yet it is naïve or disingenuous to assume that growth must (eventually) benefit poor communities, and that encouraging a strong level of growth should be the primary concrete objective of those who want to combat the destructive effects of poverty on human lives. This assumption neglects the dimension of political responsibility that is inseparable from meaningful discussions of poverty, inequality, and economic reform. We can all understand the seduction of simple theories and quick-fix solutions that would take responsibility and initiative out of our hands and assign them to some providential, invisible force (whether divine will or the mechanisms of the free market). Unfortunately, growth as such clearly does not possess the magical healing power we might like to attribute to it. Rather, the pattern of growth that shapes (and that can destroy) real human lives is to a considerable extent the fruit of political choices, which are not magical but quite mundane.

At the most basic level, to emphasize that there is a political dimension to the relationship between economic growth and the health of the poor is to argue that this is an area in which human responsibility and creativity—*our* responsibility and creativity—are engaged. The relations between growth and health are not simply programmed by inflexible economic laws over which we have no influence, though it is clear that structural factors set strict limits to what can be achieved by individual initiative. This is why those of us involved in writing this book argue for a stance of pragmatic solidarity. We seek coordinated action that takes the health of the poor as both its fundamental reference point and its concrete measure of failure or success.

Debates over poverty rates, foreign debt as a percentage of GDP, structural adjustment packages, and cost-recovery mechanisms are of course highly technical discussions of economic matters; yet the problems they raise are also political and moral. If the poor and their advocates are to be more than passive bystanders in the drama of economic transformation, then we have a responsibility to examine the implicit assumptions that guide patterns of change, and to learn about the concrete effects of these patterns on human lives.

CHAPTER THREE

Terms Reconsidered: Decoding Development Discourse

Aaron Shakow and Alec Irwin

If this is a battle of names, some of them asserting that they are like the truth, others contending that *they* are, how or by what criterion are we to decide between them?

Plato, *Cratylus*

From World Bank reports to the *New York Times* financial pages, readers will inevitably meet up with acronyms, euphemisms, and technical jargon. To grasp the impact of economic policies on poor people's lives, we first need to understand how key economic terms are used when they appear in conventional discussions of development. Then we need to step beyond or behind the standard definitions to ask where the conventional wisdom came from, how it evolved historically, and whether it neglects important aspects of the human realities it claims to describe and explain. To help with this critical reflection, we propose examining a series of key terms connected with poverty, development, and the global economy. For each term, we aim to show how the word or concept in question is usually defined, and to highlight ways in which conventional definitions and their commonsense applications may be problematic or limited.

We have not tried to explore all the major technical terms connected with discussions of global economics. Instead, we focus on a small group of closely related concepts that lie at the heart of current discussions. In doing so, we seek to emphasize the significance of words and the implications of our use of them. Myths can be perpetuated even in the seemingly objective wording of economic forecasts and policy plans.

Because of the organic connections between these terms, we treat them in a conceptual sequence, as follows: (1) Poverty (2) "Worlds" (First World and Third World) (3) Development (4) Aid (5) Neoliberalism (6) Free Markets, Free Trade (7) Market and State (8) Growth.

1. Poverty

When reading the literature on economics and development or simply scanning the newspaper, the word *poverty* is hard to avoid. "Poverty" implies, foremost, a quantitative measure. People are categorized as "poor" if their income falls below a certain numerical threshold, calculated as a function of their country's economic indicators—the *poverty line*. Conservative estimates based on such calculations show poverty to be a condition that characterizes the lives of over one billion people—approximately one-sixth of the world's population and roughly four times the total population of the United States.[1]

The quantitative character of poverty statistics implies objectivity. Yet one should be wary of assuming that poverty figures simply give an unbiased account of "the way things are." In fact, the income level at which a poverty line is set can be quite arbitrary; thresholds vary widely from one part of the world to another, and their configuration inevitably reflects political interests and particular distributions of political, social, and economic power. Poverty is a value-laden term with a heavy historical subtext; even its measurement is fraught with moral and ideological considerations. Small wonder that economists are deeply divided on the question of how poverty can be most effectively defined and measured.

Clearly, we need quantitative information to help us grasp specific aspects of poverty. Such data help show, for example, whether particular economic policies are leading to an increase or decrease in the number of poor people. Yet quantitative data only begin to describe the complex reality of poverty. A sound analysis recognizes the utility of quantitative measurements, but strives to connect numerical data with social and political dimensions of poor people's experiences that numbers may otherwise not adequately capture.

Our understanding of poverty must pay attention not only to the lack of basic economic resources (including money and food), but also to the lack of social resources, including access to education and health care.[2] Over the years, many theorists have emphasized the inadequacy of trying to grasp poverty simply in terms of income statistics. Amartya Sen, Nobel laureate in economics, has argued that poverty and wealth must be conceived in terms much more expansive than income level. For example, poverty definitions based on household incomes say nothing about uneven income distribution within a household, which leads to an "invisible" poverty affecting mostly women and children. Furthermore, most quantitative measures cannot "account for the 'double jeopardy' experienced by minority groups in which poverty is created by or exacerbated by discrimination, overt or covert."[3]

Sen's inclusive vision brings into sharper focus poverty's tragic destruction of human potential. His vision also relates economic concerns explicitly to political factors. Sen writes: "'Freedom from hunger' or 'being free from malaria' need not be taken to be just rhetoric (as they are sometimes described); there is a very real sense in which the freedom to live the way one would like is enhanced by public policy that transforms epidemiological and social environments."[4]

Eliminating poverty would require not just increasing gross domestic product (GDP), or GDP per capita, but changing the distribution of economic output, economic resources, and social services. To achieve such changes in distribution, there will have to be a shift in political power in favor of the poor. The need to modify the balance of political power in order to combat poverty is not apparent if one thinks that poverty can be eliminated simply by increasing GDP or raising a society's standard of living in broad terms. The problem of hunger exemplifies these difficulties, and under-scores the need to consider not just the existence of resources in a society but also the mechanisms that distribute these resources. Commonsense assumptions to the contrary, hunger cannot be eliminated merely by increasing food production and containing population growth—more food plus fewer mouths does not, in our complex and inequitable world, equal less hunger. Historical studies of famine demonstrate that the problem is usually not an absence of food.[5] Ending hunger requires addressing entrenched forms of structural inequality, transforming the political and economic con-ditions that prevent millions from having *access* to food or owning their own land to grow it.[6]

In trying to arrive at a more accurate understanding of poverty, theorists have developed statistical tools such as the United Nations Development Programme's (UNDP's) Human Development Index (HDI).[7] The Human Development Index goes beyond traditional definitions of poverty by including variables such as life expectancy and educational attainment, focusing on the satisfaction of a range of basic human needs, rather than simply on income or consumption figures.

In recent years scholars have tried to examine the causes and consequences of poverty and well-being by using a variety of alternative frameworks based, for example, on concepts of social exclusion and human capabilities.[8] Issues of political power—for example, the extent of grassroots organizing within poor communities—and questions about the role of public policy in poverty reduction play a more central role in these frameworks. They also remind us that economic development is a means to improve human lives, not an end in itself.

Since the 1940s and the emergence of development economics as a distinct field, a veritable industry has taken shape internationally, the function of which is to generate authoritative discourses about poverty. For certain organizations and indi-viduals, producing expert knowledge about poverty has been a profitable enterprise. Prominent institutions such as the World Bank owe much of their perceived impor-tance to their role in alleviating world poverty. "Poverty alleviation" is now one of the World Bank's stated policy objectives. The vital question, of course, is whether the Bank's policies and programs and those of similar institutions actually contribute to reducing poverty. The case studies presented in this book attempt to shed light on this question.

Perhaps one of the best ways to understand poverty and its effects is to look con-cretely at the lives of people living under conditions of material need, oppression, and vulnerability.

2. Worlds

For reasons of expediency or ideology (often both) there is an inevitable ten-dency to divide people, social groups, countries, and regions of the world into oppos-ing categories: rich and poor, developed and underdeveloped, traditional and modern, North and South, First World and Third World. None of these sets of categories is ade-quate. Yet some kind of shorthand *is* needed to underscore real differences in wealth and power between countries when we discuss issues of global inequality and health. Whatever labels we choose must be used with a critical consciousness of our vocabulary's limitations and distortions, and an awareness of the political history that lies behind the terms we use.

The term "Third World" is a good example. The concept was introduced by French demographer Alfred Sauvy in the context of post-colonial transformations following World War II. Sauvy used "Third World" to label regions that had been colonized, but not settled, by European powers. He contrasted the Third World to the industrialized communist-socialist countries (the "Second World") and to industrialized capitalist ones (the "First World").[9]

With very few exceptions, the countries Sauvy assigned to the Third World had neither well-developed industrial economies, stable political systems, nor equitable socioeconomic structures. Yet despite certain shared economic and political patterns, the Third World was never a uniform, monolithic entity. Most now recognize the enormous differences between countries conventionally lumped together under this rubric. However, an indisputable fact remains: serious inequality exists between what has been designated as the Third World and the rest of the planet. Current calculations show that 79.7 percent of the world's people live in the "Third World." Yet this population—four-fifths of humanity—enjoys less than one-fifth of total world gross national product (GNP).[10]

Until recently, Sauvy's distinction between worlds was widely adopted by scholars, intellectuals, and mainstream development institutions alike. Yet despite its wide use, opposition to the First-Second-Third World schema dates back almost to its inception. Marxists, for example, resisted what they saw as an artificial distinction among countries in a single capitalist world economy. They argued that social classes rather than states constitute the key analytic lens, individual countries' poverty and wealth being outgrowths of the same capitalist global economic system.[11] Ironically, many free-market partisans judged the First-Second-Third World categories to be anticapitalist. Critics have also taken issue with the hierarchical distinctions on which Sauvy's vocabulary seems to rely, contrasting modern, sophisticated First World people with a poor, backward, peasant Third World.

Not all concepts used to distinguish different parts of the world originate in North America and Europe. During the Cold War, the self-designated "Non-aligned Movement" was an important voice for poorer countries on the world political and economic scene. But as tensions between "East" and "West" thaw, the movement has lost much of its political potency. The Group of Twenty-Four (G-24), on the other hand, continues to provide a forum for developing country initiatives, including efforts to reform the International Monetary Fund (IMF) and the World Bank. The G-24, composed of eight representatives each from Asia, Africa, and Latin America, met for the first time in 1972. It discusses and develops proposals on financial and monetary issues promoting the interests of the developing countries. Some early successes in lobbying at the IMF in the 1980s have yet to be repeated, but the group's analysts provide sharp critiques and sound alternatives to the conventional wisdom. The South Commission also remains an important voice, although its profile is lower now than during the Debt Crisis (see Chapter 2), when the Commission played an important role in drawing attention to the social costs of debt and structural adjustment, particularly in Africa.

With the end of the Cold War, arguably, Sauvy's tripartite division of countries became moot, as the Soviet orbit disappeared. To replace it, several old alternatives re-emerged, by which states are described variously as "developed" and "developing," "dependent" and "independent," or "Northern" and "Southern." Ultimately, all such terms refer to the same basic division between countries that are mostly poor and those with greater resources at their disposal.

In recent years, the "splitting" terminology of the "First" and "Third" World has collided with the "lumping" terminology of the "world" economy. This encounter has paradoxical implications: it reinforces the ideology of poor countries' difference in a supposedly unified global economic order. The roots of poor countries' indigence are held to reside in specific *national* conditions or failings, while the role of the economic and political networks shared with their wealthier neighbors is downplayed. Meanwhile, it is argued that poor countries can improve their lot only by participating in these very international networks—the "global economy"—more fully. Yet the conditions of such participation must be considered carefully. The government policies of both rich and poor countries can help shape those conditions, for good or ill.

Although often pronounced obsolete and declared meaningless, the term "Third World" persists in popular and scholarly discussions. The alternative labels that have been proposed—"South," "developing countries," "Poor World"—all have their own problems. The gravest danger associated with employing conventional terms like "Third World" and "First World" is that the seeming neutrality of such labels can mask the violent history of colonial and neocolonial exploitation that has played an enormous role in creating this "Third World" in the first place. Similarly, such labels leave unspoken the asymmetries in power that remain between rich and poor countries, as part of the heritage of colonialism.

The editors of *Dying for Growth* have left it to the authors of each chapter to determine their own nomenclature, with the understanding that shorthand terms are necessary to make discussion possible, but that no such term is exempt from criticism.

3. Development

One highly influential alternative to the "First World"-"Third World" dichotomy has been the division of countries into "developed" and "underdeveloped." Using this distinction, programs of international assistance, bodies of economic theory, and a whole global infrastructure have evolved over the past half century with the nominal goal of helping poor countries develop. Common sense seems to suggest that development—*progress*—is a relatively simple, straightforward idea. When things "develop," they grow stronger and get better. Yet the notion of development now dominant in economics and public policy has a variety of hotly contested meanings and implications. "Development" is at once a metaphor (with echoes of Hegel's philosophy of history and Darwin's theory of evolution), an inventory of particular government strategies, an idealized model for human culture and society, and a highly political reflection of power distribution worldwide.

Originally an expression of Enlightenment ideas of progress, *development* emerged as a key economic term after World War II, orienting a series of foreign aid programs launched under the leadership of U.S. President Harry Truman. In his inauguration speech in 1948, Truman affirmed America's commitment to "a bold new program for making the benefits of our scientific advances and industrial progress available for the improvement and growth of underdeveloped areas."[12] Policy-makers divided the globe into "developed" and "underdeveloped" regions, with the latter seen as anxious to escape from their inferior condition, but needing the help of the developed powers in order to progress. While Truman insisted that "the old imperialism—exploitation for foreign profit—has no place in our plans," U.S. development-assistance programs were, from the start, connected to Cold War politics. In the West, in the Soviet sphere, and in various regional contexts, academic, governmental, and international organizations grew up to promote the geopolitical goals of the respective power blocs, using development aid to poorer countries as one way of securing strategic political and military alliances.

In the West, economists like Arthur Lewis and Walt Whitman Rostow conflated the term "development" with economic growth, usually expressed by aggregate measures like GNP. These analysts assumed that growth in the form of rising GNP and greater wealth for state-backed entrepreneurs would ultimately lead to greater economic opportunities for everyone, benefiting the impoverished majority as well as people who were already well off.

In contrast to this equation of development with growth, organizations like the UNDP and UNICEF proposed models of social development based on populations' general attainment of "basic human needs."[13] As early as 1962, the framers of the U.N.'s first "Development Decade" (1960-1970) had insisted that development and growth must not be seen as synonymous.[14] Such warnings, acknowledged in theory, have often gone unheeded in practice. Particularly after the fall of the Soviet Bloc, a neoliberal orthodoxy asserted itself in policy circles worldwide, securing the identification of development with economic growth under free market conditions. Ostensibly to correct "underdevelopment," international agencies and financial institutions like the World Bank and IMF have urged policies of structural adjustment on the governments of poor countries. Most conspicuous in the era of the Debt Crisis, this pattern continues today, as illustrated by the conditional bailout packages organized by the IMF for countries shaken by the Asian financial crisis of 1997-98. While recognizing in principle the importance of questions of poverty, wealth, and distribution, *structural adjustment* policies have worsened previously existing inequality in many countries. Under structural adjustment, poor countries have found themselves "forced to increase their integration within and dependence on the international market economy" with little regard for the human costs incurred. In many cases such countries have experienced a dramatic degradation of their social fabric through increased poverty, widespread suffering, social disorientation, and a growing gap between rich and poor.[15] Several chapters of this volume explore details of this pattern in specific instances.

In the late 1980s and 1990s, a "development with adjectives" emerged, including such catchphrases as "sustainable" development, "people-centered" development, "participatory" development, and "human" development. Terms are occasionally strung together, so that the UNDP's stated mission now is to promote "sustainable human development." This additive property of development language, however, has not led to a commensurate increase in the resources available to poor people. New vocabularies can—but don't necessarily—generate new ways of thinking and more effective patterns of action. To the extent that concepts like "sustainable human development" sharpen our awareness of the real consequences of economic and political policies on people, these terms will be useful. The final proof of their value can lie only in the action they enable.

4. Aid

It is usually assumed that disadvantaged people and nations will need strategic help from those who are better off in order to rise out of poverty. Thus, in many people's minds, the idea of combating poverty is connected with the concept of "foreign aid": financial, material, and technical assistance flowing from wealthy nations to the poor world. But what is the real scope of foreign aid? What are the modalities through which it operates? Will aid be a meaningful factor in addressing the problems of poverty and inequality in the years ahead? These questions are decisive if we are to gain a sense of poor people's prospects in the global economy.

Most Americans believe that foreign aid is a major drain on wealthy countries' economies, and in particular on the U.S. budget. However, the actual flow of aid resources from wealthy to poor nations over the past half century has been negligible, and the level of American generosity has been considerably less than overwhelming. According to several recent polls, Americans think that 40 percent of all aid given to poorer countries is contributed by the United States, and that the U.S. federal government spends 15 to 20 percent of its annual budget on aid.[16] In fact, U.S. overseas development assistance (ODA) in 1997, $9.4 billion, made up just 17 percent of the total sum contributed by industrialized countries and represented not 20 percent but 0.5 percent of American federal spending.[17] The $9.4 billion figure represents twelve one-hundredths of one percent of U.S. GNP, placing the United States solidly at the bottom of the list of wealthy nations, classed by overseas aid as a proportion of GNP. The U.S. ratio of aid to GNP was about one-ninth that of the relatively most generous donor, Denmark. Yet while the United States leads the way in stinginess, American figures point to a broader trend. Overall, development aid from wealthy nations to poor nations declined 3.2 percent from 1990-91 to 1995-96, amounting by 1997 to only one-quarter of one percent of wealthy countries' total GNP. The United States decreased its aid during that period by 8 percent, the second sharpest decline in the OECD.[18] In short, this already meager pie is steadily shrinking.

How is "aid" actually defined? Generally, it is classified under one of three categories: (1) *bilateral*—that is, arranged between two individual countries and mediated by an agency such as the United States Agency for International Development (USAID); (2) *multilateral*, involving international agencies like the World Bank, IMF, and UNDP; or (3) *independent*, meaning aid supplied by nongovernmental organizations (NGOs), such as Oxfam or Save the Children. Assessments of bilateral and multilateral assistance are complicated by the fact that the term "aid" refers not only to grants and gifts but also to loans and to partial "forgiveness" of existing debt.

It would seem reasonable to assume that aid funds would be devoted primarily to improving the lives of the poor and vulnerable, by strengthening public investment in housing and sanitation or by improving the quality and accessibility of health care and education, for example. In reality, during the Cold War a high proportion of bilateral aid went to support "friendly" regimes and their military infrastructures. Aid was sometimes also used to promote lasting consumption patterns in recipient nations, most of them former colonies, nurturing poor societies' dependence on the products of industrialized countries.[19]

Since the fall of the Soviet Bloc, the emphasis given to military technology in the aid equation has not significantly abated. According to an American arms control group, in a typical period of the 1990s in which Washington spent only about $1.25 per U.S. citizen on development and humanitarian assistance abroad, the United States exported weapons worth more than $2 per U.S. citizen, often to the same countries receiving the bulk of nonmilitary aid. By this estimate, roughly half of all arms exports worldwide from 1993 through 1995 were American.[20] As of 1997, U.S. military aid amounted to 27 percent of total external assistance, just under the American contribution for development projects.[21]

Furthermore, despite the rhetoric of altruism that surrounds them, foreign aid programs have often been dominated by wealthy countries' self-interested geopolitical strategies and by private corporate agendas. Such interests have perpetuated the phenomenon of "tied" and "conditional" assistance. According to the U.S. General Accounting Office (GAO), tied aid refers to "foreign assistance that is linked to the purchase of exports from the country extending the assistance."[22] In 1990, on average, 33 percent of aid from industrialized nations was "tied"—in Germany this figure was 66 percent. For infrastructure projects, such as road-building and power plant construction, between 45 and 91 percent of large industrial countries' aid was tied.[23] In practice, even nominally "untied" aid for such projects implicitly favors rich-country firms, since contractors in developing countries generally cannot compete with wealthy countries in winning contracts.[24] In 1994, the Clinton administration determined that the United States was not placing sufficient conditions on its assistance, and that the relatively low U.S. tied-aid level of 19 percent was hindering American commercial interests. It allocated $150 million dollars for a Tied Aid Capital Projects Fund, the stated purpose of which was to compete with other countries' use of tied aid by stepping up its American analogue.[25]

As we detail in this volume, aid has also been made heavily conditional in recent decades on recipients' economic policies. This is particularly true of multilateral institutions like the World Bank and IMF, but bilateral aid programs like USAID followed the same trend. In Haiti, for example, funds were allocated to support "processes of democratic institutional reform that will further economic liberalization objectives."[26]

As indicated by the massive IMF bailout of East Asia, the conviction that trade should ultimately replace aid doesn't mean development assistance has ceased worldwide. Rather, such assistance appears to be concentrating itself more explicitly in regions where donor countries and corporations have important financial stakes. Designed to protect heavy corporate investment in a region shaken by economic crisis, IMF loans to Indonesia, South Korea, the Philippines, and Thailand will far exceed $100 billion over the next few years.[27] Meanwhile, other poorer parts of the world are denied much-needed multilateral and bilateral support. The disparity in private financial flows is even more severe. Between 1989 and 1993, 87 percent of all private investment went to just 20 countries, of which only three were "low-income"; the 46 countries of sub-Saharan Africa attracted just 1 percent of the total.[28] In March 1998, responding to critics who complained that four relatively wealthy Asian states were getting a disproportionate share of assistance, the U.S. government legislated an Africa-wide loan fund for business start-ups—with a meager $650 million in capital resources allotted for the entire continent.[29]

A prominent belief underlying the current discourse on aid in wealthy nations is that shrinking aid budgets will eventually be compensated for by the activities of NGOs, multilateral interventions, and flows of private investment into the developing world. This notion is deeply flawed. First, NGO resources are minuscule.[30] Furthermore, both aid and private capital are selective in their flows. To focus again on the most egregious example, as the gap in wealth and health indicators between sub-Saharan Africa and the rich world continues to widen, aid to Africa in all its forms is "dropping like a stone."[31] Bilateral aid to Africa declined by 14 percent between 1994 and 1995. During the same period, multilateral aid, instead of rising to compensate, fell even more drastically, dropping by 22 percent. Overall, the proportion of aid going to the poorest countries fell from 62 percent in 1990 to 51 percent in 1995. Figures from the World Bank confirm the trend. The Bank lent $1.74 billion to sub-Saharan Africa in 1996-97, down 37 percent from the previous year's loans and credits, and its loans for education and health—crucial for Africa's poor—were down 43 percent and 65 percent, respectively. Inflows of private capital into the region, less than 5 percent of the worldwide total, have been completely inadequate to compensate for this decline. Meanwhile, what foreign investment does flow into the region is directed "mostly to industries such as oil and mineral extraction which bring little immediate benefit" to the poor.[32]

5. Neoliberalism

"Neoliberalism" is a broad term for the pattern of economic theory that has most strongly influenced American economic policies over the past two decades. While some leading industrial powers (notably Japan) resist neoliberal views, the United States and Great Britain have used their authority to ensure that neoliberal ideas inform the programs and policies of major international financial institutions (IFIs) like the IMF and the World Bank. Thus, neoliberalism, while far from uncontested in academic and political circles, has contributed decisively to shaping the current global economy.

What are the primary characteristics of neoliberal theory? At its root lies the assertion that those who exchange society's resources through market interactions are making the best possible use of those resources. Neoliberals advance a highly optimistic conception of "the market"—the mechanisms of which, if allowed to operate unfettered, purportedly will lead to optimal outcomes for society as a whole.[33] Neoliberalism is distinct from—and in some ways contrary to—"liberal" attitudes, as understood in contemporary American political parlance.[34]

Although both are outgrowths of the Enlightenment ideal of liberty, "liberal" and "neoliberal" trace their more recent historical roots to the nineteenth-century British Liberal party. Founded in 1832 by a coalition of business interests, the British Liberals espoused a *laissez faire* program, opposing trade tariffs, unions, and public relief for the poor. The party split toward the turn of the twentieth century into an economic wing committed to free trade principles and a socially oriented wing that began to endorse public welfare programs as an alternative to socialism.[35] Neoliberalism embraces the first of these attitudes and rejects the second.[36]

The term "neoliberalism" itself only became widely used in the 1990s. However, crucial elements had emerged decades earlier with the "monetarist" economics elaborated at the University of Chicago in the 1950s, as a reaction against the work of John Maynard Keynes. Keynesian theory held that an unregulated capitalist economy was susceptible to severe depressions, as illustrated by the Great Depression of the 1930s. Keynesians identified inadequate demand for goods and services as the culprit behind depressions and slow economic growth. They argued that governments could head off depressions by means of deficit spending; such government expenditures would compensate for inadequate private investment spending. Some Keynesians maintained that governments can improve long-run growth performance through such measures as social spending, which would shift resources from the rich, who save much of their income, to the poor, who spend all of theirs. Adherents of this Keynesian school maintained that putting more money into the hands of the poor would boost consumer demand, increase business sales, raise profits, and foster more investment to meet the increased demand. In contrast to the "trickle-down" economics familiar today, Keynesian economics can be described as "bubble-up" economics.

Members of the "Chicago School" and their successors—the group that would come to be known as neoliberals—challenged the Keynesian prescription. In its place, they drew from the works of immigrant Austrian economists Friedrich von Hayek and Ludwig von Mises, and from late nineteenth-century liberals like Alfred Marshall. Already in 1890, at the height of colonialism, Marshall had promoted the vision of a world "liberated" from market restrictions and characterized by tariff-free trade, unchecked investment across national boundaries, and substantial state withdrawal from the regulation of the economy.[37]

Pursuing this idea, the Chicago School, led by Milton Friedman, created models that purported to demonstrate that a free market society would achieve full employment and an optimal allocation of resources.[38] They rejected notions of democracy as "equality of condition," in favor of "equality of opportunity."[39] Such theories were woven together with Friedman's "monetarism": the contention that the supply of money in an economy—and not, for example, government fiscal policy—is the key determinant of productivity and employment. Monetarists argued that central banks (which regulate money supply) and not the executive and legislative branches of government (which set fiscal policy) should have responsibility for maintaining or restoring short-term economic stability. These claims have substantially influenced many wealthy countries' economic policies. Accepting the monetarist view, governments have given up pursuing counter-cyclical fiscal policy and have relied instead on central banks to stabilize GNP and inflation through adjustment of the money supply.

When translated into policy, neoliberal theories yield a triple prescription: *liberalization*, *privatization*, and *deregulation*. To keep price levels stable, neoliberals advocate strict limits on public spending, particularly social spending. Reduced government social spending, they claim, brings many benefits. It checks inflation, promotes private initiative and investment, and creates powerful incentives for poor people to work rather than remain dependent on public assistance.

Neoliberal theory had already begun to mark American economic policy in the later years of the Carter administration (1978-79). Yet it was the arrival of Ronald Reagan in the White House in 1981 that led to a full application of neoliberal principles. Milton Friedman himself became a key economic advisor to the Reagan administration. The neoliberal counsel of tax cuts and social service rollbacks was elevated to the status of state doctrine, and converted effectively into policy. Influenced by this convergence of policy and academic theory, development agencies and IFIs quickly renounced Keynesian prescriptions like Import Substitution Industrialization (ISI), which advocated large state outlays for industrial and social infrastructure. When poor countries fell behind in paying off the foreign loans taken out to fund their ISI programs, the World Bank and IMF intervened; however, these two institutions made their financial assistance contingent on the poor countries' acceptance of neoliberal prescriptions.

The political orientations of current leaders in Washington (Clinton), London (Blair), and Berlin (Schröder) differ from those in the Reagan era. Yet neoliberal ideas have inspired many of the policies pursued by the Clinton administration and the Blair government, particularly in the areas of fiscal and monetary policy, trade policy, and welfare policy.[40] Despite their widespread acceptance by political authorities and business leaders, however, neoliberal doctrines invite serious questions on a number of levels. For the moment, we can focus on three points. First, neoliberals rely on a fundamental presupposition that is not simply economic but moral and in a sense metaphysical: the idea that wealth and poverty, like all other aspects of economic and social life, can basically be understood in terms of individual "choices."[41] According to this view, a free, rational agent's selection from among a range of options constitutes the basic unit of economic behavior and social existence. As the later chapters of this volume show, the realities of poor people's lives call the universal applicability of this model into question. The vocabulary of "choice" distorts the nature and scope of the problems faced by the poor, and gives little insight into how these problems could be addressed.

Linked to the focus on individual choice is the neoliberals' limitless faith in the market. By this view, a free market in which economic agents make choices and pursue their interests without constraint, leads automatically to the most productive distribution of resources in society. Believing it to be "self-evident that the market should no longer be viewed as an institution which must be regulated by external social forces," neoliberals propose that the market itself should "regulate society as a whole."[42] When such a model is adopted, the suffering of the poor is acknowledged as a regrettable but unavoidable side effect of a process, the results of which will ultimately be beneficial for all: a process of economic transformation that must be allowed to run its "natural" course without interference. Through this theoretical modality, the suffering of the poor is made "understandable," predictable, and thus, finally, insignificant.[43]

In the wake of the Asian and global financial crisis that began in the summer of 1997, neoliberal theories have come increasingly under attack, not only on the basis of their brutal consequences for the poor, but because neoliberal models often fail to deliver the benefits they promise for the non-poor, as well. Critics point out that economic growth has actually been significantly slower among the advanced capitalist countries since neoliberalism gained ascendancy in the late 1970s, and that countries have often registered dismal macroeconomic performances since they adopted neoliberal prescriptions. Meanwhile, countries such as China, Taiwan, and India, which all refused to follow the neoliberal approach, have largely escaped the ravages of the most recent international financial crisis. The strongest macroeconomic performance in the world in recent decades has been registered by China, which has followed a state-guided policy dramatically different from the neoliberal model. While the causal factors at work in these various situations are of course complex, the pattern is sufficiently marked to suggest that neoliberal doctrines and the political consequences deduced from them must be submitted to fresh critical examination.

6. Free Markets, Free Trade

"Freedom" is a sacred term in American society. The expressions "free markets" and "free trade" strike us intuitively as something desirable: a free market has to be better than the alternative, and open, unfettered trade must be the optimal condition for flourishing economic activity. What public figure would dare to stand up and denounce "freedom"? Speeches by economic experts, policy-makers, and political leaders endorsing the new global economic order almost invariably connect the promised advantages of globalization with the idea of greater freedom.

In implementing the North American Free Trade Agreement (NAFTA) in 1994, American, Canadian, and Mexican officials underscored their "long-term goal...to remove barriers to trade worldwide." The trade agreement, claimed those who drafted it, sought to "reinforce free market reforms" and "stimulate cross-border economic activity" among the partner countries.[44] This aim sounds legitimate. How could freedom be a bad idea?

It is important to observe, though, that this variety of "freedom" refers to markets maintained by complex international legislation and commercial agreements and substantially dominated by the demands of transnational corporations. Under these circumstances, freedom can only partially describe the nature of economic activity. More precisely, "freedom" becomes a code word for a particular way of managing market interactions.

Our intuitive idea that a free market would be one in which firms and individuals engaged in fair, open exchange with no outside interference (above all from states) does not correspond to the realities of international trade, nor to the way in which wealthy countries have developed and prospered historically. Free trade in fact requires a complex network of legislation and framing agreements (for instance, to govern the enforcement of patents and copyrights). Moreover, trade itself and individual firms involved in it benefit substantially from "state interference" in the form of publicly funded infrastructure projects (transportation and communications networks, for example) and government financing of costly research and development programs. The development of the American computer industry from the 1950s onward represents one of the most current and spectacular examples of this pattern, more the rule than the exception among modern high-tech industries.[45] Likewise, economic historians point out that protectionist policies permitted the U.S. textile industry to thrive in its early days, while the railroad network that enabled the country's nineteenth-century economic upsurge was built with substantial public subsidies.

These considerations are important for evaluating current economic policy recommendations from supporters of "free market reforms." Through institutions such as the World Trade Organization (WTO) and the IMF, wealthy countries are today urging poorer countries to adopt free market principles, opening their economies to unconstrained foreign investment and foreign competition. This is presented as the best way for poorer countries to develop. In theory, the laws of the open market will push people and firms in the newly opened economies to seek their "comparative advantage." It is expected that people, firms, and countries will focus their productive efforts on the raw materials, goods, or services they can generate most cheaply (coffee beans in Colombia; apples—or computer software—in Washington State). They will use these products to trade for those items which could not be produced locally in an efficient manner. In this way, market forces will allow the developing economy to be more streamlined and rational.

Yet, while the free market theory appears convincing on paper, it is worthwhile to observe that this was *not* the pattern by which wealthy countries' industries developed and were able to achieve power and preeminence. Countries such as the United States and Japan made substantial and systematic use of protectionist or anti-free market devices (such as high import tariffs and other barriers to free trade) during the periods in which their fledgling industries were beginning to mature, but still remained vulnerable to foreign competition. The pattern of free market rhetoric combined with restrictive protectionist practices continued, in the American case, through the Reagan era of the 1980s. While making unrestrained market freedom the dominant theme of their political message, President Reagan and his advisors, in fact, substantially bolstered protectionist legislation safeguarding key American industries and firms from foreign competitors.[46]

7. Market and State

At the heart of today's conventional economic wisdom is the neoliberal thesis that all social actors benefit when markets operate without state interference, when the power to make economic decisions is in the hands not of politicians but of individual buyers and sellers. The neoliberal model has the advantage, according to one of its proponents, of "provid[ing] clear, consistent and, above all, simple solutions to the problems thrown up by society and the economy."[47] Yet there is no guarantee that these simple solutions are the right ones. To test these claims, we must examine the real effects of policies grounded on the assumption that all members of society will benefit when political authority withdraws from markets.

During the period when mainstream Western economic theory was dominated by the works of Keynes, it was widely supposed that regular state intervention in the operations of economic markets was necessary in order for markets to function efficiently and fairly. Given the tendency of capitalist economies to cycle through periods of recession, held Keynes, sustained active guidance by political authorities was required to maintain stability, stimulate healthy economic growth, and avoid such economic catastrophes as the Great Depression of the 1930s. This state-interventionist approach became intertwined over succeeding decades with the attempts of government administrators to mitigate the extremes of market-based distribution through social spending. The state interventionist model was challenged by *economic neoliberalism*. The roots of this reversal were already observable in the 1950s, but the neoliberal reconfiguration of the balance between market and state did not become complete until the 1980s.

Neoliberal theory tends to present "market" and "state" as forces naturally hostile to one another. For the more uncompromising forms of neoliberalism, state action in the economic sphere is inherently distorting and inefficient. Any attempt on the part of political authorities to regulate the behavior of market actors is wrong-headed. State action can never manage economic behavior more productively than the market itself; in virtually all cases, state intrusion will worsen economic performance in the long run. According to this view, as markets are liberalized and state-run enterprises privatized—that is, as state interference in citizens' economic affairs is reduced—markets will automatically function more efficiently, rewarding individual enterprise, and ultimately benefiting society as a whole (see the previous section, "Free Markets, Free Trade").

This ideal of the market as a sphere of open exchange between rational agents (buyers and sellers) acting freely as each pursues his/her own interests has deep roots in Western (particularly Anglo-Saxon) culture. Almost inevitably, this model strikes a positive chord in those of us responsive to its fundamental affirmation of individual liberty and the belief that rewards should be proportional to personal creativity, initiative, and risk. If the state operates as an arbitrary constraining force on market interactions that would otherwise unfold in a context of freedom and equal opportunity, it is hard for us not to be suspicious of government intrusions in the economic realm.

Yet, though the ideal of market freedom and the notion of the state as a perpetual threat to that freedom seem natural to us, there are good reasons to question these "truisms." As we have argued previously, effective markets are in many respects dependent on an active state, and the seemingly simple idea of unconstrained economic exchange is quite divorced from the reality of national and international trade. The buying and selling that take place both within national boundaries and across borders are never "free" in the simple (and simplistic) sense of obeying no factors other than the rationally weighed preferences of the individual actors (individuals and firms) involved. The markets defined by free trade agreements such as the General Agreement on Tariffs and Trade (GATT) and NAFTA, along with technologies like the Internet that allow investors to negotiate these markets at electronic speed, are structures created and maintained in large part by governments through their public investment, regulatory efforts, and diplomatic coordination.

In fact, states play many crucial roles in the marketplace. States usually delimit property, enforce contracts, regulate transportation and communication, and retain some control over domestic currency markets. Corporations are defined and nurtured through state legal and diplomatic conventions, which protect the rights of their stockholders, adjudicate disputes among claimants to their revenues, and otherwise regulate business transactions. Furthermore, it is most often the state that provides health and education for the population—both of which are prerequisites for effective market activity (not to mention important in their own right). It is difficult to imagine markets functioning "free" of these state activities.

The idea that markets and states are intertwined underscores an important distinction between markets as they actually exist in the real world and "the Market" as an idealized abstract, a conception people have about buying and selling.[48] In basic, nuts-and-bolts terms, a "market" can be defined as the sum total of concrete exchanges that occur between buyers and sellers of a particular category of goods or services. Yet, as economic anthropologist James Carrier has argued, over the past several decades concrete markets have been in some ways less important than "the Market" as an ideological construct: "Since around the end of the Second World War, the Market has existed primarily as a political icon or a formal economic abstraction."[49]

Central to this idealized conception of "the Market" is the axiom that, to function properly, "The Market" must be freed from constraints imposed by governments. Fair, efficient economic patterns cannot be shaped by states, but only by market forces themselves, assisted in certain cases by the timely intervention of economic specialists (for example, analysts employed by the IMF and the World Bank) whose job it is to help liberate markets overburdened by state interference. Thus, though the model of the "Free Market" belongs to the realm of speculative ideals, this abstract ideal affects the real world significantly.

An important instrument by which free market ideals are translated into concrete terms has been conditional lending by the IMF, World Bank, and other multilateral financial institutions. For example, the disbursement by IFIs of loan resources to poor countries is now predicated on their governments' reduction of state budget deficits—often in a wholly unrealistic manner, given internal economic conditions. In many cases, budget cuts have set in motion a process that "exacerbates the fiscal crisis of the [poor] state, leading to the collapse of state programmes while releasing state revenue (in the short run) for the repayment of interest on the external debt."[50] This process has destructive (sometimes deadly) consequences for vulnerable segments of the country's population as the poor state, no longer as able to allocate resources for social programs or public infrastructure, places budget decisions increasingly in the hands of the "donor community": IFIs and the wealthy countries that back them.

Recently, representatives of the IFIs themselves have begun to acknowledge the limitations of an approach that presents the relation between markets and states as inherently antagonistic.[51] In March 1998, as South Koreans staged mass demonstrations against IMF-imposed austerity programs, the IMF's managing director called for "a fiscal policy that reduces unequal income distribution and puts priority on education and health." "Promoting equity," he said, "is a basic responsibility of the state."[52] Such sentiments, however, continue to stand in tension with macroeconomic planning that channels resources from impoverished states to wealthy financial institutions and corporations. This incongruity is revealed in a recent World Bank policy paper that finds many state-run primary health-care programs in poorer countries—programs such as vaccinations and sewage treatment—"disappointing" in their lack of efficiency. The authors affirm: "It is only when markets are not working that the government can actually improve matters by intervening."[53] Yet as the studies in this volume show, the market is "not working" for poor people a great deal more frequently than officials at the World Bank and IMF admit.

There is now a widening recognition that the actual relationship between market and state cannot be fully understood in neoliberal terms. The role of the state in promoting equitable, sustainable economic growth cannot simply be a negative one—amounting, for all intents and purposes, to "getting out of the way." The World Bank's own 1997 *World Development Report* acknowledges the need to "reinvigorate the state's institutional capability" as a fundamental step to maintaining social stability and empowering development. "Public policies and programs must aim not merely to deliver growth but to ensure that the benefits of market-led growth are shared, particularly through investments in basic education and health."[54] A more balanced attitude toward state authority is necessary, one which imagines it working in tandem with market forces. As a recent UNDP discussion paper observes, more complex forms of economic strategy must now be envisaged. The authors explain that "trade protection, financial market control, corporate deals among the states, capital and labour and other non-liberal interventions [have] been associated with rapid growth" in all successful capitalist economies—including the United States, continental Europe, and Japan—and in countries of southeast Asia more recently.[55] World Bank analysts confirm that effective government policies in east Asian countries contributed substantively to the region's impressive economic development after 1960. Effective states in east Asia and the relative absence of stable state structures in much of sub-Saharan Africa may explain a portion of the contrast in the economic fortunes of these regions from 1960 onward.[56]

To describe exactly how new relationships between states and markets should be configured is perhaps not yet possible. No "one-size-fits-all recipe for an effective state" is likely to present itself, given the enormous range of differences among states and their contexts of action.[57] Yet it is clear that we must begin to move beyond the neoliberal model according to which state intervention in markets is inevitably faulty, while the unregulated "Market" can be trusted to optimize economic outcomes for all. More nuanced models for state-market relations must evolve, replacing blind faith in the spontaneous and "natural" play of the market's own intrinsic forces. As the UNDP discussion paper concludes: "History suggests that no economies developed without developmentalist states."[58] This historical insight has significant policy implications for the present: "For human welfare to be advanced, the state's capability—*defined as the ability to undertake and promote collective actions efficiently*—must be increased."[59]

8. Growth

Stimulating and maintaining economic growth is widely understood to be the primary objective of national and international economic policy, and the surest way to reduce poverty in local communities and around the world. According to the conventional wisdom, "the significance of economic growth lies in its contribution to the general prosperity of the community. Growth is desirable because it enables the community to consume more private goods and services, and it contributes to the provision of a greater quantity of social goods and services (health, education, etc.)."[60]

Indeed, growth is seen by many as the key indicator of a country's economic success. Conventionally, growth is measured by the annual percentage change in a given country's real (*inflation-corrected*) GDP. Wealthy countries consider an annual GDP growth rate of between 3 and 4 percent to be healthy. Under optimal conditions, poorer economies should be showing a more rapid rate of expansion, on the order of 5 to 7 percent annually. In general, economic policies are considered successful if they contribute to GDP growth. They are liable to be judged unsuccessful if they diminish GDP growth rates, regardless of whatever other good they may provide society. It is assumed that in the end, economic growth will benefit all segments of the population, even the poorest, to whom benefits will gradually "trickle down" in a variety of forms.

There are a number of significant problems with this model. Growth in GDP figures provide a convenient scorecard on which to base judgments about a country's economic health. However, the tendency to focus exclusively on growth figures subtly shifts our perspective from *growth* as a means of enhancing human lives to *economic growth* as an end in itself. Meanwhile, recent trends in the United States and other parts of the world show that strong economic growth does not necessarily lead to a narrowing of the gap between rich and poor, but may rather be accompanied by significant increases in the level of inequality. The "long-term" future in which the gains of growth will seep down to the poor continues to be deferred. The World Bank's own data from almost two decades of structural adjustment programs (SAPs) suggest that growth-oriented SAPs worsen inequality in many cases (see Chapter Two).[61]

Furthermore, critiques from the environmental movement challenge the notion of unlimited growth and endless productive expansion as the normative framework for the world economy. Since the 1970s, many economists and natural scientists have underscored the material constraints to economic expansion. Policies that push growth at all costs can lead to the depletion of nonrenewable resources and cause serious environmental degradation.[62] Such concerns have led to efforts to formulate a "sustainable" world development program, as well as to calls for a more equitable redistribution of resources between rich and poor countries. The language of "sustainable development" appears in documents like the proceedings of the 1992 "Earth Summit" in Rio de Janeiro, and even in the planning guidelines of the World Bank itself.

"Sustainable development," however, has yet to assert itself as a central tenet of economic policy. Moreover, proponents of sustainable development, on the one hand, and advocates of short-term action to reduce poor people's suffering, on the other, may at times find themselves opposed on particular political issues, requiring difficult forms of negotiation as they attempt to reconcile their agenda.

The editors of *Dying for Growth* concur with the view that while "economic growth cannot possibly solve all the problems" confronting the world's poor, the situations faced by poor people "would almost certainly get worse without it."[63] Yet we question the simplistic (but widespread) notion that economic growth, as such, is inherently and unqualifiedly good. In this book, we seek to give substance to such a reconsideration by exploring the relationships between economic and political policies intended to promote growth and the health outcomes of poor people in different parts of the world. Above all, this volume's authors critique the idea that stimulating strong economic growth nationally and internationally is a *sufficient* objective for those who want to respond to the economic, political, and moral challenges posed by poverty.

ACKNOWLEDGMENTS

The authors wish to thank several scholars who contributed substantively to framing the discussion of terms in this chapter: Joyce Millen, John Gershman, Jim Yong Kim, and in particular David Kotz, whose generosity, knowledge, and critical insight were indispensable.

PART II

Growth Strategies,
State Restructuring, and
the Health of the Poor

Central Plateau, Haiti. Life on one meal a day. (photo by Joyce V. Millen)

CHAPTER FOUR

Hypocrisies of Development and the Health of the Haitian Poor

Paul Farmer and Didi Bertrand

INTRODUCTION

"**L**ife for the Haitian peasant of today," observed anthropologist Jean Weise 28 years ago, "is abject misery and a rank familiarity with death."[1] Few would dispute that little has changed in this regard; by any criteria, the vast majority of the Haitian people live in poverty.[2] Since 1986, political violence has been added to the worst poverty in the hemisphere, with the expected effects on the health status of the population. Public health specialists focusing on Haiti agree that the past decade has been marked by a further decline in both Haiti's health infrastructure and in its people's health. By and large, Haitians living in Haiti have not enjoyed the fruits of twentieth-century scientific advances in medicine and public health. Few would dispute the claim that health and development, however the terms are defined, are closely linked.[3]

While there is consensus regarding Haiti's poor health, the causes of ill health are contested. Why, precisely, is there so much sickness in Haiti? Many official explanations favor local factors and local actors.[4] These analyses and commentaries assume that the high rates of poor health among Haiti's majority are caused entirely by circumstances originating *within* the country. Such explanations make reference to the country's ecology and its poverty, and also to Haitian culture and political history. In these analyses, Haiti is notable for its isolation—and its qualitative *difference*—from the rest of the world. Such views contrast vividly with opinions heard in Haiti, particularly among the poor. These opinions argue that Haiti's poor health indices are primarily the result of forces that originate from *outside* Haiti—in other words, they are caused by much broader, transnational forces, the effects of which are felt chiefly by the Haitian poor.

Although a certain complementarity exists between some of these explanations, it is nonetheless true that they cannot all be correct. Some of these models must have more explanatory power than the others; others, consequently, must involve immodest claims of causality. There are many reasons for such competing models, but before we explore them, we provide a brief overview of the health status of the Haitian people. This overview is focused by reference to clinical data from a busy facility in the hills of central Haiti, and is grounded by the comments of people served by this clinic. Many would see the area and the village in which the clinic operates as "underdeveloped." But the area's residents see their region as shaped by two developments: the loss of their land to a hydroelectric dam—touted as a "development project"—and the coup d'état of 1991. Both events are locally perceived as inextricably related to each other and to a third process—*structural adjustment*—now underway in Haiti. These events are seen not as accidents or happenstance, but rather as the results of the actions of the powerful, both Haitian and foreign. As often as not, the rural poor of central Haiti refer to these processes as consonant with their nation's history. Grounding this commentary in a broader review of the large-scale social forces that have shaped sickness and death in rural Haiti brings into relief the "hypocrisies of development."

HISTORY: HOW TO MAKE PEOPLE SICK

Haiti is Latin America's oldest nation, having declared itself independent from France after a remarkable slave revolt that began in 1791. Haiti had been France's most valuable possession, and by 1789 was producing more wealth than all 13 North American colonies combined.[5] The French were able to achieve such production, because Haiti's once-rich soil was tilled by half a million slaves. It may be argued that the French slave colony of Saint-Domingue was the template for Haiti, soon to become Latin America's first independent republic. In modern-day food shortages, it is still possible to discern the legacy of frenzied colonial production: Saint-Domingue provided sugar, coffee, and other tropical produce to much of Europe, but was unable to feed itself. Although the then newly declared United States boasted a brisk trade in foodstuffs for the French colony's half million or so slaves, then as now Haitian agribusiness was largely about *export*. Most available documentation suggests that the slave forebears of contemporary Haitians suffered immeasurably as a result:

> The slaves brought from Africa to Haiti carried with them the remnants of their cultural systems, yellow fever, yaws and malaria. The Spanish gave them sugar cane, vicious slavery, a form of Catholicism, smallpox, measles, typhoid and tuberculosis. The French, in their turn, gave the Haitian a language, traces of French culture and continued vicious servitude.[6]

The high prevalence of infectious diseases was emblematic of the French approach to public sanitation in the colonies; despite the importance of Haiti to the French economy, investments in health-care infrastructure had been negligible. On the eve of Haiti's war of independence, there were only a few miserable military hospitals. The white minority were treated by colonial doctors in their homes. Members of the black majority, if they were treated at all, received care in plantation sick-bays of varying quality. Although one historian presents data suggesting the slaves of one large plantation enjoyed robust enough health, many others have noted differential mortality rates between newly arrived Africans and island-born Creole slaves.[7] For one plantation, another historian reports that one-third of the newly acquired slaves were dead within a year or two.[8]

What were the conditions a decade later, at the close of the war of independence? Ary Bordes, author of a multivolume study of Haiti's health, offers the following summary: "Virtually all of the island's doctors and surgeons had fled. The majority of hospitals and other institutions had been destroyed; only the military hospitals in Port-au-Prince and Cap Haïtien (formerly Cap Français) remained. The towns were in shambles, without sewers or latrines." What little care could be delivered was offered by orderlies who had worked in hospitals, or by midwives, herbalists, and bonesetters. Bordes writes of a

> host of technically unprepared health workers in the presence of a population newly liberated from slavery, living for the most part in primitive huts, without water or latrines, and undermined and decimated by the infectious diseases against which they were so poorly protected. Oppressive legacy from our former masters, thirsty for profits, and little interested in the living conditions and health of the indigenous population.[9]

Just as this "oppressive legacy" was to serve as the template for subsequent Haitian production strategies, so too was the tragedy of slavery to set the tone for the new nation's public health. Although this legacy became the template for health conditions in independent Haiti, it is difficult to assess what those conditions might have been like during the new republic's first decades. The impressions of nineteenth-century visitors, certainly, were unfavorable, but it *is* clear that most European and American visitors to Haiti culled material for best-selling texts that told readers what they most wanted to hear. Invariably, the hypothesis to be "confirmed" was that blacks were incapable of self-rule. Sir Spenser St. John, British envoy to Haiti, set the tone in his 1884 memoirs, *Hayti: Or the Black Republic*: "What the negro may become after centuries of civilized education I cannot tell, but what I know is that he is not fit to govern now."[10] Haitians' presumed inability to promote public health and hygiene was yet another "manifestation" of their incapacity.

The tenor of such commentary scarcely improved during the 20-year U.S. military occupation of Haiti (1915-1934). The *National Geographic* during this time referred to Haiti's peasants as the "unthinking black animals of the interior." With curious but unsubstantiated precision, journalists noted that "it is estimated that 87 percent of the entire population were infected with contagious diseases."[11] Although such pronouncements revealed more about their authors than about the health status of Haitians, observations made during the occupation suggested the importance of infectious diseases, particularly tuberculosis. Gastroenteritis, typhoid fever, and malaria were also important causes of mortality among adults, as were gastroenteritis and measles among children; filariasis and yaws were major causes of morbidity.[12]

Finally, political turmoil—including an armed revolt against the U.S. occupation—caused significant numbers of deaths. According to U.S. sources, including the Marine Corps, between 2,000 and 3,350 rebels were killed during the 20 months of active resistance; however, the killing of peasants suspected of involvement in the rebellion led one Haitian historian to ask

> if the total number of battle victims and casualties of repression and *consequences* of the war might not have reached, by the end of the pacification period, four or five times that [figure]—somewhere in the neighborhood of 15,000 persons. This [latter] figure is all the more impressive when it is compared to the 98 dead and wounded

among the marines and the American and Haitian constabulary. This war, in many instances, must have resembled a massacre.[13]

The post-World War II arrival on the scene of representatives of the Pan American Health Organization (PAHO) and the World Health Organization (WHO) led to more scholarly statements, but even these were rarely underpinned by empirical research. Population-based studies conducted in the 1950s and 1960s suggested that infant mortality was between 200 and 250 per 1,000 live births, compared to 26 per 1,000 registered births in the United States at the time.[14] The chief causes of death among infants continued to be gastroenteritis, measles, tetanus, tuberculosis, and "debility."[15] Malnutrition was widespread, and seemed to underlie or exacerbate these pathologies.[16] (Although Haitian schoolchildren all learn to chant that "Haïti est un pays essentiellement agricole," it was the country's producers—the rural peasantry—who suffered most from food shortages.)

In recent decades, the health situation seemed to improve. The Haitian government undertook campaigns to promote oral-rehydration therapy for diarrhea and universal vaccination; both were credited for nationwide declines in infant and juvenile mortality. One study from rural Haiti showed that aggressive public health measures could be remarkably successful when diseases such as neonatal tetanus were prevented and other afflictions brought under control.[17] But these advances seemed to many Haitians to be completely undermined by a continued degradation of the country's economic and social infrastructure. Social unrest was also recurrent. In 1957, army-backed and fraudulent elections brought Dr. François Duvalier to power; he would remain in office until his death in 1971, when he was succeeded by his son.[18]

The 29 years of the Duvalier dictatorship were notable for a palpable decline in agricultural output, as deforestation and concomitant erosion each year washed thousands of acres of topsoil into the sea, and thousands more were claimed by alkalization.[19] Even as agricultural exports—which in the 1970s still accounted for more than 50 percent of merchandise exports—declined, Haiti remained inextricably tied to the world economy through its assembly plants for U.S. corporations and consumers. This arrangement has been touted as "aid" to Haiti despite the fact that almost all of the material inputs for these assembly plants are imported, and that very little other than labor is purchased from Haitians. Most of the profits generated by this brisk "industry" are, of course, repatriated.

The assembly "industry" is thus not really an industry; it is inessential to the production of goods and services. Nor is it aid in the standard sense of the term. Export-led assembly is rather a reflection of steep gradients between countries in the cost of labor. Materials produced in—or merely gathered by—a wealthy country are exported to a poor country to be assembled by the comparatively cheap and "disciplined" labor there. In this sense, the Duvaliers' Haiti offered enormous benefits for offshore assembly—generous tax holidays, a franchise granting tariff exemption, tame unions, and a minimum wage but a tiny fraction of that in the United States.

A mere decade after its arrival, the assembly sector claimed to be the "dynamic" part of the Haitian economy. By 1978, "exports" from assembly operations had surpassed coffee as the number one export. During the height of its assembly days, Haiti, the poorest country in the hemisphere, was the world's ninth largest assembler of goods for U.S. consumers, the world's largest producer of baseballs, and among the top three countries in the assembly of such diverse products as stuffed toys, dolls, and apparel, especially brassieres.[20] All told, the impact of international subcontracting was considerable: "Contributing more than half of the country's industrial exports, assembly production now earns almost one-quarter of Haiti's yearly foreign exchange receipts."[21] In terms of employment, the World Bank and the U. S. State Department estimated that, as of 1980, approximately 200 assembly plants employed almost 60,000 people, most of whom were women.[22] These factories were (and are) all located in the capital city of Port-au-Prince. "Assuming a dependency ratio of 4 to 1," add Grunwald, Delatour, and Voltaire, three assembly-sector cheerleaders, "this means that assembly operations supported about one-quarter of the population of Port-au-Prince in 1980."[23]

Unsurprisingly, this form of "industrialization" did little to arrest an economy in free fall, and Haiti sank deeper into debt. One Haitian economist reported that "in just seven years, Haiti's external public debt increased sevenfold: from $53 million in 1973 to $366 million in 1980. This represents almost twice the rate of growth of external indebtedness in Latin America, as a whole, over the same period of time."[24] In 1976, the World Bank fixed the threshold of absolute poverty at $140 per capita income per year. Even using this stringent criterion, fully 75 percent of all Haitians fell into this category. The advent of swine flu, also at about this time, led to the destruction of Haiti's important pig population, leading to increased hardship for the rural poor.[25]

By the time "President-for-Life" Jean-Claude Duvalier was firmly entrenched, the majority of Haitians had long since left behind even a peasant standard of living. In 1980, the Département de Santé Publique et Population estimated that only 1.8 percent of rural Haitians had access to pure drinking water.[26] A report released in 1981 offered the following summary: "Over 50 percent of deaths are among children under age five, with nearly 75 percent of deaths caused by or associated with malnutrition. Infectious diseases account for the majority of deaths. The major causes of childhood deaths are diarrhea, pneumonia, and tetanus; tuberculosis is the leading cause of death among adults."[27] In 1987, UNICEF announced that "one Haitian child dies every five minutes of malnutrition and related diseases."[28]

This rapid and dramatic decline occurred even as Haiti became one of the world's leading recipients of "development assistance." Throughout their tenures, the Duvaliers cynically promoted the idea of Haiti as a diseased polity that demanded rapid infusions of international aid. They appealed to every imaginable source of aid, but especially to the United States Agency for International Development (USAID), which some in Haiti have termed "a state within the state." The Duvaliers also turned to Canada, France, West Germany, and to the World Bank and International Monetary Fund (IMF), to UNICEF and the United Nations Development Programme (UNDP), and to the WHO. One study estimated that, during the 1970s and 1980s, such aid financed two-thirds of government investment and covered fully half of Haitian import expenditures. Despite obvious evidence of massive fraud, these organizations happily pumped money into the Duvalier kleptocracy:

> While [US]AID was being so charmingly credulous, the U.S. Department of Commerce produced figures to show that no less than 63 percent of all recorded

government revenue in Haiti was being "misappropriated" each year. Not long afterwards—and just before he was dismissed by Duvalier—Haiti's Finance Minister, Marc Bazin, revealed that a monthly average of $15 million was being diverted from public funds to meet "extra-budgetary expenses" that included regular deposits into the President's private Swiss bank account. Most of the "public funds" had, of course, arrived in Haiti in the form of "development assistance."[29]

Graft and thievery were only part of the story. Several studies suggested that the effects of such international largesse as has actually reached its intended beneficiaries had been deleterious to the local economy. For example, cereals donated under USAID's Food for Peace program were sold in virtually every Haitian marketplace, undermining local farmers' ability to sell their own grains.[30] In an important study of the effects of international aid to Haiti, social analysts DeWind and Kinley concluded that the chief effects of such aid have been further immiseration of the poor (by now the vast majority of Haitians) and massive emigration.[31] Another book-length study of foreign assistance examines aid to Haiti and asks, "Did the ruin of the Haitian poor occur in *spite* of foreign aid, or *because* of it?"[32]

The hypocrisies of development have been much commented upon in Haiti, and in the 1980s led many Haitians to call for an end to aid to the Duvaliers. The 1980s also saw the rebirth of grassroots political struggle against the dictatorship, which by that time was usually held, along with its foreign supporters, responsible for deplorable health conditions. By the close of 1985, popular protest was likely to comment upon the adverse effects of foreign assistance, seen chiefly as a means of propping up a U.S.-friendly dictatorship. As one widely distributed flyer would have it, "Do you wish to punish us with your aid, which serves only to strengthen the dictatorship?" The government responded with force, adding political violence to the well-entrenched structural violence and leading tens of thousands of Haitians to flee the country by boat. Many others joined the popular movements pressing for democratic rule. This struggle led, ultimately, to what was seen by many as the decade's crowning (and, for some, sole positive) achievement: the nation's first free and fair elections, held in December 1990.

Although a dozen presidential candidates ran in the 1990 election, most observers saw the contest as between Jean-Bertrand Aristide, a priest influenced by liberation theology, and Marc Bazin, former Duvalier cabinet member and World Bank official known locally as "the American candidate." The two presidential hopefuls agreed on little, but the point on which they most vocally disagreed was on the appropriate path toward development and economic recovery. Bazin advocated a World Bank-endorsed structural adjustment program (SAP) and continued reliance on U.S. aid; this plan was universally termed "the American Plan."[33] Aristide favored enforcement of taxation on Haiti's wealthy, a crackdown on corruption, and land reform to increase agricultural production. The priest was leery of rapid privatization of state-owned industries, which he felt could be profitable enough, in the absence of graft, to subvention social services for the poor. Aristide won by a landslide.

When in 1991 President Aristide initiated reform of the public health sector, he was faced with the worst health indices in the hemisphere. According to UNICEF's *The State of the World's Children*, in Haiti that year the under-five mortality rate was

137 per thousand; only 27 percent of the rural population had access to safe drinking water; only 50 percent of the population had access to even rudimentary health services; and only 31 percent of children had been vaccinated for measles. Haiti rated worst among all nations in the Western hemisphere in terms of its health indicators.[34] Aggregate data suggested a catastrophe, but may have underestimated the true dimensions of misery in Haiti. When in 1991 international health experts devised the "human suffering index" by adding other gauges of well-being—from political freedom to women's literacy—to the standard health measures, only three countries in the world were judged to be worse off than Haiti. And each of them—Mozambique, Somalia, and Afghanistan—was in the midst of civil war.[35]

Sickness and suffering are certainly recurrent and expected conditions in Haiti's Central Plateau, where a clinic (described in the next section) serves a population whose everyday lives have felt, often enough, like war. Although these miserable conditions are evident to all, there is, again, a great deal of debate as to how they came to be. We now turn to the village's experience, in order to reveal the mechanisms by which a "development project" brought misery to the peasant farmers of the lower Central Plateau. This project—fairly unremarkable, by international standards—came to be linked in the local jeremiad to a second blow, the coup d'état of 1991. It is easy to discern the same "affective tenor" in commentaries about both events, since each was perceived as the latest installment in the same bitter historical experience. Bringing this experience into view helps to reveal why there is so much resistance to conventional development projects—including current plans for structural adjustment.

THE FIRST BLOW:
ONE COMMUNITY'S EXPERIENCE OF "DEVELOPMENT"

> "We were in a bad way. Our hearts were being pulled out. But we couldn't speak. Some people just plain died from the shock. And from that day on, I've never felt right again."
>
> Mme. Gracia, on the flooding of the valley[36]

> "The rich people, the city people, bribe the bureaucrats so they can have electricity. Water makes electricity, but you need high water. So they flooded us out....And it's not the first time they've done such things. Whenever they start talking 'development,' poor people have to be careful."
>
> Mme. Lamandier, on the flooding of the valley

The village of Kay is, upon cursory inspection, just another tiny settlement in the hills, stretching along an unpaved road in the Central Plateau of Haiti. A rigorous three-and-a-half-hour drive—if only 60 miles as the crow flies—from Port-au-Prince, Kay may best be viewed from one of the peculiarly steep and conical hills that nearly encircle the village. From this vantage point, Kay appears as a collection of tiny, tin-covered huts randomly scattered on the flanks of a single, large mountainside. Most of its inhabitants live in two-room houses, many with dirt floors, and cultivate plots of land that yield slowly diminishing returns. They have no tractors, electricity, or cars. Their hillside gardens are too steep for ox plows, even if they did have oxen.

A mere decade ago, the village of Kay looked quite different from this vantage; less than four decades ago, there was not a house in sight. The history of the village, and its relationship to a "development" project, are to be found in villagers' statements about themselves: "We are Kay people, but we are not from here," explained Nosant, a man in his fifties. "We are people of the valley." The apparent paradox is resolved if the speaker gestures out over the vast reservoir that lies at the base of the hills. The history of the Kay people is submerged below the still surface of this lake.

Before 1956, the area now known as Kay was, in the words of one of the first settlers, "a desert, a dry savanna with wind and birds and grass alone." The majority of the villagers who are now over 40 years of age then lived down in the valley. They were mostly from "Petit-Fond," a fertile and gently sloping area on either side of a stream known locally as Rivière Kay. Bursting forth from a cliff face, the largely subterranean stream joined the Rivière Artibonite between the Rivière Thomonde and the Péligre Gorge, where a massive buttress dam now stands.

It is largely from oral histories that we have reconstructed both the history of the villagers' flight from the rising water and the settlement of Kay. The story is usually recounted as beginning in the mid-1950s, but irreversible steps were taken considerably earlier. The "Organisme de Développement de la Vallée de l'Artibonite" (ODVA) was born of an agreement, signed in 1949 in Washington, D.C., between the Haitian government and the Export-Import Bank. Initial plans for the dam were older still, having been drawn up during the U.S. military occupation of Haiti (1915-1934). It was during the U.S. occupation that Haiti's constitution was rewritten to abolish one of its most famous articles: the prohibition of foreign ownership of land in Haiti. This change lent a legal façade to the rapid growth of U.S.-owned agribusiness, which was even then treated as a form of development assistance to a "backward" peasant society. Inspired in part by what was to become the Tennessee Valley Authority, proponents of agribusiness in Haiti needed reliable irrigation for rice production in the fertile plains that had once been home to French plantations. In a sense, then, the dam at Péligre was an early installment of what later became known as "the American Plan."

Many North American companies had scouted Haiti for land for new plantations of rubber, bananas, sugar, sisal, mahogany, and other tropical produce. Whether the real draw was land or cheap labor, the stated goals of the ODVA were as follows:

> To use the waters of the Artibonite to irrigate the 40,000 hectares of lands deemed irrigable; to drain those areas needing to be drained in order to combat alkalinity; to protect the plains from the periodic floods that impact unfavorably on the regional economy and impoverish the harvest; to undertake, in all of these areas, a methodical agricultural development plan based on the most modern techniques; to implement a logical re-assembly of certain Valley populations in hopes of raising their standards of living through the continual enjoyment of the profits to be made from the newly cultivated and developed lands; to at last turn the Artibonite into an area of production and trade that will exert its influence throughout the country and help to normalize our commercial balance.[37]

Although the loans for the construction of the dam were received in August 1951, the news that the residents of the valley would be forced to relocate seemed not to have traveled far up river. Most of those interviewed claim that they were apprised of the impending inundation only a month before it occurred. All interviewed concur that little warning was given. The valley residents did not know, said Mme. Lamandier, "until the water was upon us. We heard only rumors, which we did not believe, until a couple of months before, when they sent someone to tell us to cooperate, that our land would be flooded. This also we did not believe." A few insist that no attempt was made to inform the valley-dwellers of their impending losses. Most recall, however, that the community was alerted at a public assembly. Absalom Kola put it this way:

> They called an assembly to say that they would be reimbursing everyone for their gardens and land....They warned us, but we all said it can't be true, it couldn't be done. We knew of nothing that could have stopped that great river. The Artibonite ran fast through the valley, and none of us believed it could be stopped.

It is striking, of course, that the residents of Petit-Fond would claim to know nothing of such an enormous project, one that took years to complete. The Péligre Gorge construction site was only a few miles away, and hundreds of locals were employed at relatively high wages. Indeed, if the rural Haitian economy of the 1950s resembled the economy of today, it is likely that some residents of Petit-Fond joined work crews in Péligre, although this is categorically denied by Mme. Gracia, one of the early settlers of Kay: "No, there wasn't anyone from Kay who went to work there. It was mostly people from Péligre or from the city [Port-au-Prince]. There were a lot of foreigners too. No one from Petit-Fond worked there."

The refugees' incredulous stance is emphatically, if apologetically, reiterated; it is reflected in accounts of their flight from the rising water. Many of those living around Petit-Fond did not move until the day the waters "chased us off our lands," as Nosant put it. But the valley residents' disbelief could not have been universal: a few landowners heeded the government's warnings, and left for nearby towns, such as LasCahobas, Thomonde, or Mirebalais. Some were said to have been reimbursed "by the State" for their lands. But most of the former valley residents interviewed stated flatly, as did Absalom Kola, that they had not been reimbursed:

> They called an assembly to say that they would be reimbursing everyone for their gardens and land. My friend, that was a lie! They came to measure the lands, and indeed a few people did receive payment—only those who were well educated, those who had secured deeds. Our lands consisted of 80 acres. This belonged to the Kola family; another 80 belonged to the Pasquet family. For these lands we received nothing. And there are many others who until this very day have received nothing.

A number of reasons were cited to explain the failure to reimburse the landholders. Mme. Dieugrand, a marketwoman who linked her lack of reimbursement to her poverty, stated that "it was the rich peasants who were reimbursed. Truly, we were all doing well back then. But some of us didn't have much land. My mother was struggling; she had no husband and seven children. That's why she got nothing." Corruption and graft were also held to have played a role. The reason most commonly invoked, however, involved a different aspect of the political powerlessness of the rural population. Although more than one informant suggested that their powerlessness was a result of their poverty, most of those who spoke of political powerlessness spoke not of lack of money, but of lack of education: "Those who were literate and who had deeds were the only ones to get paid," explained Absalom Kola.

All of those who mentioned the amount of money received for the lands spoke of the insultingly small sums offered by the government. Mme. Gracia, the one informant who stated that she had been reimbursed, attributed her recompense to the deed: "Yes, they gave me a little—$40 for 12 *karo* [over 38 acres]! Those who had the papers got a little something. Truly, there were many who didn't. But $40 wasn't a fortune back then; we were planting a lot of rice."

For many, it was clear from interviews, the years following the inundation of their lands were bitter. For some of the refugees, reaching higher ground was not enough. Their trials were not yet over: "It wasn't only the water that came after us," recalls Mme. Emmanuel, the first to settle Kay. "It was also the dynamite." The department of public works, in conjunction with the ODVA and a team of U.S. engineers, had begun building a road along the hill that looked out over the reservoir. The ledge opened up by the completion of the road was known as "the terrace." The new road was to replace an older one, also drowned by the dam, that once ran from Las Cahobas, near the Dominican border, to the heart of the Central Plateau.

Others followed Mme. Emmanuel to the stony—but safer—hills above. When asked why she came to Kay, Mme. Gracia replied, "Well, we didn't have anywhere else to go; we got out to avoid being drowned. We didn't have time to save our belongings. We built little lean-tos on the hill, and resigned ourselves to our losses." Although the land in Kay was by unanimous acclamation "without value," it was safer than the land by the water's edge. More than dynamite rendered the more fertile lowlands hazardous. The reservoir level was altered several times, and those who planted near the shore lost their crops when the water level was raised.[38] Also disturbing to the refugees who settled near the lake's shore was the state-sponsored planting of teak trees near the high-water mark. These trees were variably justified as protection against erosion and raw material for future utility poles, but many suspected that more land would be appropriated. For these and other reasons, Mme. Emmanuel's lead was followed by quite a few families. The local priest recalls that there were only "two or three" households when he first visited Kay, shortly after the basin had been filled. A 1962 mapping by photogrammetric methods from 1956 aerial photography suggests, however, that there were 15 houses in Kay within a year of the inundation.

Nineteen fifty-six was thus a traumatic year for those who had come to rely on the fertile valley. Some informants report a dazed feeling, and an inability to act decisively: "For a year, I couldn't do anything. I just sat there. My children were always crying. I didn't plant a thing," said Louis. Mme. Jolibois also reports "a heaviness, a difficulty in knowing where to go, what to feed the children. Now we're used to having nothing to offer them, but back then it was a shock." Mme. Gracia's remarks echo those of her neighbors. "We had no food and little money," she recalls. "It seemed as if we couldn't act. We planted nothing. So I sold the cows, one at a time, in order to feed the children." Mme. Emmanuel speaks, as do others, of the profound depression that followed: "My friend, everyone saw their lives ending. There were those who died of grief. This is true. My father…well, it is grief that killed him."

As deforestation and erosion whittled away at the hillsides on which the valley people now found themselves, it became more and more difficult to wrest sustenance from them. "Back then," notes Mme. Gracia, "we would never have dreamed of culti-vating land like this—it's just rocks. Back then, we used only hoes.…You see in what state we are now, but we used to be persons." The dehumanizing effect—"we used to be persons"—of rootlessness and of poverty is often referred to. "They took our land so that they could have electricity," said Mme. Lamandier, "and they don't even look to see whether we're people or animals." The comments of Louis have a stringent moral bite: "What was done to us was something that you don't do to God's children. If there's a storm, you bring in the cat. If there's a flood, you move the livestock. Even livestock they would have treated more kindly."

The dam's dehumanizing effects were keenly felt within families. In rural Haiti, the idealized living arrangements are called *lakou*, a term traditionally signifying a fam-ily compound consisting of a group of children's houses grouped around that of the *chef lakou*, or household head.[39] Many of the water refugees spoke at length of the dissolu-tion of their *lakou* by the dam. "When our *lakou* was undone," said Mme. Gracia, "my father went crazy. He kept on talking about how we all had to move over to his side of the lake so we could live together as we should and honor our ancestors. He said this while sitting on a miserable pile of rocks! He was never again right in his head."

Even among those who did not lose all their land, the dam immediately dis-rupted delicately balanced competition for scarce resources and led to overt discord. As Kola put it, "the dam turned brother against brother." Stories are told in which one member of a family turned over a deed to receive compensation, and then left the valley. Many note that the water refugees became "prone to fights" as they became more and more impoverished. These quarrels, which endure to this day, are referred to by many of the older villagers as another result of the dam.

One thing that is striking, in even a cursory reading of the interviews, is the refugees' almost unanimous appreciation of what is perceived as a central irony of the story. Each of the villagers interviewed to date has spoken of the unfairness of a "devel-opment project" that destroys a way of life and offers benefits only to Port-au-Prince. Mme. Gracia, in response to the question "Why did they build the dam?" offered the following observation: "It was in order to light up Port-au-Prince with electricity, but I get nothing out of that. Port-au-Prince has light, but I'm in darkness—and I live right next door to Péligre!" The growth of the offshore assembly industry at the time of the installation of the hydroelectric turbines led many villagers to note that these resources were monopolized by foreigners. Mme. Dieugrand observed wryly that "the American factories eat all the electricity without giving anything back. That's the way it always is."

It's clear that a project analysis of the ODVA by the former residents of Petit-Fond would be scathing indeed. What of official assessments of the ODVA? Given that its stated goals were, first, to increase "local" agricultural production by promoting agribusiness downriver, and, second, to increase Haitian electrical capacity, it should not be difficult to gauge the project's efficacy. On the first score, the ODVA did not markedly increase rice harvests, but it did concentrate land holdings in the hands of fewer and fewer. By the 1960s, agribusiness was the order of the day in the lower Artibonite valley. Shortly after the ousting of Jean-Claude Duvalier in 1986, General Henri Namphy slashed import tariffs from 150 percent to 57 percent.[40] This resulted in huge shipments of "Miami rice" and other food stuffs—amazingly, Haiti now *imports* sugar—along with significant price reductions. Local rice production was of course undermined. Peasant farmers protested that they could no longer make a living growing rice. At this writing, Haitian tariffs on food imports are now around 3 percent, and World Bank-endorsed plans call for their complete removal.[41] Haiti has become a net importer of rice. Furthermore, the region is now well known for land disputes, often with fatalities, and, more recently, for "rice wars," as cheaper imports undercut local producers.[42]

On the second score, it is true that more electricity is generated at Péligre than elsewhere in the country. But annual shortages during the dry season each year last longer and longer as the reservoir is silted-in due to deforestation and resulting erosion. Again, inequality of access is the rule: although the rural peasantry paid the price for the electricity, it is largely consumed in far off Port-au-Prince.[43] Even today, over 40 years after the construction of the hydroelectric dam, a mere 6 percent of Haitians have access to electricity, with greater than 90 percent of all national production consumed in the capital.[44]

Even the claims of officialdom cannot hide such towering failure. Writing in 1961, Paul Moral opined that the costs of the ODVA outweighed the benefits: "outside of this undeniable gain in [rice] production, the ODVA seems not to have seriously tackled the problem of transformation of...the peasant condition."[45] In six years of operation, the land dispute court heard fewer than 700 cases, whereas thousands of families clamored for justice. Once landlessness became widespread, so, too, did hunger.

If things were bad downriver, the situation was downright catastrophic in the squatter settlements behind the dam. All the standard measures revealed how tenuous was the local peasantry's hold on survival. In 1984, in the Kay region, life expectancy at birth was less than 50 years, in large part because as many as one of every five infants died before its first birthday. Tuberculosis was the leading cause of death among adults; among children, diarrheal disease, measles, and tetanus ravaged the undernourished. Although many of these trends have been reversed during the past decade, in large part through a community-based health project based in Kay, it is unsurprising that the people have a special sensitivity to the hypocrisies of development.[46]

In December 1990, the residents of Kay renounced the standard development formulae by voting, almost unanimously, for Aristide. Of 293 who voted, 289 voted for the priest—and against *le plan américain*. The strength of this victory led several of the older villagers to joke that their first request to the new president would be to knock down the dam.

THE SECOND BLOW: THE COUP D'ETAT OF 1991

"Of course they're going to persecute us. Whenever you work for the poor, you're working against them. It's not just that we're for Aristide. It's because we serve the poor."

Clinic employee from Kay, January 1992

On September 30, 1991, the Aristide government was overthrown by a military coup d'état, which, according to recently released reports from international human rights groups, led to several thousand deaths. The vast majority of those killed were civilians shot by military and paramilitary forces. Horrible as this was, the outright killing was merely the tip of the iceberg of increased morbidity and mortality. Certain afflictions were directly caused by the coup; others were the result of an interruption in medical and social services. The coup brought immediate increases in rates of interpersonal violence, ranging from rape and torture to arson. It also brought massive dislocations: hundreds of thousands of refugees fled their homes, some by sea and some by land.[47] The number of lives lost at sea is unknown; certain U.S. Coast Guard estimates ran into the thousands.[48] Still other deaths ostensibly had more mundane causes, but were nonetheless linked to social unrest. Food shortages were ubiquitous and many medications, such as anti-tuberculous drugs and even vaccines, became unavailable. During the coup, the impression inside Haiti was one of widespread and often dramatic declines in health status. Both PAHO and the WHO issued dire reports, suggesting that millions of Haitians were at risk of adverse health events due to environmental stresses.[49]

No accurate quantitative estimates of the health effects of the coup can be made, since almost no research was conducted during the three years of the coup. Given the absence of major studies, one community's experience may again be instructive. In 1985, the village of Kay became home to a large medical facility, Clinique Bon Sauveur, built to serve the region's poor; we have worked there since the clinic's founding.[50] Despite the fact that this rural clinic was tucked into the hills of Central Haiti, far from urban centers, it was far from immune to the threats that characterized the coup period. At one point, the clinic was forced to close its doors to patients. The region itself, inhabited largely by poor peasants but home to a robust community health project, was regarded by local authorities as strongly supportive of the Aristide government. But, as one clinic employee observed after he and other staff were threatened by the military, "It's not just that we're for Aristide. It's because we serve the poor."

Although clinic employees were unable to continue community-wide surveys or conduct formal research, we were easily able to discern three main types of effects of the coup: effects on community health programs; effects on morale; and effects on patterns of morbidity and mortality—or, at least, on the nature of presenting complaints to the clinic.

First, the coup's effects on local health programs were dramatic. All outreach activities, from AIDS prevention to community-based distribution of contraceptives, were interrupted, as were water protection efforts. Women's literacy projects and community organizing came to a halt. With brief exceptions, the clinic itself remained open, although there was a drop in the number of patients and, as discussed later, an increase in the gravity of presenting complaints.

Second, there was marked demoralization among health-care workers, with several resignations during the years of the coup. There seemed to be a paralysis among all members of the medical staff, a lassitude that could not always be linked to direct constraints on activities. For example, even when it became possible to resume many community-based activities, temporization was often the order of the day. Furnished with a ready supply of excuses, staff meetings were missed or canceled, research projects abandoned, and poor health outcomes shrugged off. This marked lowering of expectations endured well beyond the coup. Indeed, of all of the coup's effects, demoralization may prove the most persistent.

Third, there were the presumed effects of the coup on the health of the population. We use the word "presumed" to avoid making immodest claims of causality, for in order to make causal claims, one would need careful, population-based studies conducted before and after the coup. These, as noted, are unavailable. But in our small clinic in rural Haiti, it seemed as if the patients were sicker and had traveled greater distances to obtain care. Delays in seeking care were popularly attributed to widespread "insecurity," a code word among the poor for their fear of repression. Furthermore, we registered increased rates of certain diseases among patients presenting to the clinic.[51] Like most ambulatory clinics in rural Haiti, the Clinique Bon Sauveur predominantly sees complications of poor nutritional status, including reactivation tuberculosis, and many chronic pathologies, such as arthritis and hypertension. During the coup years, we noted a marked increase in the proportion of patients with measles, tuberculosis, typhoid, and complications of HIV infection. It was during the coup that we treated our first reported rape victims, and the number of assaults increased dramatically.

Measles

The rumor of widespread measles epidemics was certainly confirmed in the region served by the Clinique Bon Sauveur, which saw an unprecedented number of pediatric cases in 1993. This was attributable, of course, to failure to immunize: national vaccine coverage, poor at the outset, dropped from 40 percent to 24 percent during the coup years. In the northeast region, coverage plummeted from 75 percent to 17 percent. In Port-au-Prince, coverage in 1991 was 7 percent; in 1992, it was 4 percent. Despite efforts of UNICEF and WHO/PAHO to carry out vaccination campaigns during the lost years, only an estimated 30 percent coverage could be achieved in 1993, which was the level for 1990-91.[52] As we shall see, failure to vaccinate was in turn attributed to a variety of events and processes. The gravity of the resulting 1993 epidemic was clearly heightened by the marginal nutritional status of the region's children.[53]

Tuberculosis

The Clinique Bon Sauveur has always treated a large number of tuberculosis patients. In 1990, when almost 33,000 patients were seen, 448 tuberculosis cases were diagnosed. (Note that this figure includes new diagnoses only; the clinic had more than 2,000 tuberculosis-related visits in 1990.) In 1993, although little more than half the number of patients were seen as in 1990, the number of new tuberculosis diagnoses—409, to be exact—remained high. Two cases of tuberculous meningitis were registered, the first in several years. What accounts for these trends? HIV played a role, clearly, but not as large a role as is often assumed: in 1990, only 6 percent of our tuberculosis patients were seropositive for HIV.[54] With the massive movement of young people from urban slums to rural regions as a result of the post-coup repression, the number of co-infected persons likely rose. Still, much of the increase in tuberculosis can be attributed to reactivation disease as regional food supplies dwindled.[55] Furthermore, the rising number of infectious tuberculosis patients no doubt led to increased rates of transmission, as tuberculosis services became harder to obtain. Decreased coverage of BCG vaccination may have led to the return of tuberculous meningitis.

Typhoid

The water supply in the area around the clinic has exceedingly low total coliform counts, and enteric fever was diagnosed exclusively in people reporting to the clinic from elsewhere. It was our general impression that these patients were, again, sicker than in previous years. Delays in seeking care meant that many presented gravely ill or with complications, such as intestinal perforation. As previously mentioned, the coup led directly to an interruption of water-protection efforts in the region.

Sexual Violence

Little is known about rape in Haiti, although there is reason to believe it to be as serious a problem in this country as elsewhere. Politically motivated rapes, however, were not documented prior to 1991.[56] We treated four women who had been raped by soldiers and/or paramilitary "attachés." One sought care after almost three months in hiding; she was later found to be HIV-positive. Although evidence is lacking because she was not examined immediately after the assault, we believe this to be a case of rape-associated HIV transmission.

Assault

Compared with an urban U.S. emergency room, injuries inflicted during assaults have been rare in our clinic. In 1990, the majority of patients who had sustained intentional injuries were peasant farmers with machete wounds inflicted by consociates. These injuries were most often sustained in land disputes; none were fatal and few left permanent disability. In 1993, however, the absolute number of assault-related injuries almost doubled, with a marked shift toward gunshot wounds and injuries inflicted through torture.[57] Many of these were inflicted by soldiers and paramilitary forces; several of the 1993 victims were women (one of them also a victim of rape). One patient was tortured to death by police and soldiers—killed, in essence, by self-appointed officials.[58] For a variety of complex reasons, the perpetrators of many of these crimes remain unpunished.

HIV Infections

A marked increase in the number of cases of HIV disease was registered in our clinic population between 1990 and 1993. Most of these patients had been infected while living in urban Haiti. As noted, the coup of 1991 resulted in massive movements of rural-born people from Port-au-Prince back to their home regions. Because the bulk of state-sponsored violence was targeted at slum areas, such as Cité Soleil, where seroprevalence of HIV was high, it is clear that the urban exodus to low-prevalence rural areas is likely to have increased the incidence of new HIV infections in rural regions.[59]

In addition to this resurgence of diseases and injuries related to social disruption, there were other *sequelae* of the collapse of the public health system, such as it was. Significant outbreaks of anthrax, dengue fever, and meningococcal meningitis were registered elsewhere in Haiti during 1993-94. Fifty cases of meningococcal disease were reported in April 1994, in northeastern Haiti; mortality was high. As fear spread through the population, vaccines and prophylactic medications were sold on the black market, sometimes by physicians, for exorbitant prices.[60] Dengue fever has long been endemic in Haiti: in one study conducted in the 1970s, 43 percent of young children surveyed had antibodies to the etiologic agent.[61] Interestingly, the only time we could confirm our impression of widespread outbreaks of dengue fever was in 1994, when 24 U.S. military personnel stationed in both rural and urban areas became dengue cases. Immediately, rapid surveillance studies were performed, and preventive interventions implemented, for the 20,000 U.S. military personnel.[62]

On Suffering and Claims of Causality

Although population-based studies are unavailable, the trends we observed in the Clinique Bon Sauveur are suggestive, especially when note is made of the paradoxical decrease in the number of visits, attributable, in part, to the clinic's reputation as pro-Aristide (although this same attribute seems to have led to an increase in numbers of patients seeking care for injuries meted out by soldiers). One conclusion is clear: the 1991 coup d'état in Haiti led, directly and indirectly, to increased suffering for the Haitian poor.

Such intense suffering has led to a certain amount of conflicting commentary on the nature of this misery. In public health commentary on Haiti, as noted, there is both consensus and dissensus. Few contest the importance of poverty in determining the distribution of disease. The vast majority of Haiti's excess mortality is due, ultimately, to the country's historical and social conditions, and the poor remain the "sentinel chickens," announcing unwelcome trends in morbidity and mortality.

The dissensus lies elsewhere, in competing claims of causality. As is the case in other Latin American countries, Haiti's more recent increased burden of disease had both distal and proximal causes, with the latter more likely to be downplayed.[63] Take, for example, the well-known "Harvard report" on the effects of economic sanctions on the health of the population.[64] Under the headline "Study Says Haiti Sanctions Kill Up to 1,000 Children a Month," the *New York Times* ostensibly summarized the report in an article published on November 9, 1993, stating that the study "reports that although international attention has focused largely on killings and political terrorism in Haiti since the September 1991 Coup that deposed President Jean-Bertrand Aristide, 'the human toll from the silent tragedy of humanitarian neglect has been far greater than either the violence or human rights abuses.'"[65]

The effects of the Harvard report were far-reaching. Although the study's authors allowed that "the September 1991 Coup is primarily responsible for the subsequent human damage inflicted during the crisis," the report offered both the Haitian military and the U.S. press the option of focusing on a very distal "cause" of increased morbidity and mortality. On November 24, 1993, the *Boston Globe* announced that the report "has contributed to the Clinton administration's reluctance to impose further sanctions on the Caribbean nation to restore democracy."[66] Thus was it possible to elevate these sanctions—which many observers noted to be half-hearted—from effect to cause.

Responsible analyses of shifting trends in morbidity and mortality will reveal the mechanisms by which large-scale social forces come to have their effects among poor and vulnerable populations. Claims of causality are important as we face future decisions regarding health care for poor people, including plans currently under consideration in Haiti and in many other countries.

NEOLIBERAL ECONOMICS
AND THE HEALTH OF THE HAITIAN POOR

> "I don't know what is meant by 'structural adjustment,' but it sounds to me like even less for poor people. How could we possibly live on less? If privatization goes forward, they might as well just dig a big pit and shove us all into it."
>
> Peasant farmer from Kay, June 1996

Many of the people living in the Kay region view their recent history as marked by two adverse events: the building of the dam, and the coup d'état of 1991. As is clear from recent commentaries, these events are seen as related; they are also seen as consonant with the long suffering of the Haitian people. Further, both are perceived as enmeshed in "the American Plan," and both are held to be the precursors of the current SAP now underway. But it's clear from radio broadcasts, and also from the written record, that these comments are not specific to the Kay region. According to one recent overview, popular organizations are "united in their rejections of SAPs in general and privatization in particular." The report continues:

> Haitians see the coup which cut short Aristide's populist reforms and sent him into exile as part of the process of integrating Haiti into the new world economic order. 'The wealthy countries took advantage of the coup in order to advance their plan to destroy the peasant economy, to push forward their neoliberal economic model,' Haiti's largest peasant organization, MPP [Mouvman Peyizan Papay], said recently. 'They linked the return of democracy with the plan to auction off the country and its people.'[67]

Prior to the 1991 coup, Aristide pushed for a number of reforms that were directly contrary to the primary goals of SAPs instituted elsewhere. He pushed for an increase in the minimum wage, and also for bolstering the fragile health and social service safety net. Instead of selling off state-owned enterprises—one of the central tenets of neoliberal reform—Aristide cracked down on the corruption and mismanagement within them. In seven months, most of them went from large deficits to profitability.[68]

The coup changed all that, of course. Not only were the gains of Aristide's tenure reversed, but a number of components of SAPs were "implemented" during the coup years. Similarities between the *de facto* government's *laissez-faire* approach to corruption and contraband and neoliberalism did not go unremarked. Even Aristide's first post-coup prime minister, an ardent backer of SAPs, allowed that "the three years of the coup already performed 60 percent of the structural adjustment."[69] Finally, Aristide's overthrow left him vulnerable to the requisites of the international financial institutions. Most Haitians believe that Aristide was forced to sign onto the prescribed SAP as a precondition for his return.[70]

With little room to maneuver, Aristide was pushed to make concessions to the international power brokers who helped to frame policy in Haiti. There was remarkably little opposition to these concessions in the Haitian diaspora, even after the familiar outlines of "the American Plan" drifted into public view. It appeared that the largest concessions were made in a series of agreements brokered in Paris in August 1994. The World Bank and the IMF advanced an "economic recovery plan" that bore the marks of a SAP—namely, the cutting of government bureaucracies and public programs, the privatization of publicly owned utilities and industries, the promotion of exports, and an "open-investment policy" that would slash tariffs and eliminate any import restrictions that might trammel investors, especially those of the foreign variety. "Aristide Banks on Austerity," wrote Allan Nairn in the *Multinational Monitor*:

> Axel Peuker, a World Bank desk officer, says Aristide's advisers 'did consult with relevant donors' as the plan was being written, and the final product was 'well received.' He added that 'there is this tension between the public image of Aristide' and the 'rather conservative approach, financial and otherwise' adopted by his Ministers when his government was still in Haiti. Peuker noted that the new plan 'goes a step further in this direction.'[71]

Aristide's economic advisors included Leslie Delatour, the Chicago-inspired economist who had been one of the chief cheerleaders for the export-led assembly sector under Jean-Claude Duvalier. Delatour also served briefly as commerce minister under the first post-Duvalier junta, but was forced out of office by popular demonstrations against his policies. Little wonder, then, that the plan elaborated in Paris looked very much like the standard SAP favored by the World Bank, the IMF, and the governments of Japan, Korea, various European countries, and the United States—which each sent delegations to the meetings held to decide Haiti's fate. Aristide's 1991 plan to raise the minimum daily factory wage from about $2 to $4 was, according to Peuker, a "non-issue"—not up for consideration.

These policies were widely contested in Haiti when first proposed in the 1980s, and were of course contested again in 1994. One current cabinet member recently likened the imposition of structural adjustment in Haiti to "undergoing major surgery without anesthesia."[72] World Bank representatives were a bit resentful of criticism, insisting that the plan "is not going to hurt the poor to the extent that it had in other countries."[73] Why not? The Haitian poor, observed the Bank's Haiti desk officer, have so much less to lose.

The notion of a *quid pro quo* between Aristide and the international financial institutions (and the United States, to which the institutions are closely linked) had wide currency inside and outside of Haiti. There could be little doubt about the dominant ideology of the cabinet selected after Aristide's October 1995 return to Haiti. "Aristide Chooses a Premier Who Has Free-Market Ideas," ran the headline of a *New York Times* article reporting that "businessmen have been clamoring for a Prime Minister able to oversee a new economic plan acceptable to the World Bank, the International Monetary Fund and top business leaders here."[74] They got their man in Smarck Michel, described by the *Times* as "pragmatic, pro-market." *Haïti-Progrès* put a more Haitian spin on the appointment, giving it the banner headline, "Smarck Michel chargé d'appliquer le plan américain."[75]

These developments, although certainly an improvement over the bloodletting of the preceding three years, alarmed many of those most committed to democracy in Haiti. At the heart of the struggle has been the privatization of state-owned enterprises, felt to signal the return of the American Plan. Haitian-American scholar Patrick Bellegarde-Smith, speaking of the Paris agreements, complained that "the Haitian delegation to the World Bank signed away the economic independence of the country."[76] But Aristide spoke of a two-step process. Step one, the August Paris meeting, was "simply a work meeting. No agreements were signed." As for *quid pro quos*, they were Aristide's: he had attached six conditions, ranging from land reform to increased social services for employees of the enterprises in question, to plans for privatization. According to Aristide:

> These conditions were included in the Paris meetings because I insisted on it. Some members of the Haitian team were not in agreement, but I insisted that these conditions be built into the question of privatization….I had insisted to the point of having [the conditions] placed as appendices to the [documents elaborated in] the first meeting. The second step was to be taken upon my return. Smarck Michel was to return to Paris in January 1995. But from the beginning there was trouble about the six conditions. When they returned to Paris, it was still a work document; nothing had been signed….When later that year there was so much debate, I distributed this document to popular organizations. See? No signatures, I said. I plan to keep my word. If all these conditions can be met, I'm for it. If they can't keep these conditions, I said, privatization won't happen under my watch.[77]

Aristide did keep his word, stalling the privatization process because the six conditions were not being met. Smarck Michel, frustrated by Aristide's refusal to back privatization, resigned. He was replaced by Claudette Werleigh, who agreed wholeheartedly with Aristide's conditions. In retaliation, the international financial institutions—the World Bank, the IMF, and USAID—withheld approximately half of the $300 million in aid already committed to the Haitian reconstruction. Their tactics were not subtle, as the comments of the very man assigned to the task of overseeing privatization might suggest: "The international balance of forces is against us. The [Haitian] government is being forced to negotiate with a knife at its throat and its back against the wall."[78]

In effect, however, privatization did *not* occur under Aristide's watch. And this is one of the reasons that he remains so popular and would be re-elected by a comfortable margin were elections to be held today. His opposition to privatization without conditions is merely an accurate reflection of popular will. Implementation of current privatization schemes is likely to adversely affect the poor, at least in the short run. Selling off state-owned utilities, adding more user fees to publicly funded health and educational services—these actions will affect the poor directly, decreasing their access, already minimal, to clean water, to medical services, and to schooling. The push for increased efficacy through privatization may well work, but it will be efficacy at the expense of equity: improved services will be available to those who can pay.

The effects of structural adjustment on health care have been muted, it is true, by the failure of the Haitian state to provide health care. That is, the abolition of a grossly inadequate public health infrastructure would be expected to have fewer effects than the dismantling of an effective one. But it is clear that many Haitians—again, the poor majority—would prefer some legally mandated commitment to the destitute sick. Services that function more efficiently—that is, turn a profit—but have no stated commitment to the Haitian poor are not regarded as intrinsically valuable by the poor majority.

The comments of a patient who receives care at our clinic, a young woman with tuberculosis, are typical of this sort of commentary. Allowing that most goods and services in the public sector were, in effect, already beyond the reach of the poor, she nonetheless had nothing but bad things to say about privatization. "Now they won't even have to pretend they owe something to the poor," she said. "Everything's for sale. We can't buy it, and that's why we're sick all the time."[79] In other words, as bad as public services have been, they were underpinned by at least a stated commitment to the poor. No such assurances are proffered by the architects of privatization.

CONCLUSIONS: HYPOCRISIES OF DEVELOPMENT AND THE HEALTH OF THE HAITIAN POOR

What conclusions might reasonably be drawn after such a dreary review? Our essay tries to explore the long-term impact of a series of economic policies on the health not of the Haitian economy, but rather of its poorest citizens. This, it must be noted, is an altogether different exercise from those conducted by economists or policy experts attempting to gauge the success or failure of a given policy. We do not presume to deliver a verdict on the intrinsic merits of the policies often termed "health-sector reform." Nor do we assume that the introduction of user fees is intrinsically a bad idea. It is not our job, here, to offer a *post mortem* on structural adjustment and its underpinning ideologies. But it *is* our job to underline the noxious impact of many of these policies on the health of the poorest sector of a given population. In other words, ours is not a Luddite view—we have no quarrel with genuine development, and our clinic relies on quite modern technologies; we simply make an attempt to discern the effects of such policies on the group of people with whom we are most concerned.

This chapter, grounded in the experience of one beleaguered community, attempts to make three points we believe can be generalized. First, the neoliberal policies of the international financial institutions and their donors will likely have an adverse impact on the health of the poorest Haitians. Second, it is possible to trace the historical continuity of a broad variety of ostensibly disparate economic policies. These policies and processes determine, to a very large extent, patterns of morbidity and mortality among the very poor. Which leads to the third point: a broader view of public health—a geographically broad and historically deep view—is necessary if we are to understand the true nature of inferior health outcomes among the poor. Let us take each of these points in turn.

1. Neoliberal Policies and Ill Health Among the Poor: Cause and Effect

In Haiti, many of the policies endorsed by international financial institutions may be expected to have an adverse impact, at least in the short term, on the health of the poor. And the short term is, often enough, all that is left to Haiti's poor. There may well be some settings—Bolivia has often been cited as an example—where "privatization" has had a positive outcome for the majority. But we're not interested, in this chapter, in "the majority." We're interested in the most vulnerable subset of the population, who happen to be our patients. In several sub-Saharan African countries, the institution of SAPs has been associated with sharp downward turns in the health of this group.[80]

We discern several mechanisms, some direct and some indirect, through which these policies will adversely affect the health of our own patients. Direct mechanisms include decreased funding for social services, the introduction of more user fees, and decreased tariffs on the foodstuffs grown by the poor. Indirect mechanisms include all those that weaken the Haitian economy and promote social inequality.

Perhaps one of the most far-reaching and detrimental consequences of SAPs for the poor has been the lowering of trade barriers. Countries maintain tariffs on imports in order to protect domestic products and local production from the corrosive effects of cheaper imports. Certain conditions placed on SAP loans, such as the lowering of import taxes on food, may lead eventually to lower food prices. In the short term, however, these conditions worsen the plight of small-scale rural farmers who cannot compete in a global market. Surely it's ironic that Haiti, once the source of most of Europe's tropical produce, is becoming ever more dependent on foreign food. Food now accounts for 47 percent of Haiti's total imports, the highest percentile in the western hemisphere.[81] The UNDP estimated Haiti's food imports at 24 percent in 1980, but fully 77 percent in 1994. In a related trend, food as a percent of exports fell from 52 percent in 1970 to 13 percent in 1990.[82]

The effects on local food production of slashing import tariffs are clear enough. But why on earth would the rural poor in Haiti care about the privatization of industries that have never served their interests? Privatizing money-losing industries can benefit the poor wherever they are called upon, through indirect taxes, say, to subsidize such industries. This was the claim of pro-privatization prime minister Smarck Michel, who in 1995 argued that privatization will have little effect on services, because the government "doesn't do anything for anybody."[83] But recall that Aristide was able to turn a profit from state-owned industries during his brief tenure in 1991, and that he had promised to make the Haitian poor "shareholders" (*actionnaires*) in these enterprises.

The sale of the public cement and flour mills affords a clear example of selling future potential for immediate liquidity. In 1993, in the middle of the "lost years" of the coup, Ciment d'Haiti was shut down. Although it had been possible, in 1995, to delay the sale of the industry during Aristide's tenure, an equity share (65 percent) was sold for $15.6 million in December 1997, to a consortium led by companies based in Switzerland and Colombia. The Minoterie d'Haiti (the public flour mills), similarly, was sold to a U.S.-led consortium in September 1997 for $9 million. President Préval had estimated that it would cost $20 million to restart flour production.

Although these industries had not in the past served the interests of the Haitian poor—"We eat cassava, not bread," goes the refrain, "We can't afford bread"—there is little doubt that the collection of state revenues is undermined through privatization. In this manner, resources and power are shifted away from the citizenry and further concentrated in the hands of an elite (and often offshore) minority. A union leader, speaking to President Aristide in 1995, made the following argument: "To privatize the cement works along with all the other targeted enterprises is to say that we completely withdraw all economic power from the state and give it to a private sector which is against the people....All we have to do is turn the country over to the bourgeoisie so that they can do with it whatever they wish."[84]

In the eyes of many Haitians, privatization in the interests of private profit undermines the possibility of more equitable distribution of goods and services. Aid is now stalled—the World Bank estimates that $2 billion allotted for Haiti in 1998 has not been distributed—as Haiti's Congress endlessly debates the approval of a prime minister and the question of privatization. The "anti-neoliberal bloc," a small group of politicians standing against, arguably, the most powerful financial forces that have ever existed, will not hold out for long. The small group debating these changes, no matter how well intentioned, does not lack the food, health care, and other basic services that are at stake. Despite broad public resistance to privatization and other policies, structural adjustment is likely to go forward.

2. A Continuity of Structural Forces

The neoliberal policies now being foisted on Haiti have their echo in a long line of previous misadventures. It is unwise to leave unnamed the paradigmatic, forced economic policy—*slavery*—since it serves, to this day, as a template for many Haitian responses to any economic plan that promises entrenched inequality. Regardless of our thoughts on the matter, many Haitians have made clear their views on the near forced labor of post-independence plantations (deserted, more or less, for tiny hillside plots); on the agribusiness and road crews of the U.S. occupation (met with an armed uprising that went on for years); and on the more recent rise of the offshore assembly trade that has blossomed in tandem with an end to tariffs designed to protect local agriculture (stigmatized as "the American Plan").

Each of the eras comprising these activities is of course different; their policies, markedly so. Why, then, are Haitians so quick to tar them with the same brush? The terms "structural adjustment" and "privatization" are, as we have learned, used interchangeably by many Haitians; "the American Plan" has become another gloss. The reason for this apparent conflation is clear enough: from the slave plantations of Saint-Domingue to the loss of public revenue through the sale of state-owned industries, decisions taken by the powerful directly affect the fates of the poor. In fact, fluctuations in the health status of the poor are among the most sensitive indices of harmful policies. In this manner, the economically oppressed continue to serve as the "sentinel chickens" or "mine shaft canaries" of the global economy.

Our own failure to discern this continuity stems from an underestimation of the imagination of the people who brought us the successful revolution of 1804. When half of the population of Saint-Domingue perished in the Haitian revolution, it was in pursuit of ideals—liberty, fraternity, and above all, equality—much discussed but unrealized elsewhere. So it is today. The rural poor have never had electricity or telephones, but they knew that it was the intention of the country's first democratically elected government to extend such services more broadly. More to the point, poor Haitians also knew that the Aristide government planned to use profits from state-owned companies to fund desperately needed social services, including health and education. Thus selling off state assets—as a condition for receipt of the much discussed "international rescue package"—contributes to the state desertion of the social sector, unless a firm set of guarantees are put in place to keep the poor as shareholders in these industries. It was precisely this point to which Aristide clung during the so-called "intransigent phase" of his presidency, when he blocked approval of the structural adjustment package because he felt that the IMF was not keeping up its end of the bargain.

3. A Broader View of "Public Health"

If the previous arguments are true, then it is easy to assert that social forces—that is, historically given economic and cultural forces—determine, to a large extent, the health of the Haitian people. Mind you, most Haitian physicians and nurses know this; certainly, their poorer patients do. But long convinced that such matters are beyond the purview of health education, very few of us are schooled in a way that might allow us to contest the "immodest claims of causality" staked by the policy-makers.

Take physicians. We study vitamin deficiencies, but not land reform. We elaborate protocols to improve standards of care, but rarely discuss equity of access to excellent care—and almost never discuss privatization and "user fees," to say nothing of SAPs. We learn about pathophysiology, but never the embodiment of the social forces that set in motion a series of events leading, ultimately, to a critical somatic process—hemoptysis due to tuberculosis, say, or the ravaging of the distal small intestine by the bacterium that causes typhoid. And yet most physicians would concede that hunger and a lack of potable water are the root causes of these two diseases.

We are only now beginning to understand the mechanisms by which social inequality is in and of itself pathogenic. Haiti offers a series of lessons for the sort of social medicine that could offer both analysis of and remedy for at least some of the ills documented here.

One of Haiti's lessons for social medicine is that social conditions will to a large extent determine patterns of morbidity and mortality, and that the strength of this association is amplified as conditions worsen. That is, the health *sequelae* of structural violence are most severe among the poor. Unfortunately, epidemiology and public health are increasingly uninterested in such broad analyses, a trend recently bemoaned by McMichael, a British epidemiologist: "Epidemiology...assigns a primary importance to studying inter-individual variations in risk. By concentrating on these specific and presumed free-range individual behaviors, we thereby pay less attention to the underlying social-historical influences on behavioral choices, patterns, and population health."[85]

A second and corollary lesson concerns the problem of using the nation-state as the primary unit of analysis in international and public health discourse. This universally accepted approach tends to obscure three kinds of inequality. First, intranational class differentials are obscured by aggregate data of this nature, because the fact that subpopulations exist within countries—as economic classes—most often is obscured. Wealthy Haitians have health indices very similar to their North American counterparts; this was true before and during the coup. Further, intranational differences according to gender and "race"/ethnicity—themselves tightly connected to class—are also important for understanding health outcomes; yet these are also obscured by aggregate data. McCord and Freeman, physicians in a Harlem hospital, have demonstrated, for example, that age-specific mortality rates are in some age groups higher for Harlem than for Bangladesh.[86] Finally, national data suggest that nations are discrete entities, obscuring the transnational links so necessary to local epidemics of, say, AIDS and political violence. For example, when one of our patients was tortured to death, we attempted to trace the chain of command. It led directly back to U.S. foreign policy: those individuals who had tortured our patient, or ordered him to be tortured, were trained, clothed, and funded by U.S. military aid. Thus, this "sudden increase in village-level mortality" was not to be understood without a systemic analysis that included the recognition and analysis of international economic and political ties that were and remain not independent of the health status of the poor.[87]

A third lesson concerns the potential power of medical and public health interventions. Ideally, of course, the diseases we see in our clinic will be prevented by preventing malnutrition, promoting vaccination, and instituting the systematic prevention of fecal contamination of drinking water. Ideally, people will have access to employment that can satisfy their basic needs. Public health specialists, Berggren, Ewbank, and Berggren, have shown how comprehensive and well-conceived primary health-care programs can improve the health of large populations.[88] But in the interim, low-cost medical services need to be made available to the victims of structural violence. More precisely, in the current situation, the very persons most at risk for these diseases are those who cannot afford to pay for *any* health services. Thus are the poor placed at greater risk for infectious disease and then denied access to care. That this is clear to the Haitian poor is suggested by strong popular resistance to, and critique of, privatization within an economic development program that undermines the state's capacity to protect the health and well-being of its citizens.

A final lesson concerns the importance of listening to the victims of "development." Their opinions on these affairs should matter. One of the enduring contributions of anthropology has been its focus on the voices of its informants. In Haiti, this means the voices of the rural poor, cited freely throughout this chapter. Exploring the insights of the people of Kay brings into relief the large-scale social forces that have conspired to make them poor and sick. It has been their contention that their suffering has occurred less by accident, than by design. The designs, they note, are by the powerful—whether Haitian, or foreign.

We have much to learn by listening to the voices of the poor. As examples from Haiti and elsewhere show, when the poor hear about "open markets," they don't think of openness. When they hear about "free markets," they don't think of freedom. When they hear about "liberalization," they don't think of liberty, much less of liberation from want. Instead, these words are perceived, often enough, as merely the latest attempts to cloak the hypocrisies of development.

ACKNOWLEDGMENTS

This chapter has gone through several revisions, and we offer thanks: to Haun Saussy and Keith Joseph, for editing; to Evan Lyon, for substantive and bibliographic help; to Laurie Richardson, who has written some of the most incisive copy on recent developments; to Titid, who has participated in them; to Mildred Trouillot Aristide, who was kind enough to read carefully an earlier version of the manuscript; and to Noam Chomsky, the "secular saint" who inspires so many of us. We offer especially warm thanks to our coworkers at the Clinique Bon Sauveur, particularly the clinicians and the community health workers. Finally, we owe a great debt to this volume's dogged editors: Jim, Alec, John, and—never least—Joyce.

Despite harsh economic conditions and a precarious future, Senegalese children enjoy the moment. (photo by Joyce V. Millen)

Theoretical Therapies, Remote Remedies: SAPs and the Political Ecology of Poverty and Health in Africa[1]

Brooke G. Schoepf, Claude Schoepf, and Joyce V. Millen

Beset by grinding poverty, AIDS, drought, rampant malnutrition, genocide, and war, the world's poorest continent has suffered a quarter century of profound, multiplex crisis. The policies proposed to remedy Africa's ills and the theories upon which they rest are vigorously contested. Neo-classical economists, sometimes dubbed the "Washington Consensus," attribute the region's decline primarily to internal factors, such as misguided policies, mismanagement, and corruption of African governments.[2] Under the sway of Washington Consensus dicta, in the early 1980s the international financial institutions (IFIs) began to impose a series of structural adjustment programs (SAPs)[3] which they claimed would restore health to stagnant African economies.[4] The institutions' neutral-sounding, technical economic calculus actually re-presented policies that had been discredited in the late 1960s and 1970s by extensive scholarly research.[5]

Critical social scientists acknowledged the destructive effects of internal patterns within African countries. They argued, however, that these must not be understood narrowly as the "irrational" policies or individual failings of African leaders. Rather, the destructive effects of policies and practices must be understood in the context of Africa's "chains of history" and the continent's place in the world political economy.[6] The cumulative consequences of the slave trade, violent colonial conquest, and the brutal extraction of natural resources by imperial powers created an enduring legacy of structural imbalances: entrenched asymmetries between Africa and the West, and between rich and poor within Africa.[7] In this perspective, economic recovery depends upon transformation of distorted production and power structures and on reversing Africa's role in the world economy as a supplier of cheap labor and cheap raw materials.

Such critiques, however, were either systematically ignored or dismissed as "ideological" by the Washington Consensus. The claim of neo-classical economists to authoritative wisdom rests upon the power embodied in the conservative alliances that won elections in the United States and Western Europe in 1980. This political shift de-legitimated social welfare and undermined policies designed to meet the basic needs of poor people. In the aftermath, the IFIs imposed SAPs on 42 governments in sub-Saharan Africa in the 1980s and 1990s as a condition for new loans.[8]

This chapter examines the health consequences of SAPs. We present evidence to show that after two decades, more Africans are poorer and less healthy than at the beginning of the SAP era. The growth that *did* occur failed to "trickle down" to ordinary people. Not only have SAPs failed to remedy the deep causes of Africa's crises; they have visited the brunt of austerity measures on the most vulnerable and powerless people.[9] We explore how and why this has happened.

Countrywide health data are lacking for some African countries, and are inaccurate for others.[10] Accordingly, we supplement findings of epidemiological studies with personal narratives collected in our field research.[11] Together, these provide a vivid sense of how SAPs have worked in African contexts to undermine the health of the poor.

Our first narrative, the story of Nsanga, a poor woman struggling to survive in Kinshasa, capital of the Democratic Republic of Congo (DRC, called Zaire from 1971 to 1996), illustrates relations between power (or powerlessness), poverty, and disease. Disease epidemics result from social processes; the spread of infection is propelled by history, political economy, and culture.[12] The HIV disease and AIDS strike with particular severity in poor African communities that are struggling under the burdens of continentwide economic crises and two decades of SAPs.[13] Following Nsanga's story, we review historical studies and then integrate historical perspectives into our analysis of current political and economic configurations. We seek to achieve a broad understanding of SAPs and their consequences, especially their impact on the health of the rural and urban poor, the majority of whom are women.

Nsanga's Story: A Survival Strategy Gone Awry

In 1987 Nsanga was 26 years old and very poor. She and her two children, a bright and mischievous eight-year-old boy and a loquacious five-year-old girl, lived in a sparsely furnished room, one of eight such rooms grouped around a communal courtyard. The families living in the compound shared a water tap, a latrine, and a roofless bathing stall. The electric company had disconnected the hookup because the landlord failed to pay the bill for six months. The women cooked on charcoal braziers made by local artisans. When money for charcoal ran out, they reverted to the village method, setting their pots on three stones over fires of scrap wood and cardboard scavenged by the children.

Sanitation in most of Kinshasa was dilapidated or absent. Nsanga and her friends knew their neighborhood was unhealthy. Waste ran into open drains. Flies, cockroaches, and mosquitoes were ubiquitous. In the dry season, dust containing fecal matter blew about and settled on water containers and food. In the rainy season, latrines sometimes overflowed into the courtyards. Malaria, gastrointestinal disorders, malnutrition, and persistent coughs were common. Many mothers without money for adequate food or medicine had lost at least one young child to illness. A number of Nsanga's neighbors delivered their babies at home because they could not pay maternity fees.[14]

Nsanga hadn't always been the head of her household. She grew up in a village and married Lelo, a schoolteacher, when she was 18. She joined him in Kinshasa, where even on his meager salary, and despite galloping inflation, Nsanga managed to feed her family two meals a day. But soon their lives began to change.

In 1983, the international financial institutions, IFIs, instituted a series of "economic recovery" measures designed to reduce Zaire's public expenditures so that its corrupt government, which had borrowed heavily in the 1970s, could make payments on its foreign debt. The government removed price controls and sharply cut social service budgets, raising user fees for health services and education.[15] In 1984, as an additional way to cut expenses, it fired more than 80,000 teachers and health workers, further reducing poor people's access to education and health care.[16] Without a powerful patron to intercede for him, Lelo lost his job. The family lost his income, health insurance, and the subsidized rice allotted to government employees.

After six fruitless months waiting in offices in an attempt to obtain another position, Lelo's morale fell. He began to drink, selling off household goods to pay for beer and then for lutuku, a cheap but potent home-distilled alcohol. Nsanga berated him for wasting money; their relationship deteriorated. Often drunk and despondent, Lelo beat his wife and son.[17]

Nsanga tried many things to earn money. Like most poor women in Kinshasa, she had had only a few years of formal schooling. She lacked well-connected friends and family who could help her find a job cleaning offices. Forced into the "informal" economic sector, Nsanga prepared meals for the men who worked in her neighborhood. She also sold food such as dried fish when she could walk several miles across town to obtain such items cheaply. Meanwhile, prices rose with currency devaluation, unemployment mounted, and real wages fell sharply. Even men still working had little money to spend, and many skipped the noon meal. Week by week, Nsanga had fewer customers. She also faced heightened competition from other women attempting to sell similar goods. Her best efforts at petty trade brought in only pennies at a time. She grew vegetables in a vacant lot, but soldiers stole her crop. Nsanga was forced to find another way to provide money for food and rent.

One day early in 1986, after walking the downtown streets selling mangoes, Nsanga returned home to discover that Lelo had left. Stunned, because she had performed the duties of a "good, faithful wife," Nsanga rationalized Lelo's abandonment: "Good riddance! At least he won't beat me any more, and besides, now there is one less mouth to feed."

When Nsanga's children ate the food she had intended to sell, she went into debt to the landlord. She begged her elder brother for a loan, but he had a large family and no savings to lend despite his steady job on the docks. Wage freezes and sharply rising prices made it difficult for workers to stretch their incomes to the end of the month. Insulted by her brother's failure to "understand" and to help her, Nsanga ceased visiting his family. The breach of relations with her only relative in the city left her alone and vulnerable. Asked why she did not return to her parents' village, Nsanga responded:

> That's unthinkable! My relatives there are old and very poor; they barely scrape by. They would expect gifts from the city, but they would not be able to help me clear land and build us a house. Where would I get food for the children to tide us over until next year's harvest? Go to the village? Impossible! Something might happen to my children....

Desperate for cash, and without money to start a business, exchanging sex for subsistence appeared to be Nsanga's only recourse. In the first year of this new strategy Nsanga thought she was lucky. She became the second (unrecognized) wife of a government official, who paid her rent and provided regular support.[18] She also had occasional "spare tires" to buy *medicine when one of her children became sick. But then she got pregnant. Shortly thereafter, this "husband" told her his salary could not stretch farther, and he, too, left.[19]*

Nsanga had to take on more sexual partners. The rate for a "quickie" in her poor neighborhood was less than 50¢. On a good day she might find two or three partners. By comparison, the average salary for a hospital nurse at the time was about $30 per month. Nsanga and her children lived precariously, sometimes on the very edge of survival.

In mid-1987, the government and media began to acknowledge publicly the threat of AIDS. A leaflet warned men against visiting prostitutes. Most of Nsanga's clients, however, were neighborhood men who came to her each month. As her friends or "husbands," they did not label her a prostitute. Nor was Nsanga stigmatized as a "bad woman." On the contrary, as a mother fallen on hard times through no fault of her own, neighbors admired her for trying her best to "break stones" (kobeta libanga) in order to meet family obligations.[20] In the presence of HIV, however, this survival strategy had become a death strategy.[21]

In 1989, Nsanga grew very thin. She believed that people whispered about her. Indeed, neighbors were sure that she had AIDS. "But then," Nsanga reasoned, "people say this about everyone who loses weight, even when it is just from hunger and worry. All these people who are dying nowadays, are they really all dying from AIDS?"[22]

Nsanga died in 1991.[23] While her neighbors believed that she had been infected in the course of her "sex work," the time frame casts doubt on this assumption. Until the end of 1986, Nsanga had had sex with only one partner: her husband. Thus, given the long incubation period between infection with HIV and manifestation of symptoms, Nsanga's husband was more likely the source of her infection.

Many married women were disarmed by public health advice that assured people that marital fidelity would protect them from AIDS. However, most married women throughout Africa infected with HIV acquired the disease from husbands who had multiple sex partners and failed to use condom protection.[24] Nevertheless, when men fall sick, their wives are often blamed.

Nsanga's story is significant not only because it records the courageous struggle and premature death of a unique human being, but also because it mirrors conditions of life and death for millions in Africa today. Dying obscurely in a Kinshasa courtyard, Nsanga may not seem like a "historical" figure. Yet her personal tragedy embodies that of Africa, with its legacy of systematic structural and corporeal violence.

The SAP policies that played such a crucial role in Nsanga's destiny do not break with the logic of colonial exploitation. Instead, they perpetuate many of colonialism's destructive features. To understand the political and economic patterns that bring suffering and death to people like Nsanga, we must gain a sense of the background from which these patterns emerge.

COLONIALISM, VIOLENCE, AND HEALTH[25]

Conquest and Colonial Rule

African history has been decisively shaped by the colonial ambitions of the industrialized powers of Europe and the United States. In 1885, the western European nations carved up Africa, often creating artificial boundaries that divided peoples of the same cultures and kingdoms into subjects of different colonial states. For more than two decades Africans resisted conquest, but the superior military technology of the imperial powers prevailed. In some places entire peoples were wiped out by armed violence and "scorched earth" policies, or by famine when driven from their homes.[26] In the early 1890s, rinderpest, a virulent infectious disease of cattle, killed 95 percent of the cattle herds of East and Southern Africa.[27] Milk and meat disappeared from the diet; grazing land reverted to bush that provided a habitat for tsetse flies. A deadly sleeping sickness epidemic followed.[28] Increased contact with Europeans, army movements, and widespread population displacement introduced new human diseases (and new strains of old diseases) that caused severe epidemics in populations unprotected by immunity. Tremendous social disruption resulted.[29]

Colonization of Africa took place during the heyday of Western monopoly capitalism and emergent dominance of the institutions of finance capital.[30] Extensive tracts of land were expropriated to establish plantations and mines. Colonial states conceded vast monopoly production zones and trading territories to large European and American corporations. Many firms were multinationals, some with interlocking directorates that extended over wide areas.[31] State and company administrators used violence to commandeer low-cost African labor. African raw materials and crops fueled European industrial development, while little of the profit was re-invested in Africa.[32] In some areas, officials requisitioned peasants' crops or forced them to collect forest products.[33] Men in "labor reserve" areas distant from European work sites were conscripted as porters, migrant laborers, and soldiers.[34] Roads and railways needed to evacuate exports were built at great cost to African lives.[35] When paid, wages were extremely low, and living conditions unhealthy and dangerous.[36] Overworked and underfed, African workers suffered high death rates. Fatal work-related accidents were common, especially among underground miners.[37]

As young men were forced to leave their homes, women's work burdens greatly increased, while their social position and autonomy declined.[38] Elder men who remained in rural villages might marry several young women, who, with their children, were put to wielding the hoe.[39] Women in many places protested increased workloads, often by escaping to towns.[40] As planting cycles were disrupted and agriculture suffered from a lack of labor, African food production declined in many areas.[41]

Widespread hunger and periodic famines ensued, rendering populations susceptible to epidemic outbreaks of infectious disease. Colonial responses to disease often involved coercive measures, such as forced removal of populations.[42] In 1918-19 military conscripts returning to their villages brought the influenza pandemic.[43] The movement of soldiers and migrant laborers over large land areas led to the spread of sexually transmitted diseases (STDs), which lowered fertility.[44] While earlier Western writers depicted Africa as rife with disease from time immemorial, in fact the "unhealthiest period in all African history was undoubtedly between 1890 and 1930,"[45] the era of colonialists' primary capital accumulation.[46] In some areas, population declined until the end of World War II.[47]

The economic growth generated during this period mainly benefited colonial states and the European-owned plantations, mines, and trading firms.[48] Because colonial sovereignty required total subjugation through overwhelming force, no political space remained for "civil society."[49] Colonial social relations enshrined a racist hierarchy rooted in discourses of biological supremacy, with whites on top. Africans' taxes and export produce paid for continuation of the colonial endeavor on the continent, but brought few of the benefits usually granted a tax-paying citizenry.[50] When colonial governments introduced health services, they did so first to protect European agents, then to maintain those Africans directly useful to the regime, such as soldiers and overseers.[51]

Rigid "color bars," supported by a public culture of exclusionism, operated in every area of life. African workers were paid below-subsistence wages, while skilled jobs were monopolized by whites. In many cities, Africans' houses (mainly crowded shacks) remained segregated from the low-density European settlements.[52] Racism kept most Africans who obtained primary education from advancing to upper secondary schools and universities.[53] Those who did succeed were barred from higher levels of the civil service. Thus, much of Africa was deprived of critical technical and policy-making skills, and deprived of models of democratic governance, both of which would be needed upon achieving political independence.[54]

Following World War II, trade union activity and the "rural radicalism" of poor peasants increased.[55] International pressures led western European governments to open limited political space to the colonized.[56] African war veterans, miners, and railway and civil service unions agitated for a family wage and social security, then, along with educated elites and peasants, demanded independence.[57] Bent on using African raw materials to rebuild war-torn Europe, the colonial powers attempted to deflect popular demands. In the final phase of colonial rule, colonial states implemented limited reforms with "development" and welfare goals.[58] Peasants' forced labor and crop-planting quotas eased, nutrition improved, and limited biomedical health services were extended to rural areas. The new African elites obtained special status, and better-off peasants received improved agricultural services. Not yet resigned to African independence, colonial rulers sought to create a co-opted middle stratum uninterested in political independence.[59] The majority of poor Africans, however, still lacked access to primary education and health care.[60]

In sum, colonial rule came later in Africa than elsewhere. It coincided with the era of finance capitalism and multinational monopolies. Although differences existed in strategies of rule, all colonizing powers used their superior weaponry and military force to extract local resources and exploit African labor. Foreign business ventures concentrated on mines, plantations, and export-import trade. The companies, owned by white settlers and colonial states, blocked accumulation by Africans, who also were denied political and legal rights.[61] Autocratic states created a culture of systematic violence and humiliation,[62] crafting "a set of policies and a texture of relationship with subject peoples portending the difficulties…that beset African societies today."[63]

Early Independence

Most of sub-Saharan Africa won independence in the 1960s; it was the last region of the world to do so. The continent's independence is regarded by many as an achievement "of epochal dimensions."[64] Yet two closely related sets of problems were to shape Africa's future. One was political—the state and class structures broached in the preceding section—the other economic.

African governments were left dependent upon revenue generated from the export of a limited number of raw materials. Commodity prices on the world market, however, routinely encounter "boom-and-bust" cycles, over which African states have no control. During the 1960s and 1970s, many African leaders therefore sought to diversify their economies and alter their countries' place in the international economy.[65] They increased processing of domestic raw materials, created import substitution industries (ISIs) to reduce imports of manufactured goods,[66] and taxed foreign-owned businesses to provide resources for development.[67]

Most African governments also sought to meet popular expectations of expanded access to jobs, education, health care, and other services. Urban middle class constituents were favored, and urban hospitals absorbed the largest share of health budgets. In some countries, many rural people also benefited; expanded services and increased food production led to lower child death rates and gains in life expectancy. Still, most rural poor had little or no access to modern preventive and primary health care.[68] Lacking a sufficient domestic revenue base to sustain outlays for human services and development, African governments resorted to borrowing money from abroad. Private commercial banks were eager to lend, especially because lenders' home-country governments guaranteed their loans.

But whether African governments chose statism and nationalization of foreign firms or "liberalism" and "Africanization" of management, independence failed to alter European economic domination.[69] Multinational firms extracted profitable concessions from fledgling African governments and continued to repatriate their profits, leaving relatively little surplus capital for national investment.[70]

The hopeful nationalist project in newly independent African states was of short duration. As many leaders became removed from the struggles of their people, they became increasingly dependent on the "metropolitan powers," as the imperialist states are often called.[71] Foreign debt rose rapidly in the 1960s as loans funded infrastructure development. Huge sums were expended on unproductive "white elephant" prestige projects.[72] Few of the funds disbursed in loans went to poor Africans, or to programs that would have ameliorated their plight: as much as 80 percent of loan funds are estimated to have remained in the hands of Western suppliers of capital goods, management, and technical assistance.[73]

Political patterns in the newly independent countries were deeply impacted by these economic factors. Members of African countries' new "political class" had an interest in creating their own economic resource base; with most of the economy in foreign hands, their road to wealth was the state. Many individuals privatized public resources by manipulating licenses, foreign exchange, land acquisition, credit, and scarce commodities for their own enrichment.[74] Much of their ill-gotten wealth went to foreign banks and tax shelters.[75] Representatives from the World Bank and other members of the international financial community, critical of corruption in Africa, failed to acknowledge their own complicity; the loans they disbursed fueled the misuse of funds by wealthy elites, thereby creating debts that poor Africans must now repay.[76]

Widening disparities in wealth and failure to meet popular expectations for a better life brought political dissent and popular rebellions.[77] As governments were threatened with loss of control, authoritarian bureaucracy and "clientelism" won out over declarations of populist and socialist intent.[78] Often, competing elites mobilized mass ethnic constituencies to support their claims to power.[79] In some countries populist leaders and peasants sought a "second independence" through civil war.[80] As the colonizers before them had done, newly independent central governments met rebellions with force rather than negotiation. Military coups, sometimes aided by Western troops, became common.[81]

Where governments maintained control, peasants increased production for market. Many countries saw modest growth during the period; a few, such as Côte d'Ivoire, were considered growth "miracles," without regard for the inequalities engendered.[82] Relatively high rates of growth, however, failed to "trickle down" to the poor, as governments held down wages and social spending. Instead, resources generated by peasants and laborers were "sucked up" by local and foreign capitalists, and drained into the world economy. Studies conducted during early independence linked life in local communities with macro-level political economies and thus *underscored the tenacity of colonial processes and the difficulty of decolonialization.*[83]

Debt Crisis: African Initiatives and IFI Response

In the mid-1970s, as a result of quadrupled oil prices, Western banks received an abundance of "petro-dollars" from oil-producing countries. Eager to lend the petro-dollars, banks lowered their interest rates substantially, fueling further borrowing by African governments. Beginning in the same period, commodity prices became increasingly volatile. From the mid-1970s, prices of copper and agricultural commodities fell, especially in "terms of trade"—a measure that compares the prices of commodity exports with prices paid for imported manufactured goods from the industrialized countries.[84] Hard-pressed governments stepped up extraction of "rents" from the peasant sector, where farmers were often coerced to grow marketed crops for low returns.[85] As governments confronted overwhelming payments on massive foreign loans, debts were rescheduled at higher interest rates.[86] Prior to this time, African governments seldom had borrowed capital to expand production and to achieve balanced national (or regional) economies.[87]

Faced with deepening crisis, African governments, under the leadership of the Organization of African Unity (OAU) and the U.N. Economic Commission for Africa (ECA), recognized many past policy errors. They advocated a development strategy combining broadly based growth with social justice.[88] Known as the "Lagos Plan," the strategy's long-term aims included regional food security, to be realized via support for increased production by small farmers, and satisfaction of basic needs of the population through decentralized government services and local self-help. Investments would be directed toward alleviating poverty, and broadening access to health services and education. Together, these measures would slow population growth. The Lagos Plan also recommended regional integration to create wider markets for African industries using local resources.[89] Africa-centered scholars emphasized the need for redistribution of resources on a global scale.[90] Human betterment in Africa was perceived as crucial, both for social justice and for the advancement of world peace.[91]

These perspectives, however, were of little interest to international financial and corporate power holders. Instead of consulting with governments that signed the Lagos Plan, the World Bank in the same year proposed its own strategy for Africa.[92] The multiplex African crisis, exacerbated by global economic stagnation, gave the framers of the Washington Consensus an opportunity to re-create conditions for debt reimbursement and for more profitable resource extraction. These conditions would include easing foreign corporations' access to Africa's profitable oil and mineral resources and lowering import tariffs to facilitate foreign companies' access to African markets.

The key document signaling this shift in policy was the World Bank's 1981 *Agenda for Action in sub-Saharan Africa*. This report, known by the name of its senior author, Elliot Berg, shed African leaders' mid-1970s concern for social justice and "basic needs."[93] It sought to justify "production first" export policies on the grounds of economic efficiency and comparative advantage.[94] The Berg Report linked further loans to governments' acceptance of policy reforms, and required African states to devalue their currencies to make exports more competitive.[95] Governments were told to remove price controls and end subsidies for food crops to stimulate local production. The Bank demanded concessions to foreign capital, along with privatization of government-owned enterprises and public services. New investment codes included tax incentives, free repatriation of profits, elimination of tariff protection for local industries, and an end to minimum wages and labor protections.[96] The IFIs pressed African governments to trim their budgets, reduce the civil service, and recover costs by charging "user fees" for public health and education. These measures, the building blocks of SAPs, were supposed to lead to new private foreign investment and stimulate economic growth. The IFIs and governments withheld loans from African states until they signed SAP agreements. Funds previously committed were shifted away from countries that refused to sign the agreements or that insisted on designing their own SAPs rather than accepting the official models. The pattern shows how the power of the Washington Consensus rests on its command of discourse as well as financial assistance. During this period, as in the colonial era, wealthy countries and their experts claimed a monopoly of expert knowledge and exerted their power to specify the limits of policy.[97] Rather than being aided by superior weaponry and using direct military force, however, this time the metropolitan countries were buttressed by superior wealth, the promise of large loans, and the threat of Africa's further marginalization in the global economy.

The results of SAP implementation in the 1980s bore little resemblance to the predictions initially offered by IFI experts. Poor countries' economies stagnated while their debt burdens continued to increase. By the end of the 1980s, debt levels were so high that governments of most non-oil-producing countries used 30 to 70 percent of export revenues for debt service.[98] Governments required new adjustment loans in order to remain even minimally operative, while recession politics in the West diminished the amount of funds for development. Few private foreign investors appeared, except in the oil and mining industries. Commodity prices crashed.[99] Even in adjusting countries, more capital flowed out of Africa during the 1980s than went in.[100] The effects of structural adjustment further widened the gap between rich and poor nations. Within poor nations, costs fell most heavily on poor and vulnerable segments of the population. The 1980s, called "the debt decade," were a "lost decade for Africa."[101]

Crushing debt burdens and SAP conditions for new loans, coupled with the threat of popular unrest, gave foreign capital enormous leverage over policy-making. The decline in national sovereignty led some to write (and many more to speak) of the "re-colonization of Africa."[102] "The state in Africa is being recast…the power apparatus locally is increasingly being turned exclusively into an apparatus of repression…"[103]

Omissions of the Berg Report

The destructive results of SAPs came as little surprise to many African and Africanist scholars. Immediately following the Berg Report's appearance, and while acknowledging the pertinence of many of its criticisms, scholars argued that the deep historical and structural reasons for crisis in African political economies would remain untouched by Berg's prescriptions. Critics of the Report foresaw further decline in terms of trade for African agriculture largely because similar advice to increase tropical crop exports was being given to the whole of the Third World.[104] Reliance on market forces, privatization, and low-cost labor *would* allow a small number of "progressive" farmers and export-oriented large farms to increase production and profits, at least initially.[105] However, it could be foreseen that peasants with a shrinking resource base would not benefit from increased crop prices. Prices of consumer goods would rise, while diminishing access to cheap credit (where available) and the removal of subsidies for fertilizer and improved seeds, would escalate costs of production.[106] Because rising prices and unemployment prevent urban workers from sending *cash* remittances to *poor* rural relatives, the latter would suffer reduced food production, and with less income, would be unable to pay for essential food and social services.[107]

These predictions proved all too accurate.

Meanwhile, and just as foreseeably, devaluation and price "liberalization" raised the prices of imported agricultural inputs and undermined poor-country producers by exposing them to competition from larger and wealthier foreign companies.[108] Impact fell not only on industries that, on advice from an earlier generation of experts, used many imported components. Small farmers who produced for market also faced heightened competition from cheaper imported food, including subsidized grains.[109] Food security, recognized as a priority following disastrous droughts of the 1970s, was undermined by export-first policies.[110]

In addition, although SAP policies appeared to be gender-blind, they were not gender-neutral. Women's work burdens increased as they were pressed to supply an increasing share of family incomes, their earnings crucial to support children's nutrition and health as well as their own. Thus, poor women and children bore the brunt of SAP austerity.[111] The IFIs proposed to trade "short-term pain for long-term gain." They failed to acknowledge that for already vulnerable populations short-term pain could mean devastating long-term health consequences affecting future generations, and that those least responsible for the crisis would be its primary victims.[112] Yet such failure cannot be explained as mere oversight. As one critic has observed:

> Anthropologists often point to the unforeseen consequences of policies [that arise] when these are actually implemented. Sometimes the consequences are more properly viewed as undeclared goals. Critiques of the Berg Report emerged immediately following its publication [in 1981]. [Yet the policies continued.] [H]ence, we can assume that its policy prescriptions were intended to accomplish just what their results have shown.[113]

The principal goal of the original Bretton Woods Charter that established the IFIs was not to reduce poverty but to safeguard investments and profits of metropolitan firms. Because this is what SAPs actually did, it is undoubtedly what the IFIs, in fact, sought to achieve.[114]

By the mid-1980s, criticism of SAPs began to be voiced in many quarters. Independent researchers and development workers across the continent documented the suffering of communities gripped by deepening poverty and declining health.[115] Case studies by the U.N. agencies concerned with children's health and social and economic development spurred advocacy for "adjustment with a human face."[116]

In 1989, a new analysis by the World Bank recognized that SAPs had not helped the African poor and that special compensatory poverty alleviation measures were needed.[117] A new "African Initiative" sponsored by African leaders proposed substantial debt cancellation and arms reduction, the savings to be invested in health, education, and essential economic sectors.[118] The IFIs, however, were still reluctant, both to address structural imbalances or to resolve the debt issue. Leading IFI economists continued to advocate reliance on markets and privatization, although some acknowledged that much new local private economic activity was in trade and speculation, rather than in diversified production,[119] and that moreover, privatization had created new opportunities for corruption.[120] New foreign investment continued to be slow, except in extractive sectors that create few linkages to local industry—and in which foreign firms traditionally expatriate most of the profits.[121] In some countries, SAP conditions and resources were used by members of the dominant classes to reposition themselves economically and to co-opt opposition leaders as clients.[122]

Poor Africans continued under the first two decades of SAPs—and continue today—to struggle courageously and creatively to earn livelihoods. Contrary to perceptions current in rich countries, Africans do not simply accept poverty fatalistically as their foreordained condition. Yet grinding misery in the 1980s stretched and then— for many—tore apart the fabric of kinship and other social relations that serve as safety nets in times of need. The impacts have included further subordination of women, more homeless children, higher rates of malnutrition and disease, and worsening domestic and social violence.[123]

Though necessarily schematic, our survey of the historical background of Africa's current economic ills indicates the enduring forces generated by colonial conquest and the ways that recent IFI policies toward the continent perpetuate the logic of colonial exploitation. We now examine some of the consequences of SAP-enhanced economic exploitation on the health of the African poor.

PAYING THE PRICE:
SAPs' IMPACT ON THE HEALTH OF THE POOR

How do SAPs and persistent historical patterns of injustice and inequality degrade the health of Africa's poor? We examine five key areas in which SAPs, and the underlying power relations they reinforce, undermine poor people's health. First, we look at rising social and political violence, with the 1994 genocide in Rwanda as a key example. Second, we return to the spread of HIV/AIDS. Third, we document poor people's reduced access to biomedical health care. Fourth, we show the deteriorating quality of health care available to the poor and middle classes. Finally, we document the consequences of SAPs' effects on food production and nutrition. Throughout the discussion we note how SAPs have affected gender relations and have had a different impact on women than on men.

We begin by examining the most obvious challenge to health and survival for the poor: overt, systematic violence unleashed as a result of social destabilization.

From Structural to Corporeal Violence

Violence arising from political tensions and the disintegration of the social fabric constitutes one very direct way in which the health of the poor is menaced by Africa's multiplex crisis. State tyranny and civil conflict have their roots in the legacy of European colonialism, in the structural violence of poverty, and in the competition among privileged groups.[124] Anticolonial and anti-Apartheid struggles in the 1970s and 1980s were bitter and bloody, as Europeans sought to retain a monopoly of power. White minority governments in southern Africa intervened to destabilize their neighbors.

As the impoverishing effects of SAPs began to be felt across the continent, strikers and street demonstrators protested rising prices and lower real wages.[125] Termed "IMF riots," most of these actions have been met by a varying mix of force and concessions. Protesters find that even new "reform" governments deploy force against them as rulers strive to meet SAP conditions and maintain credibility with international financial institutions and donor governments.

Fear of organized social unrest ("disorder") leads some power-holders to scapegoat ethnic and regional minorities in order to weaken opposition and retain their hold on power. Coalition-building by democracy movements is thereby rendered difficult.[126] Few political elites are strongly linked to the rural poor, although some parties have included organizations of peasants, urban workers, local NGOs, and university students.

Africa's violent disputes, its civil wars, ethnic cleansing, and genocide, are not throwbacks to "centuries of tribalism," as many in the news media would have it.[127] They are similar to strategies of political and economic competition in other parts of the world. Their specific forms help to explain the level of violence in Africa over the past two decades. Struggles for control of the state as a site of enrichment have led to the "implosion" of states in civil wars; some of these have spread to encompass entire regions.[128] The conflicts have brought millions of civilian deaths, tens of thousands of rapes, and massive population displacements.[129]

The genocide of Tutsi by extremists bent on exclusive "Hutu Power" in Rwanda in 1994 is the best-known example. Extremist leaders' extensive ideological preparations, the scale of the killings, and the speed with which they were carried out were unprecedented in Africa. The organizers' basic aims, however, were not unique.[130] State and ethnic violence is a predictable result of what has come to be known as "structural violence."[131] As an illustration of how economic and political conflicts nourished by the legacy of colonialism can unleash murder on a vast scale, the case of Rwanda demands detailed consideration.

Rwandan Genocide: An Economic Genealogy

While U.S. news media continue to view genocide in Rwanda in 1994 as the result of a "centuries-old tribal conflict" between Hutu and Tutsi, the direct cause lay in political struggles.[132] Faced with having to share power, government officials used a barrage of racist propaganda and practices to mobilize their partisans. Many people were motivated to kill their neighbors by manipulation of ethnic identities; others by promises of gain.[133] Economic factors played a crucial and insufficiently acknowledged role in driving the violence. Evidence for this comes from the patterns of the atrocities themselves: houses were looted before being burned; corpses were stripped; cattle were stolen. Rather than be hacked to death by machetes, some victims with cash paid their murderers to shoot them.[134] The conflict was by no means a "purely" ethnic clash between "The Tutsi" and "The Hutu" as monolithic entities.

Ironically, in 1989 Rwanda was cited as one of the World Bank's success stories. Agricultural production had risen by 4.7 percent each year between 1966 and 1982, 1.3 percent faster than the population, and cultivated area had expanded by 37 percent. With more than 90 percent of the population living in the countryside, "Rwanda avoided the urban bias."[135] Moreover, growth was said to have taken place "without the inequities that have sometimes accompanied development elsewhere."[136]

But what the World Bank saw as an "absence of inequity" was viewed quite differently by many Rwandans.[137] The Bank ignored violations of human, economic, and political rights. Rwandan peasants chafed under decrees that in 1976 reinstituted restrictions on freedom of movement. Rwanda had "avoided the urban bias" by hampering urban growth. By the mid-1980s, an estimated one million landless and near-landless people were held "down on the farm" by pass laws.[138] Systematic discrimination against Tutsi was instituted in 1973. Tutsi were barred from the army and limited in their access to government posts. Tutsi children's ability to gain entrance to tax-supported secondary schools and higher education was restricted by quotas. Top jobs in government and *parastatals* (state-owned enterprises) went to people from the president's network and those of his wife and her brothers, without concern for competence.

In reporting on Rwanda during this era, the World Bank approvingly cited the country's erosion control programs. Yet forced labor had been used for soil protection and road building by the colonial administration. Hated by peasants, such compulsory labor (*umuganda*) was abolished at independence, but reinstated in 1976. In praising Rwanda's soil conservation efforts, the Bank had not listened to peasants who, in 1990, took advantage of weakened state power to destroy many detested anti-erosion works.[139]

With an average farm size of 1.2 hectares per family in 1984, Rwanda may have appeared from the outside to be more egalitarian than most African economies.[140] However, averages can mask significant resource disparities, even in rural areas. Most reclaimable land was already cultivated. With annual population growth at 3.7 percent and with most Rwandans confined to living on small farms, even the insufficient yields of the mid-1980s could not be sustained.[141] The result was a looming threat of hunger.

The rural crisis could only be remedied by intensifying agricultural production, redistributing resources, and reordering government priorities to include creation of labor-intensive off-farm employment.[142] The government, however, actively discouraged informal artisan production, viewing it as competition for formal sector businesses in which the political class had an interest.

The World Bank praised the fact that crop purchasing was left to private merchants and that "market forces fixed the level of food prices, which rose by 10-17 percent annually during the 1970s." Government officials, among others, found trade quite lucrative. By 1989, under the combined onslaught of land shortage and food price rises, rural incomes had fallen by 30 percent from their 1975 level.[143] A small industrial sector emerged, built by the petty *bourgeoisie*, who garnered capital from trade and corruption.

The World Bank and other foreign lenders provided funds to expand export production on large parastatal tea estates and cattle ranches. Projects, including those led by the Bank, often expropriated peasants' land.[144] Improved land was redistributed to government and army officials, their clients, and to the growing rural petty *bourgeoisie*, rather than to needy peasants. Thus, foreign assistance contributed to an accelerating crisis in the rural economy.[145] The plethora of development projects also brought conspicuous inequality: one-third of funds spent for projects in-country went to pay the salaries of technical assistants; half the remaining funds went to build these technical advisors' houses, and another one-quarter to purchase vehicles. Visible inequality heightened many peasants' sense of social exclusion—a form of structural violence.[146] Without employment in the rural areas, children of the rural poor flocked to the towns, where they tried to avoid police controls.

Government agricultural agents tended to work not with resource-poor farmers (72 percent of the population in 1984) but with better-endowed "progressive farmers" owning at least 1.5 hectares.[147] Most research and extension resources went toward increasing exports, about 90 percent of it to coffee. Except for trials of climbing coffee bean varieties and potatoes for high altitudes, little yield-increasing technology for food crops emerged from agricultural research. Peasants' processing and storage problems received scant attention.

From the mid-1970s, a chain of Swiss-funded rural banking cooperatives, intended to benefit peasants, expanded their operations. However, although their savings typically made up 80 percent of their total holdings, the majority of peasants were without collateral and therefore could not qualify for loans. Two-thirds of loans were made for trade and building activities of townsmen, thus de-capitalizing agriculture.[148]

An observer in the early 1980s described how some poor peasants fell victim to usury.[149] Beans are the preferred food staple throughout Rwanda; but poor peasants with little land cannot produce enough to last the season.[150] When they exhaust their supply, they borrow from a trader, who brings five bags of beans worth 5,000 francs. Peasants agree to repay him after the coffee harvest with five bags of coffee worth 30,000 francs. The trader reaps profits equal to five times his initial outlay.[151]

Health conditions reflected the deepening crisis. In 1988, one-third of rural children showed stunted growth, indicating chronic malnutrition, while 40 percent of women and children consumed too few calories.[152] An estimated 80 percent of women delivered their babies at home without a trained attendant. Maternal deaths were estimated at 1,530 per 100,000, among the highest rates in Africa.[153] Starting in 1978, health expenditures began to decline as a percentage of the national budget. By 1987, training and management absorbed 65 percent of public health funds.[154]

The World Bank's upbeat 1989 report on Rwanda is difficult to understand. In contrast, the Rwandan government's 1988 Development Plan recognized the imminent crisis. Its authors called for massive job creation in order to reduce growing inequality and social unrest among landless youth.[155] A 1992 evaluation found that very little had been done.[156]

In 1989, at the World Bank's insistence, the "floor price" paid to coffee growers by the parastatal *Caisse de Stabilisation* was withdrawn. Then the world market price for coffee crashed. Peasants responded by uprooting coffee and planting food crops, as they had following an earlier crash.[157] As a result, cash incomes of the peasant majority declined still further, with consequent worsening of nutrition and health.[158]

By the late 1980s, the absence of political rights in Rwanda's single-party state was under challenge from many quarters.[159] Leaders of clandestine opposition parties who sought political representation, the rule of law, and socioeconomic justice were harassed, and some assassinated. Years of negotiation by Tutsi refugees who had fled state-orchestrated pogroms and ethnic cleansing in the period from 1959 to 1973, failed to secure the right to return to their homeland. In October 1990, refugee soldiers living in Uganda crossed Rwanda's northern frontier in an attempt to claim by force what they had failed to achieve through negotiation.[160] Calling themselves the Rwanda Patriotic Front (RPF), they were joined by other exiled opponents of the dictatorial regime. The government in response straightaway arrested some 10,000 Tutsi and Hutu political opponents living inside Rwanda, many of whom were held without charge for eight months. Beatings and torture were common; sick prisoners were left untreated and many developed lasting illnesses.[161]

While these deadly human rights violations took place, international donors continued to fund development projects and to support the government financially.[162] Increasing tensions still further, Rwanda signed a new SAP agreement in November 1990. The World Bank insisted upon 40 percent currency devaluation. Prices rose and the debt grew; production stagnated, then fell. As unrest mounted, the government blamed all difficulties on the RPF invasion; officials scapegoated the Tutsi inside Rwanda. Still, sophisticated hate propaganda, pogroms led by local officials, and assassination of political opponents received little international notice, despite the plethora of resident Western development project staff.[163] A second currency devaluation, of 15 percent, took place in June 1992; coffee prices fell again.[164] With new foreign loans, the government expanded the army, and bought weapons and equipment. Extremist parties associated with the government recruited 20 to 30 thousand unemployed young men into militias. The government bought them arms; the army taught them to kill Tutsi "cockroaches" without mercy.[165] Violence grew in both rural and urban areas.[166]

Conditions in the rural areas continued to deteriorate. As population grew, farm size declined and the fertility of the soils that had been cultivated without fallow periods or fertilizers was exhausted. Poorer peasants switched from cultivating beans and maize to manioc and sweet potatoes. While the 1989 World Bank report placed a positive spin on this change, because it led to "more calories per hectare," the nutritional quality of diets suffered. A longitudinal study of a commune in rural Butare Province found that the cash incomes of 75 percent of peasants declined by 35 percent each year from 1990 through 1992. In the latter year, coffee prices fell below the level of the 1989 crash. One-fourth of peasants incurred debts and risked losing their farms. The government instituted *umuganda* work projects to drain marshes for growing rice in the dry season. While all peasant households were made to contribute labor, only officials, businessmen, and loyal peasant clients were awarded access to these plots. In 1992, only rice-growing peasants reported increased incomes.[167]

A peace accord reached in August 1993 provided for power-sharing among government and opposition leaders. Hard-liners in government and the army rejected the accords, however, and prepared, in the words of one leader, "the Apocalypse." A plane crash that killed the presidents of Rwanda and Burundi served as a pretext for a military coup that unleashed a preplanned bloodbath against all Tutsi, as well as Hutu members of opposition parties and their families.[168] The United Nations and leaders of Western governments, warned in advance of plans for genocide, refused to honor their obligations under the Geneva Convention. On television news, the world watched unarmed people hacked and beaten to death. The worldwide audience was told that tribal violence had broken out, when in fact it was genocide and political murder, planned and executed by a self-appointed rump government, whose delegate sat on the U.N. Security Council. *The extreme violence did not erupt unforeseeably, out of irrational "ethnic hatreds." It was the culmination of a long history of economic deterioration and political conflict*, every stage of which Rwanda had been observed by representatives of international financial institutions—some of whom mandated the very processes and policies that led to the bloodshed.

The Structural Violence of AIDS

The destructive impact of ongoing economic crisis on the health of poor communities takes forms less dramatic than genocide yet just as devastating. Structural and social violence have contributed decisively to the dissemination of HIV on the African continent.[169] As economic crisis intensified in the late 1970s, the HIV epidemic silently spread. Seemingly unrelated, the two phenomena are in fact intimately entwined: the effects of poverty accelerate the spread of the virus. The ravages of AIDS in turn plunge afflicted regions deeper into economic crisis.

With just 10 percent of the world's population, Africa is home to 70 percent of past and present AIDS victims in the world: 35 million people. An estimated 22 million African adults and more than 1 million children currently live with HIV/AIDS.[170] Sub-Saharan Africa was the first region to experience the effects of the prolonged crisis and, to date, remains the most vulnerable to the pandemic.[171]

Nearly 90 percent of HIV infections in Africa are transmitted during heterosexual intercourse. Untreated, classic STDs facilitate the sexual transmission of HIV, especially to women, who make up more than half of those infected.[172] In parts of Africa, cultural factors appear to limit the ability of women, married or single, to refuse sex with a steady partner, even if they suspect he may be infected.[173] Moreover, studies in a variety of contexts have shown that women's agency in determining condom use is often severely constrained.[174]

The spread of AIDS has devastated economic and social structures in the areas hardest hit.[175] Ninety percent of AIDS deaths in sub-Saharan Africa occur in adults aged 20 to 49, the prime working years; more than half those infected are aged 15 to 24.[176] As the disease proliferates, industrial firms in southern Africa face shortages of trained personnel. The impact on rural economic activities—particularly season-sensitive, labor-intensive agriculture and food processing—and on family life in affected areas is severe. Despite the efforts of extended families,[177] most are unable to cope with the material and psychological burdens of the disease[178] or with the millions of newly orphaned children.[179] Rather than strengthening families and communities to confront the AIDS onslaught, SAP policies, by failing to reduce poverty and often increasing it, have contributed to accelerating the pandemic.[180] In severely affected countries, three decades of achievement in health—including longer life expectancies and reduced mortality among infants and young children—were annulled in the 1990s due to the mutually reinforcing effects of poverty and AIDS.[181]

Response to AIDS is political in Africa as elsewhere. Public health action takes place on a terrain of contested meanings and unequal power, where different forms of knowledge struggle for control.[182] Epidemiologists and health planners in the development agencies greatly underestimated the potential magnitude of HIV/AIDS in Africa. The disease was initially "constructed" as an urban plight from which "traditional" rural areas, home to a majority of the population, would be spared.[183] Dismissing those who foresaw a catastrophic pandemic, health officials proposed to control AIDS by targeting most prevention efforts to "core transmitters." These included sex workers and long-haul transporters, recognized as having multiple sex partners.[184]

The poor themselves soon grasped the epidemic's economic roots. In 1986, people in Kinshasa dubbed AIDS (SIDA, in French) "an imaginary syndrome to discourage lovers" (*Syndrome Imaginaire pour Décourager les Amoureux*). They were aware that westerners stigmatized Africans for "having too much sex." By 1987, however, another phrase captured popular understanding of AIDS' social epidemiology: "*Salaire*

Insuffisant Depuis des Années."[185] In anglophone Africa, the same causal relationship was expressed as, "the Acquired Income Deficiency Syndrome."

Poverty and gender inequality make women particularly vulnerable to AIDS. The story of Nsanga, which introduced our chapter, shows the risks taken by a poor urban woman struggling to feed her children, her struggles sharpened by SAP policies. Nsanga's fate reflects living conditions and changes in social relations in the era of AIDS. In situations of dire poverty, the limits of "the economy of affection" are quickly reached. Family ties that might once have provided enduring support give way under the combined assault of poverty and disease. People unable to count on family solidarity incur various risks as they struggle to fend for themselves economically.[186]

Specific SAP measures, such as currency devaluation, not only shrink resources that could improve AIDS prevention and the treatment and care of persons with AIDS; they also precipitate social upheavals that accelerate the rate of HIV transmission. Poverty and SAPs have undermined the viability of rural economies, promoted mass labor migration and urban unemployment, worsened the condition of poor women, and left health systems to founder. As a result of these shifts, vast numbers of people in Africa are at increased risk for HIV infection.[187] Such economic and social factors, rather than raging hormones or a special "African sexuality," explain why HIV spreads so rapidly on the continent.[188]

The World Bank, one of the foremost architects of SAPs, is now the single largest lender for AIDS prevention efforts in Africa. Somewhat belatedly, the Bank has acknowledged AIDS as a key development issue, not simply a health problem. According to a 1998 Bank report on the worldwide AIDS situation, HIV/AIDS is exacerbating poverty and inequality, and is projected to further slow the already unfavorable per capita income growth of many countries in sub-Saharan Africa through its effects on savings and productivity. The deleterious effects of SAPs led a long-time AIDS policy advisor to ask: "Given the increased needs in terms of health on the continent, largely due to the prevalence of AIDS, why didn't the World Bank make *increasing* health budgets a condition for their loans?"[189]

Reproductive and Sexual Health

African women are greatly concerned about reproductive and sexual health: the social status of many depends on producing healthy children.[190] They are more likely than women elsewhere to die in childbirth and from pregnancy-related conditions, especially when they deliver their children unattended by trained health workers. Those at highest risk are poor women, young women under age 20, women bearing children over age 34, and women who have had five or more pregnancies.[191] In the poorest African countries 60 to 80 percent of women give birth with little or no assistance from health providers. Despite the well-known problem of high maternal mortality, many SAP countries *increased* fees for child delivery and other maternity services. In Zimbabwe, studies have shown that when maternity fees are increased, more women risk the dangers of delivering their children at home unattended by health providers.[192]

Small but growing numbers of poor women and men began to use biomedical contraceptive methods in some countries in the late 1970s.[193] By the 1990s, that increase was threatened wherever SAP-restricted health policies took hold. Family planning services were reduced, and user fees prevented many poor women from taking advantage of the services that did exist.[194] Deprived of preventive care, including health education and contraception, poor women, especially adolescents, will produce more, rather than fewer, children. As the dangers connected with unattended pregnancy and childbirth combine with poverty, malnutrition, and STDs, women's already high risks of death climb still higher.[195]

Sexual health includes freedom from STDs, which in addition to pain and increased risk of acquiring HIV, also lead to reproductive failures and serious health problems in children.[196] Women, and especially adolescent females, are more vulnerable than men to STDs, for both biological and social reasons.[197] They are also heavily stigmatized if their affliction becomes known. Because many health services primarily target married women or mothers, and are unable to provide private examining spaces, or even treat women courteously, at-risk women are often discouraged from seeking care.[198] User fees are an even greater deterrent to successful STD treatment.[199]

Declining Access to Health Care

The lack of health provider discretion and the imposition of user fees, however, are not the only barriers confronting poor Africans who seek biomedical health care. A person's ability to reach a health-care facility, to be treated by a health-care provider, or to obtain needed medicine is dependent on many factors, including proximity to the facility, transportation costs, ability to pay service and medicine fees, and sociocultural factors such as language, class, and gender.[200] Generally, the more numerous and widely dispersed health facilities and health-care providers are, the greater people's access to health care. This is especially true in Africa where the majority of poor people live in villages far from urban centers. In remote areas, distance is the most crucial determinant of health-care access.

In the 1960s and 1970s, African countries made enormous strides toward bringing health facilities and personnel to the rural majority. Since the early 1980s, however, this progress has slowed and even halted, due in large part to the economic constraints imposed by SAPs and to the costs of the AIDS pandemic. During the SAP era, governments have found it expedient to cut expenditures on services for those with little political influence. Public health outlays for the poor all too often provide such a strategy, where budget austerities are attended by only minimal political risks. As a result, public hospitals and clinics in many parts of Africa are now desperately understaffed and poorly equipped. Budget compression under SAPs reduced support for health in most countries to about 2 percent of GDP.[201]

Moreover, medical doctors and nurses throughout much of Africa either moonlight to survive or leave their countries to find employment or better salaries elsewhere. The emigration of health professionals further exacerbates the personnel shortages caused by SAP-guided government hiring freezes, salary cutbacks, and early retirement for civil servants, including health workers. In Ghana, according to a

World Bank paper, the number of doctors decreased from 1,782 in 1985 to 965 in 1991. In already underserved rural areas, these employment shifts have greatly increased the workload of the remaining doctors and nurses. At the same time that user fees were imposed, devaluation increased prices for imported medicines and supplies. Thus, SAPs "helped to precipitate a catastrophe in which virtually all economic, social, educational, and public health gains made in the 1960s and 1970s have been wiped out."[202]

Wide-ranging health, economic, agricultural, and industrial policy changes mandated by SAPs complicate access to health care for men as well as women. Inability to obtain needed health care is another way that poverty and inequality translate into suffering and premature death for the already vulnerable. The tragic effects of this pattern are illustrated in the story of Aseffa Okoso.

Okoso was a strong, imposing Ghanaian man of 43 from a small town 165 kilometers northwest of the capital city. Okoso had a wife, five children in school, and many good friends with whom he shared his extensive repertoire of jokes and songs. Beloved by neighborhood children, despite his rugged appearance and deep voice, Okoso was usually at the center of Sunday gatherings when he was at home.

Proud of his strength and skill, Okoso had worked for eight years as a manual laborer at an American-owned gold-mining company located two hours by bus from his home. In the mining town, he stayed with workmates in a rented room. So as not to spend too much on bus fare, he returned home every other Saturday after work. On alternate Saturday nights, he joined his mates at a local beer joint, where they competed to impress the young waitresses.[203]

In January 1996, Okoso suffered from extended bouts of diarrhea, with fever and night sweats. At first he thought his sickness might be due to bad water in the compound. While still on the job, he was able to pay for medicines to relieve his diarrhea. But it kept coming back. Okoso grew thin, coughed a lot, and eventually became too sick to keep up the hard physical labor his job required. He also became frightened. As his illness progressed, he was forced to leave the mine without severance pay.

At home, Okoso's condition worsened, but care at the local clinic became very expensive. When the financial burdens of Okoso's illness began to overwhelm his family, friends generously helped him cover the costs of care. But because his friends, too, were struggling, Okoso stopped asking for their assistance. Just three months after leaving the mine, Okoso gave up on his illness, choosing instead to remain at home. When asked why he no longer sought care from the clinic located just a few miles from his urban home, he responded with conviction:

> *If I went to the clinic, they would make me pay this new fee which, frankly, my family and I cannot afford. I have no work, no salary. We live day to day on what my wife can make selling vegetables in the local market or what my sons can bring home from selling things on the streets. Some days we eat only one meal and we often go to bed hungry.*

Okoso knew that the clinic nurse would give him a prescription to purchase medicines that, once again, would be too expensive. In conversation, Okoso showed a lucid awareness that his inability to afford treatment was related to the vast and rapid economic changes his country had undertaken over the preceding 13 years.

Friends suggested that he consult an African healer, but Okoso rejected that option as futile, for he was coughing blood. Miners' folklore in Africa had familiarized him, an open pit miner, with the symptoms of tuberculosis.[204] Okoso died just seven months after being diagnosed with AIDS. His two youngest children began to cough, leading the researcher to suspect that they, too, had become infected with tuberculosis.[205]

Deteriorating Quality of Health Care

Okoso's story illustrates the effects of reduced health access on people struggling simultaneously against poverty and deadly disease. Joined with the erosion of public health-sector budgets and salaries, the proliferation of such cases has had predictably negative effects on staff morale, professionalism, practitioner-patient relations, and quality of care in African countries affected by the social fallout of SAPs. The poor find less health care available to them, and the quality of the care that exists is declining.

In Côte d'Ivoire, attendance at the university teaching hospital in the country's capital, Abidjan, declined by about 50 percent following currency devaluation in 1994; the price of medicines meanwhile rose 30 to 70 percent. Physicians expressed their demoralization as, powerless to provide adequate care to poor patients, they sent them home to die.[206] Sick people consulted "traditional" practitioners, whose numbers expanded markedly.[207] While many healers have knowledge of specific herbal remedies and can treat a limited range of ailments, the claims of others to treat diseases such as cancers, tuberculosis, and AIDS suggest charlatanism.

In practice, for the poor who do access state health-care facilities, nurses deliver most of the curative as well as preventive services, usually without physician supervision. Nurses' patient loads have increased dramatically, even in poor rural and urban areas where many cannot afford services.[208] The story of Demba Djemay, a nurse from Senegal, reflects the frustration even highly motivated health-care providers feel when facing the impossible working conditions resulting from SAP-mandated economic austerity measures in the public sector.

Djemay considers nursing more than just a job; for him it is a calling. Thirty-five in 1993, he had trained for three years following primary school to become a nurse. He works in a small hospital near his hometown in Senegal. But now Djemay is unable to use his skills to care adequately for patients. His regional health center is seriously underequipped, lacking medicines and the most basic medical supplies—including disinfectants, gloves, masks, and disposable syringes. It is also short-staffed, with only one other nurse and a part-time physician. Together, these two-and-a-half professionals serve a population of more than 150,000 people. Djemay and his nurse colleague are overworked, barely compensated, and each often sees 70 patients a day—many of whom die of readily treatable diseases. Treatable, that is, were medicines and equipment available. "My work is one frustration after another," Djemay lamented. "Under these conditions, I simply cannot provide my patients the kind of care they urgently need."

Patients may wait all day, sometimes into the following day, to see him. When they finally enter his small examining room, they receive a brief, if sympathetic, audience and a prescription. Djemay said: "Most patients would have to trade away the family's food supply to purchase the medicines. Many have already sold livestock to pay for their transport to town and their hospital admission fee. So often after losing a day or more of work, patients go home empty-handed."

Djemay's patients are fortunate that he has kept his professional conscience despite adversity.[209] His frustration reflects a grim statistic: between 1980 and 1993, the number of people per nurse in Senegal rose more than six times, from 1,931 to 13,174.[210] Many other countries registered increases of two to nine times during the same period. Meanwhile, health coverage was quite uneven, with a few countries admitting declines and some making doubtful claims of improvement. Botswana, with diamonds, peace, and effective governance, was the only country with both credibly improved health coverage and a lower number of people per nurse.[211]

Shrinking access to health care and deteriorating quality of care available, both direct results of SAP policies, leave the poor increasingly exposed to suffering and death that relatively modest health expenditures could prevent. The impact of SAPs and related policy measures on food production and nutrition constitutes another critical channel through which the accumulated heritage of colonial and post-colonial economic exploitation influences the health of Africa's poor.

Food, Nutrition, and Health

Nutrition may be the single most important determinant of health. Poor nutrition is *synergistic* with disease; that is, the presence of either increases the likelihood of the other.[212] Indeed, the strongest predictors of child health are, first, broad, equitable distribution of food and primary health services, and, second, the education of women. These factors are interrelated and depend less on gross national product (GNP) figures than on governments' political choices in allocating resources to different segments of the population.[213] To show the interrelation between economic patterns, political choices, nutrition, and health, we consider data on malnutrition among poor women and children. Then we focus on World Bank agricultural policies in Africa and assess these policies' results.

Both adequate energy (calories) and "micronutrients" are required for growth and health.[214] Even moderate malnutrition increases the risk of sickness and death in young children by about 50 percent.[215] Stunting (low height for age, indicative of chronic malnutrition) affects the health of the entire body and may prevent children from ever being able to "catch up" developmentally, even if calorie intake later improves.[216] Prolonged severe nutrient deprivation may lead to mental retardation.[217] Women who had been chronically malnourished in childhood often fail to develop the bone structure needed for safe childbirth; they also give birth to more underweight babies, as do those who perform strenuous work late in pregnancy.[218] Undernourished women also produce poor quality breast milk. The consequence of these interwoven patterns is that poorly fed mothers and their infants risk chronic illness and death.[219]

Effects of economic recession and structural adjustment on the health and lives of children are monitored by UNICEF.[220] A longitudinal study undertaken in Brazzaville, the capital of Congo, used body measurements to assess nutritional status before and during the implementation of structural adjustment. As adjustment took hold, the proportion of underweight children rose, including those in families considered non-poor.[221] Among children of the poor, both acute malnutrition and stunting rose.[222] The percentage of low birth-weight babies, considered evidence of maternal nutritional stress, almost doubled.[223] The proportion of poor mothers with chronic energy deficiency increased; nearly 20 percent of mothers under age 18 did not get sufficient calories.[224] Researchers concluded that the effects of economic decline and SAPs on the health of the poor will continue to be manifested during the course of the next 20 to 30 years.[225]

Another time series comes from rural and urban samples in Côte d'Ivoire, where nutritional status worsened as poverty incidence increased between 1988 and 1993.[226] The rural poor registered the sharpest declines: child stunting rose as incomes declined. The poorest households were concentrated among small farmers in the northern savannah zone.[227] These are the people left out of the earlier growth "miracle."[228]

Most researchers did not disaggregate their data. That is, they failed to separate measurements made on children of the poor from those on children in better-off households. Even so, a study that surveyed children born in Lusaka, the capital of Zambia, found that in just two years (from 1986 to 1988), SAP policies had measurable negative effects on child nutrition and health.[229]

Increased food prices and poverty are conspicuous in big cities. However, malnutrition is generally more prevalent in rural areas, where more poor people live.[230] Food production and rural incomes have declined since the late 1970s in most of sub-Saharan Africa.[231] Inequality widened not only in incomes but in wealth and property, as ownership and access to fertile land became increasingly concentrated. Women, especially, lost land rights.[232]

Laws to encourage the privatization of land have reinforced a multilayered landholding pattern in regions where fertile land is in short supply.[233] At the top, large agribusiness estates produce for market, increasingly for export, using the labor of the landless or near-landless rural poor. The largest estates are owned by transnational corporations (TNCs); European, Asian, or local businessmen; and government officials. Since the 1980s, SAP policies have enhanced the profitability of these large export-oriented businesses, while making economies that followed SAP prescriptions even more dependent upon fewer primary products than before.[234]

The peasant (or small farm) sector is also differentiated. It includes those farmers with sufficient resources to invest in technology and labor, who produce mainly for market, and hire migrants or their poorer neighbors as temporary laborers. To the extent that government and donor programs have helped small farmers at all, in most countries it is these "progressive" or small-scale commercial farmers who have been the main beneficiaries. Middle-level peasant families are able to grow most of their food and sell the surplus. Both these types of better-off peasants have sought to educate at least one family member sufficiently to obtain a civil service job. However, as access to government employment has narrowed with SAP budget cuts, many graduates join the unemployed.

At the bottom of the land-holding pattern are peasants who produce some crops for sale but are too poor in resources to fully meet family food and other basic requirements. These households must send out members to work for wages, sometimes on farms, but also as migrant labor. In many countries, the numbers and percentage of households in this category of poor peasants expanded in the 1980s and 1990s as access to fertile land grew increasingly restricted.

Structual adjustment programs require governments to remove subsidies on food as well as on agricultural inputs such as fertilizer and fuel. Food subsidies were reduced gradually in many countries, while subsidies on fertilizer and other inputs to small farmers were removed more rapidly.[235] International advisors, nevertheless, expressed confidence that higher crop prices would create incentives for farmers to produce more. The advisors believed that farmers aiming for higher yields would continue to use fertilizer even if they had to borrow money to purchase it. The errors in this notion are demonstrated by field studies. Research with women farmers is especially telling.[236]

Even where credit is available, small producers are apprehensive about making use of it. They cannot risk being unable to reimburse loans if their crop yields suffer due to insufficient rainfall.[237] Indebted farmers may lose their land and be forced to work on others' farms. Determined to avoid this fate, small farmers struggling on the edge of survival are unwilling to adopt the entrepreneurial mentality the SAP-mandated programs assume as the "natural" inclination.

The increased vulnerability of poor farming families under the impact of SAP-mandated policies is illustrated by the story of Bintu, a forty-five-year-old Jola woman, and her family, in their village in southwestern Senegal.[238]

Bintu has difficulty pulling her slight frame out of bed each day. She explains: "When you open your eyes in the morning knowing that your day will be filled with hardship and humiliation, your desire to begin the day may wane." Before this year (1994), Bintu had considered herself fortunate. Though she had lost two children in childbirth, she had two grown children from a previous marriage who looked after her. Her daughter Sali, living in the Senegalese capital Dakar, regularly sent Bintu money, and every year after the harvest her son gave her a portion of the money he earned from selling his peanut crop. With this income, Bintu was able to meet her expenses. She was praised in the village for her cooking and for the hearty meals she served her husband and his extended family.

Bintu also felt fortunate because, despite unreliable rainfall, her husband managed to grow enough peanuts to sell in order to cover the monthly cost of purchasing subsistence grains once the familial rice stocks ran out, usually five or six months after the harvest. When Bintu was a young girl, the rice the women cultivated would last well into the next harvest season, and surplus rice could be bartered for other household necessities. But in recent decades, the rains come late and end early, and the rice fields are slowly taking on salt from nearby saline waters. Despite such trends, Bintu considered herself relatively lucky.

But in 1994 one seemingly minor incident in Bintu's household shattered the fragile balance on which the family's livelihood depended. The four-year-old son of Bintu's *brother-in-law accidentally sliced his thumb with a knife. The wound became infected, and the boy fell seriously ill. The family collected enough money to send the boy and his father to see a nurse or doctor in the hospital 45 kilometers away. At the hospital, as Bintu's brother-in-law tells the story, the boy looked dreadfully ill, barely conscious. The doctor insisted on keeping him in the hospital. He ordered the boy's father to go to the local pharmacy to purchase medicines for his son's treatment, as the hospital did not have the medicines in stock. Having spent most of the money on transportation and hospital entrance fees, the boy's father was obliged to return to the village for more money so that he could fill the prescription. After ten days, and approximately $64 in medicines, hospital fees, and transportation costs, Bintu's brother-in-law returned to the village with a healthy son.*

Most of the money for the young boy's treatment (approximately $50) came from Bintu's husband, who had stashed away half of the previous year's peanut proceeds to be able to buy rice when the family's grain stock was depleted at the end of the dry season. His remaining savings could purchase only one 50 kilo sack of rice, enough to feed the family for about 27 days. With the government's devaluation of the currency and removal of transportation subsidies for grain, the price of rice was at an all-time high. For the following two months, Bintu and her sister-in-law contributed their meager savings to purchase rice. But then with two more months remaining before the harvest, the extended household was forced to begin selling off their modest livestock.

To make matters worse, when the two men of the household went to prepare for the peanut season, they learned that the government had also ended two long-standing programs designed to encourage farmers to produce peanuts: input subsidies and a credit system that enabled farmers to receive credit for seed, fertilizer, and equipment purchases. Now, for the first time since the peanut cash crop was introduced to the area toward the beginning of the century, it was up to the individual farmers to procure their own agricultural inputs. The government promised that farmers would be paid a higher price for their peanuts after the harvest. But with no money for seeds and other inputs, Bintu's husband and brother-in-law were forced to go into debt. The family now wonders if they will break even once they sell their crop. Next year, if they incur any extraordinary expenses, the entire household is likely to "go under" altogether.

Meanwhile, the financial support Bintu had previously received from urban relatives ceased. Bintu's daughter Sali and son-in-law Bocar, living in Dakar with their baby son, had themselves fallen on desperate times, due to layoffs directly resulting from Senegal's SAP.[239] At a time when their aid was critical, they were unable to continue sending remittance money to Bintu and the family in their rural village.

The story of Bintu and her family shows how SAP policies have worked at multiple levels to increase the economic vulnerability and health risks faced by poor rural families. Bintu's family members cultivate the family's own land. Poor peasants who must work on others' land also find themselves in desperate situations. As previously noted, farm workers' wages are extremely low; for women in particular they are often insufficient to support families, even in good times. Under such conditions, any sort of health emergency can rapidly take on catastrophic proportions, forcing a family to pledge or sell their productive assets to obtain cash.[240] By selling off their land or farm animals, families exacerbate their current plight, and dim their future prospects.

Single events requiring an unexpected outlay of money can push entire families to abandon the land and flock to urban squatter settlements.

The international financial institutions have imposed the privatization of agricultural marketing in the belief that state marketing boards are inherently less efficient than private sector traders.[241] Certainly, arguments could be made in defense of this claim. Parastatal marketing boards were originally designed by colonial rulers to assist white settlers in marketing their produce. They also served to tax peasant producers by holding prices down.[242] Following independence, many such boards continued to function to the advantage of officials who not only collected the state's "rent" from peasants,[243] but also seized opportunities for corruption. Nevertheless, the better-run agencies brought goods and services not otherwise available to farmers in remote areas. These goods included fertilizer and seeds, often supplied with low-cost or interest-free loans, or for the promise of a percentage of a farmer's future harvest. In Tanzania, Zambia, and Senegal in the late 1960s, and Zimbabwe in 1980, a system of state subsidies and "pan-territorial" prices enabled peasants far from markets to increase their production and to earn cash without having to migrate in search of employment.[244] However, the elimination of these structures in response to IFI pressure in favor of "free market" models imposed from outside has worked to the disadvantage of poor farmers in remote areas. The case of Zimbabwe shows how SAPs can exacerbate social inequality within a country (see Box 5.1).

Box 5.1: Free Markets and "Free Fall" in Zimbabwe

Zimbabwe's history of struggles for control of land has been long and bitter. In the late nineteenth century, conquest by European settlers was vigorously resisted for decades. When Africans lost, they were pushed off the best land and made to work the settlers' farms. In 1965, seeking to avoid Black majority rule, Europeans unilaterally declared independence (UDI) from Britain.[245] During the UDI period of white minority rule, new land laws reconfirmed white settlers' possession of 45 percent of the total land area—including the most fertile and well-watered land. Black Africans, 95 percent of the population, were confined to just half the land, much of it arid and unsuitable for cultivation. Much of the white settlers' land remained uncultivated.[246]

The white minority government pursued policies, including subsidized credit, prices, and infrastructure, to support the white-owned, large-scale commercial farms (LSCFs). The policies further marginalized the black peasant majority, many of whom became supporters of the protracted armed struggle for liberation from white domination. In the mid-1970s, indebtedness overtook many white settler farmers, and South Africa-based TNCs gained control of the sector. By the time of independence in 1980, TNC farms garnered 75 percent of profits derived from agriculture; they prospered in part by reducing workers' wages. Zimbabwe had joined the "Global Big House."[247]

The Mugabe government's ability to carry out land reform was hampered by a British-brokered peace agreement stipulating that any redistribution must compensate settler farmers at market rates.[248] Some farm purchases and redistribution took place in the early 1980s, but not enough to meet popular expectations. A 1983 survey found that 60 percent of rural households were still without land.[249] Twenty percent of the labor force worked on plantations, with the lowest wage rates of the formal sector, the worst living conditions, and the worst health status to be found in Zimbabwe.[250] In 1982, despite a pay raise, the minimum wage was 25 percent less than the cost of a bare subsistence diet.[251] By 1990, the large farm sector employed 300,000 workers, more than any other sector. Real wages fell. Migrants could no longer send home remittances; wives and children were pressed into work.

The parastatal grain marketing board (GMB), originally set up to aid LSCFs, expanded its collecting points into African farmers in communal areas (the old "tribal" reserves). The GMB provided peasants with inputs and collected the maize crop in a timely fashion, reducing post-harvest losses. For the first time, many peasants gained access to fertilizer and hybrid seeds adapted to low-potential agro-ecological zones. Production rose among African small-scale commercial farmers (SSCFs) and among peasants in the communal areas. Between 1980 and 1985, small holders nearly doubled the area planted with white maize, the staple food, as the government raised the farm price by 80 percent. In order not to increase urban wages beyond what employers would accept, however, the government subsidized the price of white maize. Small farmers could sell shelled grain to the GMB and purchase milled maize in local shops at subsidized prices. As a result of these favorable conditions, despite two years of drought (1982 and 1983), maize collected by the GMB tripled between 1980 and 1985.[252]

Gender inequality persisted. As "heads of households," men were awarded land titles and cooperative memberships, and the attention of extension agents.[253] Men, even those working in towns, received payment for crops grown by women, despite the women's heavy cash needs for household expenses, school uniforms, and clothing. Women from the new cooperative resettlement areas agitated for change, particularly for the right to hold land in their own names.[254] Peasants in the communal areas were still poor, but from their experience in the protracted war for liberation they remained organized as communities taking active part in local and national life.[255] Free government-supported rural schools and primary health care lightened the load. Infant mortality dropped by half.[256] Some NGOs assisted with water supply and maize storage facilities, without expecting reimbursement.[257] Production was unevenly distributed, however, varying with rainfall, soil quality, labor, and access to machinery.

The LSCFs still occupied nearly one-third of all cultivated land—including most of the best. Transnational corporations became the major producers of export crops. Employers provided miserable camp housing and some clinics, but health services were poor in both accessibility and quality. Prices for food and basic goods (salt, oil, soap, and so on) were higher in the shops in LSCF areas than elsewhere.[258]

In 1991, Zimbabwe signed a new SAP agreement that mandated "liberalization." Controls were removed from foreign exchange prior to devaluation. This led to speculative imports of expensive consumer goods that drained hard currency reserves. The World Bank delayed loan disbursement, apparently to hasten further policy changes. Maize and fertilizer subsidies were removed and activities of the GMB restricted. The rural poor, affected by sharply rising costs of fertilizer, food, and basic necessities, became still poorer. Zimbabwe's 1991 SAP "sent a previously moderately successful economy into free-fall."[259]

In 1991, the worst drought ever recorded struck the region.[260] The maize crop was ruined over most of the country and prices shot up, though few small farmers could benefit.[261] Introduction of "user fees" at health centers and hospitals led to sharp declines in attendance, because people could not afford to pay.[262] The worst health and living conditions were on the large farms.[263] Conditions for women workers were even worse than for men.[264]

By 1998, the government had laid off 7,000 nurses. Many physicians left the public system for private practice. In the early 1980s, Zimbabwe's formal sector workers had quite adequate health insurance for themselves and their families, but with so many unemployed due to SAP de-industrialization, the percentage of people covered dwindled. One-quarter of the adult population reported being infected with HIV, and AIDS killed 1,200 people each day. Life expectancy declined dramatically, from 60 years in 1991 to 49 years in 1997.[265]

Beginning in 1997, the urban population became more active in expressing its anger at the widening gap between their own poverty and the wealth of the political class. Strikes, stay-at-homes, and street demonstrations protested sharp consumer price hikes, government corruption, and profiteering. While President Mugabe blamed SAPs for the country's economic problems, others saw his inner circle grow wealthier by manipulating foreign exchange, import speculation, and privatization. Costly intervention in the Congo civil war, apparently to defend assets conceded to Zimbabwe officials by Congo President Kabila, is also extremely unpopular. The Congo government refused dialogue, and instead responded with force. Leaders of trade unions and religious and other civic groups called for a new constitution and began to form a new political party.[266]

Struggles over conditions of production and exchange traced in earlier sections continue across the continent today. Studies by social scientists who have observed market transactions and interviewed peasants find that, in many countries, unregulated private sector marketing has resulted in a lack of available inputs for small farmers, and in some areas, lower prices for their produce.[267] Currently, the rural poor are socially powerless, "surrounded by a dense network of public and private actors reducing their freedom of action and draining what few resources they do have."[268] Relying solely on unrestricted markets is *not* a rational policy for Africa.[269] The solution to the inefficiency and abuses of parastatals is not to eliminate these organizations entirely but to restructure them so as to make their bookkeeping transparent and their managers accountable to peasants.[270] Improving life for poor rural Africans will be less a matter of liberating free market forces than of liberating and empowering the poor themselves. The examples of Zimbabwe, Zaire, and Rwanda show that politics in peasant communities and relations between states and peasants lie at the heart of rural economic transformation.

To be effective and just, rural revitalization must also consider gender equity in land use, food production, and marketing.[271] In most of Africa, the majority of people are farmers, and women are overrepresented among farming populations. Women produce, transport, and process between 70 and 90 percent of food grown in many areas of Africa. They also work on husbands' cash-crop fields. Women spend long hours in the fields and also may walk for miles to procure wood and water, returning to prepare meals and care for children. Women's average workdays are 30 to 50 percent longer than men's, often lasting from 10 to 12 hours in slack seasons and 14 to 16 hours in peak periods, such as during field preparation, weeding, and harvests.[272]

Rural women's cash incomes, derived mainly from their own produce sales, purchase food and other family necessities such as soap, salt and oil, medicines, and school uniforms and supplies.[273] Where women control a significant share of household resources, they and their children are more likely to eat as well as men.[274] Generally, however, when families are unable to grow or purchase enough food to meet the nutritional requirements of all members, children's and women's health is the first to be sacrificed.[275]

In regions where men migrate in search of paid employment, 25 to 60 percent of household heads may be female.[276] Unless men are able to send home remittances, these households may be very poor. Beyond these generalities, however, there exist many differences. Both rural and urban women's situations vary with age, reproductive status, education, and the wealth of their families.[277]

As women's vital role in production became recognized in the 1970s, it was noted that women farmers had less access to land, labor, tools, and credit than did men. Furthermore, women were neglected by the agricultural extension services their taxes went to support.[278] Analysts urged that women be given greater access to resources, not only as an equity issue but to increase food production and national food security.[279] Pilot projects showed that women could increase their productivity when provided with small amounts of credit, training, and technology.[280] However, these promising demonstrations were not enlarged into nationwide programs.[281] Instead, in the 1980s most women's access to resources declined as a result of economic crisis and structural adjustment.[282] More women became unpaid laborers on their husbands' fields or low-paid workers on the fields of others.[283]

Structural adjustment policies favor export crops grown on farms controlled by senior men.[284] As in the colonial period, pressure to grow export crops has meant heavier work burdens for wives and daughters. Women's time and access to land, labor, and other inputs for their own independent agricultural projects have decreased. Crops controlled by women receive less fertilizer.[285] Yields of vegetable gardens and maize fields are reduced because women cannot afford to buy improved seeds. They must often choose between family meals and cash sales. Either choice may mean a decline in the quality of the family's diet and health, because women's cash is most often used to buy foods not grown at home, along with products such as soap, salt, cooking oil, fish, and other items essential to health.[286]

Tools produced with imported steel are too expensive, so women use inferior hoes made from recycled scrap. Meanwhile, bicycles, wheelbarrows, or oxcarts for daily transport of water and materials are now an impossible dream for most poor and medium-scale peasants. The absence of wheeled conveyances means still more toil for women. Men, who often would cooperate when wheeled transport was available, generally define head-loads as "women's work."[287] Many African peasant women bitterly attribute their declining status to "recolonization by SAPs."[288]

REFORMING SAPs: RHETORIC AND REALITY

Right Words, Wrong Actions

Widespread criticism of SAPs' deleterious effects on vulnerable populations in the late 1980s led the World Bank to design new loans and programs ostensibly intended to protect the poor during the years Bank officials label the "transition period" from state-planned to market economies. Yet these short-term compensation packages, or *social safety nets*, failed in most cases to mitigate the hardships of the poor. Instead, in many African countries, they became political tools used primarily to placate SAPs' vocal and politically organized opponents. In Senegal, for example, safety net projects were created after violent protests erupted in the aftermath of a national election in the late 1980s, that threatened to derail the government's compliance with SAPs. The projects provided small business management training and credit to educated, voting urbanites, *not* the rural poor.[289] Compensatory reductions in school and health service fees were often so badly publicized or cumbersome to access that little assistance actually reached those most in need.[290] The World Bank's 1995 Africa Poverty Reduction Task Force found that poverty-alleviation programs in most countries failed to adequately identify and target the neediest—the peri-urban and rural poor. Nor was the impact of such programs on poor communities adequately monitored.[291]

Poverty alleviation campaigns were potent rhetorical tools for assuaging SAPs' critics, but they were feeble in realizing their own stated objectives. Even though farm-level studies have shown that poor farmers can, with policy support, increase their production, contribute to food security, and reduce dependence on imports, the World Bank "still has not internalized or programmed enhanced production by poor people as a significant strategic element."[292] Without first altering the fundamental relationship between the IFIs and the people and governments of Africa, it is unlikely that "band-aid" remedies such as safety nets will go far in raising vulnerable populations out of poverty. What policies might induce meaningful change? Debt forgiveness offers one option.

Dogged Debt

After two decades of SAPs, the debt burdens of many African countries are unsustainable. In the 1980s, Africa, the world's poorest continent, was a net *supplier* of capital to the industrialized countries. Still, in 1993, for every dollar given to Africa in aid, rich nations took back three in debt repayments.[293] The amount of interest paid by poor countries to multilateral banks has already exceeded the original sums of money borrowed, yet the countries are still in debt.[294] In the 1980s and early 1990s, SAP-directed currency devaluation raised debt levels by 40 to 50 percent in most African countries. The effects continue to be felt. In 1996, sub-Saharan Africa received $15 billion in loans but paid out $12 billion in debt service. Despite some debt relief in the mid-1990s, debt service payments by African governments averaged 31 percent of exports.[295]

The obligation to spend so much of national budgets on debt service hinders governments' capacity to invest in health and social development. In 1994, over four-fifths of Uganda's export earnings—$162 million—went to debt and interest payments. By comparison, the country was able to spend a total of just $120 million on health and education services.[296] Between 1990 and 1993, sub-Saharan Africa transferred $13.4 billion annually to its external creditors. This is four times as much as governments in the region currently spend on health services.[297] Debt also impedes direct foreign investment, stifles employment creation, and ultimately inhibits economic growth. (See Box 5.2.)

Box 5.2: Uganda's Promise

In the 1990s, Uganda was considered to be one of the most successful adjusting countries. An initial, failed adjustment program in 1981-85 exacerbated the suffering wrought by more than a decade of death and destruction under autocratic rulers.[298] In 1986, a guerilla force calling itself the National Resistance Movement (NRM) won power after protracted struggle. The new government, headed by President Museveni, pledging to bring reconciliation and reconstruction, attracted substantial amounts of foreign aid.

The major contribution to growth in food production and agricultural exports in Uganda in the early 1990s was made by small-scale producers, rather than by large farms.[299] Peasants made up more than 70 percent of the population. Improved crop prices reduced the cross-border smuggling for which Uganda had been famous under dictatorial regimes.[300] At the same time, favorable credit and other terms for South Asian owners ousted in 1972 encouraged those now returning to Uganda to revitalize sugar and tea plantations, cotton gins, and factories, as well as trading enterprises. African-owned firms also expanded.[301] Amelioration of public sector salaries meant that peasants no longer had to send food to urban relatives.[302] Uganda regained its position as Africa's largest coffee producer.[303] Growth in the gross domestic product averaged 6 percent annually over the period 1987-1997. It included not only agriculture, but a building boom in Kampala and new manufacturing, as well as collection and processing of peasant-grown crops. Renewed hope and restored public order over much of the country appear to have been as important as policy shifts in restarting Uganda's economy.[304]

Uganda is by no means out of difficulty.[305] With average per capita income at $330 in 1997 and 50 percent of people living on less than two-thirds of that amount, the majority of Ugandans are still among the world's poorest people.[306] A few Ugandans and some foreigners have grown conspicuously wealthy. According to Uganda's vigorous opposition press, a recent boom in banking and urban construction (led largely by TNCs) fueled corruption in government and business. Rapid privatization of publicly owned assets also brought new opportunities for corruption.

Prices of Uganda's major exports—coffee, cotton, and tea—are highly volatile. Crop diversification involves exports of flowers and vegetables airfreighted to Europe. Agricultural growth slowed to 1.3 percent in 1997, well below the 3.1 percent increase in population.[307] Food production levels are precarious. Inequality in land ownership and land shortages are severe. Insurgents terrorize peasants living along the borders of Sudan and Congo and abduct children to serve them. In western Uganda, insurgents, operating from bases in Congo, include remnants of the army and militias that carried out genocide in Rwanda, and unemployed Ugandan youth.[308]

While donors have expressed concern about corruption and increased military expenditures, they appear willing to make concessions in hopes that President Museveni can maintain the stability necessary to sustain Uganda's growth.[309] A documentary film crew followed several months of SAP negotiations in 1997. Their video shows the African leader making his country's loan priorities prevail over those of the World Bank advisory team.[310]

Heavily Indebted Poor Countries (HIPC) that meet SAP "conditionalities" can, in time, obtain some relief from debt service payments and IFIs. Debt relief is not the same as outright cancellation. Relief may also include rescheduling payments on loans made by foreign governments and private banks. By allowing debtor countries a longer time to pay, and given probable inflation, drawing out the debt period should reduce total expense. While private and bilateral loans rescheduled in the 1980s and 1990s required higher rates of interest than the original loans made in the 1970s, the IFIs will lower their rates to offer "concessional" terms.

Uganda spearheaded the call by African leaders for debt cancellation. The first (and only) African HIPC to conduct successful debt relief negotiations with the IFIs to date, Uganda obtained approximately a 20 percent reduction in overall external debt service payments.[311] Burkina Faso, Côte d'Ivoire, and Mozambique are the other African countries that met debt relief conditions in April 1998. Their SAP compliance will be monitored for three additional years, however, before action is taken. A portion of bilateral and private loans made to African nations may yet actually be cancelled, rather than merely stretched out. If creditor governments agree to buy up private debts at current market value (an estimated 10 percent of face value), thereby in effect bailing out the banks, Africans could benefit. To date, there has been more talk than action.

Growth for Whom?

From the late 1970s, the IFIs gave optimistic assurances of prospects for short- and medium-term economic recovery through SAPs. Yet despite two decades of adherence to IFI-designed programs, sustainable economic growth continues to elude many African countries. The IFIs are themselves forced to concede that the current situation gives little grounds for hope.

The World Bank's 1995 Africa Poverty Reduction Task Force estimated that at least 7 percent annual GDP growth would be needed to make "a substantial impact" on poverty. What did the authors mean by "substantial"? The Task Force calculated that at that rate, it would take 30 years or more to double average per capita incomes from their present levels.[312] In 30 years, debts now being rescheduled may be paid off, but debt service on new loans will remain. Growth of the magnitude needed to substantially reduce poverty and harmful inequality requires debt cancellation, economic transformation, and institutional measures of resource redistribution.[313]

By their own admission, the IFIs were overly optimistic about short- and medium-term growth recovery in Africa. The World Bank's 1998 poverty report found that the limited recovery that took place in the 1990s was not sufficient to reverse the spread of poverty. Across the continent, GDP growth remained very fragile at between 4 and 5 percent, just 1 to 2 percent greater than population growth. "The outlook for sub-Saharan Africa in 1998 and beyond is more uncertain than was the case in 1997," the Bank reported. It recognized that where growth has occurred, its benefits have been unevenly distributed.[314] The report also emphasizes that gender makes a difference: women have borne the brunt of SAP-induced poverty. Bank analysts are silent, however, about the effects on African food producers, most of them female, when Western agribusiness firms dump food exports onto African markets.

The 1998 Bank report offers a new list of factors that limit growth in African economies. These include weak governance, high policy volatility, poor public services, high transport costs, poor soils, disease, climatic risk, export concentration in commodities, and violent conflict. There is little explicit recognition of the crippling effect of debt or the stubborn heritage of colonial abuses, and no acknowledgment of advisors' policy errors. No mention is made of the need to transform Africa's distorted structures of production. The study does not discuss how the pressure brought to bear on poor countries by powerful international corporations restricts African governments' capacity to protect their citizens or effectuate meaningful economic change.[315]

Studies focused on the actual effects of policies, rather than policy-makers' rhetorical justifications, reveal SAPs' principal goals and hidden agenda. The first goal is debt reimbursement. The World Bank used the notion of "comparative advantage" to press for increased export production rather than for diversification. Though exports and budgetary austerity have helped governments make debt service payments, government expenditures continue to exceed revenues. Hence the need for new loans. Consequently, no surplus remains to invest in human or economic development.

The Washington Consensus has demonstrated little concern for family or regional food security.[316] This suggests a second, unstated goal associated with SAPs. American, Canadian, and European agribusiness firms are major exporters of grain and meat. Their lobbyists seek wider, unprotected markets for agricultural products abroad. Exports to Africa, including sales of food aid, are especially attractive to the industrialized nations, in the face of today's shrunken markets in Asia. That region's current crisis and SAPs have reduced Asian consumers' incomes and ability to purchase imported food. Supplying their governments with food to aid Africa is a profitable alternative for agribusiness.

A third goal of SAPs is to improve the "investment climate"—in fact, to enhance the profitability and security of TNCs in Africa. Most such firms are involved in extraction of oil and minerals, others in the sale of technology and capital equipment, and some in manufacturing. In the future, more manufacturing firms may find Africa to be an attractive outlet for surplus capital. This once again bodes ill for the poor in Africa, as private investment requires guarantees of high profits, low taxes, an end to worker protection, publicly financed infrastructure, and free repatriation of capital.[317]

The studies cited in the present chapter show that growth under these conditions cannot bring long-term socioeconomic improvements to the majority of Africans. The World Bank's remedies prescribe more of the same SAP-with-poverty-reduction advice. Yet neither credit to support survival strategies in the urban informal sector nor free rural health services and schools can remedy the structural conditions that breed poverty, disease, powerlessness, hopelessness, and violence.[318] Given that the governments of wealthy nations wield financial and political power within the World Bank and the IMF, their objectives, rather than those of the African poor, guide these institutions' decisions with respect to Africans' futures.[319]

CONCLUSION

In this chapter we have examined the complex crises of African economies and societies over the past quarter century. We demonstrated how Africa's exploitation by the European powers shattered earlier social patterns and governance institutions. Colonialism established new economic and political relations based on authoritarianism, brutality, racism, and ethnic and class stratification to ensure the profits of multinational firms and white settlers' ventures. Although Europeans claimed a "civilizing mission," Africans were forced to finance their own domination through taxes and forced labor. The roots of the economic crisis that predated SAPs reside in a combination of internal and international processes that continue to shape the realities of life in Africa today. Crises in the world economy have had deep and lasting effects on an Africa made vulnerable by colonialism's legacy of distorted internal production structures and authoritarian states that extract wealth from Africa.

Africa's ills are, of course, not only externally derived. Unable to achieve economic independence, many leaders of the new states acquired a vested interest in maintaining the old relations of domination. In order to accumulate capital and enjoy lifestyles commensurate with ruling classes elsewhere, they squeezed poor producers and plundered their countries. In the process, leaders rendered operating conditions less profitable for foreign firms. Forced to share their profits, many companies shifted operations elsewhere. In the 1980s, international financial and corporate interests sought to regain their ascendancy in Africa through SAPs. We have shown how SAPs help re-create internal and international conditions that had earlier led to economic growth without development. Africa's working poor have been made to endure wage freezes, unemployment, hunger, and ill-health so that funds might be directed to pay foreign debts and restore or enhance corporate profitability. With emphasis on export-led growth and reliance on private firms subsidized by public investment, SAPs benefit TNCs and their partners, the wealthy few within Africa.

This complex weave of history and SAPs has rendered poor Africans more vulnerable to disease and more likely to die unnecessarily. Low levels of health and education restrict the capacity of societies to develop, and undermine the long-term future of poor families. The heavy social costs of failure force increasing numbers of Africans to live in abject poverty, worse off at the end of the century than at any time since 1960. Nearly two decades of SAPs that were supposed to trade "short-term pain for long-term gain" have not halted the deterioration. Although presented by the IFIs as the only road to growth, SAPs in fact embody political choices. Deregulation and privatization are technocratic, neutral-seeming ways to redistribute wealth upward and outward.

This chapter demonstrates that the "short-term pain" of SAPs means that for many poor Africans *there will be no long term*. Case studies of hunger, malnutrition, and disease show the silent struggles for survival unfolding daily on the African continent. The 1994 genocide in Rwanda illustrates an extreme consequence of Africa's colonial legacy, as this heritage interweaves with contemporary political and economic crises exacerbated by the immediate effects of SAPs. Nsanga's story reveals how, in the deadly synergy between poverty and disease, AIDS inflicts further tragedy on poor Africans and devastates already vulnerable communities.

In order for positive economic and political transformations to take root, it is essential to cancel debt, increase investment in public services, expand productive employment at a living wage, and support sustainable, high-yield production by small-scale cultivators. These shifts would enable poor Africans to focus on something *other* than mere survival. Yet in the absence of a still more profound transformation of African economies and of the ways African wealth is redistributed, even these reforms can do little but extend the agony to future generations. However, structural transformation enabling hundreds of millions of struggling poor people to truly improve their lot would mean there would be lower profits for foreign and local firms. Therein lies the problem: conflict, as yet unresolved, between the health needs and human aspirations of poor people, and the economic agenda of the IFIs, corporate interests, and their allies among African rulers.

ACKNOWLEDGMENTS

The authors are grateful to Alec Irwin for his advice on successive versions of this chapter, his reworking of several sections, and his careful editing of the endnotes. Evan Lyon shifted our extensive references to the general bibliography and helped locate missing reference data. Jim Kim, Julie Rosenberg, Jon Welch, Aaron Shakow, Joel Brenner, Heather Rensberry, and Cassis Henry also provided valuable assistance. We thank them all.

Lima, Peru. In one of the city's many shantytowns, children await their parents in the doorway of a shop.

(photo by Catherine Crosland)

CHAPTER SIX

Sickness Amidst Recovery: Public Debt and Private Suffering in Peru

Jim Yong Kim, Aaron Shakow, Jaime Bayona, Joe Rhatigan, and Emma L. Rubín de Celis

"Señora, you have to buy these medicines, or die—you choose."
"Doctor, I want to live—but I can't afford to buy them…"

> —Peruvian patient with multidrug-resistant
> tuberculosis and her physician, 1997

Rats and roaches live by competition under the laws of supply and demand; it is the privilege of human beings to live under the laws of justice and mercy.

> —Wendell Berry[1]

Benedicta Sanchez[2] started coughing during the winter of 1994, but at first she paid it little attention. Born in a rural province north of Lima, the 38-year-old woman had moved to the shantytown district of Carabayllo, on the northern fringe of the Peruvian capital, when her husband found agricultural work nearby. From the time of their arrival, amid the economic austerity imposed by President Alberto Fujimori in 1990, the couple and their two adult daughters had teetered on the brink of starvation. Some weeks, Benedicta and her husband were able to earn as much as 20 soles (US$8), but this income was unpredictable, and often the two of them brought in far less, or nothing at all. Anticipating sporadic shortfalls, they struggled to save what little money they could.

But Benedicta had more than a cold. For months she'd been losing weight and waking up at night with drenching sweats. One Monday evening, Benedicta's oldest daughter Maria returned from night school to find her mother coughing up blood-streaked sputum. Maria had just heard a radio announcement that described the symptoms of tuberculosis and that urged people experiencing them to seek help. Maria decided to stay home from work the next day in order to take her mother to the nearest public health center, a 15-minute bus ride away. Although patients are charged two soles (US$0.80) for most visits to this clinic, tuberculosis checkups are free. This, as Benedicta and Maria were told, is because the Peruvian Ministry of Health sees tuberculosis as a very serious problem.

After taking her mother to the clinic for various tests three days in a row, Maria began to worry that she might lose her job if she didn't return to work. That Friday, after receiving *inconclusive TB test results from the clinic's lab, Benedicta went alone to the nearest public hospital, a half-hour bus ride and 20-minute walk from her home. There, health workers informed her that she needed to purchase saline solution, surgical tubing, gloves, and a syringe before a definitive diagnosis could be made. Benedicta was also told that the national tuberculosis program would not cover the cost, which amounted to almost 10 soles (US$4).*

Benedicta panicked. She had been told at the clinic that her treatment would be free. She explained to the nurse that she had only enough money for bus fare home, one sol.

"Señora, how can you leave your house and come all the way here with just one sol?" the nurse asked her.

"Señorita," replied Benedicta, "if I had known I was going to have to pay, I would not have come at all."

Benedicta returned home without even being diagnosed. When Maria asked her mother that evening what the doctors had said, Benedicta told her that she was fine, that she didn't have TB after all. Benedicta knew that Maria would force her to return to the hospital if she learned the truth. And she knew that to purchase the supplies for her treatment, she would have to deplete the family's meager savings, and perhaps threaten its survival. So Benedicta made a calculated choice: she said nothing, and went on coughing.

PUBLIC AND PRIVATE IN THE NEW WORLD ORDER

Over the last twenty years, Benedicta's experience has become commonplace in developing countries. Her aborted contact with the Peruvian health-care system typifies the way in which state abdication of responsibility for certain services can lead to the propagation of illness. In the literature of health and public administration, such displacements of responsibility are known euphemistically as "cost shifting," "cost sharing," or, as we will illustrate in the case of Peru, "funding demand but not supply." Through these displacements, many social and economic functions paid for previously by government agencies are privatized—transferred to nongovernmental organizations (NGOs), private companies, and sometimes, with tragic results, to impoverished individuals like Benedicta Sanchez.

These decisions, of course, are not arbitrary. Often they are mandated by state planners in developing countries under great pressure to reduce costs and bring greater "efficiency" to health-care systems. The term *privatization*, though imprecise, is now the gloss most widely used to describe the broad range of initiatives that confine governments' fiscal obligations in the health sector.

Privatization of health-care services differs from its analogues in other sectors, where state-owned industries such as telecommunications or mining are sold to for-profit companies. Health care is rarely privatized by a purchase and sales agreement. Rather, what ensues is a privatization of *responsibility*. No longer are states the originators and executors of health policy; initiative shifts to groups and corporations whose primary aims may have little to do with the public's health. Fundamental to this shift is the assumption that "market forces" will improve the operation of health-care systems by infusing them with often-invoked but ill-defined qualities like "efficiency" and "choice."

The privatization of health services in Latin America and elsewhere affects rich and poor people quite differently. In recent years, hospitals from Miami to southern California have engaged in aggressive marketing campaigns in Latin America, targeting wealthy consumers who can afford to pay top dollar for private health insurance plans.[3] Meanwhile, for those who survive on less than two dollars per day (about half the Peruvian population), the privatization of health can have cruel consequences.

The trend in developing countries like Peru to transform state-run social services into "market-driven" systems governed by profit and competition raises fundamental questions about human priorities. Social sector privatization in Peru and elsewhere has been undertaken within a policy framework in which freeing government funds to pay interest on foreign loans is a primary objective. The international financial institutions that oversee poor countries' debt have played a leading role in designing the neoliberal model of "structural adjustment," which counts privatization as a central element.

The design of neoliberal reforms is driven by the state's need to cut costs. Whatever might be done with the proceeds of fiscal realignment, whether they are expended on debt service or reinvested in the social sector, the structure of reform has been guided by fiscal outcomes. Such a concern is not insignificant. But if the purpose of health-care reform is to improve health outcomes—particularly for poor citizens who suffer inordinately from preventable disease and mortality—then "reforms" must be examined in a completely different light.[4]

THE PRIVATIZATION OF HEALTH CARE IN PERU

The Peruvian government, like its analogues in many other poor countries, has limited agency in determining social policy. When in the late 1980s former president Alan García set a limit (10 percent of export earnings) on the sum that could be applied to yearly debt service payments, the international financial institutions led a retaliatory campaign against the Peruvian government, with devastating effects on the populace.[5] Poor countries considering unilateral reductions in debt service payments could not help but get the message—the price of resistance would be far higher than the savings from withholding payment.

In 1990, Alberto Fujimori, a relatively unknown professor who had been the president of the National Agrarian University outside Lima, astonished the Peruvian *cognoscenti* by winning the presidential election on a populist platform. Donning a poncho and other peasant garb and taking his campaign directly to the poor, Fujimori distinguished himself from his opponent, acclaimed author Mario Vargas-Llosa, who maintained close ties to the oligarchy that had ruled Peru for many decades. During the campaign, Fujimori promised his supporters that any plan to re-initiate debt payments would be gradual, and sensitive to the most vulnerable members of Peruvian society. Just after his stunning victory, the president-elect flew with several of his top advisors to New York for a meeting with the executives of the International Monetary Fund (IMF), World Bank, United Nations, and other multilateral agencies. When one of his economic planners laid out the new administration's sketch for a gradual approach to correct Peru's hyperinflation, those across the table put their collective foot down.

> 'He was talking about Howdy Doody and the others talked to Fujimori about the facts of life,' a dismissive participant recalled. The president-elect emerged from the meeting convinced that the only feasible approach to Peru's economic recovery—or to renewed IMF and World Bank help, at any rate—involved a monetarist shock treatment.[6]

Persuaded by this forceful approach, the Fujimori government acted quickly, sparking a deliberate recession, slashing price supports for food and fuel, devaluing the currency, and imposing a 14 percent sales tax on all domestic purchases. The year after this structural adjustment program—"Fujishock," as Peruvians called it—was implemented, the consumer price index (CPI) shot up at a rate of 7,650 percent, and the value of wages dropped precipitously.[7] Health sector inflation was the highest of all consumer spending categories: the cost of care rose 8,400 percent during 1990-91.[8] Meanwhile, the population officially classed as "poor" jumped from seven to 12 million, even as state social spending plummeted.[9]

Over the next three years, however, Peru staged an "astonishing recovery."[10] Having put his country, in the words of one admiring journalist, "back on the world map," Fujimori's IMF-inspired austerity measures reduced annual price inflation to 23 percent by 1994, and boosted growth in the gross national product (GNP) to over 12 percent, the highest growth rate in Latin America.[11] Foreign direct investment, *negative* $7 million in 1991, picked up briskly as overseas financiers began "crawling all over Peru," pouring $2.86 billion into the Peruvian economy.[12]

One crucial component of the "shock therapy" implemented in 1990 was Fujimori's privatization initiative. Selling off assets and unlocking state obligations gave the government an immediate source of liquidity to resume debt payments. As a reward for the government's compliance, the IMF granted Peru a one-year grace period on late interest payments—provided that it continued to pursue the inflation-busting "stabilization package" and reform its systems of law and taxation along free-market lines. With direct assistance from the United States, Japan, and several European countries, Fujimori initiated regular debt service to the IMF; by 1996, he closed on an agreement to reschedule $10.5 billion in commercial debt, and signed new contracts with nearly all of Peru's international creditors.[13]

Ironically, the privatization of Peru's state industries was heavily promoted by many of the same multilateral agencies that had urged the government to buy them in the first place. During the 1950s and 1960s, World Bank officials strongly supported state investment in industries like telecommunications and transportation. Two and a half decades later, President Fujimori—prodded again by the World Bank and IMF—sold much of its share in the Peruvian telephone system to pay a fraction of the interest on some of the very loans which had been taken out to build it. Between 1991 and 1998, the government privatization agency Copri liquidated 97 percent of the state's assets in fisheries, 90 percent of its banks, 85 percent of its factories, and 70 percent of its interests in mining and energy.[14] While privatization did provide Peru with sufficient cash flow to get back on the world map and in investors' good graces, it proved completely insufficient to pay down the country's loan principal, which increased from $16 billion to an estimated $27.5 billion between 1990 and 1997.[15] In fact, it has not even been enough to pay debt service. During 1996, which saw more state enterprises sold than any other year to date, debt service exceeded the proceeds of privatization by $300 million.[16]

Several elements of Peru's neoliberal reform ensured that an inordinate share of its burden would fall on the shoulders of the poor. Almost immediately after it assumed power, the Fujimori government moved to cut tariffs and personal income tax; by 1997 both corporate and individual tax rates had fallen by 60 percent from their 1986 levels.[17] The slack in state budgets was taken up, in part, by value-added taxes on consumer products. This trend, in fact, was regionwide, and resulted in a highly regressive tax structure that has made poor people disproportionately responsible for public fiscal obligations—most prominently, such high-budget items as debt service.[18]

Cuts in social spending could not help but severely impact the quality and quantity of state health sector funding. According to the Peruvian National Planning Institute (INP), health spending in the early 1990s remained at levels well below those of a decade before.[19] While some initiatives like the National Tuberculosis Control Program were well funded, spending and support for health care as a whole was inconsistent. In November 1997, under pressure from creditors and aid agencies, the Peruvian government officially implemented a realignment of national health-care financing strategy.[20]

The privatization of state enterprise had first encroached on health institutions early in the 1990s, in the first wave of Fujishock. Many private companies ceased to underwrite health-care benefits that state employees had taken for granted, and other workers were pushed into the informal economy, where benefits were nonexistent. The government's reform plans, first drafted soon after Fujimori's assumption of power, formalized the trend away from direct central government involvement with health care.[21] As health ministry officials took care to point out, the plans' culmination in the Health Law of 1997 was "a change in the rules of the game." This was in effect the canonization of a model that claimed "to improve the quality of life of Peruvians" by "improving productivity and eliminating unnecessary spending on health."[22]

The 1997 Health Law was foreshadowed in a series of planning documents, texts of which bore a striking similarity to two decades of pronouncements from Washington, D.C. "The Ministry of Health," the model stated, "will remove itself from the administration and direct provision of health-care services."[23] Individuals would thereafter be required to purchase their own health insurance, selected from among a competing array of providers. The individual citizen's obligation to purchase insurance was designed to erase any potential for what economists term "moral hazard," the risk that people to whom services are provided free of charge will use them unnecessarily. While the state would offer assistance to those who could not afford basic insurance coverage, all health costs not covered by this "basic package" would have to be assumed by the individual.[24] In this fashion, the state would move from "financing the supply of health services" to "financing the demand."[25]

In keeping with Peru's 1994 constitution, both the planning model and the 1997 Health Law itself claimed to "promote and defend the individual's right to health."[26] The form in which this right was to be realized, however, was strikingly limited to "the exercise of free choice" among a range of services.[27] While in a broad sense the "protection of health" was seen to be in the public interest—mandating state regulation, surveillance, and promotion—the actual provision of curative or rehabilitative health care was not expressly guaranteed by this "right." While Peruvians would be entitled to "unrestricted access to health services and to choose the provisional system of their preference,"[28] there was no statement on how the state would ensure that the poor majority would be able to pay for these services.

In attempting to decipher the rationale behind the Health Law of 1997, we find that the *ideology* of privatization played an extremely important role. The most influential consultants in international health settled on privatization as their policy instrument of choice, despite lacking any real evidence that its health benefits or fiscal advantages would accrue to the entire population. Their leap of faith, it seems, drew upon a deep cultural cache, a powerful investment in free market prescriptions.

INTELLECTUAL ANTECEDENTS

The basic idea of privatization is quite simple: a transfer of assets or responsibilities from the public to the private sector. Governments have been doing this since the earliest days of the "public sector" itself, but as a pillar of neoliberal ideology, privatization had special importance to the right-wing coalitions that brought Margaret Thatcher and Ronald Reagan to power.[29]

In the Tory and Republican triumphs of 1979 and 1980, proponents of privatization saw a broad mandate to pursue activist initiatives on the neoliberal model. "The American people," wrote the President's Commission on Privatization in 1988, "have often complained of the intrusiveness of federal programs, of inadequate performance, and of excessive expenditures. In light of these public concerns, government should consider turning to the creative talents and ingenuity in the private sector to provide...better answers to present and future challenges."[30] On the principle that "a free people should be responsible for their own development," the commission went on to identify instances of waste and inadequacy, and instances where private enterprise was impeded from supplying a service by "excessive regulation."[31] This anecdotal argument led the authors into a seeming logical fallacy: without presenting any evidence, they concluded from samples of state inefficiency that "privatization is growing because it delivers major savings or improved service quality, or both."[32]

The extent to which services were improved or made less expensive by privatization remains deeply ambiguous; the growth of the privatization phenomenon, however, was indisputable. The 1980s saw rapid acceleration worldwide in the sale of state-owned companies: the World Bank recorded a total of 6,832 such transactions between 1980 and 1992.[33] By 1997, the global proceeds from privatization had reached $153 billion.[34]

But the "growing" trend toward private ownership of public resources was not overtaking wealthy countries alone. Historically, the governments of poor countries have owned and overseen large sectors of their economies, partly to promote social goods like employment, and partly because the state was often the only local actor with the funds and motive to promote essential industries. Some government-controlled enterprises turned a profit; many others, however, cost far more to maintain than they earned in revenue. There were several reasons for this inefficiency, including corruption, outdated technologies, and a poorly educated workforce. Subsisting on minuscule salaries, which they frequently received regardless of productivity, managers of state enterprises often had limited funds to invest in new equipment or training and saw few incentives to change. Institutions like the U.S. Agency for International Development (USAID) under President Reagan insisted that by selling off such enterprises, poor countries' governments could acquire badly needed cash, shed costly obligations, and render industry more efficient through the operation of market processes.[35] Other development agencies along with USAID moved rapidly to prod governments in this direction with specific incentives, including assistance in renegotiating the commercial loans on which many countries had fallen into default.[36] By 1991, developing-country governments had sold 2,162 state enterprises, about one-third of the world total.[37]

The stance of Reagan-era aid officials, however, had numerous critics—particularly in and around the developing world. Many planners and economists, even at the World Bank, contended that privatization of state-owned enterprises tends to concentrate wealth and to exacerbate economic inequalities.[38] As of 1991, one journalist noted, 37 Mexican businessmen, who together controlled 22 percent of the country's GNP, were the primary stakeholders in all but one of the country's public sector sell offs. "Few nationals," she reported, had access to "the money or international contacts to buy government-owned companies. This constrains the number of eligible bidders, weakens bids, and means that the few who are able to purchase previously state-owned enterprises can extend their economic reach."[39] Others, noting the efforts of USAID to secure an American interest in newly privatized industries, have contended that the agency's advocacy of privatization in poor states is designed primarily to benefit U.S. private and corporate investors.[40]

Certainly, there are instances in which money-losing "white elephants" must be let go in order to free up scarce resources in poor countries, yet a government can often earn more over the long run by implementing measures to render public enterprises more efficient.[41] But this difficult calculation is abstract—it fails to capture the *social* costs of privatization policies. By relinquishing control of industries and services, governments lose their ability to ensure an equitable distribution of the resources they generate. To Benedicta Sanchez, for example, platitudes such as "financing demand but not supply" have a deadly ring. Unable to afford the price at which health care was offered, getting sicker was the only currency she had left.

Benedicta's experience is emblematic of a conflict at the heart of privatization debates, particularly in the social sector. This conflict is not over the real-world efficiency of market-oriented social policies, but about fundamental beliefs concerning the proper relation between individuals and the state. Always contentious, allocation of expensive resources like housing, health care, and education is perennially subject to hierarchies of wealth and social standing.[42] For this reason, many argue, the distribution of basic goods and services must not be left up to the vagaries of the market; doing so would exacerbate existing inequalities within society, significantly curtailing poor people's access.[43] Resources like health care, in this view, must be seen as a basic human right, for which society, operating through the organs of government, is collectively responsible.[44] The role of the state is precisely to overcome the inequalities of the market, "either by regulating it or displacing it as a mechanism for allocating resources."[45]

The notion of a human *right* to health care and other essential social goods is seldom contested overtly by those who draft privatization strategies. Nevertheless, their prescriptions for decentralization and market autonomy are underwritten by a neoliberal ideology that may ultimately be incompatible with social rights. During the mid-1970s, Robert Nozick, an influential libertarian political philosopher, summed up this emerging attitude in a pithy revision of the old socialist motto, "To each according to their need, from each according to their ability." "From each as they choose," wrote Nozick, "to each as they are chosen."[46]

Nozick's concept of volition, arguably, is the very spirit of privatization policies in the social service sector. In poor countries like Peru, it takes on a deeply paradoxical edge. There, for large segments of the population the choice being exercised is between life-sustaining food and life-preserving medicine; and the reforms which have forced this "deliberation" are being implemented, to a significant degree, in order to maintain loan regimes entered into by no choice of their own. Volition seems almost incomprehensible when juxtaposed beside the raw need of poor people for essential resources like food and health care. In a market economy, one should note, poverty is exactly tantamount to "not being chosen."

MARKETING THE STATE

By the formulations of bodies such as Reagan's Commission on Privatization, the rationale for privatizing practically everything seemed self-evident. In "shedding" state service loads, or exposing previously closed markets to competitive pressures, reformers hoped to reduce the direct burden on taxpayers.[47] Effectively, what this mechanism implied was not so much a distinction of "public" from "private" but rather, one of *monopoly* from *competition*.[48] Two decades after such policies began to be implemented in the United States, researchers have yet to find consensus on partisans' efficiency claims. As one recent review observes, "private service delivery is [not] inherently more effective or less effective than public service delivery....There are examples of success and failure in both sectors."[49]

Although sometimes privatization initiatives dictate the sale of state interest in mines, telecommunications systems, or transportation networks to a private entity, their highly politicized context frequently dictates a more subtle approach. In many cases, state enterprises will simply be "marketized" without the government relinquishing its legal ownership; this can entail contracting out public functions to profit-making companies, instituting "voucher" programs that give taxpayers certificates for private services, or imposing user fees. Privatizing states may also reduce the services that they provide. For example, they may replace government agencies with publicly funded, privately administered systems, or deregulate industries subject previously to tight central control.[50]

The various configurations of privatization are governed by two basic suppositions: "markets" and "states" are seen to be in binary opposition, and private administration is held to be intrinsically more efficient than its public analogue.[51] These axioms have far-reaching implications, not least for the most vulnerable sectors of any given population.

Theoretically, if a private party pays market price for a state-owned enterprise, there is no net transfer of wealth, because the government has exchanged an asset for liquidity (that is, cash). The appropriate price for an enterprise should include its present worth, plus some calculation of potential future profits. By selling it, the government gives up these profits in exchange for present liquidity—this is similar, but not identical, to the trade-off experienced with government-issued bonds.[52]

The previous description, however, presumes that governments will calculate accurately the value of the enterprise they are selling. In reality, there is high uncertainty regarding the true worth and future profit-making potential of a given venture, making these sales risky both for governments and for private buyers. Incomplete knowledge on either side can make for enormous profits or losses. In developing countries, especially in situations where cash-strapped governments are negotiating with wealthy, well-informed, and powerful transnational corporations, it should come as no surprise that buyers often come out on top. Not infrequently, privatized concerns reap years of handsome dividends from formerly public resources, while the government's proceeds from their sale dissipate rapidly. Moreover, efficiency and competition are often sacrificed amid the cronyism and nepotism so prevalent in countries like Mexico and Indonesia.

Peru provides a striking example of the imbalance in cost and benefit. Soon after taking office in 1990, pointing to losses among state-owned corporations of $1.685 billion between 1985 and 1989, President Fujimori targeted 81 state-owned companies for sale.[53] Two years later, the legislature approved 22 such transactions, and in 1996 the Peruvian government gleaned $2.3 billion from the sale of public companies, much of which was to be paid out over several years.[54]

Notwithstanding Peru's volatile political climate, numerous foreigners moved to purchase privatizing enterprises. Taking advantage of low prices and wages, multinational investors were further attracted by Fujimori's policies toward organized labor, which have been strategically obstructive. As of 1998, six years after the passage of a comprehensive labor law (which, among other things, reduced severance pay by 300 percent), less than six percent of the workforce is unionized, strikes have declined "markedly," and benefits are "readily sacrificed for regular employment."[55]

In an important sense, privatization synergized with other facets of structural adjustment to create a climate where nearly all quadrants of the Peruvian landscape were for sale. One venue of the new liberal investment policies was the Yanacocha gold mine, in the Andean province of Cajamarca, about 300 miles north of Lima. Until the 1990s, the government had restricted direct foreign involvement in mineral extraction, and had levied high royalties on exports. Under Fujimori, however, this stance changed dramatically. In 1993, Denver-based Newmont Mining Company bought a controlling share in the Yanacocha, along with Buenaventura, a Peruvian concern, and—ironically, in light of the ideology that had induced the sale—the French government-owned Bureau de Recherches Géologiques et Minières (BRGM). Capitalized with $34 million, the mine was estimated to contain 3.8 million ounces of gold, worth nearly $1.5 billion.[56] At the inauguration ceremony, President Fujimori declared proudly, "We now have the legal framework so that foreign firms like Newmont Mining come here with confidence to work alongside Peruvians to help create jobs."[57]

It is undeniably true that jobs were created through the sale of the Yanacocha mine. As of 1997, the operation had a workforce of 1,633, more than 95 percent of which was Peruvian. The disparity in salaries between locals and foreign nationals, however, was striking: while the company paid an average annual salary of $11,635, according to internal statistics, the daily wage of mineworkers was just $5.60 per day or approximately $1,400 per year.[58] In its first year of operation, it produced approximately $90 million worth of gold at a cost of $40 million, thus recouping its original investment in less than a year.[59] By the end of 1995, Minera Yanacocha—owned 51.5 percent by Newmont, 43.5 percent by Buenaventura and 5 percent by the private investment arm of the World Bank—was the twelfth largest company in Peru, with assets of $166 million.[60] It is presently the largest gold producer in all of Latin America, having extracted over 1 million ounces in 1997—at less than half the cost of Newmont's own mining operations elsewhere.[61]

The lopsided benefits of the Yanacocha initiative are in many ways representative of the merits and demerits of privatization policies in general. In a country where unemployment and underemployment are together estimated at greater than 71 percent, companies that were privatized laid off, on average, 52 percent of their workers.[62] After being bought by a U.S firm for $35 million in 1993, for example, the Cerro Verde copper mine cut its workforce by 40 percent (from 1,300 to 785). Centromin, Peru's largest mining company, between 1996 and 1998 fired 29 percent of its workers (5,000 of 17,000) after privatization of its seven mines.[63] According to estimates by CEDAL, a Peruvian research foundation, the combination of public sector downsizing and privatization after 1990 resulted in 400,000 layoffs—a full 40 percent of Peru's officially employed population.[64]

Beyond this direct effect on employment, privatized companies' contributions to the Peruvian economy as a whole are debatable. Earnings were frequently transferred offshore under liberalized capital flow regulations, and large disparities existed in the salaries paid to Peruvians and to foreign workers. Moreover, the high-tech equipment that was purchased to improve production was almost invariably manufactured outside Peru. The U.S. Department of Commerce now advertises mining equipment as the "best prospect" for U.S. exports to Peru; sales are projected to reach $694 million in 1999, a 100 percent increase over 1996, and no local industry exists for the manufacture of this commodity.[65]

Much new investment in Peru since 1990 has been in extractive industries such as mining, oil, natural gas, and fishing; between 1995 and 2000, foreign companies are projected to pump $6.5 billion into mining alone.[66] In the process of pursuing these enterprises, investors have acquired huge tracts of land. Between 1990 and 1994, 37 international mining and energy companies purchased 6 million acres in Peru, double the area bought by foreigners in the previous 40 years.[67] In many cases, these properties were acquired from individual owners for a fraction of their value. One farmer, for example, was paid $42 a hectare for his plot, in an area where land costs $2,000 a hectare on the open market.[68] Such abuses have contributed to the sharp decline of subsistence and staple-crop agriculture since Fujimori's accession. Peru was projected to import 88 percent of its wheat supply and more than half of its corn in 1998.[69]

Meanwhile, permissive environmental laws shaped to encourage investment have led to significant ecological degradation from deforestation, oil spills, and poisoned waterways. In mining towns, villagers reported mass deaths of fish and livestock as a result of copper and sulfate stream contamination.[70] This trend was regionwide. As one Canadian mining executive put it, "You don't have the special-interest environmental groups in Latin America that you have in North America." In Latin America, he beamed, "they don't think of mining as a negative thing."[71]

Finally, privatization in Peru has sacrificed long-term public resources for short-term liquidity. During 1996, even as the government took in $2.6 billion for the sale of its industrial infrastructure, privatized companies made almost $1.5 billion in earnings for foreign investors.[72] In the entire six-year period of 1990-96, Peru gleaned only $7 billion in proceeds from its various auctions, while buyers frequently gained enterprises with nearly limitless profit potential. As the abortive example of Haiti's Aristide seems to indicate, it is quite possible to increase public sector efficiency through the imposition of purely administrative changes, and by resolute pursuit of progressive taxation.[73] In Peru and other countries like it, however, such efficiencies were not even attempted. Sell-offs were a foregone conclusion, and, for many, a profitable one.[74]

ADJUSTMENT AND DISEASE

Many advocates of neoliberal macroeconomic programs understood from the start that such plans would weigh most heavily on the poor. Writing for the Brookings Institute—the group which first articulated the tenets of the "Washington Consensus"—Carlos Paredes and Jeffrey Sachs noted in 1991 that stabilization programs "will probably reduce consumption most for middle-income groups, whose demands for compensation will likely be loudest. But any absolute decline in the purchasing power of the extremely poor may create serious and irreversible physical deterioration. It is to this that the government should direct scarce fiscal resources."[75]

As Fujimori's reforms were being implemented, the detrimental effect of structural adjustment on lower-income populations was becoming clear even to mainstream observers. In 1992, an OECD analysis called into question many central tenets of the "Washington Consensus," asserting that the combination of large price hikes in basic staples and mass public sector layoffs was highly damaging to the poor. Such policies, said the authors, exacerbated income inequality much more dramatically than did often necessary currency devaluations. Reductions in capital expenditures, they argued, should never be across-the-board or borne disproportionately by rural invest-ment and primary health-care budgets. Finally, they recommended that privatization be accompanied by effective compensation or retraining programs.[76]

Several very influential groups in the international development community have concurred in the notion that targeted social spending can buffer the harshest effects structural adjustment has on the poor. In 1987, UNICEF argued in *Adjustment with a Human Face: Protecting the Vulnerable and Promoting Growth* that even under the severe resource constraints caused by adjustment, the vulnerable members of society can (and must) be protected through relatively low-cost programs.[77] Fujimori's World Bank advisors understood that such "effective compensation" was as much a matter of politics as of economics and social welfare. A system of "safety nets" would safeguard not only vulnerable members of the population but also the viability of the reforms themselves.[78]

In the first days of Fujimori's administration, concern with possible resistance to his austerity program led the government to develop a social emergency program of sorts, placed initially under the control of prime minister Hurtado. Fujimori's political rivalry with the prime minister, however, led him to consolidate control over the pro-gram's budget allocations. Hostage to this tug-of-war, the fund remained a dead letter, and only 14 percent of its original allocation was spent in the first year. "During the hardest moments of economic adjustment," Julio Gamero observes, "the country lacked a social policy. From August 1990 until the end of 1991 there were no resources." Everything was subordinated to "the adjustment of macroeconomic accounts."[79]

Few were surprised, then, when it became clear several months into Fujishock that austerity-related "physical deterioration" of the Peruvian poor was affecting their health. As the Health Ministry itself pointed out in 1992, "The health situation of the population depends on what happens with the world of labor, with consumption, with the environment, and with health care. Health and disease are the result of an inter-sectoral action."[80] But *any* stabilization plan increases the prices of subsidized com-modities and decreases government services; therefore the people most hurt by the adjustment policies are those with the fewest resources. Meanwhile, the shrinking of government payrolls, benefits, and social budgets removed a crucial safety net for many Peruvians. Amid Peru's newfound status as "one of the world's most open invest-ment regimes" the resources available to low-income Peruvians were increasingly at the whim of market competition.[81]

Sharply declining health indicators in the early 1990s suggested to many that the increasing inequality of economic distribution under Fujimori had contributed to a parallel disparity in susceptibility to disease. A survey of 400 low-income house-holds between June and November 1990 showed that rates of sickness increased 20.6 percent, while spending on the purchase of medicine fell 50.7 percent in the same period.[82] By the end of 1990, the infant mortality rate reached 84 per thou-sand live births, putting Peru almost in a class with Bolivia (105 per thousand) and Haiti (94 per thousand) in that category. As late as 1993, 36 percent of all infants received no prenatal care and more than half of all births were unattended by health services personnel.[83] A 1991 cholera outbreak in Lima and environs that left 2,400 dead was perceived as further evidence of the convergence of macroeconomics and mortality.[84]

The point to be made though is not that Fujimori's reforms, privatization in particular, were intrinsically bad. In many cases, social indicators and health outcomes along with them were markedly improved from the chaos that prevailed under an isolated and disintegrating García administration. Peru's National Tuberculosis Program, for instance, is recognized by the World Health Organization (WHO) as one of the very best in the world, and a model of its kind.[85] Likewise, government officials could point with pride to drops of nearly 25 percent in infant mortality from 1991 to 1996, and a reduction in chronic pediatric malnutrition of almost one-third.[86] A critique of Peru's health policy must be more considered than simple rejection of its underlying precept—the marketization of state functions, and facilitation of the government's liquidity. Our question is more particular: when neoliberal ideology is conjoined with health policy, what happens to poor people's health outcomes and access to care?

Peru's rapidly disintegrating social safety net in the early 1990s prompted certain external donors to pressure the government for a more effective response. In 1991, the National Fund for Development and Social Compensation (Foncodes) was formed with a grant from the Inter-American Development Bank (IDB). Funding under its auspices did not reach any significant scale until 1993, during the run-up to the referendum on President Fujimori's revised constitution. Between January and May 1993, Foncodes lavished $125 million on 7,100 different projects—144 percent of the 1992 figure ($87 million).[87] In subsequent years, the fund consumed 50 percent of the government's social budget—becoming, in the eyes of many critics, a direct tool of Fujimori's campaign machine. In one region where the 1993 constitutional referendum won only 20 percent of the vote, mammoth outlays through Foncodes helped boost Fujimori's credibility to the point where he polled 67 percent in the 1995 presidential elections.[88]

While sometimes scattered or instrumental, however, Fujimori's social policies could in many cases point to significant achievements—particularly in the light of conditions that prevailed in 1990 upon his assumption of power. In 1990, an estimated 50.7 percent of the populace was making two dollars a day or less, only 18 percent of the workforce was adequately employed, inflation had reached 2,778 percent, and wages had lost their purchasing power by over 50 percent relative to 1985.[89]

But whatever Peru's successes over the last decade, there is a cost when vital social obligations become subject to the same standards that prevail in other sectors. The policy model that Peru adopted under Fujimori has only recently come to its logical conclusion: the 1997 Health Law, mandating subcontracting of state health services, fee-based care, and a private insurance model. In Peru, as elsewhere, the contours of policy were suggested from abroad, and it remains to be seen how this policy graft will take. It must be observed, however, that results in other venues are mixed at best, and horrific, at worst. This erratic performance has not exempted the United States itself: the most vigilant adherent of—and oldest experiment in—privatization of health services.

PRIVATIZATION IN THE U.S. HEALTH-CARE SYSTEM

In the United States, health care has long been much more decentralized and market-oriented than in other industrialized countries. During the 1970s, however, the spread of privatization was greatly accelerated by changes at the national legislative level. As early as 1973, Congress moved to further free market competition in the health sector through the Health Maintenance Organization (HMO) Act of that year, which gave HMOs (which at the time were mostly nonprofit cooperatives) a number of tax advantages.[90] Health maintenance organizations were a product of the baby boom; charging cheaper premiums than traditional health insurance plans, they paid doctors and hospitals a fixed amount per patient, giving them financial incentives to reduce expensive procedures and decrease the length of hospital stays. This arrangement separated health care's fiscal administration from its actual provision, pitting providers (doctors or hospitals) against each other in direct competition for patronage, while HMOs themselves competed for the business of consumers who, presumably, had sufficient information and discretionary power to choose among practitioners and between health-care plans. As congressional proponents observed, this notion of "managed competition" was the cornerstone of any attempt at health-care privatization.[91]

Spurred by the congressional incentives, "managed care" spread widely, as enrollment in HMOs increased from 5 million in 1970 to 18.9 million by 1985.[92] This trend accelerated considerably under the Reagan administration, as cost-cutting principles of managed care began to find application in the public sector as well. In 1982, Medicare guidelines were revised to establish a network of privately-run HMOs capitalized with social security funds.[93] Drained by the 20 percent cutbacks in public sector funding pushed through by the Reagan administration in 1981, as well as the loss of wealthy patients to for-profit health-care chains, many hospitals were unable to stand up beneath the fierce competition of managed care. Between 1980 and 1990, 635 closed nationwide because of financial distress.[94] By the mid-1990s, private HMOs were a dominant form of provision nationwide, with over 75 million members enrolled in 1997.[95] Large profits left them increasingly in a position to consolidate control over hospitals and other previously public resources. As of 1985, about 140 public hospitals were managed under contract by investor-owned systems.[96] Ten years later, local politicians had sold off 585 of the 2,175 health facilities that were publicly owned in 1980; 40 percent of the buyers were for-profit ventures.[97]

National divestment from the social sector and local privatization of health systems proceeded in lockstep. Together they acted to superimpose market values onto medical care, and to promote direct corporate investment. Frequently, though, the immense profitability of such investment came not through managerial efficiency—as supporters claimed—but simply by charging more for premiums, or by reducing expenditures on medical care.[98] When executives reached the limits of these savings, both private and nonprofit HMOs began to lose millions.[99] In the end, the radical changes in administration seem only temporarily to have slowed rising health costs, which federal analysts project will double between 1998 and 2007.[100]

Most troubling of all is the impact such changes have on society's most vulnerable members. Research has shown that privatized health providers, nonprofit and for-profit alike, go to some lengths to avoid expensive care and uninsured patients, shifting that particular responsibility to public providers.[101] Investor-owned companies in particular, it seems, actively avoid low-income people by screening out those unable to pay.[102] One study showed that 75 percent of for-profit agencies, and 61 percent of nonprofits, limited access to some types of poor clients.[103] If a health facility was located in an area where the low-income population was too high, companies often closed it down. "We simply can't have a hospital on every corner," rationalized a top executive for Columbia/HCA, the nation's largest private hospital chain. "We just can't afford it."[104]

Despite America's massive health expenditure, the highest level of spending (per capita) on earth, this form of organization has led to some disturbing outcomes. Out-of-pocket medical costs, particularly for fixed-income elderly people, have risen astronomically over the past decade and a half: 150 percent during one six-year period in the 1980s. Those pierced most brutally by this spike on the graph, of course, were the uninsured, whose numbers rose from about 27.5 million in 1978 to 37 million in 1986 to the 1997 figure of approximately 43.4 million, fully 16.1 percent of the population.[105] Poor people have been buffeted from two sides: first by the revocation of direct benefits like Aid to Families with Dependent Children (AFDC) and then by cuts in subsidies to local health authorities, who are responsible for an ever-increasing proportion of their care.[106]

Even when low-income people have some coverage through government agencies, there is evidence to suggest that outcomes at HMOs are distinctly worse for poor patients with chronic health problems than for wealthier consumers.[107] One reason for this differential may be that private insurers have increasingly refused to cover the Medicare and Medicaid recipients who were steered into their plans during the 1980s and early 1990s, leaving exclusive responsibility for their treatment to already beleaguered public hospitals.[108] The result is high rates of disease and morbidity among the American poor in some de-industrialized urban zones approximating those of nation-states with far fewer resources. During the last two decades, these indicators have worsened significantly. Several epidemiologists have tried to gauge the relationship between income level and early mortality; according to one of these studies, poverty led to over 91 thousand U.S. deaths during 1991, a rate of 82.3 per 100,000 people, and an 11 percent increase over 1973. Among African-American men the rate was 355 per 100,000, up 39 percent over 1973.[109]

The exodus of private HMOs from Medicaid is a direct outgrowth of their failure to deliver on promises of cost and efficiency benefits, which, during the 1980s and 1990s, convinced state agencies and private employers to shift 85 percent of American consumers into HMO plans. A recent report by the Department of Health and Human Services (DHHS) projects that total U.S. health-care expenditures will increase $1.1 trillion between 1997 and 2007, an average annual rise of 10 percent.[110] Indeed, the failure of "managed competition" to hold down costs in the long term indicates a structural flaw in the notion that free markets can deliver more cost-efficient medical care. Over thirty years ago, Nobel Prize-winning economist Kenneth Arrow observed that health is the classic example of an "imperfect market," where consumers cannot understand fully the product, nor producers entirely their clients' needs.[111] In the meanwhile, under the supervision of international finance institutions like the World Bank and IMF, privatization was made an explicit condition of poor countries' debt rescheduling. Although the health sector was relatively peripheral to the IFIs' prescriptions, their impact on the sector was nonetheless profound.

THE WORLD BANK, HEALTH CARE,
AND THE DRIVE TO PRIVATIZE

Most recent critiques of World Bank policy in poor countries have focused on the *ideological* content of Bank-sponsored publications rather than documenting the precise *mechanisms* by which the organization exerts its influence.[112] Susan George and Fabrizio Sabelli, for example, argue sardonically that World Bank planning today is as fundamentally governed by dogma as that of the medieval Catholic Church. Like the Church, they say, the Bank is built upon three pillars: a basic doctrine, a rigid hierarchy that preaches and imposes this doctrine, and a theological mode of self-justification.[113] To George and Sabelli, the impact of the World Bank lies in its ability to state and add small refinements to the received wisdom. In order to remain in existence, the World Bank must maintain an ideology consonant with that of its most important funders.[114] In a pungently ironic sense, it has little "choice" in the matter.

The limitations set by its role in the development masque have given the World Bank a rather schizophrenic public presence. At the same time that it officially promotes privatization initiatives, it produces studies demonstrating that such initiatives lead inherently to inequality and immiseration of the poorest social strata.[115] Even as it lends its institutional support to deflationary structural adjustment packages as a "poverty reduction" technique, it observes that such policies often exacerbate or leave unchanged the poverty in exactly those countries where it is worst.[116] And even as it claims to be assisting poor countries with strategies for improving primary health care, its researchers contend that evidence for the utility of primary health care is "uneven."[117] In fact, this apparent schism points up a conflict of interest so far as the low-income majorities in poor states are concerned; notwithstanding its ostensible dedication to "poverty reduction" since 1990, the World Bank's function has been and remains that of a finance institution.

Box 6.1: World Bank and WHO in Global Health-Care Finance

Less than two decades ago, the World Bank had no health policy role whatsoever. Global health-planning was overseen by the World Health Organization (WHO), an independent branch of the United Nations formed in 1948 to coordinate and conceptualize the provision of health care in poor countries. Together with regional arms (such as PAHO, the Pan American Health Organization) WHO served for several decades as the institutional fulcrum of international health policy.[118]

The prominence of the WHO was never clearer than in September of 1978, at the International Conference on Primary Health Care held in Alma-Ata, Kazakhstan. In the course of that meeting, cosponsored with UNICEF, most U.N. member countries declared together that health was a "human right," and that the inequality in the health status between poor and rich countries was "politically, morally, and economically unacceptable." They resolved that such inequalities were to be resolved by the year 2000.[119]

Even in 1978, the Alma-Ata Declaration's timetable was clearly naïve. Since then, the prospects for "health for all" have taken a dramatic turn for the worse. Mounting debt obligations have forced planners in poor countries to put repayment ahead of domestic priorities, thus contributing to an inequality of health outcomes between the rich and poor that in some respects is even more dramatic than at the time of the Alma-Ata Declaration.

As an arm of the United Nations, the WHO serves an important conceptual function through a wide range of activities that include writing health policy. But its ability to directly impact health-care programs in developing countries is limited by the fact that its annual operating budget was only $900 million in 1998, a figure that has been almost unchanged throughout the 1990s.[120] Much of that sum, moreover, is necessarily allocated to administrative overhead; for all of North and South America, the WHO's regional office was slated to spend $19 million for administrative services over 1998–99, 12 percent of its total budget and roughly equivalent to its outlay for disease control and prevention.[121] In poor countries, the WHO retains its respected role as the foremost authority on health issues. Without material resources, however, the effective power that it wields is clearly limited.

In the void left by U.N. belt-tightening, the World Bank has become a trendsetter in international health policy. This development is quite a recent one. Through the 1980s, Bank outlays for poor-country health programs were minuscule; in 1990, however, the World Bank's lending for health programs jumped suddenly by about 500 percent, to a level nearly double the WHO's entire budget allocation.[122] In 1996, the Bank issued $2.5 billion in loans for various health-care projects in poor countries, $700 million for HIV/AIDS programs alone.[123] This investment transformed the Bank, by default, into "the largest single source of health-care finance in developing countries," with an unparalleled degree of policy-making authority.[124] Bank officials are now invariably consulted on health sector reforms—if they do not design them in their entirety.

The World Bank's fundamentally pecuniary role is evident in its health sector policy. In the models recommended by the Bank to those nations that accept its loans or grants, expenditures for health-care programs are inevitably seen as a secondary component of reforms in productive economic sectors—or worse, a palliative to potential unrest caused by increased misery under structural adjustment.[125] Nonetheless, the World Bank's stance on privatization in health care is now more important for poor countries than that of any other organization. Backed by its budget, the Bank's voluminous literature on the provision of health services is tangible in the structure of health-care systems all over the developing world.

A close reading of the World Bank's publications indicates numerous contradictions in its health policy directives. While these contradictions sometimes give the impression of ideological diversity, they ultimately serve to highlight the troubling incompatibility of the Bank's guiding neoliberal policy logic and its ostensible support of "development with equity." In public pronouncements and reports, officials state repeatedly that the market is an imperfect delivery mechanism for essential social services.[126] For example, the 1993 World Development Report, *Investing in Health*, affirmed that governments must play a role in the provision of health care. Health-related services, it declared, are public goods, and "because private markets alone provide too little of the public goods crucial for health, government involvement is necessary to increase the supply."[127] Moreover, it went on, "private markets will not give the poor adequate access to essential clinical services or the insurance often needed to pay for such services. Public finance of essential clinical care is thus justified to alleviate poverty."[128]

Beneath these sometimes dramatic calls for public responsibility, however, is an ideology with quite different implications. The "common approach to health care in developing countries," wrote the World Bank's health planners in 1987, "to treat it as a right of citizenry and to attempt to provide free services to everyone...does not usually work."[129] Consequently, the 1993 report advocated a three-pronged approach to reforming the health sector in poor countries: higher levels of spending on health care were to be achieved within "an economic environment that enables households to improve health," through state policies which "promote diversity and competition." Central to these strategies was the overarching imperative to foster market growth. While growth-oriented policies were ostensibly of "direct benefit" to the poor, they were to be implemented in a way that put such benefits at a low priority; including, parenthetically, "adjustment policies that preserve cost-effective health expenditures."[130]

Indeed, cost efficacy had been a guiding precept of the World Bank's health sector policy for nearly a decade before *Investing in Health*. A 1985 paper by David de Ferranti—now head of the World Bank's social services initiatives—gave much attention to this imperative, stressing the need to "reconcil[e] goals of maximizing investment for economic growth with the demands of health programs for public funds." De Ferranti criticized health sector planners in poor countries for inadequate consideration of "the incentives they create or reinforce, or of the ensuing impact on the behavior of service providers, households, and government agencies...especially with respect to containing costs, utilizing cost-effective technologies, and minimizing inappropriate utilization of services."[131] An "essential theme" of new health initiatives, he concluded, should be that users bear a larger share of health-care costs through imposition of fees and private insurance plans—precisely the solutions employed by the Peruvian Ministry of Health a decade later.

The argument for cost recovery, De Ferranti noted, was based on an assumption that demand for health care was not *price-elastic*; that is, that people would just as likely seek treatment if fees were increased by public and private providers.[132] This supposition was stated even more emphatically in the World Bank's influential 1987 pamphlet, *Financing Health Services in Developing Countries: An Agenda for Reform.* There, the authors argued that free health care prevented the government "from collecting revenues that many patients are both able and willing to pay," and that, by increasing the price of health care to market-determined levels, more consumers would be served, quality would improve, and additional resources would be generated.[133] These assertions proved to be based on scant data. Soon after the publication of *Financing Health Services*, Bank policy-makers met with a barrage of in-house research indicating that, in fact, demand for health services was highly price-elastic, and moreover, that the degree of elasticity was heavily contingent on income level.[134]

But while mechanisms were devised to allow for low-income users by means of graded fee exemptions, the "cost shifting" prescription was essentially unchanged, despite evidence that such exemptions did not achieve their aim.[135] "Since 1987," according to one recent assessment, "virtually every World Bank pronouncement on health finance has asserted the feasibility and desirability of increased cost-recovery."[136]

The principle governing World Bank health-care policy design continues to be that governments should reconsider their roles as providers and insurers, and look to private agents to provide health care more efficiently. The most recent incarnation of this view is the slogan, "financing demand but not supply." Jacques van der Gaag, for example, describes the goals of World Bank-sponsored programs as poverty reduction on the one hand, and on the other, improvement of poor people's health through market reforms that encourage economic growth and efficiency. He expressly attacks the notion that governments can provide equitable and efficient social services: "Although many countries cite equity as the reason for strong government controls, public sector controlled policies do not have a good record of accomplishment on equity." Furthermore, van der Gaag goes on to assert that while "numerous informal comparisons...virtually always favor the private sector...the few controlled studies that do exist also seem to confirm the private sector's superiority in providing cost-effective social services in most cases."[137]

Van der Gaag never cites the studies to which he refers, and his argument against government control of health services is almost completely anecdotal. Indeed, his most widely read work provides neither significant data nor even convincing case studies to suggest that the private provision of health services (state-funded or not) would be any more equitable or cost-efficient. Such *a priori* determinations, one should recognize, are not made in a vacuum. While the efficiency rationale for privatization of health care may be dubious, government divestiture undoubtedly frees up funds for other purposes. In the absence of evidence that "cost recovery" policies benefit the health-care consumer, one might reasonably class them as distinctive, if somewhat peripheral, components of an effort to maximize the funds available to service external loans.

The World Bank does not and cannot directly force poor-country governments to reduce spending in the public health sector. But, as a lending institution charged with ensuring repayment of debt, the Bank is in a position to offer guidance on how poor countries can best "streamline" their economies to meet their debt service obligations. As a result, in recent years, the World Bank has had an enormous impact on the health of impoverished populations. The design of privatization policies, and their manner of implementation, suggests that bettering poor people's health outcomes is often incidental to their budget-cutting function.

Still, an important question remains. Whatever their ultimate intention, is it possible that privatization policies are ultimately beneficial to the health of the poor? If we base our answer on currently available data from both rich and poor countries, the answer seems to be "no." Here as elsewhere, the structure and ideology of health-care privatization can be lethal to society's most vulnerable members.

HEALTH PRIVATIZATION AND POOR STATES

In wealthy communities, we have argued, the various elements of health privatization are riddled with inequities and contradictions. They focus the resources of a highly developed and well-funded medical system on an increasingly narrow segment of the population. For those unable to afford fees and premiums associated with private HMOs, they ensure inferior service at more inconvenience and greater out-of-pocket cost. In many cases they fail to guarantee that all citizens will have access to even the most basic health services.

But if such grave flaws are endemic to the privatized American model of "managed competition," then their potential impact on countries with weak health systems and vastly more impoverished populations is far worse. Nevertheless, in Peru and many other poor countries that have implemented structural adjustment programs, policies with striking affinities to those of North America are being imposed. Such planning, by one assessment, has four primary elements: decentralization of health planning, finance, and procurement; promotion of private insurance plans; contracting out to nonprofit entities for primary health care; and the imposition of sizable user fees for drugs and curative care.[138] As in developed countries, these all conspire to reduce the resources available to free public health institutions. And, in fact, undermining free health providers is partly a strategic decision by those who design health privatization policies. In the words of one proponent, "If people can obtain health care for free or at a uniformly low cost, they will not have much incentive to pay insurance premiums to cover unexpected health hazards."[139]

The claims, meanwhile, are expansive. Policies such as private insurance are held to "mobilize more resources for health-care delivery," and to "promote equity, improve economic efficiency, raise the quality of medical services, and allow consumers more choice in selecting and paying for their treatment" in the bargain.[140] Even in utterly impoverished countries like Uganda, one article reported, mission hospitals were able to recoup as much as 95 percent of their operating costs through the imposition of user fees. This development, argued the authors, would "mobilize revenues, promote efficiency, foster equity, increase decentralization and sustainability, and foster private sector development."[141]

In a setting like Uganda, where the average person lives on 55 cents daily, the quality of services provided to the poor must be suspect if 95 percent of its cost is paid directly by the consumer. Moreover, the studies that suggested full cost-recovery from user fees rarely accounted for ancillary expenses such as administrative costs; as Hammer and Gertler note, "There is little if any credible data on this important issue."[142] Finally, data from many other settings indicate that the collection of user fees have generally contributed little to the actual financing of health care, yielding, on average, only five percent of service costs.[143]

Even when a concerted effort is made to reinvest funds appropriately, it remains ambiguous whether the revenue stream from user fees is indeed sustainable in poor countries. The most fully developed experiment to date is the Bamako Initiative, launched jointly in 1987 by the WHO and UNICEF, which envisioned a network of revolving drug funds financed by charging patients for essential pharmaceuticals. These funds were to be managed at the village level, and stocked by purchases from commercial manufacturers.

The Bamako design has been implemented throughout sub-Saharan Africa, and has been rather successful at maintaining a stable supply of medications in some venues—mostly very small institutions that dispense drugs for a limited range of ailments.[144] According to several analysts, the success of these smaller, rural sub-centers at recovering costs owes more to the fact that they are residents' only health-care alternative than to their true "affordability."[145] And even in these venues, Bamako Initiative funds were far from self-sustaining, in part because they suffered under a flood of inappropriate and expensive drug exports to Africa from pharmaceutical companies in industrialized countries.[146] In the end then, decentralization of this kind has not proved sustainable; it has, however, accelerated the push toward private economies among people who often can ill afford them.[147] This is apparently true *even for public services that are supposed to be free*, as underpaid government employees supplement their income through informal charges.[148]

Ironically, just as Peru and many other countries were implementing health sector privatization on the basis of their recommendations, de Ferranti and some of his World Bank colleagues had begun to back away from their earlier stance on privatization in general, and cost recovery in particular. The Bank's official strategic document for health and nutrition noted in early 1998 that "direct out-of-pocket health expenditure continues to be a distinctive feature of many low- and middle-income countries." This reality—which the Bank, of course, had long been promoting—was seen to "undermin[e] the social protection that could be provided by the HNP [Health, Nutrition, and Population] sector even in low-income settings." Shifting to private providers, they went on, was even less advisable: "Because of cost and the pronounced market failure that occurs in private health insurance, [it]…is not a viable option…in low- and middle-income countries."[149] Meanwhile, countries like Peru were proceeding with their reform packages, which included just such prescriptions.

As in Peru, recent data from around the world suggest a quantifiable correlation between policy innovations such as "cost shifting" and the incidence of public health failures. One study traced a relationship between increased maternal and infant mortality in Zimbabwe and sharp declines in the use of prenatal health facilities after user fees were imposed.[150] Another found that fee increases and the incidence and duration of infectious diseases were directly related; the authors theorized that "prices hurt health…by delaying treatment to the point of reducing the efficacy of medical intervention."[151] A researcher working in Indonesia has even shown that a 100 percent fee hike had a negative effect on health sufficient to reduce labor force participation among women.[152] World Bank health economists do not dispute such findings, but minimize their importance, arguing that they are "anecdotal," or that any slack in consumption at public health facilities is usually taken up by private practitioners and "self-treatment"[153]—a category that bears troubling resemblance to suffering in silence.

The 1997 Peruvian Health Law's replacement of government functions with private enterprise makes evident that user fees at public health facilities are only the surface of the privatization model. In a more general sense, market efficiency, the ability to "choose," is rapidly becoming the governing standard of access to care. This is a matter of immediate interest to others beside the Peruvian populace. As early as 1995, foreign insurance companies and HMOs were already looking eagerly southward to the opportunities presented by neoliberal reformers. In the words of one industry publication, "A new generation of pioneers is emerging as U.S.-based insurers embark on a journey to compete in a Latin American market still in the throes of democratization and privatization." The author went on, "This will open doors to multinational insurance providers with expertise in underwriting and loss control. The forecast, according to many industry experts, calls for a broad acceptance of products and services already developed and delivered by American and European providers."[154] By 1997, private U.S. concerns had purchased public facilities in settings as diverse as Puerto Rico and China.[155]

As recent history in wealthy countries has shown, however, this trend is a serious problem for the most vulnerable segments of the population. Just as with home mortgage loans and grocery stores, private health care is subject to considerations that often have little to do with people's needs—and everything to do with companies' bottom lines. When profit margins dictate, it is all too easy to "red line" impoverished areas, rendering the notion of "choice" a bitter falsehood.[156] The plight of the 40 million uninsured and underserved in the United States is nothing in comparison to what awaits the poor of Peru, a country whose poverty is much deeper and whose needs are concomitantly greater. As we have seen, even limited implementation of private payment schemes can lead directly to potentially deadly outcomes. To a significant segment of the population, the intensified privatization of health will be almost as bad as no health care at all.

THE HUMAN FACE OF PRIVATIZATION

For the residents of impoverished urban communities like the shantytown neighborhoods of Lima, Peru's health-care system presents an interesting paradox. On the one hand, due to poverty, geography, demographic transience, and political neglect, these areas are beset with high levels of disease and mortality. On the other hand, because of their relative proximity to urban infrastructure, residents of these neighborhoods are in a position to be affected by health-care privatization policies.

The shantytown district of Carabayllo, home to Benedicta Sanchez, is located on the northern periphery of metropolitan Lima. Founded in 1821, it is one of the oldest districts in the metropolitan area. Ninety percent of its residents speak Spanish as a first language; the remainder, by virtue of their origins in rural provinces such as Ancash and Canta, to the north of the capital, speak Quechua. Ninety percent of Carabaylleños are literate, and their grassroots political institutions are highly developed.

Over the last 50 years, Carabayllo has been at the forefront of a far-reaching social phenomenon: mass migration from rural provinces to the megalopolis.[157] Like many other squatter communities in Lima, Carabayllo is situated in the desert hills surrounding the city; as suggested by Benedicta Sanchez's story opening this chapter, basic electricity, water, and sewage are limited in such communities, the least developed and the most distant from public and private social services. For reasons of practical logistics, official inattention, and central economic planning priorities, essential health resources like safe drinking water, sewage systems, and primary care clinics tend to cluster around the wealthier, more completely urbanized areas of the Lima megalopolis.

The daily lives of its residents are ruled almost wholly by inequities of resource distribution. Meanwhile, central government budget-cutting has at once decreased their earning power and increased their expenses to the point where even urgently needed medical treatment is beyond their grasp.

Alejandrina's Story

After Alejandrina Huaman gave birth to her youngest child, employees of a government-sponsored family planning program encouraged her to have a tubal ligation. "Look how many children you have already, Señora Alejandrina," said one. "A tubal ligation is effective and free."[158] Their point was well taken. In 1992, Alejandrina, her husband Pedro and their three young daughters had moved from the central highlands of Peru to a one-room shack in Carabayllo.[159] Subsequent to her arrival, Alejandrina had worked mostly as a street vendor, selling plastic bags in markets throughout Lima. Traveling more than an hour each way, she sometimes earned as much as eight soles (US$3.50)—just enough to feed her family. Other days, she didn't even cover her transportation costs. Pedro, meanwhile, had been unemployed since five months before their last child was born.

After a lengthy discussion, Alejandrina decided to undergo the tubal ligation. Following surgery, she was allowed a few hours of bed rest, and then sent home. For several days after that she felt too sick to work; by the time Pedro took her back to the health center, she was weak and feverish. The attending physician prescribed a course of antibiotics, but the drugs cost 25 soles (US$10) at the center's dispensary and the couple, having barely enough money to pay for the visit, was unable to purchase the medicine. They simply went home again.

Tipped-off by field workers, a local NGO sent a physician and nurse to Alejandrina the following day. When they arrived, Alejandrina was breathing at more than twice the normal rate, barely able to care for her children because of weakness, fever, and malaise. The nurse accompanied her to an area hospital, where she was found to be septic; her infection had spread to her bloodstream. Despite this life-threatening condition, she was given intravenous antibiotics only after representatives of the NGO signed a contract to pay her medical expenses. After a month-long hospital stay, she returned home, to eke out a living selling plastic bags.

PRIVATIZATION AND THE NGO

Though precise details differ, the stories of Benedicta Sanchez, Alejandrina Huaman, and many people like them share several basic elements. On the one hand, they point up often fatal consequences that even minimal privatization of primary health care provokes in impoverished communities. The obvious inability of people at the economic margins to afford out-of-pocket fees for health services and medicines recommended by "free" medical facilities shows how spurious is the claim that privatization can improve health care in poor districts like Carabayllo. On the other hand, these stories highlight just how important a role private NGOs have come to play in filling the vacuum left by government divestiture from health services. Were it not for their intervention, Alejandrina and many others would be dying on the thresholds of public institutions, the resources of which have been allocated to other sectors of the economy.

But, although timely attention from outside the public sector led to a successful outcome for Alejandrina, NGOs are very far from sufficient to remedy the iatrogenic properties of privatized primary care. For one thing, however well-organized, their limited resources necessarily restrict coverage to a tiny fraction of the population. The total annual worldwide expenditure for health care by private foundations has been estimated recently at $1.44 billion—less than half the sum Peru paid in debt service during 1996.[160] Despite these basic limitations, the World Bank, USAID, and other development institutions have pointed increasingly to NGOs as the linchpin of their funding delivery strategies.[161]

The increasing centrality of nongovernmental agencies to the privatized health-care system has seemed to many people within the NGO ranks a perilous gamble. As a matter of both principle and practicality, official enshrinement of NGOs as service delivery mechanisms appeared, to these observers, to be an abdication of state responsibility. Five months before the Peruvian General Health Law was implemented, several large public forums were held to debate its terms, in which representatives of NGOs were vocal participants.[162] One group of Lima-based organizations in particular levied withering criticism against the proposed legislation. The law, they said, reflected a global precedent, underneath which lay a set of fundamentally ideological principles.[163] Joining with church groups and concerned health professionals, they denounced the pending shifts to private insurance, to liberalized pharmaceutical patent regulation, and to principles of "market efficiency" as misguided in principle and dangerous in application. In the words of one such critic, the poor "have remained entirely outside the realm of possibility [as] ethical obligations disappear from consideration, or are subjugated before a fate considered practically inevitable."[164]

CONCLUSION

The worldwide adoption of privatization strategies in recent years has gone forward with great fanfare. Free competition and the profit motive, proponents argue, are inherent guarantors of market efficiency, national economic well-being, and even improved health outcomes. When consumers have the right to choose between numerous options, they will invariably pick the best combination of savings and quality; the health-care system, along with the rest of the economy, will become less expensive, more effective, and more productive.

In fact, as we see repeatedly, the world in reality lays such optimistic projections to rest. Even President Reagan's Commission on Privatization was forced to admit that health care was a potentially inappropriate venue for competitive markets, given a tendency toward "adverse selection" of good insurance risks in preference to the elderly and poor.[165] Despite this concern, the commission did not substantially modify its recommendations to push forward with the privatization of the health-care system. As many poor and elderly Americans have discovered, the most pertinent choice afforded by health-care privatization consists largely of insurers' tendency not to choose *them*.

In developing countries, the principles of privatization have been applied to health services with similar disregard for the health of the poor and marginalized. The apparent failure of "cost recovery" as a means of funding health care in poor nations, acknowledged in passing by development specialists, has meant only that this strategy would give way to more fully private provision, under the slogan "financing demand but not supply." The capriciousness of such policy shifts highlights the lack of accountability with which multilateral agencies have designed, disseminated, and implemented their models. The penalties for failure have been borne by the poor, the infirm, and the vulnerable in poor countries that accepted the experts' designs.

As in most indebted countries, debt service is now one of the Peruvian government's largest budget items, amounting in 1996 to about 24 percent of total expenditures.[166] Given its external debt obligations, the Peruvian government has limited latitude in setting social policy. The successful campaign by international financial institutions to undermine the García government in the 1980s has served subsequent administrations, in Peru and elsewhere, as an inviolable object lesson. Judging, however, that juxtaposing debt service and reductions in health-care expenditures would not be well received, Peruvian health-care planners attempted to convince poor citizens and their advocates that cutting overall expenditure on health was desirable. To this end, the Health Law of 1997 was offered. Through it, and through the "efficiency" and "choice" which it claimed to promote, the Peruvian health-care system would function better and more fairly.

Where the country's poor are concerned, this contention is suspect. Amid the deep misery of districts like Carabayllo, we see once again that the poor of Latin America are being enlisted to help make up budget shortfalls they did nothing to cause, so that debt they did nothing to incur can be repaid endlessly. Not only is this inequity a moral wound in the Peruvian polity, but also, with the inexorable logic of disease and mortality, a physical wound as well.

Indeed, opposition to policies like Peru's health reform should not rest solely on abstract moral grounds. Benedicta's illness, tuberculosis, is a mortal threat to the public health, and acts as a significant brake on overall productivity.[167] In recent years it has grown markedly in poor countries worldwide, largely among the most vulnerable members of the population.[168] The case of Benedicta Sanchez makes clear that even partial privatization of the responsibility for health services can lead to nontreatment and the propagation of a deadly disease—this, even though Benedicta lives in a country that boasts one of the finest tuberculosis control programs in the world. Though the actual cost of treatment for her disease would have been borne by the state, Benedicta "chose" to forego a definitive diagnosis of tuberculosis, so that her family could eat. By imposing the criterion of *choice* on people who are in no position to exercise it, health-care reformers have prioritized financial outcomes over health outcomes, and further imperiled the health of the poor.

The case of Alejandrina Huaman is more complex. Pawn in an intricate struggle over reproductive rights, religious prescriptions around the use of birth control, and most importantly political power, Alejandrina points out the imprecision with which public and private responsibility for health-care delivery are allocated in a privatizing system. The national program that urged and performed her tubal ligation saw no explicit obligation to monitor her condition, nor provide her with follow-up care. Without the intervention of a local NGO, she might have died—because she would never have been able to "choose" to pay for the antibiotics that saved her life.

Are there alternative paths? Does it matter that the poor were not a party to the debt burden assumed by Peru's elite rulers over the last 30 years? Would it be unjust to hold those who stood to profit most from the loans responsible for their repayment?[169] Such an "historical accounting" of national debt is by no means an unprecedented notion. In the former Zaire, for example, negotiations with international finance institutions have been intertwined with the effort to unseal the Swiss bank accounts of Mobuto Sese Seko's kleptocracy. Alternatively, the banks that participated in the "orgy of lending" to Latin American governments in the 1970s and 1980s could be held accountable for their imprudent loans—a solution applied as a matter of course in the First World.

Another much more modest proposal would be to extend to poor debtor states the progressive bankruptcy exemptions that residents of wealthy countries take for granted. In the United States, for instance, bankruptcy laws ensure that someone who owes $5,000 to a credit card company need make payment on that debt only in amounts that permit the debtor to buy essentials like food, shelter, and medical care. Meanwhile, in Peru and other poor countries, public indebtedness has caused whole populations to go hungry. Recent moves by the IMF and World Bank to enshrine on an international level the principles of bankruptcy laws such as the Highly Indebted Poor Countries (HIPC) Initiative have been sharply limited in scope and ambition.[170]

In Peru, as elsewhere, drawing the boundaries between the public and the private is a contested endeavor. Millions throughout the world die every year because they cannot pay for essential medical treatments. The debate over health-care privatization, then, should open up a larger, more difficult question: the need to understand the process by which burdens in human social life come to be considered public or private responsibilities. To Peru's policy-makers, at home and abroad, it is clear that the country's external debt will remain a public burden. Meanwhile, even the poorest Peruvians are finding sickness and health to be increasingly private affairs.

ACKNOWLEDGMENTS

The authors would like to express deep gratitude to Shelly Errington and Haun Saussy for their authoritative editorial insights; to Alec Irwin, Joyce Millen, Mercedes Becerra, Dave Harrison, and Carole Mitnick for lending their keen eyes to the manuscript; to the team in Carabayllo for their skill and dedication; and above all, to "Benedicta," "Alejandrina," and other members of their community, for continuing to fight in the face of daunting—though emphatically not impossible—odds.

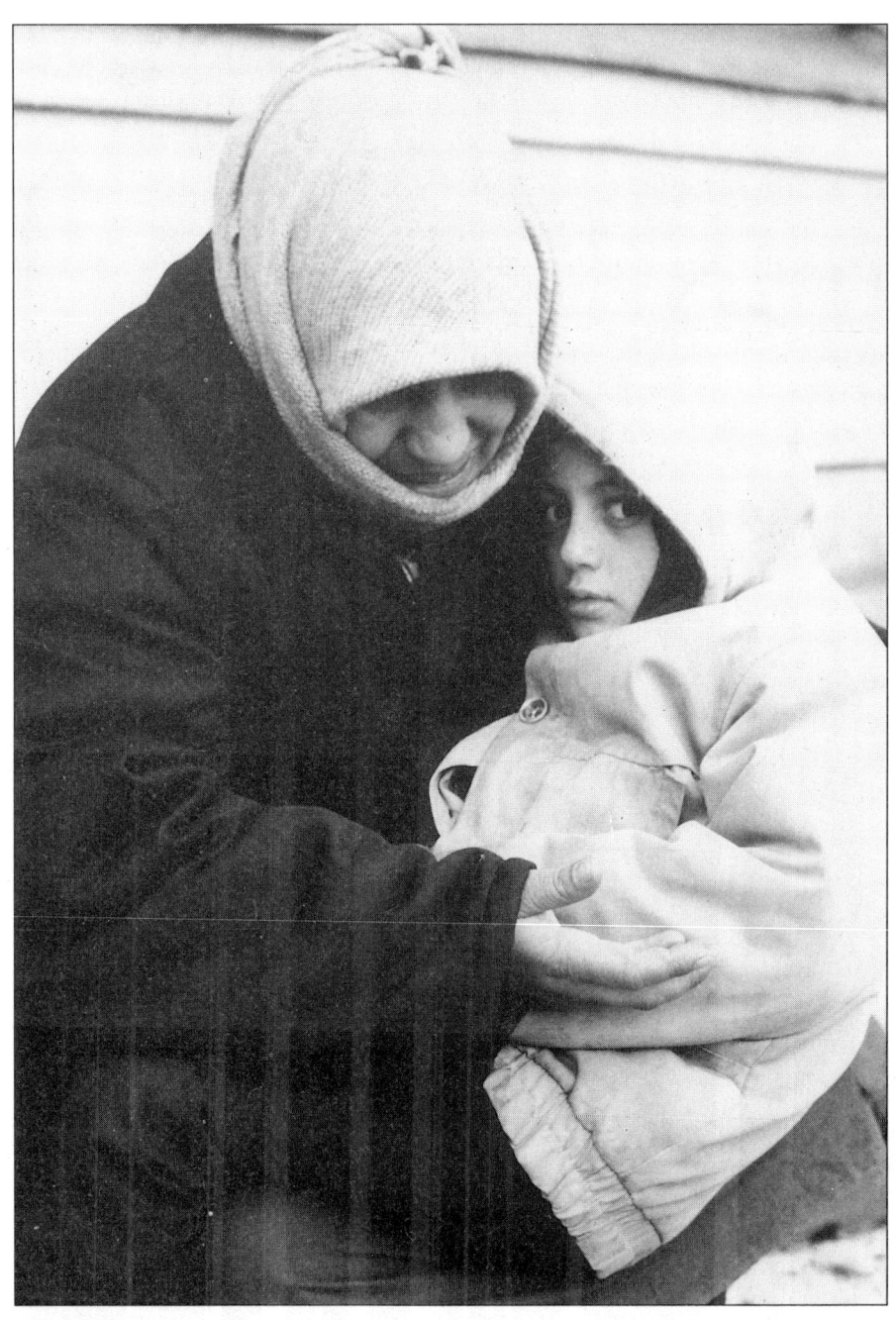

The Russian Federation. Grandmother with grandson begging for money to buy food in Red Square, Moscow. (photo by Richard Lord)

CHAPTER SEVEN

Neoliberal Economic Policy, "State Desertion," and the Russian Health Crisis

Mark G. Field, David M. Kotz, and Gene Bukhman

I n May of 1995, *Meditsinskaia Gazeta*, the biweekly journal read by health workers in Russia and most other states of the former Soviet Union, published a cartoon to illustrate the deteriorating health-care system (Drawing 7.1). It shows an ocean liner labeled "*zdravookhranenie*" ("Soviet socialized medicine") sinking into the water as its passengers jump overboard. The passengers attempt to swim, but most are drowning. One man, however, floats serenely on a raft made of 5,000 ruble notes. Oblivious to the plight of the others, he is well dressed and hatted, holding an attaché case and wearing a smug smile. He epitomizes the insouciance of the affluent few who can afford to pay for their health care—through private physicians, hospitals, and clinics—while the less fortunate "go under." The cartoon symbolizes the growing polarization of the Russian population and the relationship between money and health in the "new" Russia. In contrast to a small, wealthy elite, an increasing number of destitute people—those with no rafts of bank notes to buoy them—find themselves largely abandoned by a state that, in the past, promised free and universal health care as a constitutional right.

This is not the place to examine the nature, outreach, and quality of Soviet socialized medicine. That system was riddled with major problems. It was consistently underfunded, and it was stratified into a variety of subsystems, from the superb facilities reserved for Kremlin officials and their families to the primitive care available to the farmers and the lower orders of Soviet society. But for all its shortcomings, the old system epitomized the idea that all citizens were entitled to medical care, free of charge, at the expense of the state.

In and of itself, the demise of the Soviet system of socialized medicine cannot, however, be entirely faulted for deteriorating health in the Russian Federation (and other former Soviet republics). It is generally accepted that medical care *per se* accounts for only a small part of the variance in disease and death. According to the World Health Organization (WHO), this variance can be explained in part by health services, but other factors must be considered as well, including living conditions and life style, environmental factors, and genetics.[1] This means that a broader way of

Drawing 7.1: *Meditiskaia Gazeta* No. 39, 26 May, 1995.

accounting for Russia's current health crisis must be sought. This chapter provides elements of such an explanation by shedding light on the health effects of policies pursued by the Russian government—with the approval and guidance of Western economic experts—since Russia became an independent state at the end of 1991.

In 1992, the Russian government set out to transform a state socialist system into a capitalist market system through an economic and political agenda known as the "neoliberal strategy." This chapter explores the implications of the neoliberal program for the health and welfare of the Russian people. First, we examine the main dimensions of health in Russia. Second, we look at the neoliberal strategy pursued by the Russian government since the beginning of 1992 and the effects that strategy has had on the Russian economy and society. Last, we attempt to correlate the particular set of health problems afflicting the Russian population today with the procedures and results of the neoliberal program.

As we shall see, the policies of Russia's government are transforming an already problematic public health situation into a full-blown health crisis with disastrous consequences. In fact, the severe health crisis in Russia bears some resemblance to conditions found in many impoverished Third World nations. Unlike the health crisis in the Third World, however, Russia's difficulties cannot be attributed to decades of poverty and underdevelopment. Russia, whatever its economic problems in the Soviet era, had become a developed, industrialized country. Hence, the Russian health crisis provides a case study of the potentially harmful health effects of misguided economic policies, even in relatively wealthy, technologically advanced societies.

DIMENSIONS OF THE RUSSIAN HEALTH CRISIS

There is general agreement that following the Second World War and the introduction of antibiotics, mortality in most countries went down and life expectancy consequently increased. The Soviet Union experienced this phenomenon in the early postwar decades. During the Brezhnev years (1964-1982), however, the progress apparently slowed. Western observers' first awareness of the difficulties came with the unexpected rise in infant mortality reported by Soviet statisticians in the early 1970s.[2] This was followed by several years of an embargo on the publication of vital statistics, a sign that something was amiss.

The limited data made available by the Soviet authorities make it difficult to pinpoint the causes of the apparent decline in public health after the 1960s. The Soviet gross national product (GNP) and household consumption rose steadily throughout the post-World War II period, until the very end of the Soviet regime in 1990-91.[3] Rising living standards are normally associated with improvement in the health status of a population.[4] However, with economic growth, between 1960 and 1980 consumption of cereals declined in the Soviet Union while consumption of sugar and red meat grew. This dietary pattern is associated with increased cardiovascular mortality.[5] Furthermore, the percentage of GNP devoted to health-care spending in the Soviet Union declined from greater than 6 percent of GNP in the mid-1960s to about 3 percent, and probably less, at the time of the demise of the Soviet Union.[6]

Recent estimates of health-care spending as a proportion of GNP vary from 5 percent to as low as 1.4 percent, although these estimates usually do not include "under the table" payments, tips, or various other forms of black market medical spending. The decline in relative spending on health in the later years of the Soviet regime may have been partly a consequence of Soviet efforts to match the rapidly growing military budgets of the United States. With a GNP only a fraction of that of the United States, heavy Soviet military spending appears to be a classic case of sacrificing butter for guns. The mounting environmental costs of Soviet economic growth may also have played a role in health difficulties that developed in the latter part of the Soviet era.[7]

This history indicates that the current health problems in Russia and other republics of the former Union of Soviet Socialist Republics (U.S.S.R.) did not begin in 1992. Yet the demise of the Soviet state and the policies pursued by the successor Russian Federation have worsened the health situation to such an extent that many observers view recent developments as a catastrophe, and the term "*katastroika*" has come into use.[8] A survey of a number of specific features of the health crisis that has emerged during this period of social upheaval and rapid economic decline serves to detail the health consequences of the demise.

Mortality Rates

The Russian Federation has been more generous than the former U.S.S.R. with the publication of vital statistics, beginning in October 1992 with two white papers, one on the state of health of Russia's population, the other on the state of the environment.[9] Both paint a discouraging picture, and there is every indication that since the preparation of these documents the situation has deteriorated further.[10]

Table 7.1 shows Russia's death rate since 1980. During the Soviet years of 1980-1991, the mortality rate varied between 10.4 and 11.6 per thousand live births. Then from 1991 to 1994 mortality grew very rapidly, rising by 38 percent (from 11.4 to 15.7 per thousand), before registering a modest decline in 1995-96.

Table 7.1

Vital Statistics of Russia

Year	Births per 1,000 People	Deaths per 1,000 People	Natural Increase/Decrease per 1,000 People
1980	15.9	11.0	4.9
1981	16.0	10.9	5.1
1982	16.6	10.7	5.9
1983	17.5	11.1	6.4
1984	16.9	11.6	5.3
1985	16.6	11.3	5.3
1986	17.2	10.4	6.8
1987	17.2	10.5	6.7
1988	16.0	10.7	5.3
1989	14.6	10.7	3.9
1990	13.4	11.2	2.2
1991	12.1	11.4	0.7
1992	10.7	12.2	-1.5
1993	9.4	14.5	-5.1
1994	9.6	15.7	-6.1
1995	9.3	15.0	-5.7
1996	8.8	14.3	-5.5

Source: Goskomstat rossii, 1994, p. 43; Goskomstat rossii, 1997, p. 7.

The Russian birth rate declined after 1987, when economic reform under Mikhail Gorbachev first began to create significant uncertainty about the future of Soviet society. The decline continued through 1993, marking a total drop of 45 percent from 1987-1993. Taken by itself, a decrease in a country's birth rate is not necessarily problematic. Indeed, in most European countries the birth rate is lower than in Russia. However, Russia's plummeting birth rate, combined with its rising death rate, turned what had been a sizable natural rate of population increase into a *decrease* in 1992, the first year of Russia's independence. Since 1993, deaths in Russia have exceeded births by five to six per 1000, a demographic pattern usually seen only in times of war, famine, or plague.

One of the most worrisome mortality trends in Russia involves adult male mortality. Since 1990, adult male mortality rates have risen sharply for most age groups. For males ages 15 to 24, the annual death rate in 1981 stood at 258.7 per 100,000 population. By 1990, this figure had dropped to 209.4. But in 1993, the rate climbed to 289.3. For males ages 45 to 54, the 1981 death rate was 1,586.3 per 100,000 population, decreasing to 1,443.4 by 1990, but then surging upward to 2,173.4 in 1993.[11] The age classification reveals that the abrupt rise in mortality rates has been registered among an active and experienced segment of the adult male population.

One result of these mortality trends has been a large drop in the life expectancy of males, which fell from 63.8 years in 1990 to 57.6 years in 1994.[12] This sharp decline placed Russian male life expectancy below that of some impoverished Third World countries.[13] Female life expectancy in Russia decreased in the same period, but less precipitously, from 74.3 in 1990 to 71.2 in 1994.[14] There is now a gap of approximately 13.5 years between male and female life expectancy: Russia is on its way to becoming a country of widows and fatherless children.[15] At present rates, about half of all males now aged 16 will not reach the official retirement age of 60.[16]

Infectious Diseases

Infectious diseases that had earlier been controlled have been making a troubling comeback. Diphtheria, for example, which has almost disappeared in most wealthy countries, has seen a spectacular rise in Russia. In 1989, there were 603 reported cases of diphtheria in Russia (0.4 per 100,000 population). In 1993, a total of 15,229 cases were reported (10.3 per 100,000 population). In 1994, 39,703 cases (26.6 per 100,000 population) were reported—again, rates in excess of some Third World countries.[17] The incidence of childhood measles, fairly stable in 1990-92, increased by almost 300 percent between 1992 and 1993.[18] That of whooping cough rose 63 percent during the same period.[19] Tuberculosis is also re-emerging as a widespread health menace. The incidence of tuberculosis in Russia was relatively stable in 1990-92, but rose by 11 percent in 1993. Deaths from tuberculosis, which fell continuously until 1989, rose by 4 percent in 1990, 3.6 percent in 1991, and 15 percent in 1992. By 1992, the incidence of tuberculosis per 100,000 population was 16.5 times greater in Russia than in the United States.[20] The impact of tuberculosis on children provokes special concern, and in 1993, compared with the previous year, there was a 12.7 percent increase in the number of children suffering from active tuberculosis.[21] Most frightening of all is the rapid rise in the number of cases of multi-drug resistant tuberculosis (see Box 7.1). Meanwhile, other infectious diseases are also on the rise, including hepatitis B, cholera, typhoid, anthrax, salmonellosis, and syphilis.[22]

Box 7.1: Smoking Gun? The Resurgence of Tuberculosis in Russia

Tuberculosis is on the rise in communities and prisons throughout Russia. Prior to 1991 and the breakup of the Soviet Union, the country had decreased its tuberculosis rates by 5 to 7 percent per year.[23] Since then, the number of reported cases in the country has more than doubled, and active cases are increasing by 10 percent each year.[24,25] According to Russia's deputy minister of health, 2.5 million people in a population of 148 million currently suffer from the disease.[26] For decades, Russia made gains against tuberculosis through an extensive, centralized prevention and treatment system that included mandatory x-ray screening and a network of more than 1,000 TB hospitals, clinics, and sanatoria.[27] Now, Russia has one of the worst tuberculosis problems in the world.[28] And no improvement is in sight: in the first ten months of 1998, tuberculosis prevalence in Russia increased by 8.5 percent over 1997 levels.[29]

According to an internal document prepared by staff in Russia's Ministry of the Interior, mortality from tuberculosis increased by 89.6 percent between 1989 and 1995. The same report describes the increasing material limitations for resolving the crisis: 50 to 90 percent of the equipment in Russian TB hospitals no longer functions and several geographic areas can only meet 20 percent of their current drug needs.[30] Cure rates for tuberculosis have also dropped dramatically in some areas. For example, it dropped from 67 percent in 1987 to 44 percent in Kemerovo oblast in 1997.[31] During the same period, death rates among those receiving treatment also increased from 9 percent to 30 percent.[32] The situation in some areas is even worse. In western Siberia, the tuberculosis incidence jumped from 54 to 116 cases per 100,000 population, from 1985 to 1997.[33] In one semiautonomous Siberian state, Buryati, the 1997 incidence rate was 211 per 100,000 population, or more than two and one half times the rate in all of Russia (79 per 100,000 population).[34,35] Anticipating worsening tuberculosis outcomes and diminishing state support, the director of TB control in Buryati called the situation "a genocide...a holocaust."[36]

The incidence of tuberculosis in prisons is especially alarming, with rates far higher than those found in the general population. In 1997, in a prison in Tomsk, tuberculosis incidence was 7,000 cases per 100,000 population, and the risk of infection with the organism that causes tuberculosis was reported to be 40 times greater in prison than in the general public.[37,38] An estimated 50 percent of the 1 million prisoners in Russia are reported to be infected with Mycobacterium tuberculosis.[39] Of these, 100,000 are believed to suffer from active disease, and it is estimated that between 40 and 80 percent of all deaths in prisons are due to poorly treated or untreated tuberculosis. Overall TB mortality among prisoners is estimated at 484 per 100,000 population, one of the highest rates in the world.[40] The risk to the general population has increased with the release of sick, inadequately treated prisoners. In one prison outside Moscow, a doctor reported that 90 percent of all prisoners being released the following month were still infectious.[41] It is estimated that tens of thousands of people with infectious tuberculosis are released from prison each year throughout Russia.[42] A significant proportion of them are likely to carry strains of M. tuberculosis resistant to the two most effective anti-tuberculosis drugs, adding to the difficulties in treating the disease.[43] Recent data reveal that a shocking 30 percent of prisoners with tuberculosis have this multidrug-resistant form (MDR-TB).[44] In the Mariinsk prison in Siberia, only 25 percent of the 164 patients receiving retreatment therapy had strains of the disease that were susceptible to all first line drugs used in standard therapy.[45] These reports led Dr. Richard O'Brien of the U.S. Centers for Disease Control and Prevention to declare: "This is probably the worst situation for multidrug resistant tuberculosis ever documented in the world."[46]

The high rates of new tuberculosis infection and the increase in death attributed to the disease in Russia are symptoms of a country in crisis, contending with increased social problems, diminishing public resources to address them, and a deteriorating public health infrastructure. Tuberculosis has long been linked to poverty and homelessness, both of which have risen rapidly in Russia. Medical experts warn, "Tuberculosis is out of control in Russia because of a collapse in the health system and a lack of funds for medicines and care."[47] The disruption of funds previously devoted to health has interrupted drug supplies, possibly causing the increases in resistance to anti-tuberculosis drugs.[48] Not only has funding for tuberculosis decreased every year since the early 1990s, some regional TB programs have actually *received* less than one-third of officially allocated funds. The high TB-related death rates in prisons are attributed to the extensive deterioration of prison living conditions and infrastructure. Prisons are overflowing with inmates, sometimes to more than double capacity. Sanitation, heat, food, and medicines are virtually unavailable.[49] In several prisons, the amount of funds received from Moscow is but a tiny fraction of what is actually needed to feed and clothe patients.[50,51] Under such circumstances, it is unlikely that tuberculosis in prisons will be brought under control.

A leader of Russia's tuberculosis control efforts offers an explanation for the dire situation. The Soviet system prioritized public health and allowed for the costly, labor-intensive practice of isolating infectious patients by placing them in sanitoria and providing them with generous nourishment, rest, and some antibiotic therapy. Now, however, "We have lost certain assets of socialism." "Russia," however, "has not acquired the assets of capitalism," including large health-care budgets.[52] Another source concurs, "When the Soviet Union and its command economy collapsed, so did tuberculosis prevention. As state funding for medicine dwindled, x-ray equipment [the foundation of the diagnostic system] fell into disrepair." The enforced regular screening of millions of workers will no longer be possible as more and more people enter private sector employment. As job insecurity becomes the norm, patients are less able to spend the necessary amount of time in sanitoria.[53] Russia is faced with a full-blown public health crisis—for a disease it had come so close to conquering less than ten years ago.

Nutrition

The increasingly poor nutritional status of people living in Russia has been documented by many researchers.[54] In a 1992 study of elderly persons receiving pensions, half the people surveyed reported losing five or more kilograms in the previous six months; 57 percent stated that they did not have enough money to buy food; 40 percent reported consuming less than half a kilogram of meat per week; and 33 percent reported consuming less than half a liter of milk per week.[55] Poor nutritional status has contributed to the re-emergence in some cities of long-forgotten illnesses, including scurvy, pediculosis, and rickets.[56] Some surveys show that more than 60 percent of mothers judge themselves unable to feed their children properly because food products are either unavailable or too expensive for purchase. In many cases, children suffer from a deficiency of vitamins, such as ascorbic acid and folic acid.[57] In one survey, greater than 60 percent of children under age eight exhibited signs of nutritional deficiencies, and more than 7 percent suffered from anemia. As one author notes, "The situation with respect to children's nutrition in Russia has to be judged critical."[58] Furthermore, as people lack adequate nutrition, their immune systems perform poorly, and they become more vulnerable to other forms of infection, further compromising the health of the population.[59]

Environmental Health

Although environmental conditions in Russia prior to the demise of the Soviet Union were in many areas deplorable, the transition to a market-based economy has not led to improvements in this sector. With increased privatization and deregulation of industries, health and environmental authorities lack both the power and resources to enforce industry compliance with regulations and pollution abatement requirements.[60] Currently, 40 percent of Russia's urban population live with extremely high air pollution levels. According to a recently published environmental and health atlas of Russia: "The maximum allowable concentration of many substances is exceeded fivefold in more than 150 cities and tenfold in 86 cities, thus affecting the lives of 95 million people. Almost all reservoirs close to cities are contaminated and 75 percent of all surface water is polluted, with only half of all water safe for drinking even after treatment."[61] A report from the Interdepartmental Commission of the Russian Federation's Security Council on Ecological Safety found that, in an area of Moscow affected by emissions from the Likachev automobile plant, the average weight of newborns was 400 grams lower than the average weight of newborns in an area of the capital not affected by the emissions. The report concluded that 20 percent of the overall morbidity rate was related to environmental pollution, and that in some areas the figure was considerably higher.[62]

Russia's Health Decline: Summary

As we have seen, a variety of data point to the striking decline of health in Russia.[63] Although public health may not have been optimal under the Soviet system, most indicators suggest that Russians' health status has worsened substantially since the fall of the Soviet Union. The roots of these developments are complex—involving medical, political, economic, and social elements—and they add up to a crisis of systemic dimensions.[64] Although a variety of factors have contributed to the alarming degradation in public health in Russia, many of these factors can be traced to the neoliberal economic policies that began in 1992. We now turn to an examination of the specific details of those measures.

THE NEOLIBERAL ECONOMIC STRATEGY AND ITS EFFECTS

The neoliberal strategy was promoted by Russian economists who were the crucial economic policy-makers in the government of President Boris Yeltsin during 1991-92.[65] It was strongly endorsed by influential Western economic advisors to the newly independent Russian government, and by the organization that has arguably exerted the greatest influence over recent Russian economic policy, the International Monetary Fund (IMF).[66,67]

Russia inherited from the Soviet period an economic structure based on state ownership of nearly all enterprises; central administration of resources based on economic planning; and a comprehensive system of social protection. In addition to free health care, the social protection system included guaranteed employment, guaranteed retirement pensions, free education, inexpensive housing and food, and subsidized child care and vacations. This centralized system was to be replaced with a capitalist market system similar to that found in western Europe and the United States. The Yeltsin government's neoliberal economic policies were aimed at completing the dismantling of the centralized socioeconomic structure, a process initiated as early as 1990, when Russia was still a part of the Soviet Union.

The neoliberal strategy that Russia has followed is often identified with a triad of specific economic policies: 1) liberalization (that is, freeing) of prices; 2) stabilization of the price level through cutting government spending and keeping a tight rein on the growth of money and credit; and 3) privatization of state enterprises. But the neoliberal strategy of transition is actually broader than these three policies. The term "shock therapy," often used to describe this strategy, derives partly from one of its most important features: the call for a very rapid transformation of the economy. The huge job of transforming Russia's state socialist system into a capitalist market system was to be carried out as rapidly as possible—within a few years. An entire set of radically new policies was to be introduced simultaneously, rather than in sequence.

A second feature of the neoliberal strategy is the very limited role assigned to the government in creating the new capitalist market system. In Russia, the government's basic contribution was to abolish the old central-planning system, sell off its assets, and draft a new legal framework appropriate to a system based on private property and market exchange. It was left to private initiative to create the new market relations and restructure existing businesses, with little government guidance, support, or regulation of the process. This feature of the neoliberal strategy is based on the belief, held by free market economic theorists, that a market economy will spring up more or less automatically if the state simply gets out of the way. In this view, a market economy is the "natural" or "normal" state of the economy in human society, and fails to function only when state actions prevent it from operating.

Along with the calls for rapid transition and limited government management of the process, the neoliberal strategy includes a set of economic policies for the transition period. The aforementioned triad—liberalization, privatization, and stabilization through cutting government spending and keeping money and credit scarce—are the most widely cited specific elements of the neoliberal approach. However, two other important policies were part of the plan. The first was the elimination of the comprehensive system of social guarantees that characterized the former Soviet system. The second was the removal of barriers to international trade and investment.

The aforementioned set of policies was supposed to lead to the rapid development of an efficient, technologically progressive capitalist market system in Russia.[68] These changes were billed as a means to construct a prosperous consumer society on the ruins of state socialism. Economists painted a rosy scenario postulating that the immediate lifting of state price controls would, through the action of supply and demand in newly freed markets, cause prices to rise for those goods that consumers really wanted, while the prices of unwanted or inferior goods would fall. This would lead producers to cut back production of undesired goods while stepping up production of the goods consumers sought, making Russia's economy responsive to consumer wishes. Because suddenly freeing prices would generate inflation, the macroeconomic stabilization policy was intended to quickly bring inflation under control. Privatization, by placing enterprises in the hands of private owners, would ensure that producers would respond to the market signals generated by the new free-pricing system, and have an incentive to produce efficiently and adopt the most up-to-date technologies. Eliminating the comprehensive system of social guarantees—cutbacks in public spending were key in bringing inflation under control—would prod the overly secure Russian population into working harder. Finally, free trade and investment would subject Russian producers to healthy competition from foreign firms while also attracting foreign capital and expertise to the Russian economy.

The aforementioned policies have been followed quite rigorously by Russia since January 1992.[69] Nearly all prices were freed on January 2, 1992, a few days after the demise of the U.S.S.R. left Russia an independent state. The prescribed macroeconomic stabilization policy has been vigorously pursued since the beginning of 1992, as successive reports by the IMF have confirmed.[70] Public spending declined rapidly, falling from 47.9 percent of gross domestic product (GDP) in 1991 to 38.7 percent in 1992 and to only 26.9 percent by 1995.[71] Monetary policy has varied somewhat from month to month, but the growth of the money supply was kept well below the rate of price increases for every year during 1992-95.[72]

Privatization had been expected to be the slowest of the policies to be carried out, but it has proceeded with surprising alacrity. Most small state enterprises were privatized quickly during 1992, and by mid-1994 about two-thirds of all public enterprises had been privatized. By the end of 1994, private enterprises accounted for 78.5 percent of industrial output.[73]

While selling off state enterprises at a rapid pace, the Russian government also quickly set about relinquishing its role as provider of a comprehensive social safety net. The state stopped guaranteeing Russians a job. Subsidies for housing and food were reduced or phased out. The underfunding of publicly provided medical care only grew more pronounced as hospitals and clinics converted to a fee-for-service basis. The shortfall in the provision of funds for medical care was to be made up by an insurance system, partly obligatory and partly optional. At the present time, however, the insurance system is not working well, further compromising access to medical services.[74] Inasmuch as most of the funds available to medical directors of hospitals and clinics go to pay personnel, very little, if anything, is left for equipment, medication, instruments, food for patients, capital repairs, or other expenses.

The free trade and investment plank was also closely observed in many respects. Foreign imports have flowed freely into Russia, with tariff levels no higher than those of Western nations. Foreign investment has been welcomed, and the previously state-controlled value of the ruble has been largely left to supply and demand in the international currency markets.[75] Some controls have remained on exports of goods and capital, but they have been ineffective and readily evaded with impunity.

Although Russia has closely followed the tenets of the neoliberal economic strategy of transition, the results have been vastly different from those promised by the plan's Russian and Western promoters. Since the policy was inaugurated, Russia has experienced severe economic depression with no end in sight as of the middle of 1997. Compared to already depressed 1991 levels, by 1996 GDP had fallen by 45 percent, industrial production by 49 percent, and agricultural output by 32 percent.[76] The decline in GDP significantly exceeds what the United States experienced at the depth of the Great Depression of the 1930s. While policy-makers expected declines in some areas, every sector of the Russian economy contracted, including consumer goods, producer goods, and services.

The freeing of prices set off a runaway inflation that has proved very difficult to control, despite the tight fiscal and monetary policies followed by the government. Consumer prices rose by a factor of 26—or 2,500 percent—during 1992.[77] Inflation gradually slowed over the following years, but consumer prices were still rising at a 19.6 percent annual rate in the fourth quarter of 1996.[78] The savings of the population were wiped out in the first months of raging inflation.

Wages and pensions failed to keep pace with rising prices, and by 1995 the average real wage had fallen to 51 percent of its 1991 level and the real value of the minimum monthly pension had declined to 40 percent of the 1991 level.[79] Even these rapidly falling wages were often paid with a delay of many months.[80] Various estimates have been made of the percentage of the population that was plunged into poverty, ranging as high as 50 percent.[81] Chen, Wittgenstein, and McKeon report that the poverty rate for families grew from 2 percent to 50 percent between 1987-88 and 1995, and the fraction of family income devoted to food grew from 28 to 40 percent between 1991 and 1994.[82] Furthermore, the impoverishment of a substantial part of the population was accompanied by drastic cutbacks in public services.

In the chaotic conditions created by the neoliberal strategy, some people were able to become quite rich, by obtaining state assets at bargain prices (sometimes for free); illegally exporting valuable raw materials; speculating in foreign currencies and other financial assets; or extorting money from new private businesses. Thus, income inequality increased dramatically. According to official statistics, by 1995 the income of the top 10 percent of households was 13.5 times as great as that of the bottom 10 percent; in Soviet times that ratio was about 4.5 to 1.[83]

As the Russian state withdrew into a *laissez-faire* stance, and as state employees charged with maintaining public order found the buying power of their salaries dissipated by price inflation, the authority of the state largely collapsed. Organized crime stepped in to fill the vacuum. A 1994 study estimated that 70 to 80 percent of private banks and businesses in major cities were forced to make payments to organized crime.[84] Ordinary crimes such as murder, assault, and robbery also increased rapidly in the new Russia.

The neoliberal strategy turned out to be effective at destroying the old socioeconomic system in Russia, but it has proved powerless to create a viable new one. In its wake have come economic collapse, impoverishment of the population, an enormous growth in inequality, and a breakdown of public order. Whenever a highly touted new economic policy fails to perform as advertised, its adherents typically complain that the policy was never really followed (while usually simultaneously asserting that the policy actually worked better than is generally believed). This excuse cannot work in the case of Russia, which, as we have shown, followed the neoliberal prescriptions very closely.

Why the neoliberal strategy has produced these disastrous results has been analyzed in detail elsewhere.[85] The major problem with the neoliberal program is its false assumption that a prosperous capitalist market system can be rapidly built, essentially by individual initiative, in a country that had a radically different kind of socio-economic system for the previous 70 years. Historical experience shows that constructing a modern market system takes decades, and all successful cases in the twentieth century have involved an active role for the state in the process (examples being Japan, South Korea, and more recently China).[86] A modern market system does not arise simply by the state getting out of the way. In Russia, dismantling the pre-existing economic system before anything had been created to take its place has predictably produced chaos, depression, impoverishment, sudden enrichment of the few at the expense of the majority, and a collapse of public order.

The specific policies associated with the neoliberal strategy all failed to match expectations. Price liberalization produced rapid inflation, rather than an efficient re-allocation of production. The cuts in state spending and the rigorously tight monetary policy contributed to the severe depression and denied needed funds to Russian enterprises seeking to modernize. Hasty privatization turned state enterprises over to influential insiders but produced no improvement in business performance. Demolishing the social safety net left individuals bereft of any security, and the expected "work incentives" were irrelevant, given the absence of employment opportunities in the collapsing economy. The superior financial and marketing power of foreign producers enabled imports to rapidly establish a dominant position over locally produced goods in Russian urban markets, further undermining Russian industry. And very little foreign investment flowed into the country, due to the unstable conditions created by the neoliberal policies. Instead, tens of billions of dollars of capital flowed out of Russia, as the newly rich sought to safeguard their recent gains by placing them in Swiss bank accounts and the New York real estate market.[87]

LINKS BETWEEN THE NEOLIBERAL STRATEGY AND THE HEALTH CRISIS

How is Russia's current health crisis related to the methods and effects of the neoliberal economic program? We cannot conclusively demonstrate direct causal links, in large part because sufficient data have not yet been collected. Yet we will argue that the aggressive implementation of the neoliberal program in Russia since 1992 has contributed in a variety of ways to the widespread deterioration of public health, a deterioration that can be expected to continue unless a radical shift in public policies is made.

Data on mortality and life expectancy show a temporal pattern that is consistent with the claim that the neoliberal policies introduced at the start of 1992 bear major responsibility for Russia's health crisis. But before we examine the period directly following the neoliberal policies, it is important to consider the health patterns just prior to their introduction. Between 1984 and 1987, the Russian death rate dropped from 11.6 to 10.5 per thousand (see Table 7.1). This drop coincided directly with Gorbachev's 1985-87 anti-alcohol campaign, when the Soviet government reduced per capita state sales of alcohol from 10.5 liters of pure ethanol per capita to 3.9 liters. During this time, real alcohol consumption declined 25 percent.[88] After the anti-alcohol campaign was called off, the death rate gradually rose back up to 11.4 per thousand by 1991. This was not a trend so much as a policy-specific change. The more significant change occurred between 1992 and 1993, directly after neoliberal policies were implemented, when the death rate jumped by 2.3 per thousand—a rate of increase almost *three times* higher than any yearly change in previous decades. The death rate continued to rise, reaching as high as 15.7 deaths per 1,000 population, before decreasing slightly to 14.3 in 1996.

Life expectancy data show a similar pattern (see Table 7.2). Male life expectancy improved somewhat in the early 1980s, followed by a further gain during the anti-alcohol campaign. It then declined, reaching approximately the pre-campaign level by 1991. Starting in 1992, the precipitous fall in male life expectancy, which was noted earlier, began. Between 1991 and 1994 male life expectancy fell by 5.9 years. Female life expectancy was affected less by the anti-alcohol campaign and its aftermath; in 1991-94 it fell by 3.1 years, a significant decline, if only about half that registered among males.

Table 7.2

Life Expectancy at Birth in Russia (years)

Year	Men	Women
1979–80	61.5	73.0
1980–81	61.5	73.1
1981–82	62.0	73.5
1982–83	62.3	73.6
1983–84	62.0	73.3
1984–85	62.3	73.3
1985–86	63.8	74.0
1986–87	64.9	74.6
1988	64.8	74.4
1989	64.2	74.5
1990	63.8	74.3
1991	63.5	74.3
1992	62.0	73.8
1993	58.9	71.9
1994	57.6	71.2
1995	58.3	71.7

Source: Goskomstat rossii, 1996.

Several potential causal links can be postulated for the "coincidence" in timing between the implementation of neoliberal policies and the health crisis. The following consequences of the neoliberal strategy, also detailed earlier, are likely to have had direct effects on health: 1) the sudden impoverishment of a large part of the population; 2) the large increase in inequality; 3) the loss of security due to the dismantling of the social safety net; 4) the decline in public order; and 5) the reduced quality and availability of health care. To this list should be added the "shock" effect of the sudden disappearance of the economic, political, and cultural institutions that had organized life in Russia until 1992—that is, the dissolution of the world to which people had become accustomed.

Let us take each development in turn. Sudden impoverishment on the scale that took place in Russia involved, as noted, significant reduction in food consumption. This can have a negative impact on health, although the effects might be mitigated if diets shifted away from red meat toward more grains. Research has similarly shown that inequality in the distribution of income has, quite apart from generalized poverty, implications for public health.[89] Recent work carried out in the United States suggests that increased income inequality is linked to higher mortality rates.[90] Kaplan, Pammuk, Lynch, and coworkers found that "income inequality increases death rates at all ages, from infant mortality to deaths of the elderly." They add: "[I]ncome inequality affects all segments of the population because it affects the rate of violence and disability, as well as public spending on police protection, education, welfare, and health care."[91] If this is true of the United States, there is no reason why it should not apply, perhaps even more directly, to the contemporary Russian situation. The mechanisms by which inequality impacts health have not yet been elucidated, but some feel inequality may exert its effects through psychosocial stress or behavioral risk factors that influence accidents and cardiovascular death.[92] In addition, increased economic insecurity, the decline in public order, and the shock effect of sudden social system demise also have potential effects on health.[93] Decreased public order also involves increases in violent crime, which directly affect health. Finally, a large reduction in health-care quality and availability should have some impact on survival rates from injuries and diseases.

An examination of causes of death sheds light on connections between the recent socioeconomic changes and the increased mortality that is a striking feature of the health crisis. Table 7.3 shows the death rate and the major causes of death in 1991 and 1993, with 1985 also included for comparison to the late Soviet period.[94] Injuries and poisonings show the largest percentage increase during 1991-93, rising by more than 50 percent.[95] Deaths due to infectious and parasitic diseases also rose sharply, by 44.9 percent. Significant, although fewer, increases were recorded for respiratory, digestive, and circulatory diseases. Deaths due to neoplasms showed little change.

The last column of Table 7.3 shows the relative importance of various causes of death to the 1991-93 rise in mortality. Circulatory disease was by far the most prevalent cause of death in 1991, and it accounted for 45.2 percent of the increase in mortality rate. Death from circulatory disease, however, did not increase as rapidly as other causes of death in the 1991-93 time period. The 57.9 percent increase in deaths from injuries and poisonings made those kinds of fatalities the second largest contributors

Table 7.3

Standardized Death Rates by Causes of Death in Russia (per 100,000 population)

	1985	1991	1993	Percentage Increase 1991–93	Percentage of 1991–93 Increase in All Deaths
All Causes of Death	1,226.2	1,198.1	1,473.4	23.0%	100.0%
Circulatory Diseases	718.7	658.5	782.9	18.9%	45.2%
Neoplasms	173.2	204.8	207.4	1.3%	0.9%
Injuries and Poisonings	139.8	143.6	226.8	57.9%	30.2%
Respiratory Diseases	86.1	58.8	76.4	29.9%	6.4%
Digestive Diseases	32.5	30.1	38.9	29.2%	3.2%
Infectious and Parasitic Diseases	17.6	12.7	18.4	44.9%	2.1%

Source: Feshbach, 1995a, Table 3.9, pp. 3–25.

to the increased mortality rate, accounting for 30.2 percent of the increase in deaths. Respiratory, digestive, and infectious and parasitic diseases together accounted for another 11.7 percent of the increased deaths.

In addition to examining mortality data, it is also instructive to look at what is known as "loss in working potential," measured in thousand person-years of working activity lost due to various causes of death. This takes account of the age at which a particular cause of death typically strikes, assuming a "normal" life expectancy of 70 years, as well as a condition's frequency of occurrence in the overall population. In 1993, deaths due to injuries and poisonings accounted for the greatest loss of working potential, representing 57.7 percent of the total loss of working potential for men and 33.9 percent for women.[96]

Table 7.4 presents data on death by injury or poisoning in 1991 and 1993, based on loss of working potential. Among men, loss of working potential due to alcohol-related deaths increased rapidly, rising by 153 percent during 1991-93. Among men, loss of working potential due to murders increased by 83 percent and loss due to suicides by 47 percent. For women, loss of working potential due to alcohol-related

Table 7.4

Loss of Working Potential (person-years) of Russia's Population from Individual Causes of Injuries and Poisonings

	Men			Women		
Causes of Death	1991	1993	Percent Change	1991	1993	Percent Change
Suicides	184,000	271,000	47%	38,000	69,000	82%
Murders	142,000	260,000	83%	38,000	49,000	29%
Alcohol-related	124,000	314,000	153%	26,000	81,000	212%

Source: Feshbach, 1995a, Table 3.13, pp. 3–38.

deaths increased 212 percent, and due to suicides, 82 percent. While these increases were faster for women than for men, the absolute numbers of these losses remained much lower for women.

The rapid increase in alcoholism and violence in Russia has been a decisive contributor to rising death rates and declining life expectancy, especially for men. The rising incidence of diseases, both infectious and noninfectious, is also a factor. Given the complex changes that have occurred in practically all aspects of Russian society, assessing the causes of Russia's worsening mortality statistics is difficult, and the entire blame cannot be laid at the door of the neoliberal strategy.[97] It is clear, however, that the effects of the neoliberal strategy have played a major role. Surging rates of alcoholism and suicide dramatically reflect the psychosocial stresses generated in Russia by an abrupt increase in poverty, inequality, insecurity, and the sudden system demise.[98] The rapid rise in the murder rate may in part reflect the withdrawal of the state from the management of public life and the resulting collapse of public order.[99] The major role played by cardiovascular disease in the increased death rate is consistent with the psychosocial stress effect associated with the neoliberal strategy.

If increased alcohol consumption is a proximate cause in rising mortality and morbidity statistics, alcohol abuse itself is a result of deeper economic shifts and psychosocial tensions. As Ellman suggests, "Even if impoverishment does not lead medically to an increase in the death rate, it may do so behaviorally," by prompting, for example, violent behavior and dangerous levels of drug and alcohol abuse.[100] Irrefutable causal relationships are difficult to establish in such areas. Yet it is intuitively persuasive that in a situation of rapidly proliferating poverty, crime, and insecurity, the ultimate cause of death in many alcohol-related deaths must be sought beyond the proximate factors, in "the general state of economic, social, and political disintegration" afflicting the country.[101]

Although as mentioned earlier the impact of the medical system on mortality and morbidity may be more limited than is often assumed, it still plays an important role. The structure of Soviet socialized medicine, funded from the state and regional budgets, has to a significant extent been dismantled, but still remains to provide a modicum of care to the population. As noted earlier, the insurance principle that has been mandated by the government is still in its formative stage. It is based on a payroll deduction of 3.6 percent paid by the employee and is widely considered a failure. Many are confused about its provisions and benefits—others consider it a scam.[102] And yet the typical family budget cannot support the additional costs of voluntary insurance. Thus, medical care often has to be sacrificed to meet more urgent needs, such as food and housing. According to Rimashevskaia, "the population, by and large, will have to forgo paid medical care."[103] In the state system, physicians and other health personnel are paid a pittance, and less than industrial workers.[104] The private sector is limited to those few who can afford it.

Alternative Explanations

Three objections might be raised to our claims about the health effects of the neoliberal strategy. One is the possibility that the dramatic worsening of health indicators after 1991 might be an artifact of changes in data collection methods (including more accurate reporting of mortality) after the demise of the Soviet Union. The second is that the rising death rate might reflect the immigration to Russia of elderly ethnic Russians from other former Soviet republics. The third is the possibility that long-standing environmental damage dating back to the Soviet period might account for a major part of the current health crisis.

Two recent reports confirm the reliability of observed mortality trends during the past two decades.[105] A comprehensive evaluation of Russian mortality data by Anderson and Silver concludes that any inaccuracies in Russian death rates result only in global underestimation of mortality among infants and the elderly. The report denies the emergence of any unpublished data after 1991, and shows that the collapse of the Soviet Union did not suddenly improve data quality.

Migration also fails to explain the decline in life expectancy since 1991. Following the collapse of the Soviet Union, many ethnic Russians returned to Russia from central Asia, the Baltics, and the Caucasus. Migration could have inflated mortality rates in 1992 and 1993 if population estimates failed to include these immigrants while their deaths were recorded. Leon, Chenet, Shkolnikov, and coworkers deny the importance of this effect based on the absence of cancer as a contributor to the increase in age-specific death from all causes between 1987 and 1994. Additionally, they note that only a migration of more than 40 million individuals could explain the mortality increase between 1987 and 1994.[106] Last, the crude mortality rates reported in this chapter increase as the population ages (due to the in-migration of elderly Russians), even if the mortality rate for each age-group remains unchanged. Shapiro has estimated that this aging would only account for 3 percent of the 18.9 percent growth in death rate in 1993.[107]

Finally, environmental decay does not appear to have played a *major* role, despite Russia's well-publicized pollution problem.[108] In fact, emissions in the country have declined with the industrial collapse. On the other hand, as we noted earlier, other observers have pointed to alarming evidence of the impact of pollution on newborns and on morbidity in general. So the prognosis in this area is guarded, but hardly a cause for optimism.

Concluding Comments

As we have shown, neoliberal economic initiatives have contributed to negative health outcomes for Russians in a variety of ways and at a number of levels. Of course, the specific policy decisions associated with the neoliberal program are not the only factors that have played a role in the multifaceted destabilization of Russian society, nor in the rapid decline in health indicators among the population. Other factors have contributed to this result, including the inadequacies of the Soviet health system. Yet the Russian and foreign designers and promoters of Russia's neoliberal strategy bear a major responsibility for this health crisis, a responsibility heightened by their continued rejection of any major deviations from the neoliberal program, despite the mounting evidence of its disastrous effects on the well-being of the Russian people.

Our goal has been to focus attention on the *concrete human costs*—the acute physical and psychological suffering and the catastrophic regression in public health—associated with the particular mode of economic transition implemented in Russia since 1992, under the guidance of Western economic experts and with the blessing of leading international financial institutions. We have tried above all to provide a sense of the scope and seriousness of Russia's health disaster, and to question implicitly the neoliberal claim that "there was—and is—no other way." The Russian case offers a stinging refutation of the neoliberal assumption that an efficiently functioning market system will develop quickly and "naturally" if the state is simply prevented from interfering. Developments in Russia offer painful proof that a more nuanced and context-sensitive model of economic transition is required. The benefits of the neoliberal program, it is conventionally and ritually affirmed, will in the end outweigh and render negligible the short-term social costs. The current situation in Russia reminds us that the degree of comfort to be drawn from such assurances varies, depending on whether one is going down with the ship of state protection, floating on a raft of bank notes, or watching from the safety of the shore.

The demise of the Soviet system and the effects of the neoliberal strategy have created a sharp and growing division between the bulk of the population and a small group able to exploit the crisis to its own advantage. This elite group has rapidly achieved a luxurious standard of living. Its members can afford the best medical care available in Russia, or abroad, if necessary. In contrast to this privileged minority, an increasingly large and impoverished population can be found: alienated, embittered, and nostalgic for the stability and predictability of the former regime.

At the present moment, the polity is continuing to dissociate itself from many of the commitments that had been assumed by the past regime, thereby leaving a void that, in theory at least, should have been filled by the market, competition, and efficiency. But this dissociation has had disastrous consequences for the welfare of the population, consequences reflected in the demographic and health data. The neoliberal policies and the withdrawal of the state have increased the stress on the poorer members of the population and provoked growing discontent and alienation. The fact that under the previous regime the Communist Party did not allow the existence of other parties or sources of autonomous power meant that the collapse of the Soviet regime left a void that could *not* readily be filled in the absence of civil society. According to Andreev, the "U.S.S.R. was a paternalistic state, and in the process of reform, responsibility for personal welfare in increasing measure has been transferred to the individual and the family, which is also a source of stress."[109] Traditionally, the population saw the state as both "father" and "mother." The father was stern, exacting, often cruel, always demanding sacrifices from the people. But the state was also a supportive mother, who provided (or promised to provide) important social supports and safety nets such as housing, kindergartens, old-age and disability pensions, and free medical care. Thus, paternalism *and* maternalism have been abruptly swept away, leaving dependents orphaned and ruled by economic laws they do not understand—or perhaps understand too well.

The poverty and inequality in Russia today has a different history from that of the Third World. Russia's neoliberal policies, supported by Russian economic officials, Western advisors, and the international financial institutions, have rapidly created extreme poverty and inequality in a country that has not been accustomed to them. One consequence has been the escalating health crisis discussed in this chapter. Another is likely to be a high degree of political instability in the near future. Russia may well at some point veer off onto a path of political and economic development quite different from its present course. Whether such a change in Russia will be for the better or for the worse is difficult to predict.

UPDATE

The data in this chapter reach up to 1995 and 1996. Since that time, there have been some improvements in Russian health indicators. The most significant have been a modest decline in mortality and some increase in life expectancy. However, the Russian health crisis as described in this chapter remains acute at this writing (January 1999), and is not likely to be ameliorated following the events of August 1998 and the economic turmoil that ensued. Indeed, as this volume goes to press, current research "gives grim support to the growing concern over Russia's falling birthrate, low life expectancy, and unusually high male mortality rate." Current findings support the link between increased morbidity and mortality and "the transition to a market economy," attributing "most of the deaths to widespread human insecurity, the main factors being a loss of earnings, a rise in economic uncertainty, job losses, and a decline in social services."[110]

ACKNOWLEDGMENTS

The authors are grateful for the assistance of Alec Irwin, Joyce Millen, Jennifer Furin, Sally Zierler, Sarah Pomerantz, Carole Mitnick, Evan Lyon, Jim Yong Kim, and Jennifer Singler.

PART III

Powerful Players,
Harmful Consequences:
Transnational Corporations,
Inequality, and Health

Vietnam. Young women dressed in Marlboro outfits distribute cigarettes for Philip Morris. (photo by Debra Efroymson, courtesy of INFACT, Boston)

CHAPTER EIGHT

Dying for Growth, Part I: Transnational Corporations and the Health of the Poor

Joyce V. Millen and Timothy H. Holtz
with assistance from Dorothy Fallows and Ruth Rosenbaum

The institution that most changes our lives we least understand or, more correctly, seek most elaborately to misunderstand. That is the modern corporation. Week by week, month by month, year by year, it exercises a greater influence on our livelihood and the way we live than unions, universities, politicians and the government.

John Kenneth Galbraith[1]

Written over 20 years ago, Galbraith's words have never been truer than they are today. Of all modern corporations, it is the large global firms known as transnational corporations (TNCs) that most profoundly affect the lives of individuals and communities in virtually every corner of the world.[2] People living in the most remote rural villages and the largest cities consume TNCs' products, work in or live near their plants, and are swayed by their seductive marketing campaigns. Transnational corporations *directly* impact the well-being of workers who toil in their factories, fields, and mines, and they *indirectly* affect the quality of life for all of us through their environmental practices, promotional activities, and political influence.[3]

To understand the complexity and magnitude of health problems currently facing the poor we must know something about large global corporations—the dominant institutions of our time. By exploring the impact of TNC activities on the health of poor and marginalized people, this chapter and Chapter Nine offer a view into these corporate entities. More importantly, they suggest a vantage point from which to assess specific tenets of neoliberalism, and evaluate the current global political and economic environment in which TNCs function.[4] Though we recognize that many extraordinary medical and technological innovations of the last century are products of national and transnational corporations, our two chapters do not aim to compare positive and negative aspects of TNCs.[5] They focus instead on the observable harmful health consequences of TNC operations, arguing that for poor communities TNCs' total social costs often far exceed their social benefits.

After an introductory section describing the worldwide growth and expansion of TNCs, the present chapter includes detailed studies of three interrelated areas. Taken together, the three sections outline health effects on individuals and communities of TNC activities, including the transnational extraction, processing, manufacturing, exportation, promotion, and sale of raw materials, hazardous by-products, and goods.[6]

1) *Labor practices:* In their factories, fields, and mines, in their storage facilities and processing plants, and in their subcontracting factories, TNCs have a direct influence over the well-being of hundreds of millions of individuals throughout the world, through the wages they pay and the rights and working conditions they accord workers.[7]

2) *Environmental impact:* Throughout the world, TNCs release solid, liquid, and gaseous waste into the environment. Transnational energy, mining, forestry, fishing, manufacturing, and agricultural corporations affect human life on every continent by flooding huge tracts of land, depleting natural resources, eliminating fish stocks, and destroying vegetation and wildlife.

3) *Advertising and promotional activities:* Even among individuals who reside in remote areas far from TNC facilities, transnational corporations can have a profound and often detrimental impact on health and well-being through their aggressive advertising and promotion of products such as infant formula, cigarettes, pesticides, pharmaceuticals, and weapons.

Following the three main sections, we assess various local, national, and international efforts to render TNC operations more "socially responsible," hold corporate executives accountable for their actions, and limit corporations' growing political power. We conclude the chapter by addressing the question of responsibility. Given that we, the public—through our political representatives—set parameters within which TNCs are supposed to operate, should we consider ourselves accountable for the unsafe working conditions, contaminated water sources, cigarette addiction, illnesses, and premature deaths brought about by TNC activities? Who must ultimately assume responsibility when the excesses of corporations threaten the poorest members of society?

In the following chapter, Part II of our discussion systematically analyzes how TNCs use political power to expand their influence and limit their legal and financial obligations to states and to society. As the locus of power shifts from governments to "the market," TNCs further consolidate their authority in political arenas.[8] While this fundamental process remains unchanged since the beginning of private corporations, today's large TNCs have succeeded in globalizing their political agenda and their authority.

Most private corporations obtained their legal right to exist from governments. Yet from their inception, firms have resisted, and to a considerable extent eluded, political control. For a brief period between the late nineteenth and early twentieth centuries, it appeared governments would be able to constrain corporate activities and even channel corporations' productive capacity for national ends (see Box 8.1).

Box 8.1: The Rise of U.S. TNCs[9]

Early American businesses were dominated by family farms, craftsmen shops, worker-owned enterprises, cooperative and neighborhood stores, and businesses owned by cities and towns. After the American Revolution, states began to issue charters of incorporation to companies. But because the revolutionaries had feared and distrusted English corporations, which were chartered and controlled through the "divine authority" of English kings, the early Americans decided that their corporations would be different. American corporations would not be controlled by appointed governors, judges, or generals like the kings' corporations. Rather, the U.S. founding citizens chose to keep the control of banks and businesses in the hands of the people, by giving the authority and oversight of corporations to their legislators.

During the first hundred years after the American Revolution, citizens governed corporations and directed the nation's economy by controlling the chartering process through their state legislators. The early charters of incorporation were basically contracts that defined corporations' rights and obligations, limiting, for example, how many years corporations could exist, how much they could borrow, how much land they could purchase, and even how much they could profit. In some states, legislators used this process to set the price rates that railroad, turnpike, and bridge corporations could charge; to exempt farmers, the poor, and worshippers from paying road tolls; to limit charters for mining to 40 years and bank charters from three to ten years. Through this power to issue and also to revoke charters of incorporation, state legislators were able to monitor corporate affairs. But charters of incorporation were not the only mechanisms states used to govern corporations; state constitutions and laws also detailed the rules and operating conditions of corporations. When a corporation violated the conditions of its charter, the state would revoke the charter and dissolve the corporation. By 1860, thousands of manufacturing, mining, railroad, and banking corporations had been chartered in the United States.

The years of the U.S. Civil War marked an important shift in the relationship between corporations and the state. Local and national government helped to enrich corporations during the war years by purchasing from them mass quantities of clothing, tents, weapons, food, and dozens of other items needed for the war effort. Using the profits earned from military procurement contracts, business owners and corporate managers took advantage of the considerable civil unrest and political turmoil that prevailed throughout the war "to get the tariff, banking, railroad, labor and public lands legislation they wanted."[10] During this period, corporate executives began to hire lobbyists to influence Congress and state legislators, and little by little were able to dismantle citizen authority over corporate governance, production, and labor. With their newfound freedoms and privileges, U.S. corporations expanded their ventures and began to realize greater and greater profits. Following the war and the assassination of President Lincoln, the economy was depressed and the country in disarray. Unemployment, corruption, and a weakened government created even more opportunities for corporate influence inside the halls of government.

These were the days of men such as John D. Rockefeller, J.P. Morgan, Andrew Carnegie, James Mellon, Cornelius Vanderbilt, Philip Armour, and Jay Gould. Wealth begat wealth as corporations took advantage of the disarray to buy tariff, banking, railroad, labor and public lands legislation that would further enrich them....Gradually corporations gained sufficient control over key state legislative bodies to virtually rewrite the laws governing their own creation. Legislators in New Jersey and Delaware took the lead in watering down citizens' rights to intervene in corporate affairs. They limited the liability of corporate owners and managers and issued charters in perpetuity. Corporations soon had the right to operate in any fashion not explicitly prohibited by law.[11]

A Supreme Court ruling in 1886, *Santa Clara County v. Southern Pacific Railroad*, marked perhaps the greatest legal victory for the corporations to date. This ruling held that a private corporation is a natural person under the U.S. Constitution and is thereby entitled to the protections of the Bill of Rights, including the right to free speech and other constitutional protections granted to individuals. With newfound freedoms at home, U.S. corporations began to branch out into other countries.[12]

In the United States since the end of the nineteenth century, business executives have had every incentive to expand their operations. When the markets for their goods or services have become saturated at home, the U.S. government has given corporations tax incentives to seek new markets abroad. The government also protects U.S. corporations against foreign business and interests, and it gives corporations preferential tax treatment, especially during times of war and economic stress. Over the past 100 years, corporations have grown and expanded: successful local companies became interstate corporations, interstate corporations became national corporations, and many national corporations became multinational companies with subsidiaries overseas.

More recently, multinationals have become *transnational corporations*, which source, produce, and market their goods in many countries simultaneously, claiming nationality in the countries that offer the most favorable tax structure or trade policies. The largest among today's TNCs describe themselves as *supranational* corporations, larger than nation-states, operating under no single jurisdiction, accountable to no governmental agency.[13] Thus, with both limited government and limited popular oversight, a lack of effective multinational labor opposition, and only fragmented citizen resistance, the supranational corporations have become the dominant institutions of our time, increasingly able to operate anywhere, and often in any way, they choose.

However, the present global situation confirms TNCs' growing ascendancy over states: TNCs can relocate their operations and redefine their jurisdiction; they routinely pit states and regions against each other; and corporations often determine the extent of their own responsibilities toward their workers, the environment, and society at large. Increasingly, their economic and political power undermines governments' efforts to make policy independent of corporate interests. Under such circumstances, governments' ability to protect their own citizens diminishes, and the poorest members of society tend to suffer first and most.

Although TNCs' political influence is less conspicuous than their labor, environmental, and advertising activities, it is central to an understanding of TNCs' role in the health of vulnerable communities and poor populations. Part II (Chapter Nine) shows how corporate leaders employ their considerable financial and human resources to sway national, regional, and global policies on economic development, trade and investment, health, labor, and the environment. It examines the mechanisms through which TNCs harness their political influence to realize maximum profitability—even when achieving these goals may also undermine the health of their workers and of the communities in which they operate.

Though the influence of TNCs on health is not new to this era, the health-compromising effects of corporate labor, environmental, advertising, and political activities have greatly intensified during the 1980s and 1990s. The reason is to be sought in an environment hospitable to the TNC and its goals. During this time, modern communications technology facilitated the rapid movement of money in and out of countries, and more and more countries lessened or abandoned restrictions on movements of capital, goods, and services. Concomitant with these transformations was a dramatic expansion of TNCs.

THE GROWTH AND EXPANSION OF TRANSNATIONAL CORPORATIONS

> Corporations have emerged as the dominant governance institutions on the planet, with the largest among them reaching into virtually every country of the world and exceeding most governments in size and power. Increasingly, it is the corporate interest more than the human interest that defines the policy agendas of states and international bodies, although this reality and its implications have gone largely unnoticed and unaddressed.[14]

Over the last quarter century, TNCs have grown enormously in size, number, and share of global wealth. This growth has brought about an unprecedented consolidation of private power. Whereas approximately 7,000 TNCs were in operation worldwide in 1970, by 1996 this number had grown to over 40,000. Today, the size and wealth of these entities are mind-boggling. A commonly cited measure of their magnitude pithily notes that "of the world's 60 largest economies, only 17 of them are actually countries—the remaining 43 are transnational corporations."[15] Transnational corporations currently control over 70 percent of the products in international trade, 80 percent of the world's land cultivated for export crops, and the vast majority of world technological innovation.[16] Largely due to the U.S. government's long history of protecting its businesses from foreign competition and granting privileges to its corporations through the institutionalization of elaborate tax incentives, three-fifths of all the world's TNCs are still officially based in the United States.[17]

The largest corporations today control vast resources and are more powerful than most countries in terms of their ability to affect lives through expenditure of funds.[18] Each of the 15 largest global corporations has a gross revenue greater than the gross domestic product (GDP) of more than 120 countries.[19] General Motors, currently the fifth largest TNC in the world, generates a total annual revenue greater than the combined GDPs of Pakistan, Nepal, Bangladesh, and Sri Lanka, which together account for over 280 million people.[20] In fact, the top 200 corporations' combined sales exceed the combined economies of all but the largest nine countries in the world. The combined revenue of the top 200 corporations, now over $7.1 trillion, dwarfs the economic activity of the poorest four-fifths of humanity, $3.9 trillion for over 4.5 billion people.[21]

Given this rapid growth in TNC numbers and wealth, the owners and managers of these corporations enjoy enormous and expanding power. They not only benefit financially from the global expansion of neoliberal capitalism, they also are able to redefine the system of international trade and investment to suit their own interests. Through their substantial influence on international trade and development organizations, including the World Trade Organization (WTO), the World Bank, and the International Monetary Fund (IMF), corporate leaders have lobbied for deregulation, privatization, and liberalization so that TNCs can maximize profits and growth, largely unencumbered by the regulatory efforts of national governments.[22] A reporter from *Business Week* described the phenomenon in these terms: "As cross-border trade and investment flows reach new heights, big global companies are effectively making decisions with little regard to national boundaries. Though few companies are totally untethered from their home countries, the trend toward a form of 'stateless' corporation is unmistakable."[23]

In the absence of effective international regulatory bodies, the erosion of state control over TNCs has grave implications for health and safety. Under such circumstances, community and state governments have difficulty implementing effective labor and environmental policies to protect their citizens, and livelihoods may be threatened.[24] This has been especially true for the governments of poor and indebted countries (see Box 8.2).

Box 8.2: TNCs and Trade in Poor, Indebted Countries

How can a national government make an economic plan with any confidence if a board of directors meeting five thousand miles away can, in altering its pattern of purchasing and production, affect in a major way the country's economic life?

—Former U.S. Under-Secretary of State George Ball[25]

During the 1990s, most of the world's poor nations were integrated into the interdependent global economy. While this increasing integration brings its share of promises, such as the transfer of new technologies and new markets, integration also means increased vulnerability and new forms of economic subordination and dependence.

When at the end of the 1970s most poor and highly indebted nations declared they could no longer continue to make payments on their foreign debt, the IMF and World Bank stepped in with a program to guarantee that the debtor countries would earn enough foreign exchange to service their debt to European and American banks. The plan typically involved the imposition of draconian economic austerity measures. To secure the cooperation of indebted countries, the IMF and the World Bank began placing strenuous conditions on their lending: debtor nations would not have access to loans unless they agreed to implement sweeping structural adjustment policies, known as SAPs, profoundly altering their previous economic patterns and social priorities.[26]

The main elements of these economic adjustment programs (outlined in Chapter Two) are the promotion of export-oriented development strategies, liberalization of trade, deregulation of the market, and privatization. By placing such conditions on their loans, international financial institutions (IFIs) pushed poor, indebted governments to "liberalize" their economies in order to encourage investment by foreign firms. Transnational corporations' investments would serve to counterbalance the continued decline of development assistance by increasing host countries' foreign exchange earnings and capital flows. It would also, in theory, benefit poor countries with new technology, wage-earning employment, and transfers of intangibles such as organizational and managerial skills and marketing networks.[27]

Beginning in the early to mid-1980s, the ruling elites of most poor-country governments began to implement the IFI prescription. They opened their economies to create "free" market environments, largely because they were fearful of long-term global reprisal if they did not follow the IMF and World Bank loan conditions. Meanwhile, as TNCs continued to win new concessions and unprecedented privileges through the General Agreement on Tariffs and Trade (GATT), poor-country governments were forced to adopt new trade and investment measures. A GATT agreement on trade-related investment measures (TRIMS), for example, made it more difficult for poor-country governments to control TNC activities or implement measures to guarantee some benefits to the local population and economy. Some government leaders were convinced of the need for such measures and believed in the export-led development strategy. Other political elites signed on to the plan because they saw in it the possibility for personal enrichment.

To implement the IFI-recommended, export-led development strategy, states had to become *less* involved; governments had to remove restrictions placed on TNCs and essentially relinquish their authority to coordinate, regulate, and control the operations of foreign corporations within their borders.[28] Governments lowered tariffs, abolished quotas, and dismantled regulatory mechanisms that had been in place in most countries to protect local industry and agriculture from foreign competition. They also lowered their labor and environmental standards and the amount of taxes foreign companies were required to pay. By adopting these measures, governments were supposed to be creating "more hospitable" investment environments to which TNCs would flock.

Because so many poor countries were adopting the same export-led strategy, competition for foreign investment became stiff, and these measures alone were found insufficient, in many cases, to attract TNCs. Therefore, in their effort to lure foreign companies to their borders, governments began to engage in a downward, standard-lowering bidding cycle, or "race to the bottom," whereby the needs of their citizens, especially the poor, were typically subordinated to the needs of the foreign companies. The "competition" among poor countries was further intensified because, contrary to popular perception, TNCs are still more interested in investing in wealthier, less politically "risky" countries.[29]

Foreign investors are attracted most to countries experiencing rapid economic growth. Therefore, investment initially flowed to south, east, and southeast Asia. Among the poorest nations, such as the majority of African countries, the export-led development strategy has not had the effect promised by its designers. Despite broad efforts made by many African governments to liberalize trade, thereby rendering their local farmers and industries vulnerable to the flood of foreign foods and goods, foreign investment has barely increased on the continent.[30] The promises of increased employment and economic growth have not materialized.

Instead, these processes further marginalized the poorest nations. As economist and educator Marcos Arruda suggests, "If SAPs succeeded at all it was in submitting Southern [poor] governments to macroeconomic decisions designed abroad and integrating them further in the global Market economy as subordinate, unequal partners."[31] Poor countries are reduced to the role of suppliants for foreign investment; and even when TNCs *do* invest in the poorest countries, they are usually conscious of their bargaining advantages over poor-country governments. Large TNCs possess the capital, access to world markets, technology, and other resources that governments in the developing world want or need. Companies have a further distinct bargaining advantage because in many poor countries, foreign investment accounts for a large percentage of the stock of local investment, production, and sales. In addition, TNCs tend to dominate key sectors of the economy that are critical to the host countries' economic development. Because TNCs in poor countries are involved most often in highly concentrated industries—petroleum, mining, chemical, food products—they also tend to have oligopoly power and, hence, the ability to control supply and price.[32] All these factors enable TNCs to take advantage of investment practices—"transfer pricing," restrictive business practices, and excessive profit repatriation—that tend to maximize their profits to the detriment of local industries and populations.[33]

In the name of "enhancing global competitiveness," TNCs will continue taking advantage of the vast inequalities within and among countries and the desperation felt by poor-country governments in need of foreign capital and fearful of being left out of the global economy.[34] As one scholar asserts: "When a strong party insists that a weaker party subject itself to the 'free flow of goods and services, trade and investment,' it does not take an expert to predict that the weak party may grow even weaker whilst the majority of the benefits accrue to the strong."[35]

The implications of this vast expansion of corporate power remain obscure to the public, apparent only as occasional (rather than systemic) problems. A few high-profile cases have brought media attention and increased public awareness of TNC activities at home and abroad. A landmark case, the subject of Chapter Ten in this volume, was the 1984 Union Carbide toxic gas leak that killed at least 3,000 people and injured well over 200,000 others in Bhopal, India.[36] In the 1990s, outrage erupted over the inhumane working conditions endured by young seamstresses of subcontractors in Honduras and New York City, who were hired to make shirts, pants, and skirts for Wal-Mart and the Kathie Lee Gifford fashion line.[37] The Nigerian government's execution of the teacher, author, and activist Ken Saro-Wiwa in 1995 brought worldwide attention to the ruthless activities of Royal Dutch Shell Oil Company in Nigeria.[38] The marketing craze during Disney's release of *Pocahontas* revealed that Disney was paying Haitian slum dwellers less than 30¢ per hour to sew Mickey Mouse and Pocahontas pajamas, while paying its chief executive officer $97,000 per hour.[39] Michael Jordan's retirement heightened public awareness that an Indonesian worker would have to work approximately 60,000 years to earn a sum equal to the athlete's 1998 earnings from Nike.[40] Also drawing public attention currently are the millions of children under the age of fourteen who work for a pittance in manufacturing plants, laboring up to 14 hours a day, with no opportunity for an education that could open possibilities of a better future.[41] These stories are covered in the media and have begun to generate public discussion. A narrow focus on specific cases, however, tends to distract people from the systemic political-economic conditions that permit such abuses, and it encourages us to adopt short-term, case-specific remedies. These stories also represent only the tip of the iceberg.

Ironically, media emphasis on these major cases helps obscure the scores of similar TNC violations of local and international labor laws, health and safety regulations, environmental standards, marketing codes, and their own corporate and industry codes of conduct. Often, TNC contractors and managers excuse their business transgressions by asserting that they uphold higher standards than the nationally owned companies of the countries in which they operate. While such claims are often (lamentably) true, it is also true that large TNCs have vastly greater resources than their host-country counterparts. Should TNCs be exempted from criticism or accountability on the grounds that their standards are slightly more rigorous than those of struggling local companies?

The opportunity costs for workers and the effects on labor markets of TNC hiring and subcontracting are probably not best understood through the arguments of public-relations spokespersons. We can better grasp what is at stake for workers by considering TNC labor practices, particularly the wages and working conditions they offer in poor communities.

TNC LABOR PRACTICES

The real incomes of working people throughout Latin America, Africa, and much of Asia are declining, along with laborers' rights, entitlements, and protections. Meanwhile, competition for adequate employment is escalating, pitting workers against one another in a desperate struggle to get or keep jobs. In this international weakening of labor, TNCs are both a cause and a principal beneficiary.

Many of the difficulties that have plagued labor at the end of the 1990s began two decades earlier, with the institution of *labor market flexibility*. Labor market flexibility has been an essential element of neoliberalism and a key component of the structural adjustment programs (SAPs) promoted by the IMF and the World Bank in poor indebted countries throughout the 1980s and 1990s. During this time, international financial institutions (IFIs) considered some forms of government intervention in labor, such as minimum wage laws and job security protections, to be impediments both to labor mobility and to a competitive investment climate; by "flexibilizing" their labor markets, governments could create more friendly business environments in their countries. The improved business climate was then expected to attract corporate investment, spur competition, create new and better jobs, and ultimately promote growth.

In some parts of the world where governments indeed have dismantled worker protections and cut wages to attract foreign investment, economic growth rates in fact have increased since the 1980s[42]; in other areas, such as Africa, where most governments also have rendered their labor markets more "flexible," growth has not been restored. However, even in countries where GDP has expanded, it has come at an enormous cost to workers and the poor. The legal and economic losses associated with "flexibilizing" often cancel out any gains to come from increased foreign investment— at least as far as workers are concerned: labor market "streamlining" acts to insulate them from the new wealth they help create.

In practice, a flexible labor market means cracking down on unions, dismantling wage and benefit protections, and loosening the rules for hiring and firing—changes that strengthen the hand of managers over workers. This trend also encourages corporations to hire subcontractors and to replace full-time employees with part-time workers. The most flexible labor markets are found in the export processing zones (described in detail later in this chapter) that governments set up to attract TNCs and their foreign currency.

Even though labor market deregulation was promoted by the IFIs as a set of policies that would help alleviate poverty in the long term, most countries implementing the policies have experienced a rise in unemployment, a significant shift to informal sector employment, and deterioration of working conditions. A longtime observer of Latin America explains the paradox: "It seems a particularly twisted form of economic logic to argue that the poor's pay packet must be forced down and their working conditions deteriorate in order to reduce their poverty."[43]

The dismantling of worker protections has come at a terrible time for workers already overwhelmed by a heightened competition for jobs. Part of the problem stems from a growing supply of qualified workers due to long-term trends such as urbanization, greater access to education, and the entrance of women into the workforce. The surplus of labor has also been driven by the effects of other neoliberal policies, such as massive public sector layoffs and the lifting of import restrictions. The public sector layoffs have meant that former civil servants have been forced to enter *en masse* into the private sector workforce. Lower import tariffs likewise caused farmers to leave the land and led to job losses in local industries, as local firms could not compete with the cheap, imported foodstuffs and goods flooding the markets.

Heightened competition for jobs has been further compounded by other requirements of structural adjustment, such as currency devaluation, cuts in basic social services (including health and education), and cuts in subsidies for grains and basic food items. These measures have seriously eroded the real purchasing power of already low salaries. In such a setting, those lucky enough to have a job find they must hold on to it at any cost, especially as workers become responsible for the welfare of more and more unemployed family members, and the increasing cost of putting food on the table leaves less and less money available for school and health-care expenses.

Transnational corporations have taken part in the design of this labor market transformation, and in its wake are taking advantage of the worsening plight of workers. The deregulation of labor markets is now firmly in place in countries throughout the world. In light of this, and in light of the growing influence TNCs exert over national governments, the future does not look promising for workers. An editor for the NACLA *Report on the Americas* explains: "Since labor rights, entitlements, and protections are typically fought for and won through state legislation, the assault on state sovereignty by the transnational institutions of capital has in reality been an assault on the working class and the poor."[44] The following sections explore some of the mechanisms of this assault.

Manufacturers Without Factories

Retailers such as Wal-Mart, Sears Roebuck, JCPenney, Nike, Reebok, Liz Claiborne, and The Limited design and market their brand-name products, but often no longer make them. These "manufacturers without factories" have separated the physical production of goods from the design and marketing stages of the production process.[45] Such companies avoid "troublesome legislation" by paying middlemen to do the manufacturing for them. When corporate retailers (buyers who put their labels on products) decide to contract out cutting, sewing, and pressing, they seek bids from local manufacturers—bids that are competitive with the lowest prices on the international labor market. In poor countries, the bids often presuppose the use of child labor, significantly lower health and safety standards, and sweatshop working conditions, for all of which the contracted agent, *but not the company*, is usually held accountable.

The subcontracting arrangement ensures the lowest possible costs for the production of a company's product. It also enables the parent company to avoid responsibility for improving working conditions and paying benefits to those who supply the company with its goods and services.[46] It is the means by which large companies obtain extremely cheap labor without compromising their own corporate image and name. Even though parent TNCs often pressure their subcontracting companies to cut costs—where ever and how ever possible—the sub-contracting system enables parent firms to turn a blind eye to both the actual production process and the working conditions of the workers making their products. As John Fread, an Adidas spokesperson, describes it: "We do not own any factories. We license our ball-making through Molten (a Japanese sporting goods company). They in turn do the actual factory-sourcing and production. It's all subcontracted out."[47] Despite the often deplorable working conditions in their facilities and the low wages they offer, most subcontractors have little difficulty finding workers because of the very competitive labor market described previously.

Export Processing or Free Trade Zones[48]

Another way TNCs avoid national regulatory measures is by setting up their operations, or those of their subcontractors, in *export processing zones* (EPZs). In these zones, millions of people in Mexico, El Salvador, Haiti, Honduras, Mauritius, Sri Lanka, Indonesia, Vietnam, and other countries work for meager wages in unhealthy and dangerous conditions, producing goods for export.[49] In fact, export activities in many poor countries today are based largely on the labor-intensive assembly of manufactured goods in such EPZs or free trade zones.

Countries create these zones to attract export-oriented manufacturing investment by setting aside a physical area in the country where investors are given a range of incentives. The zones are usually located on the outskirts of large cities, and often on the banks of large rivers. Most EPZs offer foreign companies a combination of tax exemptions, near complete profit repatriation, waivers of industry regulations, special exchange systems, strict assurances against expropriation, and lax social, environmental, and labor regulations. Often, labor unions are forbidden to organize in EPZs.

The first EPZs, created in the early 1970s, were promoted as a means of attracting foreign investment to "underdeveloped" areas.[50] By the mid-1990s, over 200 EPZs employed over 2 million workers in more than 50 countries. Around 80 percent of the workforce in EPZs are women, the majority of whom are single and between the ages of 18 and 25.[51]

Conventional wisdom tells us that governments create EPZs to attract TNCs, which in turn supply needed foreign currency and jobs to the local economy. However, these jobs often do not provide laborers with enough salary to adequately feed themselves and their families. In Haiti, for example, a market basket survey among EPZs showed that wages were not sufficient to meet workers' immediate needs for food, clothing, minimal shelter, and cooking fuel. According to the study's authors, the salaries allowed only enough money for workers to purchase carbohydrates, which can stave off hunger but prevent neither protein malnutrition nor diseases due to vitamin deficiency. Without resources to purchase protein, fruits, and vegetables, workers could not maintain their health.[52] The same authors reported similar findings in Mexico and Indonesia.[53]

According to sources as varied as the National Labor Committee, the popular press, the business press, the U.S. Agency for International Development, and academic journals, workers employed in these zones suffer many types of abuse. Working hours in EPZs are 25 percent longer than elsewhere, and in some cases reach up to 90 hours per week. Wages paid women are from 20 to 50 percent lower than those paid to men.[54] Mandatory production quotas set above achievable limits are common, forcing employees to work overtime without extra compensation. In many plants, ventilation is poor, and drinking water is not available. Workers in many plants report being denied legally permitted leave and being fired for taking it. According to one observer in Haiti, "Many [workers] face a real risk of starvation if they lose their jobs, and are therefore compelled to do whatever their boss asks of them, which for many women involves sexual favors."[55] In El Salvador and Guatemala, women workers report being beaten, sexually harassed, and cursed at by supervisors.[56] Workers in the zones complain of sheer exhaustion. As one fifteen-year-old seamstress in a Guatemala City EPZ explains:

> The starting bell for work rings at 6:15 and I can feel pretty tired the first hour, but I have to work fast anyway—we have quotas. When the bell finally rings at 6:30 p.m. [over 12 hours later], you are ready to go home—but it is not always possible. If there is more work, the owners tell you they need people to stay for the night shift. If not enough people say yes, the supervisor sits in front of the doors and no one can leave. They let you rest a few minutes, and work starts again at 7:00 p.m. When the bell rings at 3 a.m., they pass out cardboard from old boxes. I look for my friends, and we put our cardboards next to each other and sleep under the tables. Then you go back to work whether you are tired or not. This happens two or three times a week. Do you think I would do this if we didn't need the money? I liked school. I would like to be a bilingual secretary, sit in front of a computer, answer telephones and say, "Just a moment, please, I'll see if he is in."[57]

According to the National Labor Committee, many girls and women who work in foreign-owned manufacturing plants in Honduras are forced to take birth control injections or pills so they won't get pregnant and cost the company money.[58] According to Human Rights Watch, many female workers in the Mexican EPZ factories known as *maquiladoras* undergo mandatory pregnancy tests and are summarily fired if they test positive.[59] And in Saipan, which is part of the U.S. commonwealth of Northern Mariana Islands, pregnant apparel workers in U.S.-based TNCs have reported being forced to have abortions so they would "remain productive."[60]

Witnessing the labor and environmental conditions in EPZs, an outraged writer reported: "Part of the 'incentive' package that a government offers to companies when it creates Free Trade Zones is the right to despoil the environment, the right to flout basic standards of social welfare, and the right to poison workers."[61] Furthermore, he contends, EPZs "illustrate the social, ecological, and human consequences of almost total deregulation, which we now seek to achieve globally as a means of maximizing world trade."[62]

Despite the difficulties faced by TNC employees who toil in EPZ factories, however, workers have no recourse to improve their situation. Labor unions in most zones are either tightly controlled or entirely forbidden. Naturally, under such conditions, labor unrest has occurred repeatedly with violent consequences.

Union Busting

In TNC-owned or controlled factories across the developing world, worker activism has been crushed: workers have been harassed, detained, attacked by police and hired thugs, and even assassinated by death squads. In Sri Lanka, when 7,000 workers from Colombo's free trade zone marched peacefully to deliver a grievance to their prime minister, they were met by a police blockade, fired upon, and attacked with truncheons. Several workers suffered gunshot wounds and many more were beaten.[63]

An extreme example of brutal suppression waged against workers who attempt to organize occurred in Mexico in 1987. In the midst of a two-month labor strike, Ford Motor Company unilaterally nullified its union contract, fired 3,400 of its workers, and cut wages by 45 percent. When in response workers at a Ford Motor Company plant rallied around dissident labor leaders and tried to organize a union independent of the state-sponsored Confederation of Mexican Trade Unions (CMT), "gunmen hired by the official government-dominated union shot workers at random in the factory."[64] In 1997, the International Confederation of Free Trade Unions (ICFTU) concluded its annual report with a telling statement on the potential for workers to organize in EPZs: "Anti-union repression is an integral part of the export processing zone concept. Potential investors see the absence of trade unions as a major advantage of the zones, and their preference for women workers is a deliberate part of their anti-union policy."[65]

In July 1998, Mexican workers at an automotive parts production facility, Echlin, Inc., were intimidated and threatened with dismissal, beating, and rape if they voted to join a branch of an independent union. Fifty workers accused of being union activists were summarily fired and forced to accept "voluntary departure." Although an arbitration board ordered the company to reinstate the workers, the latter were fired again after they returned to work.[66]

Another visible and ongoing labor dispute in Mexico is at the Han Young *maquiladora* plant in Tijuana; the plant makes parts for the Korean automotive TNC, Hyundai. Since the beginning of 1998, workers at the plant have been organizing a new union, independent from the CMT. Despite the new union's victory in two elections, the Hyundai company refuses to recognize it. The second election was necessary after the Tijuana arbitration board refused to register the union, and workers from the plant went on a hunger strike. The conflict between the workers and the TNC captivated the press, but despite the public attention, the corporation continued to harass, fire, and attempt to bribe workers not to vote for the new union.

Though the data are not presented in terms of transnational versus national corporations, the 1998 Annual Survey of Violations of Trade Union Rights compiled by the ICFTU illustrates the difficulty faced by would-be union organizers throughout the world. The report counts 4,210 cases of trade-union worker harassment and 2,330 arrests or detentions of workers involved in union-related activities in 1998 alone. In the same year, the ICFTU reported 299 documented murders of trade unionists; in virtually all cases, the perpetrators were not punished.[67]

Winners or Losers?

The direct labor cost to assemble a $90 pair of Nike sneakers [in Indonesia] is approximately $1.20, which means that the workers' wages amount to just 1.3 percent of the retail price. If Nike was to raise Indonesian workers' wages by 50 percent, the labor costs to assemble the same $90 pair of sneakers would be just $1.80, still only two percent of the sneakers' retail price.[68]

It is not so simple to calculate who most benefits—the companies or the nation-states—when TNCs set up operations in poor or less industrialized countries. Often, when local, state, or national governments go out of their way to offer appealing incentives to TNCs,[69] they operate under the premise that their community or state will necessarily gain in the exchange either financially or in terms of skills, technology transfers, and linkages to domestic industry. In fact, government elites often rationalize the exploitative behavior of their foreign investors and frequently turn a blind eye to labor abuses, because they believe a net gain will accrue to the country or to themselves.[70] However, the elites' assumption does not always hold true. Especially in EPZs, where foreign companies rely on imported materials and make few linkages with domestic sectors, the actual benefits to a host country may be minimal. In a World Bank discussion paper, the authors suggest that "poorer countries will always be at a disadvantage if the relative attractiveness of fiscal incentive packages in different countries determines investment locations."[71] And as a report written by the secretariat of the WTO argues:

> The more intense the competition among potential hosts, the greater is the proportion of potential gains which is transferred to the TNCs....If a country offers $185 million in incentives to obtain an FDI [the investment of a foreign company or *foreign direct investment*] project that brings $135 million in total benefits, the country as a whole is $50 million worse off with the FDI....Such incentives are nothing more than a transfer of income from these countries to the investing firms.[72]

With the new rules of international trade under the tutelage of the WTO, EPZs no longer exist solely within delineated boundaries; they have, in fact, begun to "encompass the entire globe."[73] Where historical and geographical circumstances are favorable, and where governments are able to regulate TNC entry and operations, these zones can help fuel developing economies. The "Asian Tiger" economies before the 1997 economic crash were able to advance economically by taking advantage of protectionist policies and pursuing an export-oriented strategy at a time when most other nations were still looking inward. Their success may not be repeatable, however, as today most developing nations are forced into a global competition for foreign investment. The greater the competition to attract foreign firms, the more elaborate and "generous" the incentive structures governments offer to TNCs. In Cameroon, for example, foreign investors receive a 100 percent tax exemption for ten years, followed by a 15 percent tax ceiling thereafter, and free repatriation of profits. In Cameroon's industrial free zone TNCs also receive flexibility in hiring and firing workers, and an exemption from the nation's standard wage classification scheme.[74] In other words, they are officially permitted to pay their workers less than the minimum wage.

For workers who come from rural areas and for various reasons are unable to return to their land, and for those who have no other means of earning a living, work in TNC facilities represents survival, and not only for themselves.[75] On their meager salaries, workers in less industrialized and poor countries often support several, and sometimes many, unemployed members of their extended families. When a person's life and the lives of family members depend upon continued employment in a factory, field, or mine, such a worker will tend to silence complaints and accept all manner of hardships just to keep the job.[76]

What if a government chooses to protect its workforce from exploitative working conditions? Transnational corporations may opt to pick up and move elsewhere, to wherever conditions are more "favorable." Ultimately, protected workers lose their jobs. And if a country does not compete for TNCs' foreign investment using the same low standards as its neighbors, it risks "falling out" of the global economy. But with such standards, workers are left unprotected from labor abuse and may have little or no job security. The current rules of the global economy that allow TNCs to move rapidly from one country to another, coupled with surpluses of people in desperate need of employment, leave workers in a no-win situation.

TNCs AND THE ENVIRONMENT

Every morning in the southern Peruvian town of Ilo, Pedro and his youngest son Jaime wake up coughing and wheezing. Often they do not sleep through the night because they are awakened by their labored breathing. Pedro never experienced health problems before coming to work in the copper smelters of Ilo, six years ago. He worries now because he has seen several fellow workers die from lung cancer and other respiratory complications.

But what troubles Pedro most is his ailing child. When his wife took eight-year-old Jaime to the local medical clinic, the doctor gave the boy cough medicine and vitamins. But the remedies did little, and Jaime's cough is often so bad he is forced to stay home from school. Many of Jaime's young friends complain of similar symptoms.

Pedro suspects that if he could afford to quit his job and move to where the air is clean, he and his son would be spared their chronic breathing difficulties. Yet he knows he is among the few in Peru who are fully employed, and he is in no position to give up this privilege.

In Ilo the dark, acrid smoke from the copper smelters is so ubiquitous motorists must use their headlights during the day to see the road. Among the residents of the town severe respiratory ailments are common, and few escape the chronic coughing and wheezing that arise from continuous exposure to the toxic dust.[77]

Pedro and his son Jaime are but two among hundreds of town dwellers whose health suffers from the careless industrial practices of the TNC operating in their backyard. Every day in the town of Ilo, 2,000 tons of sulfur dioxide are spewed into the air from the smelters of American-owned Southern Peru Copper, the largest mining company in Peru. This level of emissions is well over ten times the legal limit for similar plants operating in the United States.[78] Farmers in valleys outside the town center complain that the air pollution has affected their alfalfa, maize, rice, sugar, and olive crops. The smoke causes native vegetation to wilt and often die. According to company data, the air quality around the smelter is routinely 20 times worse than the maximum levels recommended by the U.S. Environmental Protection Agency (EPA). Peruvian environmental experts report that the actual emissions could be as much as 100 times greater than those permitted in the United States.[79] The double standard typifies the ability and willingness of a TNC to take advantage of differences in social and environmental standards existing between wealthy and poor countries.[80]

Whether through normal production processes or through accidents such as chemical spills, fires, and explosions, many TNC activities have a detrimental impact on the environment and people's health. While domestically based corporations also cause environmental damage and health problems, agricultural and industrial TNCs are the major users of hazardous materials and generate a significant source of pollution worldwide.[81] TNCs and their subcontractors use increasingly large quantities of dangerous raw materials in advanced and complex production systems that are beyond the technical reach of most national corporations. Enormous quantities of explosive, toxic, and radioactive materials are stored, transported, utilized, and disposed of by TNCs.[82] Transnational corporations dominate oil extraction and refining—as well as the extraction, refining, and marketing of gas and coal. They have virtually exclusive control of the production and use of ozone-destroying chlorofluorocarbons (CFCs) and related compounds. Large global corporations manufacture most of the world's chlorine, which is at the base of many of the most toxic chemicals known, such as PCBs, DDT, and dioxins. Transnational corporations also account for about 90 percent of worldwide sales of hazardous pesticides.[83] And despite international laws banning such practices, TNCs continue to transport and dump tons of hazardous waste in poor countries.[84]

Occupational health and environmental laws are usually more lax in developing countries than in wealthier nations, where strong political support for protective regulations is more common. Even when poor countries have environmental laws, monitoring and enforcement are expensive and often inadequate.[85] Conducting business transnationally allows corporations to take advantage of this situation and, in foreign subsidiaries, to carry out activities that would be illegal in the parent companies' home countries. Compared with national firms, whose historic ties to local areas may lead to good neighborly commitments, TNCs have little social accountability to the communities in which their subsidiaries operate. Thus, where legal accountability is lacking, community pressure weak, and local consumer advocacy undeveloped, TNCs have little incentive to regulate their environmental practices.

Transnational corporations tend to locate near low-income areas where people are not well-organized politically. When they locate in populated areas such as poor towns in Bangladesh or India, their arrival can exacerbate already overcrowded, substandard living conditions. In less populated areas, TNCs tend to invite the spread and growth of urban squatter settlements, as in many parts of southeast Asia and Central and South America. In communities along the U.S.-Mexico border, where hundreds of TNCs are in operation, higher than average rates of hepatitis A, dysentery, and shigellosis have been observed.[86] Transnational corporations in the agricultural, timber, and extracting businesses naturally locate where arable land or other natural resources are most abundant. Through deforestation, contamination, or erosion, their activities often devastate rural lands and disrupt local subsistence patterns.[87] Perhaps no case better illustrates this pattern than the environmental degradation provoked by more than 40 years of oil extraction in the Niger River Delta by TNCs such as Royal Dutch Shell, as described in Box 8.3.

Box 8.3: Black Gold, Black Death:
Royal Dutch Shell in Nigeria

In 1958, Royal Dutch Shell began oil production in one of the most densely populated regions of Nigeria, an area in the Niger River Delta named "Ogoni" after the dominant ethnic group living there. Nigeria is now one of the world's largest oil exporters and a major supplier to the United States; nearly all of its oil reserves are located along the coastal river delta.[88] Nigeria's annual oil revenue is $8 billion; the contribution of the Shell corporation alone amounts to 45 percent of the Nigerian government's foreign earnings.[89] Though oil production has enabled Nigeria's GNP to grow substantially, this growth has come at a deadly cost to the 6 million people living in the Niger River Delta. Not only have the inhabitants' lands suffered enormous environmental destruction, but residents of the Ogoni region who protested for fair treatment were subjected to systematic violence at the hands of a military dictatorship.

The delta and coastal wetlands of Nigeria include both rainforest and mangrove habitats, and have been described as one of the world's most fragile ecosystems. Within Ogoni alone, an area of just over 400 square miles, there are eight oil fields, more than 100 oil wells, and four flow stations.[90] Industrial operations practiced by transnational oil companies in the delta would be illegal under the environmental laws of most industrialized countries: constant gas flaring, open and unlined toxic waste pits, aged and corroding pipelines carrying oil above ground at high pressure, chronic oil spills....According to independent records, 27 incidents between 1982 and 1992 resulted in a total of 1,626,000 gallons of oil being spilled from Shell's Nigerian operations.[91] Gas flares have also wreaked havoc. As of 1996, "flaring in the delta oilfields of 2,000 million standard cubic feet of gas daily [was] equal to one-quarter of U.K. consumption."[92] Soot and air pollution from gas flares have wiped out much of the wildlife in the area and caused respiratory problems among the local population.[93]

Public health has suffered and villages have become impoverished as a result of the massive pollution of farmlands, fishing areas, and water supplies. In contrast to operations in the United States or Europe, not a single independent environmental impact assessment has been made available to the public.[94]

In 1990, to protest the continued environmental damage in Ogoni and to demand just compensation, several activist groups coalesced to form the Movement for the Survival of the Ogoni People (MOSOP), under the leadership of author Ken Saro-Wiwa. Though the organization explicitly adopted a Gandhian approach of nonviolent civil disobedience, MOSOP became the target of frequent violent attacks by the government.[95] To date, over 2,000 people have been killed and 27 villages destroyed in the struggle.[96] A special *rapporteur* to the U.N. Commission on Human Rights describes many abuses by the Nigerian government, including illegal detentions and extrajudicial executions.[97] The same document expresses concern that Shell's subsidiary in Nigeria is maintaining an armed force. Shell has admitted importing arms for the army but denies any connection with the atrocities.[98] Whether or not Shell is directly involved, the Nigerian government has clearly targeted activists protesting environmental damages due to oil exploration and production. In 1995, in an act universally condemned for its arbitrary brutality, Ken Saro-Wiwa and nine other tribal leaders were arrested by the government on trumped-up murder charges and hanged.

At the Worksite: In Plants and Factories

In almost every corner of the globe, workers employed by TNCs—as well as by national firms—are at risk for job-related health problems. Occupational risks to these employees include toxic exposures to lead, mercury, and other metals; increased chance of developing occupational respiratory diseases such as asthma and byssinosis; exposure to excessive noise levels; and physical injuries resulting from industrial accidents.[99] Specific cases of work-related injuries and diseases illustrate the problems that can occur in TNC factory operations.

Twenty years ago, Pennwalt Incorporated, a U.S. transnational chemical firm in Nicaragua, was found to be releasing mercury effluent into Lake Managua. When workers in the Pennwalt plants were examined, 37 percent of them were identified as suffering from symptoms of mercury poisoning such as tremors, memory deficits, and numbness. Levels of airborne mercury in the plants were measured at six times the legal limit set by the U.S. Occupational Safety and Health Administration (OSHA).[100]

Bayer, the Swiss transnational known for its aspirin, is a major manufacturer of industrial chromates. Since 1936, lung cancer from occupational chromate exposure has been well documented in the public health literature. Nonetheless, until recently, Bayer continued to ignore the dangerous, substandard working conditions in its overseas chromate manufacturing facilities. In both Mexican and South African Bayer plants during the 1980s, clinicians found that nearly 50 percent of the workers had perforated nasal septa, a classic sign of exposure to high levels of chromate. Bayer finally closed its South African plant in 1990, in the face of public outcry over the discovery of increasing cases of lung cancer among its employees. To date, Bayer has refused to offer compensation to any of these cancer victims.[101]

With heightened public awareness of the harmful effects of asbestos in their home countries, Western transnationals are moving the manufacture of asbestos products overseas, causing heated debates between public health experts and industry groups.[102] In some poor countries, asbestos is now a major cause of disability, ill health, and death among miners and construction and asbestos workers.[103] Similarly, the processes of lead smelting and refining and the recycling and production of lead-containing products such as batteries, paints, dyes, and gasoline, are now being shifted by TNCs from wealthy to poor nations. The latter are often unprepared to handle the occupational and environmental hazards created by lead.[104] In Indonesia, workers producing Union Carbide batteries suffer from severe kidney disease.[105] And in TNC textile plants around the world, workers continue to use banned benzidine dyes, despite research clearly linking these chemicals to bladder cancer.[106]

In Bhopal, India, workers at the Bharat Zinc waste processing plant toil under deplorable working conditions. In this plant, used car batteries from Europe and zinc ash from the U.S. transnational Ruby Metals are processed to extract zinc. Despite the dangers of inhaling the toxic metal dust being generated, workers are not provided with masks or gloves. After processing, the residual material, containing toxic levels of zinc, lead, aluminum, and copper, is dumped in an open area behind the factory. The lead waste is of particular concern because it can cause metabolic, neurologic, and neuropsychiatric disorders after acute and chronic exposure. Environmental lead exposure is strongly correlated with poor mental development in children, which is the reason for strict regulations on the use of lead paint in the United States. According to Greenpeace calculations, 450 tons of lead are dumped each year by the Bharat Zinc plant into the open, where it readily contaminates the air, water, and soil of the local community.[107] These are but a few examples of occupational hazards faced by TNC workers.[108]

Agricultural Production

With export-led growth now being promoted in most developing nations and monetary devaluations changing the terms of trade, large-scale agricultural production for export expanded considerably in the 1980s and 1990s. Throughout Latin America, Africa, and south Asia, small farmers continue to lose their land to large-scale, mostly transnational agribusinesses and commercial fisheries. The quick returns most TNCs seek on their investments often lead to environmentally unsound practices. In India, Bangladesh, Thailand, Malaysia, Ecuador, and Mexico, for example, commercial projects produce tiger prawns and other "exotics" such as eels for export to rich countries. These commercial aquaculture schemes have been ecologically disastrous to coastal zones, damaging fragile mangrove and wetland systems and polluting sea water. They also tend to deplete groundwater and poison the farmlands of surrounding villages, ruining previously rich agricultural land for generations to come.[109] Because farmers are rarely compensated sufficiently for their losses and have no other sources of support, one net result of agro-industrial growth in developing countries has been greatly increased landlessness and rural impoverishment. The disruption of traditional subsistence agriculture in many parts of the world has been accompanied by massive migrations of displaced farmers into urban squatter settlements and slums.[110]

Major changes in farming methods occur when native crop plants are replaced with imported species not well adapted to regional soils and climates. Moreover, produce intended for export markets must be in near-perfect shape to satisfy Western consumers. In order to carry out large-scale production of export-quality fruits and vegetables, agricultural TNCs tend to use enormous quantities of pesticides and herbicides. Most of these compounds are themselves produced by transnational agrochemical corporations operating aggressive marketing campaigns in developing countries. Many of the most commonly used pesticides in poor countries are banned from the wealthy countries that export them because of demonstrated toxicities.[111] In fact, 25 percent of all pesticides exported from the United States in the late 1980s were chemicals that were unregistered, banned, canceled, or withdrawn in the United States.[112] The wide use of these toxins, especially in poor countries, leads to significant occupational and environmental health risks for farm workers and their families.[113]

Particular problems occur in developing nations lacking regulations and guidelines for pesticide use and disposal, and technical resources for monitoring.[114] Surveys suggest that TNC agribusiness laborers often receive little training in the risks of exposure and the appropriate techniques for safe handling of these toxins.[115] Pesticides are often handled without protective gear or may even be applied by hand. In poorer areas where literacy is low and little information about pesticides' dangers is available, farmers have been known to take small quantities of the toxic substances home from the farm areas where they work to spray on their beds and even in their children's hair to kill bed bugs and other annoying pests.[116] In the Philippines, women agricultural laborers suffer sustained exposure to toxic pesticides. They work eight to ten hours in the rice fields, "planting, uprooting the seedlings, transplanting, weeding, and picking up golden snails. They inhale pesticide residues, transport pesticide-laden seedlings on their heads, and transplant with their hands pesticide-laden seedlings into the pesticide-laden mud in which they soak all day up to their buttocks."[117]

The pesticides chlordane and heptachlor were banned from use in the United States long before manufacturers exported more than 5 million pounds to 25 countries from 1987 to 1989.[118] Dichlorodiphenyl trichloroethane (DDT), dibromochloropropane (DBCP), and the methylmercuric fungicides were also widely sold by TNCs in poor countries long after being banned in the United States. Male agricultural workers using DBCP have shown significantly increased rates of sterility or reduced fertility.[119] Several pesticides have also been associated with elevated risk for spontaneous abortions and fertility problems in women.[120] Known carcinogenic pesticides such as aldrin, hexachlorobenzene, lindane, and benzenehexachloride (BHC) are still widely manufactured by TNCs and sold in the developing world.[121]

Growing public awareness about the health risks of persistent exposure to certain pesticides has led researchers and farmers to develop alternative methods for crop protection. The use of integrated pest management and biological control programs is expanding rapidly in parts of Western Europe, the United States, and elsewhere. In a study conducted in Israel, reduced pesticide use and alternative pest control programs have resulted in improved yields of cotton per unit area of cultivated land, indicating that alternative methods *can* be economically sustainable.[122] As demand for organic produce increases and chemical pesticide use is reduced in wealthier countries, transnational chemical manufacturers are likely to continue shifting their production facilities to poor areas, and expanding their markets to consumers in poor countries.[123]

A controversial subject currently receiving considerable public attention is agricultural biotechnology.[124] Since the late 1970s, plant biologists have been working to develop new crop varieties through the technology known as genetic modification. Genetic modification goes beyond traditional techniques of hybridization and selective breeding, by employing direct genetic manipulation to custom-tailor crops through the insertion of desirable genes from one organism into the genetic material of another organism. In less than a decade, this technology has exploded. The total area of land planted with genetically modified crops went from zero acres in 1990 to an estimated 100 million acres by the end of 1999—an area larger than three times the size of England. The majority of land cultivated with genetically modified crops is in the United States,[125] and large TNCs, such as Monsanto, DuPont, and Novartis, are conducting the preponderance of new research and development in the field. With so much invested in the new technologies, the agricultural TNCs are also aggressively campaigning to frame the parameters of a rapidly intensifying international debate concerning the safety of genetically modified crops and foods.[126]

The potential positive and negative effects of genetic modification farming in poor countries are still unclear. The development of new crop plants capable of higher yields and more resistant to drought and other environmental conditions could help boost the worldwide food supply considerably. Similarly, crops modified to improve the nutritional value of foods could help prevent certain diseases and alleviate much malnutrition in the world. These are not, however, the sort of crop modifications most companies are developing. Rather, TNCs are genetically modifying crops to further enhance commercial interests and sell more seeds; they create seeds with sterile progeny, crops with resistance to insect pests or commercial herbicides, potatoes with better starch content for improved french fries, and other produce with delayed ripening to prolong transportability. Occasionally, though not necessarily intentionally, companies' commercial interests overlap with efforts to resolve the wider, aforementioned health and social problems.

Despite the fact that genetically modified products are being grown and sold in countries around the world (including the United States, Argentina, Australia, Canada, China, and Mexico) the potential risks associated with genetic modification technology are not well understood and have been only minimally evaluated.[127] The European Union is adopting rigorous regulations for the production, release, and marketing of genetically modified crops, but a striking lack of consumer attention and public oversight is more common in the rest of the world. There are two basic categories of concern: the risks posed to individuals who consume genetically modified foods, and the potential impact of releasing such plants into the environment. Vulnerable consumers of genetically modified foods could risk severe health consequences if food allergens are introduced into crop plants or if genes with antibiotic resistance transfer to pathogenic microorganisms. With respect to environmental consequences, it is almost impossible to predict potential outcomes without further testing under controlled conditions. However, it is clear that the widespread use of genetically modified insect- and herbicide-resistant crop varieties could have profound long-term effects on both local and global biodiversity. Loss of biodiversity is of particular concern to poor communities in Asia, Africa, and Latin America, where most of the global centers of crop origin and diversification are located. A further loss of plant biodiversity, critical for sustainable agriculture, could endanger already precarious food supplies. Beyond these concerns, farmers in poor countries are likely to incur additional social and economic costs. One new genetic modification technology, for example, causes seed sterility after a single generation. When farmers plant this "terminator" seed, the plant grows, but its seeds cannot be used in the next planting cycle. By forcing farmers to purchase seeds annually, this process severely disadvantages those farmers who traditionally stored seeds for future use.[128]

Now that TNCs have obtained greater ease of entry into developing countries and expanded international property rights protections as a result of GATT/WTO policies, agricultural biotechnology TNCs are bringing genetic modification experiments to poor countries. Until these countries develop relevant precautions and safety regulations, this practice could prove hazardous: "There is a well-justified concern that the new biotechnologies will develop food products which would displace the traditional export [crops] of the [poor countries of the] South."[129] As farmers everywhere become increasingly dependent on the products of biotechnology firms, the TNCs are beginning to assert far-reaching monopoly rights over seed stocks, while showing little inclination to shoulder the economic or social responsibility that ought to be associated with such large-scale environmental experiments.[130] The TNCs are globalizing the corporatization of agriculture and, in the process, changing forever humanity's relationship to agriculture and food.

Environmental Exposures

Even more troubling than occupational hazards are the risks associated with environmental pollutants—because they can affect many more people at once.[131] Once they are released into the environment, toxic materials from industrial emissions or agricultural runoff can infiltrate local water sources and contaminate air and soil.[132] When this occurs, not only workers but entire communities are put at risk as they breathe the air, drink the water, and eat produce grown in the soil of a polluted environment. Unlike toxins confined within the workplace, toxins in the environment may affect any and all vulnerable members of a community, such as children and pregnant women, and may lead to increased birth defects and developmental problems in growing children.[133]

The most insidious environmental pollutants are toxins that remain stable in the environment or are taken up into the food chain. Such pollutants continue to exert their poisonous effects for years. In one study, children living near a former copper smelter in Montana were found to have elevated levels of arsenic—a toxin associated with a variety of cancers—*12 years after operations had ceased.*[134] Mercury is another toxin that persists in the environment, putting communities at risk for neurologic damage many years after industrial and mining operations have closed down. One recent study revealed elevated blood levels of mercury in a Native American population living near a cinnabar mine in California; the mine has been closed since 1957.[135]

On the U.S.-Mexican border, TNCs (mainly U.S.-owned) take advantage of the world's largest export processing zone. The *maquiladoras* in this region import most of their raw material from the United States and are supposed to repatriate the waste for disposal. But, according to the EPA, only a tiny percentage is actually returned north. An Arizona-based environmental group, the Border Ecology Project, found that the *maquiladoras* were unable to account for 95 percent of the waste they generated between 1969 and 1989. Not surprisingly, the U.S. National Toxics Campaign detected high levels of pollutants outside the plants and in the communities where the *maquiladoras* operate. In drainage water, one such pollutant, the industrial solvent xylene, was measured at concentrations of 6,000 times the U.S. drinking water standard. Moreover, tests conducted by an EPA-certified laboratory "reveal[ed] levels of xylene up to 50,000 times what is allowed in the United States, and of methylene chloride up to 215,000 times the U.S. standard."[136] The same study found that in 17 out of 23 sites studied, *maquiladoras* contained high concentrations of toxic discharges such as lead, chromium, mercury, nickel, and other metals. Severe health problems caused by exposure to these pollutants and observed in populations living near the plants include anencephaly (babies born without a brain), other severe physical deformities, and mental defects. The health effects of TNC activities in the border zone are described in further detail in Chapter Eleven.

Over a span of almost 30 years, national and transnational oil companies— U.S.-based Texaco chief among them—have extracted over 2 billion barrels of crude oil from the Ecuadorian Amazon. This region is known as one of the most biodiverse zones on earth. It is home to over 500,000 indigenous people and settlers. In the course of oil extraction, the oil companies have released billions of gallons of untreated toxic wastes and oil directly into the environment. After visiting the region, Robert Kennedy, Jr. reported:

> We met with the center's chief clinician and with the representatives of fourteen communities accounting for about 40,000 people from the Aguarico River basin. Each of them told the same story. Sick and deformed children, adults and children affected with skin rashes, headaches, dysentery and respiratory ailments, cattle dead with their stomachs rotted out, crops destroyed, animals gone from the forest and fish from the rivers and streams.[137]

Despite epidemiological reports linking the widespread oil contamination in the region to a substantial increase in the occurrence of miscarriages, birth defects, child diseases, and other health problems, the Ecuadorian government continues, under the advisement of the World Bank and IMF, to offer attractive incentives to private petroleum-extracting TNCs. The business concessions undermine efforts to monitor and regulate oil-extracting activities in the region, exacerbating the socioeconomic and health problems faced by the affected communities. Furthermore, as in the Ogoni case detailed earlier, most of the benefits derived from oil development in Ecuador have gone to a small segment of the population. Very little profit has been reinvested to help improve life quality among the poor communities in the Amazon region where the oil is extracted.[138]

Mining

Perhaps no industry is more destructive to the environment and more damaging to the long-term health of local populations than mineral extraction, and TNCs conduct the vast majority of mineral extraction in the world. Recent technological advances enable companies to mine deeper into the earth at a faster pace for less money. Though mining is not usually counted among the leading threats to people or the environment, its cumulative impact on ecosystems and the livelihood of farmers may be more destructive than the international timber trade or agribusiness.[139]

Through erosion, siltation, deforestation, and desertification, mining destroys rivers, mountains, forests, and agricultural lands. The most severe human consequences of mining operations affect mine workers and those living in close proximity to the mines, including subsistence farmers and indigenous groups. Mining firms appropriate land from local communities for their extracting operations and often cause massive displacements of people, especially in poor countries.[140] For laborers, mining has long been one of the world's most hazardous sectors. According to the International Labour Organization (ILO): "Mine workers are continually exposed to risks such as extremes of noise, vibration, heat and cold, repetitive task strain and harmful chemicals, radioactive materials, dangerous gases and dust inhalation. Worse still, they often face combinations of many of these risks at the same time."[141] Some of the more common health problems associated with large-scale mining operations include various cancers; brain damage; respiratory illnesses such as tuberculosis, silicosis, and asbestosis; skin diseases; gastrointestinal disorders; and reproductive problems such as frequent miscarriages and congenital defects.[142]

Health and environmental problems associated with mining have become more severe today, especially in poor countries implementing SAPs and adopting strict, export-led development strategies. By the end of 1995, for example, 35 African countries had radically rewritten their mining codes, incorporating incentives for foreign investors that include reduced taxation, import tax exemptions for equipment, and liberal immigration laws for expatriates.[143] The incentive measures in the mining sector appear to have worked; TNCs are now spending more money than ever before on mineral extraction in poor countries. Sixty percent of Africa's foreign direct investment in 1997 went to the mineral extraction sector. Exploration in West Africa doubled between 1993 and 1995, and several new mines have been opened. In Latin America spending on the exploration of metals went from $200 million in 1991 to $1.7 billion in 1997. And in the Philippines, over 25 percent of the country is now open to foreign-owned exploration and extraction concessions, due to the government's adoption of new investment regimes and mining laws.[144]

While, in theory, the foreign investment from TNC mining operations *could* benefit local economies and bring improved living standards to local people in poor countries, in practice, it rarely does so. This is in part because governments often deliberately relax the enforcement of social and environmental regulations as an additional incentive for investors.[145] According to a paper written for an international conference on mining in Ghana in 1997: "Presently, the benefits from mining tend to stay with the TNCs, while the negative consequences like pollution of water and soil, which may threaten the livelihood of surrounding communities, stay within the country."[146] With respect to job creation, some analysts contend that mining actually hurts employment because of the increasingly mechanized nature of the work and the massive displacements of people in mining areas. Furthermore, the clean-up costs from mines are externalized and left to future generations, rather than being paid by the TNCs responsible for the environmental degradation.[147] According to an international observer of the mining industry: "The economic model is clearly one of extraction and export to core countries—not one of enrichment for producing nations."[148]

Though similar processes are unfolding in countries such as Namibia, Ghana, the Philippines, and Zimbabwe, a case in Indonesia is illustrative of mining's complex problems.

Grasberg Gold Mine, operated by PT Freeport Indonesia, is a subsidiary of New Orleans-based TNC Freeport McMoran, and is the world's largest gold mine. Every day it dumps 130,000 tons of waste rock ("tailings") into local rivers as a means of disposal. In 1995, U.S. federal government consultants, working for the Overseas Private Investment Corporation (OPIC) conducted a detailed assessment of the mine. They concluded that PT Freeport's "tailings management and disposal practices have severely degraded the rainforests surrounding the Ajkwa and Minajerwi Rivers," and that "the project...continues to pose unreasonable or major environmental, health, or safety hazards" for "the rivers, the surrounding terrestrial ecosystems and the local inhabitants."[149] This form of riverine tailings disposal has been banned in wealthy countries now for more than 15 years. Although the company and the Indonesian military do not allow independent monitoring of river water quality, there is evidence from subcontractors at PT Freeport that poisons such as mercury exist in these waters at four times the level considered safe for human consumption. Long-term environmental damage from the chemical-weathering process by which sulfites in the tailings are exposed to air and water could become a "perpetual pollution machine," slowly leaching sulfuric acid into the ecosystem. Some believe that the worst environmental consequences of PT Freeport's operations are yet to come: the effects of acid mine drainage will potentially destroy the ecology of local river systems by raising acidity to dangerous levels and by releasing dissolved heavy metals into the river system.[150]

Another disturbing trend in the mining sector, though not limited to the extractive industries, is the increased collusion of governments, military, and commercial interests. To protect mining sites from disgruntled locals and resistance groups, TNCs have been indirectly, and sometimes directly, involved in some of the worst human rights abuses recently registered. These include arbitrary arrest and detentions, "disappearances," torture, hamletting of villages, aerial bombings, rapes, village burnings, and murders.[151] Already marginalized populations such as indigenous groups and poor communities are the chief victims of such atrocities. The most heinous crimes tend to occur in countries where repressive regimes rule.[152] Certain TNCs have a long history of colluding with such regimes, supporting them economically and politically—even when international embargoes or trade sanctions were levied against them.[153]

Toxic Waste Export

The health and well-being of poor and marginalized people is further compromised by the export of toxic waste for disposal in poor countries.[154] The last 50 years have seen enormous growth in the production of hazardous wastes, from an annual production rate of less than 10 million tons in the 1940s to a current rate in excess of 350 million tons per year.[155] Sometimes the illegal exportation of unsafe products or toxic waste into poor countries occurs when tougher environmental regulations are passed in wealthier countries.[156] However, most dumping occurs because it is simply cheaper for companies to dump waste than to treat it.[157] Until the international outcry of the 1980s, poorly paid government bureaucrats in developing countries were known to accept fees or bribes from foreign corporations for permission to dump toxic materials in their countries.[158]

Not surprisingly, such dumping occurs chiefly in the world's poorest countries. According to a U.N. publication, eight of the ten most targeted countries rank among the world's poorest nations.[159] In the late 1980s, Swiss Intercontrat offered

Guinea-Bissau, then the fifth poorest nation in the world, $140 million annually for five years to receive 3.5 million tons of hazardous waste. This amount exceeded the country's GNP.[160]

Only recently has it become illegal to transport hazardous wastes for the purpose of dumping. Until the U.N. Basel Convention on the Control of Transboundary Movements of Hazardous Wastes and Their Disposal was passed in 1994, TNCs were permitted to dump or pay officials in poor countries to accept their hazardous waste.[161] In a notorious 1991 memo, then World Bank Chief Economist and current U.S. Deputy Secretary of Treasury Lawrence Summers argued: "Shouldn't the World Bank be encouraging more migration of the dirty industries to the LDCs [less developed countries]? I think the economic logic behind dumping a load of toxic waste in the lowest wage country is impeccable and we should face up to that. I've always thought that underpopulated countries in Africa are vastly under-polluted; their air quality [level of air pollution] is probably vastly inefficiently low compared to Los Angeles or Mexico City."[162]

Depleting the Natural Resource Base

Throughout the world, TNCs are involved in the exploitation of natural resources such as trees, minerals, and marine life. Using their enormous financial power to strike lucrative deals in poor countries, TNCs buy land cheaply from governments that lack the means to exploit their own resources, then extract raw materials under low-priced, long-term contracts. By the mid-1980s, for example, foreign corporations controlled 90 percent of all logging in Gabon and 77 percent in the Congo.[163]

Large agribusiness, aquaculture, and mining firms tend to locate where resources are abundant, which is often also where indigenous communities reside. Explaining this situation, sometimes called "resource colonialism," one author describes the problem this way: "Native peoples are under assault on every continent because their lands contain a wide variety of valuable resources needed for industrial development. From the Amazon Basin to the frozen stretches of northern Saskachewan to the tropical rainforests of Southeast Asia and Central Africa, energy, mining, logging, hydroelectric, and other megaprojects have uprooted, dislocated, and even destroyed native communities."[164]

The most harmful effects of "resource colonialism" are often visited upon the poorest people, who lack material resources as well as social and political capital to adequately protect themselves.[165] One striking example occurred on the Navajo Nation in the Four Corners area of the American southwest. From the 1940s until 1980, Vanadium Corporation (a subsidiary of Union Carbide), Kerr-McGee, and other mining companies mined much of the U.S. supply of uranium within the Navajo territory. Though the mines are now closed, the rate of cancer among the 4,000 Native Americans who worked in them is far above national norms. While the mines were operational, workers were exposed to radiation at levels thousands of times higher than recommended limits. Moreover, despite government-sponsored cleanup efforts, hundreds of abandoned mines and pits containing uranium wastes remain today, leaving much of the Navajo lands useless.[166]

Long after public health experts had publicly expressed concern about the effects of radiation exposure on these miners, the mining corporations continued to lobby Congress for lighter environmental and safety regulations. Rather than improving conditions, the TNCs took advantage of the immunity granted them by the U.S. government in exchange for the companies' role in "protecting national security."

It is no secret that corporations receive both direct and indirect assistance from their national governments. What is perhaps less widely known is that for-profit corporations also receive direct assistance from international bodies, such as the World Bank. The World Bank is currently negotiating with Exxon, Shell, and ELF to provide these TNCs with over 10 percent of the $3.5 billion they need to develop oil fields in southern Chad. This undertaking will be Africa's largest oil development project ever. The enormous project will include over 600 miles of pipeline to transport oil from Chad to the coast of Cameroon. The World Bank's involvement helps guarantee accords from the governments of both Cameroon and Chad. Critics of the project point next door to Nigeria, where 40 years of oil extraction have severely degraded the environment and destroyed the livelihoods of local inhabitants. Environmentalists fear that similar devastation will occur in the forests, rivers, farmlands, and mountains along the pipeline route from the oil fields of Chad through Cameroon to the coast.[167] The project could undermine subsistence patterns and force peasant farmers off their land. The World Bank's participation in such a socially and environmentally risky operation seems at odds with the Bank's stated mission as a "partner in strengthening economies and expanding markets to improve the quality of life for people everywhere, especially the poorest."[168]

ADVERTISING AND PROMOTIONAL ACTIVITIES

Twenty-two-year-old Sali did everything she was told after giving birth to her first child, Moussa, at the local hospital in Senegal, West Africa. For two months she diligently prepared the baby formula the nurses had given her. But ultimately she could not afford to replenish her supply of the manufactured milk product and, because she had ceased breastfeeding, her own breast milk had dried up. She tried returning to the hospital to get more formula. But the nurses, though empathetic, could not give her more formula free of charge. They could only suggest where to find it at a reduced price. With their meager monthly earnings, Sali and her husband could not even afford a month's supply of the formula.

Her grandmother had warned her against not breastfeeding, but Sali wanted to have a healthy baby. In town, along the roads, and even in the maternity wards she saw billboards and posters encouraging mothers to bottlefeed their infants. The children on the billboards were plump and healthy looking. Sali noted that the sophisticated, modern women in the cities tended to bottlefeed their babies. Even on the radio, she heard announcements confirming the same message. So, after Moussa was born, when the nurses at the hospital gave her the first batch of baby formula, Sali gratefully took it.

No one told her how expensive the cans of formula would be; she had to borrow money just to buy a single month's supply. When she began to grasp the gravity of her problem, Sali devised a system to make the powder last longer. By adding double the amount of water required to mix the formula, she could make it last for two months instead of just one. But even so, water in Sali's village was scarce and often unfit for drinking.

Although the hospital nurses had insisted that Sali use only boiled water to mix the formula, she could not always do so. The time commitment for fetching water, and wood for boiling it, was sometimes too much for her to handle—especially after long and arduous days working in the fields.

Ultimately, Moussa's diluted formula did not provide the boy with adequate nutrients to grow and fight infection. And his infant body could not endure the occasional bouts of diarrhea he would get from the contaminated water Sali sometimes used to mix the breast milk substitute. In his fourth month little Moussa died from dehydration, brought on by severe diarrheal disease and malnutrition.[169]

Infant formula manufacturers' advertising and promotional efforts in poor countries began in the 1960s. Today, despite decades of well-organized boycotts and a multitude of international regulations banning the most harmful of their marketing strategies, several infant formula TNCs continue—aggressively and at times falsely—to promote their products to poor women. Companies' advertising and promotional efforts are designed to attract new consumers. They are marketing strategies for which millions of infants like Moussa have paid with their lives.

Through sophisticated advertising campaigns now heard, seen, and felt in virtually every corner of the world, transnational corporations impact the health of individuals and communities in ways that go beyond the extraction of resources or the routine production of goods. In this section, we take a close look at advertising and promotional strategies employed by giant transnational infant formula, tobacco, and weapon-producing corporations.[170] These cases illustrate the influence and potential harm of such marketing strategies, especially in poor communities throughout the world.

The Promotion of Infant Formula

In a speech she delivered to the Singapore Rotary Club in 1939, world-renowned physician Cicely Williams declared:

> If your lives were embittered as mine is, by seeing day after day this massacre of the innocents by unsuitable feeding, then I believe you would feel as I do that misguided propaganda on infant feeding should be punished as the most criminal form of sedition and that those deaths should be regarded as murder.[171]

In response both to declining birthrates in developed countries in the 1960s and to their need to sustain long-term corporate profitability, transnational infant formula manufacturers began creating markets for their products in developing countries.[172] Aggressive marketing campaigns carried out in hospitals included advertising in maternity wards; gifts to medical personnel; and free samples to get new mothers started with infant formula immediately after delivery. Bottlefeeding was promoted as sophisticated, convenient, and healthy.

By the mid-1970s, public health workers, community activists, and the World Health Organization (WHO) began to see a disturbing trend; breastfeeding was giving way to bottlefeeding in poor countries throughout Africa, Latin America, and Asia.[173] The risks associated with bottlefeeding are grave for poor mothers and their families. Careful preparation requires fuel to boil water for sterilizing bottles and clean water to mix with the powder. Because the cost of formula is more than many families can afford, new mothers tend to dilute the formula to make it last longer. Overdilution and lack of clean water for the mixture have led to millions of infant deaths from malnutrition and severe diarrheal infections.

In Sali's case, there were no medical reasons for using infant formula to feed her newborn son; she was a young, healthy woman perfectly able to breastfeed. There were, however, compelling reasons to discourage infant formula. Most significantly, Sali's family was poor and in no position to purchase a steady supply of powdered formula.

The superiority of breast milk over infant formula has been well-established for decades. For healthy women, breastfeeding is the most nutritious and least expensive way to feed young infants. Breastfed infants benefit from the protective immunologic qualities of breast milk. They have a reduced risk of developing food allergies and contracting gastroenteritis and respiratory infections, and they are believed to have better mental development than formula-fed babies.[174] Breastfeeding is also beneficial for lactating mothers. It results in lower rates of premenopausal breast and ovarian cancer and decreased risk of osteoporosis and anemia, and plays an important role in birth spacing by inducing lactational amenorrhea.[175]

When the health consequences of infant formula sales became apparent, world attention focused on the epidemic of what one leading public health pediatrician labeled "commerciogenic malnutrition" among millions of infants.[176] Several reports in the 1970s suggested that the aggressive and manipulative marketing tactics of transnational infant formula corporations such as Nestlé, American Home Products, Abbott, and Bristol-Myers were instrumental in those infants' deaths.[177]

In 1977, the Nestlé Corporation was singled out as the most aggressive promoter of infant formula to poor mothers in developing countries. To protest the company's activities, a collection of academic, consumer, and religious groups formed the Infant Formula Action Coalition and launched an international boycott against Nestlé products. The response from Nestlé was indignation and a refusal to recognize the problem. Even after hearings before a U.S. House Subcommittee, a Nestlé representative stated that "we're not sure any changes need to be made."

In 1981, after considerable international outrage over the thousands of formula-related infant death reports, the WHO's governing body, the World Health Assembly, overwhelmingly adopted its International Code of Marketing of Breast Milk Substitutes.[178] The code set out responsibilities for corporations, national governments, and health workers in relation to the promotion and dissemination of breast milk substitutes. The WHO recognized that formula-producing TNCs strongly influenced how hospitals taught mothers about infant-feeding choices by first targeting their "educational materials" directly to medical professionals, and the WHO-sponsored Code of Marketing was designed specifically to prevent the most egregious of these marketing strategies. The United States was *the only country in the world* to vote against the code. American opposition was not reversed until 1994. Because Nestlé initially refused to adopt the WHO code, the boycott continued. It was not until 1984 that Nestlé finally agreed to adopt the principles of the code. With an apparent victory on its side, the activist community called off the boycott.

The end of the boycott, however, was not the end of the story. Breast milk substitutes *still* are big business, and a nonbinding code relying on self-regulation has not been enough to stop the TNCs' drive for profit. In 1983, the global market for infant formula was estimated at $3.3 billion; in 1991 it had reached over $6 billion.[179] By the 1990s, it was apparent that several companies were no longer abiding by the WHO code, including Nestlé and American Home Products. A second boycott was called, but by the time it had gotten underway, TNCs' promotional schemes had successfully wooed the health profession. Despite the continuing effects of infant formula promotion and use in raising infant mortality, the international outrage has been muted.

In 1993, the WHO director stated: "WHO estimates that some 1.5 million infant deaths each year could be averted through effective breastfeeding."[180] In 1997, the British Interagency Group on Breastfeeding Monitoring released a report entitled "Cracking the Code." After a thorough study of mothers and health-care workers in health facilities in four nations (Bangladesh, Poland, South Africa, and Thailand), the authors concluded that many transnational infant formula corporations continue systematically to ignore the 1981 WHO code.[181] The study found that a substantial proportion (up to one-third) of mothers reported receiving information associated with a specific company that was either promoting bottlefeeding or discouraging breastfeeding. Women in all four countries (up to one-quarter of those questioned) had received sample products, most of them from within the health-care system. In all four countries the researchers discovered posters and displays of infant formula, in violation of the code. They also found company personnel making unsolicited visits to health facilities with the stated aim of giving product information to mothers. Health workers and facilities (up to one-half of those investigated) were continuing to accept samples from companies and passing them on to new mothers. The health problems that result from targeting promotional activities through health-care systems is apparent in this study. In all countries, a strong correlation was found between the proportion of mothers receiving negative information about breastfeeding and the proportion actually bottlefeeding their infants. Despite decades of efforts by consumer groups, international public and private organizations, and local activists to curb the most egregious marketing activities, transnational infant formula corporations continue to undermine breastfeeding among the world's poor, and thus threaten the health of millions of infants worldwide.

Tobacco: Tales of Death and Disease

> Increasingly, poor people throughout the world are becoming victims of political, economic, and cultural manipulation by tobacco transnationals in what is being called the "new opium war."[182]

As new antismoking regulations and strong public health messages began to have a significant impact on reducing smoking and tobacco markets in wealthy countries, tobacco TNCs sought new regions in which to sell their products.[183] During the same period, Eastern European countries were integrating into the global economy, and the neoliberal push toward open markets and freer world trade was gaining momentum. These patterns, coupled with new regional trade agreements and IFIs' loan conditions encouraging privatization of state-owned companies, were instrumental in enabling tobacco TNCs to successfully turn their attention toward poor and less-industrialized regions of the world. Since the 1980s, tobacco TNCs have aggressively and successfully expanded their sales in Latin America, Africa, Asia, and Eastern Europe.

Between the early 1970s and 1990s, wealthy countries decreased their annual consumption of cigarettes by 9 percent, while the average annual consumption in poor nations during the same period increased by 64 percent.[184] Whereas in the early 1970s wealthy countries such as Canada, Switzerland, and the United Kingdom consumed the most cigarettes, in the early 1990s cigarette per capita consumption rates were highest in countries such as Greece, Hungary, and Korea. Over the same twenty-year period, cigarette consumption in China grew 260 percent. While cigarette sales in the United States have stagnated since the early 1990s, international sales have surged. Though the world's largest and third largest transnational tobacco corporations are U.S.-based, sales within the United States accounted for only 4 percent of the world tobacco market in 1998.[185] Transnational corporations based in the United States increased total cigarette exports 340 percent between 1975 and 1994, from 50.2 billion to 220.2 billion cigarettes.[186] Since 1990, the largest U.S.-based transnational tobacco corporation, Philip Morris, the maker of Marlboro cigarettes, increased its tobacco sales to foreign countries by almost 80 percent.[187] Since 1993, Philip Morris has increased its profits by 73 percent. As of 1998, the two largest U.S.-based tobacco TNCs were each selling cigarettes in over 170 markets.[188] Of the 26 countries with the highest percentage of smokers, only one, Japan, is not a developing country.[189]

According to the WHO, about one-third of the world's population over the age of 14 smokes. Nearly 10,000 people worldwide die every day from tobacco-related illnesses, and in 20 years these illnesses are expected to be the world's leading cause of death. Seventy percent of all those deaths will occur in poor countries.[190] Worldwide, tobacco's death toll is expected to increase to 12 million per year by the middle of the next century, with most of the increase occurring in the developing world.[191] One epidemiologist has estimated that of all the people alive today, 500 million will die of smoking-related diseases.[192] Based on current rates, this means that tobacco will prematurely kill almost 10 percent of the world's population. These grim prospects are due in large part to the spectacular U.S. infiltration of overseas markets.[193]

In 1981, Philip Morris, R.J. Reynolds, and Brown & Williamson formed the U.S. Cigarette Export Association to compete more effectively in foreign markets. The efforts of these three large TNCs (which together account for 99 percent of all cigarette exports) were assisted by the 1974 Trade Act passed by President Nixon to promote free trade. The companies' cause was boosted in 1984, when Section 301 of the act was strengthened into "Super 301." This new trade policy called for mandatory imposition of U.S. trade sanctions on countries that failed to eliminate "unfair trade practices" that limited market access for U.S. products. The policy included tobacco products.

During the 1980s, with the aggressive use of Section 301 of the trade act and the threat of retaliatory trade sanctions, the U.S. trade representative forced countries in Latin America and Asia to open their markets to U.S. tobacco corporations.[194] The most notable cases have been Japan, Taiwan, South Korea, and Thailand. Under threat, countries were forced to lift bans on foreign imports, to lower tariffs, to change import quotas, and to allow advertising of foreign cigarettes. With the removal of these barriers and the securing of advertising guarantees, the tobacco TNCs were able to launch slick advertising campaigns that today still glamorize smoking and promote Western consumer culture in host countries. These campaigns have been successful. One year after Western tobacco TNCs gained access to the Korean market in 1986 and began a massive advertising campaign there, the smoking rate among male Korean teenagers rose from 18 to 30 percent. In Taiwan, where cigarette advertising was minimal before the entry of foreign tobacco corporations and where a downward trend in smoking had begun, smoking among Taiwanese high school students increased by 10 percent two years after U.S. corporations entered the market.[195] In Argentina, per capita cigarette consumption rose three times faster than before the introduction of cigarettes made by U.S.- and European-based TNCs. When U.S. tobacco TNCs entered Japan in 1987, they forced local Japanese cigarette companies to intensify their marketing efforts, in order to compete with the U.S. corporations.[196] The increased advertising expenditures have apparently paid off for both Japanese and foreign companies: especially among teens, whose cigarette consumption rose 16 percent between 1987 and 1993.[197] The same scenario is currently unfolding in China, where cigarette consumption has risen precipitously with the entry of U.S. and European tobacco giants. The rapid increase in cigarette consumption in China has become a major public health crisis: tobacco will kill a third of all young Chinese men if current smoking rates continue.[198]

Tobacco Advertising and Promotion

Until recently, many countries sold cigarettes through government-held monopolies that made little or no attempt to persuade people to buy their products. However, today cigarette advertising even in these countries is particularly insidious. Most developing countries lack the public health infrastructure to effectively educate people on the dangers of smoking. As a result, most people in poor countries are bombarded with cigarette advertisements but are still unaware of the links between tobacco and disease.

Though most countries in the world today have at least limited restrictions on tobacco advertising, tobacco TNCs are able to promote cigarettes more aggressively in some countries than they can at home. Standards for content, labeling, and advertising in most poor countries are still significantly less rigid. There are exceptions, however, and some countries such as Thailand, Mongolia, and Singapore have bans on advertising and promotion that are broader and more restrictive than current U.S. laws. But even in areas where advertising bans are in place, the corporations create new and clever ways of promoting their products. Moreover, when public health authorities in Asia have attempted to regulate the labeling of imported cigarettes, they have received letters from the U.S. embassy, forewarning that such regulatory efforts conflict with international trade agreements laid out under the WTO.[199]

To dodge bans on direct advertising, the tobacco TNCs have begun to advertise through event and sports sponsorship, giveaways and product sampling, and logo or brand-name promotion on non-tobacco products such as school bags. To promote a friendly image to African people, the transnational conglomerates compete to sponsor sporting and cultural events and to support public universities and even health-care facilities. In Kenya, the British American Tobacco Company (BAT) provides road signs for towns, villages, schools, and hospitals.[200] In Malaysia, a popular comic book for elementary school students carried a Lucky Strike advertisement, and Christmas trees in discos are adorned with balls and stars bearing the Kent logo. In Manila, journalists have reported finding cigarettes sold at snack stands operated by the local Boy Scouts.[201] In China, tobacco TNCs sponsor motorcycle and dance troupes. In Russia, the Camel Trophy Cup was sponsored by R.J. Reynolds, and in Warsaw, trolley cars are covered with Marlboro logos.[202] In Pecs, Hungary, BAT promotes social welfare by contributing 25 percent of the town's homeless shelter budget. To win over the public and public officials and to promote a "good citizen" corporate image, foreign tobacco money in Hungary also goes to local hospitals and schools, student scholarship programs, and the Red Cross. Cash-strapped government officials are reluctant to enact tough anti-tobacco legislation when the industry contributes so much to their social welfare system.[203]

The sophisticated cigarette advertising campaigns are tremendously successful in persuading people to become smokers. Though the tobacco TNCs argue that their main objective is not to recruit new smokers but to encourage brand switching, evidence reveals that after the entry of TNCs into foreign markets, the total number of smokers increases. In a study published in 1996, the National Bureau of Economic Research found that, besides increasing the market share of U.S. cigarettes in Asia, the Section 301 cases resulted in per capita cigarette consumption nearly 10 percent higher in 1991 than it would have been had markets remained closed.[204] Moreover, the cigarettes sold by TNCs in poorer countries often contain higher levels of tar and nicotine, and thus are more addictive, than those produced for wealthier countries.[205] With more people addicted to more harmful cigarettes, it is no wonder that the WHO projects rapid increases in rates of emphysema, heart disease, and cancer among the poor.

Six Western transnational tobacco conglomerates control 40 percent of the world cigarette trade and 85 percent of the tobacco leaf sold on the world market.[206] Transnationals based in developing countries also contribute to the global trade in tobacco, but with the exception of six countries, the tobacco trade results in a negative balance of trade for developing nations. Any short-term gain made by selling tobacco will be offset by long-term costs to the community and the surrounding environment. Purchase of foreign cigarettes causes a loss of foreign exchange—with profits benefiting Western shareholders. Additionally, money spent on tobacco is not available for health necessities, such as food and medical care.[207]

The ironies of the transnational tobacco trade have been duly noted. In his final speech as U.S. surgeon general, C. Everett Koop stated: "It is the height of hypocrisy for the United States, in our war against drugs, to demand that foreign nations take steps to stop the export of cocaine to our country while at the same time we export nicotine, a drug just as addictive as cocaine, to the rest of the world."[208] Peter Bourne, former president of the American Association for World Health, adds: "Despite our great concern about the effect of Colombian cocaine on young

Americans, more Colombians die today from diseases caused by tobacco products exported to their country by American tobacco companies than do Americans from Colombian cocaine."[209]

The Indefensible Marketing of Weapons

The defense industry has always been nationalistic. Defense company production facilities, managers, and even shareholders have been mostly home-based.[210] Yet due to the liberalization of world trade, shrinking defense budgets in the 1990s, and advances in weapons technology with greater industry links to nonmilitary commercial sectors, defense companies the world over are casting off their isolationist inclinations. Now striving to become more global in orientation, many firms, especially in the United States, have restructured their operations and merged with other arms makers and electronics firms. Much of the cost of these mergers has been borne by the U.S. government under a 1993 Defense Department policy that enabled companies to claim reimbursements for the cost of their mergers.[211]

Another method companies have used to pay for their restructuring is to sell their weapons abroad. Until the Clinton administration, U.S. presidents had occasionally tried to restrict arms exports, especially to repressive regimes and dictators likely to use weapons indiscriminately to maintain power. In the 1970s, President Carter enacted restrictive policies on arms exports, partly in an effort to prevent arms races between Latin American military dictatorships. During the Reagan and Bush administrations many of these policies were flagrantly ignored. From his campaign speeches in the early 1990s, it appeared that Clinton would move back to restricting arms exports. In a campaign address he said: "I expect to review our arms sales policy and to take it up with the other major arms sellers of the world as a part of a long-term effort to reduce the proliferation of weapons."[212] Once in office, however, Clinton abandoned human rights concerns for the promises of the arms makers: namely, job creation and economic growth. During President Clinton's first year in office, U.S. arms sales more than doubled.[213]

Unlike the marketing and promotional campaigns of cigarette or infant formula manufacturers, weapons makers have come to rely heavily on the U.S. government to help promote their goods overseas. In May 1993, Secretary of State Warren Christopher, a former director of Lockheed, instructed U.S. overseas diplomats to "support overseas marketing efforts of American companies bidding on defense contracts."[214] In 1996, Congress created an export-finance scheme, called the Defense Export Loan Guarantee program, to help finance U.S. weapons sales to foreign countries. These efforts seem to have paid off handsomely for the top arms exporters. From the late 1980s to the mid-1990s, the U.S. share of the world market in arms rose from 25 to 30 percent to greater than 50 percent.[215] Between 1988 and 1995, the United States sold $134.9 billion of arms to developing nations, many of them repressive regimes. By contrast, Russia sold $73.6 billion and the United Kingdom, $40.3 billion, to poor and less-industrialized nations.[216]

American arms manufacturing TNCs such as McDonnell-Douglas successfully win support for their international sales by convincing the public that such sales carry with them the potential for job creation and economic growth. The public "support" comes in the form of U.S. taxpayer subsidies—worth several billion dollars annually—to promote U.S. weapons sales abroad.[217] During the Persian Gulf War, the Cable News Network (C.N.N.) used Pentagon video footage to beam images of U.S. attacks on Iraqi targets around the world; one critic likened the coverage to "infomercials" advertising the infallibility of U.S. weapons. Not surprisingly, in the aftermath of the war, international demand for U.S. weapons reached new heights. The Saudis wanted 72 McDonnell-Douglas Corporation F-15s. To secure U.S. government approval and garner public support for the sale, the corporation made the claim that the sale was worth 40,000 aerospace jobs and $13 billion. The proceeds, McDonnell-Douglas claimed, would benefit 345 congressional districts and 46 states. Even though, according to the Federation of American Scientists and other groups, the company's job creation and monetary benefit claims were highly inflated, public officials were duly impressed and backed the deal.[218]

In a number of volatile areas in the world, the United States has been the major arms supplier to governments that are involved in ongoing conflicts. From 1993 to 1994, in 45 of the 50 largest ethnic or territorial conflicts, U.S.-supplied weapons were used on either one or both sides. American-made weapons have killed millions throughout the world, particularly in middle income and very poor countries—Haiti, Guatemala, Somalia, Liberia, Sierra Leone, Indonesia, Mexico, Colombia, and the Philippines, to name a few.[219] Between 1993 and 1997, the U.S. government sold, gave away, or let industry sell $190 billion in weapons to almost every country in the world.[220]

The global trade in weapons affects the health of the poor in multiple ways. The most obvious impact is the use of arms to maim and kill.[221] Since the Second World War, wars kill more *civilians* than soldiers; noncombatants, in fact, suffer 90 percent of the casualties of current conflicts.[222] In the 150 conflicts fought since the end of World War II, more than 14 million civilians have been killed.[223] These civilian casualties are not simply accidental. For strategic reasons, military leaders sometimes target defenseless civilian populations; hence, the proliferation of antipersonnel weapons in the past 20 years. With more than 100 million land mines sown around the globe, these weapons of war are among the most pernicious.[224] In the past three decades, more than 26,000 casualties have resulted from land mines in countries such as Cambodia, Afghanistan, Angola, Mozambique, and Somalia, reeling from the devastation of war.[225] Often these casualties are farmers returning to re-plow their fields, or rural inhabitants going about their daily chores.

The transnational weapons trade has multiple harmful effects.[226] They include environmental damage from weapons production, testing, and storage; psychological effects produced by threats to use weapons; and social and economic effects faced by countries that choose to purchase weapons by diverting funds from human services or economic development.[227] Globally, the nearly $1 trillion annually spent on arms in the 1980s was equivalent to the combined annual incomes of 2.6 billion people in the 44 poorest nations, one-half of the world's population during this period.[228]

The denial of essential nutrition, housing, education, and health services to the poor must be considered in the context of the diversion of money to armaments. In 1992, for example, Nigeria purchased 80 battle tanks from British arms TNCs at a cost that would have immunized all of the 2 million unimmunized children in the country and provided family planning services to 17 million families. Pakistan ordered 40 Mirage 2000I fighter jets from French TNCs at a cost that could have provided potable water for two years for the 55 million Pakistanis who lack safe water; essential medicine for the 13 million Pakistanis without access to medical care; *and* basic education for 12 million Pakistani children. India ordered 20 MiG-29 fighter jets from Russia, disbursing funds that could have provided basic education to all of the 15 million Indian girls who were out of school at that time.[229]

These cases, which describe the extraordinary influence of transnational infant formula, cigarette, and armament corporations, clearly illustrate how the sophisticated promotional activities of TNCs—activities not infrequently backed by governments—are able to manipulate the wants and perceived "needs" of people and nation-states throughout the world. But these are just a few of the industries that use such tactics. The pharmaceutical industry now spends in excess of $10 billion annually on advertising alone. This industry, again largely transnational, brings along with its promises new risks to individuals and communities.[230] The pesticide industry markets its products in questionable ways, often creating farmer dependence on specific formulations and exaggerating claims concerning the efficacy of the product and its relative safety.[231] Likewise, the promotional strategies of purveyors of soft drinks, alcohol, fast food, automobiles, cosmetics, and a host of other industries that are now focusing their efforts in densely populated and poor areas of the world have also been shown to undermine efforts to promote health.[232]

EFFORTS TO COUNTER TNC ABUSES

Given the international reach and expanding political power of TNCs, what structures exist to help ensure that corporations produce and sell goods and services without damage to people's health and the environment? We can identify three main mechanisms that seek to guarantee TNCs' compliance with basic labor, occupational safety, human rights, and environmental standards. These are *corporate self-monitoring, national laws,* and *NGO oversight.* We discuss these factors in turn, then focus briefly on the role of international agencies, international law, and consumer activism in setting limits on corporate power.

Company Self-Enforcement

The first level of accountability is that supplied voluntarily by corporations themselves. As noted, the executives of some TNCs show sensitivity to ethical considerations, particularly as they affect public image and reduce litigation. For such firms, implementation of labor, environmental, and human rights standards can occur in the absence of strong government enforcement. Often, the standards take the form of company "codes of conduct" and "sourcing guidelines" that stipulate ethical criteria to which the firm pledges adherence. In 1994, the Levi Strauss Company paved the way by producing its "Global Sourcing and Operating Guidelines," outlining terms of business engagement between the corporation and its Asian and Latin American contractors. These guidelines briefly sketched standards for wages, working hours, child and prison labor rules, discrimination, and health and safety requirements for business partners. Gap, Reebok, and JCPenney quickly followed suit. By 1999, under the scrutiny of NGOs such as Amnesty International, even Royal Dutch Shell had produced its own guidelines for ethical business practice. Few if any TNCs, however, devote significant resources to enforcement of these guidelines. Moreover, when workers in contracting firms eventually do attain the rights outlined in such "Global Sourcing and Operating Guidelines," the same companies that claim to promote the guidelines have often abandoned them. Nike, Reebok, Phillips-Van Heusen, and even Levi Strauss have abandoned factories and countries when local workers organized and began to demand their legal rights.[233]

Most analysts agree that such voluntary efforts are at best patchy and often serve as a smoke screen. Without independent monitoring and enforcement, ethical codes are like building façades on Main Street in a Western movie: they may fool the casual observer, but they ultimately have no substance. The mere existence of codes of conduct is insufficient to ensure non-exploitative work practices.[234]

Such codes do not affect the fundamental logic by which corporations operate. Firms seek to enhance the revenues of their (usually geographically distant) shareholders. As long as debt-ridden governments urgently seek foreign investment, and industry self-monitoring mechanisms remain fragmentary, TNCs are unlikely to seriously consider the interests of local communities and their workers unless economically or legally constrained to do so.

In the 1990s, the TNCs that came under the sharpest public scrutiny for their labor practices also saw decreased profits and additional threats to their shareholders' returns. Most of these firms were in the apparel, shoe, and toy industries. Probably because the executives of TNCs in these sectors discovered the direct correlation between a "clean" public image and increasing profit share, these industries have made the most progress in advancing social accountability through what is called independent social or ethical auditing. It is now standard practice for many TNCs in the apparel industry to contract independent professional auditors such as Pricewaterhouse Coopers and Ernst and Young to conduct social audits. Even though TNCs undertake and pay for these audits voluntarily (an obvious conflict of interest), this method has had a positive influence on some companies' social and environmental practices. It remains to be seen, however, whether such audits will become routine enough to have significant long-term effects on TNCs' social practices.[235]

National and Local Governments

National and local governments constitute important mechanisms for influencing TNC behavior. In some areas, such as Canada, the United States, and Europe, labor practices are strongly regulated, and standards are enforced through regular government inspection and union supervision. The Occupational Safety and Health Administration (OSHA) was created in the United States in the early 1970s as the main government authority on worker safety. Although by no means a perfect system, OSHA does have the authority to inspect workplaces, from automobile and apparel plants to electronics factories, and it has the power to fine companies for violations.

The Occupational Safety and Health Administration has no jurisdiction, however, over U.S.-based TNCs manufacturing or sourcing products abroad, where the most flagrant safety and human rights violations occur.

In many poor and less industrialized countries where local labor laws have already been lacking, governments now have fewer standards than a decade ago. This is because these countries have had to render their labor markets "flexible" and dismantle social and environmental protections to meet IMF and World Bank loan conditions. Due to their desperate need for the foreign currency TNCs bring, poor-country governments are unwilling to exert social pressures on foreign TNCs.[236] For example, not one member of the U.N. International Labour Organization has agreed to ratify Convention 174, drafted to prevent major industrial accidents following the gas explosion at the Union Carbide chemical factory in Bhopal, India.[237] Furthermore, recent GATT and WTO rulings markedly limit governments' ability to impose minimum environmental and social standards on companies. For example, the GATT Uruguay Round liberalized trade without providing protective mechanisms that might have guarded against industrial hazards in settings where state mechanisms are likely to be weak.[238]

Corporations commit egregious acts even in countries such as the United States that have strong, established, government-backed regulatory agencies. A close reading of the history of U.S. federal regulatory agencies reveals that these agencies, which are perceived by most to be in the business of protecting citizens, were first created in the late nineteenth century by prominent corporate leaders. The Interstate Commerce Commission (ICC), established in 1887, was actually the brainchild of railroad corporation tycoons worried about the rate-cutting wars sparked at the time by the fierce competition among railroad companies. The goal of corporate chiefs was to have the public pay for the coordination of their industry and for the maintenance of industry quality control through standards, inspections, and enforcement mechanisms. Subsequent regulatory agencies, such as those established for insurance, environment, and banking, were based on the ICC model, often enabling corporate leaders to avoid the rigors of competition by having the government manage the market and bear the costs of infrastructure and quality control. Despite successive waves of public scrutiny and efforts to render regulatory agencies more independent, many of today's agencies operate in much the same way. They create large bureaucracies that act as barriers between the corporations and people. Although they implement important regulations to protect workers, consumers, and the environment, they also tend to deflect attention away from corporations as the source of problems by shifting public attention toward efforts to improve or reform the regulatory agencies themselves.[239]

Nongovernmental Organizations

An increasing number of nongovernmental organizations (NGOs) have expanded their mandates to include investigating and publicizing the activities of nonstate actors such as TNCs. Many NGOs now regularly report on the social and environmental practices of TNCs, circulating their findings to governments, international agencies, and the public.[240] Prominent organizations such as Human Rights Watch,

Oxfam, Rainforest Action, Greenpeace, Christian Aid, and Global Exchange, as well as smaller groups like the International Labor Rights Fund, the National Labor Committee, the Campaign for Labor Rights, and the US/Guatemala Labor Education Committee are all involved in overseeing the activities of TNCs. Other groups, such as Amnesty International, the U.S.-based Interfaith Center on Corporate Responsibility (ICCR), and the Rome-based Permanent Peoples' Tribunal have produced guidelines for TNCs to use in their efforts to improve the health, human rights, and environmental impact of their activities.[241] As a reporter for the *Economist* notes: "Without independent activists the world would know much less about working conditions in the developing world."[242] The same may be said for the environmental and promotional activities of corporations.

Despite these NGO efforts, observers have noted that the NGO sector is a relatively loose-knit constellation of disparate agents with often conflicting goals, and limited capacity to provide comprehensive accountability. The limited effectiveness of NGOs in holding TNCs accountable was underscored during the latter half of the 1990s when the U.S. government attempted to bring a consortium of labor rights activists and corporate representatives to agreement regarding binding regulations against sweatshop exploitation. Beginning in 1995, revelations of labor rights abuses in plants manufacturing clothing for Gap, Wal-Mart, and many other TNCs began to draw heavy media attention—and to circulate on the World Wide Web. Responding to these incidents, the White House formed the Apparel Industry Partnership (AIP) to investigate garment sweatshop issues. The Apparel Industry Partnership included representatives from the apparel industry, unions, and human rights groups.[243]

Under pressure from President Clinton and Secretary of Labor Robert Reich, the AIP produced the "Workplace Code of Conduct" and "Principles of Monitoring" in April 1997. The two documents were immediately criticized on two main points. First, it seemed doubtful that the "Principles of Monitoring" would afford sufficient independence to those assessing compliance. Second, critics pointed out that the "Code of Conduct" determined minimum wages by *local* pay standards—ignoring the fact that in some regions of the world the legal minimum wage is not sufficient to meet workers' basic needs. The Apparel Industry Partnership went back to the drawing board but could not hammer out a consensus among all participants. In late 1998, nine of the groups' centrist members—led by executives from Nike and Reebok—began a separate negotiation. This truncated group released a "Preliminary Agreement" on November 4, 1998.

The largest U.S. apparel union, UNITE (the Union of Needletrades, Industrial, and Textiles Employees), as well as ICCR, quickly attacked the accord. The agreement authorizes companies to continue employing children as young as 14 years of age if the country of manufacture allows employment at that age (as is quite common in developing nations). It permits companies to use apparel factories, in countries such as China, that regularly repress unions and violate worker rights. Most importantly, the agreement does not require companies to ensure that their minimum wage rates are actually adequate to meet the basic survival needs of workers and their dependents. In the words of Rev. David Schilling, "The agreement...does not commit participating companies to pay a sustainable living wage in apparel and footwear plants around the world. A factory may be clean, well organized and monitored, but unless the workers are paid a sustainable living wage, it is still a sweatshop."[244] The context of the agreement was put into perspective by Tim Bissell, director of the Campaign for Labor Rights: "The intransigence of the industry representatives…makes sense when we consider that the AIP was formed to protect corporate reputations and to prevent a backlash against free trade, not to protect worker rights."[245]

Shortly after the release of the partial AIP task force's "Preliminary Agreement," a class action lawsuit was filed in January 1999 against several U.S. apparel companies manufacturing clothing in Northern Marianas Islands (Saipan), an American commonwealth near the Philippines.[246] In the sweeping triple lawsuit, Global Exchange, the Asian Law Caucus, Sweatshop Watch, UNITE, and several thousand nonunion apparel workers accused some 18 well-known companies like Tommy Hilfiger, Gap, J. Crew, and The Limited of exploiting young Asian workers from China, the Philippines, Bangladesh, and Thailand employed in factories in the Marianas. The lawsuits claim that 15,000 workers, predominantly young women, are forced to work twelve- to sixteen-hour days, seven days a week, in dreary conditions for low pay. The minimum wage in the Marianas is $3.05, far lower than the $5.15 federal minimum wage. More than $1 billion in apparel is shipped every year from the Marianas to the U.S. mainland. By producing in the Marianas, companies save more than $200 million per year in import duties, because the islands are U.S. territory. As of this writing, several settlements are being negotiated. The settlements include not only compensation for workers whose rights have been violated, they also include prospective relief requiring companies to adhere to a new, comprehensive Saipan Code of Conduct, and to comply with strict, new monitoring provisions.

As the Saipan case will likely demonstrate, workers can, and more and more often do, win small victories against enormous TNCs. However, the three monitoring structures we have just surveyed—TNC self-regulation, local and national governments, and NGOs—have not as yet succeeded in effectively checking the growing *power* of transnational corporations, nor in compelling companies to alter their *fundamental* goals and policies. We now consider briefly some other factors that may to some degree influence corporate behavior.

Other Checks on TNCs:
International Agencies and Consumer Awareness

Ideally, international bodies such as the ILO and trade monitoring organizations such as the WTO should impose international accountability mechanisms to ensure acceptable labor practices and occupational health standards throughout the world. Indeed, since its formation in 1919, the ILO has done much to monitor, document, and report poor working practices. However, ILO conventions on core labor rights have not been signed by all countries, and they do not carry the weight of binding international law.[247] The United Nations is also increasingly unable and unwilling, for reasons outlined in the following chapter, to respond comprehensively to challenges posed by new technologies, and by the policies and politics of GATT and the WTO.

It is significant that the United Nations Commission on Transnational Corporations (UNCTC), established by resolutions of the Economic and Security Council in 1974, was effectively dismantled during the 1980s. The administration of

President Reagan pressured U.N. member states (many of them dependent on investment from U.S.-based TNCs) to oppose the commission's proposed TNC Code of Conduct. This code would have been the first international agreement authorizing U.N. monitoring of TNC activities. Its defeat, like the failure of other U.N. and NGO-sponsored efforts to provide checks and balances on the activities of TNCs, reflects the dependence of the U.N. member states on foreign investment, and the formidable lobbying power TNCs exert on the U.S.—and other—governments.[248]

Meanwhile, the mechanisms of international law also possess limited authority for dealing with TNCs. International agreements, including human rights treaties, address only crimes and violations committed by nation-states, not by nonstate actors such as TNCs. In the absence of state sanctions against exploitative activities by companies, there is little the international legal system can do to address even egregious harm imposed on vulnerable populations. The 1948 United Nation's Universal Declaration of Human Rights (UDHR) does apply worldwide to state and nonstate actors alike, yet only nation-states were asked to ratify the declaration. The same pattern holds for conventions and recommendations such as the International Covenant on Civil and Political Rights (ICCPR) and the International Covenant on Economic, Social, and Cultural Rights (ICESCR).

Covenants such as the ICCPR and the ICESCR do not clearly stipulate how states and nonstate agents should ensure minimum health and environmental protection for vulnerable people, despite the fact that such protection is often critical to poor people's survival. Human rights standards have until recently been applied only to countries, not used to measure exploitation by nonstate actors. Much of the environmental and health damage associated with TNC practices of the sort examined in this chapter is not covered by any human rights treaties *at all*. Where legal protections exist, they are often fragmentary and piecemeal, engaging one area of possible abuse while leaving others unaddressed. As we have seen, labor laws to protect workers against exploitation in the workplace fail to shield communities from destruction of their land and water, and therefore from the loss of their means of survival.[249]

Consumers have had a modicum of success in some cases in encouraging TNC accountability. Well-informed consumers can exert pressure on companies to change exploitative practices through public criticism and boycotts. The International Organization of Consumers Unions (IOCU) currently monitors and publicizes negative and positive practices of TNCs around the globe. Product labeling is one way to help consumers assess and compare the environmental impact of goods. Using this system, companies that adhere to certain environmental standards are allowed to label their products as being environmentally friendly. Similarly, some carpet manufacturers that do *not* use child labor have begun to label their carpets with the "Rugmark" logo, signaling to consumers that the product was made by adults, and not children. (Oversight of companies using the Rugmark logo is scant, however.) Labeling or similar initiatives informing consumers about how products were made, extracted, or grown might provide a means of checking exploitative labor practices in other industries as well. However, the process of getting governments, companies, and international trade organizations to agree on "fair" criteria for labeling is politically charged and usually extremely difficult.

Consumer-oriented approaches and campaigns succeed in their efforts to inform the public about specific TNC abuses. However, they rarely succeed in achieving real, long-term changes in corporate practices. The first well-publicized and truly international boycott was against Swiss-based Nestlé and U.S.-based American Home Products in response to the two corporations' irresponsible marketing of infant formulas. For years the campaign was touted as a success. It had succeeded in informing the public about the catastrophic consequences of the TNCs' marketing strategies in poor countries, and it helped bring political pressure to bear on the companies by passing new international marketing codes of conduct. Years later, however, despite decades of organizing against the TNCs and boycotting their food products in supermarkets, many of the infant formula producers have returned to their old marketing tactics.[250] As in the case of cigarette advertising, the imperative of TNCs to sustain growth seems to promote in corporate managers a remarkable ability to sidestep regulations, bad publicity, and other forms of adversity.

More than most TNCs in recent years, Nike has been the subject of rather animated public rebuke. For this reason, the company's executives are continually making strides to improve their image and their human rights record. During one such effort to respond to public pressure, in March 1999 the company announced that it would increase the minimum monthly wage package for entry-level workers in its Indonesia footwear factories. These workers would receive a 6 percent pay increase, from 250,000 to 265,000 Indonesian rupiah per month. Another consumer-driven success? Not exactly, especially if one examines the wage increase in relation to inflation in Indonesia, which was as high as 80 percent in the months prior to Nike's wage increase announcement. Moreover, the Indonesian currency had lost 70 percent of its value against the U.S. dollar in 1998: Nike actually paid in early 1999 about half the wages it paid in 1997.[251] This case helps to demonstrate why the relative success of labeling and consumer boycott campaigns must be ascertained over many years, with careful attention paid to political and economic forces concurrently unfolding.

CONCLUSION

In this chapter, we have presented evidence suggesting that transnational corporations play a role in exacerbating the already precarious health conditions of poor communities throughout the world. We began by describing the growth and worldwide expansion of TNCs over the last two decades. The remainder of the chapter traced the impact of corporate activities in three distinct but interrelated areas: labor practices, the environment, and the effects of advertising and promotion. Our findings suggest a broad correlation between the economic and political ascendancy of TNCs and the increased vulnerability of poor communities.

Health-Related TNCs

Our discussion, however, has not up to this point focused *specifically* on health-related TNCs, nor on the health sector. We first wished to demonstrate that even industries having little to do with health *per se* powerfully influence people's well-being, especially in an increasingly deregulated trade and business environment. Yet it should not go unmentioned that large pharmaceutical, biotechnology, for-profit health-care providers, and health insurance corporations *have* played an enormous role in the corporatization and commodification of health. Though medically related TNCs have great potential to improve the health of the world's sick and poor, these corporations are in fact driving the medical field's shift in attention from public health to commercial concerns.

Health-care provision, biotechnology, medical therapies, and even human blood and organs for transplantation are considered among the last great profit frontiers: "dynamic growth markets" for business. To ensure full exploitation of these markets, several medically related TNCs have joined forces with their partners in the World Bank and other global institutions to design policies that shift focus away from public and community health to emphasize private and individual health with a strong reliance on medical technologies. In so doing, health businesses create new markets for their goods and services.

This shift toward the privatization of health-care services (discussed more fully in Chapter Six), coupled with the removal of trade barriers through the WTO and treaties such as NAFTA, enables U.S. for-profit managed care and health insurance companies to expand their operations in countries like Argentina, Brazil, Chile, and Ecuador.[252] American managed-care corporations, such as Aetna and CIGNA, and insurance companies, including Principal Financial Group and American International Group, entered the Latin American managed-care market as would any business seeking higher rates of return in promising new overseas markets. Unlike many of the government health programs they are beginning to replace, these health and insurance businesses do not seek to provide services to vulnerable groups. Rather, they seek healthier, wealthier patients and clients. The trend does not bode well for the poor, who, even when enrolled, face restricted access to care and expensive co-payments. The same problems that have plagued managed care in the United States, such as reduced spending for clinical services as funds are diverted to administrative costs, are now appearing in Latin America.[253]

As health services are privatized and made increasingly subservient to market forces, and as the health industry worldwide is increasingly deregulated, we move farther from protecting the health of the most vulnerable populations. Amidst these new trends, the commitment to treat health as a fundamental human right, set forth in Article 25 of the Universal Declaration of Human Rights, seems an evermore remote ideal.[254]

The largely transnational pharmaceutical companies could, in theory, dramatically improve the health of poor people, especially as their profits skyrocket and they have greater overall capacity for the research and development of new drugs. In 1995, the worldwide sale of drugs topped $700 billion. Since then, with the rising preeminence of hot-selling prescription drugs such as Viagra, Prozac, and Claritin, between 1996 and 1998 the Dow Jones Pharmaceutical Index has climbed 110 percent—a rise more than double that of the Dow Jones Industrial Average.[255] Yet this industry growth has *not* translated into lower drug prices for vulnerable populations, nor affected the production of new drugs for the old diseases that plague the poor. Rather, because achieving high returns for shareholders is of greater priority than protecting the public's health, the commercial interests of pharmaceutical TNCs are deemed more urgent than conquering disease.[256]

Nonetheless, transnational pharmaceutical firms have assisted the world in inventing and distributing the technological "know-how" to prevent, control, and even eradicate a wide range of deadly ailments.[257] Moreover, the large pharmaceutical firms have recently brought about rapid advances in sophisticated therapies that can dramatically improve the lives of people suffering from mental illness, and prolong the survival of people suffering from cardiovascular disease, Alzheimer's, and cancer.

As important as these medical advances are, however, most pharmaceutical TNCs do not research or produce remedies *for the diseases that routinely afflict the world's poor*. They focus most of their research and development on improving drugs already in use, or on drugs (such as psychotropic and cardiovascular) needed most by wealthier consumers. Despite ongoing efforts by governments, the WHO, the World Bank, and pharmaceutical associations to encourage leading pharmaceutical TNCs to develop new treatments for the world's most threatening infectious diseases (malaria or tuberculosis, for example), few corporations have actually committed to such research.[258] In fact, research on infectious diseases that occur mostly in poor areas "has been a major casualty of the consolidation of the [pharmaceutical] industry over the past decade, with companies tending to concentrate their resources on fewer—and potentially more profitable—areas."[259] Even for drugs that are produced to treat diseases that disproportionately afflict poor people, such as new AIDS medicines, the benefits of these new therapies are quite unevenly distributed, and the vast majority of people who are today in need of the lifesaving treatments will never have access to them.[260]

The Question of Responsibility

To criticize transnational corporations is easy enough. On a daily basis, the media deliver reports of TNCs' destructive activities: working in collusion with repressive national security forces; paying workers salaries below the minimum needed for survival; taking part in internationally banned and unethical promotional activities; dumping toxic wastes. *Yet TNCs cannot be adequately analyzed or criticized in isolation from the social, political, and economic framework in which they operate*. Nor should they be considered as something other than what we have collectively enabled them to be. As a commentator observed at the end of the nineteenth century:

> We are all calling upon [those who control corporate] power and property, as mankind called upon kings in their day, to be good and kind, wise and sweet, and we are calling in vain. We are asking them not to be what we have made them to be. We put power into their hands and ask them not to use it as power. [261]

When we accuse TNCs of exploiting workers and degrading the environment, how and where should we target our criticism: at the individual firms perpetrating egregious acts? At the development strategy that encourages privatization and export-led growth? At global trade and investment policies that promote the unchecked movement of capital, goods, and services? But what about the larger structure of "market competition" that impels countries to offer TNCs the lowest possible labor and environmental standards, letting companies operate in ways that harm people and communities? What of the inequalities between rich and poor that directly contribute to TNCs' capacity to exploit differences in social and environmental regulations between countries and regions? And mustn't we consider the complicity or greed of government officials? If we condemn TNCs alone, without regard for these other factors, we may indeed be "asking [corporations] not to be what we have made them to be." And yet, TNCs cannot be considered mere passive cogs in the framework within which they operate. For, as we will see in greater detail in the following chapter, corporate agents themselves play a decisive role in shaping and maintaining the global economic order.

Binary thinking may seem to offer a way out. We may hope to pit "the state" or "responsible government" against "business" or TNCs. If TNCs do not protect the health of their workers, the communities where they function, or the people to whom they sell their goods and services, we can argue that government can and must take on this protective role. Yet in practice, these matters are rarely so simple. As in the case of Nigeria, government and corporate interests may be so symbiotically interwoven as to be virtually inseparable; this pattern is especially prevalent in poor countries dependent on the revenue generated by a few foreign firms. If we dichotomize corporations in terms of "they and we," we may miss pragmatic opportunities to influence corporate leaders toward policies that actually improve poor people's health.[262]

Furthermore, we must realistically acknowledge the abilities of corporate marketers to cultivate trust, even among disadvantaged populations. Private corporations can often deliver goods and services—food, telephones, or electricity, for example—more inexpensively and efficiently than the public sector (at least to those who have the means to purchase such goods). Moreover, the harmful consequences of TNC activities in already disadvantaged areas often occur in tandem with improvements to upper income and wealthier neighborhoods. As the greatest beneficiaries of TNCs' lucrative activities, middle-income and wealthy people are, therefore, corporations' natural allies. Yet not only the rich but also the poor are easily swayed by corporate claims. As the majority of people in poor countries see their resources dwindle as a result of structural adjustment, they tend to blame their own governments for the increased economic vulnerability they experience. At the same time, friendly promotional images of TNCs have entered people's daily lives, leading many to renounce their trust of government as provider and protector in favor of a faith in what corporations promote in their advertising—material satisfaction, individuality, love, freedom, sex. Efforts to win broad public support for reining in corporate powers and preventing corporate abuses must come to terms with these shifting allegiances—ironic though the situation may be, given that "friendly corporations" have often been at the root of poor people's increased economic vulnerability.

This chapter has suggested that the expansion, consolidation, and rising power of TNCs are a major—in many contexts *the chief*—obstacle to improving health among the poor. The following chapter makes the case that the institutionalization of corporate influence in national and global organizations contributes to expanding the gap between those who gain from corporate-led economic growth and those who do not. If current trends continue, poor communities will likely become even more vulnerable, embittered, and, not surprisingly, politicized. Viewing the situation in this light, many will agree that something must change. But how, and by what mechanisms? Scholars, political activists, and other citizens groups are currently debating these questions. Should, for example, efforts be focused on trying to control TNC activities and contain corporate power? Or must legal frameworks first be restructured to redefine the relationship between corporations, citizens, and the state? To be effective, efforts must unfold simultaneously on several levels.[263] Longtime observer of corporations and author of *Corporation Nation*, Charles Derber offers a comprehensive recipe:

> A true movement of corporate responsibility must unite populists, unions, environmentalists, and community groups with visionary businesses to regulate the global financial casino that fuels corporate irresponsibility; recharter corporations as nonpersons accountable to real people; limit the manic corporate takeover of schools, health care, and media; fight for employee/community ownership and sustainable growth; and contest all undemocratic forms of corporate power.[264]

Ultimately, we must maintain the keen awareness that all efforts could be in vain if they do not address the extreme inequalities in the distribution of resources and economic power that make possible the corporate practices that harm people.

ACKNOWLEDGMENTS

The authors of the chapter shared not only consternation about corporate excesses but also an inability to narrow the focus of this piece. It was, at one point, well over 100 pages. Alec Irwin and Dorothy Fallows masterfully culled, chopped, and edited it down to its current size. We suspect readers will be as grateful to them as we are. For offering sound critique from their respective disciplines—progressive social theory, occupational health, and business—we thank Sayres Rudy, Chuck Levenstein, and Vipul Vyas. We are grateful to Evan Lyon, John Gershman, Jim Kim, Aaron Shakow, Joel Brenner, and Carole Mitnick for providing insightful suggestions, and to Anna Donald for contributing to an earlier version of the chapter. Appreciation also goes to Shelly Errington and Haun Saussy for their timely and careful editing, and to Ruth Rosenbaum and Richard Grossman for their healthy cynicism, and inspiring lessons. Our most sincere gratitude is reserved for Dave Harrison—ever patient environmentalist, physician, realist, critic, and friend.

Buenos Aires, Argentina. An auditor from Avon examines the records of one of the company's subsidiaries. (photo by Richard Lord)

Dying for Growth, Part II: The Political Influence of National and Transnational Corporations

Joyce V. Millen, Evan Lyon, and Alec Irwin

We would not long tolerate a government without accountability, a dictatorship answerable to no one. But we allow unaccountable corporations to control more of our lives than government has ever attempted.

Ralph W. Estes[1]

In the previous chapter, we elucidated specific ways activities of transnational corporations (TNCs) harm poor and vulnerable people. Having described some of the most injurious of corporate excesses, we now ask why such practices are permitted to continue under the law and in the face of public scrutiny. The basic answer is simple, but its consequences are far-reaching: TNCs can hurt people and the environment with relative impunity because corporate leaders themselves are pivotally involved in shaping the political framework and formulating the rules that define permissible behavior for companies. By exerting continual political muscle, corporations and business groups secure economic dominance and their license to function with little external accountability. This growing corporate influence over political decision-making at multiple levels is a defining feature of today's global political and economic landscape.

By its very nature, political influence is not always easy to detect, document, and analyze. Few of us have access to the settings in which such influence is brought to bear most directly: centers of governance from the state to the national and international level, and the formal and informal networks that proliferate around such centers. Moreover, those working to influence political processes for the benefit of corporations and industry groups tend to value discretion and avoid publicity. As a result, it is often difficult to assess how much political clout individual companies or industry groups actually wield. Lines of causality in specific instances are hard to establish; to assert baldly that a particular corporation's lobbying efforts caused a particular Senate bill to fail is generally to overstate the case, or at the very least to offer a hypothesis extremely difficult to prove.

Yet, while the degree of corporate influence over a specific policy decision may be uncertain, the pervasive effects of TNCs' economic and political power are increasingly apparent today. As national and transnational corporations expand their share of the global economy, they consolidate their powerful position vis-à-vis governments and international institutions, in turn further enhancing opportunities for growth. This cycle of corporate expansion and increased political leverage does not occur by accident. "The history of corporate-government relations has been one of continuing pressure by corporate interests to expand corporate rights and to limit corporate obligations."[2] Corporate leaders work systematically to push these processes forward and to protect their interests within the corridors of government. In recent years, as regulatory mechanisms limiting their activities have been scaled back, and as social forces (such as organized labor) that once counterbalanced corporate demands have lost ground, TNCs and other large companies have attained a degree of power over our political decision-making and legislative processes that a short time ago would have been unimaginable.

Corporations' political involvement and public support are today based on the view that what corporations do is ultimately good for everyone, that large firms give back to society—for example, through job creation and the payment of corporate taxes—at least as much as they take from it. However, this widely shared assumption requires serious questioning. Transnational corporations and other large companies routinely use pledges of job creation to win generous incentive packages from political authorities; yet once the community has paid the bill, the number of promised jobs often fails to materialize. And even as corporate profits mount dramatically, the share of profits companies return to the public in the form of taxes has sharply declined. In other words, corporate leaders often use public resources for their own ends (the enhancement of private profit), while evading the costs involved in maintaining public infrastructure and institutions. This strategy of enlisting political power and public resources in support of private gain has enabled many TNCs and other large companies to greatly increase profits in recent years. But gains for corporate shareholders have often meant increased suffering, exclusion, illness, and premature death for the poor.

In the pages that follow, we look at what motivates corporate leaders to become involved politically, and we examine standard political strategies TNC representatives employ. Then we highlight specific patterns of corporate political involvement, including a disturbing new effort by international business leaders to institutionalize their influence at the United Nations. Our survey can provide no more than a rapid sketch of these complex, often frustratingly opaque phenomena. Yet the data brought together in this and the preceding chapter provide a sense of corporate leaders' determination to influence political processes, and of the extent to which TNCs are involved in local, national, and international institutions of governance. The question of what should be done to change these patterns is one we cannot presume to answer in this context. But it is vital at the very least to recognize that the patterns exist, and that they pose ethical and political challenges we cannot responsibly evade.

MOTIVES AND METHODS OF CORPORATE RULE

Corporate representatives are active in electoral, legislative, and judicial processes in all wealthy, industrialized countries. Transnational corporations also seek a voice in the internal political affairs of the less affluent countries where they set up subsidiaries. And increasingly, TNCs are integrally involved in the deliberations of international political and economic institutions.

In wealthy countries like the United States, corporate managers hire professional lobbyists and lobbying firms to make direct contact with legislators. They collaborate with executives of other TNCs in trade associations so they can lobby collectively, and they give money directly to candidates and to political parties—in the United States, through political action committees (PACs). Despite recent legislative efforts in the United States to limit lobbyists' influence peddling, the largely corporate-backed lobby industry in Washington, D.C., grew by a staggering 37 percent between 1997 and 1999. More than 20,000 lobbyists—roughly 38 for each member of Congress—and their lobbying firms spent $1.42 billion in 1998 to influence legislators. Many of Washington's registered lobbyists are themselves former members of Congress: a revolving door connects the offices of government to the boardrooms of corporations.[3] Furthermore, to reinforce their direct lobbying efforts, lobbyists often also use their advertising expertise to sway public opinion and policy on issues that concern their operations and affect their pursuit of profit.[4]

Corporate leaders influence politicians and political processes for many reasons, but primarily to create favorable trade and investment environments to minimize costs and expand markets. Sometimes their approaches are direct, as when they are lobbying representatives of Congress for handouts such as tax breaks and other corporate subsidies. Since 1990, for example, corporate representatives for the world's largest agricultural commodities firm, Archer Daniels Midland Company (ADM), have exerted consistent political pressure on both Democrats and Republicans in the U.S. Congress, contributing nearly $3 million to campaign funds for both parties. For its efforts, this high-grossing TNC collected more than $3 billion in corporate welfare in the 1990s, by way of an ethanol tax break and other government subsidies. By the close of 1998, ADM, with sales of $13.9 billion in 1997, was receiving more than $1 million in corporate welfare every day.[5]

Transnational corporation lobbyists and their industry trade representatives work proactively to prevent governments from regulating their facilities and operations. They keep abreast of, and try to influence, any legislation that might impede corporate efforts to minimize costs. Labor laws such as the minimum wage, workers' entitlements and benefits, worker health and safety rules, environmental protection, and food and drug safety regulations all fall under this rubric. Even when the public strongly supports proposed legislation, as in efforts to improve air and water quality, corporations can foil a bill's passage simply by outspending those who support it. Between 1989 and 1994, some 267 political action committees for many of the largest and most environmentally destructive American TNCs, such as Chevron Corporation, Dow Chemical, Exxon, and Freeport-McMorRan, contributed over $57 million to political candidates. Their investment paid off; the TNCs were able to limit the authority of the Environmental Protection Agency (EPA) and erode many U.S. environmental laws including the Clean Water Act.[6]

At the international level, TNCs realize their cost-cutting, market-expanding goals by pressing governments, trade organizations, and international institutions such as the World Health Organization (WHO) and the International Labour

Organization (ILO), for increased deregulation of trade, investment, labor markets, and the environment. Corporate representatives "advise" the leaders of these organizations on complex scientific matters and intricate trade deals by providing them with the findings of corporate-sponsored scientific research. This use of corporate expertise to set norms for industrial and trade practice leads to highly questionable situations, as when chemical manufacturers, including DuPont and Hoechst, helped draft safety reports on chlorofluorocarbon refrigerants and the fungicide *benomyl* for the International Program on Chemical Safety of the WHO. Essentially invited to police themselves, TNCs become central players in undermining worker and environmental protection measures.[7]

As in the case of tobacco discussed in the previous chapter, TNCs expand their markets by persuading international trade organizations and their countries' trade representatives to dismantle trade protections and pry open previously closed markets. Transnational corporations also lobby to prevent new legislation on advertising and promotion that might restrict corporations' ability to create an appetite for their products at home and abroad. The issue of intellectual property rights is also central to many TNCs' international agendas. American and European pharmaceutical manufacturers, along with the film and music industries, have played an influential role within the World Trade Organization (WTO) in its efforts to "harmonize" trade-related intellectual property rights—essentially obligating the rest of the world to adopt North American and European-style patent systems. In doing so, they undermine the ability of many poor countries to acquire lifesaving drugs for their citizens through the local manufacture of "generics" that can be made available at low prices.[8]

Sometimes corporations approach politics not primarily to create positive business environments in the long term, but to get immediate handouts of public money and other forms of support, as in the ADM case mentioned previously. While corporate political involvement is complex and multifaceted, this aspect of TNCs' political influence has important implications for the health of the poor. Vast quantities of public resources are channeled from local, state, and national governments to national and transnational corporations every year: money that could have been directed to improvements in water, sanitation, housing, health, and other essential services that crucially affect poor people's (and other people's) health and well-being.

Freedom from regulation and oversight (except in those few cases such as patents, where regulation and enforcement directly benefit powerful corporations); cash handouts and other material incentives; and opportunities to use publicly funded infrastructure for private ends: these are some of the factors which motivate representatives of TNCs and national firms to take an interest in politics. We now examine some of the specific ways corporate political concerns play themselves out at different levels: from the state and local, up to the international.

CORPORATE POLITICS AT THE STATE LEVEL

Today, as the market reigns and corporations are seen as the essential engines of growth, towns, cities, states, and national governments throughout the world compete to lure TNCs. In the United States, states and municipalities vie to bring companies to their areas for the promises of jobs and increased revenue. Both U.S.-based and foreign

TNCs pit states against one another and lobby local or state politicians for the most advantageous subsidy packages, including tax exemptions, property and sales tax reductions, investment credits, grants, training funds, infrastructure improvements, and other incentives. The situation is analogous to what transpires between countries competing to attract foreign investors. In some cases, the subsidies offered to the corporations are reasonable, and both the corporation and the local community benefit. In other instances, especially in poorer areas, the subsidies are so high that little benefit actually accrues to the "winning" state or municipality. When this happens, everyone in the community pays. As economic analyst Greg Leroy explains:

> Mushrooming state and local subsidies have fed the rising inequality of wealth and income in the United States, as consumers, wage-earners, homeowners and small businesses are forced to pay higher taxes to make up for large corporations' deal-making tax dodges. Such subsidies are a root cause of many states' and cities' chronic budget crises, which undermine public education and other services.[9]

In the early 1990s, Alabama gave Mercedes-Benz aid worth $253 million (an estimated $170,000 per job created); Kentucky gave Canadian steelmakers Dofasco, Inc., and Co-Steel, Inc., $140 million in aid for a 400-employee "mini-mill"—$350,000 per job. Yet such sums do not guarantee the jobs or the increased revenue. In the 1980s, for example, Hammond, Indiana, had granted tax abatements of more than $15 million to 16 companies. The companies promised 804 new jobs, but created only 74, at a cost of more than $200,000 per job.[10] A team of journalists investigating corporate welfare and the job-creation claims made by corporations concluded: "Almost without exception, local and state politicians have doled out tens of billions of taxpayer dollars to businesses that are in fact eliminating rather than creating jobs."[11]

As the public has learned more about such deals and their consequences, the subsidies offered to corporations have come under increased public scrutiny. Cities and states are adopting measures to hold corporations accountable; some have passed protective legislation that requires companies to deliver on their promises of job creation or risk having their subsidies taken back.[12] Yet, as cities and states become more skilled at protecting their interests through legal mechanisms, corporations become more aggressive in their efforts to influence legislators sympathetic to their needs.

Far more than those who may oppose their operations—consumer, labor, or environmental groups, for example—corporations possess the resources to monitor and sway policy. In the United States, it is not difficult to find examples of demonstrably sound environmental and health policy proposals and ballot initiatives defeated because they challenged corporate interests. The case of Montana is instructive.

In 1990, 50 Montana physicians worked together to place on the state election ballot a public initiative that, if passed, would have added a 25¢ tax to the price of each pack of cigarettes sold in the state. The physicians hoped to dissuade Montanans from smoking and to provide extra funds to teenage cigarette prevention and maternal and child health programs. The initiative was defeated after nine out-of-state cigarette corporations spent $1.5 million on a media blitz against the measure. In terms of political contributions that year, the nine firms outspent the entire population of Montana. In 1996, the state of Montana placed another initiative on the ballot to prohibit mining corporations from discharging toxic wastewater into state rivers and waterways without first bringing the discharge up to state water standards. The initiative had clear health and environmental benefits and broad public support leading up to the vote. But, in a last-ditch effort to defeat the proposal, the mining industry in Montana spent $3 million on an advertising campaign that effectively convinced the majority of citizens to vote against the initiative. The large transnational mining corporations' advertising blitz negated the exhaustive efforts of a consortium of environmental groups that had spent $300,000 to educate the population about the initiative and its health and environmental concerns.[13]

The efforts and setbacks of Montana's concerned citizens are not isolated or unique. Comparable scenarios play out yearly at local, state, and national levels. Big corporate money in the political arena is, as some have put it, "like a megaphone that amplifies the speech of a few while drowning out the speech of the many."[14] Yet such amplification is legal in the United States as a result of the controversial 1976 Supreme Court decision *Buckley v. Valeo*, which classifies unlimited political spending as a form of free speech.[15]

Within the health sector, Health Maintenance Organizations (HMOs) and hospitals have an enormous stake in policy formulation at the state level. In Massachusetts in 1997, the state's largest HMOs doled out over $500,000 to powerful lobbyists working the corridors of state government. The lobbyists were hired to block or change a House bill intended to improve the quality of HMO health care in the state through a new system of quality monitoring. Part of the bill called for the creation of a new state regulatory agency operating on behalf of HMO consumers; the agency would oversee patients' appeals and issue HMO report cards.[16] The industry attacked the proposal fiercely. Yet, in this case, consumers' and citizens' groups were able to win a limited victory. Despite the industry's strong and well-organized resistance to the imposition of new government oversight, a comprehensive, though watered-down, bill to regulate Massachusetts HMOs eventually passed in the state House and Senate.

CORPORATE OBJECTIVES AT THE FEDERAL LEVEL: BIGGER HANDOUTS, SMALLER TAXES

I see in the near future a crisis approaching that unnerves me and causes me to tremble for the safety of my country....Corporations have been enthroned.... An era of corruption in high places will follow, and the money power of the country will endeavor to prolong its reign by working upon prejudices of the people...until all wealth is aggregated in a few hands...and the Republic is destroyed.

Abraham Lincoln[17]

Government handouts to corporations are not, of course, limited to states and localities. "Corporate welfare" is even more pronounced at the federal level, where political leaders often justify their bounteous giving to corporations as necessary incentives to promote growth in the economy. Such support takes diverse forms: direct grants, corporate tax deductions and loopholes, giveaways of publicly funded research and development contracts to private for-profit companies, and discounted user fees for public resources.[18] The combined worth of these handouts totals more than $100 billion per year.[19]

One might think that as TNCs continue to consolidate and as their profits reach record levels, they would be required to pay more taxes. The contrary is true. In the United States in the 1950s, corporations on average paid 45 percent of their profits in taxes to the federal government. By the mid-1990s, the portion of corporate profits paid in taxes had diminished to an average of only 24 percent.[20] Corporations obtain tax breaks by working the political system to their advantage. In 1993, during the battle over the federal budget, Senator Bill Bradley of New Jersey attacked the "loophole writing" industry in Washington, noting that the insertion of a single sentence into the tax laws can save millions, even billions, of dollars in taxes for particular corporations.[21] Without such loopholes and billion-dollar sentences, corporations would have to pay their share of taxes[22]—providing federal revenue that could be used to combat deadly diseases, to end hunger in the United States, to offer assistance and homes to the homeless, or to provide the 43 million currently uninsured Americans with health insurance.

In some cases, corporations contribute to political campaigns in order to gain advocates on the House and Senate committees charged with overseeing federal agencies, which in turn oversee corporate activities. Either individually or in collaboration with other corporations through trade associations, company lobbyists attempt to influence how agencies such as the EPA, the Department of Health and Human Services (DHHS), the Food and Drug Administration (FDA), and the U.S. Department of Agriculture (USDA) interpret federal statutes and design regulations. During the first half of 1998, well in advance of that year's congressional elections, industry contributed over $136 million to candidates and parties. The pharmaceutical and health products industry alone gave $2.7 million—a sum that exceeds all the combined contributions made by groups explicitly concerned with education, gun rights, gun control, abortion policy (both "for" and "against"), environmental issues, women's issues, and foreign and defense policy.[23]

In addition to making direct campaign contributions, corporations use a wide array of other mechanisms to influence legislators and effect political change. Experts in promoting their goods, modern corporations use their advertising skills in the political arena.[24] To promote favorable policy measures or to rally opposition around unfavorable ones, they take out large ads in newspapers and magazines and run campaigns on radio, television, and the Internet (itself a creation of publicly funded scientific research, now generating vast profits for industry). Corporations cover the media spectrum—from handbills, transit advertisements, and mass e-mail to company-produced films—in defending their causes to their own employees and the wider population.

During the Clintons' attempt to pass health-care reform measures in 1993, the I.B.M. Corporation circulated an internal electronic mail memo to 110,000 of its employees, urging each individual to send a personal message to Congress opposing the proposed health-care package. The message was written by I.B.M.'s vice chairman. Mobil corporation and DuPont acted similarly, "inviting" employees to register their opposition to the health reform measures by contacting Congress. General Mills held meetings to show employees a company-produced video that urged workers to contact Congress to oppose health-care reform measures that would require employers to pay for health coverage.[25]

Corporations increase their power and influence by pooling their resources and efforts through trade associations. Health-related trade associations—those representing hospitals, pharmaceutical companies, HMOs—are particularly powerful. In 1997, the drug and medical device industry successfully influenced Congress to pass legislation overhauling operations at the FDA. The resulting bill now enables pharmaceutical companies to increase sales by promoting second uses of FDA-approved products, even when these secondary applications have not yet been given the agency's "green light." The bill also allows medical device manufacturers to receive official approval for their products from accredited organizations other than the FDA—despite obvious conflict of interest concerns. The drug and medical device industry lobbied extensively for this new legislation and contributed over $2.6 million to federal candidates and parties during the election cycle in which the bill was debated. A year later, still more than a month before the 1998 election, the pharmaceutical and health products industry had already contributed over $8.2 million to candidates and parties.[26] Managed-care companies are also politically aggressive. They spent millions on a successful advertising campaign to thwart efforts in the 105th Congress to improve both patients' access to medical specialists and their ability to sue their health plans.[27]

INFLUENCE IN THE POLITICAL AFFAIRS OF NATIONS

We have already documented ways TNCs exert influence over the national political affairs of sovereign countries. A corporation's power is "naturally strongest if it is dealing with a small, very poor country desperate for industrial development," notes one writer.[28] Usually, TNCs influence the political affairs of poor nations directly. As illustrated in the previous chapter, petrochemical and mining TNCs in Africa and Indonesia further their interests simply by putting influential government and military officials on their corporate payrolls. By these and other means, companies exert leverage within countries by participating in important national economic policy-making committees and making financial contributions to political parties. Some corporate leaders are less subtle: they bribe officials.[29]

Since the early 1980s, TNC leaders have also impacted the affairs of national governments by exerting influence upon and within institutions such as the International Monetary Fund (IMF) and the World Bank. These two international financial institutions have made their lending to indebted countries contingent on countries' adoption of TNC-friendly policies such as corporate tax breaks and subsidies; inexpensive privatization sales; and the lowering of wages through labor-market deregulation. In so doing, the international financial institutions (IFIs) helped facilitate the entrance and increase the power of TNCs in less industrialized countries throughout the world.[30] However, the most flagrant way TNCs influence the political affairs of nations is by recruiting their own home-governments to intervene on corporations' behalf to protect corporate interests on foreign soil. Such intervention has sometimes entailed the use of military force.[31]

TNCs IN INTERNATIONAL POLITICS

Large TNCs today have expanded their exploring, processing, refining, manufacturing, and marketing to most regions of the world. The largest corporations now operate in over 100 countries. Along with their geographical expansion, large corporations have expanded their spheres of influence. Most TNCs no longer influence only the legislative efforts of individual nations. Corporate managers have found that they can more expeditiously realize their cost-cutting, market-expanding goals by also monitoring and exerting their political influence at the international level—within the deliberations of regional trade meetings, in the WTO, the World Bank, the IMF, the Organization for Economic Cooperation and Development (OECD), the Group of Eight (G-8), the United Nations, and other international organizations. Especially since the early 1980s, by increasing their involvement in these international assemblies, TNC leaders and representatives have played a decisive role in shaping the current global economic system. In fact, many analysts characterize the system as one of "corporate-driven globalization."

Corporate Interests and Influence in Trade Agreements

When TNC representatives successfully press international organizations for increased freedoms on the movement of capital, technology, and goods and services, they undermine the efforts of individual governments to regulate TNCs within their borders. Thus, international corporate power limits national governments' ability to protect their citizens. In the current global trade system, which began to take shape at the beginning of the Uruguay Round of the General Agreement on Tariffs and Trade (GATT) in 1986, TNCs successfully lobbied to have a vast array of environmental, health, consumer, and worker-safety standards categorized as non-tariff barriers to trade. Because these quotas and standards ostensibly inhibit trade, they may be considered illegal under the WTO. Any WTO member country may now challenge the laws and regulations of any other country on the grounds that the laws in question impede free trade. Such complaints are addressed by unelected WTO bureaucrats in secret tribunals, and they cannot be appealed. By signing on to the WTO, 134 member nations have effectively agreed to limit their own powers, vis-à-vis the TNCs operating within their country.[32] Ralph Nader, founder of Public Citizen, and Lori Wallach, the director of the group's Global Trade Watch, explain: "The concept of nontariff barriers being illegal gives corporate interests a powerful tool to undermine safety, health, or environmental regulations they do not like." Speaking more generally about the WTO and regional trade agreements, they assert:

> Approval of these agreements has institutionalized a global economic and political situation that places every government in a virtual hostage situation, at the mercy of a global financial and commercial system run by empowered corporations. This new

system is not designed to promote the health and well-being of human beings but to enhance the power of the world's largest corporations and financial institutions.[33]

Trade liberalization is the primary goal of most current regional trade agreements, such as the North American Free Trade Agreement (NAFTA). When trade is liberalized between countries of unequal size and wealth, however, the benefits of liberalization accrue largely to the TNCs of the wealthier trading partner, sometimes at the expense of poor communities in both countries.[34] Efforts to address this extensively documented problem currently occupy the agendas of many human rights, economic justice, and environmental groups, whose members tend to witness firsthand the effects of growing trade liberalization on local communities, industry, and environment. These groups and a growing number of national-level political leaders affirm that "the benefits of trade must be widely shared by the majority of the common working people in every participating society, not just benefit the business and financial interests of an elite few."[35] To render trade fair in this way would require *increasing* social, labor, and environmental protections, not reducing them. But in regional trade negotiations, social concerns and the problems that are inherent in trade between vastly unequal partners are considered peripheral issues, if they are addressed at all. This results in part from the identity and loyalties of those officially asked to participate in trade talks. While grassroots nongovernmental organizations (NGOs), consumer groups, labor, and representatives of the communities most impacted by the agreements are rarely invited to participate in such negotiations, corporate representatives are often integrally and officially involved at virtually every stage.

Through the trade advisory committees previously described, as well as through powerful trade groups, lobbying firms, and business coalitions, corporate leaders have had significant influence over debates on U.S. trade relations with China and in the planning of trade agreements such as NAFTA. The Boeing Corporation, now the United States' second largest arms contractor and largest arms exporter, with annual sales of $50 billion, retains seven lobby organizations and an entire army of *influence peddlers* to advocate for open commercial relations with China. China is a primary purchaser of Boeing's arms products, and accounts for 10 percent of the company's business. The country also offers Boeing a cheap labor pool from which the company engages increasing numbers of Chinese workers to manufacture its products—workers employed for a pittance, and often under the aegis of the People's Liberation Army. For Boeing to retain its attractive commercial ventures and labor advantages with China, it has had to become a dominant force in Sino-American trade policy. The company's legions of lobbyists press legislators and the office of the U.S. Trade Representatives to scale back pertinent trade barriers with China and resist efforts to link China's "most favored nation" trade status with human rights.[36]

The largest American business coalition, U.S. Business Roundtable, was conspicuously involved in official policy debates on NAFTA: "All but four (of 200) Roundtable members enjoyed privileged access to the NAFTA negotiation process through representation on advisory committees to the U.S. trade representative."[37] One of the aims of the pro-NAFTA Business Roundtable was to convince the negotiators and the public that the treaty would raise environmental and labor standards in the participating countries. Ironically, many of the Roundtable corporations most active in NAFTA negotiations were known for their environmental and labor abuses. Several had produced products in Mexico that were banned in the United States, or exported such products to the Mexican market. Others had been cited for violating workers' rights in Mexico and for failing to comply with worker safety standards.[38] As detailed in Chapter Eleven, NAFTA has facilitated the continuation of such practices. Yet despite reports revealing deleterious social, health, and environmental consequences for vulnerable populations during the first half decade of NAFTA, U.S.-based TNCs are pressing the U.S. government to expand NAFTA to all of the Americas and to create a similar trade agreement with African governments. The latter proposal has been labeled by some of its critics, "NAFTA for Africa."

New U.S.-Africa Trade Policy: In Whose Interest?

President Clinton's visit to five African countries in March 1998 was the most extensive visit by a U.S. president to the continent. One of the main goals of the tour was to begin to formulate an economic policy with the only region of the world with which the U.S. government has no official trade policy. The conviction Clinton brought to Africa, reflected in the administration's new Africa policy, was that development was to be best realized through market-led economic growth; through trade and investment liberalization; and through integration of African economies into the global economy.[39] In other words, the U.S. government was (and as of this writing, still is) recommending that Africa—the world's poorest continent, one still struggling to overcome legacies of slavery, colonialism, and enormous resource expropriation—should embark upon a path of development likely to undermine local industrial development and render nascent African economies even more vulnerable to the vagaries of the international economy.[40] The policies defining the path to development the Clinton administration advocates for Africa parallel the agenda the IMF and World Bank have been pursuing on the continent for two decades. Not coincidentally, the administration's recommendations also mirror the interests of large American corporations, impatient for unregulated business and investment opportunities in resource-rich areas of the African continent.

The proposed "Africa Growth and Opportunity Act," or H.R. 434, written in the aftermath of President Clinton's Africa visit, is being extolled as a means to assist the poor continent and achieve mutually beneficial economic aims for both the United States and African nations. Upon closer examination, however, less humanitarian motives become apparent. Rather, it seems that U.S. business and political leaders are more concerned that American TNCs might be losing out to European companies in the race to benefit from Africa's riches. In terms of foreign direct investment on the continent, European TNCs are already more than five times as active as American corporations. European investment is also considerably more diverse. Whereas U.S. firms are narrowly concentrated in only a few industrial sectors, European, Canadian, and Australian businesses are invested in everything from finance and insurance to food, beverages, tobacco, rubber, petrochemicals, mining, and other natural resource extraction.[41] American commerce officials attribute their inferior position in this race to Europe's strategic use of old colonial ties. In a U.S. Commerce Department policy paper, officials lament: "foreign governments continue to use their ties with African countries to maintain influence and win business."[42]

Meanwhile the continent is vulnerable to a new round of resource and human exploitation. With two decades of neoliberal, export-led growth and development strategy behind them, most African economies today are relatively open to foreign investors. Also, despite 20 years of IMF- and World Bank-designed structural adjustment programs to assist African governments in repaying their debts, most African governments continue to be heavily burdened by external debt and in need of the foreign currency TNCs promise. As part of structural adjustment programs, many African governments are in the process of privatizing the state sector and selling off utilities, water systems, and telecommunications to the highest bidders. These privatizations offer, according to the deputy U.S. trade representative, "very attractive opportunities for American and other large telecommunications companies."[43] Moreover, political changes such as the death of the president of the former Zaire have opened up lucrative opportunities in regions of Africa where sizable proportions of the continent's known mineral reserves are concentrated.

After two decades of austerity measures and government cutbacks, most sub-Saharan Africans are worse off. Annual economic production per person in Africa has declined in the past 20 years from an average of $752 per capita in 1980 to an average of $500 per capita in 1999.[44] For nations facing appalling rates of poverty and unemployment, TNC promises of new jobs and technology transfer are hard to dismiss. However, despite optimistic official predictions of benefits for ordinary Africans, the timing and content of the currently proposed U.S. trade agreement with Africa have led skeptics to ask in whose interest the bill was actually drafted.

American-based TNCs stand to profit a great deal from the trade arrangement. This is why passage of the proposed trade act is being pushed by a coalition of corporate heavy hitters, comprised of U.S.-based oil companies and other TNCs. Among the coalition's active members are Texaco, Mobil, Amoco, Caterpillar, Occidental Petroleum, Enron, General Electric, Chevron, and Kmart.[45] One of the primary goals of the trade act is to ensure greater access to the African market for these and other American businesses. The proposed act contains provisions to promote U.S. private investment on the continent and to establish U.S.-Africa free trade areas.[46]

Though African business and political elites stand to benefit from the proposed trade bill, African industry, workers, and vulnerable populations are likely to lose far more than they will gain. According to the Washington Office on Africa, provisions in the trade policy would "obstruct equitable development by requiring countries to adopt market-oriented policy changes analogous to those imposed under the devastating structural adjustment programs of the World Bank and IMF: government spending cuts, reduced corporate taxes, wholesale privatization, removal of trade barriers, and diminished protection for national industries."[47] The crushing social consequences of several of these policies have been widely documented, and even the World Bank now admits that this strategy has failed average Africans and exacerbated poverty in many areas of the continent.[48]

Recognizing the likely social consequences of the proposed trade bill, a number of organizations, including African civil society groups, scholars, and unions, have joined forces to challenge it. Most groups opposing H.R. 434 concede that a rapid influx of foreign investment into Africa could be good for African economies in the short term. But they also maintain that the bill seeks to advance U.S. corporate interests at the expense of the long-term development goals of African people. Similarly, opponents recognize that many of the terms of the proposed act, and the principles of trade liberalization in general, may be helpful for advancing business competition among advanced capitalist countries. Yet such terms are not appropriate between wealthy countries like the United States on the one hand and poor regions in vastly different stages of development on the other. In fact, according to a critic reporting from Ghana, several measures of the proposed trade policy will "take away from African countries the very mechanisms available to them to develop strategies which ensure that foreign investment does not undermine but rather helps the development of local industrial and general economic capacity."[49] The current executive director of the Washington Office on Africa, Leon Spencer, explains in an open letter to U.S. members of Congress and the Clinton administration that nascent African nations must maintain their sovereignty and ability to chart their own development course. He writes:

> An African nation, faced with extremely high poverty levels, with stunning unemployment rates, with limited health and other social services, and with an overwhelmingly young population without access to extended education, must discern for itself how "freely" the marketplace should operate in light of the demands of a legitimate and pressing social agenda that that nation faces.[50]

As the claims of its humanitarian goals are debunked and the corporate-designed and -promoted nature of H.R. 434 becomes public knowledge, increasing numbers of American and African economists, trade specialists, development workers, scholars, politicians, and social justice advocates have come to denounce the proposal. This mounting dissatisfaction has led members of the Congressional Black Caucus and Democratic leaders to draft an alternative U.S.-Africa trade bill. In a press release introducing the HOPE (Human Rights, Opportunity, Partnership, and Empowerment) for Africa bill, Congressman Jesse Jackson Jr. stressed: "The policies regarding Africa that the Congress sets now will deeply affect the economic future of the continent and, thus, the future of the African people for decades to come."[51] In the alternative bill, the United States still seeks to increase trade and investment with Africa. But this trade would be promoted within a framework of substantial debt forgiveness and increasing rather than diminishing foreign assistance to the continent. The backers of this alternative bill claim that trade with Africa will only begin to meet the social needs of Africa's people when it accomplishes these other urgent tasks and promotes the rights of African nations to regulate corporate excesses and to author trade and investment rules for the benefit of their people.

The Influence of TNCs at the United Nations

A striking development that has the potential to substantially strengthen the influence of TNCs at the international level is the new "partnering" between the business community and the United Nations. In the recent past, as late as 1993, TNCs and the United Nations had an antagonistic relationship. This was in part due to the existence of the now-defunct U.N. Centre on Transnational Corporations, which was charged with developing a worldwide TNC "Code of Conduct." By 1998, however, the climate between business and the United Nations had changed so radically that the U.N. secretary-general and other U.N. officials had begun to meet regularly with business leaders in gatherings sponsored by the International Chamber of Commerce (ICC), the World Business Council on Sustainable Development, and other international business organizations.

In June 1997, the chief executive officers of ten TNCs met with U.N. leaders and several senior government officials to discuss avenues for a formalization of corporate involvement in the affairs of the United Nations. The luncheon took place at the United Nations in New York City and was co-hosted by the president of the U.N. General Assembly and the executive director of the World Business Council on Sustainable Development. Two scholars and two representatives from NGOs were also invited to attend. David Korten, formerly a business school professor, was one of the academics on the panel. Reflecting on the idea of using public resources—through the United Nations—to advance unrestrained global corporate expansion, Korten wrote in a letter about the meeting: "The defining structure of fascist regimes is a corporate dominated alliance between big business and big government to support the expansion of corporate empires."[52] While Korten's reference to fascism may appear misplaced, the emerging patterns that are crystalized in the *rapprochement* of U.N. leadership and corporate powerholders suggest, at the very least, that the grounds for Korten's concern must be examined carefully.

Even the United Nations Development Programme (UNDP), the branch of the United Nations charged with addressing inequality and serving the world's poor, is now being courted by global business leaders. A proposed joint venture between the UNDP and TNCs, called the "Global Sustainable Development Facility," would give corporations unprecedented access to the UNDP's global network and the high-level government representatives with whom the UNDP collaborates. In response to this plan, NGOs from around the world drafted a letter to both the UNDP administrator and the U.N. secretary-general, calling for the UNDP to "halt its Global Sustainable Development Facility and in so doing preserve the credibility of its mission to serve the world's poor."[53]

The International Chamber of Commerce, which counts among its members such corporate giants as General Motors, Coca-Cola, Rio Tinto Zinc, Mitsubishi, Shell, Bayer, and Nestlé, has for several years lobbied for global economic deregulation within the WTO, the G-8, and the OECD. The commission is now attempting to ally itself with the United Nations. In the aftermath of a meeting sponsored by the ICC in February 1998, the ICC and U.N. Secretary-General Kofi Annan issued a joint statement to the press affirming that "broad political and economic changes have opened up new opportunities for dialogue and cooperation between the United Nations and the private sector."[54] The two groups pledged to "forge a close global partnership to secure greater business input into the world's economic decision-making and boost the private sector in the least developed countries."[55] One of the projects the ICC and the U.N. Conference for Trade and Development (UNCTAD) agreed to undertake was a jointly produced series of business investment guides to the world's poorest 48 countries.

The president of the ICC, Helmut Maucher, has explained what motivates him to organize international meetings between the United Nations and the world's largest TNCs. He seeks to "bring together the heads of international companies and the leaders of international organizations so that business experiences and expertise is channeled into the decision-making process for the global economy."[56] In a guest column for the *Financial Times*, Maucher laid out his plan for the ICC to work within the WTO and the United Nations to push for "a framework of global rules."[57] In the joint statement issued by the ICC and the U.N. secretary-general, the ICC reveals its agenda: "Business has a strong interest in multilateral cooperation, including standard-setting through the United Nations and other intergovernmental institutions and international conventions on the environment and other global and transborder issues."[58]

Some political analysts speculate that the United Nations and its branches are seeking political and economic support from corporations because the organization faces financial difficulties in light of the U.S. government's refusal to pay the $1.6 billion it owes the United Nations. John Cavanagh of the Institute for Policy Studies suggests that the U.N.'s fiscal constraints—stemming substantially from the unpaid American bill—push agencies such as the UNDP to "serve the short-term interests of corporate shareholders rather than foster the long-term goals of sustainable human development."[59] Others question the logic of encouraging TNCs—some of which have committed significant human rights, labor, or environmental abuses—to play a primary role in standard setting and in defining the rules of international development and business. Ward Morehouse of the Council on International and Public Affairs suggests, rather, that "the United Nations should be *monitoring* the human rights and environmental impacts of corporations in developing and industrialized nations, not granting special favors."[60]

One can reasonably assume that the collaboration between the United Nations and business is being driven by corporate leaders, some of whom have expressed concern at the close association between the United Nations and increasingly outspoken labor, human rights, and environmental groups. Many NGOs from around the world are, in fact, organizing to place limits on the political powers of corporations.[61] A growing number of groups are working within national and international political frameworks to design new and legally binding systems to hold TNCs accountable for their harmful impact on the environment and on the communities where they operate. The efforts of these organizations threaten the corporate world.[62] Speaking in an interview about the sway of environmental and human rights groups within the United Nations, ICC President Maucher warned: "We have to be careful that they do not get too much influence."[63] In an international meeting, the Geneva Business Dialogue, organized by the ICC, Maucher actively attempted to de-legitimate the scientific claims of environmental groups, urging U.N. and WTO representatives, national leaders, and his own business colleagues to refuse such groups' "emotional and irrational arguments."

Moreover, in his concluding remarks to the Geneva Business Dialogue, Maucher recommended to his colleagues that: "Broader efforts should now follow in order to foster rules-based freedom for business." Rules-based freedom for business meant, according to Maucher, that governments should refrain from regulation where possible, but also set and strictly implement rules that help enhance the performance of TNCs.[64] On this view, a truly rules-based freedom for corporations would require universal adoption of policies such as the controversial Multilateral Agreement on Investment (MAI), or what Maucher describes as "a truly global framework of rules for cross-border investment."[65] See Box 9.1.

Box 9.1: Multilateral Agreement on Investment

The Multilateral Agreement on Investment (MAI) could become the corporate world's crowning political achievement. This controversial agreement to further loosen foreign investment and regulatory restrictions on TNCs has been under consideration by the WTO and the OECD since 1995. If adopted, the MAI would grant TNCs expanded "investor rights," nullifying the rules governments have established to regulate foreign businesses investing in their countries. The agreement would grant TNCs greater leverage to buy land, currency, natural resources, telecommunications, and other services. It would prevent governments from placing restrictions on the movement of capital, including repatriation of profits, and would ban any uncompensated expropriation of actual or potential assets. Moreover, the MAI would require "national treatment" for all member countries, so that foreign investors would be given the same privileges as domestic investors. To guarantee the agreement's enforcement, TNCs would have the right to sue governments directly and seek compensation in the event that a local law violates investor rights established by the MAI.[66] It is, in short, a generous set of privileges—a "Bill of Rights" for foreign investors.

The Multilateral Agreement on Investment has significant implications for the protection of health and human rights in the areas of international labor standards, environmental protection, health and safety regulation, the right to development, and other economic and social rights. By further undermining national sovereignty and democratic control over national policy, the agreement could stifle government efforts to counterbalance many of the harmful consequences of two decades of neoliberal economics. In essence, the MAI represents a radical transfer of power from states to TNCs.

This is not a proposal designed by and for governments; it has been corporate-designed and corporate-led from its inception. Some have come to call the MAI the "final pillar in the architecture of corporate economic globalization."[67] Among the groups directly involved in MAI negotiations have been the influential Business Roundtable, a group of CEOs from many of the largest U.S. corporations; the International Chamber of Commerce; the United States Council for International Business; the Office of the U.S. Trade Representative; and the Business and Industry Advisory Council of the OECD.

The potential benefits of the MAI to the many corporations involved in the negotiations—including Philip Morris, Mobil Oil, and RJR Nabisco—are tremendous. Meanwhile, the potentially harmful effects on the environment and on health in poor communities are also staggering. The MAI could undermine efforts to control the international expansion of transnational tobacco corporations. Moreover, the MAI would grant TNCs the right to challenge national health regulations and even sue governments directly for loss of future potential profits related to such regulations.[68]

The Multilateral Agreement on Investment would also weaken living wage laws, local incentive contracts, and other local- and state-level efforts to improve standards of living. National environmental laws and standards and even multilateral agreements on environmental protection and sustainability could be challenged. International health conventions and declarations, such as the Alma Ata Declaration, the World Health Assembly Declaration on Health for All, the Convention on the Rights of the Child, and the International Labour Code, could all be rendered ineffectual. Unlike NAFTA and the draft MAI, these health and labor conventions and agreements contain no enforcement measures: investors can easily override them.

Although the first three years of MAI negotiations were held behind closed doors, once the "veil of secrecy" around the proposal was lifted in 1998, significant international pressure—largely from Canada, France, and New Zealand—stymied the momentum of the proposal. What the agreement intends is so extreme, one observer noted, "it requires a high level of ignorance to succeed."[69] Once the public became aware of it, several major U.S. cities and five Canadian provinces declared themselves MAI-free zones. In France, tens of thousands of protesters forced the government to retreat from negotiations.[70] With mounting international opposition, the proposal lost its home in the OECD in December 1998. As of this writing, the MAI, with the urging of the European Union and Japan, is looking longingly to return to its place of origin in the WTO. Whatever its fate, one thing is clear. In the face of the international outcry against it, the proposal is going undercover. The core principles and fine elements of the MAI model are showing up in various international institutions, including the IMF and the WTO, and in regional trade agreements, such as the Free Trade Agreement for the Americas and the newly proposed TransAtlantic Free Trade Agreement. The same principles have also filtered into the Asian Pacific Economic Organization (APEC) meetings and elements of the Clinton administration's proposed Africa trade bill.

TNC POLITICAL INFLUENCE
AND THE HEALTH OF THE POOR:
POSSIBILITIES FOR CHANGE?

Having made the case that TNCs exert significant and growing influence on national and international political processes, we conclude by returning to how this influence affects the health of poor people. The political issue differs from concerns about the health and safety of workers in TNC manufacturing plants, and about health problems in communities in the vicinity of TNC facilities. The political influence of TNCs has a less direct, yet perhaps even more pervasive, effect on health. This influence can touch virtually all aspects of poor peoples' lives: what they eat, the conditions of the land they live on, what crops they can cultivate, the air they breathe, and the water they drink.

Consider the concrete example of food. The World Trade Organization's global health and safety standards are set by the Codex Alimentarius Commission, or Codex, an intergovernmental body run jointly by the WHO and the Food and Agriculture Organization (FAO) of the United Nations. Codex is charged with setting international standards on a wide variety of products that affect health, such as pesticide residues, additives, veterinary drug residues, and labeling. The organization is highly influenced by TNCs, which tend to promote the least rigorous standards of protection. For example, Codex safety levels for at least eight widely used pesticides were up to 25 times less strict than current U.S. standards.[71] Meanwhile, 140 of the world's largest transnational food and agrochemical companies participated in Codex meetings between 1989 and 1991. Of the 2,587 individual participants in attendance, only 26 came from public-interest groups, while 37 came from a single transnational food company—Nestlé.[72]

Transnational corporations have actively participated in defining the current economic philosophy that guides international relations and shapes government policy in most of the world's nations. This corporate-led, market-determined philosophy gives primacy to the needs of corporations as the entities best fueling economic growth, and it forces the state to retreat so that business can be free from government intervention. As local, state, national, and global governments put this philosophy into practice throughout the 1980s and 1990s, corporations were accorded business freedoms and political powers they had not enjoyed since the colonial era. During this period, corporations have been empowered to disregard the sovereignty of nations; to undermine the efforts of governments to protect their citizens; and to compromise the efforts of communities to retain their land and cultural heritage.[73] At the same time, TNCs garner public favors: they are given tax breaks and receive outright billions of dollars of public money annually. Although the public monies funneled to TNCs are intended to provide "business incentives," many of the TNCs receiving these resources require no special incentives to do business: they are already among the most financially successful corporations in the world! Often, the public monies have been withdrawn from efforts to improve the environmental, health, economic, and social conditions of poor and vulnerable communities, and redirected to the enhancement of corporate wealth.

To be fair, not all TNC executives eschew efforts to render corporations more socially and environmentally responsible. In fact, in the latter part of the 1990s corporations from diverse sectors began a publicized effort to heed the concerns of their *stakeholders*—individuals affected by a company's operation and who are not shareholders. In the wake of public attention focused on several of the companies highlighted in our chapters, some TNCs have improved their environmental records, and others have amended labor practices and increased wages. Executives of TNCs have also begun to take part in a dialogue about creating a "triple bottom line," or a merging of financial with social and environmental objectives. In March 1999, senior executives from leading TNCs such as I.B.M., British Telecom, Levi Strauss, and Kodak met in London to share their concerns for businesses' and societies' future. In the meeting, they examined the potential for business to take part in addressing world poverty, mounting inequality, and environmental concerns. Via this gathering and other similar meetings, many ideas have been put on the table, among them: pressing corporate executives to be more accountable to company stakeholders; incorporating quantified assessments of social and environmental performance into corporate annual reports; and enforcing ethical trading practices.

Despite the public image concerns manifest in TNCs' efforts to clean up their practices (poor public image directly impacts profits), optimists welcome what appears to be a modest sea change toward increased social contributions from the corporate world. Pessimists, on the other hand, dismiss corporate statements about social responsibility as hollow rhetoric and doubt corporations' efforts will yield substantive improvements for those most in need. As one author asks, "Is it progress if cannibals start eating their victims with cutlery instead of using their hands, if oil companies start worrying about the environment while still pumping billions of gallons of carbon dioxide into the air?"[74]

Corporations have succeeded in creating an economic and cultural landscape in which their abusive, exploitative practices appear to many as simultaneously deplorable, banal, inevitable. This sense of inevitability is the first barrier to overcome in seeking change, or even in seeking to ask whether change is genuinely desirable. If current patterns of corporate behavior are to be challenged, what would appear to be necessary, as authors like Korten have argued, is a fundamental critique of the values of a consumption-driven society, accompanied by intelligent, coordinated efforts to limit corporate power legally and politically.[75] People from "less developed" nations often observe that corruption comes in many forms. Whereas European and U.S. leaders frequently ascribe the problems plaguing poor countries to the "endemic corruption" of government officials, many Third World activists and intellectuals trace a considerable portion of their countries' difficulties to the materially and morally corrupting power of wealthy nations and corporations driven by relentless greed. The destructive effects of corporate behavior must of course be documented on a case-by-case basis,[76] and we have attempted such documentation in this and the preceding chapter. Yet even as we wait for more evidence to come in, we can affirm broadly that TNCs have currently succeeded in institutionalizing a particular brand of corporate influence peddling within national and international bodies. The aggressive efforts of TNCs to influence decisions in national legal systems and foreign policy regimes, U.N. programs, and the WTO (to name only a few examples) are now viewed as routine. However, destructive, immoral routines *can* be broken. Reversing this form of corruption through a moratorium on aggressive corporate lobbying within national and international bodies would constitute a significant step toward enabling countries and international organizations to design legal, regulatory, financial, and political structures that genuinely and effectively protect the poor.

Bhopal, India. Survivors' art show on December 3, 1994, commemorating the tenth anniversary of the Bhopal disaster. (photo by Gary Cohen)

CHAPTER TEN

Tragedy Without End: The 1984 Bhopal Gas Disaster

Timothy H. Holtz

How the new Prime Minister deals with the gas disaster in Bhopal will tell much about India's prospects for future development. Calcutta-style scenes of human deprivation can be replaced as fast as the country imports the benefits of the West's industrial revolution and market economics. It's also true that economic progress is not without its risks. The saving grace is that the benefits outweigh the costs. As a Georgia Tech doctor told the *New York Times*, 'Of those killed, half would not have been alive today if it weren't for that plant and the modern health standards made possible by the wide use of pesticides.' We don't need cost-benefit analysis to know the truth of that.

Editorial, *Wall Street Journal*, December 10, 1984

INTRODUCTION

J ust after midnight on December 3rd, 1984, 40 tons of poisonous substances leaked from the Union Carbide pesticide plant in Bhopal, central India. The resulting cloud exposed half a million people to multiple toxic liquids and gases and awakened the community of Bhopal to an industrial horror never before seen on the planet. Many never woke to the foul odor; they died in their houses from a penetrating gas that hung over the city for hours. In the days immediately following, approximately 180,000 outpatients and 11,000 inpatients sought help in a crowded, understaffed, unprepared 1,000-bed hospital.[1] Acute respiratory distress syndrome (ARDS) killed several thousand in the first few days after the disaster; many died before they were able to reach medical assistance. Others suffered from gastrointestinal symptoms (nausea, vomiting, abdominal pain), neurologic problems (altered consciousness and coma), and gas effects on the reproductive system (spontaneous abortions). The precise number of dead and injured remains controversial, and is still unknown to this day. The Indian government claims that 1,754 died and 200,000 were injured. Local eyewitness accounts, hospital figures, and voluntary agency calculations estimate that almost 10,000 died and 300,000 were injured.[2]

The accident drew international media attention for several weeks. *Time* and *Newsweek* featured cover stories replete with pictures of dead children and sickened adults, yet the unfolding stories from Bhopal quickly dissipated from public discourse. The corporate press was lenient on Union Carbide, and quite sanguine about the death toll one week after the largest industrial disaster in modern history. In the financial community, Wall Street quickly chalked up the event as an inevitable cost of development. Accrued benefits to corporate industry clearly outweighed the costs of the disaster; ongoing stories of human suffering were therefore not worth the page copy.

For those who were maimed, or who lost family members to Union Carbide, a different cost-benefit analysis must be used. The story of Bano Bi reflects the ongoing tragedy that continues to unfold in Bhopal. It is a tragedy that still haunts this large, central Indian industrial city, and it serves as a metaphor for the human costs of the transnationalization of capital and development in a highly unequal world.

The night the gas leaked, I was sewing clothes sitting next to the door. The children's father came in and asked me, 'What are you burning that makes me choke?' The children sleeping inside began to cough. Outside we started coughing even more violently and became breathless. There were people shouting, 'Run, run, run for your lives.'

We left our door open and began to run. We reached the Bharat Talkies crossing where my husband jumped into a truck full of people going to Raisen, and I jumped into one going towards Obaidullahganj. It was early morning when we reached there. As we got down, there were people asking us to get medicines put on our eyes and to get injections.

They said the people who [were] seriously ill had to be taken to the hospital. I was kept inside for a long time and the children were getting worried. Then Bhairon Singh, a Hindu who used to work with my husband, went in and found me among the piles of the dead. He put me on a bench and ran around to get me oxygen. The doctors would put the oxygen mask on me for two minutes and then pass it on to someone else who was in as much agony as I was.

Bhairon Singh hired a taxi to take me back to Bhopal. My husband also had come back by then. He was in a terrible condition. His body would get stiff and he had difficulty breathing. We took him to a hospital. When the doctors saw me, they said, 'Why don't you get admitted yourself, you are in such a bad state.' I told them that I was all right. I was so absorbed with the suffering of my children and my husband that I wasn't aware of my own condition. But the doctors got me admitted and since there were no empty beds, I shared the same bed with my husband. We were in that hospital for one and a half months.

My husband used to carry sacks of grain at the warehouse, and load and unload railway wagons. After the gas, he could not do any work. His friends gave him five or ten rupees and we survived on that. He used to be in the Nehru Hospital most of the time. He remained in that condition after the gas disaster forever. He was later admitted to the special MIC [methyl isocyanate] ward and never came back. He died there.

Before he died, my husband had severe breathing problems and he used to get into bouts of coughing. When he became weak, he had fever all the time. He was always treated for gas-related problems. He was never treated for tuberculosis. And yet, in his post-mortem report, they mentioned that he died due to tuberculosis. He was medically examined for *compensation but they never told us in which category he was put. And now they tell me that his death was not due to gas exposure, that I cannot get the relief of 100,000 rupees (approximately $3,000) which is given to the relatives of the dead.[3]*

The 1984 gas leak in Bhopal was the largest accident in the history of industrialization around the globe. Thousands of people perished from exposure to toxic chemicals as a result of a deadly series of events that could have been prevented. Union Carbide failed to meet even minimal standards of business safety and accountability, instead emphasizing economic over social performance criteria in the course of running their Bhopal facility. In the aftermath of the immense tragedy that enveloped the city of Bhopal, Union Carbide launched a public relations campaign to downplay the medical impacts of the leak; blame the incident on others; and minimize the impact on themselves. Every step of the way, the corporation delayed interim relief payments, dragged its feet in court, and used legal maneuvers to avoid full responsibility for the effects of the gas leak on the survivors. Union Carbide effectively developed this strategy of containment to portray itself as victim rather than victimizer, and to blame the plight of the survivors on their poverty and environment, rather than on the corporation.

Fifteen years after the accident, Union Carbide appears to have succeeded on the public relations front. Though meager compensation *is* finally being paid, suffering among the survivors in Bhopal continues to this day. In the wake of corporate negligence that took thousands of lives, not one person has been sentenced for criminal wrongdoing. In what has become a watershed event in the history of corporate industrial hazards, a transnational chemical corporation and the government of a poor country have converted an emblem of foreign, investment-driven development into a mass injustice against the poor. How did such a tragedy occur? Given poor countries' increasing reliance on direct foreign investment during a time of growing inequalities between wealthy and poor people and nations, is it likely that such disasters will remain completely exceptional—or are they likely to become more and more frequent?

AN ACCIDENT WAITING TO HAPPEN

The story begins in the 1960s. Union Carbide India Limited (UCIL), 50.9 percent owned by the U.S.-based Union Carbide and Carbon Corporation (UCC), diversified its operations to produce pesticides for the Indian government's national plan for agricultural self-reliance and crop export. This strategy, modeled on the "green revolution" of other Third World countries, relied heavily on "monocropping," mechanization, and heavy fertilizer and pesticide use. In 1979, a new plant to produce methyl isocyanate (MIC), used as the precursor in the production of the pesticide Sevin, was built near the center of Bhopal, a large industrial city in the center of India. The plant was constructed under an agreement between the central Indian government and UCC, against the wishes of the local officials and UCIL.[4] In the end, the corporate management from the United States prevailed, locating the plant near an existing pesticide facility adjacent to a populated section of Bhopal. This area was selected over a designated, unpopulated, hazardous industrial site outside of town because it was the less expensive of the two options.

Strikingly, there did not exist then, nor are there even now, enforceable international standards concerning construction and safety in hazardous industries.[5] What is clear is that the standards used for the Bhopal plant and its sister MIC facility in Institute, West Virginia, were remarkably different.[6] Problems at the Bhopal plant included: poor and inadequate facility design; substandard construction materials; dangerous and irresponsible operating procedures; neglect of internal safety audit recommendations; and failure to communicate and develop adequate emergency procedures with local authorities and the surrounding community in case of a major disaster. Most of the residents of Bhopal were unaware of what was happening behind company walls; the plant was shrouded in secrecy.

Senior UCC management knew about a majority of the problems at the Bhopal plant, and gave approval for much of the substandard construction from the beginning.[7] Their goal was to develop an export market for MIC in Asia. To do this cheaply, they cut corners in plant development and construction, neglecting to use the safer "closed-loop" system that could have prevented the disaster. (A closed-loop system would not have allowed excess gases to escape into the atmosphere.) The most egregious structural error was the storage of MIC in enormous 15,000-gallon tanks, when smaller containers would have been safer. Although the operations manual stated that the tanks were to be filled to no more than 50 percent of capacity, at the time of the accident they were filled significantly beyond that level, to 75-87 percent capacity. In addition, the tanks were unrefrigerated (the cooling system had been disconnected because the freon for it was being used elsewhere), increasing the chances that the MIC thusly stored at ambient temperature would react with water and the outside air.

Other ongoing operational problems known to senior UCC management in the United States included an inoperative flare tower—with no backup system to take its place—and a faulty chemical vent gas scrubber. (At the height of the gas leak, MIC was flowing through the scrubber at more than two hundred times capacity; the flare tower served to burn off excess MIC gas if the tank pressure ever rose too high.) These flaws came to light in India only *after* the explosion, but they were known to the higher management of UCC long before. An internal audit team from the sister West Virginia Sevin plant warned UCC about these deficiencies, and the possibility of a runaway reaction involving the large MIC storage tanks, just three months before the Bhopal tragedy. Remarkably, the report was never sent to India.[8]

Moreover, worker safety in plant operation was severely substandard at the Bhopal plant from the beginning. Six major accidents occurred there between 1978 and 1982, causing multiple injuries and one death.[9] Additionally, when the pesticide market faltered in the early 1980s, UCC headquarters in Connecticut told their Asian subsidiaries to cut costs in order to justify continued production of Sevin and other pesticides.[10] Safety was the casualty. Subsidiary managers cut the work crew for the MIC unit *and* the maintenance crew in half, shortened safety training for officials, and eliminated the night maintenance supervisor shift. With such cutbacks, a major accident was all but inevitable.

A LEAK BEYOND IMAGINATION

During the night of December 2-3, 1984, workmen began washing out the lines that led to one of the 15,000-gallon MIC tanks. Through an unsafe extra "jumper line" (which connects the tanks) installed that year after authorization from UCC, water entered one overfilled MIC tank, triggering a heat-generating reaction involving 40 tons of MIC. Within hours, after an uncontrollable build-up, the high-pressure MIC liquid and gas swept past relief valves and safety systems, and burst into the night air over Bhopal. Though the work crews escaped at the sound of an internal alarm, the public siren did not sound long enough to wake any residents.[11] Without warning, the toxic cloud descended as a white mist over the sleeping city.

The residents of the impoverished shantytowns near the plant were the first to feel the burning sensations in their eyes and lungs and smell what they described as the acrid fetor of burnt chili peppers. It was among these people, the poorest of Bhopal, that the exposure was greatest and the deaths most extensive.[12] Thousands fled in all directions in darkness as the cloud spread over a 25-square-mile area. Half the population of the city was exposed to the toxic gas, and by sunrise local hospitals were overrun.[13]

Methyl isocyanate had been a little-studied chemical. It is a colorless liquid with a boiling point of 102.2°F. In 1964, Kimmerle and Eben first reported on the acute toxic effects of inhaled MIC on the lungs of animals.[14] Up until the day of the accident, data provided by industries using MIC in pesticide manufacturing mainly dealt with chemical properties, rather than toxicology. Union Carbide and Carbon Corporation had not informed the workers at the plant—let alone, the general public—about the dangers of MIC. No material safety data sheets (MSDS) were available to workers at the plant (standard protocol in U.S. industry), and UCC failed to provide to local officials and emergency workers toxicological information on MIC and other hazardous chemicals.[15] It took a human tragedy to launch investigation into the toxicology of this widely used pesticide precursor.

The exact composition of the gas and liquid cloud that formed that night is still unknown: it dissipated within hours. It *is* known that contact of MIC with water produces heat and other compounds such as carbon dioxide and methylamine gases. Contact with metal causes a violent chain reaction, and fire involving MIC produces hazardous decomposition products such as hydrogen cyanide and carbon monoxide.[16] Early medical reports from Bhopal noting that the blood of deceased victims was cherry-red suggested the presence of cyanide in the gas cloud, but the issue is still unresolved.[17] Because of the uncertainty of the actual content of the cloud, the deadly agent is now generally referred to as the "Bhopal gas."

LOST AND SHORTENED LIVES

The official government figure on the number of people exposed to the gases stands at 521,262. One month after the accident, the government directed the Indian Council of Medical Research (ICMR) to begin following a cohort of survivors to determine the long-term effects of the gas on those exposed.[18] The council terminated its studies in December 1994; to date, no official data have been published. According to ICMR data leaked to activists in 1989, studies indicated the occurrence of gas-related symptoms in 27 percent of exposed persons, putting the persistent number of affected individuals between 120,000 and 200,000. But the ICMR did not include in these figures the 50,000 permanently injured or disabled, nor the estimated 10 to 15 people who have died each month since the tragedy from the effects of the gas.[19]

The main health effects of the liquid/gas cloud, thought to be mainly composed of MIC, were on people's eyes and respiratory systems. Medical studies conducted several years after the accident found persistent corneal opacities, ulcerations, and cataracts.[20] Epidemiologic studies on survivors into the 1990s revealed chronic obstructive lung disease (emphysema), *bronchiolitis obliterans* with organizing pneumonia (BOOP), and pulmonary fibrosis.[21] A 1996 study revealed long-term, disabling respiratory symptoms such as cough, phlegm production, and shortness of breath to be significantly higher in gas-exposed residents of Bhopal than in the general population. Measured lung function by spirometry among the survivors was also much lower than among those who were not exposed to the gases.[22]

Very few treatments other than steroids and inhalers are available for these disabling conditions. Analgesics, antibiotics, antihistamines, tranquilizers, and tonics are all still given in excess to survivors in Bhopal with very little effect.[23] The widespread and inappropriate use of pharmaceuticals and lack of evidence of their efficacy are of major concern to local health workers. Low-cost interventions that would potentially be very useful for the survivors, such as respiratory physiotherapy, are not widely available to the poor in India.

The social repercussions of the accident go *far* beyond anything imagined in the immediate aftermath of the event. Epidemiological evidence strongly suggests that the Bhopal gases were toxic to the reproductive system and continue to be so. Hundreds of stillbirths were delivered after the leak, and the fetal loss rate among exposed fertile women remains high (9 percent) into the 1990s.[24] Sources in Bhopal report a general public attitude that females living in the gas-affected areas are likely to be infertile, and families are increasingly unable to marry their daughters to "suitable" men.[25]

Frequent and consistent complaints among survivors also include symptoms of neurological injury, such as loss of memory and concentration, altered smell and taste, headaches, vestibular problems (abnormal balance), and sleep disturbances.[26] A 1996 study among survivors found decreased ability to perform simple tasks and difficulties with fine motor skills.[27]

The most understudied health problem related to the disaster has been the mental health of the survivors. Immediately after the accident, depression, anxiety, and post-traumatic stress disorder were diagnosed in many residents.[28] Many struggle, living in constant pain and increasing impoverishment. Contributing to the ongoing mental health stress is the deteriorating socioeconomic situation experienced by most of the survivors. Disability insurance is nonexistent. Bhopal residents who once earned incomes (albeit meager) as laborers, porters, or small shopkeepers now find themselves unemployed, and without wages, forced into a constant struggle for survival.[29]

Despite the enormity of the disaster and the numbers of individuals affected, there is surprisingly little in the medical literature regarding Bhopal. In a 1997 editorial following a newly released study in the *British Medical Journal*, Garner reports searching Medline (1991-95) and finding only three articles about diseases related to Bhopal.[30] Given the lack of official Indian research, the survivors must depend on these few Western occupational health studies to tell their tale to the wider community. There continues to be an urgent need for sound epidemiologic research about the long-term effects of the gas exposure.[31]

CORPORATE "MORAL RESPONSIBILITY" AND THE COURTS

Weeks after the unfolding tragedy, UCC announced that it took "moral responsibility" for the accident. Exactly what this meant was difficult to determine. Within three months after this concession, UCC management adopted a strategy of "containment," by means of which the company downplayed the seriousness of the accident, minimized the adverse effects on health, refused to pay immediate relief to the victims, and eventually attempted to implicate others in responsibility for the deaths.[32] As it turned out, "moral responsibility" meant neither legal responsibility nor moral accountability; UCC sent emergency medical and financial relief only after being ordered to do so by a U.S. court.

Expecting a long court battle, the U.S. corporate press was quick to defend its industry with a cruel calculus. The suffering victims of Bhopal did not sway the *Wall Street Journal* toward compassion, nor convince the paper to assign substantive moral responsibility to UCC. [33] When, in its December 10, 1984, editorial, the *Journal* reflected that "economic progress is not without its risks," we were being told to believe that the benefits of a pesticide plant outweighed the cost of several hundred thousand damaged lives. With such solid cost-benefit theory, there was no need to challenge wildly unsubstantiated claims, such as the questionable assertion that "half of those killed would not have been alive today if it weren't for that plant." The deaths of thousands became acceptable in the march toward progress: permissible dying for growth.

These neoliberal values appear to have prevailed, given the legal battles won by the corporation. The Bhopal case was initially fought in Federal District Court in New York with a bevy of lawyers expecting a windfall. However, the U.S. judge moved the case to India on the basis of *forum non conveniens* (inconvenient forum).[34] The decision marked the transformation of this once-unconstitutional doctrine into a powerful barricade protecting U.S. transnationals from having to answer in American courts for the consequences of their negligence abroad.[35] In effect, the court protected UCC from exposure to damages on a scale that could have been expected in a U.S. court.[36] This new judicial attitude today acts to lessen the vulnerability of U.S. transnationals to the "inconvenience" of responsibility for their overseas operations. It enables the transnationals to in large part escape potential obligation by setting up subsidiaries in the developing countries where they invest. Transnationals can still, in most cases, be held accountable in foreign courts, *but judicial systems in developing nations are often unable to match the massive resources available to transnational corporations.* In the wake of Bhopal, UCC spent close to $100 million on legal and public relations efforts in India.

Initially, the Indian government strongly opposed moving the UCC case to its own courts. Prior to the Bhopal suit, Indian tort law had never been challenged by the dilemmas posed by mass disaster situations (unlike U.S. tort law). The Indian common law system inherited from the British colonial rulers was designed to serve the interests of the rulers, not the ruled. After the Indian government initially impugned the ability of its own justice system to handle the case, a thaw occurred in U.S.-India relations, and the Indian government changed its position, supporting dismissal of the case from U.S. courts.

The case wound its way through Indian courts for years. In February 1989, the government of Rajiv Gandhi, representing all the claimants injured, agreed to a settlement of $470 million ordered by the Indian Supreme Court against the protest of citizens groups.[37] This sum, which averages to $800 per person filing a claim, is not even enough to cover the expected medical costs of the victims, let alone lost wages and earning power, restitution, and punitive damages. In addition, the government agreed to defend Union Carbide in any future suits against its local subsidiary. To demonstrate their disgust with the unjust decision, Bhopal survivors—in a symbolic protest—used brooms to sweep the dirt off the Supreme Court steps. A day later, when word of the highly favorable settlement for the corporation reached New York's Wall Street, UCC's stock rose $2 per share.[38]

The settlement provoked widespread international protest and was immediately challenged in appeal by the survivors. In October 1991, after the Congress (I) Party[39] lost and regained power through the presidential elections, the Indian Supreme Court upheld the initial settlement figure but revoked immunity granted in 1989 to Chief Executive Officer Warren Anderson and the other nine UCIL officials. The Indian government was ordered to make up any difference if the settlement money proved insufficient over time, and UCC was instructed to contribute $17 million to finance a new hospital for the victims in Bhopal.

Criminal charges against nine Indian UCIL officials and C.E.O. Warren Anderson continue to this day in the Bhopal Magistrate Court; the charges are for culpable homicide and grievous harm. Warren Anderson has not appeared in an Indian court since 1984, and the Indian government has no intention of extraditing him from the United States. Such a move would send a perilous signal to other foreign investors whom India is keen on attracting. Since the "New Economic Plan" in 1991, India has followed neoliberal designs for economic growth by opening its economy to attract foreign investment and marketing its large, cheap labor force and educated professional class to the world's transnational corporations.[40] The goal is to ensure the survival of transnationals, including Union Carbide, in India. And despite the legal battles, Union Carbide not only survived, but prospered.

CORPORATE SURVIVAL IN THE MARKETPLACE

At the time of the disaster, Union Carbide was the thirty-fifth largest industrial corporation in the United States, with production in 38 countries, sales in over 100 countries, and employees numbering 99,500. Its assets were worth more than $5 billion. Foreign sales accounted for 31 percent of the $9 billion in sales in 1983.[41]

The public knows UCC by its products. Glad bags, Eveready batteries, and Prestone antifreeze are household names in the United States.

Soon after the accident, UCC began a financial restructuring that reduced its equity from over $5 billion to about $2 billion one year later. It bought back its own stock, refinanced its debt, and paid equity to shareholders. This ostensibly occurred at the same time as a failed takeover of UCC by GAF Corporation, a company one-twentieth the size of UCC.[42] Thus, the divestment to lenders and shareholders had the happy consequence of providing UCC with a bankruptcy defense. In addition, in 1986 UCC sold off its more profitable divisions, including the consumer products division and agricultural products division, with shareholders reaping $33 per share from this sale, an extraordinary dividend.[43] Management insisted it was part of the game plan to resist any hostile takeovers, though activists suggested that the sale was made to insulate UCC from a possible consumer boycott of Eveready batteries and Glad bags.

Union Carbide's financial restructuring in response to the disaster was customary for a TNC whose profits and shareholders' assets become threatened through negligence of its own making.[44] In addition to securing financial protection, UCC launched an aggressive public relations strategy to shore up its tarnished image. In 1986, UCC lawyers concocted a "sabotage theory" to explain the entry of water into the MIC tanks.[45] They abandoned the theory in court when the legal defense team realized it held no weight in the liability trial. However, Union Carbide still zealously clings to the sabotage theory in public, to shift attention from its own accountability. In response to letters sent to the present C.E.O., William Joyce, during a 1996 drive asking UCC to take more full responsibility for the suffering of the poor, activists received a letter containing the following points:

> The plant has been constructed and managed by Indians in India. No Americans were employed at the plant at the time of the accident. In the five years from 1980 to 1984, although more than 1,000 Indians were employed at the plant, only one American was employed there and he left in 1982. No Americans visited the plant for more than one year prior to the accident, and during the five-year period before the accident the communications between the plant and the United States were almost non-existent.
>
> The cause of the gas release was an act of industrial sabotage by a disgruntled employee of Union Carbide India. A reconstruction of the event demonstrates clearly that a large quantity of water was deliberately introduced into a storage tank, where it reacted with the stored chemical, resulting in tragic injury and loss of life.[46]

Ironically, the UCC containment strategy soon became a subject for case studies in corporate public relations in U.S. business schools. In 1986, the Industrial Crisis Institute at the School of Management of New York University hosted the International Conference on Industrial Crisis Management. Warren Anderson, the UCC chief executive officer at the time of the gas leak, had this to say about UCC's response to the Bhopal tragedy:

> First of all, even when a crisis grabs the attention of the world, and demands the full attention of the CEO and the board, it's essential to carry on the main business of the organization. The crisis was bound to be a powerful distraction no matter what we did, but we let people know insofar as possible, it was business as usual at Union Carbide.[47]

Business as usual, indeed. By 1988, UCC had "downsized" its workforce by half, and profits had soared to a record $662 million. At the annual meeting in April 1989 in Houston, stockholders were presented with an upbeat 1988 Annual Report: "The year 1988 was the best in the 71-year history of Union Carbide, with a record $4.88 earnings per share, *which included the year-end charge of 43 cents per share related to the resolution of the Bhopal litigation.*"[48] One shudders at the inhumanity of this stark corporate cost-benefit analysis. Shareholders of UCC lost a mere 43¢ per share, against dividends of $4.88 per share over a single year, in exchange for the death of up to 10,000 people and the suffering of 200,000 more.

UNJUST COMPENSATION

Compared with the gains made by UCC shareholders, compensation to the victims of the accident and their families has been too little and too late. Interim payments to those living in gas-affected municipalities began in 1989 at a rate of approximately seven to ten dollars per month per person. After a long and complicated compensation process, adjudication of survivors' claims began in 1992. Disability is largely being determined by respiratory function. The disability scoring method devised by the court denies the existence of multi-system damage (damage to more than one organ system), reproductive disorders, injury to the nervous system, and psychological problems such as depression and anxiety. As of May 1996, the government had passed rulings on only 302,400 of 597,000 claims for compensation, with awards given to 288,000 Bhopalis.[49] The government has disbursed only $240 million of the $470 million awarded for damages (plus interest since 1989). Of 15,310 claims of death, the courts have awarded compensation to 10,237, with an average amount of $3,000. For claims of personal injury for serious and permanent disability, the courts have given awards to only 55 percent of applicants, paying an average of roughly $1,500 per person.[50] For temporary injuries, $800 per claimant is paid. Subtracted from these amounts, however, are the monthly interim compensation awards already disbursed and various bribes to clerks and bankers that the poor have no choice but to provide.[51]

These compensation awards are insufficient to cover medical care costs for survivors, estimated at more than $600 million over the next 20 years. Originally, conservative estimates for a just settlement began at $3 billion, which included the cost of epidemiologic health surveys and surveillance; health-care costs; compensation for death; business and animal losses; job and wage losses; sanitation; housing; water supply; and vocational rehabilitation.[52] Clearly, Union Carbide is getting away cheaply.

In addition, though thousands of children were exposed to the gas, until December 1996 the Indian government denied permission to any child under the age of 18 years at the time of the leak to file for compensation. Researchers are finding children, exposed as toddlers, complaining of loss of performance in school; fatigue; loss of strength; and higher susceptibility to lung infections. Their capacity for education and the acquisition of vocational skills, and thus their ability to earn a living wage, are severely compromised.[53]

In 1996, UCC began construction of a modern tertiary-care hospital, as required by the Indian Supreme Court, seven miles from the old Union Carbide plant. Bhopal survivors insist that another hospital is not necessary, that what are desperately needed are community health clinics where health workers can monitor outpatients. The discordance is yet another example of how UCC and the Indian judicial system are out of touch with the community. To finance the project, UCC set up the Bhopal Hospital Trust and chose as its head Sir Ian Percival, former solicitor general for Prime Minister Margaret Thatcher of Great Britain. Percival, who was paid millions for his tireless efforts, convinced the Indian government to sell $20 million of UCIL stock that had been held by the Bhopal court pending appearance by Warren Anderson to face his criminal charges. The remaining UCIL stock value, estimated at $70 million, is today the only leverage the victims of Bhopal have left in the criminal case against UCC officials. The court will not release the stocks to UCIL until those charged with crimes show up in court. Sir Percival, however, has asked the court to release the remaining stock assets to be used toward "treatment" for the survivors.[54]

Economic and environmental rehabilitation is urgently needed in the poor areas of Bhopal. Beyond the one-time exposure from the Bhopal gases in December 1984, people living near the plant fear toxic waste buried there will lead to additional health problems. Analysis of sediment from a Union Carbide waste storage area, surface soils, and local drinking water have revealed the presence of multiple toxic compounds, including methylene chloride and dichlorobenzenes.[55] The average cost for such a cleanup in the United States under the Superfund Program would be $20 million. The Bhopal plant is now idle, and UCC has no long-term plan for decontamination of the site. In 1995, the Madya Pradesh Pollution Control Board considered removing the contaminated soil around the plant for incineration, but the plan was scrapped after an emergency Greenpeace assessment warned that this procedure would result in the formation of dioxins, some of the most toxic chemicals known to modern science.[56]

The Indian government has spent $13 million on "environmental rehabilitation" of Bhopal. Most of this went to "beautification" of the city, including the bulldozing of one housing area of gas-exposed survivors to make room for new roads.[57] The government's record of economic rehabilitation is not much better, despite expenditures of $8 million. In July 1992, the government closed down sewing centers, which once employed 2,300 women, for no apparent reason. Work sheds built for survivors who have lost the capacity for other gainful employment employ only a few hundred people, far fewer than the numbers in need of work.[58] The records of both the government and UCC in rectifying the long-term consequences of the gas leak are nothing short of abysmal.

In spite of UCC assertions that adequate compensation has been paid, the poor of Bhopal know otherwise. Though the government and UCC agreed upon a settlement, from the point of view of Bhopal's poor and disenfranchised, justice has not been served. Bano Bi, the Indian survivor who lost her husband to the gases, states it plainly: "I believe that even if we have to starve, we must get the guilty officials of Union Carbide punished. They have killed someone's brother, someone's husband, someone's mother, someone's sister. How many tears can Union Carbide wipe? We will get Union Carbide punished. 'Til my last breath, I will not leave them."[59]

The reason for Bano Bi's anguish is clear. No officials from Union Carbide have yet had to answer for their role in the tragedy, and the U.S. transnational corporation has never made a formal apology to the Indian people. Rather, the survivors of Bhopal have had to accept implicit and explicit excuses and justifications of the tragedy in the impersonal debate over costs and benefits of transnational corporations doing business in India. At first, Bhopal was described as an aberration, a momentary deviation from the norm. As UCC's record of double standards in other plants around the world surfaced, the accident in Bhopal was explained away as the regrettable result of small but unavoidable risks in an inherently hazardous industry.[60] The Bhopal tragedy has become a telling symbol of the levels of risk the poor must bear in the course of their country's development; a vivid reminder that those who roll the dice and reap the benefits of such corporate games of chance are rarely the people who must suffer the consequences of failure.

THE FIGHT FOR JUSTICE

Though UCC claims to have washed its hands of the Bhopal tragedy and its responsibility to the victims of its negligence, activists are pursuing the corporation to hold it accountable for the continued suffering and poverty of the survivors. The Campaign for Justice in Bhopal, based in New York City, has launched a movement to convince the state of New York to revoke Union Carbide's corporate charter.[61] (Governments define "corporations" through *charters*—certificates of incorporation. In exchange for a charter, a corporation is obliged to obey all laws, serve the common good, and to cause no harm. Section 1101 of the New York Business Corporation Law provides for the dissolution of any corporation that causes mass harm or acts "contrary to the public policy of the state." By any reasonable standard, UCC appears to meet such criteria.) Though it has been more than 50 years since a corporation was dissolved in the United States, a charter revocation would be a catalyst toward greater corporate public accountability.[62]

Medical activists have also not forgotten the human suffering of the Bhopal poor. In January 1994, the International Medical Commission on Bhopal, a group made up of internationally respected occupational health professionals, convened in the city to study the ongoing problems and unmet needs of the survivors. In December 1996, the commission released its findings, specifically calling for:

(1) The establishment of a network of community-based clinics to provide equitable primary medical care as well as health education and rehabilitation to survivors;
(2) The expansion of recognized disease categories related to the gas exposure for use in treatment and compensation, to include such disorders as neurotoxic injury, mental health problems, and immune system dysfunction;
(3) Full disclosure of all data collected by the ICMR and the establishment of an independent medical commission on Bhopal to study the long-term effects of the gas on the survivors, with specific attention paid to women and children;

(4) The creation of an independent "commission of inquiry" into the problems faced by patients, the incompetence and malpractice of physicians, the unavailability of medicine, and the corruption in hospitals; and
(5) The cleanup of the Bhopal plant site.[63]

In addition, the Bhopal Gas-Affected Working Women's Union has offered proposals to the government for: equal disbursement of compensation based on geographic indicators of exposure; income generation projects, rather than cash relief that fosters dependence; and a decentralized health-care system that maximizes patient control.[64] As of late 1999, no recommendations of the International Medical Commission had been adopted or acted upon by the government. Care of the survivors continues to be erratic, bureaucratic, and unorganized.

LESSONS

Twelve years after the accident, the lessons from Bhopal are painfully clear. For one, history has shown us how transnational corporations can be above the law in both rich and poor countries, and that despite a disaster of enormous magnitude, these corporations continue to enrich their shareholders. In the grand "trade-off" between foreign investment and economic development on the one hand, and environmental and human safety on the other, the elite reap the monetary awards while the costs to human health are visited upon the poor.[65] In short, the externalities of development growth are incurred by those least capable of paying.

Second, the formal judicial institutions allegedly in place to protect the rights of Indians were actually irrelevant to the poor. The domestic legal tort system operated on a cost-benefit business analysis, with those living in poverty simply left out of the equation.[66] The poor will continue to suffer under rules set up to serve the political and economic alliance between government and transnational business. In the end, Indian law and UCC "moral responsibility" had *nothing* to do with social justice.

Last, government and business leaders were willing to sacrifice the poorest of the population for the supposed future benefits of economic liberalism and international investment.[67] Despite the number of lives lost, the tragedy had no discernable impact on the Indian government's determination to maintain a favorable business environment for foreign investment. As long as poor countries feel that foreign-directed investment projects are the indispensable engines for their development, the deck will remain heavily stacked against poor people.

WHAT THE FUTURE HOLDS

Foreign investment-driven growth was never the design for development of the founding fathers of the modern Indian state, led by great thinkers such as Mahatma Gandhi and Jawaharlal Nehru. Among other nations in the developing world, India prides itself as being traditionally concerned with the plight of its poor majority. Its five year development plans have centered on using national resources to develop local infrastructure. The profound changes in global economics, however, have affected even "socialist" India. Having recently embraced the neoliberal agenda, with its export-led growth strategy and increased reliance on foreign investment, the Indian government now allows market considerations to override concern for the rights of the poor. The story of Bhopal shows us that even at low levels of foreign investment, such as those operative during the early 1980s, India could not (and did not) protect its poor majority. Now that neoliberalism, with its emphasis on deregulation, has captured the attention of the elite in government and business in the subcontinent, monitoring the unhealthy practices of transnational corporations will be even more difficult.

Yet, hope and activism abound in India. The country's recent history includes numerous examples of local attempts to thwart the expansion of transnational investment. When the chemical giant DuPont was negotiating to begin manufacturing nylon in the state of Goa in 1994, their contract with the local subsidiary included a limited liability clause that exempted the parent company in the event of a major chemical accident or pollution problem. Local activists eventually forced DuPont to scrap its factory plans.[68] In 1995, farmers in Karnataka broke into a Cargill seed warehouse and destroyed genetically modified Cargill seeds that were impervious to Cargill pesticides; the corporation had been trying to sell the seeds to the farmers. Later that same year, the Karnataka Farmers Association threatened destruction of Kentucky Fried Chicken restaurants in Bangalore, claiming that transnational fast-food chains favor big farmers and hurt small ones.[69] In May 1995, hundreds of villagers in Maharashtra state stormed the site of a proposed Enron 2,015-megawatt, $2.8 billion gas-fired power plant, arguing that effluent from the plant would destroy fisheries and coconut and mango groves.[70]

Yet despite these and other small setbacks to transnationals in India, the liberalization of India's economy continues to move forward. The Enron plant is now back on schedule, Cargill is expanding operations, and Kentucky Fried Chicken restaurants can be seen in most major cities. Royal Dutch Shell, Time Warner, and General Motors have all signed deals to enter into the Indian economy.[71] Meanwhile, occupational and environmental health standards continue to stagnate. The Indian chemical industry continues to have safety problems and periodic leaks of toxic substances. A 1993 International Labor Organization (ILO) report identified 6,000 hazardous installations under surveillance by a mere 903 inspectors. Industrial fatalities in India continue to occur at four times the rate of those in North America,[72] so that the possibility of another disaster like Bhopal's is very real to the millions of poor Indians who live in the shadow of these plants.

The saga of the 1984 Bhopal gas leak is far from over. The human scale of suffering remains vast, the individual stories poignant, and the paths to justice tangled. The lives of the poor of Bhopal are not much better than they were before the accident, nor before the presence of the Union Carbide corporation. Permanent relief or "development" remain remote ideals. Union Carbide has returned to making profits and benefiting its shareholders, while the poor continue to pay the price for the corporation's presence and for the alliance between the Indian government and a transnational corporation driven by the amoral logic of the bottom line. As the Indian economy liberalizes and foreign investment continues unchecked, sequels to the accident in Bhopal are sure to follow.

ACKNOWLEDGMENTS

The author gratefully acknowledges the aid of several people who helped pull together information related to the story about Bhopal, including but not limited to Ward Morehouse, Gary Cohen, Satinath Sarangi, and Gordon Blake Wood. Thanks also go to Shelly Errington, Alec Irwin, and Joyce Millen for their help in editing this chapter.

El Paso, Texas. Having lost her job when the factory in which she worked moved to Mexico, a woman stands with her child at a rally for workers displaced by NAFTA. (photo by Richard Lord)

Neoliberal Trade and Investment and the Health of *Maquiladora* Workers on the U.S.-Mexico Border

Joel Brenner, Jennifer Ross, Janie Simmons, and Sarah Zaidi

In 1965, Mexico established the Border Industrialization Program (BIP), a set of policies designed to attract foreign capital to the area along its border with the United States and to relieve a labor surplus in the region. The program created an export-processing zone (EPZ) along the border, granting foreign corporations incentives to build assembly plants there. In time, the BIP came to serve as a template for Mexico's industrialization; the plants, no longer confined by law to the border (although still highly concentrated there), became known as *maquiladoras*, and employed increasing numbers of Mexicans.[1] Under the *maquiladora* program, foreign companies are permitted to establish assembly plants in Mexico, to import parts and materials duty-free, and to pay export taxes only on the value added. During the late 1980s and early 1990s, despite competition for investment from all over the world, foreign transnational corporations (TNCs), the vast majority of them U.S.-owned, established new *maquiladoras* in Mexico at an increased pace. Since the 1994 debut of the North American Free Trade Agreement (NAFTA), the *maquiladora* sector has grown explosively, adding roughly as many new workers in five years as during the previous 30. By 1998, what had once been a backwater of Mexico's economy had become one of its driving forces, even as many other sectors of the country's economy were stagnating, or worse.

An important part of the *maquiladoras'* rapid growth and other sectors' stagnation can, we suggest, be traced to Mexico's economic liberalization during the 1980s and 1990s, which culminated in NAFTA. Proponents of liberalized trade and investment argue that the number of new jobs in the *maquiladora* sector are a sign that Mexico's bid to join the global economy is succeeding, and that the years of liberalization summed up in NAFTA have been good for Mexico. We cannot agree. Liberalization has not benefited the majority of Mexicans, and the *maquiladora* sector's growth has too often been secured at the expense of workers and the environment.

This chapter opens with the story of one *maquiladora* worker. It then seeks to explain how Mexico's neoliberal reforms of the 1980s and 1990s have contributed to the "maquilization" of Mexico; that is, to the growth of the *maquila* sector at the expense of other sectors. "Maquilization" has shaped the conditions—often brutal—under which *maquiladora* workers live and labor. The second part of the chapter describes these conditions and puts them into historical perspective. It concludes that many *maquiladora* laborers earn insufficient and declining wages, work under unsafe and unhealthy conditions, suffer the effects of an environment degraded by industrial pollution, and contend with the diseases that plague crowded populations lacking adequate sanitation and other infrastructure.

SOLEDAD'S STORY

Soledad has known difficulties throughout her life. She was very young when her mother died, and was later abandoned by her father when he could no longer provide for her and her siblings on the family farm. Soon after her father's departure, Soledad and two other young girls traveled to the border town of Nuevo Laredo and attempted to swim across the Rio Grande. Midway, Soledad became intimidated by the current and turned back; her two friends disappeared over the other bank.

After weeks alone scavenging for food on the streets of Nuevo Laredo, Soledad was taken in by a distant aunt in exchange for her labor. A year later, she found work in Nuevo Laredo's bustling maquiladora sector, at Magnéticos de México, a subsidiary of Sony Corporation. A few months afterward, she met her future husband. They soon married, and Soledad joined her husband's family in one of Nuevo Laredo's shantytowns, or colonias. When we met Soledad, she had been working for six years at Magnéticos de México. She was a productive and disciplined employee, and had more seniority than most of her colleagues.

Soledad took one month's leave before giving birth to her first child, Manuel. Because her husband's intermittent work as a day laborer was insufficient to provide for the family's basic needs, Soledad was forced to return to work almost immediately. When Manuel began to suffer severe respiratory problems only a few months later, Soledad wanted to remain at home to care for him. Again, financial constraints compelled her to keep working, for her job gave her access to the state-run, employer-financed national health program, el Seguro Social, without the assistance of which Soledad could not have afforded health care for Manuel, who required frequent hospitalization.

One day, Soledad requested leave to take her son to the hospital. She received verbal permission from a supervisor, and took Manuel to the hospital. She returned to work to find herself accused of taking a day off without permission. The supervisor who had granted her permission denied ever having given it, and Soledad was docked one week's pay and threatened with firing. Aware of her precarious position, Soledad sought an interview with another maquila, whose managers promptly informed her Sony employers of her action. Soledad's supervisors now harassed her incessantly at work. After weeks of this harassment, Soledad finally "consented" to "resign." Her forced resignation made her ineligible for severance pay and health benefits.

Pregnant with her second child, Soledad eventually found work, at a third of her former wage, cleaning for a school teacher. She received no medical benefits from this informal work. She and her husband were unable to accumulate any savings on their meager wages. Without access to medical care, Soledad was ineligible to deliver her baby at the Seguro clinic, and the couple could not afford the fees at Nuevo Laredo's private hospital. Soledad's employer, aware of the family's difficulties, made only one "gesture of support"—an offer to purchase Soledad's second child at birth.[2]

THE MAQUILIZATION OF MEXICO

The trajectory of Soledad's life raises many questions. Why had her father been unable to make ends meet on the family farm? Why did Soledad travel to the border, rather than to another area of Mexico? And why, when it seemed that all odds were against her, did she stay in Nuevo Laredo and seek work in a *maquiladora*? Why was Soledad, an employee with considerable seniority, forced to leave work over a trivial infraction? After being fired, why was she able to find only inadequately paid informal work without any benefits?

We cannot precisely answer these questions in Soledad's case; we do not know all the facts. But a central part of the answer to each of these questions—and to similar questions that arise for many of Mexico's 40 million poor—is to be found in the fact that over the last 18 years, the *maquila* sector is the only sector of the Mexican economy to have created jobs at a rate greater than that of the growth of the economically active population (EAP); in all other sectors, job creation lagged behind growth of the EAP.[3] So if we want to understand Soledad's trajectory, we will need to explain the growth of the *maquiladora* sector on the one hand, and the paucity of jobs in Mexican agriculture, manufacturing, and services on the other. The growth of the *maquiladora* sector, in turn, however, has been spurred by changes in the global division of labor, changes which directly influenced the conditions under which Soledad held, and lost, her job. In the following two sections, we argue that Mexico's liberalizing reforms of the 1980s and 1990s, culminating in NAFTA (see Box 11.1), have played an important role in *both* the expansion of the *maquiladora* sector and the relative contraction of the other sectors of the Mexican economy. We turn first to the story of the *maquiladora* sector.

Box 11.1: Mexico's Neoliberal Turn—
From Import Substitution to Export-led Growth to NAFTA

Mexico's commitment to economic liberalization was forged in the events of the 1960s and 1970s, during which Mexico sought and attained rapid economic growth through import-substitution industrialization (ISI). Yet under ISI, Mexico developed an unsustainable current-account deficit, high inflation, and a heavy load of foreign debt.[4]

In 1976, the severely indebted government was compelled to seek an International Monetary Fund (IMF) loan. The loan was granted on the usual condition that the Mexican government implement strict austerity measures.[5] But the discovery of 72 billion barrels of oil in 1978 led the government to eschew austerity in favor of a borrowing and spending binge, which shortly led to another

---

balance-of-payments disequilibrium.[6] By early 1982, Mexico's foreign currency reserves were nearly depleted and its economy was on the brink of collapse.[7] The government responded by dramatically devaluing the peso, placing a moratorium on debt payments, and nationalizing the banks.[8]

Miguel de la Madrid became Mexico's president in late 1982, and was faced with the task of extricating Mexico from a financial crisis of enormous magnitude. Under an IMF-designed structural adjustment program (SAP), de la Madrid's government implemented strict austerity measures.[9] The 1980s also saw a radical opening of the Mexican economy to international business interests. Between 1981 and 1991, Mexico unilaterally cut import tariffs on many goods in half, to an average of 12 percent. The fraction of domestic output protected by import licensing was also reduced, from 75 percent in 1981 to 20 percent by 1991.[10] In 1986, four years into de la Madrid's term, Mexico joined the General Agreement on Tarriffs and Trade (GATT).[11]

Carlos Salinas succeeded de la Madrid in 1988, pledging to extend his predecessor's neoliberal policies. Salinas privatized many state-owned enterprises, solicited foreign investment, and built up the export sector.[12] His government relaxed restrictions on foreign ownership and adapted Mexican legislation in certain areas to international standards.[13] The Salinas administration's 1990 decision to pursue a free trade agreement with the United States and Canada was simply a logical continuation of Mexico's general liberalization during the 1980s.[14]

NAFTA is "an agreement between the governments of Mexico, the United States, and Canada to phase out restrictions on the movement of goods, services, and capital between the three countries over a period of ten to fifteen years."[15] The NAFTA parties agreed to a complicated set of reciprocal tariff reductions.[16] Provisions on services outlined in NAFTA opened many Mexican markets to U.S. and Canadian insurers, banks, and telecommunications firms, among others.[17] The agreement also reduces or eliminates many restrictions on investment, and strengthens the rights of intellectual property holders.[18]

If NAFTA is more than a trade agreement, it is much less than a common market or a full political and economic union. Unlike the European Community, for instance, NAFTA retains the previous restrictions on movement of labor; it is not a monetary union; and it promulgates no regionwide regime of environmental or labor law.[19]

The agreement does, however, crystallize Mexico's neoliberal policies beyond the realm of domestic politics, effectively locking them in no matter who holds power in Mexico. In the United States, large corporations, supported by many Republicans and by Clinton Democrats, welcomed this prospect, while unions, supported by pro-labor Democrats and right-wing populists, opposed it. In Mexico, the ruling party (the PRI) naturally supported the agreement, and the mainstream opposition opposed it, although more in its particulars than in its fundamental conception.[20]

Canada, Mexico, and the United States began negotiations on the agreement in June 1991.[21] The next year, President-elect Bill Clinton made his support for

NAFTA plain, but insisted that he would not implement it without supplemental agreements on environmental and labor standards.[22] During President Clinton's first eight months in office, these supplementary agreements—the North American Agreements on Environmental Cooperation (NAAEC) and Labor Cooperation (NAALC)—were in fact negotiated, and all three countries granted NAFTA legislative approval in time for it to come into effect on January 1, 1994.[23]

The Demand for Maquiladora *Labor*

The *maquiladora* sector has grown phenomenally since its origins nearly 35 years ago. As Table 11.1 shows, the sector expanded slowly until the mid-1980s, then grew at accelerating rates. Since 1994, it has roughly doubled in size, adding almost as many workers in five years as in the previous 29. More than 2000 new *maquiladoras* have been established in Mexico since 1992. There are now more than six times as many *maquiladoras* as in 1980.[24]

The sector has become a critical one in Mexico's economy. The foreign exchange it generates is second only to that from oil exports, and may soon surpass oil-generated foreign exchange. The sector accounted for 45 percent of all of Mexico's exports of goods in 1997.[25] As a share of manufacturing employment, *maquiladora* work grew from 5 percent in 1980 to 40 percent in 1996. In some cities, the *maquiladoras* are virtually the only formal sector employers: for example, in 1998, 74 percent of jobs in Ciudad Ancuña were *maquiladora* jobs.[26]

Table 11.1

Growth of Mexican *Maquiladora* Sector, 1970–1998

Year	Total Plants	*Maquiladora* Employment (Annual Average)
1970	120	20,300
1975	454	67,200
1980	620	119,500
1985	760	212,000
1990	1,938	460,300
1993	2,172	541,000
1994	2,432	583,044
1995	2,897	648,263
1996	3,445	754,858
1997	3,850	898,786
1998*	4,050**	994,397

*Through Q3 1998
**Estimate

Sources: Galhardi, 1998; STPS, 1998a

How do we account for this stunning growth? Our starting point is the observation that TNCs will not assemble or manufacture in Mexico if it is more profitable for them to do so elsewhere. Mexico's proximity to the United States, and the infrastructure in the border region even before 1980, were undeniable advantages to foreign TNCs. Moreover, the crash of the *peso* in 1995 reduced the cost of Mexican labor for foreign manufacturers. But proximity, infrastructure, and exchange rates do not tell the whole story.

Two other kinds of causes require consideration. The first consists of several recently introduced inducements to investment. Beginning in 1988, the government negotiated annual wage "pacts" with unions and employers. These have acted to confine wage growth to levels lower than inflation in many sectors. The pacts' stated purpose is to control inflation.[27] They in fact have had this effect. Yet equally important to the government, they have put downward pressure on wages as a whole, and kept Mexican labor "competitive" on the international market.[28] For Mexican workers, the pacts amount to impoverishment by design. Mexico also removed many barriers to foreign investment in the late 1980s, as it consolidated its switch from import-substitution industrialization to export-led industrialization.[29] The North American Free Trade Agreement further lowered barriers to investment by eliminating "local content" and "local ownership" requirements, and by guaranteeing investors from any NAFTA country reimbursement in case of expropriation by a foreign NAFTA-member government.[30] The trade agreement also gave TNCs new flexibility, by allowing their *maquiladora* subsidiaries to sell an increasing proportion of output in Mexico. Whereas before NAFTA, *maquiladoras* were required to export most of their production, NAFTA provided for a gradual relaxation of the export requirement, and its eventual elimination.[31]

A second explanation for the recent growth of the *maquiladoras* is Mexico's poor enforcement of its environmental and labor laws. To the extent that they are enforced, Mexican environmental and labor laws act as impediments to investment. NAFTA's proponents argued that the agreement would oblige Mexico to enforce its laws, which are in many respects as strong as their U.S. counterparts. But the agreement's mechanisms for ensuring such enforcement have proven inadequate to the task. They have failed to make TNCs pay more of the environmental costs of production, and they have failed to uphold basic labor rights, which, if respected, would result in higher wages for workers (and thus, higher costs for manufacturers).

Proponents of NAFTA promised that the agreement and its side agreements—the North American Agreement on Environmental Cooperation (NAAEC) and the North American Agreement on Labor Cooperation (NAALC)—would improve Mexico's environment and labor standards. In Mexico, then-President Carlos Salinas was unequivocal: "With this agreement, we will raise environmental and labor protection."[32] His attorney general for the environment likewise had no doubts about NAFTA: "Certainly NAFTA will be working to the advantage of the environment because of the extra resources that will be available."[33] President Clinton, putting his pen to the agreement, declared that the side agreements would make NAFTA "a force for social progress, as well as economic growth" by, among other things, requiring

Mexico "to enforce its own environmental laws and labor standards, [and] to raise the cost of production...by raising wages and raising environmental investments."[34]

Five years after NAFTA's implementation, these promises ring hollow. In the environmental realm, the NAAEC has not put an end to illegal pollution, or even slowed it. No one disputes the *maquiladoras'* ubiquitous violations of Mexican environmental law prior to NAFTA. In fact, a 1992 Government Accounting Office (GAO) survey of U.S. factories in Mexico found that 100 percent were in violation of Mexico's environmental laws.[35] The Commission for Environmental Cooperation (CEC), established under the NAAEC, was charged with redressing this state of affairs, but has so far proven an utter failure—some would add, a failure by design. The CEC is to carry out its mission by administering a grievance procedure under which any person or nongovernmental organization (NGO) may charge its country with failing to enforce its environmental laws.[36] Yet by the end of 1998, only six complaints had been filed against Mexico. Five of these were still under review, and in the sixth, the CEC applied the most severe penalty available to it in that instance: it developed a written record of the case.[37] With penalties such as this, it should hardly come as a surprise that despoilment of the Mexican environment continues uninterrupted.[38]

On the labor front, the story is similar: Mexico routinely disregards its labor laws, and the NAALC has led to little or no improvement in enforcement.[39] We have noted that the government's wage-price pacts have contributed to keeping Mexican labor competitive internationally. In order to attract foreign investment, Mexico has in effect chosen to keep wages low, even as productivity has grown, rather than to invest in workers' skills and education.[40] Keeping wages low in turn requires suppressing independent unions: "What we won't permit," says the labor minister of the state of Coahuila, "are the unions who chase away the sources of employment. We once had unions who disturbed the peace in this state...."[41] On the other hand, Mexico's government-affiliated unions, grouped under the Mexican Workers' Confederation (CTM), are an essential part of the low-wage strategy, and have consistently supported the government's anti-inflation wage-price pacts.[42]

Maquiladora workers, like Mexican workers in other sectors, thus tend to have either no union representation, or representation by a union that is government-affiliated and -controlled.[43] In Ciudad Acuña, for example, two *maquiladoras* are unionized and 58 are not. In 1998 in Ciudad Juarez, the city with Mexico's largest single concentration of *maquiladoras*, only 15 out of more than 300 *maquilas* were unionized, all of them by government-affiliated unions.[44]

Some workers have attempted to form or join independent unions.[45] Governments and companies have variously responded with acceptance, legal maneuverings, firings, and acts of violence.[46] A 1994 drive to form an independent union by workers at Soledad's erstwhile employer Magnéticos de México provides a not untypical example.

In April 1994, Magnéticos de México employed 2,000 workers manufacturing floppy disks, videotapes, and audio tapes in Nuevo Laredo. Between 80 and 90 percent of these workers were women.[47] Tensions began to rise at the plant when the company increased working hours from 40 to 48 hours per week (as Mexican law permits), and demanded that employees work on weekends. Mexican law requires one day off per week, usually Sunday. Since many employees had young children, the introduction of weekend shifts was especially resented, and sparked antimanagement sentiments. Some workers began to organize an independent union in the plant.

At 11:00 P.M. on April 14, Sony's CTM union representatives announced an election allowing workers to choose between the CTM union and the nascent independent union, and scheduled the election for 7:00 A.M. the following day, leaving independent unionists only eight hours to organize their own slate of delegates. The election was a fraud. Workers were forced to line up publicly in support of one slate or the other. Some workers reported being pushed onto the side supporting the company's slate of delegates. The following day, April 16, workers organized a nonviolent protest in front of the plant gates to demand new, secret ballot elections so that those who had been intimidated during the previous day's election could vote without fear of reprisals. Police arrived with riot gear and shields and beat many of the employees with billy clubs; one woman was hospitalized with head injuries.

During the next two days, about 300 workers blocked the entrance to Sony's plant. The company attempted to break up the blockade with busloads of workers, but was unsuccessful. On Tuesday morning, state police were called in, and 100 workers were forced to leave. Production resumed, even though the majority of workers did not return to the plants until the following day, April 20. Workers who did not take part in the protest still feared being seen with independent union delegates or their supporters. By the end of April, 36 workers who had taken part in the demonstrations were cited on criminal charges relating to "loss of production," threatened with firing, and demoted. In addition, many employees were fired outright after the strike.[48]

The supplementary NAALC agreement was supposed to require NAFTA countries to enforce their labor laws by means of a grievance procedure similar to the one established under the NAAEC, with two crucial differences that make it, if anything, less friendly to plaintiffs than its NAAEC counterpart. First, under the NAALC procedure, individuals or organizations alleging that a NAFTA member government has persistently failed to enforce its labor laws must first file their complaint with a national government office in one of the two other NAFTA countries. Only if the national office admits the complaint may it proceed. Furthermore, unlike the environmental agreement's commission (which can at least in theory apply sanctions for violations of *any* environmental law) the commission established under the labor agreement can only apply sanctions for violations of laws *concerning occupational safety and health, child labor, or minimum wages.*

Unions, NGOs, and others have filed a total of 12 complaints against Mexico under the NAALC procedure since 1994. Of the 12, only three have resulted in consultations with the Mexican Ministry of Labor and a plan of action for resolving the dispute. (Three cases are still pending.) But what did agreeing to a plan for resolving the dispute really mean for the parties?

The efforts to organize an independent union at Magnéticos de México became the third submission under the NAALC's grievance procedure. The submission alleged that Mexico had failed to enforce its labor law on union registration. Labor officials at the highest levels of the U.S. and Mexican governments undertook consultations, and developed and implemented an action plan to resolve the dispute.[49] President Clinton's 1997 report to Congress on NAFTA cited the case as a success of the system.[50]

On the ground in Nuevo Laredo, the case takes on a different cast. The action plan resulted in several international seminars on union registration for labor ministry officials and others. It also charged the Mexican government with convening a panel of independent experts on Mexican labor law to report on its union registration provisions. Finally, it required the Mexican labor ministry and others to meet with Magnéticos de México workers, union representatives, and managers, in order to explain the remedies available to workers under domestic law, and to discuss the action plan.[51] These abundant colloquies and reports changed nothing at Magnéticos de México, however. The workers who had been fired or beaten were not rehired or compensated. Workers later tried again to organize an independent union, but their attempt was blocked by the government's Arbitration Board, which included members of the sitting CTM union and the government.[52]

We have seen how, beginning in the late 1980s and continuing under NAFTA, decreased restrictions on investment and trade, the institution of wage-price pacts, and government acceptance of (or, in some cases, complicity in) violations of environmental and labor laws have contributed to the growth of the *maquiladora* sector and increased its demand for workers. Next, we examine how Mexico's neoliberal trade and investment regime has contributed to the stagnation or decline of other sectors of the Mexican economy, and contributed to increasing the supply of potential *maquiladora* workers as well.

Supply of Maquiladora *Labor*

Under the neoliberal reforms capped off by NAFTA, Mexican agriculture has, at best, stagnated. Since 1980, agricultural production has grown at an average annual rate of less than 1 percent, lagging behind population growth.[53] Farmers as a whole have had nearly 20 lackluster years, but basic grain producers—Mexico's most numerous and culturally important group of farmers—have suffered greatly. According to José Luis Calva, an agricultural economist and early student of NAFTA, the majority of such farmers has been unable to subsist on their earnings in post-NAFTA Mexico, causing "an exodus toward overcrowded cities within Mexico and the United States."[54] Estimates of the number of peasant farmers and their dependents who have been or will be permanently displaced by the transformations underway in Mexico vary from 1 to 15 million.[55] One architect of the recent agricultural policy reforms predicted that Mexican agriculture would lose "one million farmers each year for ten years."[56] A 1995 Oxfam report estimated that 2.4 million farmers and their dependents would be permanently displaced.[57] However many people are eventually displaced, a large proportion will find their way to Mexico's urban shantytowns, including the *colonias* of the *maquiladora* towns along the U.S.-Mexico border.[58]

A series of neoliberal reforms largely explains the looming rural exodus. During the late 1980s and early 1990s, the Mexican government lowered its guaranteed prices for grains, ultimately pitting Mexican grain farmers against U.S. agribusinesses. Many farmers invested in technology in order to increase their productivity, only to find themselves deep in debt and still unable to compete. Defaults on agricultural loans mounted, and by 1993 the farm sector was in crisis, as banks attempted to foreclose on between $1 billion and $4 billion in bad loans.[59]

In 1991, partly in response to U.S. government pressure, Mexico reformed its land-tenure laws.[60] Since the Mexican revolution in 1917, a significant portion of Mexico's arable land had been held communally by groups of farmers in the form of *ejidos*.[61] As late as 1988, 75 percent of agricultural land was *ejido*-held.[62] Until 1992, these lands were operated collectively, and individual parcels could neither be bought, sold, nor rented.[63] Furthermore, banks and other creditors could not repossess land when debtors were unable to pay. A December 1991 constitutional amendment gave *ejidos* the right to buy, sell, mortgage, and rent parcels, and to enter into joint ventures with Mexican or foreign firms. *Ejidos* also gained the right to dissolve themselves and redistribute the land to parcel holders.[64] At the same time, parcel holders lost protections against repossession by creditors.[65]

Two years later, the government largely ended subsidies for the production of corn and other crops.[66] Other programs have been cut back or eliminated, including technical assistance for grain farmers, subsidies for fuel and chemicals, and finance consulting. By 1997, Banrural, the national rural development bank, had almost completely withdrawn its support of corn farmers: it financed just 3.4 percent of their production, compared with the 40.3 percent it had financed in 1988.[67]

Largely shorn of government assistance, indebted, and exposed to the threat of repossession in case of default, Mexico's grain farmers suffered a crushing blow under NAFTA due to the opening of markets to products of high-yield U.S. agribusiness. In agriculture, as elsewhere, NAFTA merely extends a line drawn little by little throughout the 1980s and early 1990s. The agreement's provisions on agriculture amount to a further opening of Mexican markets to U.S. grain and meat in exchange for the opening of U.S. markets to Mexican produce.[68]

Corn is Mexico's most important grain; in fact, its most important crop. Of 3.2 million basic grain growers in Mexico, 2.3 million grow corn. In 1994, corn was the major crop of half of all Mexican farmers. Many corn farmers are poor: more than 9 out of 10 work five hectares or fewer; nearly 7 out of 10 work two or fewer hectares; and 4 out of 10—nearly 1 million farmers—work one hectare or less;[69] five hectares is the minimum area required for a family's subsistence. The vast majority of Mexico's corn farmers are accordingly "infra-subsistence" cultivators; that is, they do not have enough land in cultivation to be able to subsist on their production.

Mexican corn culture is woefully unproductive compared with U.S. corn culture. Average Mexican yields at the beginning of the 1900s were 1.6 tons per hectare for subsistence and infra-subsistence farmers, and 2.4 tons per hectare for commercial farmers. In the United States at the same time, corn yields were eight tons per hectare.[70] Early-1990s comparisons of labor productivity show that the United States produced 137 times more corn per worker-hour than Mexico.[71] As a consequence of lower land and labor productivity, Mexican corn is at least one-third more expensive to produce than U.S. corn.

The effect of such great differences in productivity in the low-barrier North American market has been just what one would expect. The total value of corn and other grains imported by Mexico since 1994, $9 billion, is almost as great as the total from 1982 to 1993.[72] In 1998, Mexico imported an estimated 5 million tons of corn, or between one-quarter and one-third of the amount of the domestic harvest.[73] Meanwhile, prices for Mexican producers have fallen by between 40 and 60 percent since NAFTA took force.[74]

Many subsistence and infra-subsistence farmers will not be directly affected by the previously noted crisis of debt and credit or by depressed prices for local corn. But because they and their dependents rely on work as farm laborers for cash, when Mexico's commercial farm sector suffers, subsistence farmers and their households are left without local sources of revenue. The same is true of landless peasants, who, in the absence of local jobs, are under even greater pressure to migrate to an urban area, or to leave Mexico for another country.[75]

What of Mexico's urban economy? A rural exodus would be less disturbing if job markets in the cities were growing rapidly. However, the actual story of job creation under NAFTA hardly resembles the rosy picture painted by its boosters. Just as Mexico's small farmers have found it impossible to compete with U.S. agribusiness, many of Mexico's small-scale manufacturers, artisans, and retailers have found it difficult to compete with large producers from north of the border. By 1997, 28,000 small businesses in Mexico had gone bankrupt as a result of competition from TNCs and their Mexican partners and subsidiaries.[76]

Unemployment and underemployment figures for 1998 were essentially equal to those for 1994. Yet according to the government, the proportion of workers earning insufficient income grew by 3 percent between 1994 and 1998. As the government measure of insufficient income is not inflation-adjusted, the real increase is larger. Wage data, as shown in Table 11.2, support such a picture. Minimum-wage workers

---

Table 11.2

Purchasing Power of Average Manufacturing Wage and Minimum Wage, 1980–1998

	Dec. 1993	Dec. 1998
Purchasing Power of Average Manufacturing Wage, Change from Dec. 1993	—	–19%
Purchasing Power of Average Manufacturing Wage, Change from Dec. 1980	–8%	–25%
Purchasing Power of Minimum Wage, Change from Dec. 1993	—	–20%
Purchasing Power of Minimum Wage, Change from Dec. 1980	–60%	–68%

Source: Banco de Mexico, 1998

have fared poorly under NAFTA: the purchasing power of the minimum wage in December 1998 was 20 percent lower than in December 1993. And the same workers have fared much worse than workers as a whole over the period between December 1980 and December 1998, during which time the minimum wage lost an astounding 68 percent of its purchasing power.[77] As measured by the average manufacturing wage, wages as a whole also suffered declines during the 1980s and 1990s. Between December 1980 and December 1998, real wages fell 25 percent; taking December 1993 as the baseline, real wages declined 19 percent.[78]

A related trend is an increase between 1994 and 1998 in the size of Mexico's large and poorly paid informal sector.[79] Mexico's economically active population has expanded faster than the number of net new formal sector jobs created each year since at least 1980.[80] The job gaps in 1994, 1995, and 1996 were larger than the gaps in the early 1990s.[81] People unable to find formal sector jobs can either leave Mexico, return to farming (where they are not counted as unemployed), join the ranks of the unemployed, or seek work in the informal sector. The number of people who have availed themselves of the first three options is known to be smaller than the job gap since NAFTA took effect.[82] As a consequence, the number of Mexicans working in the informal sector has grown.

A rise in insufficiently paid work, broadly falling real wages, and increased amounts of informal sector work all increase pressure on urban workers to seek work in the *maquiladoras*—the one sector of the economy in which there has been net job creation. *Maquiladora* jobs, as we see later in this chapter, at least pay more than the minimum wage and offer protections informal sector work does not.

In rural as well as urban areas, neoliberal policies have contributed to the creation of an expanding supply of potential *maquiladora* workers, many of whom lack any other prospects for formal employment. As we saw earlier, the same policies have, if by different means, contributed to a rapid increase in the number of *maquiladoras*, and thus to the demand for *maquiladora* workers. These neoliberal policies remain. Now encoded in NAFTA, they will likely continue, even should a left-of-center government come to power in Mexico. Continuity of policy has so far led to continuity of results: each month 50 new *maquiladoras* are established in Mexico. We can expect thus a further maquilization of Mexico in the years to come.

THE HEALTH OF *MAQUILADORA* WORKERS

Throughout this book, we have measured the success of national economies by assessing the health of workers and the poor. Mexico's economy is undergoing a vast transformation. An important part of this transformation is the dynamic we have dubbed "maquilization." To understand maquilization from the perspective adopted in this book, one needs to understand the working environment that exists in a *maquiladora*, and what life is like for those who live in a *maquiladora* town. Occupational and environmental conditions affect workers' health in various and mutually reinforcing ways: wage levels, labor conditions, environmental conditions, and disease patterns along the U.S.-Mexican border (where *maquilas* are most-densely concentrated) are all relevant to our assessment.

Wages and Health

The health of poor workers such as Soledad (and that of their families) depends crucially on wages. Small differences in wage levels can, for instance, spell the difference between adequate and inadequate nutrition. The broader correlation between health and wealth has been well documented in various populations, and is neither discussed nor defended here.[83] Rather, we examine actual wage trends for *maquiladora* workers.

We have seen that the liberalization of Mexico's economy has been accompanied by sinking real wages for Mexican workers. One might expect that the wage trend would be different in the border cities' booming *maquiladora* sector, where workers are in high demand. This is not the case. As Table 11.3 shows, strong wage growth in 1997 and weak growth over the first three quarters of 1998 together gave workers back only 10 percent of the 23 percent loss in purchasing power they had suffered in 1995 and the first half of 1996; real wages are now still 13 percent lower than at the end of 1994. Workers in five of Mexico's six border states have suffered real wage declines since the implementation of NAFTA. Only in Nuevo León (which has relatively few *maquiladora* workers) have workers fully recouped the losses since the end of 1994.[84]

The average wage for *maquiladora* laborers was 59.7 pesos per day over the first three quarters of 1998, around US$6 at the then-prevailing exchange rates. These wages were between 30 and 40 percent below the mean Mexican wage, depending on the state.[85] Laborers earned on average twice the minimum wage, although in some states, they earned as little as 1.4 times the minimum wage. Such multiples of the minimum wage are no cause for celebration, for several reasons. First, the minimum wage is *not* a living wage; even the Mexican government does not claim it is. Second, the relatively high cost of living along the border takes a significant bite out of workers' wages. Third, by dint of having rare formal sector jobs, many *maquiladora* workers find themselves required to support large extended families. The truth is that most *maquila* workers simply can no longer afford more than the most basic necessities. One

---

Table 11.3

Mean Wage and Change in Purchasing Power of Wages, Mexican *Maquiladora Obreros* (Non-supervisory Workers), 1994–1998

	Consumer Price Index: Change from Dec. 1994	*Maquila Oberero* Mean Wage (pesos/day)	*Maquila Obrero* Mean Wage: Change from Dec. 1994	Purchasing Power of Mean *Maquila Obrero* Wage: Change from Dec. 1994
Dec. 1994	—	26.20	—	—
Dec. 1995	52%	31.90	22%	−20%
Dec. 1996	94%	38.95	49%	−23%
Dec. 1997	125%	49.73	90%	−15%
Dec. 1998	152%	57.14	118%	−13%

Sources: Banco de Mexico, 1998; STPS, 1998

Magnéticos de México worker in Nuevo Laredo compared her purchasing power in 1984 with her purchasing power in 1995:

> In 1984, I earned 300 pesos [per week], and with that money I was able to buy the weekly *mandado* [groceries] at a cost of 50 pesos, pay a woman to take care of my children, and still have money left over. Now, after accumulating 10 years of seniority, I earn 408 pesos [per week]. It is not enough. I have to pay rent, gas, electricity, and my weekly *mandado* alone costs 200 pesos. If I have enough for meat, I buy it; otherwise I don't.[86]

Occupational Health and Safety

Wages affect workers' health indirectly, but occupational hazards can affect health directly. In this section, we review a number of studies that show a relationship between work in Mexico's border *maquiladoras* and poor health.

A 1995 study of 497 *maquiladora* workers in Nogales, Sonora, found that workers who reported having a doctor or nurse at their work site were less than one-third as likely to have had a work-related accident in the previous six months than were workers who reported having no doctor or nurse at the work site.[87] Almost one-fifth of workers reported having no doctor or nurse at the work site. The study also found that workers whose plants offered them no information about occupational risks were 2.6 times as likely to report having had a work-related disease or illness in the previous six months; almost one-third of workers reported that their plant offered no information about occupational risks.

More significantly, the study found high rates of occupational injury and illness: over 12 percent of subjects reported having had an accident on the job in the previous six months, and 18.3 percent reported an episode of work-related sickness or disease during the previous six months.[88] As Table 11.4 shows, workers sustained injuries resulting in loss of work at almost twice the rate of U.S. manufacturing workers. To be sure, injury rates vary widely among manufacturing industries. Yet, the majority of Nogales workers were employed in manufacturing industries with below-average risk of injury. Fifty percent of the workers manufactured electronics components, employment which in the United States carries about one-half the risk of injury of manufacturing on the whole. Another 30 percent were employed in "diverse manufacturing," a category that excludes manufacture of foodstuffs, wood and metal products, automotive equipment, mechanical machinery, and other products the manufacture of which carries above average risk of injury. The incidence of occupational illness in the study population was also many times higher than that of U.S. manufacturing workers as a whole. For the electronics components industry, which employed half of Nogales *maquiladora* workers in 1991, the difference between the study population and U.S. workers was still greater.[89]

A recent study surveyed 267 workers from 50 different Matamoros and Reynosa *maquiladoras* for exposure to chemical, physical, and ergonomic hazards.[90] Ninety-four percent of these workers were involved in production work, and the majority worked in the electronics industry. In the area of chemical hazards, nearly half of the workers reported skin contact with chemicals during part or all of their shifts; 43 percent

Table 11.4

Annual Incidence of Nonfatal Occupational Injury and Illness Resulting in Loss of Work, Nogales *Maquiladora* Workers and Selected Categories of U.S. Workers, 1991

	Incidence of nonfatal occupational injury resulting in loss of work (/100 workers)	Incidence of work-related illness resulting in loss of work (/100 workers)
Nogales *Maquiladora* Workers	9.3	2.9
U.S. Workers		
Manufacturing, average	5	0.6
Electronic equipment, average	3.1	0.6
Electronic components and accessories	2.5	0.3

Sources: Balcazar, Denman, and Lara, 1995; OSHA 1991

reported direct exposure to chemical dusts; 46 percent reported direct exposure to gases or vapors; and 38 percent reported exposure to airborne organic compounds. By way of comparison, a 1993 study of 1,770 electronics workers in India found that 9 percent of workers were exposed to chemical dusts, 55 percent to gases or vapors, and 10 percent to organic solvents.[91]

The study of *maquiladora* workers also found strong and significant correlations between reported exposure to airborne chemicals and nausea or vomiting, stomach pain, urinary problems, and shortness of breath. Furthermore, chest pressure, unusual fatigue, and numbness or tingling in the extremities were significantly correlated with exposure to airborne organic compounds.[92]

Subjects also noted ill effects from physical and ergonomic hazards. The majority of subjects spent long weeks doing repetitive, machine-paced work; workers averaged 45.1 hours per week on the job (27 percent regularly worked 50 hours or more). This is broadly in line with Mexican manufacturing workers as a whole, who worked on average between 45 and 46.1 hours per week in each of the years between 1994 and 1998. Twenty percent of the subjects reported pain, numbness, or tingling in one or both hands during the course of the previous year; such pain was significantly related to the amount of forceful manual work employees carried out, to repetitive work, and to work in uncomfortable positions.[93] Twelve percent of subjects reported elbow/forearm pain during the previous year, and 14 percent reported shoulder pain.

One might take these findings as evidence of the hazards of exacting industrial assembly work in general, rather than of work in *maquiladoras* specifically. For instance, a 1995 study of 3,175 workers in the U.S. semiconductor industry found that the proportions of assembly workers having experienced at least one week of daily hand/wrist, elbow/forearm, and shoulder pain in the previous year were 23 percent, 12 percent, and 25 percent respectively.[94] Yet the *maquiladora* workers in the Matamoros/Reynosa study were on average substantially younger than the U.S. semiconductor assemblers. The rates seen among the *maquiladora* workers are thus unexpectedly high according to occupational health specialists.[95]

One weakness in the literature on the health of *maquiladora* workers is a lack of studies on the long-term effects of workplace exposure to various substances. There is, however, a limited literature on the reproductive outcomes of women *maquiladora* workers. A 1993 study compared the reproductive outcomes of women employed in three different industries: garment *maquiladoras*, electronics *maquiladoras*, and service industries. Women were asked about their pregnancy history, including the outcome of each pregnancy (live birth, miscarriage, stillbirth, or premature birth) and for how long they had been trying to conceive, employment status at the time of the pregnancy, and the weight of each child at birth.[96] The study found that the sector in which a woman worked more closely predicted her babies' birth weights than her age, education, smoking history, or number of previous deliveries. Service sector workers' babies were heaviest, followed by electronics *maquiladora* workers' babies (weighing on average 312 grams less than those of service workers), followed by garment *maquiladora* workers' babies (weighing on average 591 grams less than those of service workers). All other outcomes, including rates of fetal loss and length of time to conceive, were similar across the groups. The study was not able to establish a specific cause for the variation in birth weights. Possible explanations include chemical exposures, ergonomic factors, and sociodemographic variables, such as lower wages, longer hours, and lower rates of union membership among *maquiladora* workers. Nonetheless, the study was able to conclude that "reduced birth weight [appeared] to be a specific health consequence associated with *maquiladora* work."[97]

Environment and Health

Many of the toxins the *maquilas* produce affect not only workers, but also much broader populations, as the toxins are distributed into the border region's water and air. Indeed, no one disputes that the border region is terribly polluted, one of the most contaminated regions in the Americas. Opponents of NAFTA worried that increased industrialization and population would result in further degradation of the border environment, while even NAFTA's *proponents* recognized that lessening the environmental impact of the *maquiladoras* would require the dispersal of plants into the country's interior.[98]

The border between Mexico and the United States extends 2,100 miles, from the Pacific Ocean to the Gulf of Mexico, defining the northern boundary of six Mexican states: Baja California, Sonora, Chihuahua, Coahuila, Nuevo León, and Tamaulipas. The U.S. and Mexican governments define the "border zone" as the area within one hundred kilometers north and south of the international boundary, an area roughly one and one-quarter times the size of France.

Twelve million people live in this vast area, approximately 6 million on each side. The region has North America's fastest-growing population. The Mexican border population, for instance, expanded from about 3,889,000 in 1990 to 5,344,000 in 1995; the population of the border zone as a whole is expected to double between 1997 and 2010.[99] Although a large share of the region's population remains rural, growth is overwhelmingly an urban phenomenon. For example, the population of Ciudad Juarez (across the border from El Paso, in the state of Chihuahua) has grown at an average annual rate of almost 7 percent over the last 35 years.[100] Between 1980 and 1990, the eight most populous border cities grew by 43 percent. This corresponds to an average annual growth rate of 3.6 percent. During the same period, Mexican cities in the interior grew by only 22 percent, an average annual rate of about 2 percent.[101] Growth did not slacken during the 1990s. To take one example, the border town of Ciudad Acuña grew from 56,000 to 120,000 between 1990 and 1998. This amounts to an average annual growth of 10 percent.[102]

Much of this growth can be attributed to the *maquiladoras*. In June 1998, there were more than 3,900 *maquiladoras* in Mexico, employing 1,000,304 people. Some 80 percent of these people worked along the border.[103] Proponents of NAFTA promised the agreement would spread the growth of *maquiladoras* into Mexico's interior, relieving population and environmental pressures in the border zone.[104] The first part of this promise has been fulfilled: as Table 11.5 shows, *maquiladora* employment in Mexico's interior states grew by over 140 percent between 1994 and 1998.[105] But the second part of this promise has not come to pass: in five years of trade subject to NAFTA's rules, the *maquiladora* sector as a whole has grown almost as much as over the previous 28 years; so that in spite of the establishment of an increasing proportion of new

Table 11.5

Maquiladora Sector Growth, Border States and Interior States, 1970–1988

	Year	*Maquiladora* Employment (Annual Average)	*Maquiladora* Employment, Increase over Previous Year	New *Maquiladora* Employment
Border States	1994	500,811	—	—
	1995	545,660	9%	44,849
	1996	619,313	13%	73,653
	1997	727,085	17%	107,772
	1998*	796,839	10%	69,754
Interior States	1994	82,233	—	—
	1995	102,603	25%	20,370
	1996	135,545	32%	32,942
	1997	171,701	27%	36,156
	1999*	197,558	15%	25,857

*Through Q3 1998

Sources: Galhardi, 1998; STPS 1998a

maquilas in Mexico's interior states, employment in border *maquilas* grew much more quickly after NAFTA than in the early 1990s.[106] The bottom line for the border zone is that it absorbed more than twice as many new *maquiladora* jobs in 1998 as in 1994; if pre-NAFTA evidence of deteriorating air, water, and soil quality is any guide, border environmental quality will be further damaged.[107]

The unregulated growth of the *maquiladoras* has put entire communities at risk for environmental accidents. A 1994 study polled 22 community leaders in Reynosa and Matamoros about environmental incidents due to *maquiladoras*. Sixteen of 22 leaders reported one or more incidents of fire, explosion, or release of toxic gases that caused health problems for workers or community residents.[108] Subjects reported incidents including electrical fires, gas leaks, and chemical leaks.[109] There were, for instance, 15 separate "serious chemical releases" in Reynosa and Matamoros during the five years prior to the survey. In one incident, at a Deltronics plant in Matamoros, the company did not alert authorities for fear of bad publicity. Instead, "workers were kept inside the plant, communication lines were cut, Red Cross workers and fire-fighters were not permitted entry, and the incident was written off as 'mass hysteria' on the part of workers."[110]

Industrial accidents are acute examples of environmental damage with consequences for human health. Yet the slow and silent erosion of the U.S.-Mexico border zone's water quality due to industrial pollution and inadequate infrastructure for human settlements arguably represents a greater risk to human health. The great increase in population at the border since 1965 has seriously degraded the fragile ecosystem around the Rio Grande, which runs from Colorado to the Gulf of Mexico and forms nearly half the border between the United States and Mexico. As two health researchers with experience in the region remark, "No one anticipated this nearly-overnight flood of people, and government officials of the border area (on both sides) did not properly prepare for the prospect of deterioration of the scarce water supplies by sewage, industrial effluent, and agricultural and mining wastewater."[111]

The contamination of the Rio Grande may have several distinct effects on human health.[112] First, the river both supplies water for irrigation and collects wastewater and runoff; in consequence, by the time it reaches Mexico, the Rio Grande is "not a plentiful or clean source of water."[113] Downstream cities on both sides of the border cope with the surface water shortage by relying on polluted ground water for municipal needs.[114]

Second, industrial contamination of the Rio Grande and its tributaries may cause long-term damage to the health of local populations. A 1991 study found that the four major border waterways of the Lower Rio Grande Valley were contaminated with hazardous wastes.[115] High levels of toxic organic discharge, as well as metals such as mercury, chromium, nickel, and lead, were detected in sewer lines from the various industrial sites. Two out of three samples from Nuevo Laredo exceeded levels of 20 times either the ambient or drinking water standards. In fully half the sites sampled, acidity levels were so high that contact would cause burns to the skin.

More recently, a binational study of water quality in the Rio Grande from El Paso/Ciudad Juarez to Brownsville/Matamoros screened for toxic chemicals in the water and measured concentrations both upstream and downstream of each screening site.[116] Researchers from the United States found that of 21 toxic chemicals, 14 exceeded a criterion or screening level. The same study also reported that "arsenic was detected in 33 of 37 samples analyzed and exceeded criteria/screening levels in all 33."[117] While arsenic was the predominant chemical pollutant, many other contaminants were also found.[118]

The study examined the potential for both short- and long-term toxicity to humans that might arise from the consumption of fish or drinking water taken from the river. Short-term risk from water pollution was observed at one site near Laredo and Nuevo Laredo, where levels of mercury in fish exceeded U.S. Food and Drug Administration safety levels. The main long-term result was that, "low-level human health criteria were exceeded in water and/or edible fish tissue at 37 of 47 test sites."[119]

Many *maquiladoras* dump their waste into the Rio Grande's tributaries, which by their nature carry less volumes of water than the mainstream. It is thus not surprising that the study found that more than half the tributaries contained a greater variety of toxic chemicals at higher concentrations than the mainstream. In addition, the study found a "gradual increase in downstream concentrations of conventional and metal pollutants."[120]

Third, the Rio Grande has likely acted as an important conduit for disease.[121] Although industry contributes the lion's share of contamination to the border region's water supply, human waste from unincorporated settlements (*colonias*) is also an important contaminant. Border *colonias* often lack septic tanks, sewers, or running water.[122] In 1995, it was estimated that 350,000 people in Ciudad Juarez lived in *colonias*.[123] Until the mid-1990s, no sewage treatment existed in Nuevo Laredo, and 70 percent of the approximately one-half million residents flushed their toilets directly into the Rio Grande.[124] Twenty-five million gallons of raw sewage were flowing into the Rio Grande from Nuevo Laredo each day; in consequence, the river was considered unsafe for 25 miles downstream. It should thus come as no surprise that the other segments of the Rio Grande have been contaminated by high levels of human waste in sewage, especially near industrialized areas. Samples of tap water and raw groundwater from wells in El Paso/Ciúdad Juárez were tested for evidence of fecal indicator bacteria and nitrates, which signify possible contamination by sewage.[125] Sixty percent of tap water samples and 91 percent of raw well water samples tested positive for fecal coliform bacteria.[126]

The region's polluted water is complemented by polluted air and soil. In a 1994 study of the Lower Rio Grande Valley's soil and air, nine households were chosen to obtain maximum variation in exposure sources: three were located within the city of Brownsville, Texas, and were serviced by municipal sewage and water systems; two were located in *colonias* on the Brownsville city limits; and four were located in rural, agricultural areas of Cameron and Hidalgo counties in Mexico.[127] The study showed that pesticide residues were common in air, dust, blood, urine, and food. Levels of pesticides were elevated during the summer, when the application is usually heavier. Heptachlor and DDT, both banned toxins in the United States, were detected at low levels in residents' blood and urine samples. Elements such as zinc, sulfur, calcium, iron, bromine, and manganese occurred in the air and dust sampled at *every* household. Urinary arsenic levels were typically higher than those seen across the United States. Indoor and outdoor air samples were analyzed for 78 volatile organic compounds, of which about 80 percent showed up in measurable concentrations. Lead levels in the diet were found to be above accepted exposure limits.

One study has compared the U.S.-Mexico border area to Bhopal, India, prior to the 1984 explosion of Union Carbide's pesticide plant, which left thousands dead or injured (see Chapter Ten).[128] The study cites such similarities as numerous small chemical leaks, inadequate safety procedures, an untrained workforce, poorly maintained equipment, and large numbers of poor people living immediately adjacent to industrial plants. The border has yet to produce an incident as violent as the one in Bhopal, and may never do so. That it has not obscures from public view the magnitude of the toll industry is taking on both humans and the environment. There is a Bhopal taking place in the border zone; it is merely taking place over months and years, rather than seconds and minutes.

Disease

Crowding, lack of sanitation, and pathogens borne by water or air interact to affect the health of populations on the U.S.-Mexico border. Over 70 percent of the border zone's population is crammed into 14 sets of "twin cities" along the border. As noted previously, the area has witnessed rapid population growth. This growth has come without comparable improvements in infrastructure, particularly on the Mexican side of the border.[129] Partly in consequence, at least 500,000 border residents live in squatter settlements.[130] Judging by the Mexican border zone's morbidity and mortality rates for a variety of conditions, the public health implications of the border's rapid urban growth have been profound. In this section, we first compare mortality rates in the Mexican border communities to mortality rates in their U.S. counterparts and in Mexico as a whole. We then examine differentials in morbidity due to certain infectious diseases, to cancers and congenital abnormalities, and to depression.

Mexican border communities usually have a far greater burden of disease than their American counterparts. The increased burden of disease is evident in one of the most sensitive indicators of population health—infant mortality. Border counties in the United States had an infant mortality rate of 7.0 deaths per 1,000 live births over the period 1989-1991, compared to 25.2 deaths per 1,000 live births in Mexican border municipalities.[131] "Twinned" border cities often exhibited great disparities in infant mortality. The Mexican cities had infant mortality rates as great as five times higher than the U.S. cities: for instance, between 1989 and 1991, infant mortality was 6.9 deaths per 1,000 live births in El Paso and 36.2 per 1,000 across the border in Juarez.

Mortality differences between U.S. and Mexican border populations are troubling, but not unexpected, given the vast differences in wealth existing between the two countries. What *is* more surprising is that the Mexican border municipalities' infant mortality and age-adjusted mortality rates are higher than the corresponding rates for Mexico as a whole, in spite of the border zone's greater wealth. In 1996, the six border states had six of the seven highest per capita incomes in Mexico, and in aggregate, per capita income was well above the Mexican average. Nuevo León, Mexico's wealthiest state, had a per capita income almost four times that of the poorest, Guerrero. Yet the infant mortality rate for the period 1989-1991 was 25.2 deaths per 1,000 live births in the border municipalities versus 23.1 deaths per 1,000 births in Mexico as a whole. During the same period, as shown in Table 11.6, age-adjusted mortality was slightly higher in the border municipalities than in Mexico as a whole. It is interesting to note that age-specific death rates for ages 1 to 14 years are lower in the border municipalities than in Mexico as a whole, and mortality is approximately equal for ages 15-44 years; yet among those 45 and older, mortality is higher along the border. The causes of this pattern are surely too complex to disentangle here, but this much is clear: the above-average incomes of Mexico's border states have not clearly resulted in better adult health when compared to Mexico as a whole.

Some of the most widely acknowledged health problems in the border region are infectious (or communicable) diseases.[132] Tuberculosis (TB) and Hepatitis A are among the most important of these. Tuberculosis is an airborne disease caused by a mycobacterium. In adults, it most often manifests as infection of the lung. When patients have active disease, the tubercle bacillus can be transmitted to people nearby through coughing, or other contact through which airborne droplet nuclei containing the organism are transmitted. Family members and close associates of a person with active disease are in particular danger of becoming infected. In this way, crowded living conditions exacerbate the spread of tuberculosis. Given the crowding of the Mexican border zone, it is hardly surprising that incidence of tuberculosis is higher there than in Mexico as a whole;[133] in fact, Mexican border municipalities had fully twice the incidence of the country at large. Populations on the U.S. side of the border also suffer from tuberculosis at rates that far exceed the national average. In 1990, for instance, incidence of tuberculosis was almost twice as high in the U.S. border zone as in the United States at large.[134] Again, the problem is a great deal worse on the Mexican side of the border, where the 1990 incidence of tuberculosis was almost twice as high as in the U.S. border zone.

As bad as tuberculosis morbidity differentials are between the U.S. and Mexican border zones, they pale in comparison to differences in mortality rates. Table 11.7 shows tuberculosis mortality over two consecutive three-year intervals between 1989 and 1994 in border municipalities and states. Mortality rates fell on both sides of the border, but fell faster in the U.S., with the result that tuberculosis mortality in Mexican border municipalities, expressed as a multiple of U.S. border municipalities' tuberculosis mortality, grew from 7.8 in 1989-1991 to 9.3 in 1992-94. In comparison to the rest of Mexico, border municipalities' tuberculosis mortality was nearly 40 percent higher in 1989-1991, and remained nearly 30 percent higher in 1992-94.

In contrast to tuberculosis, hepatitis A is a viral illness transmitted through water contaminated with human waste. Several studies have documented the high prevalence of hepatitis A in both U.S. and Mexican border populations. A 1989 study found seroprevalence rates of 33 percent for eight-year-old children living along the

Table 11.6

Age-Adjusted Mortality, Mexico and Mexican Border Zone, 1990

Mexico

Ages (years)	Age-Specific Death Rate (per 1,000 population)	Population	Distribution of Population (%)	Number of Deaths
<1	33.8	1,927,827	2.4	65,165
1 to 4	2.4	8,267,351	10.2	20,085
5 to 14	0.6	20,951,326	25.8	11,872
15 to 44	1.9	37,362,583	46.0	71,543
45 to 64	8.9	8,871,452	10.9	78,964
65+	50.8	3,376,841	4.2	171,399
Unknown	5.5	492,265	0.6	2,708
All Ages		81,249,645	100	421,736

Mexican Border Zone

Ages (years)	Age-Specific Death Rate (per 1,000 population)	Population	Distribution of Population (%)	Number of Deaths
<1	30.6	83,671	2.5	2,557
1 to 4	1.5	320,860	9.5	470
5 to 14	0.4	740,334	21.9	324
15 to 44	2.0	1,688,326	49.9	3,304
45 to 64	10.6	360,456	10.7	3,837
65+	59.2	118,593	3.5	7,023
Unknown	2.2	70,429	2.1	154
All Ages		3,382,669	100	17,669

	Mexico	Mexican Border Zone
Crude Death Rates (per 1,000 population)	5.2	5.22
Standardized Death Rate using Mexico, 1990 (per 1,000 population)		5.56

Source: PAHO, 1994.

Table 11.7

Tuberculosis Mortality, U.S. and Mexican Border States, 1989–1994

Region	Tuberculosis Mortality (per 100,000 population) 1981–1991	Tuberculosis Mortality (per 100,000 population) 1992–1994
Baja California	11.7	10.6
California	0.7	0.5
Sonora	7.1	8.0
Arizona	0.7	0.4
Chihuahua	8.8	8.9
New Mexico	0.7	0.5
Coahuila	9.7	9.3
Nuevo Leon	7.4	7.7
Tampaulipas	9	9.2
Texas	0.7	0.5
Mexican Border*	10.2	9.3
U.S. Border*	1.3	1.0
Mexico	7.4	7.2
United States	0.7	0.4

	1989–1991	1992–1994
Mexican Border Zone Mortality as a Multiple of Mexican Mortality	1.4	1.3
Mexican Border Zone Mortality as a Multiple of U.S. Border Mortality	7.8	9.3
Mexican Border Zone Mortality as a Multiple of U.S. Mortality	14.6	23.3

*Mean value for municipalities

Sources: PAHO, 1994; PAHO, 1995

Mexican border and approximately 90 percent for adults by age 34.[135] These rates are higher than equivalent rates in less industrialized and less populated U.S. counties.[136] The two industrialized areas surveyed had hepatitis A incidence rates between 18.7 and 27 per 10,000 population, while the less developed areas had incidences of only 3.7 to 4.2 per 10,000.[137] In 1990, U.S. border counties' incidence of hepatitis A was more than three times that of the United States as a whole; El Paso's hepatitis A rates have been as high as five times the U.S. rate.[138] On the Mexican side of the border, meanwhile, 1990 incidence of hepatitis A was two-and-a-half times higher in border municipalities than in the country at large.[139]

Table 11.8

**Morbidity from Selected Infectious Diseases,
Mexican Border Zone, Mexico, and U.S. Border Zone*, 1989–1991**

Disease	Cumulative Cases, Mexican Border 1989–1991	1990 Incidence per 100,000 population			Mexican Border Zone Incidence as a Multiple of Mexico Incidence	Mexican Border Zone Incidence as a Multiple of U.S. Border Incidence
		Mexican Border Zone	Mexico	U.S. BorderZone*		
Brucellosis	669	5.4	5.1	0.6	1.1	8.6
Dengue	2,394	59.4	11.7	0.0	5.1	—
Hepatitis A	4,299	50.1	19.4	45.1	2.6	1.1
Leprosy	128	2.5	0.2	0.1	12.5	25.0
Measles	7,465	148	84.7	42.2	1.7	3.5
Salmonellosis	18,802	147.4	116.4	18.6	1.3	7.9
Primary and Secondary Syphilis	2,670	27.7	4.5	3.5	6.2	7.9
Tuberculosis	4,127	35.7	17.8	25.3	2.0	1.4
Typhoid Fever	4,691	36.1	18.4	0.4	2.0	90.3

*Excludes San Diego

Source: PAHO, 1994

Hepatitis A and tuberculosis are only two of many communicable diseases with disproportionate morbidity in the Mexican border zone; others are shown in Table 11.8, and include measles, rabies, salmonellosis, syphilis, and typhoid fever.

Noncommunicable diseases are also a growing concern among border populations. Mortality from all cancers combined was 62.9 per 100,000 population in the Mexican border zone in 1990, compared with 50.8 in the country as a whole; mortality due to cancers of the trachea, bronchi, and lung was 70 percent higher in the border municipalities.[140] These differences were not clearly attributable to different age structures of the population, as cancer mortality rates were higher for the border dwellers in every age group.

Cancers are not the only noncommunicable conditions that burden the Mexican border population disproportionately. As Table 11.9 shows, 1992-94 mortality due to congenital anomalies was marginally higher in the Mexican border zone than in the rest of Mexico, and substantially higher than in the U.S. border zone.

One might intuitively expect to find elevated levels of infectious diseases, cancers, and congenital abnormalities among newly urbanized, poor populations living in the shadow of environmentally noxious industries. Our intuitions about neuropsychiatric conditions in these same populations are much less well developed. Yet these conditions are now among the diseases most characteristic of development: in 1990, no other category of illness revealed a greater difference in the share of burden of disease between developed and developing countries.[141] Depression is by far the most burdensome of these conditions, and it is accordingly a large and growing source of ill health for adults throughout Latin America and the Caribbean. In those regions, as elsewhere, women suffer disproportionately from depression. The Global Burden of Disease report estimates that Latin American and Caribbean women aged 15 to 60 years lost almost 2 million disability-adjusted life years (DALYs) to major depression in 1990; this is roughly twice as many as were lost to tuberculosis; six times those lost to HIV/AIDS; and slightly more than those lost to all cancers combined.[142] The report projects that in 2010, major depression will cause about 50 percent more lost DALYs than all communicable, maternal, and nutritional diseases combined for

---

Table 11.9

U.S. and Mexican Mortality due to Congenital Anomolies, 1992–1994

	1992–94 Age-Standardized Mortality per 100,000 population	
	Male	Female
Mexican Border Zone	8.8	8.6
U.S. Border	6.0	5.1
Mexico	8.6	7.9
United States	6.7	6.0

Source: PAHO, 1994

Latin American and Caribbean women aged 15 to 60 years. Put another way, major depression will cause, among women aged 15 to 60, about 20 times more lost DALYs than tuberculosis; six times more than HIV/AIDS; and one-and-a-half times more than all cancers combined.[143]

In many populations, including populations of Mexicans and Mexican-Americans, depression has been shown to disproportionately affect poorer and less well educated people.[144] We might therefore expect to find higher rates of depression among the relatively poor and uneducated women working in *maquiladoras* along the rapidly developing U.S.-Mexico border than we would find among representative samples of Mexican and Mexican-American women. This is in fact what has been found—but with a twist.

A 1992 study surveyed 480 Tijuana women for symptoms of depression.[145] The study compared *maquiladora* workers (subdivided into electronics and garment workers) to service industry workers, and to women with no history of employment. There were no statistically significant differences in symptoms of depression among the four groups. This was a somewhat surprising result, given that the *maquiladora* workers were less educated and less well paid than the service workers.

The authors and other commentators have noted several possible sources of bias in the study. First, possible selection bias: informants might have avoided listing workers who were hospitalized, on medical leave, or nervous about being interviewed for the study. Second, women who had stopped working (for health or other reasons) were not included in the study. Third, *maquiladoras* may be especially good at screening for and hiring healthy workers. Fourth, women who seek (the often physically demanding) work in *maquiladoras* may belong to an especially healthy subgroup of the population.

Let us put aside these possible sources of bias, and provisionally accept that the *maquiladora* workers were *not* significantly more depressive than either service workers or women with no history of employment. Even given that assumption, the study points to something important and alarming about Mexico's rapid maquilization: depression scores for *all* groups were unusually high, between 15.3 and 17.6 out of a possible highest score of 60 on the Hispanic Health and Nutrition Examination Survey version of the Center for Epidemiologic Studies Depression scale (CES-D).[146]

These scores are far higher than the average scores, recorded in three recent studies, of Mexican-American and northern Mexican women. A 1988 study of 3,118 Mexican-American adults found a mean CES-D score for women of 9.3, while a 1989 three-generation study of 1,074 Mexican-American adults found a mean score of 9.7 for the youngest generation of females.[147] Finally, a 1987 study of depression in 991 Tijuana adults found a mean score of 12.6 among women.[148] In short, women residing in Tijuana in 1992 had much higher levels of depressive symptoms than comparable populations of Mexican-American women. Furthermore, those same women had much higher rates of depressive symptoms than women residents of Tijuana surveyed five years earlier.

Still more troubling, an extremely high proportion of women in the 1992 Tijuana study scored high enough on the CES-D to count presumptively as *depressed*. In the three other studies cited, the proportions of women meeting this criterion were 18.7 percent, 19 percent, and 33 percent, respectively. In contrast, the 1992 Tijuana study found case rates of 40 percent in electronics workers, 54 percent in garment workers, 51 percent in service workers, and 50 percent in non-wage earners.[149]

LIBERALIZED TRADE AND INVESTMENT, MAQUILIZATION, AND HEALTH: TODAY MEXICO, TOMORROW THE HEMISPHERE

During the 1990s, many *maquiladora* workers on the U.S.-Mexico border earned insufficient wages, becoming poorer even as their country became richer. They often worked under unhealthy and unsafe conditions, breathed polluted air, drank polluted water, and lived in conditions that encouraged the spread of disease and other forms of ill health.

Yet for some, Mexico's liberalization of trade and investment has not been without clear benefits. First, even though considerable trade liberalization had taken place before NAFTA, the agreement resulted in further large increases in two-way foreign trade: exports grew by 124 percent between 1994 and 1998, an average of 17.7 percent per year; imports grew almost as quickly, rising 89 percent, or 13.6 percent annually, during the same period. By lowering the costs of some foreign goods, the growth in trade has arguably helped those Mexicans wealthy enough to consume such items (although today, a concurrent weakening of the peso has destroyed many, if not most, such gains). Second, the growth of foreign direct investment (much of it in the *maquiladora* sector) combined with the growth in portfolio investment, in spite of its unevenness, has further enriched a minority of previously wealthy Mexicans. Third, foreign corporations have benefited. The distinct effects of Mexico's neoliberal turn on the (mostly North American) TNCs that produce in the *maquiladoras* are uncertain. For instance, conditions in the wealthy consumer economies have greater effects on TNCs' revenues and profits than specific Mexican policies. Furthermore, the weak peso has played an important role in convincing foreign TNCs to produce in Mexico. But the intensity with which such corporations lobbied for liberalization and the use they have made of the freedoms it offers them are enough to show that corporations expected gains from liberalization and that liberalization has delivered the expected advantages.[150]

Will economic liberalization eventually deliver broad benefits to Mexico's middle classes, working classes, and rural poor? The evidence suggests otherwise; despite ample opportunity to prove that it could deliver the promised benefits, liberalization has done nothing of the kind. Indeed, to the contrary: *under NAFTA, both the number and proportion of the extremely poor have grown.*[151] In 1994, there were roughly 17 million Mexicans living in extreme poverty, accounting for less than 20 percent of the population.[152] In mid-1998, there were 26.3 million, representing almost 28 percent of the population.[153] During the course of the longer period beginning in 1989, extreme poverty first declined slightly as a percentage of the population; but the steep increases after 1994 mean that there are today almost 10 million more Mexicans living in extreme poverty than in 1989.[154]

Thus, the maquilization of Mexico's economy has been accompanied by even deeper impoverishment of the country's poor, and we have seen that the forces behind the growth of the *maquiladora* sector are of a piece with those that have played a part in impoverishing many wage-earning and rural Mexicans. *Maquiladora* workers, though hardly the poorest of Mexico's poor (and sometimes not even technically among the poor), have grown poorer under the country's liberalization.

Securing workers' health is not a matter of stopping the growth of the *maquiladoras*, which, even were it possible, might not be desirable. The pre-1980 economy, in which almost 40 percent of Mexicans were employed in agriculture, is steadily dissolving. For many Mexicans, there is no longer any family farm to which they might return. Lacking other or better options for formal sector employment, many *maquiladora* workers are grateful for the economic opportunity and social protection that *maquiladora* work affords, even as they suffer from their employers' violations of Mexico's laws and from the government's indifference to or complicity in those violations. It is not easy to judge whether Soledad is better or worse off than she would have been had a border *maquiladora* job not been an option, and she had remained on her family's farm. It is in any case not a judgment we can make; Soledad herself might have difficulty making it.

The question, then, is how to advance *maquiladora* workers' health. And here it is easier to imagine what might have been done under a different kind of trade and investment regime; one under which the choices faced by Soledad and millions like her might have been less stark. A slower liberalization of Mexico's agricultural sector might have greatly softened the dislocations generated by the more abrupt transformation; minimizing dislocations would, in turn, likely have resulted in higher wages for *maquiladora* workers. Another North American trade and investment regime might have given international bodies real power to ensure that nations enforce their labor and environmental laws, or (better still) might have developed international labor and environmental standards with binding force. (Even today, such enforcement would likely result in the growth of unions that represent workers, and in higher wages and cleaner workplaces.) A different North American regime might also have included forceful commitments to cleaning up existing pollution along the border; to fostering the growth of *maquiladora* suppliers in Mexico by means of credits and incentives, thus linking the wider Mexican industrial economy to the *maquiladora* sector; and to encouraging TNCs to fund the education of Mexican workers. These are some of the paths to an economy that *promotes* the health of workers.

Would such concessions to internationally recognized rights, domestic law, and human decency raise costs to such a degree that TNCs owning *maquiladoras* would establish fewer of them in Mexico, or not establish new *maquiladoras* there at all, or perhaps even uproot existing ones? The first of these possibilities is certainly plausible; other things being equal, any increased cost of production in Mexico will result in *some* reduction in the proportion of global foreign direct investment that flows to Mexico. The second and third seem much less likely. Mexico is simply too convenient to U.S. firms and others producing for both the North American and, increasingly, the Central and South American markets. Mexico has a relatively well-developed infrastructure; U.S. multinationals already know how to establish themselves there (if, as in the case of General Motors, a company already has several dozen plants in Mexico, establishing a new one there will be much easier than elsewhere); transport costs are low for exports to the United States; and managers can in some cases commute from the United States.

Additionally, improved working and environmental conditions might neither reduce nor curtail investment by TNCs, given that such improvements often benefit employers despite the costs of making those improvements. For example, a workforce with high rates of occupational illness and injury, high rates of depression, and high turnover is *not* optimally productive.

We do not have to resolve here the complicated question of the cost to humanity of a hundred or a hundred thousand jobs; and our argument is emphatically not that workers' health should be well maintained so that a plant can produce at a marginally higher rate. It is, rather, that corporations often do not have the incentives to invest in workers' well-being in ways that would profit both shareholders and workers in the long run. Corporate managers are understandably preoccupied with short-term profitability. For this very reason, legislators and the architects of international trade regimes, both of whom must provide for entire societies over the long run, must compel businesses to pay the costs that will allow workers to maintain their health.

The North American Free Trade Agreement is for practical purposes not subject to repeal. But governments throughout the Americas will have many chances to demonstrate whether they have learned anything from its shortcomings, for they negotiate new trade agreements with regularity. For example, since the implementation of NAFTA, Mexico has pursued a full complement of new bilateral and multilateral free trade agreements. As of the end of 1998, bilateral negotiations were underway with Belize, Ecuador, Israel, Panama, Peru, and Trinidad and Tobago. Mexico began negotiating an agreement with the European Union during the summer of 1998, and was also negotiating a quadrilateral agreement with El Salvador, Guatemala, and Honduras.[155] The Clinton administration, for its part, negotiated more than 260 trade agreements during its first six years, and as 1998 drew to a close, announced its own plan for a trade agreement with the European Union, dubbed the Transatlantic Economic Partnership.[156]

Most of these trade agreements have relatively narrow agendas. Not so the Free Trade Area of the Americas (FTAA), which is currently being negotiated by every nation in the Americas other than Cuba. Despite a halting advance during 1998 (due to the U.S. Congress' refusal to grant President Clinton "fast-track" negotiating authority; generalized jitters over economic globalization; and delays in setting up the FTAA secretariat), the FTAA will likely unite the Western Hemisphere under a single economic umbrella, by 2005.[157]

Some will see the FTAA as an opportunity to improve upon NAFTA's weak mechanisms for protecting workers' health and the environment. An ideal FTAA would provide for common, legally binding labor and environmental standards,[158] for an international body with the power to see those standards enforced could go a long way toward eliminating injustices, such as those suffered by Soledad and other Magnéticos de México employees.

As with NAFTA, the negotiating parties have made elaborate declarations of principle concerning workers and the environment.[159] Yet, like NAFTA, the proposed hemispheric agreement contains no provisions on either labor rights or environmental protection; it is likely to be a "super"-NAFTA without NAFTA-like side agreements.[160] Under such a regime, we can look forward to maquilization of the entire hemisphere, to the depredations of Mexico's border zone writ large across it.

ACKNOWLEDGMENTS

The authors wish to thank the many people who assisted in the preparation of this chapter, including Evan Lyon, Joyce Millen, Jim Kim, Alec Irwin, Heather Rensberry, John Gershman, Tim Koechlin, Haun Saussy, Eve Mosciki, Kyriakos Markides, Rafael Moure-Eraso, Shelly Errington, Dorothy Fallows, Julie Rosenberg, Jill Petty, Aaron Shakow, Joaquim Salcedo, Mary Kay Smith Fawzi, William Vega, Mary Bachman, Asha George, Jason Fortier, Héctor Sáez, Eric Brenner, and Alicia Ingalls.

PART IV

Illicit Growth:
U.S. Drug Policy and
Global Inequality

South Dallas, Texas. Kids learn to play by watching the police.

(photo by Mary Ellen Mark)

CHAPTER TWELVE

The Drug War in Perspective

Arnold Chien, Margaret Connors, and Kenneth Fox

I n August of 1996, the *San Jose Mercury News* published a series of articles that would reverberate well beyond its usual readership.

The series presented evidence for the following picture. During the 1980s a San Francisco Bay Area drug ring supplied Colombian cocaine by the ton to Ricky Ross, the largest crack dealer in Los Angeles. The ring was headed by Norwin Meneses, an operative for the Contras, the Nicaraguan guerilla force then being run by the C.I.A. in order to overthrow Nicaragua's government. The ring's operation involved flights by Salvadoran air force planes between Colombia and a U.S. air force base in Texas. Drug proceeds were laundered through a Florida bank and then channeled to the Contras, providing them with funding at a time when Congress had cut off official U.S. aid. Meneses and Danilo Blandon, Ross's contact, were protected by the Justice Department when the Drug Enforcement Administration (D.E.A.) and local authorities attempted to investigate the drug ring. The *Mercury News* concluded that, inasmuch as crack cocaine originated in South Central Los Angeles and was largely introduced by Ross, the national crack epidemic was largely the responsibility of the C.I.A. and other elements of the U.S. government committed to maintaining the Contras.

Though neglected at first by the mainstream media, the series became a hot topic on Internet newsgroups, Black radio talk shows, and in Black communities around the country. This was made possible by some canny planning on the part of the series' author, Gary Webb. In anticipation of the neglect, a sophisticated website was designed to provide the original articles and supporting documents available for downloading (text totaling over 200 pages). By several weeks after the original publication date, the site was registering over 100,000 hits a day.[1]

Still, the Internet was just the medium for a story with scandalous implications. Could it be that the U.S. government, which had spent billions to wage a "war on drugs," was itself implicated in the drug trade? In urban communities ravaged by crack, the issue was urgent. Black civic and religious leaders organized town hall meetings, panel discussions, and press conferences to air evidence of the U.S. government's role in drug trafficking. Protest rallies were held in Los Angeles and Washington, D.C. U.S. Congresswoman Maxine Waters, who represents South Central Los Angeles, joined with Jesse Jackson and the Congressional Black Caucus to demand investigations by the Justice Department and the C.I.A.

By early October the mainstream media began to take notice. Two themes dominated the coverage. The first was that the *Mercury News* got it wrong. Initially the *Washington Post, New York Times*, and *Los Angeles Times* all ran lengthy front-page articles concluding that there was no evidence of C.I.A. involvement, Meneses's ring was responsible for only a small amount of cocaine, and his relationship to the Contras was low-level.[2] The second theme concerned the reaction in Black communities—centrally, how widely Blacks believed the government conspired to supply their neighborhoods with crack, though the *Mercury News* itself had never made this claim. The implication was clear: Blacks are irrational. The *Boston Globe* ran a typical story, which read in part:

> News accounts alleging CIA links to crack-cocaine sales are pulsing through [Los Angeles'] Black neighborhoods like a shockwave, provoking a stunning, growing level of anger and indignation....What is striking about this conflagration is that White residents have focused little attention on it, again illustrating the racial divide in Los Angeles and elsewhere, and that, even though there is no conclusive evidence that the story about the Central Intelligence Agency is true [the *Globe* article later cited the *Washington Post* report], Blacks here almost unanimously said they believe it.

The story quoted a Los Angeles grade school teacher named Lissa Washington, who explained that Blacks in poor neighborhoods have long sought to improve their lot without much success, and had come to the conclusion that the institutional barriers in their way were too high. While acknowledging that Blacks may be led in frustration to accept "unreasonable" explanations for their problems and should assume more responsibility in solving them, the teacher added that this "doesn't negate the real sense among us that the Supreme Court, the Republican Congress, the CIA, and other parts of government regularly take actions that frustrate our progress or set us back."[3]

These themes became orthodoxy as they were picked up and widely repeated by other major news organizations in the print and broadcast media.[4] But they were hardly conclusive. Despite appearances the *Washington Post* did not actually dispute Webb's main claims, and skirted a large body of evidence that had been available for years implicating the C.I.A. in the drug trade.[5] Similarly for the *Los Angeles Times*, which took the additional step of contradicting its own prior coverage of the local crack trade so as to downplay Ricky Ross's role. A reporter later confirmed the paper's lack of curiosity: "It was clear from the start that we weren't supposed to find out what really might be going on. We were encouraged to attack the *Mercury News*."[6] Like the others, the *New York Times'* attack relied on such sources as "current and former intelligence and law-enforcement officials, former rebel leaders, and Contra supporters," prompting one critic to remark: "Now there's hard-hitting impartial journalism for you. The [*New York*] *Times* runs the case by the accused, who deny the charges."[7] Meanwhile, the *New York Times* made no mention of the conclusions reached in 1988 by Senator John Kerry's Senate subcommittee about the C.I.A.'s complicity in drug trafficking. Along with the other papers, the *Boston Globe*, Kerry's home newspaper, was studiously avoiding them as well.[8]

In the midst of the controversy, a former D.E.A. agent testified during a press conference that a U.S. air force base in El Salvador was used during the 1980s for drug flights into the United States. Two months later, a Miami grand jury indicted the former head of a Venezuelan National Guard unit for smuggling tons of cocaine into the United States; according to officials involved in the case, the unit was C.I.A.-funded and the smuggling operation C.I.A.-approved. In these cases the story was reported well away from the front page, and was not repeated over time and taken up by other news outlets.[9] In similar fashion, the *San Francisco Examiner's* report a decade before on many of the matters described in the *Mercury News* series had been buried, as had the original reports on Contra drug dealing by Robert Parry and others, as had the conclusions of Kerry's subcommittee.[10] The mass media's slighting of evidence was the continuation of a pattern.

In May 1997, *Mercury News* editor Jerry Ceppos apologized for the series. While maintaining that it "solidly documented [that] a drug ring associated with the Contras sold large quantities of cocaine in inner-city Los Angeles in the 1980s at the time of the crack explosion there...[that] some of the drug profits from those sales went to the Contras [and that] given our government's involvement with the Contras...this is a major public policy issue worthy of further investigation," Ceppos wrote that the series nonetheless "did not meet our standards." He claimed this was because it omitted certain court testimony by Blandon, didn't label certain estimates of money as estimates, "oversimplified" the issue of how the crack epidemic grew, and implied C.I.A. knowledge without sufficient evidence. The *New York Times, Washington Post*, and other mainstream media immediately responded with prominent stories and editorials to the effect that the main thrust of the series had been discredited. Ceppos was praised for his "courage" in owning up to his failure (though some complained that an apology was not enough to undo the damage that had been done).[11] Since Ceppos had written that the series raised a "major public policy issue worthy of further investigation," a naïve observer might have expected him to protest the media reaction—or, perhaps, to publish Webb's follow-up investigations, which according to Webb further documented the story including the issue of C.I.A. knowledge. But the courageous Ceppos did no such thing; on the contrary, Webb was removed from the story a month later, told his new articles would not be published, and was transferred to a bureau 150 miles from his home.[12]

So the *Mercury News* would now keep to the standards of the mainstream media by re-burying the "major public policy issue." The issue was not just possible government involvement in the cocaine trade. The third installment of Webb's series pointed out that of all the criminal protagonists in the story, only the Black man from the streets, Ricky Ross, faced a life sentence (a few months later, he received it). Webb noted that this was in keeping with a general feature of the War on Drugs—namely, that it had disproportionately hurt Black communities. The on-line version of the installment included downloadable information on sentencing guidelines that treat crack cocaine, whose users are often urban Blacks, far more seriously than powdered cocaine, whose users are often suburban Whites. The series thus suggested a relation between U.S. foreign policy and the War on Drugs' effects at home. While the exact relation was not made clear, the whole issue was worth "further investigation" and wide public discussion. But because of the mainstream media, an opportunity for such discussion was lost.

In this chapter we propose to pick up where the *Mercury News* series left off. Specifically, we will attempt a full critical analysis of the War on Drugs. It is no small task. By the "War on Drugs" we mean the federally-initiated programs purportedly aimed at reducing the use and supply of illegal drugs. These programs—dating from the Nixon era, but revived under the Reagan and Bush administrations and continued under Clinton—have included myriad efforts of legislation, prosecution, interdiction, and public relations undertaken by federal agencies, the Pentagon, Congress, the courts, the media, and other institutions. The complex of issues is large and intricate, with strands leading in many directions. But we believe that Gary Webb was right to connect the War on Drugs to wider U.S. policy, and that in fact the connections are extensive and systematic. We propose to make sense of the complexity by displaying these connections.

First we examine the relation between the international drug traffic and U.S. foreign policy, and the relation of both to the War on Drugs as conducted abroad. Then we turn to the domestic front. We examine factors linking poverty and drug involvement and discuss the disproportionate effect that drug laws and law enforcement have had on poor and minority communities. What we find is that the War on Drugs both abroad and at home consistently serves not the interests of public health and safety, but those of the U.S. private sector. We conclude by summarizing the reasons why the War on Drugs has been widely considered a failure. We suggest that, on the contrary, it has been successful insofar as private interests have been served, which explains why it continues.

1. THE WAR ON DRUGS ABROAD

Drugs and Covert Action

We can begin to understand the nature of the War on Drugs by reviewing the history of ties between drug trafficking and U.S. foreign policy, as implemented through covert operations. From 1948 to 1972, the U.S. heroin market was supplied primarily through the "French Connection," a smuggling operation controlled by Corsican syndicates based in Marseille. As detailed by Alfred McCoy, the operation was largely a by-product of U.S. foreign policy. With generous C.I.A. funding, the syndicates and their political allies were encouraged to beat up striking dock workers, suppress the Marseille labor movement, and curtail the influence of the French Communist Party. The success of these efforts left the gangsters in a position of considerable power, which they used to expand their heroin operations. Marseille's first heroin laboratories opened months after the syndicates had seized control of the waterfront from the unions.[13]

Today heroin in the United States comes primarily from Burma, part of the infamous "Golden Triangle" of opium-producing highlands also encompassing areas in

Laos and Thailand.[14] United States covert operations were again instrumental in the development of the region's drug trade. In the early 1950s, the United States extended crucial material and logistical support to the remnants of Nationalist Chinese (Kuomintang, or KMT) troops who had been driven to Burma by Mao's army. Though its attempts to retake Chinese territory failed, the strengthened KMT did establish itself locally. In particular, it became the de facto government of Burma's major opium-producing region, forcing levies on the natives and assuming control of the opium traffic. Under the KMT the opium was delivered to Northern Thailand and sold to the head of the Thai police, a well known C.I.A. client. By 1973, KMT cadres controlled almost a third of the world's opium supply.[15]

Beginning in 1960, the C.I.A. pressed Hmong tribesmen into service to combat the Pathet Lao, a nationalist movement committed to land reform. To sustain the clandestine army, agency operatives delivered rice and supplies into the Laotian highlands where the Hmong cultivated poppy fields, and by 1965 were flying out opium to market. The C.I.A. and the U.S. Agency for International Development (USAID) further fueled the trade by subsidizing the Hmong army leader's formation of a private airline, which was used to ferry opium and heroin between Long Tieng and Vientiane.[16] Heroin laboratories in the region and in Burma multiplied with the build-up of U.S. ground forces in Vietnam, contributing to an addiction problem among the troops that reached epidemic proportions. Leading military and political figures in the South Vietnamese ruling elite were also active in the lucrative business, as U.S. officials knew but attempted to conceal.[17]

Another major source of heroin has been Afghanistan and Pakistan. In the mid-1980s, Afghanistan was the largest single heroin exporter in the world, responsible for more than half of the heroin in Europe and the United States.[18] The problem had been foreseen: in 1979 a member of the White House Drug Council warned to no avail that "we were going into Afghanistan to support the opium growers in their rebellion against the Soviets. Shouldn't we try to avoid what we had done in Laos?" Indeed Afghan guerillas greatly expanded their drug operations with the onset of C.I.A. support, which continued for ten years. After the Soviet invasion of Afghanistan, many of those operations were moved to Pakistan, a military dictatorship also subsidized by Washington ($3 billion in 1981). A surge of heroin exports from the region ensued, as well as an addiction epidemic in Pakistan that reached 1.3 million users by 1983. For years reports of widespread heroin smuggling by the guerillas—particularly by the leading recipients of U.S. aid—and by the Pakistani military were provided to U.S. officials, who took no action.[19]

United States covert action has also figured in the international cocaine traffic. Ninety percent of the world's coca leaves are grown in the Andean regions of Peru and Bolivia. For many years these regions supplied the cocaine-manufacturing cartels in Colombia, from which the finished product made its way to the United States by various routes through Central America and the Caribbean.[20] As the Congressional subcommittee chaired by Senator Kerry found, during much of the 1980s the traffickers included the Nicaraguan Contras. The C.I.A. (with the assistance of Argentine intelligence) had organized the Contra army from remnants of deposed dictator Somoza's National Guard scattered after the Sandinista revolution, then trained, funded, and directed it while fabricating its political leadership.[21] The Contras' links to the drug trade were especially close in Costa Rica, where cohorts of a Contra commander became major traffickers.[22] Also heavily involved was John Hull, an American rancher assisting the Contras who was evidently either an agent or asset of the C.I.A.[23] In 1989 a commission of Costa Rica's Legislative Assembly charged Hull, lieutenant colonel Oliver North, admiral John Poindexter, U.S. ambassador Lewis Tambs, and others with orchestrating the "infiltration of international gangs into Costa Rica that made use of the [Contras]...[opening the country] for trafficking in arms and drugs," thanks to efforts by North in cooperation with Panama's General Noriega.[24]

These illicit operations were known to high-level U.S. officials, who attempted to keep them hidden. The White House ordered federal agencies not to cooperate with an attempted probe by the General Accounting Office (GAO) into the role of drugs in U.S. foreign policy. Attorney General Edwin Meese instructed the U.S. attorney in Miami to suspend his investigation of trafficking in Central America. The D.E.A.'s office in Honduras was ordered to shut down even as the local drug trade was burgeoning with the heavy participation of the Honduran military; enormous amounts of cocaine were making their way into the United States from this source alone.[25] As a D.E.A. agent later told a reporter, "The Pentagon made it clear that we were in the way. They had more important business."[26] Indeed: Honduras received major U.S. subsidies to serve as a base for the Contras and a staging ground for the U.S. military.[27]

It is no accident that drug trafficking so often coincides with covert operations, as a former head of the U.S. Southern Command acknowledged: "If you want to go into the subversion business, collect intelligence, and move arms, you deal with drug [movers]."[28] Such activities require untraceable funds and often the cooperation of criminal elements willing to do the dirty work. Permitting or abetting drug traffic achieves both objectives.[29]

But it is important to not overstate the role of covert activity. In none of the cases just reviewed did the C.I.A. act contrary to high-level policy. Nor have high-level U.S. officials been known to sever strategically important links to drug smuggling; on the contrary they have been instrumental in shielding them from public scrutiny and prosecution, as we've seen. Abetting the drug traffic has served not a rogue C.I.A., but rather longstanding U.S. foreign policy aims.

Counternarcotics or Counterinsurgency?

United States aid and military activity under the War on Drugs have continued this history. In particular, they have often served to repress popular or revolutionary foment against U.S.-supported governments rather than to combat the drug trade. We will consider here the cases of Mexico and drug-producing countries in the Andes.

For decades the United States has been a major supplier of military aid to Mexico. During the 1970s the United States supplied $95 million in the form of helicopters, planes, guns, and other equipment. From 1988 to 1992, the United States sent over $214 million in military hardware, 16 times as much as France, the second leading supplier during the period. The Clinton administration has also been generous, disbursing not only weapons but modern reconnaissance technology.[30] There is evidence this aid has not been used particularly to combat drug traffickers. For example, in 1978 thousands of Mexican soldiers with the assistance of D.E.A. advisors attacked marijuana cultivators after the Direccíon Federal de Seguridad (D.F.S.), the vast Mexican agency for internal security, had already moved out the main traffickers under its protection. Those remaining were Indian peasants: according to the U.S. Catholic Conference, they were the true targets.[31] In Guerrero, Chiapas, and other states, military operations including outright massacres have been regarded by the impoverished locals as political repression in the guise of antinarcotics.[32] In early 1994, U.S.-supplied helicopters were used against the Zapatista rebels, widely regarded within Mexico as representative of peasant and indigenous rights.[33] Political analyst Eric Olson comments that "the risks of U.S. equipment being misused for counterinsurgency efforts are very real, since a major focus of Mexico's antinarcotics efforts is in Chiapas, often in areas of conflict with the Zapatistas." He cites as an example an incursion by the Mexican army into a conflict area subsequent to an operation officially intended for marijuana eradication.[34]

The United States sides with the Mexican ruling party in the civil war because, as a professor at the U.S. Army's War College puts it, a revolutionary government "could put U.S. investments in danger, jeopardize access to oil, and produce a flood of political refugees and economic migrants to the north."[35] Accordingly, the United States has not put a priority on seeing to it that equipment earmarked for antinarcotics actually be used for that purpose. According to a Mexican source, the U.S. State Department has informed the Mexican government that arms shipments need not be used only in drug operations, and that U.S. monitoring would occur only once a year and with advance notice.[36] Meanwhile staff and funding for monitoring has been reduced, and the transfer of military hardware is expected to be more expeditious following an agreement signed in April 1996.[37]

United States complicity has extended to the Mexican drug traffic. The Mexican D.F.S. masterminded the Guadalajara Cartel, which had been sending more cocaine to the United States than any other syndicate, providing logistics and political protection in exchange for a quarter of the profits. The United States was aware of D.F.S. criminality from the early 1970s, but did not suspend "antinarcotics" aid. On the contrary, the C.I.A. protected the D.F.S. from D.E.A. investigations so as to preserve its access to Mexican intelligence on indigenous revolutionary movements and East bloc diplomatic activity. At the trial of the accused killers of D.E.A. agent Enrique Camarena, government witnesses revealed that the C.I.A. protected some of the leading Mexican drug lords in exchange for their financial support of the Contras.[38]

From the late 1980s the Pentagon steadily built up its military presence in the Andean region for "the only war we've got," as the head of the U.S. Southern Command termed it, taking advantage of the Pentagon's share in the budget for the War on Drugs, which grew from $439 million in 1989 to $1.2 billion by 1992.[39] The effort has ostensibly been to provide intelligence, training, and equipment for armies fighting drug traffickers on the ground. But again the enemy on the ground generally turns out to be political dissidents, peasants, or revolutionary movements rooted in the peasantry. In Peru, U.S. military assistance has gone to a local army which has repeatedly stated that its priority in the "drug war" is fighting the Sendero Luminoso ("Shining Path") guerillas. Though the guerillas are involved in the drug trade, they are neither drug producers nor drug traffickers; on the contrary, their involvement is primarily as intermediaries negotiating prices with traffickers on behalf of coca-producing peasants.[40] More fundamentally, whereas "traffickers are members of a monolithic underground social organization with purely economic interests [and] no ideological and emotional identification with national problems...[Sendero Luminoso] and other political groups have their *raison d'être* in the ongoing abuses and social injustice against the Indians and the peasantry at large," as anthropologist Edmundo Morales observes.[41] The Peruvian military understands the distinction, being quite willing to fight Sendero Luminoso but not traffickers, sometimes even firing on counternarcotics police.[42] (Today Sendero Luminoso is virtually defunct.)

The story in Colombia is similar. There the local army has shown little interest in fighting drug traffickers, and indeed has advised and armed traffickers allied with right-wing paramilitary groups and local landowners. Meanwhile it has continued and intensified its decades-long effort to suppress popular movements and the political opposition.[43] At just the time when President Bush announced his campaign in the War on Drugs, with aid to Colombia as its centerpiece, the Andean Commission of Jurists reported that the military was using antidrug measures as a pretext to arrest and murder union leaders, grassroots organizers, and activists in the Patriotic Union political party. The aid did not go to the Colombian national police, which is in charge of almost all counternarcotics operations, but to the military. By the early 1990s Colombia was the leading recipient of U.S. military aid in Latin America, aid which increased under the Clinton Administration and was expected to reach record levels in 1997.[44] One of the most important unreported stories of the day is the generous U.S. support for a Colombian regime in which formal democracy masks an ongoing, large-scale campaign of harassment and murder against the civilian population.

The point is worth dwelling on. Father Javier Giraldo, head of a church-based human rights commission in Colombia, writes:

> Consider the following. On January 30, 1993, a car bomb exploded on a downtown street in Bogota, killing 20 people. Almost immediately, news of the bomb, which was attributed to drug traffickers, was circulated worldwide by international press agencies. During the same month of January, 1993, our human rights data bank registered 134 cases of political murder and 16 cases of enforced disappearance in the country....In other words, while a crime committed by drug traffickers which claimed 20 lives was widely reported by the international news media, 130 victims of state or para-state violence were ignored outside Colombia....Between May 1989 and June 1990, the period during which the most drug-related terrorist bombings were carried out, Colombian non-governmental organizations registered 227 drug-related fatalities. During the same period they registered 2,969 politically motivated murders, not counting deaths in combat between the army and guerillas.

Giraldo's commission reports upwards of 20,000 political murders between 1988 and 1995, secret victims of the real war underlying the War on Drugs.[45]

United States officials have repeatedly claimed that the War on Drugs abroad is not counterinsurgency. But the recipients openly admit that U.S. aid is used for this purpose, which translates into repression of the perceived supporters of armed insurgents: that is, much of the general population.[46] For example, Colombian military officials informed U.S. Congressional investigators in 1990 that most of "counternarcotics" military aid for the year was to be used for counterinsurgency.[47] Assistant Secretary of State Bernard Aronson explained in 1992 that:

> The programs we support in Peru today are not counterinsurgency programs....But they also contribute to strengthening the government's economic, administrative, and military capacity to confront and defeat Sendero [Luminoso]....The plain fact is that while drug trafficking is our top interest in Peru, the Sendero Luminoso is a direct threat to the government's survival. Peru's insurgencies...threaten democracy in Latin America and the prospects for regional economic integration and trade.

A year earlier the Bush administration had signed a bilateral agreement with Peru committing the United States to the war against Sendero Luminoso.[48] The official denials do not seem, then, to be very meaningful. But they do achieve a purpose: to give the appearance of compliance with the International Narcotics Control Act of 1990, which prohibits the diversion of funds earmarked for counternarcotics efforts.[49]

Issues of legality aside, Aronson's rationale is not entirely plausible. While anti-government guerillas have been guilty of human rights abuses—Sendero Luminoso reportedly killed over 15,000 people in the 1980s, overwhelmingly civilians—these abuses do not explain U.S. priorities since abuses by the Colombian and Peruvian armies have been as bad or worse (the Peruvian army's abuses being so bad as to prompt a Congressional cutoff of aid in 1991).[50] United States complicity in the repression in Colombia and Mexico, as well as its record in Guatemala, El Salvador, and elsewhere, suffices to show how much concern there is for "democracy in Latin America." What does cause overriding concern, however, are "the prospects for regional economic integration and trade"; that is, compliance with existing economic arrangements from which the U.S. private sector benefits, and which indigenous political movements potentially threaten.[51]

The Economic Order

What fuels the drug economies of Peru, Bolivia, and Colombia? One factor is debt. Governments must earn foreign exchange in order to stay in good standing with the International Monetary Fund (IMF) and other international creditors. If only one domestic product brings in sizable amounts of foreign exchange, there is pressure to produce it: coca in Peru and Bolivia, cocaine in Colombia (though other illicit drugs are now on the rise in these countries as well, as we later discuss).

But why are the options so limited to begin with? The main reason is that the international patterns of "economic integration and trade" are essentially colonial in nature, persisting despite the demise of overt colonialism. The poor countries have for the most part continued to perform a service role to the rich countries and the corporations that dominate their private sectors, by providing markets, cheap labor, and resources. By and large, poor countries import subsidized and protected goods from the North (usually finished products) while producing and exporting their own goods (usually raw materials) under market conditions imposed by the IMF or other Northern institutions, with local allies. The result for poorer nations has been reliance on imports for essentials and the prevention, weakening, or destruction of indigenous enterprises, which are unable to compete in domestic markets with the subsidized imports, and are victimized by low prices driven by competition with other poor countries in the global market.[52] Hence poor countries have few and unreliable means to earn foreign exchange even as they are compelled to do so.

So, for example, in prior years two of Bolivia's most important exports were tin and natural gas. But in the mid-1980s, world prices for these resources collapsed. Legal exports fell by 25 percent. Happily, Bolivia emerged from an IMF-imposed regimen with a modestly growing economy and exports back up. The secret to this success? Coca, which by the early 1990s was generating as much foreign exchange as all other exports combined.[53] Bolivian peasants earn between $1,000 and $2,500 per hectare of coca plants, about four times what could be earned by growing oranges and avocados, the next most profitable crops (with coca having the added advantages of growing in poor soil, yielding four or five crops per year, and being easy to transport). The story is similar in Peru, where coca exports earn an estimated $1 billion a year, equal to a third of all other exports combined, and national unemployment and underemployment has reached 90 percent. For Andean peasants, the survival alternatives to coca are few.[54]

Third World producers have sometimes attempted to subsidize prices of their exports in order to ensure stable incomes, just as rich countries do. These efforts have mostly failed (a significant exception being the Organization of Petroleum Exporting Countries [OPEC]) because of prevailing market forces and opposition by the rich countries. A price agreement among coffee-exporting countries, for example, was suspended in 1988 by U.S. initiative. This quickly led to a price drop of 40 percent for Colombia's leading legal export (its wheat exports having been undermined decades ago by U.S. subsidies for agribusiness firms). Similarly, even as the U.S. provided narcotics assistance aid to Colombia in 1990, it was maintaining tariffs on coffee and cut flowers despite Colombia's continuing requests for open markets. On the preferred patterns of "economic integration and trade," subsidies and protectionism are not permitted for poor countries, only rich ones.[55] The patterns reflect not free trade or free markets, but the balance of power.

So it is not just debt: as researcher Kiaran Honderich remarks, "The Latin American nations profiting from cocaine need to be given real alternatives. This means writing off much of their debt, ensuring stable markets and fair prices for other exports, and allowing them autonomy in their choice of economic systems."[56] But the problem is that these strategies would disrupt the preferred neocolonial arrangements. Autonomy, in particular, could lead to economic nationalism, or what a 1954 U.S. planning document described as policies geared toward "immediate improvement in the low living standards of the masses," and responsive to needs of local populations. United States policy-makers saw such policies as the prime danger to the overriding

U.S. interests, which are "a political and economic climate conducive to private investment," repatriation of profits, and "protection of our raw materials."[57] Accordingly, U.S. policy in Latin America (what is called "anticommunism") has consistently featured subversion of any manifestation of economic nationalism. For instance, Guatemala under Arbenz, Chile under Allende, Cuba under Castro, Grenada under Bishop, and Nicaragua under the Sandinistas had as their common denominator economic development that departed from the neocolonial model by aiming for "improvement in the low living standards of the masses."[58] It hardly seems likely that these long-standing and entrenched interests would be discarded for the purpose of weaning Andean countries from illicit exports.

Indeed, even to raise the possibility assumes that the War on Drugs is meant to be a war on drugs. What we've seen so far, however, is that it has served above all as a tool for the pursuit of elite interests. The targets of the campaign on the ground have been peasants and peasant-based reform or revolutionary movements in Mexico and the Andean countries. Even where such movements are absent or vanishingly weak, the War on Drugs still serves to strengthen the military and other local sectors with which the United States has traditionally been allied.[59]

These conclusions would not be telling if the War on Drugs aimed also at targets friendly to elite interests. But we've already seen in connection with the C.I.A. record that, on the contrary, the United States has been willing to abet or even initiate drug traffic when it serves the right interests. Let's now consider further evidence in this regard.

As part of its IMF-mandated "reform" of 1985, the Bolivian government introduced laws facilitating the movement of coca profits into the banking system. These laws enabled the buildup of foreign exchange, which consequently boosted the local currency and checked inflation. In Peru and Colombia as well, official policy is that no questions are asked and indeed tax amnesty is granted on repatriated revenues. What Melvin Burke notes of Bolivia is true elsewhere as well: "[D]rug launderers and their bankers...are not targets of the military in its brave new drug war."[60]

Nor, for the most part, are they targets of the United States. Whatever its entry point, laundered money once in the international banking system may easily make its way into U.S. banks, which are treated with respect. As far back as 1976, U.S. officials were aware of large-scale money laundering undertaken by U.S. banks, as indicated by currency surpluses channeled through the Federal Reserve. In 1979 an interagency task force known as "Operation Greenback" was formed to investigate. But within a few years, it had floundered after limited successes. There were too few bank examiners and Internal Revenue Service agents available, and no impetus from the administration. Vice President George Bush, who was named "drug czar" in early 1982, "wasn't really too interested in financial prosecution," according to Operation Greenback's chief prosecutor at the time. The task force was downgraded to a unit under the U.S. attorney's office in Miami, and by the late 1980s was defunct. By then many drug bankers had evidently moved their operations to California, where in 1988 the Justice Department attributed a $3 billion currency surplus to money laundering in Los Angeles. When an $8 billion surplus was reported for Miami and Los Angeles banks a year later, drug czar William Bennett did not investigate. Instead he expedited the eviction of low-income public housing residents in Washington, D.C., who were reported to have used drugs.[61]

To be sure, there is a U.S. law dating from 1970 which requires banks to report all large-sum transactions, and to some extent it has forced money launderers toward alternative schemes. But as of mid-1995 there was still not even a coordinated federal effort to respond to the reports, much less to monitor compliance.[62] Rather, banks are relied upon to police themselves, an arrangement under which prosecutions have been rare.[63] Even under the assumption that most individuals are honest, the arrangement is inherently unreliable given the financial incentives and competitive pressures. These are made especially clear by U.S. banks' continued offering of "private banks" catering to the wealthiest customers. Michael Zeldin, former chief of the Justice Department's money-laundering section, explains: "In private banking, the whole rationale is confidentiality, so there is a war of cultures. Private bankers will tell you that if the government requires all these disclosures and inquiries and maintenance of records, then there will be no private banking in the U.S. because it will all move offshore."[64] That is, any bank which is not subservient to affluent customers risks losing business to competitors. In a largely unregulated environment, detecting illicit money is consequently not a priority. The Organization of Economic Cooperation and Development (OECD) has estimated that in 1993 drug-trafficking revenues were at $460 billion, of which $260 billion resided in the United States via the banking system and other venues.[65]

Other U.S. corporations involved in the drug trade are also treated gingerly. The manufacture of cocaine from coca paste requires chemicals which are not produced in Colombia or elsewhere in Latin America. They are imported from multinational chemical firms. Between 1983 and 1986 imports of acetone, toluene, and other substances by Mexico, a transit point in the pipeline, increased by 1160 percent (as the Mexican economy grew by only 2.6 percent). United States corporations were the main suppliers: at the time, U.S. exports of these chemicals to Latin America greatly exceeded the amounts necessary for making foam mattresses, cosmetics, and other legal products for which they are normally used. In 1989 a drug policy advisor at the Congressional Research Service estimated that more than 90 percent of the chemicals used for cocaine production came from the United States.[66] In early 1990 the D.E.A. began taking action, halting some of the exports. But a top D.E.A. administrator testified before Congress that "we haven't done most of what we have to do," for lack of funding.[67] The D.E.A. introduced new controls in 1996, requiring advance notice of Colombian shipments and documentation of purpose. According to the Council on Hemispheric Affairs, the controls are a break from past years "when most [illicit] chemical transactions...were insufficiently regulated" because notice could be given as late as the day of shipment; this despite the War on Drugs through two presidential terms, during which the exports were known.[68] Again, law enforcement and criminal prosecution, not to mention publicity, have been lacking when it comes to white-collar suspects.

Since regulation of illicit commercial activity limits business autonomy, it has been further compromised by recent trade agreements. For example, inspections of commercial border traffic between the United States and Mexico have been dramatically reduced since passage of the North American Free Trade Agreement (NAFTA), obviously making matters easier for traffickers. International banking rules have also been relaxed, a boon for bank profits and money laundering. United States officials did not raise the drug issue during negotiation of the agreement, though they were aware of it: as one observer put it, it was "too hot to handle."[69] The Clinton administration also attempted to hide the issue from the public. According to a former D.E.A. intelligence chief, "We were prohibited from discussing the effects of NAFTA as it related to narcotics trafficking."[70] Public knowledge might have threatened the agreement, overwhelmingly supported by the business community.

The U.S. government is not a monolith. Among those who carry out policy under the War on Drugs are those whose honest efforts have included prosecution of elements friendly to U.S. economic and strategic interests. In fact, such individuals are often good sources for identifying the obstacles to a genuine war on drugs, as we've seen.[71] The point is that the topmost, most powerful, and most lavishly funded elements of government have held sway in overall policy direction, continuing a history in which the U.S. has tolerated, assisted, or protected the drug trade as a means to achieve other policy objectives.[72] At this level the fundamental objective is the promotion of U.S. private sector interests, for which the War on Drugs abroad has served as a vehicle.

2. THE WAR ON DRUGS AT HOME

We now turn to the domestic front of the War on Drugs. We first consider the relations between drug use, poverty, and the availability of treatment. Then we discuss the nature of drug dealing in poor areas. Finally, we analyze mandatory sentencing guidelines and their role in filling prisons with low-level, poor, and minority offenders. Throughout, we see once again how the War on Drugs and other policies have the effect of selectively punishing the lower classes while favoring elites, a pattern we will attempt to explain in the next section. We begin, however, with one woman's story.

April's Story

April is a 23-year-old African American woman who looks twice her age.[73] She lives in the Roxbury section of Boston, where she was born and raised. Roxbury was once an important manufacturing center. But between the 1950s and 1980s manufacturing jobs became scarce, leaving only low-paying service-sector jobs, often part-time and without benefits. Tax breaks, federally financed highway construction, and readily available business, home, and auto loans fueled a corporate exodus and subsequent White flight from the area. Urban renewal in Boston depleted the stock of low-cost housing and dislocated the poor on a large scale, while speculators on massive development projects profited enormously.[74]

April lives with her boyfriend DJ, now a night manager at McDonald's, and two of her three children. Joy, the new baby—her third—cries in the next room. April does not relate her persistent homelessness to the economic degradation of her neighborhood. She feels lucky to have gotten the Section 8 housing she is in after only a two-year wait.[75] She is also thankful that Joy was born before the first of September 1996. If the delivery had been a few *days later, new state welfare laws would have made her family ineligible for the additional $67 per month in benefits they now use to pay for milk, food, and diapers. At her kitchen table, April begins to tell her story of addiction and treatment. "I've been through a lot," she says. "I feel so old."*

April grew up in a large public-housing development in Roxbury. Her own mother struggled with drug abuse there. A high school dropout at 17, April ran away from home with a boyfriend. It was only after they broke up that she realized she was pregnant with her first child. Her mother having been evicted for drug use, April had nowhere to go and so made her home in an abandoned building. After the birth of her baby, April became addicted to crack. As her habit worsened she drifted from shelter to shelter. She recounts her survival strategies as she bounced between the street and the shelter and from one treatment program to another, amidst the sprawling squalor of her neighborhood:

> I was messin' with this dude named Calvin. We stayed in abandoned buildings. He'd hustle, rob, steal, anything. I'd eat, sleep, wait for him to come back with the coke. They had just put up this McDonald's [in one of the new empowerment zones], and they'd put boxes of garbage out. So usually we ate out of those. One day we broke into the Redemption Center— you know, the place where you turn in cans and bottles for money. We changed the bags and cashed them in again. Another day, Calvin had broke into this Chinaman's store. He stole a baby carriage and filled it with stuff he could sell. The police caught him pushing the carriage down the street. I was pregnant with Brittany [her second child] when Calvin went to jail.

In time, April fell in love with Calvin's brother DJ, who was also her regular dealer, and soon after she and the baby moved in with him. When he was arrested for drug trafficking, April and her children were homeless once more. April's addiction deepened and she began to leave the baby for longer and longer periods of time with her mother. But after a while her mother concluded, "You don't want him and I don't either." Speaking from her own experience, April's mother insisted that she get on the waiting list to enter a drug treatment program. After several months, April got a slot:

> But I didn't want to be there. I had an attitude. I had three demerits and it was coming close to my check day. So I called the bank and the check was there [by direct deposit]. I left the program and immediately went to get high. I didn't call my mother or nothin'. I disappeared for a month. So my mother called the DSS [Department of Social Services] on me.

The DSS then took legal custody of April's son:

> They made a temporary placement with my mother and said I wasn't allowed to take him out. If my mother let me take him out, they said they would take him away from us forever. That's when I really went on a smoking spree. I lived in the street. I got lost. I was angry. More angry than anything. It was built up inside me.

Eventually, DJ got out of jail and April and he got back together. "At first," April says, "I didn't want him to know I was gettin' high. But after a while I started askin' him for money. I would say, if you don't give it to me, I'll go out and make the money myself the best way I can—sellin' my behind. Then I got a place in another program."

When we asked April what part of her treatment experience made the most difference to her, she named the parenting classes. April is now raising the two children that remain in her care, in a three-room subsidized apartment in a town north of Boston she knows little about. She claims it's for the best. "The only time I go out is to go to the grocery store and come right back," she says. April fears that if she gets to know this place, she will also learn where drugs can be found. Her solution to her greatest fear is self-imposed seclusion.

April's story dramatizes some of the relations among poverty, race, drug involvement, and social malaise. It is a portrayal of drug dealing as economic opportunity and drug use as a symptom of an impoverished and demoralized community, in which scarce social support such as treatment and affordable housing can make all the difference.

Poverty and Drug Use

We now consider these and related issues in more detail, beginning with the relation between poverty and drug use. It is not that most drug users are poor. As former drug czar William Bennett has pointed out, "The typical cocaine user is White, male, a high school graduate employed full-time and living in a small metropolitan area or suburb."[76] Nor, of course, is it that all poor people use drugs. Many factors other than poverty put people at risk for drug use.

But the existence of other risk factors should not make us lose sight of the fact that poverty is a key factor. Though overall drug use nationwide has declined over recent years, the downward trends are unequal for different social and economic groups. Further, there are countervailing upward trends in use and abuse of illegal drugs, especially cocaine, in economically vulnerable sectors of the U.S. population.[77] In general, prevalence of use rises as incomes decline. Unemployed persons have higher rates of drug use than employed persons.[78] The prevalence of use among men earning less than $10,000 a year is four times higher than the rate among those earning more than $35,000 a year.[79] Drug-related illness and death are more prevalent in poor, marginalized populations such as the homeless and prisoners, and in "hyper-segregated" areas of concentrated poverty.[80] Researchers have found that age, income, and employment status are all better predictors of drug use than race or ethnicity. However, Blacks and Latinos are disproportionately poor and unemployed.[81]

Within economically disadvantaged groups such as Black adult males, drug abuse is not only more prevalent (though overall lifetime prevalences are similar across racial and ethnic groups), but also has graver consequences. Data collected in hospital emergency rooms and drug treatment programs demonstrate that Blacks suffer disproportionately from drug-related (particularly cocaine-related) disease and death.[82] This data is especially telling given that Blacks tend more often to be uninsured and to have less access to medical care and drug treatment than Whites. From 1984 to 1990, the percentage of Blacks among those admitted to emergency rooms for cocaine-related emergencies increased from approximately 40 percent to 54 percent, while the percentages of Whites and Latinos declined by 6 percent each.[83]

Poverty is an especially important factor for drug use among women. While male drug users still outnumber female users by two to one, national and state data confirm that women drug users (especially pregnant women) have considerably higher risk profiles than men. Among arrestees in the 23 cities where data were collected for a Drug Use Forecasting (DUF) report, female prostitutes were consistently more likely than any other kind of offender to be using illicit drugs. In the majority of cities surveyed, between 90 and 100 percent of these women tested positive for drugs.[84] In Massachusetts, for example, women are entering drug treatment with more severe problems in every category measured. They are more likely than men to be unemployed, to have earnings of less than $10,000 annually, and to use "hard-core" drugs (those that are supposed to be particularly addictive and to instill in the user a resistance to behavioral change). In fact, women admitted to treatment in 1995 were over a third more likely than men to be users of heroin, cocaine, or crack. The differences between pregnant and non-pregnant women drug users are even more alarming. Pregnant women users are younger, less educated, poorer, more likely to be reporting crack, cocaine, or heroin as their drug of choice, and to *already* be parenting a child.[85]

We re-emphasize that poverty is only one among many risk factors for drug use. Anthropologists Waldorf, Reinarman, and Murphy studied over 200 current and former compulsive cocaine users and concluded that it wasn't fear of the law but rather "a stake in a conventional life...jobs, family, friends—the ingredients of a normal identity—[which] turned out to be the ballast that allowed many users to control their use."[86] Another study has found school absence, truancy, failure, and dropout to be directly related to risk for drug involvement.[87] Another has identified the importance of such factors as idleness, a lack of social ties, and loneliness in renewed drug use following the completion of drug treatment.[88] But poverty is often intertwined with these factors. Because poverty means unemployment or underemployment, insufficient income, decrepit and unstable housing and neighborhoods, and limited access to quality education and health care, the poor are at greater risk for drug use than those with more resources. Poor people have fewer defenses against the temptation of drugs: as ethnographic evidence shows, this is often less the temptation of pleasure than of escape from despair.[89] One recovering addict puts it this way:

> A drug addict is a person who has feelings that they don't understand. A drug addict learns that drugs can take away those feelings. They become comfortable with the drug erasing those feelings whether those feelings are coming from alcoholic families, or an abusive childhood, or just coming from poverty and not thinking you can prosper in life, basic belittling of oneself. It's much easier to become a drug addict than to feel the things that we feel.[90]

The Paucity of Treatment

Being poor not only makes drug use harder to resist, it also makes escape from addiction harder to achieve. Poor addicts have great difficulty recovering on their own, though many strenuously try.[91] Their chances are worse if treatment is not even available.[92] Annual federal funds for drug treatment fell $75 million between the mid-1970s and the early 1980s. Over the same interval, state and local funding plunged over $100 million.[93] The 1997 drug-control budget has almost doubled since

1990, but 70 percent of the budget is for enforcement and interdiction and only 30 percent for prevention and treatment, a proportion that has not changed in over a decade.

These trends have coincided with the growing perception of drug use as a problem in the workplace. Over the last 15 years, public discourse on the "epidemic" of drug use has led many to believe that what had long been a "plague" among the lower and marginalized classes would spread to able-bodied workers and even to the privileged classes unless drug treatment was made widely available to the American workforce.[94] During this period, many employers found in substance abuse a compelling explanation for limited productivity and other economic ills. Thus, employee drug testing and employee-assistance programs (EAPs) gained increasing prominence. By the end of the 1980s about one-third of large businesses were testing workers for drug use, and over three-fourths of all workers with insurance coverage had benefits that included at least short-term substance abuse treatment.[95]

Cuts in government funding and increased drug testing by employers have together resulted in the growing privatization of drug treatment.[96] What has evolved is a two-tiered system: a growing sector which admits privately-insured addicts, and a shrinking one which admits indigent and Medicaid recipients. In this system, access to care depends on ability to pay.

The consequences for those without private insurance is the unavailability of treatment on demand and increasing scarcity of treatment of any type.[97] The numbers are revealing. In New York City alone, there are only 38,000 publicly funded treatment slots (mostly methadone maintenance) for an estimated 200,000 injection drug users.[98] In Baltimore, since Mayor Kurt Schmoke has been in office, all forms of treatment programs have been cut while more money than ever has been funneled to developers.[99] The Drug Abuse Services Research Survey documents that almost half of treatment facilities in a national survey reported more requests for treatment than they could accommodate.[100] The 1988 Presidential Commission on the HIV Epidemic noted that addicts who commonly ask AIDS outreach workers to help them access treatment often go unhelped due to extensive waiting lists nationwide, leaving them "otherwise ready to receive help with virtually no options."[101] Despite these conclusions, the problem has only worsened over the ten years since this report was issued.[102] In some instances drug users will resort to high-risk crimes, where the chances of arrest are particularly great, as a way of managing an expensive or out-of-control habit. In such cases, legal interception and consequent time in jail become the most efficient and sometimes only accessible means for desperate drug users to manage their addiction.[103]

Ability to pay determines not just access but also the quality of treatment and length of stay for those who gain access. Most indigent heroin addicts enter into federally funded methadone maintenance programs (a legacy of the Nixon administration).[104] But many such programs are now for-profit, and thus have incentive to maintain clients for years with little or no emphasis on recovery.[105] Relatively few indigent addicts gain entrance to programs that emphasize recovery.[106] Such programs depend almost entirely on a reasonable length of stay for their success, and addicts with less income don't stay as long, tending more to receive only outpatient counseling and short-term detoxification.[107] On average, users who have been addicted for fifteen years receive only three months of treatment.[108] One dimension of this problem is illustrated by the following testimony of a White, middle-class heroin user:

> I got on the methadone program to have a little more consistency and predictability in my life. New York City is the only place I've taken methadone and it's a purely maintenance deal, meaning they're not interested in detoxing anyone. The only way I could get off the program was to refuse to pay and then they had to detox me because they're not allowed to cut you off flat. My counselor had instantly taken a dislike to me because I had said that my goal was detoxing not maintenance. She thought I was being unrealistic and made it clear that she thought I should stay on methadone for many many years before even thinking of detoxing....She tried to get me health insurance without my consent so my bill could be paid for. That way I could stay in the program.[109]

Poor women with drug problems are marginalized to even greater extremes. Just eight years ago, the vast majority of drug-treatment programs in this country did not admit pregnant women.[110] Until a successful class action lawsuit in 1992, the only recourse for pregnant women seeking treatment was often imprisonment. Consequently many thought of jail time as detox time. A recent study of the accessibility of treatment for women in five major U.S. cities found that while most programs will now accept a pregnant woman, her options for treatment are severely restricted if she requires child care or is a Medicaid recipient.[111]

Furthermore, there are new efforts to criminalize a pregnant woman's addiction. Thirty-four states have already prosecuted women for ingesting drugs when pregnant, and for murder if their unborn children died. The number of such prosecutions tripled between 1990 and 1992, with poor Black women making up the majority of those prosecuted. The presumption in these cases is that pregnant addicts have a responsibility: specifically, in the words of the judge who presided over the first case in which a woman was convicted, "Pregnant addicts...have a responsibility to seek treatment." Yet the convicted woman had sought treatment several times but found none available.[112] And this is typical. A number of studies suggest that female drug users most want to recover when they are pregnant.[113] In the current system, however, they will be pushed to fail and then punished when they do.[114]

Women's exclusion from drug treatment has grave consequences. More and more children are being born to HIV-infected mothers. In New York City between 1991 and 1993, the number of foster children born to infected mothers increased 26 percent.[115] Based on a collection of studies, the GAO reports that 78 percent of foster children in New York City, Pennsylvania, and Los Angeles are at high risk for HIV based on a single risk factor: injection drug use by their mothers.

Nowhere is the discriminatory system of treatment delivery more evident than in the federal prison system. Over the past ten years, the number of inmates has nearly tripled, due primarily to the growing influx of drug offenders. Drug offenders have increased from 30 percent of all inmates to over 60 percent, and their length of incarceration has almost tripled. But treatment is scarce. Formal drug treatment in correctional settings canvassed by the National Institute on Drug Abuse fell by one-third between 1977 and 1982. According to the Institute of Medicine, this figure was nearly unchanged in 1987 despite the number of inmates having more than doubled in the meantime.[116] A 1992 survey of prisons revealed that only 28 percent offer treatment programs, and only 19 percent fund them.[117] In fact, more than 80 percent of existing programs are operated by volunteers. In 1995 a mere 6.7 percent of inmates received treatment while in jail.[118]

A dramatic case in point is the Oklahoma State Reformatory, where 60 percent of prisoners are in for drug use, possession, or distribution. The number climbs to 90 percent when those incarcerated for drug-related crimes are added. Yet there is no treatment facility. There is only one program in the entire state for prisoners with drug problems, and the waiting list is so long that it often takes years to be approved and admitted.[119]

Treatment will become even less available as small and decreasing amounts in the War on Drugs' appropriation are earmarked for treatment.[120] Furthermore, the funded modalities of treatment vary widely: they include drug education and/or counseling, self-help groups (either client-initiated or -maintained), and residential units dedicated to drug abuse treatment. According to the National Institute of Justice, the most typical alternative to incarceration is probation with a mix of counseling, support, and surveillance (electronic monitoring and urinalysis).[121] As the ineffectiveness of such approaches is evident even to nonprofessionals, chronic relapse is no surprise. Nor is what is in store: as President Clinton proclaimed in accepting the Democratic Party's 1996 nomination, "We should say to parolees, 'We will test you for drugs. If you go back on them, we will send you back to jail.'"

Not everyone is worse off in the new two-tiered system of treatment. By a variety of mechanisms, third-party payers have systematically excluded difficult, costly, or indigent patients, further straining the public facilities to which such patients then turn (as in other domains of the health-care system), while boosting earnings of the for-profit institutions to unprecedented levels.[122] On their own terms they have therefore succeeded, since their commitment is not to the general public but to shareholders.[123]

Drug Dealing as Economic Survival

Just as poverty is a significant factor for drug use, so it is for drug dealing. In poor areas, jobs are hard to find and even when found are "dead-end" and low-paying. These circumstances give rise to an underground economy. While estimates as to its size nationwide vary widely, no one doubts that the drug trade is a large chunk. Underground economies thrive especially in U.S. cities, where residential segregation is an enduring feature. By the early 1990s, seven of eight persons living in the slums of major cities were from ethnic minority groups.[124] Extreme residential separation (hypersegregation) persists at a much higher level among urban Blacks than among other racial or ethnic minority groups.[125] Up to one-half of Blacks live in hypersegregated areas where they are unlikely to have any direct contact with other ethnic groups that is not necessitated by work.[126] In the ten largest U.S. cities, the proportion of Blacks who live in extremely poor areas (more than 40 percent below the poverty line) increased from about one-third to almost one-half between 1980 and 1990.[127] These minority, low-income areas are highly stigmatized, and avoided by outsiders and mainstream businesses. They become urban "deserts": work, health care, and educational opportunities are withdrawn, tax bases erode, and a downward spiral begins toward complete deterioration.[128]

So the "legitimate" life options for the residents of such areas are very limited. As much research has confirmed, the drug trade offers economic opportunities that would not otherwise exist.[129] Of course, being poor does not inevitably lead to drug dealing, any more than it inevitably leads to drug use. But the incentives to become involved in drug use or drug trade are very strong. By one estimate, nearly half of all Black men born in 1967 in Washington, D.C., were engaged in drug dealing before reaching age twenty.[130] The point is that poverty, and in particular poverty within hypersegregated and stigmatized areas, makes the drug trade harder to resist.

It is not that the street drug trade offers riches. Journalist Clarence Lusane describes the organization of global drug distribution as a pyramid.[131] At the top are the international drug cartels which design and control international production, manufacturing, and export. On the next level, middle managers (suppliers) run regional distribution, marketing, security, and money laundering operations. In the cocaine trade, the lowest and largest level includes peasant farmers, street retailers, and their "crews" of salesworkers and shooting gallery/crack house supervisors. As drugs move from hand to hand through the trade network, profits and risks are generated and distributed in patterned ways. As one moves down the pyramid of this unregulated market, the number of exchanges increases, the units of exchange get smaller and smaller, unit prices fall, and drug purity declines as products are increasingly adulterated in order to wring out greater profits. Thus the cartels reap the highest returns, while on the streets profits are meager and work is tedious, labor intensive, and risky. Moreover, trade at the street level is by definition "public" and thus more likely to be detected and punished.[132]

Lusane's image is missing an important component: governments, "whose civilian and military intelligence agencies recurrently afford *de facto* protection to drug kingpins beneath them," as political analysts Scott and Marshall point out.[133] As we've seen, the U.S. government is not an exception. The current point, however, is the meager status and income of those at the bottom of the pyramid. Even at this level, profits and burdens are unevenly distributed; the largest profits are concentrated in the hands of a few. According to Bruce Johnson, "fewer than one-fifth of drug dealers have a net-worth cash return of more than $1,000/month."[134] A RAND study set in Washington, D.C., categorizes dealers as either regular (selling more than one day per week) or occasional (one day per week or less). Over 90 percent of all street-level net income was collected by the regular dealers in the study (however much of the money from these earnings was redistributed up the business pyramid). Notably, the study also found that regular selling was not incompatible with employment in the legal economy. Earnings from the drug trade represented only one-fourth of the total earnings of dealers in the study. Further, dealers were more likely to earn money from wage labor in the legal economy than to commit a property crime.[135]

Several researchers have documented additional details on the earnings and working conditions of the lowest-level crack and cocaine dealers.[136] First, earnings are unstable. Sustained periods of steady income are unusual, with workers usually plying their trade part-time, in the late evening and on the weekends. Second, payment is often on a consignment basis. Suppliers "front" drugs to street retailers; that is, they lend the commodity "on credit." How much the retailer and his crew earn depends on how much they sell. Third, brief periods of high earnings (up to ten times the hourly minimum wage) infrequently punctuate a more mundane course in which traffickers earn on average between $7 and $8 per hour. Fourth, "wages" and assets are lost during police busts and during time injured or in jail. Street salesmen often become users themselves and sometimes take their pay in the form of the drugs they sell. In all, the opportunities to accumulate wealth are very small.

Working conditions are bad as well, even aside from the regular dealer's risk of being killed, injured, or imprisoned.[137] This is how anthropologist Philippe Bourgois describes one crackhouse, where his informants worked day in and day out: "There was no bathroom, no running water, no telephone, no heat in winter, no air conditioning in summer...the paint on the walls was peeling, windows were pasted over...and a red forty watt bulb hung from an exposed fixture in the middle of the room...the smell of urine and vomit permeated the locale."[138]

So why do street dealers stay on the job? Because they want to survive. For all its risks, wretchedness, and income instability, drug dealing is an entry-level opportunity for otherwise marginalized surplus labor.[139] As sociologist Terry Williams writes, "The drug business is a safety net of sorts, a place where it is always possible to make a few dollars."[140]

This "safety net" has become more vital with the shredding of the legal safety net. In 1970, benefits under food stamps and Aid to Families with Dependent Children (AFDC) averaged $68.50 and $136 per month, respectively. These benefits declined by 20 percent (in constant dollars) over the next two decades.[141] With the 1996 "welfare reform" law, AFDC was eliminated and replaced with block grants to the states. The total amount of the grants is frozen at 1994 AFDC levels through the year 2000, with no adjustment for inflation or population growth. However, states are allowed to impose any number of restrictions, such as a cutoff after two years to parents who are not working or being trained. They are also allowed to use grant funds for purposes other than welfare. All in all, the law entails substantial reductions in benefits. And it is not just the former AFDC that is affected: in fact, most of the projected $55 billion in cuts over the next six years will come from other programs, including food stamps, assistance to legal immigrants, and Supplemental Security Income (SSI) for the elderly and disabled.[142]

The reduction of benefits, as well as new work requirements for recipients ("workfare"), will inevitably result in a larger labor pool. Many predict that this will have negative effects on both wages and the availability of jobs. These are effects not just on the poor but on the working population generally, since the new workers will be competing with existing workers at the lower ends of the wage scale. In New York City for example, there are a projected 91,000 job openings per year and 750,000 looking for jobs—some on welfare, others not.[143] Municipal employees in particular will be at risk of either losing their jobs to workfare workers who earn less (a quarter of what municipal workers presently earn), or else having their wages cut to remain competitive. According to the Urban Institute, 11 million families will lose income in one way or another because of the new law, over half of them working families. Not only will poor people become 10 percent poorer, but 2.6 million will become newly poor. The Economic Policy Institute estimates that absorbing the extra workers created by the new law would depress wages for the bottom third of the workforce by 11 percent nationally.[144]

This depression would continue a trend: wages fell 14 percent between 1973 and 1993.[145] Before "welfare reform," full-time minimum wage jobs were insufficient to lift a family out of poverty. Two-thirds of U.S. citizens in poor families with children were living with at least one taxpaying worker.[146] The squeeze on families headed by single women is especially severe, since women earn about two-thirds as much per hour as men and must pay for child care in order to work. This may explain why, of the 68 percent of welfare recipients who are back in the workforce within two years, between two-thirds and three-quarters return to welfare within five years.[147] The new law will make returning more difficult and continued work even less tenable.[148] So it will also make avoiding underground economies like the street drug trade more difficult.

More Time for Less Crime

When those who enter this trade are arrested, new laws mandate their imprisonment for long periods of time. One such law is that which established mandatory minimum sentencing (MMS) in 1986. According to its proponents, MMS has two main goals: that a person convicted of a crime serve a minimum prison sentence, and that the threat of a long sentence deter potential offenders.[149]

The crime of most concern is not murder, rape, or money laundering, but small-time drug involvement. In a report of the Federal Judicial Center, Vincent and Hofer note that in 1992 more than half of those convicted under MMS were drug offenders, half of whom were considered to be in the lowest criminal history category: that is, no record of violence, no evidence of sophisticated criminal activity, and no prior criminal confinement. Seventy-seven percent of convicted drug offenses involved no weapons. Only 5 percent of the convicted were organizers or leaders of an extensive drug operation, while over 85 percent neither managed nor supervised drug traffic. Overwhelmingly, convicts were poor, with 81 percent judged at sentencing unable even to pay a fine.[150] In other words, the least dangerous offenders make up the fastest growing segment of the prison population. Many are the weakest of the weak: "mules," used by small-time dealers for transporting drugs so as to lower their own risk. Often these are destitute foreigners and children, who sell or deliver drugs for a pittance. This may explain why juvenile arrests for drug sales in Washington, D.C., increased by 500 percent between 1985 and 1989, while drug arrests of adults increased by only 10 percent.[151]

Punishment under MMS is systematically disproportionate to severity of crime. Researchers Vincent and Hofer explain that since "mandatory minimums ignore many relevant sentencing factors, they give disproportionate weight to the factors they do consider—amount of drugs, particular types of prior convictions, and especially the government's power to move for a reduction of sentence based on a defendant's substantial assistance in the prosecution of another person." The latter means that the most peripheral participants receive the harshest sentences, because they have nothing to offer prosecutors. In one typical case, a woman with no prior record and who neither bought nor sold drugs was sentenced to ten years because she knew her two sons were dealing drugs and did nothing about it. Her codefendant, an active street dealer, had a prior record and was serving a sentence for manslaughter, but was sentenced to 57 months because he cooperated with authorities.[152]

While the least dangerous criminals end up in jail, more dangerous criminals increasingly avoid it. In New York State, where MMS is used extensively, the percentage of violent offenders among prisoners was 34 percent in 1992, down from 63 percent in 1982. In Florida thousands of offenders, many of them violent, have been released to make space for drug offenders. Under MMS, court resources have been diverted away from higher-level offenders toward low-level ones.[153]

"Three Strikes and You're Out" state and federal laws have effects similar to those of MMS. These laws are popular because they hold the promise of locking up repeat violent offenders for longer periods of time. In principle, they require that offenders convicted of a third violent offense be sentenced to life in prison without the possibility of parole.[154] But the legal definition of a "violent" crime has been extended to such a degree that in 68 percent of crimes classified as "violent," there was no physical injury to the victim.[155] What constitutes a "serious" felony or a "violent" crime is determined by state penal codes which often differ from F.B.I. crime classifications. In California, for example, a "third strike" can occur if the first two strikes are nonviolent felonies and the third is violent or if the first two strikes are "serious" or violent and the third a felony. A "violent" crime is classified as anything from murder to first degree burglary and a serious felony is anything from murder to robbery and a prisoner assault on a non-inmate. As the law is written, it is entirely possible to receive 25 years to life without committing a violent crime. For example, two robberies (considered a serious felony) and a car theft (a minor felony) would qualify as three strikes. In one highly publicized incident, a pizza theft counted as a third strike resulting in a life sentence.[156] A RAND study concluded that three-strike laws "cast too wide a net and catch a lot of little fish—nonviolent offenders and older felons who no longer pose much threat to society but who are going to spend the rest of their lives in prison getting geriatric care at the state's expense."[157] Many of the "little fish" are small-time drug offenders. If drug possession is either one's third felony or one's first or second felony preceding two violent crimes, a life sentence is imposed. The result has been further and longer incarceration of those at the bottom of the drug trade pyramid.[158]

In the context of increasing poverty and fewer legitimate options, MMS and "three strikes" as well as a host of other new laws have triggered a flood of drug offenders into the prison system.[159] In a mere 13 years the proportion of drug offenders in the system has grown from 25 to 60 percent.[160] The Bureau of Justice Statistics reported that in 1993, drug offenders constituted 61 percent of federal inmates, up from 38 percent in 1986 and 25 percent in 1980.[161] In state prisons, the proportion of inmates convicted of a drug offense went from one in 16 in 1980 to over one in five in 1993.[162] And these are lengthy sentences, even for the smallest offenders. In 1990, 88.9 percent of all drug offenders appearing in federal courts with no prior convictions were sentenced for an average term of 68.4 months.[163] By 1993, the average drug-offender prison sentence had increased to 82 months.[164]

Accordingly, the prison system itself has been expanding astronomically. According to the Sentencing Project, the United States has in recent years been second only to Russia in its rate of incarceration, with the number of inmates in prisons and jails having quadrupled in the past 20 years.[165] Federal spending on incarceration increased by almost 300 percent in the ten years between 1984 and 1994, with the current figure at $27 billion for the 1.4 million Americans in federal and state prisons and jails.[166] At the start of 1996, the Justice Department reported a record increase in the prison population, nearly 90,000 more inmates than the previous year. Commenting on these trends, the Deputy Director of Harvard's Criminal Justice Institute remarked that "a different sort of million man march" has put more than a million men and women behind bars, "enough to require 1,725 new beds each week."[167] And there is no end in sight. According to a 1995 survey of corrections officials, inmate populations will rise by another 51 percent over the next five years and annual prison operating costs will total $36 billion by fiscal year 2000.[168] Virtually all of this expansion is to handle new drug convicts, the majority of whom are neither repeat nor violent offenders, at least, not violent in any usual sense.[169]

Meanwhile the racial makeup of the new prison population is glaringly obvious. One-third of all Black men in their twenties are now in prison, on probation, or on parole. Blacks, who represent only 12 percent of the population, account for over half of all state and federal prisoners.[170] The Justice Department's explanation for why Blacks have been so overrepresented among those convicted under the new sentencing laws is that, because of "socio-economic factors," most crack dealers are Black.[171] The grain of truth here is that street crack dealing is an occupation of poor people, as we've seen, and poor people are disproportionately Black. From the 1940s to the 1970s, a period of dramatic economic growth, median incomes for Blacks and for Latinos rose to 52 percent of Whites' median income. But in the past two decades, this gap has not budged.[172] Furthermore, racial and ethnic minorities account for only 9 percent of businesses owned even though they are 25 percent of the population; and this 9 percent accounts for only 4 percent of sales.[173] In 1994, the unemployment rate was 5.3 percent for Whites and 11.5 percent for Blacks. Taking into account those who had dropped out of the job market and those working part-time who could not find full-time work, the numbers are 13.3 percent and 25 percent.[174] These discrepancies are largely explained by institutional racism, which many researchers have demonstrated in bank and insurance company policies; in the choices of individual and corporate consumers; in the evaluation of job applications; and in the workplace itself, where Blacks are twice as likely as Whites to occupy low-skill positions, and where Blacks earn less money than White peers in high-skill positions.[175]

But more to the present point is the racial discrimination inherent in arrest patterns and sentencing guidelines themselves, the issue skirted by the Justice Department. Most of the nation's cocaine dealers and 80 percent of its consumers are White. But more Blacks are arrested, because Black neighborhoods and schools are the ones that law enforcement targets. As the supervisor of the Chicago Police narcotics division commented: "There's as much cocaine in the Sears Tower or in the stock exchange as there is in the Black community. But those guys are harder to catch." And more capable of defending themselves if caught. Criminologist William Chambliss explains:

> Arrests of White male middle class offenders (on college campuses for example) are guaranteed to cause the organization and the arresting officers strain, as people with political influence and money hire attorneys for their defense. Arrests of poor Black men, however, create only rewards for the organization and the officer as the cases are quickly processed through the courts, a guilty plea obtained and the suspect sentenced....In a class society, the powerless, the poor, and those who fit the public stereotype of "the criminal" are the human resources needed by law enforcement agencies to maximize rewards and minimize strains.[176]

Even if one of "those guys" is caught and convicted, sentencing guidelines ensure that he will not be punished as severely as a Black man. Notoriously, possession of five grams of crack cocaine carries a mandatory five-year prison sentence (a packet of sugar in a restaurant weighs about one gram), while possession of the same amount of powdered cocaine carries a minimum 10 months of probation. Why is this so, if it is the same substance with essentially the same physical effects?[177] Powdered cocaine is the drug of choice in the suburbs, while crack is the main choice in the ghetto.[178] Not coincidentally, in 1990 the average sentence under MMS for Blacks was 49 percent higher than that for Whites. At the end of 1990, Blacks were 21 percent and Hispanics 28 percent more likely than Whites to receive at least the mandatory minimum prison term.[179]

With new laws such as MMS and three-strikes swelling the prison population, massive prison building projects are underway in nearly every state. The need for prison expansion has gone hand in hand with a strong trend toward its privatization. Typically, prisons are now privately financed and built (usually without voter ratification, because private investment lessens the short-term public cost). Furthermore, they are increasingly run by private corporations. Beginning in the 1980s, for-profit corporations began operating entire prisons (both juvenile corrections facilities and adult prisons). A 1991 census of private corrections enterprises found that 44 facilities were operated by 14 companies and housed about 13,000 inmates.[180] Lately, there have even been cases in which county and municipal agencies such as the sheriff's department or city police department contract with the state to run prisons for profit. The cost of housing a prisoner might be weighed against the revenue-generating capacity of prison labor. In Massachusetts and Maryland, for example, prisoners are paid between 90 cents and $3.50 a day to produce such items as license plates, furniture, and plastics. Contracting agencies then sell these products for competitive prices. A drug user who spent two years in a Massachusetts prison opted for work at 40¢ an hour in order to avoid the temptation to use drugs readily available in the jail. There was a five month wait for receiving any kind of drug treatment services.[181]

It may not be a coincidence that we are seeing correctional privatization in conjunction with the harshest sentencing in U.S. history. Historian Feely writes that such privatization has historically resulted in "the generation of new and expanded sanctions and forms of social control."[182] In any event, it is clear that profit incentives have distinct consequences on the perceived objectives of incarceration. As criminologist David Shichor points out, "private correctional companies do not have an intrinsic interest in rehabilitation. Because private prisons make their profits on their occupancy rate, there is no incentive for them to institute meaningful rehabilitation programs in prison."[183] The incentive rather is to keep inmates in jail for as long as possible.

Recall the similar incentive of private treatment programs to keep heroin addicts in subsidized treatment for as long as possible. Prison privatization has in some cases even given rise to an analogous two-tiered system where money makes all the difference in access to and quality of care.[184] To be sure, there had already been such a system: convicted inside trader Ivan Boesky and other rich outlaws are sent not to prison in the usual sense but to "minimal security" facilities without fences or cells, where they can play softball, tennis, and golf amidst expansive lawns and manicured hedges.[185] But there is now a new twist, where preferred conditions are made available to anyone able to pay. In Fullerton, California, which has its own city jail system, a convicted felon can apply for jail time in a safe, quiet, environment free of hardened criminals for $65 a night. The "hotel jail," as it's called, can handpick its clients. As a police captain whose department has been accepting money for jail space for over ten years says: "Jail is real business now...people want alternatives for the better living conditions."[186]

Indeed it is. As a former warden of the Oklahoma State Reformatory puts it, "The war on drugs is a failure and a success. It's a failure because it has not stopped drug use in this country. It's a success because it's the best economic boom we've ever seen. Prisoners are big business. It's the growth industry of the '90s and the profits are overriding the expenses....The poor folks are the clients of the system."[187] There is good reason to believe that the burgeoning prison industry, like any other big industry, will emerge as an obstacle to any policy initiatives which interfere with its prerogatives. For example, the director of research of the conservative New Citizenship Project, specializing in crime issues, reacted in the following way to the innovation of "drug courts" featuring alternative (non-prison) sentencing for small-time offenders: "There is a danger with drug courts that people would not make the required contribution to support sufficient jail and prison capacity."[188] The "danger," of course, is to the profits.

It is not just the prison industry which profits, but a wider "crime control industry." The sale of tax-exempt bonds for prison construction is a major new business for large financial firms, worth $2.3 billion a year. Companies in construction, transport, health care, food service, and other areas also benefit increasingly from taxpayer expenditures on prisons. Not least is what a *Wall Street Journal* reporter has described as the "defense establishment...scenting a logical new line of business" in products such as "smart guns" and high-tech listening devices.[189] Another boon to the private sector is prison labor, with over 90,000 convicts nationwide currently working as they serve time.[190] At state-run institutions pay is generally minimum wage; at private prisons, it can be as low as 17¢ per hour. Employers can freely dismiss and recall workers, need not deal with unions, and do not have to pay for benefits or even work facilities, as these costs are borne by taxpayers. For example, in its quest for cheaper and more malleable labor, aircraft manufacturing giant Boeing has set up production lines in China and in Washington state prisons; many other companies have taken advantage as well in a growing trend.[191] Just as with "workfare," cheap prison labor has the additional effect of keeping down wages everywhere, as companies can use the threat of outsourcing to discipline workers. The overall economic payoffs have had the effect of co-opting entire communities, especially in rural areas where jobs are otherwise scarce.[192]

3. SOCIAL CONTROL AND THE BUSINESS AGENDA

We have seen that poverty and unemployment are significant factors in much drug involvement, an item of common sense which is confirmed by much research (including the ethnographic record, which is replete with stories like April's). The temptations of escape and extra income through drug use and sales are harder to resist when no constructive alternatives are available. Under the War on Drugs and other policy, the alternatives are further narrowed as treatment, child care subsidy, food stamps, and other assistance for the poor become less available, while jobs in poor areas remain scarce and pay—often already below subsistence—erodes further. Under mandatory sentencing guidelines, drug offenders coming from such circumstances have been herded into a huge and expanding prison system, while more affluent and lighter-skinned offenders remain free.

Perverse though they may be, these outcomes make a certain sense once we understand government policy. The key is to recognize overall business interests. Take for example "welfare reform." On the surface, it seems anomalous that while there is a concerted federal effort to eliminate subsidies to single mothers, subsidies to corporations continue almost unabated. The latter include not only direct subsidies—for building plants overseas, borrowing money to finance corporate mergers, advertising in foreign markets, and many other activities—but also indirect subsidies hidden in the tax code ("tax expenditures"). Hidden, but not neglected: for example in 1991, the last year for which figures were available, 60 percent of U.S. corporations exploited enough exemptions to reduce their taxes to zero. The estimated $150 billion in corporate welfare is around nine times the size of the former AFDC. In fact, the latter is eclipsed by the amount lost to the single tax exemption for inherited property, totaling $20.5 billion per year.[193]

But as economic analyst Doug Henwood points out, there is no inconsistency here: cutting subsidies to poor families and preserving those to well-heeled corporations both "accomplish the same goal of fattening profits and cheapening the cost of labor."[194] Big business does not like welfare for the poor because it "allows people to remain out of the labor market, thereby tending to elevate wage rates; it interferes with managerial control over the workplace; it costs money in the form of payroll and other taxes to fund retirement, medical, and welfare programs; and it strengthens the power of government as an agent serving ordinary people."[195] Private sector interests are also served by NAFTA and other trade agreements, and by profits generally, be they of banks, chemical companies, firms with Pentagon contracts, or prisons. Accordingly these thrive under the War on Drugs, whatever the consequences on the drug trade or public health and safety. We've seen that even when money is spent on drug treatment, beneficial effects are compromised by privatization.

It is not that business interests are necessarily hostile to social welfare. A truce between business and labor existed for many decades, dating from the New Deal policies of the Roosevelt administration. But in the 1970s, international competition ended an era of U.S. dominance, making it more difficult for U.S. firms to pass on to consumers the costs of the social contract. A rebellion ensued. By a variety of means including plant relocation and suppression of union activity, businesses across the board began reducing labor costs (as noted previously, wages have been spiraling downward since 1973). For example, reported violations of a federal law prohibiting the firing of employees for union activity doubled during the period from 1970 to 1980. In addition, a large and well-financed political campaign was initiated, built upon public relations machinery that had been in place for decades: lobbying, advertising, and sponsoring of think tanks, legal groups, and journals, all geared toward attacking regulation and other constraints on business. By the end of the 1970s corporate spending on such activities was up to $1 billion a year.[196]

The major political parties followed the lead—immediately, in the Republicans' case. The Democrats lagged behind slightly because of their lingering commitment to the New Deal, in which there was a certain populist element because of the inclusion of labor interests. Crucially, however, the New Deal also had the support of certain industrial sectors, namely capital-intensive businesses such as oil companies whose labor costs are minimal. So when these sectors bolted, it posed a test: who did the Democrats really represent? It was no contest. The Reagan administration—largely carrying out policies initiated under the Carter administration—encountered little Democratic resistance in Congress, and the mainstream of the party was soon explicitly remaking itself in the Republicans' image via the Democratic Leadership Council (whose principals included Bruce Babbitt, Charles Robb, and Bill Clinton). With business unanimously pushing it, a bipartisan consensus emerged for an agenda of lower business taxes, less regulation, higher military spending (since World War II the favored approach for channeling taxpayer money to the private sector—see note 193), and cuts in social spending across the board. In short, it was not public opinion but private sector opinion which initiated the narrower political spectrum we see today, in which "liberal" is a bad word. On the contrary, the general public remained consistently "liberal" throughout the shift in the business climate, favoring many social programs, environmental regulation, and decreased military spending.[197] But it is the business agenda which prevails.[198]

The drug war's function with regard to military spending in particular is suggested by the timing of President Bush's announcement of a new initiative in September 1989. At the time, high-level policy-makers were greatly concerned about how to maintain current levels of military spending after the Cold War: the "unsettling spectre of peace" (as the *Wall Street Journal* termed it) was extensively discussed in Congress, the press, and elite policy journals. That the spectre of a drug "enemy" conceived in martial terms has been used in part as a pretext to justify the Pentagon budget (even apart from the military portion of allocations to the War on Drugs) may seem a cynical notion, but it fits the evidence and historical patterns over the past five decades.[199]

The presentation of private interests as public ones ("jobs," "defense," and so forth) constitutes a kind of social control, circumventing genuine pursuit of public interests. The War on Drugs also enables social control in a less subtle sense: the imprisonment of "undesirable" sectors of the population.

At the time the Bush administration declared its War on Drugs, ample data showed that overall drug use nationwide had been declining since the early 1980s, part of a broader trend that included decreased use of unhealthy substances generally, such as tobacco, beef, and coffee. Cocaine use had been a temporary exception, but it too had been declining since the mid-1980s. Though none of this was common knowledge among the general public, drug war architects knew the data well. As criminologist Michael Tonry remarks, "The white-shirted-and-suspendered officials of the Office of National Drug Control policy [knew this and other data] better than anyone else in the United States." They therefore knew that a drug war was not needed.[200] Nor was one compelled by public opinion. Rather the declaration and concomitant media campaign—including drug czar William Bennett's deceitful claim that frequent cocaine use had doubled since 1985—created a crisis atmosphere which manufactured opinion, causing a sudden increase in the number of Americans concerned about illegal drug use. The declaration of victory a few months later was likewise disingenuous; it was based on data showing a decrease in overall drug use since September, which however was simply a continuation of the known decline that had been going on for years.[201]

More to the present point, the data available in the late 1980s showed another trend: drug use among disadvantaged populations, especially minority inner-city communities, had not been declining (for reasons we've discussed). Tonry argues that the planners of the drug war knew all along what would happen:

> They knew that drug use was falling among the vast majority of the population. They knew that drug use was not declining among disadvantaged members of the urban underclass. They knew that the War on Drugs would be fought mainly in the minority areas of American cities and that those arrested and imprisoned would disproportionately be young Blacks and Hispanics.

He further argues that the planners are therefore accountable for the destruction of minority communities, whether they intended this destruction or merely knew it would occur. Guilt would be the same in either case, as is dictated by both common sense and criminal law.[202]

Again we find continuity with the historical record. The first federal antidrug law was the Harrison Act of 1914, which taxed and regulated opium, heroin, and cocaine. It was motivated in part by Chinese immigrants having outlasted their usefulness building railroads to become surplus labor; many of these immigrants smoked opium. The cocaine ban was added in order to ensure support of the law by Southerners, among whom myths were played up of cocaine-sniffing Black men raping White women. The prohibition of marijuana effectively began in 1937, at a time when Mexican immigrants considered under its influence were enlarging a pool of unskilled labor. As historians Bonnie and Whitebread conclude in their history of drug prohibition, drug use is most likely to be criminalized when the using population "is already perceived as a criminal class" and when it is an ethnic minority.[203]

In the case of marijuana, there was a backlash against prohibition when use became widespread in the 1960s among the children of the middle- and upper-classes. For the first time, there was a movement among judges, legislators, doctors, and other professionals which challenged the harsh penalties for users and official claims of marijuana's dangers. Their efforts resulted in milder penalties and a lapse in overall enforcement. Still, the prohibitionists did not surrender. Rather, as Bonnie and Whitebread remark, marijuana laws "were often used selectively as a vehicle for removing radical irritants from the body politic and lazy hippies from the streets."[204] This explains the fate of President Nixon's commission on marijuana (consisting largely of conservative doctors), which concluded in a 1972 report that marijuana had minimal health effects, was not a "gateway" to heroin and other drugs, did not lead to criminal behavior, and ought to be legalized. Nixon ignored the report (as did the national media). He and his drug warriors were aware, as the rest of the country was aware, that pot had political significance: in particular, that it was the drug of choice within the youthful counterculture and antiwar movement. Accordingly the marijuana laws were valued as a potential means of suppressing these undesirable elements. So, for example, J. Edgar Hoover instructed his agents that "since the use of marijuana and other narcotics is widespread among members of the New Left, you should be alert to opportunities to have them arrested by local authorities on drug charges." More generally, it was well known within the Nixon administration that the War on Drugs was to be used as an instrument against the objects of middle-class resentment: as *Newsweek* put it, "the incendiary Black militant and the welfare mother, the hedonistic hippie and the campus revolutionary." Nixon's marijuana commission did not understand that the enemy was not marijuana's perceived effects on health or safety, but who was smoking it.[205]

The "incendiary Black militant," the "hedonistic hippie," and the "campus revolutionary" have become scarce, but not the "welfare mother" or the poor generally. On the contrary. As public constraints on the mobility and power of corporations have continued to diminish, the ranks of those who are superfluous from a business standpoint have only swelled. The War on Drugs is an imperfect but workable instrument for keeping the masses under control, heading off any unreasonable demands.[206] This function is the same in Latin America, where it is implemented with not only prisons but also attack helicopters and death squads: to assist the suppression of popular movements seeking "immediate improvement in the low living standards of the masses," so as to ensure "a political and economic climate conducive to private investment"(see note 57). Here and worldwide, investors are on guard against those whose alternatives for survival have been systematically closed off.

4. CONCLUSION: FAILURE OR SUCCESS?

How should we evaluate the War on Drugs? Many analysts claim that it has been a complete failure. The case seems an easy one to make.

To begin with, drug use statistics tell a largely discouraging story. Some data show that drug use is decreasing nationwide; though as we've seen, the trend began well before the most recent War on Drugs was declared in the late 1980s.[207] Meanwhile a 1993 Drug Use Forecasting (DUF) report cautions: "If we focus only on what is happening in the general population we may wrongly conclude that the drug epidemic is subsiding."[208] In economically vulnerable and "high risk" populations there are countervailing upward trends in drug use for cocaine, crack, heroin, LSD, and PCP. These trends show up in the inner cities, where one finds hypersegregated areas of concentrated poverty. In major urban areas across the country there has been a mean increase of 17 percent in cocaine use and 7 percent in heroin use.[209] The use of cocaine nearly doubled in Newark (96 percent), Atlanta (88 percent), and San Francisco (106 percent).[210] Total drug abuse episodes (as measured by emergency room cases) increased about 20 percent from 1988 through 1993; cocaine use accounted for 23 percent of that increase, while heroin use had nearly doubled.[211] As of 1996, there is a notable leveling off of the cocaine epidemic but a steady increase in mentions of heroin use in a majority of emergency rooms as well as rapidly increasing heroin mortality rates in 50 percent of the 20 biggest urban areas nationwide.[212]

Drug use among children and adolescents has increased. A 1996 national survey found that drug use among high schoolers and eighth graders had increased since the previous year. By a year later, drug use in grades 6-8 had apparently increased again, from 10.9 to 11.4 percent, while stabilizing among high schoolers—albeit at almost 25 percent.[213] As early as 1989, arrests for the sale and possession of controlled substances in New York City among children ages 13 to 17 years were climbing.[214] A report on drug use among male arrestees found that of the 12 sites where data on juvenile arrestees was collected, two-thirds found cocaine use higher in 1994 than in earlier years.[215] In Massachusetts, drug use by the young is steadily rising, as reported by the Department of Public Health in Boston. Use of illicit drugs for adolescents in grades 7-12 increased in just three years from 38 to 46 percent.[216]

Seven years after the war declared by President Bush, there is no evidence of a decline in cocaine imports into the United States. It is commonly noted that drug production is like a balloon, with suppression in one area resulting in increased production elsewhere. For example, coca formerly confined to Peru's Upper Huallaga Valley is now grown in many other locales throughout Peru, and coca production has skyrocketed in Colombia, formerly only a producer of cocaine. The reason is that coca plants do not require good soil. So producers have many location options; in Peru and Bolivia, coca is being cultivated on less than 1 percent of the land that it could be. Meanwhile poppy production is on the rise in Colombia and Peru. Downstream production of both cocaine and heroin has also adapted. The Colombian Cali cartel benefited from the crackdown on the Medellin cartel, Mexican druglords from the crackdown on Cali. Drug mafias are now spreading as well in Bolivia, Venezuela, Brazil, and Peru, where heroin is now being produced for the first time. The abundance of supply and suppliers is reflected by low prices. The street price of cocaine has declined over the past 15 years. Heroin prices have dropped by 75 percent over the past five years, with heroin arriving highly pure on the streets of U.S. cities because dealers have no need to stretch supplies.[217]

Though the War on Drugs' effects on drug use and drug traffic have been minimal, the monetary costs have not. President Clinton requested $15 billion in 1997. This was an increase of over $1 billion from each of the two previous years, while maintaining two-thirds of the overall budget for law enforcement, prisons, and interdiction, and one-third for harm reduction (that is, treatment and reducing demand).[218] Despite Clinton and drug czar McCaffrey having recently admitted that U.S.-backed drug war activity in Latin America has been ineffective and even unwelcome, there is a 67 percent increase ($92 million) for such activity (almost two-thirds of which is paid for by cuts to UNICEF, U.N. Development Programs, and other international development aid efforts).[219] More goes to the U.S. military just to pay for the high-tech equipment it uses in the service of drug interdiction than would be required to provide drug treatment for every American in need.[220]

Considering that drug use has increased among those in urban neighborhoods and among the young, that the supply of drugs has not diminished, and that the costs of current policy are high and increasing, it is understandable that the War on Drugs has been widely deemed a failure. By now it is not just researchers and pundits who have so concluded but also some elite policy-makers.[221] The apparent failure is not hard to explain. Law enforcement cannot curb drug use if social and economic forces driving demand and the drug trade are not addressed. Stiff sentencing laws and the threat of prison are no deterrent for desperate people, for whom the possibility of getting caught pales in comparison to the day-to-day challenges of survival.[222] Meanwhile eradication and interdiction efforts are no match for numerous mobile suppliers driven by large demand. A RAND study estimates that widely available treatment would be seven times more cost-effective in reducing cocaine consumption than the best supply reduction program.[223]

Notice, however, that the conclusion of failure assumes the War on Drugs is supposed to reduce the use and supply of illegal drugs. This is a near-universal assumption but an assumption nonetheless, standing in need of proof. What is the proof? We have argued that there is none: on the contrary, we think the assumption is false. The overriding interests of the War on Drugs are revealed by the systematicity of its effects. While the War on Drugs only occasionally serves and more often degrades public health and safety, it regularly serves the interests of private wealth: interests revealed by the pattern of winners and losers, targets and non-targets, well-funded and underfunded. That these are the main interests of U.S. foreign and domestic policy generally, and that the private sector has overriding influence on policy, confirms our conclusion.

We therefore propose to evaluate the War on Drugs by different criteria, namely to what extent these interests have been served. Consider, then, that peasants and grassroots democratic openings throughout Latin America have suffered increased repression, enhancing the stability of business-friendly regimes. The poor in the United States have been further impoverished and repressed. Corporate profits in recent years have reached record levels as workers' wages and benefits decline, global mobility of capital is enhanced, and public subsidies to corporations remain high. Costs such as taxpayer expenditures and increased drug use and supply are no problem for the private sector, because they are shouldered by the public. In fact expenditures on private prisons and the crime control industry, corporate welfare, the Pentagon (see note 193), and social control not only are not a problem, but foster a favorable business climate. In contrast, negative effects on public health and safety are "externalities," not figuring into calculations of profit or economic "growth." The War on Drugs has, to be sure, been only one of many policy vehicles which have contributed to these outcomes. But to the extent it has contributed, it has been a success. This success explains why the policies continue, despite the conclusive and well-known evidence of their failure to combat drug use and supply.

But countercurrents do exist. By the second half of the Bush administration, bar associations in Boston, Rochester, and elsewhere were criticizing the War on Drugs as unjust and wasteful. Judges began to speak out against the strains placed on courts by the inordinate pursuit of small-time offenders.[224] In Minnesota, the state supreme court rejected as discriminatory the state's version of the federal law imposing heavier penalties for crack than for powdered cocaine. The National Association of Counties passed a resolution demanding the replacement of the War on Drugs with a fully funded drug treatment program. Even the press has rebelled somewhat. Local newspapers across the country have run front-page stories on the unfair effects on Black Americans. The *New York Times* and *USA Today* have published critical articles as well.[225]

These are encouraging trends. Still, we believe that any optimism should be tempered. Arguably these countercurrents stem from the fact that fallout from the War on Drugs affects not only the poor. Dysfunctional court systems, the potential of civil unrest, and the general erosion of legal and privacy rights (see note 159) are matters of concern to everyone, including elites. There is potentially a long-term business concern as well. According to the Labor Department, the children of minorities will constitute a third of the workforce before long, and will require technical skills that will not be learned on the streets or in prison.[226] Some sectors of big business may revert to qualified support of social priorities which address this need, such as public education. To say that the War on Drugs primarily serves business interests is not to say that it does so perfectly, or that these interests are monolithic or unchanging (recall for instance the partial business support of New Deal policies). It is only to say that the War on Drugs satisfies perceived business interests ascendant at a given time. What would be more encouraging than the aforementioned trends is grassroots backlash, with the potential for forcing pursuit of different interests entirely: those of communities and public well-being.

Which brings us back, finally, to South Central Los Angeles. Nowhere have the War on Drugs and accompanying broader forces hit more severely. Beginning in the late 1970s companies in Southern California (including ten huge manufacturing plants) relocated en masse to the suburbs or offshore, resulting in the loss of 75,000 unionized, well-paying jobs which had been held largely by Black men in South Central.[227] Under Reagan, the Federal Comprehensive Employment and Training Act (CETA) and Job Corps programs were curtailed. The cumulative effects were dramatic: in 1985 a housing survey found that in some South Central projects only one household in ten had an employed breadwinner. It was under such circumstances that crack and gangs appeared in the mid-1980s. Two years later, the Los Angeles City Council diverted money for South Central parks and recreational centers to wealthier districts, eliminated the Los Angeles Summer Job Program, and allocated no money for drug treatment. The answer to South Central's problems was to be the Los Angeles Police Department (L.A.P.D.): for example, "Operation Hammer" rounded up more than 1,400 people, mostly young Black men, on charges ranging from illegal weapons to parking tickets to violations of curfews that applied only in poor neighborhoods.[228]

This was the background for the riots that followed the acquittal of the L.A.P.D. officers who beat Rodney King. Basically it was also the background for the *San Jose Mercury News* series in August 1996.

Lissa Washington, the Los Angeles grade school teacher interviewed by the *Boston Globe*, explained it clearly. To residents of South Central, it made sense that the same government which had been cutting jobs programs, AFDC, and drug treatment while subsidizing corporations and enhancing their global mobility, at every turn making it more difficult for those in urban Black communities to lead productive, healthy, and drug-free lives, would turn out to have been aiding and abetting the drug traffic itself. And it does make sense. To be sure, there is no conspiracy to supply these or other communities with crack. The fundamental explanation does not have to do with conspiracy, but with the nature of our political and especially our economic institutions. The U.S. political system is dominated by the private sector, which is driven by the imperative to maximize profits. On this basis—and also considering U.S. power and global influence—many of the effects of U.S. policy can be predicted and explained without speculating on the machinations or psychologies of policy-makers.[229] We can for example trace much of the degradation of workers and poor people in this hemisphere to their status in the reigning economic system merely as potential means for generating profits, not as human beings whose rights and needs are ends in themselves. The residents of South Central thus have common cause not only with poor communities and working families of all colors around the country, but also with coca growers in Peru, peasants in Nicaragua, and union leaders in Colombia.

But even if many of Lissa Washington's neighbors go too far in their conclusions, or in another way not nearly far enough, they are closer to the truth than those who listen only to official voices. As the *Washington Post*, the *New York Times*, and other "respectable" media trivialize and disparage them, community activists in South Central and elsewhere have mobilized around the underlying larger issues: not only U.S. ties to the drug trade, but the broad nature of the War on Drugs.[230] It should come as no surprise that those who have been most victimized by it should have special insight into its hypocrisy.

As "conservatives" often say, we are all responsible for our actions. Even victims have alternatives. Despite their problems, residents of decaying inner cities should try to make the best of their circumstances and lead lawful and constructive lives. That is just what many (like April) are trying to do. But unfortunately not everyone can resist illegal or immoral behavior. While those from poor neighborhoods including teens and pregnant women serve long prison sentences for even the slightest involvement in drugs, bank executives offer discreet accounts useful to money launderers; Justice Department bureaucrats protect major drug traffickers from prosecution; C.I.A. operatives foster alliances with drug rings; trade negotiators ease regulations that hinder the global drug traffic; State Department officials oversee military aid to governments which use it to murder the political opposition; editors of prominent newspapers choose to shield such activities from public scrutiny. The powerful are as responsible for their actions as the poor, though with the difference that they have a wider range of alternatives. And there are these differences: their crimes are more consequential overall, are not on public display, and are not punished.

Those in charge are unlikely to punish themselves, however, or even to stop what they are doing. The import of analyzing the War on Drugs as serving elite interests is that change will not come by trying to persuade elites. It is not just a matter of citing studies, or of putting better people in charge. History teaches that meaningful social change comes of organization and activism from below. The significance of the *Mercury News* fallout lies in the contribution of inner-city activists to the activism of many others on fundamentally related issues over many years.[231] As Congresswoman Maxine Waters put it, "We can't wait for anybody else to do it."[232]

ACKNOWLEDGMENTS

The authors are grateful for the assistance and support of many people, including Joyce Millen, John Gershman, Noam Chomsky, Alec Irwin, Shelley Errington, Evan Lyon, Paul Farmer, Jim Kim, Kevin Batt, Jenn Ross, Bill Rodriguez, Joe Rhatigan, Steve Lamola, Philippe Bourgois, and Rebecca Wolfe.

PART V

Alternatives to the Agenda

Havana, Cuba. Children at play in a public day care center.

(photo by Timothy H. Holtz)

CHAPTER THIRTEEN

"The Threat of a Good Example": Health and Revolution in Cuba[1]

Aviva Chomsky

Cuba's lower per capita expenditure to achieve health indices similar to those of the developed countries suggests that health care is not as expensive as one might imagine. It also suggests that health care alone does not improve a population's well-being, but that meeting the entire population's basic human needs, including medical services, through resource distribution does. Money is necessary but not sufficient to improve a people's health. Government intervention is essential to guarantee access to health care and to guarantee, therefore, greater effectiveness of the medical system. Comparisons of Canada, the United States, and Britain 'suggest that among these three countries health is inversely related to health-care costs, but directly related to the degree of governmental intervention in health-care delivery.' Cuba's government is the sole provider of health care, and gives high priority to allocating resources—fiscal, physical, and human—to achieve its health goals.[2]

Julie Feinsilver

How it must pain them that...we can speak of an infant mortality rate of under ten, and even under nine, after a minimum of five years of the special period! How painful must be the news that life expectancy has increased, that, in spite of the shortage of resources and medicines, our doctors are constantly making ever greater advances! How can this Cuban miracle be compared with what we know is occurring in other parts of the world and particularly in Latin America? And they've wanted to destroy our country, they have even wanted to charge us with human rights violations, when the lives of approximately one million children and young people have been saved by the work of the Revolution....It is the reverse of what happens everywhere else and of what is advised everywhere else by the World Bank, the International Monetary Fund, and the United States: all those neoliberal theories that you're familiar with, all those practices, throwing out tens of millions of workers onto the streets, closing schools, closing hospitals, eliminating essential public services...what capitalist country has achieved the level of social security, of social justice that our country has attained, of respect for the people attained in our country?[3]

Fidel Castro

Most of the chapters in this collection explore the ways in which the so-called "New World Order," and in particular the economic programs associated with neoliberalism and structural adjustment, have undermined the health of the poor. They show that from the most basic humanitarian perspective, structural adjustment and neoliberalism are simply unacceptable alternatives. This chapter seeks to show that the results of neoliberalism are not only morally unacceptable, but also completely unnecessary. It is in fact quite possible for a poor, Third World country to protect the health of its population, even under circumstances of extreme economic privation. It is no accident that the country that disproves the assumptions behind the argument, Cuba, is virtually always left out of mainstream analyses that attempt to defend neoliberal reforms.[4]

A close examination of health and revolution in Cuba brings into sharp relief some of the false assumptions underlying current discussions of economic adjustment and health. Where mainstream studies argue that "development" in standard terms—that is, an increasing GNP—is a prerequisite for improving the health status of a country's population, the Cuban example suggests that distribution of resources within a country is more important than the overall GNP in affecting health outcomes.[5] Where mainstream approaches argue that *any* of the economic choices available to poor countries will require sacrifices in the area of health care for the poor, the Cuban example shows that in fact there are economic options that distribute the sacrifices differently. Where many analysts argue that structural adjustment can be made acceptable by targeting vulnerable sectors with specific programs, the Cuban example shows that massive social change is much more effective than targeting for improving the health of the poor. Cuba shows that First World health standards are indeed possible in a Third World economy.[6,7] For precisely this reason, most studies of economic reform through austerity and adjustment ignore the example of Cuba.

HEALTH AND REVOLUTION

At the time of the 1959 revolution, Cuba's health profile, and its health-care delivery system, were fairly good by Third World standards, although aggregate statistics masked enormous regional, racial, and class inequalities. Access to adequate food and shelter, as well as to medical care *per se*, was dependent on one's economic standing. In their study of food and nutrition in Cuba, Medea Benjamin, Joseph Collins, and Michael Scott summarize the situation in the 1950s:

> While Cuba had the highest ratio of hospital beds to population in the Caribbean, 80 percent were in the city of Havana. Havana province had 1 doctor for every 420 persons, but rural Oriente province had 1 for every 2,550. Unsanitary housing and poor diets made curable diseases widespread. The World Bank reported in 1951 that between 80 and 90 percent of children in rural areas suffered from intestinal parasites. In 1956, 13 percent of the rural population had a history of typhoid and 14 percent tuberculosis.[8]

Large sectors of the population had access neither to medical care nor to adequate food and shelter.

The 1959 revolution aimed at liberating Cuba from the dictator Batista, but more profoundly from the relationship with the United States that many Cubans felt had replaced Spanish colonialism with U.S. neocolonial political and economic domination. The Cuban independence leader José Martí (1853-1895) had spoken of the dual goals of social equality and national independence as one. But these hopes were dashed by the U.S. invasion of Cuba in 1898. Although the United States eschewed direct political rule, its subsequent control of the island stifled the Cuban independence project of the nineteenth century—the project of building a nation "with all and for the good of all."[9] The 1959 revolutionary project aimed at fulfilling, concurrently, the goals of national independence and social justice.

Julie Feinsilver argues in her study of health and revolution in Cuba that "the central metaphor in Cuba's anti-imperialist struggle...is that of health. The health of the individual is a metaphor for and a symbol of the health of the 'body politic'.... Medical doctors...are warriors in the battle against disease, which is largely considered a legacy of imperialism and underdevelopment."[10] While there are certainly political and perhaps even symbolic reasons for the Cuban government's prioritizing the health of the population, this chapter focuses on the real impact of the revolution's commitment to health. Propaganda aside, the government has been extraordinarily successful in promoting the health of the population.

The Cuban revolution's commitment to the health of the country's population is notable in several respects. First, the government understands health to be the responsibility of the state. Second, the government approaches health as a social issue that includes health-care delivery but is far from limited to it. Thus, the state is responsible not only for building, maintaining, and ensuring universal access to doctors, clinics, and hospitals, but also for guaranteeing and sustaining the social conditions necessary for health: universal access to education, food, and employment. Feinsilver paraphrases a 1961 Cuban Health Ministry report entitled "Economic Underdevelopment, the Principal Enemy of Health: How the Cuban Revolution Combats It," which argues that:

> The true eradication of misery and real improvement in health would occur only through revolution, that a band-aid approach would not eliminate disease.... [M]edicine alone will not improve the overall health of the population. What will improve it...is embedding medicine within a significant transformation of the socio-economic structure to eliminate the problems of underdevelopment: the legacy of hunger, illiteracy, inadequate housing, discrimination, and the exploitation of labor.[11]

Third, the government has insisted that health is a national project, with popular participation an integral element. Block committees and mass organizations participate in sanitation, vaccination, and education campaigns. Community workers collaborate closely with health professionals in overseeing clinics, diagnosing health problems in the community, promoting people's health schools, and designing future health strategies.[12]

Finally, Cuba has rejected the idea that Third World governments must settle for an "appropriate" level of health care, in which cost-effective public health and preventive measures are emphasized to a greater degree than more costly hospital-based and curative care. The Cuban revolution succeeded in developing both an effective public health, preventive, and primary care system and an advanced tertiary care system. In addition to being up-to-date, well-staffed, and involved in cutting-edge research, the tertiary care system is free and universally available to the country's population.[13]

Table 13.1

Select Health and Social Indicators for Cuba and Other Latin American Countries

Country	Real GDP per capita (PPP$)	Infant Mortality (per 1,000 live births)	Under 5 Mortality (per 1,000)[a]	Number of People per Physician[a]	Percentage of Population with Access to Health Care	Life Adult Expectancy at Birth (M/F, years)	Literacy Rate (percent)	Daily per capita Calorie Supply (percentage of requirement)[b]
Bolivia	2,598	71	96	2,348	67	59/62	83	84
Cuba	3,000	9	10	275	100	74/78	95.5	135
Guatemala	3,208	45	58	3,999	57	63/68	55.5	103
Peru	3,654	52	62	939	44	65/70	88.5	87
Dom. Rep.	3,933	38	44	949	78	68/72	82	102
Brazil	5,362	45	57	844	N.A.	63/71	83	114
Mexico	7,384	32	41	615	93	69/75	89.5	131
Argentina	8,937	23	27	330	71	69/76	96	131
Chile	9,129	13	15	942	97	72/78	95	102

Source: United Nations Development Report, 1997

a: World Bank, 1997
b: Bread for the World, 1998

Thus, the Cuban revolutionary approach to health has involved several different levels; radical social and economic transformation has created an egalitarian society in which the entire population is guaranteed access to food, employment, and education.[14] In addition, the government has rebuilt a health-care delivery system aimed at both public and preventive health *and* at universally accessible, high-tech, hospital-based care.[15] The results of these state policies are clear to any observer who cares to look at the statistics: Cuba, a country with a Third World economy, boasts a first-world health profile. It demonstrates that excellent social and particularly health outcomes are possible *without* major economic "development" as measured by GNP or other standard measures.[16]

As illustrated in Table 13.1, Cuba stands out among Latin American countries with respect to its health and social indicators. Despite its low per capita GDP, Cuba has the lowest infant mortality and under 5 years old mortality rates in Latin America. These indicators are, in fact, comparable to those found in the world's wealthiest countries. Cubans have a longer life expectancy at birth and are more educated than most of their Latin American counterparts. They enjoy one of the highest daily per capita calorie supplies in the world. Though Cuba is indeed poor in purely economic terms, Table 13.2 demonstrates that health has been an important priority for the country. Cuba's public sector spending on health as a percentage of GDP exceeds that of most countries. Other health and social indicators are more comparable to high-income countries than to other low-income countries.[17]

Cuba also stands out for its regional equality. Over the last 15 years, the government has invested considerable effort in mitigating social and health discrepancies among regions of the country. Although income levels among provinces still vary, Cubans from every province, even the poorest, are well provided for in terms of health. These efforts, as illustrated in Table 13.3, are apparent when Cuban health outcomes are examined by region.

The role of the state has been key in Cuba's socioeconomic transformation and in its health-care delivery system. State control of the economy has meant that resources can be allocated, distributed, and shifted, based on ongoing assessment of needs. Excellent information gathering systems and government commitment to the health of the population have allowed problems to be systematically identified and resources channeled to address them. The Pan American Health Organization (PAHO) noted in a 1994 report that Cuba's health profile has been surprisingly resistant to the economic crisis which the country has suffered since 1990. The report summarized the reasons for Cuba's ability to sustain good health in these terms: "the great capacity and effectiveness of the National Health System; the high cultural level of the Cuban people and their active participation in social and health programs...the health consciousness of the population, who consider health one of the country's greatest social triumphs; and Cuba's social and health policies, which have maintained their priorities despite the current difficult conditions."[18]

The importance of centralized planning in translating the government's commitment to health into effective outcomes can be seen with particular clarity in the Cuban response to three important health problems during the past 20 years: an

Table 13.2

Select Economic and Health Indicators

	Cuba	United States	High-Income Countries	Low-Income Countries
GDP per capita (PPP$)	3,000[a]	26,980	21,698	2,023
Public Sector Health Expenditure as Percentage of GDP	7.9	6.3	6.0	1.4
Number of People per Physician	275	421	522	4,627
Number of People per Hospital Bed	184	194	159	1,152
Life Expectancy at Birth in years (M/F)	74/78	74/80	74/81	62/64
Infant Mortality per 1,000 Live Births	9	8	7	69
Percentage of Population with Access to Safe Water	94	90	94	53

Source: World Bank, 1997

a: United Nations Development Report, 1997

Table. 13.3

A Comparison of Cuba's Provinces

Province	Monthly Salary per capita (in pesos)	Life Expectancy at Birth (in years)	Infant Mortality (per 1,000 live births)	Average Years of School
Pinar del Río	52	75.5	10.4	9.0
Habana	67	76.0	11.1	9.1
Ciudad de la Habana	72	74.2	8.8	9.9
Matanzas	65	75.5	8.6	9.3
Villa Clara	57	76.0	8.0	9.2
Cienfuegos	69	76.0	8.8	9.0
Sancti Spíritus	57	76.0	9.3	9.0
Ciego de Ávila	65	75.5	13.3	8.6
Camagüey	55	74.2	10.1	9.0
Tunas	54	76.0	11.5	8.7
Holguín	44	76.0	9.7	9.1
Granma	46	75.5	11.5	8.7
Santiago de Cuba	46	74.2	10.1	9.2
Guantánamo	43	75.5	10.6	9.2

Source: Angela Ferriol Muruaga, *Situación social en el ajuste económico.* Instituto Nacional Investaciones Económicas, February, 1995.

outbreak of dengue fever in 1981, the discovery of AIDS in Cuba in 1986, and an epidemic of neuropathy in 1993. In all three cases human, material, and scientific resources were mobilized rapidly and successfully to confront these illnesses. Because these cases illustrate so well ways in which political, social, and health factors interrelate, I briefly discuss each here.

DENGUE FEVER[19]

Dengue fever is a mosquito-borne viral illness. There are four known strains of the dengue virus (labeled dengue-1 through dengue-4), any of which can lead to dengue hemorrhagic fever (DHF) or dengue shock syndrome (DSS). Ordinary dengue is characterized by high fever, vomiting, and intense and debilitating muscular, abdominal, and head pain. For DHF and DSS, recent studies suggest that these potentially lethal complications of dengue may be partially immune-mediated and are seen most often in patients serially infected with two different strains.

Dengue outbreaks have occurred in the Caribbean since the 1950s, but Cuba did not have a case of the virus until 1977, when a Caribbean epidemic of dengue-1 struck the island. Although the epidemic struck hard and spread rapidly, it did not develop into cases of either DHF or DSS. In fact, both DHF and DSS had rarely occurred outside southeast Asia and the western Pacific and never (at least in this century) in the Americas. However, when a dengue-2 strain hit Cuba in 1981, it led to numerous DHF cases and fatalities. Cuban researchers hypothesized that a combination of relative lack of immunity among the population, heavy infestation with the Aëdes aegypti mosquito carrier, and the sequence and timing of exposure to the different strains of the virus contributed to the outbreak and severity of the epidemic.[20]

When dengue-2 appeared in Cuba in May of 1981, it spread rapidly, reaching epidemic proportions within a month; 344,203 cases were recorded during the four-month period (June-September) that the epidemic lasted. Of these, 9,203 were classified as World Health Organization (WHO) level III, or "serious," and 1,109 as level IV, or "very serious." A total of 158 people died.[21]

The Cuban government mobilized against dengue on two fronts: in identifying and providing supportive medical care to those affected by the disease, and by organizing a massive popular sanitation campaign to eradicate the mosquito that carried the disease. As Feinsilver describes it, "the nation was put on war footing to do battle against dengue."[22] The media, schools, workplaces, mass organizations, and neighborhoods were mobilized all over the country to eliminate breeding places and apply larvicides, and to identify people with symptoms of dengue and ensure that they received medical care. Under what Cuban doctors called a "liberal hospital admission policy," 116,151 patients (37 percent of those infected) were hospitalized. This was probably an important factor in reducing fatalities: "In other epidemics elsewhere, where the index of hospitalization was typically much lower, patients were hospitalized when they were already in shock, and the indexes of mortality and lethality were higher."[23]

In addition to curative care, the government launched "an intense anti-Aëdes campaign."[24] In June the government initiated a massive spraying of malathion and an education campaign to eliminate breeding areas.[25] On July 26 Castro announced the second phase—the fumigation of every house in Cuba and the treating of all water deposits with insecticides. A "health army" of over 13,000 was trained to operate 5,000 backpack larvicide sprayers to inspect and eliminate breeding places. In mid-August, the Soviet Union donated a fleet of fumigation trucks. The director general of the WHO lauded Cuba's efforts on a visit to the island in August, stating: "The strategy defined by the Cuban government is highly valid, and I am sure that it will be crowned by success."[26] And it was. Within four months the disease had been eliminated: the last case was recorded on October 10.[27] "No government in the Third World and few in the developed countries could have achieved as much as rapidly as the Cubans did, because most lack this national capacity to mobilize," concludes Feinsilver.[28] In fact, the Latin American dengue pandemic continues elsewhere with record-breaking numbers of cases and record-breaking mortality.

The dengue campaign demonstrated how a national commitment and a national mobilization could successfully contain a disease. Feinsilver argues that the mobilization was fueled by Cuban accusations that the C.I.A. had deliberately introduced dengue into the country. Thus, the battle against dengue was of symbolic importance in Cuba's battle against the United States; it was promoted in Cuba as a struggle against imperialism.[29] Whatever the true cause of the epidemic, Cuban medical professionals and the Cuban health system focused on confronting and eradicating it. Cuba's battle against dengue could have served as a model to other countries for dealing with a public health emergency; it could have been lauded as an example of a successful public health response. However, it was not. The U.S. media concentrated on ridiculing Castro's suggestion that the C.I.A. may have been behind the epidemic, and celebrating the fact that the U.S. government had generously made an exception to its embargo and granted the PAHO permission to purchase insecticides produced in the United States for use against the dengue-bearing mosquito in Cuba.[30]

HIV/AIDS

If the success of Cuba's anti-dengue campaign was overlooked by the U.S. media, its AIDS policies have not been. In fact, Cuba's policies on AIDS tend to receive greater media coverage than the rest of its health system—even though as of January 1996, Cuba had only 1,196 diagnosed HIV-positive cases, making it one of the least important health problems on the island.[31] Cuba's policies have also received much greater coverage than the AIDS policies of neighboring Caribbean islands where the prevalence of AIDS is from ten to over one hundred times greater.[32] Because Cuba's AIDS policies are so controversial, they merit special attention. I will go into some detail regarding the ways Cuba's AIDS programs have been discussed abroad, the evolution of the policies themselves, and what Cuba's AIDS policies— along with foreign responses to them—reveal about politics and health.

HUMAN RIGHTS AND AIDS

United States attention to Cuba's AIDS programs has been framed as a denunciation of human rights violations rather than a discussion of health care.[33] Key themes in U.S. media accounts have been Cuba's initial policy of quarantine for those diagnosed as HIV-positive (discussed in detail later in this chapter) and, in particular, Cuba's discriminatory policies against homosexuals. United States media accounts have been fairly consistent in focusing on the issue of freedom for those diagnosed HIV-positive and the ethical issues surrounding mandatory testing, rather than the health aspects of Cuba's AIDS programs. Ethical issues, however, have been narrowly defined by the U.S. media as individual independence from state interference. In this formulation, access or lack of access to medical treatment (much less to minimal standards of nutrition and shelter) is not an ethical issue—thus, few articles discuss the ethics of U.S. AIDS policies.

To Cubans, it seems absurd that U.S. critics could bring up the issue of human rights in discussing *Cuba's* policies toward AIDS. "It seems very important to define our concepts of discrimination, exclusion, and human rights," explained Vice Minister of Health Héctor Terry:

> In Cuba, nobody lacks economic resources because of being an AIDS carrier. In Cuba, no one dies abandoned on the streets for lack of access to a hospital. In Cuba, we haven't had to open hospices so that patients who have been abandoned have a place to die in peace. In Cuba, no one's house has been set on fire because its inhabitants are people with AIDS. In Cuba, no homosexual has been persecuted because he's

assumed to be likely to spread the virus. In Cuba, we don't have the problem of national minorities or drug addicts with high rates of AIDS.[34]

United States health-care professionals have been much less sensationalist in their assessments of Cuba's AIDS policy than has the mass media. A member of the first delegation of U.S. health professionals (from Columbia University), which visited Cuba's Santiago las Vegas Sanitarium in late 1988, described the sanitarium as "a complex of homes near Havana airport, modest by U.S. standards, but not by Cuba's, with air-conditioners and color television. The medical staff was large...." Another member of the visiting delegation stated that the facility comprised "groups of non-descript apartments that looked like typical Cuban suburban housing. It was neither barracks-like nor dungeon-like."[35] However, the U.S. media seized upon words like "involuntary"; "quarantine"; "human rights violation"; "totalitarian"; "prison"; and "rigid surveillance." They chose to focus upon the "ethical" issues involved—failing themselves to discern any ethical problems in the U.S. government's unwillingness to provide adequate medical care for many of those infected with HIV or to take any significant steps to halt the rapid spread of the disease.

HOMOSEXUALITY, THE EPIDEMIOLOGY OF AIDS IN CUBA, AND THE POLITICS OF BLAME

There is some disagreement among those studying the infection as to whether HIV/AIDS in Cuba is primarily a disease of homosexuals or of heterosexuals and in particular whether discrimination against homosexuals is connected to Cuba's AIDS policies. This is a question of political as well as epidemiological import since the issue of human rights is so intimately tied with U.S. studies of Cuba's AIDS policies. Many U.S. studies critical of Cuban AIDS policies in human rights terms argue, implicitly or explicitly, that these policies are part of a larger societal and governmental discrimination against homosexuals. There is often a hidden assumption that somehow the charge that Cuba's policies violate human rights is more credible, or is magnified, if HIV/AIDS is shown to be associated with homosexuality.

The results of the extensive testing carried out in Cuba and follow-up statistics on the characteristics of those testing positive for HIV can give us some idea of the epidemiology of HIV and AIDS in Cuba. First, and most strikingly, the rate of HIV and AIDS infection in Cuba is quite low by international standards.[36] Among those tested by May of 1988, the highest rates were, predictably, found among sexual contacts of HIV seropositive people (4.5 per 100). Among other "high risk" groups the HIV positivity rate was low compared to the rest of the Americas: among STD patients it was 0.016 per 100; among hospitalized patients it was 0.003 per 100; among prisoners, 0.01 per 100.[37]

Nancy Scheper-Hughes wrote in 1993 that "a large number of Cuban soldiers returning from Africa" were found seropositive in these initial tests.[38] Scheper-Hughes defends Cuba's policies by emphasizing that Cubans first encountered HIV in 1986 among soldiers returning from Africa. This was the reason the AIDS sanitarium was at first under the authority of the military: it was a facility for soldiers. Later, in 1986, the disease was discovered among civilians through testing at neighborhood clinics.

Many among this second group of seropositive civilians were homosexuals. Thus, in 1987 the sanitarium was transferred to the Ministry of Public Health:

> AIDS is not viewed as a disease of the sexually stigmatized. Over 60 percent of seropositive Cubans are heterosexuals, many of whom were infected overseas on military duty...or were the sexual partners of such people on their return. AIDS tends to be viewed in Cuba as an occupational hazard of internationalists, and these are hardly a stigmatized population.[39]

Héctor Terry, however, did associate AIDS with homosexuality, at least initially. As Vice Minister of Health, he reported that, in the first round of massive testing, none of the pregnant women and a "low number" of returning soldiers diagnosed positive for the infection. The Cuban media reported in 1986 that HIV had entered the country in 1982 through a Cuban who had become infected in New York, a claim repeated by Terry in 1987.[40] It then spread, according to these sources, among the homosexual community and through bisexual men to heterosexuals.[41] It is not certain, however, that identifying homosexual transmission of AIDS is inherently homophobic. A political scientist who has studied the situation, in fact, makes contradictory arguments to imply the homophobic nature of the debate about AIDS transmission in Cuba. He gives some examples where officials identify homosexual transmission, and others where they *fail* to identify homosexual transmission, and labels both of these phenomena as examples of homophobia.[42]

The debate about how HIV/AIDS got to Cuba is complicated by a number of factors. Given the history of U.S. bacteriological warfare against Cuba, some Cuban officials almost automatically assumed and explicitly argued that AIDS was another weapon in the U.S. arsenal against the island.[43] United States officials, in response, have blamed Cuban "military adventures" in Africa. And Cubans, in defending their African policies, have downplayed the African connection. Using arguments about the prevalence of AIDS among volunteers who had served in Africa, Scheper-Hughes attempted to defend Cuban policies against charges that they constituted discrimination against homosexuals. However, I have found no Cuban sources which agree with her interpretation of the origin of AIDS in Cuba. If there is any "politics of blame" in Cuban medical or popular culture, it is against foreigners in general and the United States in particular, rather than against homosexuals *or* Africa. It tends to be foreign human rights activists and gay rights activists who emphasize the association of homosexuality and HIV in Cuba.[44]

To shed further light on the epidemiology of AIDS in Cuba, let us examine the available statistics. Sexual transmission accounts for virtually all cases of HIV infection in a country in which injection drug use is rare and the blood supply has been tested for HIV antibodies since 1985, shortly after the development of serologic testing. In late 1988, the gender breakdown of those testing HIV-positive over the prior two years was 170 men and 70 women; in April 1989, it was 195 men and 73 women; about 65 percent of the men were homosexual or bisexual.[45] A 1989 study of risk factors among those infected with HIV showed that of the 315 men infected with the virus, 105 were gay or bisexual, while sexual contact with foreigners was the principal risk factor in 217 cases. A visitor in 1989 was told that "about a third of the 171 male residents [in the Santiago las Vegas sanitarium] were homosexual or bisexual."[46]

In September of 1990, there were 497 total cases of HIV infection, 362 male and 135 female; 150 had acquired the infection through homosexual contact, and 325 through heterosexual contact.[47] July 1992 statistics showed 579 men and 233 women infected with HIV[48]; at the end of 1992, the director of the AIDS Advice and Information Center in Havana stated that of the 703 people in the sanitaria, 41 percent were homosexual or bisexual and 57 percent were heterosexual.[49] In March 1994 Ministry of Health statistics showed 1,011 total cases of HIV, 71 percent of these men and 29 percent women, with 446 (44.1 percent) identified as acquired through homosexual or bisexual transmission, 549 (54.3 percent) through heterosexual transmission, and the remaining 16 through transfusions, hemophilia, occupational, or perinatal transmission.[50] Lumsden notes that the proportion of seropositive males who are homosexual or bisexual rose from 41 percent in October 1990 to 62.8 percent in December 1994.[51] Thus there exists evidence both for the importance of homosexual transmission, and for noting that it is not the *primary* means of transmission.

More important than determining the degree to which HIV/AIDS is a disease associated with homosexuality in Cuba is examining how the real, though not exclusive, association between AIDS and homosexuality has affected Cuba's AIDS policies. The opinion of U.S. medical experts who have studied Cuban AIDS policies is virtually unanimous in arguing that Cuban policies toward AIDS are absolutely consistent with its policies toward other diseases and epidemics and with its health-care system as a whole.[52] Both critics and cautious admirers of the policies agree that "Cuban health officials have viewed the AIDS-control program as an extension of the postrevolutionary health-care system."[53] Lumsden writes that "the quarantine measures were quite consistent with Cuba's radical response to other epidemics such as dengue and African swine fever."[54] Swanson, Gill, Wald, and co-workers argue that "from the outset, Cuba treated HIV/AIDS as a health problem rather than a social or political problem. Cuba's response to the AIDS epidemic was no different from the response of the country to any other outbreak, such as meningitis or gastroenteritis."[55] Scheper-Hughes goes further and argues that the tendency in the United States to approach AIDS as a social rather than a medical problem severely limited the public health response and contributed to the spread of the disease:

> In the United States and Europe human rights issues were seen as central from the very start of the epidemic. Arriving as it did on the heels of the sexual revolution and the feminist, gay rights, and patients' rights movements, AIDS was seen as a major test of our commitment...the rights agendas already in place provoked a 'hands off' response so virulent that we lost sight of the real threat. As Stephen Joseph, former Commissioner of Public Health for the City of New York told me in May, 1993, 'We came to think of AIDS as fundamentally a crisis in human rights that had some public health dimensions, rather than as a crisis in public health that had some important human rights dimensions.' This perception is reflected in the mountain of uninspiring social science literature on AIDS, a morass of repetitive, pious liturgies about stigma, blaming, and difference. These writings conceal a collective denial of the impact of AIDS....

In the United States blood screening was delayed because of the implications of asking donors to identify sexual practices and drug habits. HIV testing was not added to the work-up of every newly admitted hospital patient, and neighbourhoods with a superabundance of HIV seropositivity were not targeted for intensive treatment and prevention programmes for fear of stigmatising certain postal code districts. To this day the U.S. and other public health systems put no demands on individuals to be tested and none on those found HIV positive. The prevailing view is that to demand testing and partner notification would be to treat HIV-positive individuals like criminals....The refusal to recognize that there were real 'risk groups' meant that public health and educational resources were spread thinly...a more aggressive public health response at the very start of the epidemic might have saved countless lives....

Individual liberty, privacy, free speech, and free choice are cherished values in any democratic society but they are sometimes invoked to obstruct social policies that favour universal health care, social welfare, and equal opportunity. Until all people, and women and children in particular, share equal rights in social and sexual citizenship, an AIDS programme built exclusively on individual and private rights cannot represent the needs of all groups.[56]

EVOLUTION OF CUBA'S AIDS POLICIES

While quarantine is the best-known aspect of Cuba's AIDS program internationally, it is in fact only one element of a policy that is simply part of Cuba's overall health system. In addition, Cuba's AIDS policies have developed and evolved considerably over time. The goals have been similar to Cuba's public health objectives during the dengue epidemic: identifying and providing medical care to those affected by the disease, and preventing its spread. In 1983 Cuba established a National Multidisciplinary Commission to advise the Ministry of Public Health on AIDS. Its initial step was to ban imported blood derivatives.[57] By producing its own less efficient but safer blood derivatives, Cuba was able to protect transfusion recipients and in particular hemophiliacs—in 1989 only 4 out of 500 hemophiliacs in Cuba were HIV positive.[58]

In 1985 when tests to diagnose HIV became available, a program of massive testing began. Thorough screening of all blood donors was the first step.[59] In 1987 Cuban health officials announced that 1.1 million tests had been carried out, including every Cuban who had been out of the country between 1975 and 1986 (including soldiers, students, participants in cultural exchanges, diplomats, and foreign aid workers[60]) and in particular Cubans who had served in Africa, as well as 23,000 pregnant women.[61] State agencies and neighborhood block organizations (CDRs) compiled a census of all who had traveled outside the country, approximately 380,000 people, to identify them for testing.[62] Plans were in the works to extend testing to everybody who entered a hospital or a physician's office.[63]

By the middle of 1988, the Cuban health ministry reported that close to one-third of Cuba's sexually active population and 20 percent of the entire population had been tested, uncovering a total of 230 seropositive persons (including the 147 reported in 1987). This program involved mandatory testing of 103,500 residents of Havana's port area, only two of whom were found to be infected with HIV.[64] In late

1988 Cuban health officials said that testing was being done on all patients admitted to hospitals, on all Cubans returning from abroad, and on all Cubans likely to have contact with foreigners because of their residence or work.[65]

In 1992 the director of Cuba's Institute for Tropical Medicine (which coordinates the AIDS program) listed sexual partners of persons testing positive for HIV, blood donors, hospital patients, pregnant women, tourism employees, merchant seamen, and persons who return from abroad as those receiving routine testing for HIV.[66] Homosexuals as a group have never been identified or singled out for testing.

"QUARANTINE"

Since it is probably the most controversial aspect of Cuba's AIDS policies, the quarantine system and its evolution over time are worth describing in detail. Beginning in 1986, persons found to be HIV-positive were sent to a sanitarium outside Havana. Initially, the sanitarium was run by the military for returning soldiers from Africa, but in 1987, as the infection was found among more and more civilians, authority was transferred to the Ministry of Public Health.[67] It was only during the first months that the sanitarium maintained an actual quarantine: patients could not leave the facility at all, although some visits were allowed.[68] One resident told an interviewer in 1989 that "at the beginning we found ourselves almost totally isolated from society because the visits from relatives were restricted, because the means of transmission were not completely known. This isolation lasted a few months, and a system of passes and structured leaves was established and perfected over time."[69] After three months, the "quarantine" was modified to allow patients to leave on overnight passes with a chaperone approximately once a month.[70] Terry explained in 1987 that "the interned Cubans are allowed home visits...but are warned that if they have sexual relations, they need to protect their partners." He added: "If his wife wants to have sex without that protection, it is her problem."[71]

It is clear that the quarantine system was never directed particularly against homosexuals *per se*. Both Leiner and Lumsden argue, however, that there was discrimination against homosexuals within the sanitarium in its early days. Lumsden writes that

> gay internees...were subject to discriminatory policies within the Havana sanatorium. They initially lived in segregated quarters and were subject to greater restrictions than other residents with respect to the external passes that allowed them to make brief visits outside the sanatorium. They had to wait longer for such passes and were subject to greater supervision by the nursing staff, who chaperoned them to ensure that they had no opportunity to infect others.[72]

Scheper-Hughes attributes the segregation of homosexual residents to "conflicts [which] arose between these new arrivals and the defensively homophobic soldier patients," and says that it was protests by these new residents that led to the first reforms in the system and the eventual transfer of authority from the Ministry of Defense to the Ministry of Public Health.[73]

The first U.S. visitors to the sanitarium were a group of health professionals from Columbia University in late 1988. Sanitarium physical conditions were "pleasant," they reported, and residents confirmed in interviews that "they maintained their original salary, they could go to the movies in town occasionally, could go home on weekends accompanied by a chaperon." Married couples could live together and were also allowed unchaperoned excursions away from the sanitarium. Their uninfected children remained outside the sanitarium.[74]

Addressing the U.S. visitors' concerns about the "ethics" of mandatory testing and quarantine, Cuban health officials told them that "no coercion was necessary" for testing "since eventually all Cubans come into contact with the medical system in the workplace, at school, or during treatment for disease....Informed consent for such testing was deemed unnecessary." According to Vice Minister of Health, Héctor Terry, "Physicians undertake the tests that they consider crucial. It is not for patients to make such determinations."[75] Swanson, Gill, Wald, and co-workers confirm that:

> Routine screening for a number of health concerns is widely accepted by the population as an ongoing part of the public health program that reaches the entire population....Support for HIV screening, as well as screening for other health concerns, is buttressed by strong social pressure, whether at work or elsewhere in the community, and has been widely accepted. Most persons who are in a priority-risk category passively accept testing as a routine part of their regular blood testing.

However, "documented reports show that the wishes of individuals who have refused when asked to submit to a test at the workplace or in the community have been respected."[76] Santana, Faas, and Wald wrote that during the general screening conducted in municipalities, significant numbers of individuals (130 in Old Havana and nearly 3,000 in Sancti Spíritus) refused to be tested.

> They are not forced to provide a blood sample, but they are counseled about safe behavior on the assumption that they may be seropositive. However, it is clear that pressure from peers, neighbors, co-workers, and health officials is very strong, and many who would have preferred not to be tested have, nevertheless, agreed to it.[77]

Terry also informed visiting U.S. health professionals that:

> If people refused to enter the sanatorium, every effort was made to convince them of their obligation to do so and of their need for medical supervision. Friends, family, and neighbors were enlisted to help with the effort. Offered an opportunity to acknowledge that coercion was necessary at times, Dr. Terry demurred, noting that one woman had adamantly refused to enter the quarantine and that he had chosen not to invoke sanctions.[78]

The authors noted that this information conflicted with exiles' accounts (which they said could not be confirmed by human rights organizations) of physical coercion and concluded that only further study could determine the truth of the level of coercion involved. The authors also point out that Cuban officials "told us of a constant search for less harsh alternatives—such as permitting children to reside with their parents, allowing family members to assume responsibility for surveillance in some instances, and building new facilities more accessible from other parts of the country."[79]

In February of 1989, *New Scientist* magazine reported on Cuba's sanitarium, noting that it was "surrounded by high wire fences...to dissuade inmates from leaving," but that residents "are allowed out to local shops, although they must be accompanied by a sanitarium attendant, and are given five-day passes to stay with their families, again with a chaperone. But they must sign a promise to abstain from sexual relations." (Héctor Terry confirmed the chaperone system to another U.S. visitor but wryly noted that "the technicians do not accompany them into the bedroom." Pérez-Stable noted that "at least one woman has been documented to seroconvert following weekend visits by her quarantined husband."[80] Santana, Faas, and Wald write that "chaperones cannot prevent behavior leading to new infections, but have a strong inhibiting effect on the resident."[81]) Housing was provided for married and for gay couples. The magazine quoted the director of Cuba's AIDS testing program as saying: "Anyone in Cuba found to be HIV positive is asked to leave their job and home and is sent to the sanitarium. We send doctors and nurses to convince these people it is better to go. We create the conditions in which they will want to go. But no one puts a straitjacket or handcuffs on them."[82] Santana, Faas, and Wald documented one case where a seropositive woman refused to enter the sanitarium: "In that case, a woman with small children remained at home, closely monitored by the medical staff."[83]

After Dr. Jorge Pérez took over administration of the sanitarium in early 1989, he initiated further reforms. He tore down the wall and barbed wire surrounding the sanitarium and began a series of measures aimed at integrating residents into the community rather than isolating them.[84] By September of 1989, residents—including doctors—were permitted to practice their professions inside the sanitarium.[85] A visitor in late 1991 noted that among the staff of the sanitarium were five doctors, eight nurses, and four medical students who were all HIV-positive, and quoted Pérez as saying that "this makes the level of trust very deep with other patients."[86]

Also in 1989, officials introduced a system to evaluate residents after six months in the sanitarium, allowing those judged responsible to leave the sanitarium without a chaperone.[87] Those who left without permission were subject to a 50-peso fine by Cuban law. Knowingly infecting another could be punished with imprisonment.[88] In 1991 Terry announced that some residents were being permitted to work outside the sanitarium, returning to the complex only to sleep. He stated that, "As time goes by the restrictions could become more flexible, but it will all depend on how responsible each patient proves to be."[89]

New facilities were built in central and eastern Cuba to allow patients to be interned closer to their homes: in 1991 there were five sanitaria;[90] in 1992, there was one in each of Cuba's 14 provinces.[91] In a speech at the University of California, Berkeley, in late 1992, Pérez told listeners that residents could leave the sanitarium essentially whenever they wanted. "There are no machine guns and guards," he said.[92] By 1993 the system of "quarantine" had been modified so that after a six-month probationary period, residents were evaluated by a team of health professionals. Those judged to show adequate understanding of the need and the way to prevent transmission of the disease were allowed to spend weekends and some weeknights away from the facility. Approximately 80 percent of the residents who had been there over six months were in this "guaranteed" category.[93]

Since 1993, ambulatory care rather than mandatory sanitarium residence has been the primary strategy of Cuba's AIDS program. Since the new policy was approved in the spring of 1993, family doctors have been educated about AIDS, and arrangements made for providing care in the home community. In January of 1994, the policy was implemented, and since then, "the sanitaria have operated as a geographically based network of ambulatory care centers as planned. This policy provides initial education and continuing ambulatory care in a person's home community by the neighborhood doctor and nurse."[94] Persons diagnosed as HIV-positive are initially admitted to a sanitarium and for a period of six months provided with treatment and education about the disease and methods for preventing its spread. After the six-month residence, patients are assessed by a team of health-care professionals, and most are given the option of ambulatory care in their communities. A conflict between the rights of the individual and the rights of the community (to be protected from the disease) is resolved in favor of the community in the case of those who are judged to be unwilling or incapable of engaging in responsible behavior to prevent the spread of the disease: they are obliged to remain in the sanitarium.[95]

Interestingly, however, the majority of those given the option to leave have decided to remain. In Havana's Santiago de las Vegas' sanitarium, 75 percent of the 300 residents have been given the option, but only 68 had chosen to leave by late 1994. (In the country as a whole, 136 of the 1,077 HIV-positive citizens had chosen to receive ambulatory care.[96]) By April 1995 170 had chosen the outpatient plan; by November, 184.[97] Residents cited the benefits of sanitarium residence including special diets, comfortable living conditions, and acceptance by the community as advantages of remaining there.[98] One homosexual resident told an interviewer that "there is less repression of gays in Los Cocos [the sanitarium] than anywhere else in Havana."[99] Foreign visitors to the sanitaria have emphasized the comfort and home-like atmosphere there.[100]

It is also interesting to note that few Cubans have objected to Cuba's approach to AIDS. In a generally unfavorable assessment of Cuba's AIDS policies, Eliseo Pérez-Stable, a physician of internal medicine, acknowledges that "although I discussed the HIV quarantine policy with other health authorities, family members, friends, and many regular working citizens, I detected not a hint of disagreement. I found this attitude impressive given the spectrum of public opinion on many issues voiced by the Cuban people."[101] Lumsden writes:

> Some gay critics abroad interpreted the quarantine as further evidence of Cuba's repressive discrimination against homosexuals. Yet in Cuba it was not perceived as either unusual or discriminatory. The program seems to have been supported from the outset by the majority of the Cuban population, including a majority of homosexuals, whose experience with Cuba's health system has led them to place enormous trust in the country's medical policies.[102]

RESEARCH AND DEVELOPMENT

Cuba has also devoted its scientific and technical—and as a result, considerable financial—resources toward the battle against AIDS. Cuban health officials estimate HIV-related expenses as approximately $15 to $20 million per year,[103] or one percent of Cuba's health budget.[104] Cut off from collaboration with U.S.-based scientists and technologies and from medications produced in the United States or by U.S. companies,

Cuba relies on importing from afar and developing its own products. During the first year of HIV screening (1986), Cuba spent approximately $3 million importing equipment, but by 1987 the island had developed its own serologic test, reducing the cost substantially.[105] In 1991 there were 45 laboratories on the island that could perform the test, and by 1993 there were 52 such laboratories.[106] While some critics have questioned the reliability of the Cuban test, the accuracy of the testing system is enhanced by using a combination of the ELISA and the Western blot tests. A study conducted in collaboration with the Oswaldo Cruz Foundation in Brazil and Sweden's Ministry of Health confirmed the accuracy of the Cuban system.[107] To increase testing among those wishing anonymity the country has also initiated a test-by-mail program whereby people send a drop of blood to a state-run laboratory and receive the results by mail.[108]

Nancy Scheper-Hughes described the care and treatment of HIV-positive residents in the sanitarium in 1993 in a very positive light:

> All residents are treated with individually tailored regimens including interferons, transfer factor, and low-dose zidovudine. Those who do not respond well or who prefer alternative medicines are offered one of several antiviral herbal medicines currently being tested at the sanitarium. A small infirmary handles patients with AIDS-related illnesses but the very sick are transferred to the Medical Institute for Tropical Medicine in Havana, where they are cared for with patients suffering from other serious communicable diseases. Exercise and a diet rich in calories (5,000 kcal daily) and protein are integral parts of the regimen—indeed sanitarium residents are better fed than the average Cuban worker and each one costs the Cuban state about $15,000 a year.[109]

Patients who become ill with AIDS also receive free hospital care as well as AZT and other medications at an estimated cost of $7,000 per patient per year. (Leiner notes in comparison that no facilities in Puerto Rico offered AZT since "if we give it to one, we should give it to everybody, and that would consume the [AIDS] Institute's whole budget."[110]) Cuban researchers have also achieved promising results in a study using recombinant interferon alpha to slow disease progression in asymptomatic HIV carriers.[111]

Cuba has also been at the forefront of international efforts to develop a vaccine against AIDS. In 1995 Cuba announced plans to begin testing a genetically engineered vaccine on chimpanzees.[112] In June of 1996, Dr. Jorge Pérez announced that animal trials had been "promising," and in December 1996, 24 Cuban scientists carried out the first human trials on themselves.[113]

NEUROPATHY

The U.S. media and policy-makers were ostensibly less concerned for the well-being of the Cuban people when a mysterious epidemic of optic and peripheral neuropathy struck the island in 1991, affecting 50,862 people by January 1994—about 50 times more than the numbers affected by HIV.[114] While many medical professionals were quick to point out a relationship between U.S. policy and the outbreak, neither the U.S. role nor the Cuban success in coping with the neuropathy epidemic has attracted much U.S. media attention. This is in part because this disease does not fit into any ready-made U.S. categories about Cuba, like the "human rights violation" category.[115]

In fact, Cuba's response to the neuropathy epidemic was similar to its response to dengue and AIDS. By the end of 1992, 472 cases of optic and peripheral neuropathy had been diagnosed, and in early 1993—with 3,000 to 4,000 new cases appearing every week—the Cuban government launched a full-fledged effort to test for and study the disease. The Civil Defense for Disaster Relief, the Ministry of Public Health, and the Cuban Academy of Sciences coordinated a task force to research and test for the disease, mobilizing 18,000 family doctors; by May of 1993, 45,584 cases had been uncovered. During April and May, the government began a program of vitamin distribution to the entire population of the island, and beginning in June, the number of new cases started to decrease dramatically. By the end of the year, the epidemic was essentially over.[116]

The disease appeared first in the western, tobacco-growing province of Pinar del Río, primarily in rural areas, among adult men between 25 and 65. Most were users of both tobacco and alcohol. This province had the highest incidence of cases overall (1,332.8 per 100,000), but as the disease spread to other provinces and to urban areas, it also spread to adult women. In the end women were *more* affected than men: of the total of 50,862 cases, the national cumulative incidence was 566.7 per 100,000 women, and 368.5 per 100,000 men.[117] As of June 1993, only 57 children under 14 years of age had been diagnosed with the disease; 81 percent of these were between the ages of 10 and 14.[118] Pregnant women and young children—all of whom receive extra food through the ration—were rarely among those affected.[119]

As in the cases of dengue and AIDS, Cuba's response to the neuropathy epidemic was characterized by a generous commitment of resources for identifying, studying, and tracking the disease, curing those afflicted by it, and preventing further cases once its nature was illuminated. Vitamin deficiencies, especially of B vitamins, were identified early in 1993 as an important risk factor, even while the precise etiology of the disease remained unknown. The government obtained materials for the manufacture of vitamin supplements to include 2.5 mg thiamine, 1.6 mg riboflavin, 20 mg niacin, 2 mg B6, 6 µg B12, 250 µg folate, and 2500 IU retinol, with half-dosages for children. These were distributed through family doctors to every citizen in Pinar del Río in March and to the rest of the country in April and May. This distribution of vitamin supplements has continued on a monthly basis through the late 1990s. Most of those affected responded positively to the vitamin treatment, and there were no fatalities. Once the supplement program began, the number of new cases dropped sharply.[120]

The case of neuropathy illustrates several interesting aspects of the relationship of health to politics. First, the epidemic was triggered by nutritional deficiencies and curtailed by government distribution of vitamins.[121] As Dr. Gustavo Román, who studied the epidemic for the WHO, pointed out, epidemics of this sort have historically occurred in the context of extreme deprivation caused by war. In Cuba, however, the deprivation was due to an economic crisis that had direct political causes in the collapse of Cuba's Soviet-bloc trading partners and the tightened U.S. blockade of the country. "I found profound injustice in the occurrence of this huge epidemic of nutritional cause in a population not at war. Although the U.S. economic embargo against Cuba was not the primary cause of this epidemic, it certainly contributed to its development, complicated its investigation and treatment, and continues to hamper its prevention."[122] A joint Cuba-U.S. study that compared the epidemic to a similar outbreak a century ago in Cuba—which also occurred during a U.S. blockade of the island, during the Spanish-Cuban-American war—concluded: "Although we do not believe that the U.S. embargo is the only cause of the epidemic, we concur with the assessment of its significance made by Kuntz: that 'it is the only one factor that was deliberately devised and is the only one that could easily be reversed.'"[123]

Román summarized the direct relationship of the embargo to the epidemic as follows:

> Feed and grains, including soybean meal for human protein supplementation, must be imported from places as distant as China, with resulting higher cost; bibliographic searches are almost impossible since Cuba cannot use the National Library of Medicine's MEDLARS system; mail, telephone, and fax transmissions are unreliable; books, scientific journals, and information on science and technology are scant and outdated; and laboratory equipment, reagents, and materials for vitamin production are all covered by the embargo and can be purchased only at excessively high prices.[124]

Adds Richard Garfield, professor at Columbia University:

> The recent epidemic in Cuba...is not an incidental result of the breakdown of a weak government in a poor country but the intentional result of political measures taken by the United States....In 1992, the U.S. embargo was extended to prohibit Cuba from purchasing foods or medicines from U.S. firms and their subsidiaries abroad and to limit such sales from other countries. This extension of the embargo is a major contributing cause of the Cuban people's miseries. Many food imports were cut off; others became far more expensive. Because of the embargo, Cuba spends approximately 30 percent more for the medicines it purchases in the international market than it would if those medicines were purchased in the United States, and many modern medicines, produced only under U.S. patents, are unavailable for purchase at any price. The vitamins that were used as the initial intervention in the epidemic of peripheral neuropathy cost Cuba $151,000; they would have cost $56,000 and would have been available far more rapidly if they could have been purchased in Miami.[125]

The Cuban government's response to the economic crisis has been to *increase* rather than decrease its protection of vulnerable sectors. Thus, pregnant women, children, and the elderly were all able to rely on nutritional supplements and were less affected by the epidemic. Neuropathy struck primarily healthy adults—that is, the strongest sector of the population—because they had not been targeted for protection. One health professional who studies the Cuban situation asked, "How many places do you know where the strongest, the biggest, the male population will give up what it has for the weaker population?"[126]

HEALTH IN THE "SPECIAL PERIOD"

Economic crisis struck Cuba with the fall of the Soviet bloc in 1989. Cuba was very much part of the "old world order" and was dramatically affected by its replacement with a "new world order." In the context of U.S. hostility to the 1959 revolution, Cuba turned to a close alliance with the Soviet Union, and Cuba's economic development, especially from 1970 on, followed models advised and promoted by the Soviets. In some ways the relationship paralleled classic dependency: Cuba produced sugar for the Soviets and received manufactured goods in return. But unlike capitalist colonial or neocolonial powers, the Soviet Union was not seeking a profit from its dependency. The Soviets paid higher than world market prices for Cuban sugar—what they referred to as a "fair price" for political and strategic reasons. Thus, capital and resources flowed from the Soviet Union to Cuba, rather than the reverse, as is typical for capitalist metropole-colony relations.[127] The impact of the U.S. economic blockade imposed in 1961 was mitigated by Soviet trade and aid.

Although Cuba benefited economically from its relationship with the Soviets, there were economic drawbacks too, especially in the long term. The island remained dependent on the production of a single primary export: sugar. Fully 70 percent of Cuba's trade was with the U.S.S.R., and 85 percent was with the Soviet bloc. Cuba was heavily dependent on imported petroleum products for its agriculture and industry, on imported manufactured products, and even on imported food.[128]

When the Soviet bloc began to disintegrate, Cuba's economy entered a crisis. Cuba lost 85 percent of its foreign trade; it lost the ability to import the petroleum products needed to maintain, not to mention build and diversify, its agriculture and industry. Factories were closed, and sugar production collapsed. Cars and buses disappeared from the streets, electricity vanished from people's homes and food from their tables. The impact of the U.S. economic blockade had been mitigated by Cuba's ties with the Soviet bloc; suddenly the effects of the blockade were felt with full force. In 1991, the Cuban government declared a "special period in time of peace" and began to impose emergency economic measures. And in 1992, the U.S. economic blockade was strengthened by the Torricelli Bill, which explicitly extended the embargo to foods and medicines.

This prohibition has had direct consequences for the Cuban health system. One study summarized the effects:

> Some essential medicines and supplies are produced only in the United States and thus can no longer be purchased. These include the only effective treatment for pediatric leukemia, x-ray film for breast cancer detection, U.S.-made replacement parts for European-made respirators, and Spanish-language medical books from a firm recently bought by a United States conglomerate. Most medical products are also produced in other countries but cost more and require 50-400 percent higher shipping charges (estimated total of $4-5 million extra) than required for the same goods purchased in the United States. Production of the 24 most common pharmaceutical products produced in Cuba with imported primary materials is estimated to cost an additional $1 million per year due to the embargo. An estimated $181,000 was spent to transport vitamins to Cuba during the optic neuropathy epidemic of 1992-93; the cost would

have been approximately $56,000 had they come from the United States. In all, the Ministry of Foreign Trade estimates excess costs to the health system at $45 million per year.[129]

However, because of the character of Cuba's social and economic system, economic crisis there had very different kinds of impacts than have comparable crises elsewhere in Latin America. Since the state controls the economy, it has been able to distribute the impact of the crisis equitably throughout the society, so that potentially vulnerable sectors have not been disproportionately affected. Overall, Cuba's health indicators have remained very strong despite six years of economic crisis. Key indicators, such as infant mortality, have continued to decline. In 1989, Cuba's infant mortality rate was 11/1000 and by 1995 it was 9/1000—roughly the same rate as that currently found in the United States.

Cuban officials note proudly that not a single school nor hospital has been closed, and that rationing has ensured that the population has equal access to what scarce food and products have continued to be available. In a capitalist economic system falling supply of basic goods would lead to rising prices, a sort of market rationing which grants access to those with wealth and deprives the poor. In Cuba, the state rations according to need. Milk, for example, was removed from the parallel market when supplies fell, and is available only through the ration card or *libreta* to children under seven, to the elderly, and to those suffering from certain illnesses.[130]

At the same time, Cuba has been undergoing a process of economic opening, which in some ways seems completely at odds with the redistributive economic logic of the country. In 1993, the dollar was legalized, and several government-owned chains of dollar stores were opened to draw hard currency away from the black market.[131] The government has encouraged foreign investment and tourism as means of attracting much-needed capital to the country. In 1994 "free" *farmers' markets* (conducted in pesos) were opened, where prices are governed by supply and demand. In 1995 many new forms of self-employment became legal. Cuban economists explain and defend these measures as necessary to revive production and help the country survive in the new world order. They emphasize that the market will be kept under strict limits, and that key sectors like health and education will never be subject to market forces. Nevertheless, the economic reforms, while indeed bringing in much-needed capital and increasing production, have also introduced a level of inequality unknown since the revolution. Cubans with access to dollars, either through relatives living abroad or through links (both legal and illegal) with the tourist and foreign investment sectors, have access to food, products, and entertainment ordinary Cubans only dream of.

The crisis—and the contradictory measures taken to relieve it—have inevitably had a substantial impact on public health and health-care delivery in Cuba. Many basic food items are scarce or available only for dollars; food available through the *libreta* covers only about half the month's needs. Especially during the difficult years of 1993-94—before the economic recovery began—hunger was the norm. Still, hunger in Cuba meant weight loss for virtually the entire adult population rather than malnutrition among children and the poor. In fact, as noted above, it was healthy adults who were the main victims of neuropathy caused in part by undernutrition.

In strictly medical terms, some U.S. analysts have argued that decreased food consumption had its benefits since obesity was a serious health problem prior to the Special Period. However, Cuban health officials are more concerned about nutritional deficiencies than obesity.[132] In addition to the neuropathy epidemic, the consequences of inadequate food supply have been seen in increases in the incidence of low birth weight (which rose from a low point of 7.6 percent in 1990 to 9.0 percent in 1993), the number of women underweight at the beginning of pregnancy (8.7 percent in 1900, 10.0 percent in 1993), and in the frequency of insufficient weight gain during pregnancy (the percentage of women affected rose from 5.5 in 1990 to 6.1 in 1993).[133]

It should be noted, however, that these rates are still extremely low by international standards,[134] and they have *not* translated into increased infant and child mortality; they *have* provoked a concerted government attempt to counteract the trend. In 1994 a National Low Birth Weight Program was initiated to attack the problem on several fronts. The program seeks: to carry out studies identifying preconceptional and obstetrical risk factors for low birth weight; to work with the National Mother-Infant Department to increase the number and utilization of "maternal homes" which provide four meals a day and a residential option to pregnant women[135]; to make meals for pregnant women available in hospitals, workplaces, and agricultural cooperatives; to work with UNICEF to provide multivitamin and iron tablets for women during pregnancy and for four months after delivery.[136]

Despite such initiatives, the impact of the economic crisis on health has not been insignificant. Medications, hospital supplies, and equipment, ranging from the most basic—sheets, pens, and aspirin—to the most advanced, are all in desperately short supply. Infectious disease and parasite morbidity and mortality rates have risen since the 1980s, due primarily to material scarcities affecting public sanitation. In particular, there has been little chlorine available for water purification. The portion of the population with access to chlorinated water declined from 98 percent in 1988 to 26 percent in 1994.[137] Tuberculosis and typhoid fever rates have risen slightly, as has mortality from diarrheal diseases.[138] Nevertheless, these figures remain quite low by international standards: infectious and parasitic diseases accounted for 2 percent of deaths in 1993 while 74 percent of deaths were due to chronic and degenerative diseases and accidents.[139]

Lack of food has also seriously affected the health of the population. Some of the measures Cuba has taken to increase food production and importation are inevitably at odds with efforts to guarantee equity in food distribution. Fidel Castro described these contradictions in April of 1996:

> Measures were adopted, such as the farmers' markets, to give impetus to food production, to open up the possibility of being able to buy some things which were impossible to obtain, given the situation we were in, although clearly, they weren't the methods we used before, when we could distribute pork, chicken, eggs, milk, etc., at minimum prices, which was a better way....Nevertheless, we had to find a way of making that [excess] money circulate a little, to collect a little money and, moreover, many people were absolutely convinced that the farmers' markets were a solution, and since people with a lot of money in their pockets, who didn't have anything to

spend it on, were saying, 'It's better to have somebody supplying something, never mind the price.'

However, making imported food available in dollars meant that while the overall supply increased, inequality in access also increased. At the same time, though, the government strictly limited the free market in food in the interests of equity.

> One of the sacred things that we had to defend was the ration system still available to the population, to guarantee that [people receive] minimum amounts of garden and root vegetables, and other food products where possible [even though] a significant proportion are imported foodstuffs. This meant guaranteeing rice [and] guaranteeing specific quantities of beans....[140]

With respect to the availability of medical services, one analyst summarized the situation this way:

> The spectrum of medical services available has been maintained, although quantitatively the numbers of services provided have diminished. The population is affected by the intermittent supply of medications, the absence of some medications, limits in the diagnostic tests available because of lack of supplies, decreasing quality of hospital services, in particular in the area of food and hygienic conditions for patients in the hospital, and even by difficulties in transportation to get access to medical services that are not available in the community.[141]

Several factors have contributed to the ability of the health sector to survive the economic crisis. In addition to trying to distribute the impact of the crisis equitably and to protect vulnerable sectors, the Cuban government has attempted to take advantage of the strengths of its system. One of the greatest of these strengths is the human capital Cuba has built up over the past 40 years. In the area of health, despite material scarcities, Cuba has an enormous number of trained professionals.[142] In the mid-1980s the country began to implement the *family doctor program* in an effort to move primary health care out of hospitals and clinics and into the neighborhood. One of the program's goals was to shrink health sector costs by increasing preventive and diagnostic care and reducing the perceived over-use of hospitals and clinics for problems treatable outside these institutions. Family doctors live in the immediate community they serve and are responsible for the health of the community in both preventive and curative terms. A doctor and nurse team cares for approximately 100 families. The nationwide implementation of the family doctor program has been a significant part of Cuba's attempt to carry out an "adjustment with equity." Cuba now has approximately one doctor for every 200 inhabitants—one of the highest rates in the world.

In addition, the Cuban government has taken advantage of the country's "comparative advantage" in advanced medical technology with low labor costs to produce biotechnological and pharmaceutical products for export. The government also fosters "medical tourism," offering low-cost medical services to foreigners.[143] Profits from these exports have contributed to maintaining Cuba's health sector. Some hard currency earned in other sectors is also funneled into health.[144]

A delegation from the American Public Health Association described the extraordinary commitment of health professionals in Cuba who continue to provide necessary services under conditions of extreme scarcity:

> Doctors in the major children's hospital meet each morning to assess patients' needs and resources available for that day. As a result, the use of x-rays (the results of which were normal in 99 percent of cases) has been reduced by 75 percent....The same children's hospital administrators report spending a considerable amount of time on the telephone calling colleagues in other countries to urgently request enough pills to get a particular patient through the week....Medical personnel have increased home visits and are releasing patients from hospitals for follow-up care in the home. Health providers are increasingly using herbal remedies, acupuncture, and other non-Western procedures. However, in spite of their greatest efforts, the health workers are stretched to the limit. They are working long hours in highly stressful circumstances. Physicians and nurses, forced to severely ration resources, must count every pill and measure every drop of medicine they use. Difficult decisions must be made concerning which patients get diagnostic tests or medicines. So far, the health providers have been able to maintain health services. However, their ability to further ration scarce resources and resort to alternative procedures is extremely limited.[145]

On a visit to the Diez de Octubre hospital in May 1996, doctors described to a visiting delegation some of the same conditions and went on to detail experiments in their Pain Clinic with therapies ranging from acupuncture to mud. One delegation member asked, "How can you keep such a spirit of dedication that keeps you working when you could earn so much more by leaving the health sector and working in tourism?" The doctor smiled wearily. "You're asking that question in the wrong place," he told her. "If you want to know how we build our spirit of dedication, you have to go back to the day-care centers."

Just as important as cost-reduction measures, however, has been the overwhelming governmental commitment to the health sector. All of the factors described previously show how the government was able to maintain good health outcomes with less input of resources. However, when the epidemic of neuropathy hit the island, it was clear that only a major commitment of resources (in the form of vitamin supplements) would stem the epidemic—and that commitment was immediately made.

LESSONS OF THE CUBAN CASE

The first lesson of the Cuban case is that equity in health care and outcome is achievable, even under conditions of material scarcity. Cuba has attained excellent health outcomes with comparatively low levels of resources, and has maintained a strong health profile in the midst of a severe economic crisis exacerbated by economic warfare and blockade.

The second lesson is that Cuba's outcomes are possible because of a governmental commitment not only to health in the narrow sense but to social equality and social justice. Merely devoting resources to the health sector would not have achieved the same results. In Britain the health-care delivery system offers universal access, yet equity in health outcomes has not been achieved.[146] In Cuba the commitment to equality and human development has allowed the country's achievements in the area of health to withstand the most appalling material scarcities.

These first two lessons are hopeful ones. The third lesson is less encouraging. An inevitable conclusion for anybody studying the Cuban case is that the "New World Order" in general and U.S. policy toward Cuba in particular are unalterably opposed to the project of social justice and improved health Cuba has carried out over the past 40 years. As one U.S. policy-maker mused in 1959, "There are indications that if the Cuban Revolution is successful, other countries in Latin America and perhaps elsewhere will use it as a model. We should decide if we wish to have the Cuban Revolution succeed."[147] The decision was made within months of the revolution. In July of 1959, the director of the Office of Inter-American Regional Economic Affairs informed the State Department that "Castro's Government is not the kind worth saving," and a program to overturn it began.[148]

United States officials were quite open about the fact that Cuban success in ˌachieving economic independence and social justice would threaten U.S. profits not only in Cuba but also elsewhere in the hemisphere. The United States wished to avoid showing any "weakness" before Castro's "provocations." If the United States did not crush the Cuban revolution, continued one high-level U.S. official to another, this failure could:

> give encouragement to communist-nationalist elements elsewhere in Latin America who are trying to advance programs similar to those of Castro. Such programs, if undertaken…[could expose] United States property owners to treatment similar to that being received in Cuba and…prejudic[e] the program of economic development espoused by the United States for Latin America which relies so heavily on private capital investment.[149]

The Cuban revolution's redistributive policies threatened the explicitly stated U.S. goals of maintaining Cuban "receptivity to U.S. and free world capital" and safeguarding "access by the United States to essential Cuban resources."[150]

United States policy toward health in Cuba has explicitly aimed to deny and undermine the revolutionary government's attempts to improve the health of the population.[151] Through economic blockade and sabotage, through chemical and biological warfare, and through outright invasion and subversion, the United States has for 40 years pursued its goal of destroying the "threat of a good example" that Cuba's successes in health and social justice provide.[152] Development scholars have to a large extent echoed the U.S. position that the economic development model the United States supports for Latin America is the best answer to the region's social problems. Many scholars deny the Cuban experience by simply leaving it out of their comparative studies. Some dismiss Cuba's obvious successes by embedding them in discussions about "human rights"—narrowly defined as individual political freedoms. Those who do discuss Cuba often downplay or ignore the fact that the Cuban experiment has been carried out in the context of unremitting hostility and aggression from the United States, situated only 90 miles from Cuba's shores. The U.S. travel ban and the distorted portrayal of Cuba in both popular and scholarly media ensure that the majority of North Americans do not learn that a poor, Third World country, gripped by economic crisis, and under constant attack from the most powerful nation in the world, is still able to achieve health standards higher than those in the capital of that powerful nation, Washington, D.C.[153]

ACKNOWLEDGMENTS

I would like to thank Alfredo Prieto, Richard Garfield, and the core team of the IHSJ New World Order project for their innumerable contributions to this essay; Elaine Ardia and Laura Juraska of the Bates College Library for their help with references and interlibrary loans; and Sylvia Hawks of Bates College for secretarial support.

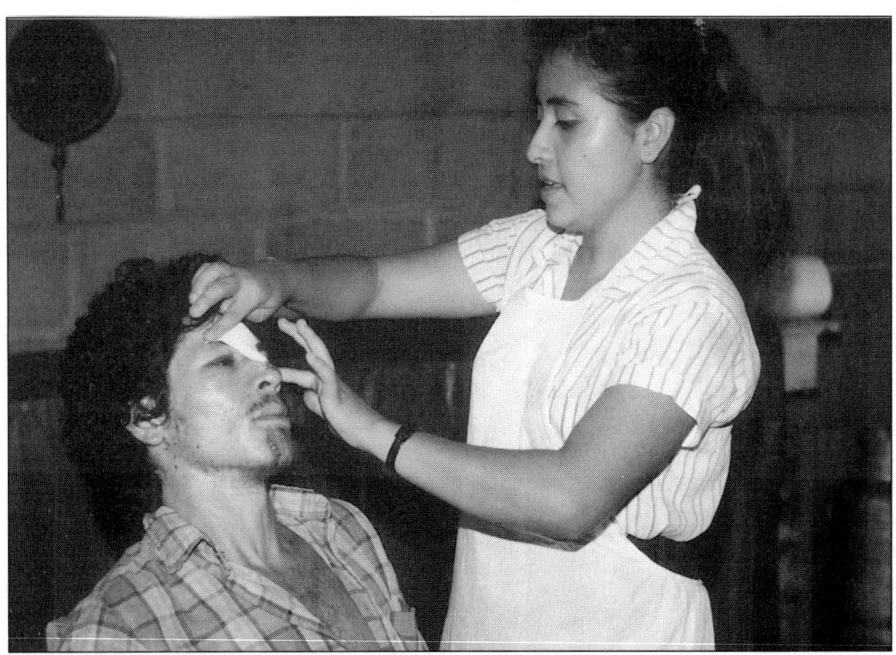

Rural Chalatenango, El Salvador. Health promoter changes the dressing on a wound of a villager. (photo by Sandy Smith-Nonini)

The Smoke and Mirrors of Health Reform in El Salvador: Community Health NGOs and the Not-So-Neoliberal State

Sandy Smith-Nonini

INTRODUCTION

In the 1990s, Third World governments in search of foreign aid have had to pledge allegiance to neoliberal reform agendas that include reducing public provision of social services and becoming more reliant on the private sector. In line with this logic, major donors such as the World Bank and the U.S. Agency for International Development (USAID) now advise health ministries in poor countries to contract with nongovernmental organizations (NGOs) for delivery of basic health services to the poor. Applying a cold geopolitical calculus, Robert Greenberger discussed the changing focus of foreign aid in a *Wall Street Journal* article entitled "Developing Countries Pass Off Tedious Job of Assisting the Poor":

> During the Cold War foreign aid was used as a weapon in the East-West struggle. Huge amounts were spent to win political loyalty, with little regard for whether it helped the poor or lined the pockets of leaders. Now, with the Soviet threat dissipated, the U.S. and many other donor nations have neither the inclination, nor the resources to be lavish with foreign aid. Thus, more governments are tapping into NGOs, paying what amounts to block grants in the hope they can deliver services more efficiently.[1]

Greenberger noted that the Clinton administration, feeling pressure from the foreign aid-slashing GOP-led Congress, planned to deliver 40 percent of foreign aid through NGOs in 1996. The World Bank, now the largest external funder of developing countries' health sectors, began linking health finance policy to conditionality for loans in 1987.[2] During the 1980s, multilateral development funds going to voluntary agencies rose tenfold.[3] And in its 1993 World Development Report *Investing in Health*, the World Bank explicitly called on countries to prioritize health interventions that have proven cost-effective. In particular, the World Bank prescribed decentralization and contracting with NGOs to increase efficiency of service delivery, citing preliminary data from Africa comparing NGO and public sector productivity.[4]

Thus, NGOs are becoming important new political actors on the international scene, a prospect which carries both dangers and opportunities for organizations concerned with grassroots health work. Many advocates for primary health care have spoken of the need to decentralize inefficient, urban-based, curative-care-oriented health ministries in poorer countries. Yet the neoliberal push to link decentralization with privatization poses a serious danger to equity—especially if governments delegate responsibility for health services to private entities without the necessary funding, technical support, regulatory oversight, or mechanisms for local accountability.

When we consider the case of Latin America, the irony is that in many countries NGOs have already been substituting for states in providing basic, often constitutionally guaranteed health services to poor populations. This chapter, based on case studies in El Salvador (see Map 14.1), examines international and national health NGOs that have supported community-based health work, with a focus on their problematic relations with the Salvadoran Ministry of Health and its neoliberal reforms in the post-war period. El Salvador offers a useful example of the complex politics involved when bi- and multilateral donors pressure a conservative ministry of health to restructure itself internally and to give up control over some services to non-state providers.

The United States Agency for International Development (USAID), the largest bilateral donor of health aid to poor countries, practically kept El Salvador's health ministry afloat during that country's recent civil war between a military-dominated government and rebels of the Farabundo Martí National Liberation Front (FMLN).[5] USAID also served as the conduit for most of the $250 million in reconstruction aid pledged by the United States since the 1992 cease-fire, $55 million of which was slated to be dispersed through NGOs.[6] The World Bank made El Salvador a structural adjustment package (SAP) loan of $100.3 million in 1992 (a small portion of which was earmarked for social services) and in early 1996 was still negotiating with the Ministry of Health about a loan to finance health sector reforms in cooperation with the Inter-American Development Bank (IDB).[7]

But donor agencies have been hesitant to make post-war reconstruction aid conditional on internal reforms. Nor have Salvadoran government leaders been willing to cut military spending—which remains at twice as high a proportion of gross domestic product (GDP) as in the pre-war period—or to levy higher income taxes to help finance reforms agreed to in the peace talks with the FMLN. Instead they have relied entirely on foreign donors, primarily the United States, to pay for reforms. A shortfall in foreign aid, combined with right-wing political opposition in El Salvador, slowed crucial peace programs like land transfers, training of the civilian police force, and justice system reforms.[8] Reform of the social service sector played second fiddle to other peace plan goals. As this study demonstrates, there is little evidence to date that Ministry of Health promises, such as decentralization of its authoritarian structures or contracting with the many NGOs currently serving the poor population, will actually make their way into practice.

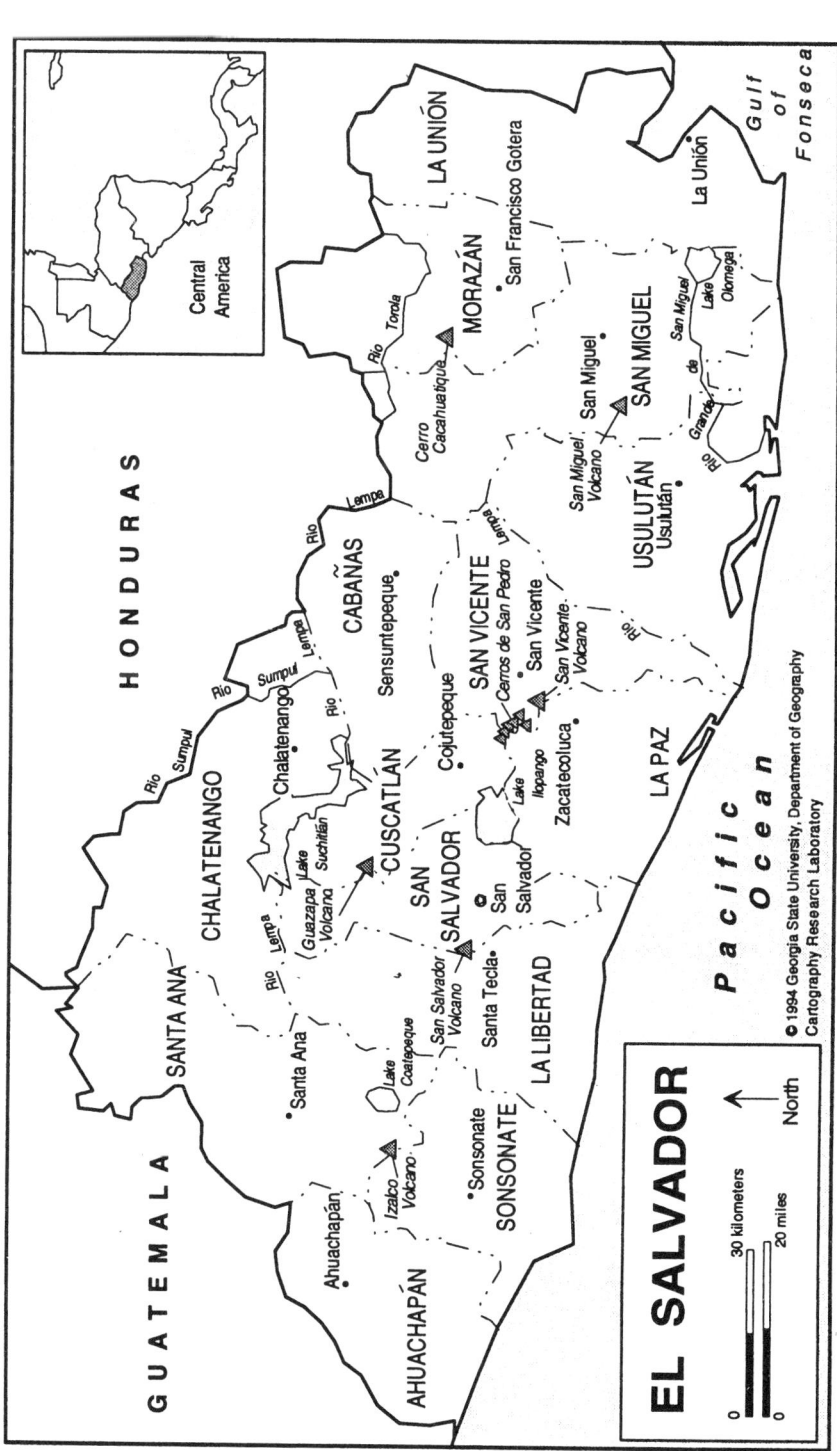

Map 14.1: El Salvador

This chapter presents a look at health reform in post-war El Salvador from the ground up. The findings suggest that although the country's ruling ARENA party is very receptive to neoliberal macroeconomics and eager to attract loans for economic development, its leaders have a vested interest in maintaining the state's clientelist structures, within which they have built their bases of power. They resist reforms they fear might erode their positions of influence. Further, in the aftermath of civil war and a decade of U.S.-financed "nation-building," ARENA's power base appears secure, and its leaders have little interest in collaborative relations with NGOs doing social development work with poor populations. After all, until a few years ago, the country's ruling elites regarded groups that advocated for the poor as the enemy.

WAR AND THE PROLIFERATION OF NGOs IN CENTRAL AMERICA

Many social justice-oriented NGOs in Latin America grew out of movements protesting governments' structural adjustment policies of the late 1970s and 1980s. As states cut back social programs (and distanced themselves further from constitutional guarantees for the poor), local self-help movements developed their own advocacy organizations, and in many cases found allies among progressive Northern development foundations seeking alternatives to corrupt governments.[9]

International NGO responses to the human misery resulting from the Central American civil wars of the 1980s gave rise to hundreds of grassroots initiatives. The activity of NGOs in the region is directly related to Washington's (and the Guatemalan army's) "low-intensity conflicts" on behalf of regional elites—a strategy that Nelson-Pallmeyer has called a "war against the poor."[10] By 1992 there were at least 300 development NGOs in Nicaragua, 700 in Guatemala, and around 700 in El Salvador.[11] The picture is complicated by the diverse political and religious groups involved in nonprofit development. While a plethora of international NGOs such as Oxfam, American Friends Service Committee, and Catholic Action supported liberation theology-style initiatives on behalf of grassroots organizations, USAID and the region's military governments responded by encouraging a wave of conservative and evangelical NGOs to begin or expand ongoing Central America programs.[12] Some right-wing NGOs in El Salvador and Guatemala even worked closely with national armies, offering one-day food giveaways and medical consultations in rural areas where anti-government rebels were active. Thus, NGOs have many faces, and policies of diverting public funds into NGO activities can cut either way on the political spectrum.

Nevertheless, the last decade of NGO-supported grassroots activism succeeded in drawing an unprecedented level of international attention and resources to populations that had suffered under decades of repression. In the case of El Salvador, the dollar value of NGO interventions sometimes rivaled that of pro-government development projects. For example, the Diaconía, a Salvadoran ecumenical organization which funded many NGO programs of humanitarian assistance for displaced peasants, received a total of $65 million in donations from abroad between 1982 and 1992, a level of funding that approached the $75 million USAID spent in the same period on its displaced persons program.[13] Unfortunately, not long after Central American peace processes got underway in the early 1990s—creating opportunities for post-war reconstruction—many major donors began redirecting their attention and funds to other global hot spots, like Bosnia and Eastern Europe, forcing national NGOs in the region to seek out new sources of support.

What remains unclear in the post-Cold War period is the degree to which NGOs in the South can continue to be effective advocates for the poor, given the onslaught of global neoliberal policies, and the many pressures to align with powerful donors or governments. The efficiency and high level of patient acceptance of many NGO health operations is directly tied to their local, grassroots orientation, and may be compromised by rapid expansion. The local participation in health work that some NGOs have nurtured within the communities they serve is likely to be shaken if the organization suddenly shifts from a combined advocacy/service role to provision of the vertically administered, selected services favored by many large donors (maternal and child health, for example). Further, few NGOs at present have the institutional infra-structure for managing basic health services on a large scale.

Nevertheless, the rhetoric of neoliberal reforms (such as collaboration with NGOs) may serve a Third World health ministry well by shoring up the government's domestic and international legitimacy and helping it attract foreign investment. The reality of promised reforms may be another matter—as members of community health NGOs discovered in El Salvador.

While the Salvadoran peace process is unique, I believe the difficulties encoun-tered by the various NGO health initiatives described here carry lessons for health NGOs in many Third World settings where traditions of democracy and state support of public services are poorly established.

SAVING ROSITA: REPLACING THE STATE IN EL SALVADOR

Four months after the 1992 cease-fire, I began a study of a so-called "popular" community health system that had developed (with assistance from a Catholic NGO) in a former war zone repopulated by refugees in El Salvador's northern province of Chalatenango. On the night of August 31st, I was asleep in the back room of a clinic in a settlement I will call Amatique when I was startled awake by a baby's cries.[14]

In the examining room I found Esperanza, a peasant woman who had arrived the previous afternoon, wringing her hands while three health workers bent over her tiny infant. Tears ran down Esperanza's cheeks as Sally, a Catholic sister trained as a pediatrician, and two community health "promoters" (locally known as *promotores*), attempted to start an intravenous line. Sally tried repeatedly to slip the needle into a tiny vein on the infant's foot. Each time, the baby squawked and twisted in the hands of the young promoters, jerking the needle out again in a trickle of blood. The promoters, Elsa and Lucía, yawned and blinked in the glare of the generator-driven lightbulb. They were exhausted, having been awakened repeatedly this night as one after the other they took turns trying to spoon-feed *suero* (oral rehydration fluid) into the dangerously dehydrated baby. The feverish infant, far too small for her age of nine months, had swallowed less and less of the lifesaving fluid, letting it drool down her chin onto her mother's soiled apron. When the effort began to seem hopeless Lucía had reached for her flashlight and struck out into the darkness to awaken Dr. Sally.

In a few weeks of fieldwork in these repopulated villages, I'd already seen about a dozen severely dehydrated babies like this one brought to popular clinics, their mothers desperate, because they lacked money for transport and medicines, and feared their country's overcrowded and underequipped urban public hospitals. They feared all government institutions.

The history of relations between the state and rural peasants in El Salvador is an ugly one, and Esperanza had just lived through the worst outbreak of rural violence in 50 years. Military repression against peasant movements has been a fact of life in this small country for over a century. This pattern was exacerbated by U.S. anti-communist policies during the 1960s when USAID sponsored the training of Latin American police forces in suppressing internal "subversion."[15] The unrest leading up to the 1980 rebellion followed a period of massive land expropriation by foreign aid-supported modernization projects such as cattle ranching and mono-crop agriculture. The dissent was greeted by rising levels of military and paramilitary terror. Members of social democratic and leftist parties seeking social reforms were forced underground by the repression, and joined forces to form the FMLN—an umbrella organization for five armed factions representing distinct political groups. In the aftermath of Nicaragua's revolution in 1979, the newly elected Reagan administration "drew a line in the sand" by aggressively backing the Salvadoran military regime in its war against the FMLN.[16]

Over the course of the 12-year war, the United States pumped an astounding $7 billion in military and economic aid into the Salvadoran regime, making tiny El Salvador the third largest recipient of U.S. aid, after Israel and Egypt. The United States became heavily involved in orchestrating both El Salvador's hasty transition to civilian rule and the war effort itself. The consequences of the prolonged war for civilians have been brutal. An estimated 75,000 Salvadorans lost their lives during the war; tens of thousands were wounded or disabled.[17] An estimated 1.6 million civilians were directly affected, by being displaced from their homes or living in a conflicted area.[18] According to the 1993 report of the United Nations Truth Commission, the armed forces, police, and allied death squads were blamed for 85 percent of the political murders, torture, and other human rights abuses that characterized this struggle.[19]

Between 1981 and 1986, the United States supplied the Salvadoran air force with planes and training for an aerial bombing campaign directed against remote rural areas where guerrillas were active.[20] It was this scorched earth campaign that forced Esperanza and her neighbors to flee their homes. The bombing was a key strategy for separating FMLN combatants from their civilian supporters. In addition to bombs and rockets, the Salvadoran military used locally made napalm against crops and civilian settlements. As with other wars, such aerial bombardment resulted in high numbers of civilian casualties. Between 1983 and 1985, hundreds of thousands of rural Salvadorans like Esperanza fled to urban refuges or into exile. Most of the peasants who repopulated northeastern Chalatenango spent these years in Honduran refugee camps.

The mass repopulations of their home villages beginning in 1986 had been a risky undertaking. With the war still going on, this was a no-man's-land. Even after the cease-fire, the simplest needs—growing food, obtaining clean water, and health care—were life or death struggles in these hardscrabble hills.

During our vigil that August night in 1992, it took thirty minutes and three more attempts to establish an IV line in a tiny vein on top of Rosita's foot. I returned to my bedroll, leaving the exhausted mother with Elsa to monitor the baby. The next day I talked with Esperanza; her tale was a familiar one. Rosita, her first child, had fallen ill with fever, diarrhea, and vomiting two days earlier. Mother and baby had hitched a ride on the back of a pickup to the clinic, a forty-minute drive on a rocky mountain road. There were no government clinics in this area, and a trip to the urban public hospital would have taken twice as long; Esperanza did not even consider it. "They ask 10 colones (US $1.20) for a consult," she exclaimed when I asked. She then expressed doubt that a government doctor would have seen Rosita on a weekend night.[21]

Esperanza was aware that her daughter came close to dying. Only a few years before, when she and her neighbors returned to their old village, 16 children had died in a diarrhea epidemic caused by the contaminated water supply. Acting quickly, local health promoters made up dozens of homemade packets of *suero* and taught all the mothers how to use it, averting a larger death toll.

Diarrhea, along with acute respiratory infections and preventable childhood diseases like measles, are the leading causes of death for El Salvador's children. The under-five mortality rate has remained stubbornly high (approximately 87/1000 live births in 1990).[22] About half the under-five population is malnourished. These hungry children get sick and die at higher rates than well-fed children.

The refugees, who began returning to Chalatenango after 1986, turned to the Catholic church for help in training more health promoters and supplying basic medicines. The church formed an NGO, referred to in this account as Salud Católica, to assist the repatriated population in building what was to become an extraordinary alternative health system. By 1995, this system had expanded beyond the conflicted area, with over 300 village-based health promoters serving eighty rural villages and towns which previously lacked access to government health services.

While it is one of the larger and more comprehensive examples, the Chalatenango popular health system is only one of dozens of health projects initiated since 1980 by grassroots organizations and NGOs in rural El Salvador. A 1995 Ministry of Health survey found 171 health-related NGOs operating. If we consider only primary health-oriented programs in which lay workers receive significant training, are village-based, and can count on a referral system for resolving residents' more serious health problems, studies suggest that in 1996 such NGO-supported community health workers numbered more than 2,000 and served more than half a million Salvadorans living in underserved rural communities.[23]

This proliferation of NGO-initiated health work came about in part because U.S. military intervention drew the world's attention to the extraordinary need of this peasant population—devastated first by death squad terror, and then by a decade of low-intensity conflict. The need, however, predated the war. In the late 1970s rural Salvadorans suffered under the most extreme situation of disparity in land tenure in Latin America. Less than one percent of the country's landowners controlled 39 percent of the land, leaving 87 percent of peasant farmers together controlling less than a fifth of the country's arable acreage. A full 41 percent of the population was landless.[24] Worse, the rural two-thirds of the population had been abandoned by their government—four out of five rural peasants lacked potable water, and 60 percent had no access to health services. Meanwhile, the Ministry of Health was directing two-thirds of its budget to urban hospitals.[25]

Many of the villages where the popular health system evolved had been sites of liberation theology-inspired Christian Base Communities in the 1970s. Here, peasants inspired by liberation theology began organizing themselves, first in participatory Bible groups where they started to reflect on their political reality, and later in myriad initiatives for self-sustaining development, peasant unions, and—as military repression intensified—self-defense. The situation worsened during the civil war, when government services such as public health clinics pulled out of many rural areas due to intensified fighting between government troops and nascent rebel groups. When the United States began training and arming the Salvadoran army, tactics of low-intensity conflict were adopted, and up to a quarter of the country ended up cut off by roadblocks and designated "free fire" zones, where anyone who had not fled was considered "subversive." As in Vietnam, civilian villages became frequent targets of air attacks and army sweeps. Isolated in this fashion, northeast Chalatenango went without government health services or other regular food or medical aid *for more than 13 years.*

Some of the young, predominantly female health promoters of the Chalatenango popular system got their initial health training from foreign (mostly European) physicians who volunteered with the FMLN rebel army. The FMLN set up a network of physicians and lay *sanitarios* who responded to both guerrilla and civilian health needs in rural areas under FMLN control. Other promoters in today's popular system got their initial training in Honduran refugee camps where some peasants who fled Chalatenango's killing fields lived for up to seven years during the 1980s.

It is a tribute to the effectiveness of the popular health system that after the war, local volunteer health professionals affiliated with Salud Católica considered the highly organized repopulation villages in the former war zone *healthier* than their less organized neighbors in rural areas that remained under the control of the Salvadoran government. Preliminary epidemiological evidence supports this assessment: (1) UNICEF surveys in 1988-89 showed vaccination coverage of 80-85 percent in conflicted areas of Chalatenango where church-trained promoters and FMLN paramedics worked, compared with rates as low as 55 percent in several government-controlled regions; (2) a 1988 short epidemiological survey in a repopulation village revealed that most local mothers knew how to feed and rehydrate infants with diarrhea (responsible for 20 percent of El Salvador's child mortality), and made frequent use of the promoter-run health clinic; and (3) in a survey by this author of five years of clinic records (1987-1992) in the repopulated village of Loma Seca there were significant and consistent declines in the percentages of clinic visits for treatment of four preventable conditions: diarrhea (including parasitic infections), malaria, conjunctivitis, and skin infections.[26]

Since the 1992 cease-fire, Salud Católica has redirected its efforts to training and supporting health promoters in more needy, formerly *government*-controlled areas that have been devastated less by war's violence than by the structural violence of neocolonial economic realities.

POST-CEASE-FIRE HEALTH NEGOTIATIONS
IN CHALATENANGO

Hoping to integrate health services in the ex-warzone of the central north, the Pan-American Health Organization (PAHO) and the United Nations Development Program (UNDP) helped initiate and mediate a series of negotiations between the Salvadoran Ministry of Health and the Chalatenango popular health system following the cease-fire. In the talks, the popular health system was represented by a committee made up of both lay health promoters and health professionals, including the coordinator (a *promoter*) for health in the repopulated communities and representatives from Salud Católica and the Fundación para Salud Comunitaria (FUNSALCO), my pseudonym for an FMLN-affiliated health NGO that is active in the popular system.

The community-based design of the popular system and its attention to both preventive and curative care resembled PAHO's favored model of an "integrated" local health system, known by its Spanish acronym, SILOS. The Ministry of Health, long associated with a highly centralized, physician-centered approach to care, had recently agreed to adopt the SILOS model, which called for collaboration with NGOs on primary health care in rural areas—so the talks soon focused on how jointly to put this model into effect.

In early talks, the PAHO representative praised the effectiveness and community participation achieved by the popular system, calling it "a great opportunity for the Ministry." But it became clear over time that the ruling right-wing ARENA party was more interested in taking over services in the former guerrilla-controlled zones than it was in collaboration with the community-based lay workers who made up the heart of the popular system.

The ministry's political will to collaborate with the popular health system appeared weak from the beginning. Early negotiations were hostile encounters. The ministry often canceled meetings without notice, or sent representatives to the talks who had no decision-making power. At first, the ministry's strategy was to push for permission to send periodic one-day mobile medical aid caravans into the ex-war zone, a proposal that was rejected by spokespersons for the popular system as a propaganda effort. Despite this, the government sent several medical aid caravans for one-day visits to repopulation villages without coordinating with local leaders. The well-organized repopulation villages boycotted the caravans; the ministry health workers were allowed to set up their tents, but no patients showed up. The boycotts angered the ministry's regional director, who then refused to deliver vaccines for Salud Católica's next immunization drive. The vaccines were released only after several hundred promoters demonstrated outside the ministry's Chalatenango headquarters.

Ministry negotiators repeatedly refused to consider proposals from popular health NGOs for legal recognition and minimal salaries for lay promoters. Instead, the ministry spokespersons pushed for permission to station government physicians in popular clinics. Aware that Salvadoran government physicians assigned to rural areas traditionally only come to town irregularly to offer consults, the popular system negotiators countered with the proposal that only permanent physicians residing in the villages be allowed to serve in popular clinics. The talks stalled over this issue for several months, then in early 1993, the ministry adopted a new policy and diverted reconstruction funds into expanding rural physician services. Ministry negotiators offered to place their physicians in six repopulation communities where they would work together with the NGO-trained community health promoters.

At this point, promoters in one repopulation village drew up guidelines on how physicians and promoters should interact. They specified that promoters should serve as primary care gatekeepers, referring only more serious cases to physicians, and that physicians should act like technical consultants and teachers, rather than authority figures. The guidelines also charged physicians with duties of coordinating with local health committees and making visits to outlying hamlets to offer medical consultations. These were the ideals that Salud Católica and FUNSALCO had long promoted in the popular health system, but ministry negotiators balked at these rules, and conceded only to a vague clause in the agreement that physicians would observe both popular system and ministry "norms."

In light of their long-term needs for more physicians and medicines, the popular health negotiators agreed to the plan. Although this plan was reviewed and approved by assemblies of health promoters, many workers in the popular system were skeptical, and their fears of ministry co-optation have indeed been partially borne out. In the last two years of this collaborative effort, health promoters in many villages have been sidelined by the new ministry physicians, who, accustomed to more authoritarian practice styles, took control over consultations, administration, and clinic pharmacies, and refused to coordinate with promoters, community leaders, or the popular health NGOs. Highly skilled lay health workers—some of whom had five to nine years experience, routinely handling births and minor surgical procedures—became relegated to low-status tasks like cleaning, and strenuous chores the urban-born physicians disliked, such as hiking long distances to vaccinate. The physicians came to town to see patients only two to three days per week, and most refused to extend services to the remote hamlets, known as "*cantones*"—whereas serving the poorer peasants in *cantones* had been a central concern of the popular system. Several ministry health workers assigned to the repopulations told me that they felt pressure from their supervisors *not* to collaborate with the popular promoters.[27]

In 1992, when I began my study, many residents of repopulated villages feared the return of government ministries. But by late 1995, the patients had become accustomed to the ministry doctors. The more authoritarian ministry physicians offended some, and at least two villages sent letters of protest to the ministry over physician-related problems. Nevertheless, the presence of a ministry physician and medicines was seen by many villagers as a social gain from years of struggle; after all, the FMLN always maintained that the government had a responsibility for public health.[28] This led many popular health promoters to fear that in a showdown with the ministry they might not have their communities' support. Local citizens, by and large, while supportive of the promoters, did not wish to risk losing access to local physicians.

Reference to a map of government clinics, however, makes it clear that the ministry agreed to an unusually high concentration of personnel and facilities in formerly rebel-held areas, while neglecting other underserved areas. This led popular health system leaders to wonder if the new state services would be pulled back once the popular system was no longer a threat to ministry sovereignty.

PROBLEMS FACED BY POPULAR HEALTH SYSTEM NGOs IN NEGOTIATIONS WITH THE GOVERNMENT

Over the four years that I followed the Chalatenango health negotiations, efforts were made by the NGOs to boost participation by community-based promoters in the talks. Promoter representation on the negotiation committee approximately doubled between 1992 and 1993. The status of negotiations and proposed decisions were frequently reviewed in community-level meetings. Nevertheless, three ex-FMLN physicians affiliated with FUNSALCO, and two or three promoters elected to positions as coordinators in the popular health system, remained the most influential decision makers. Because of the Church's officially "neutral" political position, Salud Católica health volunteers attended the talks as (active) observers, rather than full participants. This was sometimes awkward since the Church had by far the greatest personnel and financial investment in the day-to-day operations of the popular health system.

Although health promoter projects existed in other rural areas, Chalatenango's popular health system was by far the largest and most comprehensive grassroots-based system in the country. This was due in part to the local rebel faction's philosophy of promoting civilian organizations and in part to the material and educational support of the local diocese through Salud Católica. Given Salud Católica's and FUNSALCO's history as advocates for peasant populations considered to be enemies of the state, it is not surprising that their negotiators distrusted the Salvadoran Ministry of Health. Ministry negotiators correspondingly distrusted popular system leaders. Unfortunately, the Chalatenango NGOs' negotiating position *vis-à-vis* the ministry was undermined by a lack of political coordination nationwide among health workers in formerly FMLN-controlled areas. Attempts by ex-FMLN health workers from the five rebel factions to achieve unity and present a common front to the government failed, in part due to continued rivalry between political factions, and in part because of regional differences in degrees of community development in health.

The Chalatenango popular health workers' fears that the government would attempt to co-opt their years of organizing around health at the community level were well-founded. In the province of Morazán, another FMLN faction with less experience in community organization had essentially allowed the Ministry of Health to take over the area's health clinics shortly after the cease-fire. The area's rural health promoters trained during the war were quickly displaced by government physicians. In fact, the hasty compromises being reached with the ministry in other regions of the country contributed to making the ex-FMLN physicians working in Chalatenango appear as stubborn and inflexible bargainers. As the peace process—endorsed by FMLN leaders—gained momentum in early 1993, the FUNSALCO representatives to the talks felt pressure from within their own organization to reach a compromise with the ministry on accepting physicians in the former war zone.

Many popular system supporters were unhappy with the agreement signed with the ministry, which failed to specify how physicians and promoters would interact; their fears proved justified as the collaboration proceeded. The choice of Salud Católica to remain officially neutral carried a cost as the final decision about the negotiated agreement with the ministry fell to FUNSALCO. Despite its dedication to participatory community health, FUNSALCO was a physician-dominated organization whose members had specialized in training promoters as paramedics during the war. In contrast, Salud Católica volunteers tended to be more heavily committed to grassroots, long-term community development than to professional-centered services. For example, the Church physician with the most years of experience in Chalatenango had redefined his role from traveling for rural consults to project coordination, in part to subvert the persistent physician mystique and encourage greater local reliance on community-based promoters.

Amazingly, even four years post-cease-fire, Salud Católica's (mostly progressive European) funders had stayed the course, supporting long-term community development work in these ex-refugee communities for close to a decade. This is the only sort of timescale that makes sense in comprehensive approaches to primary health care. In contrast, FUNSALCO's presence in Chalatenango shrank due to the financial collapse of an Italian foundation that had committed to support the U.N.-mediated peace process. Unfortunately, neither the Chalatenango NGOs nor the ministry were able to offer a long-term solution to promoter financial needs. The repopulation communities' regional NGO supported about 100 full-time promoters with minimal living stipends from 1992 to 1995, but the funding remained unstable. In late 1995, given the post-war return of the cash economy bringing high inflation for basic goods, many promoters feared they would have to cut back on their health work.

THE MINISTRY-RUN HEALTH PROMOTER PROGRAM: A STUDY IN DISEMPOWERMENT

Clearly, the Ministry of Health's apparent intransigence on community health policies in Chalatenango was in part a product of the strained political relations between the ARENA government and its former enemy the FMLN, whose leaders remained popular in this former rebel stronghold. To gain a wider perspective, in 1995 I examined the government's policies on rural community health work in less controversial parts of the country. I chose to focus on a new ministry health promoter program that had been designed and largely funded by USAID since 1989, with the goal of bringing primary health to remote villages that lacked access to services.

It is one of the ironies of U.S. intervention in El Salvador that USAID began embracing community-based health care at such a late date. During the 1980s, the USAID mission tailored its development programs to strengthen the Salvadoran government at any cost—including massive funding of the inefficient, urban hospital-centered Ministry of Health. During the early years of the war, budget cuts caused the productivity of public health services to decline drastically. Rural clinics gained a negative reputation with poor Salvadorans due to irregular and short physician consultations and shortages of medicines. Since the end of the war, the ministry, in theory, covers health needs for 85 percent of Salvadorans. Yet, a recent USAID household survey revealed that only 40 percent of citizens say they go to public health clinics when they get sick.[29]

Ministry physicians in El Salvador saw their real wages plummet during the 1980s, and most responded by cutting back their hours of service (a practice that has been condoned by the ministry). Likewise, the ministry budget for pharmaceuticals shrank, a situation that disproportionately affected rural facilities. The fiscal crisis was caused both by the war (as funds were shifted from social spending to defense), and by a gross diversion of health funds into staffing donor-built infrastructure.[30] USAID found itself pumping millions into the Ministry of Health's operating budget after 1985 to make up its pharmaceutical purchasing shortfall, a situation that deepened dependency on foreign aid—by the end of the war USAID was buying three-quarters of the country's medicines—and relieved pressure on ministry administrators to institute reforms.[31]

According to a recent USAID health sector review, between 1987 and 1992 significant declines occurred in many ministry preventive services, including percentages of pregnant women registered in prenatal care, well-child coverage, enrollment of malnourished mothers and children in feeding programs, and immunization coverage for DPT (diptheria, pertussis, tetanus), measles, and polio.[32]

Since the 1992 cease-fire, the USAID mission officers have been frantically backpedaling in an effort to distance themselves from the Frankenstein they helped create. In interviews, they emphasized USAID efforts to upgrade and reorganize the ministry's cost accounting, and optimistically predicted that the ministry would be able to take over 100 percent of drug purchases and the health promoter project as USAID funding was phased out in 1994-95—goals that outside evaluators have called unrealistic.[33]

Predictably, the physician-administrators at high levels in the ministry were less than committed to the USAID-inspired health promoter program. Through interviews and attending meetings of an unusual (USAID-initiated) in-house evaluation of the ministry's promoter program in 1995, I learned that many ministry physicians opposed the policy of training lay promoters. As a result, both the program of promoter training and promoter duties ended up being far more restricted than for promoters in NGO-operated community health initiatives. Ministry promoters' primary duties are well-child care and education of mothers, though they have neither the training nor supplies to solve the most common health problems that rural families encounter. A 1995 USAID proposal that promoters' duties be broadened to include emergency use of sulfa drugs or antibiotics for serious respiratory infections was denied at top levels of the ministry before the evaluation got underway.[34] Insiders in the ministry told me that government physicians resented ministry promoters' relatively high salaries (equal to more than a third of the salary of physicians in their social service year), and regarded them as inadequately trained for responding to patients' curative needs (a conclusion also reached by outside evaluators).[35]

In a community meeting I attended in a *barrio* outside San Salvador, mothers complained to local-level ministry administrators about this, asking why promoters were not trained to suture cuts and evaluate fevers in small children. The mothers were hushed up by a ministry physician who chided them: "You're asking for a miracle….If (the promoter) intervenes too much she can make sickness worse. She's not a doctor!" Community members also asked if their local promoter could help organize emergency transport of sick patients and mosquito eradication in response to an ongoing dengue epidemic, but they were told such organizing lies outside promoters' jurisdiction.

Promoters are likewise hampered in promoting the construction of latrines by the Salvadoran government's requirement that peasant families pay for them, a cash outlay few poor families can afford.

The promoter program received a lukewarm review in a recent USAID-funded evaluation by outside experts, and members of a multilateral donor mission, which traveled to rural areas to evaluate the ministry promoters, described the program to me as "almost dysfunctional," noting that personnel in rural health clinics could not even tell the mission how many promoters worked in the area, or where they were based. When villagers living in towns where ministry promoters were based were interviewed by the mission, many could not describe what promoters did, and when asked whom they consulted the last time they were ill, most reported seeking care from private or NGO clinics. Ministry promoters, though present locally, were rarely consulted.[36]

At the end of 1994, when USAID turned over to the ministry full responsibility for promoter salaries, the program entered a crisis because of lack of political support at high levels of the administration.[37] Despite USAID enthusiasm for the program, Health Minister Eduardo Interiano insisted that promoters lacked the skills needed to deliver health care properly. By November 1995, plans were under way to quietly lay off most promoter supervisors, while funds were shifted into hiring more physicians and raising physician salaries.[38]

THE WORLD BANK, THE MINISTRY, AND THE NGO NETWORK: BETWEEN REFORM AND "ANTI-REFORM"

The year 1995 was a time of ferment in other ways for the Ministry of Health. As noted previously, the ministry faced pressure to assume responsibility for programs that had been instigated and heavily subsidized by USAID. At the same time, the civil service bureaucracy—which had grown bloated and corrupt from the incessant flow of U.S. economic and military aid—was under pressure from major foreign donors to downsize and rationalize public-sector expenditures. In terms of health, this translated into a new system for fee collection from public patients, the privatization of some ancillary hospital services, contracting with NGOs for community health, and *departmentalización*—the local term for decentralizing decision-making in the ministry's notoriously rigid and politicized central office.

A physician who had directed a regional office of the ministry (and whom I had known since 1992) shocked me shortly after I arrived in June 1995 with his upbeat predictions of more autonomy at the regional level and future ministry collaboration with health NGOs. "This is quite a change of heart for the ministry," I remarked. "Yes," he replied with a wink, "two years ago it would have been a sin to talk about these things." But in the months to come it became clear that "talking" was about as far as things would go.

In 1994-95, the Salvadoran Ministry of Health hosted a stream of high-powered advisors from bilateral and multilateral donors, and dutifully played along, setting up a reform office and issuing white papers. The carrot in this relationship was a proposed joint loan package from the World Bank and the Inter-American Development Bank (IDB). The ministry presented the proposed reforms that would extend services to the 37 percent of the population estimated to lack any health coverage and create a safety net insurance system for the poor. Details on how this would be done remained unclear.

Health advocates for the poor were wary of the ministry's privatization talk, fearing it might provide a rationale for the government to further shirk responsibility for public health, an obligation that, despite constitutional guarantees of rights to basic services, had never been taken seriously in El Salvador.

On the other hand, many of those working in grassroots health initiatives were hopeful that the promises would mean more autonomy and efficiency in regional health offices, and ministry financing for NGOs providing basic public health services. Like the government, many NGOs have seen their foreign donations shrink in the post-war period, while the actual level of need in the countryside remained acute. (The cost of living for peasants has risen dramatically, even compared to the difficult pre-war years, while per capita income has fallen sharply. And many promised peace process reforms, such as transfers of land, have been delayed.)[39]

But things have not worked out as either the health NGOs or the neoliberals had hoped. In fact, one development expert who had been involved in advising the ministry laughed at my naïveté when I kept asking when the reform office would publish its long-delayed, much discussed reorganization scheme. Officials in the ministry's reform office had just told me they were expecting a $40 million loan from the World Bank and IDB that they planned to use to upgrade regional health centers to small hospitals. Expansion of hospital capacity is, from a public health standpoint, a questionable prioritization of funds, given El Salvador's large underserved rural population and recent history of expanding hospital infrastructure.[40] But putting that question aside, I wondered aloud, "Doesn't the Ministry have to put these reforms into effect to get that loan?" The development consultant replied, "The reform office is to please the banks, but they're never going to follow through. The banks just emphasize reforms to maintain their international image."

Around that time, the government budget for 1996 became public. Instead of the much heralded downsizing, the national budget actually grew by several thousand jobs, a fact that generated a flurry of derisive newspaper articles. The Ministry of Health also grew, as it should have, given President Armando Calderon Sol's pledge to dedicate more funds to El Salvador's neglected social services. This new influx of funds, however, did not translate into better health care for the 37 percent of predominantly rural citizens whom the ministry fails to reach. In fact, in Chalatenango, historically one of the most underfunded provinces, the regional health director claimed that his budget had been *cut*. He had been ordered to freeze administrative hiring, and was forced to lay off a dentist and several sanitation inspectors.

Likewise, *departmentalización*, the reform intended to give more autonomy to ministry administrators in regional offices, was proving to be, as one observer put it, "a map on paper." Representatives of the Chalatenango popular health system had been assured that after the reforms the regional health director would be empowered to hire popular health promoters to work in collaboration with ministry clinics. In a formal negotiation session, however, the director claimed that *departmentalización* meant little. "The reality is that, administratively, we're totally dependent on the minister's decisions. There is no money. Who knows when there will be?" he said, throwing up his hands before frustrated popular health system negotiators.

Hopes of collaboration with the ministry were especially high for a network of 35 NGOs involved in an innovative Maternal and Child Health (MCH) program that USAID had been funding since 1989. Known by its Spanish initials PROSAMI, the program had trained 1,500 community-based promoters and was serving an estimated 10 percent of the country's population in 1995. The primary health-care orientation of PROSAMI promoters is very similar to that of the Chalatenango popular promoters, except that PROSAMI promoters have more limited prescribing and curative duties (although they *do* handle antibiotics in cases of severe respiratory infection). While they are based in historically underserved *cantones*, most PROSAMI promoters do relatively little community organizing, although a number of administrators of PROSAMI NGOs believe this aspect of their work should be expanded. Preliminary evidence from an evaluation by international health consultants showed decreasing infant death rates from diarrhea and acute respiratory disease in areas served by PROSAMI promoters when compared with areas served only by the ministry.[41] The reviewers also gave the NGO network high marks for efficiency in providing a wide array of educational and preventive MCH interventions with a high degree of community acceptance.[42] Many observers credit the NGO network's success to the fact that the program circumvented the government's rigid health bureaucracy and patronage system.

With USAID funds for PROSAMI promoters slated to run out in early 1996, advocates for rural health waited impatiently for favorable news from the ministry about future collaboration. But Dr. Interiano, the minister, disagreed with development experts from USAID and PAHO on the viability of community-based health models, and challenged the findings of the PROSAMI evaluation (which, although carried out by outside consultants, had been paid for by USAID). He favored policies of hiring more physicians for regional hospitals and increasing physicians' salaries.[43] His stance frustrated advocates for community health. One consultant advising the ministry predicted to me that the hidden support costs for each new physician brought into the system would effectively double that professional's base salary—a sum adequate to support six promoters. "If the Ministry really had cost-benefit at heart," she said, "it would be much more cost-effective to hire promoters."

Dr. Interiano also made no secret of his distrust of NGOs, many of which have long been regarded by El Salvador's government as "leftist." "We are not enemies of the NGOs, but we are friends of order," the minister told the *Wall Street Journal's* Robert Greenberger.[44] As those who are familiar with El Salvador's bloody history know, the term "order" (*orden*) has long served as a right-wing code for authoritarian policies. An insider to the health reform negotiations told me, "The Minister thinks all NGOs are guerrillas, but most of the PROSAMI network NGOs' politics are more like those of Jimmy Carter."

A health planner close to these discussions in the ministry told me that high administrators were "afraid to deal with NGOs because their funders are leaving, and NGOs will begin to pressure the ministry for full support." There were, in his opinion, no serious plans to contract with NGOs; shaking his head, he predicted, "Most of this NGO work will disappear."

To their credit, World Bank and IDB officials took the advice of their health teams and balked on the planned loan once the minister's attitudes about reform became clear. An observer at the November 1995 meeting between the ministry and representatives of the World Bank and IDB later reflected on the meeting: "They wanted hospitals. [The Minister] said 'I want four hospitals in time for the next elections.' And he wanted them in areas where the ARENA party was weakest! Imagine telling that to a joint bank mission!…He really showed his colors. The Minister is not interested in reform."

The observer said the banks considered ministry collaboration with NGOs "part and parcel of our program," but that the ministry never seriously evaluated NGO health promoter activities or looked at how to coordinate with NGOs to maximize effectiveness of rural coverage.

Members of the joint bank mission, however, noted that higher level bank administrators were not pleased with denial of the loan, and planned to send another mission to El Salvador to "try and make something work." In the months that followed, the World Bank pulled out of the joint bank loan plan. After some minor reform concessions by the ministry, the IDB extended the Salvadoran Ministry of Health a loan for slightly less than half the original ($40 million) amount considered. The ministry continued to resist reforms that involved collaboration with community health NGOs.

In summary, the first year of serious attention to neoliberal health reform in post-war El Salvador brought a larger national budget; but in rural areas, regional health administrators complain that their share of the pie continues to shrink. Decentralization of ministry decision-making is turning out to be a paper reform with little reality in practice. Instead of collaborating with existing NGO networks based on promoters whose effectiveness and low cost had been demonstrated, the Ministry of Health rejected contracting with NGOs for political reasons and is downsizing its own community health promoter program while shifting funds to doctor salaries.

COMMUNITY HEALTH NGOs
AND THE NOT YET NEOLIBERAL STATE:
DEVELOPMENT AS POLITICAL STRUGGLE

An ongoing and fertile, if frustrating, debate among Salvadoran health activists over the last five years has centered on what kind of strategies small NGOs aligned with grassroots struggles should pursue during this period of transition. During the last half of the war in particular, hundreds of professionals and community-level health workers had registered their disgust with discredited public services by forming NGOs, through which they sought political support, human rights protections, and funds from foreign donors to promote more people-oriented health care. The goal of replacing the government through revolution failed, although the rebellion did succeed in dismantling the repressive apparatus that, in William Stanley's words, had functioned for so long as a "protection racket" for the country's tiny elite.[45]

Now, with the war over, it was clear that a second phase of struggle would be needed to achieve the social reforms so many had fought and died for. It was apparent to all the community health advocates with whom I spoke that in the case of a country like El Salvador, with a highly centralized and clientelist health ministry, some aspects of neoliberal reforms such as decentralization and contracting with NGOs could work in favor of their struggle.

Unfortunately, the Ministry of Health was also aware of these possibilities. Dr. Interiano's opposition to reforms recalls Weyland's study of failed health reform in Brazil.[46] Weyland concluded that clientelist politicians opposed health reforms in Brazil for fear that if decentralized services succeeded in improving the health of the poor, this would weaken peoples' dependence on patrons, and undermine dominant politicians' electoral position.

Peter Sollis sees this intransigence as a regional pattern:

> The dilemma for urban elites who monopolize political and economic power is that organized beneficiary participation creates conditions for greater grassroots democracy and broader local autonomy at the same time as it facilitates smaller, cheaper and more cost-effective government. A consensual solution to this contradiction is the problem of governance in Central America today.[47]

For Salud Católica and FUNSALCO, the NGOs aligned with the grassroots health movement in Chalatenango, the strategy chosen in the early post-war period was one of officially confronting the ministry at the local level. This played to the strength of this locally based health system, allowing popular system leaders to reinforce solidarity at the community level through continuing "a kind of war" with the government, while showing off their model of community health to international observers from the United Nations and PAHO. But then outside donors let FUNSALCO down, at the same time as Salud Católica and the FMLN shrank from political confrontation during the uneasy stages of the peace process. This facilitated the ministry's efforts to re-establish its physicians in the formerly conflicted areas, with the end result of significant co-optation since 1993.[48]

Influenced by the impact of the low-intensity war on the ex-refugee population they serve, neither Salud Católica nor FUNSALCO trusted USAID overtures, and both boycotted invitations to join the PROSAMI network when it was being formed, despite the attractions of its funding. Interestingly, as the negotiations with the ministry broke down once again in late 1995 (at the same time that the ministry failed to follow through on promises of *departmentalización*), Chalatenango organizers began brainstorming on how to take their struggle to the ministry's central headquarters. The popular promoters formed their own regional union and began organizing a national-level union. However, their plans were hampered by delays in obtaining legal recognition from the Salvadoran government and the difficulty of organizing promoters from a variety of health initiatives around the country.[49]

Some other FMLN-aligned health NGOs did join the USAID-funded PROSAMI network, as did health groups affiliated with more social democratic factions. These groups reaped the benefits of several years of financial support and training for their promoters, and in many cases they extended their outreach into new communities that lacked health coverage. The trade-off was PROSAMI's requirement that they adopt a more service-oriented approach, with less emphasis on community development or health problems other than in projects related to maternal and child health. (Many NGO promoters and their supervisors also found it a burden to manage the USAID paperwork.) But the primary downside for most, barring a breakthrough in the ministry's policy of keeping NGOs at arm's length, was the looming cutoff in funds. Unlike the Chalatenango popular system in which promoters began as volunteers and have never counted on more than nominal stipends, PROSAMI network NGO administrators feared that their more recently recruited promoters thought of their work as "a job" and would discontinue health work when the funds ran out.

To the credit of some particularly savvy leaders in the PROSAMI NGO network, the member organizations began meeting together in 1995 and were in the process of forming an NGO health coalition—a strategy that would both facilitate economies of scale (for instance, a joint pharmaceutical purchasing initiative) and strengthen the chances of obtaining funding abroad. As it became more and more evident that they had interests in common and were duplicating efforts in some areas, the leaders of the NGO health coalition also began meeting with their health counterparts in the Catholic church. Nevertheless, as I went back and forth between health programs in Chalatenango and San Salvador in late 1995, I was constantly struck by the failures in communication between programs—a tendency that grows out of overwork and understaffing, rivalry over constituencies and resources, and the persistent distrust of other organizations that civil conflict engenders. Overcoming this fragmentation will be essential to building coalitions responsive to grassroots concerns on a national level. In any event, it is becoming more and more clear that such a broad-based campaign for social reforms will be necessary for confronting both the ARENA regime and the international neoliberal program.

Another lesson from the Salvadoran experience is that the nongovernmental sector in any developing nation should achieve a level of unity and coordination prior to contracting with a government ministry to deliver basic services. Primary health care ideally needs to be carried out at the national level to have an impact on equitable planning and resource allocation. Decentralization can serve as a political maneuver allowing state leaders to abandon burdensome functions through privatization and/or funding cuts once the state is no longer directly held accountable by citizens; Chile's recent health reforms provide an illustration.[50] In Colombia, geographic decentralization of sanitation services was used to defuse political protest and reinforce the power of local authorities and private landowners.[51] These examples illustrate the dangers involved when individual community health NGOs contract with the state to provide services. A contractual relationship carries the additional risk of diverting a grassroots NGO from a social justice orientation toward an exclusive focus on direct service delivery.

Despite speculation by some theorists about the disappearance of the state as a power base (relative to increasingly unfettered transnational corporations), Sunkel argues that states will continue to be important strategic power blocs in their own right, as well as sources of legitimacy for capitalist projects.[52] In the absence of revolutions, most social movements will continue to channel their demands for a more democratic order through states, and NGOs will be increasingly critical actors in this struggle, precisely because of their potential to extend strategic alliances across borders. Without these alliances (involving volunteers, resources, and human rights scrutiny), dissident Salvadoran peasants would have found it much more difficult to build model health systems that challenged government models.

The viability of the state as an equitable service provider and the importance of incorporating health struggles into multisectoral struggle are well illustrated by Kerala, the Indian state in which health expenditures per capita are 35 times the national norm, yielding exemplary morbidity and mortality indices.[53] But no single health initiative or campaign can take credit for Kerala's enviable statistics, which reflect decades of land reform, relatively high minimum wages, high female literacy, a popular health education movement, and a declining birthrate. Ratcliffe argues that the causes of social development in cases like Kerala must be thought of as "synergistic"—in this case involving a 40-year tradition of social activism and mass organization that has forced even conservative state administrations to adopt strong social programs.[54] And, contrary to the neoliberal paradigm, this case of development progress is not a result of economic growth—Kerala remains a relatively poor state within India—but is related to more equitable distribution of existing resources.

It is an important caveat that Kerala is not a nation-state (or its reforms might long ago have been destroyed through counter-revolutionary war). Nevertheless, Kerala offers an impressive demonstration that equitable development need not be primarily resource-driven, but can proceed from struggle and the establishment of traditions of social democracy. The consequences are felt in surrounding states: Kerala now exports locally trained health workers to all parts of India. This is what Skalnick calls "evolutionary revolution"—continuous innovations in political culture and social order in a situation in which leaders are responsive to the changing expectations of the population.[55] Such advocacy models may prove more fruitful for community health NGOs in the Third World than the "replace the state" service delivery functions envisioned for NGOs by proponents of neoliberalism. As networks, health NGOs can also be effective at advocating for reforms in the policies of major donors.[56] Arguments for donor attention to such concerns is strengthened by studies like that of Michael Cernea who, in a review of 25 World Bank projects, found a strong correlation between project success and participation of grassroots organizations.[57]

NEOLIBERAL "REFORM" AS PERFORMANCE: THE END OF POST-WAR DEVELOPMENT AS WE KNOW IT?

Many of the reforms that USAID and the World Bank recommended to the Salvadoran Ministry of Health follow from the prescriptions for cost-effective health development outlined in the World Bank's 1993 World Development Report *Investing in Health*.[58] In a review of that document, Marc Epprecht, professor of modern world history, points out some of the contradictions posed when public health is bent into a neoliberal mold. He notes that the report pointedly ignores data showing that Africans' health has been damaged by SAP loans and free trade policies that favor Northern exports of high-priced pharmaceuticals, tobacco, and polluting industries. *Investing in Health* conveniently blames Africa's declining health indices on corrupt governments, without mentioning colonialism, unfavorable trade policies, arms exports, failed development projects that contributed to famine, or the wholesale destruction of Mozambique's infrastructure and health system by South African-backed guerrillas.[59]

I would add to Epprecht's critique the observation that cost-effectiveness criteria lead the World Bank to promote questionable public health priorities. For example, the World Bank now advises countries *not* to spend loan monies on rural water and sanitation infrastructure, the very interventions that community health NGOs in Chalatenango had found to be *most important* in preventing diarrhea—one of the largest killers of rural children.[60] Citing a history of ineffective water project loans, *Investing in Health* blames corrupt public ministries for siphoning off funds instead of providing responsive services. The report then goes on to acknowledge that "demand-driven" water initiatives seem to be more efficient than "supply-side" projects. But rather than use this evidence to argue for more development work at the grassroots level, the report's authors simply conclude that in rural areas "health benefits alone do not generally provide a rationale for public subsidy of water and sanitation." The report's own statistics fail to support this conclusion given that it finds diarrhea, primarily due to poor sanitation and water supplies, to be responsible for 10 percent of the disease burden in developing countries.[61]

In a conversation with a USAID staffer about El Salvador, I noticed that cost-benefit seemed to have replaced epidemiology as the criterion for evaluating health development: instead of basic health and sanitation services for the poor majority, the emphasis was on downsizing Ministry of Health staff and implementing user fees and financial tracking systems. When I asked about evidence showing that privatization would improve services in rural areas, the official curtly reminded me: "Look, first you have to accept the premise that this is all based on; that Ministry-delivered health nationwide is not the cheapest and best way to do it." Minutes later I asked if USAID projected future profitability for basic services. My notes show this reply: "The idea that health care is profitable anywhere is not true. After all, we subsidize health in the (United) States." No argument there, but I couldn't help wondering, if not the state, and not business, then to *whom* are impoverished rural peoples of the Third World supposed to look for basic health services? To charities? An answer for the nineteenth century, perhaps; but at the end of the millenium, it is a stretch to call this "development."

One might assess the Salvadoran Health Ministry's intransigence as a failure of neoliberal reform. However, the reforms only "failed" if the stated goals (decentralization and subcontracting rural health to NGOs to obtain more efficient services for the poor, for example) are taken to be the real aims of structural adjustment under the Bretton Woods institutions. Certainly, limited redistribution of wealth was a major goal of World Bank policies during the McNamara era, and there is no doubt in my mind that the middle-level staff of major donors who talked to me are sincere in their efforts to alleviate poverty; nevertheless, it is more and more apparent that solving the problem of poverty is not a goal of the enforcers of neoliberal programs (that is, the elites of the G-7 nations).

This is particularly apparent when one tallies the human consequences of structural adjustment policies (SAPs). A study reviewing a decade of neoliberal SAP policies in eight Latin American countries found that in the name of extracting interest payments for Northern banks—amounting to a sum several times the size of the Marshall Plan in constant dollars—social expenditures were drastically cut across the board, including reductions in health budgets over ten years that averaged 67 percent of what was spent in health in 1980.[62] This in an ex-colonial region which in the last 30 years has come to have the worst disparity in income between rich and poor anywhere in the world.[63] Epprecht cites similar erosion of essential services in Africa, including declining life expectancies since 1986 in 11 countries with SAPs.[64] In the end, neither Latin American nor African countries reaped higher national GDPs for all that reform; most countries with SAPs saw GDPs fall.

After all the talk of economic growth as the key to development, one is forced to ask, "Where is the development in this picture?" In practice, it seems, structural adjustment, in combination with the neoliberal forms of modernization and economic growth it facilitates, functions to undermine social welfare for the majority. Neoliberal policies thus pervert the very meaning of development when they harness the tools of intervention in a way that creates poverty, rather than alleviating it.

Given the major donors' "pressure to lend" and track records of approving loans even for governments with abysmal human rights and development records, we can understand why El Salvador's minister of health was not rushing to implement reforms that would damage his own power base.[65] The rhetoric of reform serves ARENA very well in giving the new civilian government a badly needed veneer of social responsibility, both for domestic consumption (in El Salvador's new era of electoral politics) and in reassuring foreign donors and investors, many of whom had previously been put off by ARENA's history as the party linked to death squads. But like high-level administrators in many formerly colonized states, Dr. Interiano had his own patronage hierarchies to protect. He saw no reason to jeopardize them by contracting for community health with the "wrong kind of NGOs." Boosting ministry physicians' salaries turned out to be a more pleasing and politically feasible option.

Dr. Interiano also was no doubt reassured by USAID's decade-long history of pumping funds into his government's social services as the pacification arm of U.S. low-intensity war strategy.[66] Such a history makes it sound a bit disingenuous when the USAID and World Bank officials I spoke with blame the failures of reform on "a bad egg" of a minister, instead of on a history of policies that undercut democratic forces seeking to oust "bad eggs" from power.

Hence, the development establishment's turn to NGOs notwithstanding, this tale of health "anti-reform" adds to a long stream of evidence that decision-making by large donor institutions pursuing neoliberal goals is often less concerned with the outcomes of proposed reforms, or even their cost-effectiveness, than with the political stability of Third World governments allied with major donor nations.

Health NGOs concerned with social justice in developing nations cannot afford to ignore these geopolitical realities in their planning. The new turn to NGOs may well open up opportunities for channeling funds and expertise into grassroots projects. But the benefits will be short-lived if, in the rush for funds, NGO health planners sacrifice community development goals and become mired in the role of charitable "service provider." Just as true social development is always based on participation, so in the long run the leverage an NGO is able to wield in the political arena will always rest on the organization and political participation of its constituents.

ACKNOWLEDGMENTS

This research was supported in part by a dissertation fieldwork grant from the Inter-American Foundation, and two travel grants from the Tinker and Mellon Foundations, administered through the Duke University of North Carolina Program in Latin American Studies. The study would have been impossible without the rich collaboration I enjoyed with many dedicated community health development workers in El Salvador—people who are truly "fighting the good fight" and rarely receive the resources or credit they deserve. Special thanks are also due to colleagues who read this manuscript and offered helpful feedback and editorial assistance during its preparation, including my dissertation advisor Catherine Lutz, Alec Irwin, Aaron Shakow, Evan Lyon, John Gershman, and Rebecca Wolfe. I am especially grateful to Joyce Millen and Jim Kim for their thoughtful and careful editing. They were always a joy to work with. The author takes responsibility for any errors that have escaped their scrutiny.

CHAPTER FIFTEEN

Conclusion: Pessimism of the Intellect, Optimism of the Will[1]

Joyce V. Millen, Alec Irwin, and Jim Yong Kim

We began this book by describing the living situation of the little girl on the volume's cover. For this girl, hunger and illness are a daily norm, scraps of spoiled food a precious find, and learning to read a luxury she can only dream of. Her harsh world may seem remote from our own daily experience. Yet her world is also ours. This incongruity spurred the writing of *Dying for Growth* and moved us to explore the elusive but crucial connections between this young girl's existence and the policies and strategies of powerful international financial and political institutions.

The preceding chapters include stories of individuals whose lives illustrate the linkages among health, illness, and current political and economic forces. Though they are living—*or dying*—on different continents and are influenced by different cultures and traditions, Bintu in rural Senegal, Benedicta in a Peruvian shantytown, and April on the streets of Boston share certain commonalities. They struggle on the edge of survival, where just one poor harvest or an additional charge at a health center can have disastrous consequences. Along with a billion people worldwide, they lack adequate food and health services. All three women will likely die prematurely from an easily preventable or treatable disease.

How and why have such different personal histories led to grimly similar predicaments? The factors most routinely cited to account for the poor's vulnerability to disease—individual behavior, cultural issues, and weakness of national leadership—reveal only part of the picture. The common root of Bintu's, Benedicta's, and April's vulnerability is an entrenched poverty that is as much a product of policy measures originating from global institutions as it is of local or individual circumstances.

This book has examined the complex interactions among local, national, and global policies and institutions, and it has analyzed the effects of these interactions on poor people's health. We have scrutinized specific organizations, development approaches, and economic policy measures, arguing that many fail to relieve—and in some cases actually exacerbate—the conditions of social, physical, and economic adversity under which poor people worldwide struggle to survive. We have looked closely at strategies such as export-led growth, privatization, and trade liberalization, linking the intended and unintended effects of these policies to declining health outcomes among vulnerable populations.

The stated aim of many of these policies is economic growth. Powerful economic actors have long argued that the net effect of enhanced growth is significantly improved quality of life for all. Contesting this claim, we have presented evidence of enduring ties between the precarious state of the world's poor and the pursuit and realization of growth in three intertwined but distinguishable forms. Through a series of specific cases, we have demonstrated how growth—the market-led economic growth sought by governments, the growth in profits celebrated by businesses, and the growth in power and influence of transnational financial and corporate interests—often comes at the expense of the disenfranchised and vulnerable, including urban slum dwellers, rural subsistence farmers, the unemployed, low-wage and informal sector workers, poor women and children, the weak and ailing, and the elderly. As the imperatives of growth at any cost increasingly determine economic and social policy and the behavior of global corporations, more people join the ranks of the poor and greater numbers suffer and die.

To formulate concise conclusions at the end of a complex, wide-ranging book is difficult. A series of key themes do, however, emerge from the studies included in this volume. These points summarize some of the principal lessons of *Dying for Growth* and may, we hope, help orient further inquiry and committed action:

- Despite unprecedented world wealth, rapid technological innovation, and significant gains in international health during the last half century, hundreds of millions still suffer and die unnecessarily from hunger and preventable diseases.

- The causes of this suffering and premature mortality are integrally tied to the character of the current global economy, shaped by the pervasive influence of transnational financial and corporate interests.

- Economic growth is often promoted as a means to alleviate poverty; yet even when growth does materialize, its benefits are unevenly distributed and rarely accrue to the poor.

- The neoliberal economic policies promoted throughout the world during the 1980s and 1990s by international financial institutions and their main donors have intensified inequalities among and within countries.

- Austerity programs implemented in poor countries and justified on expectations that they would reduce foreign debt have not only failed to reduce debt in many countries, they have also worsened living conditions and health outcomes among the poor.

- As transnational corporations (TNCs) grow, expand, and consolidate their enormous resources, they wield ever greater influence in the institutions that shape national economies, international relations, and world trade. As TNC operations take on an increasingly supranational character, it becomes virtually impossible to control TNC activities, however damaging their effects on people and the environment.

- When trade and investment are liberalized between countries of greatly unequal size and wealth, small farmers, urban workers, and poor communities in the weaker country often suffer grave consequences.

- Economic privatization, and in particular the privatization of health care, will likely amplify existing social inequities in poor countries, rendering the poorest populations even more vulnerable.

- Even in industrialized countries with elaborate health infrastructures, increases in life expectancy and other public health advances can be reversed when social services are sacrificed as part of narrowly conceived, hastily implemented economic measures to expand markets and promote growth.

- Certain high-profile public health campaigns, such as the War on Drugs, have not only failed to accomplish their stated mission, they have diverted public attention from underlying social problems that exacerbate the public health threat (for example drug addiction) they claim to remedy.

- Public health and well-being are not determined solely by the quantity of resources available to a country's government, or the size of its health budget. With the political determination to put health and equity before private and corporate interests, even poor countries with limited resources can achieve high health standards and excellent health outcomes.[2]

- History repeats itself. While the names may change, the fundamental relations between rich and poor remain the same. Yesteryear's colonialism laid the foundation of today's neoliberalism, doubtless soon to be replaced with a new "ism" for the new millennium. Today's preferred euphemisms and slogans—for example, "free markets," "sustainable development," "poverty alleviation"—will also be replaced as the beneficiaries of the current system sense threats to their power and a corresponding need for at least superficial alterations of current practice. Unless the fundamental relations change, however, the poor will probably continue to suffer a disproportionate amount of violence and disease.

Given the impact of these trends on our collective future and the number of human lives affected by them, one would expect the themes listed here to figure prominently in academic discussion and in the public health and development literature. Usually, however, this has not been the case. Many of the points discussed here are acknowledged in debates about the imperatives of growth and globalization. And certainly among the people most adversely affected by them, these themes often figure prominently in day-to-day discussions. Yet the overall attention paid them has been partial and inconsistent. Isolated aspects or particular local manifestations of these issues are addressed, but often with little recognition of the patterns that connect events and trends in different parts of the world.

Part of the explanation for this failure lies in the complexity and scope of the problems themselves. Part lies in the inertia and resistance of economic powerholders, including commercially owned media. Yet those of us who work within academic institutions and nongovernmental organizations (NGOs) must also consider ways in which our own institutional positioning and habits of thought may make it more difficult for us to appreciate both the gravity and the common roots of much suffering in the world. What are some of the institutional and intellectual obstacles that have hindered our own recognition—as scholars, students, health providers, or people working within NGOs—of the scope and sources of this global crisis? In responding to this question, we point to ways we can improve our collective analysis and render our practice more useful. Academic institutions and NGOs have vital roles to play in addressing the multiple forms of inequality and suffering to which this book draws attention. But to contribute effectively, those of us working in these settings must recognize ways our thinking and practice can become distorted. And we must acknowledge the unmet challenges.

IN THE ACADEMY

The highly specialized nature of contemporary scholarship renders our efforts to engage these issues more difficult. As teachers dispensing training in one or another specific discipline—and as students *receiving* this training—we tend to lose sight of global patterns whose origins and effects defy neatly drawn, disciplinary boundaries. To grasp the social consequences of trade agreements between countries, for example, we need to understand not only economics, but also the relevant issues in geography, history, labor relations, agricultural production, health systems, and environmental policies. If we limit our questioning to a single narrowly defined topic, the "big picture" easily escapes us.

Furthermore, in recent decades, postmodern fashions in the academy have to some degree reinforced the tendency toward moral paralysis and indifference. When understood as a call to radical relativism, postmodern thought has fostered moral resignation. Brute facts—such as death, disease, and iniquitous health outcomes—tend to be effaced within certain postmodern discourses, or alternately relativized as merely one among many competing descriptions of the world, none of which is inherently more accurate than any other, and from which no binding moral imperatives can be derived. As an anthropologist who has worked in poor communities on four continents puts it: "Interpretive and post-modern approaches to the social sciences [call] into question the epistemological status of the 'objects' and the 'realities'" scholars study. The body, illness, disease, and even death become mere "constructed notions that are necessarily partial, uncertain." We lose touch with the principle that, while reality is indeed "complex, contradictory, and elusive," certain forms of human experience, above all suffering and death, "remain incontestably factual."[3]

In another dimension of postmodern discourse, well-intentioned and important efforts to emphasize particularity and to honor the unique character of specific cultures, traditions, and identities can be pushed to the point where all sense of solidarity and shared meaning is lost: "We are asked to believe that human beings are now so speciated by gender and race—though we are silent about class—that there can be no universal knowledge, politics or morality." Significantly, it is usually not among the victims of oppression and prejudice themselves that such ideas have gained dominance. "It is not [oppressed people] who have abandoned idealism, universalism, truth and justice. It is those who already enjoy these things who have denounced them on behalf of the others."[4]

Another urgent challenge faces today's scholars and researchers. In order to move global economic and political practice in the direction of justice, we need reliable data about the real effects of past and current policies on human communities in general and on the poor in particular. Yet, such data are still sketchy, approximate, difficult to obtain, or, in certain cases, simply nonexistent. This situation inevitably discourages challenges to existing practices and limits our ability to plan future policies responsibly. The dearth of reliable data on vital questions relating to economic policy and health represents both one of the greatest obstacles faced by scholars, policymakers, and activists, and also one of the greatest opportunities for researchers and students to make a meaningful contribution.

Fundamental research still needs to be undertaken on relations between poverty and health in general and, more specifically, on the links between particular policy measures and health outcomes among vulnerable populations. *Dying for Growth* attempts to raise these questions, but in the process of writing the book we were forced again and again to confront the yawning gaps in basic research on such questions as structural adjustment and health; the health consequences of TNC activities; and the effects on health of particular instances of privatization and trade deregulation. As teachers, we need to encourage our students to fill these gaps. As students, we should demand of our mentors the same commitment. All in the academic environment recognize the daunting complexity of designing, pursuing, and interpreting such research programs: the presence of confounding variables, difficulties in reliably determining causal connections, and numerous other factors. Yet we have a moral duty not to forsake urgently needed research simply because it is difficult and because the results may be challenged.

IN THE NGO COMMUNITY[5]

While scholars may be too distant and detached, those of us who work "on the ground" with impoverished communities in crisis often have the opposite problem. We have noted in our own work that it is easy for us to lose perspective through our very closeness to local situations. Our intense loyalties to the people we seek to serve and to the organizations within which we work can prompt us to dismiss wider structural questions and global or theoretical perspectives as irrelevant—or we may simply find no time left to consider them. The members of the *Dying for Growth* team who work within NGOs are acutely conscious of this difficulty.

The personnel of local NGOs must often struggle to reconcile competing commitments. We seek to improve the lives of those with whom we work, yet we must also observe an imperative of self-preservation, working to assure the stability of our organizations and our projects. In our efforts to justify our continued existence to potential funders, we sometimes define health problems in narrow, apolitical terms and overstate our capacity to resolve health crises through local interventions. In so doing, we perpetuate the tendency to view poor communities as intrinsically weak, while also causing health problems in these communities to appear as purely local phenomena without historical context.

Like academics, well-intentioned NGOs often "miss the revolution"—fail to appreciate broad trends operating nationally and transnationally—by remaining too stubbornly focused on the single local issue or problem a given organization was created to address.[6] As difficult as it may be, those of us working for NGOs need to expand our vision, combining intensive commitment to local communities and issues with critical awareness and analysis of national and global factors. As this principle is easier to state than to put into practice, the need for persistent self-critique, as well as for constructive questioning of one another, becomes clear.

The relationship between NGO activities and state withdrawal from commitments in the social and health sectors must be considered carefully. Increasingly, NGOs in poor countries have been co-opted into a system that condones governments' abandonment of those who cannot provide for themselves. Nongovernmental organizations should not assist governments in this abdication of responsibility. In general, we should do our best to draw government (back) into health work.[7] Indeed, shouldn't our ultimate goal be to render the need for assistance like our own unnecessary? Yet a cynical cost-cutting strategy that transfers responsibility for public welfare to "charity" simply perpetuates foreign assistance and facilitates the transfer of wealth away from the poor. We must find ways of refusing this disturbing bargain without abandoning the populations we serve.

The NGO-government link is fraught with compromise, but governments are not our only partners. To the fullest extent possible, we should work mutually with local communities to set agendas for action. People living in poverty usually have a clear understanding of the roots of their difficulties and how best to remedy them. And we have found they often have profound lessons to teach us. Attention to global forces ought not lead us to discount the voices and insights of the poor nor the challenges faced by local communities. On the contrary, we have found that the analyses of the poor are often very much attuned to global forces.

We can begin to grasp, then, some of the institutional traits, ideological patterns, and intellectual habits that have hampered our own full understanding of the themes this book seeks to address. And although we challenge ourselves first to remove these blinders, we also believe that the recommendations outlined previously have relevance beyond the circles of academics and NGO workers. Policy analysts, development workers, financial officers, corporate representatives, and government officials face similar challenges. Even more than our own, their work affects—and can transform—vulnerable communities.

But what is the way forward? Faced with the complex and often tragic realities discussed in *Dying for Growth*, how can we resist the temptation to resignation, numbness, and retreat? Certainly not by striking poses of moral superiority. This book contains many critical observations regarding policies initiated or approved by institutions like the World Bank and the International Monetary Fund (IMF). Yet we do not question the moral integrity of the individuals who work within these institutions. Most men and women working for the World Bank, the IMF, and international development organizations are committed to reducing human suffering and enabling the majority of people to lead more satisfying lives. However, in many cases a sharp disjunction can be observed between these humane commitments and the actual effects of the policies and practices of these organizations. Our doubts concern not personal motives, but collective decisions and institutional policies. Too often, we believe, such policies are based on faulty premises and bring with them harsh social consequences, the brunt of which must be borne by the poor. These destructive effects may take the framers of the programs by surprise. Yet often the consequences could have been foreseen.

An effective way to narrow this gap between theory and practical consequences would be to assess the real value of economic policies by their effects on the health of poor people. In the case of the neoliberal economic models that have dominated the last two decades, using the health of the poor as our evaluative criterion forces us to conclude that these models have failed. The continued dominance of comparable approaches in the years ahead would represent a grave risk (indeed a certain disaster) for large numbers of vulnerable people around the world. Unfortunately, the same prediction will also likely hold for "new," post-neoliberal policy orientations now beginning to emerge. In the absence of serious debate over a more equitable distribution of global resources, such new frameworks will surely continue to neglect the effects of policy choices on poor people's lives.

Yet, as these new frameworks are being formulated, there is a window of opportunity for more substantive transformations. Building on today's widespread perception that the architecture of the global economy must change, we offer the following proposal. We urge that, in the future, the health of poor people become a central, systematic, and binding criterion according to which new policies and strategies are designed; new political and economic relations between institutions and countries are forged; and new trade and investment regimes are established.

What we are recommending is something akin to the environmental impact assessments carried out, for example, before the start of work on an industrial construction project. To consider in advance the potential effects a policy, program, or business venture may have on vulnerable populations is hardly unprecedented. In fact, the World Bank occasionally conducts social impact assessments largely for this purpose. Yet such exercises are rarely undertaken systematically, conducted by independent analysts, or calculated with the same painstaking precision that routinely goes into reckoning projected economic gains. Most important, the voices of the people directly affected by the proposed measures generally receive only a cursory hearing, or none at all.

Financial institutions, development agencies (public and private), and companies should be required to conduct independent poverty impact statements for all their major financial, political, and business endeavors in poor communities and countries. Had such statements involving the substantive participation of poor communities themselves been a decisive component of World Bank and IMF policy during the course of the last two decades, structural adjustment policies promoted as "short-term harm for long-term gain" would have taken very different forms in many poor countries. Policies such as rapid currency devaluations, certain privatization schemes, labor market deregulation, and social sector spending cuts would have been rejected or modified. As a result, human lives would have been spared. For, as we have demonstrated throughout *Dying for Growth*, short-term harm for people living on the edge of survival involves more than petty inconvenience; it often means impaired fetal development, malnutrition, protracted illness, and premature death.

Some will argue that such impact projections would be too complicated to be realized in practice. Certainly, these studies will never attain flawless accuracy. Yet, by working in close collaboration with poor communities, and by using historical data, tools of social and health forecasting, and the ingenuity of researchers from multiple fields, we believe it would be possible, in most instances, to model with reasonable accuracy the health costs and benefits likely to be associated with specific policy measures and business ventures.

Projecting the health patterns of poor communities is more complicated than measuring the environmental and health effects of pollutants. Yet the two operations exhibit important conceptual parallels. And it is worth noting that before environmental impact statements became institutionalized, critics doubted their feasibility as well. We can learn from the example of scholars and activists who promoted environmental impact studies in an era when most experts judged the widespread use of such instruments to be both technically and financially impracticable.

Of course, to assess the health consequences of economic policies requires reliable data. This principle applies to the poverty impact projections we hope to see instituted by international development organizations, corporations, governments, and NGOs. It also applies to our own work in *Dying for Growth*: How does a rural community fare when its government, pressured to meet foreign debt payments, cuts social sector spending and food subsidies? Do its members modify their use of medical services after the government initiates cost-shifting mechanisms, such as user fees in local clinics? Do patterns of morbidity and mortality change? Can causal connections be demonstrated compellingly? In the present state of our knowledge, the answers to such questions in many cases must remain tentative. While working with the best data currently available, we are nonetheless aware that in many parts of this volume, the data presented do not permit absolutely unambiguous conclusions. However, this does not mean that no reasonable conclusions can be drawn from the available information, nor that we should refrain from discussing the consequences of economic policies for poor people's health until those consequences have been documented with a rigor that all analysts will deem unassailable. In drawing inferences from fragmentary data, we take professional risks. Yet the risks for poor people are vastly greater if we fail to draw these inferences and to engage the public debate they demand.

As we have questioned the interpretations put forward, for example, by the analysts of prominent international institutions, so we can expect to be questioned and criticized in our turn. This is as it should be. Our intention in *Dying for Growth* has not been to present ironclad and irrefutable claims, but to advance the discussion on issues that concern the health of millions of people around the world. Focusing attention on links between economic and political policies and the health of the poor, we strive to interpret the available data accurately and to formulate sound, explanatory hypotheses. Yet, a key part of the message of *Dying for Growth* is a call for expanded and intensified research into the nature of the connections we have discerned and attempted to delineate. If certain aspects of our claims about the effects of specific policies on poor communities can be proven inaccurate on the basis of carefully conducted new research, we will consider this gain in knowledge a victory; the point is not for us to be right. The point is that the health of the poor should become a central evaluative criterion for framers of economic policy, and that the research community should commit itself to investigations that will clarify with increased precision how health outcomes in poor communities are influenced by such factors as World Bank policy orientations, health care and social service privatization, and TNC self-rule in the developing world.

Far from constituting grounds for retreat and resignation, the facts presented in *Dying for Growth* should be a stimulus for committed action. As Noam Chomsky has insisted, the immense power of TNCs and the opacity of international financial and political dealings are no reason for ordinary people to surrender to economic fatalism. Today, Chomsky notes, we see widespread "efforts to make people feel helpless, as if there is some kind of mysterious economic law that forces things to happen in a particular way, like the law of gravitation." Yet belief in such an immutable law is simply "nonsense." "These are all human institutions, they are subject to human will, and they can be eliminated like other tyrannical institutions have been."[8]

Therefore, having provided throughout *Dying for Growth* ample reason for a pessimism of the intellect, we conclude the volume by offering reason to cultivate an optimism of the will. We believe that the practice of "pragmatic solidarity" indicates a way to move beyond fatalism and inertia. Through the work of solidarity with and for the poor—acknowledging primary accountability to poor communities and their needs—effective action can be undertaken to resist the multiple forces that threaten the health and survival of poor people today. The final chapter of this volume offers a list of organizations that are carrying on this work in a variety of different settings around the world. These groups' struggles are difficult, and their successes are often modest. Yet, any victory over indifference and unjust suffering is a victory worth celebrating.

CHAPTER SIXTEEN

Pragmatic Solidarity

Heena Patel, Joyce V. Millen, and Evan Lyon

Throughout the preparation of *Dying for Growth*, the book's contributors relied upon the generous volunteerism of interns and students who read—and then reread—sections of the volume to offer feedback, both on details and broader issues. The questions most often asked by our student editors were practical: "So if this is what's happening, what is being done about it?" As they read chapters showing how current political and economic policies negatively affect the health of poor people throughout the world, students became hungry for solutions. They shared a common concern, asking us in different ways: "In the face of such complex and daunting problems, what can we do?" Because we suspect, or at least hope, this pragmatic line of questioning will also resonate with this volume's wider audience, we have included this final chapter.

The following pages introduce organizations that are explicitly committed to working in solidarity with the poor for the cause of social justice. Some of these groups specifically target health issues. Others focus primarily on topics such as economic justice or hunger. The decision to include a range of social justice organizations with different areas of concern reflects our conviction that people's health outcomes are decisively conditioned by economic and social factors. Work toward narrowing the economic gap between rich and poor is also "health" work; it is a path to saving lives.

The 62 social justice organizations we list are diverse in membership, method, and scope of service. Yet they share the common goal not only of addressing the effects of poverty, but of seeking to understand and respond to poverty's deeper causes. In determining which groups to include, we have focused on those whose work engages the topics and regions discussed in *Dying for Growth*. The choice of organizations also reflects the backgrounds and experiences of contributors to this volume. Initially, contributors were asked to identify groups pursuing social justice work in their respective areas of experience. This list was expanded through "brainstorming" sessions and systematic research. In the end, we received and reviewed information from more than 300 organizations. We identified those groups whose activities corresponded most closely to the problems addressed in *Dying for Growth*, then drafted capsule profiles of these groups, which were forwarded to most of the organizations for approval. The result is a list we hope reflects the impressive number and diversity of groups around the world struggling to understand and redress the injustices that afflict the lives of the poor.

Of course, the network of organizations working alongside the poor extends far beyond those we have been able to highlight here. Many groups are allied with other like-minded organizations. Thus, when you find one such group, you may find others. For example, you can obtain a list of member organizations from the Fifty Years is Enough Campaign, or a list of Oxfam America's grassroots partnerships. The World Wide Web is a formidable resource for information about organizations from every corner of the globe. Most group websites provide links to other organizations. Essential Information and the Institute for Global Communications have websites that list organizations and provide links to their home pages. Finally, many nongovernmental organizations publish useful guides for those seeking ways to get involved in social justice work. For example, Food First publishes *Alternatives to the Peace Corps*, which should be available at most libraries.

We hope the following list will prove to be a useful resource, helping bridge the gap between knowledge about poor people's suffering and action to address that suffering through pragmatic solidarity.

A key for each organization's general activities is included for quick reference, as follows:

Publishes/Produces:		Provides/Offers:	
A	articles	**CO**	community outreach services
AU	audio	**FD**	forums for discussion (e.g., symposia, conferences)
B	books		
E	essays	**HC**	health-care services
EP	educational packets	**L**	lobbying (government, corporate)
JM	journal, magazine	**MM**	mass media (e.g., radio shows, television programs)
NL	newsletters		
R	reports	**O**	overall organization/management (e.g., work done by an umbrella organization on behalf of other groups)
V	videos		
		S	speakers
		ST	skills training (e.g., health, languages, economic literacy)
		T	tours (travel for education or to provide assistance)
		$D	loans/grants for grassroots development projects
		$R	research grants

American Friends Service Committee (AFSC)

1501 Cherry Street
Philadelphia, PA 19102
(215) 241-7000
FAX: (215) 241-7275
afscinfo@afsc.org
www.afsc.org

Publishes: NL
Provides: CO

Since 1917, the American Friends Service Committee has worked to relieve the suffering caused by war and poverty, to foster peace and reconciliation, and to promote social and economic justice. A Quaker organization, AFSC operates programs in 22 countries and 43 locations in the United States, often in cooperation with other religious and grassroots community organizations. In the United States, the Committee's work includes advocating for the rights of documented and undocumented immigrants, organizing to abolish the death penalty, and countering the growth of military influence in public high schools. Internationally, many AFSC programs focus on developing self-sustaining agricultural and economic systems. For example, AFSC coordinates an irrigation project in Vietnam, a women's economic cooperative in Mozambique, and a community marketing project in Honduras. The Committee also organizes against the proliferation of nuclear weapons, fights for the rights of indigenous people, and seeks nonviolent solutions to conflicts around the world.

The Aristide Foundation for Democracy

B.P. 806
Port-au-Prince
Haiti

P.O. Box 490271
Miami, FL 33149

Publishes: —
Provides: CO, FD, MM, ST, $D

Founded by former Haitian President Jean-Bertrand Aristide, the Aristide Foundation works to sustain democracy and promote the active political participation of all Haitians. In its efforts to break down class and social barriers to employment, health care, education, peace, and justice, the Foundation sponsors symposia, debates, conferences, and training workshops that serve as a forum for Haiti's poor majority to voice their views on issues of national importance. Specific topics of debate and discussion have included disarmament, the Haitian police force, and the implications of structural adjustment programs. The Foundation also supports two radio programs: one features ordinary Haitians discussing issues affecting their daily lives; the other, run entirely by street children, focuses specifically on issues facing the next generation of Haitians. The Foundation also sponsors Creole literacy projects to enable Haiti's poor majority, 85 percent of whom cannot read or write, to participate in the democratic process. It also provides loans, skills training, and technical assistance to community-based food and income-producing projects. The fundamental goal of the Aristide Foundation is to help Haitians meet their pressing material needs while addressing the root causes of poverty.

Baby Milk Action

23 St. Andrew's Street
Cambridge CB2 3AX
UK
44-01-223-464420
FAX: 44-01-223-464417
babymilkacti@gn.apc.org
www.gn.apc.org/babymilk

Publishes: A, EP, NL, R, V
Provides: FD, L, MM, S, ST

Baby Milk Action works to promote breastfeeding and to raise awareness of the dangers of artificial feeding. Data have shown that breastfed babies have a lower risk for morbidity and mortality than bottlefed babies. Baby Milk Action's campaigns for accurate labeling and against irresponsible marketing of breast milk substitutes are aimed at enabling mothers and health workers to make well-informed decisions regarding infant feeding while being free from commercial pressures. In keeping with its goal to ensure the highest level of health and well-being for the world's women and their children, Baby Milk Action also fights to improve maternity rights and for strong legislation in line with the World Health Assembly's *International Code of Marketing of Breastmilk Substitutes.*

Bhopal Action Resource Center (BARC)/
International Coalition for Justice in Bhopal (ICJIB)

Suite 3C
777 United Nations Plaza
New York, NY 10017
(212) 972-9877
FAX: (212) 972-9878
cipany@igc.apc.org

Publishes: B, R
Provides: $D

A joint effort of the International Center for Law in Development and the Council on International and Public Affairs (see Chapter Ten), the Bhopal Action Resource Center was founded in 1985 to monitor developments in the United States related to the Union Carbide tragedy. The Center maintains contact with victims organizations and voluntary groups in India, and lobbies to have the voices of victims heard in their struggle for justice in the aftermath of the Bhopal disaster. Since its foundation, BARC has held the watch against the Union Carbide Corporation. More recently, it has become active in monitoring other groups' efforts to protect themselves from corporations that are conducting hazardous operations in their communities. In 1989 and again in 1994, BARC sponsored a delegation of victims of the Union Carbide disaster to tour North America and Europe. The Center has also helped raise funds for the International Medical Commission on Bhopal, a consortium of medical and community health specialists from 12 countries. To date, the commission has carried out clinical evaluations of survivors and urged the establishment of community health centers for those who continue to bear the emotional and physical burden of the Union Carbide gas leak.

In 1986, BARC came together with six voluntary organizations in Japan, Hong Kong, the Netherlands, the United Kingdom, and the United States in the International Coalition for Justice in Bhopal. The sole mission of the coalition was to hold Union Carbide accountable by instigating a worldwide movement for justice. To this end, the ICJIB successfully petitioned the Permanent People's Tribunal in Rome to hold a series of sessions on industrial hazards and human rights.

Bhopal People's Health and Documentation Clinic (BPHDC)

44 Sant Kanwar Ram Nagar
Berasia Road
Bhopal 462 001
INDIA
(91-755) – 530914
sathyu@bhavna.unv.ernet.in

Publishes: R
Provides: CO, HC

In 1995, the Sambhavna Trust started the Bhopal People's Health and Documentation Clinic. The trustees sought to assist the victims of the gas leak who have suffered both physically and emotionally since the 1984 Union Carbide disaster. Despite exceeding the World Health Organization's recommendation for the number of hospital beds per capita, the city of Bhopal has continued to see a rise in exposure-related morbidity and mortality throughout the 1990s. Located in a poor neighborhood on the fringes of the Union Carbide plant, the BPHDC exists to aid victims in their struggle for justice and a disease-free, dignified life. The project counts the deaths and monitors the long-term health consequences that have resulted from exposure. It also aims to finally achieve full disclosure of the chemicals that were present in the leaked gas.

Persons seeking care at the clinic have access to a primary care provider as well as other services, including modern medical care, Ayurveda, yoga, and other alternative therapies. Treatment at the clinic is geared toward the management of chronic disease and the achievement of a satisfactory quality of life for those living with chronic disease and/or permanent disability. Community health workers walk through affected areas to contact victims whose needs may be met at the BPHDC. The Clinic also actively lobbies for public health projects that will improve living conditions, for example, by securing water supplies, building permanent dwellings, or improving infrastructure. In the near future, the Clinic will also train individuals to run community health units in their own neighborhoods.

Bread for the World

1100 Wayne Avenue, Suite 1000
Silver Spring, MD 20910
(301) 608-2400
1-800-82-BREAD
FAX: (301) 608-2401
bread@bread.org
www.bread.org

Publishes: EP, NL, R, V
Provides: FD, L, MM, ST, $D

Bread for the World is a nonpartisan Christian citizen's movement—comprised of more than 44,000 individuals and 3,500 churches from 45 denominations—that works to end hunger. Bread for the World lobbies Congress, sponsors media campaigns, and supports grassroots activism to raise hunger awareness and to promote related advocacy. Bread for the World develops educational resources aimed at promoting the anti-hunger movement; trains leaders to help carry the movement forward; and encourages concerned individuals from all denominations to take an active role in affecting policies to end hunger.

The Bread for the World Institute issues policy briefs, study guides, and an annual report on the state of world hunger. The Institute's **Annual Report on the State of World Hunger** is a valuable resource for activists working with hunger and development issues. It sponsors the **Transforming Anti-Hunger Leadership Program**, a community-based endeavor aimed at strengthening anti-hunger leadership in the United States. The **Institute's Development Bank**

Watchers' Project monitors and reports on changes in World Bank policies and practices in a quarterly bulletin. The project also produces educational materials and contributes to advocacy campaigns that influence World Bank policy, especially those policies related to poverty and hunger.

Campaign for Labor Rights (CLR)

1247 "E" Street
Washington, DC 20003
(541) 344-5410
FAX: (202) 544-9359

clr@igc.apc.org
www.Summersault.com/~agi/clr/index.html

Publishes: EP, NL
Provides: O

Serving as a bridge between local activists and organizations struggling for labor rights nationally and abroad, the Campaign for Labor Rights produces a newsletter, maintains a website, posts frequent alerts on the Internet, and runs an electronic mail Labor Alerts/Labor News Service. Through these media, CLR provides information about the many projects around the world in which it is actively supporting efforts to secure more rights for workers. CLR also assembles and distributes action packets that lay the groundwork for launching specific labor rights campaigns. The Campaign mobilizes grassroots support in the United States and Canada for the campaigns of CLR's partner organizations. Currently, CLR is involved in the labor struggles of workers in Guatemala, Mexico, Nicaragua, and El Salvador against corporations such as Nike, Disney, and Guess. CLR also works with farm and poultry-processing workers in the United States, and on behalf of child laborers throughout the world.

Center for Cuban Studies

124 West 23rd Street
New York, NY 10011
(212) 242-0559
FAX: (212) 242-1937

cubanctr@igc.org
www.cubaupdate.org

Publishes: B, EP, NL, V
Provides: O, T

In 1972, a group of scholars, writers, artists, and other professionals came together to form the Center for Cuban Studies. They hoped to counter the effects of U.S. policy toward Cuba that have occurred since the 1961 ban on trade and travel and the severing of diplomatic relations. Through publications, organized tours of Cuba, library services, exchange programs, art programs, and other educational activities, the Center serves as a vital link between the United States and Cuba. The ultimate goal of the Center's activities is to witness the normalization of U.S.-Cuba relations.

The Center publishes a bimonthly magazine covering U.S.-Cuba related politics, economics, and arts. Its **Information Service** provides up-to-date and accurate information about Cuba and has an extensive library on Cuba that is open to the public. The public can also learn firsthand about Cuba through the Center's **CUBA Update Tours**. These provide opportunities for professional research, news-gathering, and educational study. With funds raised through these activities and through donations of needed material goods, the Center's **Lifeline Fund** offers people and institutions throughout Cuba educational materials and medical, office, art, photographic, and dental supplies and equipment.

Center for Economic and Social Rights (CESR)

25 Ann Street, Sixth Floor
New York, NY 10038
(212) 634-3424
FAX: (212) 634-3425
rights@cesr.org
www.cesr.org

Publishes: NL, R
Provides: CO, FD, L, S

The Center for Economic and Social Rights treats systemic poverty and environmental degradation as violations of established international law. Founded in 1993, CESR grew out of an interdisciplinary campaign that documented the long-term health consequences of the Gulf War and the sanctions that were imposed on Iraq in its aftermath. The organization's work uses a "bottom-up" model of human rights activism that relies on collaboration with social scientists to document rights violations. It also works with a coalition of community and social justice organizations to raise public awareness and advocate for policy change.

For its human rights campaigns, CESR collects scientific and legal evidence on violations of economic and social rights; produces educational materials and disseminates them to affected communities; releases human rights reports to pressure those in government and industry responsible for the violations; and advocates at local, national, and international levels for policy changes to redress the violations.

Center for Reflection, Education, and Action (CREA)

P.O. Box 2507
Hartford, CT 06146-2507
(860) 586-0705
FAX: (860) 233-4673
crea-inc@concentric.net
www.crea-inc.org

Publishes: R
Provides: FD, S, ST

The Center for Reflection, Education, and Action provides faith-based tools for the socioeconomic analysis of globalization. It produces Purchasing Power Index (PPI) studies to document the social effects of inflation, currency devaluation, and changing wages and to objectively measure the impact of corporate practices on individuals and communities across the United States and in developing countries around the world.

The Center has co-published PPI studies for Haiti, Mexico, Indonesia, and major urban areas of the United States. CREA also promotes economic literacy, and offers groups and communities workshops and structured reflection on faith-based ways to integrate the work of social justice within our rapidly changing global economy.

Coalition for Justice in the Maquiladoras

3120 West Ashby
San Antonio, TX 78228
(210) 732-8957
FAX: (210) 732-8324
mtorig@igc.org
www.pctvi.com/laamn/cjm.html

Publishes: EP, NL, R
Provides: CO, FD, L, O, ST

The Coalition for Justice in the Maquiladoras comprises community, religious, environmental, and women's groups, individuals, and labor unions from the United States, Mexico, and Canada. Its mission is to ensure safe working conditions and humane wages for *maquiladora* workers. In support of worker and community struggles for social, economic, and environmental justice along the United States-Mexico border, the Coalition pressures corporations to adopt socially responsible practices and to work toward undoing the damage done by years of corporate negligence. The coalition also provides direct support to local worker initiatives.

The Coalition has developed the *Maquiladora Standards of Conduct* to outline minimum standards corporations should follow to alleviate health and environmental problems on the border. It has spearheaded a sustainable wage campaign that calls on transnational corporations to pay wages that allow not only for basic daily survival but also for long-term family savings and sustainable community development. To aid workers and their advocates, the Coalition produces grassroots educational tools that clearly explain Mexican federal labor laws. It also sponsors workshops to train activists to lobby for Mexican legislative reform. Efforts to end on-the-job sexual harassment and employer control of reproductive rights are additional steps the Coalition has taken to realize its goal of ensuring the physical, social, and emotional well-being of all maquila workers.

Committee for Health Rights in the Americas (CHRIA)
(formerly *Committee for Health Rights in Central America*)

474 Valencia Street, #120   *Publishes:* B, NL, V
San Francisco, CA 94103   *Provides:* CO, FD, L, S, ST, T
(415) 431-7760
FAX: (415) 431-7768

chria@igc.apc.org
www.brown.edu/Courses/Bio_Community_Health168C/chria.html

In response to the suffering imposed by the World Bank and International Monetary Fund on communities worldwide, CHRIA works to promote universal health rights. With regard to U.S. policy, the Committee hopes to see the billions of dollars spent on military and harmful foreign intervention redirected to health care, housing, and education for underserved populations throughout the Americas. Through advocacy and outreach, CHRIA works to ensure access to quality health care for immigrants and refugees. The Committee offers education and information on the medical, social, and psychological needs of immigrants and refugees. The organization's **Immigrant Health Committee** was instrumental in the San Francisco Department of Public Health's decision to stop requiring patients to reveal their immigration or documentation status prior to receiving care. In California, CHRIA is confronting the consequences of policies, such as Proposition 187, that deny health rights to immigrants and refugees. The Committee's objective is to reframe the immigration debate by making links between U.S. foreign economic policy and its effects on immigrant and refugee health.

CHRIA sponsors professional exchanges between the United States, Nicaragua, and El Salvador to improve the skills of local health workers in medical treatment, midwifery, mental health, dentistry, and rehabilitation. CHRIA cosponsors the **North American-Nicaraguan Colloquium on Health**, during which North American and Nicaraguan health professionals share their knowledge and skills. This experience enables North American health professionals to observe the effects that global and political changes have on health care.

Committee for Studies on Women, Family, and Environment in Africa (COSWEFEVA)

BP 5906
Fann, Dakar
Senegal, West Africa
(221) (8) 25-36-20
(221) (8) 20-20-85

cnare@metissacana.sn

Publishes: R
Provides: CO, FD, ST

From all West African nations, women with expertise in disciplines as diverse as anthropology, environmental science, economics, law, sociology, health studies, and communications have come together under COSWEFEVA to promote the participation of African women in the development process. COSWEFEVA works with women of all ages and collaborates with organizations that aim to ensure basic human rights for all women. COSWEFEVA hopes to empower women and expand their political influence by improving their research skills and encouraging their engagement in research projects. Members conduct research in social sciences, population studies, the environment, reproductive health, and family planning.

The organization monitors and evaluates health-related development projects, and implements programs that aim to raise awareness about poor women's lack of access to health and education. The Committee also organizes seminars for African women and provides training on how to manage income-generating endeavors.

Community Works

25 West Street
Boston, MA 02111
(617) 423-9555
FAX: (617) 338-3075

cwworks@channel1.com

Publishes: NL
Provides: CO, O, S, ST

Thirty Massachusetts-based organizations working for social and economic justice have come together as Community Works, a cooperative fundraising effort. The organizations involved in Community Works have a vision of a future in which peace replaces violence, and where human dignity and respect render discrimination and despair obsolete. Through collective fundraising, in the form of payroll deduction campaigns in workplaces, the organizations which make up Community Works increase their self-sufficiency and their ability to combat the problems facing their communities. These community-run, action-oriented groups tackle issues as diverse and complex as affordable housing, child care, health care, domestic violence, public education, AIDS education, youth outreach, homelessness, cancer awareness, gay and lesbian rights, and community capacity building. In addition to collaborating in their fundraising efforts, the members of Community Works also share their resources and skills as together they struggle for social and economic justice.

Council on International and Public Affairs

777 United Nations Plaza
Suite 3C
New York, NY 10017
(212) 972-9877
FAX: (212) 972-9878

cipany@igc.apc.org

Publishes: A, B, R
Provides: FD

The Council on International and Public Affairs operates several programs focusing on public policy issues, a few of which are of particular relevance to the health and well-being of poor people. For example, the Council operates the **Apex Press (TAP)**, which publishes books providing critical analyses of and innovative approaches to economic, social, and political issues in the United States and throughout the world. TAP is especially interested in economic and social justice and in the impact of technology on contemporary society. The Council's **Program on Economic Democracy (PED)** provides a framework for addressing issues of economic and social rights and links research with action. The Program on Economic Democracy presses for change that will alleviate economic and environmental injustice and broaden economic opportunities for all Americans. Through its **Corporate Accountability Project (CAP)**, the Council tracks citizens' struggles against corporate power. Council members actively work against the undemocratic policies and procedures embedded in the North American Free Trade Agreement (NAFTA) and the General Agreements on Tariff and Trade (GATT). The **Citizen Participation in Public and International Affairs Program** expands public dialogue on global problems. The Council's **International Toxics Project** seeks to increase public awareness of the worldwide, and often unregulated, increase in trade, manufacturing, and use of unsafe products, such as pesticides. The Council collaborates with the **Bhopal Action Resource Center**, the **International Group on Grassroots Initiatives, Communities Concerned About Corporations**, and the **Third World Leadership Development Project**.

Criminal Justice Policy Coalition (CJPC)

99 Chauncy Street, Room 310
Boston, MA 02146
(617) 482-3170 x 319
FAX: (617) 451-0009

stevesrag@aol.com

Publishes: —
Provides: FD, L, O

The Criminal Justice Policy Coalition was formed to promote progressive reform in the Massachusetts criminal justice system. The CJPC brings together grassroots activists, families of prisoners, church-based volunteers, lawyers, academics, criminal justice professionals, lobbying organizations, and concerned citizens for joint action through forums, meetings, and work with the media. The CJPC advocates for alternatives to incarceration for all but the most serious crimes. It opposes mandatory minimum sentences and the death penalty. Choosing to address drug addiction as a health concern rather than a criminal problem, the CJPC argues for the redistribution of resources from interdiction and law enforcement to prevention, education, and comprehensive drug treatment. The CJPC also works to expand prisoner education, job training, and drug and mental health treatment within institutions. In addition, the CJPC promotes increased utilization of family and community links, such as work-release, pre-release, furloughs, and halfway houses.

The Development Group for Alternative Policies
(The Development GAP, DGAP)

927 Fifteenth Street, NW
4th Floor, 3 McPherson Square
Washington, D.C. 20005
(202) 898-1566
FAX: (202) 898-1612
dgap@igc.apc.org
www.developmentgap.org/

Publishes: A, NL, R
Provides: CO, FD, L, O, S

The Development Group for Alternative Policies is a center for analysis, advocacy, and action toward constructive change. Since 1977, the Group has worked to ensure that the knowledge, priorities, and efforts of people from poor countries inform the international policy choices of wealthy countries. The DGAP assists developing-country grassroots efforts and nongovernmental organizations to develop the institutional capacity necessary to engage in effective advocacy, policy analysis, and policy development. It also aims to educate U.S. policy-makers, the media, and the public about the economic reform measures that contribute to ecological and economic devastation in poor countries. With its partners in poor countries, the DGAP defines and promotes alternative approaches to development that are environmentally, socially, and economically sustainable. For policy-makers and program officials who also aim to promote development that is rooted in local realities and priorities, DGAP provides resources, guidance, and examples of successful development projects.

Educación Popular En Salud (EPES)

Casilla 360-11
Santiago, Chile
(56-2) 274 3442
FAX: (56-2) 274 3442
EPES@Chilesat.net
www.intac.com/~blenderm/K_Anderson_Letter2.html

Publishes: A, B, EP, NL, V
Provides: CO, FD, L, ST

In 1982, during a time of military dictatorship, a group of health workers began the Educación Popular en Salud project under the auspices of the Evangelical Lutheran Church in Chile. The aim of EPES is to seek justice and equity in health care for the poor and oppressed. EPES trains and organizes those directly affected by poverty and social discrimination to serve as community health promoters. Community health workers learn to diagnose and prioritize their communities' problems, with the goal of becoming autonomous health teams. EPES responds to immediate problems while working to build long-term strategies to address the political, economic, and social forces that influence the health and well-being of people in poor communities.

EPES designs and produces health education materials for local community groups and grassroots organizations throughout the world. It sponsors internships for those training to become health professionals. In addition, EPES has led training workshops in El Salvador, Honduras, Guatemala, Uruguay, and Argentina. Since the transition to democracy in Chile, the organization has been able to work more closely with government-run health clinics. EPES is now working to expose the "myth of the Chilean miracle."

Essential Information (EI)

P.O. Box 19405
Washington, D.C. 20036
(202) 387-8030
FAX: (202) 234-5176
EI@essential.org
www.essential.org/EI.html

Publishes: A, B, EP, R
Provides: FD, O, ST, $D, $R

Ralph Nader founded Essential Information in 1982 to support projects and grassroots efforts that encourage citizens to become active in their communities. Essential Information operates the **Multinationals Resource Center (MRC)** to provide activists, journalists, academics, and interested individuals with information on the activities of transnational corporations. This information is too often ignored by the media and policy-makers. On a case by case basis, MRC responds to individual requests for information on particular industries and corporations: their history, environmental and safety records, structure and size, ownership, and their connections with international financial institutions. The Center educates the public on efforts to attain corporate accountability and end destructive operations. MRC's **Skillshare Program** brings activists together to share information, discuss common problems, and develop campaign strategies. The MRC also provides financial support for advocacy efforts and grassroots operations.

The *Multinational Monitor*, Essential Information's monthly magazine, tracks corporate activity, especially in poor countries. It covers issues as diverse as the suppression of unions, labor violations, export processing zones, product safety, export of hazardous substances, worker health and safety, and environmental health. Essential Information provides an additional service through its **Geographic Information Systems Project (GIS)**, a computerized approach to analyzing data based on location and demographic characteristics. Essential Information uses GIS to reveal patterns of discrimination in banking and lending, crime, congressional district mapping, and environmental degradation.

Fifty Years is Enough, U.S. Network for Global Economic Justice

1247 "E" Street, SE
Washington, D.C. 20003
(202) 463-2265
FAX: (202) 879-3186
wb50years@igc.org
www.50years.org

Publishes: E, NL, R
Provides: CO, FD, MM, O, S, ST

Formed in 1994 on the occasion of the fiftieth anniversary of the World Bank and International Monetary Fund (IMF), the Fifty Years is Enough Network is working to bring about profound change in the policies and practices of these two institutions. The network counts more than 200 organizations working on issues concerning the environment, agriculture, labor, health, women in development, trade policies, and social and economic justice. It has a five-point platform for reform of the World Bank and IMF: 1) institutionalize openness, full public accountability, and the participation of affected populations, with particular attention to women, in decision-making; 2) refocus economic programs to support equitable, sustainable, and participatory development that addresses the root causes of poverty; 3) end environmentally destructive lending and increase support for self-reliant, resource-conserving development; 4) reduce the power of the World Bank and IMF and redistribute financial resources to alternative development assistance; and 5) reduce multilateral debt to free up additional resources for sustainable development.

The Network is committed to increasing people's capacity to shape the global economic policies that affect them. To that end, it is working to increase public pressure for radical restructuring of the institutions that shape the global economy.

Fondasyon Kole Zepòl (Fonkoze)

Ave Jean Paul II, #7 (A Lenteryé)
Port-au-Prince, Haiti
B. P. 13062, Delmas, Haiti
(509) 21-7631
FAX: (509) 21-7641
ahasting@acn.com

Publishes: —
Provides: O, ST, $D

Fonkoze USA
P.O. Box 53144
Washington, D.C. 20009
(202) 667-1277
FAX: (202) 986-3949
LeighCarter@compuserve.com

An economic alliance of peasant organizations, cooperatives, women's collectives, credit unions, Ti Machann (women street vendor) groups, and religious communities, Fondasyon Kole Zepòl is Haiti's "Alternative Bank for the Organized Poor." Its mission is to sustain democracy through grassroots economic development. Fonkoze fills a critical void in Haiti, where poor people and their organizations are otherwise unable to access financial services, earn interest on savings, or take out loans at reasonable interest rates. The alliance offers a multifaceted program of savings for individuals, member organizations, and Haitians living in the United States. Fonkoze makes loans for income-producing activities to member organizations. It also offers financial services, such as currency exchange, to both members and nonmembers, and invests in businesses and infrastructure projects in every region of the country. Fonkoze also offers technical and legal services to its members and operates a **Literacy and Business Skills Training Program** for grassroots organizations.

The François-Xavier Bagnoud Center for Health and Human Rights

Harvard School of Public Health
651 Huntington Avenue, Seventh Floor
Boston, MA 02115
(617) 432-0656
FAX: (617) 432-4310
fxbcenter@igc.apc.org
www.hri.ca/partners/fxbcenter

Publishes: B, E, JM, R
Provides: FD

The François-Xavier Bagnoud Center for Health and Human Rights, founded at the Harvard School of Public Health in 1993, was the first major academic institute to focus exclusively on human rights aspects of health issues. The Center's work combines the strengths of academic research and teaching with a commitment to service and advocacy. Scholars at the Center advise and collaborate with other academic institutions, international agencies, health practitioners, human rights advocates, and governmental and nongovernmental organizations. The Center publishes the *Journal of Health and Human Rights*, hosts international conferences on health and human rights, and offers educational programs throughout the world.

The Center is composed of two principal program components. The **Human Rights Program** focuses on international human rights related to reproductive and sexual health, the right of children to health, and HIV/AIDS. The **International AIDS Program** focuses on expanding global and national responses to the AIDS pandemic, including the evaluation of trends, programs, and consequences.

Freedom from Debt Coalition (FDC)

34 Matiaga Street
Central District
Quezon City 1100
Philippines
(632) 924-6399
FAX: (632) 921-4381
fdc@skyinet.net

Publishes: E, R
Provides: FD, MM

The Freedom from Debt Coalition came together in 1988 to raise a strong voice calling for debt relief in the Philippines. Today, the group represents individual members, member organizations, and chapters from throughout the country, all united in a mission to see the Philippines recover from debt and structural adjustment programs. In advocating for debt policy reforms and working to prevent policies that would reignite a debt crisis, the FDC has been at the forefront in challenging anti-poor and anti-development World Bank/International Monetary Fund policies in the Philippines. The Coalition integrates environmental, ecological, and feminist perspectives in its work (addressing the gender dimensions of structural adjustment, for example). In addition to research, FDC provides venues for the discussion of debt reform and sustainable development. Outside of the Philippines, the FDC also participates in the global campaign to undo World Bank/IMF-induced social, economic, and environmental damage.

Friends of the Earth International (FoEI)

Secretariat
P. O. Box 19199
1000 GD Amsterdam
The Netherlands
31-20-6221369
FAX: 31-20-6392181
foeint@antenna.nl
www.xs4all.nl/~foeint/

Publishes: A, B, JM, R
Provides: FD, L, MM, O

1025 Vermont Avenue, NW, Suite 300
Washington, D.C. 20005-6303
(202) 783-7400
FAX: (202) 783-0444
foe@foe.org
www.foe.org/

A worldwide federation of national environmental organizations, Friends of the Earth International works to protect the Earth against further deterioration and to restore environments already damaged by human activities and negligence. Member organizations within

FoEI are autonomous groups. However, they share information, knowledge, skills, and resources. All comply with the federation's guidelines. Member organizations independently engage in grassroots activism as well as in national and international campaigns to preserve the Earth's ecological, cultural, and ethnic diversity. FoEI campaigns also address issues pertaining to deforestation, energy consumption, climate change, mining, ozone depletion, and wetlands destruction.

The FoEI's **Sustainable Societies Programme** uses the concept of "fair shares in environmental space" to counteract detrimental social and environmental trends that have been shaped by the wasteful production and consumption patterns of industrialized countries. In addition to creating practical alternatives, the program has created new, environmentally and socially sensitive indicators that are being adopted by policy-makers and institutions worldwide. The FoEI's **International Financial Institutions Group** publishes reports on the activities of groups such as the World Bank and the IMF. It considers not just the economic impact but also the social and environmental impact of these institutions' policies. With this comprehensive view, the Group actively campaigns against specific aspects of World Bank and IMF policies and projects.

Global Exchange

2017 Mission Street, 303
San Francisco, CA 94110
(415) 255-7296
FAX: (415) 255-7498
info@globalexchange.org
www.globalexchange.org

Publishes: B, NL
Provides: CO, S, T, $D

Global Exchange works for social justice through education and the creation of economic opportunities. Using varied approaches, Global Exchange educates the public on the political, economic, and human rights status of countries such as Cuba, Haiti, South Africa, Ireland, Brazil, and Vietnam. The Exchange publishes newsletters and sponsors speakers, conferences, and media appearances. Expanding on issues of general concern, "Action Alerts" detail specific human rights violations and "Reality Tours" enable concerned individuals to meet with farmers, human rights and peace activists, church workers, environmentalists, government officials, and opposition leaders in the developing world. Global Exchange promotes alternative trade that benefits low-income producers and artisan cooperatives. Two craft stores operated by Global Exchange support fair trade and provide income for thousands of craftspeople from more than 30 developing countries while at the same time educating Americans about foreign cultures and international trade. To ensure human rights protection, Global Exchange monitors elections, reports on human rights violations, and sends volunteers to conflict zones such as Chiapas, Mexico.

Global Exchange often adopts themes around which many of its activities are focused. The **Cuba Program**, for example, offered study seminars involving trips to Cuba to explore Cuban film, arts, and music, and to examine the country's development projects and public health system. Recently, Global Exchange has been active in international efforts to protect workers' rights and encourage corporations to adopt socially responsible practices.

Grameen Foundation USA

1709 New York Avenue, NW
Suite 101
Washington, D.C. 20006
(202) 628-3560
FAX: (202) 628-3880

info@grameenfoundation.org
www.grameenfoundation.org/about.html

Publishes: —
Provides: ST, $D

In 1976, Muhammed Yunus initiated the entrance of the rural poor into a viable banking system in Bangladesh. He convinced state-run banks to lend money to the poor, offering himself as the guarantor. The success of such credit programs in rural Bangladesh ultimately led to the creation of an independent bank in 1983. The Grameen Bank approach involves disbursement of small loans, requiring no collateral or guarantors, to poor rural households for income-generating activities. Like-minded women and men from similar backgrounds receive loans for small enterprises. The "peer pressure" among the borrowers helps to guarantee successful fund utilization and loan repayment. Prior to loan disbursement, the Grameen Bank educates borrowers as to its philosophy, rules, and procedures. The Bank encourages them to focus on improving their social and health conditions. The Grameen Bank has challenged conventional banking practice by creating a banking system based on mutual trust, accountability, and creative participation. And it has succeeded: the Bank has served over 2.1 million borrowers, 94 percent of whom are women, with a 98 percent repayment rate.

Grameen Trust (GT)

Mirpur 2, Dhaka 1216
BANGLADESH
880-2-801138

g_trust@citechco.net
www.grameen-info.org/grameen/gtrust/

Publishes: B, EP, JM, NL, R, V
Provides: FD, HC, ST, $D

Due to the success of the Grameen Bank (see previous entry), Muhammed Yunus began the Grameen Trust in 1989 to provide guidance, training, technical assistance, and even financial resources to organizations interested in opening a similar bank. The Grameen Trust's **Grameen Bank Replication Project (GBRP)** supports and promotes Grameen Bank replication projects throughout the world. The Project organizes **Dialogue Programs** to introduce Grameen Bank principles and assist in the design of replication projects, while encouraging innovation and self-reliance. The GBRP produces training materials for replication projects and reports on their progress in monthly publications. The Grameen Trust further assists replication projects through its **Computer Services Unit**, which provides computer-related training and education. This unit has designed banking software and introduced computers to many rural areas.

Through its **Programme for Research on Poverty Alleviation (PRPA)**, the Grameen Trust pursues an agenda that has immediate benefits for the poor and promotes decision-making by poor people themselves. The PRPA provides funds for research and maintains a library on materials related to poverty reduction. Based on the observation that ill health prevents approximately 20 percent of Grameen Bank borrowers from adequately utilizing or repaying their loans or improving their life quality, the Grameen Trust started the **Grameen Health Programme (GHP)**. The GHP provides affordable primary health-care services to Grameen Bank borrowers and non-borrowers and it promotes community-based health-care programs.

Grassroots International
(GRI)

179 Boylston Street, 4th floor
Boston, MA 02130
(617) 524-1400
FAX: (617) 524-5525

grassroots@igc.apc.org

Publishes: A, NL, R
Provides: CO, L, MM, $D

Grassroots International began in 1983 as an independent development and information agency. Its goal is to support those working for equality and social justice in poor countries. GRI recognizes the inherently political nature of "development" and supports social and economic projects sponsored by movements for democratic social change in developing countries. GRI has partnerships in areas such as Haiti, the Horn of Africa, the West Bank and Gaza, Eritrea, and Mexico for projects as diverse as emergency relief, public health programs, literacy campaigns, and worker-managed production cooperatives. Playing a critical investigative role, GRI draws media attention to crises in an attempt to catalyze action by other groups on behalf of its partners. GRI also advocates for change in U.S. government and corporate policies that negatively affect poor people.

Haitian Women for Haitian Refugees
(HWHR)

319 Maple Street
Brooklyn, NY 11225
(718) 735-4660
FAX: (718) 735-4664

Publishes: —
Provides: CO, FD, ST

After the 1991 coup d'état that overthrew Haiti's first democratically elected president, the United States began admitting Haitians fleeing their country's political crisis. Although the United States acknowledged that the Haitians had a credible fear of persecution, it did not grant them refugee status. As a result, Haitians found themselves in the United States living in deplorable conditions without health, educational, or financial assistance. Two Haitian-American women, who first became involved in the crisis of Haitian refugees as interpreters for the Immigration and Naturalization Service in Guantanomo, Cuba, started Haitian Women for Haitian Refugees after witnessing the appalling conditions in a transitional housing site in Brooklyn. Since then, HWHR has been working with refugee communities, sponsoring literacy and English-as-a-second language programs, crisis intervention, and legal/immigration referral services. HWHR also offers educational programs for children, free health fairs, assistance in obtaining state and federal social services, and computer skills training for both documented and undocumented refugees. In addition, HWHR sponsors workshops and special events on HIV/AIDS, work and housing discrimination, health awareness, domestic violence, and immigration issues.

Harm Reduction Coalition (HRC)

22 West 27th Street, Ninth Floor
New York, NY 10001
(212) 213-6376
FAX: (212) 213-6582
hrc@harmreduction.org

Publishes: EP, NL
Provides: CO, FD, O

3223 Lake Shore Avenue
Oakland, CA 94610
(510) 444-6969 x 16
FAX: (510) 444-6977

www.harmreduction.org

The Harm Reduction Coalition is a union of activists, community and spiritual groups, and professionals who have come together out of a commitment to reduce drug-related harm to individuals and communities. To nurture recovering and active drug users' ability to protect themselves, their loved ones, and their communities, HRC initiates and promotes local, regional, and national harm reduction education, interventions, and community organizing. It promotes alternative models to conventional drug treatment and health and human services while challenging traditional client/provider relationships. HRC provides health professionals, drug users, and their communities with educational materials and support for programs of rehabilitation, needle exchange, abstinence-oriented drug treatment, safe and responsible drug use, and chemotherapeutic drug treatment.

Health Action International (HAI)

c/o HAI-Europe
Jacob van Lennepkade 334-T
1053 NJ Amsterdam
The Netherlands
(31)-20-683-3684
FAX: (31)-20-685-5002
hai@hai.antenna.nl
www.haiweb.org

Publishes: A, B, E, EP, R
Provides: FD, L, MM, O

Health Action International is a nonprofit, global network of health, development, consumer, and other public interest groups located in more than 70 countries and working for a more rational use of medicinal drugs. HAI represents the interests of consumers in drug policy and believes that all drugs marketed should meet real medical needs and should be acceptably safe, effective, and affordable. HAI also campaigns for better controls on drug promotion and the provision of balanced, independent information for prescribers and consumers. The group supports the Essential Drug Policy of the World Health Organization (WHO) which concentrates on the supply and use of some 250 drugs considered to be the most essential. The HAI believes that access to these essential drugs should be the guiding principle used to assess the effects of intellectual property rights on pharmaceuticals and that public health interests should have primacy over commercial interests in questions of trade.

HAI has published extensively regarding the need for transparency and accountability in drug regulation. The group's publications include the edited volume *Power, Patients, and Pills*, which grew out of the need to provide an alternate viewpoint on national drug policies as initially envisioned by a planned cooperation between the WHO and the World Trade Organization. HAI's information package titled *Problem Drugs* provides material that highlights examples of unethical actions and double standards in drug marketing for various categories of pharmaceuticals, along with special prescribing needs for women, children, and the elderly. The HAI affiliate in Penang, Malaysia, produces a bimonthly newsletter featuring international health issues and news from HAI groups worldwide.

Hispanic Health Council (HHC)

175 Main Street
Hartford, CT 06106
(860) 527-0856
FAX: (860) 724-0437

mariam@hispanichealth.com
www.hispanichealth.com

Publishes: A, AU, B, EP, R, V
Provides: CO, HC, L, S, ST

The Hispanic Health Council was founded in 1978 to address the health-care and educational needs of Hartford's Latino community. Today, HHC is a community-based research, education, and advocacy organization that serves oppressed communities in and around Connecticut's capital. The organization comprises bilingual and bicultural health educators, social scientists, public health specialists, and concerned individuals. HHC has developed a comprehensive approach to improving the physical, emotional, and social well-being of community members by linking research with direct service. The Council develops innovative, culturally appropriate programs while also making policy recommendations. The Council's research focuses on health (including mental health), dietary beliefs and practices, help-seeking patterns, treatment experiences, and effectiveness of interventions. It shares its research findings with urban organizations throughout the United States through publications, conferences, and workshops.

HHC directly serves its constituents through several programs. **Family Health Promotion** includes violence and abuse prevention projects, school liaison services, elderly services, and general health education. **Maternal-Child Health** projects offer gynecological and family planning services, breastfeeding promotion, immunizations, and breast cancer detection education. **Women and Chemical Dependency** projects provide linguistically, socially, and culturally appropriate treatment, counseling, support, and shelter services to dependent women, their children, and their partners. HHC runs several **HIV/AIDS Prevention and Support** programs that also directly serve the community. **Youth Development and Prevention** programs offer leadership and pre-vocational training as a means toward promoting education and reducing violence among young people. In all of these activities, HHC offers training opportunities to health practitioners and community leaders. Finally, the Council is involved in policy debates and advocacy for the improvement of services at the local, state, and national levels.

INFACT

46 Plympton Street
Boston, MA 02118
(617) 695-2525
FAX: (617) 695-2526

infact@igc.apc.org
www.infact.org

Publishes: A, B, EP, R
Provides: L

INFACT is a national grassroots organization striving to bring an end to all life-threatening abuses committed by transnational corporations. Since 1966, INFACT has been both educating the public about the abuses of power by giant corporations and organizing millions of people to take action to change corporate behavior.

INFACT has run four major campaigns. The Infant Formula Campaign helped to bring about the passage of the World Health Organization's International Code of Marketing for Breast Milk Substitutes, and brought worldwide attention to the deadly, dishonest corporate practices that had been kept hidden. The passage of this code marked the first time in history that a movement of ordinary people had forced a transnational corporation to deal directly with their concerns. The Nuclear Weaponmakers Campaign targeted industry leader General Electric for its role in promoting and producing nuclear weapons. By boycotting General Electric, the campaign caused the corporation a publicity nightmare. Through the Tobacco Industry Campaign INFACT launched in 1993, consumers and health advocates are challenging Philip Morris and RJR Nabisco to stop addicting new, young customers around the world, and to stop manipulating public policy in the interest of tobacco profits. The Hall of Shame Campaign began in 1996 by shining a spotlight on corporate influence on U.S. legislators and the entire electoral process.

Institute for Agriculture and Trade Policy (IATP)

2105 First Avenue South
Minneapolis, MN 55404-2505
(612) 870-0453
FAX: (612) 870-4846
iatp@iatp.org
www.iatp.org/

Publishes: A, EP, R
Provides: FD, S, ST, T

Since 1986, the Institute for Agriculture and Trade Policy has worked to foster economically, socially, and environmentally sustainable communities and regions around the world. The Institute hopes to make policy-making institutions more accountable, accessible, and understandable, so that citizens can effectively participate in domestic and international decisions that affect their lives. The IATP is committed to policy innovation and advocacy on food, agriculture, trade, and environmental issues at all levels. The organization's three objectives are: a more equitable and democratic world economy, with stronger local and regional economies; the adoption of socially and ecologically sustainable development that allows for environmental protection, biodiversity, and food security; and more comprehensive human rights protection. In association with farmers, consumers, unions, environmental organizations, and citizens groups from around the world, IATP's work influences food, environmental, agricultural, economic, and trade policy. The IATP analyzes the social, cultural, and economic influence of global rules and patenting around issues of food, agriculture, and biotechnology. IATP has developed Internet tools to allow access to a worldwide array of information pertaining to agriculture and trade policy. In direct support of fair trade, IATP has launched coffee-importing projects that support small producers in Mexico and Central America.

Institute for Food and Development Policy (Food First)

398 60th Street
Oakland, CA 94618
(800) 274-7826
FAX: (510) 654-4551
foodfirst@igc.apc.org
www.foodfirst.org

Publishes: B, NL, R
Provides: CO, L, MM

Food First argues that people can be free from hunger only when they have democratic control over the resources needed to sustain themselves and their families. Toward this end, Food First's strategy is to change people's consciousness so that they become aware of the possibility of social change and of their own power to make this change happen. The organization implements this strategy through research, analysis, advocacy, and education-for-action. Food First identifies obstacles to ending hunger and addresses ways to remove them, while providing tools for such change. It looks beyond population growth to the underlying causes of hunger, such as inequitable distribution of resources, environmental destruction, and poor agricultural technology. Food First also identifies, evaluates, and publicizes successful and promising alternatives to traditional means of growing and distributing food. At the grassroots level, Food First promotes diversity, local knowledge, and community participation to empower people to feed themselves. The Institute for Food and Development Policy, through its books, reports, action alerts, coalition building, and campaigns to end world hunger, hopes to inspire and mobilize people and their organizations to transform the systems and institutions that perpetuate hunger, poverty, oppression, and all forms of social injustice.

Institute for Policy Studies (IPS)

733 15th Street, NW
Suite 1020
Washington, D.C. 20005
(202) 234-9382
FAX: (202) 387-7915

www.ips-dc.org

Publishes: B, R
Provides: FD, L, MM

The Institute for Policy Studies is concerned with the global economy, international security, the assurance of economic and social rights, the environment, and the development of sustainable communities. IPS crafts policies in support of society's most marginalized sectors and provides the poor with intellectual ammunition to confront public policy. For more than 34 years, IPS has worked to inform public opinion by engaging in public debate through radio, television, and print media, and by lobbying policy-makers in local and national legislatures. As a training ground for those interested in leading movements for progressive change, IPS runs the **Social Action and Leadership School for Activists (SALSA)**. In collaboration with the **Transnational Institute** of Amsterdam, IPS sponsors a fellowship for progressive scholars who devise strategies to help the world's poor. In addition, the IPS responds to developing concerns by mobilizing activism on the heels of emerging threats.

For 22 years, the IPS-sponsored **Global Economy Project** has been a leading center for analysis and education on the social implications of corporate-driven globalization. Through coalition building, research and writing, dialogue, and popular education, the Project aims to strengthen, connect, publicize, and assess the efforts of the thousands of organizations worldwide that are working to alter the path of globalization, and to promote democracy, equity, and sustainability.

Interfaith Center on Corporate Responsibility (ICCR)

475 Riverside Drive, Room 550
New York, NY 10115
(212) 870-2293
FAX: (212) 870-2023

info@iccr.org

Publishes: B, NL, R
Provides: O

The Interfaith Center on Corporate Responsibility is a North American association of nearly 250 Protestant, Catholic, and Jewish institutional investors representing religious communities, pension funds, dioceses, and health-care corporations. The ICCR is a continuation of an effort that began in 1971, when the Episcopal Church filed the first religious investor-shareholder resolution, which called on General Motors to withdraw from South Africa.

ICCR members seek more than financial return from their investments. They want to utilize their funds to change unjust or harmful corporate policies and practices. ICCR members hold corporations accountable through shareholder resolutions, meetings with corporate managers, stock divestments, public hearings, publication of special reports, letter-writing campaigns, consumer boycotts, and testimony at the United Nations, U.S. Congress, and U.S. state legislatures. The ICCR develops and implements strategies to challenge companies to improve their practices in realms as diverse as the environment, weapons production, equal employment opportunity, business ventures in countries with policies of repression, pharmaceutical pricing, toxic waste disposal, and corporate democracy. ICCR members also make alternative investments to promote economic justice and development in low-income and minority communities. With a total invested portfolio worth hundreds of billions of dollars and bold action demanding corporate responsibility, the ICCR plays a leading role in the movement to promote socially, environmentally, and ethically responsible corporate practices.

Interhemispheric Resource Center

Foreign Policy Communications/Book Orders
P.O. Box 4506
Albuquerque, NM 87196-4506
(505) 842-8288
FAX: (505) 246-1601

Publishes: B, NL, R
Provides: FD

Foreign Policy Editorial Staff/BIOS Project
P.O. Box 2178
Silver City, NM 88062-2178
(505) 388-0208
FAX: (505) 388-0619
irc@irc-online.org

Since its inception in 1979, the Interhemispheric Resource Center has been committed to research, education, and advocacy that incorporates public concern for justice and international cooperation into the foreign policy arena. The Center's goal is to aid in the development of citizen-driven models of economic integration, and to work in the direction of higher labor standards, improved workers' rights, and alternative development strategies. The Center's publications have included critical analyses of specific U.S. foreign policy measures and examinations of international development, peace, democratization, and environmental programs. The Center's advocacy includes collaborative efforts with grassroots organizations working to ensure that public participation, democratic accountability, and issues of social and environmental justice are addressed by bilateral and multilateral institutions, such as the Border Environment Cooperation Commission and the World Bank. *Borderlines* is published monthly by the Center, in both English and Spanish, to assist those at the front lines of the struggle to achieve economic integration and sustainable development. The Center has also published and updated *Cross-Border Links,* a directory of organizations pursuing cross-border collaboration.

International Forum on Globalization (IFG)

1555 Pacific Avenue
San Francisco, CA 94109
(415) 771-3394
FAX: (415) 771-1121
ifg@ifg.org
www.ifg.org

Publishes: NL, R
Provides: FD, O, ST

The International Forum on Globalization is an alliance of activists, scholars, economists, researchers, and writers. It stimulates new thinking, joint activity, and public education in response to the changing global economy and the growth and expansion of transnational corporations. Often working with little or no public participation, the world's corporate and political leaders continue to redesign global institutions and international legal frameworks that affect most of the world's communities. Organized to publicize the effects of these changes, the IFG advocates for equitable, democratic, and ecologically sustainable economics. Since 1994, the IFG has shaped its activism with a broad view of the globalization process, rather than a narrow focus on only trade agreements or World Bank policies. The IFG promotes locally controlled, community-based economics by advocating for new international agreements that place the needs of people, local economies, and the natural world before the interests of corporations. Through its publications and teach-ins, the IFG hopes to train and educate activists who seek to undo the damaging social, ecological, cultural, and political consequences of corporate-driven globalization.

International Labor Rights Fund (ILRF)

733 15th Street, NW, #920
Washington, D.C. 20005
(202) 347-4100
FAX: (202) 347-4885
laborrights@igc.org
www.laborrights.org

Publishes: B, NL
Provides: L, O, S

The International Labor Rights Fund is dedicated to ensuring that the human rights of workers are protected throughout the world. ILRF leaders call upon their diverse experience in human rights, labor, consumer, business, religious, academic, and governmental organizations. The ILRF strives to ensure that adult working people are able to work under conditions that respect their rights, dignity, economic needs, health, and safety. The other fundamental goal of ILRF is to ensure that children are not subjected to exploitative, unhealthy, or dangerous work. The **International Labor Rights Advocates,** a branch of ILRF, is a group of lawyers, law professors, and law students who voluntarily conduct legal research and litigation, and who provide representation in support of the ILRF's work. As a coalition member of the **Alliance for Responsible Trade**, ILRF also works on issues related to the North American Free Trade Agreement. The Alliance brings environmental, labor, consumer, religious, development, and agricultural groups together to advocate for trade policies that protect social and environmental standards.

International People's Health Council (IPHC)

CISAS (global coordinator)
Apartado #3267
Managua, Nicaragua
505-2-661662
505-2-666711

cisas@ibw.com.ni
www.healthwrights.org/iphc/index.htm

Publishes: A, B, E, R,
Provides: FD, L, MM, O, S

The International People's Health Council works toward fundamental social change in the struggle for health and against poverty, hunger, and unfair socioeconomic structures. The work of IPHC is geared toward poor and disadvantaged people in both underdeveloped and industrialized countries. In addition to the coordinator's site in Nicaragua, other IPHC offices are located in Africa, Asia, India, Israel, Mexico, England, and the United States. IPHC facilitates the sharing of information, ideas, experience, methods, and resources among a wide range of persons and coalitions involved in community health work. By establishing and collaborating with grassroots movements around the world, IPHC serves as a vehicle for expanding solidarity among groups committed not only to health care but also to education, workers' and minority rights, participatory democracy, environmental issues, consumer advocacy, disarmament, human rights, and the accountability of governments and corporations.

International Physicians for the Prevention of Nuclear War (IPPNW)

727 Massachusetts Avenue
Cambridge, MA 02139
(617) 868-5050
FAX: (617) 868-2560

ippnwbos@ippnw.org
www.healthnet.org/IPPNW

Publishes: A, AU, B, E, EP, JM, NL, R
Provides: FD, L, MM, O, S

International Physicians for the Prevention of Nuclear War is a global federation of physicians' organizations dedicated to safeguarding health through the prevention of war, the promotion of nonviolent conflict resolution, and the minimization of war's effects on health, development, and the environment. The chief focus of the federation is the elimination of nuclear weapons. By putting political ideology aside, IPPNW physicians sound the medical warning to humanity: nuclear war is the final epidemic, with no winners, no cure, and no meaningful medical response. This message is backed by meticulous scientific research into the consequences of nuclear warfare. For this work, IPPNW was awarded the 1985 Nobel Peace Prize.

In today's world, freed from East/West conflict, IPPNW's antinuclear work is paired with promotion of alternatives to violence and armed conflict; demilitarization of the global economy and an end to the global arms trade; the reallocation of resources from military to civilian needs, especially health care and basic human necessities; and sustainable, ecologically sound economic development. IPPNW is also a member of Jubilee 2000, a global campaign to cancel the unpayable debt owed by the world's poorest countries by the year 2000.

Jubilee 2000/USA

222 East Capitol Street, NE
Washington, D.C. 20003-1036
202-783-3566
FAX: 202-546-4468
coord@j2000usa.org
www.j2000usa.org

Publishes: R
Provides: FD, L, MM

Jubilee 2000/USA is part of a worldwide movement to cancel the crushing debt of impoverished countries by the new millennium. Recognizing that many of the debts carried by poorer countries are unpayable and exact a great social and environmental toll, the **Jubilee 2000/USA Campaign** advocates for lifting the debt burden. The group's name and central organizing ideas come from the Biblical tradition calling for a Jubilee year every 50 years, when slaves are set free and debts canceled.

Jubilee 2000/USA is calling for a definitive cancelation of international debt. This call is aimed at benefiting those most affected by the debt burden; namely, the poor. The movement is striving for an unconditional debt cancelation, accompanied by an admission of responsibility for the current crisis by both borrowers and lenders.

The Jubilee 2000/USA Campaign, launched in June 1997 at the Summit of the Group of Eight Governments in Denver, continues to publicly and visibly protest international governance and lending agencies. In addition to its grassroots organizing and informational media campaigns, Jubilee 2000/USA also helps to coordinate a massive protest petition intended for the governments of the world's wealthiest and most influential countries.

Just Act (Youth ACTion for Global JUSTice)
(*formerly* Overseas Development Network [ODN])

333 Valencia Street, Suite 330
San Francisco, CA 94103
(415) 431-4204
FAX: (415) 431-5953
info@justact.org
www.justact.org/

Publishes: A, B, EP, NL, V
Provides: CO, FD, L, S, ST, $D

Created in 1983 as the Overseas Development Network, Just Act is a national, student-based organization that addresses global issues such as hunger, poverty, and social injustice. The Network's continuing mission is to inspire a lifelong commitment in students to work for global justice through sustainable community development. ODN has served more than 170 high school and college campus groups united in their belief that people can meet basic needs, strengthen communities, and contribute to global welfare through grassroots action. The Network's **Partnership Program** facilitates the exchange of ideas, information, and resources while linking students with community groups that work toward sustainable, locally initiated development. Through ODN's **Development Education Program**, student groups help their campus communities respond to the challenges of international development by sponsoring discussion groups, action campaigns, workshops, seminars, films, speakers, fundraisers, and conferences. Nationally, the program hosts a **Working for Global Justice Conference** and a **Summer Leadership Conference**. To enable students to gain firsthand experience in the field of international development, ODN's **Opportunities Program and Clearinghouse Services** provide information and placement services for internship and volunteer opportunities in the

United States. Finally, every year, ODN organizes the multifaceted **Bike-Aid** event. Cyclists ride across the country, raise funds for community-based projects around the world, participate in community service activities, and deliver educational materials concerning the environment and development to the communities on their route.

The Lambi Fund of Haiti

Avenue Lamartiniere, #94
Port-au-Prince, HAITI
(509) 459445 (fax also)

P.O. Box 18955
Washington, D.C. 20036
(800) 606-9657
(202) 833-3713
FAX: (501) 376-7190/(202) 829-0852
lambi@igc.apc.org

Publishes: R
Provides: S, ST, T, $D

The Lambi Fund of Haiti directly assists Haitians in building a self-determined and democratic future. The Fund raises monetary and material aid to promote local and national democratic efforts in Haiti. It channels resources to programs conceived, planned, and implemented by the Haitian people. In partnership with community-based peasant organizations and neighborhood associations, the Lambi Fund provides a positive alternative to international development assistance. To promote sustainable resource management, the Fund sponsors rural projects such as tree-planting, agricultural stores, grain storage, mobile water pumps, and grain mills. Women's ventures increase access to food, housing, and basic family needs, so that women can earn an income and build their vocational and managerial skills. The ventures include projects for artisans and market women, the Women's Popular Restaurant, and credit banks for women. Projects aimed at community development and organizing also receive Fund resources; they are seen as the keys to democracy, equitable economic growth, and sound environmental resource use. These projects include popular community banks, fishing cooperatives, and community stores. Skills training is a major element of these Lambi Fund projects because such training improves collective earning power while ensuring project accountability and success. The Fund supports other programs and initiatives that develop leadership skills, provide literacy, promote environmental and human rights education, and advocate for democracy and constitutional rights. In all cases, the projects' recipients determine the Lambi Fund's direction and activities.

Maquila Solidarity Network/Labor Behind the Label Coalition

606 Shaw Street
Toronto, Ontario M6G 3L6
CANADA
(416) 532-8584
FAX: (416) 532-7688
perg@web.net
www.web.net/~msn/

Publishes: NL
Provides: CO, L, O

Corporate agenda, designed for maximum profit and market competitiveness, increasingly demand that workers accept lower wages, reductions in social services, and substandard health, safety, and environmental conditions. The Maquila Solidarity Network challenges these terms of "free" trade by supporting and uniting labor and social movements. The network's membership includes more than 300 organizations and individuals across Canada, with partner groups in Mexico and Central America. The Network's priorities are to support innovative organizing strategies that connect community and workplace issues; address health and environmental problems; and tackle the specific problems of women, who make up the majority of the *maquiladora* workforce. Network members lobby corporate and government officials to improve workplace policies and practices, and support the projects of *maquila* workers and community activists. The Network publishes newsletters with up-to-date information on the struggles of *maquila* workers and community organizations in Mexico and Central America. They also put out urgent action alerts to publicize the ongoing violations of *maquila* workers' rights.

Maquiladora Health & Safety Support Network

P.O. Box 124
Berkeley, CA 94701-0124
(510) 558-1014
FAX: (510) 568-7092

gdbrown@igc.apc.org
www.igc.apc.org/mhssn

Publishes: —
Provides: CO, FD, O, S, ST

When corporate management and government regulatory enforcement fail *maquiladora* workers, the Maquiladora Health and Safety Support Network fills the gap by offering information, training, and technical assistance. The Support Network currently has more than 300 occupational health professionals in Canada, Mexico, and the United States who donate their time and expertise. Volunteers respond to requests for information and technical assistance from Mexican labor organizations and community groups on the border. The Network offers health and safety training in Spanish for workers, community organizers, and physicians from Tijuana to Matamoros. The Support Network has also sponsored a peer-administered survey of *maquila* workers from Tijuana in order to document the adverse health effects of their working conditions. Its quarterly electronic newsletter is available from <ishmaelMD@aol.com>. Additionally, the Network helped establish a clearinghouse of Spanish-language health and safety materials; these materials are currently housed at the Labor Occupational Safety and Health Program (LOSH) at the University of California at Los Angeles.

Médecins Sans Frontières (MSF)/Doctors Without Borders (DWB)

6 East 39th St., Eighth Floor
New York, NY 10016
(212) 679-6800
FAX: (212) 679-7016

dwb@newyork.msf.org
www.msf.org

Publishes: NL,
Provides: CO, HC

Recipient of the 1999 Nobel Peace Prize, Médecins Sans Frontières/Doctors Without Borders—the world's largest independent medical organization—is dedicated to bringing effective and impartial medical relief to populations in distress. Staffed with committed volunteers from around the world, MSF/DWB sets up operating rooms and clinics, provides basic public hygiene assistance, and trains local health workers during war and conflict. During prolonged conflicts and in refugee camps, the organization also provides primary health care, nutrition services, epidemic control and vaccinations, and means for clean water and sanitation. MSF volunteers respond to natural disasters by distributing drinking water, medicine, and other medical supplies. For countries with inadequate medical infrastructures, MSF works in collaboration with existing health and social services to build stable and self-sufficient local health-care systems. Throughout the world, relief organizations use MSF-developed field kits for emergency medical treatment.

National Labor Committee (NLC)
(Education Fund in Support of Worker and Human Rights in Central America)

275 7th Avenue, Fifteenth Floor
New York, NY 10001
(212) 242-3002
FAX: (212) 242-3821
nlc@nlcnet.org
www.nlcnet.org

Publishes: A, B, EP, NL, R, V
Provides: L, MM

Established in 1980, the National Labor Committee began by forming direct ties with non-governmental organizations based in Central America. The Committee sent labor delegations on fact-finding missions, circulated detailed reports on labor conditions in the region, and initiated campaigns for the protection of trade unionists and human rights activists. Today, the NLC is an independent labor and human rights advocacy group. While continuing to advocate for worker protection, the NLC has now expanded to examine the economic issues that shape conditions for democracy and social justice throughout the hemisphere. The NLC researches, publishes, and distributes reports and other materials that link issues concerning internationally recognized worker rights and labor standards with free trade policies, job exports, foreign assistance programs, and declining living standards in both the United States and foreign countries. Seeking more effective measures for monitoring and enforcing international labor laws, the NLC organizes public education campaigns and support networks. The Committee also responds to emergency appeals from workers whose rights and lives are endangered by their pursuit of improved living and working conditions. The NLC has been at the forefront of the battle to wipe out sweatshop-like conditions and hold many of the world's largest and most influential apparel manufacturers accountable. To prevent and address labor abuses, the NLC also works toward independent monitoring of employment conditions.

NETWORK, A National Catholic Social Justice Lobby

801 Pennsylvania Avenue, SE
Suite 460
Washington, D.C. 20003-2167
(202) 547-5556
FAX: (202) 547-5510
network@networklobby.org
www.igc.apc.org/network

Publishes: EP, JM
Provides: FD, L, O

NETWORK was formed in 1971 when 47 Catholic sisters organized in Washington to campaign for civil rights, promote the cause of peace and justice, and encourage people to participate in the political process. Currently, NETWORK comprises more than 10,000 groups and individual members from various faiths. The organization mobilizes grassroots lobbying efforts throughout the country to influence legislation on critical issues affecting poor individuals and communities. NETWORK strives to influence public policy debates, change federal budget priorities, secure just access to economic resources, and transform global relationships. It advocates for policies that foster conservation, the maintenance of global resources and ecosystems, and the development of a just, participatory, and sustainable world community. NETWORK also seeks to build the political will to dismantle unjust public policy and to create alternatives that foster social justice. To this end, the organization publishes the bimonthly magazine, *NETWORK Connection*; sends action alerts to members via mail or telephone; and releases annual reports of Congressional voting records. In addition, the NETWORK Education Program offers legislative workshops, seminars, and resource materials.

New Economics Foundation (NEF)

Cinnamon House
6-8 Cole Street
London SE1 4YH
ENGLAND
44 0 20 7407 7447
FAX: 44 0 20 7407 6473

info@neweconomics.org
www.neweconomics.org

Publishes: B, JM, R
Publishes: CO, L

The New Economics Foundation is an international center that explores how a just and sustainable world would work in practice. NEF does not accept rising world poverty, environmental degradation, nor community breakdown. Rather, the Foundation devises practical and creative alternatives that put people and the environment first. NEF has developed new measures of wealth and progress that account for social and ecological factors. To achieve corporate accountability, NEF carries out social audits of large corporations and distributes a workbook on social auditing to smaller organizations that wish to follow suit. The Foundation's research and reports on corporate codes of conduct spread the values of social justice and ecological sustainability into business practice. To aid local activists who want to increase the autonomy of their communities, NEF sponsors the **Programme on Community Economics**, which integrates community and economic development in a manner that ensures sustainability. Through its **Centre for Community Visions**, NEF harnesses people's energy and creativity for social and environmental change in their own communities. Finally, NEF strives to establish viable new programs on sustainable consumption, social entrepreneurs, and education for a new economics. To that end, the Foundation has recently established the **Value Based Organization**, a project that provides organizational and developmental support to four major development and finance initiatives in India.

Oxfam America

26 West Street
Boston, MA 02111-1206
(800) 77-Oxfam
(617) 482-1211
FAX: (617) 728-2594

info@oxfamamerica.org
www.oxfamamerica.org

Publishes: NL, V
Provides: CO, L, $D

Founded in 1970, Oxfam America is a member of Oxfam International, which currently counts ten autonomous Oxfam organizations around the world. The original Oxfam began in England in 1942 as the Oxford Committee for Famine Relief. Oxfam America works in partnership with communities around the world to implement long-term solutions to poverty and hunger. Through the grants and technical assistance it provides to partner organizations in Africa, Asia, Latin America, the Caribbean, and the United States, Oxfam America supports the efforts of poor and marginalized people striving to better their lives. When disaster strikes, such as during hurricanes in Central America, the Rwandan refugee crisis, and cyclones in Bangladesh, Oxfam America provides emergency aid. The organization also supports small-scale projects that serve as examples to other groups. In partnership with Oxfam America, local organizations strive for social change, economic justice, and the kind of long-term development that will lead to safer and healthier communities. Oxfam America also lobbies the U.S. government and multilateral bodies to adopt policies that support long-term development.

Partners in Health (PIH)/
The Institute for Health and Social Justice (IHSJ)

113 River Street
Cambridge, MA 02139
(617) 661-4564
(617) 441-6288
FAX: (617) 661-2669
pih@igc.org
www.pih.org

Publishes: A, B, E, NL, R, V
Provides: CO, FD, HC, O, S, ST

Founded in 1987, Partners in Health is committed to improving health in poor communities. Its goal is to make a "preferential option for the poor in health care" by working with community-based organizations on projects designed to improve the health and well-being of people struggling against poverty. The efforts of the organization are rooted in a vision of social justice that regards health as a basic human right.

The partner relationship is the central core of PIH and is reflected in the organization's commitment to struggle alongside vulnerable communities, and against the economic and political structures that create their poverty. PIH provides its partner programs with administrative, technical, and financial assistance.

PIH works among landless peasants in rural Haiti with **Zanmi Lasante** on projects addressing malnutrition, diarrheal disease, tuberculosis, AIDS, maternal mortality, and illiteracy. In an urban squatter settlement outside Lima, Peru, PIH works with **Socios en Salud** to operate a community health center, a community health worker project, a children's nutrition program, and a tuberculosis control project. **Apoyo a Mujeres** and the **Guatemalan Refugee Project** are PIH's partners in Chiapas, Mexico. These two programs work with refugees and indigenous *Chiapanecos* to provide women's health care and develop community health training programs and support services. In Roxbury, Massachusetts, PIH has joined forces with community leaders to launch **Soldiers of Health**, a community-based project to improve the health and well-being of local residents who lack access to quality health care. With Haitian young people in the Boston area, PIH runs **Haitian Teens Confront AIDS**, a peer outreach program that enables teens to develop leadership skills and provides a forum for teens to discuss HIV prevention and issues of discrimination and racism.

In 1993, PIH formed the **Institute for Health and Social Justice (IHSJ)** which is the research, education, and outreach wing of the organization. The IHSJ works to redress the lack of critical analyses in biomedical and public health literature and to reveal the mechanisms by which poverty has an overwhelming effect on the health of poor people. Through seminars, colloquia, international conferences, and an internship program, the IHSJ examines the influence poverty and inequality have on disease by linking scholarly analysis with community-based experience. The Institute brings a critical perspective—grounded in anthropology, political economy, epidemiology, and medicine—to bear on the health problems that most afflict the poor, and it translates these scholarly investigations into meaningful health-care improvements for the disenfranchised.

The People-Centered Development Forum (PCDForum)

International Secretariat
14 East 17th Street, Suite 5
New York, NY 10003
FAX: (212) 242-1901

pcdf@igc.apc.org
iisd1.iisd.ca/pcdf

Publishes: B, EP, JM
Provides: CO, O

The PCDForum is an international alliance of individuals and organizations dedicated to the creation of just, inclusive, and sustainable human societies. The Forum proposes viable, community-based, people-centered alternatives to traditionally unequal and exploitative methods of development. Its **International Board of Contributing Editors** brings together views from more than thirty countries for its educational outreach efforts. In seven countries, PCDForum affiliates are engaging in networking, policy analysis, advocacy, public education, and constituency-building. These efforts are geared toward promoting equal opportunity for all people to meet their physical and mental health needs and to participate in the decisions that shape their lives. The PCDForum's **Program Center** in Rome carries out cooperative programs with international organizations to unite them in voluntary citizen action. A sister center in New York supports programs that advance education for global citizenship. The PCDForum's International Secretariat oversees numerous public outreach efforts. Through these programs, the Forum promotes the use of indicators that measure progress in quality of life rather than in quantity of consumption. A founding member and current president of PCDForum authored the influential book, *When Corporations Rule the World.*

Program on Corporations, Law, and Democracy (POCLAD)

P.O. Box 246
S.Yarmouth, MA 02664-0246
(508) 398-1145
FAX: (508) 398-1552

people@poclad.org

Publishes: A, B, R
Provides: FD, L

The Program on Corporations, Law, and Democracy encourages debate on the proper role of corporations in society by enlisting individuals and civic organizations to challenge the power and authority of these giant entities. The Program emphasizes a critical approach to understanding the meanings of public and private property, personhood, legalized violence, labor rights, and the historic authority of sovereign, self-governing people to determine the nature of incorporation. POCLAD uses a historical approach to examine the mechanisms through which governmental and legal structures protect the interests of giant corporations, even when these interests undermine the health and well-being of entire communities. The Program publishes reports, convenes conferences, holds "Rethinking the Corporation, Rethinking Democracy" seminars, and works with civic groups to craft creative strategies that challenge corporations in every aspect of civil society.

Specifically, POCLAD works toward ending corporate involvement in political elections, judicial appointments, lawmaking, and education. It calls for the withdrawal of judicially bestowed civic, political, and property rights, as well as a ban on corporations owning stock in other corporations. Its affiliates from around the country also collaborate to reveal many of the fundamental flaws and problems inherent in corporate charitable giving.

Finally, the Program examines the worthiness of local, national, and international efforts to control corporate behavior through regulatory means and codes of conduct. In their final analysis, to effectuate change, the POCLAD affiliates recommend a persistent and escalating confrontation with corporations and government officials to challenge constitutional interpretation, state codes, and state corporate chartering and de-chartering processes.

Project New Life Day Treatment Program/Bromley-Heath (PNL-BH)

964 Parker Street, First Floor   *Publishes:* —
Jamaica Plain, MA 02130   *Provides:* CO, HC, ST
(617) 983-8466

Working at the community level, Project New Life/Bromley-Heath encourages an atmosphere that invites community members to partake in healthy lifestyles free of drug use. The organization works to build extended "family" support networks, and stimulates broad-based participation in overcoming other public health issues. (Bromley-Heath is a housing development located in Jamaica Plain, Massachusetts; Project New Life Day Treatment Program is a partnership between the Martha Eliot Health Center, which is affiliated with Children's Hospital of Boston, and the development's Tenant Management Corporation.) The Project provides a continuum of services—medical, psychological, and social—to substance abusers and their families. For individuals, PNL-BH offers a six-month, comprehensive day treatment program, including acupuncture detoxification, urine screening, medical examination, psychiatric evaluation, individual and group therapy, Narcotics Anonymous meetings, and educational and vocational counseling. Through family counseling and individualized case management responsive to the recovering addict and his or her family, PNL-BH strengthens the ability of families to cope with and recover from a family member's use of drugs. In addition, PNL-BH has a metropolitan agenda to improve Bromley Heath's reputation and increase educational and occupational opportunities for its residents. Project New Life hopes that its combined individual/family/community-based treatment program will serve as a model for housing and public health groups nationwide.

Redefining Progress

One Kearny Street, Fourth Floor   *Publishes:* A, E, R
San Francisco, CA 94108   *Provides:* S
(415) 781-1191
FAX: (415) 781-1198
info@rprogress.org
www.rprogress.org

Redefining Progress emerged as an activist think tank in 1994 with the view that the United States' economic and political culture is increasingly at odds with democratic values and aspirations. A public policy organization made up of politically diverse economists, policy analysts, lawyers, writers, and organizers, Redefining Progress seeks to develop and promote new policy approaches that integrate economic opportunity, social cohesion, environmental conservation, and fiscal responsibility. The **Fiscal Policy Program** and the **National Indicators Program** are examples of approaches created to this end. The former, a proposal to "tax waste, not work," aims to reduce existing taxes on work and enterprise and to replace them, in a revenue-neutral manner, with fees on pollution and the use of finite natural resources. The latter program is a research and education strategy to advance social, economic, and environmental development indicators in order to replace currently used but often misleading measures, such as the gross domestic product (GDP).

Redefining Progress is critical of the GDP as an economic indicator because it gauges only the quantity of market activity without accounting for the social and ecological costs involved. The gross domestic product ignores the non-market economies of households and communities; it ignores income distribution; and it ignores the drawbacks of living on foreign assets. Redefining Progress has lived up to its name in devising the *Genuine Progress Index* (GPI). Unlike GDP, the GPI incorporates personal consumption data and the value of natural and social capital. For example, the new index adds in the value of unpaid domestic work and volunteerism, while subtracting the costs of crime, pollution, and natural resource depletion.

South African Health and Social Services Organization (SAHSSO)

Western Province
225B Lower Main Rd., Observatory
Capetown, SOUTH AFRICA
(027) 21-448-3300
(027) 21-448-3301
FAX: (027) 21-448-3367

Publishes: —
Provides: CO, L, O

The South African Health and Social Services Organization formed in 1992 as a consortium of five progressive, anti-apartheid health and social service organizations. The Organization unites people experienced in human services, grassroots health outreach, national human rights campaigns, anti-apartheid work, and international lobbying. The mission of SAHSSO is grounded in the internationally accepted standards of primary health care and people-centered development. The Organization strives to transform health and social services in South Africa from an apartheid-based, hospital-centered, politically controlled system to a more holistic system that puts the community and patients first. SAHSSO shares its insights and experience with trade unions, civic groups, women's organizations, religious bodies, and political parties that are working toward similar goals. Through these partnerships, SAHSSO promotes education, equitable housing, improved sanitation, a living wage, and access to social recreation.

Third World Network (TWN)

228 Macalister Road
10400 Penang
MALAYSIA
01-60-4-2266728
01-60-4-2266259
FAX: 01-60-4-2264505
TWN@igc.apc.org
twnpen@twn.po.my
www.twnside.org.sg

Publishes: A, B, E, JM, NL
Provides: L, MM, S

A coalition of individuals and organizations involved in development in poor countries, the Third World Network focuses on global inequalities, health concerns, the environment, culture, human rights, and international affairs. The coalition conducts research, publishes books, and hosts conferences and seminars. TWN also produces the magazines *Third World Resurgence*,

Third World Economics, and the daily *South-North Development Monitor (SUNS Bulletin)*. It operates the **TWN Features Service**, providing three features a week to magazines and newspapers worldwide to better address the needs, rights, and concerns of people in developing countries. *Third World Resurgence*, published monthly, is currently the only magazine on international affairs published by and in the developing world. *Third World Economics*, a bimonthly magazine, focuses on the General Agreement on Tariffs and Trade, the World Trade Organization, the World Bank, and the International Monetary Fund. *SUNS Bulletin* provides daily updates on North-South development issues. TWN is also a voice at major international proceedings of the United Nations and the World Bank.

Treatment on Demand Coalition (TOD)

Veterans' Memorial Building
181 Hillman Street
New Bedford, MA 02740
(508) 999-0888
FAX: (508) 991-6233

Publishes: —
Provides: CO, MM, O, ST

Treatment on Demand was founded in 1989 with a mission to combat substance abuse and HIV/AIDS by building a broad, community-based movement to work for effective drug prevention and accessible treatment. TOD hopes to offer the "real" cure for drug abuse in low-income and minority communities: an end to poverty on one hand and the promotion of egalitarian economic development, social justice, and political equality on the other. The Coalition's target group is not limited to active and recovering addicts; its outreach is extended to all those in the New Bedford community who suffer disproportionately from the burden of HIV/AIDS, substance abuse, and crime. The Coalition's constituency includes people of diverse cultural background, class, creed, gender, sexual orientation, and age. Moreover, the directors, organizing members, and volunteers at TOD are individuals who themselves have been profoundly affected by the issues that TOD strives to address. They are all involved in TOD's education program, skills-building, diversity awareness, and membership enrichment aimed at accessible drug treatment. In addition, TOD is committed to coalition-building with other New Bedford area organizations: it joins forces with groups as diverse as human service providers, consumer advocates, neighborhood associations, and crime watch groups to articulate the importance of a continuum of care, and to incorporate treatment-related concerns into the concept of prevention. TOD activities include an ongoing campaign for a local detoxification center; presentations to other drug treatment and outreach groups; distribution of literature; organization of community rallies; street outreach; voter education programs; and a cable access program about addiction, HIV/AIDS, and related issues.

United for a Fair Economy (UFE)

37 Temple Place, Second Floor
Boston, MA 02111
(617) 423-2148
FAX: (617) 423-0191
stw@stw.org
www.stw.org

Publishes: B, E, NL, R
Provides: FD, ST

United for a Fair Economy is a national organization dedicated to drawing public attention to burgeoning income, wage, and wealth disparities in the United States. UFE aims to shed light on the massive concentration of income and wealth that has developed in the United States during the course of the previous 20 years. UFE compares past policies to present-day policies and combines this knowledge with current research to develop practical, comprehensive solutions to the growing divide between the rich and the rest of the nation.

The organization's goal is to educate a body of activists who can advocate for just economic policies. To accomplish this mission, UFE has developed interactive educational workshops, launched legislative campaigns, and created artistic performances to focus on the negative implications of increased wealth and wage inequality. UFE brings together all sectors of the American public, including the wealthy, to speak out against economic injustices in the belief that people from all economic backgrounds have an interest in creating greater economic security for all. The organization is also developing new programs on globalization, race and inequality, and corporate power. United for a Fair Economy encourages immediate action while building long-term strategies that tackle the root causes of growing economic insecurity.

Workgroup for People's Health and Rights (HealthWrights)

P. O. Box 1344
Palo Alto, CA 94302
(650) 325-7500
FAX: (650) 325-1080
healthwrights@igc.org
www.healthwrights.org

Publishes: A, B, NL
Provides: CO, O, S

Founded by David Werner, author of *Where There is No Doctor*, HealthWrights has been a leader among nongovernmental organizations committed to advancing the health, basic rights, social equality, and self-determination of disadvantaged people and communities. The organization's work includes: community health projects, both in developing countries and, increasingly, in disadvantaged communities in the industrialized world; advocacy for the rights of the disabled and the appropriate use of technologies; and a commitment to critical analysis of health and social policies and programs, as well as to education regarding the effects such policies hold at all levels of society. David Werner and HealthWrights have numerous publications focusing on grassroots health-worker education, disabled children, and the analysis of the structures and politics that affect health. HealthWrights' *Newsletter from the Sierra Madre* reaches more than 130 countries and includes stories and reports of health and disability programs from around the world. HealthWrights works in close partnership with the **International People's Health Council (IPHC)** in Nicaragua, the **Third World Network (TWN)** of Malaysia, **PROJIMO (Program of Rehabilitation Organized by Disabled Youth of Western Mexico)**, and **Project Piaxtla**, out of which PROJIMO grew. With the IPHC, HealthWrights maintains a library on the politics of health, as well as the *Politics of Health Reading List*, available at HealthWrights' website.

ACKNOWLEDGMENTS

We extend our appreciation to Moupali Das for initiating the NGO information-collection system and database, and we thank Rebecca Wolfe for organizing the beginning phase of this chapter project. For contacting organizations and checking correspondence information, we thank Sarah Pomerantz, Caitlin Clark, and Ian Costello. We are grateful to the many individuals who drafted profiles of their organizations for this chapter. The chapter's first author is grateful to Thomas J. White and the folks at the Institute for Health and Social Justice, who stimulated and challenged her throughout the duration of her summer internship. We thank Monica Lowell and the Office of Community Programs at the University of Massachusetts Medical Center for supplying financial support. And for their final edits, we gratefully acknowledge the assistance of Peter Smith, Vaughn Mankey, Dave Harrison, Jim Yong Kim, and John Gershman.

Endnotes

Evan Lyon, editor

FOREWORD
by Paul Farmer

1   In borrowing this expression from Arthur Kleinman, we pay tribute to someone who has served as an "intellectual godfather" and patron of the Institute while remaining, all the while, one of our most thoughtful interlocutors.
2   Budd, 1931, pp. 174-175.

CHAPTER 1
Introduction:
What is Growing? Who is Dying?

1   Although the complex relationship between *poverty* and *ill health* has been a subject of debate in industrial North America and Europe since the early eighteenth century, in this book we take the relationship as given. Our purpose in preparing the volume is not to rehash the debate, but rather to move beyond it. In *Dying for Growth* we examine institutions, policy measures, and development strategies that exacerbate poverty, thereby rendering the poor more vulnerable to ill health.

    For concrete examples of the relationship between poverty and infectious disease, see Chapters Four and Five of this volume. For cases illustrating the relationship between poverty and ill health among women, and poverty and nutrition-related illness, see Chapter Five.

    Several books published in the 1990s investigate interconnections between poverty, social inequality, and illness. For an exploration of the concrete connections between poverty, gender, and AIDS, see the first volume in this series, Farmer, Connors, and Simmons, 1996. For an examination of poverty and child health, see Spencer, 1996. For a study of violence and poverty, see Gilligan, 1996. For an analysis of health, poverty, and world systems, see Baer, Singer, and Susser, 1997. And for an examination of poverty, infectious disease, and inequality, see Farmer, 1999a.

    Friedrich Engels, Rudolf Virchow, and Louis Villerme were among the earliest to describe and analyze the relationship between poverty and health. For more current analyses on the subject, several scholars stand out. Notable among them are Hans Baer, Ray Elling, Paul Farmer, Elizabeth Fee, Stephen Feierman, Ronald Frankenberg, Jack Geiger, David Himmelstein, Nancy Krieger, Richard Levins, Peter Lurie, Lynn Morgan, Soheir Morsy, Vicente Navarro, Randall Packard, David Sanders, Brooke Schoepf, Amartya Sen, Merrill Singer, Nick Spencer, Ida Susser, Meredeth Turshen, Howard Waitzkin, David Werner, Richard Wilkinson, and Stephie Woolhandler. Works by many of these authors are included in the bibliography.

2   WHO, 1998e, pp. 2-3.
3   Gro Harlem Brundtland, Director-General of the World Health Organization, "WHO Boss Sets out Stance on Health and Human Rights," WHO Press Release, December 8, 1998.
4   UNDP, 1997.
5   WHO, 1998e, p. 154.
6   WHO, 1998e, p. 124.
7   WHO, 1998e, p. 127.
8   WHO, 1998e, p. 1.
9   The infant mortality rate was 6 per 1000 live births in the 26 wealthiest countries and 100 per 1000 in the 48 least developed countries. If we were to measure the rates between the 26 wealthiest and 26 poorest countries the disparity would likely be even greater, but rates for many of the poorest countries are not available.

    Enormous health disparities also exist within countries—even within the wealthiest countries. In the United States, for example, life expectancy in neighboring communities can vary greatly: In Washington, D.C., life expectancy in 1990 was 62 years, while in Fairfax County, a few miles away, it was 77 years. The average life expectancy in 1990 for black men in Washington, D.C., was 58 years, below the average life expectancy in India, Pakistan, Nicaragua, Zimbabwe, and many other poor countries for the same year (Murray, Michaud, McKenna, *et al.*, 1998). Moreover, while life expectancy for men in the United States was 72 years in 1990, during that same year a boy of 15 in Harlem had only a 37 percent chance of surviving to the age of 65 (Geronimus, Bound, Waidman, *et al.*, 1996). In the United States, despite an overall decline in death rates since 1960, poor people still die, on average, earlier than those with higher incomes or better education; this disparity increased between 1960 and 1986 (Pappas, Queen, Hadden, *et al.*, 1993). Such disparities arise from the synergistic effects among historical factors, socioeconomic predictors such as income and education, and ethnicity, geographical residence, gender, and age.

    For specific works on race and health, see Krieger, Rowly, Herman, *et al.*, 1993; Geiger, 1997a; Geronimus, Bound, Waidman, *et al.*, 1996; McCord and Freeman, 1990; Nickens, 1995; Otten, Teusch, Williams, *et al.*, 1990; S. D. Watson, 1994; Williams and Collins, 1995; Williams, Lavizzo-Mourey, and Warren, 1994.

    For studies that examine relationships between income inequality and mortality, see the April 20,

1996 issue of the *British Medical Journal* dedicated to the subject. For a thorough examination of ethnic, income, regional, gender, and age disparities in the United States, see United States Department of Health and Human Services, 1998.

10 WHO, 1998e, p. 1.

11 Bread for the World, 1999.

12 WHO, 1998e, pp. 130-132.

13 For an in-depth examination of these interconnections, see Chapter Five of this volume.

14 WHO, 1998e, p. 93.

15 UNAIDS, 1998. See also "A Global Disaster," *Economist*, January 2, 1999, p. 42.

16 Curtis, 1998.

17 Feshbach, 1999, p. 26.

18 According to Dr. Alexey Priymak, one of the leaders of tuberculosis control efforts in Russia (Garrett, 1997).

19 In 1991, 50,407 cases were reported; in 1996 this figure was up to 111,075. Compare the number of reported cases in Russia, with a population of approximately 150 million, in 1996 (111,075), with the 26,000 reported in the United States, which has a population of 270 million (WHO, 1998e, p. 114). See also Meek, 1998.

20 Although this is of course due to the very real problem of population growth, we should not assume that rapid population growth causes hunger and disease. It does not. Rather, as the authors of the seminal book *Food First* wrote over 20 years ago: "Both hunger and rapid population growth turn out to be symptoms of the same disease...If we are really serious about eventually balancing this planet's population and resources, we must now address the disease that causes both hunger and high birth rates: the insecurity and poverty of the majority that results when a minority controls a country's productive resources" (Lappé and Collins, 1977, p. 64).

It is also important to consider the fact that population growth is actually slowing in the world. The world annual population growth rate during the period 1955-1975 was 1.98 percent; from 1975-1995 it had decreased to 1.67 percent. The rate is expected to decrease even further to 1.16 percent during 1995-2010 (WHO, 1998e, p. 117).

Some suggest that it is more important for rich industrialized countries to stabilize their populations than for developing countries, because the former overconsume and overpollute and are thereby responsible for the greatest increase in the impact of human activities on the already overtaxed environment (Goodland, 1996, p. 214).

21 In policy discussions and in practice, the technical sense of the term "growth" is consciously or unconsciously interchanged with other possible meanings: growth in profits for corporations, or other major economic actors, for example.

22 For a more detailed discussion of central economic concepts, including GDP, see Chapter Two.

23 Our claim is not that growth in and of itself is bad or unnecessary. On the contrary, growth can benefit the poor. For many poor countries and communities, expansion in economic activity and GDP may be a key component of programs for improving health and life

quality. Yet as our studies suggest, *if growth is to benefit poor communities, the health and well-being of poor people cannot be dealt with only as an afterthought*, relegated to the rhetoric of poverty alleviation, the prevention of social unrest, or the repair work of social safety nets. Rather, the goals of ending poverty and decreasing inequality must be integrated and prioritized within the institutional and policy mechanisms that promote growth and distribute its benefits.

24 For a more detailed analysis of the roots, claims, and consequences of neoliberalism, see Chapter Three.

25 Notions of growth "trickling down" and the belief that poor countries must experience "short-term pain for long-term economic gain" were justified in part by the works of two economists: Walt Rostow (*The Stages of Economic Growth*, 1960) and Simon Kuznets (author of Kuznets' law). Both scholars' analyses were built on meager and sketchy data and were ideologically based to help promote the Cold War economic interests of wealthy American and European countries. For more on this subject, see Herman, 1995.

26 UNDP, 1996, p. 1.

27 WHO, 1998e.

28 The UNDP calls this form of growth "pro-rich." In its 1998 annual report, the UNDP provides examples of pro-rich growth. Each year throughout the late 1980s, the Honduran economy grew by 2 percent per capita; but during the same period income poverty doubled in the country. New Zealand, the United Kingdom, and the United States all experienced economic growth between 1975 and 1995, yet during the same period each country saw an increase in the proportion of its population living in income poverty (UNDP, 1998, p. 37). For more on growth, human development, and poverty, see Chapter Two of this volume and the 1996 UNDP Annual Report.

29 United for a Fair Economy, 1998, 1999. "Private wealth" refers to assets and holdings (stocks, real estate, etc.) that are not owned by public institutions.

30 UNDP, 1998, p. 30.

31 See, for example, the series of detailed articles published in the *New York Times*, February 15-18, 1999, under the title: "Global Contagion: Networked Economies, Stunted Lives." See also the global finance survey in the *Economist*, January 30, 1999, p. 54 and following.

32 Social and economic indicators can be highly political devices, adjusted upward or downward depending upon the aims of the various governments and international agencies that prepare them. Because of the politicized nature of national statistics, we have opted whenever possible to use the conservative figures of established international institutions such as U.N. organizations and the World Bank. Also, where feasible, we have tried to examine policies in their own terms, in light of their intended consequences and proposed time frames, even though for some policy measures the time frames are vague, at best.

33 Social science data are never complete; in the case of living populations, to wait until "all the evidence is in" is unthinkable.

34 Chomsky, 1996a, p. 14.

CHAPTER 2
Getting a Grip on the Global Economy

1   Sen, 1995, p. 21.

2   A subset of IFIs are sometimes referred to as multilateral development banks (MDBs). These include the World Bank Group, the Inter-American Development Bank, the Asian Development Bank, the African Development Bank, the European Bank for Reconstruction and Development, and the North American Development Bank. The latter is technically not a multilateral bank, but a bilateral bank, for its only members are the United States and Mexico. For information on these banks, see their websites: www.worldbank.org, www.iadb.org, www.afdb.org, www.adb.org, www.ebrd.org., and www.nadbank.org, respectively.

3   Several recent articles have also revealed some dissention in the ranks of leading IFIs, particularly between the World Bank and IMF. A recent article quoted World Bank president James Wolfensohn as saying that the IMF must change its policies so that "mathematics" does not "dominate humanity" (*International Herald Tribune*, December 10, 1998). See also "World Bank Turns Up Criticism of the IMF," *Washington Post*, December 3, 1998. For a further discussion of the notion of "free markets," see Chapter Three, "Terms Reconsidered," in this volume.

4   Friedman, "Is Free Market a Casualty of the Economic Crisis? Some Fear Backlash Could Imperil Globalization," *International Herald Tribune*, October 8, 1998, p. 1. See also Krugman, 1998; Krugman, 1999; Sachs, 1997; Stiglitz, 1998; Soros, 1998. For the conflict between the World Bank, the IMF, and the U.S. Treasury, see World Bank, 1998b.

5   These figures are calculated in terms of purchasing power parity (or PPP). Purchasing power parity is defined as the number of units of a country's currency required to buy the same amounts of goods and services in the domestic market as one dollar would buy in the United States. Converting incomes to PPP corrects for problems caused by calculating incomes in U.S. dollars, using exchange rates. To minimize the impact of prices prevailing in the United States on the relative PPP in other countries, overall GDP per person is calculated at "regional prices," representative of, for example, South Asia or East Asia. Afterward, the regions are linked together to enable global comparisons of the GDP per person and of its components, such as private consumption per person. This is very important for attempts to compare average GDP per person between countries. It may not make much sense to do so between India and the United States, because the average U.S. national's "bundle" of goods and services is so different from the average Indian's bundle. But between two countries in the same region, such as India and Pakistan, such differences should be much less significant, and comparisons accordingly more sensible. Comparing GDP per person in PPP terms is not the same as comparing poverty in PPP terms. To do the latter, we need to know the proportion of persons in a given country who fall below some PPP-constant poverty line of private consumption per head and, if possible, the extent of such persons' shortfalls below the poverty line. The poverty lines are conventionally set at $30 per capita GDP and $21 of private consumption per month in 1985 U.S. purchasing power parity. These estimates have problems. For example, PPP is estimated upon average consumption or GDP, not upon the consumption of the poor, which comprises a bundle much more heavily weighted toward staple foods. The PPP comparisons are reliant upon the Penn World Tables, the latest released in early 1996 and designated as PWT 5.6. These new tables have revised dramatically the real GNP of some economies (such as China's). All these comparisons, therefore, should be taken as approximations. Some analysts argue that in order to compare poverty among places (within or between countries) or times, as one must in order to evaluate antipoverty policies and priorities, a standardized method of poverty comparisons that does not depend on PPP data is required. These analysts offer the capacity to afford the basic food, or food-energy, bundle as one means of measuring extreme poverty.

6   UNDP, 1998, p. 2; UNDP, 1997, p. 5.

7   UNDP, 1996; UNDP, 1998, pp. 30, 37, 50; UNDP, 1999.

8   UNDP, 1998, pp. 2, 29; cf. UNDP, 1999, pp. 3-4; UNDP, 1997.

9   WHO, 1995.

10 Desjarlais, Eisenberg, Good, *et al.*, 1995.

11 After adjusting for inflation, hourly wages stagnated or fell between 1989 and 1997 for the bottom 60 percent of all workers. (Wages over the 1990s did increase 1.4 percent for workers at the 10th percentile.) In real terms, earnings of the median worker in 1997 were about 3.1 percent lower than they were in 1989. Between 1989 and 1997 (projected), the share of wealth held by the top 1 percent of households grew from 37.4 percent of the national total to approximately 39.1 percent. Over the same period, the share of all wealth held by families in the middle fifth of the population fell from 4.8 percent to 4.4 percent. What is even more disturbing is that, after adjusting for inflation, the value of this middle group's wealth holdings actually fell between 1989 and 1997, due primarily to a rise in indebtedness. Between 1989 and 1995 (the latest year for which data are available), the share of households with zero or negative wealth (families with negative wealth owe more than they own) increased from 15.5 percent to 18.5 percent of all households. By 1995, almost one-third (31.3 percent) of black households had zero or negative wealth. Data from Mishel, Bernstein, and Schmitt, 1999.

12 For discussions of the concept of development, see Sachs, 1992; Sen, 1988; and the various issues of the *Human Development Report* published by the UNDP.

13 See note 5.

14 World Bank, 1997c, p. 53.

15 Figures cited from Buvinic, Gwin, and Bates, 1996, pp. 16-18. See also the special issue of *World Development* on Gender, Adjustment, and Macroeconomics edited by Çagatay, Elson, and Grown, 1995; Sparr, 1994; and Sills and Morris, 1993.

16 Sen, 1995, p. 17. See also Sen, 1992, ch. 6-7. For related issues see Rodgers, 1995.

This perspective, known as the 'capability approach,' examines how income and other goods and services contribute to people's capabilities, enabling them to meet their goals in living a dignified, satisfying life. The concept of capabilities was an inspiration for the Human Poverty Index used in the UNDP's 1997 *Human Development Report*. See the citations in Sen, 1997, p. 201, footnote 136. The roots of this approach are ideologically heterogeneous. For example, Adam Smith wrote of the importance of 'appearing in public without shame' (1776, pp. 351-352). Income-based poverty measures may also miss elements of intra-household dynamics of poverty (particularly on generational and gender lines), with significant implications for health outcomes and for the distribution of costs and benefits associated with particular patterns of growth and development. For other classic articles, see Seers, 1972. Indicator debates may also be significant (e.g., the debate over the Disability-Adjusted Life Year (DALY) presented in Harvard's *Global Burden of Disease* study and promoted by the World Bank as a universal metric for determining resource allocation in health policy). For a discussion, see Murray and Lopez, 1994; Anand and Hanson, 1997; and Chapter Six on Peru in this volume.

17 Streeten, 1994.

18 Definition from the European Foundation for the Improvement of Living and Working Conditions, cited in de Haan and Maxwell, 1998b, p. 2. See also de Haan and Maxwell, 1998; and Wilkinson, 1998, for application of the concept to health. See also the discussion in "Terms Reconsidered," Chapter Three of this volume.

The United Nations Development Programme, in its 1995, 1997, and 1998 *Human Development Reports*, presents four new indicators that try to respond to the multidimensional nature of poverty. The first two new indicators were introduced in 1995 to develop a more gender-sensitive measure for development and empowerment, respectively. The first, known as the *Gender-related Development Index* (GDI), captures inequalities between men and women on the traditional Human Development Indicators for longevity (life expectancy at birth), education (adult literacy and combined school enrollment ratios), and standard of living (per capita income in purchasing power parity terms). The second indicator, called the *Gender Empowerment Measure*, focuses on the percentage of women in key decision-making institutions (such as parliaments and the professions). In 1997, UNDP introduced the Human Poverty Index-1 (HPI-1) for developing countries. The index measures deprivation by slightly different criteria (percentage of people not expected to survive to age 40; illiteracy rate; persons deprived of access to water and health services; and the percentage of children under five who are underweight). In 1998, the UNDP introduced HPI-2. This scale was more appropriate for already industrialized countries and sought to capture elements of social exclusion. Its dimensions include: the percentage of people not expected to survive to age 60; the func-tional illiteracy rate; the percentage of people living below an income poverty line set at 50 percent of median disposable income; and the long-term unemployment rate (those unemployed for 12 months or longer). For more details, see UNDP, 1998, pp. 14-15.

19 For countries that rely upon migrant labor, for example, income from workers' remittances can be significant. Similarly, countries that have a high level of foreign-owned companies as their production base can see substantial funds depart in remitted profits.

20 As two recent critics argue, the use of GDP as an exclusive measure of progress is not merely incomplete but "perverse" in that it "not only masks the breakdown of families and communities and the depletion of the natural environment; it actually makes this breakdown—as reflected, for example, in such things as car crashes, divorces, and new prison construction—appear as economic gain. It denies what people intuitively know—that just because more money is changing hands does not mean that life is getting better." (Halstead and Cobb, 1996, pp. 198-199) Cf. the discussion with Herman Daly in Greider, 1997, pp. 451-459; Daly, 1987.

21 UNDP, 1997, p. 71. Emphasis added.

22 UNDP, 1997, p. 72.

23 The labor or capital intensity is a measure of the extent to which production utilizes greater amounts of human labor or capital per unit of production. Sometimes people think it is a contrast between agriculture and industry, but in fact both can be either: agriculture can be labor-intensive (generally, small-scale family farming) or capital-intensive (plantations); industry can be labor-intensive (generally, garment factories) or capital-intensive (high-tech auto plants).

24 See Lipton and Ravallion, 1995 for a discussion by economists, and Escobar, 1995 for a postmodern reading.

25 *Physical capital* consists of buildings, machinery, and any other material structures that are intended for some productive use. The term is used in contrast to *human capital*, which includes skills, education, and health; *social capital*, such as networks of trust that facilitate cooperation and collective action; and *environmental capital*, such as land, water, forests, and air.

26 For discussion of the development strategies of the East Asian Newly Industrialized Countries (NICs) see Bello and Rosenfeld, 1990; Deyo, 1987, 1989; Johnson, 1982; Wade, 1990; World Bank, 1993a.

27 The GATT operated from 1948 onward as an agreement among nation states committed to reducing tariff (and later non-tariff) barriers to trade. Reductions were to take effect as the result of agreements reached in rounds of negotiations, typically named for the locations where a particular "round" began. In the case of the decisive Uruguay Round, negotiations began in 1986 in Punta del Este, Uruguay, and the agreements were signed in April, 1994, in Marrakesh, Morocco. By the late 1980s, the GATT framework, which focused primarily on manufactured goods, could not address the concerns of corporations and states interested in promoting freer trade in agricultural products and services (among other items). The agreement to

form the World Trade Organization was a key product of the GATT's final round.

28 Driscoll, 1998.

29 George and Sabelli, 1994, p. 10.

30 Helleiner, 1994; Ruggie, 1985.

31 The United States, as the world's dominant economic power in the postwar period, was the architect and *primus inter pares* in shaping the policies and practices of the postwar international economy. In 1950, the United States accounted for almost half the world's GDP, and U.S. per capita income was more than twice that of Europe and six times greater than that of Japan. The United States sharply opposed national development strategies that violated liberal capitalist orthodoxy. America intervened in countries from Chile to Zaire to ensure that geopolitically strategic nations would not stray from the true path by succumbing to "the stupidity of [their] own people" (Henry Kissinger's comment concerning Chile). The United States was willing to tolerate some deviation from orthodox free market policies in countries on the front lines of the Cold War (e.g., Taiwan and South Korea), but was much less forgiving in Latin America.

32 This process was represented using an analytic tool called the *Kuznets' curve* (Kuznets, 1955, pp. 1-28; cf. Lipton and Ravallion, 1995, p. 2605). The general idea was that poor countries had low average income and low income inequality in the rural, agricultural sector of the economy, while displaying higher average income and at the same time higher income inequality in the urban industrial sector. During modernization, the distribution of income would first become more unequal as people migrated from the countryside to the city. The need for investment, and savings to fund investment, would also exacerbate inequality, as there would have to be a concentration of wealth to enable savings and investment to occur. As industrialization continued, however, income inequality would eventually decline. This dominant view thus posited a trade-off between growth and inequality in the early stages of development.

33 UNDP, 1997, p. 73.

34 Several international meetings initiated during this period, including Alma Ata, were held to respond to, and ultimately diffuse, demands for fundamental social transformation. Declarations resulting from these meetings tended to appropriate the language of the more radical movements (e.g., "Health for All," "primary health care") but ignored radicals' call to address inequalities in power and wealth.

35 In reality, the causes of the economic decline were more complex. They appear to have had (and to continue to have) more to do with the dismantling of the Bretton Wood system and the reckless liberalization of financial dealings begun in the early 1970s than with any real effects of the oil crisis itself.

36 Formed in 1961, the OECD is a group of the world's 29 wealthiest nations dedicated to building strong economies in member countries and expanding free trade. OECD countries account for more than two-thirds of the world's production of goods and services, but represent a much smaller portion of the world's population. For more information, see the organization's website: www.oecd.org.

37 The anti-statist, free market rhetoric of these administrations was significantly at odds with their actual practice in certain areas of economic policy, which tended in many cases to reinforce protectionism. While in areas of domestic social and economic policy, and for developing countries, the rollback of state responsibility was clear, in U.S. economic policy there was a decided turn toward attacking organized labor, demanding restraints on exports from trading partners like Japan, and actively promoting U.S. business interests abroad. In a review of the 1980s, Shafiqul Islam describes the Reagan Administration as having "presided over the greatest swing toward protectionism since the 1930s," shifting the United States from "being the world's champion of multilateral free trade to one of its leading challengers" (Islam, 1990, p. 174). Examples of Reagan administration protectionism include: reducing access to the U.S. market for Japanese producers of steel, automobiles, semiconductors, etc.; bailing out the Savings and Loans as well as Chrysler; undertaking one of the largest bank nationalizations in history (Continental Illinois); initiating huge subsidy increases for high-tech industry (semiconductors, telecommunications, and the Internet, etc.). The Thatcher government was also highly statist. According to the *Financial Times*, U.K. public spending as a proportion of GNP was "precisely the figure in 1978-79" that "Thatcher inherited from Labour" (January 17, 1997). The same is true for many other rich countries. The World Bank's 1997 *World Development Report* shows a continual rise in central government spending as a percentage of GDP in OECD countries, with the sharpest rise coming in the early 1980s (much higher than in the "developing countries").

38 "Structural Adjustment" is the formal IMF term to describe the programs it designs for Third World debtors. Others call them *austerity programs*. George, 1990, p. xiii.

39 *Debt service* is the sum of principal and interest payments actually made.

40 The literature on the Debt Crisis is voluminous. See Lissakers, 1991, and Devlin, 1989, for good discussions of the supply side of the Debt Crisis. See also Debt Crisis Network, 1986, and George, 1992, for accessible introductions to the political economy of the crisis.

41 See, for example, the influential work by Cline, 1983.

42 For a more specific discussion of the origins of these terms, see Chapter Three in this volume. These terms reflect particular contexts and uses. "Neoliberalism" is the favored term in Latin America. We will use "Washington Consensus" and "neoliberalism" interchangeably. See John Williamson, 1990, 1996.

43 Toye, 1993, among others, has noted how the neoclassical, public-choice school of political economics, also known as the *New Political Economy* (NPE), has imported "vulgar" Marxist arguments regarding the role of the state in capitalist economies. Neoclassical economics has discarded some of the more interesting insights of classical economists like Adam Smith, who saw the importance of embedding markets within a

socio-political framework of laws and regulations, and who also stressed cultural norms of solidarity ("fellow-feeling").

44 See Bauer, 1972; Bauer, 1981; and Bauer, 1984. This section has drawn extensively from Toye, 1993.

45 The first test case for this program was launched in Chile after the 1973 coup brought dictator Augusto Pinochet to power. His economic team of "Chicago Boys" (affiliated with the economics department at the University of Chicago) launched a wholesale restructuring of the relationship between the Chilean state and the economy. This first experiment ended in the early 1980s with a massive banking failure and state bailout.

46 Stabilization and structural adjustment programs were promoted by the World Bank and IMF through conditionality mechanisms. The funds from a stabilization or adjustment loan were usually disbursed in discrete segments (called *tranches*) over a period typically ranging from 18 months to three years. The disbursement of each tranche was made conditional on policy changes. These conditions could take the form of numerical targets connected with the inflation rate, the government deficit as a percentage of GDP, or the money supply. Loan conditionalities could also require specific policy changes: e.g., reducing tariffs to a prescribed level or selling state enterprises in the energy sector. See Mosley, Subasat, and Weeks, 1995.

47 See Woodward, 1992.

48 The most recent emphasis of adjustment programs is to increase the "flexibility of labor" by deregulating labor markets. Typically this means reducing minimum wages, shifting from industrial to enterprise-level collective bargaining, and facilitating the ability of firms to hire workers on a temporary or subcontractual basis. See Oxfam, 1994, and World Bank, 1995b.

49 Oxfam, 1995, p. 74.

50 In 1997, the net long-term private flows rose to $256 billion. See World Bank, 1998a.

51 See Chapter Five in this volume.

52 World Bank, 1998a.

53 Because exports are a key source of the foreign exchange needed to make debt service payments, a high debt service ratio indicates that more foreign exchange earnings are being used for debt repayments, as opposed to other uses, such as purchases of imported machinery, medicines, or food.

54 World Bank, 1998a, p. 160.

55 World Bank, 1998a, p. 161.

56 World Bank, 1998a, pp. 167, 173. The numbers are $179.2 billion in long-term debt for sub-Saharan Africa, of which $133.0 billion is owed to official creditors ($55.0 billion to multilateral agencies and $78.0 billion to bilateral creditors). For Latin America and the Caribbean, long-term debt is $537.6 billion, of which $163.1 billion is owed to official creditors ($72.7 to multilateral agencies and $90.5 billion to bilateral creditors).

57 Some debts have been canceled on the grounds that they were unfairly or unjustly levied. Nongovernmental efforts such as Jubilee 2000 (see Chapter Sixteen) have recently increased public awareness of these cases.

58 Oxfam, 1998, p. 1.

59 For first point see Oxfam, 1995, p. 179; for all other data, see Oxfam, 1997.

60 Until the Heavily Indebted Poor Country (HIPC) initiative (discussed later in this chapter), creditor governments had agreed in a series of negotiations to various terms for debt reduction for the Severely Indebted Low-Income Countries, or SILICS. The most recent of these is the Naples Terms, which provide for a two-thirds reduction (in present-value terms) of certain categories of official debt.

61 Of the 41 countries, 33 are in Africa, with four each in Asia and Latin America. For more details see www.jubilee2000.org and www.oneworld.org/eurodad.

62 For a critical overview of the G-7 Cologne Initiative, see the website of Jubilee 2000/USA (www.j2000usa.org). For an avowedly partisan but nontheless significant perspective on the debt situation, see the issue of *Third World Resurgence* on "Breaking the Chains of Debt," number 107, July 1999.

63 World Bank, 1988a; World Bank, 1992a; World Bank, 1994c; World Bank, 1994d. See also the review by Jayarajah, Branson, and Sen, 1996.

64 Lipton and Ravallion, 1995, p. 2569, fn. 14.

65 See Mosely, Subasat, and Weeks, 1995, and Castells, 1996. See also Stewart, 1995; Taylor, 1988; and Taylor, 1993. Also see Chapter Five of this volume.

66 Gibbon, 1992.

67 See, for example, Conway, 1994, p. 381.

68 See Chapter Four of this volume.

69 Bird, 1996, p. 1758. Bird cites a series of previous studies, including Edwards, 1989; Khan, 1990; Killick, Malik, and Manuel, 1992; and Conway, 1994.

70 Bird, 1996, p. 1758. See also Killick, 1995a.

71 World Bank, 1990a, p. 103.

72 Lele, 1991, and Bourguignon and Morrisson, 1992. The terms of trade are the ratio of one country's (or sector's) export price to the import price paid by that country (or sector). For example, if the amount of corn a farmer needs to produce in order to buy a tractor falls from 100 bushels to 50 bushels, then the terms of trade for agriculture are said to have improved. The terms of trade may improve through an increase in prices paid for produce (due to eliminating taxes on farm products, for example) and/or through a decline in the prices of industrial goods (due to, perhaps, the elimination of tariffs or other trade restrictions on farm inputs). The question is, however, *who* captures the gains from changing terms of trade. Often, wealthier farmers with access to capital and roads reap the benefits, not poorer farmers or farmworkers.

73 Killick, 1995b, p. 314.

74 Pastor, 1987.

75 The Economic Commission for Latin America and the Caribbean (ECLAC) argues that, with a few exceptions, growth rates have settled at a level lower than historical rates (3 percent annually from 1990-1996, as opposed to 5.5 percent between 1945 and 1980). In addition, the majority of the economies of the region

remain vulnerable to external shocks, with macroeconomic stability dependent upon current account deficits, sometimes financed with volatile foreign capital. On average, the incidence of poverty declined from 41 percent to 39 percent of households in the first five years of the 1990s. However, this has not been enough to recover the ground lost in the 1980s, when the incidence of poverty increased from 35 percent to 41 percent. The absolute number of poor—210 million—is the highest ever. Between 1990 and 1994, nine of 12 countries saw a reduction in poverty, but 1995 brought that process to a halt in Mexico and Argentina. The real minimum wage in 1995 was lower than in 1980 in 13 of 17 Latin American and Caribbean countries. See ECLAC, 1997. The Inter-American Development Bank (IDB) contends that 150 million Latin Americans are poor. IDB, 1997, pp. 40-41.

76 IDB, 1997, p. 18.

77 Oxfam, 1995, p. 179.

78 Oxfam, 1995, p. 184.

79 For examples of both types of political factors, see Mehrotra and Jolly, 1987; Watkins, 1998; Ribe, Carvalho, Liebenthal, et al., 1990; and World Bank, 1990b, ch. 7. For a more general discussion of the role of the State and development policy, see Shapiro and Taylor, 1990.

80 Birdsall and Londoño, 1997; IDB, 1997; Killick, 1995a; Killick, 1995b; Londoño and Székely, 1997; Lustig, 1995; Pastor, 1987; Taylor, 1993; and Vivian, 1995.

81 The soft-loan or concessional windows include: International Development Association (IDA) at the World Bank, Fund for Special Operations (FSO) at the Inter-American Development Bank, African Development Fund (ADF) at the African Development Bank, and the Asian Development Fund (ADF) at the Asian Development Bank. The concessional windows provide funds at no interest, attaching a small service charge. Unlike the banks' regular loan operations, these funds are not raised from the capital markets, but rather through appropriations from the rich-country members.

82 Ayres, 1983, p. 226.

83 See Gershman and Fox, 1996, and Lipton and Maxwell, 1992.

84 World Bank, 1996b.

85 Carvalho and White, 1997.

86 World Bank, 1996b, p. 84.

87 See Birdsall and James, 1990, p. 13, and Angell and Graham, 1995a, 1995b.

88 *Investing in Health* acknowledges the economic roots of ill health and states that improvements in health are likely to result primarily from advances in non-health sectors. The study calls for increased family income, admits that the market is not perfect in shaping health-care systems, and acknowledges that structural adjustment programs were "indiscriminate" in their impact on health services. *Investing in Health* encourages increased health spending, focuses on violence against women as a major health problem, advocates essential drug programs, and argues that smoking cessation is integral to the achievement of health goals.

The endorsement of essential drug programs and the antismoking position are especially striking in light of the Bank's history of enforcing substantive measures to preserve the tobacco and pharmaceutical industries' liberal access to Third World markets.

89 Buse and Gwin, 1998.

90 The 7 percent figure is from fiscal 1997. Since the mid-1980s, HIV/AIDS and safe-motherhood projects, and in the 1990s early childhood development projects, have grown as a percentage of the health portfolio.

91 World Bank, 1987a.

92 *Economist*, October 7, 1995: A two-year study in Indonesia found that an increase in user fees at public health centers led to declining use of health care and to reduced labor force participation among the test population. WHO, 1999, Box 1.3, p. 10.

93 World Bank, 1990b, 1992a.

94 See Lennock, 1994.

95 See Lennock, 1994, p. 14.

96 Bank economists' arguments for cost recovery are based on four principal claims: (1) The poor are already paying. In Africa, out-of-pocket expenditures already account for over 40 percent of total health spending (Shaw and Griffin, 1995). In the World Bank's eyes these expenditures reflect a willingness and ability to pay for health services. (2) Cost-recovery financing improves services. Cost recovery increases the resources available for health care, and if used for improved services, can improve public health. (3) Cost recovery improves efficiency. This goes along with the idea that a pricing system, particularly one that increases as the scale of care increases, will lead to more "rational" decisions on the part of patients to choose the lowest level of care appropriate for their illnesses. Prices, as the means of allocation in a market, determine efficient outcomes by definition. (4) Cost recovery is consistent with equity. If the poor are exempted from user fees and finances from cost-recovery systems are directed into primary care services, then the cost-recovery system will serve a redistributive function and promote equity.

As one might imagine, the devil is in the details as countries attempt to implement these policies in the real world, where needs are not always translated into effective demand because people lack resources, and where the logic of fund-raising undermines attempts to exempt the poor from user fees. On several points, the World Bank's principles and prescriptions reveal themselves as out of touch with real-world patterns.

We must question the notion that because the poor already pay, they must be able and willing to pay. This idea stems in part from what is known as the *price-elasticity of demand* for health services. In plain English, this is a measure of how price-sensitive the demand for a good or service is (the service in this case being health care). A low elasticity of demand suggests that price increases will not significantly alter the demand for health services, while a high elasticity of demand suggests that price increases will reduce demand for health services. Many studies rely upon average price elasticities, which may disguise significant differences between the elasticities in poor and wealthy households. In fact, the elasticities can be four times higher for poor households than for wealthy ones. The reason is straightforward: poor families have to balance insufficient resources among food, shelter, health care, and other necessities. Price increases in health services turn health care into a luxury, pricing poor families out of the market. User fees, then, can worsen pre-existing inequalities in access to health care (see the studies cited in Watkins, 1997).

It must not be ignored that in chronically underfunded sectors, the logic of revenue maximization often overrides the logic of equity, leading to cases where the poor are not freed from user fees. In Zambia, for example, the statutes on fee exemptions are very clear, exempting all children under five, those in chronic poverty, all those with infectious diseases, and patients suffering from life-threatening diseases. The World Bank's poverty assessment for the country found that while senior medical staff were aware of the rules, the clerks and administrators responsible for fee collection were not! In reality, the guidelines were ignored and exemption provisions minimal. As Kevin Watkins of Oxfam UK&I asked, "Are people incapable of acting in an economically rational manner in response to market forces, or are economists incapable of understanding the real constraints under which poor communities operate?" (Watkins, 1997) For a more in-depth discussion of the impact of user fees and other cost-recovery mechanisms, see Chapter Six on Peru in this volume.

97 Two types of errors are generally identified in the targeting literature. Type I errors involve excluding some of the poor (the intended targets) from the beneficiaries. Type II errors involve including the non-poor among the poor, intended beneficiaries. For more on targeting, administrative costs, and errors, see Ahmad, 1993, and Stewart, 1995. Also see Skocpol, 1995, for a discussion in the U.S. context.

98 See Grosch, 1991, 1993.

99 Ahmad, 1993, p. 374. See also Nelson, 1992.

100 See Fox and Aranda, 1996; Graham, 1994.

101 Graham, 1994, p. 252.

102 Buvinic, Gwin, and Bates, 1996, p. 64.

103 Those interested in reading an early draft outline of the next *World Development Report* on poverty can see it at the World Bank's website: www.worldbank.org/-poverty/wdrpoverty/index.htm.

104 Lipton, 1985, p..4.

105 Lipton, 1996, p. 73. Land reform, understood as redistribution of land rights to the rural poor, can play a major role in poverty reduction, if combined with other policies like agricultural extension and credit. The benefits include generally greater farm output, as well as an enhanced capacity among the rural poor to raise their voice in debates over economic and social policies. The key seems to be redistributive policies that strengthen productivity.

106 Birdsall and Londoño, 1997, p. 36.

107 For details, see Gwin, 1997.

108 For a fascinating discussion, see Wade, 1996.

109 Catherine Conaghan's and James Malloy's evaluation of the relationships between local elites and the international financial institutions in Andean Latin America captures the essence in Latin America, if not elsewhere: "It would be a gross oversimplification to view the neoliberal experiments of the Central Andes as policy packages that were unilaterally imposed by external agents such as the IMF and the World Bank. These entities did indeed play a critical role in shaping economic policy, both by providing technical assistance to local economic teams and by exercising their powers to grant or deny aid to these debt-ridden countries. Yet they were not the sole authors of neoliberalism. In all three countries, business interest groups laid the groundwork for the development of domestic neoliberal coalitions with their antistatism campaigns that began during military rule" (Conaghan and Malloy, 1994, p. 216).

110 For more on these historical ideas, see Chapter Three of this book, "Terms Reconsidered," as well as Sachs, 1992.

111 In 1996, the U.S. poverty rate settled from 14.5 percent (1994) to 13.7 percent, but it was still well above the 12.8 percent trough in 1989, the peak of the last business cycle. In 1995, approximately 36 million Americans lived below the poverty line ($12,158 for a family of three). Nearly 24 percent of children under the age of six now live in poverty, and the child poverty rate has been stable, at or above 20 percent, since the early 1980s. The number of people with no health insurance in 1998—41.7 million, or about 15.7 percent of the U.S. population—remained unchanged since 1994. Between 1989 and 1996, America's poor households saw their real income decline by 3.2 percent. Middle-income households lost 3 percent, while rich households showed a gain in real income of more than 15 percent during the same period. See the websites for the Center for Popular Economics (www.ctrpopec.org) and United for A Fair Economy (www.stw.org).

112 See Chapter Three, "Terms Reconsidered," in this volume.

113 WTO, 1998, p. 12.

114 See UNCTAD, 1995, cited in WTO, 1996a. UNCTAD figures are a result of extrapolations, as there is virtually no data on this breakdown of world trade, with the significant exception of the United States. UNCTAD's intrafirm trade estimate is based on U.S. data. The estimates for sales involving TNCs' foreign affiliates are extrapolated from data from France, Germany, Italy, Japan, and the United States.

115 The original *Maquiladoras* were factories established at the U.S.-Mexico border, which assembled U.S. manufactured components for re-export to the United States, primarily in the electronics and garment industries. Now the term *maquiladora* has come to mean almost any labor-intensive assembly operation in almost any country. WTO, "World Trade Expanded Strongly in 1995 for the Second Consecutive Year," Press Release, March 22, 1996. For more on the *maquiladoras*, see Chapter Eleven in this volume.

116 See Overseas Development Institute, 1995, and Coote and Lequesne, 1996, ch. 2. It was widely believed that, following the global recession of the early 1980s and the recovery of the mid-1980s, commodity prices would return to something approaching their late-

1970s levels. This never occurred, despite the World Bank's consistently optimistic forecasts. Commodity export earnings were roughly equal in 1992 and 1973, in real terms (Overseas Development Institute, 1995, p. 1). Growth in services and manufacturing increased far more rapidly than in commodities, and the terms of trade continued to decline throughout the 1980s. Prices for non-oil primary commodities fell by more than half relative to prices for manufactured goods from 1980-1993 (World Bank, 1994c, p. 32).

Commodity-exporting countries' difficulties are compounded by protectionism among developed countries. Wealthy countries restrict access to their markets for processed goods. For example, Malaysia can export unrefined palm oil to the European Union (EU) at a tariff rate of 2 percent. If that oil is processed and turned into margarine, the tariff is 25 percent. The average industrial country tariff on chocolate is more than twice that on cocoa beans (see Cable, 1987, cited in Oxfam, 1995).

The long-term solution to commodity dependence is, of course, diversification of the economy. This is what took place in early primary-commodity producers like the United States and Australia. But that diversification took place behind tariff walls that allowed local industry to develop, and involved significant levels of investment (private and public). Trade-restricting policies are anathema in the age of free trade. And with structural adjustment's significant negative impact on investment rates, combined with the large portion of export earnings going to debt service, the prospects for the poorest countries seem limited.

117 DeJonquiers, "Survey of Global Economy and Finance," *Financial Times*, October 6, 1995, p. 21. All but three members of the WTO (Japan, South Korea, and Hong Kong) are members of such an agreement.

118 Lawrence, 1996a, p. 17.

119 See UNCTAD, 1994, pp. 163-164, and Bailey, Parisotto, and Renshaw, 1993, cited in Kozul-Wright, 1995, p. 157. For a more specific discussion of TNCs and employment, see Lall, 1995, and Chapter Eight in this volume.

120 Why do corporations transnationalize? That is, why do they move, rather than just export or license their technology to foreign companies? The interaction of three factors seems essential: (1) the firm owns assets that can be profitably exploited on a comparatively large scale; these assets include intellectual property (such as technology and brand names), organizational and managerial skills, and marketing networks; (2) utilizing these assets, it is more profitable for these corporations if their production takes place in different countries than it would be were the corporations to produce in and export from their home country exclusively; (3) the potential profits from "internalizing" the exploitation of the assets are greater than those from licensing the assets to foreign firms, and are sufficient to make it worthwhile for the firm to incur the added costs of managing a large, geographically dispersed organization.

121 The evidence includes the phasing-out of local content provisions required under the WTO as a result of the TRIMs (Trade-Related Investment Measures)

agreement of the GATT Uruguay Round. In 1992, the World Bank adopted "Guidelines on the Treatment of Foreign Investment," described in UNCTAD's *World Investment Report*, 1993 as generally promoting liberal entry and nondiscriminatory treatment, which can enhance poorer countries' access to foreign investments, but whose framework promotes the deregulation of such investments.

122 For background on the MAI, see Clarke and Barlow, 1997.

123 See Reich, 1992, and Ohmae, 1990, for the view that corporations are essentially de-nationalized or global. For an alternate view, see, for example, Stopford and Strange, 1991, p. 233, and Streeten, 1993. The "footloose" global model is at best a partial one and may apply to American-based TNCs more than others. First, most TNC operations remain within the advanced countries (the OECD states, or the so-called Triad of Europe, United States/Canada, and Japan). Second, the hundred largest TNCs (by size of foreign assets) account for about one-third of the combined outward foreign direct investment of their home countries. All 100 of the world's largest multinationals—ranked by assets abroad compared with those at home—are based in the rich countries. More than 30 are American, while 19 are Japanese. UNCTAD, 1996.

124 See Sassen, 1990; Shapiro, 1996; and Yoffie, 1993.

125 World Bank, 1998a, pp. 3, 20.

126 Net Official Development Assistance (ODA, or *foreign aid*) from the wealthy countries fell in 1996 to its lowest level since 1970. See World Bank, 1998a, p. 50.

127 See Krugman, 1998, and Stiglitz, 1998, for example.

128 The foreign exchange estimates are calculated after correcting for the double-counting resulting from local and cross-border inter-dealer transactions and for estimated gaps in reporting. The average daily turnover in "traditional" global foreign exchange instruments includes *spot* transactions, outright *forwards*, and foreign exchange *swaps*. Although the rate of growth in other over-the-counter foreign exchange derivative instruments (*currency swaps* and *options*) was considerably higher than in traditional ones, (from $45 billion in 1995 to $97 billion in 1998), they constitute a small fraction of overall trading. The other component of derivative instruments, *interest rate derivatives*, grew from $151 million in 1995 to $265 million in 1998. See Bank for International Settlements, 1998. Also see the *Economist*, October 10, 1995, p. 10 (special section on world economy), and the Triennial Central Bank Survey of Foreign Exchange and Derivatives Market Activity published by the Bank for International Settlements.

129 *Economist*, "Survey of the World Economy," October 7, 1995, p. 10.

130 Cited in the *Economist*, "Financial Indicators," April 26, 1997, p. 109.

131 In 1984, there were 29 global and international funds; by October 1995, there were 658. Over the same period, the assets of these funds grew from $5.2 billion to $264 billion. (*Global funds* invest anywhere, whereas *international funds* invest only outside the United States. See Fishman, 1995, p. 36.) British

Invisibles, a financial and business services export promotion firm, estimated that the global fund management industry's assets topped $22 trillion in 1995, with $8.2 trillion in pension funds, $5.3 trillion in mutual funds, and $6.4 trillion controlled by insurance companies. However, ownership of and trading in securities still remains overwhelmingly domestic. U.S.-based mutual funds alone are estimated to exceed $3 trillion in value. Data from "Global Fund Management," *Financial Times*, April 24, 1997.

132 Kindleberger, 1996.

133 Strange, 1998.

134 Importantly, the Mexican and Asian crises have different roots. In Mexico, government bonds (i.e., public debt) were at issue, while in the case of Asia private debt precipitated the crisis (private corporations owed foreign banks money, or owed domestic banks debts denominated in foreign currencies).

135 Singh and Weisse, 1998, p. 609; World Bank, 1998a, p. 3.

136 Currently, privatization is stretching into what were once considered the most essential responsibilities and prerogatives of the state: e.g., the monopoly on the sanctioned use of violence. One of the best known cases is that of Executive Outcomes, the first corporate private mercenary army, available to wage war on behalf of paying clients. To date, this corporate fighting force has acknowledged working for the governments of Sierra Leone and Angola. Its troops are former elite commandos of the South African apartheid military. A U.S. defense expert speculates that firms like Executive Outcomes may constitute the "small wave of the future in terms of defense and security, because the international community has abdicated that role." The same analyst notes: "You already see more and more people hiring private security firms to keep the Third World away from suburban America."

137 OECD data cited in the *Economist*, March 22, 1997, p. 129.

138 *Economist*, "The seismic shift in American finance," October 21, 1995, p. 75. While the share of households owning stock has risen in the 1990s, by 1995 almost 60 percent of households still owned no stock in any form, including mutual funds or defined-contribution pension plans. Moreover, many of those new to the stock market have only small investments there. In 1995, for example, fewer than one-third of all households had stock holdings greater than $5,000. In the same year, almost 90 percent of the value of all stock was in the hands of the best-off 10 percent of households. Not surprisingly, then, projections through 1997 suggest that 85.8 percent of the benefits of the increase in the stock market between 1989 and 1997 went to the richest 10 percent of households. See Mishel, *et al.*, 1999.

139 IMF, 1995, p. 165.

140 Koppes, 1999; Global Corporate Governance Research Center, 1999. For a useful discussion of the role of institutional investors see IMF, 1995, and Harmes, 1998. For a good, irreverent discussion of Wall Street, see Henwood, 1997. For a discussion of stock markets in developing countries, see Feldman

and Kumar, 1994; Singh, 1995, 1996, and 1997; and Singh and Weisse, 1998.

141 Useem, 1996, pp. 255-256.

142 Useem, 1996, p. 5.

143 Data from the Conference Board, cited in "Institutional investors lift equity holdings," *Financial Times*, August 20, 1998, p. 5.

144 For a discussion of the Tobin tax, see Ul Haq, 1996. See also Stiglitz, 1998.

145 Stiglitz, 1998.

146 Wade, 1998c, p. 23. See also Bhagwati, 1998; Krugman, 1994a; Stiglitz, 1998; UNDP, 1999, pp. 84-90; Wade, 1998a, 1998b; and Rodrik, 1998.

147 *Jakarta Post*, December 26, 1998. cf. UNDP, 1999, Box 1.5, p. 40.

148 *Jakarta Post*, October 11, 1998.

149 Krugman, 1996, p. 732. Krugman argues that the "Washington Consensus" policies bear a striking resemblance to the pre-Great Depression conventional wisdom. His conclusion is worth quoting at length: "There have been many warnings from researchers that at least some elements of the Washington consensus are unwarranted; but bankers and finance ministers think they know better. They don't. There is no wisdom on economic development, and there are no wise men. There is only economic theory, imperfect as it is, and empirical evidence; we should try to use them."

CHAPTER 3
Terms Reconsidered:
Decoding Development Discourse

1 UNDP, 1997.

2 Sen, 1985; Lappé and Collins, 1977.

3 Spencer, 1996, p. 4.

4 Sen, 1993, p. 44.

5 Nikiforuk, 1996; Giblin, 1992.

6 Van de Walle, 1997; Sen, 1985.

7 See also the "Human Poverty Index" (HPI), introduced in UNDP, 1997.

8 On the concept of "capabilities" see, e.g., Sen, 1993.

9 Sauvy, 1961. A "Fourth World" later emerged in the development literature to describe the very poorest and least developed countries, or those almost entirely reliant on foreign assistance. In other contexts, "Fourth World" has been used to designate indigenous minorities deprived of political autonomy and identity: "people without nations." Fourth World then implies a critique of the division of communities into nation-states. See Ponnampalam, 1992.

10 U.S. Bureau of the Census, 1996, p. 9; World Bank, 1998e.

11 See Frank, 1997.

12 Cited in Esteva, 1992, p. 6.

13 United Nations, 1993, p. 2.

14 United Nations, 1962.

15 Berthoud, 1992, p. 70.

16 Longworth, "Americans' Aid Views Foreign to Washington," *Chicago Tribune*, November 17, 1997. Cf. Moffet, 1995a, 1995b.

17 *Economic Report of the President*, 1998, p. 377.

18 OECD, 1998.

19 See, for example, Chossudovsky, 1998; Lappé and Collins, 1977. For examples of food aid, see Chapter Four in this volume.

20 Lobe, "Half of U.S. Foreign Aid Is Being Devoted to the Military Sector," *Interpress*, July 31, 1998.

21 U.S. State Department, 1999.

22 U.S. General Accounting Office, 1994, p. 1.

23 U.S. General Accounting Office, 1994.

24 U.S. General Accounting Office, 1994, pp. 12-13.

25 U.S. General Accounting Office, 1994, p. 15.

26 Vitalis, "Dreams of Markets, Nightmares of Democracy," unpublished manuscript cited in Chomsky, 1994, p. 1. See also Chapter Four in this volume.

27 President Clinton, press conference, Dean Acheson Auditorium, Washington, D.C., December 16, 1997.

28 ACTIONAID, 1995.

29 Schmitt, 1998.

30 For further information about aid—how it is disbursed, the official assistance given by individual donor countries—as well as information on NGO-giving, see ACTIONAID, 1995.

31 "Smallest Slice of a Smaller Cake," *Economist*, October 18, 1997.

32 "Smallest Slice of a Smaller Cake," *Economist*, October 18, 1997.

33 Friedman, 1962.

34 It is worth noting, however, that many North American political liberals support neoliberal economic policies for developing countries in which they have a financial stake.

35 Neill, 1953.

36 Somewhat confusingly, the convergence of neoliberal free trade doctrine and traditional conservative views on limited government has led some commentators, mostly in England and Canada, to use the term "neoconservative" in reference to politicians like former British Prime Minister Margaret Thatcher. The "neoconservative" label is then occasionally attached to these leaders' social and economic policies, as well. Meanwhile, many Latin Americanists have thought that "neoconservative" was a better description of the authoritarian governments that usually implemented "neoliberal" trade policies in that region. In most instances, the terms are used interchangeably, although some make an explicit distinction.

37 Marshall, 1890.

38 Friedman, 1962.

39 Friedman, 1962.

40 Germany's recently elected Chancellor Gerhard Schröder has been outspoken in critiquing certain aspects of neoliberal doctrine and practice. At this writing, however, it remains unclear whether his government's actual policies will depart dramatically from those of former Chancellor Helmut Kohl.

41 See Routh, 1989, pp. 218-231; Robbins, 1994, pp. 30-37.

42 Berthoud, 1992, p. 70.

43 When the economists who popularized the Washington Consensus imagined those Poor World officials best suited to implement the model, they pictured people very much like their own colleagues—"technocrats who have taken the risk of accepting political appointments" (Williamson, 1994). Neoliberal policies have been designed by a fairly narrow transnational coterie. It is not surprising that the hardship they cause among the poor is seen to be peripheral.

44 Epping, 1995, pp. 82-83.

45 Chomsky, 1996b, pp. 104-105.

46 Chomsky, 1996b.

47 John O'Sullivan, quoted in Carrier, 1997, p. 2.

48 Carrier, 1997, p. vii.

49 Carrier, 1997, p. 1.

50 Chossudovsky, 1998, pp. 60-61.

51 An important marker of this shift was the publication of the World Bank's widely discussed *World Development Report 1997*, entitled *The State in a Changing World*. The *Report* argues for recognition of the positive contributions that an effective state can—indeed, must—make to development and the "long-term health and wealth of a society." "Good government is not a luxury—it is a vital necessity for development" (World Bank, 1997d, p. 15).

52 Osava, 1998.

53 Filmer, Hammer, and Prichett, 1997, pp. 4, 38.

54 World Bank, 1997d, pp. 7, 4.

55 Taylor and Pieper, 1996, p. 94.

56 World Bank, 1997d, pp. 32-33.

57 World Bank, 1997d, pp. 2-3.

58 Taylor and Pieper, 1996, p. 95.

59 World Bank, 1997d, p. 3. Emphasis in original.

60 *Harper Collins Economic Dictionary*, 1991.

61 World Bank, 1995; Ravallion, 1997.

62 Meadows, Meadows, Randers, *et al.*, 1972; see also Daly, 1987; Daly and Cobb, 1989.

63 Epping, 1995, p. 93.

CHAPTER FOUR
Hypocrisies of Development and the Health of the Haitian Poor

1 Weise, 1971, p. 38.

2 A 1996 report from the Washington Office on Haiti (WOH) estimated that 85 percent of the Haitian population lives below the poverty level (Washington Office on Haiti, 1996). The most recent World Bank figures available for poverty in Haiti, however, list 65 percent of the population below the national poverty line in 1987 (World Bank, 1997c). Considering the critique of measures of poverty found in the previous chapter and the authors' experience working in rural Haiti, the WOH estimate seems more plausible.

3 For an early, influential statement, see Bryant, 1969.

4 This type of analysis has a long history in Haiti, as we discuss later in the chapter. For a recent example of how

miserable conditions may be attributed to local factors, see the work of Lawrence Harrison, who was director of USAID in Haiti and the author of an influential article based on the hypothesis that Haiti's *culture*, rather than the country's history and political economy, is to blame for Haiti's poverty (Harrison, 1985, 1993). A more thorough critique of Harrison, and of this mode of analysis, is to be found in Farmer, 1994.

5 For more on the history of the French colony of Saint-Domingue, see Madiou, 1989; Moreau de Saint-Méry, 1984; James, 1963; Farmer, 1992, 1994.

6 Weise, 1971, p. 38.

7 Cauna, 1984.

8 Foubert, 1990.

9 Bordes, 1979, pp. 16-17. Paragraphing altered. Bordes fails to note that many of the health workers were not allowed to "bleed or to bandage" white patients. See Moreau de Saint-Méry, 1984, p. 559.

10 St. John, 1884, p. xi.

11 Grosvenor, 1920.

12 Swan, 1921.

13 Gaillard, 1983, pp. 261-262. For a review of these and other data, see Farmer, 1994.

14 The figure for infant mortality in the United States is from 1960 (U.S. Department of Commerce, 1970).

15 For a review of these data, see the report by Sebrell, Smith, Severinghaus, *et al.*, 1959. These authors felt that the infant mortality rate of 250 was likely to be an underestimate.

16 See the following surveys: Jelliffe and Jelliffe, 1961; Sebrell, Smith, Severinghaus, *et al.*, 1959; King, Dominique, Uriodain, *et al.*, 1968; Beghin, Fougère, and King, 1965; LaRoche, 1965; Klipstein, Samloff, Smarth, *et al.*, 1968.

17 Berggren, Ewbank, and Berggren, 1981.

18 The abuses of the Duvalier dictatorship have been much commented upon, and are the subject of several books. Some of these—for example, Trouillot, 1990; Dupuy, 1996; Nicholls, 1996—are excellent; others are informative but echo the lurid exoticism seen in mainstream commentary on Haiti and Haitians.

19 As those flying over the island know, the border separating Haiti and the Dominican Republic is starkly traced. The eastern third of the island of Hispaniola is a corrugated, treeless expanse of brown and red dry hills; the Dominican side of the dividing line remains green. Most of the tropical rain forest in Haiti was destroyed in the nineteenth century; by 1954—before François Duvalier came to power—only 8 to 9 percent of the country remained forested (Lewis and Coffey, 1985). Under continued economic stress, rural Haitians have been left with little option but to cut down the few remaining trees to produce charcoal for the domestic market. For the diminishing forested lands that remained, the World Bank estimated an annual deforestation rate of 5.2 percent between 1980-1990. Forest cover in 1998 stood at less than 1.5 percent (*Caribbean Insight*, July 1998, p. 7). With the destruction of trees comes increased erosion and soil loss. Between 1980 and 1994, the amount of arable land per capita declined by 25 percent (World Bank, 1997c).

20 Farmer, 1988.

21 Grunwald, Delatour, and Voltaire, 1984, p. 232.

22 The number of Haitians employed by the assembly sector peaked above 100,000 in 1991 and has since declined to about 23,000 (EIU, 1998a). Of the nearly 200 plants in operation in 1980, approximately 60 are still in operation—more than half of which violate Haiti's "generous" minimum wage laws (see National Labor Committee, Press Release, January 30, 1996). Recent pressure from a U.S.-based campaign against the Disney Corporation's treatment of Haitian laborers in its garment assembly plants resulted in public embarrassment for Disney and the loss of 2,300 jobs in Haiti. One reading of this event would be that worker exploitation is a condition for investment; when Disney was pressured to improve working conditions they decided it was easier to pack up and leave for friendlier shores (EIU, 1998a).

Commenting on lender promotion of export-led growth in a highly volatile political situation, Camille Chalmers, a prominent Haitian economist, notes: "To base development on the illusion of massive foreign investment would be criminal. Despite government efforts to attract investment, capital is actually flowing out, not in" (Richardson and Chéry, 1995, p. 10).

23 Grunwald, Delatour, and Voltaire, 1984, p. 232. The dependency ratio is a measure of how many people are supported by each worker. Considering the recent population growth in Port-au-Prince and the declining assembly sector, Grunwald, Delatour, and Voltaire's 25 percent becomes a mere 7 percent.

24 Cited in Lawless, 1992, p. 116.

25 Diederich, 1985. For discussion of the effects of the U.S.-initiated pig extermination project on one community, see Farmer, 1992.

26 In a devastating review of the recent literature, Jean-Louis, 1989, states that 5 percent of rural Haitians have access to potable water. More recent reports list a figure of 28 percent of the Haitian population with access to safe water. This is to be compared to figures for the neighboring islands: 79 percent in the Dominican Republic; 93 percent in Panama; 86 percent in Jamaica; 97 percent in Trinidad and Tobago; 96 percent in Cuba (UNDP, 1997; Bread for the World, 1998).

27 Feilden, Allman, Montague, *et al.*, 1981, p. 1.

28 Reported in the *Miami Herald*, April 25, 1987. See the reviews by Beghin, Fougère, and King, 1970; Feilden, Allman, Montague, *et al.*, 1981.

29 Hancock, 1989, p. 180.

30 Lappé, Collins, and Kinley, 1980, p. 97; Richardson, 1997.

31 See DeWind and Kinley, 1988.

32 Hancock, 1989, p. 180.

33 See Wilentz, 1989, p. 270, for more on popular impressions of the "American Plan." These are also discussed in Farmer, 1994, Part I.

34 UNICEF, 1993b.

35 Population Crisis Committee, 1992.

36 All quotations are drawn from interviews conducted between 1985-1996 by the first author. To protect the people of Kay, we have used pseudonyms for the name of the village and its residents.

37 Moral, 1961, p. 325.

38 During the dry season, however, many peasants of the region still run the risk of planting corn, tobacco, beans, yams, and other crops below the high-water mark. They often lose bountiful harvests to early rains, which fill the reservoir just as the crops are ripening.

39 For more on the *lakou*, see Bastien, 1985; Laguerre, 1978.

40 Richardson, 1997.

41 Kennedy and Tilly, 1996; Richardson, 1997.

42 For more on the effects of neoliberalism on Haitian agriculture, see "Producers Struggling," *Haiti Info*, August 19, 1995, and "Neoliberalism in Haiti: The Case of Rice," *Haiti Info*, September 16, 1995. It must be noted that there is precious little in the way of systematic research on food production and consumption in rural Haiti. For a review of available data, and a summary of his own mixed-methods research on food security in Haiti, see Woodson, 1997.

43 It is estimated that 30 percent of the original capacity of the lake above the Péligre dam has been lost to soil eroding into the basin (Lewis and Coffey, 1985). In a layer of irony added to the tragedy of the dam project for the people of Kay, the dam has become such an inconsistent source of electricity that most assembly plants in Port-au-Prince have their own generators (EIU, 1998a, p. 39).

44 Washington Office on Haiti, 1996.

45 Moral, 1961.

46 More recent, locally directed development efforts are described in Farmer, 1992, chapters 4-5.

47 For reviews of some of the health problems in Haiti and among Haitian refugees during this period of time, see Chelala, 1994; Centers for Disease Control, 1993; Bawden, Slaten, and Malone, 1995.

48 This number does not include the 2,000 persons drowned with the foundering of the *Neptune*, a passenger ferry, on February 16, 1993. This may have been the worst disaster in modern maritime history. It went largely unnoticed.

49 See PAHO, 1993, as cited in Chelala, 1994.

50 For more on how we came to work in Kay see the description of Partners in Health in Chapter Sixteen of this volume. See also Farmer, 1992, chapters 4-5.

51 Changes in Patient Profile, Clinique Bon Sauveur:

	1990 (N=32,744)	1993 (N=17,428)
Measles	16 (0.0005%)	352 (0.020%)
Tuberculosis	448 (0.014%)	409 (0.023%)
Typhoid	240 (0.007%)	286 (0.016%)
Rapes	0	4 (0.0002%)
Assaults	26 (0.0008%)	47 (0.0027%)
HIV Infections	94 (0.003%)	145 (0.008%)

52 PAHO/WHO-Haïti, 1993.

53 Harvard Center for Population and Development Studies, 1993. For a discussion of the high level of efficacy estimated for measles vaccine in the prevention of mortality in young children in a poor community in Haiti, see Holt, Boulos, Halsey, *et al.*, 1990.

54 Farmer, Robin, Ramilus, *et al.*, 1991.

55 For a recent review of the literature concerning nutritional stress and tuberculosis reactivation disease, see Farmer, 1999b; Mitnick, Furin, Henry, *et al.*, 1998.

56 For an analysis of 76 rape cases reported to the UN/OAS Mission Civile Internationale, see their 1997 report.

57 The shift observed in our patients coincides with evidence of nationwide massacres of civilians at the hands of government soldiers. See Glanz, 1995; Skolnick, 1995.

58 For an account of this politically motivated murder, see Part I of Farmer, 1994.

59 Farmer, 1995.

60 "Haiti—Health Goes Underground," InterPress Service, June 8, 1995.

61 Ventura and Ehrenkranz, 1976.

62 Centers for Disease Control, 1994.

63 Weil and Scarpaci, 1992.

64 Harvard Center for Population and Development Studies, 1993.

65 Howard French, "Study Says Haiti Sanctions Kill Up to 1,000 Children a Month," *New York Times*, November 9, 1993.

66 One of the study's authors later participated in a critique of the report. See "Physicians' group says a Harvard study erred on dying Haiti children," *Boston Globe*, November 24, 1993.

67 Cited in Richardson and Chéry, 1995, pp. 31, 32.

68 René Préval, prime minister under Aristide, brought nine state enterprises from deficit into surplus prior to the 1991 coup. Profits from Teleco, the state-owned telephone company, sustained the Aristide government during its three years in exile. Kennedy and Tilly, 1996, p. 11.

69 Prime Minister Smarck Michel, quoted in Richardson and Chéry, 1995, p. 32.

70 Some foreign observers agreed. According to Marie Kennedy and Chris Tilly, "Aristide's government was compelled to sign onto a preliminary version of the neoliberal plan in August 1994 as a precondition for U.S. support for Aristide's return, and accepted a more detailed agreement in January 1995 to keep desperately needed aid flowing" (Kennedy and Tilly, 1996, p. 10).

71 See Allan Nairn, "Aristide Banks on Austerity," *Multinational Monitor*, July/August, 1994, pp. 8-9. It is of note that Nairn's excellent reporting from Haiti appeared well outside of the mainstream.

72 Leslie Voltaire, cited in *Haïti-Progrès*, April 3, 1996, p. 1.

73 Alex Peuker cited in Nairn, 1994.

74 *New York Times*, October 25, 1994.

75 "Smarck Michel to apply the 'American Plan.'" *Haïti-Progrès*, October 26-November 1, 1994.

76 See "Patrick Bellegarde-Smith" (interview), *Progressive*, November, 1994, p. 32.

77 Quotations from Aristide are from an interview accorded the first author in October, 1996.

78 Cited by Richardson and Chéry, 1995, p. 31.

79 We hear comments like this all the time, and not only in Haiti. A week previously, we had been seeing tuberculosis patients in Peru, where a woman—living in Lima but from a family of *campesinos*—said much the same thing. "I keep relapsing," she said, through angry tears, "because I have nothing to eat. So please don't give me medicines without any food." She further linked the worsening of her situation to *fujishock*, the structural adjustment program discussed in Chapter Six of this book.

80 Cornia, Jolly, and Stewart, 1987. For more information, see the extensive annotated bibliography contained in Part Two of Costello, Watson, and Woodward, 1994.

81 Bread for the World, 1997, p. 106.

82 UNDP, 1997.

83 *Caribbean Insight*, September, 1995, p. 3. Even some of privatization's cheerleaders suggest that "those who advocate it on ideological grounds—because they believe that business is always superior to government—are selling the American people snake oil" (Osborne and Gaebler, 1992). Those who advocate privatization on the grounds of its increased efficacy are also making immodest claims, as recent studies suggest: "Evidence increasingly indicates that instead of providing cost-effective government services, private contracting by government produces exactly the opposite effect of helping private enterprise and special interests to benefit unfairly and sometimes unscrupulously from government" (Orthoefer, Empereur, and Bacon, 1995).

84 Richardson and Chéry, 1995, p. 33.

85 McMichael, 1995.

86 McCord and Freeman, 1990.

87 For further analysis, see Farmer, 1992.

88 Berggren, Ewbank, and Berggren, 1981.

CHAPTER 5
Theoretical Therapies, Remote Remedies: SAPs and the Political Ecology of Poverty and Health in Africa

1 In this chapter, we use "Africa" to refer to sub-Saharan Africa (SSA).

2 The "Washington Consensus" refers to a loose alliance including leading international financial institutions (IFIs) such as the World Bank and the International Monetary Fund (IMF); the U.S. Government, as the IFIs' major financier; and the network of scholars and development experts whose work defined the conventional economic wisdom of the SAP era and translated that wisdom into policy.

   In undertaking a chapter on Africa, we recognize, of course, that a regional overview cannot do justice to the many differences among countries, their resources, histories, current policies, and political forces.

However, space constraints forbid us to do more. Nor can we conduct a sector-by-sector review of SAPs and their impact on the health of the poor. Nevertheless, we hope that this chapter, drawing upon the authors' experience in 20 different countries, will orient readers to the issues, and stimulate them to consult references. We have omitted from consideration the two most populous sub-Saharan states (Nigeria and Ethiopia) and South Africa, because none of us has the indispensable firsthand knowledge needed to analyze recent literature.

3 The origins of SAPs are detailed in Chapter Two.

4 For the earlier growth strategies and the effects of austerity measures imposed by the IFIs on profits and poverty in Africa, see Seidman and Makgetla, 1980. One African scholar notes that as historians have neglected the fundamental causes of the continent's crisis, an "active process of rewriting history has occurred…[making African leaders' policies] of the 1960s and 1970s appear highly irrational" (Mbilinyi, 1994, p. 43). This is hardly surprising. For centuries Africans were considered peoples without history worthy of study, except as they appeared on the European stage (Hopkins, 1973, pp. 1-3). Also see Williams, 1944; Wolfe, 1982. Meanwhile, Professor Ali Mazrui (1991) argues that the state still has an important role to play in African economies that cannot be replaced by privatization.

5 "Neo-classical economics is unable to treat power as an intrinsic part of economic life or to analyze the importance of economic interests to the exercise of power. Hence many economists call on detached and disembodied governments to make decisions about 'the economy' for the benefit of 'the society'" (Cooper, 1993, p. 87).

6 The phrase is from Moore, 1958.

7 With respect to her country of origin, anthropologist Christine Obbo formulates a paradigmatic metaphor of external/internal dynamics: "Colonial policies… sowed the seeds of the weeds that have now overrun Uganda. However Ugandans must take blame for nurturing rather than uprooting and destroying the weeds" (Obbo, 1991a, p. 205). Obbo's exemplary ethnography, published from 1980, documents the everyday practices of survival strategies and shows how structural violence turned into corporeal violence at different political junctures. To critical scholars like Obbo, the power wielded by IFIs, Western governments, and transnational corporations over African governments, economies, and people remains decisive.

8 One critical new element in the 1980s was the enhanced power of the Washington Consensus to exert direct influence over African states' economic and political policy choices, as private banks and lending governments were persuaded to act in concert with the IFIs. Neo-classical theory became dogma in the "conservative revolution" that elected right-wing governments in Western Europe, Japan, and the United States. Firmly under the sway of large corporate interests, these governments also dominated IFI policy. The IFIs became African governments' most important source of foreign funds, and the "enforcer"

of debt repayment to foreign private banks and governments. The IFIs in effect operated "bailouts" for banks that had made bad loans and governments that insured banks' losses. The "debt overhang" and the ideology of the "conservative revolution" increased the IFIs' ability to convince other lenders to act in concert with them. Debt and "la politique de concertation" (the politics of concertation) are discussed later in this chaptetr.

9 Another new feature is that instead of blaming "traditional peasant mentalities" or culture (see Seidman, 1977), attention in some countries is directed toward official corruption as a major obstacle to development. Zaire and Uganda were prime examples from the 1960s; Central African Republic, Togo, and others were not far behind (Gould, 1980; Young and Turner, 1985; Young, 1996). We return to this subject later in this chapter.

10 In Zaire, for example, health and agriculture data were often "cooked" at three levels (at least): local reporting, regional offices, and the capital, according to exactly what purpose the data were destined to fulfill.

11 The dearth of reliable country-level health data renders this methodology particularly appropriate. It also allows us to understand the interplay of "structure and agency"; that is, how the efforts of individuals and groups to affect their circumstances may be constrained by wider conditions that they are powerless to overcome (Marks, 1987; Schoepf, 1991a, 1998).

12 See Sigerist, 1951; Rosenberg, 1962; Schoepf 1988b, 1991b; Farmer, 1999a.

13 Schoepf, 1988b, 1991a; Schoepf, Rukarangira, Schoepf, et al., 1988. Useful analysis of interconnections between AIDS and society and the effects of the pandemic on peoples' lives are found in Miller and Rockwell, 1988; Berer, 1993; WHO, 1994; Reid, 1995; Farmer, Connors, and Simmons, 1996.

14 In some places, women deliver at home by preference, or due to cultural proscriptions (see Sargent, 1989). In Kinshasa, however, women reported that poverty and user charges kept them from seeking out maternity services, despite such a decision being illegal (Schoepf, Walu, Russel, et al., 1991; Walu, 1991). Hospitals and maternity centers required mothers to pay their fees before they could take their babies home. The longer the delay, the larger the bill. Some mothers and babies were actually held prisoner. Dangerously unsanitary conditions and staff corruption at Kinshasa's public hospital continued, perhaps even worsened, under the Kabila regime (Tangua, 1998).

15 Unlike countries such as Tanzania and Mozambique, which provided free primary services, prior to SAPs neither health nor education were free in Zaire. Only higher education, from which the poor were blocked by lack of access to adequate secondary education, was free in the 1980s. Private schools and clinics mushroomed in the 1980s.

16 The term used to describe these cuts, assainissement, is unintentionally ironic; it means "cleaning up" and, by extension, making healthy. Bringing health to the budget, this "housecleaning" also brought malnutrition, illness, and worry to low-paid government employees, their families, and those whom they formerly served. Retrenched civil servants and their families no longer had access to free health care. Not only high-level officials, but thousands of nonexistent "ghost workers" (fantômes), whom a housecleaning might have been expected to sweep from the payroll, remained in place. The phantoms were a boon to needy administrators, who collected their pay packets. Although Zaire (now Congo again) has been viewed as a worst-case scenario, many of the processes of corruption—some linking internal and external actors—came to be found in other countries as the crisis deepened. In fact, Zaire was a harbinger of crisis—with all its attendant processes—rather than an exception (Schoepf, 1981).

17 There are no statistics, but African social scientists, as well as Oxfam and UNICEF, agree that alcoholism and domestic violence have soared during the crisis. Raikes, 1989; Sheikh-Hashim and Gabba, 1990; Wakabi and Mwesigye, 1991; Dédy and Tapé, 1995; Turshen, ed., 1999.

18 The term commonly used for such a relationship is deuxième bureau ("second office"). The family of a socially recognized second wife generally concurs in the arrangement, and receives a gift from the husband.

19 This was another sign of hard times.

20 Leaders of a churchwomen's club pointed to abandonment, divorce, and widowhood, and especially a child's medical expenses, as circumstances forcing women without other resources into commercial sex work.

Nsanga's new baby was sickly and died before her second birthday, following prolonged fever, diarrhea, and skin rashes; Nsanga believed the death was due to semen from so many men that spoiled her milk. She blamed herself for ignoring the abstinence period following the baby's birth.

21 Nsanga reported a few bouts with sexually transmitted diseases (STDs), for which she bought some pink tetracycline pills from the drugstore. In 1988, she had abdominal pains for several months, but without money to consult a doctor, she again self-medicated. Nsanga said: "What else could I do? The European nuns at the [neighborhood] dispensary do not treat STDs. They call them 'immorality sickness.' If you go to the University Hospital [nearby] they charge you more than you make in a month." The cost was $15 at the time; patients who did go to the hospital were told to return the next day for lab tests that cost as much again. Antibiotics likewise had to be purchased in the private sector. At the time, tetracycline—prescribed because strains of organisms resistant to cheaper antibiotics were said by physicians to abound—cost another $12. Although they did not blame patients for failure to buy the full course of medications, physicians expressed frustration at their inability to practice good medicine (B.G. Schoepf, fieldnotes, Kinshasa, 1987).

22 Nsanga's defensiveness was shared by many women. Denial was a stratagem for coping with situations that women saw no way to change. Avoidance, denial, and notions of propriety combined with poverty and gender inequality to increase young women's vulnerability. For many adolescent women, desire does not enter in; they are socialized for submission and frequently

coerced into sex. Abusive or not, anatomical and physiological immaturity of the adolescent reproductive tract renders sex with older men, who may be HIV-infected, extremely risky for these women.

23 Nsanga's death had serious implications for her children. Poor, orphaned children are at especially great risk for HIV, but they are not alone. With many wealthy men looking for ever-younger partners whom they believe less likely to be infected, the temptation for poor families to betroth and marry off their girls is very strong. The deepening crisis leaves less money to pay school fees, buy clothes, and bribe poorly paid teachers to give children passing grades (TGNP, 1993; Dédy and Tapé, 1995; Schoepf, 1998). In the cities and market towns, poor girls may be forced into commercial sex work to help their families survive, while boys sell notions on the streets, run errands, or pull heavy carts. Even in the small market centers, "bicycle boys," who have left school, work in the informal sector, transporting produce to market. In Rwanda, where bikes are beyond most rural people's means, men and boys push wooden scooters up and down the steep hills. Those with money in their pockets might share it with girls in exchange for sex. Youngsters will take up condoms if adults allow them to gain access to free supplies (B.G. Schoepf, field observations: Kinshasa, Zaire, 1987-1990; Lusaka, Zambia 1990; Dar-es-Salaam and rural Pemba, Tanzania, 1991; Kampala and rural Rakai and Mbale Districts, Uganda. See also Schoepf, 1992; Setel, 1996).

24 In 1992, B.G. Schoepf debated with the director of a development agency in Uganda who argued that *abstinence* would protect youth, including girls and young women, and therefore there was no need for his agency to promote condoms.

25 We begin with colonization but are mindful that the trading history of Europe and Africa extends far back in time. In the late Middle Ages, Africans produced an estimated two-thirds of the world's gold. Blatant European exploitation began in the 1500s, when the trans-Atlantic slave trade that propelled Western capitalist accumulation disrupted earlier internal African trade and economic growth. Africa lost an estimated 30 million people, many more than the conservatively estimated 12 million who actually arrived in the New World. Africa also was burdened with tremendous destruction of property, dismantling of socio-political institutions, and loss of cultural coherence.

Williams (1944) documented the contribution of slavery to the development of capitalism, primarily in England. Wolfe (1982) analyzed relations between Europe and the "People without History." Additional sources offer diverse views of the slave trade. For example, Ly, 1957; Curtin, 1968, 1969; Rodney, 1970; Hopkins, 1973; Lovejoy, 1986; Miller, 1988.

26 "Scorched earth" refers to the policy of systematically setting fires to destroy villages and fields. In Tanganyika (now mainland Tanzania), cultivators forced to grow cotton revolted in 1905. The Maji Maji rebellion spread across southern Tanganyika. Germans prevailed by brutal mass killings, burning homes and crops across the region. About 75,000 people are estimated to have died from starvation (Iliffe, 1969, pp.

294-296). In the Congo (Zaire) the Tetela carried on a rebellion from 1895 to 1907. In SouthWest Africa (Namibia) the Germans killed 60,000-70,000 Herero people (more than 80 percent of the total population) in 1904. They also killed large numbers of Nama who disappeared as a people. These were the first genocides of the 20th century (Boahen, 1990). In Kenya the coastal Giriama rebelled in 1914; in Nyasaland (Malawi) the Chilemba rising occurred in 1915 (Leys, 1973). Pro-independence demonstrations and strikes continued to be met with killing force until the end of colonial rule (Hopkins, 1973).

27 *Rinderpest* was believed to have been introduced by infected European donkeys brought to Somalia by Italian conquerors.

28 Ford (1971) traced the relationship between ecological change and *trypanosomiasis* in East Africa. Later, colonial expropriation restricted Africans' access to grazing land, so that only the wealthy could maintain their reconstituted herds (Dawson, 1987a, p. 89).

29 Mortality is generally high in these "virgin soil epidemics." See Onoge, 1975; Hartwig and Patterson, 1978; Turshen, 1984. Samarin (1989, p. 78) traced the spread of sleeping sickness to paths taken by colonization—along the navigable rivers. Norman Leys (1973, p. 303) noted that migrants' feces spread disease to villages along the roads. Originally published in 1924, Leys' work is the earliest political ecology of health we found for Africa. Also see Feierman, 1985; Feierman and Janzen, eds., 1992.

30 Young, 1996.

31 Long-lived examples of giant firms that reshaped African economies from the beginning of the twentieth century include Firestone Rubber in Liberia, Anglo-Dutch-owned Unilever (manufacturer of palm products in Congo and Southeast Asia, and of soap, oil, and margarine in Scotland), and Unilever's subsidiary, United Africa Company, which conducts trade across Africa (Fieldhouse, 1978). Mulambu (1971) recounts the extreme, enduring brutality of this latter company, which became a target of popular rebellion in the 1960s. Mining and primary processing firms such as Anglo-American and later Lonrho had interlocking directorates and a web of subsidiaries across southern Africa to Congo. Wolf (1963) called them "the Cape to Katanga miners." Bookers', the British-based firm trading in West Africa and the Caribbean, also owned sugar estates. Belgian-based DeBeers Diamonds, with mining interests from southern Africa to Congo and Sierra Leone, still controls the world diamond market; its advertisements currently air on U.S. television. The Belgian-based Union Minière had interests in Congo and Australia; its directorate included directors of other corporations based in southern Africa, the United Kingdom, and the United States, as well as in the Belgian Société Générale (Merlier, 1962). For late colonial and post-independence activities of multinationals in Congo, see Willame, 1980; for Sierra Leone, see Kilson, 1969; for Zambia, see Sklar, 1975; for Kenya, see Kaplinsky, 1978.

32 Wild products collected by forced labor included rubber, beeswax, and copal resin. Cotton was one of the first crops to be cultivated by forced labor.

33 On crop requisitions, see Painter, 1987.

34 On the effects of extraction of forced labor from "labor reserves," see Leys (1973, pp. 294-305). Leys' discussion focuses on Kenya, where more than half the adult men were absent from agricultural villages at any one time in 1910-1925. For villages of the Sahel, in what is now Burkina Faso, see Skinner, 1960; also Davies, 1966; Painter, 1987. For Rhodesia, see Malaba, 1981; for French Equatorial Africa, see M'Bokolo, 1982. Similar practices were used in South Africa from the mid-nineteenth century (Bundy, 1970; Atkins, 1993).

Two fictions maintained the justification that withdrawal of men's labor would not cause harm. One was the myth of the "female farming system," in which women performed all agricultural labor. The second was the myth of the "lazy African" (man) who would benefit from work (performed for Europeans). In fact, when so many young men *were* withdrawn, men's work fell to women and children, and because they could not perform all tasks, much work went undone. Houses stood in poor repair. Fallow periods on which soil fertility depended were reduced because women could not clear forest re-growth. Weeds proliferated in old fields. Yields declined; hunger and famines resulted. "It is absurd to pretend that the absence of more than half the able-bodied male population…is not the chief cause of this chronic scarcity" (Leys 1973, p. 304).

35 The Congo-Ocean railroad was estimated to have caused one African death per tie laid, and one European death per kilometer of track (Coquery-Vidrovitch, 1972). Liberia offers a glaring example of export-oriented infrastructure: railroads link northern iron mines with seaports, but to get from the capital to the east of the country one must fly (B.G. Schoepf, fieldnotes, 1981).

36 A Health Officer in Kenya found "the conditions of life of laborers in Nairobi are inferior to those prevailing in the villages, and in Mombasa…[they] are inferior to those prevailing in slavery times…" (Leys, 1973, p. 292). In Nairobi in 1923, the death rate among Europeans was 8.4 per 1,000; for Asians 16.5 per 1,000; and for Africans 33.5 per 1,000, despite the fact that most Africans were healthy young workers when they arrived (Leys, 1973, p. 289, note 1). Segregated housing was the key, according to Leys, with Africans confined to unsanitary, densely packed shacks. Poor diet and overwork were also contributing factors.

37 Leys, 1973; Gann, 1963; First, 1982; van Onselen, 1976; Perrings, 1979; Painter, 1987; Cooper, 1996. Villagers in the Congo Copperbelt believed that whites were cannibals, because so many African men failed to return from the mines (C. Schoepf, fieldnotes, 1976).

38 Colonial administrators and male elders crafted new "customary" law-courts and "traditions" that removed kin-group protection and reduced women's status and autonomy (Channock, 1982, 1985; contributors to Hay and Wright, 1982; Schoepf, 1987; contributors to Parpart and Staudt, 1989; Mandala, 1990).

39 The hoe is the main agricultural implement among poor peasant women and men, a symbol of lack of technological progress. While some men obtained oxen or horses and plows, Rodney (1972) noted that Africans went into colonization wielding the hoe and emerged still using it. In many areas, hoe use is gendered, however (see Bryceson, 1995).

40 Roscoe, an early observer of Uganda, described Busoga women who refused to cultivate their gardens in protest over forced labor requisitions (cited in Leys, 1973, p. 304). The "Aba Women's War" in eastern Nigeria protested the administration's introduction of a tax on women (Van Allen, 1972). Women escaped their hardship and the drudgery of rural life working for old men by fleeing to the towns, where because wage work was unavailable, they developed an "informal economy." Their occupations included selling cooked and raw food, prostitution, and providing "the comforts of home" to migrant men (Little, 1973; Stichter, 1990a, 1990b; Stichter and Parpart, 1990; White, 1990).

41 Although in theory limited to 25 percent of able-bodied men, conscript migrant rates in the Belgian Congo were often higher.

42 Belgian colonial response to sleeping sickness is one example (Lyons, 1985). Also see reviews in Schoepf, 1991a; Vaughan, 1991; Comaroff, 1993.

43 Death tolls in hunger-weakened populations were high. For example, an estimated 50 to 80 thousand people in Tanzania (Turshen, 1984, p. 137).

44 Male migrant labor and "temporary wives" are cited by Leys (1973) in relation to low fertility in early colonial Kenya. Infertility induced by STDs would quite likely have had high rates of incidence earlier, as well, particularly among women slaves routinely subjected to sexual abuse. Disease is more likely than dangerous, induced abortion to explain slaves' low reproductive rates. For colonial concerns with low rates of population increase, see Schoepf, 1991a.

45 The slave trade in coastal West Africa had brought new epidemics of infectious disease a century or more earlier, thus partly accounting for the earlier writers' views. The quotation is from Patterson and Hartwig, 1978, p. 4. This essay, and the case studies and bibliographic survey (Patterson, 1978), along with Ford (1971), and Hughes and Hunter (1970), marked a new departure in history studies of health and disease in Africa.

On the health effects of slaving within Africa, see Williams, 1944; Rodney, 1970, 1972; Robertson and Klein, 1983. On Western perceptions, see Schoepf, 1991a; Comaroff, 1993. Dawson (1987b) cites the anti-yaws campaign of the 1920s, as an example of misguided public health action in Kenya. He argues that people infected with yaws early in life apparently developed immunity to syphilis. Thus, vaccination against yaws increased people's susceptibility to syphilis, a more severe treponema disease for which there was no vaccination nor cure until the diffusion of penicillin after 1940. As in the case of HIV/AIDS, socioeconomic and biological factors interacted to produce an epidemic.

46 Administrators and development planners in the Congo asserted that coercion was needed to induce Africans to work, and that because regular labor was the hallmark of civilization, forced cultivation was "educational" (Schoepf and Schoepf, 1981). Also see M'Bokolo (1982) for a related discussion on French Equatorial Africa.

47 The Belgian Congo was a particularly harsh extractive regime, but others were not far behind in their exploitation. Professor Vansina (1989, p. 344) estimated that during the early period of colonial rule, the population of Central Africa declined by between one-third and one-half. On the other hand, population *growth* should not necessarily be taken as a sign of prosperity. In many African settings, peasants' need for labor drives fertility, despite high rates of malnutrition (see Cordell and Gregory, 1987).

48 Profits from African labor and natural resources went to develop the "metropolitan" (European) countries, while Africa was "underdeveloped" (Rodney, 1972; Amin, 1974). The study by Williams (1944) cited earlier, while not using the same terms, provides ample documentation supporting this view.

49 Mamdani, 1996. Rebellions took place throughout the period (see Rotberg, 1971).

50 Although the colonial powers claimed a "civilizing mission," "African subjects were compelled to finance their own domination through labor and taxes." Professor Crawford Young calls the colonial state a "frugal gourmet" (Young, 1996, pp. 171, 223). Head taxes (collected everywhere but in the Gold Coast/Ghana) were used primarily to pay salaries of the repressive apparatus. In one colony, 63 percent of collected taxes went to salaries, with only 1 percent each for health and education. Taxes and forced labor conscription increased over time. As we discuss later, this situation was reprised in the 1980s.

51 Mining companies also established health services, initially to screen out the least healthy migrants, then (in the face of labor recruiting difficulties) to reduce death tolls. Considered expensive, these efforts were sketchy at first (Packard, 1989a, 1989b; Packard and Epstein, 1991; Vaughn, 1991; Feierman and Janzen, 1992).

52 The pretext was to prevent contagion, much of which actually spread in the other "direction," as noted previously.

53 African elites in British-ruled states of the West African coast and in the French-ruled "communes of Senegal" were exceptions; the Belgian Congo (later, Zaire/DRC) had a total of eight college graduates at independence in 1960. Everywhere, Europeans were on top, and Africans far below. In some regions, people of Mediterranean, Lebanese, and South Asian origin—all of whom the whites denigrated as "wogs" or "half-whites"—served as intermediary traders. Policies based on racialized perceptions of Africans created hierarchies between ethnic groups. Some, perceived as "smart," were trained to staff lower levels of the colonial administration and large exporting firms; others became skilled workers, replacing more highly paid European labor. Groups considered "warlike" were conscripted into the military; those considered "dumb" but strong were channeled to manual labor. In situations of "indirect rule," one group might be "born to rule," while a servile mentality was ascribed to others. The most flagrant and tragic example of delineation along these lines has been in the Great Lakes area of Central Africa; Sanders (1969) traces the origins of German racialist theory in the region. In Rwanda and Burundi, both German and Belgian administrators placed Tutsi in the

"ruler" category and Hutu among the servile, despite the fact that the Germans and the Tutsi aristocracy waged war against independent Hutu-ruled states in the north, and the Belgians removed Hutu chiefs and subchiefs from office in the interest of efficiency.

54 Again, coastal West Africa was an exception. Trader elites of the nineteenth century sent their sons to missionary schools and college. Some even traveled to Britain and France for advanced degrees. Hopkins (1973) is a useful introduction to the economic history of West Africa.

55 The new elites sometimes represented themselves as the only force able to contain rural protest.

56 Davies, 1966.

57 Agitation for independence by the Pan-African Movement began in 1910. In 1936, the French Popular Front government instituted the right to organize trade unions, and after the war the left governments supported further change in the colonies. The British colonies, too, were pressed to make improvements (Cooper, 1996, ch. 7-8). Also see Hodgkin, 1957, for an early optimistic view of independence, and Hodgkin, 1968, for the same author's more realistic commentary a decade later.

58 While vastly expanded bureaucracies incorporated Africans in the lower and middle ranks, many colonies still barred Africans from commerce in all areas but petty trade. Furthermore, colonized peoples had to pay for their own subjugation. *Parastatal* (state-owned) trading monopolies and price controls, for example, were introduced during World War II as a way to increase peasants' taxes for the war effort, and compulsory crop cultivation increased (often doubled) in French and Belgian colonies; state revenues rose between 50 and 100 percent during the war years (Young, 1996, p. 185). This mode of taxation endured following independence; post-war development doctrines favored state planning and bureaucratic expansion, currently under attack by the IFIs.

59 "The essence of the strategy was to capture emergent political forces and temper their militance" (Young, 1996, p. 192). An "identity of interest" between the new elite and the colonial oligarchy facilitated the transfer of power. According to one participant-observer: "Once the capitalist mode of production was firmly in place and the appropriate indigenous elements had been formed, colonial domination became superfluous" (Nyongo, 1978, pp. 7-8).

60 "In claiming knowledge to be the justification for continued imperial rule, [colonial powers] were also saying that Africa's forms of knowledge were irrelevant.... Control of knowledge was the raison d'être of colonialism." (Cooper, 1996, pp. 16, 275). This stance, we argue later in this chapter, was re-assumed with the Berg Report (World Bank, 1981), when Western advisors claimed to hold a monopoly on economic wisdom for Africa—wisdom they dispensed in the form of SAPs.

61 Africans were "subjects" rather than citizens (Mamdani, 1996).

62 Cooper, 1996. Also Ake, 1996; Mamdani, 1996; Young, 1996. In addition to the data and diverse ana-

lytical perspectives they present, these scholars also provide extensive bibliographies. See also Iliffe, 1987.

63 Young, 1996, p. 76. The Washington Consensus ignored the enduring effects of the colonial model of centralized, bureaucratic, authoritarian states. Intended or not, strategies that divided people in order to rule them and that co-opted local elites helped create post-colonial states unaccountable to their peasant majorities. For the transition from colonial rule to independence in Zambia, see Meebelo, 1971; for Congo, see Merlier, 1962.

64 Young, 1996, p. 242. Ghana, formerly the Gold Coast, gained independence from Britain in 1957. In the Portuguese colonies, wars of liberation continued until 1975; and not until 1980 and 1994, respectively, did liberation struggles in Zimbabwe and South Africa put an end to brutal white minority rule.

65 In a number of countries, following independence the small indigenous petty *bourgeoisie*—mainly traders, successful farmers, and civil servants, and some who straddled two or more activities—aided by state regulations, expanded their economic activities into plantations and small-scale industrial production (Illife, 1983). Country studies include Côte d'Ivoire (Campbell, 1984); Kenya (Kitching, 1980; Cowen, 1981); Swaziland (Harris, 1993); Zimbabwe (Weinrich, 1979). Some industries and infrastructure were state-owned enterprises (*parastatals*), funded by foreign loans, and often planned by foreign advisors from both private firms and development agencies. *Foreign* firms did very well under "nationalization" (Seidman, 1974b; Bates 1981a). Start up and operating costs for parastatal enterprises were often raised by TNCs' transfer pricing policies. For example, ISIs, with plants heavily dependent upon imported machinery, materials, and spare parts, were overcharged, while their exports were undervalued, as were commodities sold by foreign-owned trading companies on European markets. See Seidman and Makgetla, 1980. In Zaire, foreign technical and managerial experts were typically hired at salaries inflated by "hardship" bonuses, and given allowances for family travel, housing, and school expenses, and other perquisites; when Africans qualified for these posts, they sought the same level of remuneration. Although they were generally paid much less, it was still more than the industries wanted to bear. When salaries were eroded by inflation, work performance suffered. Then, highly paid expatriates were called in, to run the firms once again (B.G. Schoepf and C. Schoepf, fieldnotes, Lubumbashi 1977, 1979, 1981).

66 For a critique, see Seidman, 1974a; Seidman, 1974b.

67 Often, this "nationalization" of major firms meant the state's assuming the role of a junior partner while at the same time stabilizing monopoly industries and trading companies (Hopkins, 1973; Davidson, 1974, p 10).

Seidman (1974a, pp. 243-255) discusses the respective roles and interests of foreign firms, African elites, and urban workers. Foreign firms hired Africans in prominent positions to ensure against nationalization. Directors of (African) personnel were often the first to be "Africanized," with attendant possibilities for patronage. Places on boards of directors helped to make loyal supporters of economists and ministers, and engaged them to hold down wages. The absence

of an indigenous capitalist class led governments to develop infrastructure and basic industries under national control. Many states took more than a 51 percent (or greater) interest in the monopoly firms, then spent the profits of the next few years paying compensation, by which time the firms required substantial new investment to retain productive capacity. Governments then borrowed heavily, or allowed industrial capacity to deteriorate.

68 This was an aspect of African elites' Western orientation. Even in "socialist" Tanzania, donor-provided hospitals drove budget allocations, and "European" standards of care were sought by the elite, leaving very little for the rural health centers and dispensaries (Segall, 1973). Although these facilities were supposed to serve as referral hospitals for the hinterland, in practice, most users lived close to the hospitals. This pattern remained until the end of the 1960s, but began to change in the 1970s.

69 Despite socialist, even revolutionary rhetoric, former nationalist leaders capitulated to capitalist policy imperatives, so that most countries created mixed economies (Mazrui, 1991; Mamdani, 1996; Young, 1996). For the case of Zaire, see Mukenge, 1973.

70 Green and Seidman (1968) provide evidence of the interlocking directorates, monopolistic control, and political lobbying with respect to concessions to foreign investors. Pressured by the IFIs to accept these investment practices in the post-independence period, many leaders found their hands tied. Green and Seidman's proposals for regional economic integration remain pertinent today.

71 Ake, 1992, p. 34. The terms 'metropolitan powers' or 'metropoles' designate the former colonial rulers plus the United States and Japan. Other euphemisms include "the West" and "the North," while the term "Third World" distinguishes the South from East (the former Soviet bloc) and West, designations now outdated.

Some leaders played strategic cards to their advantage. For example, Mobutu used the U.S. plan to support Jonas Savimbi's UNITA forces in Angola with $15 million in arms transiting through the Kamina airfield in southern Zaire as a bargaining chip to acquire new resources for himself.

72 Such projects were often urged upon African rulers by commercial interests, designed by Western consultants, and carried out by Western contractors, who also benefited handsomely. Until the mid-1970s most loans were for "capital projects," that is, for infrastructure such as roads, ports, power, and communications to attract foreign investment (see, for example, World Bank, 1979; B.G. Schoepf, interviews, USAID, Kinshasa, 1975). Pean (1988, p. 9-12) suggests that corruption escalated throughout the Third World as a result of the huge projects, as rulers and intermediaries received illegal "commissions" (bribes).

Perhaps no officials were more venal than those in Zaire, which under Mobutu was a paradigm of corruption (Gould, 1980). Highly placed officials employed the use of embezzlement, theft, and threats, while private firms often operated by means of bribery. The ethical gangrene that spread throughout the system discouraged some foreign investors. For example, a Dutch engineer stated that he would recommend that his firm not bid on an infrastructure project in Zaire because "political overhead" was likely to cost as much as three times the 15 percent required in Côte d'Ivoire (B.G. Schoepf, interview, April 1975). Some NGOs, like the Rockefeller Foundation, withdrew their ventures, as did the TNC consortium put together by Maurice Templesman for a new copper and cobalt mine at Tenke-Fungurume. Each year, U.S. officials would say about the regime's corruption: "things are getting better" (B.G. Schoepf, conversations, Lubumbashi 1974-1981). A decade later, projects typically budgeted 50 percent of funds spent in-country for "unforeseen expenses" (B.G. Schoepf, interviews, Kinshasa, 1985-1987). For more interviews with local and foreign businessmen, see MacGaffey, 1991.

Some Western governments belatedly acknowledged that during the Cold War they supported a number of authoritarian, oppressive rulers who plundered their peoples. Support for these despots, undertaken for strategic reasons, was in effect support for human rights violations and economic ruin. Patrice Lumumba, the Congo's first elected prime minister, was actually deposed and murdered with the help of the Central Intelligence Agency (C.I.A.) (Stockwell, 1978). Milton Obote's second presidency was marred by corrupt practices that were pioneered in his first (1962-1972). To these practices, his second regime added state terror, which killed as many, if not more, people than had Idi Amin. In 15 years, government forces killed an estimated 300,000 people (see contributors to Hansen and Twaddle, 1991a). The IFIs and Western governments nevertheless continued lending to Obote's government, exacerbating the debt of Uganda's new government. Some case studies of complicity of institutional lenders and elites in other countries are documented by Campbell, 1984; Reyna, 1996; Uvin, 1998.

73 African intellectuals in the mid-1970s asked: "Who is aiding whom?" ("Qui Aide Qui?")

74 By the end of the 1970s, the "political class" was accused by foreign investors, economists, and diplomats of having carried on an "economy of plunder." Corrupt leaders took too large a share of wealth at the expense of maintaining the infrastructure and investment climate for profitable international business. The fraction of officials who actually acquired substantial assets is relatively small. Lower officials (or their relatives) run small businesses. Thus they form a "petite bourgeoisie," often termed an "elite" due to their privileged access to higher education. The size of the elites may be estimated from the fact that in 1988, only 1 percent of households had access to a motor vehicle (Bryceson and Howe, 1996, pp. 192-193). The true upper class is probably less than half that.

75 Deregulation of banks and currency markets allowed developed countries to recuperate laundered "hot money," including much of the capital loaned to underdeveloped countries (Naylor, 1987, cited in Hoogvelt, 1990; also Sayed, 1986; Hoogvelt, 1997).

76 To date the Bank has failed to acknowledge its part in that collaboration. Close reading of agency documents and interviews provides a general idea. For example, profit-making subterfuges by foreign firms were noted in a World Bank (1979, p. 62) report on the results of stabilization in Zaire, where "transfer pricing and unrecorded sales render the task of verifying and registering back-taxes by large companies very difficult."

77 The new class is often called a "state bourgeoisie," or more properly, a "politico-commercial bourgeoisie," because it includes government officials and private entrepreneurs, many with a foot in both camps (Schatzberg, 1980). Its members accumulated capital through privileged access to the state and foreign loans. Whatever terms they use, scholars agree that the post-independence period fostered increasing class differentiation, including increasing rural inequality. For analyses of state control, capital accumulation, and class formation, see Cohen, 1974; Williams, 1976; Leys, 1978; Mamdani, 1976; Seidman and Magetla, 1980; Bryceson and Howe, 1996.

Much accumulation derived from agricultural pricing controlled by parastatals, some inherited from colonial administrations, others instituted by post-independence governments. Presented as an attempt to wrest control of their economies from foreign trading monopolies, they continued to extract peasant resources, although sometimes at a lower rate (e.g., between 30 and 70 percent). Instead of providing capital for diversified development, however, many became notorious for inefficiency and corruption.

78 As Young (1996, p. 242) puts it: "The silent revenge of the colonial state was surreptitiously to embed in its post-independence successor the corrosive personality of Bula Matari." The latter was the name given by Africans in the Lower Congo, first to H.M. Stanley, then to the colonial state. Translated as "breaker of rocks," it signifies the brutality of naked power.

79 C. Leys, 1978, for Kenya; Vail, 1991, p. ix, for Malawi.

80 See Young, 1978, for a summary of rebellions in the former Belgian Congo from 1964; also Weiss, 1966 for lengthier treatment. Meebelo (1971) is an interesting source for the prelude to independence in Zambia's Northern Province. See Joseph (1977) for Cameroon.

81 First (1970) analyses early military coups. Years of wars of regional secession and civil war in the ex-Belgian Congo (1961-68), coups in Ghana and secession in Nigeria (1968) wrought tremendous hardship for the populations. In these and other countries, the military used civil disorder as a pretext for taking power and using the state for personal enrichment.

82 Considered highly successful until 1979, Côte d'Ivoire's main exports were cocoa and coffee. The Ivoirian "miracle" was made possible by continuing expropriation of peasant lands by a "planter class" composed of bureaucrats and rural merchants. This class expanded from 500 families in 1950 to 20,000 wealthy planters who, by 1965, controlled about one-fourth of all cultivated land (Campbell, 1984). Labor was supplied by the exodus of migrant labor from the impoverished, drought-prone North and from the Sahel, especially Mossi from Burkina Faso (see Skinner, 1960). Celebration of capitalist development did not refer to growing differentiation between various regions and categories of farmers. Peasants growing cotton in the northern savannah remained far outside the miracle (Campbell, 1984).

Côte d'Ivoire also attracted considerable foreign private capital for plantations. French investors, associated with Ivoirians, created ISIs that, protected by tariff barriers on imports of finished goods, used high levels of imported components and repatriated their profits. Some small farmers also made modest gains: incomes of wealthier peasant export producers rose by 2.8 percent per year between 1960 and 1975 (Dédy and Tapé, 1995). Coffee and cocoa prices rose in 1976-77, then fell in 1978. From 1978 through the mid-1990s, living standards declined steadily. The North continued in poverty under adjustment with over 60 percent classed as poor and one-fifth as "hard-core poor" in 1990. More than one-third of all export crop-producing peasants (36.4 percent) remained poor compared with 30.1 percent of a national sample (Kanbur, 1990, p. 41).

83 See contributors to Heyer, Roberts, and Williams, 1981; see also most contributors to Schoepf, ed., 1981. We criticized attempts to lay the burden of responsibility for past failures solely on the shoulders of local elites. We failed, however, to foresee the degree to which Africa's pain would unleash forces of mass destruction on the continent as elites competed for a share of a shrinking resource pie, and arms sales from more industrialized nations flooded the continent.

84 Prices for Ghana's exports of diamonds, manganese, and bauxite fell by 50 precent or more in 1975-1980. Although gold prices rose, Ghana's production fell, so that export revenues declined and economic crisis deepened (Rothschild and Gyimah-Boadi, 1986). World market prices for Africa's exports declined by an average of 20 percent from 1979 to 1984, and by 50 percent between 1985 to 1990, descending to levels not seen since the Great Depression of the 1930s (Helleiner, 1985; Clement, 1996). Metal prices (excluding gold) fell drastically. In particular, copper plummeted in 1975, throwing Zaire and Zambia into a tailspin. When tin prices fell in 1985, Rwanda lost 25 percent of its export revenues, and coffee thenceforth accounted for 90 percent. Then coffee, too, declined in the second half of the 1980s and early 1990s.

85 Post-independence governments in Zaire and Rwanda reinstated compulsory planting quotas; the Portugese continued these and forced plantation labor until the successful conclusion of wars of independence in 1975.

86 Adedeji, 1989.

87 Seidman, 1974a, p. 281.

88 OAU, 1980. Rereading source materials for this chapter, we were reminded that a decade earlier African governments had attempted to prevail upon the West to establish development policies favorable to broadly based growth and to stabilize terms of trade (cited in Seidman, 1974a, 1974b).

89 The Lagos Plan was criticized as a compromise political document that embodied a utopian wish list, rather than a set of priorities with strategies geared to meeting either general goals or specific quantified targets (Ravenhill, 1986). Notwithstanding, the Lagos Plan and subsequent proposals by the ECA and the United Nations presented practical short- and medium-term policy measures (see Browne and Cummings, 1984; Onimode, 1992).

90 Some argued that Africa's past contributions to Euro-American industrial development, and the destruction it entailed within Africa, warranted grants-in-aid rather than loans, as a form of reparations (Onimode, 1992). A stronger case could have been made by emphasizing the cost to Africa of capital flight and other financial manipulations studied by Seidman, 1977; Seidman and Makgetla, 1980.

91 Skinner, 1981.

92 World Bank, 1981. The report (p. 4) nodded in the direction of Africa's history, then turned away. Recommendations for Africa were much the same as those imposed on the more developed economies of Asia and Latin America (see Chapter Two), despite considerable structural differences between the regions' economies.

93 Led by then President Robert MacNamara, the pro-poor focus nevertheless resulted in integrated rural development projects (IRDs) that, like those of the late colonial period, advanced the capacities of better-off farmers and their relatives in government. By 1989, the Bank acknowledged that half its projects had failed (World Bank, 1989).

94 A number of economists and anthropologists supported this policy. For example, Fleuret, 1990; Cleaver and Schreiber, 1994.

95 Predicted by Ambassador Walter Carrington (1981) with respect to U.S. government lending at the 1980 Tuskegee Conference, it soon became clear that IFIs intended to impose conservative "Reaganomics" policies on the global economy.

96 African taxpayers were further burdened by increased *public* debt resulting from new SAP loans taken out to improve infrastructure, attract foreign investment, and ultimately raise *private* sector profits (World Bank, 1995a, p. 78).

97 Cooper, 1996, p. 18.

98 George, 1988; George, 1992; Onimode, 1989; Adedeji, 1990; Adedeji, 1996. Onimode (1992) presents figures in support of the claim that most African countries had already repaid their debts by the end of the 1980s.

99 "The real international prices of Africa's two major export crops—cocoa and coffee—dropped almost 70 percent between 1980 and 1990, and the real price of cotton, the third major export crop, 28 percent" (World Bank, 1994, p. 77). The Bank nevertheless continued to advise "putting exports first" (1994, p. 11).

100 Capital flows are difficult to document since only official debt and imports are recorded in national accounts. Neither transfer pricing overcharges nor private profit repatriation are included; often, corporations and wealthy citizens are able to disguise their transfers abroad (Green and Seidman, 1968; Willame, 1980; B.G. Schoepf and C. Schoepf, fieldnotes, various years; Schoepf, 1975). Transfers to developing countries went from a positive $37 billion dollars in 1980 to a negative $1 billion in 1989 (Watkins, 1995, p. 179).

101 The "debt decade" (Hoogvelt, 1990) was a "lost decade" for the U.N. Economic Commission for Africa (Adedeji, 1990, p. 3).

102 "Never before have the international financial institutions wielded such pervasive influence on policy formulation in Africa: not since the days of colonialism
have external forces been so powerfully focused to
shape Africa's economic structure and the nature of its
participation in the world system" (Campbell and
Loxley, 1989, p. 1). Structural adjustment programs
brought foreign advisors *en masse*; in the 1990s, there
were more technical assistants than the 1950s, before
independence.

103 Mkandawire, 1992, p. 45, comment on presentation
by the late Claude Ake, 1992. Also see Mamdani
(1992); Mkandawire and Olukoshi (1994); and contributors to Kennett and Lumumba-Tukumbe (1992).

104 Browne and Cummings (1984) compared the Lagos
Plan and Berg. Concerned researchers began to examine the Berg Report in the light of field data at conferences from 1982. See contributors to Barker, 1984; to
Lawrence, 1986; to Sen and Grown, 1987; to
Onimode, 1989; to Gladwin, ed., 1991. Also Adedeji,
1990. In addition, research in industrialized nations
led to substitutes for many of Africa's mineral exports,
while the U.S. maintained tariff and quotas against
African exports (Onimode, 1992).

105 The Berg Report's use of dubious statistics to make
sweeping generalizations was criticized by Hill, 1986.
Schoepf and Schoepf (1984); Berry (1993b); Hill
(1986); and Russell (1988) show that assumptions of
"perfect competition" in African markets are unrealistic. In fact, "the market" is a screen behind which
hides a new round of resource redistribution—away
from African producers upward and outward
(Schoepf, Walu, Russell, *et al.*, 1991).

106 An end to parastatal crop collection and "pan-territorial pricing" (government-established countrywide
prices) would make it difficult for peasants in remote
areas to market their crops advantageously, given that
traders are unlikely to travel long distances over
impossible roads.

107 Remittances serve as working capital for seeds, labor,
and tool replacements, as well as investment in livestock, land, and buildings. They are the only social
security for the elderly and the sick.

108 Import Substitution Industries (ISIs) in textile,
footwear, and garment manufacturers would be especially hard-hit, to the point of "de-industrialization."

109 Franke and Chassin, 1980; contributors to Downs and
Reyna, 1988; Russell, 1988. This is exactly what took
place over nearly two decades of adjustment.

110 IFAD, 1992; Berry, 1993a. Domestic food production
and food security are burning issues in Africa, with
which neither the Bank nor USAID are in sympathy.
See Wilcock, 1995.

111 A Bank consultant showed how poor women farmers in
Zambia would be harmed by adjustment (Safilios-
Rothschild, 1985, cited in Staudt, 1987.) Also see Jolly,
1985; Daniel, Green, and Lipton, 1985; Obbo, 1991b.

112 J. Millen, interview with A. Edward Elmendorg, the
World Bank's lead health specialist for Africa, March
1998. Also see Green, 1993. In response to the World
Bank claim that SAPs have no discernible impact on
health spending in Africa, Peter Lurie explains:

"While the bank may not require cutbacks in health
and social spending, they do require cutbacks in general government spending—knowing full well that
health will bear a disproportionate cut. Governments
know that wiping out corruption and cutting back on
military budgets are more risky to stability and less feasible than reducing social services such as health to
disempowered people" (J. Millen, interview with Peter
Lurie, M.D., research scientist, March 1998).

113 Schoepf, Walu, Russell, *et al.*, 1991, p. 164.

114 Southall, 1988, p. 2.

115 We stress the qualifier "independent," because the
findings of much "command research" commissioned
by funding agencies tend, not surprisingly, to support
agency goals and strategies. Research that does not
tends to be shunted aside (see Lemarchand, 1982, and
Uvin, 1998, with respect to the Bank and other funding agencies in Rwanda).

116 Cornia, Jolly, and Stewart, 1987.

117 World Bank, 1989.

118 UNECA, 1989. For details and reasoning of the AAF-
SAP see Onimode, 1992, pp. 74-101.

119 The Bank argued that the poor would have been even
worse off without SAPs (World Bank, 1994a).

120 Mazrui, 1991; Goheen, 1991; Raikes and Gibbon,
1996.

121 More than 90 percent of new foreign investment went
to raw materials' extraction, nearly 75 percent went to
oil. Thus, the 1990s re-created the colonial pattern.
The authoritarian military rulers executed Dr. Ken
Sara-Wiwa and other leaders of the movement that
protested against Shell Oil's environmentally destructive practices and brutal repression of workers in eastern Nigeria. Shell, by failing to use its considerable
influence to halt the hangings, is fully complicit. See
Chapter Eight of this volume.

122 Beckman, 1992.

123 Obbo, 1992; Dédy and Tapé, 1995.

124 Young, 1996.

125 For example, in Zambia in 1985 and 1987; Zaire, in
1988. Protestors in Zimbabwe in 1998 and 1999
attacked the government for military spending of
more than $1 million per day to defend the interests of
wealthy Zimbabweans in Congo, while poverty deepened at home. The Zimbabwe government attempted
to repress dissent by force and arrested journalists. The
opposition countered by organizing a new political
party. See "Zimbabwe: Morgan's Third Way," *Africa
Confidential* 40(6), 1999; "Zambia: Mining the
Depths," *Africa Confidential* 40(6), 1999, p. 3; R.W.
Johnson, "Diary Zimbabwe," *London Review of Books*,
March 4, 1999; Chris McGreal, "Zimbabwe Sliding
into a Police State," *Manchester Guardian Weekly*,
February 14, 1999.

126 The unraveling of Kenya's pro-democracy movement
in the face of state-sponsored ethnic cleansing is
charted by Holmquist and Ford, 1992. For Rwanda,
see Longman, 1995.

127 Many of what were known as "tribes" actually were
created by colonial administrators for purposes of control. See Southall, 1988; Vail, 1991; Young, 1996.

128 Chretien, 1991a, p. 19. Achile Mbembe (1988) wrote of the state's claim to a monopoly on truth, the quasi-totalitarian control of power symbols by "l'état théologien"; Jean-Francois Bayart, 1989, wrote of "le gouvernement du ventre," the consuming state that "eats" society's resources. For analysis of the roots of violence in Africa, see Reyna and Downs, 1999; Zack-Williams, 1990, 1995, for Sierra Leone; Azevedo, 1998, for Chad.

129 Rape is a weapon of the military in peace and war, a means of terrorizing women and humiliating the civilian population. Genocide leaders and their troops in Rwanda systematically raped Tutsi women, frequently in front of family members, before killing them (African Rights, 1995; Human Rights Watch, 1996b). The killers continued raping in the refugee camps in Zaire. Infection with HIV in Rwanda's rural population was 11 percent in 1997, up from 1 percent a decade earlier.

With an estimated 6 million refugees and 17 million displaced persons, Africa is the world's most heavily burdened region. As in Zaire, refugee camps often are sites of violence, especially when soldiers move freely among women and children. On the special brutality of violence against women and girls in genocidal conflicts and in situations where refugees live among armed men, see African Rights, 1995.

130 In the face of growing popular discontent due to deepening poverty and criticism of a small ruling class believed to have grown wealthy through corruption, Rwanda's Supreme Military Council warned in July 1992 that anyone who attempted to turn race war into class conflict would be considered a traitor (Republic of Rwanda, Ministry of Defense, "Definition and Identification of the Enemy," September 21, 1992, p. 2. Quoted in African Rights, 1995, p. 39, note 43). The "international development community's" role in increasing inequality while ignoring the effects of support for a corrupt, authoritarian regime is examined in Uvin, 1998. International agencies' and institutions' role in exacerbating violence in 1994-95 is documented by a multinational joint evaluation task force of scholars in the 5-volume "DANIDA Report" (Millwood, 1995). Ideological preparation is documented by Chretien, Dupaquier, Kabanda, et al., 1995.

131 The concept of *structural violence* includes severe, multidimensional deprivation and socio-political marginalization of a significant portion of society (Galtung, 1969).

132 For example, a recent front-page article in the *Washington Post* states that: "The two tribes have competed for centuries, frequently with bloodshed, for control of Rwanda" (Goshko, 1998, p. 1). In fact Tutsi and Hutu were not tribes, but socioeconomic categories within a kingdom who shared the same language and culture. Struggles among the aristocracy were common, but there was no history of systematic violence between Tutsi and Hutu as such (Newbury, 1988; Prunier, 1995; de Lame, 1997; Des Forges, 1999).

133 Mukagasana, 1997.

134 African Rights, 1995.

135 World Bank, 1989, p. 105.

136 World Bank, 1989, p. 105.

137 See Chretien, 1991b, for an account of critical newspaper articles and the jailing of their authors in 1990. Also, references cited in the notes that follow later in this chapter, and various issues of the journal *Dialogue* for the late 1980s.

138 "Influx control" was instituted by the colonial rulers and revived by the second post-independence dictatorship (Bourdon and Ngango, 1988).

139 Ntezilyayo, 1995, pp. 324-325.

140 One hectare equals 2.5 acres. In 1984, the average holding in the densely populated northwest was only 0.8 ha. The majority (57 percent) of peasant households nationwide lived on plots of just over 0.5 ha, and 26 percent on less than that amount. The 16.5 percent who held more than 2 ha, held 43 percent of all land. Land around the capital was particularly subject to accumulation: in Kigali Prefecture, the 28 percent of holdings of over 2 ha took up 56 percent of the total cultivated land. The poorest 10 percent of the population were estimated to have obtained 3 percent of national consumption; the wealthiest 10 percent, 24 percent (République du Rwanda, ENBC, 1984a, p. 68; Bourdon and Ngango, 1988, p. 5). In the first half of the 1980s, average farm size declined by 30 percent and population density on arable land increased by 28 percent (Ntezilyayo, 1986).

In the two northwestern provinces with the most fertile soils, where many of the most powerful and wealthy government officials originated, land pressure was most acute. Their estates were worked by tenant farmers. "When a political regime restricts access to land through an institution like ubukonde [tenancy], it creates fundamental social inequality" (Pottier, 1993, p. 29). The north had the highest illiteracy rates, with half the men and three-fourths of women unable to read (UNICEF, 1988, p. 88).

In 1989, drought in southern Rwanda brought severe hunger to an estimated 17 percent of the population, while the north had bumper crops (EIU Country Report, Rwanda, 1990). Data-sets from these USAID-funded surveys fail to provide information on the wealth of the small group of millionaires—political and military officials with ranches and farms of 500-1,000 ha, nor about their holdings abroad.

141 Our sources include survey reports from the World Bank and USAID. Jones and Egli, 1984; Robins, 1990.

142 Ntezilyayo, 1986.

143 Marysse, de Herdt, and Ndayambaje, 1994, p. 35, T. 2.9. Coincidentally, 1975 was the year that new laws favored the involvement of government and military officials in produce trade (Bezy, 1990, p. 40). Services, mainly trade, increased markedly as a percentage of GNP to 36 percent in 1984 (UNICEF, 1988, p. 8).

144 For example, Lemarchand, 1982, whose evaluation of a World Bank project was quietly shelved.

145 Ntezilyayo, 1986. Dr. Ntezilyayo was minister of agriculture in the Habyarimana government from 1984 to 1990.

146 Schoepf, 1996; Uvin, 1998, p. 146. Notwithstanding, Rwandan bankers, parastatal managers, businessmen, and high-level government officials were even more conspicuous. Claude Schoepf comments about his role

in a legume project in the mountains of eastern Kivu: "Not only was the inequality flagrant, but the project did not meet the need women expressed for increased bean yields on the dwindling plots allocated by husbands. It tried to convince them to grow soybeans in which they had no interest."

147 Bart, 1993, p. 508.

148 Bezy, 1990; Uvin, 1998, pp. 147-148, asks, whether, given this situation, donors can be considered neutral.

149 Runyinya, 1985, in a thesis on Butare Prefecture, cited in Bezy, 1990, p. 38. In another example, peasants sell some of their sorghum harvest in July/August to obtain cash, at 10 francs per kilo. But in October, when stocks run out, they purchase sorghum at double the harvest price. A trader who buys 2.5 tons for 25,000 francs and resells it 2-3 months later nets a quick risk-free profit of 67 percent (calculating in an expense of 5,000 francs for transport and storage).

150 Alternatively, they may seek to avoid post-harvest losses to insects and mold.

151 The first author was able to verify this type of usury in interviews with (Hutu) peasants in rural Butare in March, 1996. Traders' practices were cited as a major element in peasants' opposition to the Habyarimana regime. At the Catholic Mission of Save, also in Butare Prefecture, low-cost storage was provided to peasants from surrounding communes, and peasants were able to avoid the merchants' usury (Bart, 1993, p. 112; B.G. Schoepf, interviews, 1996). Privatization, recommended by the World Bank and USAID, is not typically favorable for peasants.

152 One-third of peasant land was devoted to plantain bananas, a high-energy crop eaten as a staple, as well as made into beer, which is processed, sold, and consumed by men; one-third of food expenditures in poor households went to banana beer (1983-84 data from République du Rwanda, ENBC, cited in UNICEF, 1985; UNICEF, 1988, p. 72). For consideration of the consequences for nutrition and health, see Schoepf and Schoepf, 1988.

153 Only 45 percent had help from a family member; 35 percent had no help at all (UNICEF, 1988, p. 82). The situation remained unchanged in 1992, as no new maternity centers opened (UNICEF, 1992a).

154 UNICEF, 1988, p. 83.

155 République du Rwanda, 1988.

156 République du Rwanda, 1988; République du Rwanda, 1992; also Bezy, 1990.

157 EIU Rwanda Country Report, 1990. A lesser fall in 1986 led peasants to uproot coffee bushes (Schoepf, 1987). Many Rwandan peasants hated to grow coffee, forced upon them by the state. When state control diminished as a result of political protest in 1990, peasants in Butare uprooted their bushes in favor of food crops (Marysse, de Herdt, and Ndayambaje, 1994a, 1994b).

158 UNICEF, 1992a.

159 Reviewed in Schoepf, 1988b.

160 Watson, 1991. Most were Tutsi whose parents had fled during ethnic cleansing from 1959 to 1973. Others were Hutu labor migrants, while still others had fled political repression. All were political opponents of the Habyarimana regime. The leaders had served as officers in the Ugandan Army.

161 The Habyarimana government eventually admitted to 8,047 prisoners, but others put the number at more than 10,000 (B.G. Schoepf, interviews with International Committee of the Red Cross and Red Crescent Societies (ICRC) officials, and with former detainees and relatives who survived the genocide, March-May 1996). A Red Cross official spoke of starvation despite their attempts to deliver food; detainees spoke of torture, hunger, and refusal of medical treatment, sometimes resulting in death or permanent disability. An elderly priest told of his solitary confinement in a small chamber for several months. He had conducted an unauthorized funeral service for an inmate. He was taken out of the hole only for regular beatings and carried a deep indentation on one side of his skull, the result of a fracture from which he had nearly died (B.G. Schoepf, interview, April 1996).

162 B.G. Schoepf, interviews, 1996; Uvin, 1998. Donors were aware of the arrests; some carried on negotiations for release of their jailed employees.

163 The propaganda themes resembled those used by the Nazis against Jews in Germany (Chretien, 1991a, 1991b; Chretien, Dupaquier, and Kabanda, et al., 1995). Ironically, the new Rwandan government finds itself saddled with repaying loans obtained to finance the killing of government members' relatives and colleagues.

164 Marysse, de Herdt, and Ndayambaje, 1994a, 1994b.

165 "The social aspect of the killings has often been overlooked" (Prunier, 1995, p. 231). Poor young men in Kigali, including those displaced when officials removed the population from the North to "dry up the sea" of the guerillas, formed the first recruits. Eventually, every commune had its contingent. Desensitization techniques were adapted and killings practiced from that time in rural pogroms and sporadic attacks in the cities (B.G. Schoepf, interviews with survivors, Feb-May 1996). "As soon as they went into action, they drew around them a cloud of even poorer people, a lumpenproletariat of street boys, rag pickers, car washers and homeless unemployed. For these people the genocide was the best thing that could ever happen to them....Social envy came together with political hatred to fire the Interahamwe [militia's] bloodlust" (Prunier, 1995, pp. 131-132).

166 See de Lame, 1997.

167 All consumption of peasant households was reduced, including health care. One-quarter of peasants had less than 0.3 ha (1 acre = 0.4 ha). Household incomes, which had averaged $550 per year in 1984, had declined to $250 per year, most of which was spent on food. Increased farm size was linked to increased crop sales, but not to increases in food consumption (Marysse, de Herdt, and Ndayambaje, 1994a).

168 Among the first to be killed was the prime minister, a Hutu woman of the MDR party's opposition wing, along with ten Belgian soldiers of the U.N. peace-keeping force assigned to protect her. The massacres of the Hutu opposition and their families went unnoticed at the time by U.S. journalists for whom the paradigm of African conflict ended with ethnicity.

169 Schoepf, Rukarangira, Schoepf, *et al.*, 1988. Early in the epidemic, the female partners of wealthy and important men were at very high risk (e.g., Allen, Lindan, Serufila, *et al.*, 1991). However, poverty is a decisive risk factor. Relationships between poverty, gender, disease, and AIDS are documented in Bassett and Mhloyi, 1991; Farmer, Connors, and Simmons, eds., 1996. Also see the special issue of *African Urban Quarterly* (5:1-2 [1991]) on AIDS, STDs, and Urbanization in Africa.

170 Ninety percent of the more than 47 million people who have contracted HIV/AIDS to date reside in less developed countries. All figures, UNAIDS, 1997; UNAIDS, 1998; WHO, 1998d.

171 Mann, Tarantola, and Netter, eds., 1992. By 1985 life expectancy had begun to decline in three of six African countries severely impacted by AIDS for which data are available. Three others registered slower rates of increase than in the previous three decades. By 1990, the remaining three experienced declines, and all continued to 1995. Projections for the year 2000 are more optimistic—in three countries, declines should continue, but at slower rates. In a fourth country, Malawi, life expectancy is forecast to descend to the 1955 level of 40 years (United Nations Department of Economic and Social Information and Policy Analysis, Population Division, 1995).

172 Cohen, Plummer, Mugon, *et al.*, 1999.

173 For example, 86 percent of a sample of 1,458 pregnant women seen in Kigali in 1988 had been married for an average of eight years, and two-thirds had had a single, lifetime partner, yet 25 percent were HIV+. Overall prevalence was 32 percent; among those age 19 to 24 years, 38 percent were infected (Allen, Lindan, Serufila, *et al.*, 1991, p. 1660). Also Bond and Dover, 1997. Adolescent girls are especially biologically and socially vulnerable to infection by older men; up to ten times more girls 15-19 years are infected than boys of their age; infection is high among married as among unmarried sexually active women (Konde-Lule, Wawer, Sewankambo, *et al.*, 1997). AIDS-related diseases are the leading cause of death in young adults. For prevention methods that enhance women's ability to prevent becoming infected with AIDS, see Schoepf, 1992, 1993a, 1993b; de Bruyn, Jackson, Wijermars, *et al.*, 1995. For important discussions of the dynamics of gender and age in HIV transmission and control, see Obbo 1993a, 1993b, 1995a.

174 See Farmer, Connors, and Simmons, eds., 1996.

175 Hunt (1989) analyzes aspects of the relationship between economics, labor practices, and the spread of the epidemic.

176 Tuberculosis, driven by HIV, malnutrition, and poverty, is the leading cause of death worldwide in young women. About one-third of AIDS deaths in Africa are attributable to tuberculosis (UNAIDS, 1998). While tuberculosis is treatable, diagnosis and care must be available and accessible. Most African health systems rely on "passive surveillance," that is, they wait for patients to visit clinics when they cough. Between the time that active infection begins and the moment when a person seeks care, additional household members—especially young children—are likely to become infected (Deuschle, 1967). Health and social infrastructures weakened by more than two decades of crisis and regressive social spending exacerbated by SAPs cannot cope adequately with pandemic tuberculosis.

177 Heroic coping efforts made by Ugandan women are described in Obbo, 1995b. Assistance to families with orphans has been adopted as a mission by a number of religious and other NGOs, especially women's groups. Also see the UNDP's HIV and Development Program (Parnell, Hernandez, and Robbins, 1996).

178 Sophisticated drugs and monitoring are not now widely available apart from research projects; their high cost makes them prohibitive for all but the wealthy few. Death generally occurs within two years following the onset of AIDS. Neither cures nor vaccines are likely to emerge in the near future. When they do become available, access will be limited by inability to pay. Even if pharmaceutical companies offer reduced prices, AIDS drugs will not be affordable for the poor or middle classes. Nor would there be enough physicians or nurse-practitioners to monitor treatment.

179 In poor families most care of the sick falls upon women who themselves may be suffering or elderly and without resources. In poor families where parents are incapacitated, children receive less maternal care, and there are fewer resources to maintain health (Ryder, Kamenga, Nkusu, *et al.*, 1994; Parnell, Hernandez, and Robbins, 1996). Deaths of productive adults leave impoverished orphaned children and elders who depended upon them for survival. By the year 2000, an estimated 10 million African children under 15 years will have lost either their mothers or both parents. When a mother dies the chances of her young child dying increase by about 50 percent (World Bank, 1993b, p. 113, box 5.1). Due to the stigma surrounding the deaths of their parents, AIDS orphans may be shunned and left to roam the streets. Even when they are accepted by relatives, poverty makes many of these children vulnerable to HIV infection in their turn (UNDP, 1997).

180 Lurie, Hintzen, and Lowe, 1995.

181 Ten percent of AIDS deaths occur in young children. One-third of infants born to HIV-positive mothers become infected in utero, during birth, or through breast-feeding. Many children die before the age of two years because their parents cannot afford effective care. Previous gains made by child survival programs began to be reversed by 1990 (UNICEF, 1990b). Without AIDS the average under-5 mortality rate (U5MR) in the affected countries was projected to decline from an average of 158 per 1,000 live births in 1980 to 132/1000 by the year 2000. Instead, U5MR in the heavily impacted countries remained at 155-157/1000 in 1990 and were projected to rise to 189 by 2000. (Corresponding increases were expected in countries where the HIV pandemic began later.) Projections made in 1990 by the WHO and others underestimated the current situation (UNAIDS, 1998). Rises of one-third to three-fourths were predicted for Central/East and Southern Africa, respectively, with maternal infection at 30 percent (Nicoll, Timaeus, Kigadye, *et al.*, 1994). Instead, in very high prevalence areas, mortality in children under five

years rose by two to three times (UNAIDS, 1998). More African children die from AIDS than from either malaria or measles, which, compounded by malnutrition, formerly were the major killers.

182 In Uganda, Tanzania, and Senegal, resistance from many religious leaders and community elders was strong into the early 1990s. Alarmed governments nevertheless instituted imaginative forms of education and made free STD treatment and condoms widely available. These, and growing awareness of deaths from "a long and painful illness," understood as AIDS, rendered protection acceptable and possible among young people. The incidence of new infections reported in people aged 15-29 years began to decline in these countries in 1996. Elsewhere, the virus continues to spread, not only in cities where the epidemic is well established, but to rural areas and to countries apparently HIV-free in the 1980s. On the cultural politics of AIDS research and control, see Schoepf, 1995a, 1998.

183 This interpretation was challenged from the outset by many African and Africanist social scientists and public health workers, as well as by ordinary Africans. The brief historical review presented earlier gives an indication of the types of changes that took place. See contributors to Miller and Rockwell, et al., 1988.

184 Further references and critique are found in Schoepf, 1991a, 1992, 1993a, 1993b, 1998.

185 Meaning "insufficient salaries for many years."

186 See TGNP, 1994. "When people lose their jobs and their wages, while at the same time the price of their food and other basic necessities increases, they are forced to seek other ways to survive. Increasingly in Africa today we see young boys leaving school to work in the informal sector, selling trinkets on the streets while young girls may be forced into commercial sex work to help their families survive. The extended family that provided Africans with a social safety net is breaking down as people struggle for fewer resources." Dr. Joseph Lugalla, medical sociologist, interviewed by J. Millen, March 1998.

187 Lurie, Hintzen, and Lowe, 1995.

188 Many poor people's remittances to rural parents have disappeared, as has the custom of sending foodstuffs to relatives in town (Schoepf, Walu, Russell, et al., 1991). Nsanga's story underscores the need for productive activities that effectively increase women's financial independence and their sense of self-worth, leading to social empowerment in the long term. Such developments are impossible in the context of an authoritarian state.

189 Dr. Daniel Tarantola, director of the AIDS program at the Harvard School of Public Health's Francois-Xavier Bagnoud Center for Health and Human Rights, personal communication with J. Millen, March 1998.

190 See Schoepf, 1988, 1991b; Schoepf, Rukarngira, and Schoepf, et al., 1988, and references cited therein, on the issue of children as a factor influencing women's status.

191 In several of the poorest countries, the rate exceeds 1,550 women per 100,000 live births each year. Even in the least poor countries some 500 to 800 women die for 100,000 live births. With the decline of traditional post-partum sexual abstinence and reduced length of breast-feeding, women without biomedical contraception become pregnant at closer intervals than did their grandmothers.

192 Bijlmakers, Bassett, and Sanders, 1996, pp. 54-55.

193 In the 1980s, eight countries of sub-Saharan Africa registered declines of more than one percentage point (15-20 percent) in total completed fertility (World Bank, 1997b, pp. 6-8, T1.1).

194 The most effective promotion of family planning takes place at the community level, carried out by trained local people.

195 Figures on maternal mortality, cause of death, and the like are guesstimates, at best, but appear to confirm observers' reports.

196 Schultz, Cates, and O'Mara, 1994.

197 Voeller and Anderson, 1992. Many women and men may not experience symptoms in early stages of infection, or may not be aware that the itching or burning they suffer are STD symptoms. Additional reasons for failure to seek treatment are the expense and the social stigma associated with STDs.

198 Dr. Christine Minja-Trupin, who led the AMREF STD program in Tanzania in 1991, reported that from her experience, "the most difficult aspect of health worker training is the psycho-social one. Many are not comfortable talking about sex. Or making visual, let alone hands-on examinations. They generally have little experience using condoms themselves, are inept teaching condom use, and have no idea how to teach negotiation with a partner. What is still worse, many health workers share the stigmatizing attitudes of lay people toward people with STDs." She concluded that to omit culturally informed training for health workers in STDs and AIDS is a grave error (B.G. Schoepf, interview, Dar-es Salaam, October 1991).

199 Introduction of user fees in a Nairobi research clinic in 1988 was found to cause declines in attendance by both women and men: 65 percent fewer women and 40 percent fewer men sought care. When fees were removed, rates rose again, but many fewer men used the services (Moses, Manji, Bradley, et al., 1992). The health officer at USAID, an agency that promoted the fees policy, maintained that the study was deficient (B.G. Schoepf, interview, Boston, February 1993). Where biomedical treatment is unaffordable or unfriendly, people who recognize the symptoms of an STD self-medicate or seek advice from folk ("traditional") practitioners. Both forms of care are likely to be inadequate, and may lead to drug-resistant organisms and to further spread of infection.

200 Moses, Manji, Bradley, et al., 1992.

201 World Bank, 1997b, pp. 74-75.

202 Evans, 1995. On the impact of SAP policies on primary health care, see Obbo, 1992.

203 Called "bar girls" in East Africa, they are at high risk for HIV.

204 See Packard, 1989b.

205 J. Millen, interviews, Ghana, March 1989 and March 1992.

206 B.G. Schoepf, interviews, Abidjan, May 1997; Professor Seri Dédy, personal communication to B.G. Schoepf, June 1997.

207 B.G. Schoepf, interviews, Abidjan, May 1997; Professor Seri Dédy, personal communication, June 1997. See Schoepf, 1986, 1991b.

208 The extent to which services remain concentrated in urban areas varies greatly. On average, in 1995 health services were accessible to an estimated 50 percent of rural and 81 percent of urban dwellers—an average parity of 63 percent. In Tanzania and Zimbabwe, however, special efforts were made. Coverage rates were 73 percent and 80 percent for rural and 94 percent and 96 percent of urban populations, with parity rates of 78 percent and 83 percent, respectively (UNDP, 1996, pp. 152-153).

209 Djemay's case is from interviews collected by J Millen between 1992 and 1994 in southwestern Senegal.

A study in Zimbabwe in 1993 found that both patients and staff recognized reduced quality of services, dearth of medicines, and ever-increasing user charges. Nurses, frustrated by seriously eroded salaries, lamented that their social standing had declined as a result and that they no longer enjoyed the community respect due their calling. While nurses blamed increased patient loads for long waiting time, patients believed that nurses—whom they said were sometimes rude, arrogant, "rough" (meaning *brusque*), and neglectful—spent too much time on tea breaks (Bassett, Bijlmakers, and Sanders, 1997). Staff who feel let down by their organization are likely to lose their sense of moral obligation to play by the rules. This is especially the case when employees believe that higher-ups receive outrageously high salaries, or are skimming the budget for themselves. Those below them tend to take whatever options they can to increase their incomes and social status. They may pilfer supplies and medicines to use in private practice after hours, demand unofficial payment for routine services, report late for work or not at all, and vent their frustrations on patients. Alternatively, they may conduct other business on the side—sometimes coming to work tired and impatient, as did the nurses studied in Zimbabwe. This situation, widespread in Zaire (DRC) and Uganda from the mid-1970s, became common elsewhere in the 1980s as a result of SAPs (Schoepf, 1986; Kanji, Kanji, and Manji, 1991; Whyte, 1991). Because SAP-policies have undermined wages and prestige in the health professions (and education), a Ugandan researcher finds it "plausible to argue that loss of professionalism is due in part to adjustment" (Munene, 1995).

In many public health facilities, inpatients must bring their own medicines, bandages, disinfectant, soap, towels, and bedding—or go without. Women who cannot bring these things are barred from some maternity services. A relative—often a child whose labor can be spared—must come to care and cook for the patient. This practice causes crowding; strains water and sanitation facilities; and adds clutter, debris, and vermin.

210 Data on nurses and health-care coverage are from World Bank, 1997b, pp. 74-80, T2.11, T2.12.

211 Botswana's reported 87 percent access rate is bolstered by a decline in population/nurse ratio of 700:1 to 480:1. Malawi claimed an 80 percent access rate. With population/nurse ratios of 3,024:1 in 1980 and 28,951:1 in 1993, however, this seems doubtful.

Countries that reported declining coverage included Angola, devastated by prolonged civil war, and Cameroon, where the deterioration (from 20 percent to 15 percent) is attributable to SAPs, debt service, and widening disparities in wealth (see Goheen, 1991).

212 Malnutrition lowers resistance to disease; the presence of disease lowers the utilization of nutrients by the body, so that the immune system requires additional food to fight infection (Scrimshaw, Taylor, and Gordon, 1959). See Latham, 1965, for a readable text, most of which is still valid.

213 For example, see the case of Cuba in Chapter Thirteen. Several other areas of the world that have favorable health indicators despite low GNP include China, Sri Lanka, Costa Rica, and Kerala State in India (the only state with a communist government) (Halstead, Walsh, and Warren, eds., 1985).

214 Vitamins, calcium, iron, and other minerals in the absence of supplements can be provided only by a varied and balanced diet. The critical importance of calcium—understood in the West since the 1930s—is ignored in current UNICEF and WHO recommendations (for example, UNICEF, 1990a, 1990c).

215 Risk increases exponentially, at a compound rate of 7 percent for each percent deterioration in weight for age (World Bank, 1995, p. 30).

216 Stunting can to some extent be overcome by providing micronutrients, but weight gain also requires calorie-rich foods (London School of Hygiene and Tropical Medicine, 1994, p. 86). Vitamin A supplementation also contributes to growth recovery, according to a study reported in *Journal of the American Medical Association*, which, curiously, failed to test for the effects of calcium (Voelker, 1998).

217 UNICEF, 1990c.

218 In addition, the breast milk production of overworked, underfed women is less plentiful than that of mothers who are better fed and work less. An excellent review of interrelated aspects of women and children's health and nutrition is the 1990 UNICEF Situation Analysis for Tanzania (UNICEF, 1990d), prepared by Valerie Leach in collaboration with numerous Tanzanian researchers.

219 UNICEF, 1990c. Low birth weight also can be caused by heavy farm work carried on in the final trimester of pregnancy, as the energy-carrying blood supply is directed to working muscles and to the skin to dissipate heat, instead of to the fetus (London School of Hygiene and Tropical Medicine, 1994, pp. 85-86).

220 Nutrition surveillance undertaken in child health programs in the 1980s is among the preventive services abandoned in the 1990s, often along with immunizations. Reduced immunization led to resurgence of diseases such as measles, polio, and tuberculosis (UNICEF, 1993b, 1994).

221 Cornu, Massamba, Traissac, *et al.*, 1995.

222 Acute current malnutrition, termed 'wasting,' is measured as low weight for height.

223 For an opposing view, see Bantje, 1995.

224 Calcium intake was not mentioned. The authors, Cornu and colleagues (1995), point to the need to disaggregate results by socioeconomic status of mothers, because overall malnutrition rates may go down, as

they did in Congo, while rising among poor children and their mothers. With increasing rural differentiation, there is need to disaggregate results there, as well. Neither procedure is routinely followed by governments nor international donors (Cornu, Massamba, Traissac, *et al.*, 1995).

225 Costello, Watson, and Woodward, 1994.

226 World Bank, 1998d, pp. 2-3. A problem arises when researchers without knowledge of local circumstances reject the data discovered. For example, a sharp rise in poverty in households in the cocoa-producing West Forest Region of Côte d'Ivoire may be the result of socioeconomic differentiation among households. Acute differences are obvious to even the casual visitor (B.G. Schoepf, fieldnotes, 1997). See World Bank, 1996. An interview with the deputy minister of health in April 1995 suggested that poverty had risen in the West as a result of self-settled refugees from Liberia. Those who lived with relatives without working for wages reduced per capita resource availability; on the other hand, their availability as farm labor had driven wages down (B.G. Schoepf, fieldnotes, April 1995). These two processes contributed to increasing poverty in 1995.

Poverty was reported to have increased overall in Côte d'Ivoire from 18 percent in 1988 to 32 percent in 1993 and 37 percent in 1995 (World Bank, 1996a, 1998). Government and NGO officials in four regions, interviewed in June-July 1997, reported that neither rural nor urban poverty had been reduced by the recent upturn in economic growth (B.G. Schoepf, fieldnotes).

227 Kanbur, 1990. Peasant producers of food and export crops (49.5 percent and 36.4 percent, respectively), were counted among the poor by the Bank in 1985, using a line that tends to understate poverty. Since that time, the situation has worsened considerably.

228 Campbell, 1984.

229 The policy measures most destructive to living standards included the removal of government subsidies on maize and cooking oil, currency devaluation, the dismantling of labor protections, and the introduction of user fees for health and education (see Seshimana and Saasa, 1993; Mutukuwa and Saasa, 1995).

230 This pattern was discovered in the Congo Copperbelt in the 1950s, and continued in the 1970s (Schoepf, 1987).

231 In most countries the percentage of rural families living in poverty rose even with rising GDP. One exception to the trend was Tanzania, where rural poverty declined 8 percent as a result of public health and education policies designed to benefit poor peasants. Nevertheless, the number of people living in poverty more than doubled (IFAD, 1992).

232 See contributors to Davison, ed., 1988; Downs and Reyna, ed., 1988; and Gladwin, ed. 1991; also Cleaver and Schreiber, 1994, pp. 46-55.

233 World Bank economist Uma Lele described the situation in Malawi (Lele, 1990).

234 The World Bank has been unwilling to recognize that its major agricultural policy advice, concentration on export-led growth, emerges from the same logic that failed to lead to development prior to independence and failed again in the 1970s. See, for example, World Bank, 1989.

235 Some governments reinstated food subsidies in order to cushion the blow to city dwellers, generally in response to demonstrations and "IMF riots."

236 Increased crop prices do not lead to increased fertilizer use among small producers for a number of reasons, mainly because small farmers cannot afford fertilizer, and are often understandably reluctant to incur debt in order to purchase it.

237 Drought or poorly distributed seasonal rainfall occurs in one year in five in many regions and one year in three or four in the Sahel.

238 The following narrative is drawn from interviews conducted by J. Millen in Dakar and the Department of Bignona, Senegal, 1993-1994.

239 Sali's husband, Bocar, was laid off from his job at the local textile plant where he had worked for five years. He was given little warning, minuscule severance pay, and no possibility to collect unemployment benefits. The couple later learned that everyone in the factory had been laid off and the entire plant had to close down: it could no longer compete with the new foreign-owned corporations popping up as a result of Senegal's New Industrial Policy (NIP). Introduced as part of the Senegal's SAP, the NIP eliminated national labor laws instituted to protect workers. It also reduced the tariffs that were in place to protect Senegalese industries from foreign competition. Shortly after his last day at the textile plant, Bocar reflected: "We are told that this New Industrial Policy was created to promote trade 'liberalization.' But as I see it, the only thing workers are liberated from is their work" (J. Millen, interviews, Dakar and Department of Bignona, Senegal, 1994).

240 In Rwanda, 20 percent of peasants sold land in the late 1980s and early 1990s; most did so as a direct consequence of illness (Bezy, 1990, p. 33; Marysse, de Herdt, and Ndayambaje, 1994a, 1994b).

241 Bates, 1981a, 1981b.

242 As noted previously, state control increased markedly during World War II (Young, 1996, p. 171). Also see Bates (1976) for Zambia. Parastatals often require subsidies, sometimes because they are inefficient, but often, too, because the functions they perform are in the public interest. These would not otherwise be under public control, or might not be performed at all. There is nothing inherently wrong with parastatals, unless one makes a religion of providing public support for private profit-making (Green and Allison, 1986).

243 Ly (1957, p. 73) comments that "the technical role of the state in production should not make us lose sight of its class or national character."

244 Eicher (1986, p. 175) argues against parastatals but nevertheless sees small farmers as the key to increased production because they will work for very low returns to family labor. In the southwestern districts of Tanzania under *Ujamaa*, peasants who formerly had to rely on labor migration for cash, increased maize and other crop production in the late 1960s and 1970s (Mbilinyi, 1994). Eicher (1986) criticizes pan-territorial pricing as inefficient. But until new technology makes it possible for the poor to increase production of high-value, low-bulk crops, such a means of pricing may be the only alternative to poverty.

245 In 1965, faced with demands by Africans for independence from Britain, white settlers illegally issued a Unilateral Declaration of Independence (UDI). In control of the state, the settlers maintained an apartheid system nearly as rigid as that in South Africa.

246 Murapa, 1981, examines political dynamics; Kadhani and Green, 1985, give an historical overview as background to their tightly reasoned policy analysis.

247 The "Global Big House" symbolizes the shift in control of large plantations from the local owners' Big House on the hill to TNC directors in corporate boardrooms from New York to Johannesburg (W. Johnson, 1981). The latter include the multinational mining conglomerates, Lonrho and Anglo-American (Stoneman, 1981). Farm wages remained level between 1940 and 1960, then declined by 17 percent until 1973. See Cross, 1976; Riddell, 1979, cited in Loewenson, 1991, p. 36.

248 Brokered by Britain, the Lancaster House peace settlement recognized the success of the struggle for Black majority rule. Economic victory eluded the majority, however. A ten-year moratorium was imposed on expropriation of settler estates, with British promises of loans as the carrot. Before the end of the decade, political and economic conditions had shifted. The government made threats and promises of land reform that, responsive to the claims of the LSCF lobby and IFI pressures, it failed to implement. Most owners are whites, but some 600 Black Africans acquired farms following independence (Gibbon, ed., 1995).

249 There were 5,400 LSCFs remaining. The differentiated ownership pattern continued. Twenty percent of farms held 50 percent of land (the best), while 10 percent owned half the cattle (Chinemana and Sanders, 1993). Concentration of stock ownership deprives rural children of milk, important to prevent stunted growth (see notes 212 and 216).

250 Chinemana and Sanders, 1993. Government ministers are among the LSCFs, some with multiple holdings. For example, former opposition leader, now Vice President Joshua Nkomo, is reported to own 17 large farms, a former guerilla commander and leading government "marxist" has 16. Privatization did not need to be imposed from outside.

251 In response to pressure from LSCF owners, the new government legislated a minimum wage that was less than that set for workers in other sectors (Loewenson, 1991, p. 37).

252 The World Bank's (1989, p. 106) account of the situation uses the dates 1979-1985, rather than 1980, when the new government made significant policy changes. This minimizes the impact of the end to White minority rule on peasant production. The report states that the increase was caused "by rapid expansion of the input and marketing infrastructure and a rise in producer prices." These were due to government policy, which expanded the activities of the GMB parastatal to serve Black African farmers. The new competitive context for private traders is not mentioned. To acknowledge the GMB's usefulness for small peasant producers would have undercut the Bank's rationale for dismantling its activities. The politically powerful LSCF sector was able to retain GMB services to avoid

selling directly to the oligopolistic milling companies that fix low prices where they can. There are seven large mills for all of Zimbabwe; one firm controls half of all production (Gibbon, 1996, p. 369).

253 Cheater, 1981.

254 B.G. Schoepf, notes on Women and Agriculture Conference, Harare, June 1983 (see details in Schoepf, 1991b).

255 Werner and Sanders (1997, pp. 138-141) show the effects of women's collective child-feeding stations during the drought of 1981-83 (observed at the time by B.G. Schoepf and C. Schoepf, fieldnotes, Masvingo District, 1983). These grassroots structures were reactivated in the drought of 1991-92.

256 From 110/1,000 in 1980 to 53/1,000 in 1988. The role of improved nutrition was clear. The proportion of severely underweight children dropped from 17.7 percent in 1980 to 1.3 percent in 1988. The level of stunted growth, indicating chronic poor diets, however, remained high: 35.6 percent in 1982, 29 percent in 1988. Werner and Sanders (1997, p. 141) comment that while lower mortality probably resulted from expansion of PHC, with immunization, oral rehydration for diarrhea and treatment of malaria and pneumonia, recession, and SAP reduced real incomes for many. Thus, "even relatively comprehensive health services and feeding programs could not offset the effects of growing poverty and difficulty in obtaining enough food." We concur, with the further observation that enough good quality food, with calcium, vitamin A, and other micronutrients, is necessary for normal growth.

257 For example, AFRICARE, whose representative in Zimbabwe, the late Marie Chambliss, facilitated our field research.

258 B.G. Schoepf, C. Schoepf, field observations, 1983; Chinemana and Sanders, 1993.

259 Green, 1993, p. 65.

260 Two years of severe drought in 1981-83 led the new government to stockpile grain in years of good harvest to avert the danger of famine (B.G. Schoepf, interviews, Ministry of Agriculture, Harare 1983.) Bank economic advisors, with their focus on getting governments out of agriculture, prevailed upon the government of Zimbabwe to sell off surplus maize it had stored from the bumper harvests of 1990 and 1991 as a drought/famine reserve. With maize a glut on the market, the government took a substantial loss. The drought that struck the following year was the worst ever recorded. The maize harvest fell by 80 percent, obliging the government to purchase 1.5 million tons to stave off famine. Combined losses on sales and purchases amounted to an estimated ZWD$800 million (Gibbon, 1996, p. 367), or about US$160 million at the time. The government, consequently, exceeded its planned budget.

The Bank's economists may not have studied the details of Zimbabwe's agricultural history. They failed to consider the regularly recurring risks associated with agriculture in the African savannah, where rains are touch-and-go and severe drought occurs every 6-10 years. Apparently they were so committed to reliance on market forces that they would have left the "imprudent," resource-poor peasants living in the driest areas to starve. Thanks to SAP-induced de-industrialization, there were no off-farm jobs to provide income to purchase food at prices driven up by scarcity. This is an example of the problems that can arise when uninformed foreign advisors base policy advice on textbook theories rather than on situated field data.

261 Those SSCF farmers with the most and best lands, generally working with hired labor (some 20 percent of peasants), had enough to sell, and could take advantage of increased crop prices (Sachikonye, 1995).

262 Chinemana and Sanders, 1993.

263 Lacking first-hand experience of the miserable conditions of estate workers, SAP economists still believe that plantations' low-wage, labor-intensive methods and export production are appropriate and essential ways to achieve GNP growth.

264 This is the case not only in Zimbabwe, but in Côte d'Ivoire, Tanzania, Zaire, Zambia, and elsewhere (Mbilinyi, 1988, 1991; Schoepf and Schoepf, 1988; B.G. Schoepf, interviews, Côte d'Ivoire 1995, 1997).

265 WHO, 1998d.

266 According to reporters, some 11,000 troops plus airmen are in Congo (DRC); casualty figures are high, and costs are said to be on the order of $1 million per day. More than 50 troops and officers were arrested for refusal to serve in Congo on the grounds that the war is unconstitutional and that therefore their obligation to fight is rendered invalid. News is heavily censored and independent Zimbabwean editors and reporters have been arrested and tortured. At least one striker was killed in Mutare when soldiers fired live ammunition. The deputy secretary of the Zimbabwe Confederation of Trade Unions is attempting to lead a pro-democracy coalition. See "Zimbabwe: Morgan's Third Way," *Africa Confidential* 40(6), 1999; "Zambia: Mining the Depths," *Africa Confidential* 40(6), 1999, p. 3; R. W. Johnson, "Diary Zimbabwe," *London Review of Books*, March 4, 1999; Chris McGreal, "Zimbabwe Sliding into a Police State," *Manchester Guardian Weekly*, February 14, 1999.

267 Stein and Nafziger, 1991, demonstrate the incompatibility of declared objectives and actual outcomes in the Bank's strategy. Case study examples from the 1980s are provided in Gladwin 1991; Schoepf, 1986; Lawrence, 1986. For the 1990s, see, for example, Márysse, de Herdt, and Ndayambaje, 1994, focusing on coffee farmers in Rwanda.

Transport of crops to markets is difficult in areas located far from all-weather roads. Few traders come to such areas. Those buyers who do so can set prices at virtually any level they please, over and above transport costs, clearly placing small farmers at a disadvantage. Traders may also bring consumer goods from the city to remote areas. Due to the scarcity, they can charge high prices for essential goods like salt, soap, oil, and matches, as well as fertilizer. Between 25 and 50 percent of cultivator households must purchase significant amounts of food before the harvest, when prices are highest. Price gouging by traders is common, whereas well-managed parastatals can even out the costs.

268 Jazairy, 1992, p. 20.

269 Most of the critical studies cited in this chapter support this claim, and most independent senior African social scientists agree (for example, Mazrui, 1991).

270 Yusuf Bangura, a political scientist, offers recommendations for peasant control of parastatals that would make it possible to prevent these agencies from serving as a means for officials to accumulate rent (Bangura, 1994).

271 See the extensive citations in reviews by Strobel, 1982; Schoepf, 1992, 1993b. Also see references cited in notes following here.

272 Contributors to Hafkin and Bay, 1976; Bay, 1982.

273 Women and men often keep separate accounts, grow different crops, and exchange labor on unequal terms. Men's income is often spent on such items as taxes, personal consumption, and additional wives. The degree to which husbands compensate their wives varies with local custom and the negotiation strengths of the women involved. Women's groups can sometimes weigh in the balance, as can governments and local leaders (Newbury and Schoepf, 1989; contributors to Davison, 1988; to Parpart and Staudt, 1989; Mbilinyi, 1994).

274 Schoepf, 1987.

275 Schoepf and Schoepf, 1988.

276 Despite being primarily responsible for their households, many women may not be locally or nationally recognized as decision-makers (World Bank, 1995d).

277 In some coastal West African nations, such as Ghana, women's tradition of trade marks an exception to the general rule (Robertson, 1984). An excellent review of debates over the meanings and status of female-headed households is provided by Peters, 1995.

278 Boserup, 1970.

279 Afonja, 1986; Staudt, 1987; contributors to Davison, 1988; Peters 1991.

280 Anderson, 1985.

281 The Bank and USAID launched a new round of pilot projects to support women's "micro-enterprises" in the mid-1990s. B.G. Schoepf developed a training manual for one such project in 1996 in Rwanda. The criticism of earlier efforts still applies.

282 Mikell, 1997; contributors to Gladwin, ed., 1991; Gladwin, 1991; Mbilinyi, 1990, 1994.

283 Meena, 1991; Zuidberg and Djire, 1992; Steady, 1992. The Mali study concerns the status of women peasants in the cotton monopoly instituted in the colonial period.

284 Schoepf, Walu, Russell, *et al.*, 1991; other contributors to Gladwin, ed. 1991.

285 Gladwin, 1991; Goheen, 1991.

286 Schoepf, 1987.

287 Women served as porters in pre-colonial East African trade, but colonizers shifted this burden to male conscripts. When they were able, men shifted head-loading back to women for both marketing and domestic chores (see Muchena, 1982).

288 Schoepf, Walu, Russell, *et al.*, 1991; TGNP, 1994.

289 Graham, 1994, pp. 116-147.

290 In Zimbabwe, for example, researchers found that few of the needy avail themselves of these provisions. Instead, children—especially girls—are withdrawn

from school, or attend irregularly when parents are unable to pay fees (UNICEF, 1990a, 1990b).

291 World Bank, 1995a, p. 77.

292 Green, 1993, p. 64.

293 Watkins, 1995, p. 179.

294 Watkins, 1995, p. 179.

295 In 1994, the ex-French colonies of the CFA zone devalued by 50 percent. Debt as a percentage of government revenue reached an average of nearly 73 percent and greater than 85 percent in the Central and West African states, respectively (Clement, 1996).

296 Simmons, 1995, p. 20.

297 Watkins, 1995, p. 179.

298 See Hansen and Twaddle, 1991a, 1991b; Jamal, 1991; Mazrui, 1991; Obbo, 1991a; Stein and Nafziger, 1991; Macrea, Zwi, and Birungi, 1993; Brett, 1996; Brown, 1997.

299 Brett, 1996.

300 The informal/irregular/illegal economy known as the *magendo* became a way of life (Green, 1981; Prunier, 1983; Nabuguzi, 1991).

301 Many businesses were capitalized by profits from *magendo* trading under previous regimes.

302 B.G. Schoepf, fieldnotes, February 1992.

303 World Bank news release, "Uganda to Receive US$650 Million in Debt Relief," April 8, 1998. The extent to which this reflects Uganda's position as a recipient of coffee smuggled from Congo/Zaire is not known. It certainly indicates that coffee is no longer smuggled to Zaire as it was in considerable quantities (estimated at 6,000 tons/year) in the early 1980s (Vwakyanakazi, 1991, p. 50; also B.G. Schoepf and C. Schoepf, interviews with coffee traders, 1982, 1985, 1989). Nevertheless, illegal cross-border trade continues into Zaire and Sudan.

304 Most peasants worked only with hand tools; about one-third were able to hire labor in peak seasons. Pressure on the most fertile land is growing, with significant shortages in the southwest and southeast (Jamal, 1991; Kasfir, 1991; Brett, 1996). These were the regions of highest labor migration and, in the 1990s, the highest incidence of AIDS. In 1992-93 Uganda had a fairly favorable Gini coefficient of .41, indicating moderate inequality in household consumption, and the Bank indicates that poverty declined by some 18-20 percent from 1986 (World Bank, 1997, pp. 56-57, T2.6). Nevertheless, poverty remained deeply entrenched among 70 percent of the rural population, and property is increasingly concentrated in the hands of a small elite. For a discussion of the health impact of Uganda's ambiguous renewal, see Macrea, Zwi, and Birungi, 1993.

305 Coffee prices rose in 1994, with the result that currency devaluation failed to produce its intended effect.

306 World Bank, 1999b.

307 This may reflect the beginning of a labor crisis in peasant agriculture, for Uganda is the country most severely impacted by AIDS to date.

308 Prunier, 1998. On March 3, 1999, eight U.S. and British tourists and four Ugandan park rangers were killed in the region. Their deaths imparted international credibility to concerns in Uganda and Rwanda about the security danger posed by the genocider remnants sheltering in Congo/Zaire. African peasants and public servants and their families have been subjected to attacks by the genociders since they created bases in the refugee camps in Zaire.

309 Prunier, 1998.

310 Leymaire, 1998.

311 World Bank news release, "Uganda to Receive US$650 Million in Debt Relief," April 8, 1998.

312 World Bank, 1995, p.78. See the much higher UNDP, 1997, estimates cited in Chapter Two, note 35.

313 ECA, 1989; U.S. African Studies Association Task Force on Sustainable Development, published as Seidman and Anang, 1991; UNDP, 1997; Oxfam, 1998.

314 World Bank, 1999, p. 1. Focusing principally on agriculture and the rural sector, this report states that "one of the factors constraining growth and poverty reduction in SSA is gender inequality in access to and control of a diverse range of assets. In this more uncertain environment, giving attention to removing gender-based obstacles to growth is timely." The Bank should have acknowledged this at least a decade ago and adapted its lending strategy accordingly (see Jolly, 1985; contributors to Gladwin, ed. 1991). Two fairly senior Bank economists took part in the 1990 Conference on Structural Adjustment and African Women Farmers, which gave rise to the volume edited by Gladwin. Advisors can go back to the drawing board. In the meantime, however, millions of people will have needlessly suffered and died.

315 World Bank, 1999b, p. 1.

316 We reported Bank advisors' flagrant disregard of food security in Zimbabwe, in note 110 earlier.

317 For details, see Chapter Eight.

318 We are mindful that we have not adequately pursued considerations of the state in our analysis. We recommend that readers consult Seidman and Anang, 1991; Mamdani, 1996; Ake, 1992; Ake, 1996; and other works cited in earlier sections. Senior African political scientists warn that democratization requires more than multiparty elections and reform of civil society. In the presence of the institutions of the autocratic state, multiparty elections will, at best, lead to alternation of ruling cliques and military rule. Democracy in Africa demands a new kind of state that can generate and sustain broad political participation. This "requires the crystallization of different forms of power...a dismantling of the mode of rule organized on the basis of fused power, administrative justice and extra-economic coercion....[To] create a democratic solidarity requires joining participatory self-rule [in peasant communities] with representational politics....So long as the rural is not reformed, the perversion of civil society is inevitable" (Mamdani, 1996, pp. 297-298).

319 Stott, 1999, pp. 822-823. For a detailed, critical examination of the World Bank's role in development, see Caufield, 1996.

CHAPTER 6
Sickness Amidst Recovery:
Public Debt and Private Suffering in Peru

1   Berry, 1990, p. 135.

2   Names of all individuals described in the case studies have been changed.

3   See Hemlock, "Health Insurer Moves In; Miami Office Covers Hospital Care for Brazilians," *Sun-Sentinel* (Fort Lauderdale), September 9, 1998, 1D; also see Hall, Kevin G., "HMO Hopes Miami Is Gateway to Brazil," *Journal of Commerce*, February 27, 1998.

4   We must make clear, however, that we are not offering up any simplistic programmatic solutions for health-care systems in Peru or anywhere else in Latin America. Simply persisting with an inefficient, uncaring or inaccessible state health-care system is not the objective. As clinicians who have cared for patients in Latin America under government-run systems, several of us have seen firsthand the indifference and poor quality that too often characterize those systems. However, as illustrated in this volume, certain governments have done much better than others in ensuring health care for the entire population, including—and especially—the poor.

5   In 1985, Peru's total external debt was US$12 billion, with debt service of $1.4 billion annually. About one-third of this sum was owed to multilateral and bilateral lenders. By 1988, when García cut annual debt service to $347.1 million (9.7 percent of GDP), external loan principal had risen to $15 billion, and multilateral institutions held approximately half of this total, with an interest in arrears of $2.97 billion (IDB, Economic and Social Database). This afforded agencies like the IMF a great deal of leverage, as they withheld short-term cash infusions until policy changes were implemented.

6   Guillermoprieto, 1994, p. 84.

7   Análisis Tributario, 5(51):1992; PREALC estimates cited in Jiménez, 1996. The CPI is a measure of the average change over time in the prices paid by urban consumers for a fixed "market basket" of consumer goods and services. A normal annual rise is in the vicinity of two or three percentage points.

8   Iguiniz, Basay, and Rubio, 1993.

9   Attempts to determine precise poverty figures in Latin American countries are famously difficult (see Chapters Two and Three; also Mejía and Vos, 1997). By government assessments, using the World Bank's "absolute poverty" threshold ($300/month for a family of five), 50.7 percent of Peruvians were beneath the poverty line in 1997, down from the 1991 high of 57.4 percent (Cuanto, *Perú en Numeros*, 1998). After five years of economic growth under Fujimori, according to the Lima newspaper *Gestion*, 4.5 million Peruvians, 19 percent of the population, were living in extreme poverty as of 1997, without access to sanitation, water, or electricity (cited in Schemo, 1997).

10 Scott, 1994.

11 Harding, 1992, p. 12; IDB, Economic and Social Database.

12 Vogel, "Peru's Big Rebound Sets Off Foreign Investors' Enthusiasm," *Wall Street Journal*, September 15, 1994.

13 U.S. Department of Commerce, 1997.

14 Luxner, "Peru's Poor Need Shield from Asian Flu," *Washington Times*, September 29, 1998.

15 IDB, Economic and Social Database.

16 U.S. Department of Commerce, 1998; IDB, Economic and Social Database. Privatization proceeds were $2.6 billion, while debt service amounted to $2.9 billion.

17 IDB, 1998a, p. 44.

18 Lacey, 1996; see also IDBb, 1998, pp. 181-186.

19 Republic of Perú, National Planning Institute, 1992, p. 87.

20 Between 1994 and 2000, the World Bank, IDB, and several bilateral aid agencies are slated to supply half of the funding for the Ministry of Health's three highest priority initiatives, in infant health, women's health, and infectious disease control (CAME, 1998).

21 See Republic of Perú, 1996b.

22 Republic of Perú, 1996a; Republic of Perú, 1996b, p. 1.

23 Republic of Perú, 1996c.

24 Republic of Perú, 1997a, p. 4.

25 Republic of Perú, 1996b, p. 4.

26 Republic of Perú, 1995; Republic of Perú, 1996b, p. 2. See also Oscar Ugarte and Jose Monge, "Equity and Reform in the Health Sector," address at the "Poverty and Social Policy" seminar of the Social Sciences Network, Líma, October, 1998.

27 Republic of Perú, 1996b, p. 2.

28 Proyecto ley, cited in Republic of Perú, 1997a, p. 5.

29 On the historical roots of privatization in the social services, see Bahmueller, 1981; also Gurin, 1989.

30 Linowes, Anderson, Antonovich, *et al.*, 1988, p. vii.

31 Linowes, Anderson, Antonovich, *et al.*, 1988, p. viii.

32 Linowes, Anderson, Antonovich, *et al.*, 1988, p. 3. As of 1992, three World Bank researchers were brought to conclude that "much of the divestiture debate has been intuitive, theoretical and even ideological" (Kikeri, Nellis, and Shirley, 1992, p. 27).

33 Kikeri, Nellis, and Shirley, 1992, p. 22.

34 OECD, 1998, p. 150.

35 USAID, 1986.

36 USAID, 1987. The Agency for International Development established its Private Enterprise Bureau in July 1981, just after Reagan took office, with the stated purpose of promoting "global integrated capitalism" by reducing aid-recipients' levels of public sector ownership. Subsequently, the agency's loans and grants were made conditional on implementation of privatization strategies. In Costa Rica, for example, funds were not released until 42 of 47 state-owned enterprises had been closed, transferred, or liquidated under AID supervision. In Panama, to repair damage from the 1989 U.S. invasion, the agency conditioned "program assistance" on formulation of a blueprint to reduce tariffs, curb government spending, and sell off state industries. Meanwhile, AID was constructing an international network of enterprise funds, designed to ease American investment "in new private businesses, joint ventures or recently privatized enterprises" (Martin, 1996, p. 148).

37 Kikeri, Nellis, and Shirley, 1992, p. 23.

38 See, for example, Ferreira, 1997.

39 Carlsen, 1994, p. 18.

40 Martin, 1996.

41 The IDB, for example, has been able to detect little appreciable effect of privatization on Latin American growth indicators (IDB, 1998, p. 56). The authors presumed that their measures were inadequate.

42 The inequity in access to health care exists both within and between nations. According to one estimate, countries with per capita annual incomes greater than $8,500 accounted for 89 percent of global health expenditures in 1994, even though they comprised only 16 percent of the global population; residents of poor countries, meanwhile, lost 1.3 trillion disability-adjusted life years to disease, 93 percent of the worldwide total (Schieber and Maeda, 1997; cited in Iglehart, 1999).

43 See Lappé, Shurman, and Danaher, 1987.

44 Harvard Law School, Human Rights Program, 1995.

45 Watkins, 1997; also Gilson, 1989; WHO and UNICEF, 1978.

46 Nozick, 1974, p. 160.

47 Smith and Lipsky, 1992.

48 Nightingale and Pindus, 1997.

49 Nightingale and Pindus, 1997.

50 See Linowes, Anderson, Antonovich, et al., 1998; also Smith and Lipsky, 1992.

51 For example, President Reagan's Commission on Privatization began its report with the assertion that the federal government had become "too large, too expensive, and too intrusive into our lives" (Linowes, Anderson, Antonovich, et al., 1988, p. 1).

52 Adam, Cavendish, and Mistry, 1992, p. 9.

53 Boloña, 1996, p. 240; U.S. Department of Commerce, 1997.

54 U.S. Department of Commerce, 1997.

55 IDB, 1998, pp. 46-47; U.S. Department of Commerce, 1997.

56 "Peru: Construction of $40,000,000 Leaching and Metallurgical Facilities," 1994.

57 "Peru's Fujimori Inaugurates Yanacocha Gold Mine," Reuter Business Report, August 11, 1993.

58 Newmont Gold Company, 1997; Chatterjee, 1997.

59 Everest, 1994.

60 U.S. Department of Commerce, 1997.

61 Schiffer, 1995.

62 Cuánto, 1997, pg. 445.

63 U.S. Department of Commerce, 1998; Everest, 1994.

64 Cited in Diebel, 1997. Fujimori's privatization initiatives had the added effect of swelling the Peruvian informal-sector workforce—which already amounted to about two-thirds of the economically active population in 1990 (Mauceri, 1995). As of 1994, 73 percent of Lima's population was completely outside the formal economy, compared with 26 percent in 1980 (Scott, 1994). By 1995, according to UNDP estimates, 60 percent of the country's work hours, 70 percent of its housing, and 95 percent of its mass transport were provided via the informal sector—whose workers did not receive even the minimal benefits offered by private formal-sector employers ("Much of Peru's Employment Sector is Informal," 1995).

65 U.S. Department of Commerce, 1997, 1998.

66 U.S. Department of Commerce, 1997.

67 Everest, 1994.

68 Chatterjee, 1997.

69 U.S. Department of Commerce, 1998.

70 Chatterjee, 1997.

71 Quoted in Molinski, 1997.

72 U.S. Department of Commerce, 1997.

73 See Chapter Four.

74 Widespread complaints in the early 1990s that foreign investors were profiting from privatizations at the expense of Peruvians were of some concern to the Fujimori government. In 1994, the state privatization agency, Copri, launched a campaign to sell small shares in privatized companies to the general populace, targeting lower-income segments of the population in particular. Not surprisingly, while the program did distribute some 18,000 of these shares by 1996—at $200 to $1400 apiece—most of the participants were relatively well-off, and attempts to involve Peruvians earning less than $250 a month failed entirely. Copri planners, however, were seemingly undaunted; as the Wall Street Journal reported, "Opinion pollsters for the project are currently conducting extensive market surveys to determine how to include this group in the process" (Graham, 1996).

75 Sachs and Paredes, eds., 1991.

76 Bourguignon and Morrisson, 1992.

77 Cornia, Jolly, and Stewart, 1987.

78 Malena, 1997; Sachs and Paredes, eds., 1991.

79 Gamero, 1996.

80 Republic of Perú, Ministry of Health, 1992.

81 U.S. Department of Commerce, 1997.

82 Cuánto, 1991, p. 232.

83 Republic of Perú, Ministry of Health, 1992, p. 12.

84 See, for example, Bird, "Peru: A Nineteenth-Century Tragedy Reborn in Latin America," Manchester Guardian, May 17, 1991.

85 WHO, 1998e.

86 Ricardo V. Luna, Letter, Washington Post, August 24, 1997.

87 Burt, 1996.

88 Burt, 1996.

89 Rudolph, 1992, pp. 133–34.

90 Gates, 1996.

91 Enthoven, 1988.

92 Gates, 1996.

93 Zarabozo and LeMasurier, 1995; cited in Gates, 1996.

94 Fleming and Boles, 1994; cited in Gates, 1996; on "cherry picking" by for-profit chains, see Baxter and Mechanic, 1997.

95 Trager, 1998; this number has been projected to exceed 100 million by the year 2000 (Zaldivar, 1996).

96 Johnson, 1985; cited in Bergthold, Estes, and Villanueva, 1990.

97 Calculated from Hudson, 1997, p. 22.

98 This was suggested by several studies in the early 1980s (for example, Pattison and Katz, 1983). By the end of 1998, amid reports of heavy corporate losses, researchers were projecting HMO premium increases

of up to 20 percent for consumers whose insurance was issued by their employers, and 40 percent for those with individual policies (Kilborn, 1998c). Meanwhile, a 1997 survey by the California Medical Association indicated that of the state's 15 largest HMOs, medical expenditures averaged only 82.6 percent of the total, with administration and profits accounting for the remainder (Sinton, 1997).

99 Abelson, 1999.

100 Smith, Freeland, Heffler, et al., 1998; see also Iglehart, 1999.

101 Gray, 1986.

102 Marmor, Schlesinger, and Smithey, 1987; see also Dumont, 1992.

103 Cited in Bergthold, Estes, and Villanueva, 1990, p. 25.

104 Eckholm, 1994, p. A1.

105 Freeman, Blendon, Aiken, et al., 1987, pp. 6-18; Sulvetta and Swartz, 1986; Kuttner, 1999.

106 Baxter and Mechanic, 1997.

107 Ware, Rogers, Davies, et al., 1986.

108 Kilborn, 1998a; see also Pear, 1998; Kuttner, 1999.

109 Hahn, Barker, and Teutsch, 1996; see also Hahn, Eaker, Barker, et al., 1995; Lynch, Kaplan, Pamuk, et al., 1998.

110 "Rising Costs in Health Care," 1998.

111 Arrow, 1963; Smith and Lipsky make a similar point in concluding that "[If government health] professionals often find it difficult to evaluate the quality and cost of health care...surely the citizenry will find the task equally if not more problematic" (1992, p. 237). Arrow has argued in a recent interview for a "single payer" centralized health-care system as the most rational way to allocate scarce resources ("Interview with Kenneth Arrow," 1995).

112 See George and Sabelli, 1994; Chossudovsky, 1997; Rich, 1994; Caufield, 1996.

113 George and Sabelli, 1994, p. 5; also Robert Wade, "Japan, the World Bank, and the Art of Paradigm Maintenance," New Left Review 217 (May-June 1996), pp. 3-36.

114 See Chapter Two.

115 Ferreira, 1997.

116 Ravallion, 1997.

117 Filmer, Hammer, and Pritchett, 1997.

118 Brown, 1997

119 WHO and UNICEF, 1978.

120 WHO, 1998e; the U.S. is currently an estimated $145 million in arrears of its obligation to WHO.

121 WHO, "Provisional Draft of the Program Budget of the World Health Organization for the Region of The Americas for the Financial Period 1998-1999," available at www.paho.org/english/ opsreso2.htm.

122 Brown, 1997.

123 IOM, 1997; United Nations Joint Programme on HIV/AIDS, 1995.

124 Kumar, 1997, p. 1233.

125 Most World Bank publications treat improved health as something that should flow naturally from a growing economy. See, for example, Pritchett and Filmer, 1997.

126 Richard Feacham, senior health advisor to the World Bank, in an address to the Department of Social Medicine at Harvard Medical School, 1996.

127 World Bank, 1993b, p. 5.

128 World Bank, 1993b, p. 5.

129 World Bank, 1987b, p. 1.

130 World Bank, 1993b, p. 6.

131 De Ferranti, 1985, pp. 20, 22.

132 De Ferranti, 1985, p. 38.

133 World Bank, 1987a.

134 Gertler and Van der Gaag, 1990; Waddington and Enyimaywe, 1990; Gertler and Van der Gaag, 1988.

135 Watkins, 1997; Gilson, 1995.

136 Watkins, 1997.

137 Van der Gaag, 1995, pp. 18-20. Emphasis added.

138 Turshen, 1999, p. 47.

139 Shaw and Griffin, 1995, p. 3.

140 Shaw and Griffin, 1995, p. 8.

141 Shaw and Griffin, 1995, pp. 13-14.

142 Hammer and Gertler, 1997, p. 5.

143 Creese, 1991.

144 Shaw and Griffin 1995, p. 17; see also McPake, 1993.

145 Hammer and Gertler, 1997.

146 Goodman and Waddington, 1993.

147 Hammer and Gertler, 1997, p. 12.

148 Okuonzi and Macrae, 1995; cited Turshen, 1999, p. 50.

149 World Bank, 1998c, p. 8.

150 UNDP, 1997, p. 175.

151 Hammer and Gertler, 1997.

152 Gertler and Molynueax, 1997.

153 See, for example, Filmer and Pritchett, 1997.

154 Schwartz, 1995, pp. 36-40.

155 Pallarito, 1997; "Hurdling a Great Wall," 1997.

156 See, for example, Himmelstein, Wolfe, and Woolhandler, 1993.

157 Carabayllo Rural: Tierra, Agua, y Vida, 1993.

158 In fact, this recommendation was a policy directive from the highest levels of state power. In 1995, President Alberto Fujimori announced that an important reason for poverty in Peru was overpopulation; to combat it, he launched a campaign to encourage tubal ligations and vasectomies. Part of this campaign involved prominent Peruvians appearing on national television, expressing their delight with the results of these procedures; it also involved monetary incentives for health workers to encourage tubal ligations and vasectomies at public health facilities.

159 This case was written in December of 1996.

160 IOM, 1997, Appendix; IDB, 1998a.

161 See, for example, World Bank, 1996c; Malena, 1997.

162 Republic of Perú, 1997b, Appendix 1; Jameson, 1991.

163 Coalition of Peruvian NGOs, 1997.

164 Iguiñiz, 1995.

165 Linowes, Anderson, Antonovich, et al., 1988, p. 194.

166 Calculated from IDB, Social and Economic Database.

167 World Bank, 1993b.

168 WHO, 1998b.

169 See Iguiñiz, 1995.

170 For a review, see Chapter Two.

CHAPTER 7
Neoliberal Economic Policy, "State Desertion," and the Russian Health Crisis

1 Cited in Rimashevskaia, 1993.

2 Davis and Feshbach, 1980.

3 Kotz, with Weir, 1997, chapter 3. The steady rise in Soviet aggregate economic output and consumption shows up in Western estimates as well as in official Soviet statistics.

4 For further reading, see *Daedalus*, Volume 123, Number 4, 1994, titled "Health and Wealth."

5 Popkin, Zohoori, Kohlmeier, *et al.*, 1997, pp. 327-328.

6 Davis, 1993, estimates the figure at 2.3 percent for 1992.

7 See Feshbach, 1995a, 1995b; Feshbach and Friendly, 1992; Stewart, 1996; and cf. Tulchinsky and Varavikova, 1996, p. 317.

8 Ellman, 1994. According to Ellman, the term "katastroika" was coined by A. Zinoviev, combining *katastrofa* (catastrophe) and *perestroika* (restructuring).

9 *Gosudarstvenii doklad o sostoianii zdorovia naselenia Rossiiskoi Federatsii v 1991 godu*, 1992b; and *Gosudarstvenii doklad o sostoianii okruzhaioushchei prirodnoi sredi Rossiiskoi Federatsii v 1991 godu*, 1992a.

10 In a later section, we consider the possibility that the worsening health data are a statistical artifact resulting from changes in data collection methods and/or reporting procedures.

11 U.S. Department of Health and Human Services, 1995.

12 *Goskomstat*, 1996.

13 See, for example, Ellman, 1994, pp. 334-336.

14 *Goskomstat*, 1996.

15 *Sevodnia*, 1995.

16 Eberstadt, in press.

17 Centers for Disease Control, 1995, p. 178; cf. Ellman, 1994, pp. 344-345; Fontanarosa, 1995.

18 Feshbach, 1995a, cited in Stewart 1996, p. 203.

19 Ellman, 1994, p. 345.

20 Ellman, 1994, p. 345.

21 Rybinskii, 1996, p. 83.

22 Ingram, 1995; Tulchinsky and Varavikova, 1996.

23 According to Dr. Alexey Priymak, one of the leaders of tuberculosis control efforts in Russia (Garrett, 1997).

24 In 1991, 50,407 cases were reported; in 1996 this figure was up to 111,075. Compare the number of cases reported in Russia in 1996 (111,075) to the 26,000 reported in the United States, which has a population of 270 million, nearly twice that of the Russian Federation (WHO, 1998b, p. 114).

25 Meek, 1998.

26 Filipov, 1998.

27 In the 1970s, the Soviet Union had brought tuberculosis under control (WHO, 1998b).

28 Arata Kochi, director of the WHO Global Tuberculosis Program, said, "The number of tuberculosis cases in 1996 in Russia alone equals those reported in Ethiopia and Sudan, combined. We have never seen such an increase before." Garrett, "TB Surge in Former East Bloc," *New York Newsday*, March 25, 1998.

29 Loguinova, 1998.

30 Garrett, 1997.

31 Nikolai Grisoriench Mednikov, personal communication, 1998.

32 Farmer, 1998.

33 Nikolai Grisoriench Mednikov, personal communication, 1999.

34 Garrett, 1997.

35 Filipov, 1998.

36 Garrett, 1997.

37 Wares and Clowers, 1997, p. 957. Infection with the *Mycobacterium tuberculosis* does not imply that one is *actually* ill with tuberculosis. Once infected with the organism, risk for developing active disease is related to many factors, among the most important of which are the viability of one's immune system (especially cell-mediated immunity) and nutritional status. In the absence of HIV coinfection, only about 10 percent of individuals infected with the organism that causes tuberculosis ever develop active disease.

38 Paul Farmer, personal communication, September, 1998. Alex Goldfarb and Michael Kimerling (PHRI-SOROS Russia Program: An Initiative of the International Center for Public Health for the GORE-PRIMAKOV Commission, March 23, 1999) argue that the rate of tuberculosis is 60 times greater in prison than in the general public.

39 Franchetti, 1997.

40 Farmer, 1998.

41 Farmer, 1998.

42 Franchetti, 1997.

43 Multidrug-resistant tuberculosis (MDRTB) is an especially alarming problem in countries without strong health sectors, as it is both extremely difficult to treat—the treatment course is at least three times as long as for drug-susceptible tuberculosis—and much more expensive, requiring expenditures of up to $10,000 per year per patient. For reviews of the global problem of MDRTB, see Farmer and Kim, 1998; Farmer, Bayona, Becerra, *et al.*, 1998; Farmer 1999b.

44 Filipov, 1998.

45 Retreatment therapy, which is provided to patients who fail the initial treatment with four drugs, contains five drugs and lasts eight months instead of six (Kimerling, Kluge, Vezhnina, *et al.*, 1999; Farmer, 1999b).

46 Englund, "Resistant Tuberculosis Strains Spreading from Russia," *Baltimore Sun*, September 14, 1998.

47 Loguinova, 1998.

48 Williams, "Tuberculosis Treatment from Soviet Era Hinders Healing," *Los Angeles Times*, November 28, 1997.

49 Stanley, "Russians Lament the Crime of Punishment," *New York Times*, January 8, 1998.

50 Warren, "Diet of Despair in Russia's Cash-starved Jails," *Daily Telegraph*, November 17, 1998.

51 Meek, 1998.

52 Priymak, in Garrett, 1997.

53 Filipov, 1998.

54 Tulchinsky and Varavikova, 1996; Centers for Disease Control, 1992; Rush and Welch, 1996.

55 Rush and Welch, 1996.

56 Rimashevskaia, 1993, pp. 23, 32. See also Rybinskii, 1996, p. 83.

57 *Moscow News*, 1995.

58 Rybinskii, 1996, p. 83.

59 Field, 1995, p. 1473.

60 Tulchinsky and Varavikova, 1996, p. 317.

61 See Stewart, 1996, p. 203.

62 *Draft Document on Effects of Pollution on Health of Russian Population*, 1994. See Field, 1995, p. 1473.

63 Although the focus of this chapter is on the striking decline in health outcomes in post-Soviet Russia, it is important to note that the Russian government has succeeded in making some positive public health changes in recent years. In particular, the rights of patients are expanding, physician access to new medical research is increasing, and medical ethics overall are improving with the 1993 implementation of new public health laws. However, because most of the increased mortality and morbidity seen in Russia today is due to factors outside the purview of the public health sector, these positive changes are not likely to have a discernible impact on health outcomes of the population. For an examination of the current state of health care, medical practice, and medical ethics in Russia, see Cassileth, Vlassov, and Chapman, 1995.

64 See Field, 1995, p. 1476.

65 The main figure in the design of Russia's economic policies in 1991-92 was Yegor T. Gaidar, whom President Yeltsin took on as his chief economic advisor in the fall of 1991. Gaidar served as deputy prime minister in charge of the economy and as Prime Minister at various times during 1991-94. Other influential Russian economic officials who promoted the neoliberal economic strategy included Boris Fyodorov, who served as Finance Minister, and Anatoly Chubais, who was in charge of the privatization program.

66 Professor Jeffrey Sachs of Harvard University and Anders Aslund of the Carnegie Endowment in Washington, D.C., who were probably the most important Western economic advisors to the Yeltsin government, both strongly recommended that Russia follow the neoliberal strategy.

67 Not only has the IMF directly supplied about one-fourth of the total financial aid coming from the West, but the major Western nations have made their own individual grants and loans to Russia conditional upon IMF approval of Russia's economic programs. The World Bank has played second fiddle to the IMF in Russia.

68 The rationale for this approach has been sketched out in a host of books and articles; a good example is World Bank, 1996e.

69 Kotz with Weir, 1997, chapter 9, provides detailed evidence for the claim that Russia closely followed the neoliberal economic strategy during 1992-95.

70 The only exception to this was during the months immediately preceding the June 1996 presidential election. During that period the Yeltsin government, with Western (and IMF) blessing and financial backing, spent billions of dollars to make good on wage and pension arrears owed to millions of workers and retirees. The government also practically stopped collecting taxes during that period.

71 IMF, 1992, p. 70; IMF, 1995c, pp. 5, 21. The figure for 1995 is an estimate for the first six months of that year. By 1995, Russian government spending relative to GDP had fallen significantly below that of the United States.

72 IMF, 1993, pp. 88, 100; IMF, 1994, pp. 73, 98; IMF, 1995c, pp. 8, 26.

73 IMF, 1994, pp. 56, 128; *Goskomstat Rossii*, 1995a, p. 41.

74 Burger, Field, and Twigg, 1998.

75 The Russian central bank does intervene in the currency markets to reduce the short-run fluctuations in the value of the nation's currency, a practice followed by the central banks of most nations.

76 *Goskomstat Rossii*, 1997, p. 10; IMF, 1993, p. 85; IMF, 1995b, p. 1; OECD, 1997, p. 88. The figure for agricultural output is through June 1995.

77 IMF, 1993, p. 88.

78 *Goskomstat Rossii*, 1997, p. 52.

79 IMF, 1993, pp. 88, 91; IMF, 1994, pp. 73, 78; *Goskomstat Rossii*, 1995a, pp. 45, 59, 61; *Goskomstat Rossii*, 1995b, pp. 44, 60, 62.

80 Unpaid wages were estimated at 36.5 trillion rubles ($6.8 billion) in September 1996, which represented approximately 66 percent of the nation's total monthly wage bill (Open Media Research Institute, 1996a, and OECD, 1997, p. 88). Pension arrears amounted to 13.3 trillion rubles ($2.5 billion) in October 1996 (Open Media Research Institute, 1996b).

81 See, for example, Ellman, 1994, p. 341. The rapid impoverishment had a particularly brutal impact on children. Ellman cites governmental and nongovernmental Russian sources indicating that, "In 1992, 46-47 percent of all children below the age of 15 were living in poverty" (1994, p. 341).

82 Chen, Wittgenstein, and McKeon, 1996, p. 521.

83 McAuley, 1979, p. 57; *Goskomstat Rossii*, 1995b, no. 12, p. 58.

84 Bohlen, 1994.

85 For example, see Amsden, Kochanowicz, and Taylor, 1994; Goldman, 1994; Kotz, with Weir, 1997.

86 See especially Goldman, 1994; Kotz, with Weir, 1997.

87 During the three-year period 1992-94, gross direct foreign investment in Russia was $3.9 billion (Economic Commission for Europe, 1995, p. 148). During those same years, capital flight from Russia has been estimated by knowledgeable observers at between $50 and $100 billion (see Open Media Research Institute, 1995).

88 See Shkolnikov and Nemtsov, 1997, p. 243.

89 See Chapters One and Two of this volume; Farmer, 1999a.

90 Kennedy, Kawachi, and Prothow-Stith, 1996.

91 Kaplan, Pammuk, Lynch, *et al.*, 1996.

92 Chen, Wittgenstein, and McKeon, 1996, p. 522.

93 Shapiro, 1995.

94 The data on overall death rate shown in Table 7.3 from Feshbach, 1995a, contain slight differences from the official Russian death rates shown in Table 7.1.

95 "Poisoning" refers to death due to the ingestion of one or more toxins. It includes alcohol poisoning.

96 Feshbach, 1995a, Table 3.11, pp. 3-35.

97 Ellman, 1994, p. 349.

98 Avraamova, 1994, p. 24.

99 See UNICEF, 1993a, p. 46.

100 Ellman, 1994, p. 343.

101 Ellman, 1994, p. 343.

102 For example, see *Literaturnaia Gazeta*, 1994.

103 Rimashevskaia, 1993, pp. 33-34.

104 Tulchinsky and Varavikova, 1996, p. 315.

105 Anderson and Silver, 1997; Leon, Chenet, Shkolnikov, *et al.*, 1997.

106 Leon, Chenet, Shkolnikov, *et al.*, 1997, p. 386.

107 Shapiro, 1995, pp. 149-178.

108 See Feshbach and Friendly, 1992.

109 Andreev, 1994.

110 Michael Binyon, "Russia's Health Crisis Strikes the Weaker Sex," *The Times* (U.K.), August 23, 1999.

CHAPTER 8
Dying for Growth, Part I:
Transnational Corporations and
the Health of the Poor

1 Galbraith, 1977, p. 257.

2 *Transnational corporations* are firms that operate in more than one country, and are sometimes called *multinational corporations, multinational enterprises, international corporations,* or *global corporations.* Most of the differences among terms are strictly technical, but between "multinational" and "transnational" additional ideological and analytical factors come into play. Whereas the subsidiaries of multinational corporations are more tied to local economies and maintain relatively autonomous production and sales facilities in individual countries, the operations of transnational corporations are more fluid—based on vertically integrated supplier networks—and less integrated into the individual local economies in which they operate (Korten, 1995). The term "multinational" denotes a company owned by citizens of several countries and implies a certain coequality among them. "Transnational" more accurately describes the hierarchy now common in most global operations and a certain degree of "domination" between the parent firm and its subsidiary, subcontracting, and supplier offspring.

Transnational corporations extend their reach through foreign direct investment (FDI) and operate in several countries through affiliates or subsidiaries that are subject to a degree of central control. Distinct from firms that produce in one country and export to overseas markets, FDI involves the transfer of a package of resources (e.g., technology, equipment, management skills, and organizational capacity) across national boundaries, the *de jure* governance of which remains largely in the hands of the transferring firms (Dunning, 1993). The level of involvement parent firms have in the operation of their foreign affiliates differs significantly from company to company. Parent firms exercise their influence in a wide variety of ways, including through control of crucial aspects of the affiliate's operations, such as production and pricing, selection of technological inputs, determination of markets, and hiring of key personnel. Transnational corporations are involved in manufacturing, extracting, and processing activities, and in industries including textiles, agriculture, food, mining, oil, metals, coal, and petroleum products. They are also involved in communications, construction, transportation, real estate, and biotechnology. For an in-depth examination of the history of transnational corporations, see Jones, 1993.

3 A limited number of peer-reviewed articles and books have been published on the health effects of TNC activities in marginalized communities. Yet nongovernmental organizations (NGOs) and community activist groups have written prolifically on this subject. Throughout the preparation of Parts I and II of this chapter, the authors relied on scholarly literature whenever possible. In other instances, they consulted NGO reports and studies, or what is known as "gray literature." All gray literature data and sources have been cross-checked, and whenever possible the authors provide reference citations in the notes to assist readers who wish to conduct their own research.

4 For a description of the history and elements of neoliberalism, refer to Chapters Two and Three.

5 Transnational corporations can positively affect the health of populations when, for example, they provide remunerative employment and resources to people who previously had neither. In the United States from the 1950s to the 1970s, when unions were strong and many companies still operated in one or a few locations, corporations sometimes provided well-paid jobs, health care, and pensions to unemployed people, including women and minority populations. When company operations were fixed in one locale, and the corporation's owners and managers lived in the same community, business leaders tended, at least in some cases, to take an active role in promoting the health, education, and welfare of the local population. But today most large corporations are no longer based in one place. Rather, their operations are widely dispersed in every corner of the globe. As of 1993, for example, the Swiss electrical engineering giant ABB had facilities in 140 nations. Royal Dutch Shell explored for oil in 50 countries, refined in 34, and had markets in 100. Cargill, the U.S. grain company, operated in 54 countries, and H.J. Heinz was on six continents (Hoover's Handbook of World Business, 1993). By 1996, General Motors was operating in 190 countries (see the company's official website: www.gm.com).

In other circumstances, the impact of transnational corporations can be decisively negative. This is because TNCs are, of course, first and foremost profit-seeking entities that prioritize their commercial interests over the needs of the environment and the public's health. This is evident when, for example, their operations deplete the natural resource base or pollute the ground, water, and air; when their promotional activities influence consumers to adopt harmful practices; or when their lobbying efforts and political influence undermine the tools that democratically elected national governments use to protect their citizens and environment.

For people in the world's wealthy communities at least, the benefits provided by TNCs occur in tandem with their negative effects. After all, large TNCs bring us many of our creature comforts and make possible our unprecedented variety of consumer choices. However, for poor communities, the negative aspects of TNC operations and influence can outweigh the positive effects in important ways. Where people are politically less vocal and economically less influential, the consequences of TNC activities can be lethal—for present and for future populations.

6   Transnational corporations have not cornered the market on practices that harm the health of individuals and communities. Long before the dawn of industrialization, workers were exploited and environments degraded by state, religious, private, and public ventures. Many, if not most, large national corporations throughout the industrial era exploited workers and the environment. But today, with the massive and growing inequities between nations, and increasing deregulation of trade, labor, and markets, it is large, transnational corporations that most systematically take advantage of differential labor and environmental standards between wealthy and poor communities.

Transnational corporations are not intrinsically more prone than national companies to act in harmful and exploitative ways. It is simply easier today for them to do so—especially where workers, communities, and local governments have limited means to hold TNCs accountable for labor excesses and environmental negligence.

7   UNRISD, 1995, p. 154. Although TNCs control over 33 percent of the world's productive assets, they are largely concentrated in capital-intensive industries and they employ directly or indirectly only about 5 percent of the total global workforce. Yet TNCs affect the welfare of many times this number, because companies have additional links to the local economy, and most workers support at least two dependents.

8   Debate persists on the respective roles of the market versus the state. For more on this artificial dichotomy, see Chapter Three.

9   For the preparation of this box, we relied on Grossman and Adams, 1993, 1996.

10   Grossman and Adams, 1993, p. 16.

11   Korten, 1995, p. 56. See also Grossman and Adams, 1996.

12   Contrary to popular perception, U.S. multinational corporations are not a post-1945 phenomenon. As early as the 1850s, U.S. gun manufacturer Colt had built a factory in Britain. In 1867, Singer Sewing Machine's factory in Glasgow became the first sustained U.S. transnational investment. By 1914, over 40 U.S. companies—including Coca-Cola, Gillette, H.J. Heinz, Quaker Oats, and Ford—had built factories overseas. In the post-World War II era, however, the Marshall Plan, by design, helped to advance U.S.

TNC investment. For a literature review of the history of TNCs, see Jones, 1993.

13   Ruth Rosenbaum, paper presented for Health and Social Justice Seminar, Department of Social Medicine, Harvard Medical School, April 1998.

14   Korten, 1995, p. 54.

15   Calculated from the World Bank, 1999b, and "Fortune's 500 of 1998," Fortune, April 5, 1999.

16   Cited in Interfaith Center for Corporate Responsibility, 1995.

17   Though the picture is gradually changing, transnationals of American origin are still the most imposing in the world: of the world's five hundred largest corporations, over three hundred are American (Heilbroner and Thurow, 1994).

18   Estes, 1996, p. 88.

19   UNCTAD, 1994.

20   UNCTAD, 1994.

21   Anderson and Cavanagh, 1996. This "apples and oranges" comparison is made simply to illustrate the enormity of resources involved.

22   For more details, see Chapter Nine.

23   Danaher, 1996, p. 17, and Korten, 1995, p. 124 citing Business Week, May 14, 1990, p. 98.

24   It is not always the case that political leaders seek to implement policies to protect their citizens. Some, such as malevolent dictators, make little or no effort to do so, while other leaders fail to because of political and economic reasons.

25   As quoted in Heilbroner and Thurow, 1994, p. 246.

26   For more detail, see Chapters Two and Five.

27   Caves, 1996; WTO, 1996a.

28   Solutions to economic problems are often discussed in terms of more or less state involvement. But as some scholars recognize, this simple theoretical calculation may miss the real issues, especially for poor countries. Not only the quantity, but also the quality and kind of state intervention must be considered. According to Chilean economist Osvaldo Sunkel, "It is widely recognized that underdeveloped countries have special characteristics and that several of the assumptions of neoclassical economics do not pertain or do so only slightly. There is a strong case for government interventions to foster development....The state must perform regulatory and strategic coordination and guidance functions in interaction with the private sector." Ultimately, he asserts, "A dialectical, mutually reinforcing process between the state and the private sector must be worked out, its nature highly dependent on the concrete circumstances of each country, including in particular the strengths and weaknesses of the state apparatus" (Sunkel, 1995, p. 66). See also Simmons, 1995, p. 15.

29   Goodman, 1987. The bulk of TNC activity still takes place among the world's richest nations; the countries that are home to the most TNCs are also the leading hosts to foreign companies (WTO, 1996a). Though the poorest nations do not represent a major investment interest for TNCs, poor countries have seen a significant increase in foreign direct investment over the last several years. Furthermore, most analysts project that this form of investment in developing nations will continue to increase in the foreseeable

future. Even though poor countries receive a relatively small share of the world foreign direct investment total, its impact on the lives of those living in these countries is, as we shall see, enormous.

30 UNCTAD, 1994, p. XIX.

31 Arruda, 1994.

32 Tarzi, 1995.

33 Poor-country governments most object to the use of "transfer pricing," which is an accounting scheme that takes advantage of the immense inequalities between wealthy and poor countries. When TNCs exchange goods among their different branches or subsidiaries located in different countries, they can avoid taxation by adjusting prices on this intrafirm trade in order to shift profits from subsidiaries located in high-tax countries to those residing in low-tax countries. Alternatively, they can circumvent restrictions on the repatriation of profits imposed by host-country governments using similar accounting strategies. Transfer pricing not only tends to reduce host country revenues from foreign investors, it also contributes to the maintenance of the world's great economic divisions.

Surveying the often hollow promises of FDI as an engine for economic growth in poor countries, Robert Caves (1996, p. 237) concludes: "The relationship between a least-developed country's stock of foreign investment and its subsequent economic growth is a matter on which we totally lack trustworthy conclusions." Caves suggests that the literature on the topic has been highly biased, and that "the statistical studies on this issue bear strong imprints of their authors' prior beliefs about whether a negative or positive relationship would emerge." Even when a strong link is made between the level of increased direct foreign investment and economic growth, as was the case among the fallen Asian Tiger countries during the early and mid-1990s, there is no guarantee that the trend will be durable.

34 LeQuesne, 1996.

35 Martin Khor, quoted in Breslow, 1995, p. 111.

36 No one knows with precision how many people died or were injured in the accident. The official figure given by the government of India in its lawsuit against Union Carbide counts 1,754 dead and 200,000 injured. A senior UNICEF official suggests, however, that as many as 10,000 may have died. This estimate is based on the number of shrouds and the amount of cremation wood sold in the weeks following the accident (Morehouse, 1994, p. 165).

Disasters such as these are often glaring demonstrations of the discrepancy of standards TNCs permit between plants in their home countries and their subsidiary plants overseas. The "double standards" are the norm rather than the exception. More often than not, transnational corporations are not as careful or thorough in their handling of industrial hazards in their foreign affiliates as they are in their home countries (Castleman, 1995). In the case of the Bhopal disaster, double standards were pervasive in both the design of the plant and in its operation. Compared to Union Carbide's U.S.-based plants, their Indian facilities were simply unsafe. In India, dangerous raw materials were kept in storage facilities larger than officially allowed, safety controls were inadequate or inoperative, insuffi-

cient numbers of people were employed in maintenance and safety, management was poorly prepared and inadequately trained, and untrained employees were charged with carrying out complex production procedures (Castleman and Purkavastha, 1985). In the wake of Bhopal, the United Nations Center on Transnational Corporations found numerous examples where worker and community health protection measures were far weaker in the developing-country affiliates of TNCs than in their home country (United Nations Center on Transnational Corporations, 1985).

37 The popular news media have covered these issues. See, for example, Steven Greenhouse, "Live with Kathie Lee and Apparel Workers," New York Times, May 31, 1996; William Branigin, "Honduran Girl Asks Gifford to Help End Maltreatment," Washington Post, May 30, 1996; Jean Seligmann, "A Dustup Over a Dressing Down," Newsweek, May 13, 1996; "Kathie Lee Defends Herself on Sweatshop Charges," Philadelphia Inquirer, May 2, 1996; Eyal Press, "No Sweat: The Fashion Industry Patches Its Image," Progressive, September, 1996, pp. 30-31.

38 "Interview with Ledum Mitee, Deputy President of MOSOP," 1996; Cayford, 1996; Kretzmann, 1995; Lewis, 1996; Shelby, 1996. See Box 8.3.

39 National Labor Committee, 1996; Verhoogen, 1996.

40 Joyce Millen, personal communication with Jeff Ballinger, January, 1999. Ballinger has written extensively on Nike in Indonesia. For information about Nike's and other TNCs' labor practices, contact Global Exchange, National Labor Committee (see Chapter Sixteen), and Press for Change in Alpine, New Jersey.

41 Schanberg and Dorigny, 1996; Mehra-Kerpelman, 1996; Green, 1999. Some estimate that as many as 200 million children work worldwide as "bonded laborers" (a euphemism for slavery), factory and agricultural workers, domestic help, and sex workers (UNDP, 1996). Many of these children are sold by their parents, while others are kidnapped from poor communities by slave dealers who sell them to manufacturers seeking cheap labor. Compared to the number of children working in local industries, the number of children at work for TNCs is small—but these numbers are on the rise as TNCs increasingly use subcontractors, which in some cases rely heavily on child labor. Children under 14 years of age work in industries such as carpet weaving, apparel, glass manufacturing, brick making, mining, and smelting. For a study of child labor in India's export industries, see Harvey and Riggin, 1994.

Although it is difficult to determine with precision how many children are in the global labor market, UNICEF reported in 1991 that approximately 80 million children between ten and 14 years old were engaged in work so taxing to their young bodies that their development was impaired (UNICEF, 1991). According to the International Labor Organization (ILO), two-thirds of working children are employed in Asia, where they are exposed to pesticides, herbicides, fertilizers, heavy loads, industrial machines, loud noise, poor lighting, toxic fumes, and asbestos (ILO, 1996).

Children are not only sought after as laborers because they are considered cheap or because they have small and nimble fingers. They are preferred by employers because they do not engage in labor disputes, they accept longer working hours, and they are easily subdued (Mehra-Kerpelman, 1996, p. 9). Though most governments have laws prohibiting child labor, rarely are such laws actually enforced. Even if governments were able to enforce antislavery and child-labor laws, many would not do so because, as a report on the state of world mental health states: "The industries in which these children work often bring in well-needed foreign revenue, and many governments are thus willing to ignore the exploitation" (Desjarlais, Eisenberg, Good, et al., 1995, p. 161).

42 Vilas, 1999, p. 15.

43 Green, 1995, p. 96.

44 "Tough Times: Labor in the Americas," 1999, p. 14.

45 Gereffi and Hempel, 1996.

46 Barten and Fustukian, 1994; Cameron and Mackenzie, 1994.

47 Schanberg and Dorigny, 1996.

48 The terms are used synonymously.

49 For examples, see Cavanagh, Gershman, Baker, et al., 1992; Henwood, 1996; Gereffi and Hempel, 1996; Ratnapriya, 1995; Clifford, Shari, and Himelstein, 1996; Herbert, 1996a; Herbert, 1996b; Zimmerman, 1995; Harris and McKay, 1996.

50 Goldsmith, 1996.

51 Gereffi and Hempel, 1996.

52 Rosenbaum, Charkoudian, and Wrinn, 1996.

53 Rosenbaum, 1994.

54 Gereffi and Hempel, 1996.

55 Verhoogen, 1996, p. 10.

56 Verhoogen, 1996.

57 From an interview by Mary Jo McConahay with Myra Esperanza Mejia, which appeared in "In Their Own Words," Boston Globe, June 15, 1997.

58 National Labor Committee, 1995.

59 Human Rights Watch at www.hrw.org. See also Chapter Eleven.

60 Steven Greenhouse, "18 Major Retailers and Apparel Makers Are Accused of Using Sweatshops," New York Times, January 14, 1999.

61 Goldsmith, 1996, p. 269.

62 Goldsmith, 1996, p. 267.

63 Ratnapriya, 1995, p. 32.

64 Korten, 1995, p. 129.

65 ICFTU, 1997.

66 ICFTU, 1997.

67 ICFTU, 1997. Among the more prominent, ongoing cases of detention is the case of Liu Jingsheng, founder of China's Free Labor Unions, arrested in 1992 and sentenced to 15 years in prison for union activities, and the case of Dita Indah Sari, the leader of an independent trade union in Indonesia, detained since 1996 and sentenced to five years in prison for "subversion."

Union organizing in many parts of South America has become extremely hazardous. After Colombia topped the list of most dangerous countries in which to organize in 1997, with 160 murders of trade unionists, 1998 continued to be a brutal year for Colombian workers fighting for the right of free association. When in October 1998, Jorge Ortega Garcia, the vice president of the largest Colombian umbrella trade union body, was found shot in the head three times, newly elected President Pastrana was heavily criticized by the ICFTU for "failing to ensure even minimal protection standards to trade union leaders." One month later, on November 14, 1998, Oscar Artundaga Nuñez from the Public Sector Union in Cali was murdered. Just five days before the fiftieth anniversary of the United Nations Declaration of Human Rights, the body of Saul Canar Pauta, a senior trade unionist and human rights advocate in Ecuador, was found (ICFTU, 1998).

68 National Labor Committee Statement, "Raising Wages a Penny an Hour," March 29, 1999. Available at www.nlcnet.org.

69 This is distinct from decisions made as a result of bribes offered by TNCs to governmental elites.

70 Political, business, and social elites in poor countries can benefit from TNCs in many ways, including stock ownership, partnership agreements, and consultative or executive positions within the companies (Lippman, 1992, p. 392).

71 Low and Subramanian, 1995.

72 WTO, 1996a.

73 Goldsmith, 1996.

74 Weissman, 1996b, p. 13.

75 The same is true for workers in national facilities.

76 It is often assumed that people in poor countries choose to migrate to urban centers and work in free processing zones in order to improve their living standards and increase their degree of personal freedom. However, workers in many regions migrate because they have little choice: either they have been forced off their land by (often transnational) agribusiness, or they were pushed to abandon their farms when their crops could no longer compete in markets flooded with cheaper foreign foods. The question of volition is important because foreign employers tend to argue that their workers are not being forced to work in the factories and that workers would leave if they did not want to be there. The idea that remuneration from their work in the factories has improved their living standards or personal freedom needs to be assessed in light of conditions previous to TNC penetration.

77 Calvin Sims, "In Peru, A Fight for Fresh Air: U.S.-Owned Smelter Makes Residents Ill and Angry," New York Times, December 12, 1995.

78 Calvin Sims, "In Peru, A Fight for Fresh Air: U.S.-Owned Smelter Makes Residents Ill and Angry," New York Times, December 12, 1995.

79 The EPA standards recommend that the average amount of sulphur dioxide in the air should not exceed 30 parts per billion. Daily levels should not exceed 140 parts per billion more than once a year. The company numbers show that in 1995, levels of sulphur dioxide in Ilo exceeded 300 parts per billion on 20 days in the month of May alone. Local environmental groups such as Labor of Ilo brought a lawsuit against the company in Texas courts to force it to pay for the pollution. They were unsuccessful. See Association Civil Labor, Ilo, Peru, November 17, 1998, in "Peruvian Activists

Oppose Cuajone Copper Mine Expansion," *Drillbits and Tailings Newsletter*, December 21, 1998. Available from Project Underground's website, www.moles.org.

80 It is important to note that the phrase "double standard" is not meant to endorse the standards TNCs practice in their home countries, which may also be harmful. In the United States, for example, innumerable cases of corporate negligence, deception, abuse, and labor and environmental exploitation have been reported. Two recent books recall classic examples. The first provides a history of Love Canal and the political movement that grew out of the corporate atrocities that caused the disaster (Gibbs, 1998). The second book describes the history of and legal proceedings around the discovery of a leukemia cluster in a small Massachusetts town (Harr, 1995). For a critical examination of the U.S. chemical industry, see Fagin, Lavelle, and the Center for Public Integrity, 1996.

81 Dunning, 1993, p. 539.

82 Cairncross, Hardoy, and Satterthwaite, 1990.

83 Jeb Greer and Kavaljit Singh, "A Brief History of TNCs." Available on Corporate Watch website, www.corpwatch.org.

84 Cairncross, Hardoy, and Satterthwaite, 1990.

85 LaDou, 1997, p. 315.

86 Warner, 1991. Air pollution from border factories, large-scale farming, and automobiles is on the rise on both sides of the border, raising concerns about exposure to particulates, sulfur dioxides, and acid aerosols. Especially among the poor of the region, whose living conditions are already substandard, these pollutants are expected to further increase overall morbidity and mortality by decreasing lung function and elevating childhood and adult asthma rates. When the results of longitudinal epidemiological studies begin to show the deleterious effects these pollutants have upon the inhabitants of the region, the corporations will be hard pressed to deny their awareness of the causal links between environmental pollutants and diminished human health. These relationships have been examined for several decades in U.S. industrial cities and are well documented (Dockery, Pope, Xiping Xu, *et al.*, 1993).

87 Although not covered in this chapter, the activities of transnational forestry corporations continue to contribute to the loss of biodiversity, and to diminish global ecological sustainability. Forestry TNCs have displaced thousands of indigenous communities in Central and South America, Africa, and Asia. Two factors are fueling these processes. Many new free trade agreements contain energy and resource codes designed to facilitate the rapid development and export of natural resources, such as minerals and trees. Also, the export-led growth strategy promoted by the World Bank, IMF, and other IFIs leads poor countries with resource-based economies to lower their existing environmental protections and open their doors to forestry TNCs. Several groups have focused considerable attention on this topic. For more information, contact the Rainforest Action Network, Resource Conservation Alliance, and Greenpeace.

88 USEIA, 1997.

89 Brian Anderson, Shell Advertorial (a paid commercial article), *Africa Today,* May/June, 1996.

90 Testimony of Dr. Owens Wiwa before the Maryland Senate Subcommittee on Economy and Environment Affairs, February 29, 1998. Available at www.sierraclub.org/human-rights/owenstes.html.

91 Greenpeace International Report, "Shell Shocked: The Environment and Social Costs of Living with Shell in Nigeria," July, 1994.

92 Brian Anderson, Shell Advertorial (a paid commercial article), *Africa Today,* May/June, 1996.

93 "Interview with Ledum Mitee, Deputy President of MOSOP," 1996.

94 Greenpeace International Report, "Shell Shocked: The Environment and Social Costs of Living with Shell in Nigeria," July, 1994.

95 "Interview with Ledum Mitee, Deputy President of MOSOP," 1996.

96 Testimony of Dr. Owens Wiwa before the Maryland Senate Subcommittee on Economy and Environment Affairs, February 29, 1998. Available at www.sierraclub.org/human-rights/owenstes.html.

97 U.N. Commission on Human Rights, 1997.

98 Cameron Doudu, "Shell Admits Importing Guns for Nigerian Police," *London Observer,* January 28, 1996.

99 Jeyaratnam, 1992; Cullen, Cherniak, and Rosenstock, 1990.

100 Hassan, Velasquez, Belmar, *et al.*, 1981.

101 Castleman, 1995.

102 Bates, 1994, p. 36.

103 LaDou, 1997, p. 320. Despite the severe occupational and environmental hazards posed by asbestos, the asbestos industry continues to promote their products in poor countries, where demand for low-cost building materials is high and information about the dangers of asbestos is often low.

104 LaDou, 1997, pp. 320-321.

105 Castleman, 1995.

106 Averill and Samuels, 1992.

107 Leonard and Rispens, 1996.

108 For a thorough overview of recent work on U.S. and international issues in occupational health and safety, see Levenstein and Wooding, 1997.

109 Khor, 1998, p. 6. See *Third World Resurgence*, 59, July 1995, in which eight articles are dedicated to exploring the damaging social and environmental effects of aquaculture.

110 Christiani, Durvasula, and Myers, 1990, p. 397.

111 Forget, 1991.

112 From "Pesticides: Export of Unregistered Pesticides is not Adequately Monitored by the EPA," General Accounting Office of the U.S. Congress, April 1989. Cited in "Unregistered Pesticides: Rejected Toxics Escape Export Controls," Greenpeace International and Pesticide Action Network-FRG, October 1990, p. 2.

113 Levy, 1995.

114 El Sebae, 1993.

115 Wesseling, McConnell, Partanen, *et al.*, 1997.

116 Joyce Millen, interview transcripts with farmers in Senegal, The Gambia, Togo, Burkina Faso, and Ghana, 1987-1989. According to Judith Achieng ("Pesticides Pose Risk to African Farmers," *Inter Press Service*, Feb 16, 1998), "The organization, which acts as a watchdog for pesticide poisoning in East Africa—Kenya, Uganda, and Tanzania—claims the rising trend of poisoning cases in the region is a result of manufacturers cashing in on farmers' ignorance of the health effects of exposure to dangerous pesticides."

117 B. See, "Pesticides and Cordillera Women: The Right to Health and Sustainable Development," undated, p. 6.

118 Levy, 1995.

119 Thrupp, 1991.

120 Sharara, Seifer, and Flaws, 1998.

121 Moses, 1992.

122 Richter and Safi, 1997.

123 Organochlorine pesticides are no longer in use in most industrialized nations because of their low biodegradability and their tendency to accumulate in biologic tissues (Al-Saleh 1994).

124 See, for example, Michael Pollan, "Playing God in the Garden," *New York Times Magazine*, October 25, 1998, pp. 44–92; Mark Arax and Jeanne Brokaw, "No Way Around Roundup: Monsanto's Bioengineered Seeds Are Designed to Require More of the Company's Herbicide," *Mother Jones*, Jan/Feb, 1997, p. 40–42.

For detailed information on GM technology and a review of current scientific findings, see Union of Concerned Scientists on Agriculture, Biotechnology and the World Food Supply (www.ucsusa.org/agriculture).

125 *Economist*, June 19, 1999, page 19.

126 Since the mid 1990s, efforts have been underway to set global standards for the safe transfer, handling, and use of living modified organisms (LMOs). An international biosafety working group comprising officials from about 100 countries has met several times to develop protocols for the protection of biodiversity, environmental safety, and public health. The meetings have been contentious, and progress in developing universally acceptable protocols slow—due largely to the opposition of the biotechnology industry, represented in the meetings by delegates of wealthy countries, where the industry is strongest. The United Nations Environment Programme, likewise influenced by industry, is also working toward the implementation of International Technical Guidelines for Safety in Biotechnology. See Chee Yoke Ling, "An International Biosafety Protocol: The Fight Is Still On," *Third World Resurgence*, 93, May 1998, pp. 2-5.

127 "The Need for Greater Regulation and Control of Genetic Engineering." Penang, Malaysia: Third World Network, 1995.

128 See "Terminator Seeds," *Multinational Monitor*, November, 1998. For a review of current scientific findings, see Union of Concerned Scientists on Agriculture, Biotechnology, and the World Food Supply (www.ucsusa.org/agriculture). See also Mae-

Wan Ho and Ricarda Steinbrecher, "Fatal Flaws in Food Safety Assessment: Critique of the Joint FAO/WHO Biotechnology and Food Safety Report." Penang, Malaysia: Third World Network, 1998.

129 Khor, 1998, p. 7.

130 In letters to *Nature* (329, April 23, 1998, p. 751), for example, several scientists make the case for assessing the socioeconomic impact of genetically modified organisms prior to their transboundary movement. A journalist for India's *The Hindu* explains: "This one-sided system in which seed companies have all the rights and bear no social or environmental responsibility, and farmers and citizens have no rights but bear all the risks and costs, can neither protect biodiversity nor provide food security" ("Sowing the Seeds of Conflict," March 23, 1997).

131 The risks associated with environmental toxins can be difficult to measure because routes of exposure may be uncertain. Moreover, because risk analysis traditionally involves the evaluation of one potential hazard at a time, it tends to underestimate the risks populations face when exposed to several hazardous materials simultaneously (Brickey, 1995).

132 Averill and Samuels, 1992.

133 Upton, 1990. Polychlorinated biphenyls from industrial sources and organochlorine pesticides used in agriculture have been found in breast milk of women in many areas throughout the world as a result of the women eating fish taken from contaminated waters. In Kazakhstan, near the shrinking Aral Sea, for example, women were found to have elevated levels of toxins in their breast milk (Hooper, Hopper, Petreas, *et al.*, 1997), as were Mohawk women residing near hazardous waste sites in New York (Fitzgerald, Hwang, Bush, *et al.*, 1998). A recent literature review describes diverse sources of evidence linking exposures to environmental pollutants with adverse effects on female reproduction, such as reduced fertility, birth defects, and spontaneous abortions (Sharara, Seifer, and Flaws, 1998). A recent study reported an increased risk of congenital birth anomalies among families residing near hazardous waste landfill sites in Europe (Dolk, Vrijheid, Armstrong, *et al.*, 1998).

134 Hwang, Bornschein, Grote, *et al.*, 1997.

135 Harnly, Seidel, Rojas, *et al.*, 1997.

136 Goldsmith, 1996, p. 269.

137 Cited in Center for Economic and Social Rights (CESR), "Rights Violations in the Ecuadorian Amazon: The Human Consequences of Oil Development," March 1994, p. 9. The report provides a legal investigation and includes the results of a health study comprising an analysis of local drinking, bathing, and fishing waters; the results of interviews; and medical examinations.

138 Center for Economic and Social Rights (CESR), "Rights Violations in the Ecuadorian Amazon: The Human Consequences of Oil Development," March 1994. For information on CESR, refer to Chapter Sixteen.

139 Kennedy, 1998.

140 Tauli-Corpuz, 1998.

141 Panos Briefing Paper, 19, May 1996. See also *Africa Agenda*, 15, 1997, which is devoted to the topic of mining in Africa.

142 Tauli-Corpuz, 1998. Workers in gold and silver mines throughout the world face a high risk of chronic over-exposure to mercury, which in miners can be absorbed through the lungs, skin, or digestive track. Chronic exposure to mercury deleteriously affects the brain, the central nervous system, the kidneys, and the reproductive system. See "Public Health Reports, 1998," U.S. Department of Health and Human Services, 113:8; and *Africa Agenda*, 15, 1997, p. 12. An extensive public health literature exists on the consequences of copper, gold, coal, and asbestos mining.

143 Abugre, 1998.

144 Kennedy, 1998.

145 Abugre, 1998.

146 Machipisa, 1998.

147 Abugre, 1998.

148 Kennedy, 1998.

149 As quoted in Kennedy, 1998, p. 18.

150 Kennedy, 1998.

151 Atrocities have been documented in mining and oil drilling projects in South Africa, Nigeria, Burma, Sierra Leone, Solomon Islands, Zambia, Indonesia, Chile, Ecuador, Equatorial Guinea, to name a few. Kennedy, 1998; Abugre, 1998; Machipisa, 1998; Tauli-Corpuz, 1998; Mokhiber, 1988. For detailed descriptions contact Project Underground at www.moles.org; Human Rights Watch at www.hrw.org; and Multinational Monitor at www.essential.org/monitor/monitor.html.

152 For a particularly somber example of corporate collusion with a repressive regime and corporate excesses within marginalized indigenous communities, see the activities of U.S. petroleum giant Unocal and its French partner, Total, in southern Burma. Greer, 1998; Aceves, 1998; Strider, 1995.

153 TNCs collude with such regimes in many ways. Transnational banks have made loans to support the military buildup of repressive governments, as when U.S. banks loaned to apartheid South Africa in the 1970s, enabling the government to stockpile military equipment and oil, and to build major transportation, communication, and energy facilities. Transnational corporations have broken or circumvented embargoes and sanctions intended to weaken the reign of repressive regimes, as when Mobil Oil, Shell, British Petroleum, and others circumvented the U.N. trade embargo on Rhodesia in the 1960s. Despite international efforts to contain Uganda's Idi Amin in the 1970s, coffee, sugar, and cocoa TNCs continued to prop him up by purchasing primary commodities from the brutal dictator. Such trading accounted for more than 90 percent of the country's foreign exchange. Weapons manufacturers have in the past sold riot and counterinsurgency equipment to repressive governments in, for example, the Philippines, Indonesia, Brazil, Argentina, and South Africa. Transnational corporations such as ITT have intervened in the political affairs of host countries such as Pinochet's Chile (Lippman, 1992). Transnational corporations such as Royal Dutch Shell and Chevron have collaborated with military dictatorships and their security forces in Nigeria with deadly consequences for local populations (see Box 8.3 and citations). For details on the role of mercenaries in mining, see *Africa Agenda*, no. 15, pp. 20-21, 1997.

154 Castleman, 1979; Ives, 1985; LaDou, 1991; Castleman and Navarro, 1987.

155 Singh and Lakhan, 1989.

156 Dunning, 1993, p. 540; Ayadike, 1988.

157 Waste treatment can be extremely expensive. In the United States, industries spend billions of dollars per year on hazardous waste management. Depending upon the toxicity of the waste, treatment can cost anywhere from under $200 to over $3,000 per ton. Waste management firms save extraordinary amounts of money by dumping materials in developing countries for as little as $2.50 per ton or a fee of $100 per month for 2,500 tons of PCB waste (Anyinam, 1991).

158 It should be noted that TNCs are not the only toxic waste dumping culprits; townships, national industries, and even federal governments have also dumped toxic waste into poor countries. The waste is often delivered with labels hiding its true identity, as was the case with 275 drums of "cleaning fluids" shipped to Zimbabwe from the United States. The drums actually contained hazardous, U.S. armed forces waste and were imported to Zimbabwe with U.S. tax dollar money under the guise of a U.S. Agency for International Development project (Anyinam, 1991; MacKenzie and Milne, 1989).

159 They include: Sierra Leone, Guinea, Guinea-Bissau, Senegal, Benin, Liberia, Sudan, and Nigeria. United Nations, 1991.

160 Dufour and Denis, 1988.

161 The original Basel Convention was adopted in 1989 amid criticism that it did not go far enough to protect poor nation-states from toxic waste dumping. Fierce debate ensued concerning both the intent and effectiveness of the original Convention. In 1994, a revised and broader Basel Ban agreement was promoted by a coalition of developing countries, a few Western and Eastern European States, and Greenpeace. In 1995, the Basel Ban Amendment passed, despite opposition from the United States, South Korea, Australia, and Canada. This agreement banned—as of January 1, 1998—all forms of hazardous waste exports from the 29 wealthiest, most industrialized countries of the OECD to all non-OECD nations.

162 Lawrence Summers, internal World Bank memorandum dated December 12, 1991, p. 5. The excerpts quoted from this memo appeared in the *Economist*, February 8, 1992, p. 62. This memo has become possibly one of the most notorious documents in World Bank history. In response to widespread criticism, Summers claimed that the ideas in the memo had been inserted as an ironic counterpoint rather than an actual proposal. For a discussion on economic rationalism as illustrated in the Summers memo, see Korten, 1995, pp. 83-86. Summers has replaced

Robert Rubin as Secretary of the U.S. Treasury as of the summer of 1999.

163 UNRISD, 1995.

164 Gedicks, 1993.

165 Though many indigenous communities throughout the world are indeed poor, many are not. The term "indigenous" is *not* synonymous with "poor."

166 Eichstaedt, 1994.

167 Horta, 1997.

168 World Bank Mission Statement.

169 Pieced together from the transcripts of in-depth interviews conducted by Joyce Millen, with rural women in a village in southwestern Senegal, between 1992 and 1994.

170 *Advertising* refers to paid media such as billboards and television, magazine, and radio ads. *Promotions* are gimmicks such as contests, giveaways, sponsorships, and the like.

171 "A Chronology of the Infant Formula Controversy," Action for Corporate Accountability, Washington, D.C., 1996; Chetley, 1979.

172 Bader, 1979.

173 "Pushing Infant Formula in the United States: An Attack on Health, Human Rights and the Environment," Action for Corporate Accountability, Washington, D.C., 1994.

174 Howie, Forsyth, Ogston, *et al.*, 1990; Wright, Holberg, Martinez, *et al.*, 1989.

175 Newcomb, Storer, Longnecker, *et al.*, 1994; Howie, 1991.

176 Jelliffe, 1972.

177 For example, Bill Moyers' half-hour C.B.S. television documentary "Into the Mouths of Babes," viewed by more than 9 million people on July 5, 1978, focused on health problems in infants caused by formula use in the Dominican Republic. The program also revealed a kickback scheme involving the formula companies paying a percentage of their formula revenues to the Dominican Medical Association.

178 WHO, 1981.

179 Anand, 1996.

180 WHO, 1993.

181 Interagency Group on Breastfeeding Monitoring, 1997; Taylor, 1998.

182 Chen and Winder, 1990.

183 TNCs control 70 percent of world tobacco production and dominate international trade in tobacco products (INFACT, 1998, p. 10).

184 WHO, 1996a.

185 INFACT, 1998, pp. 10, 94.

186 U.S. Department of Agriculture, 1995.

187 INFACT, 1998, p. 10.

188 INFACT, 1998.

189 Connolly, 1992.

190 INFACT, 1998, p. 10.

191 Council on Scientific Affairs, 1990.

192 Peto, Lopez, Boreham, *et al.*, 1994.

193 For greater detail, see GAO, 1990, 1992. For a brief history of U.S. trade policy and cigarette smoking in Asia, see Chaloupka and Laixuthai, 1996.

194 INFACT, 1998, p. 24; Stebbins, 1994; Barry, 1991.

195 INFACT, 1998, p. 25; Connolly, 1992.

196 Cigarette advertising expenditures tripled in the two years after the United States pushed open the Japanese market. By 1989, U.S. tobacco TNCs had exported nearly four times more cigarettes to Japan (INFACT, 1998, p. 24).

197 INFACT, 1998, p. 24.

198 INFACT, 1998, p. 10, citing "The Smoking Epidemic—'A Fire in the Global Village,'" World Health Organization Press Release, August 25, 1997. In the twenty-year period during which time U.S. and European tobacco TNCs established their presence and their brand names in China, cigarette consumption in the country increased 260 percent (INFACT, 1998. p. 10). Even though the increased consumption is probably not linked *exclusively* to the presence of TNCs and their enormous advertising—the striking timing of events merits attention.

199 Nelson, 1996.

200 Nkuchia, 1995; Nkuchia, Giovino, and Malarcher, 1996.

201 "America's New Merchants of Death," *Reader's Digest*, April, 1993, pp. 50-57.

202 Connolly, 1992.

203 Ernest Beck, "Tobacco: Big Tobacco Uses Good Works to Woo Eastern Europe," *Wall Street Journal*, November 10, 1998.

204 Chaloupka and Laixuthai, 1996.

205 Yach, 1986.

206 Connolly, 1989.

207 MacKay, 1994; Stebbins, 1991.

208 Pierce, 1991, p. 383.

209 Bourne, 1988, p. 4.

210 "Global Defence Industry: Linking Arms," *Economist*, June 14, 1997. One journalist even likened defense industries to national virility symbols.

211 "Global Defence Industry: Linking Arms," *Economist*, June 14, 1997.

212 "U.S. Arms Sales: Arms Around the World," *Mother Jones* website, www.motherjones.com/arms.

213 According to the FAS publication *Arms Sales Monitor* (20 and 25), the United States sold in fiscal year 1992 $16 billion in weapons and related services and construction to foreign countries. An additional $16 billion worth of commercial sales were licensed by the State Department. The following year, the U.S. government sold $33.2 billion in weapons and related services and licensed $26.5 billion worth of commercial sales. Over 80 percent of the U.S. government sales in fiscal 1993 went to developing countries. By 1997, arms sales had dropped significantly, to $8.8 billion, with $11 billion worth of licenses issued.

214 "U.S. Arms Sales: Arms Makers' Cozy Relationship with the Government," *Mother Jones* website, www.motherjones.com/arms.

215 Calculated from U.S. Arms Control and Disarmament Agency, 1995, and "Global Defense Industry: Linking Arms," *Economist*, June 14, 1997.

216 Congressional Research Service, "Conventional Arms Transfers to Developing Nations, 1988-1995," August 15, 1996. Also see, "Support the Arms Transfers Code of Conduct" (U. S. Senate-July 25, 1997), available at www.cnie.org/book/congress.htm.

217 Wheat, 1995, pp. 16-17. For the most common arguments heard in favor of U.S. arms sales and a rebuttal of these claims, see "Point/Counterpoint" in Lumpe and Donarski, 1998. Also available on-line at www.fas.org/asmp/library/handbook.

218 Wheat, 1995, p. 17.

219 Hartung, 1995.

220 "U.S. Arms Sales: Arms Makers' Cozy Relationship with the Government," *Mother Jones* website, www.-motherjones.com/arms.

221 Levy and Sidel, 1996.

222 UNICEF, 1996.

223 Sivard, 1993.

224 Human Rights Watch/Arms Project and Physicians for Human Rights, 1993.

225 Ascherio, Biellik, Epstein, *et al.*, 1995; Stover, Keller, Kobey, *et al.*, 1994.

226 Sidel and Shahi, 1997.

227 Sidel, 1995.

228 UNICEF, 1992b; Lumpe and Donarski, 1998.

229 UNDP, 1994; see also Lumpe and Donarski, 1998.

230 In many poor countries, where national drug policies are new or do not yet exist, pharmaceutical medicines are sold incrementally in local markets by vendors or company sales representatives with no pharmacy or medical training. The risks are especially acute for non-literate people who are unable to read labels. In preliterate and poor areas, people tend to hoard medicine for years beyond their expiration dates. People in poor communities also tend to share drugs with their neighbors and family members, even when the drugs are indicated for an ailment other than what the neighbor or family member may have. For greater detail see Van der Geest and Whyte, 1988.

231 See, for example, Arax and Brokaw, 1997.

232 Adolescents are particularly vulnerable to corporate advertising and promotional schemes. In the United States, Coca-Cola and other soft drink companies now pay millions of dollars for marketing rights in public schools. Coca-Cola is also paying a reported $60 million to the Boys and Girls Clubs of America to give its products a high profile in more than 2,000 clubs nationwide. According to the Center for Science in the Public Interest, the average 12- to 19-year-old male American now drinks 868 cans of soda per year (Russell Mokhiber, "Corporate Bullies: The 10 Worst Corporations of 1998," *Multinational Monitor*, 19(12), December, 1998, p. 11). Transnational soft drink companies are among the most aggressive advertisers in poor countries. In many of the world's poorest countries they have succeeded in shifting young people's tastes away from healthier,

cheaper, indigenous juices that were enjoyed before the arrival of soft drink companies.

233 Naomi Klein, "Trying to Feel Good about Nike," *Toronto Star*, April 2, 1999.

234 Gleckman and Krut, 1995, p. 8; Cavanagh, 1996.

235 "Sweatshop Wars," *Economist*, February 27, 1999, pp. 62-63.

236 UNRISD, 1995.

237 International Labour Organization ILOLEX: the ILO's Database on International Labour Standards. C174 Prevention of Major Industrial Accidents Convention, 1993.

238 Cavanagh, 1996.

239 Jane Anne Morris, "Sheep In Wolf's Clothing," Program on Corporation, Law, and Democracy, Fall 1998, pp. 3-6. For more on this subject see POCLAD in Chapter Sixteen.

240 Cameron and Mackenzie, 1994.

241 See the Interfaith Center on Corporate Responsibility's "Principles for Global Corporate Responsibility: Benchmarks for Measuring Business Performance," *Corporate Examiner*, September 1, 1995; Amnesty International, 1998b; Cavanagh, 1996.

242 "Sweatshop Wars," *Economist*, February 27, 1999, pp. 62-63.

243 The AIP was composed of the following organizations and businesses: Interfaith Center for Corporate Responsibility (ICCR), Business for Social Responsibility (BSR), the Lawyers Committee for Human Rights, the National Consumers League, the International Labor Rights Fund (ILRF), the Robert F. Kennedy Memorial Center for Human Rights, the Union of Needletrades, Industrial and Textile Employees (UNITE), the Retail, Wholesale, and Department Store Union, Liz Claiborne, Nike, Reebok, Phillips-Van Heusen, Kathie-Lee Gifford, L.L. Bean, Patagonia, Nicole Miller, and TWEEDS.

244 Rev. David Schilling, Director of Interfaith Center on Corporate Responsibility, Public Statement, November 5, 1998.

245 Tim Bissell, director, Campaign for Labor Rights, Public Statement, November 8, 1998.

246 Steven Greenhouse, "Suit Says 18 Companies Conspired to Violate Sweatshop Workers' Rights," *New York Times*, January 14, 1999. For current updates, see "Saipan Sweatshop Litigation," available on Sweatshop Watch's website, www.sweatshop-watch.org, and Global Exchange's website, www.glob-alexchange.org.

247 The year 1998 marked the fiftieth anniversary of the Universal Declaration of Human Rights (UDHR), and a most important document in the labor rights movement, Convention No. 87 of the ILO. Freedom of association, the right of workers to form and join trade unions for the protection of their interests, is a fundamental, internationally recognized right of all workers. It is mentioned in the 1919 ILO Constitution, the 1944 ILO Declaration of Philadelphia, and is codified in ILO Convention No. 87 on Freedom of Association and Protection of the Right to Organize, and ILO Convention No. 98 on

the Right to Organize and Bargain Collectively. Article 23 of the UDHR specifically delineates what can be called "internationally recognized worker rights," including the right to just and favorable conditions of work, equal pay for equal work, just remuneration worthy of human dignity, and the right to form and join trade unions. Still, greater than half of the world's population lives in countries that have not ratified ILO Convention No. 87; these countries include China, India, and the United States.

The ICFTU, comprising 174 member nations, recognizes countries that have ratified other core ILO conventions covering forced labor, child labor, and discrimination. Convention No. 29 on Forced Labor has the highest rate of ratification (145 nations), followed by Convention No. 98 on Collective Bargaining (138 nations), Convention No. 100 on Gender Equality at Work (137 nations), Convention No. 111 on Discrimination in Employment (130 nations), Convention No. 105 on Abolition of Forced Labor (128 nations), and Convention No. 87 on Freedom of Association (122 nations). Convention No. 138 on Child Labor, also known as the Minimum Age of Employment Convention, has an abysmally low rate of ratification, with only 59 nations signing onto the document.

248 Cavanagh, 1996.

249 Permanent People's Tribunal, 1992.

250 Interagency Group on Breastfeeding Monitoring, 1997.

251 National Labor Committee Statement, "Raising Wages a Penny an Hour," March 29, 1999. Hourly wage rates for Nike workers in Indonesia, according to the NLC, have actually *fallen* from 27 cents an hour to the current 15 cents an hour.

252 Stocker, Waitzkin, and Iriart, 1999. As U.S. managed care markets have become saturated through the expansion of managed care in the United States, U.S. for-profit managed care companies have needed to create new markets overseas. As quoted in Stocker, Waitzkin, and Iriart, 1999, the president of the Association of Latin American Pre-paid Health Plans explained: "By the year 2000, it is estimated that 80 percent of the total U.S. population will be insured by some sort of MCO [managed-care organization]. Since 70 percent of all American MCOs are for-profit enterprises, new markets are needed to sustain growth and return on investment."

253 Stocker, Waitzkin, and Iriart, 1999.

254 Article 25 of the Universal Declaration of Human Rights states: "Everyone has the right to a standard of living adequate for the health and well-being of himself [or herself] and of his [or her] family, including food, clothing, housing and medical care and necessary social services, and the right to security in the event of unemployment, sickness, disability, widowhood, old age or other lack of livelihood in circumstances beyond his [or her] control."

255 Bradford, 1998.

256 Gerard O'Neill, Mitchell Zuckoff, Alice Dembner, *et al.*, "Cashing in at Public Expense," *Boston Globe*, April 5, 1998.

257 Large U.S.-based pharmaceutical TNCs profit handsomely from their innovations, even though the government finances much of the research and development required to produce highly profitable drugs. According to the National Institutes of Health (NIH), federal, state, and local government from 1986 through 1991 doled out more support for health research and development than did the industries that profit from new biotechnologies. By 1992, industry began spending slightly more on health research and development than the U.S. government, and this trend has continued (NIH Extramural Data, Fiscal Year 1996).

For an exposé on the public handouts that enrich drug makers, see the three-part *Boston Globe* series beginning on April 5, 1998. For more detail, contact the Consumer Project on Technology at www.cptech.org.

258 Williams, 1997, p. 1704. Malaria threatens 40 percent of the world's population in more than 90 countries. Between 1985 and 1994, the level of U.S. research funding going into vaccine and other therapies for malaria was halved, from about $65 million to $35 million (Attaran, 1999).

259 "Can Industry Be Wooed Back into the Act?," 1997, p. 540.

260 For example, the common multidrug therapy used to prolong the life of persons with AIDS costs approximately $15,000 per year. This figure is many times the average GDP per capita of 128 developing countries (Attaran, 1999).

261 Henry Demarest Lloyd, *Wealth Against Commonwealth*, 1894; cited by Richard Grossman of the Program on Corporations, Law, and Democracy in his keynote speech at the 1996 Public Interest Environmental Law Conference, Eugene, Oregon. See Bleifuss, 1996.

262 Tim Lang of the Center for Food Policy, speaking at a symposium about the environmental, political, medical, and social dangers of "corporate rule," in Toronto, 1997 (see Chapter Sixteen). The symposium was sponsored by the International Forum on Globalization (IFG). He asserts: "We need to get away from they and we thinking and understand the brilliance of TNCs and how they get to exactly what people want."

263 Tony Clarke of the IFG's Working Committee on Corporations (see Chapter Sixteen) has written a booklet (Clarke, 1996a) to guide students and social activists on what to do about the emergence of corporate rule. In the booklet, Clarke summarizes current policies and strategies, including: revoking corporate charters, decentralizing corporate power, overhauling corporate welfare, destabilizing corporate politics, re-regulating corporate investment, rebuilding sustainable communities, renegotiating trade deals, and restructuring global institutions.

264 Quoted in "Can Corporations be Good Citizens?" *Sierra Magazine*, May/June 1999, p. 96.

CHAPTER 9
Dying for Growth, Part II:
The Political Influence of National and Transnational Corporations

1 Estes, 1996, p. 77.

2 Korten, 1995, p. 55.

3 In the United States, big business spends many times more than other groups, including labor, investing in its favorite candidates (The Center for Responsive Politics, www.crp.org). As of summer 1999, some 138 of Washington's registered lobbyists were former members of Congress. With such a political system, the founding democratic principle of "one man, one vote" has been overshadowed by a new equation: "thousands of lobbyists plus multimillions of dollars equals access and influence out of the reach of ordinary citizens" (Arianna Huffington, "See Lobbyists Feast on the System," *Boston Herald*, August 21, 1999).

4 Corporations also sponsor large fund-raising and entertainment events to encourage potential donors. Increasingly, industry groups representing numerous companies launch nationwide ad campaigns to influence voters and legislators on specific policy measures. In 1994, when the Clintons were attempting to reform the U.S. health-care system, corporations spent more than $100 million through special interest groups to combat the plan. Much of this money paid for slick television advertisements, the "Harry and Louise" commercials, designed to "inform" so-called "average" Americans of the dangers inherent in the proposed health-care package (Folbre and the Center for Popular Economics, 1995). It is generally acknowledged that special interests such as the health insurance industry were the primary obstacle to the Clintons' thwarted 1994 health-care reform efforts. See Miller and Kehler, 1996, p. 26.

5 Barlett and Steele, 1998.

6 Levathes, 1995, p. 16. See also Bates, 1994.

7 Castleman and Lemen, 1998a, 1998b.

8 Weissman, 1996a; Weissman, 1998, p. 5. For details on the history and current issues of pharmaceutical access in poor countries, contact Health Action International (highlighted in Chapter Sixteen) and the Consumer Project on Technology in Washington, D.C., at www.cptech.org.

9 Leroy, 1995, p. 39.

10 Leroy, 1995, p. 39.

11 Barlett and Steele, 1998.

12 Leroy, 1995, p. 39.

13 John Motl, Attorney General's Office, Helena, Montana. Personal communication with Bonnie Gestring, community organizer at Montana Environmental Information Center.

14 Miller and Kehler, 1996, p. 23.

15 Miller and Kehler, 1996. Shortly after Congressional passage of the 1974 Election Reform Act, a diverse coalition of plaintiffs filed suit in federal court challenging several of the Act's provisions as unconstitutional. The plaintiffs argued that the spending limits constituted a "restriction on communication violative of the First Amendment, since virtually all meaningful political communication in the modern setting involves the expenditure of money" (Raskin and Bonifaz, 1993). The *Buckley* decision still stands, despite challenges. Meanwhile, there is little doubt that the amount of money spent on campaigns can determine the outcome of elections: senators who win elections outspend their opponents by a ratio of 1.36

to 1, and winning representatives outspend losers by 1.87 to 1 (Ronald Dworkin, "The Curse of American Politics," *New York Review of Books*, October 17, 1996). The *Buckley* decision also allows wealthy individuals unlimited spending on their own bids for office, provided they do not take election money from the federal government.

For information on the legal framework of campaign finance reform in the aftermath of *Buckley v. Valeo*, see the website of the National Voting Rights Institute (www.nvri.org). For tracking money in American politics, see the website of the Center for Responsive Politics (www.crp.org). Other industrialized countries avoid the problems of corporate interests in the electoral process by publicly funding their campaigns. For comparative information, see Hogan, 1992.

16 "Managed-Care Firms Brace to Fight Flood of Bills: Congress Considering New Rules, But HMOs Warn Health Care Costs Would Rise," *Boston Globe*, March 29, 1998; "Senate Vote on HMO Bill Due Today," *Boston Globe*, July 29, 1998.

17 As quoted in Harvey Wasserman, *America Born and Reborn*. New York: Collier Books, 1983, p. 83.

18 Sometimes the tax breaks or handouts come from business incentive programs created to respond to the economic problems of a previous era. For example, as an incentive to corporations to sell their goods abroad, companies that export can create foreign sales corporations (FSCs), which enable these corporations to shelter 15 percent or more of their export profits from the federal government. While such a device may have been useful in an era of relative commercial isolationism, most of the companies that create FSCs today would export even without the tax break, which has cost taxpayers in the 1990s about $10 billion dollars. Another corporate welfare program designed for the needs of a previous era, the Export-Import Bank of the United States, was created in 1934 during the Great Depression. Today, the "Eximbank" offers the countries' largest TNCs below-market rates for loans, guarantees, and insurance. The bank has subsidized $11 billion worth of Boeing's sales to some 30 countries (Barlett and Steele, 1998).

19 Collins, 1995, p. 66; Barlett and Steele, 1998.

20 Folbre and the Center for Popular Economics, 1995, p. 5.12. See also Mark Breslow and John McDermott, "Disappearing Corporate Taxes," in *Real World Macro*, Somerville, MA: Dollars and Sense Economic Affairs Bureau, Inc., 1995, p. 69.

21 Collins, 1995, p. 66. Many special favors corporations win from the federal government—such as permission for miners to dump hundreds of tons of waste on federal lands; for loggers to cut timber in national forests; and for oil companies to keep hundreds of millions of dollars in royalties owed to the public—sneak through Congress as "riders" attached to other bills. Legislators tack on such riders to spending bills when they fear their proposed law or amendment would not be acceptable to the public. Laws that pass through Congress as riders, "sometimes impenetrably written, [can] be enacted without the usual public hearings and public debate, or public disclosure of their legislative

22 Again, as the public becomes more interested in reforming tax codes and eliminating tax loopholes, corporate leaders work more diligently to get pro-business advocates into positions of power.

23 In fact, the pharmaceutical industry spends more on lobbying and campaign contributions than most other industries. In 1997 alone, U.S. drug companies spent $74.8 million to lobby the federal government. See the Center for Responsive Politics website at www.crp.org.

24 To date, only Montana has passed (albeit temporarily) a law limiting corporate spending on ballot measures. The law, written to force big money, for-profit corporate interests out of the electoral process on ballot initiatives, was extant less than two years before corporations sued the state, and effectively rescinded the law.

25 Estes, 1996, p. 105.

26 Center for Responsive Politics website (www.crp.org) and personal communication with political analyst Jennifer Shecter.

27 In mid-1998, a single managed-care corporation, Blue Cross and Blue Shield Association, had already made over $1 million in contributions to federal candidates and the national parties. Blue Cross/Blue Shield and its affiliates provided these contributions through their PAC.

28 Greider, 1996, p 81.

29 One egregious example was Lockheed Martin's 1995 decision to pay an Egyptian legislator a $24.8 million bribe to obtain a $79 million sale (Edmund Andrews, "29 Nations Agree to Outlaw Bribing Foreign Officials," the *New York Times*, November 21, 1997). Admitting the problem, national governments within the OECD have debated the issue of bribery with no clear consensus (Glen Simpson, "Foreign Deals Rely on Bribes, U.S. Contends," the *Wall Street Journal*, February 23, 1999).

30 Again, these conditions included export-led growth policies such as tax breaks and subsidies, inexpensive privatization sales, and the lowering of wages through labor market deregulation.

31 For example, in 1954 the United States invaded Guatemala to prevent the Guatemalan government from taking over land from the United Fruit Company to redistribute to peasants. See Barnet and Muller, 1974, pp. 81-83.

32 Countries failing to comply with WTO legislation face trade sanctions, which can devastate the economies of poor countries.

33 Nader and Wallach, 1996, p. 97.

34 This is the subject of Chapter Eleven.

35 From a press conference introducing a new trade bill to the U.S. House of Representatives Committee on Ways and Means, Sub-Committee on Trade, Description of H.R. 434, The African Growth and Opportunity Act. See the next section of this chapter for an analysis of the proposed bill.

36 From the *Mother Jones* website (www.mother-jones.com/arms).

37 Korten, 1995, p. 145. The Business Roundtable, counting approximately 200 members including the CEOs of most of the largest U.S.-based TNCs, took on its current form in 1972 with the merger of three separate lobbying groups. The Roundtable's promotional literature states that members of the U.S. government "respect the fact that business leaders care enough to study issues in detail and spend time to present their views to government." The Roundtable's nominal goal is "to present government and the public with knowledgeable, timely information, and with practical, positive suggestions for action." For more about the activities of the Business Roundtable, see their website (www.brtable.org).

38 Korten, 1995.

39 This message was in stark contrast to what President Carter had recommended to Africa during his briefer visit to the continent in the 1970s, when U.S. officials had emphasized human rights and efforts to meet the basic needs of the "poorest of the poor" (Douglas Tilton "U.S.-Africa Economic Initiatives," *Corporate Watch*, May 1998, www.corpwatch.org).

40 During the corresponding phases of its own economic development, the United States followed a strikingly different path from the one it now urges on poor countries. The newly industrializing United States defended its nascent industries through quotas, tariffs, and other forms of protectionism. For a thoughtful discussion about the benefits of protectionism in the era of economic globalization, see Lang and Hines, 1993.

41 Hormeku, 1997.

42 Believing these aspirations to be among the real reasons for the new trade act, Representative Jesse Jackson Jr. called HR 434 the "Africa Recolonization Act." A similar debate escalated into the "banana war" between the European Union and the United States in early 1999. Policies prescribed by the European Union favor the purchase of bananas from former British and French colonies in the Caribbean, although bananas from those nations are more expensive than those produced in large, mostly U.S.-owned plantations in Latin America. The U.S. government first brought complaint against the European Union through the WTO in September, 1995, prodded in part by the Chiquita Company, a U.S.-based TNC and a major campaign contributor (Larry Elliot and Charlotte Denny, "Colonial Loyalties Beneath the Split; World Trade Organization fails to stop U.S. and EU Moving Toward Disaster," *Guardian*, January 26, 1999). While the banana debate reveals a colonial legacy, potentially more important is the apparent weakness in the WTO's power to enforce its rulings. Even though the European Union's protective trade regime was deemed illegal, it remains in place.

43 Hormeku, 1997.

44 Jesse Jackson Jr., "HOPE for Africa," *Nation*, March 15, 1999, p. 6.

45 See "Meet the Multinational Corporations Behind the Lugar-Crane Africa Bill," *Corporate Watch* website (www.corpwatch.org). See also Douglas Tilton, "U.S.-Africa Economic Initiatives," *Corporate Watch*, May, 1998. Available at www.corpwatch.org. Virtually every one of the companies involved has a long-docu-

mented record of environmental, labor, human rights, worker health and safety violations, or other abuses.

46 Efforts to promote U.S. business in Africa had actually begun in early 1996, when Ron Brown, the late U.S. secretary of commerce, accompanied planeloads of U.S. businesspeople to several African countries to meet with government officials and prepare for U.S. companies to do business there (Hormeku, 1997).

47 Douglas Tilton, "U.S.-Africa Economic Initiatives," *Corporate Watch*, May, 1998. Available at www.corp-watch.org.

48 See Chapter Five for a detailed discussion of this subject.

49 Hormeku, 1997. The author cites five specific examples: (1) Opening up government procurement to international bidding results in contracts for supply going to foreign, not local, contractors. (2) Free movement of goods, services, and factors of production from the United States to Africa at low or zero tariffs means, in effect, that cheap American products will be dumped on local markets and stunt local production; the same effect is produced in agriculture by agricultural market liberalization. (3) Compliance with World Bank commitments is simply a means of prolonging the devastating effects of foreign intrusion into African countries' domestic politics. (4) National treatment for foreign investors implies that any incentives a government gives a local investor to promote a particular sector (e.g., rural banking) must also be accorded to foreign companies, thus undermining the strategy as a means of nurturing local business initiatives. (5) Removing restrictions on foreign investors means their investments cannot be appropriately regulated or oriented in accordance with an overall national development strategy.

50 "Economic Justice and the African Trade Bills Before Congress," open letter from the Washington Office on Africa to Members of Congress and President William Jefferson Clinton," February 24, 1999.

51 Introducing H.R. 772, "The Hope for Africa Act of 1999," statement by Congressman Jesse Jackson Jr., February 23, 1999.

52 David Korten, "The United Nations and the Corporate Agenda," *Corporate Watch*, June, 1997. Available at www.corpwatch.org. Korten observed: "Those of us who have been studying these issues have long known of the strong alignment of the World Trade Organization, the World Bank, and the IMF to the corporate agenda. By contrast, the United Nations has seemed a more open, democratic, and people-friendly institution. What I found so shattering was the strong evidence that the differences I have been attributing to the U.N. are largely cosmetic."

53 From "Key United Nations Agency Solicits Funds from Corporations," available at www.corpwatch.org-/trac/undp/undppress.html.

54 From "Key United Nations Agency Solicits Funds from Corporations," available at www.corpwatch.org-/trac/undp/undppress.html.

55 From "UN-Business Partnership to Boost Economic Development," ICC Statement, February 9, 1998.

56 Helmut Maucher, "Ruling by Consent," *Financial Times*, December 6, 1997.

57 Helmut Maucher, "Ruling by Consent," *Financial Times*, December 6, 1997.

58 From "Key United Nations Agency Solicits Funds from Corporations," available at www.corpwatch.org-/trac/undp/undppress.html.

59 From "Key United Nations Agency Solicits Funds from Corporations," available at www.corpwatch.org-/trac/undp/undppress.html.

60 From "Key United Nations Agency Solicits Funds from Corporations," available at www.corpwatch.org-/trac/undp/undppress.html.

61 See literature from the International Forum on Globalization (in Chapter Sixteen). For example, Clarke, 1996a.

62 Representatives of TNCs are particularly defensive in their response to environmental groups and international efforts to improve the environment. Prior to the 1992 United Nations Conference on Environment and Development (UNCED) in Rio de Janeiro, TNCs successfully lobbied government officials to have selected items removed from the UNCED agenda. These topics included efforts to regulate TNCs' environmental practices.

63 Reported in the *Corporate Europe Observer*, May 1998.

64 "The Geneva Business Declaration," available at www.iccwbo.org/Geneva_Business_Declaration.htm.

65 "The Geneva Business Declaration," available at www.iccwbo.org/Geneva_Business_Declaration.htm. See also Amnesty International, 1998a.

66 Large TNCs control greater assets than are available to many countries. As explored later in this chapter, even a wealthy nation like Canada can be intimidated by a large corporation's threat of legal action. One can imagine how less affluent countries would fare in the face of such pressure. See Clarke and Barlow, 1997.

67 Chantell Taylor, "Rage Against the MAchIne," *Dollars and Sense*, July/August, 1998, p. 10.

68 A case brought under NAFTA investment protections, which resemble those in the draft MAI, may presage the consequences of corporate ability to sue national governments. In April 1997, the Canadian Parliament acted to ban the importation of MMT, a known health threat. MMT is a manganese-based additive, used to enhance gasoline octane and reduce "knocking." There is no debate that high-level manganese exposure causes Parkinson's-like tremors and premature aging of the brain (see, for example, Huang, Chu, Lu, *et al.*, 1998). Within two weeks of parliament's initiative, the U.S.-based Ethyl Corporation—a major producer of MMT—filed a lawsuit against the Canadian government for loss of "future profits" and the tarnished corporate reputation that would result from the import ban. Like NAFTA, the investment sections of the MAI require member countries to compensate investors when their property is "expropriated" or when governments take measures "tantamount to expropriation" (from the MAI Negotiating Text as of April 1998, available at www.oecd.org/daf/cmis/mai/nnegtext.htm). The Ethyl suit was settled to the corporation's advantage in July 1998. Environment Minister Christine Stewart commented that "the government believes [settling to be] in the best interest of Canadians because it avoids long,

protracted and expensive legal proceedings" (Andrew Duffy, "Canada drops ban on gas additive: MMT now permitted; manufacturer accepts $13M settlement," *Ottawa Citizen*, July 21, 1998).

The Ethyl Corporation's third quarter 1998 earnings were reported at $30.8 million, which included "a $13 million reimbursement from the Canadian government for a portion of the Company's lost profits and legal costs related to the Canadian government's decision to lift its 1997 ban on the importation and interprovincial trade of Ethyl's MMT fuel additive" ("Ethyl Corporation Reports Earnings for Nine Months and Third Quarter," *PR Newswire*, October 12, 1998). Ethyl Corporation continues to market MMT in Canada.

69 Chantell Taylor, "Rage Against the MAchIne," *Dollars and Sense*, July/August, 1998, p. 11.

70 In August 1998, even the United Nations Sub-Commission on the Prevention of Discrimination and Protection of Minorities registered protest against the MAI in a resolution expressing concern "about the possible human rights implications [of the Agreement], and particularly about the extent to which the Agreement might limit the capacity of States to take proactive steps to ensure the enjoyment of economic, social and cultural rights by all people, and in the process creating benefits for a small privileged minority at the expense of an increasingly disenfranchised majority" (Amnesty International, 1998).

71 As cited in "Power: The Central Issue," *Ecologist*, July/August, 1992, p. 159; Korten, 1995.

72 Korten, 1995, p. 179.

73 See, for example, Chartrand, 1995; Weissman, 1996a.

74 Roger Cowe, "Boardrooms Discover Corporate Ethics," *Guardian Weekly*, March 28, 1999, p. 27. Polish poet Stanislaw Lec provided the original form of the question: "Is it progress if a cannibal uses a fork?" The idea was adapted by Elkington (1998), on whose book Cowe's article comments.

75 Korten, 1995, pp. 293-324.

76 Victims of corporate excesses must be encouraged to expose specific TNC offenders by making public the circumstances of their work-related or environmental injuries or illnesses. Leaders involved in the standard-lowering competitive push to recruit TNCs to their local, state, or national territories must re-examine their strategies and share with the public information about the net gains and losses associated with corporate incentive packages. Are funds for corporate enrichment being diverted from social services like public health? Is the trade-off worth it?

CHAPTER 10
Tragedy Without End:
The 1984 Bhopal Gas Disaster

1 Verweij, Mohapatra, and Bhatia, 1996, p. 8.

2 One method of estimating deaths was based on the number of burial shrouds sold in the days immediately following the catastrophe—7,000, by one count. A senior UNICEF official, after spending a week investigating conditions in Bhopal shortly following the disaster, commented that many doctors privately reported to him that they believed the death toll to be around 10,000 persons.

3 Bhopal Group for Information and Action (BGIA), 1990, p. 3. The BGIA is a local consortium of Indian activist groups who continue to lobby their government for increased assistance for those injured by the gas: improved medical treatment, adequate compensation and rehabilitation, and improved social services such as housing, sanitation, potable water, and jobs. The 1990 publication *Voices of Bhopal* was created to give voice to survivors, as their stories had been silenced by the inadequate 1989 settlement between Union Carbide and the Indian government.

4 Morehouse and Subramaniam, 1986, p. 3.

5 Tyagi and Rosencranz, 1988, p. 1112.

6 For a full, technical review of the origins of the liquid and gas leak, see Shrivastava, 1990.

7 Dembo, Morehouse, and Wykle, 1990, pp. 87-88.

8 In July 1984, an internal Union Carbide safety audit was conducted by operational safety and health inspectors from Institute, West Virginia. The findings of the report, released in September 1984, warned plant managers that a runaway reaction in Bhopal could occur. As reported by Philip Shabecoff in "Union Carbide Had Been Told of Leak Danger" (*New York Times*, January 25, 1985, citing original Union Carbide company documents), the audit was not made public until after the accident, and only after Congressman Henry Waxman released it.

9 Dembo, Morehouse, and Wykle, 1990, p. 90. For more details about the history of Union Carbide's industrial accidents in India and elsewhere, see Agarwal, Merrifield, and Tandon, 1985.

10 Bhopal Working Group, 1987, p. 231.

11 Because minor leaks were so frequent at the Bhopal plant, UCIL changed the public alarm system to avoid the embarrassment of having to explain its failures. The internal plant alarm and the loud public siren were supposed to be activated in concert, but sometime in 1982 the management de-linked the siren from the alarm in order to be able to turn them off separately. According to Morehouse and Subramaniam, the siren was initially turned on with the alarm, but then turned off by the control room operator (1986, p. 20).

12 See Mehta, Mehta, Mehta, *et al.*, 1990, p. 2781; Cullinan, Acquilla, and Dhara, 1996, p. 5.

13 Sutcliffe, 1985, p. 1883.

14 Kimmerle and Eben, 1964, p. 235.

15 Heinzow, 1996, p. 5.

16 Bucher, Schwetz, Shelby, *et al.*, 1987, p. 3.

17 See letters discussed in Varma, 1989, pp. 567-568. The cyanide controversy began with the anecdotal observation that some victims improved after the administration of sodium thiosulphate, the antidote to cyanide poisoning. When health workers began giving the antidote (shipped from Germany) to patients, the Indian government confiscated all the thiosulphate and for unexplained reasons forbade its use in Bhopal.

18 Kumar, 1993, p. 1205.

19 Mukerjee, 1995, p. 16.

20 Andersson, Muir, Mehra, *et al.*, 1988; Andersson, Ajwani, Mahashabde, *et al.*, 1990.

21 For a review of pulmonary and other chronic toxic effects of MIC see Mehta, Mehta, Mehta, *et al.*, 1990; Varma and Guest, 1993.

22 Cullinan, Acquilla, and Dhara, 1997, p. 339.

23 Bhatia and Tognoni, 1996, p. 14.

24 Varma, 1987, p. 154; Kapoor, 1991, p. 243.

25 Eckerman, 1996, p. 33.

26 Cullinan, Acquilla, and Dhara, 1996, p. 8.

27 Callendar, 1996, p. 38.

28 Sethi, Sharma, Trivedi, *et al.*, 1987, p. 45.

29 Bertell, 1996, p. 3.

30 Garner, 1997, p. 342. Medline is an on-line medical reference library.

31 Dhara, 1993, p. 436.

32 Dembo, Morehouse, and Wykle, 1990, p. 93.

33 See the lead editorial, *Wall Street Journal*, December 10, 1984, p. 26.

34 Under the doctrine of *forum non conveniens*, U.S. courts may dismiss cases brought by foreign plaintiffs on the grounds that it would be inconvenient for a U.S. defendant to be sued at home in a case that has sufficient foreign components to make a foreign forum more suitable. For a more complete description, see Kapur, 1990, p. 5.

35 Hager, 1995, p. 40.

36 Hager, 1987, p. 8. American courts had just awarded $5 billion in punitive damages in the Exxon *Valdez* case and awarded Pennzoil more than $10 billion in a business dispute against Texaco.

37 Cassels, 1993, p. 74.

38 Morehouse, 1994, p. 167.

39 The Congress (I) Party was created from the Congress Party by Indira Gandhi in 1978.

40 Bidwai, 1995, p. 9. See also the July/August issue of the *Multinational Monitor*, titled "India: Open for Business."

41 Dembo, Morehouse, and Wykle, 1990, p. 18.

42 Lepkowski, 1994, p. 14.

43 The agricultural chemicals division, the section that oversaw the Bhopal plant operation via UCC's Hong Kong office, was sold to the French pharmaceutical transnational Rhône-Poulenc. Ironically, Rhône-Poulenc is also the maker of Theophylline and Azmacort, two medications used heavily around the world by patients—including Bhopal survivors—suffering from respiratory ailments.

44 Transnational corporations plan for unexpected disasters and shield their assets from liability. They do this by setting up subsidiaries in foreign countries, entering into limited liability clauses with governments, leaving their corporations capital-poor by paying out dividends, and giving "soft money" contributions to political parties as risk "insurance." When disaster strikes, the corporate image is polished by the public relations engine, and expensive, stellar legal teams are assembled to defend the soul of the corporation itself.

45 The Bhopal tragedy was due to the design and operation of the plant. The alleged saboteur named by UCC has denied all charges against him and lives at peace to this day in Bhopal. Clearly, had the people of Bhopal perceived him to be guilty of such a heinous act, he would not be safe in the town. Some feel that the sabotage theory is a public relations ploy by UCC, without legal merit, as a defense against negligence under Indian law. For a personal account from a UCC worker about plant operations prior to the accident, see Chouhan, 1994.

46 This letter, dated March 5, 1996, was written by John MacDonald, assistant secretary of Union Carbide Corporation. Based on other evidence, the letter appears to be full of half-truths and distortions. For a full deconstruction of the text, contact the Campaign for Justice in Bhopal, c/o Council on International and Public Affairs, United Nations Plaza.

47 Conference description and Warren Anderson quotes are documented in Dembo, Morehouse, and Wykle, 1990, p. 117.

48 Union Carbide Annual Report, 1988, quoted in Dembo, Morehouse, and Wykle, 1990, p. 19. Emphasis added.

49 Mehta, 1996, p. 55. Far more claims for compensation have been filed than the official governmental figure of deaths and number injured, reducing the chances that those who justly deserve compensation will receive it. One could argue, however, that all Bhopalis deserve compensation for such a huge environmental economic and cultural disaster.

50 Jaskowski, Zhengang, and Mohapatra, 1996, p. 25.

51 Mehta, 1996, p. 57, illuminates some poignant stories of poor Bhopalis who are unable to pay the required bribes, while their wealthier neighbors pay under the table whatever it takes to receive their compensation.

52 Morehouse and Subramaniam, 1986, p. 62.

53 Eckerman, 1996, p. 31.

54 Bhopal Gas Peedit Sangharsh Sahayog Smiti, 1994, p. 11.

55 National Toxics Campaign Fund, 1990.

56 Costner, December 8, 1995, *Greenpeace Letter to Satinath Sarangi*.

57 Bhopal Gas Peedit Sangharsh Sahayog Smiti, 1994, p. 10.

58 Jaskowski, Zhengang, and Mohapatra, 1996, p. 24.

59 Bhopal Group for Information and Action, 1990, p. 4.

60 Dembo, Morehouse, and Wykle, 1990, p. 81. Immediately following the Bhopal leak, Union Carbide claimed that the manufacturing processes for MIC were the same in India as they were in its Institute, West Virginia plant. However, once UCC realized the implications of this statement, they retracted, saying that the Bhopal plant had "an entirely different setup" from the one in Institute. On August 11, 1985, a leak of 500 gallons of aldicarb oxime plus an unspecified amount of methylene chloride at the Institute plant sent 135 people to the hospital. Luckily, no one was killed. The leak occurred as a result of a series of human and mechanical errors, design problems, and equipment failure—all remarkably similar to the problems at Bhopal.

61 See advertisement placed in the *New York Times*, December 5, 1995.

62 Grossman and Adams, 1993.

63 Bertell and Tognoni, 1996, p. 88; Heinzow, 1996, p. 7.

64 Described in Laughlin, 1996, p. 22.

65 Cassels, 1993, p. 38; Chopra, 1994, p. 248.

66 Reif, 1994, p. 743; Kapur, 1990, p. 14.

67 Ghosh, 1994, p. 256.

68 Cohen and Sarangi, 1995, p. 23.

69 Moshavi, 1995, p. 48.

70 Chatterjee, 1995, p. 16.

71 Jordan and Brauchli, *Wall Street Journal*, December 29, 1995, pp. A1, A6.

72 As reported by Cassels, 1993.

CHAPTER 11
Neoliberal Trade and Investment and the Health of Maquiladora Workers on the U.S.-Mexico Border

1 The word *"maquiladora"* comes from the verb *"maquilar,"* the strict meaning of which is "[for a miller] to separate out a given portion of grain, flour, or oil for milling." This "portion" was known as a *maquila*. Farmers typically did not mill their own harvests; they paid millers to process them; the strict meaning of *"maquilar"* thus extends quite naturally to cover foreign corporations' assembly-for-export operations in Mexico. So it is that *"maquiladora"* refers to the plants in Mexico and elsewhere that handle the assembly work for foreign corporations.

2 Interview with Janie Simmons. April, 1995, Nuevo Laredo, Tamaulipas, Mexico.

3 Peters, 1998, p. 69. The EAP is also known as the "labor force." It is essentially the sum of the employed and the unemployed (that is, those without work who are looking for work). It can also be thought of as total population minus children, full-time students, retired people, homemakers, and informal sector workers.

4 Brooks, 1992, p. 50; Ramírez, 1989, p. 146; Grinspun and Cameron, 1995. Import substitution industrialization built up domestic manufacturing using government subsidies and high tariffs. "Similar policies were used to promote self-sufficiency in food through government support to small-scale producers, and through agrarian reform" (Coote, 1995, p. 4).

5 Ramírez, 1989, p. 149. The austerity measures, typical of the IMF "policy-based" loans that have been offered to countries all over the developing world, involved the contraction of state expenditures on industry and social programs, and the liberalization of trade in order to gain desperately needed foreign exchange.

6 Ramírez, 1989, p. 150; Lustig, 1992, p. 3; Brooks, 1992, pp. 20, 50. The government believed that world oil prices would continue to rise and cheap external credit would continue to be available. Included in the spending spree was the development of the oil industry itself, requiring vast amounts of foreign funding that only added to the ever increasing foreign debt. The situation, similar to the crisis in 1976, was made worse by the combination of an increased dependence on oil exports for foreign exchange and, by mid-1981, a global reduction in oil prices, which further shrank government revenues (Ramírez, 1989, pp. 151-152; Lustig, 1992, p. 24). Mexico's debt increased

from \$4.5 billion in 1971 to \$19.6 billion in 1976; over the next six years, it quadrupled again, reaching over \$80 billion by 1982 (Brooks, 1992, p.50).

7 Grinspun and Cameron, 1995, p. 44; Ramírez, 1989, p. 152; Lustig, 1992, p. 25.

8 Lustig, 1992, pp. 3-4.

9 Lustig, 1992, p. 28. *Structural adjustment* is the process by which a government attempts to correct a balance of payments crisis. Structural adjustment programs sponsored by the IMF often require governments to liberalize, or open up, their economies to the outside world. As Lustig puts it, SAPs sponsored by the IMF operate on the assumption that an economy will be better off in the long run if "market forces operate, and products and services are not protected, subsidized, heavily regulated, or produced by the government." Most often, as was the case in Mexico, a government implements a SAP as a condition for receiving IMF or World Bank loans.

10 Bosworth, Collins, and Lustig, 1997, p. 4. The reduction in the proportion of Mexican production protected by import licenses meant that many U.S. and other foreign goods formerly limited by licenses could enter Mexico in quantities limited only by demand; this created difficulties for many Mexican manufacturers.

11 Lustig, 1992, p. 116.

12 Brooks, 1992, p. 51. Revenues from sales of public corporations exceeded 7 percent of GNP in the period 1991 to 1994, during which time the formerly nationalized banking system was returned to private ownership (Bosworth, Collins, and Lustig, 1997, p. 4).

13 Lustig, 1992, p. 116.

14 Holbein and Musch, 1994, p. 1.

15 Coote, 1995, p. 4.

16 Mexico agreed to reduce its tariffs on U.S. exports in such a way that half of U.S. exports would be duty-free immediately, and fully two-thirds would be duty-free by 1999. The United States agreed to a reciprocal lowering of tariffs on Mexican imports. American tariffs on Mexican goods were on average 4 percent before NAFTA, versus Mexico's 12 percent. The agreement also sought to reduce non-tariff restrictions on trade. For example, NAFTA encouraged countries to "harmonize" safety standards for materials and products (NAFTA, Articles 904-915, in Holbein and Musch, 1994). The agreement's premise was that member countries would harmonize standards upward to the level of the highest country. But downward harmonization remains a concern under NAFTA.

17 NAFTA, Articles 1201-1203, in Holbein and Musch, 1994.

18 Bello, Holmer, and Norton, 1994, p. 3. The agreement's provisions on investment allow U.S. and Canadian firms not established in Mexico to sell more freely in that country; the agreement also phases out requirements about the proportion of domestic inputs transnationals established in Mexico must use, and about the proportion of their products that must be re-exported (NAFTA, Article 1106, in Holbein and Musch, 1994). American and Canadian patent holders are granted under NAFTA protections in Mexico of equivalent force to those they enjoy under their

national laws (NAFTA, Articles 1701-1703, 1708-1709, 1714-1718, in Holbein and Musch, 1994).

19 It frees the labor market in a single important instance: the agreement eases business travel among member countries (NAFTA, Articles 1601-1603, in Holbein and Musch, 1994).

20 In the United States, large corporations lobbied hard in favor of NAFTA, seeing that the agreement would open new markets to their products, and, in many cases, reduce production costs. Unions and the pro-labor wing of the Democratic Party opposed the agreement, arguing that NAFTA would depress U.S. wages and export jobs to Mexico. Clinton Democrats and mainstream environmentalists came out for NAFTA, once the side agreements had been negotiated. They believed that NAFTA was a win-win-win proposition: workers in both countries would see more jobs and higher wages; business would profit; and NAFTA and its side agreements would protect the environment and worker's rights. Aside from the purely economic arguments they advanced in favor of NAFTA, proponents also claimed that the agreement would bolster Salinas' reforms, induce Mexican cooperation on immigration and drugs, and pave the way for a hemispheric free trade agreement. See, for example, remarks by Assistant Secretary of State Alexander Watson ("Trade Pact to Give Latin America a Big Boost," *New York Times*, October 6, 1993). The idea that NAFTA broke ground for a hemispheric free trade agreement was understood by all concerned. One of the agreement's explicit purposes was the establishment of "a framework for further trilateral, regional, and multilateral cooperation to expand and enhance the benefits of this Agreement" (NAFTA Article 102, in Holbein and Musch, 1994). Many Republicans in Congress supported the agreement on the grounds that it would have mainly salutary consequences for American businesses and consumers. Many of these same Republicans opposed President Clinton's side agreements, and voted against NAFTA for that reason. Finally, populist-protectionists in and outside the Republican party opposed NAFTA with an "Americans first" argument that echoed labor's concerns.

In Mexico, the Salinas government wanted the agreement badly enough to spend $25 million lobbying the U.S. Congress in its favor—at the time, the most ever spent by a foreign government to influence U.S. legislation. In the short term, the agreement's luster would give international investors the confidence to buy a piece of Mexico's future. Investors were needed to finance the country's current-account deficit. Indeed, investment flowed quickly into Mexico during 1993, in anticipation of NAFTA's bounty. The prestige of the agreement, coupled with the investment it would bring, would help Salinas' party retain power in the 1994 election. In the longer term, Salinas' team of liberal reformers believed, NAFTA would ensure open markets for Mexico's exports and lock in the preconditions for a continuous flow of foreign investment (Coote, 1995, p. 28). These would lead to more and better paying jobs for Mexicans. The main coalition of parties on the left was opposed to the agreement, although, outwardly at least, more to its particulars than to its general theory. By the 1994 election, Cuauhtémoc Cárdenas, the coalition's candidate for president, who just three years earlier had proposed a North American trade and investment agreement that would have included a social charter as well as provisions on compensatory financing, labor mobility, and the environment, was saying only that he would seek to revise NAFTA if it proved "damaging to the national interests" (Cárdenas, 1992; Tim Golden, "Salinas Calls NAFTA a Test of U.S. Relations with All Latin America," *New York Times*, October 19, 1993). All things considered, there was considerable support for the agreement among elites of different political shades in Mexico and throughout Latin America. On Latin American support for NAFTA, see, for example, Larry Rohter, "Latin America Finds Harmony in Convergence," *New York Times*, November 21, 1993.

21 Holbein and Musch, 1994, p. 1. Canada and the United States had signed a free trade agreement in 1989; NAFTA can be seen as the accession of Mexico to that agreement.

22 Joel Kurtzman, "The NAFTA Bandwagon Rolls Towards Congress," *New York Times*, October 11, 1992; Anthony DePalma, "Curious Wrinkle in the Mexican Play," *New York Times*, September 12, 1993.

23 Holbein and Musch, 1994, p. 3.

24 Galhardi, 1998, Table 1.1.

25 Thomas Black, "A Milestone for the *Maquiladoras*," *Miami Herald*, January 26, 1998. Thus, although Mexican exports have grown faster than the population since 1980, growing on average 7 percent per year between 1980 and 1990, and 9.8 percent per year between 1990 and 1997, the *maquila* sector accounts for most of this growth (World Bank, 1999b). Whether over the period from 1980 to 1990 or from 1990 to 1997, average annual growth of output was less than 2 percent in agriculture, in manufacturing, and in services. Population growth has been consistently *higher* than 2 percent.

26 Rangel, 1998.

27 "Economic News: Real Wages Fall 5.2 Percent in Manufacturing," *El Financiero Weekly International*, May 11, 1997.

28 "Solving *Maquiladora* Health Problems," *El Financiero Weekly International*, August 30, 1998; Banco de Mexico, 1997, p. 36. Available at www.banxico-.org.mx/public_html/inveco/anu97/portada.pdf.

29 Herredia and Purcell, 1996.

30 "Local content rules" require that a fixed proportion of inputs be of domestic origin. "Local ownership rules" require that some proportion of stock be held by domestic individuals or institutions. *Maquiladoras* were already largely exempt from these and similar requirements. Yet the *maquiladora* program, though long established, was a mutable creature of Mexican law. The North American Free Trade Agreement gave prospective investors the security of being able to count on a continuation of favorable local content and local ownership rules.

31 Herredia and Purcell, 1996. A general caution: NAFTA's effects in inducing new investment cannot be divorced from the preceding decade of economic liberalization. Indeed, an important study of multinational

corporations' attitude toward NAFTA concluded that "the focus on NAFTA itself missed the point about what is happening today in North America's economy. The real story, we believe, is deepening economic integration in North America and the emergence of a true North American economy. This process did not begin with NAFTA or the Canada-U.S. Free Trade Agreement (CUSFTA); trade liberalization and the emergence of new cross-border business strategies preceded NAFTA. Indeed, both of these agreements can best be viewed as responses to deep, underlying change already under way in the structure of our economies. This profound change...is being driven by the interlinked forces of global competition, regulatory liberalization, and technology" (Blank and Haar, 1998, p. viii). Government trade officials lagged, rather than led, the businessmen: "[C]hanges in North American corporate organization and strategy have been more rapid than anyone anticipated. Crossborder corporate integration has been deeper and more far-reaching, we believe, than governments in particular seem to realize" (Blank and Haar, 1998, p. 2). According to a vice president at one of the largest U.S. multinationals: "Business is so far ahead of politicians on this one that it almost makes the agreement secondary" (Blank and Haar, 1998, p. 2). However much that may be true, large U.S. multinationals lobbied heavily for NAFTA.

32 Gregory Katz, "Mexico President Hails Treaty Deal," *Dallas Morning News*, August 14, 1993.

33 Randy Lee Loftis, "Dallas Firm Fined Over Toxics," *Dallas Morning News*, June 16, 1993.

34 William J. Clinton, "Remarks at the NAFTA Signing Ceremony," Washington, D.C., December 8, 1993; William J. Clinton, "Radio Address from the Oval Office," October 16, 1993.

35 Sarah Anderson and John Cavanaugh, "NAFTA's Unhappy Anniversary," *New York Times*, February 7, 1995.

36 The CEC may decide to investigate and has the option of making public the results of its investigation. A separate mechanism allows any member country to bring plaint against a second member country in cases where the second has shown a "persistent pattern of failure" to enforce its environmental laws. If an inquiry confirms the persistent pattern of failure, and if the party at fault does not correct its practice, and if a tortuous process that can be aborted at several stages is followed to the end, the commission may fine the offending country an amount no greater than 0.007 percent of the total trade in goods between the parties in the most recent year for which data are available. If such a fine were to have been imposed on Mexico at the time of writing, it would have amounted to less than $20 million dollars, or less than 0.05 percent of the Mexican federal government's annual revenues.

37 Karen Brandon, "A Vision Unfulfilled," *Chicago Tribune*, November 28, 1998. See also the Commission for Environmental Cooperation. Available at cec.org/english/citizen/index.cfm?format=2.

38 The environmental side agreement has also proven inadequate in regard to the task of cleaning up old pollution. The NAAEC established the North American Development Bank (NADBank) to fund environmental cleanup. The NADBank estimates that $6-$8 billion is required just to bring water supply, wastewater treatment, and solid waste disposal up to standard. In 1998, the NADBank had disbursed only $20 million in grants and loans (although it had approved $600 million). Furthermore, many of the communities most in need of loans are too poor to qualify for them, since the NADBank provides loans at market rates.

39 Of course, critics of NAFTA contend that the agreement was never intended to improve Mexico's execution of its labor laws. For a prescient assessment of NAFTA in this regard, see Levinson, 1993. Levinson, former general counsel of the IDB, saw clearly what was "the [Salinas] government's policy to assure a low-wage, stable labor environment conducive to attracting foreign investment, enforced by...strong-arm tactics...It is naive in the extreme to believe that American companies do not know that they can take advantage of this policy and the tactics which have been described. The United States negotiators for NAFTA, however, propose not to recognize that there is even a problem. NAFTA does not contemplate the creation of a social policy, as is the case with the European Community ("EC")....NAFTA, however, is more than a trade agreement. It is a trade and investment agreement, and part of the investment climate which Mexico has created involves this low wage labor stability, which is enforced by strong-arm tactics. It constitutes, in my view, an unfair investment incentive, which should have been addressed as an integral part of the NAFTA negotiations. The dirty secret of the NAFTA negotiations is the failure to address this question of what constitutes fair and unfair labor practices, which in turn amount to fair and unfair investment incentives" (Levinson, 1993, p. 226).

40 Fred Rosen, "Solving *Maquiladora* Health Problems," *El Financiero Weekly International*, August 30, 1998. Recent scholarship identifies gaps in education between the rich and poor as important perpetuators of poverty. Mexico is a case in point: the education gap between Mexico's top two deciles (measured in years of schooling) is greater than three years—along with Brazil and Honduras, the highest in Latin America. Between the top decile and the bottom three deciles, Mexico's average education gap is greater than nine years, which is greater than other highly unequal Latin American countries such as Brazil, Panama, and El Salvador (IDB, 1998a, p. 27).

41 "*Maquilas*, Jobs, and Peace on the Border," *El Financiero Weekly International*, March 29, 1998.

42 Support by the CTM was not always as strong as it now is; as Arizona political scientist Edward Williams has noted, the government made its case when it "purged a number of Mexican labor leaders and imprisoned others in a campaign launched by de la Madrid and intensified by Salinas...Mexico's labor leaders fell into line, pledging their support to the 'modernization' of the Mexican economy" (Edward Williams, "Discord in U.S.-Mexican Labor Relations and the North American Agreement on Labor Cooperation," paper presented at an international seminar, *Mexico y su Interacción con el Sistema Político Estadounidense*, Mexico City, January, 1996. Available at www.natlaw.com/pubs/spmxlb1.htm).

43 Mexico as a whole has seen a large decrease in union membership among nonagricultural workers. Between 1989 and 1991, the proportion of unionized nonagricultural workers declined from 54.1 percent to 31 percent (ILO, 1998, p. 237).

44 "Solving Maquiladora Health Problems," El Financiero Weekly International, August 30, 1998.

45 One organization that has helped maquila workers organize is the Coalition for Justice in the Maquiladoras. See description in Chapter Sixteen.

46 La Botz, 1994, p. 407; Meredith and Brown, 1995, p. 85; Korten 1995, p. 129; Peña, 1997, p. 107. Another way workers are hindered from organizing is by having many workers be represented by "ghost" or "phantom" unions within the CTM. Employees are often unaware that the union even exists until they attempt to form independent unions. At that point, they are informed that they have already signed a union contract (La Botz, 1994, p. 403; Meredith and Brown, 1995, p. 407).

47 Robert Bryce, "Gripe on Mexican Labor to get NAFTA Hearing," Christian Science Monitor, April 26, 1995. Many maquiladora managers have preferred women workers, considering them better-suited to repetitive tasks requiring nimble fingers; more willing to perform monotonous and exhausting work; and more docile—or at least less likely to organize against management. Managers and engineers, on the other hand, are almost always male. Nevertheless, the proportion of women workers employed in the maquiladoras has declined steadily since the program began and is approaching parity with men, although in some sectors, textiles for example, women still account for a substantial majority of workers; the sectorwide average is 56 percent (Galhardi, 1998; Fleck and Sorrentino, 1994; STPS, 1998a, 1998b).

48 This account of the elections at Magnéticos de México was compiled by Janie Simmons from her fieldnotes and interviews with several of the protagonists.

49 Human Resources Development Canada, 1999.

50 Executive Office of the President, 1997.

51 U.S. Department of Labor, 1996.

52 International Labor Rights Fund, 1997.

53 World Bank, 1997c, pp. 131-132. Mexican agricultural output grew by an average of only 0.6 percent per year between 1980 and 1990, and 0.4 percent per year between 1990 and 1995. Meanwhile, world agricultural output grew at average annual rates of 2.8 percent between 1980 and 1990, and 1.3 percent between 1990 and 1995. Rates for upper-middle income countries (Mexico's peer group) were 2.4 percent and 1.8 percent, respectively.

54 Lourdes Edith Rudiño, "Low Basic Grain Prices are Tied to Emigration," El Financiero Weekly International, February 2, 1997.

55 Coote, 1995, p. 22. For a low estimate, see Peña and Henderson, 1993, who predict 700,000 workers will be displaced, which, counting dependents, means 1 to 5 million people. "Mexico's essential task will be to create enough industrial jobs to absorb dislocated rural workers while also modernizing its agricultural sector with adequate infrastructure and technology and encouraging transition from staple to exportable crops.

NAFTA is expected to assist this effort by lowering trade barriers for United States farm machinery, pesticides, fertilizers…" For a high estimate, see Calva, 1992. In an interview for a 1997 article, Calva stood by his estimate of 3 million workers (15 million people) displaced by 2009. See also Lourdes Edith Rudiño, "Low Basic Grain Prices are Tied to Emigration," El Financiero Weekly International, February 2, 1997.

56 Martin, 1997, p. 89.

57 Watkins, 1995, p. 140. See also Martin, 1997, p. 89.

58 Migration has not been the only response of Mexico's rural poor to the dislocations of the last 15 years. The armed uprising in Chiapas (one of Mexico's southernmost states), which began the day NAFTA went into effect and has alternately boiled and simmered throughout the last five years, was a direct response to many years of broken government promises around land rights and social justice. Under the banner of the EZLN (Zapatista National Liberation Army), Chiapas' indigenous peoples and poor have demanded a re-instatement of the ejido system and progressive land-tenure reform. They have also called for democratic elections, an end to political corruption, and "a minimum wage high enough for people to adequately feed their children" (Werner and Sanders, 1997, p. 148). The Mexican government's response has ranged from negotiation to violence. The conflict remains unresolved, and the peasants of Chiapas, like many others throughout Mexico, persist in extreme poverty.

59 Martin, 1997, p. 88.

60 These reforms were partly in response to pressure from the U.S. government. Werner and Sanders, 1997, p. 146.

61 "The ejido is a community-based system of land tenure in which the government protected privately held parcels and communal lands within the community from the market" (Barry, 1995, p. 12). The ejido system came about in response to the first triumph of Mexican liberalism in the post-independence constitution of 1857. Liberals were the radicals then, and they saw decollectivization and privatization as a way to at once break the power of the church and other land-holding elites and move Indian-held lands from a pre-capitalist to a capitalist system of land tenure. The result was supposed to have been the creation of a large class of independent farmers. Instead, by 1910, under the Diaz dictatorship, privatization had created a small class of wealthy landowners, a fledgling (mostly urban) middle class, and an army of landless poor. This inequitable condition paved the way for the 1910 revolution, many of the ideals of which were incorporated into the constitution of 1917, which placed the ejido sector (first created in an agricultural reform bill in 1915) on solid ground. Ejidos were understood as a means of ensuring that the rural poor would at least have land on which to make a living; that the great concentrations of land that had existed under the Diaz dictatorship would not recur; and that farmers would be able to decide their own affairs democratically and autonomously.

Yet we should be wary of idealizing the ejido system. At least since the presidency of Lázaro Cárdenas in the 1930s, its autonomous and democratic qualities had been usurped, and the *ejido* made an instrument of political power—so much so that one contemporary partisan of the *campesinos* would write: "*Ejido* governance has reflected the paternalistic, clientelistic and self-serving character of the national political systems, and is not an instance of direct democracy" (Barry, 1995, p. 120). By the 1990s, *ejido*-held lands were 30 to 50 percent less productive than privately held lands (Gianaris, 1998, pp. 24-25). One reason for the lower productivity was that communal ownership, which protected farmers from dispossession, also disbarred them from using their parcels as collateral for loans, choking agricultural credit needed for investments in infrastructure. Most damning, by the early 1990s, 64 percent of *ejido* members held parcels of 5 hectares or less, so-called "infra-subsistence" plots (Barry, 1995, p. 120).

62 Barry, 1995, p. 14. Figures are percentages of the sum of *ejido*-held and privately-held lands in each of the categories. Federal government lands, amounting to roughly 6 percent of Mexico's area, have not been included.

63 Ramírez, 1989.

64 Coote, 1995, p. 20; Barry, 1995, p. 117. Sales of parcels to nonmembers require the majority vote of the members; it appears the real action in the short term will be internal, as wealthier farmers buy up plots from poorer ones, up to a limit of 5 percent of the area of the *ejido* (Barry, 1995, p. 121).

At the same time, the constitutional provision limiting commercial farms to 100 hectares of irrigated lands was undone, and the government gave up the practice of redistributing to landless claimants the excess land of farmers found to be violating the 100-hectare rule (Martin, 1997, pp. 83-84).

65 Barry, 1995, p. 125.

66 The removal of subsidies is technically not mandated by NAFTA, which requires only that governments not use subsidies as barriers against trade. But any subsidy will raise *some* obstacle to trade, compared to the subsidy's not being in place, so it remains to be seen whether the distinction between subsidies that do and do not block trade can be maintained.

Still, the Mexican government's 1993 reform of agricultural subsidies cannot be separated from NAFTA; the reform is in the spirit of the free trade agreement, although not technically linked to it. The new system replaces a bevy of targeted subsidies for individual crops and factors of production (such as seeds, water, and fertilizer) with a single payment based on the number of acres a farmer cultivates. In this way, farmers are discouraged from planting unprofitable crops. They must instead supply what the market wants, or stop farming (see David Shields, "Bleak Outlook for Peasant Farmers," *El Financiero Weekly International*, March 2, 1997).

Note that the main support for corn producers under the old system came in the form of price guarantees. The government bought farmers' surplus corn at prices 50 to 70 percent higher than market prices. Some 1.5 million of Mexico's farmers, representing 40 percent of the farming population, are subsistence or infra-subsistence farmers. Almost by definition, these farmers produce no surplus. Because they therefore never benefited from the government's price guarantees, they

were at least not in a position to be directly hurt by the government's abandonment of this particular program. The government even claimed that subsistence farmers would benefit, because the new program is a cash subsidy essentially proportional to the area under cultivation—subsistence farmers would at least receive *something* under the new program, the government reasoned. The subsidy worked out to about $106 per hectare in 1994.

67 Fernando Varela, "NAFTA Chokes Grain Output," *News*, October 16, 1998.

68 Barry, 1995, p. 66. Before NAFTA, there was no tariff on U.S. corn. Instead, Mexico regulated the amount of U.S. corn entering the country by issuing import permits; NAFTA simply exchanged the permits for tariffs. In NAFTA's first year, 2.5 million metric tons of corn were allowed into Mexico duty-free. The duty-free quantity increases by 3 percent each year until 2009. American corn in excess of the duty-free quantity is subject to a tariff that decreases to zero in 2009 (Barry, 1995, p. 70). See also Fernando Varela, "NAFTA Chokes Grain Output," *News*, October 16, 1998.

69 *National Survey on Costs and Technical Coefficiency*, quoted in Lourdes Edith Rudiño, "Low Basic Grain Prices are Tied to Emigration," *El Financiero Weekly International*, February 2, 1997.

70 Barry, 1995, p. 103. Subsistence and infra-subsistence farmers are those farming 5 hectares or less. See also, Coote, 1995, p. 21.

71 Barry, 1995, p. 74. Of course, labor productivity depends on degree of mechanization, land productivity, and fertilizer and pesticide use, among other things. The United States produces at lower monetary cost, but higher environmental cost. Some of the environmental cost is "externalized."

72 A drought in 1996 and the weather brought by El Niño in 1997 and 1998 damaged Mexican crops severely, and must be considered in assessing the consequences of trade liberalization on Mexican agriculture.

73 Garance Burke, "Grain Imports Rise as Farmers Look On," *El Financiero Weekly International*, September 13, 1998. Even though prices have fallen by as much as 20 percent since 1997, due to a good U.S. harvest, corn prices stood at $84 per ton in September 1998. Thus, in 1998 alone, Mexico stood to spend over $450 million on U.S. corn.

74 Fernando Varela, "NAFTA Chokes Grain Output," *News*, October 16, 1998.

75 See Barry, 1995, p. 82. "The small farmer and the farmworker are frequently one and the same person. For most *campesinos*—an estimated 80 percent—the family...parcel provides only a home base and a declining part of their survival needs....Most peasants are in fact rural proletarians who depend on seasonal planting, weeding, and harvesting work on estates that are sometimes far away from their villages."

Some of NAFTA's consequences have to be seen as unintended by the parties to the agreement. The crash of the peso in 1995 and the unabated stream of illegal immigration from Mexico to the U.S. since NAFTA are just two examples. But the displacement of several million small farmers has to be seen as an intended consequence; NAFTA has been conceived as a lever for forcing the demographic transition. As Barry makes clear, many Mexican elites on both the right and the left have viewed the peasantry as a retrograde element in Mexican society that retards the country's development as a whole.

Mexico thus presents a classic problem of development. From Stalin's Russia to present, leaders of countries with large peasant populations have reasoned that to become industrialized and wealthy, many peasants must be removed from the land and funelled into the industrial sector. Mexico is accomplishing by decollectivization and privatization what Stalin accomplished by collectivization and nationalization. The private market plays the role of the planners, but the result is similar: a brutal dislocation of the peasantry.

76 Jose Luiz Imanz, "NAFTA Damages Small Businesses," *El Barzon*, January, 1997.

77 Authors' calculations. Based on data from INEGI, 1998; STPS, 1998; Banco de Mexico, 1998.

78 Authors' calculations. Based on data from Banco de Mexico, 1998 and IMF, 1998, p. 496. The entire loss in purchasing power was sustained between December 1994 and the end of 1997.

79 A high proportion of Mexican workers is employed in the informal sector, which includes some of the self-employed, workers at many small and family businesses, and others. The informal sector's size is difficult to measure, because there is no single precise definition of "informality." Experts from the ILO who coined the term in the 1970s used it to mean whatever economic activity the urban working poor carried out: "Informal activities were defined by the way things were done and characterized by such elements as ease of entry into the marketplace, small size, scarcity of capital, and family ownership of businesses" (Fleck and Sorrentino, 1994, p. 12). Despite the difficulties of measuring the size of the informal sector, the IDB estimates that 62 percent of Mexicans in the labor force aged 25-45 are employed informally. Among men and women aged 25-45 in the lowest income decile, 97 percent and 99 percent, respectively, work in the informal sector. No other Latin American country has a higher rate. What is perhaps more surprising, among workers aged 25-45 in the lowest four income deciles, 82 percent of men and 94 percent of women work in the informal sector. Among Latin American countries, only Nicaragua, Honduras, and Paraguay have equal or higher rates for one sex or the other among their poorest 40 percent (IDB, 1998a, p. 28).

80 Overall net job growth between 1980 and 1996 was around 2 million new jobs. During this period, 17.05 million Mexicans joined the economically active population.

81 Peters, 1998, p. 67.

82 Migration accounts for only a small percentage of the gap, at most 300,000 excess job seekers per year (U.S. Immigration and Naturalization Service, 1997); returning to agriculture is not an appealing option; and unemployment rates are now as low as when NAFTA came into force.

83 As stated in Chapter One, this book takes the correlation between health and wealth as given. For references, see Chapter One, note 1.

84 STPS, 1998b.

85 STPS, 1998b.

86 Manuela, in an interview with Janie Simmons, 1995.

87 Balcazar, Denman, and Lara, 1995.

88 Balcazar, Denman, and Lara, 1995, p. 498.

89 Balcazar, Denman, and Lara, 1995, p. 498. The study also found that women had slightly higher rates of occupational illness and disease than men.

90 Moure-Eraso, Wilcox, Punnett, *et al.*, 1997.

91 Mathur, Gupta, Rastogi, *et al.*, 1993.

92 Moure-Eraso, Wilcox, Punnett, *et al.*, 1997. Subjects reported a variety of complaints: headache (55 percent), unusual fatigue (53 percent), depression for nonspecific reason (51 percent), forgetfulness (41 percent), chest pressure (41 percent), difficulty falling asleep (39 percent), stomach pain (37 percent), dizziness (36 percent), and numbness or tingling of the extremities (33 percent).

93 Moure-Eraso, Wilcox, Punnett, *et al.*, 1997; McGuinness, 1994.

94 Pocekay, McCurdy, Samuels, *et al.*, 1995. Of course, assembly workers suffer musculoskeletal symptoms at higher rates than the working population at large. For example, only 8 percent of subjects in the Occupational Health Supplement to the 1988 National Health Interview Survey reported one or more weeks of daily hand pain during the course of the previous year (Levy and Wegman, 1995, p. 241).

95 Rafael Moure-Eraso, personal communication, April 1999.

96 Eskenazi, Guendelman, and Elkin, 1993, p. 669.

97 Eskenazi, Guendelman, and Elkin, 1993, p. 674.

98 Public Citizen, 1996, p. 5.

99 Karen Brandon, "A Vision Unfulfilled," *Chicago Tribune*, November 29, 1998; Bosworth, Collins, and Lustig, 1997, p. 97.

100 Sam Howe Verhovek, "Pollution Problems Fester South of the Border," *New York Times*, July 4, 1998.

101 Williams, 1995.

102 Enrique Rangel, "Mass Production," *Dallas Morning News*, February 1, 1998.

103 Diane Lindquist, "*Maquiladora* Industry Has Led Way in Jobs, Growth," *San Diego Union-Tribune*, June 28, 1998.

104 Sklair, 1993.

105 Proponents of NAFTA often ignore this trend. Since 1983, the sector has been growing faster in the interior than on the border (Blank and Haar, 1998, p. 16). See also Galhardi, 1998, Table 1.1. Galhardi notes that the proportion of *maquiladoras* on the border declined from 88.4 percent in 1985 to 72.5 percent in 1993. Because border plants are on average no larger than interior plants, the proportion of workers in border plants declined from 88.1 percent to 72.7 percent over the same period. This trend in part can be attributed to a tighter labor market in the border zones compared

to the interior (Galhardi, 1998, sec. 3.1) and consequent lower wages in the interior.

106 Even though new jobs are being created faster in the interior than on the border, the proportion of *maquiladora* jobs in the interior is now declining, because of the still-rapid growth of the much larger border sector.

107 Warner, 1991; Frumkin, Hernández-Avila, and Espinosa, 1995; Moure-Eraso, Wilcox, Punnett, et al., 1994.

108 Moure-Eraso, Wilcox, Punnett, et al., 1994, p. 320.

109 Chemical leaks included release of ethyl alcohol, pentachlorophenol, and ammonia.

110 Moure-Eraso, Wilcox, Punnett, et al., 1994, p. 320.

111 Cech and Essman, 1992, p. 1053.

112 Gamble, Jackson, and Maurer, 1988; Wells, Jackson, and Maurer, 1988.

113 Eskenazi, Guendelman, and Elkin, 1993, p. 1053.

114 Eskenazi, Guendelman, and Elkin, 1993, p. 1053.

115 Lewis, Kaltofen, and Ormsby, 1991. The study was designed to test for toxic chemical discharge from industries at 23 sites along the Rio Grande, the Nogales Wash, the New River (in Mexico), and the Tijuana River. Five of the eight most toxic sites were in Texas, with two in Tijuana and one in the Nogales Wash region.

116 Texas Center for Policy Studies, 1994. Forty-five samples were taken, 19 from mainstream sites and 26 from tributaries (13 each from the United States and Mexico). Data for this study were collected by U.S. and Mexican investigators. U.S. researchers detected 21 of 161 chemicals for which they tested. Mexican results identified only nine chemicals in water, only one of which (chromium) exceeded Mexican standards. This discrepancy in results may reflect the inadequacy of Mexican testing techniques and standards.

117 Texas Center for Policy Studies, 1994.

118 Texas Center for Policy Studies, 1994. Other chemicals considered to be of concern were placed into *high-priority*, *medium-priority*, and *low-priority* groups for the purpose of future water-management decisions; these chemicals were as follows: high priority—N-nitrosodin-propylamine, bis(2-ethylhexyl) phthalate, phenolics recoverable, Chlordane, Aroclor 1260, selenium, mercury, DDE, cadmium, unionized ammonia, silver, chromium, chloride, nickel, lead, zinc, copper, and arsenic; medium priority—DDT and chloroform; and low priority—phenol single compound, 1,4-dichlorobenzene, dibromodichloromethane, bromodichloromethane, xylene, toluene, benzene, and antimony.

119 Texas Center for Policy Studies, 1994.

120 Texas Center for Policy Studies, 1994.

121 See the next section, "Disease," particularly the discussion of hepatitis A, for evidence that the Rio Grande's contaminated water has traceable health effects.

122 Warner, 1991. While the *maquiladoras* reap profits from the region, they assume no responsibility for the infrastructure of the *colonias*. A 1990 study of 80 Nuevo Laredo *maquiladoras* found that they were

assessed "only $279,000 in payroll taxes that year—hardly enough to pay for the social services needed by the *maquila* workers, to say nothing about the costs of infrastructure construction."

123 PAHO, 1995.

124 Bruce Selcraig, "From Great River to Foul Gutter: The Descent of the Rio Grande," *Los Angeles Times*, May 19, 1994; U.S. Environmental Protection Agency and Secretaria de Desarrollo Urbano y Ecológica, 1992.

125 Cech and Essman, 1992. The sites were chosen to reflect variations in population density, land use, and elevation. The authors classifed households' access to water in one of three ways: 1) *direct access*—water is delivered via indoor plumbing or a water hose connected to an outside source; 2) *indirect access*—water is delivered via a community water distribution point on the street or by truck delivery on average one in eight days (with storage in barrels near houses); and 3) *without access*—households collect rain water (Cech and Essman, 1992, p. 1056).

126 Cech and Essman, 1992, p. 1057.

127 U.S. Environmental Protection Agency and Secretaria de Desarrollo Urbano y Ecológica, 1994.

128 Moure-Eraso, Wilcox, Punnett, et al., 1994.

129 Public Citizen, 1996, p. 8

130 Frumkin, Hernández-Avila, and Espinosa, 1995, p. 98; "The Sewer Wars," *Economist*, August 8, 1998.

131 United States-Mexico Border Health Association, 1994, cited in Bruhn and Brandon, 1997, p. 41.

132 Bruhn and Brandon, 1997; Warner, 1991; Public Citizen, 1996; Frumkin, Hernández-Avila, and Espinosa, 1995; Skolnick, 1994; Redlinger, O'Rourke, and VanDerslice, 1997.

133 *Incidence* refers to the number of new events (of infection, disease, or some other measure) occurring in a given year.

134 Cech and Essman, 1992.

135 Sawer, Brown, Folke, et al., 1989. A more recent study in the same community found a seroprevalence rate of 16.9 percent in children aged 3-7 years (Redlinger, O'Rourke, and VanDerslice, 1997).

136 Varady and Mack, 1995.

137 Cech and Essman, 1992.

138 Skolnick, 1994, p. 1480.

139 PAHO, 1994.

140 PAHO, 1994.

141 Murray and Lopez, 1996, p. 261.

142 The DALYs lost to a given condition for a given population are (very roughly) the sum of the number of years of life lost by the population due to the condition (relative to a standard life expectancy for that population) and the number of years lost to disability in that population due to the condition. The number of years lost to disability depends on complicated judgments about both the numerical weight to be given to different kinds and degrees of disability *and* the value to be assigned to a given level of disability for a year as compared to a year of life lost. In recent years, DALYs have emerged as one of several standards for quantifying the burden populations carry as a result of illness and disease on populations. See Murray and Lopez, 1996.

143 Murray and Lopez, 1996, p. 602, p. 750.

144 Vega, Kolody, Hough, *et al.*, 1987; Mendes de Leon and Markides, 1988; Moscicki, Locke, Rae *et al.*, 1989.

145 Guendelman and Silberg, 1993.

146 Guendelman and Silberg, 1993.

147 Mendes de Leon and Markides, 1988; Moscicki, Locke, Rae, *et al.*, 1989. This score is adjusted for marital status, years of education, and employment status.

148 Vega, Kolody, Hough, *et al.*, 1987. This score was age-adjusted.

149 The significance of this disparity is open to the objection that the 1992 Tijuana subjects (Guendelman and Silberg, 1993) were in some ways unrepresentative of the female Mexican and Mexican-American populations; they were, among other things, younger, less likely to be married, and much more likely to work full-time. Yet, as such, they disproportionately belonged to some groups with above-average symptoms and some groups with below-average symptoms. For instance, three studies of depression in Mexicans or Mexican-Americans found less depressive symptoms among married women than among unmarried women (Mendes de Leon and Markides, 1988; Moscicki, Locke, Rae, *et al.*, 1989; Vega, Kolody, Hough, *et al.*, 1987). On the other hand, all three studies found strong and significant differences between the employed and the unemployed; in all three studies, full-time workers had less depressive symptoms than virtually any other subgroups. A further counter to the objection comes from an analysis of 1,000 Mexican migrant workers in California (Alderete, Vega, Bohdan, Kolody, *et al.*, "Depressive Symptomatology: Prevention and Risk Factors among Mexican Farm Workers in California," 1996 data, unpublished paper), which found a rate of 24 percent for women aged 18 to 25 years. The demographics of the women in this study population much more closely approximate those of Guendelman and Silberg's population than do those of the three broader studies already cited; notwithstanding a substantial "healthy worker" effect in Alderete, Vega, Kolody, *et al.* (i.e., the sample included only women healthy enough to perform hard, physical labor), they give an idea of just how high Guendelman and Silberg's rates are.

150 Even though the noneconomic arguments for NAFTA (which included promises of a reduction in illegal immigration from Mexico to the United States; more fruitful cooperation between the two countries on drug-trafficking; and improvements in labor and environmental conditions in Mexico) have so far proven hollow, charitable observers may be inclined to find political benefits in economic integration. Certain segments of the U.S. and Mexican populations will increasingly live and work together, and this increased commerce arguably spells the end of the "us and them" divisions between Anglo-Americans and Latin Americans. Of course, as the history of the United States so amply shows, the melding of many cultures into one is sometimes a less accurate depiction of cultural integration than the assimilation of less dominant cultures by a dominant culture. To the extent that the second of these pictures is the more accurate one, the integration cannot be wholly salutary.

151 Persons living in *extreme poverty* are those without access to the minimal market basket of food (as defined by the Mexican government). This should not be confused with international measures of absolute poverty, usually defined as $1 per day in 1985 dollars at purchasing power parity. Using the international standard, approximately 15 percent of Mexicans were absolutely poor in 1992. This is certainly a smaller share of the population than that living in extreme poverty according to the Mexican definition, which was approximately one-fifth of the population. See World Bank, 1999b, p. 197.

152 "Mexican Poverty on the Rise," *Miami Herald*, International Edition, July 15, 1998.

153 Garance Burke, "Extreme Poverty Increases 73 Percent in Six Years," *El Financiero Weekly International*, August 2, 1998. Eleven million of the extremely poor belonged to indigenous groups. By 1996, the ranks of the extremely poor had swollen to 22 million, or 24 percent of the population (Blank and Haar, 1998, p. 70). The Mexican economy grew strongly in 1997, but by early 1998, there were 24 million Mexicans in extreme poverty.

154 Mexico's basic poverty rate tells a story that is hardly less discouraging. Poverty in Mexico declined marginally between 1989 and 1998, from 50 percent of the population to 48 percent, but the number of poor people increased by approximately five million over the same period. In sum, whether considered since NAFTA took effect or since 1989, the liberalization of the Mexican economy cannot be said to have reduced poverty, and by several important measures, poverty has increased. For 1998 ILO estimates of the number of Mexicans in poverty, see G. Gatsiopoulos and L. Acevedo, "Finance Ministry Cuts Away at Social Spending," *El Financiero Weekly International*, May 17, 1998.

155 EIU, 1998b.

156 Charlene Barshefsky, U.S. Trade Representative, "Remarks at Meeting of the President's Export Council," Washington, D.C., November 10, 1998.

157 In a November 1998 speech, U.S. Trade Representative Charlene Barshefsky reported that: "[W]e have now formally launched the actual negotiation of the Free Trade Area of the Americas [FTAA]. We have a hemisphere very much engaged in this exercise, a hemisphere very much committed to concluding it no later than 2005. And we see in all of the…negotiating groups a very aggressive and highly particularized work agenda…including in some of the working groups beginning to draft annotated chapters of what a FTAA would look like" (Charlene Barshefsky, "Remarks at Meeting of the President's Export Council," Washington, D.C., November 10, 1998).

Proposals for a Pan-American free trade zone have rich origins in U.S. history. In 1889, U.S. Secretary of State James Blaine got from Congress what he had been wanting for almost ten years: the go-ahead to convene a Pan-American conference, with the stated aims of preserving the peace and promoting the prosperity of the American states, and of establishing an agreement "under which the trade of the American nations with each other shall…be promoted" (U.S.

Senate, 1890, p. 1-3); this was the First International Conference of American States (1889-90). The conference founded the International Union of American Republics (later to become the Organization of American States), but the governments in attendance voted down a hemispheric free trade zone. One hundred and one years later, George Bush repeated Blaine's call, inviting American heads of state to "begin the process of creating a hemisphere-wide free-trade zone" (Chasteen and Tulchin, 1994, p. 338).

The *idea* of a hemispheric trade zone predates Blaine's proposal by at least 70 years. In 1820, Henry Clay addressed Congress: "It is in our power to create a system of which we shall be the center, and in which all South America will act with us. In respect to commerce, we should be most benefited...Our citizens engaged in foreign trade...must seek new channels for it, and none so advantageous could be found as those which the trade with South America would afford..." (Annals of Congress, 16th Congress, 1st sess., 2225-2228).

158 These should, of course, be minimal standards, and countries should be encouraged to exceed them and be rewarded for so doing.

159 For instance, just as NAFTA's preamble proclaims that one of the agreement's purposes is to "protect, enhance, and enforce basic workers' rights," one of the FTAA's stated objectives is "to further secure...the observance and promotion of workers' rights" (San José Ministerial Declaration, Summit of the Americas Fourth Trade Ministerial, San José, Costa Rica, March 19, 1998. Available at www.alca-ftaa.org/English-Version/costa_e.htm).

160 Labor and environmental provisions are unlikely to be worked into a final agreement, either in its main text or in side agreements. Forces in both the United States and Latin America are arrayed against such protections. For instance, Mexico has been at the forefront in opposing any environmental provisions in the FTAA, arguing that they could be exploited by foreign interests, including protectionists in the United States (Kevin G. Hall, "Mexico Adamant about Keeping Environment out of Trade Talks," *Journal of Commerce*, January 11, 1999).

CHAPTER 12
The Drug War in Perspective

1   Webb recalled that "afterward I didn't get a single call from the *Los Angeles Times* reporters asking me how I got my sources or asking for phone numbers or for ideas for following up local angles. But I did get a call from the *Times* on-line people, asking me how I created that neat Web page." From Jill Stewart, "Just Another Big Embarrassment," *Phoenix New Times* (electronic edition), October, 1996.

2   Roberto Suro, and Walter Pincus, "The CIA and Crack: Evidence is Lacking of Alleged Plot," *Washington Post*, October 4, 1996; also Michael Fletcher, "Conspiracy Theories Can Often Ring True," *Washington Post*, October 4, 1996; Jesse Katz, "Tracking the Genesis of the Crack Trade," *The Los*

Angeles Times, October 20, 1996; Doyle McManus, "Examining Charges of CIA Role in Crack Sale," *Los Angeles Times*, October 21, 1996; John L. Mitchell and Sam Fulwood, "History Fuels Outrage over Crack Allegations," *Los Angeles Times*, October 22, 1996; Tim Golden, "Though Evidence Is Thin, Tale of CIA and Drugs Has a Life of Its Own," *New York Times*, October 21, 1996.

3   Adam Pertman, "CIA-Drug Link Stories Outrage Blacks in L.A.," *Boston Globe*, October 6, 1996. Also see Haygood, *Boston Globe*, December 15, 1996.

4   Some examples: television host Charlie Rose had as guests on one episode of his show a coordinator of the *Los Angeles Times* articles; a *Time* correspondent who echoed Tim Golden's *New York Times* article skeptical of *Mercury News'* claim; and a correspondent from *Wired* magazine who commented on the *San Jose Mercury News'* use of the Internet (PBS, October 22, 1996). No one who would defend the *Mercury News* series was invited. Mary McGrory wrote in the October 27, 1996, *Washington Post* that "the San Jose story has been discredited by major publications including the *Post*." On October 31, National Public Radio claimed that the series had been "debunked" by other respectable newspapers. The Associated Press reported on November 7 that "media critics and other newspapers have questioned the *Mercury News'* findings." *Newsweek* reported that "the Merc started getting trashed—by its peers. In turn, the *Washington Post*, the *Los Angeles Times*, and the *New York Times* poked holes in the story, exhaustively and mercilessly" (November 11, 1996). For more details, see Solomon, Norman, "Snow Job: The Establishment's Papers Do Damage Control for the CIA," *Extra!*, January/February 1997.

5   In the October 4, 1996, edition of the *Washington Post*, Walter Pincus wrote an accompanying article headlined "A Long History of Drug Allegations" that devoted all of thirty (printout) lines to the "long history," referring always to "allegations" of C.I.A. drug involvement while barely presenting the evidence (which we consider in detail later in this chapter). Not only did the *Post* not address Webb's evidence that Blandon and Meneses were protected from prosecution by the C.I.A. and the Justice Department, it did not dispute that Blandon and Meneses were drug dealers with Contra connections (though the *Post* protested that Blandon handled "only five tons during a ten-year career"), nor that some drug profits did in fact go to the Contras. This was pointed out in a letter from a *Mercury News* editor that the *Post* encouraged, but then refused to publish; see Jerry Ceppos, "In the Eye of the Storm: Series Prompts Journalism Debate," *San Jose Mercury News*, November 3, 1996. For more detailed criticism of the *Post* story, see Alex Cockburn and Ken Silverstein, *Counterpunch*, October 16-31, 1996. Commenting later on coverage by the *Post*, the *New York Times*, and the *Los Angeles Times*, the *Post* ombudsman aptly observed that the three newspapers "showed more passion for sniffing out the flaws in San Jose's answer than for sniffing out a better answer

themselves" (an understatement); see Geneva Overholser, "The CIA, Drugs, and the Press," *Washington Post*, November 10, 1996. This criticism struck a chord within the *Post* newsroom, with one editor reporting that "there was a lot of frustration. Why pick on the *Mercury News?*" (Peter Kornbluh, "Crack, the Contras and the CIA: The Storm Over 'Dark Alliance,'" *Columbia Journalism Review*, January/February, 1997).

6   See Rick Barrs, "A Barracuda Tries to Eat the Messenger," *New Times Los Angeles*, October 31, 1996. Another reporter said: "The discussion is not about which major stories we should peel off from the Webb series and hit hardest now that we know what happened, but about the perceived 'holes' in Webb's story. You know, how much of this Contra cocaine/South-Central thing is really new, and a lot of questions as to whether it's of much interest nowadays. Basically, we are in complete denial." See Jill Stewart, "Just Another Big Embarrassment," *Phoenix New Times* (electronic edition), October, 1996. One *Los Angeles Times* reporter, Jesse Katz, had to upend his own reporting of two years previous in order to discredit the *Mercury News*. (Thanks to Mark Adkins for research on this subject.) For example: in his article of October 20, 1996, Katz downplayed the importance of Ricky Ross, writing that: "the story of crack's genesis and evolution...is filled with a cast of interchangeable characters, from ruthless billionaires to strung-out curb dealers, none of whom is central to the drama....How the crack epidemic reached that extreme, on some level, had nothing to do with Ross. Before and after his reign, a bewildering roster of other dealers and suppliers helped fuel the crisis. They were all responding to market forces that many experts believe would have created the problem whether any one individual sold crack or not." But on December 20, 1994, Katz had written: "If there was an eye to the storm, if there was a criminal mastermind behind crack's decade-long reign, if there was one outlaw capitalist most responsible for flooding Los Angeles' streets with mass-marketed cocaine, his name was Freeway Rick. He didn't make the drug and he didn't smuggle it across the border, but Ricky Donell Ross did more than anyone else to democratize it, boosting volume, slashing prices, and spreading disease on a scale never before conceived. He was...South Central [L.A.'s] first millionaire crack lord." See Barrs for more on this and other details on the *Los Angeles Times* coverage.

7   Joel Kovel, "The Big Pusher," *Anderson Valley Advertiser*, November 27, 1996 (cited in Herman, *Z Magazine*, February, 1997, p. 7), commenting on the unnamed sources described by Golden. The *New York Times* was evasive in other ways as well, as in Golden's conclusion that although Enrique Bermudez (a top Contra commander who had contact with Meneses and Blandon) "was often paid by the CIA, he was not a CIA agent." As Murray Kempton subsequently noted in *Newsday*, October 23, 1996: "The maintenance of such distinctions without any essential dif-

ference is one of the more cunning of the infinite devices the agency employs in obfuscation. The CIA identifies highly placed foreign hirelings not as 'agents' but as 'assets.'" See Norman Solomon, "Snow Job: The Establishment's Papers Do Damage Control for the CIA," *Extra!*, January/February, 1997.

8   The *Boston Globe* article cited previously (see note 3) said only that the subcommittee "sought to establish" such complicity. An earlier *Globe* article (Bob Hohler, "No Proof of U.S. Tie to Drugs in Black Areas, Kerry Says," *Boston Globe*, September 27, 1996) merely acknowledged that the subcommittee "conducted the most exhaustive inquiry to date." Similarly for a *Globe* article on October 15, 1996 (Thomas Palmer, "Kerry Wants Probe of Alleged CIA Link to Contras, Drugs"). In none of these cases did the *Globe* report the subcommittee's findings. One would have thought them relevant. For example: "It is clear that individuals who provided support for the Contras were involved in drug trafficking, the supply network of the Contras was used by drug trafficking organizations, and elements of the Contras themselves knowingly received financial and material assistance from drug traffickers. In each case, one or another agency of the U.S. government had information regarding the involvement either while it was occurring, or immediately thereafter." See U.S. Senate Committee on Foreign Relations, Subcommittee on Terrorism, Narcotics, and International Operations, 1988, p. 36. In a U.S. Senatorial campaign debate on October 15, 1996, John Kerry summarized some of these findings in response to a question, mentioning C.I.A. involvement and remarking that Black activists had reason to be suspicious. But in its coverage of the debate the next day (Aucoin, Don, and Frank Philips, "Citizens Take Round 6," October 16, 1996), the *Globe* twice printed the response of Kerry's Senate challenger William Weld to the same question, branding the question's concern as a "nutty conspiracy theory." The *Globe* did not report Kerry's response. An editorial by *Globe* ombudsman Mark Jurkowitz on November 13 similarly mentioned Weld's response, but not Kerry's. (The next day, however, the *Globe* did run a prominent column by Alfred McCoy on the history of C.I.A. complicity in global drug trafficking.) On October 23, Jack Blum, who had been the Kerry subcommittee's lead investigator, testified before Congress that while the subcommittee had found no evidence that any C.I.A. or U.S. officials had plotted to sell crack to Black communities, nonetheless "if you ask whether the United States government ignored the drug problem and subverted law enforcement to prevent embarrassment and to reward our allies in the Contra war, the answer is yes"; he also discussed the Reagan administration's obstruction of the subcommittee's investigation. A.B.C.'s *World News Tonight* later reported (on October 23, 1996) only that Blum had found no evidence of a plot against Black communities, excluding the rest of his testimony. The next day, neither the *New York Times* nor the *Los Angeles Times* story on the hearing reported Blum's tes-

timony. See Peter Kornbluh, "Crack, the Contras and the CIA: The Storm Over 'Dark Alliance,'" *Columbia Journalism Review*, January/February, 1997.

9 See, respectively, Robert Jackson, "Ex-DEA Agent Ties Contras to U.S. Drug Flights," *Los Angeles Times*, September 24, 1996, and Jose DeCordoba, "Former CIA Ally Faces Drug Charge," *Wall Street Journal*, November 22, 1996.

10 *San Francisco Examiner*, March 16, 1986. See also Scott and Marshall, 1991, pp. 106-107. (For a detailed review of the media coverage in this period, see their Chapter 11.) For more on the larger pattern of omission regarding the attacks on the *Mercury News*, see Herman, "Gary Webb and the Media's Rush to the Barricades," *Z Magazine*, February 1997. Also see Robert Parry, "Lost History: Contra/Crack Story Assailed," *Consortium*, October 28, 1996; Peter Kornbluh, "Crack, the Contras and the CIA: The Storm Over 'Dark Alliance,'" *Columbia Journalism Review*, January/February, 1997; Norman Solomon, "Snow Job: The Establishment's Papers Do Damage Control for the CIA," *Extra!*, January/ February, 1997.

11 Ceppos' apology came in an editorial, "To Readers of the 'Dark Alliance' Series," *San Jose Mercury News*, May 11, 1997. For reaction, see Todd Purdum, "Exposé on Crack Was Flawed, Paper Says," *New York Times*, May 13, 1997; Howard Kurtz, "CIA Series 'Fell Short,' Editor Says," *Washington Post*, May 13, 1997. Kurtz quotes Doyle McManus, Washington bureau chief of the *Los Angeles Times*, calling Ceppos' column "courageous," as did the *New York Times* in an editorial the next day, claiming that the public outcry following the series was based on "little hard evidence." In the *Boston Globe* ("Paper Confessions," May 19, 1997), Mary Leonard wrote that Ceppos' action seemed "inadequate next to the damage done by the 'Dark Alliance' series, which took on a sinister life of suspicion and anger all its own in the Black community. For many minorities in drug-ravaged Los Angeles neighborhoods, it confirmed what they already believed: The federal government is our enemy."

12 Howard Kurtz, "Reporter Pulled Off CIA Story," *Washington Post*, June 11, 1997. Possibly, Ceppos had been pressured by his own staff, worried about repercussions of the major media's attacks. According to Georg Hodel, who worked with Webb on the series, "young staffers feared that the controversy could hurt their chances of getting hired by bigger newspapers [and] senior editors fretted about their careers in the Knight-Ridder chain, which owns the *Mercury News*" (Georg Hodel, "Hung Out to Dry: 'Dark Alliance' Series Dies," *Consortium*, June 30, 1997). Webb subsequently resigned from the *Mercury News*, and published his accumulated work in book form (Webb, 1998). The book corroborated and further documented the themes of the original series—as in fact did two reports issued in 1998 by the C.I.A. Inspector General—reports which were prompted by the activism following the series. For discussion of these reports, see Alex Cockburn and Ken Silverstein,

"Drugs, Contras, and CIA: *Post* Defends Agency's Honor," *Counterpunch*, October 31, 1998. Also see Cockburn and St. Clair, 1998, for more on the *Mercury News* affair and the broader history of the C.I.A.'s involvement with drug trafficking and the media's complicity (the authors regret that this book appeared too late to take fuller account of in this chapter.)

13 McCoy, 1991, pp. 48-49, 53-63. (This is a revised and updated version of McCoy's *Politics of Heroin in Southeast Asia*, published in 1972.)

14 GAO, 1995b, p. 4. As of mid-1996, the rate of entry into the United States of ever-cheaper and purer heroin was on the rise, because of new trafficking routes. See "Heroin Flow from Asia Said to Increase," *Boston Globe*, June 27, 1996, based on a U.N. report.

15 McCoy, 1991, pp. 162-178.

16 USAID knew the intended purpose of the airline. McCoy, 1991, pp. 308-318.

17 McCoy, 1991, pp. 226-229, 254-259, 285-286. After the troops were withdrawn in 1973, many remained users and/or became pushers back home. Meanwhile, heroin from "Golden Triangle" laboratories followed them via Corsican and Chinese syndicates to the U.S. market.

18 McCoy, 1991, p. 447 (citing the U.S. State Department, Bureau of International Narcotics Matters); see also Scott and Marshall, 1991, p. 187; Shalom, 1993, p. 174.

19 McCoy, 1991, pp. 436 (quoting Dr. David Musto), 448-450, 453-455. See also James Rupert and Steve Coll, "U.S. Declines to Probe Afghan Drug Trade," *Washington Post*, May 13, 1990.

20 Burt and Soberon, 1993, p. 441. More recently, with the breakup of the two main Colombian cartels, cocaine producers and drug mafias have burgeoned in Mexico, Bolivia, Peru, Venezuela, and Brazil. On other recent trends, see Youngers, 1996, who is also reporting on rising heroin production in Peru and Colombia, as we later discuss.

21 For documentation and many details, see Chomsky, 1985, pp. 127-145; Cockburn, 1987.

22 McCoy, 1991, pp. 479-480; Cockburn, 1987, ch. 9-10.

23 U.S. Senate Committee on Foreign Relations, Subcommittee on Terrorism, Narcotics, and International Operations, 1988, pp. 53-58.

24 Chomsky, 1992, p. 118. Scott and Marshall argue that, detailed though it was, the Kerry report still contained numerous gaps, "the net effect of [which] was to downplay evidence linking the CIA to individuals and companies implicated in drug trafficking" (1991, p. 16; see pp. 15-19 for some examples).

25 Scott and Marshall, 1991, pp. 54-57.

26 Shalom, 1993, p. 176; McCoy, 1991, p. 484.

27 For some details see Flynn, 1984, pp. 110-112; Cockburn, 1987, pp. 17-20.

28 General Paul Gorman, quoted by Marshall, 1987, p. 166 (cited in Shalom, 1993).

29 Alex Cockburn and Ken Silverstein, "Free Trade Narco-Traffickers," *Counterpunch*, May 1-14, 1996; Chomsky, 1992, p. 119.

30 See, respectively, Marshall, 1991, p. 21; *El Proceso*, December 12, 1994; and on the Clinton administration, Alex Cockburn and Ken Silverstein, "'The Zapatistas Must Be Eliminated': An Update," *Counterpunch*, December 1-15, 1996.

31 Marshall, 1991, pp. 22-23.

32 Marshall, 1991, p. 22. The pattern of government-sponsored massacre has continued to this day. In Guerrero, a 1995 massacre by Mexican soldiers of 17 unarmed *campesinos* mobilized widespread opposition to the government, and apparently led to the formation of a new guerilla movement a year later. The new group made its first appearance on the anniversary of the massacre. Their cause was described by Orbelin Jaramillo, a local Catholic priest, as that of "40 million poor people and 20 million people who live in extreme poverty, who demand work, who demand just salaries, who demand places to live. Their cause is just." See Steve Fainaru, "Mexico's War Within: It's a Strange and Dangerous Time in this Country of Extremes," *Boston Globe*, September 15, 1996. In Chiapas, 45 people (mostly women and children) were murdered by paramilitary gunmen in December 1997. Though the Mexican government denied involvement, the National Human Rights Commission (an agency of the government) reported that senior state officials, together with police commanders, protected the gunmen; did not investigate the crime scene; and altered official documents to protect themselves. Information in the report suggested that "the local police were officially encouraged to back paramilitary groups that have sprung up in Indian villages to confront followers of the Zapatista guerilla rebels" (Julia Preston, "Mexican Police Blamed for Role in Massacre," *New York Times*, January 13, 1998). Also revealing is the Mexican government's refusal to meet with Amnesty International's secretary general; the expulsion of human rights organizers; and the prosecution of foreign journalists; see Juan Enriquez, "Why Mexico's Massacre Was No Surprise," *New York Times*, December 27, 1997.

33 See Alex Cockburn and Ken Silverstein, "'The Zapatistas Must Be Eliminated': An Update," *Counterpunch*, December 1-15, 1996.

34 Olson, 1996, p. 7.

35 Donald Schultz, cited by Alex Cockburn and Ken Silverstein, "'The Zapatistas Must Be Eliminated': An Update," *Counterpunch*, December 1-15, 1996.

36 *La Jornada*, May, 1996, cited by Alex Cockburn and Ken Silverstein, "'The Zapatistas Must Be Eliminated': An Update," *Counterpunch*, December 1-15, 1996.

37 GAO, 1996a, pp. 14-15, 19.

38 GAO, 1996a, pp. 42-43.

39 Burt and Soberon, 1993, p. 445. In a similar vein, Pentagon and C.I.A. involvement in Mexico under the War on Drugs has according to many U.S. officials, been partly motivated by "their need to find new tasks after the cold war," as a *New York Times* reporter put it (Tim Golden, "Dangerous Allies: U.S. Helps Mexico's Army Take Big Anti-Drug Role," *New York Times*, December 29, 1997).

40 Burt and Soberon, 1993, pp. 445-446, citing the Washington Office on Latin America (WOLA), 1991; see also pp. 450-451.

41 Morales, 1989, p. 135.

42 Burt and Soberon, 1993, pp. 450-451; Andreas and Sharpe, 1992, p. 78.

43 Burt and Soberon, 1993, p. 446; Andreas and Sharpe, 1992, p. 79.

44 See Chomsky, 1992, pp. 128-129; Chomsky, 1994, pp. 54-62; Giraldo, 1996, pp. 12-13; Andreas and Sharpe, 1992, p. 79. On levels of U.S. military aid under Clinton (an estimated record $123 million in 1997) see Human Rights Watch, 1996, p. 5. Little changed with the 1996 "decertification" of Colombia, which did not affect "counternarcotics" aid; in any case all sanctions were lifted in early 1998. See the Associated Press article "U.S. Waives Sanctions Versus Columbia," *New York Times*, February 26, 1998. Furthermore, even official restrictions on military aid had apparently been sidestepped by the Pentagon's Joint Combined Exchange Training (JCET) program, under which U.S. troops conducted training exercises with the Colombian military throughout the period of "decertification." The Pentagon's program was not restricted to Colombia. As Senator Patrick Leahy commented, "from Colombia to Indonesia, our Special Forces have trained foreign troops without regard for who they are or whether they turn around and torture and shoot pro-democracy students." See Dana Priest and Douglas Farah, "US Force Training Troops in Colombia," *New York Times*, May 25, 1998.

45 The number is a conservative one drawn from data presented by Giraldo, 1996, p. 17; quotation from pp. 19-20. Two recent reports confirm the general pattern. According to a Human Rights Watch study (see previous note), in 1991 the Colombian military, assisted by the Pentagon and C.I.A., set up a network of paramilitary groups responsible for intelligence-gathering and execution of civilians. The previous month, Amnesty International reported that Colombian military units, which likewise had been killing civilians, used U.S.-supplied arms. See Diana J. Schemo, "Report Says Columbia Misused U.S. Aid On Rebel War," *New York Times*, November 26, 1996. The Amnesty report was based on leaked documents that refuted the Clinton Administration's claims that U.S. aid to Colombia was not supporting political repression (Amnesty International press release, October 29, 1996).

46 The Colombian government has made this explicit, calling in 1988 for "total war against the internal enemy" including, according to a recent report, "labor organizations, popular movements, indigenous organizations, oppositional political parties, peasant movements, intellectual sectors, religious currents, youth and student groups, neighborhood organizations...." See Giraldo, 1996, p. 9 (Chomsky's introduction), and pp. 59-60. The counterrevolutionary doctrine of

killing the "fish" by drying up the "sea" is a well-practiced one, used by U.S. clients in South Vietnam, El Salvador, Guatemala, and elsewhere.

47 Andreas and Sharpe, 1992, p. 79. See also Human Rights Watch, 1996a, p. 4, on Congress's attempt in 1994 to restrict U.S. aid to military units which engage "primarily" in counternarcotics, even though there are no such units.

48 Burt and Soberon, 1993, pp. 449, 451. See also Peter Andreas, *The Nation*, August 13-20, 1988, who notes that: "U.S. officials in Washington and Peru are careful to emphasize that counterinsurgency is neither the intent nor the focus of [Condor 6, a U.S.-sponsored military operation begun in 1988]....[T]he distinction between counterinsurgency and antinarcotics operations is critical for the legitimacy of Condor 6, but several State Department officials who oversee Peruvian affairs admit that the line between the two is sometimes blurry in the war-torn valley" (p. 127). See also Joseph Treaster, "Drug War Stalled in Two Key Countries," *New York Times*, December 6, 1989.

49 The U.S. ambassador to Colombia in 1991 was even more forthcoming than Aronson in his admission that the use of "anti-narcotics" aid for counterinsurgency was not unwelcome: "...in the U.S. Congress from time to time some Senators or Representatives say that they would prefer that the arms not be utilized in objectives different from the struggle against drugs; but this is not a requirement of the United States." This contradicts the 1990 law. See WOLA, 1991, pp. 52-53. U.S. officials have sometimes claimed that the insurgents are drug traffickers, which would appear to legitimize the use of aid for counterinsurgency. For instance, in October, 1997 drug czar McCaffrey asserted: "With the unholy alliance between the cocaine industry and the revolutionary guerilla movement, the drug-trafficker threat to Colombian civil democratic society has again ratcheted up." Eduardo Gamarra, a Florida-based political analyst, commented that McCaffrey was deliberately blurring the lines between counterinsurgency and counternarcotics and that "what U.S. policy is angling toward is a greater presence of U.S. counterinsurgency advisers in Colombia." See Tom Brown, "Drug Gang, Rebel Axis Called Colombia Peril," *Boston Globe*, October 21, 1997; also WOLA, 1991, ch. 3.

50 On Sendero Luminoso abuses, see George, 1992, p. 60, citing the Peruvian National Coordination for Human Rights. On abuses by the Peruvian army, see Burt and Soberon, 1993, pp. 448-449.

51 The point isn't subtle. For instance, in 1989 when Colombia asked the United States for a radar system near its southern border in order to monitor drug flights, a system was installed on a remote island off the Colombian coast, far from any drug routes—but only 200 miles off the coast of Nicaragua. The Colombian government justifiably accused the Pentagon of using the War on Drugs as a pretext to monitor Nicaragua, merely the latest pretext used in the effort to subvert the Sandinistas. See Chomsky, 1992, p. 132, and references therein.

52 One form of subsidy is World Bank loans, which, as Cheryl Payer comments, are usually "project-tied, which means the money is paid directly to the corporations that win contracts for constructing and/or supplying projects financed by the Bank....This international 'public spending' could be regarded as a sort of international Keynesianism which, taken together with expenditures financed through bilateral aid programs and other international institutions, plays an important role in maintaining the capitalist system by providing a taxpayer-financed market for goods produced in the creditor countries" (1982, p. 35). For a capsule history tracing the continuity of global trade patterns with the colonial period, see Hayter, 1981; for many details, see Chomsky, 1993. On food, see George, 1977, ch. 1, especially pp. 16-17. George points out that the global arrangement "is a hangover from the colonial period, but the system itself has flourished at least since the Roman Empire used North Africa as its granary, and the same situation will doubtless continue as long as gross economic inequalities continue between nations" (p. 16).

53 Andreas and Sharpe, 1992, pp. 75-76.

54 See Burke, 1991, p. 67; Honderich, 1993, p. 129. On Peru, see Andreas and Sharpe, 1992, pp. 77-78.

55 Chomsky, 1992, p. 127; Falco, 1992, pp. 11-12. See also George, 1977, p. 17. On the "Food for Peace" agribusiness subsidies and their effects, see George, 1977, ch. 8; George, 1992, p. 53. On Colombian wheat exports see LaFeber, 1986. On the far-reaching extent of U.S. protectionism, see Bovard, 1991. The United States also has militated against regional trading blocs from which it is excluded, as in the case of the Southern Cone group Mercosur led by Brazil; see Diana J. Schemo, "Clinton's Envoy for Latin America Out To Show the U.S. Cares," *New York Times* (International), June 8, 1997. Incidentally, cocaine earns much more than coca, which, as George notes, illustrates another consequence of the current international economic order: the lesser value of raw materials vis-à-vis finished products, which the South has been largely prevented from developing.

56 Honderich, 1993, p. 136.

57 Chomsky, 1993, p. 33, citing a 1954 National Security Council memo and (on "our raw materials") State Department planner George Kennan.

58 Arbenz allowed the poor to unionize and vote, which are not traditions in Guatemala. Most importantly, he instituted a program of land redistribution (one which adhered closely to reform recommended by the World Bank at the time). During Chile's three years under Allende, infant mortality dropped by 18 percent, infant deaths from respiratory disease by 30 percent, and child malnutrition by 17 percent. By 1979 in Cuba, life expectancy was at 72 years, and infant mortality at 19.4 (per 1000 live births)—measures attained by few other poor countries; illiteracy had been virtually eliminated and school enrollment of

children aged 6-12 was at 99 percent by 1976. See Herman, 1982, p. 177 (on Arbenz), and pp. 91-105, and references therein, which include crucial comparisons to the much poorer social measures of countries under rulers favored by the United States. The Sandinistas are also well known for their social priorities, having implemented programs for literacy, health, and agrarian reform in the years just after revolution, programs with no parallel during the Somoza years. For a comparison of this agrarian reform with the much less comprehensive Salvadoran reform favored by the United States, see Deere, 1984. For some details on the U.S. subversion of these and a great many other nationalist movements worldwide, see Blum, 1986 (for instance, pp. 310-313 on the social achievements of Grenada under Maurice Bishop, and subsequent U.S. hostility). On recently released documents concerning the C.I.A.-backed coup in Guatemala, see Kate Doyle, "CIA Shows Its Bloody Hands," *Boston Globe*, June 8, 1997.

59   For example: "In Bolivia, where no insurgent group of significance is active, some U.S. military officials view the strengthening of the armed forces and the repression of the coca trade as essential to precluding future guerilla activity" (Burt and Soberon, 1993, p. 451).

60   Burke, 1991, p. 68; Andreas, 1993, p. 28.

61   For a review of the record, see Jefferson Morley, "Contradictions of Cocaine Capitalism," *Nation*, October 2, 1989. The record also shows that high officials in the U.S. Justice and Treasury Departments were protective of the Bank of Credit and Commerce International (BCCI), despite strong evidence of massive international money laundering activities. As Congressman Charles Schumer remarked upon the release of a 1991 report on BCCI, "it wasn't just that BCCI was rumored to be bad. It was that professional investigators in the agencies had hard evidence that they were bad, and bad in a big way, and nobody did anything about it" (cited in Scott and Marshall, 1991, p. viii). A U.S. intelligence officer partly explained the disinterest: "If BCCI is such an embarrassment to the U.S. that forthright investigations are not being pursued it has a lot to do with the blind eye the U.S. turned to the heroin trafficking in Pakistan" (Jonathan Beaty, "The Dirtiest Bank of All," *Time*, July 29, 1991). The reference is to the fact that BCCI's clients included Pakistani and Afghan allies of the C.I.A. during the period of covert action in Afghanistan, and Panama's General Noriega, at a time when he was assisting U.S. efforts against the Sandinistas. For details, see Scott and Marshall, 1991, pp. vii-ix.

62   See GAO, 1995a. On one of the alternative schemes, see Clifford Krauss and Douglas Frantz, "Cali Drug Cartel Using U.S. Business To Launder Cash," *New York Times*, October 30, 1995, reporting the use of U.S. businesses for money laundering by Colombia's Cali cartel. Another new trend is currency smuggling, whereby drug proceeds made within the United States are moved out of the country and deposited within foreign banks, from which they can be moved back to the United States with less chance of detection; see GAO, 1994.

63   It is instructive to consider the few cases that have been prosecuted. Michel Chossudovsky writes that "criminal indictments are invariably limited to local-level bank employees," as, for example, in a 1994 case brought against American Express Bank International (1996, pp. 27-28). When Bank of America was fined in 1986 for failing to report numerous large cash transfers, no criminal charges were brought. The Treasury Department sought only one-quarter of the maximum civil penalty allowed under law—a standard practice. See Nathaniel C. Nash, "Bank of America is Told to Pay U.S. \$4.78 Million Fine," *New York Times*, January 22, 1986. In a recent case, the Justice Department froze \$26 million in a Citibank account as part of an investigation into apparent laundering by the late Mexican drug lord Amado Carillo Fuentes (Mary Beth Sheridan, "Account Frozen in Mexican Cartel Probe," *Los Angeles Times*, September 13, 1997); whether there will be any criminal investigation of Citibank officials remains to be seen. No new ground was broken in May 1998 when U.S. officials announced, with great fanfare, the results of an undercover operation that had exposed systemic money laundering in Mexico. No U.S. banks or bank officials were indicted, and as the top bank regulator in Mexico pointed out, none of the Mexican bank employees were top executives. He noted, "United States authorities…made it seem as though they were announcing something terribly important. But I think this has been taken out of context. It seems much more important than it really is." See Julia Preston, "Mexicans Belittle Drug Money Sting," *New York Times*, May 20, 1998.

64   Paul Blustein, "Money Laundering Rules Can Be Hard To Apply," *Washington Post*, June 6, 1996. Blustein is sympathetic, writing that money laundering laws can raise possible "dilemmas" for bankers. Note that the dilemma is between observing the law and maximizing bank profits. The priority of the latter is clear as "financial institutions are tripping over themselves to lavish attention on the affluent and those with good prospects of becoming so" (see Kimberly Blanton, "Up and Coming Business: These Institutions Woo the Rich—and Those Who Likely Soon Will Be," *Boston Globe*, November 27, 1996, on trends in Boston, but the incentives are not peculiar to Boston). Some light was cast on the criminal potential of private banking in the recent case of Raul Salinas (brother of the former Mexican president), who moved \$100 million of illicit funds into Swiss bank accounts via his private account at Citibank. In its internal investigation of the matter, Citibank mysteriously excluded mention of its own top official overseeing safeguards against money-laundering. Meanwhile, Citibank is not the target of the Justice Department investigation into the matter (ongoing as of this writing). See Paul Blustein, "Money Laundering Rules Can Be Hard To Apply," *Washington Post*, June 6, 1996.

65 Study reviewed by Apolinar Biaz-Callejas in *Excelsior* (Mexico), October 14, 1994. On conduits into the banking system and other venues, see note 62.

66 Brook Larmer, "U.S., Mexico Try To Halt Chemical Flow to Cartels," *Christian Science Monitor*, October 23, 1989.

67 Douglas Jehl, "U.S. Solvents Helped Fuel Cocaine Trade in Columbia," *Los Angeles Times*, February 7, 1990. See also Larmer (previous note) on the lack of D.E.A. personnel.

68 Council on Hemispheric Affairs, *Washington Report on the Hemisphere*, April 12, 1996.

69 Andreas, 1993, p. 24 (quoting Gary Hufbauer, a fellow at the Institute for International Economics). See also Alex Cockburn and Ken Silverstein, "Free Trade Narco-Traffickers," *Counterpunch*, May 1-14, 1996; Tim Weiner and Tim Golden, "Free Trade Treaty May Widen Traffic In Drugs, U.S. Says," *New York Times*, May 24, 1993; Waters, 1997.

70 Phil Jordan, speaking on A.B.C. television's "Nightline," May 6, 1997 (cited in Waters, 1997, p. 3).

71 Here are some further examples. The former chief of a high-level D.E.A. enforcement unit has stated for the record that "in my 30-year history in the [D.E.A.] and related agencies, the major targets of my investigations almost invariably turned out to be working for the CIA" (Dennis Dayle, quoted by Scott and Marshall, 1991, x-xi). A former D.E.A. operations chief has said that beginning with the directorships of William Colby and George Bush, the C.I.A. regularly stole D.E.A. informants and investigative targets for recruitment as assets: "When the D.E.A. arrested these drug traffickers, they used the C.I.A. as protection and because of their C.I.A. involvement they were released. This amounted to a license to traffic for life because even if they were arrested in the future, they could demand classified documents about their prior C.I.A. involvement and would have to be let go. The C.I.A. knew full well that their assets were drug traffickers" (quoted in Marshall, 1991, p. 41). Other current or former D.E.A. employees who report obstruction by higher-ups in fighting a true drug war include Michael Levine (Levine, 1990), Celerino Castillo (see Robert Jackson, "Ex-DEA Agent Ties Contras to U.S. Drug Flights," *Los Angeles Times*, September 24, 1996), and officials who testified that Oliver North sacrificed a sensitive drug investigation for the Contra support effort (*Nation*, June 13, 1994). For more on the protection of drug smugglers by North under the supervision of high-level Reagan Administration officials, see Peter Kornbluh, "Documents Show US Condoned Drug Smuggling in Contra Operations," *Baltimore Sun*, November 18, 1996, discussing recently released documents.

72 For an account of problems faced by underfunded and understaffed federal agencies involved in interdiction, see GAO, 1995b, pp. 3, 5-6. In this context, it is important to keep in mind that involvement in the drug trade is not the most scandalous aspect of U.S. policy. For example, it is arguably less scandalous that

the U.S.-enforced economic order has driven Latin American countries to rely on drug exports than that it has caused widespread hunger in the region (see references in note 52). To take another case, a much more serious crime than the C.I.A.'s transport of opium in Laos was the U.S. Air Force's saturation bombing of that country. The United States dropped more tonnage on Laos between 1965 and 1973 than the United States dropped on Germany and Japan in all of World War II. As an American community worker in Laos wrote: "Village after village was leveled, countless people burned alive by high explosives, or burnt alive by napalm and white phosphorous, or riddled by anti-personnel bomb pellets." The destruction and terror were designed to prevent the ascension of the Pathet Lao nationalists. See Blum, 1986, pp. 155-161. Remaining mines and bomblets are being tripped off to this day, killing 10,000 people a year, according to the Lao government (Barry Wain, "The Deadly Legacy of War in Laos," *Asia Wall Street Journal*, January 24, 1997).

73 All quotes and first person accounts are based on interviews with active or recovering drug users by the authors (Connors and Fox), unless otherwise indicated.

74 For more on this history, see Medoff and Sklar, 1994.

75 "Section 8" refers to a federal housing program that has served roughly 3 million poor families by subsidizing about two-thirds of their rents through payments to private landlords. For more on the severe fiscal threats to this program that result from housing budget cuts, see Jason DeParle, "Slamming the Door," *New York Times* Magazine, October 20, 1996.

76 Sklar, 1995, p. 125, quoting Don Harris, "Blacks Feel Brunt of Drug War," *Los Angeles Times*, April 22, 1990. More telling than there being fewer Black drug users than White users is the fact that Blacks are less likely than Whites to use any particular one major drug, except heroin; see Tonry, 1995, pp. 108-109.

77 Mosher and Yanagisako, 1991; Kandel, 1991. How these data and data to follow relate to the planning of the "War on Drugs" is discussed in section 3.

78 Kandel, 1991, p. 393.

79 Kandel, 1991, cites Anthony and Helzer, 1991. Since the early 1980s, data reveal a downward trend in overall prevalence of lifetime, annual, and current drug use. However, many of these studies have shown that the declines in overall prevalence are explained by dramatic drops in casual (rather than heavy) drug use. Notably, these declines have been sharper for Whites and for middle-class persons than for racial and ethnic minorities, working-class people, and poorer people. Prevalence is higher among young male adults (18-34 years old) than among all other demographic categories. See also Mosher and Yanagisako, 1991, for more on the social demography of use.

80 For example see Wilson, 1996; Neuspiel, 1996; Clifford, 1992; Kandel, 1991; Kornblum, 1991.

81 For example, one in three Blacks lives in poverty, compared with one in ten Whites (O'Hare, Pollard,

Mann, et al., 1991). On the predictors of drug use, see Mosher and Yanagisako, 1991; Kandel, 1991.

82 Mosher and Yanagisako, 1991, pp. 288-290.

83 Kandel, 1991, cites Drug Abuse Warning Network (DAWN) data from the National Institute on Drug Abuse (NIDA), 1990a and 1990b. See also Tonry, 1995, pp. 97-101.

84 The average rate for testing positive for drugs in other arrest categories, while varied, was 40-50 percent with occasional peaks in the 80th and 90th percent range (National Institute of Justice, 1995).

85 Massachusetts Department of Public Health (MDPH), 1996d. Explanations of why women are worse off in virtually every category can head along a number of trajectories. The most obvious is that there are no differences between men's and women's severity of substance abuse nor men's and women's social conditions; rather, women are more likely to seek help for their problem, enter treatment, and thus skew the ratios. The data collected by the state fail to support this reasoning. In 1993, greater than 7 out of 10 admissions to treatment in Massachusetts were men, disproportionate to the ratio of male/female substance abuser estimates (MDPH, 1994a, p. 6). We propose that the treatment population, if anything, represents an optimistic profile of the risks women generally assume, and that it is the disadvantaged position of women from the start that explains their more severe profiles. See Miller, 1995, who documents with ethnographic data how the degradation of women takes many forms, particularly among crack-cocaine dealers and users. See also Fullilove, 1992; Goldstein, Oellet, Fendrich, et al., 1992; Ratner, 1993; Feucht 1993.

86 Waldorf, Reinarman, and Murphy, 1991, p. 10. Other studies have come to similar conclusions. See Barr, Farrel, Barnes, et al., 1993; Herd, 1994; Whitehead, Peterson, and Kaljee, 1994; Leviton, Schindler, and Orleans, 1994.

87 Mensch and Kandel, 1988.

88 Porter, 1996.

89 The phenomenon is not restricted to contemporary U.S. inner cities, but tends to be found wherever populations are oppressed. Native Americans, Australian Aborigines, and many new immigrant populations— all historically oppressed groups—suffer disproportionately from drug and alcohol abuse. Opium use among Chinese laborers in Britain's textile and agricultural industries was highly prevalent; some have written that even the babies of these laborers were drugged into silence, so that their parents could work (Berridge and Edwards, 1981 pp. 21-48, 97-109; Parssinen, 1983, pp. 22-58). Some historians argue that opium was the key to the coolie labor system; see Courtwright, Joseph, and DesJarlais, 1989, pp. 207-208. When narcotic addiction was no longer used to quell the misery of long and arduous work in factories and railroad building, it merely became the counterpoison for the misery of abject poverty. Heroin is the most common drug used among those working in the fishing industry; opiates "kill the pain" of the damp-

ness, the cold, and the muscle aches of fish cutters. See Clark, Wirth-Cauchon, and Krakow, 1995, for more details based on interviews with fishermen in Gloucester and New Bedford/Fall River, Massachusetts.

90 See note 73.

91 In a recent study of the barriers to HIV prevention among low-income, injection drug users, 97 percent of active users interviewed had attempted to end addiction on their own (Connors, 1992). Many had tried time and time again without success. Over 50 percent tried to quit "cold turkey" either by locking themselves in a room or getting themselves arrested. In their determination, many went through a long series of attempts: cutting down on their habit, substituting one drug for another, self-detoxifying, and eventually seeking formal treatment.

92 By contrast, studies conducted by such researchers as Lipton fuel fervor that drug users must be jailed to be stopped. In a 1996 publication by the National Institute of Justice, Lipton asserts: "During times when drug-abusing offenders are not incarcerated, they do not seek treatment and have no interest in it" (p. 13). Lipton goes on to argue for increasing treatment programs available to intravenous drug users (IDUs) in jail, clearly much needed given the numbers of inmates with drug/alcohol problems. But, once again, his approach emphasizes the benefits of incarceration. He quotes a study by a prison-based, long-term therapeutic care program that concludes that "'hard-core' drug users who remain in the prison-based therapeutic care longer are much more likely to succeed than those who leave earlier" (p. 15). This certainly seems reason enough to institute minimum mandatory sentencing laws in every state. Will prison soon become the state's preferred alternative to voluntary drug treatment?

93 Schlesinger and Dorwart, 1992. See also Baum, 1996, pp. 144-145.

94 McAuliffe, 1990.

95 Schlesinger and Dorwart, 1992.

96 In 1976, 95 percent of all drug treatment was publicly funded; by 1989, it had diminished to 65 percent (Schlesinger and Dorwart, 1992).

97 According to the Institute of Medicine (1990), private treatment programs had 50 percent higher reserve treatment capacity than public programs in 1987. It should be added here that while treatment centers often have plenty of slots for detoxification, the duration of a slot has been steadily decreasing, and is now five to seven days, which is grossly inadequate.

98 Philip Hilts, "AIDS Panel Backs Efforts to Exchange Drug Users' Needles," New York Times, August 7, 1991.

99 See Street Voice 43, Baltimore, Maryland.

100 Schlesinger and Dorwart, 1992.

101 Presidential Commission on the HIV Epidemic, 1988, p. 17.

102 The greatest deficit of treatment facilities is found precisely in the communities where incidence of drug abuse is rising: that is, poor, inner-city communities. The underserving of such communities and underpro-

vision of particular types of treatment has been a consistent pattern. See Schlesinger and Dorwart, 1992; Institute of Medicine, 1990. See also Porter, in press, for a thorough explanation of why neighborhood-based treatment is needed for the most marginalized ethnic minorities.

103 Research in progress by Connors confirms that male drug users in particular are prone to viewing, or at least considering, a jail stint as a needed break from their drug habit. This association functions because treatment programs are so inaccessible, especially when compared to the "accessibility" of the criminal justice system.

104 The federal system of treatment centers was initiated in 1970 by the Nixon administration, partly for political reasons. The administration's treatment of choice for heroin addiction was methadone, a treatment based on a notion of addiction as an *individual* disease, divorced from social contexts. Methadone treatment therefore served as a way to undercut calls for spending on social problems, a notion of Johnson's "Great Society" to which Nixon's drug warriors were opposed. See Baum, 1996, p. 44.

105 See MDPH, 1996b. The vast majority of clients (86 percent) in drug treatment programs in 1987 were being treated on an ambulatory basis—either methadone maintenance or outpatient non-methadone treatment—although they may have received inpatient or residential treatment in previous years. See Institute of Medicine, 1990, p. 209.

106 "Recovery" is a contested term among advocates of harm reduction. To some advocates, drug use is a choice, and those who choose to use drugs have a right to do so. These advocates see "recovery" as a mechanism of government and public health to force abstinence among "responsible" drug users. Others believe such a view evades social class differences in the use and consequences of illicit drug consumption. Both classic and recent studies show marked differences between the classes in success at "recovery" and access to these programs. See Biernacki, 1986; Pierce, n.p., n.d.

107 Bell, Richard, and Feltz, 1996; Condelli and Hubbard, 1994; DeLeon, 1993; Simpson, 1993.

108 See MDPH, 1996b.

109 Excerpt is from Pierce, n.p., n.d.

110 See Breitbart, Chavkin, and Wise, 1994; Baum, 1996, p. 269.

111 Breitbart, Chavkin, and Wise, 1994.

112 See Baum, 1996, pp. 269-270.

113 Connors, 1992.

114 Laws currently under consideration would require court-ordered mandatory drug treatment for drug-using pregnant women. See Breitbart, Chavkin, and Wise, 1994; Jos, Marshall, and Perlmutter, 1995.

115 GAO, 1995c.

116 IOM, 1990, p. 207.

117 Peters and May, 1992.

118 Lipton, 1995, p. 18.

119 Cozzone and Gray, *Prison Life*, January/February, 1996.

120 There are actually incentives in the system to *discourage* treatment options. The former warden of East New Jersey State Prison states: "Nobody can convince me that there's a county jail, a prison, or any other place where people are locked up that there aren't drugs." In fact, inmates who run up drug bills they can't pay check into protective custody to avoid retaliation. Since 1989, 13 staff members at the crowded Graterford, Pennsylvania, state prison have been arrested for drug smuggling. Monthly urine tests at the prison reveal about 20 percent of the population there to be actively using drugs. See Wynn, *Prison Life*, January/February, 1996.

121 Lipton, 1995.

122 Schlesinger and Dorwart, 1992.

123 The move of treatment into the for-profit arena has also affected the direction of research. There is now a deficit of government-funded research on treatment and a tendency for research to be biased in favor of the for-profit system by, for example, testing the hypothesis that shorter lengths of stay in in-patient, long-term treatment makes little difference in relapse rates (which would legitimate a move toward short-term treatment and therefore, in "managed care" facilities in which costs rise with length of stay, more profitable turnover).

124 Wilson, 1996, p. 51; Massey and Denton, 1993. Starobin, "The Economy You Can't See," *National Journal*, June 18, 1994, reviews estimates of the size of the entire underground economy. The studies he cites vary in their estimates from $145 billion (by the I.R.S.) to $1 trillion (by Wells Fargo).

125 Massey and Denton, 1993, p. 74, describe "hypersegregation" as a high degree of separation along at least four of five measurable dimensions of social geography: unevenness (overrepresentation of some groups in some areas, underrepresentation in others), isolation, clustering, concentration, and centralization.

126 Massey and Denton, 1993, p. 77.

127 See Wilson, 1996, p. 14, who cites Jargowsky, 1994.

128 See Wallace, 1990. A June 1998 report by the Clinton administration on the state of American cities concludes that, while urban employment rates had increased 10.4 percent since 1993, the increases paled in comparison to suburban job growth—a disparity attributed to continuing urban flight and commercial disinvestment because of crime and poor schools. The report surmised that the number of lowest wage earners would increase by 353,000 during the following five years because of welfare reform. Consequently, employers would be likely to have two applicants for every low-paying job. The report projects some cities, including Cleveland, Newark (New Jersey), and Providence (Rhode Island), will see five times that number of applicants for the same low-paying jobs. See Michael Janofsky, "An Administration Report Finds Urban Improvement, but Hardly Fat City," *New York Times*, June 19, 1998.

129 See Bourgois, 1995; Kornblum, 1991; Waldof, Reinarman, and Murphy, 1991; Williams, 1989.

130 Reuter, MacCoun, and Murphy, 1990.

131 Lusane, 1991.

132 The pyramid is international in nature. As an illustration of the dynamics, consider the following scenario. A Peruvian farmer produces 330 kg of coca leaves from a little less than one acre, bringing him $100—more than he can make with any other crop, though hardly a fortune. These leaves in turn yield 2.5 kg of coca paste. When processed by local manufacturers, the paste will eventually produce one kilogram of cocaine powder, which sells for about $2,000 in the local market. The kilo of cocaine is packed in the belly of a plane that takes off from an Army airstrip. The cargo that arrives in Miami is suddenly worth about $15,000 to a middle-tier distributor. A "transporter" moves the kilo from Florida to Massachusetts by truck. In Boston, a middle-tier supplier buys the wholesale kilo, now valued at $20,000. When cut into ounces, this same kilo is worth $50,000. Cut again by a "beeper boy" into quarters (7 grams), eighths (3.5 grams) or one-gram units, the kilo of cocaine, which brought a Peruvian farmer $100, now has a retail worth to the international cartel of about $100,000 on the streets of Roxbury, Massachusetts. Processed as crack, tiny sub-gram fractions of the original kilo are traded at the street level in small quantities that sell for as little as $7 each. (These figures are rough estimates based on Falco, 1992; Williams, 1989; Wisotsky, 1990; Bourgois, 1995; Reuter, MacCoun, and Murphy, 1990.)

133 Scott and Marshall, 1991, p. vii.

134 McFate, 1990, p. 6, cites Bruce Johnson of Narcotic and Drug Research, Inc.

135 Reuter, MacCoun, and Murphy, 1990.

136 For examples, see Williams, 1989; Bourgois, 1995.

137 About 1.4 percent of regular dealers are killed annually: a risk of work-related death ten times greater than for the highest risk law-enforcement career—namely, police work. Seven percent of dealers are injured annually and approximately one-third of a regular dealer's career is spent in jail. See Reuter, MacCoun, and Murphy, 1990.

138 Bourgois, 1995, pp. 93-94.

139 See Sklar, 1995; Reuter, MacCoun, and Murphy, 1990; Bourgois, 1995.

140 Williams, 1989, p. 8. As a Massachusetts inmate underscores: "Black men do want to take care of their families. But if the doors to higher paying jobs aren't open for you, hey, the first order of the day is survival" (Anthony Flint, "Inside Views on Black Incarceration Issue," Boston Globe, October 20, 1995).

141 Albelda and Folbre, 1996, p. 16.

142 See Gold, 1995; Havenman, 1996; and Doug Henwood, "Demote the General Welfare," Left Business Observer, October 7, 1996, p. 3.

143 Fred Kaplan, "Hope, Scarcity Collide: Workfare Thins NYC Welfare Rolls, but Jobs Remain Few," Boston Globe, November 19, 1996.

144 See Doug Henwood, "Demote the General Welfare," Left Business Observer, October 7, 1996, pp. 3, 7 (citing the Economic Policy Institute and the Urban Institute).

145 Tilly and Albelda, 1994. From 1996 to 1997, wages began to increase somewhat, although "the U.S. still has a two-tier economy, and many Americans are struggling to get ahead....A vast number of people labor in lower-skilled, lower-wage jobs that...offer few prospects for on-the-job training or advancement. Family incomes, adjusted for inflation, have recovered just half their losses from prerecession levels of 1989. Heady stock market gains primarily benefit the top 25 percent of families...and while income inequality at last has begun to narrow, the chasm between top and bottom is much wider than it was 25 years ago" (Aaron Bernstein, "Sharing Prosperity: Real Wages are Finally Starting to Rise," Business Week, September 1, 1997).

146 Center for Budget and Policy Priorities, cited by Tilly and Albelda, 1994.

147 See Pavetti, 1993; GAO, 1993; Albelda and Folbre, 1996, p. 115. Former Massachusetts Governor William Weld introduced cuts in the welfare benefits that were then available to women raising children out of wedlock, announcing stridently at a press conference on welfare policy: "Children without fathers leads to violence in everyone's life" (October 12, 1995).

148 Since child care support is not a part of President Clinton's welfare reform package, elimination of welfare benefits will further stress the already overburdened foster care system, as women struggle to both work and provide proper care for their children (Havenman, 1996, p. 23). For a recent report on these issues, see note 128.

149 See Campaign for an Effective Crime Policy, 1993, p. 1.

150 Vincent and Hofer, 1994, p. 6. Under mandatory sentencing in Massachusetts, two-thirds of all men sentenced during the course of the two-year period between 1994 and 1996 had never been convicted of a violent crime (see Zachary Dowdy, Boston Globe, November 25, 1997, citing a recent report by an assistant state attorney general).

151 Campaign for an Effective Crime Policy, 1993, p. 3.

152 Vincent and Hofer, 1994, pp. 13-14.

153 Campaign for an Effective Crime Policy, 1993, p. 6.

154 For an analysis of the high cost of these laws, see Greenwood, Rydell, Abrahamse, et al., 1994; "'Three Strikes': Serious Flaws and a Huge Price Tag," 1995.

155 Miller, 1996.

156 Bureau of Justice Statistics, 1995.

157 Peter Greenwood, cited in "'Three Strikes': Serious Flaws and a Huge Price Tag," 1995.

158 Ricky Ross, the street drug dealer highlighted in the San Jose Mercury News series, was sentenced to a life term under "three strikes." Even in his case, the judge said she would have preferred "to have more discretion to fashion a more appropriate sentence" (Webb and Kramer, The San Jose Mercury News, November 20, 1996).

159 Among the most significant legal changes has been a series of Supreme Court decisions that have hollowed out Fourth Amendment protections against unreasonable search and seizure. Since 1984, the Court has ruled in successive cases that anonymous tips may justify a search; that police may make for themselves

"good-faith exceptions" to the "exclusionary rule" forbidding the use of illegally obtained evidence (with Justice Stevens arguing in dissent that the decision made "the Bill of Rights into an unenforced honor code that police may follow at their discretion"); that police may obtain a search warrant based on spying into a house from a helicopter; and that a home can be searched with the permission of merely a visitor. For an account, see Baum, 1996, pp. 184, 202-203, 278, 302. Also see Wisotsky, 1987.

160 United States, Department of Justice, 1995. An important aside to the increasing size of the prison population is that as market forces pave new roads in the privatization of the penal system, sheriffs and others are offered stock, with profits based on full occupancy.

161 Bureau of Justice Statistics, 1995a.

162 Bureau of Justice Statistics, 1995b.

163 In contrast, 79.4 percent of first-time violent offenders were sentenced to prison. See Kopel, 1994.

164 Bureau of Justice Statistics, 1996.

165 Maurer and Huling, 1995, p. 23.

166 Shichor, 1995. In addition to the 1.3 million incarcerated, there are 2.8 million people on probation, and 671,000 on parole. Figures on costs of incarceration are from Sklar, 1995, p. 119. Statistics based on 1994 prison population and spending figures.

167 Smith, *Boston Globe*, December 10, 1995.

168 Maurer and Huling, 1995; Wunder, 1995; GAO, 1996b.

169 The F.B.I. considers robbery and burglary to be violent crimes; the state of California considers stealing when preceded by one or two violent crimes to be worthy of a life sentence (see the discussion of "three strikes and you're out" earlier in this section); the federal government deems some drug offenses to merit the death penalty, even when a murder is not involved. The Bureau of Justice Statistics reported in 1995 that the increase in drug offenders accounts for nearly three-fourths of the total growth in federal prison inmate populations since 1980.

170 Maurer and Huling, 1995. In Massachusetts, 85 percent of all prisoners sentenced for drug offenses are Black or Latino (Zachary Dowdy, *Boston Globe*, November 25, 1997).

171 Gary Webb, *San Jose Mercury News*, August 20, 1996.

172 Danziger and Gottschalk, 1995, p. 73.

173 Pincus and Ehrlich, 1994, pp. 237-238.

174 Wilson, 1996. For more, see Steinberg, 1995.

175 Steinberg, 1995; O'Hare, Pollard, Mann, et al., 1991.

176 Chambliss, 1994a, pp. 191-192. His conclusion is in part based on observations he and his students collected over several years while riding with the "Rapid Deployment Unit" (R.D.U.) of the Washington, D.C., Metropolitan Police, which revealed a clear pattern of aggressive and often abusive patrols and raids targeting poor areas only. For example, police looked for any minor infraction, sometimes even creating one, in order to have an excuse to stop a vehicle with a young Black male driver. They then typically approached the vehicle with guns drawn, called for backups, intimidated the driver until he granted permission to search the car, and issued a veiled threat even if nothing was found (which was most of the time). As one police officer described the mind-set: "This is a jungle....[W]e rewrite the constitution every day down here." In contrast, the R.D.U. did not patrol predominantly White sections of the city. There, officers stopped cars only for clear infractions: they treated drivers courteously, and did not draw their guns, search the car, nor call for backups. Sting operations ("rips") and the serving of warrants were similarly discriminatory. The overall pattern is nationwide; for a review, see Sklar, 1995, pp. 120-130.

177 As recently confirmed by researchers in the *Journal of the American Medical Association*, specifically in order to challenge the sentencing guidelines (Christopher Wren, "Less Disparity Urged in Cocaine Sentencing," *New York Times*, November 20, 1996).

178 See Anthony Flint, "Inside Views on Black Incarceration Issue," *Boston Globe*, October 20, 1995. The Supreme Court recently upheld the sentencing disparity; see Joan Biskupic, "Court Rejects Bias Claim in Crack Cocaine Sentencing," *Washington Post*, April 15, 1997.

179 Meierhoefer, 1992, p. 20.

180 Thomas and Foard, 1991.

181 Based on authors' interviews for Street Treatment Project, 1997. Not surprisingly, the problem of addiction in the jail population replicates that of the inner city. Self-reported cocaine use among arrestees was over 50 to 60 times greater than current use in the general population (Courtwright, Joseph, and Desjarlais, 1989).

182 Feeley, 1991, p. 2, cited in Shichor, 1995.

183 Shichor, 1995, p. 182. The incentives can also co-opt governments that rely on private prisons. The state of Florida pays the Wackenhut Corrections Corporation, which runs one of Florida's prisons, on a per-day and per-prisoner basis, and guarantees that the prison will never be less than 90 percent full. See Paulette Thomas, *Wall Street Journal*, May 12, 1994. See also note 192.

184 By *privatization* we do not mean simply the contracting out of specific "services," such as meal, laundry, or educational programs, to private firms. We mean, rather, the private financing and operation of a prison, where a corporation maintains day-to-day control over management.

185 Mokhiber, 1988, p. 59.

186 Mark Ehrman, "Pay $100, Go Directly to Nicer Jail," *Boston Globe*, October, 1996.

187 Cozzone and Gray, *Prison Life*, January/February, 1996.

188 As quoted in Mireva Navarro, "Experimental Courts Are Using New Strategies to Blunt Lure of Drugs," *New York Times*, October 17, 1996.

189 Paulette Thomas, *Wall Street Journal*, May 12, 1994; see also Alex Cockburn and Ken Silverstein, "America's Private," *Counterpunch*, January 1-15, 1997; Christie, 1994, ch. 7. One executive interviewed by Thomas commented: "I'm in the prison-building business, but I'm also a taxpayer. It's easier for us to build prisons than to look at the causes of crime."

190 Jeff Nesmith, "Prison Job Construction Stirs Concern," *Atlanta Journal and Constitution*, September 18, 1996, cited in Wright, 1997.

191 Wright, 1997, pp. 27-28; see also Alex Cockburn and Ken Silverstein, "America's Private," *Counterpunch*, January 1-15, 1997.

192 See Paulette Thomas, *Wall Street Journal*, May 12, 1994; for a case study, see Christian Parenti, "Rural Prison As Colonial Master," *Z Magazine*, June, 1997. Parenti discusses Pelican Bay State Prison in Crescent City, California, an area in which unemployment was 20 percent before the prison was built in 1989 by the California Department of Corrections (C.D.C.). Construction of the prison was followed by an employment and population boom, the opening of a hospital and large retail stores, and savings for the local government, as it employed inmates instead of public works crews. Apparently, the obvious incentives for keeping the prison full have affected the justice system. A spokesman for the California Prison Focus, a human rights group based in San Francisco, commented: "From our investigations it seems that the prison, in conjunction with local judges and prosecutors, is using every excuse it can to keep more people locked up for longer." According to local defense attorneys and prison whistle-blowers, the C.D.C., in cooperation with local authorities, has actively sought to prevent legal defense and even humane treatment of prisoners, who according to court papers have often been sadistically abused.

193 For details see Charles Sennott, "The $150 Billion 'Welfare' Recipients: US Corporations," *Boston Globe*, July 7, 1996; Aaron Zitner, "Tax Code Gives Companies a Lift," *Boston Globe*, July 8, 1996; Aaron Zitner and Charles Sennott, "Business' Clout Keeps the Government Breaks Coming," *Boston Globe*, July 9, 1996. On the exemption for inherited property, see Edward S. Herman, "The Assault on Social Security," *Z Magazine*, November, 1995, p. 31. The Cato Institute's estimate of corporate welfare is $75 billion, but counts only direct subsidies, not also tax breaks. But tax accountants recognize the equivalence between a targeted spending program and tax breaks conditioned on certain behavior, such as investing overseas (thus the term "tax expenditure"); these hidden expenditures are significant, as noted. Even the *Globe's* estimate of $150 billion, which *does* include tax expenditures, understates the problem, because it *doesn't* include Pentagon spending, much of which is barely disguised government support for high technology. One example is the Strategic Defense Initiative, which the Pentagon pitched to Congress on the basis not of military merit or feasibility, which is highly questionable, but on the merits of economic benefits to high-tech industry. In fact, Pentagon support has been crucial for development of almost *all* the U.S. industrial economy, including aviation, computers, telecommunications, and (of prominent significance nowadays) the Internet. The Pentagon subsidizes research and development and provides a guaranteed market without which new technology would be too risky and expensive to develop. According to an OECD report cited by the London *Economist* (September 7, 1985), the Pentagon has disbursed funds into high-tech sectors in a manner very similar to Japan's Ministry of International Trade and Industry, which operates explicitly as a strategic manager of public subsidies to the private sector. For extensive documentation and discussion, see Chomsky, 1985, pp. 202-214 (citing the business press and business historians).

194 Doug Henwood, "Demote the General Welfare," *Left Business Observer*, October 7, 1996, p. 7.

195 Edward S. Herman, "The Assault on Social Security," *Z Magazine*, November 1995, p. 31.

196 For a meticulous account of the history here, see Ferguson and Rogers, 1986, ch. 2-3.

197 See Ferguson and Rogers, 1986, ch. 1-3.

198 It might be debated that public opinion is in fact what drives policy in the case of welfare reform, given that opinion is presently *against* welfare (that is, that public opinion drives welfare policy to target the poor). However, public opinion is also against corporate welfare (Republican pollster Frank Luntz, cited in Zitner and Charles Sennott, "Business' Clout Keeps the Government Breaks Coming," *Boston Globe*, July 9, 1996), which nonetheless continues almost unabated. In both cases, policy follows what business circles want. Furthermore, public opposition to social welfare might just go to show that the public relations campaigns featuring "welfare queens" have been successful. A telling point is that majorities still favor government assistance for the poor, so long as it is not called "welfare." According to a 1992 poll, for example, 44 percent thought there was too much spending on "welfare," but only 13 percent thought there was too much spending on "assistance to the poor." (See Albelda and Folbre, 1996, pp. 108-110.) This is just one example of how the business agenda permeates general public discourse. This is accomplished by means of a vast public relations industry, proclivities of the corporate media, and the short-term dependency of most of the population on satisfaction of business demands. The business agenda is well impressed upon the population, under the guise of "conventional wisdom" or even popular will. This largely explains why implementers of policy need not consciously "conspire" in order to systematically carry out business imperatives, nor take this to be what they are doing. (On the public relations industry, see, for example, Stauber and Rampton, 1995; on the mass media, Bagdikian, 1983; Herman and Chomsky, 1988; Cohen and Solomon, 1995; on the public's short-term dependency, Cohen and Rogers, 1983. See also Schiller, 1989.)

199 See Chomsky, 1992, pp. 107-114, for a review of the concern over military spending. On the history of pretexts for increased military spending, see Chomsky, 1985, pp. 202-215.

200 See Tonry, 1995, pp. 83-91. He discusses the data in detail, from various NIDA surveys, including the National Household Surveys on Drug Abuse and the Department of Agriculture (on red meat, whole milk, and other fatty foods), suggesting the obvious explana-

tion—that many Americans had simply become more health-conscious. See also Chomsky, 1992, p. 115.

201 On polling data, see Associated Press dispatches in the *Wall Street Journal*, November 28, 1988, September 22, 1989, and September 27, 1989; see Chomsky, 1992, p. 120, and p. 115 on Bennett's claim. See also Chambliss, 1994a, pp. 190-191, who places the Bush administration's propaganda efforts within a history of U.S. politicians' attempts to create "moral panics" (a term he borrows from Stanley Cohen). Also part of the campaign was the notion that violent crime had been rising. But according to the Justice Department's own National Crime Victimization Survey, violent crime *was consistently flat between 1976 and 1992* (*Left Business Observer*, March 7, 1994). For more details see Chambliss, 1994a, pp. 184-187.

202 Analogously, one who burns down a house for the purpose of collecting on an insurance policy, with the knowledge that everyone inside would be killed, is as guilty as he would be if his purpose *were* to kill everyone inside. In criminal law this analysis is known as *mens rea*; see Tonry, 1995, p. 32. ("They knew" quotation from p. 104.) The data on drug use in poor areas are from DAWN and Drug Use Forecasting (DUF) data; see Tonry, pp. 97-101, and also note 84 to this chapter. As Tonry comments (p. 101), the significance of class on the two sets of data—the NIDA surveys on the one hand, and DAWN and DUF on the other—is well understood.

203 Bonnie and Whitebread, 1974, pp. 29-30; see also Clifford, 1992, pp. 310-311; Tonry, 1995, p. 94.

204 Bonnie and Whitebread, 1974, p. 227, and all of Chapter 12 on the "collapse of the marijuana consensus" and resulting retrenchment among prohibitionists.

205 On the marijuana commission's conclusions and how they were dismissed see Baum, 1996, pp. 71-72 (also see Bonnie and Whitebread, 1974, ch. 13, and ch. 7 for the similarly selective regard of science—i.e., *disregard*—at the onset of marijuana prohibition in 1937). Hoover's memo quoted on pp. 7-8; *Newsweek* quote from October 6 and 16, 1969, p. 21. On general motivations within the Nixon administration, see Baum, 1996, pp. 3-12, 20-21, 24-25. Some years later, Ronald Reagan's drug czar Carlton Turner revealed similar motivations, remarking that drug use "is not only a perverse, pervasive plague of itself, though it is that. But drug use also is a behavioral pattern that has sort of tagged along during the present young-adult generation's involvement in anti-military, anti-nuclear power, anti-big business, anti-authority demonstrations; of people from a myriad of different racial, religious or otherwise persuasions demanding 'rights' or 'entitlements' politically while refusing to accept corollary civic responsibility" (p. 154). Nixon did not just criminalize marijuana, he institutionalized its criminalization. Before the Nixon administration, it was the job of the surgeon general and other health officials to "schedule" drugs; i.e., categorize them according to the danger of their use. Since then, it has been the job of the D.E.A., which is a divi-

sion of the Justice Department. That is, scheduling is now the job *not* of medical professionals but of *prosecutors*. Under this regime, even the use of marijuana for proven medicinal effects in the treatment of glaucoma, AIDS, and other conditions has been disavowed, simply by fiat. When a long-standing government program for medical distribution of marijuana was terminated in 1991, a U.S. official acknowledged the political motive: "If it's perceived that the Public Health Service is going around giving marijuana to folks, there would be a perception that this stuff can't be so bad." (See Baum, 1996, p. 314, quoting Dr. James Mason. On drug scheduling and D.E.A. subversion of medical evidence, see pp. 25-26, 83, 126, 314.) It might be added that if marijuana were legalized, the number of illegal drug users would drop from about 24 million to 14 million, thus reducing the "problem" that the "War on Drugs" is supposedly attacking. This provides a certain motive for continuing the prohibition of marijuana. (See Baum, 1996, p. 126 for an account of the D.E.A.'s ulterior motives in its push for a harder line on marijuana under the Carter administration.) Under the Clinton administration, arrests for marijuana possession hit a record high in 1995. (According to an October 17, 1996, news release of the National Organization for the Reform of Marijuana Laws, the F.B.I. recorded 588,963 arrests for marijuana violations in 1995, an 18 percent increase from 1994 and the highest ever recorded by the F.B.I.) There has also been an aggressive federal effort to undercut voter-approved initiatives in California and Arizona for the medicinal use of marijuana; see the Associated Press, "Doctors Given Federal Threat on Marijuana," *New York Times*, December 31, 1996. There is, incidentally, a further institutional barrier to the legalization of marijuana: as a D.E.A. official once explained, "There's no profit incentive to develop marijuana," because anyone can grow it (Baum, 1996, p. 110). In contrast, tobacco requires special cultivation, and thrives as a major industry.

206 Drawing a similar conclusion, Christie traces the problem of idle hands to "the earliest stage of industrialization," posing two potential dangers: unrest and demonstration of independence from the labor market (1994, p. 60). From this perspective the War on Drugs is a new solution to an old problem. Likewise, William Chambliss comments: "The loss of jobs and increasing impoverishment of the lower classes increase the threat of riots, rebellions, and demands for a redistribution of wealth through education and job retraining. During these periods, social control through criminal law always increases in an effort to defuse, control, and preempt riots and rebellions" (1996, p. 113). See also Gordon, 1994, especially ch. 10, on the control of the "dangerous classes" (as the objects of social control are termed in the sociology literature). We would add that it isn't only during cyclical downturns that social control is useful. For example, the expansionary period current as of this writing has relied largely on a continuing class war (see note 145).

207 Substance Abuse and Mental Health Services Administration, 1995. These data are generated from a telephone survey of the general population, and exclude the homeless, the incarcerated, and those unreachable by phone. These data are therefore skewed toward the middle and upper classes.

208 Reardon, 1993, p. 30.

209 CEWG, 1990.

210 CEWG, 1990.

211 For these trends, see Office of National Drug Control Policy, 1995, based on emergency room surveys conducted by DAWN. The latest DAWN data, released in December 1997, show a 6 percent decrease in drug cases compared to the previous year. But the decrease was only for legal drugs; cocaine, marijuana, and heroin stayed the same. See Laura Meckler, "Emergency Room Drug Cases Reported Off 6%," Boston Globe, December 31, 1997.

212 CEWG, 1996.

213 On the 1996 survey, see Christopher Wren, "Adolescent Drug Use Continues to Rise," New York Times, December 20, 1996. More recently, the Parents' Resource Institute for Drug Education (based in Atlanta) reported that in 1996, drug use in the sixth through eighth grades had risen from the previous year, though drug use in high school had leveled off. This finding contradicted parts of a report in August, 1997, by the U.S. Department of Health and Human Services' National Household Survey on Drug Abuse, which found an overall decline among teenagers. The latter report was based on a smaller sample, and upon home telephone interviews, a technique which some have criticized on the grounds that teenagers may be less candid about drug use if they think their parents might be within earshot. See Christopher Wren, "Drug Use Up Among Younger Teens, Survey Says," New York Times, October 29, 1997.

214 New York State Division of Substance Abuse Services, 1989.

215 Feucht, 1993; National Institute of Justice, 1995.

216 MDPH, 1994b.

217 See Youngers, 1996, pp. 2-3; Matt Bai, "Colombia Cartels Pour Pure Heroin into Boston," Boston Globe, September 4, 1996, on heroin prices.

218 See Office of National Drug Control Policy, 1996, pp. 58-59. The percentages are unchanged from the Bush years. For an account of how the "narco-enforcement" bureaucracy has multiplied, see Bertram, Blachman, Sharpe, et al., 1996, pp. 126-129.

219 New York Times, August 19, 1996. In late 1997, McCaffrey attacked the Pentagon for proposing only $809 million for its 1999 drug war budget, ordering $141 million more for interdiction efforts in the Andes, Mexico, and the Caribbean (Bradley Graham, "McCaffrey Wants Pentagon to Spend More Against Drugs," Washington Post, November 7,1997).

220 See Inciardi, 1989, p. 237; Sklar, 1995, p. 132. Sklar also points out that in 1992, the United States spent four times as much on its military as on education, job training, housing, economic development, and environmental protection combined.

221 Bertram, Sharpe, Falco, Honderich, Burt and Soberon, Youngers, Andreas, D. Lewis, Wisotsky, J. Skolnick, and Baum are just a few among the many researchers. For sample editorial opinion, see "A Drug War Casualty," Miami Herald, September 2, 1996. The elite policy-makers include drug czar McCaffrey; see "Election Year Posturing on Drugs," editorial, New York Times, August 19, 1996. Chambliss' conclusion is that "almost everyone, including Attorney General Janet Reno, acknowledges [the 'war on drugs'] has been a complete and utter failure" (1994b, p. 675).

222 See Miller, 1995, for a case study of two women for whom it is evident that punitive action was not an incentive to enter treatment.

223 Study summarized in "Treatment: Effective (But Unpopular) Weapon Against Drugs," Rand Research Review, 1995b. For a related point on the economic inefficiency of incarceration see Greenwood, Rydell, Abrahamse, et al., 1994. See also J. Skolnick, 1992; Schmoke, 1995. Note that the point here isn't simply that demand-side strategies are superior to supply-side. We agree with this commonly made point, but are going further: even more superior is a strategy addressing socioeconomic conditions of both demand and supply.

224 A Gallup survey of 400 state and federal judges by the American Bar Association found that 90 percent opposed minimum mandatory sentences for drug offenders. While the American public has expressed little alarm, the judges who are sentencing small-time users and dealers to 5-10 years behind bars are in some cases refusing to follow federal sentencing guidelines. A growing number have instituted "drug courts," which provide the option for alternative sentencing and help with the problem that puts these minor offenders in the criminal justice system—their addiction. See Mireva Navarro, "Experimental Courts Are Using New Strategies to Blunt Lure of Drugs," New York Times, October 17, 1996.

225 Baum, 1996, pp. 322-324. Recently, the city of Baltimore launched a major antidrug program emphasizing treatment and prevention, as well as job training, aid for housing, and other social initiatives. The city's health commissioner remarked: "The war on drugs has been a total failure. The problem is, most politicians are terrified of looking soft on drugs if they do anything different. Maybe we'll be able to change that." See Michael Grunwald, "Mavericks in the War on Drugs," Boston Globe, November 12, 1997.

226 See Edward Fiske, "Impending U.S. Jobs 'Disaster': Work Force Unqualified to Work," New York Times, September 25, 1989, on the Labor Department projection.

227 Baum, 1996, p. 251; Jesse Katz, "Few Get Rich, Most Struggle in Crack's Grim Economy," Los Angeles Times, December 20, 1994.

228 Baum, 1996, pp. 251-252.

229 See note 198.

230 For example, the "Malcolm X Grassroots Movement" organized several events while issuing the following guidelines for participation:

- Respect for cultural, gender, sexual, and linguistic diversity;
- Opposition to racism, sexism, classism, and homophobia;
- Respect for the dignity, human rights, and cultural practices of the people in the communities in which we work; and the following "principles of unity":
- Reparations for victims of the crack trade;
- An external investigation of the problem that includes members of the affected communities;
- Grassroots hearings on the damage crack has done in our community;
- Money for drug rehabilitation programs;
- Release and treatment of all non-violent drug offenders;
- Repeal of mandatory minimums laws;
- Immediate incarceration of those involved in the CIA-Contra drug operation;
- Investigation of the influx of heroin to our community;
- Immediate return of forfeited property to those who have not been accused of a crime.

A reasonable platform overall, though the evidence and background on which it relies would not be apparent to anyone relying on the mass media for information. (The last item refers to a little-known feature of recent drug war prosecution, namely legislation permitting the seizure of assets of suspected drug dealers *without* due process—assets including those which might be used to hire a defense attorney.) "Immediate incarceration" would be a violation of due process, but a call for criminal prosecution *would* seem appropriate—more appropriate, certainly, than the usual call for official investigation, under the false premise that the matter has not already been investigated.

231 For one episode see Baum, 1996, pp. 326-328.

232 From a talk given by Waters at Morehouse College, Atlanta, GA (Kevin Merida, "Lawmaker Using CIA Controversy to Marshal Forces," *The Washington Post*, October 25, 1996).

CHAPTER 13
"The Threat of a Good Example": Health and Revolution in Cuba

1 The title phrase is borrowed from *Nicaragua: The Threat of a Good Example?* (Melrose, 1989).

2 Feinsilver, 1993, p. 97. She is quoting Hatcher, Hatcher, and Hatcher, 1984, p. 90.

3 Fidel Castro speech, April 30, 1996. Translated and published in *Granma International*, May 15, 1996; reprinted in *The Militant* 60(23), June 10, 1996.

4 There has been a proliferation of studies in recent years attempting to examine the causes and consequences of different types of economic adjustment in the Third World. Most mainstream studies assume the inevitability of structural adjustment; if they mention its devastating impact on the poor at all, it is often in order to examine (or suggest) regime strategies for defusing popular protest against adjustment. One of the few essays to explicitly address the impact of adjustment on the poor is Joan Nelson's "Poverty, Equity and the Politics of Adjustment." In this piece, Nelson notes regretfully that there is little data available which disaggregates the economic effects of structural adjustment to allow scholars to study its impact on the poor. Still, her emphasis is on policies that governments can use to overcome popular resistance to necessary adjustment programs (Nelson, 1992; see also Handelman and Baer, 1989; Hartlyn and Morley, 1986; Nelson, 1989; Nelson, 1990; Nelson, Kochanowicz, Mizsei, *et al.*, 1994; Smith, Acuña, and Gamarra, 1994; Stallings and Kaufman, 1989; Thorp and Whitehead, 1987). Most of these studies ignore the poor altogether. Rather, they look at "larger" economic issues like investment and growth and examine how different regime types cope with the rigors of imposing austerity programs. Only one of these books (Hartlyn and Morley, 1986) includes an essay on Cuba, and it essentially dismisses the Cuban experience because of its "undemocratic" nature. Even the works that highlight the deleterious social and health consequences of adjustment policies advise mitigating the ravages of adjustment—through programs targeted to specific social groups—rather than redesigning the programs to achieve equity, as Cuba has attempted to do (see Cornia, Jolly, and Stewart, 1987). An early study of U.S. attempts to promote its version of national development for Latin America through the Alliance for Progress in the 1960s noted with some perplexity that, although the goal of the Alliance was to *prevent* revolutions like Cuba's, "Cuba has come closer to some of the Alliance objectives than most Alliance members. In education and public health, no country in Latin America has carried out such ambitious and nationally comprehensive programs. Cuba's centrally planned economy has done more to integrate the rural and urban sectors (through a national income distribution policy) than the market economies of the other Latin American countries" (Levinson and de Onis, 1970, p. 309). The author's conclusion, however, was not that the United States should support the Cuban experiment, but rather that it should "recognize its limitations" and give up the goal of other Latin American countries reaching Cuba's levels of social development (pp. 321, 323).

5 A recent study of the relationship among per capita income, income distribution, and mortality rates worldwide concluded that "rather than the richest, it is the countries where income differentials between rich and poor are smallest which have the highest average life expectancy" and that "the study of health inequalities" should be "at the top of the public health agenda" (Wilkinson, 1992a, pp. 1083-1084).

6 See especially Cornia, Jolly, and Stewart, 1987.

7 As Sergio Díaz-Briquets pointed out in 1983, "the most recent Cuban evidence shows...that conventionally used measures of welfare, such as per capita income...may not be the best indicators of development. Rather than an overall summary measure of

development, what appears to be more important is the distribution of benefits of development" (Díaz-Briquets, 1983, p. 131).

8   Benjamin, Collins, and Scott, 1989, p. 6. They cite Leyva, 1972, pp. 474, 472; International Bank for Reconstruction and Development, 1951, p. 441; Agrupación Católica Universitaria, 1972, p. 201. Other studies (e.g., Díaz-Briquets, 1983, and Danielson, 1979) emphasize that Cuba's health indicators and medical services were superior to typical Third World levels even before the revolution. They do not, however, challenge the prevalence of regional inequalities and the Third World character of rural Cuba. As Feinsilver notes: "Maldistribution of health resources was acute, with Havana siphoning off most personnel and monies. Although there was a good overall physician-to-population ration, few physicians practiced outside of the cities and most were in Havana.... Malnutrition, parasites, and other diseases of poverty afflicted the majority of rural dwellers. Sanitation facilities and potable water were scarce everywhere, including the capital." (Feinsilver, 1993, p. 92. She additionally cites Danielson, 1979; Agrupación Católica Universitaria, 1972; Pan American Sanitary Bureau, 1958; PAHO, 1962; Díaz-Briquets, 1983; and Díaz-Briquets and Pérez, 1981.)

9   On Martí's ideologies of social justice, see Pérez, 1995, pp. 145-148.

10 Feinsilver, 1993, p. 22.

11 Feinsilver, 1993, pp. 27-28. Note that, unlike mainstream development literature, this document defines *development* as social transformation rather than merely as increasing the GNP.

12 A Pan American Health Organization study on community involvement in health development in 1984 looked at case studies throughout the Americas and concluded that in Cuba "the social system seems to be the major factor in the reported level of community involvement. It has furnished a solid organizational base on which the health system has been built by providing channels for participation, training for both health personnel and community representatives, and a relatively permanent professional staff. The urban case appears to be a model. It is a teaching unit and appears to have gone further in applying CP [community participation] methodology than may be the norm elsewhere." Community participation was widespread at all levels of health development. In the rural area they studied in Cuba, however, community participation was less profound and "appears to be limited to cooperation with the health staff in carrying out activities." See PAHO, 1984, pp. 18, 49-51, for a detailed description of how community participation functioned in the two communities they evaluated.

13 See Feinsilver, 1993, Chapter 5, for a detailed discussion of the state of medical research and technology in Cuba. She focuses especially on biotechnology and the development of pharmaceuticals, vaccines (hepatitis-B and meningitis-B), and medical equipment. On pp. 59-61 she describes the sophisticated medical equipment and procedures available in Cuban hospitals through 1993. See also Tancer, 1995. He describes Cuba's "cutting-edge" research and develop-

ment, and its export of products like the two vaccines mentioned by Feinsilver and a cholesterol-lowering drug, policonasol (PPG-5).

Regarding access to health care, PAHO concludes that "health care coverage" of the population is "100 percent" (PAHO, 1994, vol. 2, p. 155). This places Cuba with the United States and Canada as the only three countries in the Americas with over 99 percent of the population having access to the health system. The former British colonies also have high access (over 95 percent); the only other Latin American countries with over 90 percent access are Argentina, Costa Rica, Uruguay, and Chile. See PAHO, 1994, vol. 1, p. 11, Table 4. These last four all have gross national products double that of Cuba's. See PAHO, 1994, vol. 1, p. 9, Table 2.

14 As the Pan American Health Organization points out, even the terms and concepts we use to evaluate a country's health conditions have to be reformulated in the case of Cuba. "The health situation in the early 1990s is strongly conditioned by the socioeconomic changes that have taken place in Cuba during the past two decades....The discrepancies among various groups have been considerably reduced, and living and health conditions for the entire population are now quite homogeneous....This homogeneity necessitates a special approach for analyzing health differentials in relation to living conditions, since it is difficult to stratify the population on the basis of poverty, education levels, access to basic commodities, and other variables generally used to classify populations according to living conditions" (PAHO, 1994, vol. 2, p. 154).

15 According to PAHO, "vaccine-preventable diseases are not responsible for any morbidity among children under age 5" since vaccination rates for children under one year are 97.9 percent for BCG, 97 percent for OPV, 90.6 percent for meningococcus B, 97.9 percent for MMR, and 82 percent for hepatitis B. (Hepatitis B vaccination rate was lower because the immunization program for this disease only began in late 1992; the 82 percent figure was from December 1992!) See PAHO, 1994, vol. 2, pp. 157-158.

16 Cuba is of course not the only example of this. See, in particular, research on Kerala, India, such as Franke and Chasin, 1994.

17 Garfield and Santana calculate per capita funding for the Cuban health-care system at approximately $150 during the 1980s. It fell slightly in the early 1990s and rose again in 1993 due to the need to import vitamins to counteract the neuropathy epidemic (Garfield and Santana, 1997, pp. 18-19). Feinsilver provides per capita health expenditures by province in pesos when the official exchange rate was one peso to the dollar. For 1987 it ranged from a high of 151 pesos in the province of the City of Havana to a low of 62 in Holguín. Approximately half of this expenditure was for salaries. Her figures are from Ministry of Health documents (Feinsilver, 1993, p. 117). She also cites 1986 figures from Sivard, 1989, which show Cuba's per capita expenditure at the equivalent of $84, as compared to $784 for the United States, $521 on average for developed countries, and $31 on average for Latin America. Santana cites figures of 62 pesos

per capita in 1982 and 95 pesos per capita in 1988 (equivalent to $80 and $130, respectively, at what she calls the "somewhat artificial" prevailing exchange rate). Total health expenditures for 1987 were 922 million pesos, and for 1988, 988 million pesos (for a population of approximately 10 million). These figures do not include construction costs. She also notes that in 1982 health costs were 6 percent of the state budget and 2.6 percent of the Global Social Product (Santana, 1990, p. 266). She cites Muniz, Fabián, Manriquez, et al., 1984. Eliseo Pérez-Stable quotes Ministry of Health sources as stating that in 1983 Cuba spent 7.8 percent of its government budget on health care and in 1989, 12 percent (Pérez-Stable, 1991, p. 565). Granich, Jacobs, Mermin, et al. state that 12 percent of the Cuban national budget was devoted to health care in 1993 (1995, p. 143).

Clearly Cuban health expenditures are much lower than those in the United States in both absolute and proportional terms. However, readers should be aware that it is exceedingly difficult to compare health-care costs across countries and across social and economic systems. Currency rates fluctuate, accounting methods differ, and many factors affect costs. Most aspects of medical care are much "cheaper" in Cuba than in the United States. For example, doctors' salaries in Cuba are much lower than in the United States: doctors earn in the range of 300 pesos per month which, at the current exchange rate of 21 pesos to the dollar, converts to approximately $14 per month. Cuba produces many of its own pharmaceuticals, again at costs considerably lower than elsewhere. Of course the "cheapness" of labor in Cuba must be qualified by government subsidization of all basic goods, including food, housing, transportation, child care, education, and of course, health care. That is, labor costs are low in part because of government spending in other sectors.

If health-care costs are deflated in Cuba because of low labor costs, they are inflated in the United States because of physicians' high incomes, the enormous for-profit insurance bureaucracy (which includes health insurance and malpractice insurance), and medicine's hidden costs of advertising and administration. Prices of many pharmaceuticals are also artificially inflated in the United States, largely due to the vagaries of the U.S. patent system.

18 PAHO, 1994, vol. 2, pp. 153-154.

19 Discussion of the 1981 dengue epidemic in Cuba and Cuba's response is based in part on Feinsilver, 1993, p. 85-90.

20 See Kourí, Guzmán, and Bravo, 1986; Kourí, Guzmán, and Bravo, 1987, for detailed descriptions of the history and types of dengue and its course in Cuba. Since children under the age of two—who had not been exposed to the previous outbreak in 1977—appeared to be unaffected by DHF, Cuban scientists hypothesized that the sequential exposure to dengue-1 and dengue-2 was an important factor in the development of DHF. These two reports grew from research carried out by scientists in the program on Dengue Hemorrhagic Fever at the Instituto de Medicina Tropical "Pedro Kourí" in Havana, supported with funds from the International Development Research Center in Ottawa, Canada.

21 Kourí, Guzmán, and Bravo, 1986, p. 27.

22 Feinsilver, 1993, p. 86.

23 Kourí, Guzmán, and Bravo, 1986, p. 26.

24 Kourí, Guzmán, and Bravo, 1986, p. 25.

25 See description in Lionel Martin, Reuters dispatch, September 2, 1981.

26 This description of the anti-Aëdes campaign is based on Feinsilver, 1993, pp. 85-90 and Lionel Martin, Reuters dispatch, September 2, 1981.

27 Kourí, Guzmán, and Bravo, 1986, p. 26.

28 Feinsilver, 1993, p. 88.

29 Feinsilver, 1993, pp. 86, 98. In the midst of the epidemic, Fidel Castro made a major speech at the twenthy-eighth anniversary celebration of the revolution in which he quoted extensively from the 1975 U.S. Senate report on C.I.A. covert activities in Cuba (United States Congress, 1975) and suggested that the C.I.A. had probably not changed its course since the report was released. In addition to suggesting the likelihood that the C.I.A. had released dengue-bearing mosquitoes in Cuba, he listed recent outbreaks of sugar cane rust and blue mold on tobacco (that had severely damaged Cuba's agricultural production during the previous two years), and an outbreak of African Swine Fever in 1971 as plagues that "could have been introduced...by the C.I.A." ("Castro on the Attack Again with Hints of U.S. Biological Warfare," *Washington Post*, July 29, 1981, p. A24.) In fact several C.I.A. sources from Cuba and the United States had previously confirmed their role in passing a sealed container containing African Swine Fever virus into Cuba in 1971, shortly before the outbreak. See "CIA Linked to '71 Swine Fever," *Facts on File World News*, January 15, 1977, p. 19 D2. Western diplomats estimated that the past two years' epidemics had cost Cuba approximately half a billion dollars (*Latin America Weekly Report*, August 7, 1981, p. 31). The recent capture of five members of the Florida-based Alpha-66 group in an attempt to invade the island added weight to Castro's claim that the C.I.A. was stepping up its "secret war" since the election of Ronald Reagan. (See "Castro suspects CIA in epidemic," UPI dispatch, July 27, 1981, and Reuters dispatch, July 27, 1981.) Bill Schapp summarized the (circumstantial) evidence regarding possible U.S. involvement in the dengue outbreak in "U.S. Biological Warfare: The 1981 Cuba Dengue Epidemic," (Schapp, 1982). He noted that the United States had the capability for such biological warfare, that the disease appeared simultaneously in several distinct areas in Cuba with no clear source (i.e., dengue-2 was not prevalent elsewhere in the Caribbean at the time, and those first infected had neither traveled outside the country nor had contact with others who had), and that trying to spread diseases was consistent with other well-documented types of sabotage that U.S. forces had carried out in Cuba. In August, 1981, Castro asked the United Nations Disarmament Committee to investigate his charges about U.S. involvement with the outbreak (Reuters dispatch, August 18, 1981). These charges were lent additional weight in 1984 when a Cuban exile accused (and later found guilty by a U.S. court) of terrorist acts testified about a "mission" he was aware of in 1980: "The group that was ahead of me had

a mission to carry some germs to introduce them in Cuba to be used against the Soviets and against the Cuban economy, to begin what was called chemical war, which later on produced results that were not what we had expected, because we thought that it was going to be used against the Soviet forces, and it was used against our own people, and with that we did not agree" (Schapp, 1984, p. 35, citing the transcript of the trial of Eduardo Victor Arocena Perez, pp. 2187-2189). Cuban television renewed the charges in July, 1987, with a spectacular series of broadcasts featuring testimony by Cuban double agents and film clips of U.S. diplomats and others engaged in covert activities against Cuba. Double agents testified that their C.I.A. contacts had questioned them about dengue and other relevant issues (other diseases, pesticides and insecticides, medications, etc.) prior to the outbreak in 1981. These testimonies and some relevant documents were collected in Ridenour, 1991. The television documentaries were also described in a Reuters dispatch "Cuban TV Charges CIA Responsible for Plagues and Disease," (July 23, 1987) and in the Los Angeles Times ("Duped CIA, 'Double Agents' Claim; U.S.-Cuban Tensions Rise as Spying Charges Spiral," July 26, 1987).

United States officials were no less politicized in their statements about the possible origin of the dengue outbreak in Cuba: they suggested that Cuban troops in Africa had probably introduced the disease. See "Washington Whispers," U.S. News and World Report, August 10, 1981; "Epidemic in Cuba sets off dispute with the U.S.," New York Times, September 6, 1981.

30 Castro originally claimed that Cuba had tried to obtain the insecticide from Mexico, but since components were made in the United States, the country was not permitted to buy the insecticide there (because of the U.S. embargo) and had to import it at much greater cost from Europe. See Christopher Dickey, "Castro on the Attack Again," Washington Post, July 29, 1981. The United States later approved a request from PAHO for an exemption from the embargo to permit the export of the insecticide Abate to Cuba.

31 Reuters dispatch, January 16, 1996, citing figures from Granma. The dispatch added that in 1995, 97 people tested positive for HIV (out of approximately one million tests conducted), compared with 110 people in 1994, showing continued low infection rates. This figure corresponds with that cited by Hans Veeken in 1995, reporting 1,089 diagnosed HIV-positive cases (Veeken, 1995, p. 937). In May 1993, Cuba had 927 cases of seropositivity and 187 cases of AIDS (Scheper-Hughes, 1993, p. 965). In July 1992 the Cuban government announced 812 HIV carriers (NotiSur, July 21, 1992, from EFE, July 14, 1992); and health officials reported 676 cases at the end of 1991 (Los Angeles Times, December 8, 1991). In April 1989 Health Ministry figures showed 268 HIV positive tests (Storer H. Rowley, Chicago Tribune, April 27, 1989). In September 1987 the deputy Minister of Health reported that 147 individuals had been diagnosed HIV positive in 1.1 million tests since the virus had been discovered in Cuba (Washington Post, September 16, 1987).

32 A 1996 PAHO/WHO report tabulates the annual incidence rates of AIDS per million population in the

Caribbean for the past six years. For 1995, the figures were: Cuba, 7.1; Dominican Republic, 46.8; Haiti (last calculated in 1992), 119.3; Puerto Rico (last calculated in 1994), 184.6; Barbados, 362.6; Jamaica, 206.4; Bahamas, 1413.0. Except for the tiny islands of Anguilla and Montserrat (which had no cases in 1995), Cuba's rate was by far the lowest. See Table 2 in PAHO, World Health Organization, 1996.

33 See, for a recent example, Tim Golden, "Patients Pay High Price in Cuba's War on AIDS," New York Times, October 16, 1995; Ernesto F. Betancourt, "Cuba's Callous War on AIDS," New York Times, February 11, 1988. Betancourt was the director of Radio Martí at the time his op-ed was published.

34 Leiner, 1994, p. 145. He is citing an interview with Terry by Karen Wald in 1989.

35 Jeanne Smith, M.D., and Sergio Piomelli, M.D., letter to the New York Times, January 22, 1989, and "Cuba's AIDS Quarantine Center Called 'Frightening,'" New York Times, November 4, 1988. In fact, Dr. Ronald Bayer called the center "pleasant" but "frightening in its implications."

36 See note 32 for comparative statistics for the Caribbean, and note 107 for an evaluation of the accuracy of the Cuban testing system.

37 Compare to rates of over 10 percent found among STD patients in the United States. See Terry, Galbán, and Rodriguez, 1989, p. 67.

38 Scheper-Hughes, 1993, p. 965. Since only 147 out of the one million tests were positive, it is not exactly clear what she means by "a large number." We do not have a breakdown of those 147. Figures from 1989, however, showed a total of 84 HIV-positive results from tests conducted among the 300,000 Cubans who had returned from Africa. Altogether, 3.5 million tests had been conducted, with a total of 268 positive results. As of April 1990 there were 122 cases of HIV infection among internationalists—or their sexual partners—who had served in Africa.

39 Scheper-Hughes, 1993, p. 966. Santana, Fass, and Wald also note that foreign service and contact with foreigners are associated with privilege in Cuba, so that "the individuals at highest risk of infection are not minorities or 'underclasses' of the society as in many other countries" (1991, p. 513).

40 See Leiner, 1994, p. 136; Lumsden, 1996, p. 165. Neither author cites a source for this claim, although it does not seem implausible.

41 Héctor Terry, quoted in the Washington Post, September 16, 1987.

42 Both types of examples appear in Lumsden, 1996, p. 165. However, he also notes that the role of homophobia in the Cuban response to AIDS is far less than its role elsewhere in Latin America.

43 Jesús García, "Cuba: Charges U.S. with Waging 'Bacteriological Warfare,'" Interpress Service, November 24, 1987. He is summarizing an article from Moncada, a Cuban Interior Ministry publication. Leiner quotes a speech by Fidel Castro in 1988: "Who brought AIDS to Latin America? Who was the great AIDS vector in the Third World? Why are there countries like the Dominican Republic, with 40,000 carriers of the virus; and Haiti, and other countries of

Central America and South America—high rates in Mexico, in Brazil and other countries? Who brought it? The United States, that's a fact." Quoted in Leiner, 1994, p. 131. Some U.S. analysts have also pointed out that contact with the United States was a key factor in determining a country's HIV infection rates. See Farmer, 1994 and Farmer, 1992. See note 29 for other examples of U.S. bacteriological warfare.

44 Leiner, for example, states that although "the official position" in Cuba is that "AIDS cuts across gender, sexual preference, and age…a strong popular view tends more often to associate homosexuality and AIDS." As evidence, he states that "early educational programs on AIDS" implied that it was primarily a disease of homosexuals (although he acknowledges that "this position soon changed"), that Cuban media reported in 1986 that the first case of AIDS in Cuba was that of a homosexual who had contracted it in New York (the same case mentioned by Héctor Terry in 1987), and that "several medical students" told him that "they thought the Cuban population perceived…homosexual sex" as the cause of AIDS. All of his other evidence, strangely, comes from the United States. See Leiner, 1994, pp. 136-138.

45 Smith and Piomelli, New York Times, January 22, 1989; Storer H. Rowley, "Cuba's AIDS Center Resembles Prison," Chicago Tribune, April 27, 1989. He cites Cuban Ministry of Public Health statistics.

46 Bayer and Healton, 1989, p. 1023.

47 Santana, Faas, and Wald, 1991, pp. 519-520.

48 "Cuba: Report on AIDS," NotiSur, July 21, 1992.

49 Leiner, 1994, p. 146, citing Dr. Giselle Sanabria, quoted in Robert Bazell, "Happy Campers," The New Republic, March 9, 1992, and Reuters dispatch, December 1, 1991.

50 Swanson, Gill, Wald, et al., 1995, p. 35.

51 He does not cite a source for this: Lumsden, 1996, p. 160. There are several facts which help account for apparent inconsistencies in the figures cited, although despite small inconsistencies, the general picture remains the same. Initially all HIV-positive persons were in the Santiago las Vegas sanitarium outside Havana; as new sanitaria were built elsewhere in the country, the Santiago figures represent only a portion of those diagnosed as HIV positive. Some HIV-positive persons later developed AIDS and died, so they were no longer counted among those classified as HIV positive. In addition, as Lumsden points out, some HIV-positive men may be reluctant to report homosexual contact, so there may be underreporting on that count.

52 Santana, Faas, and Wald noted: "Almost every health worker interviewed, at all levels of the health hierarchy, immediately mentioned the dengue epidemic as an analogy to the HIV epidemic" (1991, p. 523).

53 Bayer and Healton, 1989, p. 1022.

54 Lumsden, 1996, p. 163.

55 Swanson, Gill, Wald, et al., 1995, p. 36.

56 Scheper-Hughes, 1993, p. 967.

57 The origins of Cuba's AIDS policies are described in Terry, Galbán, and Rodriguez, 1989.

58 Smith and Piomelli, letter to the New York Times, January 22, 1989. Santana, Faas, and Wald confirm that importation of blood and blood products from countries with reported AIDS cases was halted in 1983, and that since May 1986 all blood donations have been screened. They say that (by 1991) there had been seven transfusion-associated cases of HIV, all infected prior to 1986, of whom two were hemophiliacs. Santana, Faas, and Wald, 1991, p. 524.

59 Swanson, Gill, Wald, et al., 1995, p. 36.

60 Bayer and Healton, 1989, p. 1022.

61 Héctor Terry, Vice Minister of Public Health, presentation to PAHO/WHO International Conference on AIDS, Quito, Ecuador, September, 1987. Reported in the Washington Post, September 16, 1987.

62 Bayer and Healton, 1989, p. 1022.

63 Héctor Terry, as reported in the Washington Post, September 16, 1987.

64 Reuters dispatch, June 18, 1988.

65 Smith and Piomelli, letter to the New York Times, January 22, 1989.

66 Swanson, Gill, Wald, et al., 1995, p. 36, citing interview with J. Pérez.

67 Scheper-Hughes, 1993, p. 966. Granich, Jacobs, Mermin, et al. repeat Scheper-Hughes' date for the shift in authority (1995, p. 142). Ian Lumsden, however, states that the sanitarium was administered by the Ministry of Defense until 1989 (1996, p. 163). Leiner also notes that the new director (presumably Jorge Pérez) took over in early 1989 (1994, p. 140). There seems to be no evidence at all for Antonio M. Gordon's 1989 claim that "the entire AIDS campaign is under the direction of State Security (the Cuban KGB)" (Gordon and Paya, 1989, p. 829).

68 Granich, Jacobs, Mermin, et al., 1995, p. 142.

69 Interview conducted by Karen Wald in 1989, cited by Leiner, 1994, pp. 140-141.

70 Granich, Jacobs, Mermin, et al., 1995, p. 142.

71 Héctor Terry, in the Washington Post, September 16, 1987.

72 Lumsden, 1996, p. 164. He bases his analysis on interviews with sanitarium residents.

73 Scheper-Hughes, 1993, p. 966.

74 Smith and Piomelli, in the New York Times, January 22, 1989; Bayer quoted in the Los Angeles Times, November 4, 1988; Bayer and Healton, 1989, p. 1023.

75 Bayer and Healton, 1989, p. 1023. It is worth noting that popular culture in the United States seems to have a particular concern for involuntary testing in the case of HIV, perhaps because of the association of HIV with homosexuality and the general stigmatization of homosexuality. My physician, for example, did not specifically ask for my "consent" last time she tested my blood for iron and cholesterol counts; it did not occur to me to consider the tests she conducted as "involuntary."

76 Swanson, Gill, Wald, et al., 1995, p. 36.

77 Santana, Fass, and Wald, 1991, p. 526.

78 Bayer and Healton, 1989, p. 1024.

79 Bayer and Healton, 1989, p. 1024.

80 Pérez-Stable, 1991, p. 565.

81 Santana, Faas, and Wald, 1991, p. 529.

82 Origin Universal News Services, February 16, 1989.

83 Santana, Faas, and Wald, 1991, p. 529.

84 Scheper-Hughes, 1993, p. 966.

85 Leiner, 1994, p. 140. He cites an interview with an HIV-positive physician in the sanitarium conducted by Karen Wald in September, 1989.

86 Mary Jo McConahay, "Cuba's Quarantine of Victims Typifies Aggressive Campaign in AIDS," the *Los Angeles Times*, December 8, 1991.

87 Granich, Jacobs, Mermin, *et al.*, 1995, p. 142.

88 Santana, Faas, and Wald, 1991, p. 529.

89 Leiner, 1994, p. 142. He is quoting an interview with Terry published in *Granma International*, April 7, 1991.

90 Pérez-Stable, 1991, p. 563.

91 Colin Brewer, "Cuba's Key to AIDS Treatment," *The Guardian*, March 20, 1992.

92 As reported in Charles Petit, "Cuban Policy on AIDS Defended," *San Francisco Chronicle*, September 15, 1992.

93 Scheper-Hughes, 1993, p. 966.

94 Swanson, Gill, Wald, *et al.*, 1995, pp. 36-37.

95 Swanson, Gill, Wald, *et al.*, 1995, pp. 37-38.

96 Reuters dispatch, September 19, 1994; BBC Summary of World Reports, September 22, 1994.

97 Dalia Acosta, "Cuba-Health: Few HIV Patients Rejoin the Community," InterPress Service, April 20, 1995. Manuel Hernández, head of Cuba's anti-AIDS campaign, quoted by Reuters World Service, November 14, 1995.

98 Swanson, Gill, Wald, *et al.*, 1995, pp. 38-39.

99 Lumsden, 1996, p. 172. He interviewed this resident in 1995.

100 Scheper-Hughes, 1993; Swanson, Gill, Wald, *et al.*, 1995.

101 Pérez-Stable, 1991, p. 566.

102 Lumsden, 1996, p. 163. It is also interesting to consider how a Swedish infectious disease specialist compared Cuba's program to that of Sweden—a country rarely accused in the United States of human rights violations. Dr. Johan Giesecke noted in 1992 that Sweden's approach was "closer" to that of Cuba than to that of the United States: "voluntary testing has been strongly encouraged in nationwide campaigns, and a third or more of the population between the ages of 20 and 40 have been tested. Whilst seropositivity per se can never be sufficient for isolation, patients are required to maintain regular contact with their physician, and those who expose others to risk of infection may be isolated in hospital by court order." The evolution of Cuba's policies since 1992 has brought them even closer to the Swedish model as described. Giesecke went on to note that "the widespread testing could be part of the explanation for the similarly favourable HIV situations in Cuba and Sweden, but in neither country would it have been possible without previous strong public confidence in a benevolent and non-discriminatory state and health-care system" (Giesecke, 1993, p. 942).

103 Granich, Jacobs, Mermin, *et al.*, 1995, p. 143.

104 Santana, Faas, and Wald, 1991, p. 523.

105 Santana, Faas, and Wald, 1991, pp. 523-524. They report that Cuba spent $1 million on HIV screening in 1987, $400,000 in 1988, and $300,000 in 1989. These figures represent costs of importing materials with foreign exchange.

106 Granich, Jacobs, Mermin, *et al.*, 1995, p. 140; Santana, Faas, and Wald, 1991, p. 526.

107 Pérez-Stable cites Ministry of Health estimates that the cost of developing the tests and establishing the necessary facilities was approximately $3 million, and that the testing program continued to consume about $2 million per year between 1986 and 1991 (1991, p. 565). He also describes the testing system and the Brazil-Sweden study (1991, p. 564). Granich, Jacobs, Mermin, *et al.* confirm the figure of a $3 million investment in developing the test and add that tests now cost approximately 22 cents each to carry out (1995, p. 140). Bayer and Healton also describe the multiple-testing system and the international study but express concern about false-positive results, which they estimate at possibly from 21 to 53 out of the three million tests conducted by 1989 (1989, p. 1023). (This estimate does not take into account Cuba's system of multiple testing.) A 1995 study described the testing system this way: specimens testing positive in the first ELISA test are re-tested; if the second test is also positive the specimen is referred to the National Reference Laboratory, which "repeats the test using competitive and indirect ELISA systems and also runs a Western blot test." If these continue to give positive results, the patient is required to provide a second specimen, upon which the same tests are run. "Indeterminate results are followed up with a radioimmunoprecipitation test and viral culture." This study concludes that a high level of accuracy is obtained through such testing (Granich, Jacobs, Mermin, *et al.*, 1995, p. 140). Other critics have expressed the opposite concern: based on blood tests conducted on Cuban immigrants to the United States in 1980 (like Cuba's tests, presumably without the consent of those tested, though the doctors ignore this issue), they argue that Cuba's HIV rates are much higher than those suggested by the results of Cuban tests. See Gordon, 1987, p. 3387; De Medina, Fletcher, Valledor, *et al.*, 1987, p. 166; Gordon and Paya, 1989, p. 829.

108 Reuters dispatch, May 5, 1995.

109 Scheper-Hughes, 1993, p. 967. Granich, Jacobs, Mermin, *et al.* also cite the figure of $15,000 per year (1995, p. 143). Cuban doctors have reported significant successes with long-term recombinant interferon treatment, especially when begun in the early stages of HIV infection. See Rivero, Limonta, Aguilera, *et al.*, 1994.

110 Leiner, 1994, p. 125, quoting Dr. Samuel A. Amill in the *New York Times*, June 15, 1990.

111 Rivero, Limonta, Aguilera, *et al.*, 1994.

112 Jorge Pérez, quoted by Xinhua News Agency, April 18, 1995; Manuel Limonta, head of Cuba's Centre for Genetic Engineering and Biotechnology, quoted by Reuters, Limited, November 12, 1995. Limonta stated that "he would be one of the first human volunteers on which the trial Cuban vaccine could be tested."

Meanwhile, the United States and France proposed progressing from chimpanzees to human tests in Thailand, Uganda, Brazil, and Rwanda—citizens of these countries apparently being the next step up in the progression from chimps to humans in the eyes of "First World" scientists. See Cohen, 1996. The World Health Organization in 1991 proposed Thailand, Rwanda, Brazil, Uganda, and Zaire potential sites for vaccine trials. Rwanda and Zaire were eventually rejected because of political unrest, and Thailand was selected.

113 *Daily Cuban News from Havana* 138, June 6, 1996. Distributed by the Cuban Interests Section, Washington, D.C. The plan to begin tests on human volunteers was also reported by InterPress Service on July 28, 1996 (Dalia Acosta, "Cuba—Health: Tests to start on AIDS Vaccine") and by Agence France Presse ("Humans to be injected with AIDS vaccine," July 16, 1996). See also "Cuba Starts Testing Anti-AIDS Vaccine on Humans," (Reuters Dispatch, December 22, 1996) and "Sin reacciones graves participantes pruebas prototipo vacuna," (EFE Dispatch, February 28, 1997).

114 Román, 1995b, p. 531.

115 A rash of newspaper articles in the United States reported the existence of the epidemic in 1993; only a few mentioned in passing that the government was distributing vitamins as a preventive measure. See "Cuban Epidemic Spreads to Nearly 50,000," UPI dispatch, July 21, 1993; "43,412 Stricken Cubans, and Not a Single Answer," *New York Times*, June 15, 1993; "Experts Ponder Cuban Epidemic," *New York Times*, May 25, 1993; "Illness that Hit Cubans is Said to be Lessening," *New York Times*, May 21, 1993; "Mystery Nervous-System Epidemic in Cuba Easing, Doctors Say," *Los Angeles Times*, May 22, 1993; "Malnourished Cubans Flock to Hospitals," UPI dispatch, April 14, 1993. The message of most of these articles is that Cuba is collapsing and the population is starving.

116 Cuba Neuropathy Field Investigation Team, 1995. This article was the result of a collaborative study organized by PAHO with doctors and scientists from the Centers for Disease Control and Prevention, the Cuban Ministry of Public Health, PAHO, the National Institutes of Health, and the FDA. Between January and July of 1994, only 102 new cases were reported. See Cuba Neuropathy Field Investigation Team, 1994a, p. 7.

117 Cuba Neuropathy Field Investigation Team, 1994b, p. 1154. This article is a summary report by the Cuban Ministry of Health.

118 The history and epidemiology of the disease is summarized in Tucker and Hedges, 1993, pp. 350-351.

119 Lincoff, Odel, and Hirano, 1993, p. 517. The Cuban Health Ministry reported that the rate for children under 15 years of age was 4.2 per 100,000 and for adults over 65 it was 290.9. It did not report the rate for pregnant women but stated that they were among the groups least affected by the disease. See Cuba Neuropathy Field Investigation Team, 1994b, p. 1156.

120 Tucker and Hedges, 1993, p. 351; Cuba Neuropathy Field Investigation Team, 1994b, p. 1156.

121 Studies of the outbreak agree that the cause was probably a combination of sudden and severe reductions in diet with exposure to as-yet-unidentified toxins, possibly related to smoking. The Cuba Neuropathy Field Investigation Team summarized their findings as to the causes of the disease as follows: "Although we cannot assign a definitive cause to this epidemic, our findings suggest that its occurrence was linked to a deterioration in diet affecting nutrients such as methionine, vitamin B12, riboflavin, and carotenoids, in conjunction with a high prevalence of tobacco use and possibly cassava consumption" (1995, p. 1181). The Cuban Health Ministry wrote that "risk for illness was associated with tobacco smoking, lower body mass index, and lower intake of animal protein, fat, and foods that contain B-vitamins" (Cuba Neuropathy Field Investigation Team, 1994b, p. 1156). Tucker and Hedges also point out that "with the ethically necessary treatment of all patients with vitamin therapy, and the provision of vitamin supplements to the entire population, it will not be possible to prove a definitive causal relationship between specific nutritional factors and the epidemic. Still, the evidence suggests that B vitamins are centrally involved. The appearance of the epidemic shortly after food shortages began, the measured dietary and biochemical deficiencies, the response to treatment with vitamins, the recent decline in incidence with population vitamin supplementation, the parallels with other outbreaks of neuropathy, and the logic of the biochemical mechanisms are all consistent with a nutritional causal factor" (1993, pp. 355-356).

122 Román, 1995b, p. 533.

123 Ordúñez-García, Nieto, Espinosa-Brito, *et al.*, 1996, p. 742. They are citing Kuntz, 1994, p. 175.

124 Román, 1995a, p. 9.

125 Garfield, 1996, p. 1063. He is responding to the report by the Cuba Neuropathy Field Investigation Team, which he says "fails...as a public health analysis in that it does not address the more fundamental causes of the epidemic" which "are to be found in socioeconomic conditions complicated by geopolitical issues."

126 Richard Garfield, quoted in Elizabeth Oplatka, "U.S.-Cuba Stalemate Blocks Trade, Information," *AAP News*, October 1994, p. 14.

127 United States international relations do not always follow the classic "economic dependency" pattern either; for example, the U.S. relationship with Israel is closer to the Soviet/Cuba model of political convenience and economic support.

128 In the early 1980s, Cuban statistics showed that 94 percent of fats and oils, 80 percent of beans, 40 percent of rice, and 24 percent of milk were imported. See Benjamin, Collins, and Scott, 1989, p. 116, citing Food and Agriculture Organization, *Food Balance Sheets, 1979-1981*, and Comité Estatal de Estadísticas, *Anuario estadístico de Cuba, 1982*.

129 Kirkpatrick, Garfield, and Smith, 1994, pp. 681-682. They cite a study published in 1993 by the Cuban Ministry of Public Health, *Adverse Effects of the US Economic Embargo on Exercise of Human Rights in Cuba*. Several other recent and important studies have come to similar conclusions. See American Association for World Health, 1997; Garfield and Santana, 1997; Kirkpatrick, 1996; *Lancet* Editorial "Sanctions on Health in Cuba," 1996.

130 Between 1986 (when a six-year experiment with agricultural markets was ended) and 1994, all marketing of food was through state-run stores. Here, basic goods are sold at highly subsidized prices through the ration system, to ensure that they are available to all. Items plentiful enough to be removed from the rationing system are sold to the public at somewhat higher state-determined prices at state-run stores (known as the "parallel market"). For the evolution of Cuba's food policies through 1986, see Benjamin, Collins, and Scott, 1989.

131 The dollar stores are also state-run, but they sell imported goods (or Cuban goods processed for export) at prices few Cubans can afford. The fall of the Soviet bloc resulted in the loss of fuel to run Cuban factories and manufactured Soviet-bloc imports. Consequently, few manufactured goods are available in Cuba outside of these dollar stores.

132 Benjamin, Collins, and Scott criticized the government's approach to obesity in the mid-1980s as "quite feeble" and speculated that political factors as much as strictly health factors were at work: both government officials and the general population were convinced that the typical high fat, high protein Western diet was the ideal. "We don't support the idea that has been tossed around in international circles that developed countries are going to have animal protein while developing countries get vegetable protein," the Cuban vice president told them (1989, pp. 113-114). Eckstein remarks that the population "looked better" as a result of weight loss during the Special Period (1994, p. 135); Feinsilver notes that "the economic crisis may have a somewhat salutary effect" (1993, p. 76) in reducing the availability of meat. Cubans, however, rarely voice this type of analysis. A study carried out in Havana in 1993 compared anthropometric indicators including height, weight, and body mass (measured by arm circumference and arm muscle area), to national data from studies in 1972 and 1982 and concluded that "nutritional standards have been significantly affected except among young children" (Republic of Cuba, 1994, pp. 26-27).

133 Republic of Cuba, 1994, pp. 23, 25.

134 It is difficult to compare low birth weight rates to other areas in Latin America because so many births occur outside of hospitals. However, the United States' rate is similar to Cuba's low point, approximately 7 percent. See PAHO, 1994, vol. 1, p. 435.

135 There were 22 of these "homes" in 1970, and 135 in 1987 (Feinsilver, 1993, p. 232, n. 117); the *Plan nacional de acción para la nutrición* did not give figures for later dates.

136 Republic of Cuba, 1994, pp. 23-24.

137 Garfield and Santana, 1997, p. 16. They cite Republic of Cuba, 1994.

138 Deaths from typhoid rose from 0.9 per 100,000 in 1991 to 2.3 per 100,000 in 1993; from dysentery (amoebic and bacterial) from 6.4 in 1991 to 16.8 in 1993. See Republic of Cuba, 1994, p. 43, table 17.

139 Muruaga, 1995, p. 8. She cites figures from the 1993 MINSAP Statistical Yearbook. For the sake of comparison, in Honduras (with a GDP per capita of $2,000 in 1992, close to that of Cuba), communicable

diseases accounted for 18.4 percent of deaths from defined causes—and PAHO estimated that there was a 48.8 percent underregistration of deaths. In Peru (with a GDP of $3,300, and an estimated 50 percent underregistration of deaths), acute respiratory infections alone accounted for 15.3 percent of deaths, and diarrheal diseases 6.7 percent. In Cuba, PAHO estimated underregistration of deaths to be 0.5 percent in 1980, and that now "the statistics being reported at present can be considered reliable and virtually complete." See PAHO, 1994, vol. 2, pp. 156, 254, 350, and UNDP, 1995, p. 156, for GDP estimates.

140 Fidel Castro, April 30, 1996 speech quoted in *Granma International*, May 15, 1996.

141 Muruaga, 1995, p. 9.

142 With 43.3 physicians per 10,000 population in 1990 (and many more now), Cuba had the highest rate in the Americas, trailed by Uruguay (36.8), Argentina (26.8), and the United States (24.5). See PAHO, 1994, vol. 1, p. 435.

143 Feinsilver provides a 1988 price list for "health tourism" by one of Cuba's state-run travel agencies, Cubanacán, including "destruction of kidney stones through extracorporeal lithotripsy, $4,034 for one kidney and $5,020 for both"; "open-heart surgery, $8,897"; "ophthalmological microsurgery to correct myopia, $900 for one eye and $1,500 for both"; "neural transplant to treat Parkinson's disease, $14,974." These prices include hospital stays of several weeks and all diagnosis and follow-up care. She notes, for comparative purposes, that coronary bypass surgery at the University of Michigan hospital cost $21,000 for hospital and physicians' fees in 1989 (1993, pp. 213-214).

144 In May 1996 Cuba's Health Minister announced that since 1994 workers in the tourist sector had contributed $2 million from their tips to the health sector; these tips were being used for cancer treatment. Contributions from mining, fishing, and tobacco workers, meanwhile, were earmarked for the national mother-child program. Radio Havana Cuba International Shortwave Service in English transcript, May 14, 1996.

145 Kuntz, 1994, p. 175.

146 See the comparison of Cuba and Great Britain made by Susser, 1993.

147 Hill, September 18, 1959, *FRUS 1958-1960*, VI, p. 605.

148 Turkel, "Memorandum," July 1, 1959, *FRUS 1958-1960*, VI, pp. 546-558.

149 Rubottom to Dillon, December 28, 1959, *FRUS 1958-1960*, VI, pp. 716-720.

150 Rubottom, January 14, 1960, *FRUS 1958-1960*, VI, p. 742.

151 The American Association for World Health recently concluded that "the U.S. embargo of Cuba has dramatically harmed the health and nutrition of large numbers of ordinary Cuban citizens....It is our expert medical opinion that the U.S. embargo has caused a significant rise in suffering—and even in deaths—in Cuba....The U.S. embargo of food and the de facto embargo on medical supplies has wreaked havoc with the island's model primary health care system" (1997, n.p.).

152 The Bay of Pigs invasion of 1961 and the continuing economic blockade of the island, recently strengthened by the Torricelli Act (1992) and the Helms-Burton Act (1996) are only the tip of the iceberg. See Morley, 1987, pp. 149-155 for a summary of the covert war in the 1960s and 1970s. Other sources include United States Congress, 1975; Branch and Crile, 1975; Ayers, 1976; and Hinckle and Turner, 1992.

153 The American Association for World Health makes the point that Cuba's infant mortality rate is half the rate found in Washington, D.C. See American Association for World Health, 1997.

CHAPTER 14
The Smoke and Mirrors of Health Reform in El Salvador: Community Health NGOs and the Not-So-Neoliberal State

1 Robert Greenberger, "Developing Countries Pass Off Tedious Job of Assisting the Poor," *Wall Street Journal*, June 5, 1995.

2 Walt, 1994, pp. 127-130.

3 Hellinger, 1987.

4 World Bank, 1993b, pp. 163-164.

5 USAID, 1991.

6 GAO, 1992a.

7 See Boyce, 1995; Pastor and Conroy, 1995, for reviews of El Salvador's foreign aid in the post-war period. El Salvador has sought "precautionary" agreements with the International Monetary Fund, in part for the legitimization the Fund provides for seeking loans from other creditors, but the government has not drawn directly on IMF resources. The government of El Salvador enjoys a more stable economic situation than many post-conflict regimes because of a decade of generous USAID support (which allowed some sectors, including the military, to accumulate considerable cash reserves); there has also been a steady capital influx through cash remittances sent from Salvadoran refugees in the United States to their families in El Salvador (Boyce, 1995).

8 Boyce, 1995.

9 See Wignaraja, 1993; Sollis, 1996.

10 Jack Nelson-Pallmeyer, 1990, *War Against the Poor: Low-Intensity Conflict and Christian Faith*.

11 Sollis, 1996.

12 Sollis, 1996.

13 Sollis, 1996, p. 191.

14 To protect the security and privacy of those who shared their lives and work with me, the identities of all villages, individuals interviewed, and local NGOs will be protected through use of pseudonyms and in some cases minor editing of identifying characteristics. I've made no effort to disguise identities of public officials nor of nationally or internationally known agencies and NGOs.

15 For further reading, see McClintock, 1985; Siegal and Hackel, 1988.

16 For further reading, see Schoultz, 1987; Montgomery, 1995.

17 Sundaram and Gelber, 1991, p. 13.

18 See Edwards and Siebentritt, 1991, p. 18.

19 Sixty percent of those testifying before the commission blamed El Salvador's uniformed armed forces for the abuses.

20 See Montgomery, 1995; Smith, 1985.

21 Interview notes.

22 UNICEF, 1992b.

23 See: Revisión y Evaluación de Promotores de Salud Comunitaria: Ministerio de Salud Pública y Asistencia Social y Organizaciones No Gubernamentales, Informe Final (borrador), Investigaciones de Población y Mercado, San Salvador, 1995.

24 See Wilkie and Haber, *Statistical Abstract of Latin America*, Vol. 22, 1983 (Los Angeles), cited in DeWalt, 1994.

25 IDHUCA, 1992.

26 The UNICEF statistics were given to the author in a 1989 interview with staff members from the San Salvador office, and were cited in Smith, "Health Care Battle in El Salvador," *San Francisco Chronicle*, May 10, 1989. The epidemiological survey is reported in Meyers, Epstein, Burford, *et al.*, 1989. For a more detailed description of the popular health system and an evaluation of its effectiveness, see Smith-Nonini, 1997b. The declines in incidence of these conditions in clinic patients was not related to a drop-off in visits to the clinic. The number of patient visits doubled from an average of 150 per month to 300 per month during this five-year period.

27 For a more detailed analysis of the negotiations and collaboration, see Smith-Nonini, 1997a.

28 Since the cease-fire, the ministry's rural clinics in the Chalatenango area have been better stocked with medicines, due to massive infusions of USAID funds (for pharmaceuticals) and post-cease-fire budget increases. However, given that in 1994–95 USAID was pulling most of its mission and funding out of El Salvador with a relatively short transition period, there is a high likelihood that if the ministry does not restructure its accounting system (which currently gives urban hospitals control over two-thirds of the budget) the cost crisis will recur (Fiedler, Gomez, and Bertrand, 1993).

29 Gomez, 1990.

30 From 1975 to 1979, foreign aid, primarily from the Inter-American Development Bank (IDB), financed a 40 percent increase in Ministry of Health infrastructure, but no provisions were made for support of recurrent costs for staffing and maintaining the new facilities. The crisis was exacerbated by cutbacks in the national health budget due to war and a declining economy after 1980; despite these problems, the IDB building project continued into the 1980s. As a result, from 1977 to 1985 the share of the health budget directed to personnel costs increased from 56 percent of the Ministry's Centralized Agencies operating budget to 92 percent. This caused a concurrent fall in the budget for pharmaceuticals and supplies from 44 to 8 percent in the same period (Fiedler, 1987).

31 Fiedler, Gomez, and Bertrand, 1993.

32 Fiedler, Gomez, and Bertrand, 1993.

33 Fiedler, Gomez, and Bertrand, 1993.

34 Information was obtained from interviews with Ministry of Health employees and foreign-aid consultants, all of whom asked that their identities not be revealed. Over a two-month period I made multiple requests for an interview with Dr. Eduardo Interiano, the Minister of Health, in order to include his perspective and obtain responses to the many criticisms I heard of his policies from other informants. His secretary said he was too busy for an interview and referred me to the reform office.

35 This is based on several sources, including: a focus-group meeting in a community served by ministry promoters; a focus-group meeting of ministry health professionals which met to evaluate the program; interviews with evaluators of the program from consulting firms hired by USAID; and interviews with an official from the World Bank who oversaw a team charged with evaluating ministry promoters.

36 This information is based on phone interviews with health specialists from the IDB and the World Bank. The report on the evaluation was not yet published at the time of this writing.

37 Compared with the war years, USAID has had declining influence with the Salvadoran government in the post-cease-fire period, in part because the agency is rapidly downsizing its mission size and funding. A degree of resistance to USAID is also a matter of national pride, as many Salvadoran officials have long resented the United States' encroachment on their country's sovereignty.

38 This information is based on interviews with persons close to the ministry's community-health planning process, and was confirmed in interviews with people from the ministry's reform office and finance division.

39 The Salvadoran Ministry of Planning estimated in 1988 that two-thirds of Salvadorans were living in poverty, with one-third living in "extreme" poverty—a designation for families that are unable to purchase the basic food basket (canasta básica). Average per capita income in El Salvador fell by 25 percent during the war years as the economy stagnated. Although the GDP began to grow again after 1990, this growth did not translate into increased income for the poorest Salvadorans, who have been disproportionately affected by recent hikes in taxes on purchases of basic consumer goods. The San Salvador-based Center for Defense of the Consumer calculated that the cost of the canasta básica for a family of five increased by 11 percent from July 1994 to July 1995.

40 An international health consulting team (funded by USAID) expressly (and strongly) advised against regional hospital expansion in a 1993 overview of the Salvadoran health system, noting that occupancy rates for hospital beds have been "well below accepted standards, especially in the health centers where they have averaged less than 50 percent since at least 1985 and have been falling. The Ministry of Health cannot afford to build more hospital beds. More infrastructure, therefore, can only be justified by the need for greater outpatient capacity, in which case the preferred facility type is the (smaller) health unit" (Fiedler, Gomez, and Bertrand, 1993). In telephone interviews a representative from the World Bank mission said that, in contrast to ministry administrators' expectations, no exact loan amount had been agreed to, nor had the Bank reached an agreement with the Ministry of Health for projected uses for the funds.

41 Thornton, Boddy, and Brooks, 1994, pp. 121-122.

42 Thornton, Boddy, and Brooks, 1994.

43 Fiedler, Gomez, and Bertrand, 1993.

44 Robert Greenberger, "Developing Countries Pass Off Tedious Job of Assisting the Poor," Wall Street Journal, June 5, 1995.

45 Stanley, 1996.

46 Weyland, 1995.

47 Sollis, 1996.

48 Smith-Nonini, 1997a.

49 All NGOs in El Salvador are required to register with the Ministry of the Interior, a process known as obtaining their "personería jurídica." As of November 1995 the organization of health promoters in Chalatenango had been waiting more than two years for its personería jurídica from the government. An investigation of the role of NGOs in the post-war reconstruction process by the U.S. General Accounting Office (GAO) (1992) found that representatives of all five of the ex-FMLN social service NGOs on which the GAO consultants collected information complained of similar delays in obtaining legal standing. Sollis (1996) reported that new NGOs favored by the ARENA government had been granted legal status much more rapidly. One NGO waited a mere two months, while the ex-FMLN NGOs submitted their applications more than a year before, and one had been waiting since 1988.

50 Vergara, 1997.

51 For the role of the state in equitable PHC, see Collins and Green, 1994. For examples of states using decentralization to cut back health services, see Collins, 1989. See Walt, 1994, pp. 92-93 for a discussion of the forms decentralized health care can take and examples from Chile and Colombia.

52 Sunkel, 1995.

53 Franke and Chasin, 1994.

54 Ratcliffe, 1978.

55 Skalnick, 1989.

56 For examples of such advocacy, see Walt, 1994, pp. 138-140, on NGO successes in promoting new international policies on baby formula and essential drugs; Epprecht, 1994, pp. 33-34, on NGO contributions to the World Bank's "learning experience"; and Hellinger, 1987, pp. 136-137, on Oxfam (United Kingdom) and other NGOs that have challenged large donors to reform projects seen as insensitive to grassroots needs.

57 Cernea, 1988.

58 World Bank, 1993b.

59 Epprecht, 1994.

60 World Bank, 1993b, pp. 93-95.

61 Interestingly, Investing in Health (World Bank, 1993b) finds the disease burden for diarrhea (a condition which the report acknowledges is best resolved by improved water quality and sanitation) comparable to

that for malnutrition [e.g., poor nutrition accounts for 8.7 percent of total "disability-adjusted life years" per 1,000 (p. 76), compared with 9.7 percent being accounted for by diarrhea (p. 90)]; but, rather than write off the problem of malnutrition as unsolveable, the report devotes several pages to solutions such as "making supplemental feeding work." There is, of course, no mention of land reform as a strategy.

62 Petras and Vieux, 1992, p. 613.

63 For further reading, see Halebsky and Harris, 1995.

64 Epprecht, 1994.

65 For a discussion of donors' "pressure to lend," see Walt, 1994, pp. 157-159. See also Justice, 1986; Danaher, 1994.

66 Some scholars have interpreted U.S. militarism in Central America during the 1980s as being linked to a neoliberal counterrevolution on the economic front throughout the developing world (see Freysinger, 1991; Bello, 1994). While causality in international affairs is highly complex, the linkages between military governments and "unproductive" development projects are now coming under scrutiny at high levels in Bretton Woods institutions. Staff at both the World Bank and International Monetary Fund (IMF) have begun to question long-standing policies of treating military expenditures as sacrosanct relative to other government programs in the conditionality of SAP loans imposed on Third World countries (see Boyce, 1995; Pastor and Conroy, 1995).

CHAPTER 15
Conclusion:
Pessimism of the Intellect, Optimism of the Will

1 Known as *Gramsci's dictum*, from the work of Italian writer and political philosopher Antonio Gramsci (1891-1937).

2 Only a few of the chapters in the volume have addressed directly the very real problem of corruption and the direct and indirect roles that theft, graft, bribery, and capital flight play on the health of poor communities. The overt profligacy of extraordinarily corrupt Third World dictators of the mid- to late-twentieth century—Ferdinand Marcos, Jean-Bedel Bokossa, Mobutu Sese Seko, and the Duvaliers being but a few examples—may be waning. Yet, more subtle and less direct forms of corruption persist and contribute to the immiseration of the poor throughout the world. The issue has not received ample consideration here for several reasons. First, the subject of corruption already receives abundant attention in economic development literature and the mainstream press. Second, the international financial institutions often use corruption among government officials to blame countries for their failure to implement harsh economic measures "correctly." And last, the prevalence of corruption is often used to deflect attention from the fundamental flaws (and vested corporate and national interests) of economic measures imposed on poor and indebted countries.

3 Scheper-Hughes, 1996, pp. 889-900.

4 O'Neill, 1995, p. 1.

5 We are referring primarily to nonlocal NGOs that provide direct services to poor communities in countries throughout the world.

6 Starn, 1991.

7 Note, however, that in some cases, NGOs will have compelling historical and pragmatic reasons for needing to distance themselves from state authority (see Chapter Fourteen).

8 Chomsky, 1998, p. 24-25.

Bibliography

Edited by Evan Lyon and Heather Rensberry

Uncredited Articles

1984 "The Bhopal Tragedy." Editorial. *Wall Street Journal*, December 10.

1987 "Foreign Privatization of National Health Systems." Editorial. *American Journal of Public Health* 77(10): 1271-1272.

1993 *Carabayllo Rural: Tierra, Agua, y Vida*. Lima: Alternativa, Centro de Investigación Social y Educación Popular, Municipalidad de Carabayllo and Junta de Usuarios de Agua del Rio Chillón.

1993 "World Bank's Cure for Donor Fatigue." *Lancet* 342(8862): 63-64.

1994 *Draft Document on Effects of Pollution on Health of Russian Population*. Joint Publication Research Service, TEN-94-009, April 7, pp. 25-31.

1994 "Peru: Construction of $40,000,000 Leaching and Metallurgical Facilities." *Export Sales Prospector*, April.

1995 "Interview with Kenneth Arrow." *The Region*, December. Minneapolis: U.S. Federal Reserve Bank.

1995 "Much of Peru's Employment Sector is Informal." *Market Latin America* 3(7): 4.

1995 "'Three Strikes': Serious Flaws and a Huge Price Tag." *Rand Research Review* 19(1): 1-2.

1995 "Treatment: Effective (but Unpopular) Weapon Against Drugs." *Rand Research Review* 19(1): 3-4.

1996 "Interview with Ledum Mitee, Deputy President of MOSOP." *Africa Today*, May/June, pp. 8-14.

1996 "Sanctions on Health in Cuba." *Lancet* 348(9040): 1461.

1997 "Can Industry be Wooed Back Into the Act?" *Nature*, April 10.

1997 "Hurdling a Great Wall: U.S. Company Opens China's First Foreign-run Hospital After Four Years' Effort." *Modern Healthcare* 27(44): 26.

1998 "Rising Costs in Health Care." Editorial. *New York Times*, September 23.

1999 "AIDS in the Third World: A Global Disaster." *Economist*, January 2, p. 42.

1999 "Tough Times: Labor in the Americas." *NACLA Report on the Americas* 32(4): 14.

Abelson, Reed

1999 "For Managed Care, Free-Market Shock." *New York Times*, January 3.

Abugre, Charles

1998 "Mining Boon: A Gain for Africa?" *Third World Resurgence* 93: 20-23.

Aceves, William J.

1998 "Doe vs. Unocal." *American Journal of International Law* 92(2): 309-314.

ACTIONAID

1995 *The Reality of Aid 95*. Tony German and Judith Randel, eds. London: Earthscan.

Adam, Christopher, William Cavendish, and Percy S. Mistry

1992 *Adjusting Privatization: Case Studies from Developing Countries*. London: Villiers Publications.

Adedeji, Adebayo

1989 *Towards a Dynamic African Economy*. London: Frank Cass.

1990 *The African Alternative*. Addis Ababa: Economic Commission for Africa.

1996 "Institutional Restitution, Renewal and Restructuring." *Development*, June 2, pp. 68-72.

Adelman, Irma

1978 *Income Distribution Policy in Developing Countries*. Oxford: Oxford University Press.

Afonja, Semi

1986 "Land Control: A Critical Factor in Yoruba Gender Stratification." In *Women and Class in Africa*. Claire Robertson and Iris Berger, eds. New York: Africana Publishing. Pp. 78-91.

African Rights

1995 *Rwanda: Death, Despair and Defiance*. 2nd ed. London: African Rights.

Agarwal, Anil, Juliet Merrifield, and Rajesh Tandon

1985 *No Place to Run: Local Realities and the Global Issues of the Bhopal Disaster*. New Market, TN: Highlander Research and Education Center, Society for Participatory Research in Asia.

Agrupación Católica Universitaria

1972 "Encuesta de Trabajadores Rurales, 1956-1957." *Economía y Desarrollo* 3(12): 188-213.

Ahmad, Ehtisham

1993 "Protecting the Vulnerable: Social Security and Public Policy." In *Including the Poor*. Michael Lipton and Jacques van der Gaag, eds. Washington, D.C.: World Bank. Pp. 359-377.

Ake, Claude

1992 "The Legitimacy Crisis of the State." In *Structural Adjustment and the Crisis in Africa: Economic and Political*

Perspectives. David Kennett and Tukumbi Lumumba-Kasongo, eds. Lewiston, NY: Edwin Mellen Press. Pp. 29-47.

1996 *Democracy and Development in Africa*. Washington, D.C.: Brookings Institute.

Al-Saleh, I.A.

1994 "Pesticides: A Review Article." *Journal of Environmental Pathology, Toxicology and Oncology* 13(3): 151-161.

Albelda, Randy and Nancy Folbre

1996 *The War on the Poor: A Defense Manual*. New York: The New Press.

Alesina, Alberto and Roberto Perotti

1996 "Income Distribution, Political Instability, and Investment." *European Economic Review* 40(6): 1203-1228.

Alexander, R., D. Gonzalez, M. Campbell, et al.

1993 *Economic and Environmental Conditions in the Lower Rio Grande Valley Along the Texas-Mexico Border*. Report Prepared at the Request of Congressman Gephardt. Weslaco, TX: Texas Rural Legal Aid, Inc.

Allen, Susan, Christina Lindan, Antoine Serufila, et al.

1991 "Human Immunodeficiency Virus Infection in Urban Rwanda." *Journal of the American Medical Association* 266(12): 1657-1663.

American Association for World Health

1997 *Denial of Food and Medicine: The Impact of the U.S. Embargo on Health and Nutrition in Cuba—An Executive Summary*. Washington, D.C.: American Association for World Health.

Amin, Samir

1974 *Accumulation on a World Scale*. New York: Monthly Review Press.

Amnesty International

1998a *Human Rights and Proposals for Global Deregulation of Capital*. London: Amnesty International.

1998b *Human Rights Principles for Companies*. London: Amnesty International.

Amsden, Alice H.

1989 *Asia's Next Giant: South Korea and Late Industrialization*. Oxford: Oxford University Press.

Amsden, Alice, Jacek Kochanowicz, and Lance Taylor

1994 *The Market Meets its Match: Restructuring the Economies of Eastern Europe*. Cambridge, MA: Harvard University Press.

Anand, R.K.

1996 "Health Workers and the Baby Food Industry." *British Medical Journal* 312(7046): 1556-1557.

Anand, Sudhir and Kara Hanson

1997 "Disability-adjusted Life Years: A Critical Review." *Journal of Health Economics* 16(6): 685-702.

Anderson, Barbara A. and Brian D. Silver

1997 "Issues of Data Quality in Assessing Mortality Trends and Levels in the New Independent States." In *Premature Death in the New Independent States*. José Luis Bobadilla, Christine A. Costello, and Faith Mitchell, eds. Washington, D.C.: National Academy Press. Pp. 120-155.

Anderson, Mary B.

1985 "Technology Transfer: Implications for Women." In *Gender Roles in Development Projects: A Casebook*. Catherine Overholt, Mary B. Anderson, Kathleen Cloud, et al., eds. West Hartford, CT: Kumarian Press. Pp. 57-78.

Anderson, Sarah and John Cavanagh

1996 *The Top 200: The Rise of Global Corporate Power*. Washington, D.C.: Institute for Policy Studies.

Andersson, N., M.K. Ajwani, S. Mahashabde, et al.

1990 "Delayed Eye and Other Consequences from Exposure to Methyl Isocyanate: 93% Follow Up of Exposed and Unexposed Cohorts in Bhopal." *British Journal of Industrial Medicine* 47(8): 553-558.

Andersson, N., M.K. Muir, V. Mehra, et al.

1988 "Exposure and Response to Methyl Isocyanate: Results of a Community-Based Survey in Bhopal." *British Journal of Industrial Medicine* 45(7): 469-475.

Andreas, Peter

1993 "Profits, Poverty, and Illegality." *NACLA Report on the Americas* 27(3): 22-41.

Andreas, Peter and Kenneth Sharpe

1992 "Cocaine Politics in the Andes." *Current History*, February, pp. 74-79.

Andreev, E.M.

1994 "A New Demographic Catastrophe in Russia?" *Xhimia i Zhizn* 10: 229-234.

Angell, Alan and Carol Graham

1995a "Can Social Sector Reform Make Adjustment Sustainable and Equitable? Lessons from Chile and Venezuela." *Journal of Latin American Studies* 27(1): 189-219.

1995b "Social Sector Reform and the Adjustment Process." Paper presented at the Latin American Studies Association. Washington, D.C. September 28-30.

Anthony, James C. and John E. Helzer

1991 "Syndromes of Drug Abuse and Dependence." In *Psychiatric Disorders in America*. L. Robins and D. Regier, eds. New York: Free Press. Pp. 116-154.

Anyinam, Charles A.

1991 "Transboundary Movements of Hazardous Wastes: The Case of Toxic Waste Dumping in Africa." *International Journal of Health Services* 21(4): 759-777.

Arax, Mark and Jeanne Brokaw

1997 "No Way Around Roundup: Monsanto's Bioengineered Seeds are Designed to Require More of the Company's Herbicide." *Mother Jones*, January/February, pp. 40-42.

Arrow, Kenneth

1963 "Uncertainty and the Welfare Economics of Medical Care." *American Economic Review* 53: 941-973.

Arruda, M.

1994 "The New World Order: The Dominant Development Model and Democratic Alternatives."

Paper presented at the International Consultation on People-Centered Development Alternatives for the South. University of Fort Hare, South Africa. June.

Ascherio, Alberto, Robin Biellik, Andy Epstein, et al.
1995 "Deaths and Injuries Caused by Landmines in Mozambique." *Lancet* 346(8977): 721-724.

Atkins, Keletso E.
1993 *The Moon is Dead! Give Us Our Money!* Portsmouth, NH: Heinemann.

Atkinson, Anthony
1997 "Bringing Income Distribution in from the Cold." *Economic Journal* 107(3): 297-321.

Attaran, Amir
1999 "Human Rights and Biomedical Research Funding for the Developing World: Discovering State Obligations." *Health and Human Rights* 4(1): 27-58.

Auty, Richard M. and John Toye, eds.
1996 *Challenging the Orthodoxies*. New York: St. Martin's Press.

Averill, Elizabeth and Sheldon W. Samuels
1992 "International Occupational and Environmental Health." In *Environmental and Occupational Medicine*. 2nd ed. W.N. Rom, ed. Boston: Little, Brown, and Co. Pp. 1357-1364.

Avraamova, E.
1994 *Social and Demographic Dimensions of the Economic Transition Impact on Families with Children*. New York: UNICEF.

Ayadike, O.
1988 "Toxic Terrorism." *West Africa*, June, pp. 108-109.

Ayers, Bradley E.
1976 *The War that Never Was: An Insider's Account of CIA Covert Operations Against Cuba*. Indianapolis: Bobbs-Merrill.

Ayres, Robert L.
1983 *Banking on the Poor*. Washington, D.C.: Overseas Development Council.

Azevedo, Mario J.
1998 *Roots of Violence: A History of War in Chad*. New York: Gordon and Breach.

Bader, Michael
1979 "Breastfeeding: The Role of Multinational Corporations in Latin America." In *Imperialism, Health, and Medicine*. Vincente Navarro, ed. Farmingdale, NY: Baywood Publishing Company. Pp. 235-252.

Baer, Hans A., Merrill Singer, and Ida Susser
1997 *Medical Anthropology and the World System: A Critical Perspective*. Westport, CT: Bergin and Garvey.

Bagdikian, Ben
1983 *The Media Monopoly*. Boston: Beacon Press.

Bahmueller, Charles
1981 *The National Charity Company: Jeremy Bentham's Silent Revolution*. Berkeley: University of California Press.

Bailey, Paul, Aurelio Parisotto, and Jeffery Renshaw
1993 *Multinationals and Employment: The Global Economy of the 1990s*. Geneva: International Labour Office.

Balcazar, Hector, Catalina Denman, and Francisco Lara
1995 "Factors Associated with Work-Related Accidents and Sickness Among Maquiladora Workers: The Case of Nogales, Sonora, Mexico." *International Journal of Health Services* 25(3): 489-502.

Banco de Mexico
1998 *Economic and Financial Information, Prices Sector*. Available at www.banxico.org.mx/public_html/indices/indexe.html.

Bangura, Yusuf
1994 *Economic Restructuring, Coping Strategies and Social Change: Implications for Institutional Development in Africa*. Discussion Paper 52. Geneva: U.N. Research Institute for Social Development (UNRISD).

Bank for International Settlements
1998 *Central Bank Survey of Foreign Exchange and Derivatives Market Activity in April: Preliminary Global Data*. Basel: Bank for International Settlements.

Bantje, Han
1995 "Women's Workload and Reproductive Stress." In *Women Wielding the Hoe: Lessons from Rural Africa for Feminist Theory and Development Practice*. Deborah F. Bryceson, ed. Oxford: Berg Publishers. Pp. 111-130.

Banuri, T. and Juliette Schor, eds.
1992 *Financial Openness and National Autonomy*. Oxford: Clarendon Press.

Barker, Jonathan, ed.
1984 *The Politics of Agriculture in Tropical Africa*. Berkeley: Sage Publications.

Barlett, Donald L. and James B. Steele.
1994 *America: Who Really Pays the Taxes?* New York: Simon and Schuster.
1998 "What Corporate Welfare Costs: A Special Investigation by Donald L. Barlett and James B. Steele." *Time*, November.

Barlow, Maude, Bruce Campbell, Steven Shrybman, et al.
1992 "Lessons from Canada." In *Trading Freedom: How Free Trade Affects Our Lives, Work, and Environment*. John Cavanagh, John Gershman, Karen Baker, et al., eds. San Francisco: The Institute for Food and Development Policy. Pp. 34-49.

Barnet, Richard J.
1994 "Lords of the Global Economy." *The Nation*, December 19, pp. 754-760.

Barnett, Richard J. and Ronald Muller
1974 *Global Reach: The Power of the Multinational Corporations*. New York: Simon and Schuster.

Barr, Donald A. and Mark G. Field
1996 "The Current State of Health Care in the Former Soviet Union: Implications for Health Care Policy and

Reform." *American Journal of Public Health* 86(3): 307-312.

Barr, K.E., M.P. Farrell, G.M. Barnes, *et al.*
1993   "Race, Class, and Gender Differences in Substance Abuse: Evidence of Middleclass/Underclass Polarization Among Black Males." *Social Problems* 40(3): 314-327.

Barro, Robert J.
1997   *Determinants of Economic Growth.* Cambridge, MA: MIT Press.

Barro, Robert J. and Xavier Sala-i-Martin
1995   *Economic Growth.* New York: McGraw-Hill.

Barry, Brian and Robert E. Goodin, eds.
1992   *Free Movement: Ethical Issues in the Transnational Migration of People and of Money.* University Park, PA: Penn State Press.

Barry, Michele
1991   "The Influence of the U.S. Tobacco Industry on the Health, Economy, and Environment of Developing Countries." *New England Journal of Medicine* 324(13): 917-920.

Barry, Tom
1995   *Zapata's Revenge: Free Trade and the Farm Crisis in Mexico.* Boston: South End Press.

Bart, François
1993   *Terres d'Afrique, Montagnes Paysannes: le Cas du Rwanda.* Bordeaux: Universite de Bordeaux.

Barten, F., and S. Fustukian
1994   *The Occupational Health Needs of Workers: The Need for a New International Approach (Testimony).* London: Permanent Peoples' Tribunal on Industrial and Environmental Hazards and Human Rights.

Bassett, Mary Travis and Marvellous Mhloyi
1991   "Women and AIDS in Zimbabwe: The Making of an Epidemic." *International Journal of Health Services* 21: 143-156.

Bassett, Mary Travis, Leon Bijlmakers, and David Sanders
1997   "Professionalism, Patient Satisfaction, and Quality of Health Care: Experience During Zimbabwe's Structural Adjustment Programme." *Social Science and Medicine* 45(12): 1845-1852.

Bastien, Rémy
1985   *Le Paysan Haitien et sa Famille: Vallée de Marbial.* Original, 1951. Paris: Éditions Karthala.

Bates, David
1994   *Environmental Health Risks and Public Policy: Decision Making in Free Societies.* Seattle: University of Washington Press.

Bates, Robert H.
1976   *Rural Responses to Industrialization: A Study of Village Zambia.* New Haven, CT: Yale University Press.
1981a "Agricultural Policy in Africa: Political Origins and Social Consequences." In *The Role of U.S. Universities in Rural and Agricultural Development.* Brooke G. Schoepf,

ed. Tuskegee, AL: Tuskegee Institute, Center for Rural Development. Pp. 51-60.
1981b *Markets and States in Tropical Africa.* Berkeley: University of California Press.

Bauer, Peter Tamas
1972   *Dissent on Development.* London: Weidenfeld and Nicolson.
1981   *Equality, the Third World, and Economic Delusion.* London: Methuen.
1984   *Reality and Rhetoric: Studies in the Economics of Development.* London: Weidenfeld and Nicolson.

Baum, Dan
1996   *Smoke and Mirrors.* Boston: Little, Brown, and Co.

Bawden M., D. Slaten, and J. Malone
1995   "Falciparum Malaria in a Displaced Haitian Population." *Transactions of the Royal Society of Tropical Medicine and Hygiene* 89(6): 600-603.

Baxter, Elaine and David Mechanic
1997   "The Status of Local Health Care Safety Nets." *Health Affairs* 16(4): 7-23.

Bay, Edna, ed.
1982   *Women and Work in Africa.* Boulder, CO: Westview Press.

Bayart, Jean-Francois
1989   *L'Etat en Afrique.* Paris: Fayard. English translation: 1993. *The State in Africa: The Politics of the Belly.* London: Longman.

Bayer, Ronald and Cheryl Healton
1989   "Controlling AIDS in Cuba: The Logic of Quarantine." *New England Journal of Medicine* 320(15): 1022-1024.

Beckman, Bjorn
1981   "Ghana, 1951-78: The Agrarian Basis of the Post-Colonial State." In *Rural Development in Tropical Africa.* Judith Heyer, Penelope Roberts, and Gavin Williams, eds. New York: St. Martin's Press. Pp. 143-167.
1992   "Empowerment or Repression? The World Bank and the Politics of Adjustment." In *Authoritarianism, Democracy and Adjustment: The Politics of Economic Reform in Africa.* Peter Gibbon, Yusuf Bangura, and Arye Ofstad, eds. Uppsala: Scandinavian Institute for African Studies.

Beghin, Ivan, William Fougère, and Kendall.W. King
1965   "Enquête Clinique sur l'État de Nutrition des Enfants Préscolaires de Fond-Parisien et de Ganthier (Haiti): Juin, 1964." *Annales des Sociétés Belges de Médicine Tropicale* 45(5): 577-602.
1970   *L'Alimentation et la Nutrition en Haiti.* Paris: Presses Universitaires de France.

Bell, David, Alan Richard, and Lawrence Feltz
1996   "Mediators of Drug Treatment Outcomes." *Addictive Behaviors* 21(5): 597-613.

Bello, Judith H., Alan F. Holmer, and Joseph J. Norton
1994   *The North American Free Trade Agreement: A New Frontier in International Trade and Investment in the*

Americas. Washington, D.C.: American Bar Association and The International Lawyer.

Bello, Walden

1994 "Global Economic Counterrevolution: How Northern Economic Warfare Devastates the South." In *Fifty Years is Enough: The Case Against the World Bank*. Kevin Danaher, ed. Boston: South End Press. Pp. 14-19.

Bello, Walden and Stephanie Rosenfeld

1990 *Dragons in Distress: Asia's Miracle Economies in Crisis*. San Francisco: Institute for Food and Development Policy.

Benjamin, Medea, Joseph Collins, and Michael Scott

1989 *No Free Lunch: Food and Revolution in Cuba Today*. Rev. ed. San Francisco: Institute for Food and Development Policy.

Bennett, John and John R. Bowen, eds.

1988 *Production and Autonomy: Anthropological Studies and Critiques of Development*. Lanham, MD: University Press of America.

Berer, Marge, ed., with Sunandra Ray

1993 *Women and HIV/AIDS: An International Resource Book*. London: Pandora/Harper-Collins.

Berggren, W., D. Ewbank, and G. Berggren

1981 "Reduction of Mortality in Rural Haiti Through a Primary Health-Care Program." *New England Journal of Medicine* 304(22): 1324-1330.

Bergthold, Linda, Caroll Estes, and Augusta Villanueva

1990 "Public Light and Private Dark: Privatization of Home Health Services for the Elderly in the United States." *Home Health Care Services Quarterly* 11(3-4): 7-33.

Berliner, Howard S. and C. Regan

1987 "Multinational Corporations of U.S. For-Profit Hospital Chains: Trends and Implications." *American Journal of Public Health* 77: 1280-1284.

Berridge, Virginia and Griffith Edwards

1981 *Opium and the People: Opiate Use in Nineteeth-Century England*. London: Allan Lane and St. Martin's Press.

Berry, Albert

1997a *Economic Reform, Poverty, and Income Distribution in Latin America*. Toronto: University of Toronto Press.

1997b "The Income Distribution Threat in Latin America." *Latin American Research Review* 32(2): 3-40.

Berry, Sara

1993a "Coping with Confusion: African Farmers' Response to Uncertainty in the 1970s and 1980s." In *Hemmed In: Responses to Africa's Economic Decline*. Thomas Callaghy and John Ravenhill, eds. New York: Columbia. Pp. 248-278.

1993b No Condition is Permanent: The Social Dynamics of Agrarian Change in Sub-Saharan Africa. Madison: University of Wisconsin.

Berry, Wendell

1990 "Economy and Pleasure." In *What Are People For?* San Francisco: North Point Press. Pp. 129-152.

Bertell, Rosalie

1996 "Twelve Years After Bhopal." *International Perspectives in Public Health* 11: 2-4.

Bertell, Rosalie and Gianni Tognoni

1996 "International Medical Commission on Bhopal: A Model for the Future." *National Medical Journal of India* 9(2): 86-91.

Berthoud, Gérald

1992 "Market." In *The Development Dictionary*. Wolfgang Sachs, ed. London: Zed Books. Pp. 70-97.

Bertram, Eva, Morris Blachman, Kenneth Sharpe, *et al.*

1996 *Drug War Politics: The Price of Denial*. Berkeley: University of California Press.

Betts, Dianne C., Daniel J. Slottje, and Jesus Vargas-Garcia

1992 *Crisis on the Rio Grande: Poverty, Unemployment, and Economic Development on the Texas-Mexico Border*. San Francisco: Westview Press.

Bezy, Fernand

1990 *Rwanda: 1962-1989: Bilan Socio-Economique d'un Regime*. Louvain-la-Neuve, Belgium: Institut d'Etudes du Development.

Bhagwati, Jagdish

1998 "The Capital Myth." *Foreign Affairs* 77(3): 7-12.

Bhatia, Rajiv and Gianni Tognoni

1996 "Pharmaceutical Use in the Victims of the Carbide Gas Disaster." *International Perspectives in Public Health* 11: 14-22.

Bhopal Gas Peedit Sangharsh Sahayog Samiti

1994 *Bhopal Lives: Anniversary Notes*. Bhopal, India: Bhopal Group for Information and Action.

Bhopal Group for Information and Action (BGIA)

1990 *Voices of Bhopal*. Bhopal, India: Bhopal Group for Information and Action.

Bhopal Working Group

1987 "The Public Health Implications of the Bhopal Disaster." *American Journal of Public Health* 77(2): 230-236.

Bidwai, Praful

1995 "Making India Work—For the Rich." *Multinational Monitor*, July/August, 1995, pp. 9-13.

Biernacki, Patrick

1986 *Pathways from Heroin Addiction: Recovery Without Treatment*. Philadelphia: Temple University Press.

Bird, Graham

1996 "Borrowing from the IMF: The Policy Implications of Recent Empirical Research." *World Development* 24(11): 1753-1760.

Birdsall, Nancy and Robert Hecht

1996 *Swimming Against the Tide: Strategies for Improving Equity in Health*. Human Capital Development and Operations Policy Working Paper No. 55. Washington, D.C.: World Bank.

Birdsall, Nancy and Estelle James

1990 *Efficiency and Equity in Social Spending: How and Why Governments Misbehave.* Working Paper Series 274. Washington, D.C.: World Bank.

Birdsall, Nancy and Juan Luis Londoño

1997 "Assets Inequality Matters: An Assessment of the World Bank's Approach to Poverty Reduction." *American Economic Review Papers and Proceedings* 87(2): 32-37.

Bjilmakers, Leon, Mary Bassett, and David Sanders

1995 "Health and Structural Adjustment in Rural and Urban Settings in Zimbabwe: Some Interim Findings." In *Structural Adjustment and the Working Poor in Zimbabwe.* Peter Gibbon, ed. Uppsala: Nordiska Afrikaininstitutet. Pp. 215-282.

1996 *Health and Structural Adjustment in Rural and Urban Zimbabwe.* Uppsala: Nordiska Afrikainstitutet.

Black, Maureen M. and Izabel B. Ricardo

1994 "Drug Use, Drug Trafficking, and Weapon Carrying Among Low-income, African-American, Early Adolescent Boys." *Pediatrics* 93(6): 1064-1072.

Blackden, C. Mark and Chitra Bhanu

1988 *Gender, Growth, and Poverty Reduction: 1988 Status Report on Poverty Reduction in Sub-Saharan Africa.* Washington, D.C.: World Bank.

Blank, Steven and Jerry Haar

1998 *Making NAFTA Work: U.S. Firms in the New North American Business Environment.* Miami: North-South Center Press, University of Miami.

Bleifuss, Joel

1996 "The New Abolitionists." *In These Times,* April, pp. 12-13.

Bliss, Christopher

1993 "Life-Style and the Standard of Living." In *The Quality of Life.* Martha Nussbaum and Amartya Sen, eds. New York: Oxford University Press. Pp. 417-436.

Block, Fred

1990 *Postindustrial Possibilities: A Critique of Economic Discourse.* Berkeley: University of California Press.

Bluestone, Barry and Bennett Harrison

1982 *The Deindustrialization of America: Plant Closings, Community Abandonment, and the Dismantling of Basic Industry.* New York: Basic Books.

Blum, William

1986 *The CIA: A Forgotten History.* London: Zed Books.

Boahen, A. Adu, ed.

1990 *Africa Under Colonial Domination 1880-1935.* General History of Africa, abridged edition, Volume VII. London: James Currey.

Bobadilla, José Luis and Christine A. Costello

1997 "Premature Death in the New Independent States: Overview." In *Premature Death in the New Independent States.* José Luis Bobadilla, Christine A. Costello, and Faith Mitchell, eds. Washington, D.C.: National Academy Press. Pp. 1-33.

Bohlen, Celestine

1994 "Graft and Gangsterism in Russia Blight the Entrepreneurial Spirit." *New York Times,* January 30, 1994.

Boloña, Carlos

1996 "The Viability of Alberto Fujimori's Economic Strategy." In *The Peruvian Economy Under Structural Adjustment: Past, Present and Future.* Efraín Gonzales de Olarte, ed. Miami: North-South Center Press, University of Miami Press. Pp. 183-264.

Bond, George C., Joan Vincent, Ida Susser, *et al.*

1997 *AIDS in Africa and the Caribbean.* Boulder, CO: Westview Press.

Bond, Virginia and Paul Dover

1997 "Men, Women and the Trouble with Condoms: Problems Associated with Condom Use by Migrant Workers in Rural Zambia." In *Vulnerability to HIV Infection and Effects of AIDS in Africa and Asia/India.* James P.M. Ntozi, John K. Anarfi, John C. Caldwell, *et al.,* eds. *Health Transition Review* Supplement to Volume 7: 377-392.

Bonnie, Richard and Charles Whitebread

1974 *The Marihuana Conviction.* Charlottesville: University Press of Virginia.

Boote, Anthony R. and Kamau Thugge

1997 *Debt Relief for Low-Income Countries: The HIPC Initiative.* Pamphlet Series No. 51. Washington, D.C.: International Monetary Fund.

Bordes, Ary

1979 *Évolution des Sciences de la Santé et de l'Hygiène Publique en Haiti.* Tome 1. Port-au-Prince: Centre d'Hygiène Familiale.

Boserup, Ester

1970 *Women's Role in Economic Development.* New York: St. Martin's Press.

Bosworth, Barry, Susan Collins, and Nora Claudia Lustig, eds.

1997 *Coming Together? Mexico-United States Relations.* Washington, D.C.: Brookings Institute Press.

Bourdon, D. and F. Ngango

1988 "Urbanisation et Equite Sociale." *Dialogue* 126: 5-20.

Bourgois, Philippe

1995 *In Search of Respect: Selling Crack in El Barrio.* Cambridge: Cambridge University Press.

Bourguignon, François and Christian Morrisson

1989 *External Trade and Income Distribution.* Paris: Organization for Economic Cooperation and Development.

1992 *Adjustment and Equity in Developing Countries: A New Approach.* Paris: Organization for Economic Cooperation and Development.

Bourne, Peter

1988 "Colombian Cocaine and U.S. Tobacco." *World Development Forum* 6(June 15): 4.

Bovard, James

1991 *The Fair Trade Fraud.* New York: St. Martin's Press.

Bowles, Samuel and Herbert Gintis
1986 *Democracy and Capitalism: Property, Community, and the Contradictions of Modern Social Thought.* New York: Basic Books.

Bowles, Samuel, Herbert Gintis, and Bo Gustafsson
1993 *Markets and Democracy: Participation, Accountability, and Efficiency.* Cambridge: Cambridge University Press.

Boyce, James
1995 "External Assistance and the Peace Process in El Salvador." *World Development* 23(12): 2101-2116.

Bradford, Stacey L.
1998 "Sector Analysis: Drugs' Steroid-Induced Performance." *Smart Money,* November.

Branch, Taylor and George Crile III
1975 "The Kennedy Vendetta: How the CIA Waged a Silent War Against Cuba." *Harper's,* August, pp. 49-63.

Branford, Sue and Bernardo Kucinski
1988 *The Debt Squads.* London: Zed Books.

Bread for the World
1997 *What Governments Can Do: Hunger 1997.* Silver Springs, MD: Bread for the World Institute.
1998 *Hunger in a Global Economy: Eighth Annual Report on the State of World Hunger.* Silver Springs, MD: Bread for the World Institute.
1999 *The Changing Politics of Hunger: Ninth Annual Report on the State of World Hunger.* Silver Springs, MD: Bread for the World Institute.

Brecher, Jeremy and Tim Costello
1992 *Global Village or Global Pillage: Economic Reconstruction from the Bottom Up.* Boston: South End Press.

Breitbart, Vicki, Wendy Chavkin, and Paul Wise
1994 "The Accessibility of Drug Treatment for Pregnant Women: A Survey of Programs in Five Cities." *American Journal of Public Health* 84(10): 1658-1661.

Breslow, Marc
1995 "Why Free Trade Fails: The Dangers of GATT, NAFTA, and the WTO." In *Real World Macro: Twelfth Edition.* Randy Albelda, Marc Breslow, John Miller, *et al.,* eds. Somerville, MA: Dollars and Sense. Pp. 109-111.

Brett, Edward A.
1996 "Uganda." In *Limits of Adjustment in Africa.* Poul Engberg-Pedersen, Peter Gibbon, Phil Raikes, *et al.,* eds. London: James Currey. Pp. 309-346.

Brickey, C.
1995 "Relevance of Risk Assessment to Exposed Communities." *Environmental Health Perspectives* 103(Supplement 1): 89-91.

Brooks, David
1992 "Mexico's Future Hinges on Political and Economic Reforms." In *Trading Freedom: How Free Trade Affects Our Lives, Work, and Environment.* John Cavanagh, John Gershman, Karen Baker, *et al.,* eds. San Francisco: The Institute for Food and Development Policy. Pp. 50-52.

Broomberg, Jonathan
1994 *Health Care Markets for Export? Lessons for Developing Countries from European and American Experience.* London: London School of Hygiene and Tropical Medicine.

Brown, Phyllida
1997 "The WHO Strikes Mid-life Crisis (50 Years of World Health Organization)." *New Scientist* 153(2064): 12-13.

Browne, Robert S. and Robert J. Cummings
1984 *The Lagos Plan of Action vs. The Berg Report.* Washington, D.C.: Howard University, Center for African Studies.

Brownsville Community Health Center
1992 *Health Care Fact Sheet: Matamoros, Mexico and Brownsville, Texas.* Brownsville, TX: Lower Rio Grande Valley Community Health Care Network.

Bruhn, John G. and Jeffrey Brandon, eds.
1997 *Border Health: Challenges for the United States and Mexico.* New York: Garland Publishing.

Bryant, John H.
1969 *Health and the Developing World.* Ithaca, NY: Cornell University Press.

Bryce, R.
1995 "Gripe on Mexican Labor to Get NAFTA Hearing." *Christian Science Monitor,* April 26.

Bryceson, Deborah F., ed.
1995 *Women Wielding the Hoe: Lessons from Rural Africa for Feminist Theory and Development Practice.* Oxford: Berg Publishers.

Bryceson, Deborah F. and John Howe
1996 "An Agrarian Continent in Transition." In *Africa Now: People, Policies, Institutions.* Stephen Ellis, ed. London: James Currey. Pp. 175-197.

Bucher, J.R., B.A. Schwetz, M.D. Shelby, *et al.*
1987 "Introduction: The Toxicity of Methyl Isocyanate." *Environmental Health Perspectives* 72: 3.

Budd, William
1931 *Typhoid Fever: Its Nature, Mode of Spreading, and Prevention.* New York: George Brady Press.

Bujra, Janet
1988 "Taxing Development: Why Must Women Pay? Gender and the Development Debate in Tanzania." *Review of African Political Economy* 47: 44-63.

Bundy, Colin
1970 *The Rise and Fall of the South African Peasantry.* London: Heinemann.

Burbach, Roger and Patricia Flynn
1984 *The Politics of Intervention.* New York: Monthly Review Press.

Bureau of Justice Statistics
1995a *Drugs and Crime Facts, 1994.* NCJ-154043. Rockville, MD: National Criminal Justice Reference Service.

1995b *Prisoners in 1994*. NCJ-151654. Washington, D.C.: Government Printing Office.

1996 *Compendium of Federal Justice Statistics, 1993* (Executive Summary). NCJ-163171. Washington, D.C.: Government Printing Office.

Burger, Edward J., Mark G. Field, and Judyth L. Twigg

1998 "From Assurance to Insurance in Russian Health Care: The Problematic Transition." *American Journal of Public Health* 88(5): 755-758.

Burke, Melvin

1991 "Bolivia: The Politics of Cocaine." *Current History*, February, pp. 65-90.

Burki, Shahid-Javed, Sri-Ram Aiyer, and Rudolf Hommes, eds.

1998 *Annual World Bank Conference on Development in Latin America and the Caribbean, 1996: Poverty and Inequality: Proceedings of a Conference Held in Bogotá, Colombia*. Washington, D.C.: World Bank.

Burt, Jo-Marie

1996 "Alternative Poverty Programs in Peru." *NACLA Report on the Americas*. May/June: 34-35.

Burt, Jo-Marie and Ricardo Soberon

1993 "'The Only War We've Got': Anti-drug Campaigns in Washington's Latin America Strategy." In *Altered States: A Reader in the New World Order*. Phyllis Bennis and Michel Moushabeck, eds. New York: Olive Branch Press. Pp. 441-454.

Burtless, Gary

1995 "International Trade and the Rise of Income Inequality." *Journal of Economic Literature* 33(2): 800-816.

Burtless, Gary, Robert Z. Lawrence, Robert E. Litan, et al.

1998 *Globaphobia: Confronting Fears About Open Trade*. Washington, D.C.: Brookings Institute.

Buse, Kent and Catherine Gwin

1998 "The World Bank and Global Cooperation in Health: The Case of Bangladesh." *Lancet*, 351(9103): 665-669.

Buvinic, Mayra, Catherine Gwin, and Lisa M. Bates

1996 *Investing in Women: Progress and Prospects for the World Bank*. Washington, D.C.: Overseas Development Council.

Cable, V.

1987 "Tropical Products." In *The Uruguay Round: A Handbook on the Multilateral Trade Negotiations*. J. M. Finger and A. Olechowski, eds. Washington, D.C.: World Bank.

Çagatay, Nilüfer, Diane Elson, and Caren Grown, eds.

1995 "Gender, Adjustment, and Macroeconomics." Special issue of *World Development* 23(11).

Cairncross, S., J.E. Hardoy, and D. Satterthwaite, eds.

1990 *The Poor Die Young: Housing and Health in Third World Cities*. London: Earthscan Publications.

Callaghy, Thomas and John Ravenhill, eds.

1993 *Hemmed In: Responses to Africa's Economic Decline*. New York: Columbia.

Callendar, Thomas

1996 "Long-term Neurotoxicity at Bhopal." *International Perspectives in Public Health* 11: 36-41.

Calva, J.

1992 *La Agricultura Mexicana Frente al Tratado Trilateral de Libre Commercio*, [Chapingo]: Mexico, D.F.: CIESTAAM.

CAME (Consejo Andino de Manejo Ecológico)

1998 "La Situación del Sector Salud, la Cooperación Externa y las Organizaciones No Gubernamentales de Desarrollo." En *El Seminario Taller: La Reforma de Salud y El Rol de Las ONGs*. Lima: Comite Nacional del CAME.

Cameron, J. and R. Mackenzie

1994 *Implementation of Rights in Relation to Industrial Hazards (Evidence)*. London: Permanent Peoples' Tribunal on Industrial and Environmental Hazards and Human Rights.

Campaign for an Effective Crime Policy

1993 *Evaluating Mandatory Minimum Sentences*. October. Washington, D.C.: Campaign for an Effective Crime Policy.

Campbell, Bonnie

1984 "Inside the Miracle: Cotton in Ivory Coast." In *The Politics of Agriculture in Tropical Africa*. Jonathan Barker, ed. Berkeley: Sage Publications. Pp. 143-172.

Campbell, Bonnie and John Loxley

1989 "Introduction." In *Structural Adjustment in Africa*. Bonnie Campbell and John Loxley, eds. Houndmills, UK: Macmillan.

Cárdenas, Cuauhtémoc

1992 "The Continental Development and Trade Initiative." In *Trading Freedom: How Free Trade Affects Our Lives, Work, and Environment*. John Cavanagh, John Gershman, Karen Baker, et al., eds. San Francisco: The Institute for Food and Development Policy. Pp. 95-100.

Carlsen, Laura

1994 "From the Many to the Few: Privatization in Mexico." *Multinational Monitor*, May, 1994, pp. 16-21.

Carriapa, Chip A.

1997 "The Political Origins of Neoliberal Economics." Ph.D. dissertation. University of Texas, Economics Department.

Carrier, James

1997 "Introduction." In *Meanings of the Market: The Free Market in Western Culture*. James G. Carrier, ed. Oxford: Berg. Pp. 1-68.

Carrington, Walter

1981 "African Development Challenges of the 1980s." In *The Role of U.S. Universities in Rural and Agricultural Development*. Brooke G. Schoepf, ed. Tuskegee, AL: Tuskegee Institute, Center for Rural Development. Pp. 17-23.

Carvalho, Soniya and Howard White

1997 *Combining the Quantitative and Qualitative Approaches to Poverty Measurement and Analysis: The Practice and the Potential.* Washington, D.C.: World Bank.

Cassels, Jamie

1993 *The Uncertain Promise of Law: Lessons from Bhopal.* Toronto: University of Toronto Press.

Cassileth, Barry R., Vasily V. Vlassov, and Christopher C. Chapman

1995 "Health Care, Medical Practice, and Medical Ethics in Russia Today." *Journal of the American Medical Association* 273(20): 1569-1573.

Castells, Manuel

1996 *The Rise of the Network Society.* Cambridge, MA: Blackwell Publishers.

Castleman, Barry I.

1979 "The Export of Hazardous Factories to Developing Countries." *International Journal of Health Services* 9: 569-606.

1995 "The Migration of Industrial Hazards." *International Journal of Occupational and Environmental Health* 1(2): 85-96.

Castleman, Barry and Richard Lemen

1998a "Corporate Junk Science: Corporate Influence at International Science Organizations." *Multinational Monitor,* January/February, pp. 28-30.

1998b "The Manipulation of International Scientific Organizations." *International Journal of Occupational and Environmental Health* 4(1): 53-55.

Castleman, Barry I. and Vincente Navarro

1987 "International Mobility of Hazardous Products, Industries, and Wastes." *International Journal of Health Services* 17: 617-633.

Castleman, Barry I. and B.I. Purkavastha

1985 "The Bhopal Disaster as a Case Study in Double Standards." In *The Export of Hazard.* Jane H. Ives, ed. Boston: Routledge and Kegan Paul. Pp. 213-223.

Castro, Fidel

1996 "Speech given April 30, 1996." First Published in *Granma International,* May 15; reprinted in *The Militant* 60(23), June 10.

Caufield, Catherine

1996 *Masters of Illusion: The World Bank and the Poverty of Nations.* New York: Henry Holt.

Cauna, Jacques

1984 "L'État Sanitaire des Esclaves sur une Grande Sucrérie (Habitation Fleuriau de Bellevue 1777-1788)." *Revue de la Société Haitienne d'Histoire et de Géographie* 42(145): 18-78.

Cavanagh, John

1996 *Codes of Conduct on Corporations: What Appears to be Working.* Washington, D.C.: Institute for Policy Studies and the Transnational Institute.

Cavanagh, John, John Gershman, Karen Baker, et al., eds.

1992 *Trading Freedom: How Free Trade Affects Our Lives, Work, and Environment.* San Francisco: The Institute for Food and Development Policy.

Caves, Richard E.

1996 *Multinational Enterprise and Economic Analysis.* Cambridge: Cambridge University Press.

Cayford, S.

1996 "The Ogoni Uprising: Oil, Human Rights, and a Democratic Alternative in Nigeria." *Africa Today* 43(2): 183-197.

Cech, I. and A. Essman

1992 "Water Sanitation Practices on the Texas-Mexico Border: Implications for Physicians on Both Sides." *Southern Medical Journal* 85(11): 1053-1064.

Center for Responsive Politics

1998 "Who Paid for this Election? A Special Report on Fundraising Patterns in the 1998 Elections." Available at www.crp.org/pubs/index.htm.

Centers for Disease Control (CDC)

1992 "Nutritional Needs Survey Among the Elderly—Russia and Armenia, 1992." *Morbidity and Mortality Weekly Report* 41(43): 809-811.

1993 "Health Status of Haitian Migrants—U.S. Naval Base, Guantanamo Bay, Cuba, November 1991-April 1992." *Morbidity and Mortality Weekly Report* 42(7): 138-140.

1994 "Dengue Fever Among U.S. Military Personnel—Haiti, September-November 1994." *Morbidity and Mortality Weekly Report* 43(46): 845-848.

1995 "Diphtheria Epidemic—New Independent States of the Former Soviet Union, 1990-94." *Morbidity and Mortality Weekly Report* 44(10): 177-180.

Cernea, Michael

1988 *Nongovernmental Organizations and Local Development.* Washington, D.C.: World Bank.

CEWG (Community Epidemiology Working Group)

1990 *Epidemiology Trends In Drug Use—Executive Summary.* Division of Epidemiology and Prevention Research, National Institute on Drug Abuse.

1996 *Epidemiology Trends In Drug Use—Executive Summary.* Division of Epidemiology and Prevention Research, National Institute on Drug Abuse.

Chaloupka, Frank J. and Adit Laixuthai

1996 *U.S. Trade Policy and Cigarette Smoking in Asia.* Working Paper 5543. Cambridge, MA: National Bureau of Economic Research.

Chambers, Robert

1983 *Rural Development: Putting the Last First.* London: Longman.

Chambliss, William

1994a "Policing the Ghetto Underclass: The Politics of Law and Law Enforcement." *Social Problems* 41(2): 177-194.

1994b "Why the U.S. Government is not Contributing to the Resolution of the Nation's Drug Problem." *International Journal of Health Services* 24(4): 675-690.

1996 "Another Lost War: The Costs and Consequences of Drug Prohibition." *Social Justice* 22(2): 101-124.

Channock, Martin

1982 "Making Customary Law: Men, Women and Courts in Colonial Northern Rhodesia." In *African Women and the Law: Historical Perspectives.* Jean Hay and Marcia Wright, eds. Boston: Boston University African Studies Program, Papers on Africa VII. Pp. 53-67.

1985 *Law, Custom, and Social Order: The Colonial Experience in Malawi and Zambia.* Cambridge: Cambridge University Press.

Chapman, Malcolm and Peter J. Buckley

1997 "Markets, Transaction Costs, Economists and Social Anthropologists." In *Meanings of the Market: The Free Market in Western Culture.* James G. Carrier, ed. Oxford: Berg. Pp. 225-260.

Chartrand, Harry Hillman

1995 "Intellectual Property in the Global Village." *Government Information in Canada* 1(4): 1-10.

Chasteen, John Charles and Joseph S. Tulchin

1994 *Problems in Modern Latin American History: A Reader.* Wilmington, DE: Scholarly Resources, Inc.

Chatterjee, Pratap

1995 "Enron Blows a Fuse, but India Open for Business." *Multinational Monitor,* July/August, pp. 14-17.

1997 "Conquering Peru: Newmont's Yanacocha Mine Recalls the Days of Pizarro." *Multinational Monitor,* May/June, pp. 44-47.

Cheater, Audrey

1981 "Women and Their Participation in Commercial Agricultural Production: The Case of Medium-Scale Freehold in Zimbabwe." *Development and Change* 12(3): 349-377.

Chelala, César

1994 "Letter from Haiti: Fighting for Survival." *British Medical Journal* 309(6953): 525-526.

Chen, Lincoln C., Friederike Wittgenstein, and Elizabeth McKeon

1996 "The Upsurge of Mortality in Russia: Causes and Policy Implications." *Population and Development Review* 22(3): 517-530.

Chen, T.T.L. and A.E. Winder

1990 "The Opium Wars Revisited as U.S. Forces Tobacco Exports in Asia." *American Journal of Public Health* 80: 659-662.

Chetley, Andrew

1979 *The Baby Killer Scandal: A War on Want Investigation into the Promotion and Sale of Powdered Baby Milks in the Third World.* London: War on Want.

Chinemana, Frances and David Sanders

1993 "Health and Structural Adjustment in Zimbabwe." In *Social Change and Economic Reform in Africa.* Peter

Gibbon, ed. Uppsala: Scandinavian Institute of African Studies.

Chomsky, Noam

1985 *Turning the Tide.* Boston: South End Press.

1992 *Deterring Democracy.* New York: Hill and Wang.

1993 *Year 501: The Conquest Continues.* Boston: South End Press.

1994 "Democracy Enhancement II: The Case of Haiti." *Z Magazine,* July/August, pp. 52-65.

1996a "Forward: Debunking the Corporate Agenda." In *Corporations are Gonna Get Your Mama: Globalization and the Downsizing of the American Dream.* Kevin Danaher, ed. Monroe, ME: Common Courage Press. Pp. 7-14.

1996b *Powers and Prospects: Reflections on Human Nature and the Social Order.* Boston: South End Press.

1998 *Talking About a Revolution.* Boston: South End Press.

Chopra, Sudhir

1994 "Multinational Corporations in the Aftermath of Bhopal: The Need for a New Comprehensive Global Regime for Transnational Corporate Activity." *Valparaiso University Law Review* 29: 235-284.

Chossudovsky, Michel

1996 "The Business of Crime and the Crimes of Business." *Covert Action Quarterly* 58: 27-28.

1997 *The Globalisation of Poverty: Impacts of IMF and World Bank Reforms.* London: Zed Books.

Chouhan, T.R.

1994 *Bhopal: The Inside Story—Carbide Workers Speak Out on the World's Worst Industrial Disaster.* New York: Apex Press.

Chretien, Jean-Pierre

1991a "Les Racines de la Violence Populaire en Afrique." *Politique Africaine* 92: 15-27.

1991b "Presse Libre et Propagande Racist au Rwanda: 'Appelle a la Conscience des Bahutu.'" *Politique Africaine* 92: 109-120.

Chretien, Jean-Pierre, Jean-Francois Dupaquier, Marcel Kabanda, et al.

1995 *Les Medias du Genocide.* Paris: Karthala.

Christiani, D.C., R. Durvasula, and J. Myers

1990 "Occupational Health in Developing Countries: Review of Research Needs." *American Journal of Industrial Medicine* 17: 393-401.

Christie, Nils

1994 *Crime Control as Industry.* New York: Routledge.

Chu, Ke-young and Sanjeev Gupta, eds.

1997 *Social Safety Nets: Issues and Recent Experiences.* Washington, D.C.: International Monetary Fund.

Clark, Thomas, Janet Wirth-Cauchon, and Milly Krakow

1995 *Illicit Drugs in Massachusetts. Findings from Focus Groups with Methadone Clients and Outreach Workers 1994-95.* Boston: Massachusetts Department of Public Health.

Clarke, Tony

1996a *The Emergence of Corporate Rule and What to Do About It: A Set of Working Instruments for Social*

Movements. San Francisco: International Forum on Globalization.

1996b "Mechanisms of Corporate Rule." In *The Case Against the Global Economy*. Jerry Mander and Edward Goldsmith, eds. San Francisco: Sierra Club Books. Pp. 297-308.

Clarke, Tony and Maude Barlow

1997 *MAI: The Multilateral Agreement on Investment and the Threat to Canadian Sovereignty*. Toronto: Stoddart.

Cleaver, Kevin M. and Gotz A. Schreiber

1994 *Reversing the Spiral: The Population, Agriculture, and Environment Nexus in Sub-Saharan Africa*. Washington, D.C.: World Bank.

Clement, Jean A.P. with Johannes Mueller, Stephanie Cosse, and Jean Le Dem

1996 *Aftermath of the CFA Franc Devaluation*. Washington, D.C.: International Monetary Fund.

Clifford, Mark. L., Michael Shari, and Linda Himelstein

1996 "Pangs of Conscience: Sweatshops Haunt U.S. Consumers." *Business Week*, July 29, pp. 46-47.

Clifford, Patrick

1992 "Drug Use, Drug Prevention and Minority Communities." *Journal of Primary Prevention* 12(4): 303-317.

Cline, William, ed.

1983 *Trade Policy in the 1980s*. Washington, D.C.: Institute for International Economics.

Coalition of Peruvian NGOs

1997 "Ley General de Salud y el Derecho a la Salud—A las Autoridades del Gobierno Central y a la Opinión Pública." *El Comercio*, November 2.

Cockburn, Alexander and Jeffrey St. Clair

1998 *Whiteout: The CIA, Drugs, and the Press*. London: Verson.

Cockburn, Leslie

1987 *Out of Control*. New York: Atlantic Monthly Press.

Cohen, Craig R., Francis A. Plummer, Maclean Mugo, et al.

1999 "Increased Interleukin-10 in the Endocervical Secretions of Women with Non-ulcerative Sexually Transmitted Diseases: A Mechanism for Enhanced HIV-1 Transmission?" *AIDS* 13(3): 327-332.

Cohen, Gary and Satinath Sarangi

1995 "DuPont: Spinning its Wheels in India." *Multinational Monitor*, March, pp. 23-26.

Cohen, Jeff and Norman Solomon

1995 *Through the Media Looking Glass*. Monroe, ME: Common Courage Press.

Cohen, Jon

1996 "A Shot in the Dark: Thailand to Begin Testing AIDS Vaccines." *Discover* 17(6): 66-73.

Cohen, Joshua and Joel Rogers

1983 *On Democracy*. New York: Penguin.

Cohen, Michael

1974 *Urban Policy and Political Conflict in Africa: A Study of the Ivory Coast*. Chicago: University of Chicago Press.

Collins, Charles

1989 "Decentralization and the Need for Political and Critical Analysis." *Health Policy and Planning* 4(2): 168-171.

Collins, Charles and Andrew Green

1994 "Decentralization and Primary Health Care: Some Negative Implications in Developing Countries." *International Journal of Health Services* 24(3): 459-475.

Collins, Chuck

1995 "Aid to Dependent Corporations: Exposing Federal Handouts to the Wealthy." In *Real World Macro: Twelfth Edition*. Randy Albelda, Marc Breslow, John Miller, et al., eds. Somerville, MA: Dollars and Sense. Pp. 66-68.

Comaroff, Jean

1993 "The Diseased Heart of Africa: Medicine, Colonialism and the Black Body." In *Knowledge, Power and Practice: The Anthropology of Knowledge and Everyday Life*. Shirley Lindenbaum and Margaret Lock, eds. Berkeley: University of California Press. Pp. 305-329.

Commission on Health Research for Development

1990 *Health Research: Essential Link to Equity in Development*. New York: Oxford University Press.

Conaghan, Catherine M. and James M. Malloy

1994 *Unsettling Statecraft: Democracy and Neoliberalism in the Central Andes*. Pittsburgh, PA: University of Pittsburgh Press.

Condelli, W. and R. Hubbard

1994 "Relationship between Time Spent in Treatment and Client Outcomes from Therapeutic Communities." *Journal of Substance Abuse Treatment* 11: 25-33.

Congreso de la Republica

1997 "Ley General de Salud, No. 26842." *El Peruano*, July 20, pp. 151245-151252.

Connolly, Greg

1989 "The International Marketing of Tobacco." In *Tobacco Use in America Conference*. Houston, Texas: American Medical Association. Pp. 49-66.

1992 "Worldwide Expansion of Transnational Tobacco Industry." *Journal of the National Cancer Institute* 12: 29-35.

Connors, Margaret M.

1992 "Risk Perception, Risk Taking and Risk Management Among Intravenous Drug Users: Implications for AIDS Prevention." *Social Science and Medicine* 34(6): 592-601.

1994 "Stories of Pain and the Problem of AIDS Prevention: Injection Drug Withdrawal and Its Effect on Risk Behavior." *Medical Anthropological Quarterly* 8(1): 47-68.

— "Bridging the Gap Between the Street and Drug Recovery: A Rationale and Model to Limit Drug Addiction and HIV Transmission." N.p., n.d.

Conway, Patrick

1994 "IMF Lending Programs: Participation and Impact." *Journal of Development Economics* 45(2): 365-391.

Cooper, Fredrick

1993 "Africa and the World Economy." In *Confronting Historical Paradigms: Peasants, Labor, and the Capitalist World System in Africa and Latin America.* Fredrick Cooper, Allen F. Isaacman, Florencia E. Mallon, *et al.* Madison: University of Wisconsin Press. Pp. 84-201.

1996 *Decolonization and African Society: The Labor Question in French and British Africa.* Cambridge: Cambridge University Press.

Coote, Belinda

1995 *NAFTA: Poverty and Free Trade in Mexico.* Oxford: Oxfam Publications.

Coote, Belinda and Caroline Lequesne

1996 *The Trade Trap: Poverty and the Global Commodity Markets.* Oxford: Oxfam.

Coquery-Vidrovitch, Catherine

1972 *Le Congo au Temps des Grandes Compagnies Concessionaires, 1898-1930.* Paris: Mouton.

Corbridge, Stuart, Nigel Thrift, and Ron Martin, eds.

1994 *Money, Power, and Space.* Oxford: Blackwell.

Cordell, Dennis D. and Joel W. Gregory, eds.

1987 *African Population and Capitalism: Historical Perspectives.* Boulder, CO: Westview Press.

Cordes, D.H., D.F. Rea, I. Schwartz, *et al.*

1989 "Mexico Maquiladoras and Occupational Medicine Training." *Asian Pacific Journal of Public Health* 3: 61-67.

Cornia, Giovanni Andrea, Richard Jolly, and Frances Stewart, eds.

1987 *Adjustment with a Human Face: Protecting the Vulnerable and Promoting Growth.* 2 vols. Oxford: Clarendon Press.

Cornu, A., J.P. Massamba, P. Traissac, *et al.*

1995 "Nutritional Change and Economic Crisis in an Urban Congolese Community." *International Journal of Epidemiology* 24(1): 155-164.

Costello, Anthony, Fiona Watson, and David Woodward

1994 *Human Face or Human Façade? Adjustment and the Health of Mothers and Children.* London: Centre for International Child Health, University of London.

Costner, Pat

1995 "Remediation of Union Carbide Site, Bhopal." Greenpeace Letter to Satinath Sarangi. Eureka Springs, AK: Greenpeace.

Council on Ethical and Judicial Affairs

1990 "Black-White Disparities in Health Care." *Journal of the American Medical Association* 263(17): 2344-2346.

Council on Scientific Affairs

1990 "The Worldwide Smoking Epidemic." *Journal of the American Medical Association* 263(24): 3312-3318.

Courtwright, David, Joseph Herman, and Don DesJarlais

1989 *Addicts Who Survived: An Oral History of Narcotic Use in America 1923-1965.* Knoxville: University of Tennessee Press.

Cowan, Laing Gray

1990 *Privatization in the Developing World.* Contributions in Economics and Economic History No. 212. London: Greenwood Press.

Cowen, Michael

1981 "Commodity Production in Kenya's Central Province." In *Rural Development in Tropical Africa.* Judith Heyer, Penelope Roberts, and Gavin Williams, eds. New York: St. Martin's Press. Pp. 121-142.

Creese, Andrew L.

1991 "User Charges for Health Care: A Review of Recent Experience." *Health Policy and Planning* 6(4): 309-319.

Critsner, Greg

1996 "Oh, How Happy We Will Be: Pills, Paradise, and the Profits of Drug Companies." *Harper's*, June, 1996, pp. 39-48.

Cuánto, S.A

1991 *Peru en Numeros.* Lima: Cuánto, S.A.

1997 *Peru en Numeros.* Lima: Cuánto, S.A.

1998 *Peru en Numeros.* Lima: Cuánto, S.A.

Cuba Neuropathy Field Investigation Team

1994a "Cuban Epidemic Neuropathy: An Update." *PAHO Epidemiological Bulletin* 15(3): 7.

1994b "Epidemic Neuropathy—Cuba, 1991-1994." *Journal of the American Medical Association* 271(15): 1154-1156.

1995 "Epidemic Optic Neuropathy in Cuba—Clinical Characterization and Risk Factors." *New England Journal of Medicine* 333(18): 1176-1182.

Cullen, Mark R., Martin G. Cherniak, and Linda Rosenstock

1990 "Occupational Medicine." *New England Journal of Medicine* 322(9): 594-601, 675-683.

Cullinan, P., S.D. Acquilla, and V. Ramana Dhara

1996 "Long-term Morbidity in Survivors of the 1984 Bhopal Gas Leak." *National Medical Journal of India* 9(1): 5-10.

1997 "Respiratory Morbidity 10 Years after the Union Carbide Leak at Bhopal: A Cross Sectional Survey." *British Medical Journal* 314(7077): 338-342.

Curtin, Philip D.

1968 "Epidemiology and the Slave Trade." *Political Science Quarterly* LXXXIII: 190-216.

1969 *The Atlantic Slave Trade: A Census.* Madison: University of Wisconsin Press.

Curtis, Emma

1998 "Child Health and the International Monetary Fund: The Nicaraguan Experience." *Lancet* 352(9140): 1622-1624.

Daedalus

1994 "Health and Wealth." Vol. 123, No. 4.

Daly, Herman

1987 "The Economic Growth Debate: What Some Economists Have Learned But Many Have Not." *Journal of Environmental Economics and Management* 14: 323-336.

Daly, Herman E. and John B. Cobb Jr.

1989 *For the Common Good: Redirecting the Economy Toward Community, the Environment, and a Sustainable Future.* Boston: Beacon Press.

Daly, Herman and Robert Goodland

1993 "An Ecological-Economic Assessment of Deregulation of International Commerce Under GATT." Washington, D.C.: World Bank Environment Department.

Danaher, Kevin

1996 "Introduction: Corporate Power and the Quality of Life." In *Corporations are Gonna Get Your Mama: Globalization and the Downsizing of the American Dream.* Kevin Danaher, ed. Monroe, ME: Common Courage Press. Pp. 15-31.

Danaher, Kevin, ed.

1994 *Fifty Years is Enough: The Case Against the World Bank.* Boston: South End Press.

Daniel, Philip, Reginald H. Green, and Michael Lipton

1985 "A Strategy for the Rural Poor." *Journal of Development Studies* 16: 113-136.

Danielson, Ross

1979 *Cuban Medicine.* New Brunswick, NJ: Transaction Books.

Danziger, Sheldon and Peter Gottschalk

1995 *America Unequal.* Cambridge, MA: Harvard University Press.

Danzon, Patricia M.

1997 *Pharmaceutical Price Regulation: National Policies versus Global Interests.* Washington, D.C.: American Enterprise Institute Press.

Davidson, Basil

1974 *Can Africa Survive? Arguments Against Growth Without Development.* Boston: Little, Brown, and Co.

Davies, Ioan

1966 *African Trade Unions.* Harmondsworth, UK: Penguin Books.

Davies, Susanna

1996 *Adaptable Livelihoods: Coping With Food Security in the Mahalian Sahel.* New York: St. Martin's Press.

Davis, C.

1993 "Russia's Health Reform: A Complicated Operation." *Transition* 4(7).

Davis, C. and Murray Feshbach

1980 *Rising Infant Mortality in the USSR in the 1970s.* Washington, D.C.: United States Department of Commerce.

Davison, Jean, ed.

1988 *Agriculture, Women and Land: The African Experience.* Boulder, CO: Westview Press.

Dawson, Marc

1987a "The Social History of Africa in the Future: Medical-Related Issues." *African Studies Review* 30(2): 83-91.

1987b "Health, Nutrition and Population in Central Kenya, 1890-1945." In *African Population and Capitalism: Historical Perspectives.* Dennis D. Cordell and Joel W. Gregory, eds. Boulder, CO: Westview Press. Pp. 201-217.

de Bruyn, Maria, Helen Jackson, Marianne Wijermars, et al.

1995 *Facing the Challenges of HIV/AIDS/STDs: A Gender-Based Response.* Geneva: World Health Organization, Global Program on AIDS.

De Ferranti, David

1985 *Paying for Health Services in Developing Countries: An Overview.* World Bank Staff Working Paper #721. Washington, D.C.: World Bank.

de Haan, Arjan and Simon Maxwell, eds.

1998 "Poverty and Social Exclusion in North and South." *IDS Bulletin* 29(1): 1-9.

de Lame, Danielle

1997 *Une Colline entre Mille.* Brussels: Musee Tervuren.

De Medina, M., M.A. Fletcher, M.D. Valledor, et al.

1987 "Serological Evidence for HIV Infection in Cuban Immigrants in 1980." *Lancet* 2(8551): 166.

De Swan, A.

1988 *In the Care of the State.* Oxford: Polity Press.

Debt Crisis Network

1986 *From Debt to Development.* Washington, D.C.: Debt Crisis Network.

Dédy, Seri and Gozé Tapé

1995 *Famille et Education en Cote d'Ivoire: Une Approche Socio-Anthropologique.* Abidjan: Edition des Lagunes.

Deere, Carmen

1984 "Agrarian Reform as Revolution and Counter-Revolution: Nicaragua and El Salvador." In *The Politics of Intervention: The United States in Central America.* Roger Burbach and Patricia Flynn, eds. New York: Monthly Review Press. Pp. 163-188.

DeLeon, G.

1993 "What Psychologists Can Learn from Addiction Treatment Research." *Psychology of Addictive Behaviors* 7: 103-109.

Dembo, David, Ward Morehouse, and Lucinda Wykle

1990 *Abuse of Power: Social Performance of Multinational Corporations—The Case of Union Carbide.* New York: New Horizons Press.

Des Forges, Alison, ed.

1999 *Leave None to Tell the Story.* New York: Human Rights Watch.

Desjarlais, Robert, Leon Eisenberg, Byron Good, et al., eds.

1995 *World Mental Health: Problems and Priorities in Low-Income Countries.* New York: Oxford University Press.

Deuschle, Kurt W.

1967 "Tuberculosis." In *Preventive Medicine*. Duncan W. Clark and Brian MacMahon, eds. Boston: Little, Brown, and Co. Pp. 509-524.

Devlin, Robert

1989 *Debt and Crisis in Latin America. The Supply Side of the Story*. Princeton, NJ: Princeton University Press.

DeWalt, Billie R.

1994 "The Agrarian Basis of Conflict in Central America." Reprinted in *Applying Cultural Anthropology: An Introductory Reader*. 2nd Edition. Aaron Podeolefsky and Peter J. Brown, eds. Mountain View, CA: Mayfield Publishing. Pp. 117-122.

DeWind, Josh and David Kinley

1988 *Aide a la Migration: l'Impact de l'Assistance Internationale a Haiti*. Montreal: CIDIHCA.

Deyo, Frederic C.

1987 *The Political Economy of the New Asian Industrialism*. Ithaca, NY: Cornell University Press.

1989 *Beneath the Miracle: Labor Subordination in the New Asian Industrialism*. Berkeley: University of California Press.

Dhara, V. Ramana

1993 "The Bhopal Gas Disaster: It's Not Too Late for Sound Epidemiology." *Archives of Environmental Health* 48(6): 436-437.

Díaz-Briquets, Sergio

1983 *The Health Revolution in Cuba*. Austin, TX: University of Texas Press.

Díaz-Briquets, Sergio and Lisandro Pérez

1981 "Cuba: The Demography of Revolution." *Population Bulletin* 36(1): 5-6.

Diebel, Lisa

1997 "Clinging to Life: Peru's 3 Million Cliff Dwellers Struggle on the Dark Side of the Economic 'Miracle.'" *Toronto Star*, November 23.

Diederich, Bernard

1985 "Swine Fever Ironies: The Slaughter of the Haitian Black Pig." *Caribbean Review* 14(1): 16-17, 41.

Dockery, Douglas W., C. Arden Pope III, Xiping Xu, et al.

1993 "An Association Between Air Pollution and Mortality in Six U.S. Cities." *New England Journal of Medicine* 329(24): 1753- 1759.

Dolk, H., M. Vrijheid, B. Armstrong, et al.

1998 "Risk of Congenital Anomalies Near Hazardous-Waste Landfill Sites in Europe: The EUROHAZCON Study." *Lancet* 352(9126): 423-427.

Doremus, Paul N., William M. Keller, Louis W. Pauly, et al.

1998 *The Myth of the Global Corporation*. Princeton, NJ: Princeton University Press.

Downs, Robert E. and Steven P. Reyna, eds.

1988 *Land and Society in Contemporary Africa*. Durham, NH: University Press of New England.

Driscoll, David D.

1998 "What is the International Monetary Fund?" External Relations Department. Washington, D.C.: International Monetary Fund. Available at www.imf.org/external/pubs/ft/exrp/what.htm#1.

Dufour, Jean-Paul and Corinne Denis

1988 "The North's Garbage Goes South: The Third World Fears It Will Become the Global Dump." *World Press Review* 35(3): 30.

Dugger, William M.

1998 "Against Inequality," *Journal of Economic Issues* 32(2): 287-303.

Dumont, Matthew P.

1992 "Privatization of Mental Health Services: The Invisible Hand at Our Throats." *American Journal of Orthopsychiatry* 62:3, 328-329.

Dunning, J.H.

1993 *Multinational Enterprises and the Global Economy*. Wokingham, England: Addison-Wesley Publishing Company.

Dupuy, Alex

1996 *Haiti in the New World Order: The Limits of the Democratic Revolution*. Boulder, CO: Westview Press.

Dwyer, Daisy and Judith Bruce, eds.

1988 *A Home Divided: Women and Income in the Third World*. Stanford, CA: Stanford University Press.

Eberstadt, Nicholas A.

1994 "Demographic Disaster." *The National Interest*. Summer, p. 53.

ECA (Economic Commission for Africa)

1989 *The African Alternative Framework to Structural Adjustment Programmes for Socio-Economic Recovery and Transformation (AAF-SAP)*. Addis Ababa: Economic Commission for Africa.

Eckerman, Ingrid

1996 "The Health Situation of Women and Children in Bhopal." *International Perspectives in Public Health* 11: 29-36.

Eckholm, Erik

1994 "A Town Loses Its Hospital, In the Name of Cost Control." *New York Times*. 26 September, A1.

Eckstein, Susan

1994 *Back from the Future: Cuba Under Castro*. Princeton, NJ: Princeton University Press.

ECLAC (Economic Commission for Latin America and the Caribbean)

1997 *La Brecha de la Equidad. Latin America, the Caribbean, and the Social Summit*. Santiago: U.N. Economic Commission on Latin America.

Economic Commission for Europe

1995 *Economic Survey of Europe in 1994-95*. New York: United Nations.

Edwards, Beatrice and Gretta Tovar Siebentritt

1991 *Places of Origin: The Repopulation of Rural El Salvador*. Boulder, CO: Lynne Rienner Publishers.

Edwards, Sebastian

1989 *The IMF and Developing Countries: A Critical Analysis.* Carnegie-Rochester Conference Series on Public Policy, No. 31. Washington, D.C.: Holland.

Eicher, Carl K.

1986 "Facing Up to Africa's Food Crisis" In *Hemmed In: Responses to Africa's Economic Decline.* Thomas Callaghy and John Ravenhill, eds. New York: Columbia. Pp. 149-180.

Eichstaedt, Peter H.

1994 *If You Poison Us: Uranium and Native Americans.* Santa Fe: Red Crane Books.

EIU (Economist Intelligence Unit)

1990 *Country Report, Rwanda.* London: The Economist.

1998a *Country Profile, Haiti.* 2nd quarter. London: The Economist.

1998b *Country Report, Mexico.* 4th quarter. London: The Economist.

El Sebae, A.H.

1993 "Special Problems Experienced with Pesticide Use in Developing Countries." *Regulatory Toxicology and Pharmacology* 17: 287-291.

Elkington, John

1998 *Cannibals with Forks: The Triple Bottom Line of 21st Century Business.* Gabriola Island, BC: New Society Publishers.

Ellman, Michael

1994 "The Increase in Death and Disease Under 'Katastroika.'" *Cambridge Journal of Economics* 18: 329-355.

Engberg-Pedersen, Poul, Peter Gibbon, Phil Raikes, et al., eds.

1996 *Limits of Adjustment in Africa.* Copenhagen: Centre for Development Research (in association with Oxford: James Curry and Portsmouth, N.H.: Heinemann).

Engels, Friedrich

1986 *The Origin of the Family, Private Property, and the State.* London: Penguin Books. [1884.]

Enthoven, Alain C.

1988 *Theory and Practice of Managed Competition in Health Care Finance.* New York: Elsevier Science Publishing Company.

Epping, Randy Charles

1995 *A Beginner's Guide to the World Economy: Seventy-Seven Basic Economic Concepts that Will Change the Way You See the World.* New York: Vintage Books.

Epprecht, Marc

1994 "The World Bank, Health, and Africa." *Z Magazine,* November, pp. 31-38.

Escobar, Arturo

1995 *Encountering Development: The Making and Unmaking of the Third World.* Princeton, NJ: Princeton University Press.

Eskenazi, B., S. Guendelman, and E.P. Elkin

1993 "A Preliminary Study of Reproductive Outcomes of Female *Maquiladora* Workers in Tijuana, Mexico." *American Journal of Industrial Medicine* 24: 667-676.

Espinosa, J. Enrique and Pedro Noyola

1997 "Emerging Patterns in Mexico-U.S. Trade." In *Coming Together? Mexico-United States Relations.* Barry Bosworth, Susan Collins, and Nora Claudia Lustig, eds. Washington, D.C.: Brookings Institute Press. Pp. 25-58.

Espinosa-Torres, Felipe, Mauricio Hernández-Avila, and Lizbeth López-Carrillo

1992 "El TLC: Un Reto y Una Oportunidad para La Salud Ambiental. El Caso de Las Maquiladoras." *Salud Pública de México* 36(6): 597-616.

Estes, Ralph W.

1996 *Tyranny of the Bottom Line: Why Corporations Make Good People Do Bad Things.* San Francisco: Berrett-Koehler Publishers.

Esteva, Gustavo

1992 "Development." In *The Development Dictionary.* Wolfgang Sachs, ed. London: Zed Books. Pp. 6-25.

Evans, Imogen

1995 "SAPping Maternal Health." *Lancet* 346(8982): 1046.

Everest, Larry

1994 "The Selling of Peru." *Z Magazine,* September, pp. 32-36.

Executive Office of the President

1997 *Study on the Operation and Effects of the North American Free Trade Agreement.* Washington, D.C.

Fagin, Dan, Marianne Lavelle, and the Center for Public Integrity

1996 *Toxic Deception: How the Chemical Industry Manipulates Science, Bends the Law, and Endangers Your Health.* Secaucus, NJ: Carol Publishing Group.

Falco, Mathea

1992 "Foreign Drugs, Foreign Wars." *Daedalus* 121(3): 1-14.

Fapohunda, Eleanor R.

1988 "The Non-Pooling Household: A Challenge to Theory." In *A Home Divided: Women and Income in the Third World.* Daisy Dwyer and Judith Bruce, eds. Stanford, CA: Stanford University Press. Pp. 143-154.

Farmer, Paul Edward

1988 "Blood, Sweat, and Baseballs: Haiti in the West Atlantic System." *Dialectical Anthropology* 13: 83-99.

1992 *AIDS and Accusation: Haiti and the Geography of Blame.* Berkeley: University of California Press.

1994 *The Uses of Haiti.* Monroe, ME: Common Courage Press.

1995 "Culture, Poverty, and the Dynamics of HIV Transmission in Rural Haiti." In *Culture and Sexual Risk: Anthropological Perspectives on AIDS.* Han ten Brummelhuis and Gilbert Herdt, eds. New York: Gordan and Breach. Pp. 3-28.

1999a *Infections and Inequalities: The Modern Plagues.* Berkeley: University of California Press.

1999b "Managerial Successes, Clinical Failures." *International Journal of Tuberculosis and Lung Disease* 3(5): 1-3.

Farmer, Paul Edward, Jaime Bayona, Mercedes Becerra, et al.
1998 "The Dilemma of MDRTB in the Global Era." *International Journal of Tuberculosis and Lung Disease* 2(11): 869-876.

Farmer, Paul Edward, Margaret Connors, and Janie Simmons, eds.
1996 *Women, Poverty and AIDS: Sex, Drugs, and Structural Violence*. Monroe, ME: Common Courage Press.

Farmer, Paul Edward and Fiona M. Graeme-Cook
1999 "Case Records of the Massachusetts General Hospital. Weekly Clinicopathological Exercises: Case 8-1999: A 28-Year-Old Man with Gram-Negative Sepsis of Uncertain Cause." *New England Journal of Medicine* 340(11): 869-976.

Farmer, Paul Edward and Jim Yong Kim
1998 "Community-Based Approaches to the Control of Multidrug-Resistant Tuberculosis: Introducing 'DOTS-Plus.'" *British Medical Journal* 371: 671-674.

Farmer, Paul Edward, Simon Robin, St. Luc Ramilus, et al.
1991 "Tuberculosis, Poverty, and 'Compliance': Lessons from Rural Haiti." *Seminars in Respiratory Infections* 6(4): 254-260.

Feeley, M.
1991 "The Privatization of Prisons in Historical Perspective." *Criminal Justice Research Bulletin* 6(2): 1-10.

Feierman, Steven
1985 "Struggles for Control: Health and Healing in Modern Africa." *African Studies Review* 28(2-3): 73-147.

Feierman, Steven and John M. Janzen, eds.
1992 *The Social Basis of Health and Healing in Africa*. Berkeley: University of California Press.

Feilden, Rachel, James Allman, Joel Montague, et al.
1981 *Health, Population and Nutrition in Haiti: A Report Prepared for the World Bank*. Boston: Management Sciences for Health.

Fein, O.
1995 "The Influence of Social Class on Health Status: Americans and British Research on Health Inequalities." *Journal of General Internal Medicine* 10(10): 577-586.

Feinsilver, Julie
1993 *Healing the Masses: Cuban Health Politics at Home and Abroad*. Berkeley: University of California Press.

Feldman, R.A. and M.S. Kumar
1994 *Emerging Equity Markets: Growth Benefits and Policy Concerns*. IMF paper on Policy Analysis and Assessment. Washington, D.C.: International Monetary Fund.

Ferguson, Thomas and Joel Rogers
1986 *Right Turn*. New York: Hill and Wang.

Fernández-Kelly, María Patricia
1983 *For We Are Sold, I and My People: Women and Industry in Mexico's Frontier*. Albany: State University of New York Press.

Ferreira, Francisco H.G.
1997 *Economic Transition and the Distributions of Income and Wealth*. Policy Research Working Paper #1808. Washington, D.C.: World Bank.

Ferriol Muruaga, Angela
1995 "Situación Social en el Ajuste Económico." Paper given at Instituto Nacional de Investigaciones Económicas, February.

Feshbach, Murray
1993 "Continuing Negative Health Trends in the Former USSR." In *The Former Soviet Union in Transition*. Vol. 2. Washington, D.C.: JEC U.S. Congress.
1995a *Environmental and Health Atlas of Russia*. Washington, D.C.: PAIMS.
1995b *Ecological Disaster: Cleaning Up the Hidden Legacy of the Soviet Regime*. New York: Twentieth Century Fund Press.
1999 "Dead Souls." *Atlantic Monthly*, January, pp. 26-27.

Feshbach, Murray and Alfred Friendly
1992 *Ecocide in the USSR: Health and Nature Under Siege*. New York: Basic Books.

Fetter, Bruce, ed.
1990 *Demography from Scanty Evidence: Central Africa in the Colonial Era*. Boulder, CO: Lynne Rienner.

Feucht, T.E.
1993 "Prostitutes on Crack Cocaine: Addiction, Utility, and Marketplace Economics." *Deviant Behavior* 14: 91-108.

Fiedler, John
1987 "Recurrent Cost and Public Health-Care Delivery: The Other War in El Salvador." *Social Science and Medicine* 25(8): 867-874.

Fiedler, John, Luis Carlos Gomez, and William Bertrand
1993 *An Overview of the Health Sector of El Salvador: Background Paper of the Proposed Health Sector Assessment*. USAID and Clapp and Mayne.

Field, Mark G.
1986 "Soviet Infant Mortality: A Mystery Story." In *Advances in International Maternal and Child Health*. Vol. 6. D.B. Jelliffe and E.F.P. Jelliffe, eds. Oxford: Clarendon Press. Pp. 25-65.
1995 "The Health Crisis in the Former Soviet Union: A Report from the 'Post-War' Zone." *Social Science and Medicine* 41(11): 1469-1478.

Fieldhouse, David Kenneth
1978 *Unilever Overseas: The Anatomy of a Multinational*. Stanford, CA: Hoover Institution.

Filipov, David
1998 "Tuberculosis Finds Fertile Breeding Grounds in Russian Prisons." *Boston Globe*, November 1.

Filmer, Deon, Jeffrey Hammer, and Lant Pritchett
1997 *Health Policy in Poor Countries: Weak Links in the Chain*. Poverty Research Working Paper #1878. Washington, D.C.: World Bank.

Filmer, Deon and Lant Pritchett

1997 *Child Mortality and Public Spending on Health: How Much Does Money Matter?* Washington, D.C.: World Bank.

First, Ruth

1970 *Power in Africa.* New York: Pantheon.

1982 *Studies in Black and Gold: The Mozambiquan Miner from Peasant to Proletarian.* Sussex, U.K.: Harvester Books.

Fishman, Ted C.

1997 "The Joys of Global Investment: Shipping Home the Fruits of Misery." *Harper's,* February, pp. 35-42.

Fitzgerald E.F., S.A. Hwang, B. Bush, et al.

1998 "Fish Consumption and Breast Milk PCB Concentrations Among Mohawk Women at Akwesasne." *American Journal of Epidemiology* 148(2): 164-172.

Fleck, Susan and Constance Sorrentino

1994 "Employment and Unemployment in Mexico's Labor Force." *Monthly Labor Review* 17(11): 3-29.

Fleming, S.T. and K.E. Boles

1994 "Financial and Clinical Performance: Bridging the Gap." *Health Care Management Review* 19: 11-17.

Fleuret, Patrick

1990 "Food, Farmers, and Organizations in Africa." In *African Food Systems in Crisis, Vol. 2: Coping with Change.* Rebecca Huss-Ahsmore and Solomon H. Katz, eds. New York: Gordon and Breach. Pp. 269-287.

Flynn, Patricia

1984 "The United States at War in Central America: Unable to Win, Unwilling to Lose." In *The Politics of Intervention: The United States in Central America.* R. Burbach and P. Flynn, eds. New York: Monthly Review Press.

Folbre, Nancy and The Center for Popular Economics

1995 *The New Field Guide to the U.S. Economy: A Compact and Irreverent Guide to Economic Life in America.* New York: New Press.

Fontanarosa, Phil B.

1995 "Diphtheria in Russia: A Reminder of Risk." *Journal of the American Medical Association* 273(16): 1245.

Ford, John

1971 *The Role of Trypanosomiases in African Ecology: A Study of the Tsetse Fly Problem.* Oxford: Oxford University Press.

Forget, G.

1991 "Pesticides and the Third World." *Journal of Toxicology and Environmental Health* 32: 11-31.

Foubert, Bernard

1990 *Les Habitations Laborde á Saint-Domingue dans la Seconde Moitié du XVIIIè Siècle Contribution à l'Histoire d'Haiti.* Doctoral thesis: Université de Paris IV, Sorbonne.

Fox, Jonathan and Josefina Aranda

1996 *Decentralization and Rural Development in Mexico: Community Participation in Oaxaca's Municipal Funds Program.* San Diego: University of California-San Diego, Center for U.S.-Mexican Studies.

Franchetti, M.

1997 "Thousands of Russians Die in TB Gulag." *Sunday Times,* September 28.

Frank, Andre Gunder

1997 "The Cold War and Me." *Bulletin of Concerned Asian Scholars* 29(3): 79-84.

Franke, Richard W. and Barbara H. Chasin

1980 *Seeds of Famine.* Totowa, NJ: Rowman and Alanheld.

1994 *Kerala: Radical Reform as Development in an Indian State.* Oakland, CA: Institute for Food and Development Policy.

Freeman H.E., R.J. Blendon, L.H. Aiken, et al.

1987 "Americans Report on their Access to Health Care." *Health Affairs* (Millwood) 6(1): 6-8.

Freund, Bill

1984 *The Making of Contemporary Africa: The Development of African Society Since 1800.* Bloomington: Indiana University Press.

Freysinger, Robert

1991 "U.S. Military and Economic Intervention in an International Context of Low-Intensity Conflict." *Political Studies* 39: 321-334.

Friedman, A.

1995 *Crime and Punishment in America.* New York: McGraw-Hill.

Friedman, Milton

1962 *Capitalism and Freedom.* Chicago: University of Chicago Press.

Friedman, Samuel R., Bruce Stepherson, Joyce Woods, et al.

1992 "Society, Drug Injectors, and AIDS." *Journal of Health Care for the Poor and Underserved* 3(1): 73-92.

Frumkin, Howard, Mauricio Hernández-Avila, and Felipe Espinosa Torres

1995 "*Maquiladoras*: A Case Study of Free Trade Zones." *Occupational and Environmental Health* 1(2): 96-109.

FRUS (Foreign Relations of the United States 1958-1960)

1991 Washington, D.C.: Government Printing Office, VI.

Fullilove, Mindy, T.E.A. Lown, and Robert E. Fullilove

1992 "Crack 'Hos and Skeezers: Traumatic Experiences of Women Crack Users." *Journal of Sex Research* 29(2): 275-87.

Gaillard, Eduardo

1983 *Le Guerilla de Batraville.* Port-au-Prince: Imprimerie Le Natal.

Galbraith, John Kenneth

1977 *The Age of Uncertainty.* Boston: Houghton Mifflin.

Galhardi, Regina M.A.A.

1998 *Maquiladoras: Prospects of Regional Integration and Globalization.* Geneva: International Labor Organization.

Available at www.ilo.org/public/english/60empfor/publ/etp12.htm.

Galtung, Johan

1969 "Violence, Peace, and Peace Research." *Journal of Peace Research* 6(3): 167-191.

Gamble, L.R., G. Jackson, and T.C. Maurer

1988 *Organochlorine, Trace Element, and Petroleum Hydrocarbon Contaminants Investigation of the Lower Rio Grande Valley*. U.S. Fish and Wildlife Service, Ecological Services, Texas.

Gamero, Julio

1996 "La Política Social Selectiva: Una Nueva Forma de Articulación Estado-Sociedad." In *Cuestión de Estado* 19 (October/December).

Gann, Lewis H.

1963 *A History of Northern Rhodesia: Early Days to 1953*. London: Chatto and Windus.

GAO (General Accounting Office)

1990 *Trade and Health Issues: The Dichotomy Between U.S. Tobacco Export Policy and Antismoking Initiatives*. May. Washington, D.C.: GAO.

1992a *El Salvador: Role of Nongovernment Organizations in Postwar Reconstruction*. GAO/NSAIAD-93-20BR. Washington, D.C.: U.S. General Accounting Office.

1992b *International Trade: Advertising and Promoting U.S. Cigarettes in Selected Asian Countries*. December. Washington, D.C.: GAO.

1993 *Self-Sufficiency: Opportunities and Disincentives on the Road to Economic Independence*. HRD-93-23. Washington, D.C.: U.S. General Accounting Office.

1994 *Money Laundering: U.S. Efforts to Fight It Are Threatened by Currency Smuggling*. GAO/GGD-94-73. Washington, D.C.: U.S. General Accounting Office.

1995a *Money Laundering: Needed Improvements for Reporting Suspicious Transactions Are Planned*. GAO/GGD-95-156. Washington, D.C.: U.S. General Accounting Office.

1995b *Observations on U.S. International Drug Control Efforts*. GAO/T-NSIAD-95-194. Washington, D.C.: U.S. General Accounting Office.

1995c *Services for Young Foster Children*. HEHS 95-114. Washington, D.C.: U.S. General Accounting Office.

1996a *Drug Control: Counternarcotics Efforts in Mexico*. GAO/NSIAD-96-163. Washington, D.C.: U.S. General Accounting Office.

1996b *Federal and State Prisons: Inmate Populations, Costs, and Projection Models*. GGD-97-15. Washington, D.C.: U.S. General Accounting Office.

Garfield, Richard

1996 "Epidemic Neuropathy in Cuba." *New England Journal of Medicine* 334(16): 1063.

Garfield, Richard and Sarah Santana

1997 "The Impact of Economic Crisis and U.S. Embargo on Health in Cuba." *American Journal of Public Health* 87(1): 15-20.

Garner, Paul

1997 "Industry Can Damage Your Health." *British Medical Journal* 314(7077): 342.

Garrett, Laurie

1997 "Crumbled Empire, Shattered Health: Underfunded Ex-Soviets Losing Battle Against Soaring TB Rates." *New York Newsday*, October 27.

Gaston, Melchor W., Oscar A. Echevarria, and Rene F. de la Huerta

1957 *Por Qué Reforma Agraria*. 2nd ed. Habana: Agrupación Católica Universitaria.

Gates, Doris M.

1996 "Changes in Health Care Financing: Effects on the Delivery of Health Care Services in the 1990s." *Journal of Cardiovascular Nursing* 11(1):1-13.

Gedicks, Al

1993 *The New Resource Wars: Native and Environmental Struggles Against Multinational Corporations*. Boston: South End Press.

Geiger, H. Jack

1997a "Inequality as Violence: Race, Health, and Human Rights in the United States." *Health and Human Rights* 2(3): 7-13.

1997b "Racism Resurgent—Building a Bridge to the 19th Century." *American Journal of Public Health* 87(11): 1765-1766.

George, Susan

1977 *How the Other Half Dies*. Montclair, NJ: Allanheld, Osmun, and Co.

1988 *A Fate Worse Than Debt: A Radical New Analysis of the Third World Debt Crisis*. Harmondsworth, UK: Penguin Books.

1990 *A Fate Worse Than Debt*. New York: Grove Weidenfeld.

1992 *The Debt Boomerang: How Third World Debt Harms Us All*. Boulder, CO: Westview Press.

George, Susan and Fabrizio Sabelli

1994 *Faith and Credit: The World Bank's Secular Empire*. Boulder, CO: Westview Press.

Gereffi, G. and L. Hempel

1996 "Latin America in the Global Economy: Running Faster to Stay in Place." *NACLA Report on the Americas* 29(4): 18-27.

Geronimus, Arline, J. Bound, T. Waidman, *et al.*

1996 "Excess Mortality Among Blacks and Whites in the United States" *New England Journal of Medicine* 335(21): 1552-1558.

Gershman, John and Jonathan Fox

1996 "Taking On Poverty Targeting." *Bankcheck Quarterly*, No. 14, May.

Gertler, Paul and John Molyneaux

1995 *Pricing Public Health Services: Lessons from a Social Experiment in Indonesia*. Santa Monica, CA: Rand Corporation.

1997 *Experimental Evidence on the Effect of Raising User Fees for Publicly Delivered Health Care Services: Utilization, Health Outcomes, and Private Provider Response*. Santa Monica, CA: Rand Corporation.

Gertler, Paul and Jacques van der Gaag

1988 *Measuring the Willingness to Pay for Social Services in Developing Countries.* LSMS Working Paper No. 45. Washington, D.C.: World Bank.

1990 *The Willingness to Pay for Medical Care: Evidence from Two Developing Countries.* Baltimore, MD: Published for the World Bank by Johns Hopkins University Press.

Ghosh, Subha

1994 "Book Review: The Uncertain Promise of Law: Lessons from Bhopal." *Stanford Environmental Law Journal* 13(247): 251-256.

Gianaris, Nicholas V.

1998 *The North American Free Trade Agreement and the European Union.* Westport, CT: Praeger.

Gibbon, Peter

1992 "The World Bank and African Poverty, 1973-91" *Journal of Modern African Studies* 30(2): 193-220.

1996 "Zimbabwe." In *Limits of Adjustment in Africa.* Poul Engberg-Pedersen, Peter Gibbon, Phil Raikes, *et al.*, eds. London: James Currey. Pp. 347-397.

Gibbon, Peter, ed.

1995 *Structural Adjustment and the Working Poor in Zimbabwe.* Uppsala: Scandinavian Institute for African Studies.

Gibbs, Lois Marie

1998 *Love Canal: The Story Continues.* Gabriola Island, B.C., Canada: New Society Publishers.

Giblin, James Leonard

1992 *The Politics of Environmental Control in Northeastern Tanzania, 1840-1940.* Philadelphia: University of Pennsylvania Press.

Giesecke, Johan

1993 "AIDS and the Public Health." *Lancet* 342(8877): 942.

Gilligan, James

1996 *Violence: Our Deadly Epidemic and its Causes.* New York: G.P. Putnam's Sons.

Gilpin, Kenneth

1993 "Brazil Reaches an Agreement with Big Banks on Debt." *New York Times*, April 16.

Gilson, L.

1989 "Financing Health for All." *World Health Forum* 10(1): 97-99.

1995 "Management and Health-Care Reform in Sub-Saharan Africa." *Social Science and Medicine* 40(5): 695-710.

1997 "The Lessons of User-Fee Experience in Africa." *Health Policy and Planning* 12: 273-285.

Giraldo, Javier

1996 *Colombia: The Genocidal Democracy.* Monroe, ME: Common Courage Press.

Gladwin, Christina H.

1991 "Fertilizer Subsidy Removal Programs and Their Potential Impacts on Women Farmers in Malawi and Cameroon." In *Structural Adjustment and African Women Farmers.* Christina H. Gladwin, ed. Gainesville: University of Florida Press. Pp. 191-216.

Gladwin, Christina H., ed.

1991 *Structural Adjustment and African Women Farmers.* Gainesville: University of Florida Press.

Glanz, James

1995 "International Experts Help Probe Haiti's Bloody Past." *Science* 269: 1812-1813.

Gleckman, Harris and Riva Krut

1995 *The Social Benefits of Regulating Transnational Corporations.* Portland, ME: Benchmark Environmental Consulting.

Goheen, Miriam

1991 "The Ideology and Political Economy of Gender: Women and Land in Nso, Cameroon." In *Structural Adjustment and African Women Farmers.* Christina H. Gladwin, ed. Gainesville: University of Florida Press. Pp. 239-256.

Gold, Steven

1995 *The ABCs of Block Grants.* Albany, NY: Center for the Study of the States.

Goldman, Marshall

1994 *Lost Opportunity: Why Economic Reforms in Russia Have Not Worked.* New York: W.W. Norton.

Goldsmith, Alexander

1996 "Seeds of Exploitation: Free Trade Zones in the Global Economy." In *The Case Against the Global Economy.* Jerry Mander and Edward Goldsmith, eds. Pp. 267-272.

Goldstein, P.J. , L.J. Oellet, and M. Fendrich

1992 "From Bag Brides to Skeezers: A Historical Perspective on Sex-for-Drug Behavior." *Journal of Psychoactive Drugs* 24(4): 349-361.

Gomez, Luis Carlos

1990 *Household Demand for Health Care in El Salvador.* REACH (Resources for Child Health) Project.

Goodland, Robert

1996 "Growth Has Reached its Limit." In *The Case Against the Global Economy.* Jerry Mander and Edward Goldsmith, eds. San Francisco: Sierra Club Books. Pp. 207-217.

Goodman, H. and C. Waddington

1993 *Financing Health Care.* Oxford: Oxfam.

Goodman, L.W.

1987 *Small Nations, Giant Firms.* New York: Holmes and Meier.

Gordon, Antonio M.

1987 "HIV Infection in Cuba." *Journal of the American Medical Association* 258(23): 3387.

Gordon, Antonio M. and R. Paya

1989 "Controlling AIDS in Cuba." *New England Journal of Medicine* 321(12): 829.

Gordon, Diana

1994 *The Return of the Dangerous Classes.* New York: W.W. Norton.

Goshko, John

1998 "Rwandan Given Life Term for Genocide." *Washington Post*, September 5.

Goskomstat rossii

1994 *Rossiiskii statisticheskii ezhegodnik.*

1995a *Statisticheskoe obozrenie*, No. 4.

1995b *Statisticheskoe obozrenie*, No. 12.

1996 *Demographic Yearbook of the Russian Federation.* Moscow.

1997 *Statisticheskoe obozrenie*, No. 1.

Gosudarstvenii Doklad

1992a *Gosudarstvenii doklad o sostoianii okruzhaioushchei pirodnoi sredi Rossiiskoi Federatsii v 1991 godu.* Moscow.

1992b *Gosudarstvenii doklad o sostoianii zdorovia naselenia Rossiiskoi Federatsii v 1991 godu,* 1992. Moscow.

Gould, David

1980 *Bureaucratic Corruption and Underdevelopment in the Third World: The Case of Zaire.* New York: Pergamon Publishers.

Government of Malawi

1990 *Nutrition Facts for Malawian Families.* Blantyre: Inter-Ministerial Food and Nutrition Committee, Office of the President and Department of Economic Planning and Development. Available from UNICEF's New York headquarters.

Graham, Carol

1994 *Safety Nets, Politics, and the Poor: Transitions to Market Economies.* Washington, D.C.: Brookings Institute.

1996 "People's Capitalism Makes Headway in Peru." *Wall Street Journal*, April 14.

Granich, Reuben, Bradley Jacobs, Jonathan Mermin, et al.

1995 "Cuba's National AIDS Program: The First Decade." *Western Journal of Medicine* 163(2): 139-144.

Gray, Bradford H.

1986 *For-Profit Enterprise in Health Care.* Washington, D.C.: National Academy Press.

Green, Duncan

1995 *Silent Revolution: The Rise of Market Economics in Latin America.* London: Cassell and LAB.

1999 "Chile: Workers of the Americas." *NACLA Report on the Americas* 32(4): 21-27.

Green, Reginald H.

1981 "'Magendo' in the Political Economy of Uganda: Pathology, Parallel System or Sub-Mode of Production?" Discussion Paper 64, Institute of Development Studies, University of Sussex.

1989 "The Broken Pot: The Social Fabric, Economic Disaster and Adjustment in Africa." In *The IMF, the World Bank and the African Debt: Vol. I, Economic Impact; Vol. II, Social and Political Impact.* Bade Onimode, ed. London: Zed Books. Pp. 31-55.

1993 "The IMF and the World Bank in Africa: How Much Learning?" In *Hemmed In: Responses to Africa's Economic Decline.* Thomas Callaghy and John Ravenhill, eds. New York: Columbia University Press. Pp. 54-89.

Green, Reginald H. and Caroline Allison

1986 "The World Bank's Agenda for Accelerated Development: Dialectics, Doubts and Dialogues." In *Africa in Economic Crisis.* John Ravenhill, ed. New York: Columbia University Press. Pp. 60-84.

Green, Reginald H. and Ann Seidman

1968 *Unity or Poverty? The Economics of Pan-Africanism.* Baltimore, MD: Penguin Books.

Greenwood, Peter W., C.P. Rydell, A.F. Abrahamse, et al.

1994 *Three Strikes and You're Out: Estimated Benefits and Costs of California's New Mandatory Sentencing Law.* Santa Monica: RAND.

Greer, Jed

1998 "U.S. Petroleum Giant to Stand Trial for Burma Atrocities." *The Ecologist*, January/February, pp. 34-37.

Greider, William

1997 *One World Ready or Not: The Manic Logic of Global Capitalism.* New York: Simon and Schuster.

Griffin, Richard F.

1996 "Conventional Arms Transfers to Developing Nations, 1988-1995." Washington, D.C.: Congressional Research Service, Library of Congress.

Griffin, Robert A.

1997 "Inequality: Recent American Perspectives." *Journal of Income Distribution* 7(1): 109-119.

Grinspun, Ricardo and Maxwell Cameron

1995 "Mexico: The Wages of Trade." In *Free Trade and Economic Restructuring in Latin America: A NACLA Reader.* Fred Rosen and Deidre McFadyen, eds. New York: Monthly Review Press. Pp. 39-53.

Grosch, Margaret

1991 *From Platitudes to Practice: Administering Targeted Social Programs in Latin America.* Washington, D.C.: World Bank.

1993 *Administering Targeted Social Practice in Latin America.* Washington, D.C.: World Bank.

Grossman, Richard L. and Frank T. Adams

1993 *Taking Care of Business: Citizenship and the Charter of Corporations.* Cambridge, MA: Charter, Ink. and The Program on Corporations, Law, and Democracy.

1996 "Exercising Power Over Corporations Through State Charters." In *The Case Against the Global Economy.* Jerry Mander and Edward Goldsmith, eds. San Francisco: Sierra Club Books. Pp. 374-389.

Grosvenor, Gilbert Hovey

1920 "Haiti and Its Regeneration by the United States." *National Geographic* 38: 497-505.

Grunwald, J., L. Delatour, and K. Voltaire

1984 Offshore Assembly in Haiti. In *Haiti—Today and Tomorrow: An Interdisciplinary Study.* Charles Foster and Albert Valdman, eds. Lanham, MD: University Press of America. Pp. 231-252.

Guendelman, Sylvia and Monica Silberg

1993   "The Health Consequences of Maquiladora Work: Women on the U.S.-Mexican Border." *American Journal of Public Health* 83(1): 37-44.

Guillermoprieto, Alma

1994   *The Heart that Bleeds: Latin America Now.* New York: Alfred A Knopf.

Gurin, Arnold

1989   "Government Responsibility and Privatization: Examples for Four Social Services." In *Privatization and the Welfare State.* Sheila B. Kamerman and Alfred J. Kahn, eds. Princeton, NJ: Princeton University Press.

Guyer, Jane

1988   "Dynamic Approaches to Domestic Budgeting: Cases and Methods from Africa." In *A Home Divided: Women and Income in the Third World.* Daisy Dwyer and Judith Bruce, eds. Stanford, CA: Stanford University Press. Pp. 155-172.

Gwin, Catherine

1997   "U.S. Relations with the World Bank, 1945-1992." In *The World Bank: Its First Half Century.* Devesh Kapur, John P. Lewis, and Richard Webb, eds. Washington, D.C.: Brookings Institute. Pp. 195-274.

Haas, Richard N. and Robert E. Litan

1998   "Globalization and Its Discontents: Navigating the Dangers of a Tangled World." *Foreign Affairs* 77(3): 2-6.

Hafkin, Nancy J. and Edna G. Bay, eds.

1976   *Women in Africa: Studies in Social and Economic Change.* Stanford, CA: Stanford University Press.

Hager, Robert

1987   *Brief Amicus Curiae of the National Council of the Churches of Christ Regarding the Union Carbide Corporation Gas Plant Disaster to the Supreme Court of the United States.* Washington, D.C.: Fulcourt Press.

1995   "Bhopal: Courting Disaster." *Covert Action Quarterly* 53: 38-42, 56.

Haggard, Stephan and Robert R. Kaufman, eds.

1992   *The Politics of Economic Adjustment: International Constraints, Distributive Conflicts, and the State.* Princeton, NJ: Princeton University Press.

Hahn, Robert A., Nancy D. Barker, and Steven M. Teutsch

1996   "Letter to the Editor." *Epidemiology* 7(4): 453-454.

Hahn, Robert A., E.D. Eaker, N.D. Barker, et al.

1995   "Poverty and Death in the United States—1973 and 1991." *Epidemiology* 6: 490–497.

1996   "Poverty and Death in the United States." *International Journal of Health Services* 26(4): 640-673.

Halebsky, Sandor and Richard L. Harris

1995   *Capital, Power, and Inequality in Latin America.* Boulder, CO: Westview Press.

Hall, Kevin G.

1998   "HMO Hopes Miami is Gateway to Brazil." *Journal of Commerce*, February 27.

Halstead, Scott B., Julia Walsh, and Kenneth S. Warren, eds.

1985   *Good Health at Low Cost.* New York: Rockefeller Foundation.

Halstead, Ted and Clifford Cobb

1996   "The Need for New Measurements of Progress." In *The Case Against the Global Economy.* Jerry Mander and Edward Goldsmith, eds. San Francisco: Sierra Club Books. Pp. 197-206.

Hammer, Jeffery and Paul Gertler

1997   *Strategies for Pricing Public Health Services.* World Bank working paper (March).

Hancock, Graham

1989   *The Lords of Poverty: The Power, Prestige, and Corruption of the International Aid Business.* New York: Atlantic Monthly Press.

Handelman, Howard and Werner Baer, eds.

1989   *Paying the Costs of Austerity in Latin America* (*Westview special studies on Latin America and the Caribbean*). Boulder, CO: Westview Press.

Hansen, Holger Bernt and Michael Twaddle, eds.

1991a *Changing Uganda: The Dilemma of Structural Adjustment and Revolutionary Change.* London: James Currey.

1991b *Uganda Now: Between Decay and Development.* London: James Currey.

Harding, Colin

1992   "Fujimori Puts Peru Back on the World Map." *Independent*, February, 7.

Harmes, Adam

1998   "Institutional Investors and the Reproduction of Neoliberalism." *Review of International Political Economy* 5(1): 92-121.

Harnly, M., S. Seidel, P. Rojas, et al.

1997   "Biological Monitoring for Mercury within a Community with Soil and Fish Contamination." *Environmental Health Perspectives* 105(4): 424-429.

Harper Collins Economic Dictionary

1991   *The Harper Collins Economic Dictionary.* New York: Harper Collins.

Harr, Jonathan

1995   *A Civil Action.* New York: Random House.

Harris, Betty J.

1993   *The Political Economy of the Southern African Periphery: Factories, Cottage Industries and Female Labor in Swaziland Compared.* Basingstoke, U.K.: Macmillan.

Harris, John F. and Peter McKay

1996   "Companies Agree to Meet on 'Sweatshops.'" *Washington Post*, August 3.

Harrison, Lawrence

1985   *Underdevelopment is a State of Mind.* Lanham, MD: University Press of America.

1993   "Voodoo Politics." *Atlantic Monthly* 271(6): 101-108.

Hartlyn, Jonathan and Samuel A. Morley, eds.

1986 *Latin American Political Economy: Financial Crisis and Political Change.* Boulder, CO: Westview Press.

Hartung, William D.

1995 *U.S. Weapons at War.* New York: World Policy Institute at the New School for Social Research.

Hartwig, Gerald W. and David K. Patterson, eds.

1978 *Disease in African History: An Introductory Survey and Case Studies.* Durham, NC: Duke University Press.

Harvard Center for Population and Development Studies

1993 *Sanctions in Haiti: Crisis in Humanitarian Action.* Working Paper Series (November). Cambridge, MA: Harvard Center for Population and Development Studies, Program on Human Security.

Harvard Law School, Human Rights Program

1995 "Economic and Social Rights and the Right to Health." Conference proceedings, Harvard Law School (September, 1993). Cambridge, MA: Harvard Law School Human Rights Program.

Harvey, Pharis J. and Lauren Riggin

1994 *Trading Away the Future: Child Labor in India's Export Industries.* Washington, D.C.: International Labor Rights Education and Research Fund.

Hassan, Amin, Eliana Velasquez, Roberto Belmar, et al.

1981 "Mercury Poisoning in Nicaragua: A Case Study of the Export of Environmental and Occupational Health Hazards by a Multinational Corporation." *International Journal of Health Services* 11(2): 221-226.

Hatcher, Gordon, Peter R. Hatcher, and Eleanor C. Hatcher

1984 "Health Services in Canada." In *Comparative Health Systems: Descriptive Analyses of Fourteen National Health Systems.* Marshall W. Raffel, ed. University Park, PA: Pennsylvania State University Press.

Havenman, Robert

1996 "From Welfare to Work: Problems and Pitfalls." *Focus* 18(1): 21-24.

Hay, Jean and Marcia Wright, eds.

1982 *African Women and the Law: Historical Perspectives.* Boston: Boston University African Studies Program, Papers on Africa VII.

Hay, Margaret Jean and Sharon Stichter, eds.

1984 *African Women South of the Sahara.* New York: Longman.

Hayter, Teresa

1981 *The Creation of World Poverty.* London: Pluto.

Heath, Dwight B.

1992 "U.S. Drug Control Policy: A Cultural Perspective." *Daedalus* 121(3): 269-291.

Heilbroner, Robert and Lester Thurow

1994 *Economics Explained: Everything You Need to Know About How the Economy Works and Where It's Going.* New York: Simon and Schuster.

Heintz, James, Nancy Folbre, and Center for Popular Economics

1999 *New Field Guide to the U.S. Economy.* New York: New Press.

Heinzow, Birger

1996 "Results of the International Medical Commission on Bhopal." *International Perspectives in Public Health* 11: 4-8.

Helleiner, Eric

1994 *States and the Reemergence of Global Finance: From Bretton Woods to the 1990s.* Ithaca, NY: Cornell University Press.

Helleiner, Gerald K.

1985 "Aid and Liquidity: The Neglect of Sub-Saharan Africa and Others of the Poorest in the Emerging Monetary System." *Journal of Development Planning* 15: 67-84.

Hellinger, Doug

1987 "NGOs and the Large Aid Donors: Changing the Terms of Engagement." *World Development* 15 (Supplement): 135-143.

Hemlock, Doreen

1998 "Health Insurer Moves In; Miami Office Covers Hospital Care for Brazilians." *Fort Lauderdale Sun-Sentinel*, September 9.

Henwood, Doug

1996 "The Free Flow of Money." *NACLA Report on the Americas* 19(4): 11-17.

1997 *Wall Street.* London and New York: Verso.

Herbert, B.

1996a "From Sweatshops to Aerobics." *New York Times*, June 24.

1996b "Nike's Bad Neighborhood." *New York Times*, June 14.

Herd, D.

1994 "Predicting Drinking Problems Among Black and White Men: Results from a National Survey." *Journal of Studies on Alcohol* 55(1): 61-71.

Herman, Edward S.

1982 *The Real Terror Network.* Boston: South End Press.

1995 "Immiserating Growth(2): The Third World." *Z Magazine*, March, pp. 22-27.

Herman, Edward S. and Noam Chomsky

1988 *Manufacturing Consent.* New York: Pantheon.

Herredia, Carlos and Mary Purcell

1996 "Structural Adjustment in Mexico: The Root of the Crisis." In *Structural Adjustment and the Spreading Crisis in Latin America.* Washington, D.C.: The Development Gap.

Heyer, Judith, Penelope Roberts, and Gavin Williams, eds.

1981 *Rural Development in Tropical Africa.* New York: St. Martin's Press.

Hill, Polly

1986 *Development Economics on Trial: The Anthropological Case for a Prosecution.* Cambridge: Cambridge University Press.

Himmelstein, David, Sidney Wolfe, and Steffie Woolhandler
1993 "Mangled Competition." *The American Prospect*, Spring, pp. 116-126.

Hinckle, Warren and William W. Turner
1992 *Deadly Secrets: The CIA-Mafia War Against Castro and the Assassination of JFK.* New York: Thunder's Mouth Press.

Hodgkin, Thomas
1957 *Nationalism in Colonial Africa.* New York: New York University Press.
1968 "Forward" In *Unity or Poverty? The Economics of Pan-Africanism.* Reginald H. Green and Ann Seidman, eds. Baltimore, MD: Penguin Books.

Hogan, G.W.
1992 "Federal Republic of Germany, Ireland, and the United Kingdom: Three European Approaches to Political Campaign Regulation." *Capital University Law Review* 21: 501-543.

Holbein, James R. and Donald J. Musch
1994 *NAFTA: Final Text, Summary, Legislative History, and Implementation Directory.* New York: Oceana Publications.

Holm, Hans-Henrik and Georg Sørensen
1995 *Whose World Order: Uneven Globalization and the End of the Cold War.* Boulder, CO: Westview Press.

Holmquist, Frank and Michael Ford
1992 "Kenya: Slouching Toward Democracy." *Africa Today* 39(3): 97-111.

Holt, Elizabeth A., Reginald Boulos, Neal A. Halsey, et al.
1990 "Childhood Survival in Haiti: Protective Effect of Measles Vaccination." *Pediatrics* 85(2): 188-194.

Honderich, Kiaran
1993 "Cocaine Capitalism." In *Creating a New World Economy.* G. Epstein, J. Graham, and J. Nembhard, eds. . Philadelphia: Temple University Press. Pp. 123-139.

Hoogvelt, Ankie
1990 "Debt and Indebtedness: The Dynamics of Third World Poverty." *Review of African Political Economy* 47: 117-127.
1997 *Globalization and the Post-Colonial World.* Baltimore, MD: Johns Hopkins University Press.

Hooper K., K. Hopper, M.X. Petreas, et al.
1997 "Analysis of Breast Milk to Assess Exposure to Chlorinated Contaminants in Kazakstan: PCBs and Organochlorine Pesticides in Southern Kazakstan." *Environmental Health Perspectives* 105(11): 1250-1254.

Hoover's Handbook of World Business
1993 *Hoover's Handbook of World Business.* Austin, TX: The Reference Press.

Hopkins, Antony G.
1973 *An Economic History of West Africa.* London: Longmans.

Hormeku, Tetteh
1997 "U.S.-Africa Trade Policy: In Whose Interest?" *African Agenda* 12/13: 6-11.

Horta, Korinna
1997 "Fueling Strife in Chad and Cameroon: The Exxon-Shell-ELF World Bank Plans for Central Africa." *Multinational Monitor*, May, pp. 10-13.

Howie, P.W.
1991 "Breastfeeding: A Natural Method for Child Spacing." *Journal of Obstetrics and Gynecology* 165: 1990-1991.

Howie, P.W., J.S. Forsyth, S.A. Ogston, et al.
1990 "Protective Effect of Breastfeeding Against Infection." *British Medical Journal* 300(6716): 11-16.

Huang, C.C., N.S. Chu, C.S. Lu, et al.
1998 "Long-Term Progression in Chronic Manganism: Ten Years of Follow-Up." *Neurology* 50(3): 698-700.

Hudson, Terese
1997 "Faster, Stronger, Private?" *Hospitals and Health Networks* 13(7): 22.

Hughes, Charles C. and John M. Hunter
1970 "Disease and Development in Africa." *Social Science and Medicine* 3: 443-493.

Human Resources Development Canada, Labour Program
1999 "Summary of Submissions Received under the NAALC." Available at labour-travail.hrdc-drhc.gc.ca/doc/ialc-cidt/eng/e/submiss-e.html.

Human Rights Watch
1996a *Colombia's Killer Networks.* New York: Human Rights Watch.
1996b *Shattered Lives: Sexual Violence During the Rwandan Genocide and Its Aftermath.* New York: Human Rights Watch.

Human Rights Watch/Arms Project and Physicians for Human Rights
1993 *Landmines: A Deadly Legacy.* New York: Human Rights Watch.

Hunt, Charles
1989 "Migrant Labor and Sexually Transmitted Disease: AIDS in Africa." *Journal of Health and Social Behavior* 30: 333-353.

Husain, Ishrat
1995 "Adjustment in Africa: Lessons from Country Case Studies." In *Africa's Experience with Structural Adjustment.* World Bank Discussion Paper 288. Kapil Kapoor, ed. Washington, D.C.: World Bank. Pp. 28-40.

Hwang, Y.H., R.L. Bornschein, J. Grote, et al.
1997 "Environmental Arsenic Exposure of Children around a Former Copper Smelter Site." *Environmental Research* 72: 72-81.

ICFTU (International Confederation of Free Trade Unions)
1997 *Annual Survey, 1997.* Brussels: International Confederation of Free Trade Unions.

1998 *Annual Survey, 1998*. Brussels: International Confederation of Free Trade Unions.

IDB (Inter-American Development Bank)

1997 *Economic and Social Progress in Latin America: Latin America After a Decade of Reforms*. Washington, D.C.: IDB.

1998a *Economic and Social Progress in Latin America*. Washington, D.C.: IDB.

1998b *Facing Up to Inequality in Latin America: Economic and Social Progress in Latin America 1998-1999 Report*. Washington, D.C.: IDB. Pp. 181-186.

— *Economic and Social Database*. Statistics and Quantitative Research Analysis Unit and Regional Operations Department. Available at www.iadb.org/int/sta/ENGLISH/staweb. Undated.

IDHUCA (Instituto de Derechos Humanos de la Universidad Centroamericano José Simán Cañas)

1992 "La Salud en Tiempos de Guerra." Report prepared by the Instituto de Derechos Humanos de la Universidad Centroamericano José Simán Cañas. *Estudios Centroamericanos* 513-514: 653-673.

IFAD (International Fund for International Development)

1992 *The State of Rural Poverty*. Rome: IFAD.

Iglehart, John K.

1999 "The American Health Care System— Expenditures. Health Policy Report." *New England Journal of Medicine* 340(1): 70-76.

Iguiñiz, Javier

1994 *Buscando Salidas: Ensayos Sobre la Pobreza*. Lima: Instituto Bartolome de Las Casas, CEP.

1995 *Deuda Externa en America Latina: Exigencias Eticas desde la Doctrina Social de la Iglesia*. Lima: Instituto Bartolome de Las Casas, CEP.

Iguiñiz Javier, R. Basay, and M. Rubio

1993 *Los Ajustes: Perú 1975-1992*. Lima: Fundación Friedrich Ebert.

Iliffe, John

1969 "Tanzania Under German and British Rule." In *A Survey of East African History*. B.A. Ogot and J.A. Kieran, eds. Nairobi: East African Publishing House and Longmans. Pp. 290-311.

1983 *The Emergence of African Capitalism*. Minneapolis: University of Minnesota Press.

1987 *The African Poor: A History*. Cambridge: Cambridge University Press.

ILO (International Labor Organization)

1996 *Child Labor: Targeting the Intolerable*. ILO: Geneva.

1998 *World Labour Report: Industrial Relations, Democracy, and Social Stability 1997-98*. Geneva: International Labour Office.

IMF (International Monetary Fund)

1992 *Economic Review: Russian Federation*. Washington, D.C.: International Monetary Fund.

1993 *Economic Report: Russian Federation*. Washington, D.C.: International Monetary Fund.

1994 *Economic Report: Russian Federation*. Washington, D.C.: International Monetary Fund.

1995a *Economic Review: Russian Federation*. Washington, D.C.: International Monetary Fund.

1995b *International Capital Markets: Developments, Prospects, and Policy Issues*. Washington, D.C.: International Monetary Fund.

1995c *Russian Federation: Statistical Appendix*. Washington, D.C.: International Monetary Fund.

1998 *International Financial Statistics*. Washington, D.C.: International Monetary Fund.

Imig, Doug

1996 *Poverty and Power: The Political Representation of Poor Americans*. Lincoln: University of Nebraska Press.

Inciardi, James A.

1989 "Debating the Legalization of Drugs." *American Behavioral Scientist* 32(3): 233-242.

Inciardi, James A. and Duane McBride

1989 "Legalization: A High-Risk Alternative in the War on Drugs." *American Behavioral Scientist* 32(3): 259-289.

INEGI (Instituto Nacional de Estadistica, Geográfica, y Informática)

1998 "Short-Term Economic Indicators." Available at www.inegi.gob.mx/economia/ingles/fieconomia.html

INFACT

1998 *Global Aggression: The Case for World Standards and Bold U.S. Action Challenging Philip Morris and RJR Nabisco*. New York: Apex Press.

Ingram, Miranda

1995 "Russia Warned of Collapse of Health System." *British Medical Journal* 311(7010): 897.

Interagency Group on Breastfeeding Monitoring

1997 *Cracking the Code: Monitoring the International Code of Marketing of Breast-Milk Substitutes*. London: Interagency Group on Breastfeeding Monitoring.

Interfaith Center for Corporate Responsibility

1995 "Introduction to the Principles." *The Corporate Examiner: Principles for Global Corporate Responsibility*. September 1, pp. 2-4.

International Bank for Reconstruction and Development

1951 *Report on Cuba: Findings and Recommendations of an Economic and Technical Mission Organized by the International Bank for Reconstruction and Development in Collaboration with the Government of Cuba in 1950*. Baltimore: Johns Hopkins Press.

International Labor Rights Fund

1997 "NAFTA and Labor Rights." In *Failed Experiment: NAFTA at Three Years*. Economic Policy Institute, Institute for Policy Studies, International Labor Rights Fund, *et al*. Washington, D.C.: Public Citizen Publications.

IOM (Institute of Medicine)

1990 *Treating Drug Problems* (Vol. 1). Washington, D.C.: National Academy Press.

IOM (Institute of Medicine), Board on International Health

1997 *America's Vital Interest in Global Health: Protecting Our People, Enhancing Our Economy, and Advancing Our International Interests.* Washington, D.C.: National Academy Press.

Islam, Shafiqul

1990 "America and the World" *Foreign Affairs* 69(1):172-182.

Ives, Jane H.

1985 "The Export of Hazard." In *The Export of Hazard: Transnational Corporations and Environmental Control Issues.* Jane H. Ives, ed. London: Routledge and Kegan Paul. Pp. 213-223.

Izvestiia

1995 August 10, 1995, p. 1. In *Current Digest of the Post-Soviet Press,* Vol. XLVII, no. 32, p. 24.

Jamal, Vali

1991 "The Agrarian Context of the Ugandan Crisis." In *Changing Uganda: The Dilemma of Structural Adjustment and Revolutionary Change.* Holger Bernt Hansen and Michael Twaddle, eds. London: James Currey. Pp. 78-97.

James, Cyril Lionel Robert

1963 *The Black Jacobins: Toussaint L'Ouverture and the San Domingo Revolution.* New York: Vintage Books.

Jameson, Kenneth P.

1991 "In the Time of Cholera; Death and Debt in Peru." *Commonweal,* October 25, p. 609.

Jargowsky, Paul

1994 "Ghetto Poverty Among Blacks in the 1980s." *Journal of Policy Analysis and Management* 13: 288-310.

Jaskowski, J., Wang Zhengang, and S.C. Mohapatra

1996 "Compensation for the Bhopal Disaster." *International Perspectives in Public Health* 11: 23-28.

Jayarajah, Carl A.B., William H. Branson, and Binayak Sen

1996 *Social Dimension of Adjustment: World Bank Experience, 1980-93.* Washington, D.C.: World Bank.

Jazairy, Idriss

1992 *The State of World Rural Poverty.* New York: International Fund for Agricultural Development/NYU Press.

Jean-Louis, Robert

1989 *Diagnostic de l'Etat de Sante en Haiti.* Forum Libre 1. Medicine, Sante et Democratie en Haiti, pp. 11-20.

Jelliffe, Derrick B.

1972 "Commerciogenic Malnutrition." *Nutrition Review* 30(9): 199-205.

Jelliffe, Derrick B. and E.F.P. Jelliffe

1961 "The Nutritional Status of Haitian Children." *Acta Tropica* 18(1): 1-45.

Jeyaratnam, Jerry, ed.

1992 *Occupational Health in Developing Countries.* Oxford: Oxford University Press.

Jiménez, Luis Felipe

1996 "La Experiencia de Ajuste Durante la Década de los Ochenta en Latinoamérica, sus Consecuencias Distributivas y el Diseño de Políticas Sociales." In *Desarrollo con Equidad.* CEPAL/CLAD/SELA, ed. Lima: Nueva Sociedad. Pp. 14-31.

Jochelson, Karen, M. Mothibeli, and J.P. Leger

1991 "Human Immunovirus and Migrant Labor in South Africa." *International Journal of Health Services* 21(1): 157-173.

John, Stanley, Lawrence Brown, and Beny J. Prim

1997 "African Americans: Epidemiologic, Prevention and Treatment Issues." In *Substance Abuse: A Comprehensive Textbook.* J.H. Lowinson, P. Ruiz, and R.B. Millman, eds. Baltimore: Williams and Witkins.

Johns, Christina J. and Jose M. Borrero

1991 "The War on Drugs: Nothing Succeeds Like Failure." In *Crimes by the Capitalist State: An Introduction to State Criminality.* Gregg Barak, ed. Albany, NY: State University of New York Press.

Johnson, Bruce D. and John Muffler

1997 "Sociocultural Determinants and Perpetuators of Substance Abuse." In *Substance Abuse: A Comprehensive Textbook.* J.H. Lowinson, P. Ruiz, and R.B. Millman, eds. Baltimore: Williams and Witkins. Pp. 107-118.

Johnson, Chalmers

1982 *MITI and the Japanese Miracle: The Growth of Industrial Policy, 1925-1975.* Stanford, CA: Stanford University Press.

Johnson, D.E.

1985 "Investor-Owned Chains Continue Expansion, 1985 Survey Shows." *Modern Health Care* 15: 75-90.

Johnson, Jon R.

1994 *The North American Free Trade Agreement.* Ontario: Canada Law Book, Inc.

Johnson, Willard R.

1981 "The Agricultural Industrial Complex: The Global Big House." In *The Role of U.S. Universities in Rural and Agricultural Development.* Brooke G. Schoepf, ed. Tuskegee, AL: Tuskegee Institute, Center for Rural Development. Pp. 38-44.

Jolly, Richard

1985 "The Crisis for Women and Children: What Can Be Done?" *Journal of Development Studies* 16: 99-112.

Jones, Geoffrey

1993 "Introduction: Transnational Corporations—A Historical Perspective." In *Transnational Corporations: A Historical Perspective.* Vol. 2. Geoffrey Jones, ed. London: Routledge. Pp. 1-20.

Jones, William I. and Robert Egli

1984 *Farming Systems in Africa: The Great Lakes Highlands of Zaire, Rwanda and Burundi.* Technical Paper No. 27. Washington, D.C.: World Bank.

Jordan, Miriam and Marcus Brauchli

1995 "Beyond Gandhi: Economic Reforms Seem Secure in India, Election Rhetoric Aside." *Wall Street Journal,* December 29.

Jos, Philip, Mary Marshall, and Martin Perlmutter

1995 "The Charleston Policy on Cocaine Use During Pregnancy: A Cautionary Tale." *Journal of Law, Medicine, and Ethics* 23: 120-128.

Joseph, Richard

1977 *Radical Nationalism in Cameroon: Social Origins of the UPC Rebellion.* Oxford: Oxford University Press.

Justice, Judith

1986 *Policies, Plans, and People: Foreign Aid and Health Development.* Berkeley: University of California Press.

Kadhani, Xavier and Reginald H. Green

1985 "Parameters as Warnings and Guideposts: The Case of Zimbabwe." *Journal of Development Studies* 16: 195-244.

Kanbur, Ravi

1990 *Poverty and the Social Dimensions of Adjustment in Cote d'Ivoire.* Washington, D.C.: World Bank.

Kandel, Denise B.

1991 "The Social Demography of Drug Use." *Milbank Quarterly* 69(3): 365-413.

Kanji, Najmi, Nazeen Kanji, and Firoze Manji

1991 "From Development to Sustained Crisis: Structural Adjustment, Equity and Health." *Social Science and Medicine* 33(9): 985-993.

Kaplan, George A., Elsie R. Pammuk, John W. Lynch, et al.

1996 "Inequality in Income and Mortality in the United States: Analysis of Mortality and Potential Pathways." *British Medical Journal* 312(7037): 999-1003.

Kaplinsky, Raphael, ed.

1978 Readings on the Multinational Corporation in Kenya. Nairobi: Oxford University Press.

Kapoor, Kalil, ed.

1995 *Africa's Experience with Structural Adjustment: Proceedings of the Harare Seminar.* Discussion Paper 288. Washington, D.C.: World Bank.

Kapoor, Renu

1991 "Fetal Loss and Contraceptive Acceptance Among the Bhopal Gas Victims." *Social Biology* 38(3-4): 242-248.

Kapur, Devesh, John P. Lewis, and Richard Webb

1997 *The World Bank: Its First Half Century.* Two Volumes. Washington, D.C.: Brookings Institute.

Kapur, Ratna

1990 "From Human Tragedy to Human Rights: Multinational Corporate Accountability for Human Rights Violations." *Boston College Third World Law Journal* 10(1): 1-40.

Kasfir, Nelson

1991 "Land and Peasants in Western Uganda: Bushenyi and Mbarara." In *Uganda Now: Between Decay and Development.* Holger Bernt Hansen and Michael Twaddle, eds. London: James Currey. Pp. 158-174.

Kennedy, Bruce P., Ichiro Kawachi, and Deborah B. Prothow-Stith

1996 "Income Distribution and Mortality: Cross-Sectional Ecological Study of the Robin Hood Index in the United States." *British Medical Journal* 312(7037): 1004-1007.

Kennedy, Danny

1998 "Mining, Murder and Mayhem: The Impact of the Mining Industry in the South." *Third World Resurgence* 93: 15-19.

Kennedy, Marie and Chris Tilly

1996 "Up Against the 'Death Plan': Haitians Resist U.S.-Imposed Economic Restructuring." *Dollars and Sense* March/April: 8-11, 43-45.

Kennett, David and Tukumbi Lumumba-Kasongo, eds.

1992 *Structural Adjustment and the Crisis in Africa: Economic and Political Perspectives.* Lewiston, NY: Edwin Mellen Press.

Khan, Mohsin S.

1990 "The Macroeconomic Effects of Fund-Supported Adjustment Programs." *IMF Staff Papers* 37, June.

Khantzian, Edward J.

1986 "A Contemporary Psychodynamic Approach to Drug Abuse Treatment." *American Journal of Drug and Alcohol Abuse* 12(3): 213-222.

Khantzian, Edward J. and Arnold Wilson

1993 "Substance Abuse, Repetition, and the Nature of Addictive Suffering." In *Hierarchical Concepts in Psychoanalysis: Theory, Research, and Clinical Practice.* Arnold Wilson and John E. Gedo, eds. New York: Guilford Press. Pp. 263-283.

Khor, Martin

1998 "Developing Countries—Problems with Current Agricultural AID Policy." *IFG News* 3: 6.

Kikeri, Sunita, John Nellis, and Mary Shirley

1992 *Privatization: The Lessons of Experience.* Washington, D.C.: World Bank.

Kilborn, Peter T.

1998a "H.M.O.s Are Cutting Back Coverage of the Poor and Elderly; Insurers Tighten Rules and Reduce Fees for Doctors." *New York Times*, July 6.

1998b "The Uninsured Find Fewer Doctors in the House." *New York Times*, August 30.

1998c "Premiums Rising for Individuals." *New York Times*, December 5.

Killick, Tony, ed.

1995a *IMF Programmes in Developing Countries: Design and Impact.* New York: Routledge.

1995b "Structural Adjustment and Poverty Alleviation: An Interpretive Survey." *Development and Change* 26: 305-331.

Killick, Tony and Moazzam Malik

1992 "Country Experiences with IMF Programmes in the 1980s." *The World Economy* 15(5): 599-632.

Killick, Tony, Moazzam Malik, and Marcus Manuel

1992 "What Can We Know About the Effects of IMF Programmes?" *The World Economy* 15(5): 575-597.

Kilson, Martin

1969 *Political Change in a West African State*. Cambridge, MA: Harvard University Press.

Kimerling, Michael E., H. Kluge, N. Vezhnina, et al.

1999 "Inadequacy of the Current WHO Re-Treatment Regimen in a Central Siberian Prison: Treatment Failure and MDR-TB." *International Journal of Tuberculosis and Lung Disease* 3(5): 451-453.

Kimmerle, G. and A. Eben

1964 "Toxicity of Methyl Isocyanate and How to Determine Its Quantity in Air." *Archives of Toxicology* 20: 235-241.

Kindleberger, Charles P.

1996 *Manias, Panics and Crashes: A History of Financial Crises*. Basingstoke, UK: Macmillan.

King, K.W., Gladys Dominique, G. Uriodain, et al.

1968 "Food Patterns from Dietary Surveys in Rural Haiti." *Journal of the American Dietetic Association* 53: 114-118.

Kirkpatrick, Anthony F.

1996 "Role of the United States of America in Shortage of Food and Medicine in Cuba." *Lancet* 348(9040): 1489-1491.

Kirkpatrick, Anthony F., Richard Garfield, and Wayne Smith

1994 "The Time Has Come to Lift the Economic Embargo Against Cuba." *Journal of the Florida Medical Association* 81(10): 681-685.

Kitching, Gavin

1980 *Class and Economic Change in Kenya: The Making of a Petite Bourgeoisie, 1900-1970*. New Haven: Yale University Press.

Kleinman, Arthur, Veena Das, and Margaret Lock, eds.

1997 *Social Suffering*. Berkeley: University of California Press.

Klipstein, F.A., M. Samloff, G. Smarth, et al.

1968 "Malabsorption and Malnutrition in Rural Haiti." *American Journal of Clinical Nutrition* 21(9): 1042-1052.

Konde-Lule, Joseph K., Maria Wawer, Nelson Sewankambo, et al.

1997 "Adolescents, Sexual Behavior and HIV-1 in Rural Rakai District, Uganda." *AIDS* 11(6): 791-799.

Kopel, David

1994 *Prison Blues: How America's Foolish Sentencing Policies Endanger Public Safety*. Washington, D.C.: Cato Institute.

Koppes, Richard H.

1999 "Corporate Governance in the New Millennium: Concentrated Ownership Swells Activist Influence." *Directorship* 25(2): 4-5.

Kornblum, William

1991 "Drug Legalization and the Minority Poor." *Milbank Quarterly* 69(3): 415-435.

Korten, David C.

1995 *When Corporations Rule the World*. West Hartford, CT: Kumarian Press, Inc.

Kotz, David M., with Fred Weir

1997 *Revolution from Above: The Demise of the Soviet System*. New York: Routledge.

Kourí, Gustavo, María G. Guzmán, and José Bravo

1986 "Haemorrhagic Dengue in Cuba: History of an Epidemic." *PAHO Bulletin* 20(1): 24-30.

1987 "Why Dengue Haemorrhagic Fever in Cuba? An Integral Analysis." *Transactions of the Royal Society of Tropical Medicine and Hygiene* 81(5): 821-823.

Kozul-Wright, Richard

1995 "Transnational Corporations and the Nation-State." In *Managing the Global Economy*. Jonathan Michie and John Grieve Smith, eds. Oxford: Oxford University Press. Pp. 135-171.

Kretzmann, S.

1995 "Nigeria's 'Drilling Fields'—Shell Oil's Role in Repression." *Multinational Monitor*, January/February, 8-11.

Krieger, Nancy and Elizabeth Fee

1994 "Social Class: The Missing Link in U.S. Health Data." *International Journal of Health Services* 24(1): 25-44.

Krieger, Nancy, D. Rowly, A. Herman, et al.

1993 "Racism, Sexism, and Social Class: Implications for Studies of Health, Disease, and Well-Being." *American Journal of Preventative Medicine* 9(6 Supplement): 82-122.

Krugman, Paul

1994a "Competitiveness: A Dangerous Obsession." *Foreign Affairs* 73(2):28-44.

1994b "The Myth of Asia's Miracle." *Foreign Affairs* 73(6):62-78.

1995 "Dutch Tulips and Emerging Markets." *Foreign Affairs* 74(4):28-44.

1996 "Cycles of Conventional Wisdom on Economic Development." *International Affairs* 71(4): 717-732.

1998 "Saving Asia: It's Time to Get Radical." *Fortune*, September 7: 74-80.

1999 "The Return of Depression Economics." *Foreign Affairs* 78(1): 56-74.

Kumar, Sanjay

1993 "India: The Second Bhopal Tragedy." *Lancet* 341(8854): 1205-1206.

1997 "World Bank's Policy of Structural Adjustment Under Fire in India." *Lancet* 350(9086): 1233.

Kuntz, Diane

1994 "The Politics of Suffering: The Impact of the U.S. Embargo on the Health of the Cuban People—Report of a Fact-Finding Trip to Cuba, June 6-11, 1993." *International Journal of Health Services* 24(1): 161-179.

Kuttner, Robert
1999 "The American Health-Care System—Health Insurance Coverage." *New England Journal of Medicine* 340(2): 163-168.

Kuznets, Simon
1955 "Economic Growth and Income Inequality." *American Economic Review* 45(1): 1-28.

La Botz, Daniel
1994 "Manufacturing Poverty: The Maquiladorization of Mexico." *International Journal of Health Services* 24(3): 403-408.

Lacey, Robert
1996 "Pension Reform in Latin America: Current and Future Challenges and the Role of the World Bank." *Economic Notes* May 64(5).

LaDou, Joseph
1991 "Deadly Migration: Hazardous Industries' Flight to the Third World." *Technology Review* 94(5):47-53.
1997 "Global Migration of Hazardous Industries." In *International Perspectives on Environment, Development, and Health: Toward a Sustainable World*. Gurinder S. Shahi, Barry S. Levy, Al Binger, *et al.*, eds. New York: Springer Publishing Company. Pp. 313-324.

LaFeber, Walter
1986 "The Alliances in Retrospect." In *Bordering on Trouble: Resources and Politics in Latin America*. A. Maguire and J. Brown, eds. Bethesda, MD: Adler and Adler. Pp. 365-380.

Laguerre, Michel
1978 "Ticouloute and His Kinfolk: The Study of a Haitian Extended Family." In *The Extended Family in Black Societies*. Demitri Shinkin, Edith Shinkin, and Dennis A. Frate, eds. The Hague: Mouton. Pp. 407-445.

Lall, Sanjaya
1995 "Employment and Foreign Investment: Policy Options for Developing Countries." *International Labour Review* 134(4-5): 521-540.

Landes, David
1998 *The Wealth and Poverty of Nations*. New York: W.W. Norton.

Lang, Timothy and Colin Hines
1993 *The New Protectionism: Protecting the Future Against Free Trade*. London: Earthscan.

Lappé, Francis Moore and Joseph Collins, with Cary Fowler
1977 *Food First: Beyond the Myth of Scarcity*. Boston: Houghton Mifflin.

Lappé, Francis Moore, Joseph Collins, and David Kinley
1980 *Aid as Obstacle*. San Francisco: Institute for Food and Development Policy.

Lappé, Frances Moore, Rachel Schurman, and Kevin Danaher
1987 *Betraying the National Interest*. New York: Grove Press.

LaRoche, V.
1965 "Infection et Malnutrition Infantiles en Haiti." *Bulletin de la Société de Pathologie Exotique* 58(6): 1179-1187.

Latham, Michael C.
1965 *Human Nutrition in Tropical Africa: A Textbook for Health Workers*. Rome: Food and Agriculture Organization (FAO).

Laughlin, Kim
1996 *Transnationalism, Harmonization, and Ill-Effect: The Bhopal Case*. Unpublished manuscript.

Lawless, Robert
1992 *Haiti's Bad Press*. Rochester, VT: Schenkman Books.

Lawrence, Peter, ed.
1986 *The World Recession and the Food Crisis in Africa*. London: James Currey.

Lawrence, Robert Z.
1996a *Regionalism, Multilateralism, and Deeper Integration*. Washington, D.C.: Brookings Institute.
1996b *Single World, Divided Nations? International Trade and OECD Labor Markets*. Paris: OECD.

Leiner, Marvin
1994 *Sexual Politics in Cuba: Machismo, Homosexuality, and AIDS*. Boulder, CO: Westview Press.

Lélé, Sharachandra M.
1991 "Sustainable Development: A Critical Review." *World Development* 19(6): 607-621.

Lele, Uma
1990 *Structural Adjustment, Agricultural Development and the Poor: Some Lessons from the Malawian Experience*. Washington, D.C.: World Bank.

Lemarchand, Rene
1982 *The World Bank in Rwanda: The Case of the Office de Valorisation Agricole et Pastorale du Mutara (OVAPAM)*. Bloomington: Indiana University, African Studies Program.

Lennock, Jean
1994 *Paying for Health: Poverty and Structural Adjustment in Zimbabwe*. Oxford: Oxfam UK and Ireland.

Leon, David A., Laurent Chenet, Vladimir M. Shkolnikov, et al.
1997 "Huge Variation in Russian Mortality Rates 1984-94: Artefact, Alcohol, or What?" *Lancet* 350(9075): 383-388.

Leonard, Ann and Jan Rispens
1996 "Exposing the Recycling Hoax: Bharat Zinc and the Politics of the International Waste Trade." *Multinational Monitor*, January/February, pp. 30-34.

Lepkowski, Wil
1994 "Ten Years Later: Bhopal." *Chemical and Engineering News*, December 19, pp. 8-18.

LeQuesne, Caroline
1996 *Reforming World Trade: The Social and Environmental Priorities*. Oxford: Oxfam Publications.

Leroy, Greg

1995 "No More Candy Store: States Move to End Corporate Welfare." In *Real World Macro: Twelfth Edition.* Randy Albelda, Marc Breslow, John Miller, *et al.*, eds. Somerville, MA: Dollars and Sense. Pp. 38-42.

Levathes, Louise

1995 "Easy Money; Political Contributions." *National Audubon Society*, November 21, p. 16.

Levenstein, Charles and John Wooding, eds.

1997 *Work, Health, and Environment: Old Problems, New Solutions.* New York: Guilford Press.

Levine, Michael

1990 *Deep Cover.* New York: Delacorte.

Levins, Richard

1995 "Preparing for Uncertainty." *Ecosystem Health* 1(1): 47-57.

Levinson, Jerome

1993 "Comments on Labor Law in Mexico: The Discrepancy Between Theory and Reality." *United States-Mexico Law Journal* 1(1): 225-228.

Levinson, Jerome and Juan de Onis

1970 *The Alliance that Lost Its Way.* Chicago: Quadrangle Books.

Leviton, S., M.A. Schindler, and R.S. Orleans

1994 "African-American Youth: Drug Trafficking and the Justice System." *Pediatrics* 93(6): 1078-1084.

Levy, Barry S.

1995 "Occupational Health Policy Issues in Developing Countries: The Experience of Kenya." *International Journal of Occupational and Environmental Health* 1(2): 79-85.

Levy, Barry S. and David H. Wegman

1995 *Occupational Health: Recognizing and Preventing Work-Related Disease.* Boston: Little, Brown and Co.

Levy, Barry S., T. Kjellstrom, G. Forget, *et al.*

1992 "Ongoing Research in Occupational Health and Environmental Epidemiology in Developing Countries." *Archives of Environmental Health* 47(3): 231-235.

Levy, Barry S. and Victor W. Sidel

1996 "The Impact of Military Activities on Civilian Populations." In *War and Public Health.* Barry S. Levy and Victor W. Sidel, eds. New York: Oxford University Press.

Lewis, David C.

1992 "Medical and Health Perspectives on a Failing U.S. Drug Policy." *Daedalus* 121(3): 165-94.

Lewis, Laurence A. and William J. Coffey

1985 "The Continuing Deforestation of Haiti." *Ambio* 14(3): 158-160.

Lewis, P.

1996 "Nigeria's Deadly Oil War: Shell Defends Its Record." *New York Times*, February 13.

Lewis, S.J., M. Kaltofen, and G. Ormsby

1991 *Border Trouble: Rivers in Peril. A Report on Water Pollution Due to Industrial Development in Northern Mexico.* Boston: National Toxics Campaign Fund.

Lewis, William Arthur

1984 "Development Economics in the 1950s." In *Pioneers in Development.* Gerald M. Meier and Dudley Seers, eds. Oxford: World Bank and Oxford University Press. Pp. 121-137.

Leymaire, Philippe

1998 "Review of 'Nos Amis de la Banque' by Peter Chappell." *Le Monde Diplomatique*, February, p. 12.

Leys, Colin

1978 "Capital Accumulation, Class Formation and Dependency: The Significance of the Kenyan Case." *The Socialist Register 1978*: 241-266.

1996a "The Crisis in Development Theory." *New Political Economy* 1(1): 41-58.

1996b *The Rise and Fall of Development Theory.* Bloomington: Indiana University Press.

Leys, Norman

1973 *Kenya.* 4th ed. London: Frank Cass. Original 1924.

Leyva, Ricardo

1972 "Health and Revolution in Cuba." In *Cuba in Revolution.* Rolando E. Bonachea and Nelson P. Valdés, eds. Garden City, NY: Anchor Books.

Lillie-Blanton, M., J.C. Anthony, and C. Schuster

1993 "Probing the Meaning of Racial/Ethnic Group Comparisons in Crack Cocaine Smoking." *Journal of the American Medical Association* 269(8): 993-997.

Lincoff, Norah S., Jeffrey G. Odel, and Michio Hirano

1993 "Letter from Havana: 'Outbreak' of Optic and Peripheral Neuropathy in Cuba?" *Journal of the American Medical Association* 270(4): 511-518.

Link, Bruce G. and J. Phelan

1995 "Social Conditions as Fundamental Causes of Disease." *Journal of Health and Social Behavior* (Extra Issue): 80-94.

Linowes, David F., Annelise G. Anderson, Michael D. Antonovich, *et al.*

1988 "Privatization—Toward More Effective Government." *Report of the President's Commission on Privatization.* Washington, D.C.: The Commission on Privatization.

Lippman, Matthew

1992 "Multinational Corporations and Human Rights." In *Human Rights and the World Community: Issues and Action.* Richard Pierre Claude and Burns H. Weston, eds. Philadelphia: University of Pennsylvania Press. Pp. 392-400.

Lipton, Douglas

1995 *The Effectiveness of Treatment for Drug Abusers Under Criminal Justice Supervision.* Washington, D.C.: National Institute of Justice.

1996 *Prison-Based Therapeutic Communities: Their Success with Drug-Abusing Offenders.* Washington, D.C.: National Institute of Justice.

Lipton, Michael

1985 *Land Assets and Rural Poverty.* World Bank Staff Working Paper 744. Washington, D.C.: World Bank.

1996 "Comment on 'Research on Poverty and Development Twenty Years after *Redistribution with Growth*, by Pranab Bardahn.'" In *Annual World Bank Conference on Development Economics 1995.* Michael Bruno and Boris Pleskovic, eds. Washington, D.C.: World Bank. Pp. 73-79.

Lipton, Michael and Martin Ravallion

1995 "Poverty and Policy." In *Handbook of Development Economics.* J. Behrman and T.N. Srinivasan, eds. New York: North-Holland. Pp. 2551-2657.

Lipton, Michael and Simon Maxwell

1992 *The New Poverty Agenda: An Overview.* IDS Discussion Paper #306. Brighton, Sussex, U.K.: Institute for Development Studies, University of Sussex.

Lissakers, Karin

1991 *Banks, Borrowers, and the Establishment: A Revisionist Account of the International Debt Crisis.* New York: Basic Books.

Literaturnaia Gazeta

1994 "Public Health: The Patient Pays Three Times." September 21, 1994, p. 11. In *Current Digest of the Post-Soviet Press*, Vol. XLVI, No. 38, 1994, pp. 7-8.

Little, Kenneth

1973 *African Women in Towns: An Aspect of Africa's Social Revolution.* London: Cambridge University Press.

Loewenson, Renee

1991 "Harvests of Disease: Women at Work on Zimbabwean Plantations." In *Women and Health in Africa.* Meredeth Turshen, ed. Trenton, NJ: Africa World Press. Pp. 35-49.

Loguinova, V.

1998 "Russia-Health: TB Becomes Uncontrollable in Russia." *Agence France Presse*, October 20.

London School of Hygiene and Tropical Medicine

1994 *Research Report, 1993.* London: University of London.

Londoño, Juan Luis and Miguel Székely

1997 *Distributional Surprises After a Decade of Reform: Latin America in the Nineties.* OCE Working Paper No. 352. Washington, D.C.: Inter-American Development Bank.

Longman, Timothy

1995 "Genocide and Socio-Political Change: Massacres in Two Rwandan Villages." *Issue* 23(2): 18-23.

Lovejoy, Paul, ed.

1986 *Africans in Bondage: Studies in Slavery and the Slave Trade.* Ann Arbor: University of Michigan Press.

Low, P. and A. Subramanian

1995 *TRIMS in the Uruguay Round: An Unfinished Business?* Discussion Paper 307. Washington, D.C.: World Bank.

Lowinson, Joyce H., Pedro Ruiz, and Robert B. Millman, eds.

1997 *Substance Abuse: A Comprehensive Textbook.* Baltimore, MD: Williams and Wilkins.

Loxley, John

1990 "Structural Adjustment Programmes in Africa: Ghana and Zambia." *Review of African Political Economy* 47: 8-27.

Lumpe, Lora and Jeff Donarski

1998 *The Arms Trade Revealed: A Guide for Investigators and Activists.* Washington, D.C.: Federation of American Scientists.

Lumsden, Ian

1996 *Machos, Maricones, and Gays: Cuba and Homosexuality.* Philadelphia: Temple University Press.

Lurie, Peter, Percy Hintzen, and Robert A. Lowe

1995 "Socioeconomic Obstacles to HIV Prevention and Treatment in Developing Countries: The Roles of the International Monetary Fund and the World Bank." *AIDS* 9(6): 539-546.

Lusane, Clarence

1991 *Pipe Dream Blues: Racism and the War on Drugs.* Boston: South End Press.

Lustig, Nora

1992 *Mexico: The Remaking of an Economy.* Washington, D.C.: Brookings Institute.

Lustig, Nora, ed.

1995 *Coping with Austerity: Poverty and Inequality in Latin America.* Washington, D.C.: Brookings Institute.

Ly, Abdoulaye

1957 *L'Etat et la Production Paysanne ou L'Etat et la Revolution au Senegal.* Paris: Presence Africaine.

Lynch, J. W., G.A. Kaplan, E.R. Pamuk, et al.

1998 "Income Inequality and Mortality in Metropolitan Areas of the United States." *American Journal of Public Health.* 88:1074-1080.

Lyons, Maryinez

1985 "From Death Camps to 'Cordon Sanitaire': The Development of Sleeping Sickness Policy in the Uele District of the Belgian Congo, 1903-1914." *Journal of African History* 26: 69-91.

M'Bokolo, Elikia

1982 "French Colonial Policy in Equatorial Africa in the 1940s and 1950s." In *The Transfer of Power in Africa: Decolonization 1940-1960.* Prosser Gifford and William Roger Louis, eds. New Haven, CT: Yale University Press. Pp. 173-210.

MacGaffey, Janet, with M. Vwakanakazi, Rukarangira wa Nkera, Brooke G. Schoepf, et al.

1991 *The Real Economy of Zaire: The Contribution of Smuggling and Other Unofficial Activities to the National Economy of Zaire.* London: James Currey.

Machipisa, Lewis

1998 "Mining Companies Wreak Havoc in Africa." *Third World Resurgence* 93: 24-25.

MacKay, Judith

1994 "The Tobacco Problem: Commercial Profit Versus Health—The Conflict of Interests in Developing Countries." *Preventive Medicine* 23(4): 535-538.

MacKenzie, Debora and Roger Milne

1989 "If You Can't Treat It, Ship It: International Trade in Toxic Waste: Waste Shipments to Africa." *New Scientist* 122(1658): 24-25.

MacKenzie, Thomas D., Carl E. Bartecchi, and Robert W. Schrier

1994 "The Human Costs of Tobacco Use: Second of Two Parts." *New England Journal of Medicine* 330(14): 975-980.

Macrea, J., Anthony Zwi, and H. Birungi

1993 *A Healthy Peace? Rehabilitation and Development of the Health Sector in a Post-Conflict Situation: The Case of Uganda.* London: London School of Hygiene and Tropical Medicine.

Madiou, Thomas

1989 *Histoire d'Haiti.* 9 vols. Port-au-Prince: Imprimerie Henri Deschamps.

Malaba, Luke

1981 "Supply, Control, and Organization of Labour in Rhodesia." *Review of African Political Economy* 18: 7-28.

Malena, Carmen

1997 "NGO Involvement in World Bank-Financed Social Funds: Lessons Learned." *Environment Department Papers: Toward Environmentally and Socially Sustainable Development.* Washington, D.C.: World Bank.

Mamdani, Mamoud

1976 Politics and Class Formation in Uganda. New York: Monthly Review.

1992 "The Peasant Question and the Contemporary Crisis." In *Structural Adjustment and the Crisis in Africa: Economic and Political Perspectives.* David Kennett and Tukumbi Lumumba-Kasongo, eds. Lewiston, NY: Edwin Mellen Press. Pp. 49-70.

1996 *Citizen and Subject: Contemporary Africa and the Legacy of Late Colonialism.* Princeton, NJ: Princeton University Press.

Mandala, Elias C.

1990 *Work and Control in a Peasant Society: A History of the Lower Tchiri Valley in Malawi.* Madison: University of Wisconsin Press.

Mander, Jerry and Edward Goldsmith, eds.

1996 *The Case Against the Global Economy: For a Turn Toward the Local.* San Francisco: Sierra Club Books.

Mann, Jonathan, Daniel Tarantola, and Thomas Netter, eds.

1992 *AIDS in the World.* Cambridge, MA: Harvard University Press.

Mann, Kristen and Richard Roberts, eds.

1991 *Law in Colonial Africa.* Portsmouth, NH: Heinneman.

Manning, Patrick

1987 "The Prospects for African Economic History: Is Today Included in the Long Run?" *African Studies Review* 30(2): 49-62.

Marks, Shula, ed.

1987 *Not Either an Experimental Doll: The Separate Worlds of Three African Women.* Bloomington: Indiana University Press.

Marmor, Theodore R., Mark J. Schlesinger and R.W. Smithey

1987 "Nonprofit Organizations and Health Care." In *The Nonprofit Sector: A Research Handbook.* Walter W. Powell, ed. New Haven: Yale University Press. Pp. 221-239.

Marshall, Alfred

1890 *Principles of Economics: An Introductory Volume.* New York: MacMillan.

Marshall, Jonathan

1991 *Drug Wars: Corruption, Counterinsurgency, and Covert Operations in the Third World.* Forestville, CA: Cohen and Cohen Publishers.

Martin, Brendan

1996 "From the Many to the Few: Privatization and Globalization." *The Ecologist* 26(4): 145-155.

Martin, P.

1997 "Do Mexican Agricultural Policies Stimulate Emigration?" In *At the Crossroads: Mexico and U.S. Immigration Policy.* F. Bean, ed. London: Rowman and Littlefield. Pp. 79-116.

Marysse, Stefaan, Tom de Herdt, and Elie Ndayambaje

1994a *Revenus Ruraux Avant l'Ajustement Structurel. Cas de Kirambogo.* Cahiers du CIDEP, March 19.

1994b *Rwanda: Apauvrissement et Ajustement Structurel.* Paris: L'Harmattan.

Massachusetts Department of Public Health (MDPH)

1994a *Profiles of Women in Substance Abuse Treatment FY 1988-93: A Comparative Gender Analysis.* Health and Addiction Research, Inc. (December).

1994b *Tobacco, Alcohol and Other Drug Use: Trends Among Massachusetts Public School Adolescents 1984-1993.* Health and Addictions Research, Inc. (June).

1996a *Bureau of Communicable Disease Control, AIDS Surveillance Program* (April).

1996b *Indicators of Substance Use in Massachusetts 1985-1993: A Compendium.* Health and Addiction Research, Inc. (April).

1996c *Overview of the Bureau of Substance Abuse Services* (February).

1996d *Socio-Demographic Characteristics of Admissions to Publically Funded Substance Abuse Treatment by Region and CHNA for Fiscal Year 1995* (February).

Massey, Douglas and Nancy Denton
1993 *American Apartheid. Segregation and the Making of the Underclass*. Cambridge, MA: Harvard University Press.

Mathur, Neeraj, Brahma N. Gupta, Subodh Rastogi, et al.
1993 "Socioeconomic and Health Status of Electronics Workers Employed in Organized Industry." *American Journal of Industrial Medicine* 23: 321-331.

Mauceri, Philip
1995 "State Reform, Coalitions, and the Neoliberal Autogolpe in Peru." *Latin American Research Review* 30(1): 7-37.

Maurer, Marc and Tracy Huling
1995 "Young Black Americans and the Criminal Justice System: Five Years Later." Washington, D.C.: The Sentencing Project.

Mauro, Paolo
1995 "Corruption and Growth." *Quarterly Journal of Economics* 110(3): 681-712.

Mazrui, Ali
1991 "Privatization Versus the Market: Cultural Contradictions in Structural Adjustment." In *Changing Uganda: The Dilemma of Structural Adjustment and Revolutionary Change*. Holger Bernt Hansen and Michael Twaddle, eds. London: James Currey. Pp. 351-378.

Mbembe, Achille
1988 *Afriques Indociles: Chretienisme, Pouvoir d'Etat en Societe Postcoloniale*. Paris: Karthala.

Mbilinyi, Marjorie J.
1972 "The State of Women in Tanzania." *Canadian Journal of African Studies* 6(2): 371-377.
1988 "Agribusiness and Women Peasants in Tanzania." *Development and Change* 19(4): 549-583.
1990a "Structural Adjustment, Agribusiness and Rural Women in Tanzania," In *The Food Question: Profits Versus People*. Henry Bernstein, et al., eds. London: Earthscan. Pp. 111-124.
1990b *A Review of Women in Development Issues in Tanzania. Consultant's Report*. May, 1990. Dar es Salaam: World Bank.
1991 *Big Slavery: Agribusiness and the Crisis in Women's Employment in Tanzania*. Dar es Salaam: Dar es Salaam University Press.
1994 "Gender and Structural Adjustment." In *Structural Adjustment and Gender: Empowerment or Disempowerment*. Tanzania Gender Networking Programme (TGNP). Pp. 25-62.

M'Bokolo, Elikia
1982 "French Colonial Policy in Equatorial Africa in the 1940s and 1950s." In *The Transfer of Power in Africa: Decolonization*. Gifford Prosser and William Roger Louis, eds. New Haven, CT: Yale University Press. Pp. 173-210.

McAuley, Alistair
1979 *Economic Welfare in the Soviet Union*. Madison: University of Wisconsin Press.

McAuliffe, William E.
1990 "Health Care Policy Issues in the Drug Abuse Treatment Field." *Journal of Health Politics, Policy and Law* 15(2): 357-385.

McClintock, Michael
1985 *The American Connection: State Terror and Popular Resistance in El Salvador*. London: Zed Books

McCord, Colin and Harold Freeman
1990 "Excess Mortality in Harlem." *New England Journal of Medicine* 322(3): 173-177.

McCoy, Alfred
1991 *The Politics of Heroin*. Brooklyn: Lawrence Hill.

McCusker, J., A. Stoddard, J. Zapka, et al.
1993 "Behavioral Outcomes of AIDS Interventions for Drug Users in Short-Term Treatment." *American Journal of Public Health* 83(10): 1463-1465.

McFate, Katherine
1990 "Black Males and the Drug Trade: New Entrepreneurs or New Illusions?" *Focus*, May, pp. 5-6.

McGuinness, M.J.
1994 "Free Trade and Occupational Health Policy: An Argument for Health and Safety Across the North American Workplace." *Salud Pública de Mexico* 36: 578-596.

McMichael, A.
1995 "The Health of Persons, Populations and Planets: Epidemiology Comes Full Circle." *Epidemiology* 6: 633-636.

McNamara, Robert S.
1975 *Address to the Governors of the World Bank*. Washington, D.C.: World Bank.

McPake, B.
1993 "User Charges for Health Services in Developing Countries: A Review of the Economic Literature." *Social Science and Medicine* 36(11): 1397-1405.

McPake B., K. Hanson, and A. Mills
1993 "Community Financing of Health Care in Africa: An Evaluation of the Bamako Initiative." *Social Science and Medicine* 36(11): 1383-1395.

Meadows, D.H., D.L. Meadows, J. Randers, et al.
1992 *Limits to Growth: A Report for the Club of Rome's Project on the Predicament of Mankind*. New York: Universe Books.

Medoff, Peter and Holly Sklar
1972 *Streets of Hope: The Fall and Rise of an Urban Neighborhood*. Boston: South End Press.

Meebelo, Henry S.
1971 *Reactions to Colonialism: A Prelude to the Politics of Independence in Northern Zambia, 1893-1939*. Manchester, U.K.: Manchester University Press.

Meek, J.
1998 "Killer TB Threat to the World." *The Guardian*, September 23.

Meena, Ruth

1991 "The Impact of Structural Adjustment Programs on Rural Women in Tanzania." In *Structural Adjustment and African Women Farmers*. Christina H. Gladwin, ed. Gainesville: University of Florida Press. Pp. 169-189.

Mehra-Kerpelman, Kiran

1996 "Children at Work: How Many and Where?" *World of Work: The Magazine of the International Labour Office* (15): 8-9.

Mehrotra, Santosh and Richard Jolly, eds.

1987 *Development with a Human Face: Experiences in Social Achievement and Growth*. Oxford: Clarendon Press.

Mehta, Pushpa, Anant S. Mehta, Sunder J. Mehta, *et al.*

1990 "Bhopal Tragedy's Health Effects: A Review of Methyl Isocyanate Toxicity." *Journal of the American Medical Association* 264(21): 2781-2787.

Mehta, Suketu

1996 "Bhopal Lives." *Village Voice*, December 3, pp. 50-55.

Meierhoefer, Barbara

1992 *The General Effect of Mandatory Minimum Prison Terms*. Washington, D.C.: Federal Judicial Center.

Mejía, José Antonio and Rob Vos

1997 *Poverty in Latin America and the Caribbean. An Inventory: 1980-95*. INDES Working Paper. Washington, D.C.: IDB.

Melrose, Dianna

1989 *Nicaragua: The Threat of a Good Example?* Oxford: Oxfam.

Mendes de Leon, Carlos F., and Kyriakos S. Markides

1988 "Depressive Symptoms Among Mexican-Americans: A Three-Generation Study." *American Journal of Epidemiology* 127(1): 150-160.

Mensch, B.S. and Denise Kandel

1988 "Dropping Out of High School and Drug Involvement." *Sociology of Education* 61: 95-113.

Meredith, Emily and Garrett Brown

1995 "The *Maquiladora* Health and Safety Support Network: A Case Study of Public Health Without Borders." *Social Justice* 22(4): 85-87.

Merlier, Michel

1962 *Le Congo de la Colonisation Belge a l'independence*. Paris: Maspero.

Meyers, Alan, Adrienne Epstein, Doris Burford, *et al.*

1989 "Community Health Assessment of a 'Repopulated' Village in El Salvador." *Medical Anthropology Quarterly* 3(3): 270-280.

Mikell, Gwendolyn, ed.

1997 *African Feminism: The Politics of Survival in Sub-Saharan Africa*. Philadelphia: University of Pennsylvania Press.

Millen, Joyce and Bob Lederer

1998 "Banking on Disaster." *POZ*, July, pp. 98-101, 119.

Miller, Ellen and Randy Kehler

1996 "Mischievous Myths About Money in Politics." *Dollars and Sense*, July/August, pp. 22-27.

Miller, Jerome

1996 *Search and Destroy: African-American Males in the Criminal Justice System*. Cambridge: Cambridge University Press.

Miller, Joseph C.

1988 *Way of Death: Merchant Capitalism and the Angolan Slave Trade, 1730-1830*. Madison: University of Wisconsin Press.

Miller, Norman and Richard Rockwell, eds.

1988 *AIDS in Africa: Social and Policy Dimensions*. Lewiston, ME: Edwin Mellen.

Miller, Suzanne

1995 "Case Studies: Profiles of Women Recovering from Drug Addiction." *Journal of Drug Education* 25(2): 139-148.

Millwood, David, ed.

1995 *The International Response to Conflict and Genocide: Lessons from the Rwanda Experience*. Odense, Denmark: Strandberg Grafiske.

Mishel, Lawrence, Jared Bernstein, and John Schmitt

1999 *The State of Working America, 1998-99*. Ithaca, NY: Cornell University Press.

Mitnick, Carole, Jennifer Furin, Cassis Henry, *et al.*

1998 "Tuberculosis Among the Foreign-Born in Massachusetts, 1982-1994: A Reflection of Social and Economic Disadvantage." *International Journal of Tuberculosis and Lung Disease* 2(9): S32-40.

Mkandawire, Thandika

1992 "The Political Economy of Development with a Democratic Face." In *Africa's Recovery in the 1990s: From Stagnation and Adjustment to Human Development*. Giovanni Andre Cornia, Rolph van der Hoeven, and Thandika Mkandawire, eds. New York: St. Martin's Press. Pp. 296-311.

Mkandawire, Thandika and T. Olukoshi, eds.

1994 *Between Liberalization and Repression: The Politics of Structural Adjustment in Africa*. Dakar: CODESRIA Books.

Moffett, George

1995a "A Flap Over Privatizing Foreign Aid." *Christian Science Monitor*, February 27.

1995b "Foreign Aid on GOP Chopping Block." *Christian Science Monitor*, February 22.

Mokhiber, Russell

1988 *Corporate Crime and Violence*. San Francisco: Sierra Club Books.

Molinski, Michael

1997 "Mining Companies See Boom Times Again in Latin America." *Bloomberg News*, April 12.

Montgomery, Tommie Sue

1995 *Revolution in El Salvador: From Civil Strife to Civil Peace*. Boulder, CO: Westview Press.

544 BIBLIOGRAPHY

Moore, Barrington

1958 *Political Power and Social Theory: Six Studies.* Cambridge, MA: Harvard University Press.

Moral, Paul

1961 *Le Paysan Haitien.* Port-au-Prince: Les Éditions Fardin.

Morales, Edmundo

1989 *Cocaine: White Gold Rush in Peru.* Tucson: University of Arizona Press.

Moreau de Saint-Méry

1984 *Description Topographique, Physique, Civile, Politique et Historique de la Partie Française de l'Isle Saint-Dominque (1797-1798).* 3 vols. New ed. B. Maurel and E. Taillemit, eds. Paris: Société de l'Histoire des Colonies Française and Librairie Larose.

Morehouse, Ward

1994 "Unfinished Business: Bhopal Ten Years After." *The Ecologist* 24(5): 164-168.

Morehouse, Ward and M. Arun Subramaniam

1986 *The Bhopal Tragedy.* New York: Council on International and Public Affairs.

Morita, Akio

1993 "Toward a New World Economic Order." *Atlantic Monthly*, June, pp. 88-97.

Morley, Morris

1987 *Imperial State and Revolution: The United States and Cuba, 1952-1986.* Cambridge: Cambridge University Press.

Moscicki, Eve K., Ben Z. Locke, Donald S. Rae, et al.

1989 "Depressive Symptoms Among Mexican Americans: The Hispanic Health and Nutrition Examination Survey." *American Journal of Epidemiology* 130(2): 348-360.

Moscow News

1995 "It is Easier to Die than to Live in Moscow." No. 48, December 8-14.

Moses, Marion

1992 "Pesticides." In *Public Health and Preventive Medicine.* John M. Last and Robert B. Wallace, eds. Norwalk, CT: Appleton and Lange. Pp. 479-489.

Moses, Stephen, Firoze Manji, J.E. Bradley, et al.

1992 "Impact of User Fees on Attendance at a Referral Centre for Sexually Transmitted Diseases in Kenya." *Lancet* 340(8817): 463-466.

Moshavi, Sharon

1995 "Get the Foreign Devils: India's Backlash Against Multinationals Gains Strength." *Business Week*, October 23: 48-49.

Mosher, James F. and Karen L. Yanagisako

1991 "Public Health, Not Social Welfare: A Public Health Approach to Illegal Drug Policy." *Journal of Public Health Policy* 12(3): 278-323.

Mosley, Paul, Turan Subasat, and John Weeks

1995 "Assessing Adjustment in Africa." *World Development* 23(9): 1459-1473.

Moure-Eraso, R., M. Wilcox, L. Punnett, et al.

1994 "Back to the Future: Sweatshop Conditions on the Mexico-U.S. Border. I. Community Health Impact of Maquiladora Industrial Activity." *American Journal of Industrial Medicine* 25: 311-324.

1997 "Back to the Future: Sweatshop Conditions on the Mexico-U.S. Border. II. Occupational Health Impact of Maquiladora Industrial Activity." *American Journal of Industrial Medicine* 31: 587-599.

Muchena, Olivia

1982 *Report on the Situation of Women in Zimbabwe.* Harare: Ministry of Community Development and Women's Affairs.

Mukagasana, Yolande

1997 *La Mort Ne Veut Pas de Moi.* Paris: Editions Fixot.

Mukenge, Tshilemalema

1973 "Les Hommes d'Affaires Zairois: du Travail Salaríe à l'Entreprise Personelle." *Canadian Journal of African Studies* 7: 455-475.

Mukerjee, Madhusree

1995 "Persistently Toxic: The Union Carbide Accident in Bhopal Continues to Harm." *Scientific American* 272(6): 16, 18.

Mulambu Mvulaya

1971 *Contribution à l'Etude de la Revolte des Bapende (Mai-Septembre 1931).* Brussels: Les Cahiers du CEDAF(1).

1974 *Cultures Obligatoires et Colonisation dans l'ex-Congo Belge.* Brussels: Les Cahiers du CEDAF(6-7).

Munene, J.C.

1995 "Structural Adjustment, Labour Commitment, and Cooperation in the Ugandan Service Sector." In *Beyond Economic Liberalization in Africa: Structural Adjustment and the Alternatives.* K. Mengisteab and B.I. Logan, eds. London: Zed Books. Pp. 75-105.

Muniz, José G., José C. Fabián, José C. Manriquez, et al.

1984 "The Recent Worldwide Economic Crisis and the Welfare of Children: The Case of Cuba." *World Development* 12(3): 247-260.

Muntemba, Dorothy

1989 "The Impact of IMF-World Bank Programmes on Women and Children in Zambia." In *The IMF, the World Bank and the African Debt: Vol. I, Economic Impact; Vol. II, Social and Political Impact.* Bade Onimode, ed. London: Zed Books. Pp. 111-124.

Murapa, Rukudzu

1981 "The Political Economy of Zimbabwe: An Historical Exploration." In *The Role of U.S. Universities in Rural and Agricultural Development.* Brooke G. Schoepf, ed. Tuskegee, AL: Tuskegee Institute, Center for Rural Development. Pp. 155-165.

Murray, Christopher J.L. and A.D. Lopez, eds.

1996 *The Global Burden of Disease.* Geneva: World Health Organization.

Murray, Christopher and Alan D. Lopez, eds.

1994 *The Global Burden of Disease.* Cambridge, MA: Harvard University Press.

Murray, Christopher J.L., C.M. Michaud, M. McKenna, et al.
1998 "U.S. County Patterns of Mortality by Race 1965-1994." *Harvard Center for Population and Development Studies Working Paper.* Cambridge, MA: Harvard University Press.

Murray-Garcia, Jan
1995 "African-American Youth: Essential Prevention Strategies for Every Pediatrician." *Pediatrics* 93(1): 132-137.

Musto, David F.
1987 *The American Disease: Origins of Narcotic Control.* New York: Oxford University Press.

Mutukwa, Mebelo K. N. and Oliver S. Saasa
1995 "The Structural Adjustment Program in Zambia: Reflections from the Private Sector." In *Africa's Experience with Structural Adjustment.* World Bank Discussion Paper 288. Kapil Kapoor, ed. Washington, D.C.: World Bank. Pp. 73-87.

Nabuguzi, Emannuel
1991 "Le Magendo en Ouganda." *Politique Africaine* 42: 134-140.

Nader, Ralph and Lori Wallach
1996 "GATT, NAFTA, and the Subversion of the Democratic Process." In *The Case Against the Global Economy.* Jerry Mander and Edward Goldsmith, eds. San Francisco: Sierra Club Books. Pp. 92-107.

National Institute of Justice
1995 *1994 Drug Use Forecasting Annual Report on Adult and Juvenile Arrestees.* NCJ157644. Washington, D.C.: Justice Department, National Institute of Justice.

National Institute on Drug Abuse (NIDA)
1990a *National Drug and Alcoholism Treatment Unit Survey (NDATUS) 1989: Main Findings Report.* Rockville, MD: U.S. Department of Health and Human Services.
1990b *Semiannual Report. Emergency Room Data, Jan 1987-Dec 1989. Medical Examiner Data, July 1986-June 1989.* Rockville, MD: U.S. Department of Health and Human Services (Statistical Series G, No. 24).

National Labor Committee
1995 *Zoned for Slavery: The Child Behind the Label.* Video. New York: Crowing Rooster Arts.
1996 *The U.S. in Haiti: How to Get Rich on 11 Cents an Hour.* New York: National Labor Committee Education Fund.

National Research Council
1995 *Measuring Poverty: A New Approach.* Washington, D.C.: National Academy Press.

National Toxics Campaign Fund
1990 *The Lingering Legacy: Analysis of Carbide-Related Toxins at the Former UCIL Site.* Boston: National Toxics Campaign Fund.

Naylor, R.T.
1987 *Hot Money and the Politics of Debt.* Toronto: McClelland and Stewart.

Neill, Thomas P.
1953 *The Rise and Decline of Liberalism.* Milwaukee: Bruce Publishing.

Nelson, Harry
1996 "Thai Proposals for Openness Agitate Tobacco Multinationals." *Lancet* 347(8994): 112.

Nelson, Joan
1992 "Poverty, Equity, and the Politics of Adjustment." In *The Politics of Economic Adjustment.* Stephan Haggard and Robert Kaufman, eds. Princeton, NJ: Princeton University Press.

Nelson, Joan M., ed.
1989 *Fragile Coalitions: The Politics of Economic Adjustment.* New Brunswick, NJ: Transaction Books.
1990 *Economic Crisis and Policy Choice: The Politics of Adjustment in the Third World.* Princeton, NJ: Princeton University Press.

Nelson, Joan M., Jacek Kochanowicz, Kalman Mizsei, et al.
1994 *Intricate Links: Democratization and Market Reforms in Latin America and Eastern Europe.* New Brunswick, NJ: Transaction Books.

Nelson-Pallmeyer, Jack
1990 *War Against the Poor: Low-Intensity Conflict and Christian Faith.* Maryknoll, N.Y.: Orbis Books.

Neuspiel, Daniel R.
1996 "Racism and Perinatal Addiction." *Ethnicity and Disease* (6): 47-55.

New York State Division of Substance Abuse Services, Bureau of Research and Evaluation
1989 *Street Drug Alert: Street Perspective on Current Trends.* Abstracts of "What Works" Conference. October.

Newbury, Catharine
1988 *The Cohesion of Oppression: Clientship and Ethnicity in Rwanda.* New York: Columbia University Press.

Newbury, Catharine and Brooke G. Schoepf
1989 "State, Peasantry and Agrarian Crisis in Zaire: Does Gender Make a Difference?" In *Women and the State in Africa.* Jane Little Parpart and Kathleen A. Staudt, eds. Boulder, CO: Lynne Reiner. Pp. 91-110.

Newcomb, Polly A., Barry Storer, Matthew Longnecker, et al.
1994 "Lactation and a Reduced Risk of Premenopausal Breast Cancer." *New England Journal of Medicine* 330(2): 81-87.

Newmont Gold Company
1997 "Yanacocha, Peru." Available at www.newmont.com/yanacochab.htm.

Nezavisimaya Gazeta
1995 "Sick People of a Sick City." May 4, 1995, p. 9. For an English translation see the *Current Digest of the Post-Soviet Press,* Vol XLVII, No. 20, 1995, p. 15.

Nicholls, David
1996 *From Dessalines to Duvalier: Race, Colour, and National Independence in Haiti.* London: Macmillan Caribbean.

Nickens, Henry
1995 "The Role of Race/Ethnicity and Social Class in Minority Health Status." *Health Services Research* 30(1): 151-162.

Nicoll, Angus, Ian Timaeus, Rose-Mary Kigadye, et al.
1994 "The Impact of HIV-1 Infection on Mortality in Children Under 5 Years of Age in Sub-Saharan Africa." *AIDS* 8: 995-1005.

Nightingale, Demetra Smith and Nancy Pindus
1997 *Privatization of Public Social Services: A Background Paper.* Washington, D.C.: The Urban Institute.

Nikiforuk, Andrew
1996 *The Fourth Horseman: A Short History of Epidemics, Plagues, Famine, and Other Scourges.* Toronto: Penguin.

Nisbet, John David and Patricia Broadfoot
1980 *The Impact of Research on Policy and Practice in Education.* Aberdeen, Scotland: Aberdeen University Press.

Nkuchia, John M.
1995 "Milking the Last Drops: A Case of the Tobacco Industry in Kenya." In *Tobacco and Health.* Karen Slama, ed. New York: Plenum Press. Pp. 295-299.

Nkuchia, John M., G.A. Giovino, and A.M. Malarcher
1996 "Epidemiological Surveillance of Tobacco Use in Africa." *CHASA Journal of Comprehensive Health.*

Nozick, Robert
1974 *Anarchy, State and Utopia.* New York: Basic Books.

Ntezilyayo, Anastase
1986 "L'Agriculture à l'Horizon 2000 ou Comment Doubler la Production Vivrière au Rwanda." *Revue du Tiers Monde* 27(106): 395-417.
1995 "L'Agriculture: Une Priorité dans la Reconstruction Nationale." In *Les Crises Politiques au Burundi et au Rwanda (1993-1994).* Andre Gichaoua, ed. Paris: Karthala. Pp. 319-338.

Nyongo, Peter André
1978 "Liberal Models of Capitalist Development in Africa: Ivory Coast." *World Development* 3: 5-20.

Nzila, Nzilambi, Marie Laga, A.B. Thiam, et al.
1991 "HIV and Other Sexually Transmitted Diseases Among Female Prostitutes in Kinshasa." *AIDS* 5: 715-722.

O'Connor, Anne-Marie
1997 "Tijuana Union Fight Highlights NAFTA Fears." *Los Angeles Times*, November 7.

O'Hare, William, Kelvin Pollard, Tayniak Mann, et al.
1991 "African-Americans in the 1990s." *Population Bulletin* 46(1): 1-40.

Obbo, Christine
1980 *African Women: Their Struggles for Economic Independence.* London: Zed Press.
1991a "What Went Wrong in Uganda?" In *Uganda Now: Between Decay and Development.* Holger Bernt Hansen and Michael Twaddle, eds. London: James Currey. Pp. 205-223.
1991b "Women, Children and A Living Wage." In *Changing Uganda: The Dilemma of Structural Adjustment and Revolutionary Change.* Holger Bernt Hansen and Michael Twaddle, eds. London: James Currey. Pp. 98-112.
1992 *Needs, Demands and Resources in Relation to Primary Health Care in Kampala.* Kampala: Save the Children Foundation.
1993a "HIV Transmission: Men Are the Solution." *Population and Environment* 14(3): 211-243.
1993b "HIV Transmission Through Social and Geographical Networks in Uganda." *Social Science and Medicine* 36(7): 949-955.
1995a "Gender, Age and Class: Discourses on HIV Transmission and Control in Uganda." In *Culture and Sexual Risk: Anthropological Perspectives on AIDS.* Han ten Brummelhuis and Gilbert Herdt, eds. Amsterdam: Gordon and Breach. Pp. 79-96.
1995b "What Women Can Do: AIDS Crisis Management in Uganda." In *Women Wielding the Hoe: Lessons from Rural Africa for Feminist Theory and Development Practice.* Deborah F. Bryceson, ed. Oxford: Berg Publishers. Pp. 165-178.

OECD (Organization for Economic Cooperation and Development)
1997 *Short-Term Economic Indicators: Transition Economies.* February.
1998 *Development Co-Operation, 1997 Report.* Paris: OECD.

Office of National Drug Control Policy
1995 *Fact Sheet: Drug Use Trends.* Washington, D.C. (NCJ 153518).
1996 *The National Drug Control Strategy.* Washington, D.C. (NCJ160086).

Ohmae, Kenichi
1990 *The Borderless World.* New York: HarperBusiness.

Okuonzi, S.A. and J. Macrae
1995 "Whose Policy Is It Anyway? International and National Influences on Health Policy Development in Uganda." *Health Policy and Planning* 10(2): 122-132.

Olson, Eric
1996 *The Evolving Role of Mexico's Military in Public Security and Antinarcotics Programs.* Washington, D.C.: Washington Office on Latin America.

Onimode, Bade
1992 *A Future for Africa: Beyond the Politics of Adjustment.* London: Earthscan.

Onimode, Bade, ed.
1989 *The IMF, the World Bank and the African Debt: Vol. I, Economic Impact; Vol. II, Social and Political Impact.* London: Zed Books.

Onoge, Omofume
1975 "Capitalism and Public Health: A Neglected Theme in the Medical Anthropology of Africa." In *Topias and Utopias in Health: Policy Studies.* Stanley R. Ingman and Anthony E. Thomas, eds. The Hague: Mouton. Pp. 220-232.

Open Media Research Institute
1995 Daily Digest, Part I, No. 122, June 23.
1996a Daily Digest, Part I, No. 187, September 26.

1996b Daily Digest, Part I, No. 195, October 8.

Ordúñez-García, Pedro O., F. Javier Nieto, Alfredo D. Espinosa-Brito, et al.

1996 "Cuban Epidemic Neuropathy, 1991-1994: History Repeats Itself a Century After the 'Amblyopis of the Blockade.'" *American Journal of Public Health* 86(5): 738-743.

Organization of African Unity (OAU)

1980 *The Lagos Plan of Action for African Economic Development from 1980 to the Year 2000 (LPA)*. Addis Ababa: OAU.

Orthoefer, J., R. Empereur, and J.M. Bacon

1995 "Privatization in the Public Sector: Lessons for Local Health Departments." *Current Issues in Public Health* 1: 186-190.

Osava, Mario

1998 "LATAM Development: Political Reform, Today's New Challenge." *Interpress Service*, March 25.

Osborne, D. and T. Gaebler

1992 *Reinventing Government: How the Entrepreneurial Spirit is Transforming the Public Sector*. Reading, MA: Addison-Wesley Publishing.

OSHA (Occupational Safety and Health Administration)

1991 "Incidence Rates of Nonfatal Occupational Injuries and Illnesses by Industry and Selected Case Types, 1991." Available at www.osha.gov/oshstats/bls/Manuf1.html.

Otten, M., S. Teusch, D. Williams, et al.

1990 "The Effect of Known Risk Factors on the Excess Mortality of Black Adults in the United States." *Journal of the American Medical Association* 263(6): 845-850.

Overseas Development Institute

1995 *Commodity Markets: Options for Developing Countries*. Briefing Paper 5. London: ODI.

Oxfam

1994 *Structural Adjustment and Inequality in Latin America: How IMF and World Bank Policies Have Failed the Poor*. Oxford: Oxfam.

1995 *The Oxfam Poverty Report*. Oxford: Oxfam United Kingdom and Ireland.

1997 *Poor Country Debt Relief: False Dawn or New Hope for Poverty Reduction*. Oxford: Oxfam United Kingdom and Ireland Policy Department.

1998 *Making Debt Relief Work: A Test of Political Will*. Oxford: Oxfam International.

Packard, Randall M.

1989a "The 'Healthy Reserve' and the 'Dressed Native': Discourses on Black Health and the Language of Legitimation in South Africa." *American Ethnologist* 16(4): 686-703.

1989b *White Plague, Black Labor: Tuberculosis and the Political Economy of Health and Disease in South Africa*. Berkeley: University of California Press.

Packard, Randall M. and Paul Epstein

1991 "Epidemiologists, Social Scientists and the Structure of Medical Research on AIDS in Africa." *Social Science and Medicine* 33(7): 771-783; 793-794.

PAHO (Pan American Health Organization)

1962 *Health Conditions in the Americas, 1957-1960*. Scientific Publication, No. 64. Washington, D.C.: Pan American Health Organization.

1984 *Community Participation in Health and Development in the Americas: An Analysis of Selected Case Studies*. Scientific Publication, No. 473. Washington, D.C.: Pan American Health Organization.

1992 *Substance Abuse in the U.S.-Mexico Border Region*. El Paso, TX: El Paso Field Office, PAHO.

1993 *Health Situation Analysis. Haiti 1993*. Port au Prince, Haiti: PAHO.

1994 *Health Conditions in the Americas*. Vols. 1 and 2. Scientific publication, No. 549. Washington, D.C.: Pan American Health Organization, Pan American Sanitary Bureau, Regional Office of the World Health Organization.

1995 *Substance Abuse in the U.S.-Mexico Border Region*. El Paso, TX: El Paso Field Office, PAHO.

1997 "Resolutions of the XL Meeting of the PAHO Governing Council." Doc. CD40/R1. Available at www.paho.org/english/ops97cd1.htm.

PAHO (Pan American Health Organization), WHO (World Health Organization)

1996 *AIDS Surveillance in the Americas*. Quarterly Report (June 10), Regional Program on AIDS/STD, Division of Disease Prevention and Control. Washington, D.C.: Pan American Health Organization and World Health Organization.

PAHO (Pan American Health Organization), WHO (World Health Organization-Haiti)

1993 *Haiti—L'Aide D'Urgence En Santé*. Port-au-Prince: Pan American Health Organization.

Painter, Thomas

1987 "Making Migrants: Zarma Peasants in Niger 1900-1920." In *African Population and Capitalism: Historical Perspectives*. Dennis D. Cordell and Joel W. Gregory, eds. Boulder, CO: Westview Press. Pp. 122-133.

Pallister, David, Sarah Stewart, and Ian Leppe

1998 *South Africa, Inc: The Oppenheimer Empire*. New Haven, CT: Yale University Press.

Palmer, Robin and Neil Parsons, eds.

1977 *The Roots of Rural Poverty in Central and Southern Africa*. Berkeley: University of California Press.

Pan American Sanitary Bureau

1958 *Summary of Four-Year Reports on Health Conditions in the Americas, 1953-1956*. Scientific Publication, no. 40. Washington, D.C.: Pan American Sanitary Bureau.

Pappas, Gregory, Susan Queen, Wilbur Hadden, et al.

1993 "The Increasing Disparity in Mortality Between Socioeconomic Groups in the United States, 1960 and 1986." *New England Journal of Medicine* 329(2): 103-109.

Parfitt, Timothy

1995 "Adjustment for Stability or Growth? Ghana and the Gambia." *Review of African Political Economy* 63: 55-72.

Parnell, Bruce, Juan J. Hernandez, and Cindy Robbins

1996 *Developpement et l'Epidemie a VIH: Evaluation Prospective de l'Approche du Programme VIH et Developpement du PNUD*. New York: United Nations Development Programme.

Parpart, Jane Little and Kathleen A. Staudt, eds.

1989 *Women and the State in Africa*. Boulder, CO: Lynne Reiner.

Parssinen, Terry

1983 *Secret Passions, Secret Remedies: Narcotic Drugs in British Society, 1820-1930*. Philadelphia: Institute for the Study of Human Issues.

Pastor, Jr., Manuel

1987 "The Effects of IMF Programs in the Third World: Debates and Evidence from Latin America." *World Development* 15(2): 249-262.

Pastor, Jr., Manuel and Michael Conroy

1995 "Distributional Implications of Macroeconomic Policy: Theory and Applications to El Salvador." *World Development* 23(12): 2117-2131.

Patterson, K. David

1978 "Bibliographic Essay." In *Disease in African History: An Introductory Survey and Case Studies*. Gerald W. Hartwig and David K. Patterson, eds. Durham, NC: Duke University Press. Pp. 238-250.

1981 *Health in Colonial Ghana: Disease, Medicine and Socio-economic Change*. Waltham, MA: Crossroads Press.

Patterson, K. David and Gerald W. Hartwig

1978 "The Disease Factor: An Introductory Overview." In *Disease in African History: An Introductory Survey and Case Studies*. Gerald W. Hartwig and David K. Patterson, eds. Durham, NC: Duke University Press. Pp. 3-24.

Pattison, Robert V. and H.M. Katz

1983 "Investor-Owned and Not-for-Profit Hospitals. A Comparison Based on California Data." *New England Journal of Medicine* 309(6): 347-353.

Pavetti, LaDonna A.

1993 *The Dynamics of Welfare and Work: Exploring the Process by Which Women Work Their Way Off Welfare*. Cambridge, MA: Harvard University Press.

Payer, Cheryl

1974 *The Debt Trap: The IMF and the Developing Countries*. New York: Monthly Review.

1982 *The World Bank: A Critical Analysis*. New York: Monthly Review Press.

Pean, Pierre

1988 *L'Argent Noir: Corruption et Sous-Developpement*. Paris: Editions Fayard, Verschave and Boisgallais.

Pear, Robert

1996 "Elderly and Poor Do Worse Under H.M.O. Plans' Care." *New York Times*, October 2.

1998 "HMOs are Retreating from Medicare, Citing High Costs." *New York Times*, October 2.

Peña, Bert R. and Amy Henderson

1993 "Effect of NAFTA on Agriculture in the United States and Mexico." *United States-Mexico Law Journal* 275(1993) 1(1): 259-282.

Peña, Devon G.

1997 *The Terror of the Machine: Technology, Work, Gender, and Ecology on the U.S.-Mexico Border*. Austin, TX: University of Texas Press.

Pérez, Jr., Louis A.

1995 *Cuba Between Reform and Revolution*. 2nd ed., Latin American Histories. New York: Oxford University Press.

Pérez-Stable, Eliseo J.

1991 "Cuba's Response to the HIV Epidemic." *American Journal of Public Health* 81(5): 563-567.

Permanent Peoples' Tribunal

1990 "Tribunal on the Policies of the International Monetary Fund and the World Bank, West Berlin, September 26-29, 1988: Verdict." *International Journal of Health Services* 20(2): 329-347.

1992 Findings and Judgments of the Permanent People's Tribunal on Industrial and Environmental Hazards and Human Rights. Third Session. Bhopal.

Perrings, Charles

1979 *Black Mineworkers in Central Africa: Industrial Strategies and the Evolution of an Industrial Proletariat in the Copperbelt, 1911-1941*. London: Heinemann.

Peters, Cynthia, ed.

1992 *The New World Order at Home and Abroad*. Boston: South End Press.

Peters, Enrique Dussel

1998 "Recent Structural Changes in Mexico's Economy: A Preliminary Analysis of Some Sources of Mexican Migration to the United States." In *Crossings: Mexican Immigration in Inter-disciplinary Perspectives*. Marcelo M. Suarez-Orozco, ed. Cambridge, MA: Harvard University Press. Pp. 53-74.

Peters, Pauline

1991 "Debate on the Economy of Affection. Is It a Useful Tool for Analysis?" In *Structural Adjustment and African Women Farmers*. Christina H. Gladwin, ed. Gainesville: University of Florida Press. Pp. 307-320, 324-328.

1995 "Uses and Abuses of the Concept of 'Female-Headed Households.'" In *Women Wielding the Hoe: Lessons From Rural Africa for Feminist Theory and Development Practice*. Deborah F. Bryceson, ed. Oxford: Berg Publishers. Pp. 93-108.

Peters, R. and B. May

1992 "Drug Treatment Services in Jails." In *Drug Abuse Treatment in Prisons and Jails*. C.G. Leukefeld and F.M. Tims, eds. Washington, D.C.: U.S. GPO. Pp. 38-50.

Peto, Richard, A.D. Lopez, J. Boreham, *et al.*

1994 *Mortality from Smoking in Developed Countries 1950-2000, Indirect Estimates from National Vital Statistics*. New York: Oxford University Press.

Petras, James and Steve Vieux

1992 "Myths and Realities: Latin America's Free Markets." *International Journal of Health Services* 22(4): 611-617.

Phillips, Kevin

1990 *The Politics of Rich and Poor*. New York: Harper Perennial.

Pierce, J.P.

1991 "Progress and Problems in International Public Health Efforts to Reduce Tobacco Usage." *Annual Review of Public Health* 12: 383-400.

Pierce, Todd

— *Gen-X Junkie*, Ethnographic Interviews. N.p., n.d.

Pincus, Fred L. and Howard Ehrlich

1994 *Race and Ethnic Conflict: Contending Views on Prejudice, Discrimination, and Ethnoviolence*. San Francisco: Westview Press.

Plotnick, Robert

1993 "Changes in Poverty, Income Equality, and The Standard of Living in the United States During the Reagan Years." *International Journal of Health Services Research* 23(2): 347-358.

Pocekay, Dennis, Stephen McCurdy, Steven J. Samuels, *et al.*

1995 "A Cross-Sectional Study of Musculoskeletal Symptoms and Risk Factors in Semiconductor Workers." *American Journal of Industrial Medicine* 28: 861-871.

Ponnampalam, Mark

1992 *Fourth World: The Third World Within the First World: Implementing Racial Hygiene in the Late Twentieth Century*. Harpenden: United Kingdom Council for Human Rights.

Popkin, Barry, Namvar Zohoori, Lenore Kohlmeier, *et al.*

1997 "Nutritional Risk Factors in the Former Soviet Union." In *Premature Death in the New Independent States*. José Luis Bobadilla, Christine A. Costello, and Faith Mitchell, eds. Washington, D.C.: National Academy Press. Pp. 314-334.

Population Crisis Committee

1992 *The International Human Suffering Index*. Washington, D.C.: Population Crisis Committee.

Porter, Judith

1996 *The Street/Treatment Barrier: Drug Treatment Experiences of Puerto Rican Heroin Injectors*. Unpublished report for the National Institute on Drug Abuse.

Pottier, Johan

1993 "Taking Stock: Food Marketing Reform in Rwanda, 1982-1989." *African Affairs* 92: 5-30.

Presidential Commission on the HIV Epidemic

1988 *Interim report*. March.

Primm, Beny J.

1993 "Drug Abuse in the Community: Race or Racism?" *Annals of Epidemiology* 3: 171-174.

Pritchett, Lant and Deon Filmer

1997 *Child Mortality and Public Spending on Health: How Much Does Money Matter?* Policy Research Working Paper #1864. Washington, D.C.: The World Bank.

Pritchett, Lant, Deon Filmer, and Jeffrey Hammer

1997 *Health Policy in Poor Countries: Weak Links in the Chain*. Policy Research Working Paper #1874. Washington D.C.: World Bank.

Prunier, Gerard

1983 "Le Magendo: Essai sur Quelques Aspects Marginaux des Echanges Commerciales en Afrique Orientale." *Politiquue Africaine* 9: 53-62.

1995 *The Rwanda Crisis: History of a Genocide*. New York: Columbia University Press.

1998 "Forces et Faiblesses du Modele Ougandais." *Le Monde Diplomatique*, February, pp. 12-13.

Public Citizen

1996 *NAFTA's Broken Promises: The Border Betrayed. U.S.-Mexico Border Environment and Health Decline in NAFTA's First Two Years*. Washington, D.C.: Public Citizen Publications.

1997a *The Failed Experiment: NAFTA at Three Years*. Washington, D.C.: Public Citizen Publications.

1997b *NAFTA's Broken Promises: Failure to Create U.S. Jobs*. Washington, D.C.: Public Citizen Publications.

Quinones, Sam

1998 "The Maquiladora Murders." *Ms. Magazine*, May/June, pp. 11-16.

Raffer, Kunibert

1996 "Is the Debt Crisis Largely Over? A Critical Look at the Data of International Financial Institutions." In *Challenging the Orthodoxies*. Richard M. Auty and John Toye, eds. New York: St. Martin's Press. Pp. 23-38.

Raffer, Kunibert and Hans Wolfgang Singer

1996 *The Foreign Aid Business: Economic Assistance and Development Co-Operation*. Cheltenham, U.K.: Edward Elgar.

Raikes, Alanaugh

1989 "Women's Health in East Africa." *Social Science and Medicine* 28(5): 447-460.

Raikes, Phil and Peter Gibbon

1996 "Tanzania." In *Limits of Adjustment in Africa*. Paul Engberg-Petersen, Peter Gibbon, Phil Raikes, eds. Copenhagen: Centre for Development Research (in association with Oxford: James Currey and Portsmouth, N.H.: Heinemann). Pp. 215-308.

Ramírez, Miguel D.

1989 "The Social and Economic Consequences of the National Austerity Program in Mexico." In *Paying the Costs of Austerity in Latin America*. Howard Handelman and Werner Baer, eds. Boulder, CO: Westview Press.

Rangel, Enrique

1998 "Maquiladora Jobs Grow to 1 Million." *The Dallas Morning News*, January 22.

Raskin, Jamin and John Bonifaz

1993 "Equal Protection and the Wealth Primary." *Yale Law and Policy Review* 11(2): 273-332.

Ratcliffe, John

1978 "Social Justice and the Demographic Transition: Lessons from India's Kerala State." *International Journal of Health Services* 8(1): 123-144.

Ratnapriya, S.

1995 "Busting Labor in Sri Lanka." *Multinational Monitor*, January/February, pp. 32-34.

Ratner, Mitchell, ed.

1993 *Crack Pipe as Pimp: An Ethnographic Investigation of Sex-for-Crack Exchanges.* New York: Lexington Books.

Ravallion, Martin

1997 *Can High-Inequality Developing Countries Escape Absolute Poverty?* Policy Research Working Paper #1775. Washington, D.C.: World Bank.

Ravenhill, John

1986 "Collective Self-Reliance or Collective Self-Delusion: Is the Lagos Plan a Viable Alternative?" In *Africa in Economic Crisis.* John Ravenhill, ed. New York: Columbia University Press. Pp. 85-107.

Ravenhill, John, ed.

1986 *Africa in Economic Crisis.* New York: Columbia University Press.

Reardon, Judy

1993 *The Drug-Use Forecasting Program: Measuring Drug Use in a Hidden Population.* NCJ 144784. Washington, D.C.: National Institute of Justice.

Redlinger, T., K. O'Rourke, and J. VanDerslice

1997 "Hepatitis A Among Schoolchildren in a U.S.-Mexico Border Community." *American Journal of Public Health* 87(10): 1715-1717.

Reich, Robert

1992 *The Work of Nations.* New York: Alfred A Knopf.

Reid, Elizabeth, ed.

1995 *HIV and AIDS: The Global Dimension.* West Hartford, CT: Kumarian Press.

Reif, Linda

1994 "Book Review: Multidisciplinary Perspectives on the Improvement of International Environmental Law and Institutions." *Michigan Journal of International Law* 15(705): 723-745.

Renshaw, Laurie

1995 *The Impact of Structural Adjustment on Community Life: Undoing Development.* Boston: Oxfam America.

Republic of Cuba

1994 *Plan Nacional de Acción para la Nutrición.* N.p.

Republic of Perú

1997a "Dictamen en Minoría Sobre el Proyecto de Ley No. 2263/96, Ley General de Salud." Lima: June 10, 1997.

1997b "Dictamen, Proyecto de Ley No. 2263/96—CR. Ley General de Salud." Congreso de la Republica. June 3, 1997.

Republic of Perú, Ministry of Health

1992 "Un Sector Salud con Equidad, Eficiencia y Calidad: Lienamientos de Política de Salud 1995-2000."

1995 "La Reforma del Sector Salud en el Perú, 1995."

1996a "Analisis Situacional de la Gestión de los Servicios de Salud y Propuesta Etratégica, Programa de Fortalecimiento de Servicios de Salud." Lima.

1996b "La Reforma del Sector Salud, Documento de Trabajo." Lima.

1996c "Un Nuevo Modelo para el Cuidado de la Salud, Documento de Trabajo." Lima.

Republic of Perú, National Institute for Statistics and Information (INEI)

1990 "Compendio Estadístico 1989-1990." Lima.

Republic of Perú, National Planning Institute (INP)

1992 Programas de Apoyo Sectorial de Salud, Documento de Trabajo." Lima.

Republique du Rwanda

1984a Enquête Nationale sur le Budget et la Consommation des Menages (ENBC), Vol. I. Kigali: Ministére de L'Agriculture, November.

1984b Enquete Agricole Nationale (ENA), Vol. I. Kigali: Ministére de l'Agriculture, September.

1988 IV eme Plan Quinquennal de Développement, 1988-1992. Kigali: Ministére du Plan.

1992 Evaluation du III eme Plan Quinquennal de Développement, 1988-1992. Kigali: Ministére du Plan.

Reuter, Peter, Robert MacCoun, and Patrick Murphy.

1990 *Money from Crime: A Study of the Economics of Drug Dealing in Washington, D.C.* Santa Monica: RAND, Drug Policy Research Center.

Reyna, Stephen P.

1996 "The Dating Game: Subalterns and Their Knowledges." Paper presented at the 95th Annual Meeting of the American Anthropological Association, San Francisco, November 20-24.

Reyna, Stephen P. and Robert E. Downs

1999 *Deadly Developments: Capitalism, States, and War.* New York: Gordon and Breach.

Ribe, Helena, Soniya Carvalho, Robert Liebenthal, et al.

1990 *How Adjustment Programs Can Help the Poor: The World Bank's Experience.* Washington, D.C.: World Bank.

Ricardo, Izabel B.

1994 "Life Choices of African-American Youth Living in Public Housing: Perspectives on Drug Trafficking." *Pediatrics* 93(6): 1055-1059.

Rich, Bruce

1994 *Mortgaging the Earth: The World Bank, Environmental Impoverishment, and the Crisis of Development.* Boston: Beacon Press.

Richardson, Laurie

1997 *Feeding Dependency, Starving Democracy: USAID Policies in Haiti. A Report from Grassroots International.* Boston: Grassroots International.

Richardson, Laurie and Jean-Roland Chéry

1995 "Haiti's Not for Sale Yet." *Covert Action Quarterly* 53: 30-37.

Richter, E.D. and J. Safi

1997 "Pesticide Use, Exposure, and Risk: A Joint Israeli-Palestinian Perspective." *Environmental Research* 73: 211-218.

Ridenour, Ron

1991 *Backfire: The CIA's Biggest Burn.* Habana: Editorial José Martí.

Rimashevskaia, Natal'ia

1993 "The Individual's Health is the Health of Society." *Sociological Research* 32(3): 22-34.

Rivero, J., M. Limonta, A. Aguilera, *et al.*

1994 "Use of Recombinant Interferon-alpha in Human Immunodeficiency Virus (HIV)-Infected Individuals." *Biotherapy* 8(1): 23-31.

Robbins, Joel

1994 "Equality as Value: Ideology in Dumont, Melanesia and the West." *Social Analysis* 36: 21-70.

Roberts, D.E.

1991 "Punishing Drug Addicts Who Have Babies: Women of Color, Equality, and the Right of Privacy." *Harvard Law Review* 104(7): 1419-1482.

Robertson, Claire C.

1984 *Sharing the Same Bowl: A Socio-economic History of Women and Class in Accra, Ghana.* Bloomington: Indiana University Press.

Robertson, Claire C. and Iris Berger, eds.

1986 *Women and Class in Africa.* New York: Africana.

Robertson, Claire C. and Martin A. Klein, eds.

1983 *Women and Slavery in Africa.* Madison: University of Wisconsin Press.

Robins, Edward

1990 "The Lesson of Rwanda's Agricultural Crisis: Increase Productivity, Not Food Aid." In *African Food Systems in Crisis.* Rebecca Huss-Ashmore and Solomon H. Katz, eds. New York: Gordon and Breach. Pp. 245-268.

Rodgers, Gerry, ed.

1995 *The Poverty Agenda and the ILO: Issues for Research and Action.* Geneva: International Labor Organization.

Rodney, Walter

1970 *A History of the Upper Guinea Coast, 1545 to 1800.* Oxford: Oxford University Press.

1972 *How Europe Underdeveloped Africa.* Dar es Salaam: Tanzania Publishing House.

Rodrik, Dani

1997 *Has Globalization Gone Too Far?* Washington, D.C.: Institute for International Economics.

1998 "Why Do More Open Economies Have Bigger Governments?" *Journal of Political Economy* 106(5): 997-1032.

Román, Gustavo C.

1995a "Epidemic Neuropathy in Cuba: A Plea to End the United States Economic Embargo on a Humanitarian Basis." *Journal of Public Health Policy* 16(1): 5-12.

1995b "On Politics and Health: An Epidemic of Neurologic Disease in Cuba." *Annals of Internal Medicine* 122(7): 530-533.

Rosenbaum, Ruth

1992 *Market Basket Survey: A Comparison of the Buying Power of Maquiladora Workers in Mexico and the United Auto Workers Assembly Workers in General Motors Plants in the United States.* The Coalition for Justice in the Maquiladoras.

1994 *Market Basket Survey: A Comparison of the Buying Power of Maquiladora Workers in Mexico and the United Auto Worker Assembly Workers in General Motors Plants in the United States.* Newton Center, MA: Research and Report Service for Ethical and Socially Responsible Investing. F.L. Putnam Securities, Inc.

Rosenbaum, Ruth, L. Charkoudian, and K. Wrinn

1996 *In Whose Interest? Using the Purchasing Power Index to Analyze Plans, Programs, and Policies of Industrialization and Development in Haiti.* Hartford: The Center for Research, Education, and Action, Inc.

Rosenberg, Charles

1962 *The Cholera Years.* Chicago: University of Chicago Press.

Rostow, Walt Whitman

1960 *The Stages of Economic Growth, a Non-Communist Manifesto.* Cambridge: Cambridge University Press.

Rotberg, Robert I., ed.

1971 *Rebellion in Black Africa.* London: Oxford University Press.

Rothschild, Donald and E. Gyimah-Boadi

1986 "Ghana's Economic Decline and Development Strategies." In *Africa in Economic Crisis.* John Ravenhill, ed. New York: Columbia University Press. Pp. 254-285.

Routh, Guy

1989 *The Origin of Economic Ideas.* Dobbs Ferry, N.Y.: Sheridan House.

Rubin, Elizabeth

1997 "An Army of One's Own." *Harper's*, February, pp. 44-55.

Rudolph, James D.

1992 *Peru: The Evolution of a Crisis.* London: Praeger.

Ruggie, John Gerard

1985 "International Regimes, Transactions, and Change: Embedded Liberalism in the Postwar International Order." In *International Regimes.* Stephen D. Krasner, ed. Ithaca, NY: Cornell University Press. Pp. 195-232.

Rush, David and Kathleen Welch

1996 "The First Year of Hyperinflation in the Former Soviet Union: Nutritional Deprivation Among Elderly Pensioners, 1992." *American Journal of Public Health* 86(3): 361-367.

Russell, Diane

1988 *The Outlook for Liberalization in Zaire: Evidence from Kisangani's Rice Trade.* Boston: Boston University, Center for African Studies.

Rybinskii, E.M.

1996 "The Position of Children in Russia." *Russian Social Science Review* 37(2): 78-95. The original Russian text first appeared in *Pedagogika* no. 6 (1994): pp. 3-12.

Ryder, R.W., M. Kamenga, M. Nkusu, *et al.*

1994 "AIDS Orphans in Kinshasa, Zaire: Incidence and Socio-Economic Consequences." *AIDS* 8: 673-679.

Sachikonye, Lloyd M.

1995 "Industrial Relations and Labor Relations under ESAP in Zimbabwe." In *Structural Adjustment and the Working Poor in Zimbabwe*. Peter Gibbon, ed. Uppsala, Sweden: Nordiska Afrikainstitutet.

Sachs, Jeffrey D.

1985 "External Debt and Macroeconomic Performance in Latin America and East Asia." *Brookings Papers on Economic Activity* 1985(2): 523-564.

1997 "The Wrong Medicine for Asia." *New York Times*, November 3.

Sachs, Jeffrey D. and Carlos E. Paredes, eds.

1991 *Peru's Path to Recovery: A Plan for Economic Stabilization and Growth*. Washington, D.C.: Brookings Institute.

Sachs, Wolfgang, ed.

1992 *The Development Dictionary: A Guide to Knowledge as Power*. London: Zed Books.

Safilios-Rothschild, Constantina

1985 *Socioeconomic Development and the Status of Women in the Third World*. Center for Policy Studies. Working Paper 112. New York: Population Council.

Samarin, William J.

1989 *The Black Man's Burden: African Colonial Labor on the Congo and Ubangi Rivers, 1880-1900*. Boulder, CO: Westview Press.

Sanders, David and Abdulrhaman Sambo

1991 "AIDS in Africa: The Implications of Economic Recession and Structural Adjustment." *Health Policy and Planning* 6: 157-165.

Sanders, Edith

1969 "The Hamitic Hypothesis: Its Function and Origins in Time Perspective." *Journal of African History* 10(4): 521-532.

Santana, Sarah M.

1990 "Whither Cuban Medicine? Challenges for the Next Generation." In *Transformation and Struggle: Cuba Faces the 1990s*. Sandor Halebsky and John M. Kirk, eds. New York: Praeger. Pp. 251-270.

Santana, Sarah M., Lily Faas, and Karen Wald

1991 "Human Immunodeficiency Virus in Cuba: The Public Health Response of a Third World Country." *International Journal of Health Services* 21(3): 511-537.

Sargent, Carolyn

1989 *Maternity, Medicine, and Power: Reproductive Decisions in Urban Benin*. Berkeley: University of California Press.

Sassen, Saskia

1990 *The Mobility of Labor and Capital: A Study in International Investment and Labor Flow*. Cambridge: Cambridge University Press.

1998 *Globalization and Its Discontents*. New York: New Press.

Sauvy, Alfred

1961 *Le "Tiers-monde," Sous-developpement et Developpement*. Georges Balandier, ed. Paris: Presses Universitaires de France.

Sawer, J., J. Brown, L. Folke, *et al.*

1989 "Hepatitis A in a Border Community." *Border Health* 5(9): 2-5.

Sayed, Shiraz

1986 "The Multi-Billion Dollar Flight of Capital Out of the Third World." *London Observer*, September 28.

Schanberg, Sydney and Marie Dorigny

1996 "Six Cents an Hour." *Life*, June, pp. 38-48.

Schapp, Bill

1982 "U.S. Biological Warfare: The 1981 Cuba Dengue Epidemic." *Covert Action Quarterly* 17: 28-31.

1984 "News Notes: Omega 7 and Dengue Fever." *Covert Action Quarterly* 22: 35.

Schatzberg, Michael G.

1980 *Politics and Class in Zaire*. New York: Africana.

Schechter, S.

1995 "The War on Drugs: An Alternative Approach." *Rhode Island Medicine* 78(6): 154-155.

Schemo, Diana Jean

1997 "Peru's Stark Poverty Dulls Fujimori's Gleam." *New York Times*, June 10.

Scheper-Hughes, Nancy

1993 "AIDS, Public Health, and Human Rights in Cuba." *Lancet* 342(8877): 965-967.

1996 "Small Wars and Invisible Genocides." *Social Science and Medicine* 43(5): 889-900.

Schieber G. and A. Maeda

1997 "A Curmudgeon's Guide to Financing Health Care in Developing Countries." In *Innovations in Health Care Financing: Proceedings of a World Bank Conference*. World Bank Discussion Paper 365. Washington, D.C.: World Bank.

Schiffer, Craig

1995 "Newmont Touts Yanacocha Costs." *American Metal Market* 103(157): 5.

Schiller, Herbert

1989 *Culture Inc.* Oxford: Oxford University Press.

Schlesinger, Mark and Robert Dorwart

1992 "Falling Between the Cracks: Failing National Strategies for Treatment of Substance Abuse." *Daedalus* 121(3): 195-237.

Schmitt, Eric

1998 "Bill to Push Africa Trade Is Approved." *New York Times*, March 16.

Schmoke, Kurt L.

1995 "Medicalizing the War on Drugs." *Academic Medicine* 70(5): 355-358.

Schoenberger, Erica

1998 "Discourse and Practice in Human Geography." *Progress in Human Geography* 22(1): 1-14.

Schoepf, Brooke G.

1986 "Primary Health Care in Zaire." *Review of African Political Economy* (36): 54-58.

1987 "Social Structure, Women's Status and Sex Differential Nutrition in the Zairian Copperbelt." *Urban Anthropology* 6(1): 73-102.

1988a "Rwanda: Economic Hardship." In *1988 Collier's Yearbook*. New York: Macmillan. Pp. 440-441.

1988b "Women, AIDS and Economic Crisis in Zaire." *Canadian Journal of African Studies* 22(3): 625-644.

1991a "Ethical, Methodological and Political Issues of AIDS Research in Central Africa." *Social Science and Medicine* 33(7): 749-763.

1991b "Gender Relations and Development: Political Economy and Culture." In *Twenty-First Century Africa: Towards A New Vision of Self-Sustainable Development.* Ann Seidman and Fred Anang, eds. Trenton, NJ: Africa World Press. Pp. 203-241.

1992 "Aids, Sex and Condoms: African Hearers and the Reinvention of Tradition in Zaire." *Medical Anthropology* 13: 1-18.

1993a "Action-Research on AIDS with Women in Kinshasa: Community-Based Risk Reduction Support." *Social Science and Medicine* 37(11): 1401-1413.

1993b "Women and AIDS: A Gender and Development Approach." In *Women and International Development Annual.* Rita Gallin, Anne Ferguson, and Janice Harper, eds. Boulder, CO: Westview Press. Pp. 55-85.

1995a "Culture, Sex Research and AIDS Prevention in Africa." In *Culture and Sexual Risk: Anthropological Perspectives on AIDS.* Han ten Brummelhuis and Gilbert Herdt, eds. Amsterdam: Gordon and Breach. Pp. 29-52.

1995b "Genocide and Gendered Violence in Rwanda, 1994." Paper presented at the American Anthropological Association Annual Meeting. Washington, D.C. November 15-19.

1996 "When Structural Violence Goes Corporeal: The Political Ecology of Genocide in Rwanda." Paper presented at the American Anthropological Association 95th Annual Meeting. San Francisco. November 20-24.

1998 "Inscribing the Body Politic: Women and AIDS in Africa." In *Pragmatic Women and Body Politics.* Margaret Lock and Patricia Kaufert, eds. Cambridge: Cambridge University Press. Pp. 98-126.

Schoepf, Brooke G., ed.

1981 *The Role of U.S. Universities in Rural and Agricultural Development.* Tuskegee, AL: Tuskegee Institute, Center for Rural Development.

Schoepf, Brooke G. and Claude Schoepf

1981 "Zaire's Rural Development in Perspective." In *The Role of U.S. Universities in Rural and Agricultural Development.* Brooke G. Schoepf, ed. Tuskegee, AL: Tuskegee Institute, Center for Rural Development. Pp. 243-259.

1984 "Peasants, Capitalists and the State in the Lufira Valley (Zaire)." *Canadian Journal of African Studies* 18(1): 89-93.

1988 "Land, Gender and Food Security in Eastern Kivu." In *Agriculture, Women and Land: The African Experience.* Jean Davison, ed. Boulder, CO: Westview Press. Pp.106-130.

Schoepf, Brooke G., Rukarangira wa Nkera, Claude Schoepf, et al.

1988 "AIDS and Society in Central Africa: A View from Zaire." In *AIDS in Africa: Social and Policy Dimensions.* Norman Miller and Richard Rockwell, eds. Lewiston, ME: Edwin Mellen. Pp. 211-235.

Schoepf, Brooke G. and Walu Engundu

1991 "Women's Trade and Contributions to Household Budgets in Kinshasa." In *The Real Economy of Zaire: The Contribution of Smuggling and Other Unofficial Activities to the National Economy of Zaire.* Janet MacGaffey, ed. London: James Currey. Pp. 124-151.

Schoepf, Brooke G., Walu Engundu, Diane Russell, et al.

1991 "Women and Structural Adjustment in Zaire." In *Structural Adjustment and African Women Farmers.* Christina H. Gladwin, ed. Gainesville: University of Florida Press. Pp. 151-168.

Schoultz, Lars

1987 *National Security and United States Policy Toward Latin America.* Princeton, NJ: Princeton University Press.

Schultz, K.F., W. Cates, Jr., P.R. O'Mara

1994 "Pregnancy Loss, Infant Death and Suffering: Legacy of Syphilis and Gonorrhea in Africa." *Genourinary Medicine* 63: 191-195.

Schwartz, Susana

1995 "Discovering the Americas." *Insurance & Technology* 7: 36-40.

Scott, Noll

1994 "Fujimori's Peru: A State in Its Leader's Image." *The Guardian* (London), November 5.

Scott, Peter Dale and Jonathan Marshall

1991 *Cocaine Politics.* Berkeley: University of California Press.

Scrimshaw, Neville S., Carl E. Taylor, and J.E. Gordon

1959 "Interactions of Nutrition and Infection." *American Journal of Medical Science* 237: 367-403.

Sebrell, W.H., Sam C. Smith, Elmer Severinghaus, et al.

1959 "Appraisal of Nutrition in Haiti." *American Journal of Clinical Nutrition* 7: 528-584.

Seers, Dudley

1972 "What Are We Trying to Measure?" In *Measuring Development.* Nancy Baster, ed. London: Frank Cass. Pp. 21-36.

Segall, Malcolm

1973 "The Politics of Health in Tanzania." *Development and Change (1972-1973)* 4(1): 39-50.

Seidman, Ann

1974a *Planning for Development in Sub-Saharan Africa.* Dar es Salaam: Tanzania Publishing House.

1974b "The Distorted Growth of Import-Substitution Industry: The Zambian Case." *Journal of Modern African Studies* 12: 601-631.

1977 "The Economics of Eliminating Rural Poverty." In *The Roots of Rural Poverty in Central and Southern Africa.* Neil Parsons and Robin Palmer, eds. London: Heinemann Educational. Pp. 410-423.

Seidman, Ann and Fred Anang, eds.

1991 *Twenty-First Century Africa: Towards A New Vision of Self-Sustainable Development.* Trenton, NJ: Africa World Press.

Seidman, Ann and Neva Seidman Makgetla

1980 *Outposts of Monopoly Capitalism: Southern Africa in the Changing Global Economy.* Westport, CT: Lawrence Hill.

Selcraig, Bruce

1992 "From Great River to Foul Gutter: The Descent of the Rio Grande." *Los Angeles Times*, May 19.

Sen, Amartya K.

1985 *Commodities and Capabilities.* Amsterdam: North-Holland.

1988 "The Concept of Development." In *Handbook of Development Economics, Volume I.* Hollis Chenery and T.N. Srinivasan, eds. New York: Elsevier Science Publishers. Pp. 10-26.

1992 *Inequality Reexamined.* Cambridge, MA: Harvard University Press.

1993 "Capability and Well-Being." In *The Quality of Life.* Martha Nussbaum and Amartya Sen, eds. New York: Oxford University Press. Pp. 30-54.

1995 "The Political Economy of Targeting." In *Public Spending and the Poor: Theory and Evidence.* Dominique van de Walle and Kimberly Nead, eds. Baltimore and London: Johns Hopkins University Press. Pp. 11-24.

1996 *Poverty and Child Health.* Oxford: Radcliff Medical Press.

1997 *On Economic Inequality* (Expanded Edition). Oxford: Clarendon Press.

Sen, Gita and Karen Grown, eds.

1987 *Development Crises and Alternative Visions: Third World Women's Perspectives.* New York: Monthly Review.

Seshimana, V. and Thomas Saasa

1993 *Constraints to Service Delivery in Lusaka.* Lusaka: World Bank.

Setel, Philip

1996 "AIDS as a Paradox of Manhood and Development in Kilimanjaro, Tanzania." *Social Science and Medicine* 43(8): 1169-1178.

Setel, Philip, Chijene Wiseman, and Eleanor Preston-Whyte, eds.

1994 "Sexual Networking, Knowledge, and Risk: Contextual Knowledge for Confronting AIDS and STDs in Eastern and Southern Africa." *Health Transition Review* 7(Supplement 3): 1-107.

Sethi, B.B., M. Sharma, H.K. Trivedi, *et al.*

1987 "Psychiatric Morbidity in Patients Attending Clinics in Gas-Affected Areas in Bhopal." *Indian Journal of Medical Research* 86(Supplement): 45-50.

Sevodnia

1995 "Russia May Become a Country of Widows." *Current Digest of the Post-Soviet Press*, XLVII, no. 29 (July 19), pp. 17-18.

Shabecoff, Philip

1985 "Union Carbide Had Been Told of Leak Danger." *New York Times*, January 25.

Shakow, Don and Aaron Shakow

1996 *Interim Report to the Bullitt Foundation, Democratic Governance Project.* Unpublished paper. Seattle, WA: Institute For Washington's Future.

Shalom, Stephen

1993 *Imperial Alibis.* Boston: South End Press.

Shapiro, Helen

1994 *Engines of Growth: The State and Transnational Auto Companies in Brazil.* Cambridge: Cambridge University Press.

1996 "The Mechanics of Brazil's Auto Industry." *NACLA Report on the Americas* 29(4): 28-33.

Shapiro, Helen and Lance Taylor

1990 "The State and Industrial Strategy." *World Development* 18(6): 861-878.

Shapiro, Isaac and Robert Greensteinf

1993 *Making Work Pay: The Unfinished Agenda.* Washington, D.C.: Center on Budget and Policy Priorities.

Shapiro, Judith

1995 "The Russian Mortality Crisis and Its Causes." In *Russian Economic Reform at Risk.* Anders Aslund, ed. London: Pinter Publishers. Pp. 149-178.

Sharara, Fady I., David B. Seifer, and Jodi A. Flaws

1998 "Environmental Toxicants and Female Reproduction." *Fertility and Sterility* 70(4): 613-622.

Shaw, R.P. and C.C. Griffin

1995 *Financing Health Care in Sub-Saharan Africa Through User Fees and Insurance.* Washington, D.C.: World Bank.

Sheikh-Hashim, Leila and Anna Gabba

1990 *Violence Against Women in Dar es Salaam: A Case Study of Three Districts.* Dar es Salaam: TAMWA (Tanzania Media Women's Association) Research Report.

Shelby, B.

1996 "Shell Under Fire." *World Press Review*, February 28.

Shepherd, George

1990 "The African Right to Development: World Policy and the Debt Crisis." *Africa Today* 37(4): 5-14.

Shichor, David

1995 *Punishment for Profit: Private Prisons/Public Concerns.* Thousand Oaks, CA: Sage Publications.

Shkolnikov, Vladimir M. and Alexander Nemtsov

1997 "The Anti-Alcohol Campaign and Variations in Russian Mortality." In *Premature Death in the New*

Independent States. José Luis Bobadilla, Christine A. Costello, and Faith Mitchell, eds. Washington, D.C.: National Academy Press. Pp. 239-261.

Shortell, Steven M. and Edward F.X. Hughes

1988 "The Effects of Regulation, Competition, and Ownership on Mortality Rates Among Hospital Inpatients." *New England Journal of Medicine* 318(17): 1100-1107.

Shrivastava, Paul

1990 *Bhopal: Anatomy of a Crisis.* Bristol, PA: Taylor and Francis.

Sidel, Ruth

1996 *Keeping Women and Children Last.* New York: Penguin Books.

Sidel, Victor W.

1995 "The International Arms Trade and Its Impact on Health." *British Medical Journal* 311: 1677-1680.

Sidel, Victor W. and Gurinder S. Shahi

1997 "The Impact of Military Activities on Development, Environment, and Health." In *International Perspectives on Environment, Development, and Health: Toward a Sustainable World.* Gurinder S. Shahi, ed. New York: Springer Publishing Company. Pp. 283-312.

Siegal, Daniel and Joy Hackel

1988 "El Salvador: Counterinsurgency Revisited." In *Low-Intensity Warfare: Counterinsurgency, Proinsurgency, and Anti-Terrorism in the Eighties.* Michael T. Klare and Peter Kornbluh, eds. New York: Pantheon Books. Pp. 112-135.

Sigerist, Henry

1951 *History of Medicine, Volume I: Civilization and Disease.* New Haven, CT: Yale Medical Library.

Sills, Marc A. and Glenn T. Morris, eds.

1993 *Indigenous Peoples' Politics: An Introduction.* Denver: University of Colorado at Denver, Fourth World Center for the Study of Indigenous Law and Politics.

Simmons, Pat

1995 *Words into Action: Basic Rights and the Campaign Against World Poverty.* Oxford: Oxfam.

Simpson, D.

1993 "Drug Treatment Evaluation Research in the United States." *Psychology of Addictive Behaviors* 7(2): 120-128.

Singh, A.S., B. Jang, and V.C. Lakhan

1989 "Business Ethics and the International Trade in Hazardous Wastes." *Journal of Business Ethics* 8(11): 889-899.

Singh, Ajit

1995 *Corporate Financial Patterns in Industrializing Economies: A Comparative International Study.* Technical paper No. 2. Washington, D.C.: International Finance Corporation.

1996 *Pension Reform, the Stock Market, Capital Formation and Economic Growth: A Critical Commentary on the World Bank's Proposals.* CEPA Working paper Series I, Working paper No. 2. New York: Center for Economic Policy Analysis, New School for Social Research.

1997 "Financial Liberalisation, Stock Markets, and Economic Development." *Economic Journal* 442: 771-782.

Singh, Ajit and Bruce A. Weisse

1998 "Emerging Stock Markets, Portfolio Capital Flows and Long-Term Economic Growth: Micro and Macroeconomic Perspectives." *World Development* 26(4): 607-622.

Sinton, Peter

1997 "How Much HMOs Spent on Patients." *San Francisco Chronicle,* February 22.

Sivard, Ruth Leger

1989 *World Military and Social Expenditures, 1989.* Washington, D.C.: World Priorities.

1993 *World Military and Social Expenditures 1993.* Washington, D.C.: World Priorities.

Skalnick, Peter, ed.

1989 *Outwitting the State.* New Brunswick, NJ: Transaction Books.

Skinner, Elliott P.

1960 "Labour Migration and Its Relationship to Socioeconomic Change in Mossi Society." *Africa* 30(4): 375-399.

1981 "The Global Economic Order and the Poor Villages." In *The Role of U.S. Universities in Rural and Agricultural Development.* Brooke G. Schoepf, ed. Tuskegee, AL: Tuskegee Institute, Center for Rural Development. Pp. 8-18.

Sklair, Leslie

1993 *Assembling for Development: The Maquila Industry in Mexico and the United States.* University of California, San Diego: Center for U.S.-Mexican Studies.

Sklar, Holly

1995 *Chaos or Community?: Seeking Solutions, Not Scapegoats for Bad Economics.* Boston: South End Press.

Sklar, Richard

1975 *Corporate Power in an African State: The Political Impact of Multinational Mining Companies.* Berkeley: University of California Press.

Skocpol, Theda

1995 "Targeting Within Universalism: Politically Viable Policies to Combat Poverty in the United States." In *Social Policy in the United States: Future Possibilities in Historical Perspective.* Theda Skocpol, ed. Princeton, NJ: Princeton University Press. Pp: 250-274.

Skolnick, Andrew A.

1992 "Some Experts Suggest the Nation's 'War on Drugs' Is Helping Tuberculosis Stage a Deadly Comeback." *Journal of the American Medical Association* 268(22): 3177-3178.

1994 "Along U.S. Southern Border, Pollution, Poverty, Ignorance, and Greed Threaten Nation's Health." *Journal of the American Medical Association* 273(19): 1478-1482.

1995 "Forensic Scientists Helping Haiti Heal." *Journal of the American Medical Association* 274(15): 1181-1182.

Skolnick, Jerome

1992 "Rethinking the Drug Problem." *Daedalus* 121(3): 133-159.

Smith, Adam

1776 *The Wealth of Nations.* 1982 Edition. New York: Penguin Books.

Smith, David and Ruth Stewart

1994 *Annual Report: 1993-1994.* Austin, TX: Texas Department of Health.

Smith, Eva Marie

1993 "Race or Racism? Addiction in the United States" *Annals of Epidemiology* 3: 165-170.

Smith, S., M. Freeland, S. Heffler, *et al.*

1998 "The Next Ten Years of Health Spending: What Does the Future Hold?" *Health Affairs* 17(5): 128-140.

Smith, Sandy

1985 "Rain of Terror: The Bombing of Civilians in El Salvador." *Health and Medicine* 3(1): pp. 21, 26-28.

Smith, Steven Rathgeb and Michael Lipsky

1992 "Privatization in Health and Human Services: A Critique." *Journal of Health Politics, Policy and Law* 17(2): 233-253.

Smith, William C., Carlos H. Acuña, and Eduardo A. Gamarra, eds.

1994 *Latin American Political Economy in the Age of Neoliberal Reform: Theoretical and Comparative Perspectives for the 1990s.* New Brunswick, NJ: Transaction Books.

Smith-Nonini, Sandy

1993 *Insurgent Health: Contesting Biomedical Hegemony in El Salvador.* Master's Thesis. Chapel Hill: University of North Carolina.

1997a "'Popular' Health and the State: Dialectics of the Peace Process in El Salvador." *Social Science and Medicine* 44(5): 635-645.

1997b "Primary Health Care and Its Unfulfilled Promise of Community Participation: Lessons from a Salvadoran War Zone." *Human Organization* 56(3): 364-374.

Sollis, Peter

1996 "Partners in Development? The State, NGOs and the United Nations in Central America." In *Nongovernmental Organizations, the United Nations and Global Governance.* Thomas Weiss and Leon Gordenker, eds. Boulder, CO: Lynne Reinner. Pp. 189-206.

Solow, Robert

1956 "A Contribution to the Theory of Economic Growth." *Quarterly Journal of Economics* 70(1): 65-94.

Soros, George

1998 *The Crisis of Global Capitalism: Open Society Endangered.* London: Little, Brown.

Southall, Aidan

1988 "'The Rain Fell on Its Own'—The Alur Theory of Development and Its Western Counterparts." *African Studies Review* 31(2): 1-16.

Sparr, Pam, ed.

1994 *Mortgaging Women's Lives: Feminist Critiques of Structural Adjustment.* London: Zed Books.

Spencer, Nick

1996 *Poverty and Child Health.* Oxford: Radcliffe Medical Press.

St. John, Spencer

1884 *Hayti: Or the Black Republic.* London: Smith and Elder.

Stallings, Barbara and Robert Kaufman, eds.

1989 *Debt and Democracy in Latin America.* Boulder, CO: Westview Press.

Stamp, Patricia

1989 *Technology, Gender, and Power in Africa.* Ottawa: International Development Research Center.

Stanley, William

1996 *The Protection Racket State: Elite Politics, Military Extortion, and Civil War in El Salvador.* Philadelphia: Temple University Press.

Stanton, Bonita and J. Galbraith

1994 "Drug Trafficking Among African-American Early Adolescents: Prevalence, Consequences, and Associated Behaviors and Beliefs." *Pediatrics* 93(6): 1039-1043.

Starn, Orin

1991 "Missing the Revolution: Anthropologists and the War in Peru." *Social Science and Medicine* 6(1): 63-91.

Stauber, John and Sheldon Rampton

1995 *Toxic Sludge Is Good For You: Lies, Damn Lies, and the Public Relations Industry.* Monroe, ME: Common Courage Press.

Staudt, Kathleen

1987 "Uncaptured or Unmotivated? Women and the Food Crisis in Africa." *Rural Sociology* 52(1): 37-55.

Steady, Filomina Chioma, ed.

1992 *Women and Children First: Environment, Poverty, and Sustainable Development.* Rochester, VT: Schenkman Books.

Stebbins, Kenyon R.

1991 "Tobacco, Politics, and Economics: Implications for Global Health." *Social Science and Medicine* 33(12): 1317-1326.

1994 "Making a Killing South of the Border: Transnational Cigarette Companies in Mexico and Guatemala." *Social Science and Medicine* 38(1): 105-115.

Stein, Howard and E. Wayne Nafziger

1991 "Structural Adjustment, Human Needs, and the World Bank Agenda." Review Article. *Journal of Modern Africa* 29(1): 173-189.

Steinberg, Steven

1995 *Turning Back: The Retreat from Racial Justice in American Thought and Politics.* Boston: Beacon Press.

Stewart, Francis

1995 *Adjustment and Poverty: Options and Choices.* New York: Routledge.

Stewart, John Massey

1996 "No Place to Hide." *Nature* 381(6579): 203-204.

Stichter, Sharon

1990a "Women, Employment, and the Family: Current Debates." In *Women, Employment, and the Family in the International Division of Labor.* Sharon Stichter and Jane L. Parpart, eds. Philadelphia: Temple University Press. Pp.11-71.

1990b "Migration of Women in Colonial Central Africa: Some Notes Toward an Approach." In *Demography from Scanty Evidence: Central Africa in the Colonial Era.* Bruce Fetter, ed. Boulder, CO: Lynn Reinner.

Stichter, Sharon and Jane L. Parpart, eds.

1990 *Women, Employment, and the Family in the International Division of Labor.* Philadelphia: Temple University Press.

Stiglitz, Joseph

1998 "More Instruments and Broader Goals: Moving Toward the Post-Washington Consensus." The 1998 WIDER Annual Lecture, Helsinki, Finland, January 7, 1998.

Stocker, Karen, Howard Waitzkin, and Celia Iriart

1999 "The Exportation of Managed Care to Latin America." *New England Journal of Medicine* 340(14): 1131-1136.

Stockwell, George

1978 *In Search of Enemies: A CIA Story.* New York: Norton.

Stoneman, Colin

1981 *Zimbabwe's Inheritance.* London: Macmillan.

Stopford, John and Susan Strange, with John S. Henley

1991 *Rival States, Rival Firms: Competition for World Market Shares.* Cambridge: Cambridge University Press.

Stott, Robin

1999 "The World Bank: Friend or Foe to the Poor?" *British Medical Journal* 318(7187): 822-823.

Stover, Eric, A.S. Keller, J.C. Kobey, et al.

1994 "The Medical and Social Consequences of Landmines in Cambodia." *Journal of the American Medical Association* 272: 331-336.

STPS (Secretaría del Trabajo y Previsión Social)

1998a "Estadísticas Laborales, Cuadro I.6." Available at www.stps.gob.mx/302a/302_0057.htm.

1998b "Estadísticas Laborales, Cuadros III.1-III.20." Available at www.stps.gob.mx/302a/302_0057.htm.

Strange, Susan

1998 *Mad Money.* Manchester: Manchester University Press.

Streeten, Paul

1993 "Markets and States: Against Minimalism." *World Development* 21(8): 1281-1299.

1994 "Human Development: Means and Ends." *American Economic Review (Papers and Proceedings)* 84(2): 232-243.

Strider, R.

1995 "Blood in the Pipeline." *Multinational Monitor,* January/February, 1995, pp. 22-25.

Strobel, Margaret

1982 "African Women: Review Essay." *SIGNS* 8(1): 109-131.

Substance Abuse and Mental Health Services Administration

1995 *National Household Survey on Drug Abuse: Population Estimates 1994* (95-3063).

Sulvetta, M.B. and K. Swartz

1986 *The Uninsured and Uncompensated Care: A Chartbook.* Washington, D.C.: National Policy Forum.

Sundaram, Anjali and George Gelber

1991 *A Decade of War: El Salvador Confronts the Future.* New York: Monthly Review Press.

Sunkel, Osvaldo

1995 "Uneven Globalization, Economic Reform, and Democracy: A View from Latin America." In *Whose World Order? Uneven Globalization and the End of the Cold War.* Hans-Henrik Holm and Georg Sørensen, eds. Boulder, CO: Westview Press. Pp. 43-67.

Susser, Mervyn

1993 "Health as a Human Right: An Epidemiologist's Perspective on the Public Health." *American Journal of Public Health* 83(3): 418-426.

Sutcliffe, Moira

1985 "An Eyewitness in Bhopal." *British Medical Journal* 290(6485): 1883-1884.

Swan, John M.

1921 "Medical Notes on the Dominican Republic and Haiti." *American Journal of Tropical Medicine* 1: 19-27.

Swanson, Janice M., Ayesha E. Gill, Karen Wald, et al.

1995 "Comprehensive Care and the Sanatoria: Cuba's Response to HIV/AIDS." *Journal of the Association of Nurses in AIDS Care* 6(1): 33-41.

Tancer, Robert S.

1995 "The Pharmaceutical Industry in Cuba." *Clinical Therapeutics* 17(4): 791-797.

Tangua, Nelly

1998 "A l'Hopital ex-Mama Yemo, la Salle Shamukwale Est une Prison pour les Bebes Prématures et Leurs Mamans." *Le Soft* (Kinshasa), June 5.

Tarzi, Shah M.

1995 "Third World Governments and Multinational Corporations: Dynamics of Hosts' Bargaining Power." In *International Political Economy: Perspectives on Global Power and Wealth.* Jeffrey A. Frieden and David A. Lake, eds. New York: St. Martin's Press. Pp. 154-164.

Tauli-Corpuz, Victoria

1998 "The Globalization of Mining and Its Impact and Challenges for Women." *Third World Resurgence* 93: 29-32.

Taylor, Anna

1998 "Violations of the International Code of Marketing of Breast Milk Substitutes: Prevalence in Four Countries." *British Medical Journal* 316(7138): 1117-1122.

Taylor, Lance, ed.
1988 *Varieties of Stabilization Experience.* Oxford: Clarendon Press.
1993 *The Rocky Road to Reform: Adjustment, Income Distribution, and Growth in the Developing World.* Cambridge, MA: MIT Press.

Taylor, Lance and Ute Pieper
1996 *Reconciling Economic Reform and Sustainable Human Development: Social Consequences of Neoliberalism.* New York: UNDP Office of Development Studies.

Tendler, Judith
1975 *Inside Foreign Aid.* Baltimore: Johns Hopkins University Press.

Terry Molinert, Héctor, Enrique Galbán García, and Rodolfo Rodríguez Cruz
1989 "Prevalence of Infection with Human Immunodeficiency Virus in Cuba." *PAHO Bulletin* 23(1-2): 62-67.

Texas Center for Policy Studies
1994 *Binational Study Regarding the Presence of Toxic Substances in the Rio Grande/Rio Bravo and Its Tributaries Along the Boundary Portion Between the United States and Mexico.* Austin, TX: International Boundary and Water Commission, United States and Mexico.

Texas Department of Health
1993 "Anencephaly in Texas Border Counties, 1986-1991." *Disease Prevention News.* 53(19): 1-5.

Texas Department of Health and Centers for Disease Control
1992 *An Investigation of a Cluster of Neural Tube Defects in Cameron County, Texas.* Austin, TX: Texas Department of Health.

Texas Natural Resource Conservation Commission
1994 *Regional Assessment of Water Quality in the Rio Grande Basin.* Austin, TX: Watershed Management Division, TNRCC.

TGNP (Tanzania Gender Networking Project)
1993 *Gender Profile of Tanzania.* Dar es Salaam: Tanzania Gender Networking Project.
1994 *Structural Adjustment and Gender: Empowerment or Disempowerment.* Dar es Salaam: Tanzania Gender Networking Project.

Theobald, Robert
1997 "The Multilateral Agreement on Investment: An Alternative Approach." Available at www.crisny.org/not-for-profit/unions/theobald.htm.

Thomas, C. and S. Foard
1991 *Private Correctional Facility Census.* Gainsville: University of Florida, Center for Studies in Criminology and Law.

Thornton, Lewis H., Peter Boddy, and M. Roy Brooks, Jr.
1994 *Mid-Term Evaluation—Maternal Health and Child Survival Project (PROSAMI).* Project Number 519-0367. San Salvador: Prepared for the U.S. Agency for International Development.

Thorp, Rosemary and Laurence Whitehead, eds.
1987 *Latin American Debt and the Adjustment Crisis.* Pittsburgh, PA: University of Pittsburgh Press.

Thrupp, L.A.
1991 "Sterilization of Workers from Pesticide Exposure: The Causes and Consequences of DBCP-Induced Damage in Costa Rica and Beyond." *International Journal of Health Services* 21(4): 731-757.

Tilly, Chris and Randy Albelda
1994 "It's Not Working—Why Many Single Mothers Can't Work Their Way Out of Poverty." *Dollars and Sense* 196: 8-11.

Tonry, Michael
1995 *Malign Neglect.* Oxford: Oxford University Press.

Toye, John
1993 *Dilemmas of Development: Reflections on the Counter-Revolution in Development Economics,* 2nd edition. Oxford: Blackwell.

Trager, Ellen Lutch
1998 "The Health-Care Gap Between the Affluent and Poor." *Boston Globe,* October 21.

Trouillot, Michel-Rolph
1990 *Haiti, State Against Nation: The Origins and Legacy of Duvalierism.* New York: Monthly Review Press.

Tucker, Katherine and Thomas R. Hedges
1993 "Food Shortages and an Epidemic of Optic and Peripheral Neuropathy in Cuba." *Nutrition Reviews* 51(12): 349-357.

Tulchinsky, Theodore and Elena Varavikova
1996 "Addressing the Epidemiologic Transition in the Former Soviet Union: Strategies for Health System and Public Health Reform in Russia." *American Journal of Public Health* 86(3): 313-320.

Turshen, Meredeth
1984 *The Political Ecology of Disease in Tanzania.* New Brunswick, NJ: Rutgers University Press.
1999 *Privatizing Health Services in Africa.* New Brunswick, NJ: Rutgers University Press.

Turshen, Meredeth, ed.
1989 *Women and Health in Africa.* Trenton, NJ: Africa World Press.
1999 *Conference Report—African Women Against Violence.* Dakar, Senegal, January.

Tyagi, Y.K. and Armin Rosencranz
1988 "Some International Law Aspects of the Bhopal Disaster." *Social Science and Medicine* 27(10): 1105-1112.

Ul Haq, M., I. Kaul, and I. Grunberg, eds.
1996 *The Tobin Tax: Coping with Financial Vulnerability.* Oxford: Oxford University Press.

UNAIDS (United Nations AIDS Program)
1997 *Report on the Global HIV/AIDS Epidemic.* Geneva: UNAIDS/WHO.
1998 *AIDS Epidemic Update.* Geneva: UNAIDS/WHO.

U.N. Commission on Human Rights

1997 *Situation of Human Rights in Nigeria.* Fifty-fourth session. Report submitted by the Special Rapporteur of the Commission on Human Rights, Mr. Soli Jehangir Sorabjee, pursuant to Commission resolution 1997/53.

UNCTAD (United Nations Conference on Trade and Development)

1992 *World Investment Report 1992: Transnational Corporations as Engines of Growth.* New York: United Nations.

1993 *World Investment Report 1993: Transnational Corporations and Integrated International Production.* New York: United Nations.

1994a *World Investment Report: Transnational Corporations and Competitiveness.* New York: United Nations.

1994b *World Investment Report: Transnational Corporations, Employment and the Workplace.* New York: United Nations.

1995 *World Investment Report: Investment, Trade, and International Policy Arrangements.* New York: United Nations.

1996 *World Investment Report: Transnational Corporations, Market Structure, and Competition Policy.* New York: United Nations.

UNDP (United Nations Development Programme)

1990 *Human Development Report, 1990.* New York: Oxford University Press for UNDP.

1992 *The Urban Environment in Developing Countries.* New York: Oxford University Press for UNDP.

1994 *Human Development Report, 1994.* New York: Oxford University Press for UNDP.

1995 *Human Development Report, 1995.* New York: Oxford University Press for UNDP.

1996 *Human Development Report, 1996.* New York: Oxford University Press for UNDP.

1997 *Human Development Report, 1997.* New York: Oxford University Press for UNDP.

1998 *Human Development Report, 1998.* New York: Oxford University Press for UNDP.

1999 *Human Development Report, 1999.* New York: Oxford University Press for UNDP.

UNFPA (United Nations Population Fund)

1996 World Population Prospects, cited in UNAIDS 1997.

UNICEF (United Nations International Children's Emergency Fund)

1985 *Situation Analysis of Women and Children in Rwanda.* Kigali: UNICEF.

1988 *Analysis of the Situation of Women and Children in Rwanda.* Kigali: UNICEF.

1990a *Strategy for Improved Nutrition of Children and Women in Developing Countries.* New York: UNICEF.

1990b *State of the World's Children.* New York: UNICEF.

1990c *Children and Development in the 1990s: A UNICEF Sourcebook.* New York: UNICEF.

1990d *Women and Children in Tanzania: A Situation Analysis.* Dar es Salaam: UNICEF.

1991 *State of the World's Children.* New York: Oxford University Press.

1992a *Situation of Women and Children in the Republic of Rwanda.* Kigali: UNICEF.

1992b *State of the World's Children Report.* New York: Oxford University Press.

1993a "Central and Eastern Europe in Transition: Public Policy and Social Conditions." In *Regional Monitoring Report* (No. 1, November: p. 46). Florence, Italy: UNICEF International Child Development Centre.

1993b *The State of the World's Children.* New York: Oxford University Press.

1994 *The State of the World's Children.* New York: Oxford and UNICEF.

1996 *State of the World's Children, 1996.* New York: Oxford University Press.

United for a Fair Economy

1998 "Executive Excess 98: CEOs Gain from Massive Downsizing." *Fifth Annual Executive Compensation Survey.* Boston: United for a Fair Economy.

1999 Trainers Manual. Boston: United For a Fair Economy.

United Nations

1962 *The U.N. Development Decade: Proposals for Action.* New York: United Nations.

United Nations Center on Transnational Corporations

1985 *Environmental Aspects of the Activities of Transnational Corporations: A Survey.* New York: United Nations.

United Nations, Centre for Human Settlements (Habitat)

1996 *An Urbanizing World: Global Report on Human Settlements 1996.* Oxford: Oxford University Press.

United Nations, Department of Economic and Social Information and Policy Analysis, Population Division

1995 *World Population Prospects. The 1994 Revision.* New York: United Nations.

United Nations, Joint Programme on HIV/AIDS

1995 "Strategic Plan 1996-2000." Available at www.unaids.org/unaids/projects/stratigic.html.

United Nations Truth Commission

1993 *From Madness to Hope: The 12-Year War in El Salvador; Report of the Commission on Truth for El Salvador.* New York: U.N. Security Council.

United Nations/OAS Mission Civile Internationale

1997 *Haiti: Droits de L'homme et Rehabilitation des Victimes.* Port-au-Prince: MICIVIH.

United Nations, Population Information Network (POPIN)

1993 "Population, Development and Environment: An NGO Position Paper for the 1994 International Conference on Population and Development." Available at www.undp.org/popin/icpd/recommendations/other/43.html.

U.S. Arms Control and Disarmament Agency

1995 *World Military Expenditures and Arms Transfers.* Washington, D.C.: Government Printing Office.

U.S. Bureau of the Census

1996 *World Population Profile: 1996.* Report WP/96 by Thomas M. McDevitt. Washington, D.C.: Government Printing Office.

U.S. Department of Agriculture

1995 *Tobacco: Situation and Outlook Report.* TBS-231. Washington, D.C.: Department of Agriculture Economic Research Service.

U.S. Department of Commerce

1970 *Statistical Abstract of the United States.* Washington, D.C.: Department of Commerce.

1997 *Country Commercial Guide: Peru: Fiscal Year 1998.* Washington, D.C.: U.S. and Foreign Commercial Service.

1998 *Country Commercial Guide: Peru: Fiscal Year 1999.* Washington, D.C.: U.S. and Foreign Commercial Service.

U.S. Department of Health and Human Services

1995 *Vital and Health Statistics: Russian Federation and United States, Selected Years 1980-93.* Hyattsville, MD: Department of Health and Human Services.

1998 *Health, United States, 1998 with Socioeconomic Status and Health Chartbook.* Hyattsville, MD: National Center for Health Statistics, U.S. Public Health Service.

U.S. Department of Justice, Office of Research and Evaluation

1995 *Key Indicators—Strategic Support System.* December. Washington, D.C.: Department of Justice.

U.S. Department of Labor

1996 "InterAm Database at the National Law Center for Inter-American Free Trade, via U.S. Department of Labor, U.S. NAO 'Ministerial Consultations-Submission 940003: Agreement on Implementation' May, 1996." Available at www.natlaw.com/mexico/topical/laborlaw/spmxlb1.htm.

U.S. Environmental Protection Agency and Secretaria de Deserollo Urbano y Ecologia

1992 *Integrated Environmental Plan for the Mexican-U.S. Border Area, First Stage, 1992-1994.* Washington, D.C. and Mexico City, Mexico.

1994 *Lower Rio Grande Valley Environmental Monitoring Study: Report to the Committee on the Pilot Project.* Washington, D.C. and Mexico City, Mexico.

U.S. General Accounting Office

1990 *Trade and Health Issues: Dichotomy Between U.S. Tobacco Export Policy and Antismoking Initiatives.* Washington, D.C.: U.S. General Accounting Office.

1992 *International Trade: Advertising and Promoting U.S. Cigarettes in Selected Asian Countries.* Washington, D.C.: U.S. General Accounting Office.

1994 *Report to U.S. House of Representatives, General Government Division.* May. Washington, D.C.: U.S. General Accounting Office.

U.S. Immigration and Naturalization Service

1997 *Statistical Yearbook of the Immigration and Naturalization Service, 1996.* Washington, D.C.: Government Printing Office.

U.S. Senate

1890 "Senate Executive Document No. 231, 51st. Congress, 1st Session." *Minutes of the International American Conference.* Washington, D.C.: Government Printing Office.

U.S. Senate Committee on Foreign Relations, Subcommittee on Terrorism, Narcotics, and International Operations

1988 *Drugs, Law Enforcement, and Foreign Policy.* 100th Congress, 2nd session. Washington, D.C.: U.S. Government Printing Office.

U.S. State Department

1999 *Congressional Presentation for Foreign Operators, Fiscal Year 1999.* Washington, D.C.: Department of State.

U.S. Congress, Senate, Select Committee to Study Governmental Operations with respect to Intelligence Activities

1976 *Alleged Assassination Plots Involving Foreign Leaders: An Interim Report of the Select Committee to Study Governmental Operations with Respect to Intelligence Activities, United States Senate—Together with Additional, Supplemental, and Separate Views.* New York: Norton.

United States-Mexico Border Health Association

1994 *Sister Communities Health Profiles: United States-Mexico Border, 1989-1991.* El Paso, TX: Pan American Health Organization, El Paso Field Office.

UNRISD (United Nations Research Institute for Social Development)

1995 *States of Disarray: The Social Effects of Globalization (Report for the World Summit for Social Development).* London: United Nations Research Institute for Social Development.

Upton, Arthur C., ed.

1990 "Environmental Medicine: Introduction and Overview." *Medical Clinics of North America* 74(2): 235-535.

USAID (United States Agency for International Development)

1986 *A.I.D. Policy Determination 14: Implementing A.I.D. Privatization Objectives.* June 16.

1987 *Economic Growth and the Third World: A Report on the A.I.D. Private Enterprise Initiative.* Washington, D.C.: Bureau for Private Enterprise, USAID.

1991 *El Salvador: USAID Health Profile.* Arlington, VA: Center for International Health Information, USAID Health Information System.

Useem, Michael

1996 *Investor Capitalism: How Money Managers are Changing the Face of Corporate America.* New York: Basic Books.

USEIA (United States Energy Information Administration)

1997 "Energy Situation Analysis Report, Nigeria." December. Available at converger.com/eiacab/nigeria.htm.

Uvin, Peter

1998 *Aiding Violence: The Role of Foreign Assistance in the 1994 Genocide in Rwanda.* West Hartford, CT: Kumarian Press.

Vail, Leroy, ed.

1991 *The Creation of Tribalism in Southern Africa.* Berkeley: University of California Press.

Van Allen, Judith

1972 "'Sitting on a Man': Colonialism and the Lost Political Institutions of Igbo Women." *Canadian Journal of African Studies* 4(2): 165-181.

van de Walle, Dominique

1997 *Public Spending and the Poor: What We Know, What We Need to Know.* Policy Research Working Paper #1476. Washington, D.C.: World Bank.

van der Gaag, Jacques

1995 *Private and Public Initiatives: Working Together for Health and Education.* Washington, D.C.: World Bank.

van der Geest, Sjaak and Susan Reynolds Whyte, eds.

1988 *The Context of Medicines in Developing Countries: Studies in Pharmaceutical Anthropology.* Dordrecht: Kluwer Academic.

van Onselen, Charles

1976 *Chibaro: African Mine Labor in Southern Rhodesia 1900-1933.* London: Pluto Press.

1996 *The Seed is Mine: The Life of Kas Maine, A South African Share-Cropper 1984-1985.* New York: Hill and Wang.

Vansina, Jan

1989 "Deep Down Time: Political Traditions in Central Africa." *History in Africa* 16.

Varady, R. and M. Mack

1995 "Transboundary Water Resources and Public Health in the U.S.-Mexico Border Region." *Journal of Environmental Health* 57(8): 8-14.

Varma, Daya

1987 "Epidemiological and Experimental Studies on the Effects of Methyl Isocyanate on the Course of Pregnancy." *Environmental Health Perspectives* 72: 153-157.

1989 "Hydrogen Cyanide and Bhopal." *Lancet* 2(8662): 567-568.

Varma, Daya and Ian Guest

1993 "The Bhopal Accident and Methyl Isocyanate Toxicity." *Journal of Toxicology and Environmental Health* 40(4): 513-529.

Vaughan, Megan

1991 *Curing Their Ills: Colonial Power and African Illness.* Cambridge: Polity Press.

1992 "Syphilis, AIDS, and the Representations of Sexuality: The Historical Legacy." In *Action on AIDS in Southern Africa.* Zena Stein and Anthony Zwi, eds. New York: CHISA (Committee for Health in Southern Africa). Pp. 119-126.

Veeken, Hans

1995 "Letter from Cuba. Cuba: Plenty of Care, Few Condoms, No Corruption." *British Medical Journal* 311(7010): 935-937.

Vega, William A., Bohdan Kolody, Richard Hough, et al.

1987 "Depressive Symptomatology in Northern Mexico Adults." *American Journal of Public Health* 77(9): 1215-1218.

Ventura, Arnoldo K. and N. Joel Ehrenkranz

1976 "Endemic Dengue Virus Infection in Hispaniola: I. Haiti." *Journal of Infectious Diseases* 134(5): 436-441.

Vergara, Pilar

1997 "In Pursuit of 'Growth with Equity': The Limits of Chile's Free-Market Social Reforms." *International Journal of Health Services* 27(2): 207-215.

Verhoogen, E.

1996 "The U.S.-Haiti Connection: Rich Companies, Poor Workers." *Multinational Monitor*, April, pp. 7-10.

Verma, Kiran

1996 "Covert Costs of Privatization: Lessons from the Closure of Three Public Chronic-Care Hospitals in Massachusetts." *Public Budgeting and Finance* 16(3): 49-62.

Verschave, Francois-Xavier and A.S. Boisgallais

1994 *L'Aide Publique au Developpement.* Paris: Syros.

Verweij, M., S.C. Mohapatra, and R. Bhatia

1996 "Health Infrastructure for the Bhopal Gas Victims." *International Perspectives in Public Health* 11: 8-13.

Vilas, Carlos

1999 "The Decline of the Steady Job in Latin America." *NACLA Report on the Americas* 32(4): 15-20.

Vincent, Barbara and Paul Hofer

1994 *The Consequences of Mandatory Minimum Prison Terms: A Summary of Recent Findings.* Washington, D.C.: Federal Judicial Center.

Virchow, Rudolf

1848 *Die Medizinische Reform.* Berlin: Druck and Verlag von G. Reimer.

Vis, Henry L., C. Yourassowsky, and H. van de Borght

1975 *A Nutritional Survey in the Republic of Rwanda.* Tervuren: Musee Royal de l'Afrique Central (MRAC) and Butare.

Vishnevskii, Anatolii

1998 "Russkii Krest." *Novie Izvestiia*, February 24.

Vitalis, Robert

1994 "Dreams of Markets, Nightmares of Democracy." *Middle East Report*, Spring.

Vivian, Jessica, ed.

1995 *Adjustment and Social Sector Restructuring.* London: Frank Cass.

Voelker, Rebecca

1998 "Drink to Children's Health." *Journal of the American Medical Association* 279(18): 1429.

Voeller, Bruce and Deborah J. Anderson

1992 "Heterosexual Transmission of HIV." *Journal of the American Medical Association* 267(14): 1917.

Vogel, Steven K.

1997 "International Games with National Rules: How Regulation Shapes Competition in 'Global' Markets." *Journal of Public Policy* 17(2): 169-193.

Vwakyanakazi, Mukohya

1991 "Import and Export in the Second Economy in North Kivu." In *The Real Economy of Zaire: The Contribution of Smuggling and Other Unofficial Activities to the National Economy of Zaire.* Janet MacGaffey, ed. London: James Currey. Pp. 43-71.

Waddington C.J. and K.A. Enyimayew

1990a "A Price to Pay: The Impact of User Charges in Ashanti-Akim District, Ghana." *International Journal of Health Planning and Management* 4: 17-48.

1990b "A Price to Pay, Part 2: The Impact of User Charges in the Volta Region of Ghana." *International Journal of Health Planning and Management,* Vol. 5.

Wade, Robert

1990 *Governing the Market: Economic Theory and the Role of Government in Taiwan's Industrialization.* Princeton, NJ: Princeton University Press.

1996a "Globalization and Its Limits: Reports of the Death of the National Economy Are Greatly Exaggerated." In *National Diversity and Global Capitalism.* Suzanne Berger and Ronald Dore, eds. Ithaca: Cornell University Press. Pp. 29-59.

1996b "Japan, the World Bank, and the Art of Paradigm Maintenance." *New Left Review* 217 (May-June): 3-36.

1998a "The Asian Debt-and-Development Crisis of 1997-?: Causes and Consequences." *World Development* 26(8):1535-1554.

1998b "Asian Water Torture." *Financial Times,* June 23.

1998c "From Miracle to Meltdown: Vulnerabilities, Moral Hazard, Panic and Debt Deflation in the Asian Crisis." Working Paper for the Russell Sage Foundation, June 1.

Wade, Robert and Frank Veneroso.

1998 "The High Debt Model Versus the Wall Street-Treasury-IMF Complex." *New Left Review* 228 (March/April): 2-23.

Wakabi, Yeri and Hope Mwesigye

1991 *Violence Against Women in Uganda: A Research Report.* Kampala: FIDA (Federation of Ugandan Women Lawyers).

Waldorf, Dan, Craig Reinarman, and Sheigla Murphy

1991 *Cocaine Changes: The Experience of Using and Quitting.* Philadelphia: Temple University Press.

Wallace, Roderick

1990 "Urban Desertification, Public Health, and Public Order: 'Planned Shrinkage', Violent Death, Substance Abuse, and AIDS in the Bronx." *Social Science and Medicine* 31(7): 801-813.

Walt, Gill

1994 *Health Policy: An Introduction to Process and Power.* Johannesburg: Witwatersrand University Press.

Walu, Engundu

1991 *Women's Work in the Informal Sector: Some Lessons from Kinshasa, Zaire.* Master's Thesis, Institute of Social Studies, The Hague.

Ware, John E. Jr., Martha S. Bayliss, William H. Rogers, et al.

1996 "Differences in 4-Year Health Outcomes for Elderly and Poor, Chronically Ill Patients Treated in HMO and Fee-for-Service Systems: Results from the Medical Outcomes Study." *Journal of the American Medical Association* 276(13): 1039-1048.

Ware, John E., William H. Rogers, Allyson R. Davies, et al.

1986 "Comparison of Health Outcomes at a Health Maintenance Organization with Those of Fee-for-Service Care." *Lancet* 1(8488): 1017-1022.

Wares, D.F. and C.L. Clowes

1997 "Tuberculosis in Russia." *Lancet* 350:957.

Warner, David C.

1991 "Health Issues at the U.S.-Mexican Border." *Journal of the American Medical Association* 265(2): 242-247.

Washington Office on Haiti (WOH)

1996 "The Haiti Economic Justice Campaign." In *Support of Economic Justice and Self-Determined Development in Haiti.* Washington, D.C.: Washington Office on Haiti.

Waters, Maxine

1997 *Drug Trafficking on the Fast Track.* Congressional Report. November. Washington, D.C.: U.S. House of Representatives.

Waterston, Alisse

1993 *Street Addicts in the Political Economy.* Philadelphia: Temple University Press.

Watkins, Kevin

1995 *The Oxfam Poverty Report.* Oxford: Oxfam.

1997 "Cost-Recovery and Equity in the Health Sector: Issues for Developing Countries." Paper prepared for WIDER project on Provision and Financing of Public Goods in Developing Countries. Oxfam United Kingdom and Ireland Policy Department. February 27.

1998 *Economic Growth with Equity: Lessons from East Asia.* Oxford: Oxfam Great Britain.

Watson, Catherine

1991 *Exile from Rwanda: Background to an Invasion.* Washington, D.C.: U.S. Committee for Refugees.

Watson, Fiona

1994 *Human Face of Human Façade: Adjustment and the Health of Mothers and Children.* Part 2: Annotated

Bibliography. London: Centre for International Child Health, University of London.

Watson, Sidney Dean

1994 "Minority Access and Health Reform: A Civil Right to Health Care. *Journal of Law, Medicine, and Ethics* 22(2): 127-137.

Webb, Gary

1998 *Dark Alliance: The CIA, the Contras, and the Crack Cocaine Explosion.* New York: Seven Stories Press.

Weil, C. and J.L. Scarpaci, eds.

1992 *Health and Health Care in Latin America During the Lost Decade: Insights for the 1990s.* Minnesota Latin America Series, No. 3, Iowa International Papers, Nos. 5-8.

Weinrich, A.K.H.

1979 *Women and Racial Discrimination in Rhodesia.* Paris: UNESCO.

Weise, Jean

1971 *The Interaction of Western and Indigenous Medicine in Haiti in Regard to Tuberculosis.* Ph.D. Dissertation. Department of Anthropology, University of North Carolina at Chapel Hill.

Weiss, Herbert

1966 *Political Protest in the Congo.* Princeton, NJ: Princeton University Press.

Weissman, Robert

1996a "A Long, Strange TRIPS: The Pharmaceutical Industry's Drive to Harmonize Global Intellectual Property Rules, and the Remaining WTO Legal Alternatives Available to Third World Countries." *University of Pennsylvania Journal of International Economic Law* 17: 1069-1125.

1996b "Waiting to Export: Africa Embraces Export Processing Zones." *Multinational Monitor*, July/August, pp. 12-16.

1998 "U.S. Drug Imperialism." *Multinational Monitor*, June, p. 5.

Wells, F.C., G.A. Jackson, and T.C. Maurer

1988 "Reconnaissance Investigation of Water Quality, Bottom Sediment, and Biota Associated with Irrigation in Lower Rio Grande Valley, 1986." *U.S. Geological Survey. Water-Resources Investigations Report 87-4277.* Washington, D.C.: U.S. Geological Survey.

Werner, David and David Sanders

1997 *Questioning the Solution: The Politics of Primary Health Care and Child Survival.* Palo Alto, CA: Health Rights.

Wesseling, C.R., R. McConnell, T. Partanen, et al.

1997 "Agricultural Pesticide Use in Developing Countries: Health Effects and Research Needs." *International Journal of Health Services* 27(2): 273-308.

Weyland, Kurt

1995 "Social Movements and the State: The Politics of Health Reform in Brazil." *World Development* 23(10): 1699-1712.

Wheat, Andrew

1995 "Exporting Repression: Arms Profits vs. Human Rights." *Multinational Monitor*, Jan/Feb, pp. 16-21.

White, Luise

1990 *The Comforts of Home: Prostitution in Colonial Nairobi.* Chicago: University of Chicago Press.

White, Oliver, C. Campbell, and Anita Bhatia

1998 *Privatization in Africa.* Washington, D.C.: World Bank.

Whitehead, Tony, Larry Peterson, and J.L. Kaljee

1994 "The 'Hustle': Socioeconomic Deprivation, Urban Drug Trafficking, and Low-Income, African-American Male Gender Identity." *Pediatrics* 93(6): 1050-1054.

WHO (World Health Organization)

1981 *International Code of Marketing of Breastmilk Substitutes 1981.* Geneva: World Health Organization.

1993 *Infant and Young Child Nutrition.* EB93/17. Geneva: World Health Organization.

1994 *AIDS: Images of the Epidemic.* Geneva: World Health Organization.

1995 *World Health Report.* Geneva: World Health Organization.

1996a *Tobacco or Health: First Global Status Report.* Geneva: World Health Organization.

1996b *World Health Report.* Geneva: World Health Organization.

1997 *World Health Report.* Geneva: World Health Organization.

1998a "Director-General Sets Out WHO Stance on Health and Human Rights." Press Release WHO/93. December 8.

1998b *Global Tuberculosis Control: World Health Organization Report 1998.* Geneva: World Health Organization.

1998c "Questions and Answers." Available at www.who.int/aboutwho/en/qa6b.htm.

1998d *Report on the Global HIV/AIDS Epidemic (Slideshow).* Geneva: World Health Organization, June 22.

1998e *World Health Report.* Geneva: World Health Organization.

1999 *World Health Report.* Geneva: World Health Organization. www.who.org/whr/1999/en/report.htm.

Whyte, Susan Reynolds

1991 "Medicines and Self-Help: The Privatization of Health Care in Uganda." In *Changing Uganda: The Dilemma of Structural Adjustment and Revolutionary Change.* Holger Bernt Hansen and Michael Twaddle, eds. London: James Currey. Pp. 130-148.

Wignaraja, Ponna

1993 *New Social Movements in the South: Empowering the People.* London: Zed Books.

Wilcock, David C.

1995 "Cereals Marketing Policy Reform in Three African Countries: Vested Interests, Marketing Efficiency, and Food Security." Paper presented at the Annual Meeting of the American Anthropological Association. Washington, D.C., November 19.

Wilentz, Amy

1989 *The Rainy Season: Haiti After Duvalier*. New York: Simon and Schuster.

Wilkinson, Richard

1992a "National Mortality Rates: The Impact of Inequality?" *American Journal of Public Health* 82(8): 1082-1084.

1992b *Unhealthy Societies: The Afflictions of Inequality*. London: Routledge.

1998 "What Health Tells Us About Society." *IDS Bulletin* 29(1): 77-85.

Willame, Jean Claude

1980 *Le Secteur Multinationale au Zaire*. Brussels: Cahiers du CEDAF.

1995 *Au Sources de l'Hecatombe Rwandaise*. Paris: L'Harmattan.

Williams, D. and C. Collins

1995 "U.S. Socioeconomic and Racial Differences in Health: Patterns and Explanations." *Annual Review of Sociology* 21(9): 349-389.

Williams, D., R. Lavizzo-Mourey, and R.C. Warren

1994 "The Concept of Race and Health Status in America." *Public Health Reports* 109(1): 26-41.

Williams, Edward J.

1995 "The *Maquiladora* Industry and Environmental Degradation in the U.S.-Mexican Borderlands." Paper presented at the Annual Meeting of the Latin American Studies Association. Washington, D.C. September.

Williams, Eric

1944 *Capitalism and Slavery*. London: Andre Deutsch.

Williams, Gavin, ed.

1976 *Nigeria, Economy and Society*. London: Rex Collins.

Williams, Nigel

1997 "Drug Companies Decline to Collaborate." *Science* 278(5): 1704.

Williams, Terry

1989 *The Cocaine Kids*. New York: Addison-Wesley Publishing Company.

Williamson, Jeffrey

1996 "Globalization, Convergence, and History." *Journal of Economic History* 56:277-306.

Williamson, John

1990 *Latin American Adjustment: How Much Has Happened?* Washington, D.C.: Institute for International Economics.

1994 "In Search of a Manual for Technopols." In *The Political Economy of Policy Reform*. John Williamson, ed. Washington, D.C.: Institute for International Economics.

1996 "Lowest Common Denominator or Neoliberal Manifesto? The Polemics of the Washington Consensus." In *Challenging the Orthodoxies*. Richard M. Auty and John Toye, eds. New York: St. Martin's Press. Pp. 13-22.

Wilson, William J.

1996 *When Work Disappears: The World of the New Urban Poor*. New York: Alfred A. Knopf.

WIN (Women in Nigeria)

1985 *Women in Nigeria Today*. London: Zed Press.

Wish, E.D.

1991 "U.S. Drug Policy in the 1990s: Insights from New Data from Arrestees." *The International Journal of Addictions* 25(3A): 377-409.

Wisner, Ben

1989 *Power and Need in Africa*. Trenton, NJ: Africa World Press.

1992 "Health of the Future/The Future of Health." In *21st Century Africa: Towards a New Vision of Self-Sustainable Development*. Ann Seidman and Frederick Anang, eds. Trenton, NJ: Africa World Press. Pp. 149-181.

Wisotsky, Steven

1987 "Crackdown: The Emerging 'Drug Exception' to the Bill of Rights." *Hastings Law Journal* 38(5): 889-926.

1990 *Beyond the War on Drugs: Overcoming a Failed Public Policy*. Buffalo, NY: Prometheus Books.

WOLA (Washington Office on Latin America)

1991 *Clear and Present Dangers*. October. Washington, D.C.: Washington Office on Latin America.

Wolf, Alvin

1963 "The African Mineral Industry: Evolution of a Supra-National Level of Integration." *Social Problems* 10(3): 153-164.

Wolfe, Eric R.

1982 *Europe and the People Without History*. Berkeley: University of California Press.

Wood, Adrian

1995 "How Trade Hurts Unskilled Workers." *Journal of Economic Perspectives* 9(3): 57-80.

1996 "Openness and Wage Inequality in Developing Countries: The Latin American Challenge to East Asian Conventional Wisdom." *World Bank Economic Review* 11(1): 33-57.

Woodson, Drexel

1997 "Lamanjay, Food Security, Sécurité Alimentaire: A Lesson in Communication from BARA's Mixed-Methods Approach to Baseline Research in Haiti, 1994-1996." *Culture and Agriculture* 19(3): 108-122.

Woodward, David

1992 *Debt, Adjustment, and Poverty in Developing Countries*. London: Pinter Publications, in association with Save the Children.

World Bank

1977 *Economic Conditions and Prospects of Zaire*. Draft 1975. Washington, D.C.: World Bank.

1979 *Zaire: Current Economic Situation and Constraints*. Washington, D.C.: World Bank.

1981 *Accelerated Development in Sub-Saharan Africa: An Agenda for Action. (The Berg Report.)* Washington, D.C.: World Bank.

1983 *World Development Report, 1983*. Washington, D.C.: World Bank.

1985 *Rwanda: Agricultural Strategy Review*. Washington, D.C.: World Bank.

1987a *Financing Health Services in Developing Countries: An Agenda for Reform.* Washington, D.C.: World Bank.

1987b *World Development Report, 1987.* Washington, D.C.: World Bank.

1988a *Adjustment Lending: An Evaluation of Ten Years of Experience.* Washington, D.C.: World Bank.

1988b *Poverty in Sub-Saharan Africa, Status Report.* Washington, D.C.: World Bank.

1989 *Sub-Saharan Africa from Crisis to Sustainable Growth: A Long-Term Perspective Study.* Washington, D.C.: World Bank.

1990a *World Development Report, 1990.* New York: Oxford University Press.

1990b *Zimbabwe: Issues in the Financing of Health Services.* Washington, D.C.: World Bank.

1991 *World Development Report, 1991.* New York: Oxford University Press.

1992a *Improving the Implementation of Cost Recovery for Health: Lessons from Zimbabwe.* Washington, D.C.: World Bank.

1992b *World Development Report, 1992.* New York: Oxford University Press.

1993a *The East Asian Miracle: Economic Growth and Public Policy.* London: Oxford University Press.

1993b *World Development Report, Investing in Health.* New York: Oxford University Press.

1994a *Adjustment in Africa: Reforms, Results, and the Road Ahead.* Washington, D.C.: World Bank.

1994b *Better Health in Africa.* Washington, D.C.: World Bank.

1994c *Global Economic Prospects and the Developing Countries.* Washington, D.C.: World Bank.

1994d *World Development Report, 1995.* New York: Oxford University Press.

1995a *Taking Action for Poverty Reduction in Sub-Saharan Africa: Draft Report of an Africa Region Task Force.* Washington, D.C.: Technical Department of Poverty and Human Resources Division.

1995b *Global Economic Prospects and the Developing Countries.* Washington, D.C.: World Bank.

1995c *Monitoring Environmental Progress: A Report on Work in Progress.* Washington, D.C.: World Bank, Environmentally Sustainable Development Department.

1995d "Social Dimensions of Adjustment: World Bank Experience, 1980-93." Available at www.worldbank.org/html/oed/14776.htm.

1995e *The World Bank and AIDS: In Partnership to Combat an Unparalleled Threat to Society and Development.* World Bank, Human Development Department, December 5.

1995f *World Development Report, 1995.* New York: Oxford University Press.

1996a "Monitoring Poverty over Time: Some Lessons from Cote d'Ivoire." Findings, Africa Region, 75, November.

1996b *Taking Action for Poverty Reduction in Africa.* Washington, D.C.: World Bank.

1996c *The World Bank's Partnership with Nongovernmental Organizations.* Washington, D.C.: World Bank.

1996d *World Debt Tables, 1996.* Washington, D.C.: World Bank.

1996e *World Development Report, 1996: From Plan to Market.* New York: Oxford University Press.

1997a *Global Development Finance.* Washington, D.C.: World Bank.

1997b *Health, Nutrition, and Population Sector Strategy.* Washington, D.C.: World Bank.

1997c *World Development Indicators, 1997.* Washington, D.C.: World Bank.

1997d *World Development Report, 1997.* New York: Oxford University Press.

1998a *Global Development Finance.* Washington, D.C.: World Bank.

1998b *Global Economic Prospects and the Developing Countries.* Washington, D.C.: World Bank.

1998c *Health Nutrition and Population Sector Strategy Paper.* Washington, D.C.: World Bank.

1998d "Nutritional Status and Poverty in Sub-Saharan Africa." *Findings,* Africa Region, 108. April.

1998e *World Development Indicators, 1998.* Washington, D.C.: World Bank.

1999a "Gender, Growth, and Poverty Reduction." *Findings* 129.

1999b *World Bank Development Report 1998/99: Knowledge for Development.* New York: Oxford University Press.

Wright, A., C.J. Holberg, F.D. Martinez, *et al.*

1989 "Breastfeeding and Lower Respiratory Tract Illness in the First Year of Life." *British Medical Journal* 299(6705): 946-949.

Wright, Paul

1997 "Captive Labor: U.S. Business Goes to Jail." *Covert Action Quarterly* 60: 26-31.

WTO (World Trade Organization)

1996a *Trade and Foreign Direct Investment.* Geneva: World Trade Organization.

1996b "World Trade Expanded Strongly in 1995 for the Second Consecutive Year." Press Release, March 22.

1998 "World Trade Growth Accelerated in 1997, Despite Turmoil in Some Asian Financial Markets." Available at www.wto.org/intltrad/internat.html.

Wunder, Amanda

1995 "Prison Population Projections." In *Corrections Compendium.* Washington, D.C.: National Institute of Justice.

Yach, Derek

1986 "The Impact of Smoking in Developing Countries with Special Reference to Africa." *International Journal of Health Services* 16: 279-292.

Yamba, C. Bawa

1997 "Cosmologies in Turmoil: Witchfinding and AIDS in Chiawa, Zambia." *Africa* 67(2): 200-223.

Yoffie, David B., ed.

1993 *Beyond Free Trade: Firms, Governments, and Global Competition.* Boston: Harvard Business School Press.

Young, Crawford

1978 "Zaire, the Unending Crisis." *Foreign Affairs* 57(1): 169-185.

1996 *The African Colonial State in Comparative Perspective.* New Haven: Yale University Press.

Young, Crawford and Thomas Turner

1985 *The Rise and Decline of the Zairian State.* Madison: University of Wisconsin Press.

Young, David W.

1990 "Privatizing Health Care: Caveat Emptor." *International Journal of Health Planning and Management* (5): 237-240.

Youngers, Coletta

1995 *Fueling Failure: U.S. Drug Control Efforts in the Andes.* April. Washington, D.C.: Washington Office on Latin America.

1996 *The Andean Quagmire: Rethinking U.S. Drug Control Efforts in the Andes.* March. Washington, D.C.: Washington Office on Latin America.

Zack-Williams, A.B.

1990 "Sierra Leone: Crisis and Despair." Review of African Political Economy 49: 22-33.

1995 *Tributors, Supporters and Merchant Capital: Mining and Underdevelopment in Sierra Leone.* Aldershot, England: Avebury.

Zaldivar, R.A.

1996 "HMO Cost-Cutting Frays Doctor-Patient Ties." *The Denver Post*, March 28.

Zarabozo, Carlos and Jean D. LeMasurier

1995 "Medicare and Managed Care." In *Essentials of Managed Health Care.* Peter R. Kongstvedt, ed. Gaithersburg, MD: Aspen Publishers. Pp. 209-233.

Zimmerman, R.

1995 "Nike Laces Up Vietnam Factories." *Business Journal*, May 5.

Zuidberg, Lida and Tata Djire

1992 *Les Paysannes du Mali-Sud: Vers une Meilleu Integration au Program de la CMDT.* Amsterdam: Royal Tropical Institute, Bulletin 326 and Sikaso, Mali: CMDT.

Index

About the Editors

Jim Yong Kim is a practicing physician and medical anthropologist. He is Executive Director of Partners in Health (PIH), a public charity that works with sister organizations in Haiti, Peru, Mexico, Cambodia, and the United States to improve health outcomes for poor people. In this role, he works closely with Socios en Salud, PIH's sister organization in Peru, a global leader in combating the spread of multidrug resistant tuberculosis. He also directs an HIV/AIDS treatment and prevention program in Roxbury, Massachusetts. As Co-Director of the Program in Infectious Disease and Social Change in the Department of Social Medicine at Harvard Medical School, Dr. Kim teaches courses that focus on the nexus between poverty, culture, and infectious disease. His research examines the international pharmaceutical industry and pharmaceutical distribution and use in developing countries.

Joyce V. Millen is Co-Director of the Institute for Health and Social Justice and a research associate in the Program in Infectious Disease and Social Change in the Department of Social Medicine at Harvard Medical School. She is a medical anthropologist and also holds degrees in public health and international relations. She worked for seven years on health and agriculture projects in rural Senegal and has evaluated development programs in several other African countries. She has conducted extensive ethnomedical and epidemiology research among two West African ethnic groups, examining current political and socioeconomic forces that lead to changes in disease patterns and prevalence. Her current research focuses on the health consequences of corporate-driven globalization, especially for marginalized populations.

Alec Irwin is an Assistant Professor in the Department of Religion at Amherst College and a research associate of the Institute for Health and Social Justice. His scholarship and teaching explore how religious allegiances and conceptions of the sacred intertwine with economic and political factors to promote or inhibit social change. He is the author of *Eros Toward the World*, a comparison of ideas of love in the work of theologian Paul Tillich and in contemporary religious feminism. His recent articles have focused on the politics of sainthood in twentieth-century Europe. He is currently preparing a study of French philosopher and social activist Simone Weil, and is working to develop medical ethics and environmental ethics courses critically attuned to patterns of transformation in the global economy.

John Gershman is an Institute for Health and Social Justice Research Associate and a visiting doctoral candidate at Princeton University's Woodrow Wilson School. A political scientist by training, his research throughout the past 15 years has focused on United States foreign policy in Asia, nongovernmental organizations, and reform of international financial institutions, all with a special emphasis on the Philippines. He is co-editor of *Trading Freedom: How Free Trade Affects our Lives, Work, and Environment*.

FOR MORE GREAT BOOKS
AND INFORMATION

Award-Winning Common Courage Press has been publishing exposés and authors on the front lines since 1991. Authors include…

- Louise Armstrong
- Judi Bari
- Peter Breggin
- Joanna Cagan
- Noam Chomsky
- Neil deMause
- Laura Flanders
- Jennifer Harbury

- Jeffrey Moussaieff Masson
- Margaret Randall
- John Ross
- Ken Silverstein
- Norman Solomon
- Cornel West
- Howard Zinn
- and many others

Also available: the dynamite **The Real Stories Series** of small books from **Odonian Press** including titles from Noam Chomsky and Gore Vidal.

FOR BULK DISCOUNTS CALL 800-497-3207

For catalogs and updates, call 800-497-3207.
Email us at **orders-info@commoncouragepress.com**.

Write us at
Common Courage Press
Box 702
Monroe, ME 04951

Send us your email address if you want news about forthcoming books sent directly to you.

www.commoncouragepress.com